More Praise for *New York Times* *bestselling author*

Shirley Conran

And

"*LACE*...

SOARS INTO THE SAME STRATOSPHERE WHERE YOU'LL FIND *VALLEY OF THE DOLLS* AND *SCRUPLES* . . . The real fun is the entree it gives the reader into that heavenly world . . . of high fashion, big money, fast action and momentous stakes . . . the inaccessible, mysterious, hopelessly alluring world of global glamour." —*The Washington Post*

"All the women are wildly successful, and . . . their sex lives are explored in loving detail." —*People*

LACE 2

"I was up all night reading *LACE 2*. You won't be able to put it down."
—*Cynthia Heimel,*
Author of SEX TIPS FOR GIRLS

"*LACE 2* is my ideal curl-up-and-read book." —*Pat Miller,*
NEW WOMAN *magazine*

CRIMSON

"In Conran's new two-generation saga . . . readers get: the Cannes Film Festival, a palace in southern France, the New York modeling scene, swinging Sixties London, Europe during W.W.I, much discussion of love . . . and an avalanche of detail on how trust funds operate . . ." —*Kirkus Reviews*

"The crafty Conran gives us a powerful grandmother who is herself a famous romance novelist, three beautiful granddaughters, and a handsome lawyer named Adam who charms them all. . . ." —*Chicago Tribune*

Three Complete Novels

SHIRLEY CONRAN

Three Complete Novels

SHIRLEY CONRAN

LACE
LACE 2
CRIMSON

WINGS BOOKS
New York • Avenel, New Jersey

This edition contains the complete and unabridged texts of the original editions. They have been completely reset for this volume.

This omnibus was originally published in separate volumes under the titles:

This 1994 edition is published by Wings Books, distributed by Random House Value Publishing, Inc., 40 Engelhard Avenue, Avenel, New Jersey 07001, by arrangement with Simon & Schuster Inc.

Random House
New York • Toronto • London • Sydney • Auckland

Printed and bound in the United States of America

Library of Congress Cataloging-in-Publication Data

Conran, Shirley.
[Novels. Selections]
Three complete novels / Shirley Conran.
p. cm.
Contents: Lace—Lace 2—Crimson.
ISBN 0-517-10073-8
1. Motion picture actors and actresses—Fiction. 2. Women novelists, English—Fiction. 3. Man-woman relationships—Fiction. 4. Love stories, English. I. Title. II. Title: 3 complete novels.
PR6053.0512A6 1994
823'.914—dc20 94-6606
CIP

8 7 6 5 4 3 2 1

CONTENTS

LACE

This book is for
my sons,
SEBASTIAN CONRAD and JASPER CONRAD,
with love.

ACKNOWLEDGMENTS

I owe a great debt to my editor, Michael Korda, for teaching me so much and making the process so enjoyable. I also greatly appreciate John Herman's support, care and editorial involvement.

Without Morton Janklow's perception and judgment this book might never have been started, let alone finished, and I also owe a great deal to Betsy Nolan for her shrewd advice.

For reading my manuscript, I am most grateful to George Seddon, Celia Brayfield and Giorgio Sandulescu. For typing on and on . . . and on, I would like to thank Bettina Culham, who somehow managed to decipher Linear C.

For helping to ensure that this book is technically accurate, I would like to express my gratitude to Professor T. W. Glenister, Dr. Jonathan Gould, The Cancer Research Institute, Alexander Mosley, Victor Sassie, Richard Pearce, Patrick Forbes, William Frankel, Clive Carr, David O'Brien, Mike Ricketts, Peter Alexander, Michael Crawford, Lanham Titchener, Ian McAlley, Roger Wood, Alexander Weymouth, David Maroni, Patrick O'Higgins, Peter Boumphrey, Sebastian Conran, Jasper Conran, Rowland Castro, Anna Weymouth, Dee Wells Ayer, Lesley Blanch, Sandy Fawkes, Mary Quant, Tina Vanzyl-Lubner, Pat Miller, Shirley Lowe, Ruth Janner Morris, Deirdre McSharry, Anna Palmer, Myrna Shapiro, Jill Haas, and Ellie Boris.

My thanks also to Arthur Klebanoff, Jerry Traum, Anne Sibbald, Arnold Kinsman, Aimée Mikaelis, Rebecca Head, Deborah Gordis, Willow Morel, Mary Jo Valko, Joan Feeley, Anna Wintour, Nina Santizi and Mallory Andrews, who were kind enough to help me when I needed their expertise, and also to my assistant, Linda Sheridan, for what can only be described as everything.

PRELUDE

Paris, 1963

SCRAPE . . . SCRAPE . . . SCRAPE . . . The cold, hard metal dug deep into the child's body. She forced her knuckles into her mouth and bit against the bone as hard as she could to fight pain with pain. She didn't dare scream. She just mumbled, "Jesus, Jesus, Jesus," as she bit her hand.

Tears ran down her cheeks and onto the paper pillow. Her body was trembling and clammy with cold sweat. Outside she could hear the cheerful noise of a busy Paris street, but in this small brown room there was no sound except the scraping and her mumbling and the occasional clink of steel against steel. She would count to ten and *then* she'd scream! Surely it couldn't go any higher, whatever he was pushing up inside her? It felt like a dagger, persistent, cold, merciless. She wanted to vomit, to faint, she wanted to die. She couldn't bear it to go on and on and on. . . .

The man was intent on what he was doing as she lay on the hard table, her knees forced high and apart by the steel surgical stirrups. It had been horrifying from the moment she entered this place, the dark brown room with the hard, high table in the middle. A line of silvery instruments and a few odd-shaped bowls lay on another table; there was a camp bed and a cloth screen in one corner of the room. A white-aproned woman had pointed to the screen and said, "You can take off your clothes behind that." Naked, she had shivered behind the screen, not wanting to leave its protection, but the woman had taken her briskly by the wrist and tugged her to the table in the center of the room. She had been positioned on her back so that her narrow hips rested on the edge of the table, while her legs were pulled apart by the woman and lifted into the cold surgical stirrups. The shivering child felt unbearably humiliated as she gazed into the powerful overhead light.

There had been no anesthetic. The man wore a crumpled green surgeon's gown. He had muttered some instruction to the woman and then he had inserted two fingers into the child's vaginal canal; he held the cervix with his fingers as he placed his other hand on her abdomen to feel the size and position of her uterus. Then she was swabbed with antiseptic, and he pushed in a chill speculum shaped like a duck's bill, which kept the walls of the vagina apart and enabled him to see the opening of her uterus. The speculum didn't hurt, but it felt cold and menacing inside her small body. Other instruments were also inserted and then the pain started as the cervix was opened slowly with the stainless steel dilators until it was wide enough for the operation to start. The man picked up the curette—a metal loop on the end of a long thin handle—and the excavation began. The curette moved in and around the uterus, scraping the life out of her; it took only two minutes, but the time seemed endless to the suffering child.

The man worked quickly; occasionally he muttered to the woman who was helping him. Hardened though he was, he carefully avoided looking at the child's face; her little feet in the stirrups were reproach enough as he swiftly finished the job and removed each bloodied steel instrument.

As the uterus was emptied it gradually contracted back to its original size, but the child's body was jerked with agonizing cramps until the contractions stopped.

Now she was wailing like an animal, gasping as each new pain clawed her. The man abruptly left the room; the woman swabbed her; the cloying smell of antiseptic filled the air. "Stop making such a noise," hissed the woman. "You'll feel fine in half an hour. Other girls don't make such a fuss. You should be grateful that he was trained as a real doctor. You haven't been messed up inside; he knows what he's doing, and he's fast. You don't know how lucky you are." She helped the thin, thirteen-year-old girl off the table and onto the camp bed in the corner. The child's face was gray, and she shook uncontrollably as she lay under a blanket.

The woman gave her pills to swallow, then she sat and read a paperback romance. For half an hour there was no sound in the room except for the child's occasional stifled sob. Then the woman said, "You can go now." She helped the girl to dress, gave her two large sanitary towels to put in her pants, handed her a bottle of antibiotic tablets and said, "Whatever happens, don't come back here. You're not likely to hemorrhage, but if you start bleeding, call a doctor *immediately*. Now get home and stay in bed for twenty-four hours." For one moment the woman's carefully controlled, impersonal toughness weakened. "*Pauvre petite!* Don't let him touch you for at least a couple of months." Awkwardly she patted the child's shoulder and led her through the passage to the heavy front door.

The child paused outside on the stone steps, wincing in the sharp sunlight. Slowly, painfully, Lili walked along the boulevard until she came to a small café where she ordered a hot drink. She sat and sipped it, feeling the sun and the warm steam on her face as a jukebox pumped out the new Beatles hit, "She Loves You."

PART ONE

CHAPTER 1

IT WAS A warm October evening in 1978 with the distant skyscrapers sparkling in the dusk as Maxine glanced through the limousine window at the familiar New York skyline. She had chosen this route for that view. Now, in the discreet, hushed comfort of the Lincoln Continental, they stood stuck in traffic on the Triboro Bridge. Never mind, she told herself, there was plenty of time before the meeting. And the view was worth it—like diamonds sprinkled across the sky.

Her neatly folded sable coat lay beside the maroon crocodile jewel case. The nine maroon-leather suitcases—all stamped in gold with a tiny coronet and the initials M de C—were stacked beside the chauffeur or stowed in the trunk. Maxine traveled with very little fuss and at enormous expense, usually someone else's. She took absolutely no notice of luggage allowances; she would say, with a shrug of the shoulders, that she liked comfort; so one suitcase contained her pink silk sheets, her special down-filled pillow, and the baby's shawl, delicate as a cream lace cobweb, that she used instead of a bed jacket.

Although most of the suitcases held clothes (beautifully packed between crisp sheets of tissue paper), one case was fitted as a small maroon-leather office; another carried a large medicine box packed with pills, creams, douches, ampoules, disposable syringes for her vitamin injections and the various suppositories that are considered normal treatment in France but frowned on by Anglo-Saxons. Maxine had once tried to buy syringes in Detroit—*mon Dieu*, could they not tell the difference between a drug addict and a French countess? One had to look after one's body, it was the only one you were going to get and you had to be careful what you put on it and in it. Maxine saw no reason to force terrible food on the stomach merely because it was suspended thirty-five thousand feet above sea level; all the other first-class passengers from Paris had munched their way through six overcooked courses, but Maxine had merely accepted a little caviar (no toast) and only one glass of champagne (nonvintage, but Moët, she observed with approval before accepting it). From a burgundy suède tote bag she had then produced a small white plastic box that contained a small silver spoon, a pot of homemade yogurt and a large, juicy peach from her own hothouse.

Afterward, while other passengers had read or dozed, Maxine had taken out her miniature tape recorder, her tiny gold pencil, and a large, cheap office duplicate book. The tape recorder was for instructions to her secretary, the office duplicate book was for notes, drafts and memos of telephone conversations; Maxine tore them off and sent them on their way, always retaining a copy of what she had written; then when she returned to France, her secretary filed the duplicates. Maxine was well organized in an unobtrusive way; she didn't believe in being *too* well organized and she couldn't stand bustle or hustle, but she could only operate when things were orderly; she liked order even more than she liked comfort.

When Madame la Comtesse booked a reservation for a business trip, the Plaza automatically booked a bilingual secretary for her. She sometimes traveled with her own secretary, but it was not always convenient to have the girl hanging round one's neck like a pair of skates. Also, as the girl had now been with Maxine for almost twenty-five years, she was able to keep an eye on things at home in Maxine's absence; from the condition of her sons and her grapes to the times when Monsieur le Comte returned home and with whom.

Mademoiselle Janine reported everything with devoted zeal. Since 1956, Mademoiselle Janine had worked hard for the Château de Chazalle and she shone in the reflected glory of Maxine's success. She had first worked for the de Chazalles twenty-two years ago, when Maxine was twenty-five and had opened the château as a historical hotel, museum and amusement park, before anybody (except the locals) had heard of de Chazalle champagne. Mademoiselle Janine had fussed around Maxine from the time her three sons were babies, and she would have found life intolerably dull without the family. Indeed, she had been with the de Chazalles for so long that she almost *felt* like one of the family. But not quite. They were—and always would be—separated by the invisible, unbreakable barriers of class.

Like New York, Maxine was glamorous and efficient, which was why she liked the quick pace of the city, liked the way that New Yorkers worked with neat, brisk speed whether they were serving hamburgers, heaving garbage off the sidewalk or squeezing fifty cents' worth of fresh orange juice for you on a sunny street corner. She appreciated these fast-thinking people, their tough humor, their crisp jokes, and privately thought that New Yorkers had all the *joie de vivre* of the French, without being nearly so rude. She also felt at home with New York women. She enjoyed observing, as if they were another species, those cool, polite, impeccable women executives as they operated under the merciless pressure of the grab for power, the lunge for money, the lusting after someone else's job. Like theirs, Maxine's self-discipline was colossal, but—at the age of forty-seven—her grasp of people-politics was even better. Had it not been so, she would not have been traveling to meet Lili.

That gold-digging slut!

But Maxine was undoubtedly intrigued by Lili's offer and it was partly her curiosity that had brought her all the way across the Atlantic. Again she wondered whether she would accept the job. She would have thought that Lili—who must be about twenty-eight years old by now—would never have wanted to see Maxine again. Maxine remembered that long-ago expression of startled pain in the flashing chestnut eyes of the troublemaker whom the press had nicknamed "Tiger-Lili."

She had been amazed to receive the telephone call, to hear that low, sensual voice sound so astonishingly humble, as Lili had asked Maxine to meet her in New York to decorate Lili's new duplex on Central Park South. Lili wanted her new home to be a showpiece, a conversation-stopper, and she knew that Maxine could supply the correct blend of erudite elegance and spirited style. The budget would be as large as was necessary, and of course all expenses for Maxine's trip to New York would be paid whether or not she decided to accept the commission.

There had been a pause, then Lili had added in a penitent voice, "I would also like to feel that something no longer has such painful memories for you. For so many years I have lived unhappily with my conscience, and now I dearly wish to do whatever is necessary to be at peace with you."

After this apology there had been a thoughtful pause, then the conversation had turned to Maxine's work. "I understand you've just finished Shawborough Castle," Lili had said, "and I also heard about the stunning job you did for Dominique Fresanges—it must be wonderful to have a talent such as yours, to rescue historic houses from decay, to make so many homes beautiful and comfortable while they still remain a heritage for the world. . . ."

It had been a long time since Maxine had enjoyed a holiday in New York by herself, so eventually she had agreed to make the journey. Lili had asked Maxine to tell nobody of the meeting until after it had taken place. "You know the press won't leave me alone," she had explained. And it was true. Not since Greta Garbo had there been an international movie star who so intrigued the public.

As the limousine started to crawl forward, Maxine glanced at her diamond wristwatch—there was plenty of time before the six-thirty meeting at the Pierre. Maxine was rarely impatient; she disliked being late, but assumed that everyone else would be. That was life today—undependable. If a situation could be improved, Maxine would generally do it with a slight, one-sided smile, a look that combined conspiratorial charm with a hint of menace. If a situation could *not* be improved, then she folded her hands in her lap and imperturbably accepted *la loi de Murphy*.

She happened to catch sight of herself in the back mirror of the limousine and leaned toward it, lifting her jaw above the cream lace jabot and poking it sideways at her reflection. It was only five weeks since the operation, but the tiny scars in front of her ears had already disappeared. Mr. Wilson had done an excellent job and it had only cost a thousand pounds, including the anesthetist and the London clinic bill. There was no tautness, no pulling at the mouth or eyes; she simply looked healthy, glowing and fifteen years younger—certainly not forty-seven. It was sensible to have it done when you were still young, so that nobody noticed, or, if they did, they couldn't pin you down; today you never saw an eyebag on an actress over thirty, or on an actor, come to think of it. Nobody had noticed her absence; she had been out of the clinic in four days and had then spent ten days in Tunisia where she had lost seven pounds, a satisfying bonus. She simply could not understand why some people went all the way to Brazil and paid heaven knows what for their lifts.

Maxine was a firm believer in self-improvement, especially surgical. One *owes* it to oneself, was her justification; her teeth, eyes, nose, chin, breasts, all had been lifted or braced until Maxine was a mass of almost invisible stitches. Even so, she was no great beauty, but when she thought back to her girlhood and remembered the prominent nose, the horselike teeth and her painful self-consciousness, she was grateful that years ago she had been persistently urged to do something about it.

It had not been necessary to do anything about her legs. They were exquisite; she stuck out one long pale limb, rotated an elegant ankle, smoothed the blue silk skirt of her suit, then opened the window and sniffed the air of Manhattan, oblivious to the strong carbon monoxide content at street level. She reacted to New York as she did to the champagne of her estate—with happy delight. Her eyes sparkled, she felt high and ebullient. It was good to be back, despite the traffic jam, in the city that made you feel as if every day was your birthday.

Judy Jordan looked like a tiny, blonde, exhausted Orphan Annie, although she was forty-five years old. In her Chloë brown velvet suit, and a fragile, cream silk blouse, she sat in the crowded bus as it crawled up Madison Avenue. Impatient by nature, she always took what came first, a bus or a cab. She had in fact recently been photographed by *People* in the amazing act of getting on a bus. This had given Judy a great deal of satisfaction, because there had been a long period in her life when she couldn't afford anything *but* a bus.

Suddenly she felt sad. As if she were touching a talisman, she fiddled with one of the matching rings she wore on her middle fingers, each one an exquisitely carved coral rosebud on a thick gold band. Apart from these she didn't much care for jewelry—her passion was for shoes. Her walk-in shoe closet contained row upon row of exquisitely handmade boots and shoes. Judy decided she might just celebrate tomorrow by going mad in Maud Frizon. Why not? Her partner had told her only this morning that they were worth nearly two million dollars *more* this year!

It was increasingly hard to remember life in her old studio on East 11th Street, from which she'd been evicted because she couldn't pay the rent. But Judy forced herself to remember those days. They made the present all the more pleasant by contrast.

There was another reason why Judy never wanted to forget what it felt like to be short of money in a big city. That was how a lot of her readers felt. They bought *VERVE!* for its optimism, its encouragement, its sensuality, and they looked on the magazine as a *friend*. The truth was that Judy traveled by bus because she wanted to stay in touch with her readers.

Reconciling the opposite sides of her public image was sometimes difficult. On the one hand, she liked to be seen as a warmhearted, straightforward, hard-working woman who'd been known to lunch off a street corner hot dog, a working girl much like her readers. On the other hand, those same readers expected her to lead a glamorous social life, dress the way they dreamed of dressing, and be a celebrity herself. So, when Judy was not eating hot dogs she lunched at Lutèce, dieted at the Golden Door when necessary, and traveled constantly. Like New York, she set a brisk, optimistic pace. On those occasions when—suddenly—she plummeted into black loneliness, she gritted her teeth and bore it. Loneliness from time to time was the price of freedom, and freedom wasn't a stars and stripes, Boy Scout idea, it was doing what you damn well wanted to do—all the time.

The doors of the bus hissed open, sucked in more passengers and hissed shut again. A sallow, middle-aged woman collapsed into the seat opposite Judy, settled her shopping bag on her knees, then suddenly groaned. "I wish the buildings would go up in flames, then there'd be no more problems." She said it again, then yelled it. No one in the bus took the slightest notice until the woman got off; then there was a general rustle of relief, a few smiles and shrugs—just another New York crazy who didn't care what anyone thought of her.

But that was also a sign of maturity, mused Judy. You became an adult when you stopped caring what other people thought about you and started to care what *you* thought about *them*. . . . Was it a feature? she wondered professionally. She thought about a possible author, celebrities to interview, a quiz, and made a quick mental note to get one of the editors working on it. "Are You Grown-up Yet?" Not a bad title. Not a bad *question*, either, she thought to herself, unable to answer it. She still felt as childlike inside as she looked on the outside, although she would never allow anyone to know it. Vulnerability was bad for business. Judy preferred her reputation as an *enfant terrible*, a baby tycoon, the lethal little lady publisher who had already come a long way and intended to go much farther. The image that Judy projected was that of a woman to be reckoned with—a woman who made you think ten percent faster when you were with her, but also a woman with a weakness for pretty shoes.

She was making up for lost time. Until she was fifteen, Judy had worn only sensible black shoes.

Behind the lace curtains her family had been painfully poor. Her parents were devout Southern Baptists, greatly interested in sin and its avoidance. In order to avoid sin, Judy and her young brother Peter were never allowed to do anything on Sundays. They could sing in church but they weren't allowed to do so at home, they were not allowed to listen to the radio, because radio on Sunday was sinful: the big, elaborate, walnut radio, with the wooden sunray pattern over the speaker, was the focal point of the living room, but on Sundays, apart from cooking noises, the only sound in the house was the clatter of the old icebox that stood by the door to the back porch.

Naturally, smoking and drinking were sinful. Nevertheless, her Grandad, who lived with them, would disappear from time to time into the cellar for a drink from the bottle that he kept hidden behind the boiler; perhaps he justified it to himself as medicine. After his Sunday drink, Grandad always went to the back porch to his rocking chair, which creaked under his weight as he beamed at the apple tree at the end of the yard and waited for the hereafter. Judy's parents must have known about the whiskey because you could smell the stuff on his breath; her mother's mouth would tighten, and she would give a tiny, delicate, disapproving sniff, but she never said anything. Grandad was supposedly a teetotaler.

The man in the plaid shirt seated across from Judy looked uneasy and lowered his eyes furtively to check his zipper. She looked away quickly—she must have been staring again. When she was lost in thought, her dark blue eyes glared through the big tortoiseshell frames with a ferocity that was as alarming as it was unintentional.

She wondered again what the purpose of this meeting with Lili was, and why the mystery?

First there had been the contrite telephone call—and God knows, Lili had every reason to sound contrite. Ultimately, of course, the bust-up with Lili had been good for Judy's public relations business, but that hadn't been Lili's intention that night in Chicago. . . . "If you could find it in your heart to forgive me for the very bad way in which I behaved . . . " Lili had pleaded, in that deep voice with the slight continental accent. . . . "I was so ungrateful. . . . So very unprofessional. . . . I am ashamed when I think about it. . . . " In spite of herself, Judy had started to mellow; it wasn't just because of Lili's stardom or her magnetism, it was simply because Judy had enjoyed working with her. They really had been a terrific team until that night in Chicago.

Lili had said there was a special matter that she wished to discuss with Judy, "something of a very confidential nature I should like to speak to you about personally."

Judy didn't waste her time on anybody. Dozens of strange proposals were put to her each week, and most of them didn't get past her secretaries. But this was Lili, whose name had been linked to more celebrities than that of any other woman, Lili, whose waiflike beauty was a twentieth-century legend, Lili, who *never* gave interviews.

The last fact counted most with Judy. Lili was worth at least a thousand words for *VERVE!*, whatever happened at the meeting, so Judy agreed to it. Eager and charming as a child, Lili thanked her and asked her to keep their rendezvous a secret. Judy hadn't intended to tell anyone anyway. But she was intrigued; like herself, Lili had also succeeded in life fast, mysteriously and against the odds. She must be about twenty-eight or twenty-nine now, although she didn't look it.

Last month's telephone call had been followed by a confirming letter on thick, cream paper with the single word LILI centrally engraved in navy Bodoni typeface; for some reason Lili had no last name.

What could she have in mind? Judy wondered. Backing? Surely not. Publishing? Not likely. Publicity? No longer necessary.

It was six-twenty and the traffic was still motionless, so Judy jumped off the bus and walked the last few blocks. She always liked to arrive on time.

The cab smelled of stale cigarette smoke, the back seat had been slashed and the guts were spilling out. It was also stuck in traffic on Madison Avenue, but the driver, a surly Puerto Rican, was mercifully silent until suddenly he barked, "Where you from?"

"Cornwall," said Pagan, who never thought of herself as English. She added, "The warmest part of Britain," and thought that wasn't saying much. Pagan's pallor was due to poor circulation, she had always suffered from cold weather, which was eleven months of the year at home. As a child she had hated to put her naked feet out of bed on winter mornings and hurriedly plunged her chilblains into sheepskin slippers. Her first frenzied love-hate relationship was with her warm but uncomfortable winter underclothes; the scratchy, cream wool combination suit that covered her from neck to ankle, with sagging sanitary trapdoor that unbuttoned at the back; the prickly, flannel Liberty bodice, a vestlike garment that ended at the stomach with long, dangling suspenders to hold up her thick woolen stockings.

When Pagan was a child, at seven every morning a little housemaid had scurried around Trelawney to light the stoves and the fires, which were banked down or turned off every freezing winter night at eleven P.M. no matter what time everyone went to bed. Smelly cylindrical oil stoves stood before the lace curtains of the bathrooms and minor bedrooms, open coal fires smoldered in the principal bedrooms and great, glowing logs were piled in the hall and drawing room, but the long hallway and bathrooms were always freezing, and the food from the home farm was lukewarm when it finally arrived on the manor table. The uneven flagstones in the dining room always felt cold, even in summer, even through Pagan's shoes; when she thought no one was looking, Pagan used to tuck up her feet under her bottom and away from the icy floor—but it was always noticed and she would be told sharply to "sit up like a lady."

However, the worst part of winter had been getting into bed under the cold heaviness of the linen sheets. Once beyond the heat range of the oil stove, Pagan's bones would ache and her body become gradually numb until sleep mercifully anesthetized the dull pain.

At this memory, although it was hot for October, the forty-six-year-old Pagan shivered in her pink wool Jean Muir coat.

As usual, Pagan was staying at the Algonquin, where she felt oddly at home. The lobby had the slightly seedy, unwarrantedly superior air of a London club with its high-backed, shabby leather wing chairs and dim, parchment-shaded lights. Her room was small but surprisingly pretty after the calculated gloom of the lobby. A comfortable, pink velvet armchair stood on the grass-green carpet; artful lace scatter pillows, cunningly placed brass lamps, a few bird pictures in golden frames spoke of the skillful decorator's touch. The old-fashioned, newly smart brass bedstead reminded Pagan of the nursery at Trelawney and the dark-green-on-white trellis wallpaper swept her mind back to the conservatory where her grandfather used to read the *Times* every morning, surrounded by slumbering dogs, palms, ferns and tropical plants. The conservatory was heated by long, hot, brown tubes that writhed around the walls at floor level and burned your fingers if you touched them. It was easily the warmest, if not the *only* warm spot in that drafty mansion, especially when the wind was blowing straight off the sea, sweeping harshly over granite-grim cliffs to the rhododendron-encircled lawns. The conservatory was also a terrific place to hide from her mother; with a book and an apple, Pagan would slither like a lizard under jade fronds and jagged malachite spikes, concealed by yellow froth and spumescent greens.

Pagan could hardly remember her father, who had been killed in a car crash when only twenty-six. Pagan, then three years old, had been left with a vague memory of a scratchy cheek and a scratchy, tweed-kneed lap. The only traces of her father were the row of silver trophy cups, which stood on the oak shelves in the study, for school swimming matches and county golf, faded sepia photographs of cricket teams, and a group of laughing people at a beach picnic.

After his death, until she was ten and had to go to school in London, Pagan and her mother made their home with Grandfather at Trelawney, where Pagan had been both spoiled and toughened. When she was three years old, she had been taken out into the bay and lowered over the side of the dinghy in Grandfather's arms to learn to swim. When she was thirteen months old she had been put on her first pony; the reins were placed in her baby hands and her grandfather walked her around the paddock every morning so that she would learn to ride before she was old enough to be frightened; she first hunted with Grandfather Trelawney when she was eight.

It was her grandfather who had taught Pagan courtesy. He listened politely and with genuine interest to everybody, whether it was one of his tenants, the village postman or his neighbor, Lord Tregerick; the people Grandfather couldn't stand were what he called "the money chaps"—lawyers, bankers, accountants. Grandfather never looked at bills, he simply passed them on to his agent to be paid.

Pagan had always been surrounded by servants, many of whom were there because her grandfather hated to dismiss anyone. Somebody put Pagan's gloves on, somebody pulled her boots off, somebody brushed her hair at night, and somebody put her clothes away, so the little girl grew up to be compulsively untidy. Pagan always remembered the soft rustle of the housemaid's skirt as she carried brass cans of hot water to the bedroom in the early morning and stood them by the rose-patterned washbasin; the blissful warmth of the butler's pantry, where Briggs cleaned the silver and kept the flower-decorated Minton dinner service on shelves behind glass doors; the cozy warmth and fragrance of the big kitchen; the resigned, sour face of her grandfather's valet as he scratched the mud from Pagan's riding clothes in the brushing room.

Pagan seldom saw her mother, and when she did put in an appearance she was obviously bored. She hated the country; there was nowhere to go and nothing to do. Cornwall in the 1930s was hardly sophisticated and Pagan's mother certainly was. Short hair sleeked beetle-neat against heavy, dead-white makeup; the daily masterpiece, a scarlet glistening mouth, was painted over her real mouth, which was much thinner; red traces of Pagan's mother could be found on glasses, cups, towels and innumerable cigarette butts. Mrs. Trelawney often went up to London, and when she came back, she brought her London friends down for the weekend. Pagan disliked them, but nevertheless, she picked up much of their Mayfair slang, and for the rest of her life her conversation was dotted with their dated, breathless exaggerations.

Now in 1978 Pagan still missed her grandfather and regretted that her husband had never met him—or stayed at Trelawney before it had been transformed. Not that her grandfather would have had anything in common with her husband, who was interested only in books and his work. He took no interest in Pagan's fundraising—although without the money she raised, he would have been unable to continue his research. Exasperated, she sometimes scolded him. When she did, he would hug her and say, "Darling, I'm sorry white mice are so expensive."

Pagan knew that he was proud of her work, though at first her forthright business methods had alarmed him. Sometimes she suspected they still did.

She always hated to leave her husband, but after his heart attack it was unwise for him to travel; he was better off at home with help close at hand, a semi-invalid, but still one of the wittiest, cleverest and most distinguished men in the world. Although neither of them spoke about it, the past sixteen years had been a very special bonus—but sixteen years of constant care to keep him alive and working would be triumphantly worth that effort if now, as seemed likely, he might at last succeed within the next ten years. The question that they never asked each other was whether he could *last* until then. That was why Pagan hated to leave her husband, even to discuss the possibility of a major donation to the Institute.

And from such an unexpected source.

In the scarf-scattered, gumboot-glutted, coat-choked, stone-paved passage of her cottage on the Trelawney estate, Pagan had answered the telephone and heard the low, husky voice of Lili herself. As casually as if she were suggesting meeting in the next village, Lili had asked Pagan to travel to America to meet her on a matter that was both urgent and confidential. Pagan had been astonished by the telephone call. International film stars weren't in the habit of phoning her out of the blue and she had never met Lili, though of course she'd heard about her. One could hardly avoid hearing about that romantic, talented, sad creature.

On the telephone, the film star had spoken in a quiet, serious voice. "I've heard so much about your projects," she said. "I'm fascinated by the wonderful work your husband is doing and I'd like to discuss a way in which I might be of help."

When Pagan had politely pressed Lili for further details, Lili had explained that her American accountant had suggested several possible ways in which Lili might contribute, some extending over several years, and he had suggested a preliminary meeting in New York with Lili's tax advisers. It sounded as if a really big contribution was going to be made and a very generous check had then been sent to Pagan to cover her first-class travel expenses.

Sitting in the stationary cab and listening to the driver swear in Spanish, Pagan wished that she didn't feel so utterly awful. The waving mahogany hair that fell to her shoulders always looked fine, but today her face was puffy, her blue eyes dull, her eyelids swollen, and she looked all of her forty-six years.

New York time is five hours earlier than London. Pagan had arrived the previous evening, and after only a few hours' sleep, she woke at two in the morning, which was breakfast time in Britain. She wasn't able to concentrate on her book and she hadn't been able to get to sleep again. She never took sleeping pills or any other medicine, not even aspirin.

She was too terrified of getting hooked again.

Sleek black skyscrapers loomed slightly darker than the sky. You don't know how many shades of black there are until you've been in fashion or the printing business, Kate thought, as she hurried along West 58th Street, slightly late as usual. When she left the office at six-ten the sky had been pale blue and cream, but now, at six-thirty, it was dark. For a moment Kate thought nostalgically of the long English autumn twilights, then she paused at Van Cleef & Arpels. The Empress Josephine's diamond coronation tiara sat in state in one window; Kate preferred it to the tiara in the other window, the more magnificent Russian Imperial diadem which had candy-sized emeralds set in a three-inch-thick blaze of diamonds. Again Kate wondered why she hadn't let Tom pull her through the revolving doors last Monday. Most men hadn't even *heard* of Van Cleef, let alone know where it was, let alone offer to do a little shopping there. "Let's go get Josephine's tiara," Tom had said, tugging at her hand, and when she shook her head he had still tried to pull her in, pointing out that emeralds went with anything. Why hadn't she wanted to accept an expensive present from him? After all, her birthday was next week: she would be forty-six years old and she didn't care a bit. She didn't need expensive reassurance; she had got what she had always wanted—a wonderful man and a wonderful job.

Now that she was a successful magazine editor, nobody would ever guess that for years Kate hadn't known what she wanted or where she was going, that she had felt as little in control of her life as a rag doll being tossed around in a washing machine. She felt she was being pushed around, all right, but she didn't know in which direction. "Now, girl," her father always said, "remember you're as good as anyone, Kuthreen, remember that your dad's got the wherewithal and that's what *counts*. Nothing to stop you being *top* of the pile, and that's where your dad expects you to be, make no mistake about it."

The "wherewithal" had been the vast profits from the rows of identical small, squat red-brick houses that her father had built across central England. The "wherewithal" had paid for better clothes, better cars, better holidays and a better home than her schoolmates', but it had *not* been what counted; if anything, the "wherewithal" had been responsible for unspoken resentment from some of the other girls at her London day school. She had *never* felt that she was as good as any of them, and neither was she *top*. She always dreaded the arrival of the end-of-term reports, anticipating her father's rages, the punishments and—most alarming of all—her father's attempts to coach her: the more he shouted the less she could remember.

She had been a cowed girl. The anger that she had never dared to show had built up in layers of silent resentment. She knew she was a moral coward, but she was terrified that argument would rouse her father's anger. So, like her mother, Kate always said as little as possible or fled.

Once they knew her well, men were always surprised to discover how easily they could make Kate do exactly what they wanted without a word of complaint from her. But then, when they pushed her too far, she simply disappeared without a word of explanation.

As Kate couldn't stand her father when he was alive, she couldn't understand why, whenever one of her books hit the best-seller list, the wistful thought came unbidden into her head, "Wish the old bugger could have seen *that*." She couldn't understand why she wanted the ogre of her youth, dead these twenty years, to be proud of her; she couldn't understand her disappointment because her father had died before she discovered what she was top *at*, before she could shout, "Daddy, Daddy, you bastard, I've made it!" Kate didn't take much notice of her success, and neither did her friends, most of whom dated from the days when she was unknown, but her dad would have relished it, he would have cut her pictures out of the newspapers, kept all her cuttings and alerted his buddies when she was about to be on television.

Certainly this new book sounded an easy winner, another potential best-seller. Lili's story—true or false—should hit the list a week before publication. She was beautiful, romantic, irresistibly fascinating, and the public lapped up every detail of her life; for instance, *how* many times had she read that Lili always wore white, whether it was satin or silk, tweed or cotton? And of course Lili was a woman with a past—and what a past!

Before Lili had reached international status, when she had still been just another continental B-film actress who stripped in every movie, Kate had once spent some time hanging around the set in a wet wood outside London and had subsequently written the first big story to treat the teenage Lili as a potential star. Kate had not heard from Lili since the interview, but the piece had been syndicated around the world, which is why, Kate supposed, she had been summoned to the Pierre. Today, all the stars wanted an "as told to" autobiography. Nevertheless, she had been surprised when Lili had telephoned in person and asked to meet her secretly.

Kate hurried toward the Plaza, smelled hot bagels and damp autumn mist, passed a group of blank-faced, bald-headed women, swathed in silver fox and lace, spotlit in Bergdorf's window; stopped at the traffic light beyond which was a blue police car, with two cops inside, both as bald and blank as the plaster models in Bergdorf's. Kate crossed the street. Dark green, elegant awnings stretched from apartment building doors across the sidewalk to where bored chauffeurs sat in spotless dark cars. Kate nodded to the blue-uniformed doorman, who saluted her as she swung between the marble pillars of the Pierre Hotel, through the revolving doors and along the wide cream corridor.

At the reception desk they phoned up to make sure she was expected. The guests standing beside her murmured in soft Italian, the groups beyond spoke Arabic and French. Kate couldn't hear a word of English. It reminded her of Cairo. The elevator took her to the seventeenth floor and as she walked along the hushed gray corridor to Suite 1701, Kate pulled the back of her mulberry jacket down and fluffed up the purple silk bow of her blouse.

Just before she reached it, the door was opened by a thin woman with gray hair that matched her dress. Beyond her, through the open door, Kate could see into a long cream room that overlooked Central Park. A waiter was setting out ice, tongs and small dishes of olives; the secretary beckoned him out, stood aside so that Kate could enter and then softly closed the door from the hall.

Kate gasped.

"Jesus!" said Judy.

"Wrong again," said Kate, who could never resist a one-liner. Astonished, she stood in the doorway, trying to decide what this was all about. Judy and Pagan were sitting on a couple of apricot velvet couches placed at right angles to each other; at either end of the couches, huge vases of madonna lilies and imported apple blossoms stood on low, smoked-glass tables and beyond, to the right, in a beige velvet armchair, sat Maxine.

"What's this, a surprise reunion?" asked Kate.

Pagan fingered the delicate little green malachite butterfly that hung around her neck on a fine gold Cartier chain. Maxine said in a fast, low voice, "We'd better be careful what we say."

The atmosphere was tense. Kate did not have time to move over to the other women before the double doors at the far end of the room were flung open and in walked a small, gold-skinned young woman, wearing a white silk gown draped like an ancient Greek tunic.

Star quality radiated from Lili. A cloud of black, soft hair hung to her shoulders, swept back from an oval face with high, slanting cheekbones. Her small nose had a faintly predatory hook, her full lower lip was slightly too large, but when you looked at her you only noticed her eyes. They were huge shining chestnut eyes, thickly lashed, that glistened as if a crystal tear were about to fall from each one.

Tonight, however, Lili's eyes did not glisten. They glared. They projected rage and fury. For a moment the star stood silent as she surveyed the four older women: Kate in her mulberry suit by the door; Pagan in pink, sprawled across the apricot cushions; Maxine poised, porcelain cup in one hand, the saucer held on her blue silk lap; Judy in brown velvet, on the edge of the sofa with shoulders hunched, hands under her chin, elbows on her knees, scowling right back at Lili.

Then Lili spoke.

"All right," she said, "which one of you bitches is my mother?"

CHAPTER 2

"I FEEL SICK," muttered Kate, leaning back against the headboard and fastening a new lace bra over her adolescent breasts.

"Worth it," said Pagan, as she licked her fingers. Wearing orange satin boxer shorts and a pink kimono, she sat cross-legged at the end of Kate's narrow bed and looked regretfully at the white cardboard box between the two teenage girls. One chocolate eclair remained.

"We'll save this for after supper. Now shall I paint your toenails purple to take your mind off throwing up?"

The English pupils always splurged their first week's allowance on cakes, lipstick and nail polish. They had been freed from strict schools in order to be transformed into cultured young ladies by this Swiss finishing school. After years of deprivation, followed by a postwar period in which even bread and potatoes were rationed, the girls thought Switzerland in 1948 was a paradise compared to shabby, tired Britain—a paradise of cream cakes, chocolate, snow and romance.

Pagan hunched over Kate's left foot. A myopic, pre-Raphaelite beauty, she usually stooped to minimize her height. She rarely wore her glasses, partly because she was vain and partly because she kept losing them.

Lolling back on the bed, bare left foot poised in midair, Kate looked over Pagan's head. She could see the snow-topped mountains of Gstaad, framed by the white lace curtains of her open bedroom window.

"Let's go into the forest before tea," suggested Kate.

"Keep *still*, you idiot," said Pagan. "We were told to greet the new girl. We'll go after tea if she hasn't arrived. Poor thing, you've bagged the best armoire. There's hardly any hanging space in hers; she'll have to keep her stuff under the bed."

Most of the bedrooms in l'Hirondelle finishing school were for three girls, but on the top floor, under the wooden eaves of the huge chalet, the rooms were smaller. Leading off Kate's bedroom for two was a tiny, pale blue attic, with a low, sloping pine ceiling and just enough space for one narrow blue bed, a small table and a chest. Pagan had grabbed it and she was so exasperatingly untidy that it was just as well she had a room to herself. Nothing could teach Pagan to be neat. She had been christened Jennifer, but as her nanny's constant cry was "Pick it *up*, you little pagan," or "No tea until your room's tidy, you little pagan," Jennifer eventually became known as "Pagan," and the nickname stuck.

"I'm not going to waste such a lovely afternoon!" Kate jumped off the bed and pulled on a neat beige cashmere sweater and skirt. Pagan tugged a pair of old jodhpurs over the orange satin shorts and wriggled into a gigantic Fair Isle pullover, which she yanked in at the middle with a man's thick leather belt that almost went around her waist twice. They clattered down the wooden stairs two at a time, flung themselves out of the front door and half-walked, half-skipped along the steep path that led behind the school and up into the forest. After climbing about a mile over fallen pine needles, they found a notice stuck in the middle of the path that read "*Attention! Défense de passer.*"

"Probably means that the pass is defended by attentive gamekeepers," said Pagan, whose French was atrocious, and they continued to puff uphill until the path stopped in a grass clearing that ended abruptly on a cliff edge. Below they could see the brown chalets of Gstaad, encircled by the dark green forest, and beyond, a spectacular amphitheater of mountains that were snow-topped even in midsummer.

"Yoohoo . . . oooo," yelled Pagan through cupped hands. As the sound echoed back across the valley, she turned to Kate and said, "They'll expect us to yodel properly by the time we get back to—"

She stopped abruptly. Suddenly they heard an answering cry, seemingly from beneath their feet. Then someone shouted, "*Au secours!*"

"That means 'help,' " Kate said earnestly.

"And it came from beyond the cliff. *Pourquoi secours?*" yelled Pagan.

The voice yelled "*Parce que* . . . I'm stuck."

"Are you English?" yelled Pagan, starting to stride forward, but Kate yanked at her belt to stop her. They were about ten feet from the cliff edge and it might not be safe.

"No, American. Watch out. The cliff just gave way. We weren't even near the edge . . . It just suddenly crumbled."

"How many of you are there?"

"I'm the only one that fell. Nick jumped back and he's gone for help . . . aaaah!" Both girls heard the sound of slithering earth and stones.

"Are you still there?"

"Yes, but there isn't much ledge left. Oh, God, I'm so frightened."

"Don't look down!" said Pagan, lowering herself to the ground and starting to snake forward. "And don't shout any more . . . Kate, I'm going to crawl to the edge and then you lie down behind me and hang onto my ankles." Slowly Pagan wriggled to the point where the grass stopped abruptly. She peered carefully over the edge. About six feet below her, two dark blue eyes looked up, surrounded by fair, shaggy hair.

The girl was standing on a narrow ledge, arms outspread as she hugged the cliff face. "Nick just couldn't reach me," she said. "He tried and tried. He took off his shirt and tried to pull me up with it but it tore, then the ledge started to crumble and so he ran to get a ladder. But the ledge keeps crumbling, there's not enough room to sit down now. I'm so frightened."

At least a hundred feet below, the earth was starting to slide again. It made Pagan feel sick. "Oh, crumbs," she gasped. "Oh, Lord, don't look down." She tried to reach the girl with her hands but her outreached fingertips were about two feet from the upstretched hands of the frightened girl below.

"Look, hang on just a bit longer," called Pagan encouragingly, as she withdrew her head and wriggled back to Kate. She started to take off her sneakers and jodhpurs.

"These pants are tougher than the shirt," she explained, as she tied the end of her jodhpur legs with a reef knot so that the garment formed a circle; then she threaded her belt through it, pulling the buckle tight.

"For God's sake hang tight onto my ankles," Pagan hissed to Kate, as she wriggled back to the cliff face and peered over it. Some earth crumbled away beneath her breasts and she felt even sicker as she dangled the jodhpurs down to the girl below. "Can you get them over your head and under your arms like a lifebelt? *Don't look down!*"

Slowly Pagan lowered the makeshift lifebelt until it reached the girl's outstretched fingertips. "Keep your hands together and try to wriggle the jodhpurs down under your arms . . . slowly . . . slowly . . . "

Pagan wrapped the other end of the belt around her left hand and hung onto the end of it with her right hand. All the time she noticed little crumbs of earth were sliding down the sheer cliff face toward the red earth, snapped-off pine trees and roots that were piled so far below.

"Now hold onto the belt," she said in what she hoped was a commanding voice. "*Slowly*, try to walk up the cliff, like a fly."

"I can't. I *can't!*"

A chunk of earth fell from below the girl's left foot, leaving it dangling in space.

"If you fall, I'm not sure I can hold you," Pagan said. "You'll probably break my wrist and pull me over, so don't *think* about what I say. Just *do* it, when I count to three."

Kate was now lying behind Pagan with her arms hanging around Pagan's waist. "Now, one, two, *three!*" Pagan said, as forcefully as she could.

Obediently, the thin little girl—thank God she was so small—leaned out and started to scramble up the mountain. As the belt jerked taut, Pagan felt an agonizing pain in her wrist and shoulder. She wondered whether she'd dislocated it, then the whole of her left arm was in agony as, inch by inch, the girl scrambled up.

The leather belt started to slip in Pagan's sweaty hand. She was gasping for breath as she slowly wriggled backward, pulled by Kate.

Two dirty hands hanging onto the belt slowly appeared over the cliff face, followed by a frightened white face.

"Slowly," gasped Pagan, "slowly!" She thought she felt the ground move beneath her and experienced a moment of cold terror. Then the little girl collapsed over the top of the cliff and Kate quickly pulled her up over it and back to safety as Pagan's bleeding fingers released the belt.

But before Pagan could stand up, the ground beneath her fell away and suddenly she was dangling from the waist, head downward over the crumbling mountain. The ledge that the girl had been standing on had disappeared.

Kate grabbed Pagan, and together they fell backward, panting and sobbing as they crawled to safety.

Not until they reached the pine trees and the little path did Pagan feel safe. Then her knees gave way and she collapsed. Anxiously, Kate bent over her.

Suddenly a look of alarm crossed the face of the girl Pagan had rescued. "Oh, my," she said, putting both hands to her temples, "I'm going to be late. Oh, I dare not. Oh, I *must* go. Oh, dear, oh, thank you, oh, look, do you know the Chesa? Can you come there sometime so I can say . . . I mean, I can't thank you enough but . . . *I must go!*"

And she turned and half-ran, half-staggered down the path, then disappeared around the bend.

"What a cow!" Kate said. "You saved her life and she just ran off! Oh, darling Pagan, your poor hands!" Pagan's legs were filthy and her hands were bleeding. As the jodhpurs and sneakers were still on the cliff edge, she was wearing only the Fair Isle sweater and the dirty orange satin shorts.

Suddenly, from the other side of the clearing, a group of laborers appeared carrying rope, a net and a ladder. A tall, thin young man, naked to the waist, ran in front of them, but he suddenly stopped dead, ran a hand through his floppy black hair and yelled, "Christ, it's fallen!"

"The girl's all right, we got her up," called Pagan from where she was sitting. "Are you Nick?"

The young man came running over. His crooked nose was smeared with earth, his aquamarine eyes looked distraught. "She's all right? Judy's *all right?* What happened? How? . . . You're *sure* she's all right? Where is she? . . . Oh, God, I've been through such hell. . . . "

"So has Pagan," Kate said indignantly. "She leaned over the cliff and pulled your girl up—and then she rushed off when Pagan had just saved her life, saying that she didn't want to be late!"

"Well, if she's late again, she loses her job, you see. She's already been warned twice. Was she *all right*—not hurt, I mean?"

"*She* must be all right to rush off like that," said Kate scornfully, "but Pagan isn't all right. Look at her hands!"

"Stop making a fuss, Kate." Pagan wobbled to her feet. She was as tall as the young man who had jumped to help her. "I'll be perfectly fine after a bath."

"Just let me tell the rescue team there's no longer a problem and I'll see you home," said Nick, pushing his floppy black hair out of his eyes and turning to talk in rapid German to the group of men behind him. He turned back and put a supportive arm around Pagan's waist.

"I'm perfectly all right," said Pagan weakly, wincing as he touched her left arm. "Let's get out of here before more mountain disappears."

"That's unlikely," said Nick. "The rescue team said they've been dynamiting part of the mountain away because after last winter's avalanches, a dangerous overhang was left. Unfortunately, that's what we were walking on. . . . They're finishing the work next week."

"Who's that girl, the one who was *late?*" Kate's voice was heavily sarcastic.

"She's an exchange scholarship student from America and she hasn't any money, so she's working as a waitress at the Chesa," Nick explained as slowly they moved down the path. "I don't know how she does it all, she works so hard, and she never seems tired, she's always . . . oh, terrific fun."

Kate noticed that he blushed. "Are you . . . uh?"

"No, we're not, but I wish we were. She's got some fellow in Virginia. Jim." There was a pause. Both girls looked sideways at Nick and decided that Jim must be pretty sensational.

"Are you a student, too?" Nick was obviously English.

"In a way. I'm a *stagiaire.* An exchange waiter at the Imperial."

"What's an exchange waiter?"

"Well, my family is in the hotel business, so I'm learning hotel management." He pulled Pagan's arm round his shoulder. "I left school early and took the two-year course at Westminster Tech, then I was a waiter at the Savoy. I came out here on an exchange scheme; one of the Imperial waiters is taking my place in London."

"What was it like at the Savoy?" Kate asked, round-eyed at the thought of working in such sophisticated surroundings.

"Hard work. Hot. The restaurant kitchen was above ground so we had windows, but the poor bastards in the grill kitchen worked in the basement and never saw the light of day. We cooked on red-hot, old coal ranges, and there was sawdust on the floor to soak up any spilled fat so you didn't slip on it. You sweated so much that you drank anything that came your way—water and milk as well as your beer allocation—you never stopped swigging liquid."

"Why did you leave the Savoy?" Pagan asked, as they stopped on the path so that Nick could support her more firmly. Her arm was horribly painful, but Nick was taking her mind off it.

"To continue my course." Nick staggered. Pagan was no lightweight. "I'm staying here until the end of the winter season, then I'll be eighteen and have to do my National Service. I hate the whole idea of being in the bloody army, but there's no choice. Anyway, my father says it will teach me leadership, if nothing else. He's very keen on leadership."

"Goodness, do waiters *need* leadership qualities?"

"No, but hotel managers do!"

"That's our school," Kate said, pointing. "Nearly there, Pagan, only a few steps more." She and Nick were now almost totally supporting Pagan as the dirty little group staggered up to the front door.

Nick blushed, then said apologetically, "Look, I know you think Judy was ungrateful but you've no idea how hard things are for her. She's here alone and she's only fifteen. Why don't we meet at the Chesa for tea on Sunday, then she can thank you properly as I'm sure she wants to. . . . And—and, I'd like it too."

Pagan nodded as carefully he released his hold, said goodbye, then hurried down the street. She waited until he turned the corner, then gave a little groan and fell to the ground.

Pagan was propped up in bed eating the last chocolate eclair with her right hand; her left hand was bandaged and her arm was in a sling. Kate was painting her toes bright orange.

"I can't, *can't* bear it," Pagan groaned.

Kate looked up anxiously. "Is the pain still awful?"

"No, I can't feel a thing after that injection. What I can't bear is that Paul carried me upstairs and I never knew about it! You wouldn't lie to me, Kate; he really did pick me up in his strong arms and hold me to his manly chest and . . ."

" . . . No, he didn't," said Kate. "No normal man could carry *you* upstairs like that. He *staggered* up with you. I was afraid he might fall backward on Matron and me."

Pagan gave a voluptuous sigh of regret. Paul was the headmaster's chauffeur and the unofficial school heartthrob. All the girls were fascinated by his olive face, his slanting black eyes, his sleek dark hair and his erect tight-buttocked bullfighter's stance.

"Tell me again what happened," Pagan begged, as Kate dabbed Oriental Orange on her big toe.

"You were too heavy for me to drag out of the gutter so I rushed inside. Paul was leaning against the hall table with his arms crossed and his cap in one hand—waiting for old Chardin to appear, I suppose. As soon as I explained what had happened, he dashed outside, flung his cap on the pavement and put his arms around you—you made his uniform absolutely filthy, by the way—heaved you over his left shoulder in a sort of fireman's lift, with one arm around your back and the other around your orange satin bottom, then he carried you straight into Chardin's study without knocking and lowered you onto the sofa and knelt by you and lifted your eyelid and . . . I've already told you the next bit."

"Again."

"Then he felt under . . . he pulled your sweater up and yelled at me to fetch Matron and telephone for a doctor, but I was rooted to the ground." Kate giggled. "I suppose he was checking your heartbeat; he didn't seem to *notice* you weren't wearing a bra. Anyway, I rushed off and got Matron, and when we came in your sweater was down again and you were whispering, 'Where am I?' just the way you're supposed to . . ."

Suddenly the door crashed open and the Swedish matron stomped in, followed by the school porter dragging an old pigskin suitcase. Behind him stood a plump girl wearing a navy coat. Her brown eyes looked anxious as she smiled. She had buck teeth.

Matron scowled. "It's forbidden to sit on the beds. It's forbidden to eat in your rooms. It's forbidden to apply nail polish anywhere except in the bathroom." She turned on her heels and left.

"Bitch," said Pagan. *"Parlez-vous anglais?"*

"A little, but I am French and come here to learn English," the new girl said. "I am Maxine Pascale."

"But *nobody* learns English here. Or French, come to that," exclaimed Pagan. "You'll see. The English and American girls talk English, the South Americans speak Spanish, the Italians yell nonstop Italian and the Germans bark in German. *Nobody* speaks French, except one Greek girl, and that's because nobody else speaks Greek. *Mais nous pouvons practiquer sur vous.*" Pagan's French was atrocious, as if to prove she was right.

"No, I shall only speak English with you," the new girl said firmly, with a smile. She lifted her suitcase onto the bed and started to unpack, carefully pulling out and smoothing the many sheets of crisp white tissue that lay between each garment. It was more like a trousseau than a set of school-girl's clothes, and as Maxine hung them up, the girls could see the Christian Dior label.

"I say, you must be rich!" gasped Pagan. "They're divine!"

"No, I'm not rich," Maxine said. "But I *am* lucky. I have an aunt."

And indeed, Maxine's Aunt Hortense, who had made a good but childless marriage, was a shrewd realist. In her opinion there was no point in spending money on a trousseau *after* one had landed a man. Chic clothes were needed to set a girl up so she could make the best possible marriage. It was an investment in a girl's future.

So she had swept Maxine and her mother into the Dior salon, and eventually—Maxine was not consulted—the two older women decided on a midnight-blue wool coat with two huge buttons that glowed like sapphires; next, they chose a cocktail dress in blue satin covered in black Chantilly lace and a simple blue wool town suit with an alternative pleated skirt *pour le weekend* in blue and cream tartan. They also picked an apricot wool dress that flared tactfully over Maxine's ample hips, and their final choice was a floor-length, strapless gown in pale-blue silk taffeta with a little matching jacket. All the waists were tightly nipped in, all the skirts were enormous; all the garments were exquisitely stitched and fitted. It had taken three weeks to make them, with five fittings each, and Maxine had felt faint when she heard that the price of the five outfits was 750,000 francs. She would never dare to wear them, she had thought.

The girls missed tea because—with a secret view to future borrowing—Kate was trying on every stitch that Maxine had brought with her, and even though Pagan couldn't try them on because her arm was in plaster of paris, she hopped around, thrilled by the glamorous clothes. Maxine was impressed by Pagan's height, her hair and her exuberant high spirits. "I say, Kate, *silver high heels!* Oh, Maxine, your feet are sparrow-size, dammit," she cried. Kate burrowed into the suitcase, sending tissue paper flying. "Look, Kate, that's a real crepe de chine blouse—and a lace nightgown! Y'know clothes are still rationed in England, Maxine. There's nothing so ravishing as these! Oh, how I *long* for something pretty!"

Not fooled by this, Maxine could see that Pagan was used to getting what she wanted. How strange that she should be a friend of Kate, who seemed so quiet and ordinary-looking, even mousy despite the purple toes. They were obviously fond of each other, and Maxine quickly found out that they had been together at school in London since they were ten. That was not the only reason that Kate and Pagan were friends. What the two girls had in common and what had brought them together originally was that they were both, in different ways, outsiders. Kate, because her father was so very obviously so very rich, and Pagan because she had been brought up to live a life that no longer existed. Her world of privilege had disappeared forever, together with the wrought-iron gates of the manor which—like the saucepans in the mining cottages—had been melted down to make guns in 1940.

Because her speech and her background were so different from the middle-class students at St. Paul's, Pagan tended to sound arrogant without meaning to do so. And even in a school with few uniform rules, she dressed in a most peculiar fashion. No store-bought clothes ever fitted Pagan, who was five foot ten and boyish in build. During the war, when clothes were severely rationed and brides pooled their year's clothing coupons in order to buy one wedding dress for eight of them to wear, everyone in Britain wore their clothes until they fell to pieces and made new dresses out of old tablecloths, sheets and curtains.

Inspired by the general example, Pagan went up to the attic and unpacked the clothes of her dead father. First she wore his cashmere pullovers and his silk scarves with a pair of jodhpurs; then she purloined his silk shirts, which she belted and wore as dresses, and Mrs. Hocken in the village turned a white-dotted navy silk. Charvet dressing gown into "a best dress" for Sunday. Then Pagan plundered some of the other older trunks in the attic: she was never able to get into her grandmother's tiny-waisted silk dress, but she wore lace blouses that were a hundred years old with similarly ancient skirts of bottle-green velvet or dark blue silk. Soon she acquired a reputation not only for eccentric opinions but also for eccentric clothes, but because of her height, her slimness and her wonderful mahogany hair, Pagan always looked carelessly marvelous.

L'Hirondelle supper gong was rung at seven-thirty. Reluctant to leave Maxine's wonderful wardrobe, but very hungry, the three girls joined the human stream of flying hair, bouncing breasts and perceptible underarm odor as all the pupils clattered downstairs to the dining room, where old portraits hung in heavy gilt frames and brass Dutch chandeliers were suspended from dark ceiling beams above long oak tables. Above the noise, Maxine asked about the school routine.

"Morning bell at seven, breakfast at seven-thirty, lessons from eight to twelve," Pagan mumbled, as Kate cut her lambchop into little pieces. "Voluntary sport from two to four-thirty and after that, study time 'til six-thirty. Then supper and lights out at ten. No work over the weekend. Church optional. *Qu'est-ce que tu penses du nourriture de l'école?*"

"It is revolting," said Maxine with deep sincerity, "like your French."

"Never mind, Monsieur Chardin told my mother that my accent was excellent," said Pagan cheerfully. "Would you please undo the top button of my pedal pushers, Kate. . . . Have you met the headmaster yet? No? Well, he's a common little creep. Obsequious and oily, you'll see. In London he stayed at Claridge's and I went along to visit him with Mama. He was wearing a canary pullover and a big-checked suit that no Englishman would be seen dead in, especially not in town. I noticed that he didn't even *read* my school reports. Just as well, since they were absolutely grim. . . . I got the feeling that Chardin was fishing for any pupils he could *get*. He's obviously in it just for the money, don't you think, Kate?"

Kate nodded. She was slowly eating a chocolate biscuit. She could make one biscuit last two hours, nibbling nonstop at a steady pace, like a rat at a corpse.

Pagan said, adjusting her sling, "I'm rather surprised my mother sent me here, except it *is* supposed to be the best school in Switzerland and my grandfather's paying the bill, not her."

She wiped a bit of bread around her plate. "Also, dammit, I certainly *need* polishing up. I mean, I'm not good at being tidy or wearing clothes or knowing what to say to people at parties or doing *any* of the things that grown-up girls do."

Kate said, "We've been here a week and so far we've hardly seen Chardin; his apartment is on the other side of the chalet and it has a different front door. He seems to live an entirely separate life from the school. I'm certain he has better meals than *we* do, because you can sometimes smell things like roast duck coming out of the kitchen. *Not* my idea of a headmaster!"

"A couple of Brazilian girls have already been here a year and they say he's got a fearful temper," Pagan added. "But there's only one thing he really *explodes* about, and that's if you get out of school at night. Apparently *he* has hysterics—and *you're* expelled!"

There was an awed silence. Being expelled was a fate worse than death. The shame would pursue you through your whole life.

After supper, half the school squeezed into Kate's bedroom to gaze at Maxine's wardrobe until lights out. Immediately after Matron's inspection to check that all girls were in and all lights were out, Pagan crept into the adjoining bedroom, clutching around her, like an overweight redskin, the bulky, feather-filled quilt that is the only covering on Swiss beds. Pagan climbed onto the end of Kate's bed and the three girls whispered until well after midnight. Maxine told them about her three younger brothers and sisters in Paris. Kate, who like Pagan was an only child, thought that a big family sounded like fun, but Maxine's school in Paris, on the other hand, didn't sound like fun at all.

"We also had hours and hours of homework at St. Paul's," said Pagan. "Each assignment was supposed to take you only twenty minutes, and at the bottom of your work you were supposed to put how long it took you, so naturally everybody lied because they didn't want to look dumb. If your essay on Greek architecture took three hours, you put down twenty-five minutes. All Paulinas are liars, and they all have weak eyes because they do so much of their work by flashlight in bed."

"My mother complained to the high mistress once," said Kate, "and she sat Mummy in a little low chair opposite her huge commanding throne and said in her low boom, 'Of *course* Kate must not work in bed, she must work in her lunch hour or *leave* if she cannot keep up.' "

"The high mistress was a huge, commanding figure. She moved like a ship. You couldn't believe she had legs," said Pagan. "She wore pince-nez and her hair in a gray bun and very old-fashioned orange sweaters with no bra; you could see but you didn't dare notice. Somebody described her as God in drag. She thundered at us in a low majestic voice. I once came second in a reading competition simply by mimicking her. I was afraid I'd get ticked off for insolence, but nobody *noticed.* They said I showed promise."

"Why did your mother send you to that school if she was frightened of the headmistress?" asked Maxine.

"Not headmistress," said Kate, "*high* mistress. I went because my father wanted me to have . . . the best."

* * *

Kate's father had wanted her to have the sort of education he hadn't had himself. She had been sent to St. Paul's because Kate's father had read that royalty went there. Kate's father always wanted the best, so Kate's mother always asked for it, even when shopping. When she was buying plums she would ask the grocer, "Which are the best?" When she was buying chairs she would ask, "Which are the best?" When she was buying a dress she could never decide which one suited her, so she always asked the assistant, "Which is the best?" and naturally the assistant chose the most expensive, which was all right, because the more things cost, the better they were.

Kate's mother was also influenced by royalty, and dressed like the Queen. Kate's quiet, ladylike clothes came from Debenham & Freebody because the little Princesses' clothes were bought there and "By Appointment to Her Majesty" was printed on their boxes. Kate hated the place, with its pillared, echoing marble halls and the ancient, exquisitely polite assistants, all gentlewomen who had known better days. She would have preferred to shop at Selfridge, like the other girls, for the cheap cotton copies of the New Look.

Kate's mother also had the best at their home, Greenways. The antiques were expensive, but somehow the ornately carved chairs, the brocade sofas and heavy-fringed, satin curtains failed to achieve the casual look of elegance of Pagan's mother's flat in Kensington, where the simple furniture had come up from their country house and every piece was interesting and well proportioned, if a bit battered. Some of the china was chipped, but if your family had been using it for a hundred and fifty years, it would be, wouldn't it?

Kate hated the smug perfection of Greenways. On either side of the drive, the trees and foliage were spotlit at night; Kate's father thought this looked stylish and set off the pillared porch. Inside, on the ground floor, the chairs, sofas and tables were too big, the lampshades and pictures too small; the dining room was paneled in plastic wood, and the chandelier consisted of a circle of fake candles with little fake parchment hats. Upstairs, the bedrooms were surprisingly stark. After all, nobody ever went upstairs except to sleep, so Kate's father saw no point in wasting money there.

Kate was driven to school in her father's Rolls-Royce. The chauffeured car set Kate apart from her classmates. *They* didn't have a different dress for each day of the week, and *they* traveled to school by bus or on the underground. Kate always made the chauffeur stop the Rolls at the end of the road and walked the rest of the way to school. This subterfuge was general knowledge, but her fellow schoolgirls thought it right and proper that she should avoid showing off; showing off was a major school crime.

Unfortunately, Kate's father showed off rather a lot. When her schoolfriends came to the house he would show them his cars and ask them to guess how much money he'd made last year or what he had bought last week. Afterward, he would have a little chat with Kate and tell her which of her friends he preferred. Eventually Kate stopped asking people home. She started to spend her free time and eat her lunch with Pagan, who was also a loner because she was considered odd by the other girls. It was unusual for a girl of Pagan's age from a decent family to be so careless of her appearance or to be so indifferent to what people thought about her. For her part, Pagan made it clear that she considered the conscientious, hardworking girls of St. Paul's as boring as riding around a dusty London park instead of cantering over the Cornish moors, hair streaking behind her in the salty wind.

Kate's father showered invitations on Pagan and her mother—who was obviously "top drawer"—and once he invited them on a cruise to Majorca (he pronounced the j as in jug), although the invitation was politely declined. Kate knew why her father liked Pagan's mother. Kate knew her father wanted a good marriage for her, perhaps even a title: he didn't know how he was going to manage it, but after all he had the wherewithal, and he could see that Pagan's mother knew the sort of people who had titles and she also knew "the done thing." The reason Kate had been sent to l'Hirondelle was because Pagan was going. If a Swiss finishing school was "the done thing," then Kate had to do it.

Pagan teased Kate about her father's secret hopes. "When you're a marchioness, you'd better not ask the way to the loo, you'd better say bathroom."

"What does it matter, so long as it's clear where I want to go?" asked Kate crossly, but secretly she read Nancy Mitford's novels and learned what established you as "U" (or Upper Class), as opposed to "non-U." Kate said "writing paper," not "notepaper," "napkin," not "serviette," and offered visitors "a glass of sherry," not "a sherry." She also practiced altering her accent to a clipped, yet languid, drawl, but she soon realized that it was hopeless. The upper classes *seemed* to speak the King's English, but in fact they spoke a secret language full of subtle references you could learn only in the cradle. In "U" circles there was only one thing worse than not knowing these subtleties and that was *pretending* to know them, aping your betters. One little slip and this was apparent: all you had to do was to refer to the Royal Yacht Squadron as the Royal Yacht Club *once*, or hang family photographs on the walls instead of propping them on side-tables in silver frames from Asprey, and you were *doomed.*

Sometimes Kate stayed overnight with Pagan, who lived in Kensington, near St. Paul's—although after that awful Friday she always found an excuse not to do so. For some reason Kate always felt guilty when she remembered that November weekend.

Pagan lived in an apartment on the top floor of a once-elegant, now slightly seedy house on Ennismore Gardens. They had been playing hockey all afternoon and Kate was sweaty, so she decided to take a bath while Pagan went out to do an errand for her mother. Kate was naked and about to step into the bath when the door opened and Pagan's mother entered, wrapped in a white terry robe. Somehow Kate knew her presence was not an accident and she was nervous. Instead of apologizing and backing out—as one would expect—Mrs. Trelawney moved toward her, and Kate grabbed a towel as her hostess smiled, droplets of steam beading her scarlet lips. As she came closer, Kate could distinguish the aroma of gin.

"*What* lovely little breasts," said Mrs. Trelawney in a husky voice. "A girl's body is so much more *delicate* than a boy's, don't you think? *Most* men don't appreciate that, of course. They don't appreciate the exquisite *tenderness* of the breasts, the nipples."

Clutching her towel around her, Kate backed into the small space against the window, between the washbasin and the lavatory, where she was effectively trapped. "I expect you've noticed . . . " and suddenly she reached out with one manicured hand and squeezed Kate's nipple.

Kate was frozen with horror, unable to move. To her bewilderment and mortification she felt a sharp thrill in her groin. She could see the pores of Mrs. Trelawney's nose, the drooping, fleshy folds above her eyes, black-beaded with mascara. Then Mrs. Trelawney closed in on her, clutching Kate with one hand while she tried to pull away the towel with the other. She bent down so Kate could see the white line where her hair was parted. Her tongue moved swiftly, like a snake's, toward Kate's nipple, while her fingers slipped into Kate's crotch with a strength that was at once painful and exciting. For a few moments Kate felt erotically hypnotized, then her knees buckled and she slid to the floor, pushing the woman away. Gasping, she brought one knee up to her chin and prepared to kick if Mrs. Trelawney pounced again. Kate said nothing, but her eyes glittered with fear and anger.

Mrs. Trelawney got the message. She seldom made a mistake, but when she did, she knew how to retreat.

Mrs. Trelawney backed away. "I'll leave you to bathe in peace," she said in her soothing, perfect-hostess voice as if nothing had happened, and left the room.

Kate leaped into the bath and sat in it, shaking. She felt safe there and wouldn't come out until the water was cold. She spent the rest of the weekend trying to avoid being alone with Pagan's mother, and it was months before she could be persuaded to visit their home again. When she did, Mrs. Trelawney behaved so normally that Kate was tempted to think she'd imagined the scene. Could she have been mistaken?

That unfortunate few minutes was destined to have a far-reaching effect on Kate's future love life, when in the passionate embrace of a man, she felt almost unbearable sexual excitement—and then fear, repulsion and shame.

CHAPTER 3

THE NOISE OF a piano, the chink of china, an occasional clear laugh sounded above the voices in the Great Hall of the Imperial. People had been drifting in since four o'clock for tea or cocktails: under the serene gaze of an oil-painted Madonna the bridge hostess was checking her list, and at the backgammon board the first dice rattled. In one corner Prince Aly Khan was earnestly whispering into the ear of a raven-haired South American girl. Beyond him, the young, slim Elizabeth Taylor reached for her fourth slice of sacher torte.

Surrounded by a small group of impassive henchmen, Aristotle Onassis swung through the swing doors, followed by a small, blonde young woman who clutched a pile of books under one arm. It was a fatal entrance for a girl who was trying to avoid being seen, because the heads of the concierge, the headwaiter and the maître d'hôtel all turned to make sure that one of the richest men in the world was being suitably attended. Behind him, Judy Jordan tried to look like a typical hotel guest as she headed for the elevator, walking rather fast and looking straight ahead as she approached the hall porter's desk. She wore a pleated tartan skirt, a white sweater that buttoned down the back, white socks pulled to midcalf, and saddle oxfords that sank into the thick carpet. Nearly there. Fifteen more steps . . . ten . . . five . . . damn! A group of Arab bodyguards had suddenly appeared on either side of the elevator. Judy caught a glimpse of the neat, olive-skinned neck of a dark, slim young man who entered the elevator followed by an aide-de-camp in Western military uniform. For security reasons, nobody was allowed to travel in the elevator with Prince Abdullah or any other member of the Sydonian royal family, which kept two permanent suites at the Imperial while the eighteen-year-old Prince was at Le Mornay.

As Judy changed direction and headed for the stairs she felt a heavy hand on her shoulder. "*Fraulein*," hissed the concierge, "you have no business to be in the Great Hall; you are supposed to use the servants' staircase; you're not even permanent staff. This is the last warning you get before dismissal."

"I'm sorry, but they kept us late at the language laboratory and I've got to change before going on duty at the Chesa. I was trying to save time."

"No excuse is an excuse at the Imperial. Now get to the backstairs."

So instead of taking the elevator to the sixth floor, Judy had to plod up a hundred and twenty-two steps, then run the last two flights to the sloping attic under the roof that was subdivided by thin partitions into shoebox cubicles for the staff.

She flung her books on the gray blanket and wriggled into the costume that she had to wear as a waitress in the Chesa coffee shop, which was attached to the hotel. Three more days until her free Sunday, she thought, as she pulled the drawstring of the embroidered white lace blouse, dived into the red dirndl skirt and tightened the strings of the black lace corselet. Still pulling the black laces, she ran to the end of the corridor, knocked at a door and without waiting for an answer rushed in.

Nick was lying on the iron bed. His white shirt-sleeves were rolled up, his black trouser legs were crossed and a toe poked through one of his gray socks. "The year 1928 was almost as good as 1945," he said. "An exceptional vintage for Medoc, Graves, St. Emilion and Pomerol, not quite so good for the dry white Bordeaux wines, but excellent for the Sauternes." He threw his textbook down. "Vintner's exam next Tuesday. Got time to test me on the vintages, Judy?"

"Not a hope, Nick. I'm late. I only looked in to ask if you could scrounge me something to eat from the kitchen in case I don't get a chance."

"You're too young to starve," he said, swinging his legs off the bed and sitting up. "Promise to spend Sunday with me, and in my plastic-lined waiters' pockets I'll steal a meal that will last you three days."

"It's a deal. I'll test you on the vintages then."

"Okay. I'll drop into the Chesa later for a cup of coffee before going on duty. Anything to catch another glimpse of you." She blew him a kiss in reply, then dashed out, heading for the hundred and twenty-two steps down to the coffee shop.

In spite of her abundant physical energy Judy felt very tired—in fact, she would have preferred to stay in bed on Sunday. This was only her fourth month in Switzerland but already she felt exhausted all the time. The hours of the Gstaad Language Laboratory were from eight in the morning until three-thirty in the afternoon and she did her homework in the hour allowed for lunch. Then until one in the morning, six days a week, she worked as a waitress at the Chesa coffee shop with only a short break for a snack. There were no union regulations in Switzerland, but no working permit problems either. She had been lucky to get the job. Pastor Hentzen had arranged it at the start of the summer season when the hotel had needed every pair of hands it could get. She had been taken on for a couple of months, then retained, at a wage far lower than any of the other waitresses. It was hardly enough to pay her laundry bill, but she got bed and board, which was all that mattered.

Maxine, Kate and Pagan were already sitting in the Chesa with a fourth girl who had been invited for one reason only—she had a brother at Le Mornay. However, Pagan had already decided half an hour ago that if Nigel was anything like his silly cow of a sister, there was no point in getting to know him.

"Daddy says it's really *changed* Nigel, he's made *unbelievably* good contacts." Francesca droned on, "Daddy says he looks upon the fees as a good investment because he wants Nigel to have an *international* outlook and at Le Mornay you only meet people with money and names. All the oil children go there, you know. It doesn't look like a school. It's in an old castle on Lac Leman." She bit into a cream cake. "They can go into Geneva or Lausanne on their evenings off, and they're allowed away for the weekend if their parents give permission." Francesca took another *tête de nègre*. "They have plenty of work to do, but they're not cooped in, like us Hirondelles. And of course the boys can come to the Saturday night dances. Every Saturday night during the winter a public dance is held in one of the hotels, you know, although Nigel only goes to the *smart* ones at the Imperial or the Palace."

"We've never been to a dance," Kate said. "In fact, we can't dance."

"Except for the polka and the Highland fling—we learned those at school," Pagan amended.

Boys, dances, grand hotels, it was all tremendously thrilling and alarming. Lucky, lucky Francesca to have an older brother, they thought.

"When are the Le Mornay boys coming here?"

"They're in Gstaad for three months, from January to March. Mummy says it's *so* well planned—after the Christmas holiday Nigel's trunk is simply sent to Gstaad instead of Roue."

"That reminds me," Pagan said, lying quickly, "Matron asked me to tell you to go to the post office, Francesca. There's a parcel waiting there for you with three francs to pay on it."

Francesca squealed in anticipation, paid her bill and rushed off.

"I couldn't stand much more of her," Pagan said loudly.

"Neither could I," said the tiny waitress. Pagan turned around and suddenly realized that the girl in the traditional Swiss costume was the girl she had rescued on the mountain. Her short blonde hair looked as if it had been hacked with a pair of kitchen scissors, which it had. Gravely she said, "You saved my life . . ."

" . . . I'm glad you realize that!" snapped Kate.

" . . . and you've broken your arm!"

"No, only sprained the shoulder," said Pagan. "Are *you* all right?"

"Hardly a scratch, but I was really frightened. My knees wobbled for hours afterward. I don't know what to say except thank you. I know I shouldn't have rushed off . . ."

"It's okay, Nick explained," Pagan said.

"*You* may be all right," Kate snapped, "but Pagan wasn't. She fainted, and her poor hand as well as her shoulder were torn to bits. She was kept in bed for two days."

"Shut up, Kate, what's the point of making her feel guilty? After all, she didn't fall off the cliff on purpose."

"I didn't even fall off. The ground gave way beneath me. But I was almost more worried about being late on duty than ending up a corpse."

"Well, let's forget it," said Pagan, embarrassed. "Hey, look who's arrived!"

She waved to Nick, who had just opened the heavy carved oaken door. He waved back, ducking his head to pass under a low beam, blackened by hundreds of years of smoke from the hearth. The Chesa was older than the rest of the hotel and had once been a seventeenth-century farmhouse, with walls as thick as an arm's length.

"I can't talk anymore," said Judy, "but Nick and I are off on Sundays and we'd love to meet you properly—and thank you properly. And I've got something for you."

She hastily refilled the cups with hot chocolate and dashed off with her tray as Nick gazed after her, clearly besotted.

The following Sunday afternoon the Chesa door burst open and a blast of cold air came in with Judy, followed by Nick. She was wearing her Sunday uniform of blue jeans rolled up to midcalf, saddle oxfords, white socks and an American navy pea jacket. She looked around, then beamed when she saw the girls.

"Hi there!" she called. She presented Pagan with a large gift-wrapped box tied with white satin ribbon. Inside was a pair of scarlet knitted knee socks with leather soles. Pagan was delighted. "They match my red silk sling," she said, insisting that Kate put them on her immediately.

Maxine turned to Judy. "Why did your parents send you to the language laboratory and not one of the finishing schools?"

"They didn't send me anywhere. I didn't tell them I was entering for the exchange scholarship, because I never thought I'd win it—and when I did my mom was furious. She thought that fifteen was too young to leave home and anyway she can't understand why I want to learn foreign languages, but our minister persuaded her that I ought to use the talent that the good Lord gave me," she grinned. "The pastor of the Lutheran church here is supposed to keep an eye on me. He seems to think I'm going to be an African missionary so I'll need French and German for the heathens of the Belgian Congo and East Africa."

"And aren't you?" Maxine carefully smoothed the skirt of her best tangerine dress, which she was wearing because Nick was, after all, twenty-five percent her date.

"No, I'm going to Paris," said Judy in a firm voice.

"Alone? Will your parents let you go alone?"

"They won't know. I'll tell them when I get there after I've got a job. Otherwise they might say no," Judy explained.

There was an awed silence from the three girls around the table who had never thought about the future, never planned further ahead than the next holiday. As in a child's coloring book, everything in the picture of their future life was clear and simple and the responsibility of someone else. Eternal bliss awaited each of them beyond the altar, and the only bit that hadn't been filled in was Prince Charming's face. To the Hirondelles, Judy's work sounded *real*, as opposed to chopping onions for the cookery mademoiselle or half-heartedly typing, "Please believe in my most distinguished sentiments" at the bottom of a business letter copied from a textbook.

Eagerly, Kate questioned Judy about the language lab.

"Yes, the courses really *are* concentrated," Judy answered, "and it's just as well, because I've only got one year to learn fluent French and German. All the other students are in just as much of a hurry. They're all older than me, *really* old—some of them are over thirty! If they need an extra language for business, they fly into Gstaad from all over the world and sit all day in little booths with earphones. My German isn't yet good enough for conversation. I shouldn't really talk to Nick at all, I suppose. I should be practicing German instead."

Nick looked at her fondly. "We hardly get any time to talk as it is. We only get to our bedrooms to sleep. I start at seven laying tables for breakfast, then we work in the restaurant straight through until three in the afternoon. Then there's a break until six-thirty and we're back in the restaurant until eleven. Unless there's a function, in which case we work until two in the morning and *still* get up at seven."

"We're lucky to have such good sleeping quarters here," Judy said. "The student waiters who are on loan from the Lausanne Palace say that there it's five to a room under the roof, and at the Palace Saint Moritz I hear that the temporary staff have to sleep in the basement."

"Goodness, I feel as if l'Hirondelle is a rest cure," said Pagan, who rather enjoyed the slack tedium of the school routine—unlike Kate, who was exasperated by the laziness and boredom of the lessons.

After that meeting, Judy always saved a table at the Chesa for the girls on Wednesday afternoon when they each took two hours to drink one expensive cup of chocolate, and Nick took them all out for tea on Sunday afternoons when they ate their heads off.

Judy's obvious independence immediately fascinated the other three girls, who envied her her energy, her stamina and her cheerfulness, not realizing that Judy had to push herself every morning to survive the drudgery of her day. Reluctantly, the girls followed their school timetable, but Judy set her own harsh timetable, and she stuck to it grimly. The Hirondelles were also intrigued by the forceful way that Judy spoke. She said exactly what she thought, whereas the three more privileged girls had been brought up to hide their feelings and not express their own wishes and opinions.

The girls quickly realized that while Nick was besotted with Judy to the exclusion of anyone else, here was the older brother they had all longed for—to admire them, to protect them, to tease them, to provide them with introductions to other boys and to pay for their outings. Nick was safe. He wasn't part of the sexual success-or-failure, scalp-collecting game, so the three Hirondelle girls instinctively developed a special way of flirting with Nick. They could be outrageously provocative with Nick with no fear of the consequences; they could practice their act with a safety net, as it were.

Nick was flattered and delighted with his new role as escort to three attractive but undemanding girls. Brought up in the stone-cold confines of the traditional British boarding school, a timid child, living in the country, he hadn't had much chance to meet girls, attractive or otherwise. But he had beautiful manners and once his blushing was under control, he was as proud as a pasha when escorting the four of them. Playing such an important part in what the other girls at l'Hirondelle enviously christened "the Set" also meant that Nick soon lost the bashfulness of an only child and the agonized self-doubt of a British teenage male.

The girls knew that they would eventually meet other boys once the weekly dances started in mid-November, but despite Nick, they were sometimes restless and thirsty for adventure.

"Maybe we could sneak out the back door one night and go to some divine nightclub, somewhere like the Gringo," Pagan said with a yawn one Sunday afternoon, after an enormous banana split.

Nick looked up sharply and brushed his black hair back from his face. "You'd better be careful, you know. You'll get expelled if you're caught . . . and there's something else." He blushed. "Something nasty. You know old Chardin's driver, Paul?"

"Yes, the chauffeur," said Kate.

"No he's a *driver*," Pagan corrected. "Unless you're speaking French, a chauffeur is someone you hire for the evening. A driver is in your permanent employ."

"Whatever you call it, you know what I mean. Well, Chardin is a . . . er . . . homosexual and his . . . er . . . *friend* is Paul. I know it's true because Paul is also carrying on behind Chardin's back with one of the chefs at the Imperial." He turned even pinker. "The next bit is just a strong rumor, but I've heard it several times. You *all* know that what Chardin really loves is money."

Everyone nodded.

"Well, it's rumored around town that if a girl is caught outside the school with a boy, she's immediately expelled—unless her father pays hush money to avoid the disgrace. The girl might just have been out for a lark, nothing serious, but Chardin exaggerates to parents over the long-distance telephone. It's always her word against Chardin's, and the girl has to admit that she got out, so the parents usually believe the worst and pay up."

"I can't believe it!"

"How do you know?"

"Do people realize he's homosexual?"

"All the waiters around here know that Chardin's queer," said Nick. "For years he's had handsome male drivers when he doesn't need a driver at all. There's a bar at the back of town called Le Cous Cous—some pretty odd types hang out there—*I* wouldn't walk into the place, I can tell you!"

"But wouldn't he be afraid of being blackmailed?" Pagan asked.

"If the blackmail stories are true, then Chardin is playing a dangerous game, but it isn't as dangerous as it might seem. He picks his victims carefully. And there are plenty to choose from. You don't suppose for one minute that he couldn't *stop* girls from getting out at night if he wanted to, do you? The parents of the girl are always a long way off in another country, and they're rich. Chardin never asks for sums they can't easily afford. I believe the lowest rate is an extra year's tuition. On the whole, the parents can easily afford to pay their way out of a minor scandal, and because they're all from different countries, none of them are in touch with each other, so there's no danger of their meeting up."

The girls hung on his words, fascinated by these awesome, wicked possibilities. "So for heaven's sake be careful," Nick continued. "Just in case any of these rumors are true. I know it's gossip, but I *keep* hearing the same thing on the hotel grapevine. And that's not all. Some fellows say that Paul is bisexual."

There was a pause while Nick explained what bisexual meant. By now he was blushing fiercely and wished he hadn't started, but he was also enjoying this flattering attention. "It's said that if a very rich girl gets out at night and she's caught by Chardin, then she might be . . . deliberately *seduced* by Paul and photographed in . . . er . . . compromising positions. The barman at the Imperial told me that last year the father of one of the Brazilian girls had a few too many and started cursing Chardin. He said he'd flown over only because the headmaster was blackmailing him, and he couldn't go to the police because his daughter was involved and if the scandal leaked out, his wife would never forgive him. . . . He had to protect the family name and his daughter's reputation or she'd never make a good marriage, and so forth. . . . Then he said that he was never going to forgive his daughter for putting him in such a position, because he couldn't risk calling Chardin's bluff. There were photographs of his daughter with Paul."

Nick smiled. "They must have been pretty unusual pictures. He told the barman that he paid thirty-six thousand Swiss francs for them. Cash."

For Pagan, Maxine and Kate, life at l'Hirondelle passed in a charming haze of sentimental naivete. Although disguised in the bodies of women, the pupils were still children. Exuding puppylike exuberance and energy, they giggled and tittered, scampered and shrieked, and were, on the whole, rather silly. Lessons bored them, love fascinated them, passion was what they longed to study and their only ambition was to fall in love. There was a heady air of anticipation as they prepared to be—*women!* Hours were passed with magazine instructions and diagrams in one hand, costly tubes of makeup in the other, as girls decided whether their faces were oval, round or square. Much time was spent discussing, trying on and swapping clothes. All the girls yanked their waists in to minimal with wide elastic belts; they wore low ballet dancer's slippers, huge full skirts and pale pink or blue sweaters with a small strand of small pearls. The bras of the American girls divided their breasts into circular stitched cups that thrust skyward like twin ice cream cones. On their second Saturday, every new, non-American pupil rushed out and bought a French lace bra. After that, the girls endlessly compared their new bouncing breasts, measured them and worried about them. "One of mine's larger than the other. . . ." "Why are mine lower than yours . . . ?" "Serena's got *hairs* on her *nipples*. . . ." "You can get more cleavage in the middle if you stuff socks down the side. . . ." "I wish I had more. . . ." "I wish I had less."

Maxine tried hard to avoid mammary emphasis. She had large, rather low breasts, and she hadn't yet become accustomed to them. They still embarrassed her, so she pushed as much of them as possible under her armpits and gradually acquired a round-shouldered stoop. Nothing that the other girls said could convince Maxine that her splendid protuberances were an asset. She would turn scarlet as soon as she saw a group of workmen in the distance, knowing that when she drew level with them, the men's mesmerized eyes would follow her breasts as she passed. To comfort Maxine, her mother had told her that her *embonpoint* would disappear when she breast-fed her first baby, but the thought of carrying those footballs around for years until they were battened on by a baby that hadn't yet been conceived did nothing to console Maxine, who, when not wearing her expensive Dior clothes, hid under enormous, shapeless sweaters.

Maxine was wearing one of these short woolen shrouds as, one evening, she taught Kate to dance *un slow*. Humming "Slow Boat to China," she grasped Kate as they solemnly shuffled around the narrow space between the two beds. "It's better that there's no space, because that's how it feels in a nightclub," explained Maxine, who had never been to one. None of the three girls had ever had a date with a boy, wouldn't know what to talk about if they did, desperately envied all the girls with older brothers and worried endlessly about where you put your nose when you were kissed.

They talked about such matters every night. After lights out, Pagan would creep from her room, clutching her heavy goosefeather quilt as a wrap, and sit cross-legged on the end of Kate's bed while they discussed all aspects of being a woman. Always it was unanimously agreed that they would dare *all* for true love, which would instantly be recognizable as such. Next, they decided what sort of man they were going to marry and sketched their personal Prince Charming to each other. They discussed what their wedding dress would look like, and then the honeymoon was described. In the cozy darkness they would draw deep breaths and discuss the fascinating mystery that none of them had yet encountered . . . sex. This was invariably romantic and never left you sleeping on the damp patch. They never imagined Prince Charming with an erection and certainly not wearing a rubber.

The universal lack of accurate sexual knowledge in the school was surprising, but all girls at l'Hirondelle lied in their teeth about their sexual experience—which, on the whole, was nil—in order to avoid looking unsophisticated. Hitherto, Kate and Pagan's only sexual experience had been furtively fantasizing about tampons. To date, neither of them had used tampons, but Pagan had stolen the brochure from her mother's box and she and Kate had pored over the perplexing illustrations.

None of them had explored, felt or seen the area between their legs. None of them had heard of masturbation or knew that they had already experienced it. The fourteen-year-old Maxine, bored and wriggling on a chair during Scripture class, thought she had experienced religious ecstasy. Pagan, hunting on a borrowed mount with an unusually high-fronted saddle, had once felt exulted with what she thought was the divine thrill of the chase. Kate had always loved climbing ropes at gym class because of the lovely tickly sort of itch you got when, having pulled yourself up arm-over-arm, you slid down the rope with your legs crossed around it, thighs tensed and descent controlled by your feet acting as brakes. Once she'd had this feeling right at the top of the rope and had hung there swaying, blissfully frozen, unable to move and heedless of the cross, clipped voice of Miss Haydock, the instructress (who was used to girls being frozen on top of the ropes), telling Kate to come down immediately.

Maxine, being French and seventeen—a year older than Kate and Pagan—was their unquestioned and respected authority in sexual matters, especially as she had been *instructed.* Boys were all the same, Maxine's priest had explained, tomcats. They were only after one thing and you weren't to let them get it, because once they had got it, they despised you for letting them get it. Even if a boy swore that he loved you, after getting it he would spurn you (both privately and—worse—in public) because then, obviously, he wouldn't respect you any more. If a really serious boy really loved you, and tried to insist, well he was just testing you—the priest didn't say for what. In some mysterious way a man couldn't control himself, so if he went berserk with sexual passion, it was your fault for being so attractive, which was called "leading him on." This might easily lead to disaster, for then what would you tell your husband on your wedding night? Were you not to save yourself for your husband, the marriage would be a disaster from the start, and therefore your life would be ruined. Because the man could always tell.

It was strange that not one of the girls queried the sexual double standard. They accepted that a boy could be driven uncontrollably mad by passion, but it never crossed their minds that it was understandable if a girl felt the same way. They accepted that setting the sexual limit was the responsibility of the girl, not the boy; it was *her* job to control *his* lust. So girls would learn to chop off their own erotic urge, a behavior pattern was formed, and after years of cutting off their natural feelings, many of these girls later found it difficult to proceed—or even be aroused—*beyond* that permitted sexual cutoff point. Their sexuality had been programmed and warped.

Maxine insisted that Italian girls saved themselves for their husbands and at the same time let a man go all the way by using an alternative route for the journey.

"Ugh! You're inventing it, you revolting creature," said Pagan. "Anyway, *how* can a man tell?"

"If he can't get his thing in, that's proof that you are a virgin," said Maxine, "unless you are very sportive, or ride on the horse or the bicycle or do gymnastics."

Even if you had a serious beau who you thought might metamorphose into a fiancé, there were definite rules of sexual etiquette. Luckily, Maxine knew them all and shared her information after lights-out. "Nothing on the first meeting—the rendezvous," she said with authority, "except a significant look when you say goodbye." There was a pause while they all practiced significant looks in the darkness.

"Then after the second meeting you would permit him to kiss you on the cheek. And the next time, a real kiss at the farewell."

"French kiss, with the tongue?" asked Kate.

"Not until the fourth rendezvous."

Maxine had to admit that she hadn't done it and hurried on to the fifth rendezvous, where, if the boy was serious, you might wish to go to the waist, a category that had two subdivisions: over clothes and under them. Personally, Maxine would never permit either. She intended to be prudent until she was married.

A certain sort of girl allowed the man to go below the waist, in which case the two subdivisions were (1) above and (2) below the underclothes, but with his thing firmly zipped up, you understand.

"But what *happens* under the underclothes?"

"The boy strokes the fur." There was a further silence while in the dark they all furtively stroked their pubic hair and felt nothing.

The seventh stage of wickedness was letting the boy go all the way. Going all the way would be ecstasy, of course, but it would also be dreadfully dangerous.

Considering that every girl in l'Hirondelle was terrified of getting pregnant, it was surprising, when it came to the point, that they all felt a firm, almost religious conviction that pregnancy couldn't be inflicted upon them, especially not the first time. God wouldn't let it happen to you, and anyway, statistics proved it. Unless, of course, you touched . . . the stuff. All the girls were terrified of semen. It only took one microscopic egg, from all those millions, to get you pregnant and the damn things could stay alive for four days, invisibly creeping up your panty legs. So it was better to take no risks at all, and vital for the boy to take a precaution. But how revolting if he used the rubber thing!

"It's called a French lettuce," said Pagan with authority.

"No, it's called a *capot anglais*," corrected Maxine coldly.

Whatever it was called, it led to another etiquette problem. Did you look away while he was putting it on? Did you pretend not to notice? Or did he put it on before he arrived? In which case it would *prove* that he had not been carried away by your beauty, but that he'd really meant to do it all along. Anyway, how was it put on? "I think they smooth it on when the thing is pointing upward," said Pagan, "like a glove with only one finger."

Not very romantic, they thought. But they had to admit it was better than being pregnant. Being pregnant was, well, inconceivable. Any unfortunate girls at whom fate pointed the finger had to sit in a scalding hot bath and drink a whole bottle of neat gin. A true friend would sit beside her in the steam to cheer her up, stop her fainting, drowning or making loud drunken noises that might be heard by Matron. Alternatively, you had to find a relatively large sum of money and visit an old woman in a back street, who would lay you out like a plucked chicken and pull your legs apart on her grubby kitchen table. Then, *without washing her hands*, she would push a knitting needle up you. If you were rich you could go to a private clinic and have an anesthetic, and the knitting needle would be made of stainless steel and sterilized and everybody would pretend that you were having your appendix out.

Kate woke before the bell sounded and immediately realized that something odd had happened overnight. The street sounds were muffled and the room seemed unusually light. She dashed to open the window and push aside the lace curtain. The frost pressed white flowers against the glass. Barefoot in her blue nightgown, she leaned out. The trees were sprinkled with snow, the roofs of the chalets below were covered with thick white blankets that glistened in the early sun, the turrets of the Imperial Hotel shone white like a child's frosted birthday cake. Beyond the town, the pine forests looked ghostly, like gray lace.

Snow fell heavily for several nights and in a week the little town was transformed. The ski-rental shop hardly ever closed; skiers slid along the streets; children wrapped like bulky parcels pulled little colored sleighs, the milk was delivered by dog sleigh and the local stable immediately brought out its magnificent horse-drawn sleighs. It was, at last, The Season.

Overnight a new elite appeared. Any man who could ski well was attractive, and any man who couldn't, wasn't. Men who had spent the summer being ignored as farm laborers and bricklayers suddenly became gods in the form of ski instructors. Every plumber's winter hope was to marry one of the heiresses from the finishing schools, consequently the girls were given preferential treatment in ski class and a great deal more attention than they deserved. The suntanned, lithe instructors, in their red wool hats and sweaters, captured every girlish heart as they coaxed, scolded and helped the stragglers, swooping back and forth with effortless grace that every girl envied, for to ski well was the ultimate social distinction.

Also worshiped, but from a greater distance, was the Swiss ski team, in training at Gstaad. The merits of the four team members and two reserves were endlessly discussed, but the team members themselves had time for nothing except training. They lived in a chalet on the edge of the town and were hardly ever seen. Which, of course, made them even more attractive.

* * *

One morning at breakfast, Pagan interrupted the now nonstop speculation as to what would happen next Saturday at the first dance of the season. She looked up from a rare letter from her mother. "Guess what?" she asked. "My mother knows Nick's father. I told her about him in my last letter and she thinks he might have been at Eton with my cousin Toby. She says that if his surname is Cliffe with an 'e,' then he's Sir Walter Cliffe's son and he's going to inherit an enormous family hotel business."

"It *can't* be the same or he would have mentioned it," said Kate.

"If he's Sir Walter Cliffe's son then he certainly *wouldn't* have mentioned it," Pagan said, adding for Maxine's benefit, "It's British understatement, you see."

Later, in the cloakroom of the Chesa, they told Judy, who said, "No kidding! He's never said anything to *me* about it. I thought he was learning to be a waiter so he could *be* a waiter." They went back to their table. Nick edged his way over to them through tightly packed tables. To the embarrassment of the other girls Judy immediately pounced on him.

"Is it true that you're going to inherit the Cliffe hotel business one day?"

Nick blushed. To give himself time to think he pushed his hair back from his face, then stammered, "Well, yes—I'll have to *run* it, but it won't actually be mine; it's in a family trust. It'll be my job to look after it . . . for the family."

"Does that mean you're rich?" Judy asked. There was a pause.

"I'm not poor," Nick admitted unhappily, "but I'm going to have a lot of responsibility." With unusual firmness he added, "Now d'you mind very much if we don't discuss it any more?"

Later, in the cloakroom, Maxine turned to Judy and beamed. "Well, now you know about Nick, this will be the end of Jim in Virginia, I suppose?"

"Why?" asked Judy, astonished.

"Well, Nick is obviously mad about you. And it would be a very good proposition, no?" Maxine asked.

Judy laughed. "Look I'm not sixteen yet. I don't intend to get married to *anyone* now, let alone a guy I'm not in love with. I promised my mother I wouldn't even go *out* with a boy while I was here, and it was only because of that that she allowed me to come. I think it was a sensible promise, and I'm going to keep it. I know it must seem crazy to you rich kids, but *I've* got to earn my living. It's hard keeping up with the French classes as well as the German ones, and working as a waitress doesn't make studying any easier. But I'll only get this one chance, so I'm grabbing it. There'll be men around for the rest of my life. They can wait." She hesitated, then admitted, "If you want to know the truth, I don't *have* any beau at home. Jim in Virginia doesn't exist. He's just a smoke screen that I tell other guys about if they get interested in me. It lets their vanity off the hook. Men hate being told no for no's sake."

"But if you make a good marriage you won't *need* to work," said Maxine, puzzled.

"Wanna bet?" said Judy.

That evening the school supper table buzzed with excited discussions as all the girls decided what to wear for the dance. Maxine had her blue silk strapless gown, with a puffed-sleeve bolero; Kate would wear her dull, Debenham's cream moiré dress with a sash and a modest heart-shaped neckline, filled in with a lace fichu. Maxine offered to recut the front in a daring low scoop, and her offer was immediately accepted, but that didn't solve the problem of what Pagan was to wear.

"It's no use. I can't go. I haven't got a long dress," Pagan said gloomily.

"But you've got a full black taffeta skirt," said Maxine, "and your grandmother's white silk blouse. Suppose we buy a couple of meters of shocking pink taffeta and make a huge frill around the bottom of the skirt so that it reaches your ankles and pleat the leftover material around your midriff in a cummerbund, then unbutton the neckline of the blouse so that it's low?"

Pagan cheered up. In an odd way Maxine sounded just like old Mrs. Hocken in the village, and Pagan liked nothing better than converting a garment into something for a totally different sort of occasion than the one for which it had been intended.

That evening Maxine chalked a new, daringly low scoop on the cream moiré, and Kate shut her eyes and crossed her fingers as the scissors bit into it. Then, on her knees, Maxine moved around Pagan, pinning newspaper to the bottom of her skirt to make a pattern for the frill. All over the school girls were trying on their dance dresses. Some of the continental girls wore an entrancing garment called a "Merry Widow," which encased the wearer from armpit to suspendered thigh in black satin and lace. It was backed with steel strips as uncomfortable as the whalebone stays worn by Victorian women, but it was sexy.

All over the school girls without one wrote home by airmail, begging money for extra violin lessons. . . .

The Imperial, with its fairytale towers and turrets, is one of the most beautiful hotels in the world. As the unheated green school minibus drew up to the glittering glass porch, the pupils took off their unchic winter coats (few of them had evening wraps) because it was better to freeze than look dowdy. Escorted by two harassed mademoiselles they trooped across red carpet under crystal chandeliers to the ballroom, where people were already sitting at small white candlelit tables. The girls sat down in the row of dark red banquettes that had been reserved for the school and ordered gin fizzes—the girls had to pay for their own drinks, and gin fizzes were supposed to last longest. Politely formal, Nick was one of the waiters who took their orders.

All the girls were nervous; they dreaded being asked to dance, they dreaded *not* being asked to dance, they dreaded dancing badly or stepping on their partner's toes. They pretended to ignore the stag line that was beginning to form at the far end of the room as they prepared for—possibly—their first major public humiliation. Pagan was glad she was sitting down so the boys couldn't see how tall she was. She was too tall for half the men in the room, although she couldn't imagine why they hated it—she didn't mind small *men*.

"I think I'll go to the ladies' room," Kate said casually.

"No you *don't*," said Pagan. "One thing's certain, nobody's going to ask you to dance if you're in the ladies' room. Don't be in such a funk. Look at me! *That* will take our minds off this horrible ordeal. I'm terrified I'm going to step on this damned fuchsia frill and rip the whole thing off."

The band struck up "La Vie en Rose," there was a sudden scuffle and their table was surrounded by boys who all wanted to dance with . . . *Kate!* Stunned, Kate accepted the invitation of the nearest one, who led her off for *un slow* as she thanked God for Maxine's lessons. Soon all three girls were on the dance floor, saved from the awful fate of being wallflowers.

At the end of the dance they were escorted back to their table, where their partners bowed and left them. Then, as the band struck up a samba, there was the same wild rush to ask Kate to dance. She couldn't believe it as she floated around the dance floor with a handsome, loose-limbed fellow called François, a student at Le Mornay.

François was—according to prescription—dark and handsome. In the arms of this loose-limbed fellow (so confident, even when reversing in the waltz), Kate wafted around the dance floor in a haze of joy as his masterful arm pulled her closer to his white starched shirt front, and her heart thumped as she felt his unfamiliar warmth against her breasts. The second dance was a rumba, which François did with all sorts of tricky variations. Before it had finished Kate suddenly flushed. This room's too hot, she thought, then she felt an unfamiliar sensation; a simultaneous wooziness of the head, a lurch in the stomach and a weakness in the knees. She thought, I'm going to *faint*, how odd it feels. But then she suddenly realized what was happening. This must be *it*, Kate realized, bursting with happiness as she mistook lust for love.

François had a smooth, well-practiced line of small talk. As they floated around the floor, or as he bent her body back and forth against his in an increasingly close samba, he spoke very politely, as if they were having tea with his family. Kate found it was oddly erotic to feel his body hardening against hers (or was she imagining it, because he obviously hadn't noticed) as he suavely described the best forest walks, ski runs, guides, bars, hotels and ballrooms in the district.

Kate said very little. Her green eyes just looked up adoringly into his tanned face as François explained that there was one stumbling block to the Saturday night dances. After the dance was over, the girls from l'Hirondelle were forbidden to speak to the men they had met. On Saturday night you could cling to the man of your dreams through innumerable accordion renderings of "La Vie en Rose," but should you meet him on the street on Sunday morning, you were meant to ignore him, to look straight through this potential love of your life.

From the headmaster's point of view, the girls were supposed to dance perfectly by the time they were shipped back to their parents. François explained that other inadequacies could be blamed on a girl's inherent inability, laziness, pubescent nervousness or premenstrual tension, but the parents got angry if their daughters couldn't dance. A good, cheap way of finding partners willing to teach them and getting the girls to practice their French was to allow pupils to attend public dances at the expense of their parents. However, Monsieur Chardin didn't trust a single one of the pubescent young women for whom he was responsible, and he wanted no irate grandparents-to-be on his doorstep demanding compensation or (even more difficult) identification. The easiest way to ensure his tranquillity and to keep his pupils safe was to lock them in every night, like chickens.

It was an invitation to trouble.

By midnight Kate felt like Cinderella. She was, in fact, too dazed to notice that when she went to the cloakroom none of the other girls spoke to her. They were not simply jealous of Kate's success. What made them angry was that they couldn't *understand* it. Kate looked so *ordinary*. "I can't think what they see in her in that boring old dress," sniffed one girl. "It's not as if she's *pretty*. Thin hair—not even long—and those odd, green, hooded eyes."

Kate had just had the first taste of a disbelieving jealousy that she would have to endure from women for the next thirty years. Because they could not understand why men were attracted to her, women thought that Kate was sly, that she had tricked them, that no man was safe with her. In fact they were wrong; Kate was safe with no man.

With a crash of cymbals the spotlight shone on the band-leader as he announced that the competition to elect "Miss Gstaad" would take place after the next dance, during which the voting slips would be passed out to each table. "Well, it's quite obvious who's going to enter it from our table," beamed Pagan. "Kate is the belle of the ball; she'd better be Miss Gstaad as well."

"Don't be ridiculous," said Kate. "I'm not going to go up on that stage and make a fool of myself."

"I *dare* you," said Maxine. "It's not serious, it's not Miss World, after all, it's only a little village hop." She gave Kate a firm push, shoving her off the maroon velvet bench. "Don't be so bloody British."

Kate stood up. Reluctantly, she shuffled onto the dance floor and was pushed into line by the majordomo, who handed her a large card marked number 17. A couple of other finishing schools had also come to the ball, so there were about thirty girls in line on the dance floor, including a voluptuous Italian girl in a black velvet, strapless gown. Kate saw she had no chance of winning, but it was too late to back out. Slowly the girls formed a circle.

But Kate had reckoned without Nick, who walked over to the waiter responsible for passing out the voting slips, gave him a smile that meant, "I'll settle with you later," shoved a handful of slips into his own pocket, dashed into the men's cloakroom and quickly scribbled "17" on all of them. Then he walked out and picked up the top hat that was to be passed around the tables to collect the voting slips. Simple.

The lights were lowered, and an erratic spotlight illuminated each competitor as she slowly walked up the steps that led to the platform, stood center stage, beaming or looking embarrassed, held up her number and then walked down the steps.

Amid applause and wolf whistles the lights came up again as everyone dropped his voting slip in the hat that Nick held out to each table.

Each girl in the competition tried to look unconcerned. To them, the beauty contest wasn't a minor evening's diversion, decided upon by the bored-but-professionally-jolly majordomo; for each of them, it was their first taste of public sexual competition, and their hearts thumped and they found it hard to breathe until after the next samba when the majordomo stepped forward and announced that the new Miss Gstaad for 1948 was, Ladies, Lords and Gentlemen—number 17!

Kate shook her head in disbelief, Maxine flung her arms around her and hugged her, Pagan whooped with delight and a flock of knowing waiters lined her path to the little stage where, scarlet with surprise and pleasure, a pale blue sash that read "Miss Gstaad 1948" was draped around her by the majordomo, who then popped a diamanté tiara on her hair, presented her with two magnums of champagne and stood at her side in an avuncular pose as photographers' flashlights popped.

"We'll be having trouble with *that* one," muttered one of the harassed mademoiselles who had been sent to escort the Hirondelle girls.

It was an accurate forecast.

CHAPTER 4

BY THE END of November nearly all the schoolgirls had steady boyfriends and had discovered that the little town was astonishingly full of places for secret meetings. They met behind the church, in stables and in barns, crouching in the backs of cars, in the back of the ski shop, in tearooms on the outskirts of town or on top of the ski runs. On the weekends the Eggli, the Wasserngrat, the Hornberg and the Wispile each had their quota of courting couples, as did the inns and cafés of nearby villages such as Saanen and Château d'Oex, which had already catered to generations of foreign finishing-school girls suffering from the symptoms of puppy love.

After a Saturday night spent with their hair twisted up in paper curlers and their faces covered in cream or dried mud to prevent wrinkles, the Hirondelles invariably headed for the Chesa. Their show of self-confidence barely hid their uncertainty and indecision. One remark or laugh could produce an instant, hateful blush—and it was doubly humiliating to be betrayed by one's own neck. Flirtatious and pert, conscious only of their appearance and their audience, the girls appeared not to notice the young men who were sitting at nearby tables, tilting their chairs back, impatient but resigned to all this feminine play-acting, as the girls pretended to ignore them.

Unexpectedly, for the first time in their lives, the girls had discovered they possessed a sort of power. Once she realized this, each girl felt a strange pride in being able to enslave a boy—or two or three, which made a girl twice or three times as powerful. None of them realized the strength or dangers of this sudden sexual power; they never realized that it could be black magic or white magic, depending on how you used or abused it. In 1948, sex appeal was *power*, the only power these girls were ever likely to get, and you used as much of it as you had as hard as you could and full blast! Naturally, the girls knew their own prim petting cutoff points, but it never once occurred to any of them that a man might find it difficult to switch off his own powerful urges at the moment when it suited the girl to do so. It never occurred to any of them that the power they had raised in the man was not only passion but, if thwarted, the power to rape or kill. The reactions of a frustrated man had never been explained to any of them.

Judy acted as postbox for all the adolescent lovers. For the first time since term started, dictionaries were thumbed, grammars consulted and Maxine was much in demand as a translator. Judy also passed messages about meeting places, which often depended on the weather. When she placed a bill or a paper-lace napkin on a table it might well be accompanied by a note that read, "Sheila,

Nursery slope ski lift at five," or "*Hélas! Gérard chéri, impossible cette semaine. Samedi prochain à trois heures, ton Isabel.*"

Occasionally, a girl was caught talking to a boy by one of the school staff and punished by being kept in school the following weekend, but Kate was the only girl who *kept* getting caught, first, because she was besotted with the dazzling François, and second, because she was at heart a straightforward girl, unaccustomed to being devious. When challenged by Matron, she admitted meeting François in the local church. A fortnight later a jealous classmate reported Kate's rendezvous with him in a stable and the following week a mademoiselle saw them drinking *Glühwein* on the Hornberg—a major offense. Kate was increasingly anxious until one weekend François told her he had booked a sitting room in a little *pension* on the edge of the town. He wanted to be alone with her in comfort, not crouching in straw, standing half-frozen in the snow or sitting on public exhibition in a café. He wished to talk to her in private because he had something important to say. *He's going to propose,* thought Kate.

So she followed him into a green-shuttered chalet, their boots clattering up the dark, wooden stairs. François unlocked the door and Kate stopped dead at the sight of the carved wooden double bed covered with a blue-and-white checked quilt. François gently pulled her to an armchair by the window and started to kiss her. Knees melting, Kate thought that perhaps he hadn't *noticed* the bed. Perhaps the bed was a mistake, perhaps he couldn't get a room without one.

She kicked her boots off as she felt his warm tongue licking her ear, then his lips were on the back of her neck and finally she lay in his arms, eyes almost closed and mouth half open.

"*Chérie*, we're going to have a wonderful life together," François said, as he slowly undid each pearl button on her gray lace blouse and slid his hand inside it. Kate felt as if she were swimming under water in a slowed-down film as with gentle movements he pushed back her blouse, unhooked her bra and bent his lips to caress the pink tips of her nipples.

Then, naked from the waist up, she was lying languorously under the checked quilt and the wet tip of his tongue was warm in her other pink ear. She felt his hand under her skirt, a cunning, casual movement as if the hand was moving without the knowledge of its owner.

She shifted and tried to jerk her body up from the bed. François thrust her back. Quite hard. "Cock tease," he hissed. Under a sea of stiffened prickly petticoats Kate felt his grip on her thigh as he thrust his hand above her silk stocking top and then up the leg.

She tried to pull away from him. "I never have, I don't know how to, please don't, I'll do anything if you won't."

Oh, God, Kate thought, he'd undone his trousers and now she could feel his flesh throbbing against her soft inner thigh. Poised above her, François was looking at her as if he didn't know her, he was breathing hard, his eyes were glazed, intent, somehow uninvolved. "I'll be careful then," he muttered and to Kate's relief he withdrew his hand; but only so that he could roll sideways and strip his clothes off. He didn't seem to realize that his thing was showing. The lavender-pink penis reared up from its nest of black hair, balls wobbling beneath it. How *ugly* it was, Kate thought.

Kate tried to get up again, but he thrust her down on the bed then roughly pulled her breasts toward him, lunged his throbbing penis between them and started thrusting his body. Squashed beneath him, Kate felt bewildered, indignant, disbelieving. She couldn't breathe because of his weight on top of her. With a hoarse grunt François stiffened and shivered, his grip hardening painfully on her breasts. Then he collapsed on top of her and Kate felt a stickiness trickling over her collarbone and down her neck. She knew what it was and she didn't dare move in case some of the stuff got in the wrong place. She was terrified.

"You see, I told you I'd be careful, my darling," François mumbled.

Kate didn't think he'd been careful at all. How *dare* he call her his darling? On the other hand, wasn't that just what she'd *wanted* half an hour ago? To *be* his darling? His passion for her must have been uncontrollably great.

Yes, that was it, she told herself. He loved her, that's why this had happened. It wasn't what she'd expected, it hadn't been romantic and wonderful, it had been messy and uncomfortable. But perhaps making love was like skiing, painful and hard for the first couple of times. . . .

Anyway, now she'd let him go below the underclothes, stage two, so obviously he *had* to be the love of her life.

But, strangely, she felt like crying.

Two days later Kate discovered that the rest of the school wasn't speaking to her. They were ostracizing her. Smugly, theatrically, publicly, they made it clear that they despised her. "What's the matter? What have I done?" Kate asked Pagan, who looked harassed.

"Oh, they think you've gone all the way with François. Pay no attention to the jealous bitches," she said.

"But I *haven't*," Kate said, wondering whether, in fact, she really *had*. Certainly the school thought so. Kate was puzzled by the hypocrisy of a world that condemned certain actions in public but practiced or envied them in private; she had disobeyed the eleventh commandment: Thou shalt not be found out. And besides, she was being punished for being Miss Gstaad.

The following Sunday, Judy was waiting for Kate outside the Chesa, arms held across her chest and tucked in her armpits, stamping her boots in the snow to keep warm. "Listen, Kate, that creep you're going out with has told the whole town that he's slept with Miss Gstaad. The barman at the Imperial told Nick and Nick came straight to me. We thought you ought to know."

"I don't believe it," said Kate, realizing at last how the school knew. She dashed to the *pension* to meet François, where François smoothly denied telling anyone. Kate believed him because she wanted to. She felt drained of energy, forlorn, bruised. She clung to François, let him undress her completely, clung to him shivering under the warm quilt as he stroked her body, as he pushed his hand beneath her buttocks, as he felt between her legs. . . . That hurt a bit as he wriggled his finger inside her. But Kate remained passive—she didn't know what was expected of her, but since she'd already been blamed for it, she might as well do it. She could feel the hard warmth and weight of François on her stomach, there was a second of suspense, then she gasped in pain. But soon they were moving together smoothly, as if they were dancing, and she began to feel a slight warmth and excitement. But before it developed into anything even approaching an orgasm, François stiffened with a gasp, then she felt a warm wetness as his erection subsided. He seemed pleased with himself, but Kate felt oddly disappointed, wobbly and stranded. Perhaps there was something wrong with her? Perhaps she was frigid?

It did not occur to her that François was at fault. Boys, she assumed, knew how to do these things. Perhaps she just needed more practice. She supposed that she'd get the hang of it in time.

"Two to come out, the black ones in front to be capped and I have to wear a brace at night for a bit," reported Maxine that night in bed. "He phoned Papa on the spot and Papa said go ahead. Not nearly as expensive as I thought, cheaper than my tangerine dress."

"Well, now your hair," said Pagan, huddled under her quilt in the moonlight. "It grows too low on your forehead, like a Neanderthal woman. . . . I'm going to trim away a bit with my nail scissors and give you a lovely widow's peak. If you don't like it, you can loop your back hair over it, and if you *do* like it, you can have it done permanently by electrolysis." She sprang off the bed and reached for Kate's little purple underarm razor. In the face of such assurance, Maxine allowed her hairline to be shaved away by the light of her pocket flashlight. Pagan looked slightly worried after she'd done it; Maxine looked terrible, as if she were being prepped for a lobotomy.

"Maybe if you plucked her eyebrows?" suggested Kate, so Pagan attacked Maxine's bushy eyebrows. Unfortunately, she plucked too much from the left side, then attempted to match up the right side and took too much of that away, so she returned to the left for further depilation until Maxine was left with two thin odd horizontal question marks of hair under her lopsidedly shaven forehead.

Maxine looked in the mirror and burst into tears.

The following day Matron hurried her off to the hairdresser, and later that afternoon Maxine returned, beaming again. Her hairline had been properly trimmed, and the hairdresser had persuaded her to have her hair streaked and styled. Her braids had gone and in their place was a thick, blonde, shining mane.

"Now your weight," Judy said firmly the following Sunday. "Ten kilos. No more cakes. You're always saying you hate the school food, so it shouldn't be too difficult. You can buy seven hard-boiled eggs a week and have one for breakfast with black coffee, an orange and a slice of ham in your room at lunchtime, no tea break, and as little as possible for supper. And the footballs will slowly disappear."

They didn't, but the rest of Maxine diminished at the rate of a kilo a week. Fascinated, the rest of the school watched her transformation. Some tried to emulate it, but they hadn't Maxine's determination and tenacity in the face of warm bread, fresh from the oven, with strawberry preserves for breakfast or the cream cakes and steaming chocolate of the five o'clock break.

When Maxine was no longer a size sixteen but a size fourteen heading for twelve, Judy examined her thoroughly, as one might a horse on auction, and nodded with satisfaction. Then she stepped back and said, "The nose."

Surprisingly, Maxine was worried that she might appear vain, that people would *notice*, that her mother would object, that it was sacrilegious to alter the nose God had given her.

"God didn't intend you to wear a bra either," Judy said. "It's up to you to help God a bit, you know, if you want to look as good as you can."

* * *

After Christmas Maxine returned to school ten days late, with two black eyes and a perfect nose. "What a performance," she said, lifting her sunglasses to show her bruises. "I nagged and I cried and I refused to go out, oh, you would have been proud of me, I behaved so badly and with such determination. I wheedled Aunt Hortense into paying for it, provided my parents consented." She readjusted the sunglasses. "The aunt didn't expect my parents to consent, but I kept telling them that they couldn't be so cruel as to refuse such an offer. I tell you, the whole of Christmas Day I was in tears. So eventually they agreed. It only took four days, and I needed the rest after that performance!"

Maxine's new nose and figure greatly increased her self-confidence, and she now concentrated on losing more weight. She ate and drank as little as possible, she was on skis as often as possible, every night and morning she would sit on the floor of her bedroom and roll her plump thighs away with a wooden kitchen rolling-pin. "Ninety-eight . . . ow, ninety-nine . . . *il faut souffrir pour être mince*, ouch, a hundred. Pouf! Now where are my ski socks?"

"Surely you're not going to ski today?" Kate asked. "It looks like an upended paperweight outside. It's a Sunday for staying by the fire."

"I only lost half a kilo last week, look at my chart on the wall. Five more kilos to lose."

Maxine trudged off to the ski lift. She had decided to try a longer, more advanced run so she caught the *gondelbahn* cable car to the top of the Wispile. The top of the mountain was gray and threatening with black clouds lacing the sky behind. Maxine shivered and looked at the signpost, a Christmas tree of colored arrows nailed to the post that pointed to different ski runs. The yellow runs were easy, the red ones more difficult and the black runs were only for very experienced skiers.

Maxine, who had only been skiing for a couple of months, thought that the black track didn't look all that difficult—in fact it looked quite easy and much the prettiest. And so it was for the first two hundred yards, then the *piste* took a sharp turn to the left and Maxine found herself in a rutted ice path that fell steeply through the forest. For a moment she thought of climbing back, then she was going too fast and couldn't stop; her skis clattered over the ruts. She was frightened of wrapping herself around a tree; it hadn't occurred to her that there might be nobody else on the *piste*. She jerked over a bump, fir trees loomed, she floundered and fell.

She pulled herself to her feet, shot forward—again too fast—on the corrugated ice track and fell again, bruising her hip. Although she was wearing two pairs of woolen mittens inside her ski gloves, she couldn't feel her numbed hands and her cheeks and forehead already ached with the cold. She pulled herself up again and for the next ten minutes she managed to ski slowly and carefully with a great deal of side-slipping. Then it started to snow, which limited visibility until she could only see a few yards in any direction; the *piste* was quickly covered by snow and she could see no arrows. As snowflakes fluttered down remorselessly, the lack of sound was eerie and she felt frightened.

Suddenly, a lone, black-clad skier with an orange-peaked cap shot past her. She waved her ski poles after him and shouted, but he didn't stop. Maxine groped her way onward and downward, following the direction the man had taken. She found herself alone on a steeply sloping field of icy bumps, but she didn't dare take it straight. She started to traverse it slowly. Each time she reached the edge of the field, she did a laborious kick turn and clumsily levered herself down a couple of feet. Her knees started to tremble with the effort but she zig-zagged on, all thought of style forgotten. She had just reached the bottom of the field when the man with the orange-peaked cap slipped gracefully past her.

"*Au secours*," she shouted. "*Help!*" But the skier didn't seem to hear, so again Maxine followed in the direction that he had taken and soon found herself on the edge of the steepest slope she had ever been on.

She was terrified. She considered climbing back, but downhill, she reasoned, would be easier than uphill, so she took her skis off and dragged them behind her, kicking footholds with the heels of her ski boots, terrified lest she drop a ski, because it would undoubtedly shoot off down the glassy mountain and be lost forever. As perhaps she was herself. . . .

Although she was heading downhill, she had a nasty feeling that she might be going the wrong way. It was now three hours since she had left the top of the mountain. She was soaking wet, she'd got snow down the back of her neck and could no longer even feel her feet. Cold, forlorn and frightened, she sat down to rest in the snow, worrying about frostbite and peering into the thick grayness all about her.

This time, because she wasn't skiing, she heard the orange-hatted skier descend, scrambled to her feet, waved and screamed at him.

"Stop, *stop*, please *stop*."

He pulled up by her side.

"Could you please tell me the easiest way down?" Maxine asked anxiously.

He looked at her through yellow goggles and said in French, "There *is* no easy way down. You're on the black run. Why did you pick the black, why not one of the easier runs?" He sounded exasperated. "Look, you'd better follow me or you'll never get down. Put your skis on."

Slowly Maxine inched her way after him down the hellish mountain. He would ski forward then stop and wait, watching her as she jerked, slid and wobbled forward, her new teeth gritting with determination as the gray obscurity started to thicken into darkness. Then suddenly her knees gave way and she collapsed into the snow. She gave a little sob.

"I'm afraid I can't go on. I've got to rest. I'm sorry, but I can't move anymore."

The black skier's voice became gentle and persuasive as he urged her on. "Come on," he said, "you're doing wonderfully well, we're nearly at the halfway station, it's just around the next bend, then you can ride on the *gondelbahn* back to the bottom!"

So they slowly inched forward until Maxine fell again. She ached all over. "I can't go on," she muttered, then buried her face on her knees and rolled over in the snow, curled in a fetal position.

The skier sighed, unclipped his skis and stuck them upright in the snow. "Here, let me rub you warmer," he said. He rubbed each arm, then her back until she ached with the pain of it. Then he roughly rubbed her legs until she could feel them again and helped her stand.

Slowly, painfully, they progressed onward. The halfway station wasn't around the next bend or the one after that. It was almost an hour before they turned around a bend and saw it. Maxine almost crawled into the station, but her rescuer said he was going to ski down the remainder of the *piste*. He would join her in the bar at the bottom, if she liked.

Effortlessly, he slipped downhill and away from her.

At the bottom of the ski lift Maxine, slightly recovered, headed for the nearby bar and staggered to the cloakroom. She took off her cap, goggles, scarf and extra sweaters, washed her face in warm water—oh the bliss of it—and fluffed out her hair as best she could. Then she clumped into the steamy, pine-lined bar. Because no one was stupid enough to ski in such dangerous weather, the bar was empty except for a huge, husky black figure leaning against it, dangling an orange cap and yellow goggles.

"Hot buttered rum for you, I think, tea for me," he said, as she smiled her newly irresistible grin. "I must admit that I never expected to find a pretty girl under that collection of old horse blankets you were wearing."

His bronzed face was ringed with neatly curling blond hair. Maxine took one look into the clear, blank blue eyes and fell in love with him on the spot.

The added bonus was that Maxine's savior was a reserve on the Swiss ski team, and every girl in l'Hirondelle would have killed for a chance to meet any member of the team. *Wait* until she told them! she thought.

But she didn't tell them because Pierre Boursal sat with her, alone in the deserted bar, until it was time to go back to school for supper then walked her back, carrying her skis, while Maxine prayed that he would ask to see her again, and by the time he did—not to ski, mind you, once was enough—he had become too important to her to boast about. She didn't even tell Kate or Pagan in case it was tempting fate. Or Kate or Pagan.

From then on, Maxine met Pierre whenever she could—after the last ski lift stopped, of course. Pierre had not intended to get involved with a girl. He took his training seriously. He didn't smoke, didn't drink and didn't intend to be distracted by women. Maxine's virtue was splendidly safe with him, thanks to his training, she thought, longing for him as they clung to each other on some tiny dance floor or she sat with his muscular arm around her waist in the darkest corner of some tearoom. At such times she clearly saw how very, very easy it would be to be wicked.

If only she ever got the chance.

The slalom race was due to start at ten o'clock that morning. Urged by Maxine, wearing her best yellow ski jacket and her beautiful silver fox hood, the girls were again on top of the Eggli. Shepherded by the sportsmaster, they had caught the little green bus from Gstaad, up the mountain to the funicular which carried the skiers even farther up. At times the dark green pines shuddered and snow fell silently from their branches.

Although it was early, the girls shared a mug of hot, red *Glühwein* as soon as they reached the summit restaurant, for they knew they would soon be numb with cold. Their sportsmaster explained again that ski racing was a combination of trained technique, superb physical fitness, the best equipment—and favorable weather conditions. On a gray day, when visibility was low, a skier would be able to see only a short way ahead. The hazy white sky would merge with the snow and it would be impossible to see where the track ended and the sky started, whether there was mountain ahead or a vertical drop. In bad conditions, luck was more important than when the weather was perfect, for the sunlight showed up uneven ground so that every bump, ridge, dip and rut was clearly defined by shadows on the snow.

When the girls left Gstaad that morning, the steep icy slopes had glistened in what had been the first sun of the week. But by the time they reached the summit, the sun had disappeared between low clouds and it had started to snow—not hard, but just enough to reduce visibility. The officials at the top of the slalom course decided to start the race twenty minutes early before the snow worsened.

The only sound on the muffled mountain was the crunch of snow under their skis as the girls glided down to the finishing post. On either side of the course a soft beige row of fencing leaned away from them and disappeared up the quiet white mountainside. The 300-yard course with a drop of 300 feet was staked out to the right of a clump of pine trees. Fifty pairs of colored slalom poles had been driven into the snow to make fifty "gates" at five meter intervals. This race, the Men's Slalom, was an individual event. Each skier would not only be competing against the other racers but against his own best time as he skied alone down the first course, then the adjoining course. The fastest aggregate time would decide the winner.

Pierre Boursal didn't think he had much chance of winning. There were thirty-seven starters, including three members of the team and the other reserve. However, one reserve would have to qualify for a team place, because the day before Leist had broken his collarbone in a car crash.

Suddenly impatient, Pierre thought why wait when he could ski? He went up in the funicular and streaked down the *piste*. More than anything else in the world he loved silently slipping downhill on skis, using only his body and earth's gravity to flick like a hawk over the magical white surface. For him, it was the ultimate physical exultation, that thrill of constant risk and deliberate danger when he allowed himself to go a little too fast and just out of control. He had first been put on skis when he was a tiny child and quickly discovered that it was the only way he could escape from his glamorous mother and her insufferable hordes of would-be lovers, crowding the smarter parts of Saint Moritz every year. Rather than be dragged along in the wake of that mob, Pierre used to take his skis and seek the solitude and purity of the snow at the top of a mountain, and hear in that celestial silence only the faint noise of his skis as he carved his own path through the virgin snow.

Pierre was not a good scholar and by the time he was thirteen, his only source of joy and satisfaction was skiing. Afterward, carrying his skis through some village street, he loved to notice two responses from passersby; sometimes he would see a little group staring up at his trail and hear them exclaim, "Only a madman would attempt the Scharnfürts today," or "Did you see how fast his descent was?" Sometimes, in ski villages where he was known, Pierre would notice that he was being pointed at in the street, that men were muttering and turning their heads to look at him from the opposite sidewalk.

Only his mother and father were unaware that their son skied like a demon.

It was not until the president of the multinational company that was sponsoring the junior team congratulated Monsieur Boursal at a bankers' dinner in Zurich on being the father of a future champion that Pierre's father realized his son was neither untalented nor lazy—he was merely not interested in scholastic subjects.

Now, Pierre moved down the Eggli with perfect style and breakneck speed, skiing to the limit—and a little beyond. Unlimbering before the race, Pierre swung around the most difficult bumps, then veered off the *piste* and into the deep virgin snow, leaning backward so that his ski tips wouldn't catch the powder. The snow plumed up behind him, a silent diamond spray. He cut back onto the *piste*, then crouched low, elbows to knees, into a final *schuss* with skis flat and fast, head down and sticks tucked under his arms. His anxiety was forgotten. All he felt was the sheer physical sensation of his body, the snow and the heady, cold champagne-sparkle of the winter air at this high altitude.

Carrying his skis, Pierre walked up the side of the course, trying to memorize it, because competitors weren't allowed a trial run down. The right route would only become apparent when he was on it, flashing through the maze of bamboo poles. As he waited his turn, he would watch the skier before him, trying to work out the course from his movements. Total concentration was essential because the gates were pitched irregularly and often closely together; it was very easy to crash into a pole or miss a gate.

Today's course didn't look too difficult; two steep drops, both near the beginning of the descent, several sharp "V" turns, one of which was almost immediately followed by an exceptionally tight twist that would have him straining uphill to reach it. That was the bastard to watch for.

Pierre reached the top of the course and waited with the other competitors, shuffling up toward the start, breath visible in the frozen air. He had drawn number 8, a good number because the track would be defined by the seven previous racers but wouldn't have developed the deep ruts that might catch the ski tips of the last few racers.

Now he was next. Pierre checked the red knitted headband that kept the hair out of his eyes and prevented his ears and forehead from freezing. He cleared his throat, spat in the snow, then stood at the top of the run. Tense, poised, flexing his shoulders and neck, impatiently he slid his skis backward, forward, backward, waiting for the starter to touch his shoulder and his boot to start the timer.

Now!

As he leaped off, Pierre was conscious of a black, silent human hedge of spectators alongside the course. He swooped down, then took a sharp left turn above his first gate. Before he was through that gate, he would be preparing his crouching body for the next gate, and deciding where his turn would be for the gate after that. From the moment he started to train, his instructor had yelled at him to "think two gates ahead," and "Faster, faster, *faster.*" He had been taught to start cautiously, get the feel of the course, then—as soon as he had his rhythm and momentum—to move as fast as he could without losing control.

He snaked sharply to his right through the gap, legs slightly apart for balance, crouching low, then transferred his weight onto his inner leg as he leaned into the mountain. With a scraping, skating motion his lower, outer leg pushed, pushed, *pushed* him around and on.

After the steep drop at the eighth gate his body began to adjust to the rhythm of his movements. Pierre felt the tension leave him and his heart pumped unusually loudly as excitement took over from anxiety. As each gate flicked past, there was a flash of relief.

Suddenly his skis shuddered, then rattled on the sharp dip to gate 14. Pierre fought to regain control. For a few terrifying seconds he hit black ice where the racers before him had scraped away the thin covering of powder snow. Almost immediately came the third steep drop. He swung to take an awkward gate on his left. His skis shuddered badly against the ice again and for a moment he lost control. Abruptly he stopped thinking two gates ahead and saw only the couple of bamboo sticks immediately in front of him, an impassive challenge.

He made a painful effort of will, lips tight and eyes bulging as he regained his mental control, then grimly swung through the next gate, his concentration once more two gates ahead, hardly noticing—as he swept past—a blue-jacketed casualty who was crawling to the side of the course.

This was a sneaky little tight turn. He had felt a gate pole shudder against his upper arm. Almost immediately came an even tighter turn on almost the same level. He quickly pushed himself upward with his outer ski and felt his leg muscles quiver with the effort. It was going to be too much for his legs, he'd never make it.

He jerked to the left to avoid a pole that had fallen sideways and hadn't been straightened. He nearly missed the thirty-fourth gate and again his concentration faltered as he checked his speed and just missed a headlong crash into the pole. Shaken, his first reaction was to slow down, but his inherent determination urged him ahead and with the tenacity of a born champion, he skied even faster through the next ten gates.

Not *another* sharp drop? He thought, I'd like to get the bastard who laid out this course. . . . Surely, this must be the last one . . . ?

Then suddenly Pierre could hear the encouraging rhythmic roars of the crowd. He knew they yelled in time to your turns if you were going especially well. He thought, I *mustn't* listen, I *must* concentrate.

Then, dear God, *no*—there was another steep drop. . . . Recklessly, Pierre used it as a springboard, and his whole body lunged forward as he forced his skis onward and summoned up his remaining energy to propel himself past the finishing post.

He suddenly felt euphoric. *Not* bad. . . .

After all the competitors had finished the first descent, Pierre led by 1.50 seconds. Fourteen of the thirty-seven had dropped out.

The second slalom was laid out beside the first course and speeds were usually faster because the racers had loosened up, but weather conditions had now worsened; it was cold and overcast with a deceptively gloomy light. Visibility was almost at the danger point and Pierre wondered whether the race would be canceled. Please God, no, he prayed.

This time, at the end of his descent, he didn't feel euphoria, only tired anxiety. He thought his time was good, but was it good enough?

He skied over to the huge notice board where the times were marked up, and stood by it, his back to the slalom course, as he watched the figures go up. Maxine kept away from him and held her breath. The course was claiming more than its fair share of victims; one had overshot the gate when taking a steep, icy drop. Then a pole hit another racer in the face, luckily resulting only in a slight concussion and a black eye. One racer caught his ski in an icy rut and took a tremendous tumble into the fence that guarded the course scattering spectators as he broke his left leg in three places below the knee. Pierre held his breath hopefully and he couldn't help inwardly rejoicing when, three minutes later, his personal rival, Klaus Werner, neatly wrapped one ski around a pole and cartwheeled gracefully out of the race, uninjured.

Suddenly, number 8 went up on the board, with a time of 1.56 minutes. Maxine clambered through the snow to throw her arms around his neck, as she yelled, "Pierre, you've won, you've won!"

And to her surprise, and his, he kissed her with a passion that took her breath away.

Pierre whispered, "I've got to go with the team, darling. Meet you at the Chesa in half an hour." Then he was surrounded by instructors, fans and fellow racers grinning and slapping him on the back.

* * *

Maxine waited for him at the Chesa. They were both too excited to eat, although they drank from the obligatory bottle of champagne. After half an hour, Pierre—who hardly ever drank—put his arm around her and said, "Now we go to my room, eh?"

"Now?" said Maxine, doubtfully, longing to and yet afraid.

"Now."

They clumped through the streets as congratulations were shouted at Pierre. How long did it take to do it? wondered Maxine as she slunk along at his side.

The ski team chalet was empty. They clattered up the wooden stairs in their heavy ski boots.

Pierre's room contained two narrow beds. He put the ashtray outside the door before locking it—the standard signal to the roommates.

Maxine wanted to leave but she also wanted to stay.

Pierre started to undress her quickly, kissing her whenever she started to say something. She wanted him to stop but she also wanted him to go on. Should she tell him she had never been below the waist?

He flashed a careless smile, expertly unsnapping her bra hooks with one hand. "Don't worry, I have been in this situation *hundreds* of times."

"Hundreds?" said Maxine, relieved, shocked and cross.

"Well, enough." There was a struggle over her ski pants as she clutched them to her body, so Pierre started to pull off his own clothes. As he unzipped his trousers Maxine shut her eyes. Then she opened them, jumped onto the bed and hid her head under the quilt like an ostrich.

"Pierre, it's *daytime.* I'm shy. Anyone might look through the window."

"We're three stories above the ground," he laughed, but obligingly he drew the lace curtains.

Suddenly he was lying naked beside her, gently prying her hands away from her face and kissing her naked breasts in a determined manner that Maxine found wildly exciting. Torn between embarrassment and ardor, she involuntarily twisted around toward Pierre's body, burying her head against his chest so that she couldn't see anything. Then she stiffened again. Now she could feel his muscular nakedness and smell his desire. And she could feel something else. Stealthily she pulled her hand away, but Pierre firmly took it and drew her hand gently downward. Maxine tugged it back rather sharply. Softly, insistently, Pierre again pulled her hand downward and clasped it over his flesh. Maxine decided to pretend that it wasn't her hand. She was terrified of doing something wrong, of hurting him. Did you bend it forward? Did you rotate it? Could it snap off?

There was a loud knock on the wooden door. "Monsieur Boursal! Photographers downstairs."

They both froze. Pierre cursed and sat up crossly.

"Tell them . . . Tell them I'm asleep. Exhausted. Later."

There was another pause, then footsteps clattered away down the corridor.

Pierre turned back to the matter at hand. Maxine was surprised that her stroking should have such an effect on him, should render him so helpless, that she was lying here under the warm quilt sending this man berserk just by gingerly touching his thing.

"Let's get those damned trousers off," muttered Pierre as articles of Maxine's clothing went flying across the room from under the quilt.

She risked a furtive peep downward and froze again. The size! But it was an impossibility, she would be cut in half! "I'm frightened, I think we should stop," she said, stopping. With a groan Pierre also stopped.

"You're right, you're too young," he said reluctantly. Whereupon Maxine was furious and grabbed the thing again.

"I don't want to hurt you," muttered Pierre, rolling on top of her nevertheless.

Then suddenly it wasn't so painful and the thing was *in* and they were moving together.

"Am I doing it right?" whispered Maxine, worried about the rhythm. It was a bit like doing the samba horizontally, Maxine thought, but should she be moving *with* him or in the opposite direction?

"Just don't think about it; don't worry about a thing," he murmured in her ear. She lay there feeling waves of warmth lap over her. She felt a strange tingling all over her, then found herself instinctively responding to him.

Suddenly he started to move more frantically, with increased urgency. He arched his back, gave a strangled gasp as if in pain and collapsed on top of Maxine. For a moment she thought he had fainted, but after a few minutes he made a noise like a sleepy, contented puppy and then he dozed off.

All was well. Or was it? She felt a sense of relief that it was *over*, that she had crossed a hurdle and was a real woman, but she also felt strange—exhausted, but wide awake; tense and uncomfortable. Pierre's arm lay under her back and she didn't dare move for fear of disturbing him. Slowly she inched down the bed until his arm was under her neck and she was hidden by the quilt. She felt lonely. She shut her eyes and wanted to cry.

Was that *all*? All they had speculated about and hoped for after lights out, all that had been hinted at in a hundred magazine romances? This damp patch of bloody sheet under her elbow, the unfamiliar, sweaty smell of bodies, the sour smell, this sticky stuff trickling over her thighs.

All she felt was a longing to be clean, lying in her own bed in her own room with the sun shining in the window through the lace curtains. What she wanted more than anything else in the world was a bath.

She must have done something wrong . . . Or else he hadn't done something right.

"In training for some things, out of training for other things," Pierre said as sleepily he raised his head and looked at her. "Oh, Maxine, you have the most wonderful breasts," and with great concentration he pounced on them.

Soon Maxine felt more cheerful, then she was caught up in warm waves of delight. Her body started to move to his rhythm, she couldn't help it, she felt that she was melting into him, or was he melting into her? She stretched her hands around his body and pulled his hard strong buttocks against her. "Please don't stop, please don't stop, please *don't stop*," she gasped urgently. She felt poised like a frozen waterfall, then her body arched again and again and what she felt was an amazing pleasure, every bit as good as one had heard about—in fact, better.

The hammering on the door grew more frantic. Maxine woke with a start, felt the warm naked body next to hers, and jumped again.

"Maxie! Maxie!" She recognized the urgency in Pagan's voice. Stumbling out of bed, she felt her way through the unfamiliar moonlit room to the door, which she cautiously opened, shielding her naked body behind it.

Pagan stood there in her oversized green tweed coat. "D'you realize it's nearly midnight? You said Pierre would bring you back before supper, but we didn't really worry until bedtime."

"*Mon Dieu*," gasped Maxine. "I mean, sheet, then they know I'm missing!"

"No, when Matron did the lights-out round, Kate just said you were in the bathroom, then we waited until everyone had gone to bed and tossed a franc to see who'd come to look for you. I lost, so Kate crept off with her flashlight to the office and lifted the back door key off the hook and she's waiting to let us in again. Four fast knocks at the kitchen window is the signal. For heaven's sake, *hurry*!"

Trembling, Maxine scrambled into her ski clothes without waking Pierre. The two girls tiptoed along the passage, down the creaking wooden stairs and into the street. Without speaking, hands in their pockets, they ran clumsily through the snow as fast as they could, sometimes stumbling, sometimes skidding on an icy patch.

As they approached the dark bulk of the school chalet, the road was suddenly lit by the oncoming lights of a lone, slow car. Then the car stopped abruptly, and to their horror, the headlights were switched full onto them. As they drew level, a window slid down and a man leaned out. "Well, well," he said cheerily, "been visiting the nightclubs?"

It was Paul, the headmaster's driver. "Get in the back," he said sharply. They scrambled in, then Paul turned and put one arm on the back seat as he grinned at the two white-faced girls who knew they faced expulsion.

"Why go back now? Why not come out with me to a *real* nightclub? I know one where you won't be recognized and you'll be safe with me."

"No, it will only get us into worse trouble," muttered Maxine, remembering what Nick had said about Paul. But Pagan's first thought was that if she went with Paul, he'd be a fellow conspirator; he wouldn't be able to tell Chardin. They wouldn't be expelled.

She summoned up her courage. "Maxine had better go in as someone will be waiting for us. I'll come with you, but how will I get back?"

"I've got a key, of course."

With an anxious backward look, Maxine slipped out of the car and ran through the snow to the back door. The blue Jaguar slid off through the snow.

But Paul didn't drive to a nightclub. He drove right through the town and then out the other side.

"Hey!" Pagan said, sitting upright, as they drew up at a lone chalet. "Is *this* a nightclub?"

"No, it's my home," Paul said, "it's safer than a nightclub. We'll just have one drink, then I'll take you back to school."

Pagan looked out of the car. She could no longer see the lights of Gstaad, and she had no idea where she was, so she obediently followed Paul into the little chalet and found herself in a surprisingly modern living room. There were groups of low, chrome-framed chairs; abstract pictures hung in huge silver frames; a lifesize marble statue of a male torso stood candle-white against the black walls.

Pagan blinked as astonishment overcame fatigue. Still in her coat, she stood silently in the middle of the room as Paul prepared a silver cocktail shaker. He shook it, poured the contents into a tumbler and handed it to Pagan. It smelled like soap and dry-cleaning fluid, though Paul said it was brandy and vodka with a dash of something special. Better keep friendly with him, Pagan thought—but the only way she was going to be able to drink the stuff was to hold her breath and knock it back. She did so. She spluttered, felt her legs grow weak, then passed out.

Pagan wished her stomach would keep still. She didn't think she'd ever be able to lift her head again. Carefully she opened her eyes. There was a shower of bright lights. She shut them again. She was dizzy; she was going to be sick; she seemed to have no control over her limbs. She felt cold steel on her wrist and heard a click. . . . What *did* the man imagine he was doing?

Paul had handcuffed her to the bedpost.

"And now the other hand. Just so you don't do anything imprudent, miss."

Pagan felt too weak to think. She shut her eyes again, and couldn't decide whether she felt worse with her eyes open or shut. She was freezing cold and *she had no clothes on*. She wished she understood what was happening . . . wished that Paul would leave her alone. . . . What *was* the bloody man going to do?

"I'm just going to stroke you, that's all that will happen, then I'll take you back to school. You don't really want to get up now, do you? You don't really want to stop me, do you? You can't, can you? You *like* it, don't you?"

And Pagan *did* like the soothing, soft, catlike strokes on her breast, on her ribs, on her stomach. She tried opening her eyes again and saw that Paul was lying beside her, naked, on black sheets. His sleek head propped on one hand, an amused detached smile on his face, Paul was stroking her with a black feather. She shut her eyes again. Then he slid softly off the bed and Pagan felt something else, a snaking sensation on her thighs.

She opened her eyes again and got a frontal view of her first erection. Paul's naked body was poised over her, legs apart, and, no, it just wasn't possible! He was gently tickling her thighs with a black leather whip. "You have no choice, you have to do *exactly* as I say," he whispered.

She shut her eyes again. It was all too much. How her head ached! There was a sudden flash, and Pagan suddenly came to her senses.

She had just been photographed.

After that, he did it to her and it wasn't painful at all. Revolting, but not painful.

Then he sat on the end of the bed and smoked some sort of herbal cigarette. That was the faint odor she'd smelled as she entered the chalet. Paul ignored Pagan until suddenly he turned toward her, started to giggle helplessly and stubbed the cigarette out on the sheets. This alarmed Pagan so much that she became alert. She had no idea of the time, but she had to get these handcuffs off, find her clothes and get back to school before this bloody man burned the house down.

"Paul darling," she said, "*please* undo me so I can go to the bathroom." He crawled up on the bed and undid her handcuffs. Pagan groped her way into the living room, looking for her clothes. She started to pick them up, then peered into a bronze-ringed mirror over the bureau and saw her swollen face. Her eyes had almost disappeared; she must have been crying at some time.

She noticed that the top drawer of the bureau had been pulled half-open. The contents made her eyes snap wide open.

Quickly she put her hand in.

* * *

It was past dawn when Pagan crept up to her room.
"You look terrible. It's past five o'clock."
"You smell awful, where did you go?"
"What happened?"
"We went to a bar and I drank too much; now *will* you kindly *piss off*?" Pagan growled. She rinsed her mouth with disinfectant, bathed her face and staggered into bed. She didn't go down to breakfast, and when Matron saw her swollen face and red-rimmed, dull eyes, a thermometer was immediately stuck in her mouth. Though Pagan's temperature was normal, she certainly looked as if she were developing something, so she was moved to the school infirmary for two days.

CHAPTER 5

TEN DAYS LATER the resilience of youth had triumphed. Pagan had managed to convince herself that she had wiped that revolting incident out of her mind and could pretend it had never happened. Amazingly, the episode had not lowered her high spirits and one Sunday afternoon, sparkling with restless energy, she wheedled the other three into hiring the horsedrawn red sleigh for an hour.

Off clopped the horse over the snow-laced cobbles, the four girls huddled luxuriously under the ancient silver fox fur rugs. Jogging along to the jingle of the silver bells on the harness, they waved to passersby as they drove through the fields outside the town and headed toward Saanen. When they stopped, the girls took turns sitting on the driver's seat, whip and reins in hand, as Pagan photographed them with her box Brownie.

Without thinking, Judy—who couldn't ride—flapped the reins and shrieked "Giddy *yap*!" flicking the whip in the air. Unfortunately the leather thong caught the ear of the middle-aged mare. Startled, the horse reared. Judy dropped the whip in fright and clutched the driver's seat as the horse broke into a canter, swaying the heavy sleigh from one side of the track to the other. Kate and Maxine crouched in the back as they hurtled over the snow. Pagan and the driver were left behind, standing open-mouthed by the path.

For the first time in ten days Pagan really forgot that loathsome scene. She dropped her camera and dashed after the sleigh as it lurched from one side to the other of the snow-rutted path, the horse leaping ahead with unaccustomed speed.

As the sleigh passed a small group of skiers, one of the men caught at the reins, half-running, half-pulled along by the mare. Gradually, the horse slowed down, and by the time Pagan had puffed up to the sleigh, the skier was soothing the quivering horse, stroking her steaming neck and murmuring in a language that Pagan didn't understand.

"*How dare you*!" Pagan yelled to the frightened, white-faced Judy. "How dare you hit that mare! How dare you make her rear and gallop on ice, you bloody idiot! Get in the back!" Her head was thrown back, her short, straight nose pointed imperiously, her nostrils flared with rage.

Still intent upon the condition of the horse, she took the reins from the stranger, said thank you almost without noticing him, and walked the horse back to the furious stable driver, who headed for home.

Outside the stable a man was waiting for them, a dark fellow wearing ski clothes and the arrogant air of a privileged servant. With a face devoid of expression except for a hint of hauteur, he approached Pagan and gave a slight bow.

"My master, His Royal Highness the Crown Prince Abdullah, wishes to invite you to meet him at the Imperial Hotel."

"And I'm the Queen of China," said Pagan, still furious and refusing to listen to Judy's apologies.

"Abdullah certainly *is* staying at the Imperial, Pagan," Judy said. "He's got two permanent suites there, while he's at school. I've never *seen* him, but this guy certainly looks like one of his Arab bodyguards." Judy flung her pale blue scarf-end around her chin. "Look, I must go, I'm due at the Chesa, but I'd consider that invitation. How often does royalty invite you to tea?" She ran off, hampered by her heavy boots.

Remembering her previous painful escapade with Paul, Pagan hung back. She didn't want to get involved in anything else outlandish.

"No harm in going along to the Great Hall," the other two insisted. "Oh, Pagan, *royalty*," Kate added, as they followed the dark-faced man toward the Imperial.

In a corner of the Great Hall, wearing all-white ski clothes, sat Prince Abdullah, upright and impatient. Under winged eyebrows he had the watchful look of a hawk, the eyes of a man who is used to being obeyed. Without moving his head, his eyes followed the girls' approach, then he stood and said politely, "*So* good of you to come. Wonderful weather we're having, don't you think?" His English was clipped, with only the faintest trace of an accent.

The Prince waved a hand at the velvet chairs grouped around his table. They all sat down and talked about the weather, the hotel and the ski runs. The Prince's ramrod back, his arrogant, almost menacing calm proclaimed majesty but sat oddly on the shoulders of an eighteen-year-old boy. Pagan thought he would probably look more at home on an Arab horse than on that old green velvet hotel chair. She steered the conversation to horses and the Prince smiled for the first time.

From that moment, the other two girls might not have existed.

"Snap!" screamed Pagan, lying on her stomach on the polar bear rug, in front of the blazing log fire. She pulled the pile of playing cards toward her, as Abdullah, sitting cross-legged opposite her, grinned and shrugged his shoulders.

Prince Abdullah refused to go to the Chesa. He said he didn't like people staring at him and didn't want any *paparazzi* polking cameras in his face, but though he didn't say so, he considered the crowded tearoom a security risk. Pagan had at first refused to visit Abdullah's suite, but eventually, trusting his promise to "behave himself," she agreed to spend Saturday afternoons lolling on the thick maroon carpet in Abdullah's private sitting room, talking about horses or teaching him nursery card games like "racing demon" and "snap!"

In private, Abdullah dropped his invisible cloak of majesty. It disappeared as soon as his bodyguards were dismissed with a curt nod of his head.

"I'm starting to think you cheat," yawned Abdullah, who always cheated himself. His grin widened into a full-lipped smile showing white, even teeth.

As Abdullah twisted onto his side with an agile, catlike movement that was somehow lazily dangerous, there was a sharp crack from the adjoining room. With one bound, Abdullah was on his feet and as he moved, Pagan—still gathering up the playing cards—saw him pull a gleaming automatic pistol from beneath his purple sweater. He leaped to the bedroom door and kicked it open.

Except for the crack of the burning logs, the room was silent. With another catlike crouch, Abdullah jumped inside, his back to the door.

"No problem," he called after a moment. "Sorry, Pagan."

She stood up and ran into the adjoining room. In contrast to the velvet, soft-carpeted luxury of the private sitting room, Abdullah's bedroom was totally bare—it wasn't even curtained—except for a double bed that stood in the center of the room with a small low table beside it upon which stood a water carafe, a bottle of pills and another pistol.

Abdullah was standing beside the window wall, looking out. "I think a tree just fell," he said. "I'm sorry I alarmed you, but I have to be careful."

"But the bodyguards! . . ." gasped Pagan.

Abdullah shrugged. "The price of a bodyguard is low. I'm in the same position as the poorest beggar in my kingdom—if I don't look after myself, nobody else will."

"What an odd room!" Pagan said, looking around it again.

"Arabs have an uneasy, love-hate relationship with comfort and luxury," Abdullah said. "Luxury softens a man, and if I'm to survive I can't afford to be soft. I have to keep my mind as tough and hard as my body." Seemingly unperturbed, he looked at her with the steady gaze of a superbly self-confident male animal. He pushed the pistol back into his trouser band and pulled the purple sweater over it.

"Let's get on with our game," Pagan said hastily, still round-eyed as she tugged him back into the sitting room. "What were you afraid of . . . what did you think was going to happen?" Pagan asked.

"Maybe a kidnap plot, maybe an assassination." He shrugged his shoulders and looked slightly embarrassed. "Would you care for some tea?" He pressed the bell.

"You don't *really* think you might be kidnapped?"

"The first kidnap attempt was before I was a year old. My nurse was stoned to death for her part in the plot. The next attempt was when I was seven years old. I had a bodyguard who pushed me under the bed, but they hauled me out, then stabbed him five times and left him for dead. But he didn't die immediately and managed to raise the alarm before the plotters got me out of the palace." He gave a lazy grin as he looked at Pagan's incredulous face. "The next attempt was when I was fourteen. We were returning from a hunting trip. I was in the first Land Rover. We were ambushed in a gully and I was shot twice in the arm and once in the chest before our second Land Rover arrived on the scene, with guards shooting in all directions. I was shot in the leg by one of our men, but I managed to kill one of my attackers." Suddenly he looked ruthless. "From then on I trusted no one. It wasn't difficult. My heart seemed to harden overnight. To risk trust is to risk death: it was that simple. And that was the last time I was careless. From then on, I always carried a gun, slept with a gun by my pillow, and drove with my own submachine gun on the seat next to me."

There was a quiet knock at the door. Nick, wearing his waiter's uniform, opened the door. The respectful look on his face dropped for an instant when he saw Pagan lolling on the bearskin, then he resumed his waiter's mask. Abdullah ordered lemonade and tea, then, still not quite at ease, he padded nervously around the room.

"Stop prowling," ordered Pagan.

"I have a restless spirit; if you never feel secure, then naturally you feel restless."

Nick returned with a laden tray and gave Abdullah another look of servile insolence as he stiffly bent and placed the tray on a low table by the velvet couch. Pagan winked at Nick, who ignored her. He can't stand Abdullah, she thought. I wonder why?

Not by one muscle movement did Abdullah show that he had recognized Nick, but he had, and for one swift moment Abdullah remembered the most humiliating moment of his life.

The eight-foot-long green baize board that hung by the staircase had been the hub of school activity; on it was pinned much purple-stenciled information about special classes, outings, clubs and chapel together with the sports lists. Abdullah remembered his boyish exaltation when one morning on his way back to his room after school breakfast, he saw his name listed on the house team for Eton football. There it was in a handwritten scrawl—Abdullah. He was the only boy in the school without a surname. He was the only boy in the school without a friend.

Abdullah didn't understand why every boy—himself included—was of equal rank inside those ancient stone walls. To Abdullah, the centuries-old, traditional top-drawer British school was a hostile, incomprehensible world. Ignorant of the private language and rigid conventions of his schoolfellows, Abdullah did what was not done and said what—according to Eton etiquette—should not be said. But now, he had thought, all would be forgiven. *He was on the house team!* With a whoop of excitement he ran along the stone corridor to get his books for the next lesson.

Each pupil had his own small room with a scarred wooden table, two chairs, a narrow metal convertible bed, a bureau, and a chest in which he kept his sports gear. Abdullah's was pretty much the same as the other rooms with one exception: on his wall hung framed photographs of his father's yacht, his mother dressed for court, his father in ceremonial uniform being decorated by King George VI, a picture of Abdullah, aged thirteen, taking the salute from the Sydonian Palace Guard, and another picture of himself being kissed on the cheek by Rita Hayworth.

As Abdullah rummaged in his bureau for a missing Latin grammar, he heard voices that he recognized outside the door.

"Can you believe it? Look, Horton, the baboon's on the House Side."

"No! Bugger me!! Can't think why we even have to have him in Coleridge's. We certainly shouldn't have a dirty little wog representing us on the House Side. Couldn't they have kept him in the Sine?"

"I suppose he's not bad at dribbling, but he's always cornering and sneaking . . ."

"Some nigger lover will put him up for Pop next. . . . Expect he'll get a record number of blackballs. . . . Black balls, ha, ha, ha! What color balls do baboons have, royal purple, d'ye think?" There was a burst of hoarse laughter as a bell rang and the malicious voices drifted away from the notice board.

Abdullah didn't dare face them. All three were members of Debate, so it was inconceivable that he should complain about them—he would only be laughed at. Abdullah's hands started to shake with impotent fury. Why should he care what that trash thought? They were destined merely to be farmers, soldiers or politicians, whereas he was destined to be a king, the leader of his people, beloved of many tribes, cheered by his men and his women.

Suddenly he took a deep breath. . . . Women! Those arrogant nonentities hadn't been instructed for three weeks by the *hakim* in Cairo. . . . Standing there, shaking with rage, his battered Latin grammar book in one hand, a sweet revenge occurred to Abdullah.

He decided that he would have their women.

Pagan left Abdullah's suite earlier than usual. Instead of leaving the Imperial, she took the elevator to the top floor and ran up the remaining stairs to Nick's room, to which, by now, the girls had all made giggling visits. She was in luck, because Nick had just come off duty. He answered her knock in his shirt-sleeves.

"Slumming?" he inquired coldly, as Pagan pecked him on the cheek.

"No, just wondering why you can't stand Abdullah. You can't expect to have *all* the attention of all *four* of us, you know, especially when we know that you're besotted with Judy." The springs sagged as she sat on his iron bedstead. Nick looked unhappy.

"Your private life is none of my business."

"But what is it, Nick? Has Abdi already got a girl?"

"I've no idea. Anyway, it's none of my business, and I wouldn't tell you if I knew. . . . But . . . we were at school together, and I promise you that bastard Abdullah is not what he seems. Of course *women* think he's irresistible. He's obviously attractive."

"It's not only that," said Pagan with a giggle, "it's the stage props that are such fun. The bodyguards and the flowing robes and the fierce black mustaches and the . . . er . . . precautions." She suddenly wondered if Abdullah was officially allowed to carry firearms in Switzerland. Presumably he traveled on a diplomatic passport and could do anything he pleased. She sighed. "I can't *think* why I haven't fallen for him, but I haven't. He's fascinating, but I'm just not besotted, the way you are with Judy."

"Well, you're bloody lucky, because Abdullah doesn't treat women like a gentleman, he *uses* them. I mean *he doesn't care about women*. Not the maids or chaps' sisters or even their mothers."

"Nick! Surely you don't mean—?"

"What I mean is that he's oddly . . . objective about women." Nick didn't know how to say that Abdullah was calculating and deliberate in his attitude toward Western women. He used them. He learned from them. His lovemaking was to prove his power over them and their menfolk.

"Oh, Nick, he's wary about *everyone*, wary of being exploited or shot or whatever other things princes have to be wary of," Pagan said, thinking Nick merely had a case of straightforward jealousy.

"And that combination of menace and charm is just what women find irresistible," Nick said bitterly, and with a tinge of envy.

"Am I to understand that you think Abdi might deliberately play cat-and-mouse with me? Make me miserable?"

"Pagan, stop talking about silly sex games and listen to me. I'm very fond of all four of you, and you know how I feel about Judy. But I'm your *friend*. I wouldn't use any of you, and that's what Abdullah *does*. He has no respect, no understanding of chivalry and he's . . . no gentleman."

Pagan threw her head back and laughed. "Darling Nick," she said, "you are an old auntie! In the future, I'll wear barbed wire instead of knicker elastic."

What Pagan wanted to know—and what the whole school wanted to know—was whether Abdullah would invite her to the St. Valentine's Day Ball. Abdullah was rarely seen in public, especially after he had hired the horse sleigh one Sunday afternoon and a street photographer took a picture of Pagan and the Prince together. The negative was swiftly sold to *Paris-Match*, and within twenty-four hours it had appeared in newspapers around the world.

Every two days an armful of long-stemmed red roses, with no card attached, arrived for Pagan. "You said red roses were vulgar," Kate said gleefully, and had a pillow thrown at her. After the third sheaf, Pagan was summoned to the headmaster's study and told that she could not accept any more flowers. Monsieur Chardin sounded unusually agitated. Half the gossip writers of Europe had been plaguing him. No doubt the publicity was good for the school, but he was obliged to display disapproval.

A few evenings later Pagan was called down to the headmaster's study again. She returned looking bemused. "What happened?" asked Kate, lying on her bed, one foot in the air, having her toenails polished by Maxine.

"Telephone."

"*Who?*" A telephone call was always an event in their lives.

"My cousin Caspar. He's our Ambassador in the Emirates. He said that he's heard I was seeing a great deal of Prince Abdullah, and that I should be *most prudent*." She giggled nervously. "Caspar also said that in Sydon, women are regarded as possessions and once defiled they're discarded. In fact, they're sometimes stoned to death. Can you imagine?"

Maxine said, "Bloody well keep still, Kate."

Pagan flung herself on the other bed. "So I asked what had defiled Arab women got to do with me?" She was wearing a tattered Victorian nightgown that was over a hundred years old and a pair of scarlet Turkish slippers with the toes turned up.

The other two sat up and nail polish dripped on Kate's ankles as Pagan continued. "Old Caspar said that Abdi was pushed into power long before he was old enough, because his father is apparently very religious and a bit mad and lives in total seclusion. But Caspar said that although Abdi is very, very tough, he isn't nearly as sophisticated as he thinks he is, and not nearly well enough equipped to handle the twentieth century, and if he feels he's being laughed at or humiliated he can turn nasty." She giggled. "He went on and on about Abdullah really being two people—a Western-educated ruler who will negotiate diplomatically with

Western politicians and a ruthless, immensely powerful Arab leader whose word is the law and whose instincts are violent, dangerous and medieval."

She kicked off the Turkish slippers and jumped on the end of Kate's bed. Sitting cross-legged, she added, in an offhand manner, very fast, "Caspar also told me that Abdullah is engaged to be married."

"*What!*" Maxine, in her white nightgown, stopped climbing into bed. "*Who?*"

"To some Arab Princess who's only ten years old! Can you *believe?* They're going to be married when she's fifteen." Pagan tried to sound unconcerned. Her voice broke and she said unsteadily, "I hooted with laughter, so Caspar got cross and said he was going to phone Mama."

Suddenly the lights went out, switched off as usual from the headmaster's apartment, and the moonlight, streaming through the lace curtains, cast a wreath of intertwined pale gray roses on Maxine's bed as she tossed back the sheets and rushed over to hug Pagan. "Poor darling, poor darling! He is a bloody two-timer, a rat, a sheet."

"If it's true, it sounds medieval," exclaimed Kate.

"That's exactly Caspar's point. Abdi isn't like a rich Western teenager trying to behave like a man of the world. He's sort of . . . a ruthless very powerful desert hood." She paused. "I rather think that's what I find so fascinating."

"But he's certainly not to be trusted!" Maxine said. "But then of course *no* man should be trusted."

"Cut out that sophisticated act," Kate said. "Who *can* you trust?"

"We can trust each other," Maxine said firmly. So rather solemnly, they all sat on Kate's bed in the moonlight and promised lasting friendship.

"Through thick and thin," Pagan said wildly, shaking her hands over her head like a bruised but victorious boxer.

"Thick and thin," giggled Kate, "*especially* thin." She prodded Maxine's still well-covered ribs.

"Sick and sin," said Maxine, who, like all the French, pronounced "th" as "s."

"Well, yes, that too," Kate said thoughtfully.

The next morning Pagan was called out of the classroom, where chunks of Lamartine were being analyzed by Mademoiselle as, in their heads, the girls planned what to wear for the St. Valentine's Day Ball and how to get more money from home, supposedly for needlework but really for cigarettes. The lessons were a farce, Kate thought crossly as she continued (under cover of her sheet of pink blotting paper) to hack out her initials with her nail scissors on the graffiti-covered wooden table. A nimbus of lethargy hung over the schoolroom, which smelled of chalk and underarm odor; the only noise was the squeak of chalk on a blackboard and the thump of the old upright piano upstairs; maddeningly, the unseen player kept faltering, making the same mistake, then starting again.

Pagan came back giggling from her telephone call and sat down demurely.

"What was that?" The harassed mademoiselle whipped around from the blackboard just too late to see Pagan, with the top of her wooden ruler, flip a note to Kate. Kate didn't send a note in reply because Pagan's little paper pellets never needed a reply. She only sent them to relieve her boredom. The note said, "Getting ballgown, whoopee!"

When class was finished, Pagan immediately rushed over with her news. "Mama was quite agitated. She just tried to make me promise not to see Abdullah alone. I asked if she could please send me some decent clothes—which stopped her in her tracks, rather—but I explained that he might invite me to the St. Valentine's Ball and she knows perfectly well I've nothing to wear. However, I thought I'd better make sure of a dress, so after *she'd* been cut off, I phoned Grandfather and asked him if he couldn't please see that I had a proper ballgown. In fact," she added, a little ashamed, "I hinted that if I wasn't sent a dress Abdi might cough up for one. Grandfather said he'd be happy to buy me a dress, but made me promise not to accept any presents from Abdi."

A few days later a huge brown box was delivered by special messenger to Pagan. The whole school crowded behind her as she ran into the dining room, flung the box on one of the long empty tables, tore off the wrapping, plunged her arms into crisp layers of white tissue and drew out a beautiful cloud of pale gray net that sparkled with diamond droplets. It was a Norman Hartnell ballgown with a heart-shaped neckline demurely high, but not impossibly so.

The whole school sighed longingly.

After her next meeting with Abdullah, Pagan returned somewhat more subdued. "I asked whether he had a ten-year-old fiancée. He looked rather displeased and pointed his chin at me and said he did, but that it was entirely a matter of diplomacy and nothing to do with *us*. He was a bit odd for about ten minutes, then he went into his bedroom to make a telephone call and—can you imagine—about twenty minutes later there was a knock on the sitting room door and one of those grim bodyguards came in with a little man from the Cartier boutique. He handed Abdi a box and backed out of the door very fast. Then Abdi turned to me and gave me this blissful crimson velvet box lined with white satin, and in it, sparkling frantically at me, was an utterly divine diamond necklace. If I hadn't promised Grandfather, I'd have accepted it on the spot. So I told him I couldn't accept anything from him. I don't think he's used to people turning down diamond necklaces or saying no in general."

On the following four occasions when Pagan turned up at teatime in Prince Abdullah's suite, he tried to give her gifts of jewelry. Always a crimson velvet case was produced, but Pagan would never so much as try on the emerald earrings, the tiara of golden birch leaves, the bracelet of aquamarine or the enormous uncut sapphire ring. But the only thing Pagan accepted, with her mother's permission, was Abdullah's offer of his grandfather's old riding cloak, which he made her reluctantly promise to wear to the ball, as a penance for not accepting his valuable gifts. Pagan wasn't sure that she wanted to wear a smelly old Arab horse blanket to the ball, but, she thought, she could take it off in the school bus before entering the Imperial.

The following night there was another small dance, this time at the town hall. The girls from l'Hirondelle, wearing clumsy *après-ski* boots and tweed overcoats over long dresses, carried drawstring cotton bags for their dancing shoes as they climbed onto the little green school bus. As usual, Mademoiselle counted each head as they got on, as she would again when they reentered the bus to return after the dance.

Pagan had coaxed Maxine into lending her the pale-blue taffeta Christian Dior dress, although she couldn't shed the bolero because she couldn't pull the zipper completely up. Maxine had tacked up the hem a couple of inches to make it ankle-length for Pagan. As she and her partner whirled around the dance floor to the music of a gypsy band, Pagan was tapped on the shoulder by one of

Abdullah's bodyguards, ill at ease in a Western dinner jacket that was at least two sizes too large for him. "My master, the Crown Prince Abdullah, wishes to dance with you," he said.

"Well, he'll have to wait," said the Danish student who was dancing with Pagan, and moving his arm more firmly around her back, he started to dance again. The bodyguard took a swift step forward and suddenly the Danish student was sprawled on the floor.

Pagan turned around indignantly and saw Abdullah standing in the doorway. Slowly, with a small smile, she moved over to him, propelled by his bodyguard's iron hand in the small of her back. Still smiling she said, "May it please your Royal Highness to tell your thugs *never* to touch me again. And remember that I'm *not* one of your subjects. You don't own *me*, and I shall dance with whom I please."

Suddenly she dropped her hauteur and said in a quiet voice, "Oh, Abdi, why bother to humiliate Hans and draw attention to me?"

There was a pause, then Abdullah said stiffly, "Most regrettable. My servant was overzealous."

"Oh stop talking like an Indian Raj phrasebook," said Pagan crossly. "Of *course* I want to be with you, but you really can't push people around as it suits you and expect them to *like* you. I hate it when you're suddenly imperious. This is just an ordinary dance, and if you didn't want to be treated in an ordinary manner, you shouldn't have come." Wickedly she added, "I hope you aren't going to be as bossy with your poor little ten-year-old fiancée."

Abdullah's mouth tightened and his eyes blazed with anger. For a moment Pagan thought he might hit her, but instead he put his arm around her and they danced off in silence. Unseen by Abdullah, Pagan blew a kiss over his shoulder to Hans, who scowled back at her.

Suddenly, Pagan found that she was trembling as she leaned against Abdullah's muscular body—closer to him, suddenly more physically aware of him in that crowd of dancers than she had ever been when alone in his suite. Tonight, Pagan felt different, reckless, as she felt his warm breath on the side of her neck, then the tip of his tongue against it, erotic and inviting.

For the rest of the evening Pagan moved around the dance floor in an erotic trance. As the midnight curfew approached, Abdullah looked straight into her eyes and murmured persuasively, "Come back with me and let me show you what love is. I'll make you feel as you've never felt before."

"Mmmmm," sighed Pagan, as his hand lightly touched the nape of her neck. "How can you be so sure?"

"Because when I was sixteen I spent three weeks in Cairo with the *hakim* Khair al Saad, who taught me how to make love, to think only of your pleasure."

"You had lessons in *love* for *three weeks?* You studied it, like geography?" Pagan was astounded, impressed, intrigued. She longed to ask what he had learned and how it was taught. Were there real live women or a blackboard and chalk, and what was the homework and what difference had it made? Instead, she simply blurted, "How?"

He nibbled at her earlobe and purred, "Come back to the Imperial and let me *show* you."

Fascinated, Pagan couldn't stop staring into those self-assured black eyes. She found herself following Abdullah toward the main door. But then she remembered her cousin, her mother, the fiancée and the *paparazzi*, and stopping, she said with real regret, "I can't, I simply *can't*, Abdi. Look, Mademoiselle is waving us all to the cloakroom."

Aching with desire, Abdullah pulled her to him as Pagan tried to break away. "*What do you expect a man to do?*" he growled. "You arouse me and then you vanish into the night. In my country we have a name for such a woman."

"Oh, in my country too." Then Pagan couldn't resist adding, "but after all, you *are* engaged to be married."

Abdullah's black eyes blazed again, as an impatient Mademoiselle waved a beckoning finger at Pagan. Prince or no Prince, she wanted to get to her bed. Once more Abdullah pulled Pagan tight against his body and she felt his throbbing arousal. Then Abdullah turned on his heel and stalked angrily out of the room.

On the evening before the St. Valentine's dance Kate burst into the bedroom. "Pagan, you slut, you didn't clean the bath after you, there's a grubby ring around it."

"But surely a bath is for cleaning *oneself*," said Pagan, puzzled. "One does not clean *it*."

"One hasn't up to date, but one damn well will in the future," said Kate. "You really are the slut of the school."

"*O rage, o désespoir.*" Pagan yelled her new curse words and threw a tattered exercise book at Kate. "I'm sick to the withers with both of you. Kate's always criticizing and Maxine doesn't keep her promises."

"I do keep my promises, you *beech*."

"You *promised* to lend me ten francs."

"*Merde*, I mean sheet, why don't you ask your rich little Prince for ten francs? He can afford it better than I."

"Only because you spend all your money on diet food to get skinny for a stupid ski bum who likes skiing more than he likes you." Pagan pounced on Maxine and pummeled her.

"Ow, *merde*, sheet, ferk, dammit, *bloody* beech."

"Stop that sexy scuffling," Kate cried. "You know Matron already suspects that the whole school is a seething mass of lesbians. Ppppplease don't quarrel, I can't bear it. Pagan didn't mean what she said about Pierre. Of course he really loves you."

"Of course he does. I know that, because of *it*," Maxine said with dignity. She had wound up her hair in twists of toilet paper to curl it for the St. Valentine's Ball on the following night. "Especially because of the afterward, that golden glow like fireworks dying in the sky."

There was a pause, then Kate said timidly, "Afterward is the awful part for me. I feel so jittery and weepy and sort of apart from François."

"*Mon Dieu*, I feel much *closer* to Pierre." Maxine frowned thoughtfully at her hairbrush and speculated. "Maybe you haven't done it *enough*. I didn't like it the first time with Pierre, but I didn't want to upset him so I said nothing. I wanted him to *stay* with me, that's all I felt at first."

"That's the only thing I feel with François," Kate worried. "I've been doing it longer than you have, Maxine, but the last thing I feel is deep peace. When I really feel sexy and utterly marvelous and glowing is *before* we start. The afterward is just a letdown. I mean you cling to someone for hours and hours on the dance floor, you can feel his body against yours, you can smell it, and you rock to the music, wrapped around each other, and every time he moves you almost swoon, and you finally go the whole way because you know that it will be *even better*. Then he puts the thing in you and suddenly everything goes flat. He's in seventh heaven and going wild, but I'm suddenly looking down on the scene from the ceiling and that marvelous, melting-knees feeling is gone. I want to hit him and cry."

Perplexed, Maxine suggested, "Maybe you should relax more, Kate. Maybe you worry too much about what you *should* be doing, instead of what you *feel* like doing. I always feel *wonderful* afterward."

"It must be because you're French," Kate said, gloomily.

"Don't be silly," said Pagan. "Maybe François hasn't had enough practice, or maybe he's *never* been told what to do. When Abdullah was sixteen, he was sent to a special doctor to *learn* about love—for three weeks! Imagine! I didn't like to ask him if he was given tests or exams."

There was a sudden, polite, interested silence. Pagan immediately said, "You're *wrong*—we never have, and I'm not going to say another word."

"How do we know that story isn't just an upmarket brand of old Arabic bullshit if you won't talk about the consumer tests?" demanded Kate. "*We're* coming out with our secret sexual experiences in the interests of further education, and if you won't join in, then you can't listen. This is *serious* for me. Maybe I'm a freak, I'm worried."

There was another long pause, then Pagan said, "Well, if you're a freak, then I am too, because I felt the same way as you did. . . . But it wasn't with Abdi, it was with Paul, and *if you dare tell anyone, I'll kill you.*"

"So you *did.*"

"Yes," said Pagan gloomily, "and it was *beastly*. I think sex is overrated."

"I suspect it's addictive," offered Maxine, "like oysters."

There was a bang on the door. "I don't like *them* either. *Entrez!*"

The ancient porter carried in a huge box addressed to Pagan. The other two girls peered over her shoulder as she opened it. This time there was no tissue paper. The box was full of soft, dark Persian lamb. There was an awed silence as Pagan lifted it out and draped it around her shoulders and pulled the hood over her tangled mahogany hair. The wonderful cloak reached to the floor.

"Oh, Christ, I mean *mon Dieu,*" said Pagan, "this isn't what Mama expected. I'll have to check with her or she'll give me hell."

After the girls had each tried on the cloak, Pagan went to the telephone to call her mother. She came back half an hour later looking vexed.

"She says that as she agreed I could have it, I can keep it, but as the cloak is valuable, I can't wear it. I can wear it to the St. Valentine's Ball because to do otherwise would be discourteous, but after that I'm not to be seen in it."

"Well, at least it will be warmer to wear at night than that rotten old bed quilt."

So for the rest of her time at school, after lights-out, Pagan sat cross-legged on the end of Kate's bed, wrapped from head to toe in priceless Persian lamb.

CHAPTER 6

MAXINE HAD DRESSED her frizzed hair up in a topknot for the dance; it had taken nearly two hours to skewer it into place so that it stayed up. Almost painfully excited, she immediately spotted Pierre.

Kate couldn't see François. In fact it had been over a week since she'd seen François. Judy had slipped her a note in which he explained that he had to cancel their rendezvous because his father insisted that he have extra ski coaching. Kate wished that his father wasn't so ambitious for François, but it was understood that skiing took priority over anything else. His father wanted him to try for the Swiss team. Kate shut her eyes to François's faults and wouldn't hear a word against him. She had gone All the Way because she was in love with him. Or was it the reverse? She wished she knew.

As Pierre moved purposefully toward Maxine, Kate suddenly saw François. He was seated between two plump, dark girls with identical heavy-lidded, somnolent eyes. Kate waved at him but François didn't seem to notice. Someone asked her to dance so she fox-trotted around the floor and waved as she passed his table, but again François didn't seem to see her.

At the end of the dance Judy slipped over to Kate's table. She was wearing a traditional Swiss costume with white blouse, tightly laced black corselet and voluminous scarlet skirt. "I'll be glad to stop wearing this cuckoo-clock outfit—I can't stay long because I'm helping behind the bar. What's up, Kate?"

When Kate explained, Judy said, "You've got two legs and a tongue in your head. Don't just sit there, go over to him and say hello."

So Kate, a striking sight in her cream taffeta, the neckline of which was cut lower for every dance, went over to where François was sitting. He looked up and gave her a little frown.

"Ah, good evening, Kate. May I present Anna and Helena Stiarkoz?" Kate smiled at the two girls, who both inclined their heads toward her about one-eighth of an inch. One of them carefully fitted a cigarette into a long, gold holder and François snapped his lighter under it almost as a reflex movement.

Kate said, "I'm sitting in that far corner, François."

"So I noticed. I look forward to dancing with you later, perhaps."

Bewildered, Kate recognized his note of dismissal and clumsily bumped her way back through the tables to her seat.

Later? . . . Perhaps. . . . *This was the St. Valentine's Day Ball!*

"What's wrong?" Maxine asked.

Kate couldn't speak. She was afraid she'd cry. An unbecoming dull flush crept up from her neck and over her face.

"Come to the cloakroom," Maxine said quickly, tugging at her hand.

Once there, Kate burst into tears. "I think perhaps you exaggerate," Maxine said soothingly. "Perhaps they are old friends of his. I'll go over and say hello. You wait here."

So Maxine went over and greeted François. Again, he introduced the two girls and made it clear that he didn't wish to speak to Maxine.

Poor Kate, thought Maxine as she hurried back. Across the dimly lit room, Maxine saw Judy and jerked her head toward the cloakroom. Judy joined them a few minutes later. Maxine was saying, "Kate, *chérie*, you must stop these tears. There must be some reason for his behavior." But even as she spoke, Maxine knew that there were indeed *two* reasons, one sitting on either side of François.

"Look, he's a rat and you're well rid of him," said Judy, too inexperienced to know that a friend should never denigrate a jilted woman's lover. "There are two things you can do," Judy continued, taking Kate by the shoulders and shaking her. "Either have a scene with him out there—which you will lose—or refuse to let him see that he's humiliated you. Men don't like weeping, sniveling, clinging women. You've simply *got* to summon up your pride. Get back in there smiling."

"You mustn't let him know that he has hurt you," Maxine agreed. "You must deal with it properly and at the correct time when you face him with it so he can't avoid it."

"Look, François has been having lunch at the Chesa all last week with those two Greek lumps," said Judy. "They're heiresses to a shipping fortune, and don't think that François doesn't know it. So you can either snivel on or be brave and not show that he's dumped you."

Unfortunately, this conversation was overheard by another Hirondelle pupil who was in one of the toilet booths. She gleefully sped out to spread the whispered news. Miss Gstaad had received her comeuppance at last. When Kate emerged, freshly made-up, she instantly recognized that her humiliation was common knowledge. It brought out the Irish in Kate and she beckoned to the waiter. "Nick, get me a double something," she said, "there's a darling."

Nick, who also knew about the Greek twins, produced a forbidden double brandy. Kate choked and spluttered over her drink, then asked for another but Nick wouldn't let her have one. However, he kept bringing her ridiculously colorful, nonalcoholic drinks full of sliced-up fruit, for which he paid, and he kept up a cheerful stream of chat that needed no reply. It comforted Nick to comfort Kate. He knew how she felt because that was how he felt about Judy whenever he had time to think. Why didn't Judy feel the force of his love? Why didn't it *force* her to love him? Why did she constantly refuse to treat him as anything but a friend? For both Nick and Kate, part of the pain of their love lay in not realizing that it was not the only love of their lives, but only the first love of their lives.

"Look, there's the bunch from Le Mornay," Nick whispered to Kate, "all waiting to fall in love with you."

A group of dinner-jacketed adolescents had just come through the glass entrance doors. They were remarkably cosmopolitan, two Persians with arched dark eyebrows that met above their noses, a sallow Indian Rajah and a thin blond Scandinavian boy, who carried himself as if he were used to everyone else walking behind him. The group also included two current gems of Le Mornay—the immensely rich Hunter Baggs and Prince Saddrudin, the younger son of the Aga Khan.

As they sauntered over to their table, a sudden unmistakable hush fell—it was that moment of anticipation that always precedes the entrance of royalty. All heads turned toward the door where Prince Abdullah, the guest of honor, stood as stiffly as if he were reviewing a parade. Demure on his arm, Pagan floated down the steps in a cloud of sparkling, mist-gray tulle.

Kate now openly flirted with Nick, with whom she felt safe. At midnight pink-and-white balloons fell in a cloud from the ceiling and all the women guests were presented with golden heart-shaped powder compacts and a single long-stemmed pink rose. Silver streamers were hurled around the ballroom, and all formality was abandoned.

Kate could no longer bear the gaiety and headed for the cloakroom, but she was waylaid by Nick, who had been drinking although he was on duty. "Look, we're both unhappy," he whispered, "Judy won't have anything to do with me except as a friend, and she won't even *talk* to me tonight. I'm so lonely and miserable. Kate, I need you," he said simply. "Come to my room, darling Kate."

To her surprise, Kate considered it. She longed for the reassuring warmth of a man's arms after the pain of rejection. "Well, I don't know," she said, "I mean, how do we fix it?"

"Be one of the first to be counted into the front of the school bus and then nip out the back door while Mademoiselle is still busy counting at the front. Get Pagan to let you in later." Kate looked so forlorn and miserable that Nick risked a quick hug.

"All right, I'll try, but I can't promise. It depends on Pagan."

She went back to discuss possibilities with Maxine, who was slightly tipsy after two glasses of champagne. "Pierre wants me to stay, too," she said, obviously longing to do so.

"Is he going to take you to the team chalet?"

"No, he's booked a room upstairs, just in case."

Kate was impressed. "Goodness, on the off chance. How expensive!"

"Well, why shouldn't we?" The two girls looked across at Pagan pretending to be a princess as she danced around the floor. "You don't think Pagan will want to stay out?"

"I don't think she'd dare." They signaled across the room to Pagan and again rushed to the cloakroom.

"*Stay?*" Pagan exclaimed. "How can I possibly stay? Everyone would *know*. I'll let you in at five. But for heaven's sake, don't be late."

At one o'clock Kate and Maxine climbed into the bus. They were just ahead of Pagan, who created a diversion by fussing loudly as she lifted her Hartnell skirts over the grimy steps and nearly managed to knock Mademoiselle into the gutter as Kate and Maxine slipped out the other door.

Kate fled back into the Imperial and up the backstairs, slowing down as she reached the sixth floor where Nick was waiting. They hurried down the passage to the servants' stairs. Once in the security of his room, he hugged her, then unbuttoned her bulky tweed coat. Kate perched gingerly on the edge of the bed, which creaked. Nick gently pulled her head against his chest and stroked her hair for a long time until he felt her relax against his body. Then he started to kiss her hair, then her cheeks, although he didn't touch her mouth. That was still his private measure of treachery. But later Kate reached up and pulled his lips down to hers and then, with a gasp, all thought was forgotten as he kissed her with all the pent-up ardor of his eighteen years and the accumulated anxiety and pain of the last eight months. That kiss seemed to last for half an hour. He couldn't bear to leave her mouth, he felt himself drowning in her fragrance and the soft feel of her body, warm through the increasingly creased cream taffeta.

Then the taffeta was thrown on the floor and he was softly kissing her breasts. "Under the blankets," he murmured, but oddly that was Kate's measure of treachery, so they lay in a tangle of half-shed clothes, limbs entwining, writhing, gradually discarding garments and inhibitions, until at last Nick lay, triumphantly naked, on top of Kate's yearning body.

But something wasn't quite right, thought Kate, as she slid one arm down Nick's body to caress him with her hand. It was as if he had done it already. As she touched him, Nick flinched, then kissed her with renewed ardor, moving himself away from her hand.

Ten minutes later Kate again felt for him, eager to caress him as François had shown her, anxious that she should not fail some unexplained test. She felt soft little pouches and limp flesh against the palm of her willing hand, which Nick again removed. They both felt embarrassed. They neither of them knew what to do next. In a frenzy of misery, they threw their arms around each other and cuddled tenderly, as friends, warm and comforted by each other's arms.

But they both felt sad.

Maxine crunched down the snow-covered, blue-shadowed street toward Kate, who was shivering under the street lamp. Without a word they held mittened hands, ran down the road to the back door and gently tapped on it.

The door was flung open by a wrathful Matron, fully dressed in her navy uniform. "A fine pair you are," she shouted, "you should be ashamed of yourselves. You're to go to the headmaster's office immediately."

Wearing a maroon silk dressing gown, Monsieur Chardin was pacing up and down in a rage. Pagan, wrapped in her shabby, camel's hair Jaeger dressing gown—cut on the lines of a monk's habit but yanked around her waist by a purple satin sash—was sitting pale and silent, nervously picking at the arms of her chair. She looked unhappy. She had been awakened at three o'clock that morning by Matron, whose white hair hung in a long plait over her dressing gown. Pagan's mother had been on the telephone—her grandfather had suffered a massive heart attack that afternoon, had collapsed in the stables and died shortly after midnight. Pagan was to return to England immediately.

As Matron passed through Kate's room to reach Pagan's inner room she had noticed that neither Kate nor Maxine was sleeping in her bed. Dazed by the news of her grandfather's death, Pagan nevertheless admitted nothing and—as if to indicate this to them—she looked up as the two girls were hustled into the study and said, "Where *have* you been? To Gringo's?"

Now suddenly Kate and Maxine faced reality. Shivering in their overcoats in the unheated study, they trembled in front of Chardin, terrified of facing their parents. The soft, pink petals of Kate's wilting rose floated to the floor, leaving only the long, thorny stem in her hand.

Then Chardin exploded. He hurled every insult at them from ingratitude to whoredom, until he finished by pointing a chubby finger at Kate and shrieking, "And *you*, you *putain*, you chase every pair of pants in town!"

At which the Irish in Kate rose again and she replied, "So do you, Monsieur."

There was a nasty silence, then Chardin said with venom, "You will both be expelled from this school tomorrow."

"No they won't," said Pagan in a tired, oddly disinterested voice.

Chardin turned to her, "And who are you, miss, to tell me what to do?"

"I am a friend of your friend, Paul. He took me to his house and showed me lots of photographs. I didn't think he'd miss them so I stole a few and left them with a friend in town. But here's one."

She felt in her dressing gown pocket and produced a photograph of Paul in bed with the two little South African girls who had left so suddenly after Christmas. Pagan showed the photograph first to Matron, then to Chardin, then she put it back in her pocket and produced her trump card—a photograph of Monsieur Chardin himself, plump and naked as a baby, poised above the naked body of Paul.

"Happy snaps," said Pagan with disinterested weariness. Yesterday this scene would have been dramatic and terrifying. Today, it was trivial compared to her grandfather's death. "I can't help thinking that your scheme only works if you play one father at a time. If any father had seen photographs of more than one girl, it would have been apparent that you are in fact a cheap blackmailer, Monsieur Chardin, and that you deliberately set those girls up to be photographed with Paul. Anyway, he told me all about it." Nobody spoke or moved. "I think he said the going rate for fathers is six thousand francs every three months. I don't really know what to do about it, but if you take any action against Maxine and Kate, I'm going straight to the police with my story and the other photographs. So it's your decision, Monsieur Chardin."

Chardin stood silent for a moment. Then smiled. In a forced voice, he said, "Miss, you are no doubt overwrought because of your grandfather's sad death, therefore I shall take no notice of your ridiculous accusations. And because I do not want to bring disgrace upon my school, I will not punish these two foolish girls."

He cleared his throat and paused to regain his authority. "But I trust that they realize the seriousness of their folly. It is just lucky that none of your set is pregnant. Now get to bed, all of you."

The exhausted, frightened girls stumbled off to bed, weak with relief. There was no need for further anxiety, they thought, as they wearily undressed.

But they were wrong, and so was the headmaster.

Because one of the set *was* pregnant.

PART TWO

CHAPTER 7

CONSCIOUS OF HER shabby overcoat, Judy suddenly felt like a hick. She longed for the fragile, beautiful clothes, so artfully displayed in the windows of Paris, that Maxine pointed out, chattering nonstop until they reached the corner where Hermès stood. Timidly, they pushed through the glass door, whereupon Maxine adopted a haughty, nose-in-the-air attitude, examining the most expensive silken scarves and handbags in the world as if none of them was quite good enough for the two teenage girls. Intoxicated by the smell of rich leather, Judy bought a Hermès diary, a beautiful calfskin appointment book with its own gold pencil stuck in the side.

It made her feel a bit more French and a bit more grown-up. After all, she was now seventeen years old and she had been in Paris for two whole days. She was completely fascinated by the city, by the superb chestnut-lined boulevards, the glittering boutiques, the elegant, scented women, the wonderful mouth-watering restaurants and the cheerfully noisy apartment of Maxine's family, where Judy was staying for a week or two until she found a job and a place to live. She wasn't going to think about that yet; today she was going to pretend that she was able to lead the carefree, protected existence that Maxine, Pagan and Kate were able to lead. *One* day, Judy promised herself, she would live like that *always*, not just for a few days.

"Now for the Latin Quarter," Maxine said. They hurried down the streets, still snow-covered in February, and clattered under the wrought-iron art nouveau lilies of the valley that decorated the entrance arch of the métro at Palais Royal. They plunged down the steps and past the fat old flower seller huddled on a stool, a gray shawl around her head. A blast of welcome heat carried upward the fragrance of Gaulois cigarettes, yellowing newspapers, bad drains and garlic.

"We're late. I told Guy we'd meet him at twelve," Maxine worried, as they emerged into daylight at the end of their journey. "Not that he's likely to be on time, especially not for *me*. Ever since we were children he's been conscious of the fact that he's three years older than me. We only saw a lot of each other because our mothers were close friends at school, so he had to put up with me."

She hurried along the Boulevard St. Germain, tugging Judy with one scarlet glove; the American girl dawdled to peer down the winding streets that branched off the main boulevard.

"What sort of clothes does Guy make?" Judy asked.

"Mostly suits and blouses, with a few light coats."

"Does he sew them himself?"

"No, no, he has a cutter and a seamstress. They work in one room and he sleeps in the room next to it. He'll soon have to look for an *atelier*, but they're unbelievably scarce if you have no key money—and Guy hasn't."

"Then how does he pay the seamstress and the cutter?" asked Judy.

"His Papa refused to help him because he said that fashion was an occupation for *pédérastes*, so Guy got money from a few private clients. At the start he went to my mother and offered to dress her in four outfits a year for a modest annual advance payment. She accepted and sent him to her friends and *they* all signed up, even my Aunt Hortense."

Judy was still bewildered by the thought of Maxine's Aunt Hortense, who was unlike any aunt she'd ever met—or any other adult, come to that. The previous evening Aunt Hortense had taken them to dine at Madame de George, an elegant meal that had transported Judy from Rossville forever, as she ate quails' eggs, artichokes, guinea fowl and a dessert that tasted like frozen brandy. After the sumptuous meal, the lights were lowered and the floor show began, with a *frou-frou* of pink ostrich plumes covering—just—the pudenda of a line of unusually beautiful showgirls, all tall, elegant, slim-hipped and high-breasted. Suddenly, Judy noticed their wide shoulders, biceps and muscular forearms. Her mouth fell open. She couldn't believe her eyes. She pinched Maxine and said, "Are those . . . er . . . girls . . . er . . . *men*?"

"Yes," Maxine giggled.

"I'm amazed that your aunt would bring us to such a place."

"She wanted you to see something *oo la la!*" Maxine laughed. "and this is the least naughty of the naughty Paris nightspots. Aunt Hortense likes to *épater les bourgeois*—she can't stand pompous people and she likes to shock the smug."

"I'll never understand you Europeans."

"Aha, but *we* understand *you*, we know what shocks you," said Aunt Hortense. Her voice reminded Judy of gently drifting snow, raindrops splashing on an old stone fountain, the well-bred chink of china and weathered leather riding boots. Judy sensed that Aunt Hortense, while raising hell, would never raise her voice. She had a large, craggy face with a huge thrusting nose above a wide mouth drawn back in a permanent, deceptive smile, and her eyelids were painted emerald to match her emerald satin cocktail hat. She was tall, imperious and forbidding until she fixed you with her oddly enchanting wide smile.

Hurrying through the snowy streets, eventually the two girls reached the steam-misted glass walls of the café Deux Magots, where they sat down at the only empty table and ordered hot lemon punch.

"*Merde*, I mean ferk, no one I recognize," wailed Maxine. "It's different in the evening. I once saw Simone de Beauvoir having a row with Jean-Paul Sartre. And I once saw Juliette Greco. She always wears a black sweater and pants—an odd wardrobe don't you think?"

"Saves making a decision in the morning," said a small, wiry blond boy wearing a black sweater and pants. He sat down in the empty seat beside her. He looked like an unmasked cat burglar—small with a slightly hooked Roman nose, a wide sensual mouth and a shock of hemp-colored hair. "Heavens, the difference. . . .

Your face, Maxine. . . . I would only recognize you from the rear. And you're so svelte that I could use you as a model." He unwound the long black scarf from his neck and ordered three *croque-monsieur*, the fried ham and cheese sandwich that is the staple diet of French students.

"What's been happening to you?" Maxine inquired.

"I've been living here on the Left Bank in the Hôtel de Londres for over a year, being a master couturier, but nobody seems to have noticed."

"How did you become a master couturier?" Judy asked, plunging right in. "How did you get out of your *service militaire?*"

"I had TB when I was fourteen so the army didn't want me. Papa was furious, of course, but Mother was enchanted when I joined Jacques Fath because I no longer insisted on making dresses for *her*. She said it was so tedious being fitted by me—I stuck pins in her!" He giggled.

"*How* did you suddenly jump out of school and into the studio of a world-famous couturier?" Judy asked.

"Frankly, I got the job with Jacques Fath because my mother knew the head *vendeuse*. When I wasn't picking up pins, I spent every spare moment sketching the Fath clothes. As publicly as possible, you understand—I can draw wonderfully." He blew a straw at Maxine.

"When my first year was up at Fath, they took me on as a studio sketch artist, and when my second year was up, I was promoted to designer's assistant. Not assistant to Fath himself, you understand, but to one of his menials." He poured wine for all of them. "My job was to translate Fath's sketches for the workrooms, then sort out the decisions until the *toile* was made, then look after every zipper and button until the garment was ready for the first model fitting. Naturally, we never had anything to do with the clients—the *vendeuses* dealt with them. . . . Maxine, you shouldn't eat *croque-monsieur* at such a rate if you want to keep this amazing new shape."

"But how did you learn to make clothes?" Judy persisted. She wanted to know everything.

"Oh, I don't know, I just *did* it." Guy shrugged his shoulders.

In spite of his careless pose as a newly hatched genius, the real secret of Guy Saint Simon's success—apart from his talent—was the obsessive interest in fashion that had led him to spend every spare moment with the Jacques Fath tailors and cutters, learning to cut with the skill that had evolved over generations and had been passed on—only by example—from man to man (the tailors were always men, the women worked as dressmakers).

"But you *can't* 'just start,' " objected Judy.

"Well, I made some *proper* suits for my mother and she wore them. I thought she was doing it just to please me, but then all her friends wanted to buy the same suits. So—*voilà!*—I was in business! Now tell me what *you* intend to do with yourselves."

"I want to be an interior decorator and study in London," Maxine said, "but I don't dare tell Papa yet so I'm going to try and get Aunt Hortense to intercede for me."

"And I'm going to get a job here in Paris as an interpreter," Judy added, sounding far more sure of herself than she was. She knew that the job competition in Paris was almost as fierce as the traffic, and that French working hours were long and poorly paid.

"Then she's going back to New York," said Maxine gaily, "to get a job in some glamorous international company where she can use her languages and eventually, of course, marry the boss!"

"Can we see your clothes, Guy?" Judy asked, wanting to change the conversation.

"But of course. You might both marry appalling old millionaires and become my best clients. But not today; I have to see my button-maker in ten minutes. Meet me after work tomorrow, six o'clock at the Hôtel de Londres. I'll take you to dinner at the Beaux Arts afterward, because it's St. Valentine's Day tomorrow and all the students will be having a terrific party. . . . What's wrong? . . . Why are you both looking so odd? . . . Have I said something to upset you?"

"No, no," said Maxine hastily, "it's just that we had a bit of trouble at school last year on St. Valentine's Day. We . . . er . . . got back from a dance later than we should have done."

"Well, you won't be bothered by such childish things anymore," said Guy, waving for the bill and not noticing the girls' uneasy silence.

Outside, a weak winter sun was shining, the wind had dropped and it wasn't nearly so cold. The two girls drifted along the cobbled *quais*, by the stone parapets of the Seine, past the secondhand book carts and the dark green stalls.

"Does Guy like girls?" asked Judy as they walked over the Pont Royal. There had been something about the way he moved his hands.

"I don't know. Perhaps not, I've no idea. Either way, you mustn't fall for him, you know. I want to leave you with someone to look after you, someone to take the place of Nick—a brother, not a lover, for the moment. I don't want you to feel alone in Paris."

"Can't I have both?"

"But of course, you won't be able to avoid it in Paris. Just wait until the spring when the chestnut trees are flowering. Look, there are already some flowers here in the Jardin des Tuileries."

The girls hurried through the gardens, then turned left toward the Avenue Montaigne, becoming increasingly excited as they neared number 32, the salon of the greatest couturier in the world, Christian Dior.

A cloud of perfume enveloped them as they entered the pampered warmth. Aunt Hortense, whom they were to meet, was nowhere to be seen so they wandered around the boutique, fingering exquisite silk blouses in sugar-almond colors, eyeing the unbelievably fragile lingerie and stroking the suede gloves.

To Judy's relief she was ignored; but the *vendeuses* fluttered around Maxine, who was wearing her navy Dior overcoat, so she daringly decided to try on a couple of things. She put on a floor-length jackal coat, watched by an indulgent saleswoman who knew that this child had no intention of buying, but that nevertheless somebody had bought her clothes from Dior. Then she slipped on a white cotton nightgown trimmed with narrow green satin ribbon that cost the equivalent of her allowance for three months. She had just discarded it and purchased a pale blue lace garter belt—three weeks' allowance but worth it—when Aunt Hortense swept in and they went off to claim their reserved seats from the big antique reception desk.

Had Aunt Hortense not been a regular customer, the elegant receptionist would have courteously asked her name, address and telephone number, then written them in the big leather visitors' book; she would also have asked who suggested they visit the house of Dior. This procedure helped to sort out the spies and time-wasters from the genuine customers. Commercial spies rarely tried to get in after the opening of a collection because they had all the information they needed by the third day of the show, but smartly dressed women (sometimes genuine customers like cosmetic tycoon Helena Rubinstein) often visited the collection with a less well-dressed "friend," who was really a dressmaker—and whose second-rate shoes, bag and gloves invariably proclaimed the fact.

"So comfortable here," said Aunt Hortense, as they were seated in the pale gray salon in the front row of delicate gilt chairs, "although I have never understood why men think women enjoy shopping. It is a painful ordeal that has to be endured in order to acquire new clothes. The pain comes in two parts—choosing the right garment, then making sure that it fits. . . . Oh, the arguments I've had with fitters! So I come to Christian Dior because I *dislike* shopping. One isn't demoralized at a couturier, as one is in a shop where they urge you to try on clothes that make you feel fat, awkward and ugly."

"Or complain that you're not a stock size, in a way that makes you feel like a freak," agreed Judy.

"Or intimidate you, so that you end up buying something expensive merely because you don't look as dreadful in it as the other things you tried on," Maxine added.

"Quite so. It's easier to go to Dior. You pay more, but you never waste your money and you always look your best. Ha, here comes the first model!"

The audience concentrated keenly, like buyers at a horse auction, as each haughty, elegant model appeared, held a pose and then drifted back through the gray velvet curtains.

"How can that girl *possibly* have such a tiny waist?" Judy wondered, as a raven-haired model appeared in a pale gray flannel coat cinched with a wide silver-gray calf belt. "Where does her food go?"

"If you remove the belt," Aunt Hortense murmured, "you'd find that there was no flannel underneath, only silk taffeta joining the top to the skirt. That's why her waist looks so tiny. But she shouldn't carry her furs so carefully. Pierre Balmain says that the trick to wearing mink is to look as though you're wearing a cloth coat, and the trick to wearing a cloth coat is to treat it as if it were as precious as mink."

As always, the final item in the collection was a white bridal gown with a flutter of little lace frills frothing from the shoulder to form an eight-foot-long train. "Excellent," approved Aunt Hortense, "a bride should always choose something with back interest for everyone to look at when she's kneeling at the altar. A wedding service is so boringly predictable. Now for my fittings."

They moved to a dressing room where the silent fitter—silent because her mouth was full of pins—made minute alterations on an apricot silk dress with billowing gypsy violinist sleeves and a wasp waist. "Three fittings for every garment," grumbled Aunt Hortense, "but it means a perfect fit, which is one of the main attractions of a couture garment." She addressed herself to the fitter. "It needs a little more room at the waist, don't you think? . . . You want to know why I chose this dress, Judy? Because it's fairly original but not outrageous. Only the very rich, the very beautiful or the truly creative can carry off really original clothes. I am not one of them. But I know what effect I wish to give, whereas most women want to look distinctive and indistinguishable, both at the same time, which is impossible."

"That V neck doesn't plunge as low as the one in the show," Maxine criticized.

"No, Monsieur Dior kindly agreed to a high neck. Before six-thirty and after forty-five one should never show an inch of skin."

"It's very chic," offered Judy, and was immediately contradicted.

"Very *elegant*, not very chic. Schiaparelli invented the word 'chic' to mean eccentric and original. One can't be chic now and again. One either is or one isn't. I am not chic."

But Aunt Hortense *was* a perfectionist. Energetic and tough enough to know what she wanted—and get it—she never spared anyone's feelings in order to achieve perfection. Always polite, she would return a dress, coat or hat to the workroom again and again until she considered it satisfactory. Nothing was ever better than satisfactory. Aunt Hortense did not have many clothes, but they were all made of the finest chiffon, the softest silk, the most subtle tweeds and supple furs. Apart from her Dior clothes, her outfits were different variations of one ensemble that she considered suitable for her age and style of life; this was a suit, a collarless jacket worn with an A-line or pleated skirt made from silk or wool, with a chiffon blouse in the same color, and each outfit always had two hats, a small head-hugging one and a big-brimmed felt or straw. These simple outfits blazed with exquisite jewels. Although Aunt Hortense liked discretion in clothes she did not care for it in jewelry; she liked hunks of gold, heavy chains of platinum, chunks of emerald quartz spiked with diamonds, and long ropes of knobbly baroque pearls.

After the Dior show, Aunt Hortense took the girls for a cup of tea in the Plaza Athénée. The wide corridor was lined with clusters of little velvet arm chairs and smelled of expensive scent, rich cigars and well-laundered Americans.

"What did you think of the show?" asked Aunt Hortense as the pastry trolley was wheeled up.

"It was very splendid," Judy said, leaning back. She enjoyed being waited on more than could possibly be imagined by anyone who had never been a waitress. "Very beautiful and very splendid, but I think that clothes should be practical, and those weren't. Even if I could afford them, I couldn't afford to look after them, so I shouldn't buy them however rich I was." She put her fork into a meringue. "Maxine, you needn't look as if I'm insulting the Virgin Mary. How do you hand-wash a dress with five yards of fabric in the skirt? How would you dry-clean that white crèpe ballgown? And how do you keep a cream suede coat clean?"

"Your American designers can't produce anything nearly so good as our Paris collections," said Maxine indignantly. "That's why they all come over *here* to buy."

"Look, Maxine, I said the show was divine, but I also thought that for most women who haven't a lady's maid and endless credit at the cleaners, it was impractical. Your Aunt Hortense asked me what I thought and I'm telling her. I hope I'm going to be much too busy to spend half my life looking after my clothes."

Aunt Hortense, sitting bolt upright on her little velvet chair, like a Saint Cyr cadet, said, "Interesting and practical criticism. I would tell Monsieur Dior except, of course, he wouldn't take the slightest notice. There are only about eighteen thousand women in the world who are rich enough to afford couture clothes from Paris and they all seem to be queueing at his door, so he doesn't have to bother about the practical aspects of his collection. But Judy is quite right to say exactly what she thinks; I always do. When I was your age I was a timid little mouse—well, not little, but terrified of opening my mouth. Children were seen and not heard, you know, before the First World War."

"The reason I always say what I think," said Judy, "is that I don't know how to talk any other way. I know Europeans think I'm ill-mannered, but I don't understand why."

"You're tactless and you shout," said Maxine, still annoyed by Judy's criticism of Dior.

"I shout sometimes when I get excited because I had to when I was little or none of the bigger kids would have paid any attention to me."

"Don't change," advised Aunt Hortense. "You think for yourself, you don't repeat other people's opinions. You are direct and expect other people to be. Perhaps your manner seems a little brusque to people who don't know you, perhaps it may even irritate or alarm them, but you will soon pick up the social graces now that you are no longer a child. Personally, I find you refreshingly straightforward, somewhat similar to myself, in fact. This charming naiveté, this ruthless innocence I find fresh and appealing."

She took a thoughtful sip of her tea. "Losing your innocence has very little to do with virginity, you know. Loss of innocence comes when you have to deal with the real world by yourself, when you learn that the first rule of life is kill or be killed. So different from one's nursery stories."

She picked out another crystalized violet. "I realized this quite quickly during the war. It was only then, at the age of forty-two, that I learned what real life was like. The war was dreadful, but sometimes it was also exciting. I still miss the action. As Maxine knows, I prefer action to discussion. You shouldn't just sit and twiddle your thumbs and wait for something to happen in your life."

"No," said Judy eagerly. "You have to make it happen!"

"Quite so. Oh, what fun we used to have in the middle of such horror and pain! Maurice, our chauffeur, was my *chef* in the Resistance and we worked on the railways." In answer to Judy's unspoken query, she snapped her middle finger against her thumb. "Blowing them up. Then we became part of an escape route—not so much fun, but even more dangerous." Daintily, Aunt Hortense stirred her porcelain cup with a silver spoon.

"But where did you learn all that?"

"Oh, I was never taught anything useful. But you pick things up very fast when you have to."

"What do you wish you'd been taught?"

"I wish I'd been taught to expect change as a matter of course in everything including oneself. You will find that you're one person when you're seventeen, but by the time you're twenty-five you've developed into quite a different person with different aims, interests, attitudes, friends." She paused, then shrugged her shoulders. "Then ten years later you find you've changed again—and so it goes on. Finally, when you get to my age, people say you get set in your ways, but what they really mean is that you like having your own way. It is the beginning of the selfishness of old age."

She paused and lifted the silver teapot. "You two girls seem so much more adulterous than I was at your age. No? That's not the right word? Well, my English is rusting. Judy will be good practice for me." Judy nodded, and Aunt Hortense continued. "To me you both seem very grown-up. At sixteen I thought I knew nothing and it caused me great anxiety; at eighteen I thought I knew everything, then at thirty, I realized that I knew nothing—and possibly never would, which depressed me until I noticed that no one else knew anything either.

Adultery implies a certain objectivity, restraint and wisdom, don't you think?"

"I don't think you mean adultery. That's other people's husbands committing intimacy."

"Thank you, dear child, I meant adult behavior. My point was that you don't necessarily grow more adult as you grow older."

At first Judy thought Aunt Hortense a snob, but she quickly realized that Hortense was merely French and rich and old, that she was experienced and worth listening to and didn't give a damn for anyone's opinion. Judy was fascinated by her. She was so different from her mom, Judy thought with disloyalty. The thought made her feel guilty. She was still frightened by the specter of Rossville, terrified of letting her life slip away like her mother without anyone noticing—not even herself. Unlike her mother, Judy didn't intend to spend her life being frightened of doing anything.

Her mother was unable to forget her memories of the thirties, when for two bad years her husband had been out of work. She had managed to pass this fear of being penniless on to Judy, who consequently thought about financial security the way other girls did about Prince Charming. Judy couldn't help noticing that her father had not turned out to be Prince Charming. Marriage was no guarantee of money and security, she knew that. She'd have to work long and hard before she could pull a large bill out of her alligator purse and hand it to a waiter without looking at the check as Aunt Hortense had just done.

Having cross-questioned Judy about her future plans, Aunt Hortense said thoughtfully, "If you have nobody to look after you, please remember that I have nobody to look after. I am not as fierce as I look, and I remember very well what it was like to be seventeen, so telephone me if you need help. In fact, please telephone me anyway."

Maurice drove the two girls back to Neuilly. Judy looked at his broad shoulders below the black peaked cap. "Do you think intimacy was ever committed?" she whispered.

"With Aunt Hortense, who knows?" Maxine whispered back.

As the old Mercedes sped through the center of Paris, Judy felt as if she were in heaven. Like many an American before her, she was already in love with Paris.

CHAPTER 8

THE DUSTY FOYER of the Hôtel de Londres had an air of minding its own business. Faded wallpaper peeled from the top of the walls and the baseboards were well kicked.

"Where is the elevator?" Maxine asked the receptionist.

"At the Ritz." He jerked a thumb toward the staircase at the back of the hall.

The girls walked past an exhausted palm tree that sagged in a copper pot, then climbed the creaking stairs to the fifth floor where at the end of a dim passage they found Guy's workroom. Small and low-ceilinged, far cleaner than the rest of the hotel, it overlooked a small courtyard. Silhouetted in front of the window, a woman crouched over a whirring sewing machine; shirt-sleeves rolled up, a man in white apron was cutting into a length of mauve wool on a table that occupied most of the room. Bolts of fabric were stacked in a rack to the left of the door and on the right were two dressrails on wheels from which hung garments shrouded in white tissue paper.

"So now I show you," said Guy, after introducing the girls to his cutter and seamstress, who were just about to leave at the end of their day. One by one, Guy took the clothes off the rail and carefully slid off the tissue. His designs were mainly suits or separates; sensuous silk jackets and skirts in misty rose and lavender were matched to pants in darker jersey; jewel-colored velvet suits in garnet, topaz and sapphire could be worn with matching wool coats. The designs were simple, without boning or padding.

"These clothes should be worn with a lot of bold, gilt jewelry," Guy explained, as the girls tried on the clothes and then admired themselves in the big mirror. "I'm only doing one raincoat but in three different lengths; it's reversible. It can be worn over anything in the collection with or without a belt." He produced a cinnamon gabardine raincoat with a purple wool lining. "I would also like to do it in pewter gray lined with pale pink, but I can't afford to produce my designs in too many colors in my first collection."

"I love nearly everything," Judy said enthusiastically after she and Maxine in their petticoats—clothes-mad like all girls of their age—had spent half an hour trying on the garments. "They're so easy to move in—easy to live in, as well, I should think. They feel as if you're wearing no clothes at all. You're not conscious of them."

"What I'm trying to do is to produce clothes that make a woman look smart without making her feel uncomfortable. Did you notice that all my skirt bands are elasticized? And I insist that my model visit the bathroom in every single garment to make sure it's totally practical."

Guy's comfortable clothes were very different from the exquisite but constricting ensembles that Judy had seen at Dior. Although Guy's look was casual, it was nevertheless elegant because of the clever cut and the beautiful fabrics he used.

He pulled a bolt of mauve silk from the rack, draped a length over Judy's bare shoulders and started to pin it. "This isn't the way most designers work," he mumbled through a mouthful of pins. "Only Madame Grès cuts straight from the fabric and pins onto a live model."

"Do your cutter and seamstress fit people?" asked Judy.

"Never! The fit is the *most important part* of a garment and *I* do it. I don't much like doing it, but I have nobody else who can. Good fitters are born, not made, and in Paris we have the best fitters in the world. Keep still or I'll jab you. I can also make patterns and samples, cut, sew, fit and supervise a small workshop, but I'm primarily a designer and when I'm big enough I'll never do anything else, thank you."

"What about selling?" asked Judy. "Who sells your stuff?"

Guy looked worried. "To date there has been no need for a *vendeuse* because my clients know me and they bring their friends. They think it's intriguing to come to this shabby place—they feel they're getting something cheap, which of course they *are*. Also they feel they are in on a new discovery, which I hope is true. Now, how do you like that, *ma chère?*" He stepped back and Judy moved carefully to the mirror. She was wearing the classically draped dress of a Grecian goddess.

"Oh, how I long for this!"

"When I'm richer, then we shall see. At the moment every sou I spend is vital." He rapidly unpinned her and deftly caught the length of silk as it fell from her shoulders. "Now can I offer you an aperitif?"

He opened the adjoining door that led to his bedroom, a strange contrast to the immaculate, severely practical room in which they stood. Guy's personal possessions—books, underwear, shoes—were piled on the end of the bed, which was the only semiempty space in a room crammed with half-draped tailor's dummies, metal clothes racks, bales of muslin and paper patterns. Guy pushed the heap of books and shoes farther down the bed and the three of them sat cross-legged on it, sipping white vermouth from one toothmug and two paper cups as the girls listened to Guy's plans. He outlined his career and spread his life plan before them—almost as clear as the aerial view from the Arc de Triomphe had been yesterday, Judy thought wistfully as she said, "You sound so confident."

"Myself? I live in constant self-doubt, indecision and secret panic about my capability," Guy said. He added gloomily, "You have no idea what agony it is to decide whether a jacket should be double- or single-breasted—and such a decision is vital because I cannot afford to produce many garments, so it has to be the one or the other. And until I can afford an assistant, there is no one with whom to discuss *anything*. I tell you, it's lonely at the bottom."

"I know what you mean," said Judy. "I'm going to miss Maxine dreadfully. I'll have no one to chat with, not even a room to live in as yet."

"Why not move in here?" Guy suggested. "It's the cheapest decent place I could find, only five hundred francs a night—that's about two dollars isn't it? The Left Bank is full of cheap rooming hotels for students, but *this* one is clean, and they bring you breakfast in bed, if you can afford it. When I had influenza I had three breakfasts a day sent up. And there's a telephone; they take messages if you tip that surly bastard in the hall once a month."

"A wonderful idea," Maxine said. "Guy can keep an eye on you, and you can advise him on double or single breasts."

On their way to dinner, they stopped at the hall desk where Maxine negotiated with the surly porter over monthly rates and got a fifteen percent discount. Then they walked along the rue Bonaparte to the noisy Beaux Arts restaurant on the corner. Lifting her glass of wine, Judy felt much more settled. Now all she needed was a job.

Judy didn't feel so cheerful two days later when she went job hunting.

Armed with her Swiss diplomas, she was interviewed in a shabby employment office where she sat in line until her name was called. She was interrogated by a woman of uncertain age, with a typically French face—that combination of sallow skin, weary brown eyes and expensively gilded hair pulled back in a chignon. She spoke very fast and Judy stuttered when making her replies. At the end of the interview, the woman gave a long sniff to imply doubt, shrugged her shoulders to imply resignation, then pulled a large kitchen timer out of her drawer and gave Judy a typing test. In spite of the intimidating atmosphere, Judy passed. The woman gave another long sniff to imply surprise, shrugged her shoulders to imply that one never knows, made four telephone calls, handed Judy four address cards and sent her off to her first interview.

Having finally located the building, Judy took the cagelike elevator to an airless office where she was interviewed by a finicky little fat man who kept looking down and brushing his left sleeve as he asked his questions. After he turned her down, she went on to the next interview, and, in all, spent a week and a half visiting similar dingy offices. They were all painted gray or beige, smelled of dust and old biscuits and the desks were piled with overstuffed, crumpled, cream cardboard files. Finally, after being beaten down from the salary that the agency had quoted, Judy was accepted as a temporary secretary by a large, middle-aged fabric importer, with a face like a gray egg upon which had been painted a drooping black mustache. He dictated in French, but when necessary, Judy translated his letters into English or German before typing them, and struggled with the innumerable customs forms that were necessary to get tweed from Scotland and linen from Dublin to Paris, or to send silk from Lyons and lace from Valenciennes to New York. Her employer obviously regarded her as nothing more than a walking, talking, typing machine and made no effort to speak to her apart from a brief "*B'jour, mademoiselle.*"

"I wore your beautiful silk dress to a ball last night, and I danced every dance with a different young man—and I was bored limp," Maxine said gloomily to her Aunt Hortense as they sat in the small, maple-wood paneled library of Aunt Hortense's Paris apartment. Maxine, who had sought the meeting, was tense but determined.

"I can't seem to talk about this to my parents without a fight. Anybody would think we were living in 1850, not 1950. Mama can't understand that I don't *want* to go to all the right parties and dance with all the right men, then marry one of them. I don't want to marry Pierre, the god of the ski-slopes, and then have a complete duplicate of the dull, comfortable life that my mother has led."

Under her huge, green-brimmed straw hat, Aunt Hortense raised bushy eyebrows above her big bony nose and sniffed. Unlike Judy, Maxine was a bit frightened of her aunt, who now nodded without saying anything. Encouraged, Maxine continued. "Of course I love my family, but I don't want to be part of that nursery life any longer. I want to get away from them. I want to have a life of my *own*. 'You will have, if you marry the Boursal boy,' says Mama." She mimicked her mother's exasperated voice. "Pierre has already spoken to Papa, you know, but when I visit his parents in that apartment on the Avenue George V, I can't get out fast enough. It's claustrophobic and I feel trapped again. Although it's much grander than our home—white marble and a black maid—his mother leads exactly the same life as my mother, except that *she* does it in haute-couture clothes. I don't *want* to marry Pierre because I don't *want* that life."

Angrily Maxine bit her thumbnail although there was little left to bite. "And there's another more important reason. Pierre is really only interested in skiing, you know. I realize that sounds ridiculous and you're going to tell me that it will pass, but I think that with him, when it does pass, nothing else will take its place. He's rich and he likes to ski; he doesn't like to work and there's no reason why he should." She looked up at her aunt pleadingly. "But I couldn't stand being married to a rich ski bum, especially an *aging* rich ski bum. So I'm going to refuse Pierre, and then I want to leave Paris for a bit. I know Paris. I've lived here all my life. I want to visit other places—London and Rome."

Again Aunt Hortense nodded slowly in order to give herself time to think. At that age, many girls felt like Maxine, but the child was unusually impatient in this attempt to get what she wanted. In time, Maxine would learn to move slowly and carefully in order to get her own way, not to crash aggressively into a prerehearsed argument like this one. She would learn that, whoever she married.

"What exactly *do* you want?" Aunt Hortense asked.

"I want to go to London and learn to be an interior decorator, then come back to Paris and open my own concern. *You* are the one who started to educate my eye—shopping for clothes with you, shopping for antiques with you, going around museums with you. *You* have your own style. Now I want to develop one of my own. French designers are still doing the same thing that they've been doing since before the war. Stuffy, overdecorated, over-expensive interiors. This is not what I want to do." She looked up from under her lashes. "I'm going to ask Papa to let me study in London for two years. I want you to persuade him to let me go because I know I can't, and I know you can."

Aunt Hortense nodded again as she tended to when she thought it prudent to say nothing.

Encouraged, Maxine continued. "My friend Pagan says that the best London decorator is James Partridge, who's just done her mother's flat. She says he's got a marvelous understanding of color and antiques and Pagan's already talked to him. She's asked if he could find a job for me."

Aunt Hortense nodded again. It was not such a stupid idea. It was always useful if one married well. It would certainly improve the girl's eye and if she were making money, then she could hardly be spending it.

So she asked Maxine's parents to one of her smaller, grander dinner parties. She seated Maxine's father between a mildly famous, mildly flirtatious actress and a pretty little Countess who had been widowed the previous year and was rumored not to be inconsolable. Maxine's father enjoyed himself hugely. After the meal, when her guests were sitting over brandy and coffee in the library, his sister drew him to one side and said, "A little word with you, Louis, about my goddaughter. I feel that Maxine shouldn't waste any more time socializing in Paris. It's time that she continued her education."

"Well, we rather assume that she's going to marry the Boursal boy. . . ."

"Oh, surely not, surely that's not what you want for your clever daughter? That blockhead? Why, the girl is hardly out of school and you want to marry her to a brainless idiot like that! No, I think that Maxine takes after you. She is clever, she shows a definite talent for the arts. It would be a good idea if she studied them seriously."

"Well, perhaps you're right, Hortense," said Maxine's father, who really didn't think it was important what Maxine did before she married provided it didn't cost him too much. "I'll ask her mother to see what courses are available at the Beaux Arts."

"Very wise of you, Louis. And there's one other small thing that should be attended to. Her English isn't nearly good enough—not nearly as good as yours. She speaks English the way Winston Churchill speaks French—*exécrable!* What I should most like to see for her is two years in London, studying with a really good decorator. One learns so much faster in practice than in theory, don't you think?"

"*London? Two years?* You must be mad, Hortense, her mother would never let her go. She's only nineteen, remember."

"You've just implied that she's old enough to be married. Besides she has friends in London. Oh, Louis, think what a joyless adolescence *we* had. She has such talent, your Maxine! Surely you wish to allow the poor child to spread her wings a little before she has to knuckle down to the serious and often tedious business of being a wife."

There was a pause. "And if I allowed her to go to London, to whom would she go?"

"The best decorator in London, of course," said Aunt Hortense decisively, "and that is Monsieur Partridge. I have no idea whether there's a free place in his office, and I don't know if he charges for apprentices, but I can telephone him tomorrow and find out. No! No! It would be a *pleasure* for me to attend to your wishes in this matter, Louis."

She led him back to the library, quite pleased with herself. It was amazing how you could spoonfeed flattery to a grown man.

So in due course, after kissing Judy goodbye, Maxine caught the Golden Arrow to London. Kate and Pagan were waiting at Victoria Station. Kate had already rented a basement apartment in Chelsea for herself and Maxine. There were only two small, dark rooms, but it was in Walton Street, a charming little road of tiny nineteenth-century houses in Chelsea.

Every evening at six, Judy rushed from the depressing office back to her shabby, overblown-rose-patterned room at the Hôtel de Londres. The room overlooked an inner courtyard that was as full of life as a soap opera. Nobody ever seemed to draw the curtains, and beyond the other windows you could hear the fights, see the lovemaking and smell the cooking from the apartments on the opposite side.

As Guy's collection progressed, his own bedroom grew less habitable, so when he finished work he would climb two further flights of stairs to Judy's room for a glass of wine and sympathy. Sitting cross-legged on her pillow, she quickly learned about the world of French couture.

"One whole day wasted on fittings," groaned Guy one evening, throwing himself onto the bottom of the bed. "How I long to design for the boutique market!"

"What difference will that make?"

"Mass orders, *ma chère*. Mass manufacturing and *no* damned fittings. An haute-couture garment is made to order and has three sacred, time-wasting fittings, but boutique clothes are made in batches, in standard sizes, and are sold ready-to-wear. It's up to the customer or the store to alter them, if necessary."

Judy leaned under her bed for the wine bottle and filled two small glasses. "I thought you liked couture customers?"

"Only because I have to. Very few women can afford couture clothes. All of them are spoiled, and most of them are fickle. Hardly any women stick to one couture house, except the best dressed ones." He sipped his wine very slowly, then continued. "Celebrity clients often borrow ballgowns for a gala, then return them dirty, sometimes even torn, with never a word of thanks. *Zut!* I don't want to spend *my* life at the mercy of a few rich bitches who spend *their* life dressing for cocktails." Suddenly he sat up and pointed under the washbasin. "*Nom d'un nom*, what is *that*?" Standing on a strip of linoleum was a wastepaper basket, and propped up in it in a nest of aluminum foil lay an upended electric iron.

"It's my stove. I've bought a little saucepan and I cook on the flat side of the iron. It's one of the new thermostatic ones—I set it at 'linen' for boiling eggs or making toast and at 'wool' for simmering stew."

Guy rolled his eyes. "A terrible fire hazard! You're lucky to be alive! You know the hotel doesn't allow cooking in the bedrooms. They'll throw you out."

"I can't afford to eat at restaurants all the time, so I keep food in a suitcase under the bed."

"You'll have mice and cockroaches."

"No, it's all in a tin box." She dragged the suitcase out to show him. "Look, I'll boil you an egg."

"Please don't." Intrigued, in spite of his disapproval, Guy said, "You Americans are undoubtedly ingenious. I see it in your fashion industry—you're ten years ahead of us in your manufacturing and marketing and in the way you specialize. In the States, a single firm doesn't offer its customers every sort of garment from skirts to ballgowns, as we do in France. A firm that makes skirts to retail between ten and twenty dollars won't know much about skirts that retail between forty and fifty dollars. One is more likely to make money in fashion if one specializes."

Thinking of her own odious job, Judy sighed. "There must be a lot of satisfaction in being a designer."

There was a pause. "Not really," Guy said gloomily. He moved back and sat on the edge of the bed. "I'm sorry, I am in a dark mood. It's *le cafard*. It is only because I'm tired and worried, and instead of getting on with the important work, I've been fiddling about all day, letting out a quarter of an inch here, taking in a quarter of an inch there."

"You only feel depressed because you're exhausted and under pressure. You'll be in love with couture again tomorrow."

"Yes, but I repeat, I don't want to spend my life working for a few rich women. I want to produce clothes that will make *thousands* of women feel marvelous." He gave an exasperated sigh. "Today, women want to look like themselves and I want to help them." He snorted. "Haute-couture is a dwindling market—every year there are fewer and fewer rich private customers."

"Let me massage your back," Judy said, turning from the window. "It'll help you to unwind."

He stood up wearily and started to unbutton his blue cotton shirt, still thinking aloud. "Another disadvantage is that one's designs are always stolen by mass manufacturers from all over the world so one's virtually working for them, unpaid."

Judy took the pillows off the bed, straightened the cover, spread a clean towel on it and rolled up her sleeves. Guy sat on the edge of the bed, kicked his shoes off and lay down.

" . . . But one doesn't make one's name in mass production, one makes it in haute-couture." He lay face down on the bed and Judy started to work on his spine, pressing firmly with her thumbs, starting in the small of his back, as Guy continued to think aloud. As she worked on his shoulder muscles he could feel himself unwinding, breathing more deeply. "Shall I tell you my plan?" he mumbled. "I want to do something new, to specialize in high-quality mass production. My clothes won't be as expensive as haute-couture, but they won't be as cheap as most manufactured garments. My long-term ambition is to have a business that's halfway between the two, producing my own designs with my own label."

Now her thumbs were on the back of his neck, firmly pressing the tension out of it. "Mmmm, that feels better already . . . I want to make exquisite, ready-to-wear clothes that have the design, cut and fabric quality of an haute-couture garment, although the customer won't get personal fittings. The clothes will have to be carefully designed so that they're easy to alter to fit. I'm starting with a collection of separates, a lot in wool jersey . . . aaah, that's wonderful."

"Now, turn around and face the window," Judy said, "otherwise I can't get at your left side properly because the bed's against the wall. Listen, world tycoon, when will your suits be ready, and what will you do with them?"

"My sample stock will be ready in July. I'll hire a hotel suite and show the designs to stores and boutiques. The stores will order—with any luck—and the clothes will be made up by a little factory in Fauchon."

Judy gave him a gentle slap on the back and said, "You are now a new man."

Guy stood up and put on his shirt. "Thanks." He leaned forward and ruffled the ragged fringe of her new street-urchin coiffure. "Look, Judy, I'm *truly* sorry I've been in such a rotten mood, but the entire day has been unproductive. José, the seamstress, has been off for the whole week because she strained her wrist so we're behind schedule. I have to do so many jobs, even the damned deliveries."

"I'm going to take you out to dinner," Judy said.

"Judy, you're an angel, but it's not possible. I must do the bookkeeping before paying the wages tomorrow. It is the bookkeeping that drives me the most crazy—it's only about an hour a week but somehow there never *is* an hour."

"If you like, and if it's *really* only an hour a week, I'll do it for you," Judy offered. "You can pay me when you can afford it. I process orders and invoices at the office and I'll get Denise, our office bookkeeper, to show me whatever else is necessary. I could do it on Thursdays."

"Angel! Shall I pay you in advance with a suit? The blue silk with the low V neck to the breasts? You can wear it in the evening with nothing underneath, just pearls."

CHAPTER 9

"*KEEP STILL, AND* breath in," urged Judy, heaving on the zipper. "Now for heaven's sake don't breathe out."

One of the four models had let them down, so Guy was showing his first collection on only three girls. Voile curtains stirred in the slight breeze, but the July heat was still almost unendurable, even here in the Plaza Athénée. Guy was checking the accessories list and laying things out on the three trestle tables that had been set up by the hotel in place of the usual twin beds, which had been taken away for the day. Three hundred invitations had been sent out, but only thirty people were expected.

Having worked almost nonstop for the past four months, Guy was gray with fatigue and understandably tense. He was going to supervise the models. Judy, who had taken a week's vacation from her job, would usher guests to their seats and announce the models. Most of the important couture houses of Paris had already shown their collections; clothes were still pretty but uncomfortable, with voluminous skirts, boned waists and breasts squashed flat under jackets that were stiff with padded interlining; Guy's simple, comfortable clothes would certainly look different. Every evening, Judy had rushed to buy newspapers in order to read the reports of the collections that had been shown that day, and Guy anxiously telephoned around for backstage information.

First through the gilded double doors was Guy's mother with a group of friends, then, one by one, his private customers appeared. Aunt Hortense gave Judy a conspiratorial wink and whispered, "You can get your order book out, I'm going to buy two outfits even if he's showing shrouds." A couple of Guy's friends from the Jacques Fath studio also showed up, but none of the press appeared and only three of the buyers who had been invited from the smarter shops and stores of Paris.

The first model appeared from the hallway, wearing a garnet suit with a short, straight jacket and box-pleated skirt. She wore a black sailor hat on the back of her head and dragged the cinnamon raincoat. As if to an audience of thousands, she gave a radiant smile, advanced into the room with the gait of a nervous racehorse, then pirouetted very slowly. Because of the missing model, appearances were to be dragged out as long as possible in order to give the other girls time to change.

Once in the bedroom the model moved on the double. The seamstress held her second change ready to step into, the cutter snatched up the discarded clothes and Guy, standing by the door with his stopwatch to time each model's departure, held her accessories ready for her to grab.

At the end of the collection there was a round of polite applause, then champagne was handed around by a waiter who had strict instructions to keep the glasses full. Behind the scenes, Guy paid the models in cash, as was the custom, while his two helpers packed up the clothes. All the private customers gallantly placed orders. Guy's mother waited to see what nobody had ordered—a cream wool battledress-top suit that did not flatter a middle-aged figure—and then ordered it. Aunt Hortense bought the cinnamon raincoat, a saffron velvet jacket with a short skirt, a long skirt and matching chiffon blouse, but she declined the drainpipe pants. The private clients all left together, still trilling applause and encouragement.

As soon as the last one had gone, Guy slumped into a pale blue brocade armchair and buried his head in his hands. "Not *one*, not *one* order, except from friends!"

Back in Judy's room at the Hôtel de Londres he slumped on the edge of the bed, staring in despair at the blowsy roses on the opposite wall. "Lie down and I'll make you a cup of tea," Judy said, gently pushing him back on the bed, but by the time the iron had boiled the water, Guy was already asleep. Judy took his shoes off and arranged him tidily on the bed as if he were dead or drunk, then lay down beside him. She, too, was exhausted. Alas, she thought, there wasn't going to be much invoice work . . .

The following day the telephone woke them in midmorning. It was José phoning from the downstairs workshop. The Galeries Lafayette boutique buyer wanted to know when Guy could show to them.

* * *

Five weeks later Guy bounced into Judy's room, jumped on the bed and leaped up and down on it, giving Indian war whoops. "First my problem is failure, now it's success," he shouted. "We're completely sold out of the winter collection and I've had to turn down two million francs' worth of orders—that's eight thousand dollars, isn't it? The orders are *flooding* in! It's frightening because I haven't got enough money to finance a bigger turnover and I don't want to find myself in a liquidity crisis. My father says that's what generally happens if you expand too fast."

"Since when has your vocabulary included such phrases as 'liquidity crisis'? And stop jumping on that bed. The chambermaid hasn't reported my food suitcase but she couldn't avoid reporting a broken bed."

Guy sat down and stayed seated on the end of the bed. "My father has changed his tune. He's really being quite helpful. We went through the figures last night, and I think he was surprised to find I'm so businesslike—entirely due to you, of course. . . . Anyway, he says it's vital to make only a certain number of each design, and not to take more orders than I can afford to produce. I'm to tell latecomers that I'm very sorry but my production schedule is booked up. *And it is!* Put your suit on. I'm taking you to the Ritz for a glass of champagne."

"Isn't there a better way of saying no?" Judy asked slowly, as she slipped into the pale blue silk suit—suitable for all seasons—that was her only decent dress. "Isn't there some way that won't exasperate customers but will make them order faster next time? How about giving away a couple of suits to celebrities, on condition that they'll go around saying they're *mortified* that they weren't allowed to order more than two?" She pulled up the zipper. "It could make your collection seem more select. Instead of trying to hide the fact that you can't finance your orders, *flaunt* it."

"But I don't know any celebrities. And I can't afford to give away clothes. I haven't sweated for years to give presents to strangers."

Judy quickly buttoned the jacket and snapped on a gilt dog collar. "Guy, you have to pay something for publicity. Europeans *never* understand that! Nobody is going to blow your trumpet for free. Dammit, I wish you could afford to hire *me* full time!"

"As soon as I can afford it, you're hired, *mon chou*. Right now I need all my cash to buy you a drink at the Ritz. No, no, *not* the black patents, the cream pumps."

In spite of her friendship with Guy, Judy missed Nick more than she cared to admit. Although he wrote to Judy every week, Nick's letters arrived irregularly, sometimes three in two days, sometimes none for a month. Judy's replies were similarly spaced, because she only wrote when she had something special to say. Then she would scrawl a few lines in green ink, just as if she were speaking to him, with a total disregard for grammar and punctuation. She wrote to Maxine, Kate and Pagan in the same way. The only person to whom she wrote regularly, neatly and once a week was her mother, and Judy hated doing it. Writing home was like doing homework. She couldn't write freely and she couldn't say anything about the fashion business that was her growing passion, for her mother would die of shock if she knew that Judy was involved in it.

By the end of August, Paris was sweltering and the very cobblestones of the streets seemed to melt in the heat. Still, it was probably even hotter in Malaya, thought Judy, as she saw a pale blue airmail envelope in her pigeonhole and eagerly ran toward it. Standing by the wilting palm tree in the hotel lobby she tore open the envelope and then gasped.

"Darling Judy," wrote Maxine, "I have some very bad news. At first we hoped it wasn't true, but we have checked with the War Office and there is no doubt. I don't know how to tell you, but Nick has been killed on duty . . . in a Communist ambush in Malaya."

Judy read the rest of the letter with her eyes but she didn't absorb the contents. Stunned, she moved mechanically up the seven flights of stairs to her room, carefully locked the door, ran over to the washbasin and threw up. Then she carefully cleaned the washbasin, took her shoes off, lay neatly in the middle of the bed and started to shiver in spite of the heat.

The concierge, the chambermaid and Guy were arguing in the passage.

"It's true, I haven't been able to get into her bedroom for two days; it's chained from the inside," said the chambermaid. "We should break the door down."

"And she doesn't answer the telephone," agreed the concierge. "But the door is hinged from the inside—and to break the door down, well, I can't be responsible for the damage."

"I'll pay for the door," said Guy, impatiently. "We know she's in there, there's no sound, she's either ill or . . . I've been shouting out here for hour after hour. I'll break it down myself, if you won't!" Angrily, he threw his slight body against the door. "*Judy!* Can you hear me?"

"Maybe we should call an ambulance?" the chambermaid suggested.

"I should have done this yesterday," Guy grunted, heaving his body against the door. "How do we know she's alive after being locked in for two days with no sound from her?"

Suddenly, to his relief, they heard the scrape of metal as the chain was unhooked, then the door lock turned and the door slowly opened. Judy stood there in her stocking feet and the crumpled clothes she'd been wearing for two days. She looked white and dazed.

"What's wrong? Are you ill? Why did you lock yourself in?" Guy asked, furious with her now that he could see that her wrists weren't slit and she wasn't in a coma.

They all crowded into the room. Guy pushed the concierge and the chambermaid out and slammed the door. Judy scowled at him. Then she felt tears fall onto her cheeks and suddenly she was able to cry.

Guy wrapped her in his arms and held her tightly to him. Blindly, she reached one hand out to the night table and handed him Maxine's letter. Guy read it over Judy's shoulder and softly stroked her hair until she was a little calmer. "Get undressed and hop into bed," he said gently. "I'm going down to my room, but don't you dare lock this door again." He was back within minutes with a large bottle of eau-de-cologne and half a liter of milk, which he warmed for her, carefully setting the iron to "wool."

"I feel so guilty, so dreadfully guilty about *everything*. I didn't love Nick, he loved me, and *now it's too late*," Judy snuffled.

"You can't order love."

"But I can't seem to love *any* man. I go out with a few guys, yes, but I can't seem to *love* anyone."

"Judy, you're eighteen and you've told me before that you don't want to fall in love with a Frenchman. You said you didn't want to complicate your life at the moment."

He stroked her hair again, and stayed with her until, in the soft gray twilight, she fell asleep.

In the dark Guy slipped the pale blue letter into his pocket. He felt like throttling Maxine. Why hadn't she telephoned him?

Twice in the night Judy woke in tears, and he stroked her hair and soothed her to sleep again. In the morning he lifted the phone and firmly ordered *café au lait* for two, with double croissants, much to the surprise of the chambermaid, who had thought he was the other way.

CHAPTER 10

THE SATURDAY AFTER Nick's death, Aunt Hortense telephoned and immediately sensed a difference in Judy. "Are you ill, my child? Your voice sounds so flat and weary. I was hoping to swoop you off to Versailles."

"I don't think so, thank you," Judy said. "I have some paperwork to do for Guy."

Aunt Hortense immediately telephoned Guy and was told the true reason for Judy's apathy. She called Judy again and firmly said, "I'm sending the car around for you straightaway, because I'd like to see you for half an hour if it's not inconvenient. I have a present for you."

She rang off before Judy had time to think of an excuse.

Usually Judy loved to visit Aunt Hortense's beautiful old stone house with the lacework balconies, which stood on l'Isle de la Cité, the tiny island in the middle of the Seine that was the original city of Paris. But today she sat listless in the back of the Mercedes as it threaded its way through the cobbled streets, past street criers carrying big wicker baskets full of fresh butter and eggs, Romany gypsies trying to sell dried lavender or hand-carved wooden clothespins to the passersby, the wigmaker's shop and the buttonmaker's shop. And when the car passed the shop full of young girls making funeral wreaths of violets and lilies and white roses, she started to sob again.

The setting sun was gilding the walls of Aunt Hortense's drawing room as she silently handed Judy a small green velvet box. Inside was an antique necklace of seed pearls.

"But why?" Judy asked. "It's not my birthday. I can't accept. . . ."

"Yes, you can," said Aunt Hortense. "I accepted them at your age for a much more wicked reason and I want you to have them. What would I do with them now? They are for the neck of a young girl. Let me show you how the clasp works.

If you don't care for the ruby clasp, then you can choose another one from Cartier."

Judy slowly fastened the necklace and then moved to a mirror. In the old, warped, silver surface, the pearls gleamed against her skin.

"Why have you given me this, Aunt Hortense?"

"To be direct, because you are miserable, because you have lost a friend and because you are unhappy in a boring job. I think we should perhaps try and find you another job."

"Well, yes, almost *any* other job would be an improvement, but other offices seem pretty much the same."

"I wasn't thinking of an office job. I thought you might like to be an assistant saleswoman at Christian Dior. The assistants are quite young you know." Her emerald eyelids fluttered. "I cannot promise anything, you understand, but I have spoken to the *directrice* and she is willing to interview you. The pay will be terrible, of course—*if* you get a job—because the competition is fierce. I know you don't really approve of Monsieur Dior, but it is the house where I have the most, how do you say?"

"Clout?"

"Exactly. They know me there so they will interview you. But please don't offer your opinion of Monsieur Dior's work. And don't forget to use the servants' entrance, my child."

"Aunt Hortense, you are so kind."

"It is merely common sense. Something has to be done."

"Maxine and I secretly call you Aunt Horse-Sense."

"I know, *ma chère*. I have been called worse."

So Judy visited Christian Dior again, this time entering by the employees' entrance, which was heavily guarded. She wore her blue silk suit and tried not to sound overqualified. The shrewd-looking woman who interviewed her wore a perfectly cut gray linen dress and her silver hair was swept up in a French knot. "So you speak English, French and German?" she asked.

"And a little Spanish."

"And you've been handling exports and secretarial work. Why don't you want an office job?"

"Because I want to learn to sell and I want to be with *people*. I've been working in a room by myself for nearly a year. Also I would do *anything* to work at Dior."

"Most of the girls that come here say that. They want a job because they love fashion, but they don't realize what a hard job it is. It's physically very tiring."

As the interview continued, the *directrice* became increasingly surprised by Judy's technical knowledge of fashion until she mentioned that she did bookkeeping for Guy Saint Simon.

"Aha, now I understand. A young man to watch. Of course, it is not difficult to get a little publicity at his age, but if it doesn't go to his head, if he stays small for the moment, if the buyers remain confident of his ability, quality, finish and—above all—his reliability, then he could go far."

"He intends to."

There was no vacancy at Dior, but her name was taken and in early December the personnel manager telephoned to say that one of their assistant salesgirls had contracted hepatitis. Did Judy want her job, on a temporary basis, until after the collections in February? Anything to get her foot in the door, Judy thought, and immediately accepted.

* * *

All chatter stopped as Judy timidly entered the sales-women's room for the first time. It felt like her first day in high school. Terrifying. Like the other saleswomen, she was wearing a gray flannel dress that had been provided free by the house. Her first Dior! She was rapidly introduced to everyone by her boss, Annie, who then whisked her out to the salons. Annie grumbled incessantly about her feet and her commission, which she was always working out on a hypothetical basis in her little black notebook. "*If* the Countess also takes it in black . . . *if* the Ambassador's wife doesn't think it's too flamboyant . . . *if* Zizi Jeanmaire likes the scarlet feathers."

Most of the other assistants were older than Judy and got no commission, only a meager salary. They were putting in a two-year stint before getting a job as first saleswomen in second-rank couture houses, after which their next step would be to become a first saleswoman in a first-rate house.

Judy was surprised to find what a large staff was necessary in order to operate the elegant, pale gray salons. The doorman, the scent-sprayer, the boutique salesgirls, the *directrice*, the salon sales force, the publicity department, the six models and the dresser were only the visible tip of the iceberg. The huge behind-the-scenes force included the quiet, awesome, pasty-faced Monsieur Dior himself and his assistants, his design staff (all men) and *their* assistants. Also the business manager, the buyers, the accountants, the secretaries, the tailors and cutters, the head fitters, the first and second sewing hands, the *midinettes*, the stock girls and so on, down to the delivery boys.

She quickly lost her respect for the refined salon saleswomen who, behind the scenes, were always bitching over new customers or the location of seats for old customers. She acquired a new respect for the seemingly humble head fitters, such as Madame Suzanne, who had pinned the apricot silk dress on Aunt Hortense. The fitters spent the whole day on their feet or their knees and often worked until nine in the evening—or even later, before a collection—carefully pinning clothes on weary, bad-tempered models. Each head fitter was responsible for a workshop with perhaps forty workers in it, all stitching busily as they gossiped, all wearing plain black skirts and sweaters with white blouses, except on St. Catherine's Day when they all pinned on the yellow and green ribbons of their patron saint.

Behind the scenes was a constant, hurried feeling of pressure, but once through the doors that led to the quietly sumptuous salons, everyone's manner changed. Annie spoke in a calm, almost hushed voice; her manner was respectful; she was solicitous but never urged a sale; she never criticized a customer in any way, especially when invited to do so. The customer was always right. If anything was wrong, it was the color, the cut, the fit or the lighting. But once back behind the swing doors, her exquisite tact vanished in a flash. "The Countess must have put on ten pounds since her first fitting. Judee, where's my order book? You'd think an ambassadress would be able to make up her mind, without asking *me*, if cyclamen suited her. Judee, where is the list of tomorrow's fittings? That old Belgian bitch knows perfectly well that no alterations can be made to a design without the consent of Monsieur Dior. Why does every single customer think that she's the only one who wants her clothes by Christmas? Judee, what news from the workroom about number 22 in white satin for la Comtesse de Ribes?"

* * *

At the house of Dior the atmosphere became increasingly rushed and tense as the day of their big February collection drew near. Models hurried from their dressing rooms to the studios in white wrappers that kept their clothes clean and prevented anyone from seeing them until the press show. Monsieur Dior also insisted that all the studio staff wear white smocks in order to keep the clothes spotlessly clean. A hushed atmosphere surrounded the design studios, which looked like a cross between a modern church and an operating theater; no white-walled corners were unlit, there were no shadows; the cream window shades were kept pulled down all day and all night in order to prevent spying from binoculars on the other side of the street; Monsieur Dior had his own room in which he was surrounded by paints, crayons, photographs and scraps of fabric, but the designers worked in the outer studio, their drawing boards grouped around a huge central cutting table, twenty feet long and ten feet across. The walls were lined with shelves and racks neatly piled with buttons, belts, bags, shoes and jewelry and roll upon roll of fabric samples. Normally, this was where the manufacturers' reps showed their wares and often hopefully left a bolt of cloth in case it caught some designer's fancy, because if Dior used a new fabric, the whole world wanted it.

During the dress rehearsal, there was a guard on every door. Christian Dior—"The Master"—in an immaculate gray suit sat straddled on a chair, his arms folded over the chairback, his pale, aging-cherub's face showing no sign of emotion or temperament—only weariness—as, gently and quietly, he scrutinized each model that passed before him and, together with his assistants, decided which jewelry and accessories were needed to complete each ensemble.

It was drizzling on Avenue Montaigne as Judy rushed to work. By eight A.M. crowds had already gathered outside the main door. Photographers with gear hanging from their shoulder straps jostled next to the two parked film trucks; the film crew shivered farther down the sidewalk. There was a crowd around the staff entrance and a bottleneck at the door, as security guards checked each person. Inside, there wasn't much talking; everyone was hurrying, their anxious faces preoccupied.

Chaos broke out as the front doors opened and the crowd heaved inside, clutching invitation cards like refugee passports. Pandemonium swept the reception desk as each card was checked and suspects were asked to show their official *chambre syndicale* stamped press cards with their photograph attached. Security men linked arms at the doors like police at a football game to keep the crowds out. Blasts of cold air swept up marble steps and crowds shrieked as the celebrities arrived: Princess Aly Khan, once Rita Hayworth, Gene Tierney glowering at her, and the Duchess of Windsor looking like a little governess.

The approved guests surged into the main salon, where every gilt chair was numbered. Nevertheless, reporters argued over seats; neither the *chambre syndicale* (the couturiers' association) nor the fashion houses knew the relative importance of foreign journalists and they were too arrogant to find out; journalists were dragged ten thousand kilometers to stay at the Plaza Athénée, then treated like pickpockets on the New York subway; there were angry arguments when high-powered, syndicated columnists found their seats—booked weeks beforehand—occupied by Little Rock newspaper reporters with six-week deadlines. The syndicated writers were prepared to struggle ruthlessly as they claimed their places, fighting with kamikaze desperation.

It was different in the front row, which was always reserved for film stars, *Vogue, Harper's Bazaar, Women's Wear Daily.* . . . "Who's that little blonde? How did *she* get there?" someone asked Judy.

"That's Empress Miller, she's the new fashion writer for the *New York Clarion.*" Judy had met Empress at one of Aunt Hortense's parties.

The mob behind the front row were quieter now, all notebooks ready. The miasma of a thousand new perfumes grew more sickly. It was getting hotter and it would be worse when the arc lights were turned on.

The lights went on and there was an immediate hush.

Behind the scenes Judy felt she was witnessing a kaleidoscope of hissed queries, anxious eyes, strained faces and general chaos in the model dressing rooms. Naked to the waist, stockings snapped to their girdles (no models wore panties because the line would show through the clothes), the young women sat before their mirrors. The shelves below were a jumble of colored grease, half-empty pots, grubby sticks of makeup and stumps of lipsticks. The models stuck on immense eyelashes while hairdressers stabbed at their coiffures. Then the models were helped into their clothes by dressers—zippers zipped, snappers snapped and buttons buttoned. The head dresser checked that accessories were correct, hems straight, clothes properly pressed and immaculate.

Holding the accessories ready, Judy watched the models leave their *cabines*, ready to go. Timing was by stopwatch and military-precise. The presentation had been planned to contrast and counterpoint the color, cut and line of the new collection, and the clothes were grouped so that the press could see a new line or color develop. Judy had seen it all decided at the first rehearsal. Instructions were then transferred to the big pinboard outside the dressing rooms; rows of cards with each model's name and the number of garments were listed vertically in appearance order. That pinboard was the blueprint of the show: 22, 13, 71, 49, 32, etcetera; the numbers were not according to appearance but had been allocated to the garments months ago, when they were first designed.

The models were as nervous as greyhounds at the gate, fiddling with the necklaces that Judy clipped on them, pulling down jackets and smoothing their hair. There were six house models and eight free lancers—cinnamon-stick thin—had flown in from overseas; they were even skinnier than the Dior house models because it was essential that they fit every designer's clothes. They lived on Dexedrine and yogurt and frequently collapsed after the collections from exhaustion, malnutrition and stress.

The first model was announced by an oddly high, breathless voice. "Peking, *numéro trois*, nombair sree." The model wore Oriental makeup, her doe eyes lined with black crayon. The loose white linen jacket, straight black skirt and straw coolie hat were carefully calculated pointers to the theme of the whole collection—the Chinese influence. Pencils leaped, the working audience concentrated. Some journalists were incessant scribblers, but Empress Miller only noted, "No change skirt length/Chinese/b & w coolie look/fluid/no stiffening/no padding/easy move/hats straw big brim/suits sailor navy & w/skirts pleated & flat."

Journalists were allowed to take notes but not to write complete descriptions or to sketch. It was getting even hotter. A girl in a lynx coat collapsed and was swiftly carried out. A raven-haired house model in a scarlet strapless net formal gown noticed a journalist sketching; the model paused, touched her left earlobe and smiled directly at the journalist.

Annie pounced.

Sketches and notes were confiscated and the journalist's name put on the *syndicale* blacklist. Two other journalists were expelled later. Rage, threats, pleas, tears—all were useless.

An hour afterward, in the dressing room, Judy heard a sudden roar of applause. Monsieur Dior, in an immaculate pale gray suit, his face glistening with heat and fatigue, had stepped forward to bow his thanks. Judy paused as she unfastened a gold necklace from a model wearing only a feather hat and garter belt. The head dresser visibly relaxed. "Not so loud as '47 but louder than last July," she pronounced. Slowly they all grinned; then Monsieur Dior appeared in the dressing rooms and an orgy of kissing started.

"I feel like a broken spring," Judy said gloomily, five days later.

"Cheer up," said Guy, who was lying on her bedroom floor with his bare feet propped on the bed. "You always knew that your job at Dior was temporary."

"Yes, but I *hoped* they'd keep me on."

"You've still got a job until the end of February when Annie's assistant returns," he pointed out, "and you've got your gray flannel Dior dress, which would have cost over eight months' salary if you'd paid for it. If you're willing to go anywhere and do anything for the same pathetic salary as Dior paid you, you can work full time for me. The hotel says I can't continue working from here; they say it's not a sweat shop. So your first job is to find us two workrooms somewhere near here. No, don't kiss me while I'm drinking."

Judy found an adequate, skylit studio two streets away from the hotel. She was now responsible for all non-manufacturing work, saw clients, answered the telephone, did the bookkeeping and handled dispatch.

Guy designed, bought materials and supervised the workshop staff. The faithful José had now been joined by another seamstress; the new sewing hand's mother was a first hand at Nina Ricci so Marie had been trained since childhood to sew to a professional standard.

Judy was busier than she'd ever been, and happier. The buyers liked her because she didn't stand blankfaced, order book in hand, but talked and joked with them. She had a keen sense of the ridiculous and liked to make people laugh, even if she could only do it by making them laugh *at* her. A few people found this exuberance exhausting, and some found it difficult to accept her forthright attitude, for she was direct and said exactly what she thought. After watching her scold a buyer for not ordering one of their new jackets, Guy said, "You might cultivate a little tact, Judy. Why can't you behave with the buyers as you do with Aunt Hortense's crowd—with a little more respect?" He was annoyed. "I know you're just being straightforward, but the French do not understand it. They interpret you as 'tough,' which you aren't."

"More's the pity," said Judy, scowling at the clip of invoices marked "overdue" that she held in her hand, "and here is where I start. I'm going to be tough about payments. You can't afford to give these people credit. In the future they'll have to pay when they sign the order, and we won't process it until the check is in our account."

"Selling on cash terms is a nice idea, but nobody in the garment business does it. I'll lose all my customers."

"And a lot of bad debts," said Judy. "But cash was the way you started, remember? Your mother and all her Avenue George V friends paid in advance. If people want your stuff, why *shouldn't* they pay for it when they order it? Now is the time to find out whether they *really* want you—*before* you go bankrupt."

Judy earnestly tried to look older than her age. She and Guy found their youth a grave disadvantage in business because nobody took the young seriously. "I suppose it's just a nuisance to be endured," Guy complained, "like a breaking voice or General de Gaulle; in time it will pass." In the meantime, Judy didn't wear teenage clothes; she grew her hair and wore it twisted up in an unbecoming French knot; she lived in her gray flannel Dior dress and wore big hornrimmed spectacles, hoping to project an air of age, distinction and respectability.

"*Ma chère*, you quite frighten me," said Maxine. She had returned from her two years' training in London the day before and they were catching up on each other's news over breakfast in the Deux Magots. Maxine planned to ask her father for a loan to start a business.

A touch envious, Judy said, "You're damn lucky to have a rich father."

Maxine, dunking a croissant in her *café au lait*, said, "Papa isn't rich; I couldn't have gone to Switzerland if Aunt Hortense hadn't paid. Papa is *comfortable*. I hope he'll guarantee a bank loan for me. I don't think he can afford to give me the money, but he'll still be taking a risk on me." She took a large bite and flakes fell on the table as she mumbled, "Guy is the one with a rich father."

Judy put her cup down. She was astonished. "Then why is Guy always so short of money?"

"First, because he wants to make it on his own and second, because, as you know, his papa disapproves of designers. He made it plain he wouldn't help Guy. So Guy wants to show his old man he can get along without him."

Judy went straight back and asked Guy for a raise. Then they plunged into work for the July collection; they were showing a range of separates—jackets, skirts, pants and suits—each in three alternative colors, with one overcoat and one raincoat. Judy loved the colors of the new collection; subtle, seductive grays in pewter, silver, oyster and pearl blended with pale rose, burgundy, burnished chestnut, copper and bronze. Narrow toreador pants were worn with brilliant taffeta tops that had huge puffed sleeves. Judy's favorite was geranium taffeta worn with saffron velvet pants. Their smoke-gray overcoat, bias-cut like a cape, was also lined with geranium silk; the raincoat, of similar cut, was dark green gabardine lined in pink silk.

With this show Guy hoped to establish himself as a serious businessman, not just a young design prodigy playing at fashion. So this time they planned to present it in style, at the Plaza Athénée again, but with a professional stage manager in charge. It was expensive, but worth it.

For Guy, this collection was make or break.

CHAPTER II

FIVE DAYS BEFORE the show, Guy burst into Judy's bedroom. Too tired to work for another minute, she had decided to have an early night before the inevitable last-minute rush of the show. She was leaning with her elbows on the window frame as a hot July breeze stirred the white lace curtains. The couple opposite had just started their nightly fight.

"They've been stolen! Everything's gone! Even the accessories! They've cleared every damn thing off the racks, six months' work has just *disappeared!* My whole collection has vanished from the workroom."

"Have you told the police?" Judy demanded, after she realized he wasn't joking.

"Of course. Immediately. They sounded uninterested. Then I telephoned you, but the hotel phone was out of order so I ran around. Every damn thing has disappeared, but only clothes; what's odd is that the thieves didn't take my little silver coffee set or the typewriter or the bales of cloth or anything else valuable. Only the clothes."

Together they ran back to the empty workshop. "We'll have to get this door fixed tonight," Judy said. "We can't leave the cloth here for anyone to take."

"I'll sleep here tonight," Guy said wretchedly. Then the telephone rang and they both jumped. A man's voice asked for Judy.

Surprised, she took the receiver from Guy. "Judy Jordan here."

"If you want your clothes back by Friday it'll cost his dad eight million francs in cash," the man said in French.

The line went dead. Judy looked at Guy. "It's blackmail!" She repeated the man's message and added with awe, "That's nearly twenty-nine thousand dollars they want."

"How does he know we're showing on Friday?"

"Plenty of people know we're showing on Friday; everyone we've invited, in fact. Better call the *flics* again."

They spent the rest of the evening with the police. Only Parisian police could appreciate the disaster that would result to a couturier from the absence of the forty-two missing garments that constituted Guy's entire collection. If he didn't show his clothes when the buyers were in Paris and buying, then he wouldn't get any orders for them. Apart from that, there was the question of Guy's prestige. Without doubt, all the important buyers and all the important press would be turning up at Guy's next show; Guy would look like a careless amateur to a group of important people with not a minute to waste during the fortnight of the collections. And—most important of all—there was the vital question of Guy's reliability. If he couldn't produce his own collection on time, then the buyers certainly wouldn't risk his being unable to deliver their orders on time. The rumor that he was "unreliable" would be Guy's professional death knell.

Again and again, the police questioned Judy. Was mademoiselle sure that she had heard correctly? Could she describe the voice? Did either of them have any enemies? What was the business value of the collection, as opposed to the value of the clothes? And so on.

Eventually Judy and Guy returned to their hotel. A shopping bag hung on Judy's white china doorknob; inside was a geranium taffeta blouse slashed to ribbons. Horrified, she was holding the rags in her hand when the telephone by her bed rang.

"Got the red blouse? Good. Be at the café Rubis, by the meat market, at four tomorrow afternoon. They'll have a parcel for you."

Two floors down, Guy had also found a shopping bag hanging on his door handle. Inside was a pair of saffron velvet pants roughly bisected.

"Do we tell the police?" asked Guy.

"Not yet," Judy said, "they'll only give us another hundred forms to fill in. Anyway, I think I'm their chief suspect. Let's try and get more information before we go back to the police. Let's try and analyze what little we know."

Suddenly, she shook her head. "Both telephone calls were for *me*. Why not you? Everyone knows when you're showing your collection, but very few people have heard of me or know where I live. Besides, I'm a foreigner—I can't describe a French telephone voice except to say whether it's a man, woman or child. So it must be someone we know! Someone in the workshop, or a buyer, a journalist perhaps, or even one of our suppliers. . . . Let's make a list of them from the order and delivery books and the press addresses."

The next morning outside the workshop door was a parcel penciled "Judy." It contained a topaz silk shirt ripped across the middle.

Guy was distraught. "They're only showing us they're tough," Judy reasoned. "They won't cut up the whole collection or they won't have anything to sell to us. They've only destroyed two blouses and a pair of pants, not jackets. Maybe we'll have time to remake them. They're all made by Marie, aren't they?" She paused for a moment: "Now that's interesting! Not *one* of these three garments was made by José. Perhaps someone who sews as exquisitely as José couldn't bear to slash her own work."

Guy refused to believe that José, who had been with him since he started, would rob him. "How about the cutter?" asked Judy, but Guy refused to believe that he could have been betrayed by any of his tiny staff, all of whom had seen how hard he worked, how much he worried and how careful he was not to be overdemanding of them.

Then Guy suddenly remembered, "José's husband is a meat porter and the café Rubis is near the meat market! I once gave José a lift there to meet him. I took her in the delivery van. I don't suppose she'd remember."

"Hardly a coincidence with the whole of Paris to choose from."

At four o'clock that afternoon they walked into the café Rubis. As the door swung open, a blast of steamy noise hit them; violet neon lighting glared down from a ceiling supported by slim iron columns. Against a zinc bar leaned hennaed whores, bloodied, white-aproned butchers and meat porters with leather-bound wrists.

Without being requested, a plate of appetizers was put on the table before them—thick slices of aromatic spiced sausage, chunks of fresh ham and large green aspic cubes contained smoked tongue. For the next three hours they dawdled over black coffee, but nothing happened and no parcel was delivered. They grew increasingly anxious, nervous and depressed until Judy said, "I'm going to telephone Aunt Hortense and ask her advice."

Luckily Aunt Hortense was at home. Quickly, Judy told her story. There was a silence, then Aunt Hortense said, "Wait until ten o'clock, then telephone me again and if nothing has happened, come around here."

But at nine o'clock the waiter said, "*Vous-êtes Americaine, Mademoiselle Jordan? Téléphone.*"

She went to the phone booth at the back of the café, an upright, coffin-sized wooden box that smelled of old sweat and dead cigarettes. She grabbed the old-fashioned earpiece off the wall and crisply said, "Judy Jordan." *Concentrate*, she thought. Listen for the sound of his voice, write down the words as he speaks them. But there was no writing surface and one-handed she couldn't hold her notebook against the wall.

"Get the money tomorrow morning and put it in a plain white envelope, the sort that's used for letters. Then wait in your office. Make sure the money is unmarked because we'll check it. If you try any tricks with the cops, you won't hear from us until Thursday because we'll be busy with the shears."

Judy left the foul-smelling booth and repeated the message to Guy. The voice had been fairly deep, a man's voice, a rough bark. She couldn't tell more, couldn't even guess if the voice were disguised.

"He said 'shears,' not 'scissors'? Are you sure? Only workshop staff would do that," said Guy, grim.

They hurried to Aunt Hortense's apartment. She was waiting in the library and to their astonishment Maurice, the chauffeur, was sitting back in an armchair, legs comfortably crossed, sipping a whiskey and soda. Guy and Judy both refused a drink. "Then let's have some black coffee to keep us awake," said Aunt Hortense. "The staff have gone off for the night so I'll make it myself—the Nescafé, so practical."

"I'll do it," Judy said, and moved down the gloomy corridor that led to a kitchen.

When she returned with the tray of coffee, Judy was made to repeat her tale. Then Guy was asked to repeat the whole story, in case there was any slight difference that might provide a clue. After a thoughtful silence Aunt Hortense asked, "Do you know where your staff live? Do they have the telephone? No? That's good. Let us visit this young seamstress, Marie, immediately. Guy can demonstrate agitation and pretend that he wishes to know how long it will take her to sew two replacement blouses and the pants. Any excuse will do; the point is to catch her by surprise at home."

Marie, in a white cotton nightdress with her hair twisted up in curl papers, was indeed astonished by Guy's late call. She immediately asked him in and said she was prepared to sew, nonstop, all night until the replacement garments were finished.

"Cross her off the list," said Guy, scrambling into the Mercedes. "Now the cutter. I'll ask him if he's prepared to stay at the workshop tomorrow and work through the night." Again, although it was now nearly midnight, guy was invited in and the cutter immediately agreed to work throughout the following night.

"Cross him off the list. Now let's visit José."

A clearly terrified José poked her head around the gray front door of her second-floor apartment. Guy asked if he could enter, but with agitation she demurred. At this hour she was not dressed so it was impossible, her husband was sleeping and she didn't want to disturb him, he had to get up early to be at the meat market by five in the morning. Guy said that he wanted her to try to remember whether any stranger had been in the workshop the previous week. José answered that the police had already asked her twice and she'd said that delivery boys and fabric salesmen were always in and out. Again Guy asked if he could come in, and again José refused, panic in her eyes. "Tomorrow morning at the workshop I'll talk about anything you want but not now. It's too late. Not now, Monsieur Guy. I dare not wake him."

Guy said goodnight, clumped off loudly down the passage, then tiptoed back and put his ear to the door crack. He could faintly hear low, staccato voices arguing. Furious, Guy felt sure that his clothes were inside the apartment and felt like breaking the door down. Shaking with rage and impotence, he walked around the block to the waiting Mercedes and reported to Aunt Hortense.

"What do you think, Maurice?" she asked.

"It's unlikely to be a buyer or a journalist or a supplier, Madame, it's too great a risk for a mere eight million francs. It's more likely to be someone with a low income—a delivery boy or a fabric salesman or one of the staff."

"A delivery boy or a fabric salesman would never have said 'shears,' " Guy pointed out, "but workshop staff never say anything else." He hesitated. "I once gave José a lift to the café Rubis. Her husband works in the meat market. If we are going to be negotiating in that café, he won't look out of place, because I expect he's always popping in and out, and even if somebody *did* notice him, I doubt they'd say anything to the *flics*; it's a tough sort of place."

"But if the husband knows that you have taken José there he would be unlikely to use it."

"I only dropped her outside; maybe she didn't mention it or maybe she's forgotten it. She's not a master brain, you know, and tonight she was terrified; she gabbled whatever came into her head first, she wouldn't let me in and she lied to me. She said her husband was asleep, but I heard them talking two minutes later. *Why* should she lie?"

"The fact that she lied, that she didn't let Guy inside, and that she goes to the café Rubis, which is a meat-market café, and that her husband is a meat porter apply to José and nobody else," said Judy. "Apart from that there is the odd coincidence that none of José's work has been ruined. She knows my name, she knows that I'm a foreigner, she must know that Guy's father is rich and she would certainly say 'shears,' not 'scissors.' "

"And what none of you saw except me," added Guy, "was how terrified she was at the thought of letting me into her apartment tonight. She was gibbering with fright. I think she was terrified of me and even more terrified of her husband. But why should that be unless she's guilty?"

There was another thoughtful silence, then Aunt Hortense said, "If we broke into their apartment when they weren't there, what would we have to lose if they were innocent? The police wouldn't prosecute unless José pressed charges, and in such circumstances I'm sure she would prefer the cost of a new front door and a large cash bribe by way of recompense. What is your opinion, Maurice?"

"I'm inclined to think she's guilty, Madame. I suggest a surprise attack at José's apartment, at the time of the arranged rendezvous to hand over the money. By ourselves, Madame. The police will not move fast enough."

"Exactly my opinion. Oh, it's like old times! I'll drive the Mercedes as I used to. You and Guy can break in; you can hold off any attackers. Guy's job will be to get a window open, then throw the clothes out to Judy. She will be waiting on the sidewalk ready to stuff the clothes into garbage sacks and throw them into the Mercedes. If there's any trouble I'll drive off with the clothes and leave you to sort yourselves out. Wear low-heeled shoes, Judy, in case you have to run." She turned to Guy. "Maurice is very good at this sort of thing, but you *must* move fast. You'll only have five minutes, that's all you can count on. However, you'll be amazed at what you can do in five minutes."

The next morning Judy and Guy went to the workshop as usual. While Guy played the part of a distraught designer, the staff started to work again. José—who really did look terrified—apologized to Guy for not letting him into her apartment the night before.

"Forget it, I shouldn't have come. I'd had a couple of drinks."

Guy went to his bank where he obtained a few small bank notes, which he added to an envelope already full of plain white paper.

Back at the office, the sewing machines stopped whirring and everybody froze expectantly whenever the phone rang. The call came at midday, again for Judy.

"Be in front of the Odéon Cinema on the Champs Elysées at five minutes past five o'clock this evening. Come alone or we won't pick up. Face the photo stills display on the right-hand side of the cinema. Hold the money in a white letter-size envelope in your left hand down at your side. And do not move your head. The envelope will be taken from you. Don't move for five minutes after that."

"How do we know we'll get the clothes back?"

"We have no use for the clothes. Once we have the money, we'll send a message to tell you where we've stored the clothes."

This was reported back to Aunt Hortense. "Clever," she said. "The film probably ends at five, so there will be a crowd pouring out around Judy and their pickup will be in it. Judy would hardly feel the snatch and she certainly wouldn't be able to identify anyone. Of course, they have no intention of handing over the clothes; they're incriminating evidence. I expect they plan to dump them in the Seine. We had better plan the surprise attack."

At a quarter to five that evening, Maurice parked the Mercedes two streets away from José's apartment and changed places with Aunt Hortense, who wore a navy coat, navy beret and enormous sunglasses. She turned to Guy, whose face was chalk-white, and cheerfully said, "Justice depends on who is holding the scales. My dear, you have three things to remember. First, if you're caught by the police, say nothing, not even your name, just ask for my lawyer. Second, do *exactly* as Maurice says—he is in charge. Unless Maurice gives you an order, just do your own job and get out after five minutes. Ignore any fighting. With luck you'll hear me blow three blasts on my whistle when your time is up. And finally," she added in a reasonable voice, "remember that you're merely collecting your own property." She put the car in gear with a crash as Maurice winced. "We hit them at ten to five when they'll be most jumpy, when their thoughts will be at the Odéon."

Upon reaching José's apartment building, Judy—also wearing sunglasses and a navy beret—jumped out of the car and stood on the pavement, a pile of garbage bags in her hands. Guy followed Maurice under the arch into the inner courtyard, up the stairs and along a dark, narrow corridor. Maurice looked around carefully, inspected the grubby, gray door, then put his ear to it. He felt the lock with the tips of his fingers and paused. He leaned casually against the wall opposite, lifted his left foot to the level of the lock, then gave it one vicious kick. The door flew open and Maurice charged in, flinging the door flat against the wall with his left arm, then throwing his back against it.

The shutters were down and the apartment was muggy and silent except for the noise of traffic outside. There was very little furniture—a flowered sofa and two armchairs, a standard lamp with a fake parchment shade, a sideboard, a few pictures of agonized saints hanging from the wall.

Maurice stuck his head out of the door and beckoned Guy in.

"You take the left room and I'll take the right."

The right door led to a small, bare kitchen and a lavatory. The left door led to a large room containing a double bed with a crucifix hung above it, a small wardrobe, an ornate birds-eye maple dressing table with triple mirror and another fake parchment lamp, this one with maroon fringe. Leading off the bedroom was another smaller room. In the dim, shuttered light, Guy could see that it contained another small wardrobe, a kitchen chair and a single bed—upon which was piled his entire collection of clothes.

He gave a cry of triumph and wrestled open the shutters as Maurice dashed into the room.

Guy could see Judy two floors below and about fifteen feet away, anxiously looking up. He screamed at her. She heard immediately and dashed toward Guy's window. Aunt Hortense started up the motor and the Mercedes slowly followed Judy, then waited with the engine running.

Both men started hurling the clothes out of the window so they landed far too fast for Judy to stuff them into the bags. She wrenched open the near side door of the Mercedes and threw suits, dresses, hats and shoes into it as fast as she could pick them off the pavement. The few astonished passersby watched motionless until Aunt Hortense gave three sharp whistle blasts. Judy jumped into the back of the car, throwing herself on top of the clothes, the two men ran out of the doorway and squeezed into the front seat of the Mercedes. Aunt Hortense stepped on the gas and took the first corner on two wheels, leaving a pink satin shoe and a green scarf fluttering on the pavement behind.

"Steady, Madame, steady!" Maurice said. "We don't want a speeding ticket at this point." But Aunt Hortense was enjoying herself. She drove at top speed to Guy's dry cleaner, where they left Judy with the clothes. Judy felt exultant as she never had before—she now knew the exhilaration of action. She had expected to be frightened but instead she had positively *enjoyed* it. And they had won.

"Nothing seems to be missing," reported Guy, as Aunt Hortense drove to the workshop. "Only the hat brims are wrecked."

Aunt Hortense braked, then reluctantly yielded the wheel to Maurice. "No need to mention anything to the police," she said carelessly. "They don't like breaking and entering. And they might want to keep the clothes as evidence. So why not let this remain yet another of their unsolved mysteries?"

Guy nodded, then raced upstairs, two at a time, hoping to catch José before she left for the night. The other two employees had already left and José was belting her beige raincoat. One look at Guy's face told her that she had been found out. Roughly he leaped across the room, caught hold of her wrist and dragged her to the telephone. "If you don't want me to call the police, you'd better tell me why you did it and who helped you," he said, tight-mouthed with fury.

"Let me go! You must be mad, Monsieur Guy, let me go. I'll scream."

"Scream away—and someone will call the police." She tried to free her wrist, tried to kick Guy, then jerked her head in despair toward the window as she and Guy fought. He panted, "I'm not going to let you throw yourself out the window, José, what good would that do? I don't want to hurt you, I only want to know what happened. I know it wasn't your idea. I know you didn't want to do it. We've got the clothes back. They were on the bed in the little bedroom in your apartment."

Astonished, she stopped struggling and looked at him, frightened but wary. "What good will it do me if you go to jail, José? I've got the clothes back. But I want to know what *happened*. If you tell me all I want to know, I *might* not tell the police. But if you don't come clean I'll call the *flics* straightaway, and that'll mean prison. So tell me the truth, José. It was your husband's idea, wasn't it?"

"I don't know what you mean." There was a pause.

"We found the clothes in your apartment."

José burst out, "It *wasn't* my man." She paused again and Guy jerked her toward the telephone. "No! It was his pal André—he's a pickpocket. I've never liked him. My man would never have tried this by himself. Oh, Mother of God, what's going to happen to us now?"

"And who else helped you?"

"No one else! Put the phone down, Monsieur Guy! I'll tell you! There was no one else."

"Was it this André who telephoned?"

"Yes, yes, it was André who phoned."

"Liar!" He yanked at her wrist until she started to whimper again, but she still looked surly and wouldn't speak. "André would not have said 'shears.' One more lie and I call the *flics*."

She burst into tears again. Guy shook her shoulders but she only howled louder. However, when he picked up the telephone she stopped in midshriek and told him the rest of the story. It was very simple.

At five o'clock that afternoon, her husband had been waiting fifty yards from the cinema in the Champs Elysées because he hadn't trusted his pickpocket friend. Their plan was that after snatching the money both of them should dive into the métro, catch a train at random, get out and find a park. They would wait until dark, when there would be few people around, and then divide the money. José's husband then planned to post his share of the money addressed to himself, *poste restante*, at his local post office. When he felt safe, he would collect the money.

Guy could only whisper, he was so furious, so weak with rage. "Get out," he croaked, "and never, never, never come around here again or I'll call the police immediately."

José burst into fresh tears and fled.

Within twenty-four hours, the story of Guy's kidnapped and returned collection was known to the entire fashion trade of Paris, and although he denied the story to reporters, the intriguing tale drew many more journalists to his collection than might otherwise have seen it.

That collection established Guy as a serious designer to be watched, not just a rich brat dabbling in fashion. Judy suddenly found that dealing with the press was almost a full-time job.

The only person to publicize an accurate story of the theft was Empress Miller, who was so charming, so disarming, so unobtrusively efficient that she always found out the truth—which was why Judy was a little afraid of her.

CHAPTER 12

THE NEXT TWO years were breathlessly busy but packed with excitement. Success invariably involved money problems until Guy obtained support from an unexpected source—his bank manager. Having studied Guy's financial history and the profit and loss projections, his bank manager—unprompted—telephoned Guy's father and said that it seemed a pity to turn his back on a potential money-making business simply because it had been started by his own son. The result was that the bank agreed to back Guy, and his father—quite glad to be able to drop his dogmatic stance—guaranteed the loan. Nevertheless, Guy was still determined not to expand simply because he had enough orders to do so.

"I'm not interested in short-term turnover but in long-term stability," he explained to Empress Miller, who was wedged into a creaking conical cane chair perched on three thin black metal legs. Their new, modern office not only had an elevator and a tiny reception area, it also had a picture-window view of the gray rooftops and chimney pots of Paris—now covered with January snow—and a louvred cupboard, inside which was fitted a compact little kitchen. Judy hovered with the coffee pot as Guy answered Empress Miller's questions. "What I eventually want is to establish a small, good-quality ready-to-wear collection. There's no RTW fashion in Europe, as there is in the States, only cheap, manufactured garments. But on the other hand, in the States there are no name designers—which is why your manufacturers buy their designs from Paris. I want to combine the two operations."

"Yes, that's quite a good idea, Guy." Empress always praised with caution, although she did not hesitate to criticize in a manner that ranged from mildly ironic to downright acid. But she was always fair, and when she didn't like something, she explained exactly why.

Her neat blonde head bent over her notebook. "How does it feel to be so successful when you're so young? To have come so far in only a couple of years?"

Guy wriggled on his purple canvas womb chair, suspended on a thin, black metal butterfly frame. "That's the question that everybody asks me, but you might as well ask me what it's like to be a dog or a university student or a post office messenger. I am who I am, and there's no getting away from it, and I don't know what it's like to be different. I'm a fashion designer, just the way someone else is an accountant. I started young because it worked out that way and because I wasn't interested in anything else." He looked reflectively at the orange ceiling. "If you're going to do something really well, I suspect that it has to be to the exclusion of everything else. And I *haven't* been an overnight success. I'm twenty-six and I've been working hard in fashion for ten years. It's simply that people suddenly *realized* it overnight. I suspect that most overnight successes are the same."

"Nevertheless, Wool International went out on a limb for you with your last collection."

"And so did I for them. My entire collection was made from wool and nothing else."

Not without some of the noisiest rows I have ever participated in, thought Judy, who had insisted on this publicity-attracting theme.

Empress raised her eyebrows in polite query and Guy explained. "Wool jersey drapes well and is flattering to the figure—synthetic fabrics tend to be either too stiff or too limp." He heaved himself out of the purple canvas sling, pulled a bolt of dark green wool from the rack, then deftly draped and pinned the fabric around Judy, an old favorite trick to demonstrate his point. "See what I mean? And look at the color—it glows, it has depth, because a natural fiber absorbs color better than a synthetic."

"Ow," said Judy, "a little less depth to the pins please." Guy finished his work and stood back.

"See how that's going to *flow* as she walks?" The pinned material had taken the shape of a coat, flared at the back like a bullfighter's cloak. It was cut on the same lines as that mulberry coat he'd just finished for Maxine, hanging on the rail by the door, ready for them to take to her this evening. Judy was looking forward to a couple of peaceful days in the country, tramping the frozen, silent woods by day and lying in front of a crackling log fire in the evening.

"How does Pierre Mouton feel about wool?" Empress suddenly asked, looking him straight in the eye.

How does she know? Guy wondered. The Belgian manufacturer would never have told Empress of their plan, and the only other person who knew it was Judy. It had to be a factory leak. You couldn't keep a damned thing quiet in this industry, everybody knew everything within five minutes.

"The buzz is that you're producing a new RTW collection and it's being manufactured outside Brussels by Pierre Mouton. You'll show the RTW at the same time as you show your summer couture collection, then start selling the next day so that RTW garments will be selling before any couture customer can get her clothes fitted, let alone finished." Empress never took her eyes off Guy's face. "Of course this *might* turn out to be professional suicide on your part, because all your couture customers will be furious, but I can see that it could be a daring new way of linking RTW to couture designs. Do you agree?"

Guy stared at her. How *did* she know? No factory hand could possibly know that. They had calculated that the couture customers wouldn't be irritated by the RTW collection if they were offered first choice of the RTW garments. And the RTW wasn't a copy of the couture collection. He had designed two collections calculated to overlap, rather than have one a cheap copy of the other.

"Pierre Mouton has always bought from me," Guy said, affecting calm, "but you know that his factories aren't geared up to produce boutique-quality clothes."

Empress looked at him sharply. "You haven't answered my question."

"If what you say were true, you know I couldn't answer it. Pierre Mouton is one of my best customers. That's all I'm prepared to say."

"Well, that wraps it up," Empress said gaily, snapped her notebook shut and turned to Judy. "Now I'd *love* another cup of coffee. It's a joy to get a good cup of coffee in Paris. Sometimes I suspect that they're still making it out of ground acorns as they did during the war."

"It's because the French are so stingy that they won't use enough coffee. The secret is simply to use twice as many beans as they do," said Judy. She was happy to talk about anything to get the conversation away from Pierre Mouton. "But you can't do anything about French milk," she said. "I don't think French cows have blood in their veins. I still sometimes *long* for a glass of real American milk. I still get homesick for silly little things like that, although I've now been away for six years."

She got homesick for bigger things than milk. However long she lived in Paris, however much she loved it, she suspected that her character was too basically American to allow her to settle in Europe forever. She sometimes wondered if that was the reason why she never seemed to fall in love like every other woman in Paris. She didn't want to marry a European. She went out with the eligible Frenchmen that Aunt Hortense produced from time to time, but she never seemed to feel entirely at ease with them except for darling Guy. The rest were so damned suave. But that was another worry: she was certainly having a terrific time, but she didn't want to play second string to Guy all her life. What had happened to her own career?

After Empress left, Judy shook off the sudden wistful yearning that she always felt after a visit from an American journalist who knew that a cheerleader wasn't a political position and who knew the difference between a milkshake and a soda.

Judy shook her fist at Guy. "I didn't say a word! *You* practically told her. She only had to put two and two together, and she must have heard something as well. You *must* have told someone, you *must* have hinted. I knew you wouldn't be able to keep your lip buttoned. Pillow talk, I suppose."

"I swear I haven't said a word, you're the one who chatters to journalists the whole time." He grabbed her wrist, they lost their balance and both fell noisily onto the purple canvas sofa, pummeling each other, shrieking and laughing, flinging cushions—a deliberately childish reaction to the strain, the carefully casual mood of the interview.

"What will the night cleaner think if she comes in?" giggled Judy, looking up at Guy's tousled head.

"She will be totally confused, decide that all the gossip she's heard about me is a dirty lie, then she'll buy a pair of black fishnet stockings and make a pass at me. You know it's in the French blood, mixing the romantic with the practical. I'll never have a moment's peace." They were giggling at the idea of their enormous sixty-year-old cleaner pouncing on slight Guy when the telephone rang. Judy scrambled to answer it. Strange, someone telephoning the office at nearly nine o'clock at night.

But it was only three in the afternoon in Rossville. She heard her father's voice and was immediately apprehensive. It could only mean a disaster; her father would only make a long distance call in a cataclysmic emergency.

"Is that you, Judy?" Thee was a lot of echo on the line. "I've got some real bad news. It's your mother. Can you hear, Judy? You'd better come home."

At two in the morning they were still sitting in Aunt Hortense's chilly library, Judy in a red wool dressing gown, Aunt Hortense in a fragile, green lace negligée under a mink coat. The central heating had shut down at midnight.

"Your mother may well recover. A cerebral aneurysm is terrible, but not always fatal."

"It's not only that. I feel so guilty. I've been away six years."

"But you told me that you wrote every week. And you were working hard. You were doing something that your mother was going to be proud of."

"Oh, she never said a word, she never complained or asked me to go home, but however good the excuses, I know I simply didn't *want* to go home. Paris is more fun than Rossville. The weeks just dissolved into each other, it was all so exciting, and I felt that going anywhere near Rossville would be . . . an emotional trap. I was frightened that once I got back, she'd ask me to *stay*—and I was afraid I wouldn't be able to say no."

"Judy, your mother and you may not have much in common, but from what you've told me she realizes that. I don't think that she would have tried to stop you doing anything. I can't see that she ever has. She obviously loves you, just as you love her in your own way. This emergency proves it—you can think of nothing but flying back to her."

"Prompted by guilt. Knowing that I haven't flown back in six years."

"Unfortunately, I don't know what it feels like to be a mother, but if you were my child I would give you a good shake. Guilt is boring and pointless. You are going home to see your mother who is sick. Kindly do not overdramatize the situation. You will have a happy time with her; then you will return to Paris with her blessing."

But Judy didn't return to Paris. After an agonizing twelve weeks, during which her mother hung between life and death, she slowly opened her eyes and saw her only daughter at her bedside. She tried to smile and whispered with the urgency of the very ill, "That's all I wanted. To see you once again."

"Oh, thank God, Ma, thank God." She clutched her mother's shoulder and knelt at the bedside, to bring her face close to her mother. "What can I do, Ma? What can I do to make you happy? What do you want? What can I give you?"

There was a moment's silence, then that weak whisper. "I've always thought how wonderful and brave it was of you, Judy, to go off and see new things. . . . I never could. . . . I was always afraid . . . you're so different. I want to get to know you, I'm so proud of you . . . I want to know you before I die. . . . I want to spend time with you. . . . Please. Stay nearby a while. I know I mustn't keep you in Rossville, but please . . . stay in America."

Without a moment's hesitation, Judy promised.

CHAPTER 13

THE OFFICES OF most working publicity agents do not look as if they are waiting for the *House and Garden* photographer to arrive, and this one was no exception, Judy thought—in fact, it was almost as dingy as the office where she'd first worked in Paris. Outside the grimy window on her left, girls in flowered dresses on the sidewalks of New York were getting the first wolf whistles of spring; inside, opposite the window, was a row of chipped, gray filing cabinets, on top of which magazines were stacked almost to the ceiling. The wall in front of her was covered with lavishly dedicated photographs of people who had been showbiz celebrities five or ten years ago. Hanging in one corner was last year's calendar. Someone had stopped tearing off the leaves at April 5, 1954. In front of it was a gray metal desk stacked with old newspapers, more magazines and metal baskets full of old press releases. A tall, loose-limbed blonde woman, wearing a scarlet suit and ludicrously high-heeled black patent shoes, perched on one corner of it. She looked as if she belonged in a detective story.

"I guess very few people actually *decide* to be a press agent and study it in college," said the blonde. "You just suddenly find you're in it. I was a reporter until the paper folded. I was on unemployment when a friend told me that the Ice Follies was looking for an advance man. I said, 'What's an advance man?' and the next week I was in Philadelphia, being one." She dragged on her cigarette. "Just why do you want to be in PR?"

"I've done some publicity work in France. I worked fairly closely in Paris with Wool International and they suggested I apply here for a job."

Suggested, did they? Didn't this child realize that the head of WI in Paris had telephoned Lee & Sheldon to see if she could be fitted into the agency's New York office? And when the agency had hesitated, it had been pleasantly suggested to them that WI would like this unknown Miss Jordan to work on their account. Simultaneously, the agency president had received a phone call from Empress Miller herself, saying that she had worked closely with Miss Jordan, whose understanding of haute-couture was far greater than her years might suggest. Empress always underplayed things, but quite obviously this kid had friends. And although she was very young, her experience was certainly impressive. So why did she want an assistant's job? Why all this exasperating internal reshuffling just to fit in Miss Jordan?

But Judy knew she needed on-the-job experience before she could handle an account in a New York office. She didn't want to be an executive secretary; she wanted to bide her time while she sorted out her Seventh Avenue contacts and saw whether there was any chance of getting a job like the one she'd held with

Guy. PR seemed a good way to mark time while looking around.

She had stayed in Rossville for seventeen weeks, until her mother recovered—as much as she was likely to; she would never regain the complete use of her left arm and her mouth still drooped a little.

Although Judy still felt guilty about having left home, she had now made peace with her mother and as much peace as she was ever likely to make with her father, who bragged in a rather touching manner about how Judy had "flown all the way from Paris, France, *the very next day*." A child's presence in time of crisis was a form of local prestige, based on the distance that the child had to travel and how fast the child covered it.

To Judy, the town felt as claustrophobic as ever. She knew everyone, their faces, their family, their outlook and their future. The men were uninteresting, the women walked around in shapeless winter coats or shapeless pastel prints. They could only talk about recipes, the weather, their children, their last pregnancy and the last pregnancies of all their friends. The people of whom they spoke rarely had a name. Instead, they were identified by the name of their parents and where they came from, as in, "I hear Tom—Steven's boy—is going to marry Joan MacDaniel's girl," or "She's the MacDaniel girl who's marrying that fellow from Quantico."

Again, Judy felt that she had to get out—and now it wasn't only for her own self-protection. She had to earn enough to pay for the therapist and her mother's enormous medical expenses, which her father's insurance had only partly covered. She wrote to Guy and her other French friends to tell them why she couldn't return to Paris, and she also sent a note to Empress Miller asking if she could suggest a suitable job in New York.

Guy replied with an immediate, extravagant telegram:

DESOLATED LOSE MY RIGHT HAND STOP UNDERSTAND YOUR MOTIVES STOP REFUSE END RELATIONSHIP STOP HOPE YOUR NEW CONTACTS HELP ESTABLISH ME AMERICA STOP HURRY HURRY STOP ONE BILLION KISSES STOP GUY

Once in New York Judy rented a studio on East 11th Street, sent out three hundred resumés, and had telephone interviews with seventeen people, only three of whom wanted to see her when they heard she had had no previous experience in America. At times, thinking of her exciting job and the friends she had left in Paris, Judy's shoulders sagged; she felt alone and that she had thrown away a promising future for a sentimental promise.

Then she received a note from Empress Miller suggesting that she contact Lee & Sheldon, and a day later a letter suggesting the same thing arrived from Wool International in Paris.

"You realize you would have to do a lot of traveling?" asked the blonde in the scarlet suit. "Basically you would assist me on the WI account. We forecast fashion trends to the press, send out news releases, prepare press kits with photographs and sketches and twice a year, after the Paris collections, we coordinate the wool models that WI has commissioned from French couturiers. We promote any wool copies that are being produced by American manufacturers and generally plug the message that wool is wonderful and they'd better buy more." She swung an elegant nylon leg and lifted an eyebrow in query.

"I've handled all that," said Judy. "On a small scale, of course."

"We also appear on TV and give talks on wool, illustrated by photographs and sketches. None of it is nearly as glamorous as it sounds, by the way, not even taking fashion editors to lunch."

"I'm used to that," Judy said with growing confidence.

The blonde shifted position, started to swing the other shapely leg and said, "Press agents spend their careers explaining why their client is not an asshole. And mostly they are, of course." She lit another cigarette. "If you join us, we would want you to handle the truck shows. The models we buy from the Paris collections immediately tour the best stores in every important town in America. We would expect you to arrange the shows, book the models and then travel with them, looking after the girls and the clothes, carrying publicity materials, photographs, display cards, samples of the fabrics being used and inexpensive give-aways. You would be booked into a different town every day of the week for four weeks twice a year. D'you think you could stand it?"

"Try me."

"Let's both try a martini."

Judy had never worked so hard in her life. Her boss, Pat Rogers was merciless. An ex-journalist, she was demanding; she expected everyone else to work as fast as she did and she was a superb trainer. Judy quickly realized that if a thing wasn't absolutely right it was *wrong*—nearly right was not good enough.

"The easy way to be a good press agent," Pat told her, "is to realize that you can't buy good coverage with a free lunch. You have to have a good story. This isn't Paris, kid. You have to fight for every inch of coverage because the competition is fierce."

She leaned back, crossed her feet on the desk and tilted her chair. "You're trading services. What a journalist wants is the facts and fast, and maybe in return he'll publicize your product; that's the basic deal. There are *very* few really good press agents and they're mostly ex-journalists, which is why they understand what's needed. An ex-journalist knows what *news* is. News is what nobody knew yesterday, and if a story isn't news, then it won't rate good news coverage, however interesting."

One day Pat said, "About time you learned to write, kid. Don't mess around with correspondence courses. Go sleep with a journalist for a couple of months. No? Well, clear the decks for Saturday, get the Kleenex out, come around to my apartment and I'll teach you. I am the Saturday School of Compressed Journalism, smallest of its kind in the world."

After two Saturdays of crumpled paper and insults, Pat stretched and said, "You've got the rough idea, kid. People either pick it up fast or not at all, mostly not at all. You're impatient, which helps; you're easily bored, which also helps; you'll never be Ernest Hemingway, but for straight factual reporting all you need is practice. Now let's have a martini."

That September, Judy set off on her first tour, traveling two days ahead of the show to check arrangements and spread the news, just like the carnival advance men of years ago. She lugged suitcases full of advance material, straightened out the inevitable snarls in arrangements, flattered, soothed and sweet-talked her way around the country and from the moment that she staggered out of bed in the morning to the moment that she fell into the next one in the next town that night, she thought only of wool.

It was a tough and lonely life, but during the day she was too busy to care and at night she was too tired. Her life was spent rushing from airport to cheap hotel room to offices and TV studios, then back to the airport and on to the next airport. Her tiny budget didn't enable her to stay in good hotels. Try as she might, she couldn't stretch her personal travel allowance to cover her expenses as well as her food, and she couldn't get the accounts department even to discuss the matter, so she started cheating on her expenses, until Pat said that the executive vice-president had pointed out that her telephone bill was bigger than his, at which Judy exploded. She liked to eat; the accounts department never allowed for the speed with which she had to cover a town in one day, or for any deviation from her theoretical routine. She suggested that the next trip be handled not by her but by one of the junior accountants and they could see how *he* made out.

Pat said, "I can see you enjoy shouting, but it's not the way to win an argument," and went off to shout at the chief accountant, after which Judy's expenses were raised. It was still a lonely, dyspeptic life, but at least she ate.

And she produced results.

Less than six months later Judy was able to persuade Pat to fly Guy to New York to discuss a truck show. Pierre Mouton accompanied him to investigate the possibilities of selling in the United States. Guy's new collection of separates covered the blue segment of the spectrum from lavender to deep purple. The unconstricting clothes projected a pulled-together style that was easy to move in, made a woman feel as if she wasn't wearing anything and enabled her to look her best without feeling self-conscious. He had used only luxurious fabrics and refused to produce a really cheap line. "One good suit is a better investment for a woman than three so-so suits," he said firmly to Judy as they leaned against the boat rail.

From the green-gold water, Wall Street looked like strips of ticker-tape stretching toward the sky. "This is the obligatory tourist's starter trip," Judy had explained, "down the Hudson River, past the Statue of Liberty, then up the East River to circle Manhattan. After that, I'm going to march you right around this city. You have no idea how I love it."

"More than Paris?"

"Different." Within a week of being in New York, Judy had decided that this marvelous, glittering, exhausting place was where she belonged and that she would never leave it. She felt personal and possessive about the city in a way she had never felt about Paris. "I love New York and I'm starting to love my job; life isn't quite so hectic and it's a good deal more comfortable now that I travel with the show and not ahead of it." She turned toward him, squinting into the late afternoon sun. "Incidentally, Pat wants to meet us for dinner so we can discuss touring your next collection. I warn you, she wants you to travel with it—a genuine French Frenchman wiz faseenateeng accent. They'll keel over at the mere *sound* of you in Cleveland."

"I wouldn't mind a free trip around the States."

"Don't expect a vacation." Judy turned her back to the water, leaned against the rail and wagged a finger at him. "Certainly the trips look wonderful when you see the models being greeted at airports, with armfuls of cellophane-wrapped roses as they step into the limo, but that's all baloney. What really happens is that we arrive on the last night plane—six people and thirty-eight suitcases—and we're met by a truck at the airport. I drag them out of bed at dawn, then one model will zip off to do the TV breakfast show and the rest get ready for a store show where the entire fashion-conscious audience is wearing tired-looking trouser suits or limp raincoats. Then we're interviewed by every newspaper in town, and after that there's the afternoon store show, then TV again, then off to the airport. If you travel on in the evening you arrive too late to eat or drink anything anyway, except those packets of Nescafé in the hotel bedroom. I tell you, after a truck tour you need two days in bed with the telephone off the hook while your nerves and your stomach sort themselves out."

She paused and watched the seagulls swoop over the gray water. "It's a nonstop routine of packing and unpacking. The poor dresser has to get all the garments pressed before each show, then she has to lay out the accessories. They're real saints, those dressers!" she snorted. "But the models are devils, and the sexual complications never end. We had two lesbians on the last trip, they couldn't keep their hands off each other, even on the catwalk. . . . Then there's the food problem. Of course the models are terrified of putting on weight and the really skinny ones are the worst—they're all either on some diet of dried seaweed and lime flowers, which they expect the hotel to stock, or else they order champagne and caviar and try to charge it to room service. We always tell the hotels that we won't pay extras, and the girls know it. Still, they sulk when they find that they either have to pay cash for the caviar or send it back."

"So tell me more about these poor thin girls and their sexual complications. Surely they can't *all* be so tiresome."

"I suppose that some of them are basically sweet girls, but they lead very insecure lives. They're totally exterior-oriented—they don't even enjoy their good looks because they constantly worry about losing them. *No* model thinks she's good-looking. Not surprising! They're constantly being auditioned, even the famous ones, for some assignment, and if twenty girls are auditioned, then nineteen will be turned down. They have to put up with endless rejection, and consequently they're very vulnerable."

She pulled her cream knitted cap down to cover her ears. "Some girls live on uppers to cut their appetite—so they're edgy and take offense at the slightest thing. Or else they can't sleep because we move on every night to a different hotel, so they take sleeping pills. Then I can't get them up in the morning." She giggled. "Of course, sometimes I can't get them up because they aren't *there* to get up. They'll have picked up some guy in the bar and disappeared. Just keeping the photographers off them is a full-time job."

"You can't frighten me." Guy tickled Judy's button nose. "Of course I'll tour. We'll go together. You helped me to become a success in France. This time, Judy, I'm going to see that you stay a permanent part of the success! You won't escape from me so easily again. . . . Unless you insist on wearing such ridiculous hats."

He tugged off her cream knitted cap and threw it into the East River. "That is the sort of thing my grandmother used to keep her boiled eggs warm. First thing tomorrow we buy you a beautiful fox fur hat from Saks. Only tiny babies wear that sort of knit thing."

Much to his surprise, Judy burst into tears.

PART THREE

CHAPTER 14

THE FROST HUNG white lace curtains outside the window.

Elizabeth hated to get up in the freezing winter. The sky was still dark and cold, a dim sprinkling of snow topped the apple trees and beech hedge around the garden. She wanted to stay safe and snug under the feather-filled quilt, luxuriating in the warmth as she listened to her family downstairs.

"You'll be late, Elizabeth," shouted Maman from the bottom of the stairs.

Eyes still shut, the small child put her bare feet on the rug and stumbled to the foot of the carved wooden bed, where her clothes lay neatly folded on the red-lacquered lid of the blanket chest. Sleepily she fumbled into thick black tights, heavy, wool winter underwear, blue-checked frock, navy apron and then she sat on the rug to lace up her stout, stiff black boots. In 1955 this was the typical winter school uniform of a Swiss child.

She climbed onto the chair by the window, rubbed clear a chilled glass pane and peered out at the weather. There was no snow today, as light started to show above the jagged black mountains on the other side of the Alpine valley. Below her, dimly visible beyond the snow-encrusted wooden balcony of the chalet, was the garden. Underneath her window, the first-floor balcony ran right around the chalet. Under the fish-scale tiles of the roof, an old prayer had been carved:

GOD BLESS ALL WHO LIVE HERE
1751

The child jumped down from the window, clumped in clumsy boots across the wooden floor of the corridor and flung open the door. Her foster brother's small room faced the mountain, and very little light filtered through the ancient windowpanes.

"Get up, get up, lazybones." She laughed. She flung herself on the patchwork quilt as an indignant head emerged from it. "You haven't fetched the bread from the bakery."

"Felix said he'd bring it up," mumbled Roger, sleepily.

"I don't believe you. Felix is on late duty this week."

Felix was the Hungarian head receptionist at the Hotel Rosat in Château d'Oex. In 1939, Felix had been dragged from his father's farm and conscripted into the Hungarian army, then he had been forced into the German army to fight the Russians on the Eastern front. After the fall of Budapest, Felix's division fled toward Germany, at which point Felix had managed to escape into Switzerland. Felix chopped the wood and did other jobs that were too heavy for a woman; in return, Maman did his washing and sewing.

"I tell you he's coming up early, he promised." Elizabeth rushed off, her boots clattering down the wooden stairs to the kitchen, where they always sat and ate in winter to save fuel. Maman was heating chocolate in a saucepan on top of the green, enameled stove.

"Roger hasn't got the bread for breakfast."

"Well, it doesn't matter, Elizabeth, I'll just flick water across yesterday's loaf and reheat it in the oven. You won't be able to tell the difference, Miss Telltale." Her foster mother's dark hair, still in a loose braid, not yet coiled in its neat daytime bun, hung down the back of her white flannel nightgown. Her red hands, skin flaking, placed a white pot of hot chocolate on the table.

Maman's husband had been killed on the Diablerets glacier eight years before. A ski guide, he had been leading a party across the glacier when they ran into bad weather. The party had been lost in the snow. Angelina Dassin was left with a small baby, which prevented her from working as a live-in maid as she had before her marriage. Almost penniless, she took the first job she was offered, scrubbing floors at the local hospital. In the evenings and on weekends she embroidered lace-trimmed white blouses for the tourist souvenir shop. For three years life had been very hard. Then she was asked to foster a baby girl who had been born at the hospital. The extra money meant that Angelina was able to stop her back-breaking cleaning job, stay cozily at home with two babies and concentrate on her embroidery.

Elizabeth was brought up as one of the Dassin family, but she was always told by Angelina that she also had another mother, a *real* mother, and that one day—when she was older—her real mother would come and take her home. Those were her thoughts as every night Angelina softly sang "*Au clair de la lune, mon ami pierrot*" and other nursery rhymes as she rocked Elizabeth to sleep and the pines rustled outside in the dark garden.

In fact, Angelina knew little more than Elizabeth about this mythical mother. A monthly check came in an anonymous envelope from a bank in Gstaad. Angelina always began her laborious reports, "*Chère madame*," hoping that by now the poor child was married, but the replies gave no information about the sender. There were merely questions about the child's progress that were duly answered in the report.

At first Elizabeth imagined her real mother as a kind of angel in a lace nightgown. Every night after saying her prayers on the rag rug she would whisper: "*Bonne nuit, vraie maman.*" Then she hoped that her real mother was a fairy princess and the reason that she couldn't come to see Elizabeth was that she was sleeping in a forest glade until the fairy prince woke her with a kiss. How Elizabeth wished he'd hurry up! She hoped that the forest wasn't too damp and that there weren't any ants.

Roger teased her that *vraie maman* was a witch woman with long fingernails and no teeth or hair, but Elizabeth refused to believe him, and when she overheard, Angelina, for once, scolded Roger. Such unkindness to his sister when he knew that if it wasn't for her five hundred francs a month, Angelina would be on her knees with acres of wet ward floor in front of her instead of sitting in a warm kitchen and embroidering blue edelweiss around heart-shaped necklines.

"Roger said Felix is coming up early," Elizabeth said, as she gulped her hot chocolate.

"Then I'd better dress quickly—hurry up, little one." Almost in one movement, she twisted Elizabeth into her scarlet coat, guided her fingers into the gloves that were attached by a tape threaded through the sleeves, tugged on her red wool helmet, wound a thick scarf around her neck and kissed her goodbye.

Outside, Elizabeth stood on tiptoe at the top of the steps, hopefully searching for Felix. She shivered, her breath froze on her scarf, her eyes watered and ran with tears that immediately turned to ice. A piercing whistle echoed across the mountains as the blue train to Montreux swished along the track, steel-pointed plough in front to clear the early morning snow. Elizabeth heard the low lulling noise of the cows, the clanging milk pails and the clatter from the next-door farm; she sniffed the straw and dung. Except for this farm, the Dassin chalet was the last one on the mountain track. Beyond and above it, dark pine forest stretched to the summit rocks, now covered in January snow; below the chalet, the garden fell away down the mountain slope toward the frozen river that divided the snow-covered valley. The white blanket was broken only by that winding black line and the sharp dark line of the railway.

Trudging up the mountain track from the village, she saw the bulky figure of Felix, a large basket over one arm. Shrieking greetings, the frail child slithered down the track to meet him. "Felix, will you be here when I come back from school? Will you tell me stories? Will you mend my doll, her arm's hanging loose? Will you make me another igloo?"

"Yes, yes, and yes, if you're not late for school."

"Oh, I promise."

The skinny little girl slithered and slid down the hard-packed snow track; she just managed to slip through the glass doors of the village schoolroom and dodge past the blackboard as Tante Gina rang the pewter handbell. The clock chimed seven-thirty as Elizabeth scrambled to her place on the splintered wooden bench that would feel harder and harder as the day wore on, until all the blue-apron-clad children perched upon it wriggled with numb discomfort.

After prayers, the whole school always chanted their multiplication table, "*Un fois deux, deux. Deux fois deux, quatre.*" Afterward, as it was Wednesday, Elizabeth climbed the stairs to Tante Simone's sitting room for her special English lesson. She also had a special French lesson but that was on Friday.

Tante Simone's sitting room smelled of biscuit crumbs, mothballs, eau de cologne and old ladies. Dark brocade wallpaper was punctuated by the monochromatic serious stares of previous pupils. Below these photographs stood an old upright black piano, while the center of the room was dominated by a round table covered with an ink-stained Indian shawl and surrounded by faded blue velvet chairs, a white lace antimacassar draped over each high back. On one of these chairs sat Elizabeth's favorite person.

Mademoiselle Sherwood-Smith taught Elizabeth to chant traditional nursery rhymes and brought her books about a rabbit called Peter, a bear called Rupert, and the battle-scarred bloody history of the English kings and queens. She helped Elizabeth to assemble the big jigsaw puzzle that was a map of England and played a fierce game of racing demon, which was how Elizabeth learned to count in English.

Elizabeth wasn't nearly so keen on her special French lesson. She had learned to talk in the lilting French Vaudois accent of the canton, which sounded a bit like cows in a barn, as the voice was always lowered in the middle of a sentence, then lifted upward at the end of it in a gentle, musical moo. Mademoiselle Pachoud was much older than Mademoiselle Sherwood-Smith and she walked with a stick because of her bad leg. She was French from France, and she gave Elizabeth elocution lessons so that she should speak classic French, not a Swiss dialect. But after Elizabeth started to do this, the other children teased her.

They pounced on her again at midday as Elizabeth wound herself into her outdoor clothes before going home for the midday meal; one of the big girls snatched her balaclava helmet and tantalizingly dangled it just beyond her reach. Elizabeth, small for her age, jumped and jumped for it, until she was out of breath and scarlet-faced with exertion and suppressed tears.

"See, you're not so smart, skinny, in spite of your special lessons; no wonder nobody wants to be your special friend, you stuck-up show-off."

Elizabeth jumped and grabbed again but the scarlet wool was jerked away. "Think you're better than us but you're not. I heard my maman say that you're a *bastard. Skinny little bastard, stuck-up skinny little bastard.*"

Two other girls took up the taunting cry and danced around Elizabeth, tweaking her long dark plaits, until suddenly the exasperated small child put her head down and butted one of her tormentors in the stomach. Caught off guard, the girl fell to the ground, shrieking, just as Mademoiselle Gina entered the cloakroom.

"She pushed me over, Elizabeth *pushed* me, Mam'selle."

Mademoiselle Gina looked at Elizabeth, scarlet-faced, teeth bared, leg drawn back, ready to kick. "Shame on you, Elizabeth, go home immediately."

Later, over their midday soup, Mademoiselle Gina spoke to her sister. "More trouble with Elizabeth fighting again."

"Oh, dear, you don't think they tease her?"

"Even if they do, there's no need for violence. There's plenty of teasing in the playground, but Elizabeth is the only child who uses her fists. She fights like a boy."

"Well, her foster brother Roger is more of her friend than any of the girls; I expect he's taught her some rough tricks. It's a pity she seems so different from the other girls, somehow an outsider. They feel suspicious and ill at ease with her, that's why she's so difficult and that's why she has no close girl friends."

"No excuses, Simone, the child is very touchy, always ready to suspect an insult and overhasty to avenge it. She shouldn't react so violently."

"It's only when she think she's being unfairly treated that she loses control of herself; then she needs the action to get rid of her resentment. Five minutes later she's always calm again and, apart from that, she's a quiet pupil, very conscientious."

"Yes, well, she can't afford to have such a hasty temper, no matter what the reason. Life is not going to be easy for that child. . . ."

* * *

As Elizabeth ran home through the hushed snow, the cold calmed her turbulent feelings. Holding tight to the iron railing, she clambered, one foot at a time, up the high stone steps to the front door, which was above the winter snowline. She stood on tiptoe to bang the iron door knocker, then bent down to push open the letter box and sniff; diced potatoes with bacon and onion chopped into it. She always felt safe as soon as she was home.

Careful not to let the snow in, Angelina opened the door a crack. As usual, she was wearing a blue denim dress, blue apron, long shapeless black cardigan and black boots; she never wore makeup or jewelry apart from her wedding ring.

"Maman, what's a bastard? That's what they called me at school."

Angelina looked harassed as Elizabeth stamped the snow off her boots. "It's a silly name for people who haven't got a father."

"But Roger hasn't got a father, is he a bastard as well?"

"You can both have a father if you want one." Elizabeth glanced up, perplexed, as Angelina pulled her gently into the sewing room and shut the door.

"Shhh. It's still a big, big secret. But who would you *choose* for a father?"

"A fairy prince."

"No, someone you know."

"Not Roger, he's not old enough. . . . I know—*Felix!*"

"Right!"

Long dark hair and fingertips touching the cobbles, Elizabeth hung upside down in a yellow, striped bathing suit, her skinny legs wound around the ropes of the trapeze. "Now swing around and up to sit on the bar," Felix said. "Now, over again, Lili, as high up the ropes as you can get . . . Good."

Since he had married Angelina, eighteen months ago, Felix had taught the two children some of the tricks that he had practiced with his brother long ago in Hungary.

"Now a little trampoline work, Lili," he ordered, pulling the little green trampoline onto the grass. As he put Elizabeth through her paces, the setting sun slowly touched the peaks of the far mountains with a flushed red glow. Angelina leaned over the balcony to call them to supper. In front of her, a cloud of cream butterflies fluttered around the mirabelle tree and a light sweet scent rose from the pink-and-blue sweet peas that grew against the wooden lattice under the balcony. She watched Elizabeth grasp the man's hands; her thin legs swiftly ran up his thigh, then his hip, then sprang onto his strong shoulders. There she wobbled until she gained her balance, let go of his hands and slowly stood upright with knees slightly bent and arms outstretched.

"Can I walk?" called Felix.

"Not yet, I'm not ready. . . . Ow, Felix, you brute."

"Stop talking and concentrate, Lili. I want to see a beautiful leap off my shoulders and onto the trampoline with feet together and no sloppy finish."

Obediently, the small girl flew through the air, bounced on the green canvas twice and then bounced off onto the grass. She landed with her feet slightly apart. Drat! She saw Angelina above her and waved, then the child wandered off to the wooden swing under the balcony where she lazily pushed herself backward and forward as she sniffed the summer. The warm odor of earth, garden roses and pine trees in the forest rose to meet the pungent richness of the hay and liquid manure. Summer was a honey-warm smell, autumn smells were sharper and smokier; autumn was the sour smell of fallen apples stored in the cellar to make pink jelly and applesauce, hazelnuts collected from the forest, and piles of rotting pungent leaves at the bottom of the garden begging to be stomped on, kicked and scattered.

Felix carried the trampoline into the cellar. Then he and Elizabeth clattered up the flight of open wooden steps that led up to the kitchen and supper. Roger was already sitting at the table. He had been swimming in a forest stream and on his way home he had filled his cap with small, wild strawberries.

"Almost as good as in Hungary," Felix said approvingly, after a delicious meal of river trout. This remark was always greeted with jeers, but tonight he added, "Before the 1939 war, *every* Hungarian restaurant—no matter how grand—had to feature on its menu a meal for one pengö; that's one Swiss franc. So long as he had *one* pengö, theoretically any old tramp could go in and eat, no matter how dirty he was; by law the restaurateur was supposed to serve him."

Elizabeth climbed onto his lap, as she always did after supper, curling up like a kitten.

"Tell us about Gundels," begged Elizabeth, who loved hearing his stories about the gaiety and romance of prewar Hungary.

"Well, Lili, I was just a young waiter, but oh, we saw such food. Pressed boar's head in aspic, cold pike with beetroot sauce and cucumber salad, shredded marrow in dill sauce, thimble egg dumplings, smoked sausage, rich red goulash, Transylvanian goose and pancakes stuffed to bursting with fluffy orange curd, sultanas and chocolate sauce. . . ."

"Don't tell us about the food, tell us about the children and the parties in the park," demanded Elizabeth, banging an imperious little fist on his chest.

"Well, Lili, you know that the Gundel family with their ten naughty children lived over the restaurant, and the restaurant was surrounded by trees, with two huge black iron gates at the front."

"Get on to the party in the park," Elizabeth shrieked with excitement.

"Well, the first fifty tables formed the outdoor beer garden—although we mostly drank white wine—and then the next fifty tables were for more expensive meals, and then, at the back, you walked up eight shallow stone steps onto the terrace where vines trailed down from the roof, and *that* was where the aristocracy ate. The whole of Hungary ate together in that garden to the music of the brass band in the beer garden and a romantic gypsy band near the terrace."

"Show us how the gypsies played, Felix," she called excitedly.

"They wore wonderful, bright Hungarian costumes." The big man stood up, carefully put Elizabeth on his chair, draped his scarlet napkin around his neck, picked two twin-sprigged cherries from the bowl on the table and hung one over each of his ears: then he tied his red spotted handkerchief around his head and started to hop slowly around the kitchen table, like a great black bear playing an imaginary fiddle.

Elizabeth shrieked again with delight.

"Can we play the best night ever, Felix, oh, please?"

Felix looked at Angelina and asked permission with raised eyebrows. She laughed and nodded, whereupon the little girl tore out of the kitchen and dashed back in her petticoat, carrying two strips of white sheet and a traditional wide, red laceup belt. "Start, Felix, start," she cried with excitement, as Angelina indulgently knotted the two lengths of cotton over her skinny shoulders.

"The best night ever," Felix said, stroking his long, dark mustache, "was one velvet evening in 1938 when King Zog of Albania became engaged to be married to a Hungarian aristocrat. Geraldine Apponyi was her name." Angelina untied the little girl's plaits and softly fluffed up the long, dark hair. "She was dark and beautiful," Felix said, "and she was going to become Queen of Albania. They had a huge dinner party on the terrace and I served there from seven at night until seven in the morning." Taking white roses from the bowl in the center of the table, Angelina started to pin them in the child's hair, like a coronet, as Felix continued. "There was music but no dancing, and there were gay, happy speeches all night." As Angelina laced the belt around the child's slight middle, Elizabeth stood up, straight and grave, awed, and aware of all those eyes upon her.

"Was the little queen a bit frightened, Felix?"

"A bit bewildered, perhaps. But she looked stunning in a white dress with lace and diamonds sparkling in that thick, dark hair."

Beneath her wreath of white roses the child's big, dark eyes dreamed in a sun-golden face. Serene, confident and very lovely, she raised her little forehead, then gave a regal nod.

"What did I eat, Felix?"

"I served you with a dish of creamed eggs, calf's brains and mushrooms, just an ordinary in-between-courses dish," said Felix, suddenly an obsequious waiter, bending to offer an imaginary platter. "I could hardly breathe. I couldn't take my eyes off that beautiful woman. She only helped herself to a teaspoonful of the food, by the way, not like the Archduchess Augusta—that was the Emperor Franz Joseph's daughter—she had a face like a bear and an appetite like a bear, and a laugh like a bear. And she smoked huge cigars, puff, puff, puff."

Suddenly the little girl tugged the roses out of her hair, draped her scarlet napkin around her shoulders, twisted her hair up into a bun with her left hand, slumped back into her chair, grinned with her lips pulled over her teeth, nodded in a knowing fashion and with her right hand puffed an imaginary cigar. "Puff, puff, puff like this, Felix?"

"To the life, Your Highness."

"You spoil her," Angelina laughed, but then he spoiled all of them. They had led such a quiet, sedate and orderly life until Felix crashed into it with this masculine strength, exuberance and noise.

"Bedtime," Angelina said, reaching forward to unknot Elizabeth's robe.

"Maman, can I have a proper white dress, not an old sheet?"

"No, you'd only get it dirty, my little acrobat. When you're older you shall have a white dress, if you're good."

"Am I as good as you were when you were a little boy, Felix?"

"On the trapeze, Lili, yes, but not quite so good on the trampoline. But when you go to Hungary in September you can practice with Uncle Sandor on the trampoline we used together as children, and by then I expect you to do a double somersault and land *with both feet together*."

CHAPTER 15

ELIZABETH HUNG OUT of the window and waved to the people she passed. Farmworkers in blue dungarees waved back from fields of high Indian corn, luxuriant tobacco leaves or nodding yellow sunflowers. Herdsmen on horseback flourished their whips above flocks of great white oxen, lazily chewing. Like a time machine, the olive train ran through a Hungarian countryside which had changed very little over the past two hundred years.

It all looked so pretty that Elizabeth couldn't understand why Felix wasn't his usual cheerful self. He sat with his head turned away from the railway corridor, biting his lip, silent and trembling. Though he looked out of the window he didn't seem to see the flat golden fields of wheat or the lake where placid fishermen sat in flat-bottomed punts and willow trees trailed their branches in the water.

Angelina tugged at Elizabeth's cotton dress as they passed pale gray towers and battlements rising above the trees. "We're nearly there, let me comb your hair. . . . "

At Sopron, Uncle Sandor was waiting for them on the platform, waving his whip in recognition. He was dark and fiercely handsome, like a gypsy, with even longer mustachios than his brother Felix. After bearhugs of welcome, they climbed onto the flat-bottomed, dusty red farm cart. An hour's ride lay ahead of them, through poplar-lined, shady roads that cut through field after field of ripening grapevines.

They reached the farmhouse as dusk fell over the low building. Vanilla-scented pink and white oleander bushes grew along the white-washed walls, long strings of dark red peppers were hung to dry outside the kitchen window, dogs barked as the wagon wheels creaked to a halt. Grandma Kovago rushed into the yard, wiping her hands on her white apron, then drew the children into the lamplit kitchen where thin, bent Grandpa Kovago, wearing a collarless open shirt and frayed black suit, waited to greet them.

On the wall opposite the kitchen door hung a tambourine, three old shotguns and several gilt-framed pictures in which crudely colored saints rolled their eyes towards the ceiling. Two nineteenth-century sepia portraits of the Empress Elizabeth gazed seriously into the lamplight. The kitchen table was set with wooden platters and huge earthenware crocks of food. A sour smell of cheese, spices and rough wine hung over the low room. Black hams hung from the smoke-stained rafters, along with strings of sausages and ropes of dried mushrooms.

When the women were putting the children to bed and for the first time Felix found himself alone with his father, the old man's amiability was abruptly discarded.

"Why have you come back, Felix? How dare you take such a fearful risk—not only for yourself but for your wife and the children!"

Felix was silent. It had been a hard decision. Three months before, after receiving the smuggled message from his mother, he had sweated at the thought of the danger he was running into. As a war refugee, Felix hadn't been granted Swiss citizenship and was in no position to apply for a Hungarian passport. It would have been an insane risk for him even to go to the Hungarian consulate in Berne and make inquiries about the possibility of visiting his homeland. Not only had Felix fought against the Russians in the Hungarian army, but also in the German army. When Felix consulted the Hungarian anti-Communist exile group in Geneva they told him he could expect to be arrested at the frontier and sent to a labor camp for twenty years—if he was lucky!

But after some argument, the group eventually agreed to provide Felix with the necessary forged documentation, and it was agreed that he would cross the border with his Swiss wife and two Swiss children to strengthen his story of a family visit.

So far, in spite of his fright, the scheme had worked successfully. In the lamplit kitchen, he lifted his head and for the first time he addressed his father man-to-man, and not as an amiable son.

"You know why I've come back, Papa. Because Mama sent for me. Because you're . . . not going to live forever . . . And we all know it. I came back to see you both for the . . . once more . . . And I came back because Mama wants me to get Sandor out. That's why I've come back, and that's what I'm going to do."

"Does Angelina know?"

"No. Because she's safer not knowing."

"Does Sandor know?"

"Not yet, for the same reason."

There was a silence, then the old man sighed and said, "You're a brave boy and I'm proud of you, but you're foolish, and your foolishness makes me angry because of the danger."

For the next two weeks the children lived the pleasant, pastoral Hungarian life that had changed little since medieval days. They rode bareback, swam in the lake and gathered berries from the hedges to make jelly. In the brackish wet soil of the woods they picked thick, fat mushrooms beaded with dew and as big as a baby's fist.

They practiced acrobatics on the trampoline that Uncle Sandor dragged out of the stable, and he tossed, caught and instructed the two children as they leaped and turned on the canvas. Lili's small, thin frame obeyed Sandor's every shouted command, and she continued to sail through the air long after Roger had become bored and wandered off to the stables. The two children went for short walks with Grandpa Kovago or long walks through the forest with Uncle Sandor, who carried their lunch in a basket strapped to his back. One day they even went as far as the Austrian border, which lay northwest of their farm. As they sprawled on a hilltop, eating smoked sausage, Lili was a little disappointed. She had expected to see a thick red line wandering as far as the eye could see—as it did on the maps at school—but no red line led through the forests of pine that covered the hillside.

Wherever they looked outside the farm, rows of vines stretched to the horizon. They weren't waist height like Swiss vines, but were trained around twenty-foot-high poles, and they looked like rows of green-leafed wigwams. When harvesting started, Angelina worked in the fields with the other women pickers, propping a fifteen-foot-high ladder against the vines in order to reach the topmost branches. The burly male supervisor moved slowly along the lines, stooping with the weight of the big wooden container that was strapped to his back. As he passed each woman, he stopped while she tipped her bucket into the container on his back. When it was full, he climbed up the ladder that was propped against the open truck and leaned over so that the grapes fell from his container and over his head onto the golden, growing pile of fruit in the truck.

One evening Elizabeth triumphantly dashed up to Felix and threw her arms around him. "I've been practicing all day! I can do a backward somersault off the farmyard gate and onto the trampoline!"

"You *can?*"

"Well, I *almost* can."

"Either you can or you can't, Lili. Stick to yes and no; can or can't; did or didn't; will or won't; good or bad. Everyone knows what black and white is, but gray can be anywhere in between, so stick to black and white, miss. Now, let's see that somersault."

That evening the two brothers walked down to the local *csarda*, two miles distant, to meet the men they had known since boyhood. Walking back in the moonlight after a lot of gossip and far too much white wine, Sandor suddenly said, "Felix, I must admit I thought you were a fool to have left Hungary, a fool to risk coming back—most of all, a fool to have left the farm to me. But now I'm not so sure."

"Why not?" asked Felix, guardedly. "Everything looks as good as it ever did, the grapes grow, the sun shines, the children play."

"Felix, you've never been able to see more than what's under your nose." Sandor stumbled. "Nothing's wrong with God's weather, the trouble is man's tyranny. Under the surface, Felix, things in Hungary are getting worse. *You* haven't felt the fear in the cities. *You* don't notice that everyone is shabby and everything is in short supply. *You* don't notice that men have been taken off the farms to work in the new factories, so farms are producing less because now farming takes second place."

Sandor stopped on the moonlit road and with an exaggerated, tipsy gesture, he started checking off on his fingers. "Farming takes second place to the coal industry, the chemical industry, the bauxite and the dye industry. The Russians send raw materials here to be processed and manufactured in Hungary, then it's nearly all sent back to Russia and our workers have nothing to show for their work. All the farm produce is collected by the state and a lot of the food is sent out of the country, so there isn't much incentive for farmers to produce it in the first place—but if there isn't enough food to collect, then a farmer might suddenly be thrown into prison."

"But who's to know, Sandor, if you sell a pig or a goose?"

"If you're caught selling one goose on the black market, you can get a seven-year sentence. What I'm telling you is that, slowly, we are becoming Russian slaves."

They walked in silence along the moonlit road, then Sandor added, "Janos the schoolmaster says that the newspapers and radio are censored and most of the new books and plays are just crude Soviet propaganda."

"Nothing new about that, Sandor."

"No, but Janos says that even the Communist intellectuals in Budapest have now started to criticize the harshness of the Russian system. See what I mean?" He stumbled again. "Hungarian *Communists* are criticizing the Soviet Union."

"Very healthy."

"The Russians won't allow it. The secret police get more powerful every day." He hung one arm around his brother's shoulder. "Back in June, Miklos the blacksmith got drunk in the *csarda* one night and said more or less what I've just told you. Next afternoon the secret police turned up in a car, shoved Miklos into it and headed back toward Budapest."

He suddenly stood still in the moonlight, remembering. "Nobody knows what's happened to him, but someone said he was being taken to the *Avo* headquarters at Andrassy Street and everybody knows that number sixty Andrassy is where the *Avos* have their torture chambers, so we don't expect to see Miklos again. I tell you, if it wasn't for the farm and the old couple, I'd leave with you after the wine festival."

Felix kept his plans to himself as they clumped along in the peaceful moonlight. He simply observed, "Farmers never starve if they keep their mouths shut."

Vendors wandered among the tents pitched around the *csarda* tempting the peasants to buy their strings of pork sausages, cakes and sweetmeats. Inside the tents, a brisk trade flourished in hats, dresses, ornaments, pots and pans, scythes and other agricultural implements. The evening before, the land around the *csarda* had been covered only with grass, but now it was jammed with brightly dressed peasants in their Sunday best, celebrating the *szuret*, today's wine festival. Some of the women wore as many as twenty-five petticoats under green or scarlet skirts that reached to the top of their soft, scarlet leather boots; their white organdy blouses were richly embroidered, and so were their little waistcoats.

Early that morning the women had made a huge wreath of grapes mixed with wild flowers and bound it with colored ribbons. This wreath had been carried in state from the vineyards to the village, followed by a gypsy orchestra which fiddled merrily in front of the parade of vineyard workers. Jostling along in the happy, noisy procession, Elizabeth and Roger passed slowly through the town until they reached the *csarda*, where, like everybody else, they drank a glass of pale, golden wine before the feasting started. Then the gypsy leader flung his dark head back and very slowly drew his bow across the strings of his fiddle. One by one the other instruments joined in until the music grew louder and louder, faster and faster, more and more insistent. Soon boots were kicking, skirts whirling, arms twirling as dancers spun with uninhibited shouts of joy.

"No other nation can dance like Hungarians," shouted Uncle Sandor, pulling Angelina up to dance. "Dancing is in our blood and nothing can stop us."

Very different from the quiet, staid Swiss, thought Elizabeth, her eyes as big as eggcups, as she watched the whirling skirts, the flying dark hair, the flashing eyes of the dancers.

"Come on, Lili, I'll show you how to dance," cried Felix, grabbing her hand and running forward. In an open-necked, white shirt with huge billowing sleeves, a scarlet cummerbund, black open waistcoat and tight black trousers thrust into high scarlet leather boots, he looked wonderfully dashing. Felix tugged her toward the dancers, then suddenly stopped, hobbled a couple of steps, stopped again and winced.

"Damned if I can. My foot's throbbing. You'll have to wait for Sandor."

So Lili stamped and whirled and twirled with Uncle Sandor, while Felix limped to a bench, took off his right boot and winced as Angelina examined his foot. "It was a mosquito bite that I scratched; now it's septic. Nothing to make a fuss about."

He didn't want a mosquito bite to spoil the fun of the *szuret* so he painfully squeezed on his boot again, ignored his throbbing foot and contented himself with watching the dancers instead of joining in. But that evening Felix rode back to the farm with the women on the horse-drawn cart.

Angelina bathed his foot in the tin basin, while Grandma Kovago prepared the bread poultice. Grandfather ridiculed Angelina's suggestion of a doctor. The gnarled old man took the black pipe out of his mouth and laughed. "For a mosquito bite?" The gold watchchain that looped across his little belly wobbled with mirth.

The next day Felix sat outside the kitchen door. Swathed in white linen, his foot was propped on a chair seat. But by evening his leg had started to throb and the following morning Felix could hardly walk.

Angelina insisted on consulting a doctor, so Sandor set off for Sopron on horseback. By evening when the doctor arrived, Felix was sweating, with a high temperature, unable to move without pain.

"Blood poisoning. He needs penicillin, not bread poultices," growled the doctor, frowning over spectacles pulled halfway down his nose at the swollen, purple-red foot. "You're going to be in bed for a couple of weeks at least. If you're lucky."

So Angelina wrote a letter to Herr Pangloss, the manager of the Hotel Rosat, to say that Felix could not return until the end of October. But there was no cause for alarm. After all, it was merely a mosquito bite.

Early on the evening of Wednesday, October 24, 1956 (three weeks after Elizabeth and Roger should have been back at school in Switzerland), Uncle Sandor took his usual, two-mile evening walk to the *csarda* outside the village to meet Janos the schoolmaster for their usual drink, smoke and chat. The evenings were now cold so he wore his *bunda*, the traditional long embroidered sheepskin coat with fleece facing inward.

When he hadn't returned by ten o'clock, Grandma started to grumble. "Politics, politics, always talking senseless politics over too much wine." At eleven o'clock they gave up waiting and were about to go to bed when the heavy kitchen door flew open and Sandor burst in, out of breath.

"The revolution has started! In Budapest! Quick, turn on the radio! The students have captured the radio station." A flurry of scraping chairs and questions followed him as he strode over to the big, old-fashioned radio and tuned into Radio Budapest, which was playing recorded gypsy music of a markedly unrevolutionary nature.

Wakened by the noise, Elizabeth crept out of bed and peeped around the door. For once Felix ignored her as the grown-ups gathered around the wireless. Uncle Sandor burst out, "The Russians have appointed Nagy as President of Hungary again, and martial law was proclaimed at nine o'clock this evening. We heard it on the radio at the *csarda*. Later they said that Nagy had asked the Russian troops to help restore order."

There was a chorus of cries. "Nagy is a patriot, he'd never do that."

"Well, he did, I heard them say so."

"Then the Russians must have forced him to do it."

"Now sit down, Sandor, and tell it from the beginning. We're obviously going to hear nothing except music on this damned radio."

"Perhaps we should return to Switzerland," suggested Angelina, worried.

"You can't. The frontiers are closed and no one can leave without a Russian exit permit."

Horrified, Angelina looked at Felix. He limped over, hugged her and said, "There's no reason to be frightened, we're safe here. Put Lili to bed again and sit with her until she's asleep—and you go to bed as well, Mama. War is man's business."

Apprehensive but obedient, the women disappeared, then Sandor said, "Until your leg is better, Felix, you stay here and see they're safe. I'll leave you one rifle and take the other two with me to Budapest. They're broadcasting for food, so we'll start loading up the cart at dawn tomorrow. No, Papa, they're fighting for you and it's up to you to feed them. Janos and I are off to Budapest tomorrow."

In spite of Grandma's anguished tears, Sandor creaked off early the following morning, the horse-drawn cart laden with food and looking like a harvest festival float as it jerked down the steep, frozen, muddy ruts of the farm track.

In the afternoon Grandfather walked into the village for news and didn't return until nightfall. "The *Avos* in Budapest fired on an unarmed crowd of twenty thousand people that included children, women and old men," he growled, "and then they threw the bodies into the Danube."

By Sunday, only five days after the fighting had started, the tired but triumphant voice of Prime Minister Nagy announced over the wireless that Khrushchev had agreed to withdraw the Soviet troops. Unbelievably, it looked as though the country really *had* liberated itself as Russian tanks started to rumble out of the devastated streets of Budapest and—for the first time in ten years—broadcasts and newspapers were uncensored.

But Grandpa was skeptical and suspicious. "It's not like the Russians to give in so easily, they're up to something," he insisted. "When you're my age you, too, will mistrust bears who behave like lambs. The uprising must have surprised them—after all it surprised everyone—and they probably didn't think we Magyars had so much fight in us after so long."

He lit his pipe, sucked at the stem and shook his head. "You mark my words, the Russians are being meek just to stop the Western nations from joining in the fight. Once the fuss and interest has died down, the bastards will be back here with their boots on our necks again."

And Grandpa was right. On November first came the ominous news that hundreds of Soviet tanks were streaming over the border into Hungary. Thousands of Soviet troops had marched in and surrounded Budapest.

Every morning and evening at eight o'clock Grandpa rode into the village to wait at the post office at the hour when Sandor said he would try to telephone. "No news yet, Mama," he reported, "except that refugees from the cities are streaming to the Austrian border and the Russian tanks are turning them back and shooting anyone who tries to escape. Not much fun trying to escape in this weather; bitter wind, heavy snow and worse to come."

On the following Tuesday, on the evening of November sixth, Sandor got a message through to the post office. "Now don't get upset, Mama, but they were storming a Soviet tank and Sandor has been shot in the right arm and shoulder," said Grandpa, not adding that Janos had been killed at the same time. "The Russians are apparently pouring into Budapest. They're shelling buildings and shooting passersby. There's also been heavy fighting in the other cities, but it's worst in Budapest and the Russians are in control of the city again. It's just like 1945, God help us."

Grandpa continued sadly. "Sandor says that the city is starving, the Freedom Fighters have run out of ammunition and medical supplies. . . . Sandor's trying to get home, and then he thinks that we should all escape to Austria. The reprisals are going to be terrible, and any able-bodied adults might be shipped to Soviet labor camps."

Felix said, "For God's sake take the children somewhere else, Angelina."

The children had been almost ignored all weekend, and finding the strain of adult anxiety irksome, they had kept out of the way. It was too cold to go outside and there wasn't yet enough snow for play, just a thin film over the hard earth. But now Uncle Sandor had been shot and all the grown-ups looked worried.

"Hang a lantern in the window and keep it lit all night in case Sandor turns up," Grandpa ordered, then he turned to Felix and took his hands. "My son, we're too old to leave. We were born here and we want to die here when the good Lord wills it. But the rest of you must leave as soon as Sandor returns. We did not raise our two sons for the benefit of the Russians."

Unable to speak, Grandma could not take her sad, wrinkled eyes off Felix. She feared that she was seeing him for the last time.

The moon shone through the clouds, flooding the countryside with silver. The small group could see a hamlet and vineyards edged with trees as they hurried along a path between bare fields of silver snow. They wore dark, heavy overcoats, and the two children had cardboard identification labels tied around their necks, as did all escaping children, in case they were separated from the adults who accompanied them. Sandor's right arm was in a dark sling, which meant that he couldn't button his coat up to the neck and the cold wind hurt his chest. Felix walked with the help of an old shepherd's crook and carried the farm's only remaining rifle in his other hand.

It was two o'clock in the morning and they were nearing the frontier. The journey had not been difficult, mainly downhill through wooded land. Twice they had waded through icy, rushing streams over which Elizabeth had been carried on the shoulders of Felix, who was still limping badly and should not have been walking on his poisoned leg. They were heading for a path through the woods to the frontier that Sandor knew hadn't been fenced off. It ended at a barbed-wire fence. Beyond that fence lay half a kilometer of no-man's-land, then a second barbed-wire fence, which was the actual frontier. Both fences and no-man's-land were patrolled with guard dogs by the frontier police.

Paradoxically, the safe places to cross were often near the high, wooden lookout towers that punctuated the frontier and from which a single guard had a good view of all the surrounding land. These towers were undermanned and even, occasionally, empty. That was too much to hope for now, but if they crossed near one of the towers, they would be able to see what was happening and where the searchlights were probing.

Their plan was to wait in one spot until the dog patrol had passed and then make a dash for freedom. Ideally, Sandor hoped to reconnoiter the spot in moonlight, then wait to move until the moon had passed behind a cloud. He would also have preferred to have picked a cloudless night, but they had no choice: the longer they waited before escaping, the more dangerous it became.

Suddenly, they nearly walked into the first barbed-wire fence. It was almost invisible, about six feet high and with much longer, more vicious barbs than agricultural barbed-wire. Beyond it lay no-man's-land. The patchy snow was spattered over rough grass that sloped up a fairly steep bank. They couldn't see what lay on the other side.

Sandor touched his brother, and wordlessly pointed to the right. They skirted the trees until they came within sight of a wooden frontier tower. It seemed to be operated by one man who slowly rotated a single searchlight. The little group of five melted back into the trees. They had to get out of the scent range of the dogs and yet remain within earshot; luckily, the wind was blowing from the frontier into their faces. After the patrol had passed, they would move down to the fence and cut the bottom wires with their two pairs of clippers, blades carefully smeared with dirt so they didn't glint in the moonlight. They would move back into the shelter of the trees when the searchlight swept toward them, and having cut the wire, they would dash forward to escape as soon as it had passed. Roger would hang on to Sandor's coat and Elizabeth would hang on to Felix.

Sandor could no longer feel his cold feet. His arm, neck and chest were painful, but they weren't as dangerous as Felix's poisoned, painful, throbbing leg. Silently Sandor moved forward, alone, and waited under a fir tree. It shuddered noiselessly and sprinkled his shoulders with snow. Then he heard a distant crunch of boots, low growls and animal panting. He faded back into the trees to where the others were waiting and looked at his luminous watch. Two-twenty.

They stood there in the freezing cold until the patrol returned because they had to know how much time there was between each patrol. Angelina gently rubbed the faces of the children with her wool mittens to help their circulation.

Then they again heard low voices and again the panting of the dogs as the patrol returned. The wind was blowing from behind them, so Sandor waited to get a good view, when he could see the two-man patrol wearing overcoats and round Russian hats with earflaps. They carried automatic rifles.

Fifty minutes between patrols; that should be time enough.

He hurried back to the others and beckoned them forward. The moon was now hidden behind the clouds and it was difficult for them to see Sandor and follow his dim shape as he ran between the firs.

Angelina and the children waited under cover as the two brothers crept forward to the six-foot-high fence and started to cut the bottom wires. Clumsily using his left hand, Sandor started cutting the bottom wire while Felix worked on the wire above it.

The clippers seemed to make no impression on the wire. Then suddenly Felix held two slack strands instead of a taut one. Swiftly he started to cut the next wire. Panting, the men hacked fiercely, knowing that their lives depended on speed. When the searchlight swept toward them—as it did every twelve minutes—they dashed back into the cover of the trees.

The moment the searchlight had passed, they ran back again to work on the wire, cursing and panting with effort, until there was a soft scraping sound and it parted at last.

Bending low, the two men stumbled back through the snow to where the others stood and they all waited, hearts pounding, for the searchlight to pass.

A gray beam swung through the darkness, getting brighter as it approached them. It moved on, then grew gray again. Like sprinters in a race, they dashed forward, Angelina so frightened that she tried to blot everything out of her mind except the will to follow Felix.

The men held the bottom wires back as she and the children scrambled underneath. Then, in sodden boots and coats, they all ran clumsily up the escarpment.

Sandor could see that they were nearly at the top of the slope. Twenty meters . . . Ten meters . . . Felix was falling behind . . . Five meters. . . . Then they clambered over the rise and started to scramble downhill, sweating with relief, gasping painfully for breath.

But the distance from the other side of the slope to the second wire fence was much farther than they had expected. It was the greater part of that half-kilometer band of no-man's-land, and the lower slopes were covered by boulders that were difficult to climb over, although convenient to hide behind. The little group separated and scrambled for cover behind the first boulders only a few seconds before the searchlight swept over it.

At that point, for the first time, Felix allowed himself to hope that they might make it. Again they scrambled to their feet and started to stagger forward over the uneven terrain.

Suddenly Felix faltered and felt dizzy. Feeling Elizabeth clutching trustingly at his greatcoat, he willed himself to keep going. Then to his horror he heard the dogs barking in the distance, picking up the scent.

Frantically summoning up what strength remained to him, Felix dragged Elizabeth along. He now had no idea where the others were. His only thought was to get to the second fence before his throbbing leg collapsed or the dogs caught up with them.

When he reached it, he nearly ran into the wire. It was a brute—higher than the first, and with more barbs. He couldn't see it as clearly as he had the other one, because now there was no moon. He touched it, then jerked back with a gasp.

The fence was electrified.

Trembling, panting hoarsely, Felix threw away his stick, carefully put his rifle on the ground and swiftly bent down to Elizabeth, whispering urgently.

"Lili, darling. You know that an acrobat must be obedient. Now I want you to stand on my shoulders and show me your best jump *ever*, over this fence. Don't land the way you do on the trampoline. Try to go limp as you land, try to land in a ball. Do a *bad* landing for Felix. Got that, darling? A *very* good, *very* high jump and a limp, curled-up landing. Then get straight up and run down the mountain and into the first house. Don't wait for me, my darling, and *don't look back!*"

He pulled her mittens off, to improve her grip. Uncomprehending but obedient, Lili climbed onto his shoulders. Slowly, concentrating, she straightened upright, then she took a deep breath, bent her knees a little, and soared over the fence as if it did not exist.

She landed, painfully, on all fours, in the thin snow on the other side.

As she picked herself up Lili heard baying dogs and hesitated. Then she heard Felix shout, "Obedience, Lili! Run. *Run!*"

She started to run downhill, a small gray shadow against the snow.

Behind the barbed-wire fence, Felix picked up the rifle and crouched. In the dim light, he could hear the harsh panting breath, the throaty rasp of the big Alsatian before he could see it.

As the animal flung itself at Felix, he squeezed the trigger. The shot hit the animal in the shoulder in midspring, but it was too late for Felix to avoid its leap, which knocked him to the ground. With a savage growl—regardless of training instructions—the wounded, maddened animal attacked.

Felix was pinned to the ground by the heavy, writhing body. He smelled the panting, fetid animal breath on his face, then felt unendurable agony as the Alsatian tore his throat out.

PART FOUR

CHAPTER 16

THE SEVENTEEN-YEAR-OLD MAXINE started work in London at Partridge, in the chaotic studio above the calm shop off Bond Street. Mr. Partridge looked and dressed more like a City stockbroker than a famous designer. He projected a sort of charming helplessness that made people feel *they* had to do the work because *he* couldn't; this made his staff feel needed and wanted, rather than merely employed. He was a gentle, kind, learned man, but ruthlessly uncompromising about his work. His supreme virtues were an extraordinary sense of color combined with exquisite tact and discretion.

After familiarizing herself with Partridge's library of samples, Maxine's work consisted mainly of running around. She collected paint samples from here, and delivered fabric samples there; she matched up this lemon silk to that lemon yellow satin swatch. It was quite extraordinary, she thought, that there were so many different fabrics and textures and that ninety-nine percent of them were perfectly repulsive. Quickly she was promoted to doing paste-ups; this meant preparing sheets of cardboard upon which Maxine stuck square samples of all the paints, fabrics and finishes, together with photographs or drawings of all the other items that were to be used in an interior; she loved this job, which combined her gift for color with her impeccable sense of clarity. She also became very good at writing specifications. Maxine's mind was as orderly as a filing cabinet, and her practical shrewdness was invaluable in the crises that invariably filled their days.

Within a few months, Mr. Partridge discovered her passion for old furniture and sent her scouting around the more distant, dusty antique shops and little-known auction rooms, such as Austen of Peckham, where you could buy a mahogany Victorian fitted wardrobe—with a special place for opera hats—for a few pounds or, for a great many more, an *almost* Chippendale breakfront bureau-bookcase.

However, Maxine's favorite source of furniture was an esoteric antique shop next to Lord Raglan's cream-tiled dairy in Pont Street. The shop was very quiet and dark. The shop owner was a charming, elderly man called Jack Reffold, who had a high, quavery voice, discerning taste and an unerring eye for proportion.

In his shop Maxine found objects that she would never see elsewhere: the blue, feather-patterned breakfast china from Queen Victoria's yacht; a bridal doll's trousseau packed in a miniature portmanteau; a gory oil painting of the battle of Trafalgar. Most of his better pieces were sent straight to New York, but Maxine grew to be a steady customer, particularly for the simple, stripped-pine Victorian furniture that her grandmother would have thrown out as unfit for the servants.

One July evening, tired after work, Maxine walked back from Mayfair in the hazy golden sunset of a London summer. She took a route that led through the cream Grecian beauty of Belgrave Square and into Pont Street. They were working late at Reffold's, so Maxine stopped to drink a glass of sherry with Jack and his three amiable, aged assistants.

Maxine now knew a great deal about English and French furniture and the price that Americans were willing to pay for it. Jack Reffold had refined her taste and shown her what to look for, whether in a Sheraton chair or a Meissen fruit bowl. That evening he was fussing over an ornate Rockingham vase that displeased him.

"Just look at this *horror*, Maxine! Remember, always look for the *basic* shape—it *must* be good. *No* use piling decoration on a shape like *this*, which is basically *ill*-proportioned," he said in his quivering, scolding voice. "And it's *enormous! Never* buy big pieces of *anything*, darling girl, because they're *so* hard to resell." He filled her glass and continued, "*So* many people now have *small* rooms, so they want *small* furniture, they *don't* want over ornate pieces that are difficult to clean. Sir Hugh Casson *says* that if a thing's worth *having*, then it's worth dusting, but I don't suppose Sir Hugh *does* much dusting."

Afterward Maxine strolled home through the gilded evening, thinking how lovely life was. However, as she unlocked the red front door she could hear the sound of sobbing in the bedroom. She ran in. Kate was lying on one narrow bed with her head in Pagan's lap and they were both weeping. Pagan raised a blotchy red face and without a word she handed Maxine the evening paper. On the back page, a two-inch item read, "The War Office has announced that the subaltern of the Green Howards killed last week by Communist terrorists in an ambush in Panang, Malaya, has been named as Nicholas Cliffe, son of Sir Walter Cliffe of Barton Court, Barton, Shropshire."

Maxine couldn't believe her eyes. Death was not a part of her life. Elderly relatives disappeared, aged cats were taken away to be "put to sleep," but it was not something that happened to you or your friends. She, too, burst into tears.

"Does Judy know?" she asked. There was a horrified silence—they all realized that their sense of loss was minor in comparison to what Judy would feel when she heard the news.

That night they cried themselves to sleep and wept nonstop for the next two days, as almost everything from coffee cups to crumpled pillows seemed to remind them of something about Nick. Surprisingly, it was Kate's father who halted their mournful apathy. He sat in their badly lit small front room and encouraged them to talk about Nick. After listening patiently he said, "And how do you think this fine young man would want you all to behave when you heard that he'd passed on?" They all looked up inquiringly. "Would he want you to sit around weeping? No, of course not, he'd want you to carry on living and remember the happy times you had together. Now, if a doodlebug had got me in the blitz, Kate, I'd have wanted you and your mother to have one good cry and then never again remember me with tears. I'd have wanted you both to feel happy when you remembered me."

Eventually he enticed them out of the basement along to the Berkeley buttery for lunch, then as the sun was shining, he took them to look at the ducks in St. James's Park, after which they felt much better. They didn't forget Nick, but they stopped drooping and snuffling when his name was mentioned.

Pagan and Kate, who were doing the London season, both introduced Maxine to the countless young men with whom they watched polo at Windsor, tennis at Wimbledon and racing at Ascot. When not at work, Maxine was rowed in punts on the Serpentine, wore picture hats to picture galleries or watched hours of incomprehensible cricket. She stayed in English country houses, where she observed the extraordinary way that British women dressed in the country: the headscarf knotted under the chin like Princess Elizabeth, the twin set that never fitted on the shoulders and stretched across the bosom, the stockings that wrinkled around the ankle, the baggy tweed skirt (covered with dog hairs), the identical beat-up crocodile handbag. Mystifyingly, clothes that were neat, well pressed and tidy were the mark of an outsider.

At times Maxine went to dances, but not often, because she had to be in her office by nine o'clock in the morning. The drawback to dances was that an Englishman expected you to spend the whole evening with him, to the exclusion of everyone else. Having been used to Switzerland and France where both sexes at a party cheerfully changed partners until midnight, Maxine found it tedious to dance and talk and stay with one man for the whole evening until the inevitable attempt to entice her into the back seat of his sports car. She did not much care for these young men in their bowler hats and Edwardian suits or their golf caps and tweed jackets on weekends: they dressed, spoke and behaved alike—they even thought alike.

Pagan and Kate loved the London social life, but Maxine quickly grew tired of it. She was already *une sérieuse*. She preferred what was called work to what others called fun. When Maxine returned to Paris, she was determined to persuade her father to spend her dowry money on the lease of one of the small antique shops in the rue Jacob. She would paint the whole place in soft olive green and import directly into France the sort of furniture she was buying from Jack Reffold—pieces that were not quite good enough to ship across the Atlantic. She would specialize in what the French called *le style anglais*, decoration generally based on an English, eighteenth-century interpretation of antique Indian or Chinese designs, teamed with simple Adam furniture or else with comfortably upholstered Georgian chairs and sofas, so different from the uncomfortable, buttoned-satin chairs upon which Maxine's mother's friends perched in their drawing rooms. The French took these ingredients and refined the details; they manufactured fringing and braid to match the curtains and bedcovers, they wove plain upholstery fabrics that picked up the colors in the chintz patterns. With these ingredients the decorative formula was easy: you picked your basic chintz pattern, which was used for the curtains and sofas and perhaps one chair; then you picked two distinct colors from the chintz pattern and matched them to plain fabrics that were used for the rest of the upholstery and any bedcovers; walls were covered with the chintz fabric or with wallpaper in the same pattern or else they were painted in a color picked from the chintz pattern, only much paler.

By the time Maxine had finished her two-year apprenticeship in London, she could produce *le style anglais* overnight although she was careful never to let her clients know this. Clients overvalued time and undervalued talent and experience, she realized.

James Partridge offered her a permanent, paid job with him in London, but Maxine preferred to return to Paris and get on with her "career," as she now secretly called her job. "The difference between a career and a job," Judy had once told her, "is that a job gets you nowhere. If you plan a career, then a job should be a step toward a definite goal—when you accept a job you should know exactly when you intend to leave it."

"Nonsense!" Maxine had said. "Why don't you go and write a self-improvement book like Dale Carnegie?" But it wasn't bad advice, in fact, and with it in mind, she quit her job and went back to Paris where she found that Judy—instead of getting on with her own career after leaving Christian Dior—was busily helping Guy to establish his career in fashion design.

Maxine's father was delighted to see her again, proud of her English and even prouder of her new abilities. He quickly found that he enjoyed making plans with her for the simple reason that she made *sure* he enjoyed them. She treated him like a favorite customer. He was impressed with her new knowledge and seriousness, but appalled by her ignorance of accountancy.

"I don't know *why* you insisted on staying six months extra in Switzerland to take your business exams," he said. "No wonder you failed them! An absolute waste of money! Until you have been in business for a whole year, you will phone me every day, at ten in the morning, and let me know the most important thing that happened to you the day before. I never want to hear about *more* than one thing, and I never want to hear less. That will teach you to sort out your priorities. And I want to see your accounts every Saturday morning."

To her father's surprise, Maxine, in fact, had a head for business. Within a month, she had a seven-year lease on number 391, rue Jacob. It had not been difficult to find a shop in this street lined with dusty antique shops that had not yet become smart, shops that were still badly painted and dingy, visited by dealers rather than tourists. Number 391 was narrow and dark, but it was very deep and the apartment above was included in the lease. For the time being Maxine sublet it to an old Polish professor of Latin. She renamed the shop Paradis, and immediately hired an assistant, since otherwise she would never be able to leave the premises without closing. Then she found an art student to work part-time in the back of the shop, doing what she had done in London for James Partridge. Her father chose Maxine's bookkeeper, a big-boned rather ugly woman called Christina, with a long, cow face and bovine brown eyes. The two women were always in the shop by 7:30 in the morning, and Maxine kept a folding deck chair in the little kitchen, so that she or Christina could stretch out and rest for half an hour if they were going to be working late in the evening.

On Saturdays her father taught Maxine how to plan a budget and how to draw up a liquidity forecast. He also taught her how to read a balance sheet, which was much easier and more interesting than she had expected. To his surprise, and hers, Maxine turned out to have a strong streak of frugality in her and an instinctive business sense.

After she had worked at Maxine's shop for six months, Christina presented Maxine with the request to become a partner, backed by a cash investment.

Christina also had a father and she had also persuaded him that a business with an income would be a better investment than a cash dowry, especially as, at thirty-four, Christina was not entirely sure that she would ever need a dowry.

After a year Paradis began to get bigger jobs—not just a bathroom here and a kitchen there, but complete apartments, small offices, even one country house. Paradis specified everything from the door handles to the window frames, and although modern colors and lighting techniques were used, Maxine specialized in traditional design. Paradis now had two full-time designers as well as part-time assistants.

Every Monday morning, Maxine and Christina planned the next week's work and allocated the different jobs to their designers, and every Monday evening there was a short conference for all their part-time staff. This was held after the shop closed at six o'clock, and the meeting was always followed by supper at the Beaux Arts restaurant, always full of cheerful, noisy students eating hearty, traditional French food. Everybody enjoyed Monday evenings, because it was then that they felt the camaraderie, rather than the anxiety, of business; and they were able to relax and gossip with each other about the jobs.

By 1953, when Maxine was twenty-two, she had attained a small but definite success; the shop was beginning to show a profit. Her father was delighted, but Maxine's mother worried because she wasn't married and appeared to consider suitable suitors tiresome. "It's so unnatural," she wailed to Aunt Hortense, "the child's not interested in any man unless he's a designer, or a client, or a potential client, or some grubby, bearded protégé who's still at the Beaux Arts."

Hortense nodded sagely. "I'll see what I can do," she said.

A few months after this conversation, Aunt Hortense telephoned Maxine. "Maxine, my dear," she said. "I have a client for you. The nephew of a friend of mine. This poor boy has just inherited a decrepit château near Epernay; apparently it's in utter chaos; nobody has lived in it since the war, and the poor man hasn't time to deal with the house—he has to take over an estate that has been shamefully neglected for the past fifteen years. I thought it would be an interesting project for you. So, my dear, if you are willing, I shall collect you at nine o'clock tomorrow morning and we shall drive to Chazalle. I believe there's also a vineyard attached to the estate—about seven hundred acres, also sadly neglected."

The next morning Aunt Hortense collected Maxine, who wore her client-trapping outfit—a stunning peach linen suit with shoes of a slightly darker shade; her hair, a shoulder-length hank of heavy gold, was tied at the back of her head in a peach silk pussycat bow. They drove out of Paris toward Champagne. The de Chazalle estate was thirteen kilometers south of Epernay, on the edge of the Côte des Blancs region that lay south of Epernay, between Vertus and Oger, to the west.

From just below the forest on the flat hill summit, vine-covered slopes stretched down to the golden haze of corn on the plains below. The Mercedes turned off the dusty country road through a pair of rusting, wrought-iron gates, one of them sagging from its hinges, and drove for half a kilometer up a neglected, weedy drive, past overgrown flower beds. Etched against the lavender sky was the dark, turreted silhouette of a splendid château. When they came closer they could see that it, too, was shuttered and forlorn. Several smashed tiles from the roof lay in the courtyard, Maxine noticed, as she and her aunt stepped up the chipped stone steps to the front door and pulled the rusting iron bell handle. Surprisingly they heard it clang down some distant corridor.

The door was opened by a tall, thin young man, wearing an old brown sweater. His face was small and lean, with fine bones, and his gray eyes had laughter lines at the corners. He looked surprised and pleased, as if someone had just given him an unexpected present. He bowed, kissed their hands and invited them inside. "Everything is dusty, which is why I keep sneezing, but I've cleared a space in one of the salons and a village woman comes up to clean it. The place is in a terrible state."

The shuttered hall was depressingly dark and bare. The filthy paint was peeling, cobwebs laced across the corners and one of the dividing doors had been smashed and was lying on the floor. German soldiers had been billeted at the château; the beautiful carved doors had been chipped and broken, initials had been hacked in the antique paneling and obscene messages scrawled on the walls. Most of the furniture had been used for firewood except for a few pieces bricked up in the attics by the *Kommandant*, who had hoped to liberate them for himself at a later date.

"Apart from this, there are only four other good châteaus still standing in this area. Montmort is first class, so's Brugny, but Mareuil is less impressive and I don't personally care for the design of Louvrois." The Count had a slight stoop and a long neck. Occasionally, furtively, he turned toward Maxine. She thought to herself, He expected me to be older—he doesn't want to trust the job to someone so young—so look efficient. She started to make copious notes on the large pad of her clipboard.

Diffident and modest, Charles de Chazalle was attractive in his sheer helplessness. Whereas a more aggressive man might have considered Maxine too bossy, she was exactly what he needed and he admired her more as the day progressed. Maxine scribbled nonstop, and at the end of the afternoon she suggested a simple, but efficient, system for dealing with the chaos in which Charles had so suddenly found himself.

Not surprisingly, she got the job.

After that, almost every afternoon she would bump up the drive in her little white Renault van, a different Parisian expert at her side. First a surveyor and an architect, then an auctioneer, a roof expert, a drains expert, a furniture restorer and a picture valuer.

In due course all the experts made their reports, and every Friday night Maxine and Charles discussed the project over dinner in an eighteenth-century post inn at Epernay. As summer faded, there was local venison and wild boar and always the soft, white, tangy Boursault cheese; and of course they drank the local white wine, naturally dry and delicate with a slight taste of hazelnut.

Maxine might as well have been eating dry bread and water. Despite a great deal of discussion before giving their order, she was hardly ever aware of what she ate; she thought only of how she longed for him to like her.

Charles always enjoyed every mouthful of the meal. He didn't eat out much. He liked his quiet life in the country and didn't want to sparkle around Paris, prattling at smart dinner parties. During the day he worked hard, tending his neglected vineyards. On the whole he preferred to spend his evenings alone by the fire, stretching out his long, thin legs, reading or listening to music. Maxine amused and intrigued him, partly because she was *une sérieuse.*

"There's such a lot to be done," he sighed, one Friday evening as they finished their meal. "For a start, we aren't producing nearly enough wine at the moment.

The average yield from each hectare should be about 5,600 liters of champagne." He signaled for coffee. "How do I know? Well, it's not *surprising* that I know a lot about the theory of the champagne business. After all, my family has lived here for centuries. But I've only been able to put my theories into practice since my father died."

He paused as the waiter poured his glass of brandy, then laid the snifter sideways on the table to check the measure; it should almost spill, but not quite. "Most Frenchmen want their sons to join the family firm, but my father was so anxious to demonstrate his independence that he didn't let me take any real part in the business. On the other hand, he wouldn't let me work for any other firm. This was very frustrating, because he was resolutely opposed to using new methods. I knew he couldn't live for long—he'd been badly tortured by the Gestapo in the war—so I never went against his wishes."

Country restaurants closed early, and the Royale Champagne was emptying, but Charles continued to turn the empty brandy glass in both hands. "I suppose it's natural that he should have felt nostalgic for the prewar days. He liked to pretend that *he* hadn't changed, that *nothing* had changed." The bill was brought on a plate. He glanced at it (He *can't* have added it that fast, thought Maxine), signed it and continued. "Unfortunately, his business methods were also old-fashioned. When I tried to discuss work with him, I was put firmly in my place. 'There is plenty of time for you to alter things when I'm dead,' my father used to say. Those were his wishes and I respected them, but now I intend to work as hard as possible to restore the de Chazalle firm."

He hesitated, looked at Maxine and then said, "Our champagne is no longer considered one of the very best, but I'm determined to change that." As if expecting to be contradicted, he continued, speaking fast and rather defensively. "It's not such an insane ambition; the Lansons were originally a tiny firm and their premises were virtually destroyed during the First World War, but the two sons—Victor and Henry—traveled all over the world in pursuit of orders and their success has been amazing."

The waiter started to switch off the lights. Charles took the hint.

"Shall we go?" With concealed reluctance Maxine nodded, stood up and another waiter leaped to pull back her chair. Charles nodded goodnight and followed her toward the door, saying, "I don't see why I shouldn't try what the Lansons did. They made their champagne world-famous in half a century that included two World Wars—*and* a long period of depression."

Increasingly, they both secretly looked forward to Friday evenings and Maxine's return trips to Paris got later and later. She found it hard to leave Charles, who had started gently to tease her about her efficiency, and who could make her laugh at herself or at nothing at all. Charles could make her giggle as she had not done since she left school.

To other people he appeared quiet, reserved and almost dull, but not to Maxine. The power to make a woman laugh is a strong aphrodisiac, and she couldn't wait for Friday nights. She always felt excitement in the air as she dressed that morning; she always changed her mind at least three times and left her bedroom untidily strewn with clothes. Her mother cheered up wonderfully at these unusual signs. Indecision in one's wardrobe always meant a man.

And in the evening, as they sat over coffee and brandy at the Royale Champagne, she longed for Charles to touch her. But he didn't.

One Friday their conversation seemed to drag over the meal, there seemed to be a barrier of embarrassment between them. Maxine was acutely aware that, to her, Charles was no longer just a client, and she felt very self-conscious whatever she was doing, whether scratching her head with a pencil (a habit much deplored by her family) or eating and drinking with suddenly noisy swallows.

By the end of the following week, Maxine felt so agitated that she could hardly bear to stand next to Charles. That evening she had shown him a group of battered oil paintings, horse portraits that she had collected from different areas of the house and stacked in a corridor; they were very similar to the ones that Jack Reffold had started to sell in America. They were late for their dinner reservation at the hotel, but she had particularly wanted him to see them, as she wondered whether it was worth sending a couple over to Jack for appraisal.

"Why don't you come back after dinner?" Charles asked. "We can decide then which ones to send to London."

"I'll be too exhausted and I'll get back to Paris much too late and the van will probably weave all over the road on the return journey."

"I'll drive you back," Charles offered.

"It's too far, you won't get back to Epernay until dawn." Privately, she thought he might never get back—the only thing she disliked about Charles was his reckless driving.

They continued their meal. Then, after the waiter poured their coffee, Charles leaned across the table and slowly, deliberately stroked her thick, newly corn-colored hair. Maxine felt the shock waves on her scalp, in her breasts, in her groin. She couldn't breathe properly, she was panting as if at a high altitude. Charles let the strand of hair drop back into place, and a little moan left her lips. Charles noticed. "These late journeys are too much of a strain for you," he said. "Why don't you simply move in with me?"

"Because my parents would have a fit!"

"They wouldn't if we were married," Charles said, not taking his eyes off her face but lifting her left wrist to his mouth and, very softly, kissing the pale blue veins that led to her palm.

Maxine, who was always in command of a situation, who always knew exactly what she wanted to do, was speechless. She felt short of breath. She didn't dare move. She felt so weak that she didn't know whether she'd be able to walk out of the restaurant. She couldn't take her eyes off his face. He was not smiling for once; instead, he seemed oddly impassive.

After they left the restaurant, Charles drove back to the château at breakneck speed without saying a word. He grabbed Maxine's hand and—still without a word—tugged her after him as he leaped up the steps toward the main entrance, oblivious of nocturnal scents of warm earth and hot grass. He was conscious only of the tense, expectant, determined passion that passed like an electric current through their clasped hands.

Once inside the front door, Charles pulled Maxine to him and kissed her hard on the mouth, as with one hand he held her to him and with his other explored her body. Gently he traced the outline of her spine down to its base, then softly felt the shape of her buttocks. Crushing her against his body so that she could feel his mounting excitement, he slowly pulled up her skirt and she felt his hand on the naked flesh below her panties, then he slid his hand under the delicate lace. Maxine was shaking. She wanted him as she had never wanted anyone before, her knees were trembling and she didn't think that she could stand much longer. She felt him hard against her stomach as his fingers caressed her quivering white buttocks and firmly pulled her against his body.

With an effort, Charles pulled himself away, gave a great sigh of anticipation, heaved Maxine into his arms (she would never be as light as thistledown) and carried her up the curved staircase to the dusty, but magnificent, blue-brocaded state bedroom. Moonlight fell in silver shafts across the room as he gently laid her on the antique, silk bedcover, then fiercely tore his clothes off and fell upon her.

Maxine gasped with surprise. She had not expected the gentle, amiable, amusing Charles to be so masterful, so passionate, so skillful.

For the next four hours Maxine felt her body move and respond as she had never known it could. Afterward, she didn't want to leave him. Naked, she clung to him, her tangled, damp yellow hair falling over her full, milky breasts. "I don't want to go," she whispered, with tears in her eyes, resisting as he gently, insistently tugged her off the bed and helped her to dress in the moonlight.

"Your parents will be concerned," he said. "I'm driving you back to Paris now, but I shall speak to your father in the morning."

Stopping only in the hall to pick up the torn, white wisp of lace, they drove to Paris, speeding through the air in Charles' open, dark green Lagonda. They both exulted as the vintage sports car leaped through the mysterious night landscape. It seemed oddly silent, theirs alone. Clouds swept across the moon, then the night was velvet-black again, except for the golden track forged ahead of them by the headlights.

As they tore past black poplar trees, through dark tunnels of green gloom, they heard the odd, harsh animal noises of the night, so similar to the inarticulate, helpless sounds that had just been heard in the moonlit sheen of the blue brocade bedroom.

CHAPTER 17

PAGAN COULDN'T COME to the wedding, because she was in Egypt, but nothing could have kept Judy and Kate away. Kate's gift was a hunk of amethyst as a paperweight for Maxine's desk, and Judy brought a charming Steinberg etching of a nervous, blank-eyed bride clutching her gawky groom. Pagan sent a beautiful antique Damascan chest inlaid with a mother-of-pearl design.

Maxine and Charles were married at the *mairie* in Epernay almost a year after they had met. Maxine wore a pale-pink silk dress with a skirt that was layered like rose petals, and a large cream straw hat. She and Charles sat in two hard little chairs while the brief marriage ceremony was performed by the mayor, who wore his ceremonial red, white and blue sash. Then they signed the civil register, the French equivalent of signing a marriage contract. They were now officially married, and with their whole family swept off to the Royale Champagne for a lunch that lasted until six in the evening, when Maxine returned to Paris with her parents, as was the custom.

The church ceremony was held on the following day in the mellow, stone church at Epernay. A French bride normally had no matron-of-honor and no bridesmaids, but Maxine's two small girl cousins were to be *enfants d'honneur*, following her over the ancient stones.

Maxine asked Kate to help her dress. In the hotel bedroom Kate laughed as she looked at Maxine, who was wearing only a froth of diaphanous veiling and skimpy, white satin underwear. Her clothes had been laid out on the bed. "Really, Maxine, even your wedding dress is practical!" Kate picked up the cream silk calf-length coat. Designed by Raphael, it was tight-waisted, with a row of seed-pearl buttons stretching from the demure mandarin collar to the hem of the lavishly full skirt. For the wedding, the coat was worn over a strapless cream tulle ballgown, but later it could be worn by itself—as a coat or dress—to the races at Chantilly or almost any formal indoor occasion.

"Well, it's the prettiest dress I've ever had," Maxine reasoned, "so I don't want to wear it only once."

For once Maxine didn't look efficient; in fact, she looked ethereal as she floated down the aisle between solemn stone columns. Beneath the hem of the long, full cream coat billowed a froth of cream tulle, and on her head Maxine wore a simple coronet of starlike flowers. As she passed Kate, the demure Maxine gave her a quick lascivious wink.

As soon as they returned from their honeymoon, Maxine was introduced to all the notable families of the district. Christina continued to run the day-to-day affairs of Paradis while Maxine made these important new contacts. Most of all, she enjoyed her visit to the house of Moët & Chandon, whose tradition of hospitality dated back to the Napoleonic era. Like Empress Josephine, the Czar of Russia, the Emperor of Austria and the King of Prussia before her, Maxine was shown around the long, subterranean cellars to watch the making of champagne. They moved through dark vaults, gray and green with age, smelling of damp chalk, mold and sour wine. "There are eighty miles of these cellars carved from the chalk soil under Epernay," said Charles. He took Maxine's hand and scraped her nails on the crumbly surface of the cellar wall. "You see? The whole of the champagne district is composed of this special chalk; it's *only* on this ground that the vines produce grapes with the unique champagne flavor. There's nowhere else in the world like it."

By the end of the visit, Maxine thought that she'd heard quite enough about champagne for a bit, although she knew it might have been worse. She might have married a sheep farmer or a canning industry king or a railway coupling manufacturer, after all. As if reading her thoughts, Charles said, "You needn't worry. I don't intend to become just another champagne bore. My business is part of my life and my heritage—in other words, it's my responsibility—but I'm not a city businessman. I'm a countryman. I like looking after my land and walking across it with my dogs, then in the evenings I like to read or listen to music—a quiet life."

"And then at night," said Maxine, "you like to make love."

"All the time I like to make love," said Charles firmly.

The next day Charles suggested that Maxine should pay a visit to his headquarters and learn a little about champagne production. "As the wife of the owner, you have to know these things," he said, "so now for a little homework. I'll try not to make it too dull, my darling."

We're in for a boring morning, thought Maxine as, in her bedroom, she stepped into her Christian Dior going-away suit of primrose linen. It had a huge, knife-pleated skirt and a little, tight-waisted jacket that buttoned down the front and she looked charmingly demure in it. "You look prim and proper, very ladylike," said Charles approvingly, as he helped her into the Lagonda.

They screamed to a stop just outside Epernay in a stone courtyard and entered the ancient building that now served as an office. In the dim, empty entrance hall, as they climbed the worn stone steps to the laboratory, Charles explained, "What a champagne house tries to do is to produce a wine that is *always* the same taste and quality. As the weather is always different and each harvest is different, one can only achieve this consistency by blending." He paused to open a plain, white-painted door. "You are now going to meet the most important person in any champagne manufacturer's firm: my blender." He beckoned her in. "You can't blend champagne by machine. A good house must have a good blender: the reputation of the entire firm depends on his palate, eyes and nose."

They entered a scrupulously clean laboratory: in front of a row of wooden chairs there stood a few spittoons. Several unmarked bottles stood on the central wooden table. "No Smoking" signs hung on the walls. It was indeed extraordinarily dull so far, thought Maxine, as she was introduced to a pendulous-bellied man with a lugubrious face, the purple-red color of a turkey cock's wattle.

The *chef de cave* solemnly offered them a glass of non-vintage champagne. Maxine thanked him with the grace and dignity that befitted her new position, and Charles then led her back down the stairs, and along the black and white marble-tiled corridor toward the dim hall.

Suddenly he grabbed Maxine's wrist and pulled her into a dark recess under the staircase. He swiftly unbuttoned her primrose jacket, dipped both his hands into her lace bra and stopped her gasp of horror with his mouth. She felt his tongue pushing against hers. Then Charles pulled his head back and said in a normal voice, "The first bottling generally takes place sometime after April and we add a little cane sugar to the blend to start a second fermentation." He started to kiss her nipples. Maxine felt physically helpless, but as she groaned with reluctant pleasure, Charles suddenly withdrew his hands and buttoned her up as fast as a lady's maid.

Weak with desire, Maxine whispered, "You mustn't, you really mustn't . . . do that sort of thing." But she didn't sound convincing.

Charles took her by one hand and led her down more steps, saying loudly, "The second fermentation is when the champagne acquires its sparkle. That sparkle is really gas. Fermentation builds up an explosive pressure of gas. So a good cork is vital."

Still speaking smoothly, he tugged her from the bottom of the staircase and into the shadows underneath it. Then he held her against his chest as, with his right hand, he felt under the primrose pleated skirt and tugged at her panties.

"Off!" he muttered.

"Charles! You must be *mad*, someone might *see*," Maxine protested.

"Off!" Charles ordered, giving the lace a vicious tug. Nervously, Maxine wriggled out of them and tried to pick up the scrap of yellow lace, but Charles wouldn't let her bend down. "I'm not having you turn into a prim little countess who worries about what people think all the time, like my sisters," he said.

Then he froze as they heard footsteps approaching them. Maxine shut her eyes, and waited for the humiliation! The footsteps advanced and paused, then she heard a door open and bang. Charles released his grip. Maxine quickly bent down, picked up her panties and stuffed them into her linen shoulder bag. Without saying anything, Charles took her by the arm and hurried her toward the elevator at the back of the hall, saying in a normal voice, "I hope you're going to be warm enough: I warned you yesterday that the cellars are cold. Shall I get a coat from the car?"

A youth in a white overall appeared behind them and sprang forward to open the iron grille of the two-person elevator.

"No, no, Charles, stop fussing," Maxine said in a wobbly voice for the benefit of the respectful boy as he closed the grille shut behind them. Charles pressed a green button, the little lift started to jerk downward and, as Maxine half-expected, his hand was under her skirt, his thumb moving in a steady rhythm against her flesh. The lift jerked downward. Charles' other hand was clamped around her naked buttocks, the back of her skirt was caught up against the lift. She'd never get those creases out, Maxine thought, it took hours to iron. "Until Dom Perignon came along in 1668, bottles were sealed with linen bungs dipped in olive oil, and of course this didn't provide a hermetic seal," Charles explained gravely. Oh, God, she could think of nothing but his fingers. Now she'd risk humiliation rather than have him stop. Charles went on, as if he was having a conversation with his mother. "Dom Perignon's *brilliant* idea was to wet a bit of cork to make it pliable, then ram it into the neck of the bottle." Maxine jumped and quivered as he continued, "The cork sealed the bottle and stopped the gas escaping."

The elevator stopped with a swift, gentle shudder. Charles pulled back the iron grille. "The pressure inside a bottle of champagne is about the same as the tire pressure of a bus . . . so you see how important the cork is."

Maxine staggered out, smoothing down her skirt. Breathless and wobbly, she moved along the cellars, past thousands of bottles tilted neck downward in racks against the green-tinged chalk walls. Charles waved one hand toward the neat, lustrous rows, the little green soldiers of his empire. "We leave the bottles of blended wine in cellars for a year or two, then they're put in these special racks so that the sediment from the wine drains down slowly onto the cork."

"Onto the cork," echoed Maxine, in a dazed voice. A drip fell from the ceiling onto her cheek, then Charles tugged her by the wrist into one of the dim, bottle-filled bays and again unbuttoned Maxine's jacket. This time she didn't protest.

"Yes," said Charles gravely, "onto the cork." He pulled her back into the main passage and they walked down the long, wide cellar toward a row of silent men in navy sweaters and overalls, all working with their backs to Maxine as they swiftly twisted the bottles.

Maxine watched the bottles slowly move into the shining maw of a steel machine. Somewhat to her disappointment, Charles was now behaving perfectly. But he moved her closer to the machine so that it hid their bodies from the workers beyond, who could only see their heads. Then Charles grabbed her hand and held it against him, so that Maxine could feel his mounting excitement. Maxine grasped him as Charles continued to talk in a normal voice. "When the cork is removed, the frozen sediment comes out, clinging to it. Clever idea isn't it?" His body shuddered at the touch of her fingers as he droned on in the bored, sing-song voice of a tourist guide. "After that, the wine is sniffed to check that it's still in good condition, and finally, as you'll see in the next bay, these men give it a sending-off dose—that's a tiny quantity of sweetened liqueur made from old wine and cane sugar. . . ."

He gave a contented sigh. After a moment, they moved to the next bay where Charles picked up a beaker of liqueur and gave it to Maxine to sniff. "You don't add much if you want a *brut* wine, which is generally the best wine a firm makes," he said. "The liqueur content is increased, according to how sweet you want your wine to be—extra dry, dry, *demi-doux* and *doux*, which is disgustingly sweet and will never be served at my table."

"*Our* table," said Maxine as they moved on. She added, "I think I could make a batch by myself now."

"You haven't seen the last working bay. There it is ahead of us. This is where the bottles are recorked and we fit those little wire nozzles over the cork to keep them in place. After that we rest the bottles for a few years in those cellars at the far end, then we label them and send them off to customers."

Maxine looked along the high-arched tunnel; either side was lined with deep bays stacked high with champagne, the black green bottle bases facing toward them in an endless rich pattern. Suddenly, Charles tugged her into another deep bay. He pinned her shoulders against the chalk walls where they could be seen by anyone who happened to pass, but Maxine was now heedless of anything except her urgent need for Charles, and their sexual tension swiftly built up to a climax as violently explosive as the cork bursting from a bottle of champagne.

CHAPTER 18

W*ITHIN THREE MONTHS* of her marriage, Maxine found to her joy that she was pregnant. Unfortunately, she felt ill throughout her pregnancy, so all her plans for the château had to be postponed and she did the minimum work for Paradis. She thanked her lucky stars for the stolid, tough Christina, who continued to run the day-to-day aspects of their business. As Maxine grew larger and larger, she felt dull and sleepy. "I thought I was going to have a wonderful complexion and be radiantly serene," she shouted to Charles from her bathroom, "not become bovine and lethargic. No, don't you *dare* come in, I'm heaving myself into this disgusting support corset. I think I'm going to give up clothes and just lie around in a negligee on the sofa like Madame Récamier for the next few months."

In an easy birth, she had a son, Gérard. Happily she and Charles counted his toes and analyzed his features. "He's got *your* nose," said Charles fondly.

"But *your* mouth," Maxine added.

"And my hair, though not nearly enough," said Charles, tenderly stroking the soft, pale, beige silken head.

"I had no idea that being a father would make me so happy," Charles admitted four months later. He tugged at Maxine's cream lace negligee and softly kissed the base of her throat.

"Then you're going to be twice as happy, Charles."

Suddenly alert, he sat up and looked at her questioningly. "Goodness. You don't mean . . . but Gérard is only four months old!"

"Goodness had nothing to do with it," said Maxine, slyly quoting Mae West.

This time the birth was extremely difficult. She was in labor for three agonizing days, at the end of which she gave birth to another son, whom they christened Oliver.

The birth left Maxine exhausted and depressed. Her stitches were painful whenever she moved. She burst into tears over trivial matters and she snapped at Charles. As she knew perfectly well that she was a very lucky woman with no reason to feel sorry for herself, she felt secretly anxious about the melancholy that swamped her. Was there something wrong with her? Charles quietly spoke to the doctor about her tears and tantrums. She hadn't been as bad as this after the birth of Gérard. The doctor said that it would probably be a couple of months before she recovered fully from the birth. Could not her sister or her mother or a friend come and stay to cheer her up? Someone she'd known a long time and with whom she felt comfortable?

As soon as the doctor departed, Charles reached for the telephone. Pagan was still in Egypt, and there was no answer from Kate, but he got Judy on his first try. He explained the situation.

"I can't possibly drop everything and come immediately," said Judy. "I'm a hired hand, remember? But I'm due for a vacation, and anyway, I'll be over in Paris for the collections in two months' time. I could come for a couple of weeks before then, if you like."

Maxine burst into tears when she heard of Judy's visit. She didn't want to see anyone. Harassed, Charles took his dogs for a long walk in the rain. *Women!* However, as the weeks passed, his wife slowly grew stronger and more cheerful and by the time Judy arrived, Maxine longed to see her again.

Every morning Judy ate breakfast in Maxine's blue silk bedroom, while Maxine lay back against lace-trimmed pillows beneath the billowing blue silken swags that fell from the gilded coronet fixed high above her head. In the morning they went for a short, brisk walk, pushing the two high baby carriages before them over the frozen ground of the park. In the afternoon they sat and chatted in the nursery.

From the moment Judy arrived, Maxine began to recover her spirits. She loved Judy's ability to go straight to the point. "You sharpen my wits, Judy," Maxine said, with admiration and a twinge of regret. "You make me focus on what is *important*, as opposed to what is merely urgent. And you do this naturally, whereas I find it takes a great effort of will on my part. Every day when I get to my desk, I find it covered with problems. It's so tempting to avoid the big ones, and so much easier to occupy oneself with little difficulties."

"That's because you're fat, idle and happily married," said Judy.

"I'm all for marriage," Maxine yawned. "Why don't you try it?"

"Oh, because I don't like very young men or very old men: I like middle-aged men, but nobody will admit to being one."

"No, seriously, Judy, haven't you got some special fellow? You never mention anyone, but surely . . ."

"I know plenty of men, Maxine, but I can't seem to get particularly *interested* in any of them, that's all. I go out on dates but I never seem to fall in love. I see other women do it all the time, but it just doesn't seem to happen to me. Anyway, I'm on the road so much that a serious love affair would be a geographical impossibility."

"You don't think that perhaps you're frightened of giving yourself to a man?"

"Oh, shove it, Maxine. No, really, there *are* other things to life, you know. . . . I'm only twenty-two! *Men* of my age don't go mooning around and worrying if they're not in love. I suspect that women overrate falling in love."

"Only because you haven't yet!"

"If you don't shut up," Judy said amiably, "I shall feel obliged to throw this glass of champagne at you." She raised her long-stemmed tulip-shaped glass as the cold red sun touched the horizon. "Incidentally, how come you don't have real champagne glasses?"

"That *is* a real champagne glass," said Maxine, clasping her hands behind her head and leaning back against the buttoned crimson velvet of her chair. "The traditional glass is not supposed to be wide and shallow. A wide glass prevents the concentration of the bouquet, and the wine goes flat more quickly because such a large surface of it is exposed to the air." She yawned, stretched and scooped up the black cat that lay in front of the fire. "You see, I now know every bloody thing there is to know about champagne."

Judy stared into the blazing fire, glanced around the room and then looked at Maxine. "You got it all, kid," she said, grinning.

"And Heavens, I *work* for it!" Maxine suddenly looked harassed and the cat stiffened in surprise. "It's damned hard work running a home, no matter what the size is. In fact, I think it's easier to run a business, because your business shows results. Nobody notices housework unless you don't do it, then they complain. And business hours are generally only eight hours a day, five days a week, while housekeeping is sixteen hours, every damned day of the year, if you're running a home with young children." She sighed, "Well, at least I no longer have any guilt about being a mother who goes out to work—although Charles' sisters never stop sniffing about it."

She relaxed again and the cat settled down. "Do you remember after I had Gérard I also became a bit depressed for no apparent reason? Charles was working hard, running a house was no longer a novelty, I was no longer a young bride showing off. . . . I felt *guilty* because I was depressed. I thought it must mean that I was not maternal, that I was a bad mother, otherwise I would have been happy with baby, wouldn't I?"

An ironic smile shadowed her face. "So I started to cheer myself up with little snacks between meals, not exactly in secret, but when nobody else was around, you understand. . . . You remember that chocolate is my great weakness? I used to nibble chocolate cakes and chocolate ice cream, drink hot chocolate with thick cream. . . . When I put on weight, I simply stopped standing on the scales, and then I became pregnant again so fast that I had a good excuse for getting . . .

well, I never used the word 'fat' to myself, of course."

She looked up, still stroking the cat on her lap. "Then one day, walking along the street, I caught sight of myself in a shop window—and I didn't *recognize* myself! I tell you it was a real shock and I thought, heavens, I'll soon be as tubby as I was when I first went to Switzerland. That had been puppy fat and not difficult to shed, but after two babies, the doctor warned me it would be more difficult."

The cat stretched her front paws and extended her little claws and dug them into Maxine's knee. She gave it a little slap and continued, "So in order to take my mind off the diet he gave me, I went back to work at Paradis. I worked there every single day for a month, and by the end of the month, to my surprise, I found that I was happy again! I hadn't had time to eat, or feel bored or sorry for myself." She yawned. "So when I've stopped feeding Oliver, I'm going back to work. I've argued the case with myself and the doctor and we've decided that it's better the babies don't have a twenty-four-hour-a-day, depressed, overweight, worried mother. Sixteen hours a day is enough time to spend at home."

"You get top marks for sheer ingratitude," Judy said. "Here you are, twenty-four years old, with a marvelous husband, two adorable babies, a flourishing business, a title and a château. What *more* could you want?"

"Money," said Maxine simply.

"But I thought you were rich!"

"That's the other reason I went back to work. Paradis pays for all our personal expenses, although the profits really ought to be going back into the business. Christina is getting angry about it, and I don't blame her. But what can I do? We're poor. It's almost our only income."

She hesitated, and then in a rush she said, "To tell you the truth, we probably can't afford to live here much longer. That's why I'm so glad to have you staying here now. Charles is as stubborn as a mule, he refuses to sell the château, but it's going to fall around our ears at any moment. He insists that one day the vineyards are going to show a profit, but the harvest is mortgaged to the hilt, so it won't make any difference if we have a good one, and we'll be in dreadful trouble if we *don't*. Papa is going to discuss the business with Charles this weekend. He's an exporter, so it might be possible for him to improve our foreign sales. But there's so much competition in the champagne industry, and nobody's ever *heard* of de Chazalle champagne. They buy from Moët or one of the other big firms."

Judy said thoughtfully, "You must forgive me if I point out that you have six indoor servants. That's not what I call poor."

"Yes, but the two maids are essential to clean this vast place. Charles needs a secretary. The children need a nanny if I am to work. The four of them need a cook, and five servants need a butler to supervise them."

Judy raised a skeptical eyebrow, lay back against her chair and looked into the hypnotic flames of the fire. "Maxie, I *know* you're sitting on a gold mine. I can feel it. I just can't *quite* work out how you can make money, except that you've given me such a wonderful time here that I find myself thinking I would far rather stay here than at the grandest hotel. This last month has been a dream. I've never enjoyed myself so much in my life. And I've never felt so comfortable and so happy. You're a very gifted hostess, Maxine. Wouldn't it be possible to run the château as a sort of hotel, perhaps not *exactly* a hotel, but the sort that's run for paying guests who would like to experience castle life exactly as if they were private guests? For, say, sixty dollars each a weekend, you could give people a *fantastic* time!"

Maxine sat up. It was a brilliant idea! Why hadn't she thought of it? It was very much like what she was doing already, in a small way; Charles' sisters already used the place as a rest home. And perhaps she might open a branch of the antique shop in the stables.

"I could help to arrange for publicity at the American end," volunteered Judy. "What you need is a steady flow of people from the States who want to enjoy the château experience. Perhaps you should start by asking some well-known Americans to stay free."

"But I thought the idea was to make money," Maxine objected.

"Yes, but if you invite a couple of Hollywood stars—they often visit Paris—you'll get terrific coverage in the American papers and then you'll be talked about. Word of mouth! Honestly, Maxine, I know this business. You mustn't think that PR work is free; you mustn't make the same mistake as the rest of your goddamned compatriots. You pay for it, just as you do in advertising, only in a different way."

Judy rolled her eyes in mock Gallic exasperation. "It's riskier, because you can't control what publicity you're going to get, but if you've got a good, newsworthy product and the PR is handled efficiently, you get good coverage."

"I'll speak to Papa this weekend," said Maxine thoughtfully, "*before* he speaks to Charles about the vineyards."

Charles was appalled by Judy's idea and made it clear that he wanted no part of it. He found it painfully distasteful to think of strangers in his family home. He realized that something had to be done to stop the château from falling down, but he was working as hard as he could to make the estate pay and to modernize it and he simply didn't have time for any other ventures. Eventually, however, he was worn down by Judy's enthusiastic insistence and Maxine's quiet determination. Vulnerable because of his exhaustion and anxiety, knowing that something had to be done, he agreed to let Maxine go ahead, provided she committed none of his meager capital to the project—because there was simply none to spare.

Maxine was tremendously excited. She found it difficult to keep her mind on the practical aspects of the project because charming little side ideas kept popping unbidden into her mind. She was sure they could set up a little arcade of shops in that great useless stable block; she could franchise some of them the way Paris hotels did, and they could have a little shop to sell champagne by the bottle or by the crate.

When consulted, Maxine's father cautiously said that while he thought the idea had possibilities, he couldn't possibly finance such a venture himself. However, they might be able to get bank financing.

As soon as they started to draw up estimates, they realized that the restoration of the château would need far more money than they could gross by running it as a hotel. Maxine had heard that one or two English stately homes had been turned into historical entertainment areas for family outings, with museums and amusement arcades. She thought this sounded like a good possibility, but dared not mention it to Charles until she had researched her scheme; she could imagine his rage at the idea of turning the home of his ancestors into an amusement park.

After Judy had flown home, Maxine also left for a two-week trip, during which time she visited those châteaus of the Loire Valley that had been opened to the public. The interiors were almost empty and devoid of interest, except to the scholarly. She went to England and visited Longleat, an exquisite example of Elizabethan architecture, owned by the Marquess of Bath; she went to the beautiful and highly successful Woburn Abbey; then she trudged up to Derbyshire to see the Duke of Devonshire's Chatsworth in all its chilly splendor. She returned to Epernay with very decided ideas: in her own castle she did not want merely to present a tour of an old family home—she wanted to try to *evoke* history, using stage production techniques.

Maxine, her father and the estate accountant drew up a new set of figures for her ambitious project. Both men were dubious, but Maxine was determined that her scheme would be accurately assessed for financial viability. Then, filled with despair by the total figure, Maxine telephoned Judy. "We're going to need around $177,000. I don't think it's going to be possible."

"It's possible until it's proved impossible, so just look quietly confident and project assurance."

Maxine had learned a lot since drawing up her first financial forecast to extend her antique shop. Now, with the help of her father and the estate accountant she set out her business proposition, and together the four of them—for Charles had reluctantly agreed to participate in the presentation—drove to Paris to discuss it with a merchant bank. They needed to borrow 33 million francs, and if they got it, they would need to achieve a turnover of 39 million francs a year to cover running costs and show a profit. With any luck, it would take them fifteen years to get out of debt. But if they didn't have any luck they would be homeless and out of work, for the entire estate was now pledged as collateral against loans, not to speak of a further guarantee from Maxine's father.

Understandably, Charles fought against this. "I said that I would agree in principle, *provided* that none of my capital was needed!"

"This isn't capital. It's a matter of using all your unmortgaged assets as collateral for the loan."

"But if it doesn't succeed we'll be bankrupt."

"And if it *does* succeed you won't have to leave your family home. Your sons can grow up here as you did."

Maxine won.

From the day the bank loan was taken up and the interest began to mount, there was not a moment to be wasted. Maxine hired a secretary, a neat competent girl with a tight mouth, and from that moment it was difficult to tell whether Mademoiselle Janine was running Maxine or Maxine was running Mademoiselle Janine.

Charles shuddered when he thought of what could go wrong. Maxine thought only of the work to be done; she woke up remembering what she had forgotten the day before, her life revolved around a series of lists and lists of lists, but she was exuberantly excited. Judy had already designed her letterhead; in traditional script it read simply:

Le Château de Chazalle • Epernay • France

During the months that followed, Maxine couldn't spend as much time with her babies as she would have wished, but no matter how busy she was, she always spent the afternoons with them. After they had gone to bed, Maxine worked far into the night—every night—as she took over the responsibility of the château as a business proposition and continued with the work that she had abandoned when she first became pregnant.

Apart from the relatively small area in which the family lived, many of the rooms and passages were still in a depressing chaos. Forgotten treasures stood next to worthless watercolor daubs by Charles' great-aunts; everything seemed to be dirty, covered with cobwebs and fly-droppings or nibbled by mice. The attic in the west turret was filled with oil paintings—horses and dogs, sheep and prize bulls, as well as other animals treasured by Charles' ancestors; unfortunately, they had been badly stored, and many of the paintings were torn and in need of repair. It was a daunting project.

Paradis designed and superintended the rebuilding and decoration work. Maxine picked a young Parisian designer to work with her on the exhibition and together they produced a plan. Maxine didn't want crowds shuffling in and out of beautiful rooms while a bored guide chanted at them. She wanted the tour to be an exciting, theatrical event. "I want our guests to feel amazement and delight," she told the designer, who had never before dealt with such an odd demand.

Their first job was to get an accurate plan of the second floor, and once that had been surveyed, their next step was to plan the tour. For a week they pored over the plans together, scribbling over them on tracing paper and chalking out different ideas for the tour route. Then the whole family moved to a rented house in Epernay and everything in the château was cleared out to go into storage for six months while the building restoration took place. Before it went through the door and into the furniture vans, each item was catalogued and photographed. Aware of the inexorable change in popular taste—and also that the throw-outs of one generation are the antiques of the next—Maxine had resolved to sell almost nothing. "We have plenty of space," she reasoned, "so we will invest in storage. This sort of nineteenth-century picture and furniture is already selling well in America, so we will only get rid of the really big pieces, like all those armoires, which I can sell to cabinet-makers who will make fake period bookcases from them."

Maxine examined every single piece of furniture herself. Her greatest discovery was when she spotted the gracefully curved legs and fine bronze mounts of a slender pair of Boulle commodes; the handles, set in rosettes of five acorns, were the same as the Mazarine commodes in the Louvre which had been made in 1709 for Louis XIV. Only one item was sold—a cylinder-topped desk with inlaid floral marquetry by Oeben, dated 1765. Maxine hated it on sight. She sold it to the Metropolitan Museum for five million francs, to the astonishment and admiration of her husband, and it paid for the plumbing.

Then the building contractors moved into the château and Charles found it difficult to decide whether they were rebuilding it or tearing it down.

"I cannot stand much more of this chaos!" he roared at Maxine one morning, waving his arms in the middle of the gutted main salon, where doors and windows were being unblocked and partitions were being destroyed in a welter of banging rubble and dust. Maxine was used to the chaos caused by such work and she did not see the apparent muddle but only what would shortly be the exquisitely restored salon. Linking her arm in his, she led him away to the next wing, where much of the reconstruction work had been completed. But here the noise and bustle was even worse as the whole wing was being scrubbed from top to bottom by professional cleaners with huge scrubbing machines for the floor, complicated, automated ladders and arm extenders for getting into places that were otherwise impossible to reach.

Charles bolted out of the nearest door and headed for the stable block where the dogs were kenneled, but his traditional house of peace had been invaded by yet another army of workmen. The interior of the stable block was being rebuilt as an arcade of charming, old-fashioned little shops, and would also contain a coffee bar, a restaurant and a free wine-tasting cellar.

Charles threw up his arms in Gallic despair as Maxine caught up with him and tugged his sleeve. "Darling Charles, you've been so patient . . . only a few more weeks, love . . . let me show you the part that's finished—Ancestor Alley—it was completed yesterday!"

Ancestor Alley was their joke name for the History Walk on the first floor. The entire tour was electronically operated by a push-button system, with the human element introduced as extra, because Maxine wasn't sure how much human element she'd be able to rely on. Pencil-beam spotlights marked the darkened, crimson-roped route. Some of the small rooms had been completely blacked out and furnished with museum showcases of clear glass, cunningly lit by narrow beams of light, so that it looked as if the family treasures were floating in space.

One eight-foot-wide corridor was painted Chinese yellow and used as a gallery for the portraits of Charles' ancestors. Charles calmed down as he walked past the beautifully exhibited rows of de Chazalles who stretched back into history—seven-year-old Christian with a blue sash under his lace shirt was leading a donkey across the park in 1643; in 1679 Amélie de Chazalle smiled in a pale gray, low-cut moiré dress, with a parrot perched on her shoulder; in 1776 a group of seven little children (with two sets of twins) sat solemnly around the dining table eating grapes and walnuts, while their beringed and ringleted little mother fed almonds to her pet monkey.

"Poor things, they were all beheaded in the Revolution except for the youngest boy," Charles suddenly heard his own recorded voice saying. "He escaped to Geneva, disguised as a runaway lady's maid, somehow managed to marry a heiress, and their daughter married Henri Nestlé of the chocolate family."

Charles' voice also welcomed the visitors in the entrance hall and, as they moved through the house, he recited his entire family history from the twelfth century to the present; translations in twelve languages were available. Other rooms had background music—Strauss waltzes, harpsichord music, the voice of a young boy soprano floating to the arched roof of the family chapel, and the faint, animated chatter of children, which could be heard in the old nursery.

Maxine had hoped to open the château to the public on the first of July, but as always there were problems with workmen, so they were unable to open until mid-August. On the opening day they all waited, tense with anticipation. Supposing nobody turned up? Expectantly, they all waited at their battle stations at nine o'clock in the morning. But nothing happened.

In the cobbled courtyard, between the stable block and the house, a charming, nineteenth-century carousel had been erected, with carved and gilded horses, dolphins, swans and mermaids for children to ride. Children could also be taken for rides on ponies or on a trip in the old yellow-lacquered, eighteenth-century state coach, which once again would lumber up and down the drive. There were going to be as many free shows as Maxine could devise, from carousel rides to champagne-tasting—anything that was necessary to make a success of the first day, not only to boost the morale of the staff, but also because the press might be there.

Nothing happened until ten-thirty in the morning. Then as the first three coaches approached the château (Charles immediately thought, We'll have to reinforce that drive), a small cheer broke out from the excited group that was waiting for them on the front steps. In an unprecedented gesture, Aunt Hortense snatched off her scarlet pillbox hat and threw it in the air. She had been more worried than any of them. Only she knew that it had been her last-minute, behind-the-scenes arguments that had convinced Maxine's father to take the plunge.

If it failed, he would never forgive her.

CHAPTER 19

*F*ROM THE BEGINNING Judy had had no trouble in getting publicity for the château, and nearly all the first paying guests were booked in from the United States. Maxine had also invited a handful of French celebrity friends, including Guy Saint Simon, now a well-known fashion designer, in order that the Americans would feel that they were getting their money's worth.

"They're obviously all enjoying themselves tremendously," Guy commented after his first visit.

"Oh, yes, one or two have already booked up for a further visit," said Maxine happily. To her surprise, she found that she loved entertaining these strangers—she found something interesting about most of them, and their enjoyment was infectious.

Painfully, Maxine rebuilt the crumbling fabric of Charles' family home and brought it to life again. Of course, it was not possible to please everybody. Charles' sisters were icily critical, but then they always found something to complain about. They thought it vulgar that a de Chazalle should have to work and that their home should be opened to strangers. "Serves him right for marrying a bourgeoise," said his elder sister. "God knows what she'll think of next: strip shows in the drawing room or a zoo in the park."

Both sisters refused to face the fact that without Maxine's work there would no longer *be* any château, and that without her encouragement and support,

Charles would be in no position to establish the estate as one of the principal minor tourist attractions of the Champagne. Most of all the sisters deplored Maxine's vulgar American associate, the one who had flown over from New York for the opening, that young woman, Judy, who talked loudly and discussed money and business at meals.

Just before Judy flew back to America, Guy drove out to the château from Paris. It was the chef's evening off, and a cold meal had been left in the library. As she took a slice of ham, Judy felt an odd, schoolgirlish, conspiratorial atmosphere of suspense and smothered giggles, as if a secret was about to be revealed. Maybe they were going to give her a present? After all, opening the château had been her idea. . . . She took her plate and sat on the footstool in front of the log fire at Aunt Hortense's bony feet, the metatarsals bulging after a lifetime spent in too-high heels. It wasn't really cold enough for a fire but Maxine always kept one burning in the little library.

"Something's going on. What's up? What are you hiding from me?" Judy said suspiciously.

Aunt Hortense gave a smothered laugh and almost dropped her plate. Guy looked at Charles, who gave an odd grin—Charles now enjoyed Guy's company, although at first he had resented this dressmaker who had been in the nursery with Maxine and who consequently knew what she was thinking far better than her husband.

Now Guy nodded his head at Charles and turned to Judy. His face was serious. "We want to discuss a business proposition with you, Judy. We want to suggest that you open your own office and handle our publicity in the States."

Judy was astonished. "That's very . . . that's wonderfully flattering and very generous of you."

"Not at all, it would be in *our* interest," said Guy. "I need my own PR in the States, and I've worked with you for years in Paris. You know my business."

"And we are obviously going to rely on American visitors to the château," added Maxine. "So we need someone we can trust to handle us in America."

"Don't think that the idea hasn't crossed my mind! But I'm far too young and I haven't any capital. Maxine, you know I need every cent I can save for mother's medical bills. I've no money."

"We're paying other firms to do this work now," Charles said. "We might as well pay you. To be frank, I *also* thought you might be too young, but we *all* started young. You're nearly twenty-three, Judy. A woman of that age is not too young to be responsible for little children, so why not for a little business? You don't have to start immediately. We could plan for six months' time."

Judy turned to Guy. "Was this what was at the back of your mind when you first came to New York? Was this what you were hinting at on the East River?"

"Of course. You've helped us to start. Now we intend to help you." He stood and raised his flute of champagne. "To Judy!"

They all echoed his toast. And Judy cried.

Charles allocated nearly all his small publicity budget to PR rather than to advertising. He quickly became intrigued by Judy's ideas, by her straightforward approach and the impressive results. At first he found it difficult to work with a woman who talked in such a brusque, forthright fashion: Charles was used to business conversations that were more circuitous and women who flattered men, but he realized that to survive, new ideas were needed; he also realized that as Judy was starting her own business she would work as hard as she could on his account. Which she did.

It was not difficult to promote an account as glamorous as champagne; had Judy been trying to sell brushes or sensible walking shoes, she might have had a far more difficult time. From the beginning she pushed three linked words: "*Paris-Champagne-Maxine.*" She used Maxine rather than Charles because Charles hated publicity. Maxine understood it much better. She enjoyed being a professional celebrity. The second reason was that "Maxine" was very similar to "Maxim's," the name of the world-famous Parisian restaurant. When Judy devised a new letterhead that read "*Paris* • *Champagne* • *Maxine*," there was an immediate, reproachful protest from Maxim's restaurant, which felt that *they* were inextricably associated in the public's mind with Paris, and that the use of Madame la Comtesse's Christian name might confuse the public. But Judy—delighted—begged to disagree and refused to change the letterhead.

Maxine became increasingly well known as a French celebrity. She was always able to provide a quotable sentence, a joke or a shrewd comment when it was needed. Judy warned her never to talk in public about money, politics or religion and never to complain to the press about anything at all; when the odd spiteful article appeared, she was to ignore it. "Yes, I know that there are boxes and boxes of splendid press cuttings," said Maxine sadly, "but unfortunately, it's only the bitchy ones that one pays any attention to—these are the only ones that upset me."

"Well, you've got to learn to live with it," Judy said firmly. "I don't mind how loudly you voice your feelings in private as long as you don't *ever* try to get an apology out of a newspaper. Sue them or forget it."

Judy also stressed that Maxine should always be beautifully dressed. Maxine did not find this instruction difficult to obey. As soon as she could afford to, Maxine shopped at Christian Dior, although at first she could only afford a couple of outfits a year. After visiting Dior, Maxine would take a leisurely stroll up the rue du Faubourg St. Honoré to choose a few boutique items and restock her lingerie drawers.

Maxine needed a great deal of underwear for a very private reason.

Charles was an affectionate and indulgent husband. After a certain amount of initial irritability, he let Maxine take over the organization of their lives and was both proud of and quietly amused by the way she did it. Once in a while he put his foot down, but this happened rarely. Most of the time she had her own way and was allowed to win their occasional arguments, but Charles liked her to remember that this was not because he was doting or henpecked, but simply because he chose to indulge her. He had a special way of reminding his wife of this.

Sometimes on formal occasions Charles would make Maxine gasp or blush or even forget what she meant to say. He could manage this by directing one meaningful look at her. It was a power that he had over her and he enjoyed it immensely, this ability to destroy her calm with that one look that, he knew, made her heart lurch and her groin moisten. Maxine knew exactly what the look meant.

One night, shortly after they were married, Charles had murmured, "I don't want you to wear any underwear to the de la Fresange ball tonight. I want to know that if I care to feel you at *any time*, you will be ready for me." Maxine thought he was joking, but during the course of the evening he danced her out of the ballroom and onto a dark corner of the terrace, then swiftly felt beneath the pale-pink net layers of her ballgown.

Maxine was wearing panties.

Charles ripped them off and flung them to the ground and then, with his left arm, he held her pressed against the stone balustrade. From the back they looked like any courting couple, but his fingers were feeling fiercely for her. She was terrified that they would be seen, that she was going to fall backward over the low stone balustrade as he pressed against her, but she could not resist Charles' rhythmic fingers. Quickly he undid his clothes and she felt him inside her body, demanding her with a selfish fierceness that she had never felt from him before. After he climaxed, he kissed her gently on the lips and said, "Darling, in just a few matters, I expect to be obeyed by you without question."

After that, upon occasion, he would casually ask Maxine not to wear underwear, particularly if they were going to a very formal function. When this happened he gave his driver the evening off, somewhat to the man's surprise. In the car, Charles' hand would search under Maxine's skirt and feel between her quivering white thighs to find out whether he had been obeyed. Once when he hadn't been (because Maxine wanted to see what would happen), he had stopped the car and roughly told Maxine to get out. There on the grass verge of the country road he made her wriggle out of her panties, then he threw the flimsy scrap of peach chiffon over the hedge, pulled Maxine into the back seat, put her over his knee and spanked her. He was not joking.

A few days later, after they had dined *à deux* at home, Charles took her by the hand and led her to the office that they shared. The deserted room was like a comfortable drawing room, although around it were spread typewriters, tape recorders and filing cabinets. In the middle of the room was a six-foot-square green leather-covered antique partners' desk, with drawers on both sides so that two people could work at the one desk.

Charles threw himself onto his office swivel chair.

"Get your clothes off," he said softly, "*now*. I want to see you naked."

"But the servants haven't gone to bed yet. Can't we go upstairs?"

"Now! Here!"

He watched with a slight smile as Maxine undressed, then he leaned forward and tugged roughly at her neat chignon so that the blond hair tumbled forward and over her heavy breasts. Then he pulled her onto his lap so that she sat astride him, facing him, nervous, puzzled and more than a little worried. He bent his lips to one full, blue-veined breast and sucked passionately until Maxine, arching her back so that her tangled straw hair fell toward the floor, no longer knew where she was or what she was doing. Then he lifted her buttocks and pulled her body gently onto his, starting slowly to thrust inside her, until, as Maxine was about to climax, he murmured in her ear, "Do you care if the servants hear?"

"No, no," she gasped, "don't stop, don't stop!"

"Do you care if anyone sees us?"

"No!"

On another moonlit night in the office, he again made her undress and sit on the edge of the great desk. He caressed her back with silken strokes, voluptuous and oddly objective; softly he ran his fingertips over her rounded belly, tasted her warm, musky female odor. Then he gently pushed her backward so that she was quivering naked on the leather desk and strands of blond hair fell over the dictaphone as Charles bent his head and flicked his tongue over her pale body. Afterward, when she lay still and gasping, he quickly tore his clothes off and mounted her on the desk. Then he tantalizingly stopped and said, "You wouldn't *mind* if Mademoiselle Janine were to see what happens here out of office hours?"

"No! Oh, *please*, darling Charles, come back inside me."

"You don't mind if she knows that Madame la Comtesse, so correct, so elegant, turns into an abandoned hussy if I simply slip my hand between her thighs?"

But Maxine was groaning too hard with pleasure to answer.

As Maxine became more and more famous in France, as she was courted and quoted and photographed with this or that celebrity, Charles loved to think that he could shatter her poise with a single glance. He would look hard at her, across a room full of impeccably dressed, important people, and he would have the immediate satisfaction of seeing Maxine give a little jump and blush.

Later that night he would tear off her frail nightgown—he rather liked to tear fragile, lace-covered garments off his wife—and say, "*That* was what the General wanted to do to you, wasn't it?" Or he would roughly grasp her breasts and bury his head between them muttering, "Was *that* what you wanted from the Newman man?"

Maxine had never dreamed that married life would be so laced with hazard and surprise or that her lingerie bill would be so large.

She loved every dangerous moment of it.

Most of Maxine's married friends had been involved with other men, but Maxine had long ago decided to be faithful to her husband—an unusual decision for a Frenchwoman of her class. Maxine felt—hoped—that she did not need any added excitement in her life.

In spite of Charles' amiability, he turned out to be an exceedingly jealous husband, but only if he saw—or thought he saw—that some particularly handsome man was interested in Maxine. He was not the sort of husband who checked her every movement.

With one exception.

In the winter of 1956, without warning, without mentioning her intentions to anyone and only leaving a brief message with Charles' secretary, Maxine suddenly went away for a week. Just before her little green MG disappeared, there had been much long-distance telephoning in the privacy of her boudoir—a room that she rarely used.

After seven days, Maxine returned looking white and haggard, distraught and tearful. She told a furious, worried Charles that she'd suddenly decided to see Colette Joyaux, an old school friend in Bordeaux who had suddenly been taken ill.

Her husband exploded with jealous rage. She couldn't even be bothered to *lie* to him with her usual efficiency. He sarcastically said that he found it hard to believe that a friend whom she rarely saw, who was little more than an acquaintance, in fact, should suddenly be stricken with an illness that required the presence of Maxine.

What was the illness? What was the name of Madame Joyaux's doctor and his telephone number? Why did Maxine leave without warning, but with a packed suitcase? Why had she packed her own suitcase instead of asking a maid to do it? Why hadn't she told him of Colette's illness before she left? Why had she telephoned during the morning when she knew that Charles was never in the

Epernay office to say that she'd be away for a few days? Why hadn't she telephoned *once* in the morning or the evening when she might assume that he'd be at home?

Maxine tried to answer his angry barrage of questions. Clumsily she clambered out of one lie with an answer that immediately plunged her into another, but she stubbornly refused to give any explanation of her absence. She looked white and ill, and Charles had never seen her look so sad. She seemed not to care what Charles felt, thought or said. She didn't even bother to hide her indifference. Although she was physically present, Charles could see that her mind was miles away. With somebody else.

He strode out of her boudoir, charged down the circular staircase, jumped into his Lagonda and drove to Paris for a week, giving no details of his whereabouts to Maxine. After his departure she found that two photographs of Pierre Boursal had been taken from her school scrapbook and had been left, in torn-up shreds, on her dressing table.

When Charles returned after dinner one night, looking grim but smug, they had a fierce fight that ended roughly and happily in bed. The matter was never referred to again.

Charles had made his point and knew when to let well enough alone.

CHAPTER 20

AS SOON AS Elizabeth saw the dim lights in the valley below, in the safety of Austria, she felt lonely and anxious. She almost didn't want to reach those lights. Out of breath, the small, tired child paused to rub her chilled hands and then trudged on through the Austrian snow down a twisting path that led to Eisenstadt.

An hour later, she staggered up the steps of the first house she reached and wearily jumped to bang the door knocker. There was a sudden glare of light, a big man's silhouette, then she heard someone say, "More soup, Helga, here's another one." Dazed and silent, the child was only vaguely aware of a steamy kitchen and strange adults in nightclothes fussing around her. Then she went to sleep, wrapped in a blanket and huddled in an armchair.

The following day she was taken to the Eisenstadt refugee camp, a collection of bleak old army huts with a constant stream of people plodding from one to the other—some of the hundred and fifty thousand Hungarian refugees who surged over the border in 1956. Hastily recruited voluntary workers moved from hut to hut taking particulars of the forlorn, silent groups who wore overcoats with turned-up collars and clutched knobbly shopping bags, potato sacks or small attaché cases that held their only possessions.

An impatient, harassed, oily-faced woman who carried a clipboard asked Elizabeth her name. She spoke at first in broken German and the bewildered child didn't understand what she was saying until she switched to French. "Speak up, child! There's a string around your neck but no name tag on it. Was it torn off? I must have your name before your medical inspection."

Eventually the child croaked, "Lili."

"Lili what?"

"*Quoi, s'il vous plaît, madame?*"

"Your family, what's the name of your family?"

"Da . . . da . . ." No, she was no longer called Dassin. . . . Lili sobbed. "Ko . . . Ko . . . *vago*." The woman wrote "*Lily Vago (French-speaking) born 1949*" at the head of the sheet of paper and so, at the age of seven, Lili acquired her fourth surname—the name on her birth certificate, then Dassin, then Kovago, and now Vago. She was then handed a piece of soap and a piece of black bread and stood in a line of sad-eyed adults for her medical inspection. Lili felt a singing in her ears and, from far away, a chill stethoscope on her chest. "It sounds like pneumonia. Shock and exposure. Take her over to the hospital hut. Next one, please."

As soon as the child was well enough to travel, a refugee committee worker told her that she was being sent to a family in Paris. "You're a very lucky little girl, Lili. We haven't been able to find homes for half the people in this camp."

During the long, uncomfortable train journey, the child hardly said a word to the group of other anxious and exhausted refugees. When they arrived at the acrid smelling station they were met by another refugee committee worker, carrying the inevitable clipboard. She ticked them off her list, then took them to the waiting room where they sagged on hard benches as their lives were reassembled.

"Lili . . . Lili Vago, there she is, over there, Madame Sardeau. Stand up and say hello, Lili. You're going to stay with Madame Sardeau, who has generously offered you a home."

The couple who stood in front of Lili did not look generous. They were bundled up against the cold, their sharp noses and pinched mouths showing from behind their dark scarves.

Oddly formal, this middle-aged couple shook hands with the child. Then the woman said sharply, "But we were expecting a much older girl. We asked for a girl of twelve to fourteen!"

Equally sharply the refugee committee worker said, "Madame, in this situation, while we appreciate your hospitality and concern, one cannot order children as if the refugee camps were a department store."

"No luggage? No passport?" the man asked.

"No papers tonight," said the refugee committee worker in a tired voice. "If you would just sign here, and here, and there, we'll expect you at the office tomorrow—anytime—to fill in the forms and complete the other formalities."

The child walked out of the station to her new home and life with the Sardeaus. She sensed that something was wrong, that she disappointed and vexed them. In silence they caught the métro to Sablon, then hurried through darkened streets to an old-fashioned apartment building. The huge arched entrance to the inner courtyard was covered by a pair of black doors, big enough to let a wagonload of hay pass through. Lili followed her new parents, too tired to notice anything but the ache in her calves, the ache in her chest and the fog inside her head. They paused outside a door, then, as Monsieur Sardeau fished for his keys outside the apartment door, the child slid to the floor.

"Henri, you don't think they've given us one that has something wrong with her?" Madame Sardeau asked anxiously. "We didn't agree to an invalid; we don't want doctor's bills; we want a strong girl who can do the housework."

"Nevertheless, we'd better call a doctor tonight." Monsieur Sardeau picked up the fragile little body. "You put her to bed and I'll get Dutheil."

Doctor Dutheil was sympathetic. "There seems to be nothing basically wrong with her. Children are remarkably resilient. She's suffering from exhaustion, and from what she says, it sounds as if she's recently had pneumonia and hasn't fully recovered. She's also had a bad emotional shock and won't discuss it; that's also normal and understandable. She's not strong enough at this stage to relive the experience by talking about it, so please don't press her to say anything. Just leave her quietly in bed, give her good food, plenty of hot milk and keep her very quiet."

He looked uncertainly at Madame Sardeau, but could not imagine her in the role of comforter. He took off his spectacles, wiped them with his handkerchief, paused and shrewdly said, "You are a heroine, madame! You are a saint to have rescued this poor child! I will come and see her again tomorrow and until she has recovered, and there will be no charge for my visits. Pray allow me to make this contribution to your noble action."

The following morning, Madame Sardeau buttoned herself into her black overcoat, bound a thick, rust scarf around her neck, stabbed her hat into place with two pins and set off for the refugee committee central office. She gave her name to the receptionist and waited in the small, crowded office. People hurried in and out; some were officials but some were obviously voluntary workers. After an interminable wait, she was shown into a cold little cubicle piled high with files of documents.

"You're not the one I saw at the station last night," Madame Sardeau said to the small, harassed woman who faced her.

"No, Yvonne speaks Hungarian so she had to go to the station to meet a new batch that we weren't expecting. I'm sorry, madame, it is not our aim in life to inconvenience you, but everyone here suddenly has far more problems than usual. Now, where is the child?"

"Ill in bed. Being attended daily by a doctor who says she must stay in bed for at least two weeks! Imagine the expense! What a way to start!"

"Oh, dear, we're supposed to get the details directly, because we must try to trace the child's parents. We'll do the best we can for the time being, but when she's recovered, you *must* bring her in to answer for herself. Now let's try to get these forms filled in."

And thus the forms were filled in, stamped and returned to the file, which was then placed in the V drawer of the filing cabinet.

When Lili was well enough, she sat up in bed with a coarse shawl wrapped around her chest and pinned at her back. Anxiously she asked what had happened to Angelina and Felix and her foster brother Roger.

"The refugee committee is trying to locate them. When you're well enough we'll go to their office and they'll tell you what they can."

"And does *vraie maman* know where I am?"

"Aren't Monsieur and Madame Vago your real parents?"

"No, Angelina is looking after me until I can join my real mother in another land and Felix is looking after her and also Roger, although Felix isn't Roger's *vrai* papa of course. And Felix is called *Ko*vago and I am really called Elizabeth, except I prefer Lili because that's what Felix calls me. Everyone calls me Lili in Hungary, it's only in Château d'Oex that they call me Elizabeth. I like Lili best and I like Hungary better than Switzerland, I think, only I wish I could speak Hungarian properly. I only know a few words."

Was the child still delirious? Madame Sardeau wondered. Best to wait until tomorrow, until after the doctor's visit and then ask again.

The next day Madame Sardeau took the kitchen notebook and a pencil into Lili's bedroom and sorted out her story. "So you were the foster child of Madame Kovago and lived in Switzerland and were on a visit to Hungary when the revolution broke out? And you do not know any details of your real mother?"

"Yes, yes, yes, no. Can I go back to sleep now?"

Over their evening meal, Madame Sardeau discussed the matter with her husband.

"It's not our responsibility to trace her family; it's up to the refugee committee," she said. "I'm not sure I believe such a muddled tale anyway. Doctor Dutheil said this afternoon that it's possible she's living in an imaginary world, in order to avoid the real one. He says it might be the only way she can face the sudden loss of her family."

"In the meantime, my dear," said Monsieur Sardeau, slicing into the crisp onion tart, "perhaps I should write to the mayor of Château d'Oex to inquire whether there is—as the child says—a family living there called Vago or Kovago. After all, if they escaped, then they would obviously return to their home and if they have, then we can return the child and ask them for the financial compensation that is our moral right. On the other hand, if they haven't escaped, or if they've been killed, then the child might stand to inherit some property—the house perhaps. So I shall dictate a letter tomorrow morning."

The winter of 1956–57 was bitterly cold in Paris. Doctor Dutheil would not allow Lili to leave the stuffy, overheated apartment until mid-February, when Madame Sardeau returned for the second time to the refugee committee office, this time accompanied by Lili. Again, they had a long wait in the small, freezing waiting room, although this time it was not crowded. Eventually, Madame Sardeau and Lili were interviewed by a voluntary worker whom she had not seen on her previous visit.

"Your name, darling?"

"Lili Kovago."

Half an hour's harassed search followed, thirty minutes spent burrowing under beige piles of paper that covered the desk and the tops of the filing cabinets, until Madame Sardeau thought to say, "Perhaps the file is under V for Vago; there was an initial mistake. Not my fault you understand."

Indeed, the file was found under V. The interviewer then lost her spectacles and Madame Sardeau lost her temper. "It is intolerable that I should be kept waiting, that the documents should twice have been lost."

The interviewer looked more harassed. "We have received no inquiries for a child of that name."

"Idiot!" snapped Madame Sardeau. "Inquiries would have been for a child called *Ko*vago or Dassin, which was the mother's previous name, and they would be filed under K or D."

So the interviewer again burrowed into the filing cabinet, looking under K and under D, but there were no files labeled Kovago or Dassin.

"You waste my time in this chaos," Madame Sardeau snapped. "You waste your *own* time in this chaos. It is obviously a waste of time to sit here like an imbecile." And she swept out, towing Lili in her wake.

The exhausted voluntary worker put Lili's file—still labeled Vago—back into the V cabinet. Nobody searching for Lili would be likely to look under V because there was no reason to do so. Lili was now literally lost in a sea of misplaced paper.

The next morning, after hearing an indignant account of his wife's visit to the refugee center, Monsieur Sardeau dictated another letter, complaining to the president of the refugee committee. He received an apologetic, but otherwise uninformative, letter.

Six weeks after that, Monsieur Sardeau received a brief letter from the office of the mayor of Château d'Oex to say that, so far as he knew, there was no family called Vago in the town, but a Hungarian waiter called Kovago had lived in a rented chalet on the outskirts of the area. Unfortunately, he and his family had been on a visit to Hungary when the revolution broke out and the whole family had apparently been killed while attempting to escape.

The town archives held no further details.

"Don't think we're rich." Madame Sardeau gave a dainty snort as she carried her shopping bags through the big doors and into the courtyard beyond. "This apartment is rent-controlled; we were lucky, after the war."

"Don't think we're rich," was a favorite Sardeau phrase. If Lili took an extra bit of bread or forgot to switch off the light in the old-fashioned, windowless toilet or asked for anything at all, this phrase came automatically to their lips.

The Sardeaus were childless. No tyrannical baby had ever shattered their sleep or their ornaments. They had never had so much as a cat to care for and clean up after, and they soon discovered that they didn't care for the responsibility of looking after a little girl. Their reason for offering to adopt an orphan had been practical—they had no one to care for them in their old age, to push a possible wheelchair, to attend a bedside or collect a pension. They had never been able to afford a servant, Madame was now getting on in years and needed help in the home, and, yes, perhaps they could use some company, for Monsieur worked in a government statistics office and after twenty-seven shared years they had exhausted their conversation.

But although the child was small and thin, although she wasn't nearly as strong as a fully grown worker, she ate as much as a maid would. Worse yet, unlike a maid, she was often not there when required because she was at school or dawdling over her homework. Certainly, for the moment, she did not justify the cost of her keep. And she couldn't be trusted; she told lies. The child obviously had bad blood; they hoped she was not Jewish.

A docile, obedient, pale-faced schoolchild, Lili had indeed started to tell little lies in self-defense, in order to have some time to herself in which to dream of what might have been. She lied about the time she left school and whether she'd been in the park—where she wasn't supposed to wander; whether she'd been to church; whether she'd done the dusting or finished the ironing. As the Sardeaus forced Lili's imagination along this gray path of self-preservation, she turned secretive, living a life of inner fantasy in which the lonely child was always adored and a scintillating heroine. Lili became increasingly subdued and withdrawn. Increasingly, she built up her mother's identity into a romantic mystery—because the alternative was to face her mother's brusque rejection.

The apartment on the seventh floor was small, dark, uncomfortable and spotlessly clean. Every ugly china knick-knack had its preordained place, as Lili discovered when she dusted them daily. Lili lived in a cupboard-sized room off the dark kitchen that faced on to the inner courtyard.

Although her schoolwork at the lycée was hard, Lili soon realized that she preferred the cheerful, noisy school atmosphere to the claustrophobic, funeral-parlor atmosphere of the Sardeau home. Certainly, she had to work far harder at school than ever before.

Madame Sardeau had no intention of letting Lili have time off. In the holidays, she not only had to do all the light housework, but she also had to prepare the vegetables, wait on the table and do the ironing and sewing. Madame Sardeau soon discovered that Lili's stitching was exquisite and piled more work on the child. After all, she thought to herself, watching Lili slave away, the devil makes work for idle hands.

After two years Lili understood—possibly better than they did—that the Sardeaus regarded her as a poor investment, which unfortunately couldn't be liquidated in favor of something more promising. They were not unkind to the child; she was dressed, fed and given suitably improving gifts on anniversaries—a book on the lives of the saints, a sewing kit, a new vest—but the girl was never grateful.

Just before her ninth birthday, Madame showed her a newspaper picture of a huge-eyed, stick-limbed African orphan and said, "See what we saved you from!"

Lili was silent for a long time, then she said, "My mother wouldn't have let me starve."

"You know perfectly well that your mother is dead."

"My other mother would have come for me."

Madame Sardeau lost her temper. "You little liar, your fairytale stories of your other mother and sleighbells in the snow are just fantasy. The priest told me that many children have them, especially if their parents have to beat them for bad behavior. You would do better to be more dutiful to *us*. You owe a duty to *us*. It is *we* who feed you, shelter you and spend money on you. Your mother and father are dead! Get *that* into your head."

"But not my Kovago grandparents. They didn't come with us that night. When I'm old enough, I shall go back to them."

"You ungrateful little idiot! Even if they're still alive, they are now behind the Iron Curtain. You will *never* see them again."

Lili was silent, struggling with emotion and frustration. Then her anger and long-suppressed resentment surfaced and, with a glare of hatred, she spat at Madame Sardeau. There was a shocked moment of silence then—outraged—the woman yelled, "Such guttersnipe manners merely betray your low origins! I shall report your behavior to my husband this evening and he will discipline you. Now get in your room!"

Lili fled, tears falling down her school pinafore. Lying face down on her lumpy bed, she longed for Angelina, Felix and Roger. Now she had nothing. No brother, no grandma or grandpa, no uncle, no father. And instead of two mothers, she had none at all. How would her *vraie maman* even know that she was in Paris?

How could she now know where to find her, when the time came?

Lili felt as if an unseen, vindictive spirit was punishing her, crushing her, in this joyless apartment. Although she was only nine, she knew that her childhood had passed and that she now had to mark time through the gray days that lay ahead until she was old enough to run away.

CHAPTER 21

MAXINE WORKED ALMOST nonstop for three years after the château opened. By 1959 she had discovered that business progress zigzagged, with one step backward for every three steps forward. The staff of the Château de Chazalle were learning their jobs day by day and Maxine—who was in charge of them—found it hard to cope with business problems that were on a far larger scale than those to which she had been accustomed in the rue Jacob shop.

In the first year they had 92,000 visitors and they grossed 30.8 million francs. In other words, they suffered a loss. *O rage, o désespoir*, thought Maxine, grimly remembering Pagan's oft-repeated schoolgirl wail. More days were spent with accountants, there were more anxious visits to the bank and—worst of all—more borrowing, which brought more sleepless nights.

In the second year they had 121,000 visitors and grossed 48.4 million francs. Success!

But would it last?

In the third year over 174,000 people visited the château, and in the fourth year they passed the magic figure of 250,000 visitors.

Yes, *it was going to last*. But could Maxine? Guy, worried, privately told Charles that he thought she was like someone running too fast downhill, forced on by her own impetus and unable to stop. Charles agreed, and repeated his original, overall instruction to Maxine's executive secretary. Mademoiselle Janine was to keep as much work as possible away from Madame la Comtesse. She managed this so efficiently that eventually Maxine was able to delegate nearly everything except the weekly business meeting on Monday with the estate accountant, and her weekly Friday meeting in Paris with Christina to go over the design work.

Maxine no longer stayed at her desk until past midnight in order to clear it, only to be greeted by a new pile of mail the following morning. Instead of getting up at six in the morning, Maxine now had a leisurely breakfast in bed, went to her office at nine and had finished the serious business of the day by lunchtime. To her relief, she was able to see far more of her children; it was one of the advantages of living over the shop, she thought, as every cold afternoon she played in the firelit nursery with her two charming little boys and every warm afternoon they all romped around the park with the dogs. Maxine had never expected to find such simple happiness with her children, and sometimes, looking at her sons, she felt a sudden pang of guilt; she felt that perhaps she didn't deserve them, it was all too good to be true; she sometimes shivered as the thought crossed her mind that perhaps Fate was going to demand some dreadful penalty for her almost ruthless practicality and success.

Partly because of the huge success of the château, Paradis was also steadily building a reputation for rescuing and converting historic houses. After the Château de Chazalle had opened in a blaze of publicity that proved what Paradis could do, potential clients streamed into the office. Maxine had successfully restored twenty-six buildings to date.

Paradis converted historic buildings into showplaces for the public, into hotels or small apartments for several families to live in. It now employed four full-time designers. Although Maxine expected everybody to work hard, she saw to it that her designers enjoyed their jobs and frequent gales of laughter would issue from the main studio when she was working there; but Maxine still approved every scheme at the sketch stage before it was presented to a client. Nothing, no matter how minor, could escape her eye for detail.

Maxine was also irreplaceable in one other very important area. Sometimes the investment needed for the Paradis projects could be as high as fifty million francs, sometimes it was considerably less. Maxine's expertise lay in presenting a scheme to a possible source of finance. "You go off with your eyes lit up, like a bullfighter about to go into the ring," observed Charles.

To Maxine, work was fun, but this was partly because she had never had a major setback.

Then, in spite of knowing that Charles would be furious, Maxine did something that she'd been secretly wanting to do for a long time. For years she had hated her breasts. They *hadn't* diminished when the boys were born, so one day, without telling Charles, she slipped anonymously into a hospital for breast reduction.

Maxine and her Dior *vendeuse* hoped that she would emerge with the silhouette of Audrey Hepburn, but although her breasts were resited four inches higher, they still remained ample. As always, the operation was very painful and Maxine was left with a semicircle of blanket stitches under each breast and another jagged little row from beneath the breast up to the nipple. They were ugly. They would never disappear.

Charles was furious. He had particularly *liked* her breasts. "Why the hell didn't you tell me what you were going to do? You know that there's always some danger with a full anesthetic!"

"Because I thought you might stop me."

"Damn right! They're not *your* breasts, they're *our* breasts. How would *you* like it if *I* decided to have an inch or two snipped off?"

But on the whole, Maxine's life passed excitingly and successfully until she was nearly thirty years old, when two things happened—Maxine became pregnant again and Charles fell in love with another woman.

At first Maxine knew only of the first event and not the second. She was not pleased to be pregnant again. Two sons were enough. She had just got on top of her job again and for the first time in years she was enjoying her position. She felt in charge of what was happening, rather than just keeping up with the daily treadmill of work. Her organization was now highly efficient, and she was paying off the château bank loan much faster than anticipated.

Then one morning, as she handed Maxine her mail, Mademoiselle Janine said, "I noticed that Madame de Fortuny was here again yesterday. For a copywriter, that one is certainly devoted to her job. She's always on the telephone to Monsieur le Comte, and I notice that she's on the list of guests for lunch today. Myself, I find that she always smells too strongly of carnations. Too much perfume can be overpowering."

This was such an unusually long speech for Mademoiselle Janine that Maxine looked up sharply. What on earth was the girl talking about? Some copywriter's scent? Wasn't de Fortuny the woman who was working on the new champagne labels and literature? she wondered idly, then pushed the thought aside as she switched on her dictaphone and started to sort through the mail. Nevertheless, she took particular notice of pretty little Madame de Fortuny at the luncheon. She was wearing a new Chanel suit—*un vrai Chanel*, not a Wallis copy—in cream wool banded with narrow cream satin—impractical and extravagant. And Mademoiselle Janine was right, the woman *did* reek of carnations. Still, she was an intelligent and amusing guest, told particularly droll stories about her job and was generally charming to everybody.

Maxine's attention was abruptly distracted by the arrival of Sir Walter and Lady Cliffe. After Nick's memorial service, Maxine and Kate had several times visited his parents at their London home; sadly, Nick's mother clung to his friends—especially the last ones to have been with him—as a last link with her dead son.

After the other luncheon guests had departed to visit the champagne caves, Lady Cliffe asked to meet Maxine's children. As the two women sat in the sunny, yellow nursery, watching Gérard wrestling with Oliver, Lady Cliffe said wistfully, "For me, the saddest thing is that I shall never have grandchildren." She paused, then added, "Of course Walter's also concerned that there's no one to inherit the title, so it will die out, but he'd already come to terms with that long before Nick died." Maxine looked mystified. "Because when Nick was fourteen, he caught mumps, complicated by orchitis. Twice we were told he wouldn't live, but then he recovered, although the medical specialists told us that Nick would never be able to have children."

"Did Nick know?" Maxine asked, astonished.

"Yes, of course he had to be told, but I don't think he ever really accepted it—I think he always secretly hoped that somehow he would be cured."

"Poor Nick. Just as well for Judy that she didn't want to marry him," Maxine said to Charles that evening, as they were dressing for dinner. "Although," she added, "I'm not all that keen on children at the moment." She patted her heavily pregnant stomach.

Charles laughed. "Patience," he said, "you haven't long to wait." He bent and kissed the back of her neck and, as he did so, Maxine smelled the faint but unmistakable fragrance of carnations. She swept the thought to the back of her mind. After all, Charles had been with the woman for the whole day.

Two weeks later, Christina said casually to Maxine, "I saw Monsieur Charles yesterday evening at Le Grand Véfour? I must say, Maxine, he gets handsomer every year in that pale, charming way."

"At Le Grand Véfour? Are you sure?"

"Yes. With that woman from his advertising firm. Jack Reffold was over here with a new delivery and I thought I'd take him somewhere nice. Charles was at the other side of the restaurant. I waved to him, but I don't think he noticed me." She bent over her work and chattered on about the latest consignment of furniture from Reffold's. Maxine felt as if someone had thrown a glass of cold water in her face. Her fingertips were tingling and she couldn't breathe properly. She knew what Christina was telling her, that she had chosen her words so the subject could be ignored if Maxine chose to do so. Maxine had spent the previous evening quietly at home eating supper on a tray, watching ballet on television, because Charles had to entertain a group of Canadian buyers. He would have to take them out on the town, probably the Folies Bergêre, then perhaps to a nightclub, both of which, as he correctly said, would bore Maxine rigid. . . .

Christina looked up. "Are you all right, darling? Maybe you'd better lie down. Is the baby kicking? Poor darling. We all expect you to carry on as if nothing is happening, simply because you always do. Come and lie down on the deck chair in the back room."

"No, no," said Maxine faintly. She felt as if she were hearing herself from a great distance. She had to talk to someone about her suspicions. She would telephone Aunt Horse-Sense, as Judy always called her.

From the tone of Maxine's voice, so carefully casual, Aunt Hortense immediately knew that something serious had happened. "Come around straightaway, dear child. You know I'm always here."

Once inside her aunt's front door, Maxine burst into tears. Aunt Hortense led her goddaughter to a chaise longue and held both Maxine's hands in hers.

"Now, what's the matter, is it Charles?"

"Yes," whispered Maxine, "how did you know?"

"Well, it *is* your third baby, my dear, and you *have* been married eight years. I cannot tell you what to do, my child, because I know no details and I do not *wish* to know them. Is Charles trying to deceive you? . . . Yes? . . . Good! In that case, what I caution you to do is to ignore the situation, if possible, until the emotions have calmed down. Now is not the time to have the showdown."

Maxine nodded as her aunt continued, "Charles is no doubt besotted with some lady, in which case he is not thinking logically. You, my child, are suspicious and jealous so you cannot see things calmly. So you must—at all costs—not provoke an argument while emotion, rather than common sense, is possessing your head and his."

Maxine looked rather surly, but Aunt Hortense spoke firmly, as if Charles were merely a car that needed its engine tuned. "You do not want to clash with Charles. You never know with men. He might run off with this lady merely as an act of defiance. Charles obviously loves you, otherwise he would not want to hide this alliance from you. Men who no longer love their wives don't bother to hide anything, you know."

Maxine said sadly, "She's beautiful and slim."

"My poor child, it would be worse for you if she were *not* beautiful. Then you would worry endlessly as to what invisible magic she might possibly possess." Aunt Hortense released Maxine's hands and pulled the bell to order coffee. "At the moment her attraction is perfectly obvious—good looks combined with the novelty of a forbidden liaison." She shrugged her shoulders. "However much he loves you, Charles has grown *used* to you. It's a pity that brides are never warned that they will undoubtedly fall in love again with someone else, and so will their husbands. But sometimes life is too painful to explain to the young, and anyway, they would never believe it."

She turned aside to give instructions to the manservant who had appeared. "So leave Charles alone, my dear, and notice *nothing.* My child, you must behave like an angel."

She took Maxine's hands in hers again. "There is only one further thing that you should think about," said Aunt Hortense gently, picking her words with care. "A good husband is more important than a business. That is not to say that your business is *not* important. I'm saying that a good husband is much, much *more* important."

So Maxine behaved like an angel and found it very difficult, as daily she became more tense and clumsy. Charles was frequently away from the château, and when he was present he seemed preoccupied. Sometimes Maxine would glance up and catch him looking at her with a frustrated, accusing stare that made her heart fall sickeningly.

She felt ruthlessly jealous and possessive. In her head she constantly checked Charles' timetable, although she dared not question him too sharply about his movements. She tried not to nag him—she didn't want him to feel that he was hemmed in to the point where he might be tempted to run away. Sometimes her mood abruptly switched and Maxine felt violently resentful of her husband's treachery, the smoothness with which he lied to her—day after day and month after month—seemingly untroubled by conscience. Maxine suffered terribly from the strain of playing a part, of hiding her pain from her husband, of lying to him, as he did to her.

Charles was supposedly in Lyons when their third son was born, a week before he was due and after a far easier birth than Maxine had expected. She clutched her baby to her and wanted to keep him by her all the time. The tiny Alexandre was her hope for the future, her link with her husband.

This time there was no possibility of Maxine's being pregnant four months after the birth. Four months after the birth Charles had still not returned to her bed from the *lit Napoléon* in his dressing room.

By 1963, Charles and Maxine had been estranged for three years and Maxine continued to ignore her husband's infidelity. Invariably, she was only able to do this by repressing her natural instincts and relying on the formal good manners that she had acquired from her strict French bourgeois upbringing. From time to time she fled to Aunt Hortense for reassurance and sympathy.

Maxine was still behaving like an angel, but she found it a great strain. She no longer slept well, her face was gaunt, and even when she switched on her confident little smile, her brown-fringed eyes betrayed her anxiety. Sometimes she snapped at her children and at her staff, because the only alternative was to burst into tears or scream. Maxine was suffering from the intolerable strain of living a false life, of playing a false part while she waited and waited and wished she could put back the clock. "If only" became her favorite game.

If only the cobwebs of time could be swept away and they could return to that lovely warm summer before she was last pregnant.

If only she'd chosen a different advertising agency.

If only the agency hadn't assigned that homewrecker to the Chazalle account.

If only she were thinner, taller, younger, more enchanting.

If only Charles could see in her what he used to see!

Her self-confidence dissolved. She alternated between dull clothes that were too old for her and outré clothes that didn't suit her. Her *vendeuse* despaired and grumbled to her assistant, "If Madame de Chazalle can't put up with the competition then she shouldn't have married an attractive man; it's too shaming to see one of my clients lose her dignity in front of the whole of Paris. She should give Monsieur le Comte a taste of his own medicine, there are plenty of attractive young men in Paris who would adore to pluck such a ripe peach."

In May of 1963, Judy was staying at the château for a working weekend. Looking at Maxine's sad, mechanical smile, and thinking of her busy but lonely life, Judy came to a sudden decision. Charles was her client but Maxine was her friend. She chose her moment carefully and the following morning, as Charles drove Judy to the champagne office, Judy said, "Aren't you happy that both the businesses are doing so well?"

Charles nodded, absently.

"And aren't you proud of those three handsome boys of yours?"

Again he nodded casually.

"And isn't Maxine a wonderful hostess? Doesn't the whole of France know it?"

Another mechanical nod.

"And how much longer do you think she will stand this present situation, Charles? I think she's almost at the breaking point. I know divorce almost never happens in France, that husbands and wives have discreet affairs which never threaten their marriages. But Maxine loves *you*, she doesn't want some other man. So I think that eventually she won't be able to bear the duplicity of the life she's leading—and she'll leave you and live in Paris, preferring to live with loss than with pain. Then think what you'll lose, Charles." Judy was extremely careful not to appeal to Charles' better instincts, but to his Gallic instinct for self-preservation. "You'll lose your easy, comfortable life, you'll lose your children, you'll lose the hostess you're so proud of and who is such an asset to your business. And what will you have gained? That calculating little cow of a copywriter and a number one scandal."

Judy turned to look at him. Outraged and silent, Charles concentrated on the road ahead. She continued.

"Oh, Charles, *nobody* can have everything they want. You're risking so much unhappiness for such a stupid reason. In God's name, what has happened to your well-known appreciation of family, comfort and money!"

Charles' hands tightened on the wheel and he said nothing. His first feeling was shock that Judy should discuss such a personal topic with him, and his second was fury that she had dared to do so. But by the time they reached the office, Charles was already starting to consider what she had said, to imagine life without Maxine.

A week after Judy's departure, Maxine was sitting at the white lace wrought-iron table under the copper beech tree beyond the terrace. She was keeping an eye on eight-year-old Gérard, who, with a set of yellow and orange building blocks, was building a fort on the grass for two-year-old Alexandre. Maxine was idly checking the guest list for a big party they were about to give to celebrate the newly modernized champagne company's first great vintage year.

Suddenly Charles appeared on the terrace. Maxine looked up. It was odd to see him in midafternoon.

Suddenly, as Charles moved toward her, her life seemed to lapse into slow motion. He looked so purposeful.

She waited, her heart pounding.

When he reached his wife, Charles bent down and kissed her ear.

The way he used to.

Maxine turned her head sharply and looked into his eyes. Seeing his expression she felt weak with hope and joy, then she sprang to her feet and into his arms, as her chair crashed backward to the ground.

Charles hugged her tightly. Then he leaned over Maxine's shoulder, picked up her pen and crossed the name de Fortuny off the guest list. Maxine grabbed his hand and kissed it. She couldn't let go.

Some time later, Maxine lay back on her bed, her thick blonde hair streaming over the blue silk spread. It had not been the same mad, passionate frenzy as when they first made love—it had been better, a sensual, sexually charged and shared experience, in which wordlessly Charles had asked forgiveness and wordlessly Maxine had told him that it didn't matter, nothing mattered but *now*.

Charles murmured, "Feel under the pillow." Maxine felt beneath the cream lace and drew out a small, scarlet box.

"It's from Cartier! But it's not my birthday!"

"No, it's not for a birthday. It's forever," said Charles, looking guilty. Inside the small velvet box was a blazing band of square-cut diamonds.

"You got the finger size right," cried Maxine. Again Charles took her into his arms, murmuring fondly into her ear.

"You're not the only one in the family who is efficient," Charles said. And he smiled at her—just the way he had when they first made love together.

PART FIVE

CHAPTER 22

SOON AFTER HER grandfather's death, Pagan—who had immediately returned to England from her Swiss school—realized that her mother's protracted grief was not because he had died, but because he had died poor. His business affairs were in chaos. The big Cornish estate was in perfect order, but it didn't seem to belong to them. It belonged to the bank—everything was mortgaged to the hilt. When searched, the Queen Anne desk in the study revealed a moth-eaten rabbit's foot and an anonymous wedding ring in the secret drawer; other drawers contained only torn-out newspaper cuttings, a cigar box full of letters home written by Pagan's father when he'd been at Eton, a few heavily marked, ancient copies of *Horse & Hound* and a heap of yellowing letters and documents. There were no bills because bills were always automatically handed to the agent and paid immediately against the vast overdraft at the bank, guaranteed by the manor house.

The chaos took a long time to sort out. Just before Christmas 1949, Pagan and her mother visited the lawyers' office in St. Austell.

They were given the bad news straight: there was no money. Couldn't they perhaps sell the house for use as an institution of some sort, a school, perhaps?

"Impossible," said Pagan's mother. "We only have twenty-three bedrooms."

In gloomy silence the two women drove back toward the low, stone Tudor house. Pagan's mother went straight to her bedroom and telephoned London. Seventeen-year-old Pagan wandered through the house as if it had already been sold and she were saying goodbye. All over the house innumerable clocks softly ticked in different rhythms, all collected by the grandmother she had never known: marble clocks, bronze clocks, china and brass clocks, an indigo enameled bedside clock, given to Pagan's grandmother by Queen Alexandra, glittered with rhinestones around the face. Every now and then the clocks rustled and chimed.

For a week, the two women mourned their loss. Pagan never cried in the house, only in the comfort of the woods, or on top of the granite cliff, sitting with her legs stuck out in front of her like a wooden doll. Then Selma came for the week-end.

By now Pagan's mother shared her London flat ("So lonely while you were away darling") with Selma, a severe-looking woman in her early fifties who lived on a meager maintenance paid by an ex-husband who lived in Hull. Selma was a big-boned woman with cheekbones that curved down like scimitars and a rectangular mouth that also bent down above a stringy neck. She was not a woman that Pagan would have expected her mother to befriend; you couldn't imagine Selma in pearls and a little black dress. She was not chic, not at home in London society, but gruffly imperious when away from it.

One evening after Selma's departure, as the sea wind shook the windowpanes of the library, Pagan lolled against the desk, remembering the hands that last had touched the maroon-leather stationery-holder and the paperweight carved from a whale's tooth. Mrs. Trelawney, sitting by the log fire, took a quick, neat sip from her glass of sherry and said, "Do stop fiddling, Pagan, I want to talk to you seriously. About money. Selma thinks it would be possible to turn Trelawney into a health farm."

"A *what*?"

"A place where people go to get thin. Selma once worked at one in the New Forest. Actually, they specialized in drying-out socially acceptable alcoholics. Selma says it wouldn't be very expensive to set up that sort of thing at Trelawney."

"Mummy, you must be dotty if you're planning to entertain a bunch of alcoholics on the edge of a cliff," was all Pagan said.

Shortly afterward, Mrs. Trelawney packed Pagan off to visit Kate at Greenways; it would cheer her up, she explained. "It also got me out of the way," Pagan told Kate, as they were walking the Scottie dogs over the common. "I'll bet Selma moved in as soon as I'd moved out; they're both totally engrossed in this batty project."

But Kate's father didn't think it was such a foolish idea and made Pagan explain it to him. "It might work," he said thoughtfully, "I can see the advantages."

"The only advantage to me is that, as there's no money, I won't be able to be a debutante as planned," said Pagan. "It costs about two thousand pounds to do the London season, if you're going to give a dance, that is. Thank heaven Mama can't manage it. I don't fancy whooping around London from dusk to dawn in pink net ballgowns."

Kate's father said nothing, but in due course he telephoned Mrs. Trelawney and offered to sponsor Pagan's London season if Mrs. Trelawney would also launch Kate into society. He intended to give his daughter the best possible chance to meet the right sort of man, by which he meant rich and, who knows, perhaps with a . . .

Pagan's mother was delighted at the idea of having a season at somebody else's expense.

"What your papa doesn't realize," said Pagan to Kate one evening, as they sat on the floor in Pagan's London bedroom sipping mugs of cocoa, "what he doesn't seem to understand is that we aren't aristocracy. We're only landed gentry, and I'm not even sure about that. There might not be any land left by now."

"He doesn't care so long as I get married. Now, how many ballgowns d'you think we can manage on?"

The year 1950 provided an idyllic British summer. By the time Maxine arrived in London, Pagan and Kate were whirling in a scintillating social catherine wheel. They were both presented at Court. You could only be presented to the King and Queen by a lady who had herself been presented (in this case, Mrs. Trelawney), so the three of them—wearing elbow-length white kid gloves and silk dresses with the obligatory below-calf hem, high neckline and covered shoulders—sat for hours in the Mall in a chauffeur-driven Rolls-Royce with a special X label on the windscreen, as all the other cars containing all the other debutantes slowly inched up to Buckingham Palace, then crawled through the ornate black iron gates and into the courtyard. Once past the impressive stone columns of the front entrance, they queued in a red-carpeted antechamber until their name was called. Pagan might have been waiting for school tea, she was so unconcerned, but Kate felt very nervous as she mentally checked her curtsy. In a squad of about ten girls, she and Pagan had taken the necessary three curtsying lessons from the famous Madame Vacani.

Kate shot upright as her name was called. She was ushered into another red-carpeted antechamber—rather like a very wide corridor—in which the Royal Couple sat on a red-carpeted dais. One step forward on right foot, one step forward on left foot, right foot move to side, then swing left leg behind and *down* you go with your head bowed in front of His Majesty King George the Sixth. Straighten up, then right foot to the side, left foot across in front, right to the side in front and that got you in front of Queen Elizabeth, then repeat curtsy and move off to right. . . .

Kate wobbled into a palatial, chandelier-hung room in which all the girls ate cucumber sandwiches with their tea and talked to each other in unusually subdued voices.

Every day there was a plethora of different entertainments. Months before, the dates of these occasions had been anxiously checked and coordinated with Betty Kenward, the pace setter of modern London. Mrs. Kenward wrote "Jennifer's Diary" in the *Tatler* and was the unofficial arbiter of the Season. Nobody dared offend Mrs. Kenward: everybody wanted to appear in "Jennifer's Diary."

Kate and Pagan held endless lunches to entertain other debutantes and they always had tea at Gunter's or the Ritz or Brown's. They attended at least two cocktail parties a night, unless they were going to a private dinner before an important ball, when Pagan's mother would not allow them to attend a cocktail party because they might get "overexcited." After a month there were permanent bags under their eyes, but with the relentless stamina peculiar to a debutante, they managed on very little sleep and a ludicrous diet. By the end of the summer, neither girl could face another glass of champagne, another cucumber sandwich, another cold slice of ballet-slipper-pink salmon, another chicken glistening in mayonnaise, another vanilla ice cream or silver dish of strawberries.

They went to the races at Ascot and Goodwood, they watched rowing at Henley, yachting at Cowes and cricket at Lord's; on none of these occasions did they pay much attention to the sport in question (except for tennis at Wimbledon) because, like most of the other debutantes, they were busy checking each other's clothes with satisfaction or dismay. They went to the Oxford Commem-Balls and the Cambridge May Balls, when dignified and ancient college courtyards echoed to the swing music of Tommy Kinsman or someone else especially imported for the occasion. And on weekends the girls did the rounds of British country houses.

Kate's father footed all the bills, and Kate's mother kept well out of the way so that she didn't make fatally shaming mistakes, such as saying "appointment" instead of "engagement," or holding her knife so that the handle showed.

Courtesy of Kate's father, Mrs. Trelawney gave lobster lunches at her apartment for all her old friends, who were also launching *their* daughters. Meanwhile, Selma directed activities at Trelawney. She had been right. Converting Trelawney into a health farm wasn't going to involve much work. Lobster lunches were also available for beauty editors who might mention the new health farm in their columns, and bottles of vintage champagne were sent to gossip writers who might mention the girls. Pagan exasperated her mother by carelessly ignoring the gossip writers, while cultivating other friends that her mother thought unsuitable.

Both girls had a group of presentable escorts: smart young army officers, crow-dressed fledgling bankers, stockbrokers and insurance men from Lloyd's—all learning to be men-about-town, sometimes on a very limited income. Nice girls were careful not to order expensive dishes, it was back to the old gin fizz routine when you went to nightclubs after a dance (especially with the young army officers), and it was best not to take too much money in your handbag or it might be borrowed and not returned (especially by the young army officers).

As in Switzerland, purity was at a premium. All the debs pretended to adhere to severe propriety, but in reality there was much panting and gasping in taxis, much exploring under pink net and burrowing under pale blue twin sets. However, all the girls knew that too much passion would result in your name being bandied around the mess, around the clubs, even around the all-night Turkish baths in Jermyn Street, for none of the chaps liked That Sort of Girl in theory, although in fact, they all seemed to want one. How Far You Went was again endlessly discussed. Pagan still insisted that she hadn't let Abdullah go too far. Well, not below the waist. Neither Kate nor Maxine believed her. "What's the point of going to a love school for three weeks," yawned Kate, "if they don't teach you to get below the waist?"

During the summer of 1950, Kate was in *Tatler* twice and Pagan was in seven times, twice with Prince Abdullah. Normally Pagan didn't seem to give a damn about anything or anybody; thirty percent of her seemed to be absent. But when Abdullah was in London, she became excited and alive, and although she swore to Kate and Maxine that she wasn't in love with him, privately they agreed that this was a face-saver. Pagan rarely knew in advance when he was going to dash into the Dorchester for a day or two; sometimes the other girls saw him, sometimes they didn't. At this time Abdullah was obsessed by the possibility that he might be assassinated, and going out to dinner with him meant pretending to get into one car and then suddenly hopping into another one that swiftly drew up behind it at the curb; it meant being told that you were going to one restaurant and then being ushered in to a quiet table at the back of a totally different one. "Don't you think Abdi's a bit paranoid?" asked Kate. "Don't you think it's a bit melodramatic, all this cloak-and-dagger stuff?"

Two days later, Abdullah's equerry climbed into his official staff car, turned the ignition on and the vehicle exploded. Bits of the car and bits of the equerry were flung all over Kensington Square in front of the house that had been rented for Abdullah's stay in London. After that, Maxine and Kate weren't so keen on acting as Pagan's unofficial ladies-in-waiting, and Pagan never again complained about unexpected changes of plan when she was with His Royal Highness.

Together with three hundred other guests, Abdullah came to Pagan and Kate's coming-out dance, held in the ballroom of the Hyde Park Hotel. Kate and Pagan shone with excitement, Pagan in white satin, embroidered with pale green lilies of the valley, Kate in primrose tulle. Naturally, they were the stars of the evening as they danced under the proud gaze of Kate's father, her mother—looking nervous in gray taffeta—and Mrs. Trelawney, whose skinny, birdlike, dieted-to-the-bone body was sheathed in bronze silk, courtesy of Kate's father.

As she waltzed Kate suddenly stumbled: for one heart-lurching moment she watched as François, her Swiss seducer, sauntered into the ballroom, accompanied by a girl in a white lace gown. Then Kate realized that the man *wasn't* François, although he had the same sort of Cary Grant face, the same brown eyes and quizzical mouth. However, this man was even better-looking than François, taller and with broader shoulders. Kate couldn't stop looking at him out of the corner of her eye. She longed to meet him and yet at the same time she wanted to rush as far away from him as possible. Casually, she asked who the dark fellow was and was told that he was a banker's son named Robert Salter, studying at Cambridge.

For the rest of the evening Kate felt an irresistible attraction, and yet she couldn't bring herself to walk up and introduce herself—although it was her dance.

But the following morning, an orange tree was delivered to Walton Street. Attached to it was a note that said Kate had been the star of a wonderful evening. It was signed Robert Salter. Although he hadn't had a chance to dance with Kate, his girl had told Robert that Kate was an only child, her father was very rich and that they lived in a castle in Cornwall.

Robert started to shower Kate with gifts. He knew that he'd have to buckle down to work in his father's bank when he returned to Cairo, where he had grown up knowing all the pampered, eligible girls in that city. Better to choose a wife in England, he thought, and, as he watched Kate swirling happily in primrose net, he decided to have a try for her.

Though he discovered on their first date there was no castle, he experienced, close up, Kate's invisible, oddly irresistible, sexual allure. She wasn't nearly as good-looking as her friend but it was Kate he desired, Kate who filled his dreams.

Kate told nobody about their meetings except her mother, who she knew would keep her secret. Kate was dazed by Robert's good looks and his masterful sophistication. "He just seems more grown-up than the Hooray-Henrys on the stag line," she confided one morning as she and her mother were getting ready for yet another trip to Harrods for silver dancing shoes.

"I must admit that Robert knows how to treat a girl in public, which is more than those Henrys do," her mother agreed.

"There's nothing unusual about having lunch at the Savoy," Kate said wistfully, as she pulled on kid gloves, "but when you go with Robert every waiter in the place flutters around you. With Robert it's always limousines at the door and great bunches of lilies from Constance Spry every morning, and jeweled trinkets from Asprey's in those regal purple boxes, delivered with a salute by an impressive uniformed chauffeur."

She snapped open her purse and revealed a gold cigarette case and lighter, a matching compact, a platinum lipstick holder, a little jeweled pencil and a crocodile notecase. "It isn't as if Daddy couldn't have bought these for me, but to be showered with gifts like this—well, it's like Christmas every day."

"I hope you're being *sensible*," said her mother, meaning prudent.

"Oh, yes," Kate lied, snapping shut the purse.

CHAPTER 23

AFTER CHRISTMAS, PAGAN refused Kate's father's offer of skiing at Saint Moritz, cheerfully explaining, "I'd rather break my leg falling off a horse, and no man born will ever be attracted by the sight of me on skis." She stayed in Cornwall. Kate didn't want to leave Robert, so she stayed in the snug little basement apartment in Walton Street and idled the day away shopping or chatting on the telephone. She occasionally toyed with the idea of going to art school, and when this mood fell upon her she would wander off to the Victoria and Albert Museum to look at the Elizabethan jewelry or the Persian miniatures.

Maxine was surprised by the recent change in her flatmate. When not on the telephone or wandering around the Victoria and Albert Museum, Kate just lay on the carpet listening to records or else flopped on the sofa doing nothing for hours on end. Maxine couldn't comprehend how a person could spend the whole week doing nothing. Every Friday, Kate caught the train to Cambridge and reappeared on Monday, either looking wildly happy or in tears. However much she was questioned and teased, Kate refused to discuss these trips, but obviously there was a man involved—and obviously Kate didn't want her friends to meet him. It must be serious, therefore, Maxine concluded.

In the late spring the social round started again, and Kate became a little more animated, surrounded by her usual cluster of lovesick swains. But she spent Easter among the floodlit joys of Greenways, either in gales of tears or else writing letter after letter. In early summer, Kate was off again to Cambridge every weekend, but in July her interest in that ancient university town suddenly lapsed and letters with a Cairo postmark started arriving at Walton Street twice a week. "If you don't tell me about him I'm going to open the next one," said Maxine. "*Why* won't you tell us about him? I *know* why, because you want to marry him and you think that if you tell us he won't ask you."

"Bitch."

Then one September morning a radiant Kate burst into her bedroom, her dressing gown unbuttoned, an open letter in her hand. "He *does*, he *does*, he *does* want to marry me. Robert . . . Kate Salter . . . Mrs. Robert Salter . . . Mrs. Salter."

"You mean it's really *it* this time? I thought you were already engaged to be married to about fourteen men," said Pagan, who was spending a few days in Walton Street while Maxine was working at a house in Wiltshire.

"Only if they leave the country; only if their ships are posted abroad or their regiments go to Malaya; and I only say maybe, it's practically a patriotic duty."

"Yes. And look at all the scent you get and boatloads of brocade from Singapore."

"Oh shut up! He's going to phone me this evening. Robert's going to phone! *Of course* I'm going to say yes. So now I can tell you. He's been reading economics at Cambridge, but his father's a banker in Cairo, and he's going back to work there. Just imagine! *Living in Egypt*! Pyramids, rose water and a great desert moon above the sail of a *felucca* on the Nile!"

Kate then produced a sheaf of photographs of a rather portentous-looking young fellow. In none of the photographs was he smiling, and in all of them he looked as if he were about to pronounce on something important. "He looks *marv*elous," said Pagan politely. She wondered why Kate had been so secretive about Robert, he looked such a pompous old prodnose, not worth stealing, even if he was handsome as Cary Grant.

Kate sat by the telephone from six o'clock in the evening until two in the morning, when Robert got through. The line was faint and indistinct and Kate had to bellow. From the next room Pagan could clearly hear the conversation. "*Yes*, I love *you too*, oh, darling Robert, yes, yes. . . . " This went on for about twenty minutes. Jolly good thing his father *is* a banker, thought Pagan. Then there was silence.

Pagan padded into the room to find Kate in tears. "Cheer up, you're the first one of our set to get engaged, that's nothing to cry about. Remember the pyramids and the moonlight over the Nile. When's the wedding?"

"Not until summer. Robert has just started to work at his father's bank and he can't leave for a honeymoon as soon as he starts. Bad example, he says. But we can't wait *nine whole months*. He wants me to go out there. He said why don't I go with Mother, but honestly I don't think that would be much fun and she'd hate it." Neither of them could imagine Kate's mother on the pyramids under a desert moon or floating down the Nile in a *felucca*.

"Why don't *you* come with me, Pagan?" Kate asked. "If Dad stumps up for your fare."

"Well, he certainly won't let you go to Cairo on your own."

Babbling with joy after a sleepless night, Kate phoned her parents at seven in the morning. "Thought something was up," her father said, "you haven't been home for weeks."

Kate decided to fly out to Cairo immediately after Christmas. Just before they left, Kate returned from a shopping trip to find Pagan lying on the living room floor, exhausted by her determination not to cry. Kate already knew the reason. She had seen the headlines in the evening papers: "*Abdullah and Marilyn—Film Star Declares Love for Prince—Marilyn Says They'll Wed.*"

"Is it true, Pagan?"

"Don't know about the bloody 'wed,' but I've known about the love bit for some time." She kicked the brass fender. "I thought she was like the rest, you know. I mean there's always some busty wench in the background. Marilyn was just more famous than the rest."

She hesitated. Pagan hated to confess humiliation. "I know he's at the Dorchester. The happy couple was photographed in front of their damned fountain, so I've been telephoning all afternoon—using our secret code—but he won't take my calls. Utter hell."

"Be reasonable, Pagan, he might be doing something else—ordering a destroyer, or having a cup of tea at Buckingham Palace."

"No, Kate, I can tell by his secretary's voice—a certain nasty smoothness. I *know* the absolutely grim way he talks to anyone who's on the blacklist." She sighed. "It's easier for Abdi not to talk to me, so he won't. Frantically convenient, being royal."

For days afterward Pagan sat in her mother's apartment looking out over the leafy treetops of the square but seeing nothing. She didn't cry; she wouldn't see anyone; she wouldn't go to Cornwall and she wouldn't leave her bedroom. Her self-assurance had been shattered by Abdullah's behavior and it was as if one of the guy-ropes holding her upright had been cut. He had deliberately broken their special bond of intimacy and trust and seemed to consider that their friendship—which Pagan had treasured—was at an end.

Pagan only roused herself from her lethargy when it was time to pack for their trip to Egypt.

Robert met them at the Cairo airport and Kate flew into his arms. As the three of them climbed into the back of his Cadillac, Pagan gave Robert a swift, sidelong look. He was certainly good-looking, but perhaps a bit *dull*?

But Cairo wasn't dull, it was a dusty, beige, hot, urban tumult. Camels and donkey carts trotted alongside swaying trams and automobiles. Pagan saw a tent pitched next to a modern apartment building, by a clump of palm trees. The skinny brown men on the sidewalks wore black skullcaps and what looked like crumpled pajamas or white, vaguely biblical nightgowns. Fatter men were draped from head to toe in white sheets; hurrying women were shrouded to the eyes, downcast in dusty black. Fly-covered beggars hunched on the sidewalks, newsboys shrilled and sweetmeat vendors crouched, languidly wafting a flyswatter over their wares. Some shops sported neon signs, others were grimy with peeling, sun-faded paint. Any spare wall space was plastered with posters of General Naguib, the new military governor of Egypt.

Robert's widowed father's apartment hung above the city. High, cool, white rooms led into high, cool, white rooms. The servants, all male, wore white uniforms with a dark red fez, and had all been with the family for years. From the roof garden, the girls could gaze down upon the languid Nile as it wriggled through the desert on its way to the sea. Faintly from across the river they could hear the sounds of Cairo: the whine of traffic, ululations, klaxon shrieks; the *muezzin* calling the faithful to prayer over the P.A. system on top of every mosque. Above them, black kites swooped over the apartment buildings, the mosques, domes, tombs, the palaces and slums of the dusty city.

Soon Kate wore a marquise diamond engagement ring that she flashed as much as possible. She doted on Robert, repeated everything he said, followed him around like a faithful spaniel and was terrified of playing bridge with him in case she didn't bid correctly. Pagan thought this very bad for Robert, who was self-satisfied enough as it was.

Every night Kate nipped along the passage to Robert's bedroom where, to her sorrow, not much happened. Robert was out almost before he was in. She didn't even have time to feel frustrated. So she faked.

Apart from that drawback Kate loved the leisurely life of Cairo. In the afternoon the girls played tennis at the club, where all the British gathered, swam in the pool, then played bridge for very small stakes until it was time for dinner. There were dances or parties almost every night: once they went to a ball at the British Embassy, surrounded by traditional Britishers of the sort that look like film extras: peppery old colonels, balding diplomats, dowagers shrouded in black taffeta.

Sometimes they drove into the western desert for a picnic.

Naturally they visited the pyramids as soon as they could and were duly photographed on camels. Having discovered that horses were for hire, Pagan immediately mounted one of the depressed-looking nags and, much to its surprise, galloped off into the desert. When she returned, Robert was furious and said that never, *ever* were they to go anywhere alone. When he took them to the bazaar he warned them to stay very close to him. They sniffed the scent of goat, tanning hides, tobacco, mint tea, cheap jasmine and patchouli oil.

All the narrow, winding alleys looked exactly the same as the streets leading off them. Robert led the way and their driver walked immediately behind. Nonetheless, the girls were pinched and pummeled, as they threaded their way down through rows and rows of stalls and shops smaller than a European bathroom. Inside, they listened to the clack of Arabic and gazed at Persian carpets, delicate wood carvings, beautiful teak boxes inlaid with mother-of-pearl and ivory, high-piled bales of brilliantly colored gauzes. Much to their initial embarrassment, Robert bought nothing at the bazaar without haggling.

Robert didn't talk about money, but he thought about it a lot. He was a human calculator; everything he did and spent was balanced in advance against possible return; he kept a little notebook in which, unknown to Kate, he recorded every penny he spent on her—the original orange tree; every bunch of roses; every generous tip at the Savoy.

Pagan had lots of beaus. She was making a determined effort to distract her mind from Abdullah by never giving herself time to think about him. In one frenetic burst of energy she decided they ought to learn Arabic and produced a suitable phrasebook. "You can learn in only eighteen lessons," she explained to Kate, "and we can practice on the butler. If we turn up late, we can mutter *Kulli shayy fi yid Allah* (everything is in God's hands) . . . hey, listen to this. *Ma takhafush, ehna asakir inkelizi*, that's 'do not be afraid, we are British soldiers.' It's followed by *akhad el-kull we-addi lek bih wasl*—that means, 'I will take everything and give you a receipt.' No wonder the British Empire crumbled. This might be useful, *ma kuntish azunnek ragil gabih kide*. That's 'I did not think you were such an untrustworthy man.' Oh, dear. . . . "

Pagan made sure she was occupied from morning until night, although there were many times when she lay on her back, tears dripping from the corner of her eyes and trickling onto her damp pillow. She couldn't sit still and she couldn't stand being alone. When Robert and Kate went off by themselves, she immediately picked up the telephone and organized an impromptu party on the terrace; the engaged couple would return to the clink of glasses and laughter as Pagan imitated a belly dancer or whirled on the roof garden in a satirical Highland reel. She quickly became one of the most sought-after girls in Cairo, and it was obvious that Robert's father, a sardonic man with eyes like small black pebbles, was intrigued by her exuberance. In contrast to most of the languid small-talking women of Cairo, Pagan played wild tennis, wild bridge, laughed and danced through the night, was never seen on a darkened balcony. She had more style than the rest of the women put together, he decided, watching her move along the terrace with her impatient, long-legged walk, half-stride, half-swoop. By contrast, Kate trotted adoringly behind Robert, agreed with everything he said—especially if she didn't understand it—and looked a little insipid.

Eventually, Robert's father took his son to one side and, without preamble, said, "I've made a few inquiries in England and I don't know whether you realize it, but Pagan would be a far more suitable wife for you than Kate, you know. She's far better connected, and although there's no money, she owns a manor house in Cornwall."

Robert looked astonished. "That belongs to her mother, doesn't it? The health farm?"

"No, it belongs to Pagan. Her grandfather left it outright to her, and her mother pays her a token rent for the place. There's quite a lot of land with it. Poor Kate doesn't seem about to shine in society as your wife *should*. Have a think about it."

When Robert's father said "Have a think about it," he was giving an order, as Robert well understood. None of his Cambridge contemporaries would have stood for such parental interference in their love life, but Robert was neither surprised nor resentful. If his father felt that interference was necessary, then it probably was; he and his father thought in a surprisingly similar way. Besides, Robert's future depended upon his father.

A few evenings later, under the green palms of the roof garden, the two men talked again. "I've been thinking about what you said, Dad, and I see that perhaps you're right," Robert said, as he slowly sipped his whiskey and gazed at the dust-veiled citadel, a twelfth-century mountain fortress on the horizon. "Perhaps I was unwise."

His father was pleased. He wouldn't have to stop Robert's allowance and he wouldn't have to send both girls back to England.

"Well, of course, it leaves one in a slightly embarrassing position," said his father, "but I have a plan."

The following weekend, both girls had been invited to Alexandria by a rich Levantine widow with a great reputation as a hostess. At the last minute, Robert announced he wouldn't be able to go. "I've got a lot of work to catch up with after an unexpected rush this week," he explained. He also made it clear that he did not want Kate to leave him, so eventually Pagan set off alone for Alexandria.

That evening Robert drove Kate out to the Auberge des Pyramides for dinner. They watched belly dancers gyrate in their oddly determined manner to the rhythmic tinkle and clash of the gold and silver coins that hung in ropes around their rotating rumps. Then Robert suggested they watch the moonlight falling on the pyramids, as lovers have done since travel brochures first were written.

When the car drew up before the famous and now familiar tombs there was no moon. Kate looked across the car expectantly, waiting to be pounced upon. Robert thought he might as well get it over with. Adopting a pained expression, he said, "Darling, uh, I've been thinking a lot about *us*—and, darling, I hope this isn't going to hurt you dreadfully—but I don't think it's a very good idea."

Kate didn't absorb what he was saying. "What isn't a very good idea?"

"Us getting married, that is. You've been here two months now and I felt—almost as soon as you arrived—I felt that I'd made a mistake. Although at first I thought that I should go through with it." He looked sideways at her.

She was stunned. "You mean wait longer? To get married you mean?"

Slowly, firmly, Robert shook his head. "I mean, call it off, darling."

Kate was bewildered, disbelieving. "What have I done? What's different? What's happened?"

"It's nothing that you've done or that I've done, darling, it's just that, well, the *chemistry* isn't there," he said looking at her with rather theatrical regret, a touch reproachful almost.

Kate was stunned. She was also ashamed and humiliated. She didn't know what to say or do.

"I've already spoken about it to my father some time ago," Robert continued with smooth sorrow, "and he suggested that I wait until I was *quite* sure before talking to you about it. I know it's hard on a girl when a man changes his mind, but it's just as well I found out *before* we got married. Dad says he'll do anything he can to help. He was awfully decent about it, awfully thoughtful. He said you might find it humiliating to stay in Cairo when everybody knows that we're . . . well, that we've both . . . that I . . . that I don't want . . . that we're not. . . . " He didn't have to continue.

"I want to go home," said Kate in a whisper. "I want to go home as fast as possible." Suddenly Kate longed to be with her mother, someone simple, loving and undemanding. She felt soiled, rejected.

The next morning Robert came to Kate's bedroom. Her face was white and she lay limp on the bed. Robert was calm but concerned, rather as if Kate had flu. He had no idea that it would be so easy. Once again, Dad had been right. "Dad's been able to pull a few strings and he's arranged for you to fly back today if that's really what you wish," he said, "but there was only one seat on the plane, so perhaps it's just as well if you let Pagan stay here until the end of the week. After all, this isn't *her* fault. . . . "

Oh, he *does* know that I faked, thought Kate, he knows I'm frigid.

"And it won't look as odd as if you both suddenly disappeared. We don't want people to talk. Pagan can say her goodbyes and explain that you were suddenly called back on a personal matter."

Home. Oh, God. Kate dreaded breaking this news to her father. She could already hear him—"So you made a mess of it? Let him make a bloody fool of you! You went *all that way* just to be made a bloody fool of, eh? I hope you realize that everybody's going to think you're a bloody fool."

All she could think about on the long plane journey back to Britain was how her father was going to take the news. Her dread of his reaction even outweighed the misery and shame she felt as a result of Robert's behavior. And Kate was right.

Both her parents were standing waiting at the airport barrier, her mother looking sad and her father scowling. He barely said anything to Kate until they had climbed into the Rolls, when he slammed the glass panel shut so the chauffeur couldn't hear, turned to Kate and said, "I hope you realize you've made a bloody fool of yourself!"

But for once Kate's mother stood up to him. "Don't you dare say another word to that poor girl," she said quite loudly.

And for the first time since she'd heard Robert's news, Kate burst into tears.

CHAPTER 24

TO HER ASTONISHMENT, Pagan returned from Alexandria to find that not only had Kate disappeared but that she had left no message. Robert was looking desolate. "She's chucked me," he said. He unclenched his fist to show the marquise diamond ring. "She even insisted on giving me the ring back."

Pagan gasped at it. "I can't *believe* that Kate did that, it's not like her at all to be so hasty and unkind. Did you have a row?"

"No, it came as a total surprise. She just coolly told me over a drink that she'd decided the whole thing was a mistake and that she wanted to leave immediately."

"And she didn't leave a letter for me?"

"No (sigh), and although I'm *deeply* hurt, I can't help thinking that if this is the way she behaves, then it's just as well she did so before we were married, rather than after."

In fact, Kate had left a letter for Pagan, but Robert had opened it and read her painful, unhappy, accurate account of what had happened between them. He tore up the letter.

"And she didn't want me to go back to London with her?"

"No, she said she was sorry she had to hurt me, but she didn't want to spoil your holiday. She said that she had deliberately waited to tell me until you were out of the way." He put his head in his hands and his shoulders shook. Pagan felt wildly embarrassed and walked to the edge of the terrace. She couldn't stand seeing men cry.

Robert's father thought it might be more tactful if Pagan didn't telephone England; Kate would telephone if she wished to do so. It would perhaps be better to respect her wishes and leave her alone as she had asked. He thought that Pagan ought to wait for a letter from Kate before writing to her. So Pagan waited, but no letter arrived.

At the end of the week Pagan wrote to Kate as tactfully as possible telling Kate how upset Robert was and asking Kate to reconsider her decision. Robert offered to post the letter for her at the bank. After a bit, Pagan wrote more letters to Kate and one worried scrawl to Kate's mother, but she received no reply because, of course, instead of posting the letters, Robert tore them up. It never occurred to Pagan that when Robert offered to post her letters from his office—which meant that they would go by special express courier—he did this in order to check her correspondence; and it certainly never occurred to Pagan that her letters were being destroyed. With calm ruthlessness, Robert also intercepted Kate's letters to Pagan and tore *them* up; this was a simple matter of getting up in the morning before Pagan, who was always served breakfast in bed.

At first, Pagan was puzzled by Kate's refusal to write to her or even to send a postcard acknowledging the letters that Pagan wrote in her large, generous, long-looped scrawl. Then Pagan felt hurt by Kate's neglect of her and—finally—she felt worried. As Pagan was totally straightforward and honest, she never dreamed that Robert would suppress her letters and trap her in a net of lies. When Pagan asked again whether she shouldn't perhaps telephone to make sure that Kate was all right, Robert gave her a pained look and asked her whether it had occurred to her that Kate might be ashamed of herself? Otherwise, she would surely have replied to at least *one* of Pagan's letters.

From the moment Kate left, Robert made a determined play for Pagan, subtly supported by his father. Wherever they went they had the maximum attention, the best service and the best seats; flowers were showered upon her, and whatever Pagan wanted, Pagan had. She appreciated these attentions and tried to forget Abdullah in this leisurely round of pleasure. Cairo was as heavily romantic as a magnolia blossom and she was being delightfully spoiled. Pagan couldn't think of anything that urgently needed her attention in England, unless it was to work as a shop assistant in Peter Jones' department store: she wasn't academically qualified, she wasn't trained to do any job, she was too tall to be an air hostess, she wasn't thin enough to be a model.

Not only was Pagan bewitched by the luxurious life of Cairo, but Robert-in-Cairo was a much more beguiling proposition than Robert-in-London, where there was plenty of competition from other men. Cairo lacked eligible young European bachelors and the few who found themselves in the city were fiercely fought over by hostesses and flattered in the most outrageous way. Women hung on Robert's every word and responded to every joke he made with tinkling laughter. Pagan started to look at Robert with more appreciative eyes.

Robert bided his time until one evening after they'd been to a Christmas dance at the Semiramis. The creamy moon hung like a lotus in the sky. He had ensured that Pagan's champagne glass was never empty, and she was definitely giggly as they drove home. She swayed slightly as they walked toward the elevator, and Robert put his arm around her in protective fashion as they waited.

"Merry Night! Happy Night! Good Christmas!" chortled Pagan, and it seemed the most natural thing in the world to kiss him goodnight. Then she went to her room, threw all her clothes on the floor, fell on the bed, and immediately went to sleep.

Farther along the passage Robert adjusted the Japanese kimono that he affected as a dressing gown, pulled the sash firmly into place, then moved purposefully into Pagan's bedroom.

Pagan woke up the next morning wondering, as many had before her, "What *have* I done?"

Robert then concentrated all his attention on a classic, whirlwind courtship, with his benevolent father beaming in the background. He brought Pagan charming little gifts—dangling golden bell earrings, a square-cut purple amethyst as large as her thumb, a darling little pet monkey in a scarlet jacket that Pagan immediately took off the delightful little creature.

Two months later, somewhat to her surprise, Pagan and Robert were married at the British Embassy. Robert's father gave her a pale blue Rolls-Royce as a wedding present.

Almost immediately after the wedding reception, the marriage started heading for the rocks.

Pagan had never been passionately interested in sex, so at first she merely thought that all Robert needed was a bit of practice. She was wrong. A couple of months after their marriage, she tentatively said, "Could you possibly wait for me?" He immediately stiffened, said he didn't know what she meant and accused her of being frigid. Amiably, Pagan agreed that she might be. "It's just that I haven't been so far," she added. Robert turned purple with rage. Quoting the *Kinsey Report*, he said the average man took two and a half minutes to climax, which meant that she was getting thirty seconds *more* than average, didn't it?

Pagan longed to talk to somebody about it, but she felt too shy. She dearly wished she could talk to Kate to ask if it had been the same with her. Pagan wouldn't mind asking Kate, because she was too desperate to be embarrassed, and she thought that if Kate knew how agonized Pagan was, then Kate wouldn't mind talking about it. But Kate hadn't answered one of her letters.

In fact, Kate had written a violent letter to Pagan when she heard her friend had married Robert, but Robert spotted Kate's handwriting and fished the letter from the silver salver in the hall. Slitting it open with his forefinger, he gave a sniff as his eyes flew over the five pages of accusation in Kate's little, neat handwriting, every letter clear and separated, with no loops on the down strokes or any sort of flourish, and pain in every line. Robert put the letter in the inside pocket of his suit and later tore it up in his office.

That evening—wearing his pained look—he told Pagan that he'd had a short letter from Kate, saying that she hoped he could forgive her and let bygones be bygones, that she was now in love with a Twelfth Lancer called Jocelyn Ricketts and hoped soon to be a soldier's wife. Pagan eagerly asked to be shown the letter. Robert looked in his inside pocket and said dash, he seemed to have left it at the office, he'd bring it back tomorrow evening. The following evening he said, with irritation, that he'd forgotten the damn thing, and surely Pagan realized that he had more important things to think about than a couple of scrawled lines from a woman who'd hurt him so deeply.

Pagan never again asked to see the letter, but after a few days—although Robert had distinctly told her not to do so—she locked herself in her pale blue bathroom as soon as Robert had left for the office and booked a call to Walton Street. After a four-hour delay, her call was put through but there was no answer. All that Pagan heard was the little quiet hiccup of that old-fashioned heavy black telephone, thousands of miles away in London. She immediately booked another call and again there was a four-hour delay and again no answer; Pagan didn't dare book another call because Robert was due home, but she telephoned again on the following morning.

There was no reply from Walton Street.

On the third day Pagan booked a call to Kate's mother. This time there was only a two-hour delay and Kate's mother answered the phone herself on the fourth ring. Oddly stiff and formal, she said that Kate was staying in Scotland with friends. Yes, perfectly well. Yes, she and Mr. Ryan were also perfectly well, thank you.

"D'you think you could get Kate to write to me, then, or telephone?" asked Pagan.

There was a pause. The line crackled. Then, in a rush, Mrs. Ryan said, "I don't think Kate ever wants to hear from you again. Or Robert. Kindly leave her alone."

Then Mrs. Ryan carefully put down the receiver with no intention of upsetting her Kate by telling her daughter that Pagan had telephoned to beg forgiveness. What a nerve the girl had!

By Pagan's first wedding anniversary, the *Kinsey Report* had been quoted at her so much that she thought perhaps she had better check if she *was* frigid. So she had an affair with her tennis coach, a cheerful Italian with good legs, gentle hands and a voluptuous appetite. They weren't in love, so for Pagan there was a strange, embarrassing, impersonal feeling about the relationship at first, but Alfonso was a skillful lover and he adored everything about women.

Alfonso was mysteriously unavailable at siesta time (when it was too hot to play tennis) but three months later Pagan found that there was a very good reason for this—a rich Armenian widow, one of those overscented, plump, languid women of Cairo who wore tight black dresses from Paris with too much ostentatious jewelry and had their hairdressers call every morning. Alfonso beat the hairdresser to it, and his proposal of marriage was accepted. Although he suggested to Pagan that they continue their liaison, she thought it would be too complicated, however exciting.

After that, she had a couple of young diplomats from the British Embassy, but they weren't at all like the tennis coach—they were tense, elaborately polite and not at all cuddly, not very different from Robert, in fact.

Robert had now started to complain that she was not only frigid but sterile. Considering his hostility, Pagan was surprised he still wanted to make love to her. "Well, shall we have another *stab* at it?" he would suggest with a polite snarl, and poor Pagan was duly stabbed with what she privately called the marital *chippolata*, wearily wishing that Robert would stop touching her nipples as if he were turning up the volume.

Urged by Robert, who wanted a row of little Roberts, she eventually consulted a doctor, not only to check that her fallopian tubes were unobstructed, but because after Robert had made love to her, she felt a heavy turgid pain in her lower back, as if she were having a really nasty period. This sometimes lasted for hours, during which time Pagan would be tense and tearful, drop glasses, upset cups and ashtrays; she also started to suffer from insomnia. Not knowing that these were classic symptoms of a sexually aroused and then frustrated female, Pagan would eventually get up at four in the morning and slug herself to sleep with a blissful half-pint glass of neat vodka.

The doctor confirmed that there was no reason why she shouldn't conceive ("Keep practicing," he said jovially), and decided that her other physical symptoms were psychosomatic because of her concern at not being pregnant. When Pagan suggested to Robert that *his* potency should be checked, he puffed up with rage like an angry pigeon and flatly refused to take a sperm test on the grounds that it was undignified.

Outwardly, Pagan seemed exactly what Robert needed. A splendid-looking woman, a charming hostess and, as such, a business asset. But once she had acquired a wardrobe of rich clothes, once she knew all the people and had been to all their parties, Pagan started to long for the woods, the trees, the cliffs and the cold gray sea of Cornwall. Increasingly, she felt oppressed by the yellow dust of the lotus, by the rich, pointless life of Cairo, by her own rich, pointless life and by her rich, pointless husband. She couldn't stand the way that Robert kowtowed to his father, who now—for some unknown reason—didn't seem to care for Pagan. Pagan knew that Robert blamed her for their lack of children, but she didn't realize that both he and his father also silently blamed her for not having her own money. Unfairly, his father blamed Robert for having made a bad investment decision, conveniently forgetting that the marriage had been his own idea in the first place.

"More trouble over your bloody estate," snarled Robert, one evening when he returned from the office. With a nod he accepted the whiskey and soda that Mohamed silently proffered on a silver salver. "My father's spent thousands of pounds on lawyers and yet they can't upset your bloody mother's trusteeship!"

He strode over to Pagan, sitting on a flowered chintz sofa on the balcony, and spat, "The old girl's as tough as nails. That place belongs to you and she's got it for a song!"

Pagan yawned, then said in an offhand voice, "Well, it doesn't much matter, darling, does it?" She stretched both arms up and moved along the sofa so that she was directly in the breeze stirred by the overhead fan. "After all, *we* don't want to live there at the moment, and it gives Mama something to do, and she's earning her own living, you don't have to help support her."

" . . . Typical of *you*!" yelled Robert. "Just as Father says. You're totally careless about money . . ."

" . . . *You're* totally under your bloody father's thumb . . . "

" . . . At least my father doesn't exploit me . . . "

And so another row started. Pagan realized by now that Robert didn't love her. She also had painful cause to know that he was a verbal bully as he repeatedly tried to grind her down with criticism.

Robert was finishing the job that Abdullah had started—the job of wrecking Pagan's spirit. Not only did he not love her, he really wasn't interested in her. Robert was interested in presenting himself to the world as a wise, just man; and to do this he prevaricated endlessly. He was never guilty of anything; in Robert's eyes Robert could do no wrong. If the facts indicated otherwise, then the facts had to be readjusted. Certainly, Robert would never be honest enough to admit to himself that he was a rotten lover and a sham, Pagan thought.

One night, after Robert had performed his marital duty for the usual three minutes, she told him so. Robert snapped on the bedside light and sat up, glowering at her. "What exactly do you mean by saying that I'm a dishonest sham?"

Pagan realized she'd presented him with the perfect excuse for a row, but suddenly she didn't care.

"I mean that you're not only a selfish lover but you pretend not to be. *That's* deceitful and dishonest, when you turn over and go to sleep *knowing* that I'm churning inside, but pretending that you *don't* know. I loved you when we married and I didn't want to say anything to hurt you, and as a matter of fact I thought that all you needed was a tiny bit of practice. In fact, I thought we both probably did. If you were still the same as you were then, I wouldn't mention it, but you've gotten worse."

Robert grew redder.

"At first I thought you were too tired, Robert. I thought it was the strain of your job, but then I saw that it was just old-fashioned laziness and selfishness.

And there was something nastier; you didn't want to be *involved with me*. If you could press a button and have me disappear after you've come, you'd press it."

Robert turned purple. "You're the only woman who's ever complained—and that's because you're *impossibly demanding!*"

Pagan took a deep breath and said what she'd been rehearsing in her mind for months. "Robert, I can masturbate to a climax in five minutes. I checked it with the kitchen egg-timer. *That's* how long it takes to arouse me if I'm not anxious or under pressure. Not much longer than you. But you don't bother to find out what makes me come. I've hinted for a long time and now I'm happy to tell you straight, as well as show you, so that you can't go on pretending that you don't know."

"You castrating bitch!"

"No, I'm not. It's just that I'm not an acquiescent Betty Grable or whatever female fantasy you imagine you have in your arms, when it's only me. You'd *rather* fuck an imaginary Betty Grable than a real me, because she responds in exactly the way that suits you and gives no trouble. Good old Betty disappears at the touch of a button when you don't need her any longer, doesn't she? I can't compete with a myth, with an invisible, acquiescent pinup. I want reality and honesty. I want a real relationship with a real man."

"You've got a filthy whore's mouth."

"You've got a filthy schoolboy's mind. I expect my mother's generation would put it more daintily—they'd say you were insensitive or didn't understand a woman's needs or something—but for once, Robert, I'm speaking plainly because I want there to be no doubt about what I'm saying. I don't want you to double-think this conversation into something that suits you. I'm saying that I don't want to be used only for sex. I want to be loved. I want intimacy and sensuality and mutual concern. Not a quick stab, thank you!"

She thought that Robert was going to hit her, but he didn't; he merely glowered at her and stormed off to sleep in one of the other bedrooms. For three days he wore an air of righteousness and did not speak to his wife; then he returned to her bed and behaved as if their conversation had never taken place.

Pagan wept. She had hoped that after he'd simmered down, he might take some notice of what she had said. But he didn't.

And she never tried again.

CHAPTER 25

THE GLASS DOORS of the sumptuously decorated penthouse suite of the Dorchester were thrown open. Although it was early June, it was a warm day for London.

Inside the powder-blue bedroom, on the vast, rumpled, lace bedspread, the twenty-three-year-old Abdullah lay naked across a woman's half-clothed body. He slid his hand into her crumpled white silk blouse and softly pulled out her other breast. The rosy tip quivered erect in his mouth as his lips pulled on the vulnerable flesh, harder and harder on the sensitive, delicate skin. Abruptly he released it.

"Don't stop, please don't stop!"

Delicately he ran the tip of his tongue over the little jutting peak, ran it swiftly back and forth, the nipple quivering again as his tongue softly circled around it. He gently took it in his mouth and again started to suck softly, pulling at the now deep-red areola. Abruptly, he stopped again. A little cry, a gasp. Purring, he rubbed his silky, black mustache against the nipple, slippery with his saliva; gently growling, he played delicately with it.

"Oh, that's unbearable, don't stop, darling."

Softly he nipped it with his teeth, let go, then pounced again, surrounding the raspberry flesh with his sucking mouth. Again he darted his tongue over and around the soft, dark bud, drawing it gently, then with increased firmness between his moist lips, pulling, stretching taut the heavy cream breast, clasping it with both brown hands, sucking harder and harder, greedy and insistent.

"Darling, I can't stand it. I'm going to come."

Abruptly, he stopped and pulled his gleaming brown body away, poised above her, his hand holding her wrists to the bed as she writhed in frustration, trying to reach up to him. "You can't touch me," he growled softly, "you can see me, you can see what you want and you're not allowed to touch it, you can't have it . . . until I allow it."

He shifted his position, lay beside her and taking her wrists in one hand he pressed them to the pillow above her head. Then his other hand slid down her body, felt beneath the crumpled skirt, slid over the stocking top and found her warm thigh. The hand slid over to her inner, quivering warmth, and felt soft, enfolding flesh on both sides as he lightly pressed his thumb against the moist, silken hair beneath it. The body beneath him writhed in ecstasy, oblivious to all but his hands and mouth.

"Now I'm going to undress you," he purred, "very slowly." Abdullah always talked to his women, always softly told them what he was going to do, just before he did it. It was sometimes easier not to undress a woman completely to whom he was making love for the first time. There was then no time to recall a husband, to feel guilt as clothes were being removed, and besides, Abdullah sometimes liked the urgent feel of a half-clothed woman beneath his naked body, he liked to feel the sensuous slither of satin and silk, the fragility of lace beneath his fingers or, in a more tigerlike mood, to feel fine fabric tear beneath his hard hands.

The woman beneath him moaned again, "How can you . . . why don't you . . . How can you *stand* it?" But Abdullah had been instructed in the sexual customs of the East, and those special, subtle practices had taught that there could be no deep satisfaction for a man, one who was no longer a boy, without *imsak*, the control of his own fierce passion.

For an instant Prince Abdullah's mind spun back seven years to 1947, to the cool inner courtyard of the old doctor's house in Cairo, where surrounded by lemon trees the fountain splashed under the arched, white colonnades that surrounded the courtyards. There he had lain on a vast, cushion-strewn, silken divan to be instructed in the arts of love and the special, subtle sexual practices of Arabia. He remembered the soft feel of the plump, brown thighs of his first girl, the silken curve of her knee under his hand, the ever-fascinating undulations of her dimpled backside, the soft feel of it beneath him and her conspiratorial giggle as, unable to contain himself, he thrust into her with frenzy, then climaxed with a harsh, triumphant cry.

Only once was he allowed to do this, by way of introduction to the girl who for the first week was to be his partner, mentor, tease, informer and judge. Gravely, over thimblesful of black coffee, the old *hakim* explained that regular sexual intercourse was necessary to keep a man fit and healthy, but the sexual act could either be a simple one of reproduction—no more complicated than that of a beast in a field—or it could be a subtle act of love, a discipline to be learned and practiced, in order to achieve and appreciate the most sublime gift of Allah.

Abdullah remembered the air, heavy with sexual promise, that hung over those cool rooms, and the soft, ululating wail of Arab love songs, accompanied by the music of flutes. He remembered the odor of those rooms, a sultry mixture of cinnamon and spices, *kef* and coffee, warm black hair and female musk, the scent of rose and jasmine, mingling with the fragrance of vanilla that wafted in from the tubs of white olcanders that stood on the turquoise-patterned tiles of the central courtyard.

That first week was a week of eagerness and exasperation as he was made to practice *imsak*, a word that roughly translated means "to retain": Abdullah was taught that his whole aim should be to avoid losing control of his body, and that this was best and most pleasantly accomplished by concentrating his mind entirely on the woman. By the objective study and prolongation of the pleasure of his partner, a lover could stem and control his own tide until she had achieved a height of passion that left her dazed and unaware of her surroundings. Only once a day was the sixteen-year-old boy allowed to climax. By the end of the first week his body was bruised all over where plump little Fatima had sharply pinched him when she judged it necessary, but he could tell by her pouts, by the regret in her merry eyes, the sly look she gave him under her glossy lashes, that she was sorry to see him progress to the older, more experienced women in the second week, as their plump, soft hands guided him, as they murmured words of suggestion and lightly scratched their sharp almond nails upon his skin when he needed correction. Always, after the evening bath, when eunuchs poured silver pails of warm scented water between his thighs, a masseuse in white robes would bend over Abdullah's silken couch to stroke and knead, to soothe, refresh and once again stimulate every tingling muscle in his body.

It was only because of those weeks of unrelenting, skilled tuition that he could now make this blonde creature beneath his body attain heights of pleasure that she was unlikely to know with a Western man. Few Western women had experienced such consideration as Abdullah could show, such lifting of mood from gentleness to passion to wild abandon and then softly back again. Abdullah loved the primitive, musky smells of women, and he knew their bodies and their needs as he knew his own; he seemed uncannily able to read a woman's mind and know exactly what she longed for at any given moment—everything she had ever secretly desired—and he was the Nijinsky of cunnilingus. Abdullah was completely, naturally uninhibited, and so his women felt equally abandoned, which was generally what made the difference between how they felt with their stiff British husbands and how they felt about the breathless sensuality of Abdullah's body which summoned up such erotic response to what he murmured in their ears. He well knew that speech was an important part of seduction.

Prince Abdullah did not find it difficult to use Western women as his means of revenge upon Western men; he loved women as some men love horses. In almost every female he found something to admire and desire; he loved their softness, their elusiveness, their laughter. He loved small girls and big, voluptuous ones, slim bodies and rounded chubby ones; he loved dark silky hair and short blonde curls; he loved little, firm, high breasts and low, voluptuous breasts like melons; he loved slim waists, but he also loved little rounded stomachs, big rounded buttocks and thighs like soft pillows. He loved the excitement that he could summon up in that delicious, warm, sensual flesh, to see some beauty writhing out of control at his command, responding in a frenzy to his light, sure touch, while Abdullah, by contrast, stayed in complete possession of himself and could remain so for hours. He gave many women that romantic bliss that as schoolgirls they had dreamed of; he gave a few women the sort of unrestrained passion of which they had never *dared* to dream. He captivated women with his fierce, proud face, his lean, well-exercised body, and his aura of sexuality, wild as that of a stallion. Added to which, by the time he left Sandhurst, Abdullah had the carriage and savoir faire of a much older man as well as the invisible assurance provided by money and power.

However, to be loved by Abdullah was not always a bed of roses, although great sheafs of roses were, in fact, sent three times a day to his current lady. Abdullah always made it clear to all his women that, although at that moment he was completely at her command, there could be no permanent future for her in his life. He would whisper this regretfully, with heartbreaking sorrow, as if he couldn't really bear to speak of it, but felt it only honorable to say before he bent again to the distraction of her snowy breasts. So no woman could say that he had in any way misled her, although he might easily exasperate, hurt or anger her when he suddenly disappeared. No woman could say he had deceived or jilted her, or dropped her or left her, because he never really had. He hated saying goodbye to a woman; he always liked to feel that he was joined to them by an invisible silken thread that he could, if necessary, gently tug. After being loved by Abdullah, no woman ever remembered him with anger or remorse—only with nostalgia, a slight smile or a sigh and the memory of having been magically charmed. It was as if he had just appeared one night for a brief moment. Then—

equally suddenly—he wasn't there anymore and the wonderful nights were gone.

But the memories were unforgettable, if only because they were unlikely to be repeated. Abdullah, murmuring soothing words of flattery and love, encouraged most women to behave in a more voluptuously agile manner than they had ever thought possible as he led them swiftly through an erotic crash course which culminated in his sensuous pièce de résistance. With silken cords he would bind the wrists of the more adventurous ones to the bedhead and then he would dip one golden hand—his skin wasn't very dark, just a permanent sun-bronzed tone—into the bowl of golden fish that always seemed to be at his bedside. Abdullah would quickly scoop out one little fish and swiftly push the wriggling creature into the girl. At this point, she generally stiffened and shrieked with surprise, but Abdullah threw his body on top of hers and held her hard against the mattress until she relaxed and was able to enjoy the strange erotic sensations as she felt the little fish move inside her warm body. As soon as the girl started to groan with pleasure, Abdullah would slide down her body and—with great dexterity—he would languorously suck out the goldfish.

Now, as the present blonde writhed beneath Abdullah's body and her harsh little shrieks grew louder, his aide-de-camp was calling him through the ornate doors of the Dorchester Hotel. "Your Highness, Sire. The telephone, Sire. The prime minister, Sire."

Abdullah threw his head back and growled. Suliman was supposed to see that no telephones disturbed him, especially not in the late afternoon.

"An emergency, Your Highness."

Quick as a cat, Abdullah was off the bed and, in an instinctive reflex action, had grabbed his gun before the woman on the bed realized what was happening. She lifted herself on her elbows, as Abdullah backed toward the telephone, carefully lifted the receiver and had a short conversation in guttural Arabic.

Abdullah carefully replaced the receiver. In the dim light of dusk, he looked alert, wary and very upset. Suddenly the woman on the bed realized that although he was scowling fiercely at her, he had forgotten that she was there.

"Your Highness," she said, uncertainly. There hadn't been time to get on first-name terms. He blinked and looked thoughtful. "Not Your Highness," he said, "Your Majesty."

Damn, the tousled blonde thought as Abdullah strode naked to the door. Damn, damn, *damn!*

CHAPTER 26

PAGAN WAS SITTING up in bed and drinking her morning mango juice, when Robert threw the morning newspaper at her and said, "That wog boyfriend of yours is now in the hot seat." The headline read, *Young Warrior King Ascends Throne.*

Pagan said nothing until Robert had left for the office, then she went to the cocktail cabinet, took out a bottle of vodka and climbed back into bed with it. In 1954, after three years of marriage, her relationship with her husband had become one of polite, cold hate. Pagan was no longer such a good business asset. In fact, she was carelessly drunk quite a lot of the time.

The next morning, Pagan woke to see Robert, his head propped on one arm, looking at her from the next pillow with such venom that she felt frightened. Suddenly she realized that she'd always been a little frightened of him. She faced the truth—she had made a dreadful mistake; she'd married a pompous ass with an imposing exterior. Inflated by his own self-importance, Robert was as empty on the inside as a blown-up carnival balloon.

"You're thinking about that black bastard as usual, *aren't* you?" Robert threw the sheets back from the bed with cold fury and, still glaring at her with hate, roughly yanked at the shoulder strap of her topaz silk nightgown. As Pagan flinched away from him, Robert gave a strange little hiss, tore the silk from her breasts and raped her.

She cried out as she tried to push him away from her, but his fingers only dug harder into her breasts. Afterward, she saw a look of satisfaction on his face, of power and cruelty. She realized he had enjoyed hurting her and would do so again. He had become her intimate enemy.

After he had left the room to saunter to the terrace for his impeccably served breakfast, Pagan staggered into the bathroom. Silk strips fluttered from her body, and in the mirror she saw fingermarks on her breasts. Shuddering, she ran a warm bath and lowered herself into the water. With a wet hand she carefully lifted the telephone and dialed the airport.

Leaving behind her the pale blue Rolls—later much regretted for its trade-in value—Pagan caught the next plane to London.

Pagan's mother was appalled, but not surprised, to see her daughter. A cablegram had arrived for Pagan the day before and Mrs. Trelawney had opened it, thinking her daughter still in Egypt.

INTEND TO IMMEDIATELY DIVORCE YOU STOP GROUNDS DESERTION STOP ALIMONY NOT FORTHCOMING FOLLOWING YOUR DISGRACEFUL BEHAVIOR STOP PLEASE ACKNOWLEDGE ROBERT SALTER

Pagan scowled as she read it. "He makes it sound as if I'd been sacked for incompetence."

"Do you mind explaining what happened?"

"Darling Ma, couldn't we have a drink first? It's been eight hours on the train you know." Pagan's mother sniffed, took a step closer and sniffed again. "Yes, I know, I had a nip or two on the train. Medicinal. And consoling. So *cold* here after Cairo. And I was a tiny bit disappointed that you didn't meet me at the airport. Didn't you get my cable?"

"Yes, darling, but I could hardly just disappear and leave Selma on her own for two days; one has one's responsibilities. And after all, you're not a child, you only had to take a cab from the airport to Paddington Station. How long do you think you'll be here?"

"Darling, I've come *home*. *Here*. Trelawney is my home. I'm going to stay here in blissful Cornwall."

There was a pause, then her mother walked toward a wall-hung corner cupboard. "I think we both need a drink."

She poured two glasses of Amontillado sherry. "We're full at the moment," she said, after a moment of silence. "There isn't a spare guest bedroom, but one of the servants' bedrooms is vacant. It's on the top floor of the east wing."

"You mean that utterly grim *attic*?"

"Well, darling, you must admit your arrival is unexpected. We didn't know you were coming and we're fully booked up three months in advance; doing quite well since the new hydrotherapy tank was installed. Goodness, you finished that quickly, darling, are you sure you want another?"

Pagan was intrigued by the change in her mother. She and Selma wore crisp, white uniforms and called themselves the Executive Director and the Dietetic Consultant. They spoke in low, soothing murmurs, even when no one else was present. Mrs. Trelawney wore no makeup, sported a large pair of tortoiseshell spectacles, and had taken up yoga.

After four nights, during which Pagan slept in a small servant's bedroom, Mrs. Trelawney said, "I've talked things over with Selma and when it's free we're prepared to let you have one of the guest rooms—the housekeeper's old room I thought. But you'll have to behave. You know what I mean. No drink, darling. Not *one*, tiny, hidden bottle. You know that I can't risk it."

Pagan no longer wanted to live at Trelawney, where strangers in dressing gowns drifted down the overheated passages or sipped weak tea in the conservatory. She had decided to move into a gamekeeper's abandoned cottage about a mile from the house. It nestled in a dip in the woods surrounded by golden azalea bushes. Mrs. Trelawney had intended to convert the old cottage into a luxury annex suite, but when she said, "Impossible, darling, I'm afraid" Pagan looked at her coldly and said, "Darling, please remember that Trelawney belongs to *me*."

The gray stone cottage was furnished with some castoffs from the big house, and Mrs. Hocken came once a week to clean up. "What you want is a bit of company, Miss Pagan," she offered one morning, leaning on her broom. "A nice cat or a dog. Mrs. Tregerick was telling me since her Jim passed on there's not a body to exercise their dog, a sheep dog 'tis, no harm in having a look at 'un."

Buster was black and white, shaggy and the size of an armchair. Together they kept the cottage in a state of chaos—it smelled permanently of wet dog. Every day Buster took Pagan for a walk, nearly pulling her arm out of its socket as he strained at the leash. Buster meant that Pagan didn't stay alone in the cottage all day, sprawled on her chintz-covered lump of a sofa whose sagging springs creaked as she reached for the vodka bottle.

She felt bitter and frightened—a failure. How and where had she gone so wrong? Could someone else have made Robert happy? Should she have tried longer, harder? It took more energy than she could muster to think it over again and what was the point? It would all end badly anyway. Better to stay home with her darling Buster and her vodka and blot out the loveless mess.

One morning Mrs. Trelawney walked over to the cottage to find Pagan sitting on the kitchen floor wearing gum boots and a pair of old riding breeches and nothing else. She had been eating baked beans laced with vodka out of the dog bowl and could barely manage to lift the spoon to her mouth. She flung the spoon at her mother.

"Pagan! Pull yourself together!"

"People only say that when you can't."

Pagan's mother suggested she might like to talk with the clinic doctor, who was able to help people with unfortunate addiction problems.

"It's a bit bloody late to start being interested in *me*," Pagan shouted.

Pagan had arrived in Britain with only a hundred and fifty-six pounds cash, all that had remained in her account at the Ottoman Bank. After two months in Britain, this had been reduced to seventeen shillings and four pence, so Pagan decided to tackle her mother about funds. She waited until evening to walk up to Trelawney: after six o'clock her mother had no reason to give that sharp, meaningful sniff.

Mrs. Trelawney was checking diet sheets at her desk in the study. "Won't be five minutes, darling," she murmured, peering over her tortoiseshell rims. "Help yourself to . . . " But Pagan was already pouring a gin and tonic.

"Darling, haven't you any *dresses*? Since you arrived I've only seen you in gum boots and jeans."

"Well, Ma, it's such a divine change from Cairo. Wearing clothes *there* was practically a full-time career, one was always having to change. Frantically boring. Anyway, I haven't any money to spend on clothes, which is what I'd like to talk to you about."

"You mean you expect *me* to support you?"

"I don't see how else I can be supported, for the moment."

"A pity you didn't consider that before you left your husband."

"Ma, do you really want to know why I left so suddenly?"

"That's a personal matter between you and Robert."

"But do you want to know?"

"No."

Mrs. Trelawney didn't want to be involved, she never had.

"But I must have something to live on, and my only asset is Trelawney."

"No need to ram that down my throat, darling. If it hadn't been for Selma we'd have had to sell it."

"But now that you're doing very well, surely you could let me have a small allowance? After all, you'd have to pay rent to somebody else if you moved the health clinic. I'm willing to work if I can find somebody to bloody well hire me, but what can I do? I've no saleable abilities. You never trained me to earn my own living. I'm useless."

"I don't think you should have another drink, darling. If you'd only stop, we could perhaps give you a job in the hydrotherapy department."

"Pointing a hose at fat old men?"

"You can be so incredibly vulgar at times."

"What exactly *is* the position of the estate—or should I ask that solicitor in St. Austell?"

"By all means do so, but I can tell you myself. As your trustee I leased Trelawney to the health clinic on a full repairing lease for fifty years at a rental that amounts to the yearly interest on the loans secured by the estate. It's already been explained to your husband's lawyers. They plagued the life out of me for months as soon as you were married."

"Eh? Could you say that again please. . . . " Her mother did so. "Does that mean that when I'm sixty-eight I will *still* have Grandfather's debt around my neck although you will have been raking in the profits for half a century? What happens if you die tomorrow?"

Her mother looked into the fire. "Selma and I have drawn up identical wills. We both own fifty percent of the shares in the clinic, and upon the death of either shareholder the surviving shareholder may purchase the shares at par value. I saw no reason to mention that to Robert's lawyers—they were unpleasantly aggressive—but I suppose *you* ought to know now."

"You mean that if you died, then Selma would get the lease of Trelawney?"

"Darling, I wasn't trained to earn my living, either. When Grandfather died I had to accept the business proposition that Selma put to me. Of course, now that I've had five years' experience, I could run the place by myself, but don't you remember the state I was in at the time? And it's a full repairing lease. You'll get the place back in perfect condition, which will increase the value."

"Doesn't sound as if that's a bonus. Grandfather always kept it in perfect condition."

"I do wish you wouldn't raise your voice, the patients might hear. To be quite frank, the other directors and I have already discussed the possibility of paying you a small allowance."

"Who are the other directors?"

"Selma and her accountant. *Our* accountant."

"And what did they say?"

"Mr. Hillshaw thought we *might* manage three pounds a week."

"Four. Plus the running costs and upkeep of the cottage."

"Certainly *not* the running costs."

"Then I'll go to St. Austell tomorrow."

"Oh, all right then. But no telephone bills."

"No telephone, darling."

CHAPTER 27

BOTH MEN WERE sweating in the heat of the helicopter cabin. A thousand feet below, their own shadow bobbed ahead of them over the south Sydonian desert. Flying high over Sydon you could see to the north the narrow, green plain, split by the twisting silver ribbon of the river as it slithered west to the Red Sea from its source high in the magnificent mountain peaks of the eastern hills. Beyond the mountains, farther to the east, the implacable beige monotony of the desert was broken only by the roofs of Fenza.

Abdullah took the helicopter up a bit higher. He always felt happy and unfettered in the air, free from fear in a way that he could never be on earth. Both he and Suliman had learned to fly while they were at Sandhurst, and Abdullah had later qualified as a helicopter pilot. A helicopter was the ideal means for moving around his country swiftly and in relative secrecy.

They were flying south, away from Semira, his capital city. The old city stood on the north bank and upon its summit stood the Royal Palace, which overlooked closely packed, dazzling, white-domed rooftops, the narrow lanes between them and the small *souk* in the middle. All week there had been a sense of foreboding in the *souk*; the market had been unusually subdued, full of sullen, worried faces and the bark of sudden argument. Troublemakers were at work again, with all their usual slogans. Abdullah reflected that it was perhaps a mixed blessing to send young people abroad to be educated; they returned with impractical, radical ideas, loosely described as "progressive," and talked of establishing a so-called people's republic where no one would ever again fear or want for work.

The previous evening the King had granted an urgently requested audience to the United States Ambassador. Together they had strolled under vine-covered trellises, along walks planted with low herbs, where no eavesdropping was possible.

The Ambassador had warned the King that another attempt to kill him could be expected within two days and that the plot was apparently planned at a very high level. Neither man was surprised. During the previous year, the young ruler of Sydon had made it clear that he intended to make many changes, that he intended to root out the cynical corruption and lethargy with which his country was run. Unfortunately, the older politicians did not wish the old ways to be changed and the Western-educated students wanted radical changes that included ousting the King. Trouble was only to be expected.

Ostensibly, the helicopter was flying south along the brilliant azure line of the sea, toward the southern border and royal seashore palace of Dinada, that beautiful steel-and-glass building designed by Philip Johnson for Abdullah's father.

But suddenly the helicopter dipped and turned seventy degrees off course to the east, heading inland over the desert that composed seventy percent of Sydon.

Within ten minutes they spotted the low, black goathide tent and a small group of tethered camels. The helicopter landed a hundred yards away from the animals, in order to alarm them as little as possible.

One young officer of the Desert Patrol and two officers of the First Armored Regiment ran toward the helicopter and stood at the salute outside the circumference of the great blades. His gun drawn, Suliman waited until the blades were still and then jumped down.

"*Salam Alaikum.*"

"*Alaikum a Salam.*"

After the traditional greeting, the men bowed to their king, who entered the low tent, quickly sat cross-legged and motioned to the others to do likewise. There was a pause, then the usual exchange of extravagant compliments and declarations of devotion. Suliman, who had grown up with two of the officers, nodded to them.

"Your Majesty, it is said that the life of Your Sacred Majesty is in danger. This we know, for one of us was approached by a senior officer and promised higher rank if total unquestioning obedience was promised for the next few days."

He paused and looked, as if for confirmation, to his two brother officers. "Fortunes are being offered in bribes to the army, this we also know." The other officers nodded, black eyes harsh above beak noses.

"And we have been warned that the First Armored Regiment will shortly be ordered to leave on a long march, a secret night exercise." There was another pause, and again the speaker looked around, as if for support, before he continued. "Your Majesty, we fear we shall be ordered to surround the capital and bar all exits.

"If such a thing were allowed to happen, in the confusion either a civil war might start in Sydon or an outside power, such as those dogs, the Saudi, might quickly gain control of Semira, then the radio station and thus the whole country."

He drew a final deep breath. "We suspect there are traitors at all points in the army. We even doubt the loyalty of those who command us, and we wish to receive our orders directly from Your Majesty."

Except for the harsh desert wind, there was silence as all four men waited for Abdullah to speak. Conscious of the dangers risked by these men in approaching Suliman to set up the meeting, Abdullah lifted his chin. Even when sitting cross-legged in olive fatigues, he had great presence and radiated tough energy. He said firmly, "Remember, O, my brothers, that I was appointed by Allah to lead you!" He lifted his left hand and slowly pointed at each man in turn. "All of you remember the personal oath you swore to me when I became your leader. Our entire nation will applaud your action when they hear of it."

He folded his arms across his chest and slightly raised his voice. "Justice is on our side! Now we will move swiftly without mercy to wipe this menace from our land!"

There was a pause, then each man reaffirmed his loyalty, after which they discussed possible plots, suspected plotters and dates for their execution.

It was decided that all three officers would accept any offer made by the plotters and would then try to warn Suliman, by telephone or in person.

The meeting took less than a quarter of an hour.

* * *

In the darkness, small waves slapped against the hull of the sixty-foot cabin cruiser, hove-to three miles offshore and north of Semira harbor. Leaning over the bridge and straining his ears, the Greek captain could just hear the muffled oars of the two inflatable dinghies. Then he glimpsed the occasional phosphorescent flash, the occasional herring-silver glitter of their bubbling wake, as one by one the dinghies pulled away from the rope ladder that dangled from the main deck to the waterline. Even so far out, they dared not risk the noise of the outboard engines. Lucky there was no moon. Under cover of darkness, without being seen or heard, both dinghies should be able to make the harbor and nose in among the fishing boats lined up against the northern quay. They ought to be able to be there before dawn.

The captain squinted through his night glasses at the town. It seemed quiet and peaceful. There were a few lights around the port, although not many at this late hour. The dinghies had taken enough stuff aboard to blow the whole harbor to bits. Thank God it was out of his hold at last. There didn't seem to have been any new developments since yesterday afternoon when, at the seashore palace of Dinada, he had been ordered to cast off at twenty minutes' notice. His Majesty had dashed aboard with his bodyguard and ordered him to set off at full speed on a northwesterly course—final destination Cairo.

As soon as they were out of sight of shore and darkness had fallen, they had doused all lights, gone about and then, steering by compass, headed north through the night toward Semira.

Eight of Abdullah's armed guards were now in the lead boat. The best of the soldiers were with His Majesty in the second boat. Nobody knew who, how many, or whether in fact anyone awaited them at the harbor rendezvous.

The previous afternoon, one of Suliman's contact officers in the First Armored Regiment had telephoned Suliman at Dinada Palace and suggested a hunting trip to shoot partridge in the desert; he had offered to set off immediately by car for Dinada with a few friends. Suliman had his answer ready. He would prefer to go fishing. He would meet his friend just before dawn at Semira harbor, between the low customs shed and the harbormaster's office.

"Impossible, I have already agreed to a hunting trip."

"Then arrange for other friends to meet my fishermen."

Suliman had then reported to Abdullah that it sounded as if a force of armored cars was about to leave Semira barracks for the Dinada Palace, in order to kill him.

Neither King Abdullah nor Suliman had any means of knowing whether the young officer would have had time to arrange the "fishing trip" and whether a party of loyalist fighters would await them at the harbor, but both men knew that after their flight from Dinada they would never again see the young officer responsible for it. His telephone call to the palace from the barracks would have been logged automatically and he would automatically be killed upon suspicion of being an informer.

They were now close to the shoreline; there were only two hundred meters between the lead dinghy and the harbor mouth. Now they could smell the small port odors—diesel oil, rope, sailcloth, tar, rotting fish, urine, iodine.

A low whistle through the darkness and their oars were raised. Under their own momentum the boats slid into the treacle-black harbor, turned to port and nosed quietly in among the fishing boats. As they docked, a barefoot sailor from each dinghy heaved himself up onto the stone quay and lashed the painter to a metal bollard. Another low whistle and the sailors helped the soldiers to scramble up, then the men and their burdens became part of the black night.

Behind the dark bulk of the customs sheds stood two armored cars, each containing a driver and an officer. Silently the soldiers crammed into the two vehicles, leaving one on guard with the extra guns and ammunition for which there was not enough space in the cars. "To the barracks," Abdullah commanded.

Tense and silent, safety catches released, the grim band drove slowly away from the harbor and threaded its way through the winding, unlit streets that led to the northern gates; massive, iron-studded, ten-foot-high wood slabs, they were set into the six-foot-thick stone walls that surrounded the old town. As usual at night, a sentry stood on duty, and as they approached he lifted his gun and challenged them.

The officer leaned out. "We wish you to open the gates and stand aside for His Majesty King Abdullah."

"Tonight we have orders not to open the gates," said the sentry, uncertain.

"Soldier," Abdullah commanded. "It is I, your King. Advance so you may see that it is indeed your King who wishes to pass."

Slowly the sentry moved forward, still uncertain, and peered into the car. He immediately stiffened to the salute upon recognizing Abdullah's impassive face, the dark eyes staring through him, then he ran to unbar the gates, shouting to the sentry on the other side to do likewise.

After they had pushed the heavy gates back against the walls and secured them, two of Abdullah's men jumped out to replace the sentries, who were silently motioned into the second car. Both vehicles shot forward toward the Semira barracks.

Light was just dawning as the two vehicles sped toward the main entrance of the low, brick-built barracks. Already trucks were lumbering slowly from the huge inner barrack square, out through the three arched exits. Abdullah's two vehicles jerked to a stop outside the first gate. All doors were thrown open and all occupants of the cars, except Abdullah and one driver, sprang to the ground, their guns at the ready. The two officers marched briskly up to the surprised sentries and halted the stream of trucks to allow Abdullah's car to drive into the courtyard.

The car stopped against the inner wall and Abdullah's escort immediately surrounded the car, while their King leaped onto the roof of the vehicle. Wearing the impressive scarlet *kaffiyeh* of the Palace Guard, he looked a brave and fierce figure as he announced that he, their rightful King, had come to lead his men against all traitors.

There was a burst of cheering as swarthy soldiers ran to his car and surrounded it. Fierce, black-bearded, hawk-nosed faces were upturned to his: delighted shouts rang out: scimitars were flourished. It was at least five minutes before Abdullah could quell the roars of delight and continue with his speech.

"All army personnel are to obey my orders only, issued from my mouth alone and not passed through officers or NCOs," he shouted. "No one is to leave the barracks until disloyal officers have been arrested! I now declare a state of emergency, during which my army—led by me—will assume sole control of the country."

After further shouts of support, Abdullah continued, "Parliament will be dissolved and the Constitution suspended until order prevails in our land! All political meetings are banned and from tonight there will be a dawn-to-dusk curfew throughout the land. Until further notice, no political speakers will be allowed on the radio." More cries of approval. After which, Abdullah roared, "Any rioting crowds will be immediately dispersed by mounted troops with tear gas, and anyone who erects barricades or tries to stone my troops from rooftops will be shot on sight!"

Half an hour after entering the barracks, Abdullah was able to hold a staff conference, after ordering his entire army to remain in barracks or camp and expect a visit from the King. Nearly all the plotters were senior officers; very few NCOs and no rank and file seemed to have been involved. To Abdullah's lasting bitterness, the plot had been engineered by the commander-in-chief of the army and included not only two other generals, but also three members of his Inner Council of Five, including the new prime minister. This was a greater blow than he had expected.

That afternoon, at the Royal Palace of Semira, the King summoned a meeting of the remaining two members of the Inner Council as well as all army officers above the rank of major. The murmur of voices in the great cool hall was hushed as the throb, throb, throb of the drums was heard outside.

Suddenly, King Abdullah appeared in the arched doorway. This was a very different figure from the fierce, scarlet-cloaked soldier-leader who had stood on the roof of the car that morning, legs astride, brandishing a scimitar that flashed in the rays of the rising sun. Wearing an immaculate white ceremonial uniform with gold epaulettes, Abdullah moved slowly forward, a ruler rather than a leader.

Two men stood silent on the topmost terrace of the palace, looking down over the white rooftops of Sydon. The sun, a blood-red ball, was sinking below the horizon; above the dark sea, the sky was streaked with orange and yellow. Suliman risked a respectful grin. "That went well, Sire."

"Yes, I rather thought it did. Would you please arrange to have the former prime minister executed in about three days' time, and also any of the other political plotters who haven't already fled to Syria, where they will no doubt continue to conspire against me."

"It is wise to take all possible precautions, Sire."

Abdullah watched the sun disappear and the sky fade. He reached a decision. "That reminds me, will you please invite El Gawali here as fast as possible. To arrange the marriage. I can't put it off any longer. I need sons."

CHAPTER 28

CHRIST, WHAT A noise! She wouldn't answer the door! . . .

Pagan decided to ignore the door knocker and then whoever it was would go away. She was about to put her head under the pillow when she heard a female voice singing, "Happy birthday to you! Happy birthday to you!" The knocker was being thumped in rhythm with the song. *Christ* her head . . . surely . . . Could that be *Kate's* voice?

Pagan opened her eyes, sat up, shut her eyes again, staggered out of bed, opened her eyes, picked her dressing gown off the floor, tried to put it on, couldn't find the sleeves, threw it down, pulled the bed quilt around her, then carefully felt her way down the stairs and opened the door. Above a sheaf of sunny, yellow daffodils, she saw Kate's smiling face.

Kate stopped smiling when she saw Pagan's red-rimmed eyes, her puffy face and shaggy hair. She stepped forward and hugged Pagan as hard as she could. God, the smell of her breath. . . .

"Come inside quickly, it's cold. Why were you singing?"

"Because it's almost your birthday."

"Is it?" said Pagan indifferently. "When *is* the twenty-seventh? Good God, I'll be thirty. . . . I think it's thirty; if this is 1962 I'll be thirty." She led Kate down the stone-flagged passage into the sitting room. "That means I've been living down here for over eight years. Seems only yesterday I moved in. . . . Thank you, I'll stick them in a vase. . . . How did you know I was here?" She wasn't sure she wanted to see Kate, now removing the smart, khaki tweed jacket of her Mary Quant trouser suit.

Kate glanced at the sofa covered with dog hair and sat on a wooden Windsor chair. "I met that woman Phillippa last week. You remember, the big, bossy one with the fuzzy red hair that we used to play bridge with in Cairo? She told me about your divorce so I phoned your mother straightaway."

For years Kate had blamed Pagan for stealing her fiancé. But Phillippa had told Kate the gossip that most of Cairo society had known for years and thought Kate knew—the Byzantine subterfuge by which Robert had parted the two friends. It was Robert who had been traitorous, not Pagan. Now that Kate was happily married, she had immediately responded with remorse and guilt to the fact that she had been tricked into losing her childhood friend.

"I saw Phillippa about a week ago and I came as soon as I could, darling. I thought I'd surprise you. You were quite right to divorce Robert. He was my idea of a prize shit."

"You might have told me."

There was an uneasy pause and then Kate burst into tears. "I can't bear to see you like this."

"Don't *you* start," said Pagan. "I'm perfectly happy . . . I don't spray tears all over the place like you and Maxine . . . d'you remember, it was always either giggles or sobs? Can't think why women cry so much . . . I'll see if there's any tea."

She went to the kitchen, had a quick nip from the vodka bottle and eventually produced a tray of ill-assorted china with some old ginger biscuits and marmalade.

They chatted about nothing much for ten minutes, then Kate asked gently, "Why have you hidden yourself away like this, Pagan? Why don't any of your old friends in London know that you're here?"

"Because I didn't *tell* them, darling. . . . I simply didn't want to see anybody after that three-parties-a-night life in Cairo."

She gave a sad laugh. "I felt so ashamed of myself and Mama was obviously ashamed of me as well. . . . Nobody of our school year has been divorced." She poured tea from a blue tin teapot. "I just wanted to hide from people. . . . A few chums got in touch with Mama, or wrote to me suggesting a visit, but I never answered the letters. . . . The fact is, I never knew how I would react to anyone," she sighed. "I looked normal on the outside but inside my feelings were bubbling. If anybody spoke to me in a kind voice, I wanted to crumple up and cry. Idiotic, wasn't it? . . . I used to get a lump in my throat and couldn't answer them back. So I avoided talking by avoiding people. I only spoke to the villagers when it couldn't be helped and I dashed upstairs and hid when I heard the postman's bicycle bell." She added milk to the cup with a shaking hand.

Kate was stunned by the change in Pagan. How had that confident, vibrant creature changed into this confused, nervous wreck? Her speech was rambling and disconnected.

"Don't you see *anyone*, Pagan?" she asked.

Pagan shrugged her shoulders. "I've become a bit of a hermit, except for occasionally seeing Mama. . . . One day I heard Mama explain to one of her patients that I was a recluse and that's why I talk to myself. That gave me a laugh." She handed a cracked pink cup to Kate. "Matter of fact I've never understood what's wrong with talking to yourself; your jokes are always laughed at . . . you always win your arguments . . . it demonstrates a happy degree of self-acceptance." She sipped from her earthenware mug. "You don't have to finish that biscuit, it's about six months old. . . . Don't think I was unhappy. I had Buster for company and every day for the first six months I woke up and, oh, it was just utter bliss to see that Robert wasn't there on the next pillow. I'm comfortable enough here, listening to the radio and reading. I'm afraid it's not very tidy at the moment because Mrs. Hocken broke her ankle falling over a puppy, so she hasn't cleaned for a couple of months."

"Don't you still ride?"

"Well, I keep meaning to get a horse, but I always put it off until next week, like everything else. Mama sold the horses and the stables are now massage booths and a gymnasium. . . . More tea?"

She held out another ginger biscuit to Buster but dropped it. There was a moment's silence. Then Pagan said, "Oh, dear, why weren't we sent into this life with an instruction manual? My trouble is that I don't seem to learn from my mistakes. I don't just *repeat* my mistakes, I make *new* ones. . . . When I look back,

I suppose everything started to go wrong in Switzerland. Since then, everything I got involved with looked wonderful to begin with and ended in disaster. . . . Now I'm just permanently tired. Tired of everything. Tired of failure. Tired of life. So, I retired."

She put her hands behind her head and gazed up at the ceiling. Kate quickly slipped her ginger biscuit into her handbag. There was another pause, then Pagan said, "That's enough of me. You've now heard everything that I've done here for the last eight years. Nothing. . . . Unlike old Maxine. I sometimes see photographs of her in newspapers—not that I often read them, I just listen to the nine o'clock news and thank God that none of it is about me. . . . Amazing how old Maxine's sort of zoomed into being a glamour puss. One of the movers and shakers as they say. . . . Suppose the rest of us could be described as the shaken and the still shaking."

Pagan stretched her arms and yawned. "Now what's happened to *you* in the last ten years, Kate?"

"I was heartbroken over Robert," Kate said, and sipped her tea, "although it seems ludicrous now. After that, I went out on the same old round with anyone who asked me—anything rather than stay at home. It was parties, parties, parties until I met darling Toby. Then after we were married we had a far more quiet life." She took another sip. "But let's not talk about me this evening." She finished her lukewarm tea and put down the cup. "How about walking up to Trelawney? It's such a lovely day. The woods are full of bluebells."

"No need to be in such a hurry," Pagan said, picking up the tea tray. "If you wait long enough to clean the car it always rains. Old Arabic proverb." She carried the tray toward the kitchen and the vodka bottle that had been quickly hidden under a tea cozy. Whoever he was, Kate's husband could obviously afford Gucci shoes and a Hermès handbag, Pagan noticed.

While Pagan was banging away in the kitchen, Kate surveyed the living room—books piled on the floor, old newspapers piled on the chairs, half-empty teacups, a table covered with ring marks and cigarette scars, overflowing ashtrays, dog hair everywhere. Her first thought was to clean up Pagan and then the cottage; it could be a charming little home. Kate's second thought was to see Pagan's mother before taking any action. Why hadn't *she* done anything? The bloody woman was supposed to specialize in drunks, wasn't she?

They walked up the path through the woods, admiring the bluebells as they went. Past a mass of dark green rhododendrons, they crossed the steel cattle grid that supposedly stopped the deer from getting onto the main road. They climbed slightly uphill, over a muddy field of buttercups and then across the well-trimmed lawn that surrounded the beautiful stone house. In front of the conservatory was a ten-foot-high, curved, see-through, plastic shelter. "The new heated outdoor swimming pool," Pagan explained. They walked through the conservatory, now filled with glistening chrome—the bicycles and huge mechanical rubber belts for massaging the buttocks. Once past the rows of pink-faced guests, cycling hard to nowhere, they went into the hall and climbed the six-foot-wide, purple-carpeted stairs that led to Pagan's mother's study.

Mrs. Trelawney looked up from her desk, over her horn-rimmed glasses. "Nice to see you, Kate," she said, as if she'd last seen Kate yesterday. "You haven't changed a bit." With neat movements she removed her glasses, folded them and placed them in a crocodile case. They shook hands; the marmoreal temperature of Mrs. Trelawney's hand matched her welcome. She rang a bell and they drank lapsang suchong from rose-decorated Minton china. Then Kate was shown around Trelawney.

After her tour Kate managed to steer Mrs. Trelawney to one side. "I can only stay down here for a week," she said in a low voice that, nonetheless, conveyed her fury. "I want to tidy up Pagan and the cottage as soon as possible. I'm sure you can let me have a couple of your cleaners tomorrow; I'd also like to take all the treatments that you offer, and I want Pagan to take them with me. Perhaps you could give me the bill for both of us."

"Frightfully kind of you," Mrs. Trelawney said in a polite voice, as if she were commenting on the view, "but do please be my guest on the machines. I'm afraid that treatments might be a little difficult to arrange because the appointments book is already full."

"Well, cancel a few," Kate said coldly, and went back to join Pagan by the swimming pool.

They drove into St. Austell in Kate's silver Karmann Ghia. First, Kate bought food: meat, cheese, fruit, Bath Oliver biscuits, pickled onions, two tins of pâté de foie gras, a box of homemade flapjacks, a honeycomb, clotted cream, black cherry jam, stone-ground bread, some Bendicks Bittermints and (because they were so pretty) a little bottle of crystalized violets. She also bought a new set of pots and pans, some buttercup yellow towels, flowered sheets and scented soap for the bathroom. Pagan protested but Kate firmly said, "Birthday present," as she scribbled another check for a couple of yellow-striped reclining chairs for the garden. Finally, she took Pagan to Jaeger and bought her a lavender cashmere sweater and matching tweed skirt with plenty of hem to let down; then she chose another sweater and skirt in sage green.

Pagan had been fidgety since pub opening time at eleven-thirty in the morning, but Kate didn't let her friend out of her sight. In order to avoid alcohol, Kate decided not to have lunch at a hotel or a pub, so she bought a couple of steaming onion-and-meat-filled Cornish pasties, which they ate in the car. Pagan shivered as she dusted crumbs from her skirt.

"Why are you wearing that mackintosh and not a coat," asked Kate, "when you know how quickly the weather turns nasty down here? . . . I suppose you *do* possess a coat?"

"Well, I *did* have one," Pagan said, "but I left it somewhere. One didn't need a heavy coat in Cairo."

"Your mother was wearing a *mink* jacket this morning."

"Well, if she gave me something like that I'd lose it," Pagan said. "You know how untidy I am." She was not convincing.

Suddenly Kate remembered. "Whatever happened to Abdullah's cloak?"

"My God, I bet it's still in the attic. She never let me wear it, you know," said Pagan brightening. "Didn't want me to lose my reputation!" She hooted with laughter and cheered up.

They drove back to Trelawney. "If it's still there," Pagan's mother said vaguely, "it'll probably be in one of the cardboard boxes in the east wing attic. You'll see about forty boxes labeled 'clothes.' "

After looking through half the dusty cardboard boxes, Pagan gave a shout of triumph and pulled out glistening folds of black Persian lamb. "Oh, heavens, moths!"

And indeed the beautiful soft black folds were bald in patches. "But it is wearable," said Kate, "it's warm and I'll get it recut for you in the summer. *Next* birthday present."

That evening they lay on the rug in front of the fire, as they used to when they were schoolgirls, and talked. "Looking back," Kate mused, "I can't think what either of us saw in Robert. He was such a stuffed shirt behind that young-Cary-Grant mask. That awful, rigid, public school mold—all his lot, those Hooray-Henrys, were terrified of putting a foot out of line. I mean you can't imagine Robert saying piss off in public, can you?"

Pagan thought not. "I can't think how you ever fell for him, Kate. I really fell in love with Egypt, not Robert," she said dreamily. "It was so warm, so ancient and mysterious. You know I don't really like parties, but I *loved* the attention, I loved being the belle of Cairo, it was so soothing after the pain of . . . well, it stopped me thinking about Abdi."

"In one way Robert was a bit like Abdi," Kate added thoughtfully. "Unlike the Hooray-Henrys, Robert used to be very good at supplying your every want—and even wants you never knew you had. Then, just when you got used to having everything supplied—as if it were Christmas every day—he would disappear to Cairo and it would all stop so suddenly that you missed it dreadfully."

She paused, then added, "And another thing, Robert didn't try to get you into bed like all the other scalpers. Robert always wanted to stop when you wanted to stop."

"With good reason!" hooted Pagan, and they both giggled until it hurt, as they hadn't done since their schooldays.

"What about sex?" Kate asked curiously. "What have you done about that for the last few years?"

Pagan sighed. "Once I had a little fling with one of the patients. . . . I'd been to see Mama and he followed me back to the cottage. We had a jolly old time for a couple of days. He went back pissed to the gills—I've never seen Mama so furious. I was not to interfere with her patients/bread and butter/reputation/life, etcetera. Very unnerving.

"A couple of months later, I imported a hitchhiker, one of those irresistible blond hunks. That lasted for about four days and then, when he thought I'd gone for a walk, I caught him yanking open the drawers of my desk. I got the feeling he was looking for money, but I always keep cash in the toe of my spare gum boots, so I tiptoed away, then crashed in. I told him my mother was coming to stay for a few days, so he'd have to leave. He asked for money for the train ticket to London and was pretty nasty when I wouldn't give it to him . . . anyway, I thought that maybe the next pickup would strangle me, hack me up neatly with the bread knife, pack me in a suitcase and dump me in the left-luggage at St. Austell station and nobody would miss me for days. So I decided to forgo the pleasure. You know sex has never really been that important to me. There's always masturbation, but really after a bit I didn't bother. I didn't seem to need it."

The following morning when two stout cleaning ladies appeared, Kate shooed Pagan out for a walk with Buster. Four hours later the cottage was clean and tidy, food lined the cupboards, a fire was burning in the sitting room grate, and Kate had planted a little basket with primrose. Exhausted, Kate thought she would open some of the pâté when Pagan got back.

But Pagan was already back. Kate found her after the cleaners had left, when she went to get more logs for the fire. Pagan was lying asleep on the floor of the woodshed with two Guinness bottles at her side and an empty hip flask in her hand. Chill with horror, Kate shook her awake. "Darling, darling you'll catch your death out here. Come in and have a hot bath."

She helped Pagan stumble into the kitchen, then ran a bath for her. Pagan's eyes were half-closed and she was beaming as Kate washed her face. "Nanny, Nanny, mind the shope doesn't go in my eyes," she gurgled, before slipping under the water.

Pagan was an amiable drunk, but a heavy one. By the time she had been dried and lugged to bed with a hot water bottle under the patchwork quilt, Kate was exhausted and very worried. She had something to eat and then, at six in the evening, she took a cup of black coffee up to Pagan's bedroom.

"*Why do you get drunk?*" she burst out crossly. "When did it start?"

Pagan scowled; she had a headache; she felt queasy; she felt without energy or interest. Nonetheless, she sensed that it was now or never. She had never admitted to herself or anyone else that she was a drunk. But now she did.

"In Cairo," she said eventually. "That's when it started. A couple of drinks made those endless evenings with the same stuffy people a bit more bearable. And drink would blot out the reality of having to go home with Robert afterward. Then in the mornings Robert liked to start the day with a quarrel; he enjoyed a row, the way some people enjoy tennis or Canasta. Whatever I'd done, it was always because I was lazy and useless and stupid. He was very convincing." She gave a tired sigh. "I used to stay in bed until he'd left for the office . . . then I'd numb the memory by sloshing some vodka into the fresh mango juice." She felt for Kate's hand. "I never meant to get drunk when I had a drink. I still don't, I never feel I *need* it, I just feel, 'why *not?*' And then I have another, then just a little one, then another and another, until I can't remember how many." She held the hand tight. "In Cairo we never once mentioned it, but I *know* Robert knew about my drinking. He once let slip that he knew I'd been sick in the night because I'd left the seat up, so he *must* have known." She shivered.

"I mean, normal wives aren't sick in the night, are they? Of course, what he wanted was a wife who was sick in the morning, but there I was, labeled 'frigid' and 'barren.' Nothing like spiked mango juice for that particular condition, and I knew why Robert didn't want to talk about the booze. He didn't want to feel gruesomely guilty about it."

"But it's eight years since you left Robert!"

"Then my sense of inadequacy is eight years old. . . . I thought I'd feel better as soon as I left him, that the depression would be wiped away as soon as I got back to England. But it wasn't." She paused and plucked at the patchwork quilt. "I felt a sudden gulf of gloom when I left Cairo, because I knew I'd burned my boats. I stupidly expected Mama to meet me when I went through customs at London airport. . . . I hadn't seen her for two years, but I always wrote to her every week and I'd cabled her to say that I was coming back."

Another pause and this time the quilt was carefully smoothed. "But she wasn't there." Kate squeezed her hand sympathetically. "So I waited and waited until suddenly, standing there in the middle of the arrivals lounge, I completely lost my nerve. It's difficult to explain, but suddenly I wasn't certain of anything; I couldn't have told you the time, I felt so unsure and incapable. And then I suddenly felt *terrified* of being on my own."

She gulped and paused for a moment. "Odd, because I'd never been close to Mama, so why did the roof suddenly fall in when she didn't meet me at the airport?" Kate gripped the hand tighter in silent sympathy and Pagan continued. "I suppose that was the first time I realized I was alone in life and it was a moment of stark terror. As a wife I'd been a failure, as a daughter I wasn't worth meeting at the airport and as a mother I really was a nonstarter, as we all knew. . . . Darling, I think my hand's going to turn blue if you hold it any harder."

There was another long pause. "Then I found I had hardly any money and that bitch, Selma, was totally in control of my mother. She really adores the old cow. That hurt." For a moment Kate thought she was going to see Pagan in tears. "I just had a feeling of futile emptiness, a flat sensation that nothing—*nothing*—lay ahead.

"Then the feeling tilted, it became steeper and steeper and I felt as if I were running too fast downhill and couldn't stop. There was a black hole at the bottom. It got worse and worse." She clutched Kate's hands until Kate winced. "It made me panic, and when I panicked I drank. I didn't need an excuse to die, I needed an excuse to live, and I almost ran out of excuses. If I woke up in the night I felt suicidal, but if I drank, I didn't wake up in the night. So I drank. Drink blotted out the depression; it made me feel like a real person, like the person I was and the person I might have been. When I was drunk I didn't feel like a failure."

"Slower, slower," said Kate, alarmed by this sudden agitation.

Pagan took no notice and continued as if speaking to herself. "When I was small I used to hide from my nanny and escape into a fantasy world where my real friends lived; animals who talked and wore aprons and slippers and had teapots. Life became a bit like that again. Reality was too fearful, so I blotted it out. Once I fell into the bath when I was drunk and knocked myself out. I woke up in the bath with all my clothes on and my hand hurting like hell. Luckily there wasn't any water in the bath or I might have drowned."

"Oh, Pagan," Kate said, "I can only be with you a few days. Darling, won't you please, please try? Can't you stay in bed all the time and I'll look after you? Living alone here could be positively dangerous."

"Yes," agreed Pagan. "I once passed out on the sofa with a cigarette in my hand and my book caught fire. Luckily it only made a mess of the book. But I *did* manage to stop smoking, and I don't drive a car; even when I'm pissed, I'm not very dangerous on a bicycle."

"Pagan, there must be someone. Isn't there *anyone* who can help you? A local doctor? The vicar? They obviously all know you're an alc—That you drink."

"Nobody knows. I'm *very* careful. I bury the bottles. I'm very careful in the village. . . . Oh, you're right, Kate, I don't suppose I've really fooled anyone. But I'm *not* an alcoholic. You're not to say that. Alcoholics are old down-and-out tramps who sleep in city doorways at night. I like getting drunk. There's a difference."

"Pagan, how can you be so stupid? What does it matter what you call it? You're wrecking your life. Can't you go to a doctor in London?"

"I'll tell you what I'll do, Kate. While you're here I honestly will *try* not to drink. And if I lie or cheat, I'll tell you afterward. I can't offer more than that."

For the rest of the evening Pagan was restless and twitchy, drank innumerable cups of tea, and only picked at Kate's cheese omelette. The next day they walked up to Trelawney where Pagan not only had a massage, a facial and a manicure, but had her hair styled and her eyebrows plucked.

Her hands started to shake that evening. Her teeth chattered, and then her whole body started to shiver. Kate put her to bed again, spooned chicken broth into her, and crooned as if to a sick child.

"For heaven's sake," Pagan muttered weakly. "stop *henning* around me. This is what you wanted, isn't it?"

Wrapped in a coverlet, Kate spent the night in an armchair in Pagan's room. Neither of them slept much. Kate wanted to talk to a doctor, but Pagan made her promise not to. "Everyone around here knew Grandfather. I know I'm a disgrace to the Trelawneys, but I don't want everyone else to know."

The next morning Kate went to see Pagan's mother. She wasted no words. "You *must* know that Pagan's a drunk. Why haven't you taken her to a specialist or to some hospital or organization that can help her?"

"I can't see that Pagan's condition is any business of yours, Kate. Or mine," Mrs. Trelawney said in her well-bred, don't-touch-me voice. "Pagan is a grown woman. She's thirty years old. As a matter of fact, when I suggested she see a therapist she said she could never see the word 'therapist' without stopping after the 'the.' "

"But why didn't you *insist?*"

"Because there's nothing *wrong* with her. It's just that she *drinks* too much. There's nothing wrong with her head. All she needs is self-discipline. Psychiatrists are for the mentally ill and there's no mental illness in our family."

"You mean that you refuse to face the possibility of mental illness in your family."

"If there was anything I could do, then I would have done it, because, quite candidly, it's such a bad advertisement for the clinic. I've spoken to our doctor about her on several occasions, and Pagan has seen him, but the fact is that she's seemingly bent on self-destruction and I can't make her do anything about it. I never could."

"You never tried," Kate snapped, storming out of the room.

After a second sleepless night, Pagan's teeth were chattering and her body shook. Kate figured that when her body needed sleep, Pagan would sleep. Until then it didn't matter much whether or not Pagan slept. It wasn't as if she had any urgent appointments.

For three days Pagan trembled and was unable to sleep. She couldn't walk or stand without help. On the fourth night Pagan still couldn't sleep and retched horribly, but at dawn she suddenly calmed down and fell into a doze.

"I'm proud of you," Kate said gently as she dipped strips of bread into a boiled egg and fed them to Pagan in bed.

"Oh, darling, so am I. No, I can't force any more down. I never dreamed that stopping would be so absolutely grim, I had no idea that I was so dependent on the bloody stuff."

Kate worried that when she returned to London Pagan would return to her drinking. Pagan wasn't as worried as Kate. "You see, darling, for the first time I really *want* to stop. After all, what's the alternative? Do I continue to knock back cooking sherry for the next twenty years?"

"We'll put in a telephone and I'll ring you every day. At least you'll be able to phone me if you get in a panic. There's one thing I want you to promise me. That you won't be ashamed of telling me that you . . . if you can't make it."

"No, I've already said that if I lie to you, I'll own up afterward," said Pagan.

Kate went off, though not very hopefully. Until the telephone was installed she sent a telegram or a short letter to the cottage every day. She also telephoned Alcoholics Anonymous, but was told they could be of no use unless Pagan approached them of her own free will.

CHAPTER 29

THOUGH PAGAN CONTINUED to feel exhausted, the increased comfort of the cottage cheered her up. Mrs. Hocken cleaned the cottage twice a week. Pagan started to clear up the overgrown garden, for she wanted to keep herself occupied and out of the house. She went for a long walk every morning and would continue to do so until she felt strong enough to start riding again. They had both agreed that when she was again confident on a horse, Pagan might get some horsy sort of job that she would enjoy, even if she didn't earn much.

Wrapped against the wind in her ankle-length, Persian lamb cloak, Pagan walked with Buster to a weather-beaten wooden bench on top of the cliff. There she would sit in the sun, calmed by the waves slapping far below.

But one morning, as the spring wind tore at her cloak and she slowly climbed the rise, she could see that someone was already sitting on her bench. As she approached, she could make out that the figure was a man—a black figure hunched against the gray sky.

Pagan stumped up to the summit of the cliff. She muttered a brusque "Good morning," then sat down on one end of the bench and pulled her cloak around her. She felt the raw wind on her face. The water was pale gray at the horizon and gray where it dashed against the cliffs beneath her, but the rest of the sea was black.

"Do you come here often?" her neighbor asked amiably.

"Yes," she said curtly. There was silence for another ten minutes. When the wind flung the water against the base of the cliff, Pagan could feel the tremor under her feet. The gray sky was now laced with lavender streaks, in fact, there was likely to be a storm.

"Nice day," the stranger said.

She turned and looked at him. "It's my birthday."

"Do I congratulate you?"

"No."

"Well, have a humbug." He produced a paper bag from his pocket and offered her one of the sticky peppermints. She'd never seen him before. He wasn't local and he couldn't be at the clinic with that bag of candy. "May I offer you a glass of champagne in celebration?"

There was a long silence. Then Pagan fell.

"You mean you've got a bottle *here?*"

"No, but I'm staying at the Golden Lion in the village. I should think they'd have some. Are you staying in the village?"

"Not really." Pagan hesitated, not liking to say that he was on her land.

They walked back through the woods to the saloon bar of the Golden Lion. "Mornin', Miss Pagan," the landlord said, "not often we see *you* here."

The low, empty room smelled of yesterday's beer and cigarettes. Behind the bar a row of gleaming bottles hung upside down, awaiting just one word from Pagan. There was only one bottle of champagne in the cellar. It was very old and much too sweet, but as they drank it on the upright oak settle by the fire, Pagan could feel the relaxation seep through her body.

The stranger's name was Christopher Swann, and he was staying at the Golden Lion in order to finish a book. "It's not the sort of book that anyone's likely to buy to pass away the weekend. I'm a biochemist and a virologist; the book's an account of some experimental work. A group of us are trying to prevent cancer; we're trying to discover suitable vaccinations. My lab is working on a vaccine against hepatitis B, which is strongly linked to cancer of the liver."

"Vaccination? Like a smallpox shot?"

"That was the most important shot of all."

"Did a biochemist invent it?"

"No, a country doctor called Edward Jenner. Around 1796 he noticed that dairymaids didn't seem to catch smallpox, but many of them caught cowpox, which was a relatively mild infection. So Jenner thought that perhaps if everyone had a mild attack of cowpox, then they wouldn't catch smallpox. He checked his antibody theory by vaccinating an eight-year-old boy on the arm with pus that had been drawn from an infected pustule on a dairymaid who had cowpox."

Halfway through her second glass of champagne, after Pagan had listened to the stranger's fascinating conversation for nearly an hour, she invited him to supper. "It won't be an elaborate meal," she warned, aware that she had nothing in the cupboard except a tin of pâté de foie gras and a jar of crystalized violets. He offered to escort her home, but she refused. "I'll meet you here this evening at six o'clock and take you home."

Suddenly energetic and hopeful, she flew off to Mrs. Hocken.

"Darling Mrs. Hocken, will you please, please help me? Will you clean out the cottage with me today instead of Friday? I'm having a visitor!"

Since Kate had left, not much cooking had been done at the cottage, and there was nothing in the refrigerator except half a jar of mayonnaise and a large bottle of vitamin pills. Pagan cycled back to the village and bought some thick veal chops, potatoes to bake in their jackets, salad and fresh Cheddar cheese. She also bought two bottles of wine.

She was very careful while her visitor was there; only filled her glass an inch at a time, waited until his glass was empty before refilling hers, and didn't open the second bottle of wine since he didn't seem to want any more.

But after he'd left, she immediately drank the remaining bottle and woke up at four in the morning, still in the armchair, frozen and with an aching head. She burst into tears and smashed the bottle into the fireplace, where it scattered the still-warm ashes.

Next morning she suffered terribly from self-accusation but had a clear head. While lying in her bath, she considered what to do with the bottles at the back of the woodshed that she'd hidden from Kate. She considered throwing them over the cliff. She considered having a swig right there.

She dressed, piled the bottles into her big straw shopping basket, lugged them into the wood and buried them under a pile of bracken. Then she went home and looked up "biochemistry" in her dictionary.

Christopher worked in the early morning and the afternoon. For the next three mornings, Pagan met him at the bench on the cliff. They roamed the woods and the beaches and climbed over the granite rocks above the sea line at the base of the cliffs. Together, they were soaked by salt spray, splashed on the beaches by waves that broke on the sand farther up than they expected, slipped on slime and seaweed, then walked back to hot Cornish pasties and half a pint of bitter at the Golden Lion.

Every evening, Christopher came to supper at the cottage. Mrs. Hocken was bribed, cajoled and flattered to act as Pagan's private cook. She provided soups, casseroles, pastries, even a steak-and-kidney pie with Christopher's initials in golden-brown pastry.

Every evening Pagan built a roaring fire, put classical music on the gramophone, and then they talked far into the night. She found to her surprise that, although she didn't understand it all, she was fascinated by what Christopher said as he talked about his work. Watching the firelight flicker over his face, once Pagan was so absorbed by his presence that she forgot Mrs. Hocken's cottage pie warming in the oven. It was burned black.

Pagan tried to drink only one glass of beer in the mornings, and in the evening she restricted herself to one glass of wine by pouring the rest of the bottle into Christopher's glass as fast as she could. "Are you trying to get me drunk, then take advantage of me?" he half-joked on their fourth evening together.

"I don't like to drink too much," she muttered.

But the following morning, Pagan found herself scrabbling in the wet bracken, trying desperately to remember where she had buried the bottles. When she couldn't find them, she burst into tears. Looking again, she found her treasure trove, snatched off a cork and remembered no more until hours later, when she woke up stiff and damp. It wasn't the first time she'd blacked out, but it was the first time she cared. She only had fourteen days before Christopher would return to London.

She staggered back to the cottage, took an icy shower, then walked to the clinic to make two telephone calls. First she called the Golden Lion and left a message for Christopher that though she hadn't been able to see him this morning, she would expect him for supper as usual. Then she phoned Kate and confessed.

"But can't you see him without having a drink?" asked Kate. "Plenty of people do."

"But I can't, I *can't* stop. It's so shaming. I'd have to explain . . . I can't, I can't," Pagan cried miserably. "Keep sending the telegraphs and I'll keep on trying to drink as little as possible. But I can't stop, it would look odd to him."

"Might look odder if you don't stop," Kate said.

On the seventh evening, Pagan and Christopher were soaked by a sudden squall on the way through the woods to the cottage. Pagan thought she looked terrific with her hair plastered wet against her head, striding through the rain. It was an old trick of hers to suggest a walk in the rain, and besides Pagan really loved the physical sensation of getting soaked.

In the kitchen they pulled off their wet shoes and socks and shrugged off their soggy tweed jackets. The fire had gone out in the sitting room, and Christopher bent down to relight it as Pagan rubbed her purple hands. "The only way I'm going to get warm again is by having a bath." She ran upstairs and turned on the water, recklessly pouring in far too much hyacinth oil from one of Kate's bottles.

Fragrant steam filled the bathroom. "We need a Boy Scout," Christopher called up the stairs. "I can't get this fire going."

Pagan poked her head around the door. "The wood's a bit damp. Try the firelighters in the cupboard on the right of the fireplace."

She had just submerged in the blissfully hot water when he shouted up, "There aren't any left in the box."

"Well, there's a new box in the kitchen, it's on the . . . I can't remember. . . . Wait a minute, I'll get them." Snatching off her bathcap, she wrapped her new yellow robe around her, padded down the steep stairs, and found the box of firelighters under the sink. "Might as well do it while I'm here. I understand its temperamental ways."

She knelt down to poke the firelighter under the wooden kindling and then leaned forward as she lit a match. As she did so, her dressing gown gaped open and revealed one pointed breast. Christopher leaned forward and cupped it firmly in his hand.

For a moment Pagan didn't move. There was a *whoosh* as the paper caught fire. She turned her head, her hair dripping, and the buttercup robe fell back from her naked shoulders. Then his mouth was on hers and they collapsed on the moss-green carpet.

Christopher's hand felt swiftly for her other breast. She felt his body as he tugged at her robe, pulled it open, felt between her slippery wet thighs. He softly explored her until her whole being seemed to leap toward him as he slid his body on top of hers.

He pushed steadily inside her and she gasped as their bodies started to move, both driven by his hard rhythmic thrusts. His hands held her breasts firmly and Pagan felt as though she were flying as she yielded to this insistent strength. Seagulls swooped in her head, the tides sucked in and out, she felt the pull and depth of the sea, the sweet drowning of fulfillment.

Afterward they lay together on the carpet, neither wanting to leave the other's body, neither speaking. Finally, Christopher murmured, "Fire's gone out again. How about a bath?" Leaving her wet robe and his clothes strewn over the living room, they slowly mounted the narrow staircase outside the kitchen. He stood her in the warm bath and soaped her all over, his hands sliding down her body, following the soap as he explored every part of her. Then he took the hand spray that fit over the taps, and she felt the warm sting of water caressing every inch of her body. She felt as if she were coming alive again.

Christopher hopped into the bath and they rocked together languorously in the warm scented water. Then Christopher lay back against the porcelain, and Pagan sat upon him as his hands tickled her erect pink nipples. She could feel him high inside her, as he thrust against the core of her. She wanted him to stay there forever, joined to her. Then she felt his pent-up energy inside her. He pulled her down to him and a wave of warm water swept over the bathroom floor as they laughed together in the hyacinth-scented steam.

He dried her in front of the bedroom fire, fondled her with Kate's soft yellow towels. In the dim light he embraced her, wrapped his arms hungrily around her.

Then he slowly pushed Pagan backward onto the patchwork quilt and gently spread-eagled her limbs. "I want to get to know you," he said softly. He knelt at the foot of the bed and started to stroke the sole of her left foot. Gently, teasingly, he kissed her toes and slowly licked between each one, drawing each toe into his mouth as he stroked her legs with a butterflylike touch. Pagan swooned into semiawareness, conscious only of the voluptuous sensations that were flooding her body.

"My right foot's about to march in protest," she murmured.

"Tell it we've got the whole night," Christopher said, busy tickling the back of her knee. When his fingertips, featherlight, reached up from her knee to her inner thigh, Pagan pushed them away.

"Don't. I'm horribly fat there, darling, it embarrasses me, don't touch it."

"*All* women think their thighs are too fat. Shall I tell you something? Men adore plump thighs. They don't *like* stringy, boyish muscles there. Men love that soft, yielding flesh of your inner thigh." He nibbled it gently. "For most men there's nothing more erotic than slowly sliding their hand over the taut top of a nylon stocking, past the garter, feeling the warm satin-smooth flesh, then that softer warmth, that inner promise. Lace underwear feels harsh and scratchy against the voluptuous softness of a woman's inner thigh. Look, feel for yourself." He grabbed Pagan's fingertips and, with them, he gently stroked her thigh then slowly brushed her fingers over her inner leg. "There, see? Soft, baby flesh." He made love to each leg and then each arm, and when Pagan tried to pull him to her, he pushed her firmly back upon the quilt, saying, "Later."

By the time his mouth had reached her navel, she was only conscious of the response of her body to his skilled touch. She made small, birdlike sighs, her pleasure became almost unbearable. She reached out one arm to touch his shoulder and tried again to pull him to her but was firmly pushed back on the bed. She started to stroke the gray hair on his chest, but her hand was gently laid by her side. "Please don't interrupt my work," he mumbled as his tongue reached her armpit. She felt as if she were about to faint from the tickling pleasure.

Then he was inside her again, and she felt as if the brass bedstead were slowly whirling up toward the ceiling. She was soaring ecstatically, about to fly through the sky. His thrusts were slow and insistent until the moment when she gave the wild shriek of a gull as it soars to heaven; then she felt his excitement mount as he thrust fiercely into her until, with a harsh cry, he climaxed.

They lay still and silent, warm together in the little bedroom.

CHAPTER 30

PAGAN'S MOTHER COULDN'T believe her ears. "What do you mean? You're going to get married? To *whom?*" She looked at her happy, animated daughter, glowing as only physical passion can make a woman glow. Mrs. Trelawney was even more astonished when she heard that she was about to become the mother-in-law of Sir Christopher Swann, the distinguished Director of the Anglo-American Cancer Research Institute.

Kate wasn't so thrilled. "Are you going to tell him or *not?*" she asked Pagan in the cloakroom of La Popote, a small restaurant in Walton Street, where they were dining.

"Not *yet*," said Pagan.

"Is it fair?"

"I don't care."

"He's so much older than you," said Kate doubtfully, "and Pagan, he's so big and bald. Dammit, he's an *old* man! How can you marry an *old* man?"

"Darling, he's forty-nine, old is ninety. He says he's been bald since he was thirty. It's quite sexy, you know, that shiny, hard top. If you think what it's like to have the back of your neck stroked, then that's what it's like up there, he says." She leaned forward to peer in the mirror as she dabbed her lipstick. "And he's big but not *fat*; I mean, I promise you, darling, I've seen him as nature intended. That's all muscle." She screwed back her lipstick. "Do you like this new pale pink? . . . So do I. Want to try it? . . . You must admit he looks a bit like Peter Lawford, apart from the hair, that is. And don't you love that amused look in his eyes as if he can read your innermost thoughts! It turns my knees to jelly."

"I can see you're in love with him," said Kate, deciding that the pale pink lipstick didn't suit her, "so it really doesn't matter what other people don't see in him."

"And there's another thing. He is *the* most marvelous lover. Maybe it's because he's been doing it for so long, darling, maybe that's one of the advantages of old age. But all I can say is that for the last two weeks we've hardly been out of bed. I don't have any *time* to think about booze. He knows so much about me now, he can keep me out of my skull with delight for hours and hours."

Kate was impressed. She had always wanted to know what a great lover did.

"Christopher says that he's never yet met a woman who's the same as another woman. He says we all like different things, we all—oh—*respond* in a different way, and the most important thing for a man is to get a woman to tell him what exactly she likes and wants."

"But I should die of embarrassment. If Toby asks what I like most, I always say everything."

"Christopher says that most women say everything, darling, but it's just being frightfully tactful. He says it's nearly always difficult to get them to talk because they're so madly shy of saying what they want or else they're afraid it's hrrre-volting, as Maxine used to say."

She had started to tug a comb through her hair. "It's wonderful. It's not that we get into seventy-nine different positions or that he can keep it up for hours, it's just that it's so *intimate*. Once I got over that hurdle of false modesty and was able to shut my eyes and blush in the dark and talk to him truthfully, it was such a relief. For years I'd been lying because I thought I was a freak, because the magic wand left me cold, and now Christopher has proved that I'm not a freak . . . I'll tell you what he does."

"Careful, there's someone else coming in. You can't spout this filth in front of strangers."

"I'll tell you when we get back from our honeymoon, only in the interests of education, mind. We're getting married in three weeks, at the chapel at Trelawney. You *will* come, won't you? You'll *never guess* where we're going for our honeymoon. Indianapolis! Christopher has to lecture at something called St. Vincent's. He says I can lie in bed and recover while he's earning our keep. Then, thank God, we're going on to California and afterward back to New York. I'll telephone you with all the filthy details when we get back at the end of June."

"Well, be careful what you order from room service," said Kate.

"I'm going to stick to beer, nothing but beer, and drink it out of little wine glasses. But I'm definitely going to stop drinking when we get back."

Only Kate and Mrs. Trelawney were present at the wedding in the sixteenth-century chapel in the hollow below the bluebell wood. Pagan wore a pink wool Chanel suit encrusted with gold chains and gilt buttons with lions' heads on them. With it she wore a navy silk blouse with a pussycat bow, a navy Breton straw hat and matching slingback shoes. She looks electrically happy, as if she could hardly bear to get out of bed long enough to get married, thought Kate as Pagan strode down the aisle on her husband's arm to the traditional triumphant burst of Mendelssohn, played rather jerkily on the organ by Mrs. Hocken's sister.

But by the end of September, Kate still hadn't heard from Pagan.

It was mid-October before Pagan telephoned Kate.

"That was a long honeymoon."

"Well, something happened, something utterly terrifying. On our first night in New York I woke up to hear odd strangled gasps. When I turned on the light, Christopher was purple and his eyes were staring and his arms were thrashing around. So I grabbed the phone, and the doctor arrived so fast you'd have thought he was waiting in room service. He gave Christopher a horse-size injection into his chest and I was shooed out of the way. Then they took Christopher off to the hospital in an ambulance. It was a massive heart attack. He was in the hospital for three months—thank God we had medical insurance."

"I can't believe it," Kate gasped. "Where are you?"

"I'm in Christopher's apartment—I mean our apartment. It's in Onslow Gardens. Can you come around, darling? We got home last night. I've only just unpacked and I feel so utterly depressed. Christopher's in bed, and I have to be so bloody cheerful all the time. It's absolutely grim."

Kate canceled her luncheon appointment and drove straight to Onslow Gardens. Pagan's big sitting room was really an avocado-colored library with books covering the walls from floor to ceiling. There were Persian rugs, tan leather sofas, brass lamps with blue-green glass shades, and a big bay window that looked out over the elm trees in the gardens.

"How long will it be before Christopher gets better?" Kate asked tentatively.

"Well, the doctors don't exactly look at it that way," Pagan said glumly, sipping from a large mug of coffee. "They treat heart failure by correcting the imbalance between the supply and demand of the blood and by removing all the accumulated excess fluids in the patient's body."

"Eh? What does that *mean*?" Kate asked, completely mystified.

"It means that Christopher has to have a lot of rest—mental and physical. He isn't allowed to work for too long. And he has to diet, because being overweight puts so much strain on the cardiovascular system. He isn't supposed to eat salt because he mustn't retain fluid, and he takes diuretic pills to make him pee a lot. In and out of the loo all day. He's also had to give up smoking. But the really awful thing is no sex."

"For how long?"

"Forever."

"*How awful!* But I suppose he can . . . pay attention to you."

"No—it might excite him."

"But the doctors can't be serious! How does Christopher feel about it?"

"Rather selfish. He doesn't want to die. As a matter of fact, I feel the same way."

Now I'll *never* find out what a really great lover does, Kate thought. It would be too unkind to ask. Oh *damn!*

Kate immediately realized the danger of Pagan's depression. "If he needs looking after, then you simply *must* stop drinking. Even beer in little wine glasses. Suppose he had an attack when you were bombed?"

"I've thought about it," said Pagan dully. "I know I've got to stop and I know it's not going to be easy. I lived here with Christopher for a month before we were married and I can't *tell* you how unbearably fast I got hooked again. I tried to fight the yearning, but it beat me within days." She heaved a noisy sigh. "As soon as Christopher had left for the laboratory I used to set the alarm clock for four P.M., then grab the cooking sherry and sip until I passed out or was sick. The alarm clock always jerked me awake, and then I'd have at least a couple of hours to pull myself together with a cold shower, eau de cologne and aspirin. It was ghastly. I only seemed to do it when I was alone, never at weekends. Perhaps I would slink out to the kitchen for an occasional swig, but somehow the dreaded craving wasn't too strong at weekends. Look, I want that address from you again, I've lost it. That list of AA places."

"It will be no use unless you tell Christopher. Do you want me to tell Christopher for you?"

"No. I'll tell him as soon as he's got over the journey. Let's get this bloody phone call over."

The following Thursday she went to her first Alcoholics Anonymous meeting, leaving Kate with Christopher and two sheets of typed emergency instructions.

"It was grim," Pagan told her later. "Tough. No pissing about. You felt they were all desperately serious, all there for a purpose. We all had that fatal interest in common. We met in the crypt of St. Martin's-in-the-Fields, you know that church in Trafalgar Square, and we sat drinking tea and eating biscuits. They smoked a lot, after a couple of hours you'd have thought the room was full of sea fog. There were lots more men than women and a couple of them were quite shabby—they looked as if they might be just out of prison or something."

"So what *happened?*" demanded Kate.

"Someone started off by saying that willpower was about as effective a cure for alcohol addiction as it is for cancer. If your system can tolerate ethyl alcohol, then alcohol can give you harmless pleasure, the way it does for you, Kate. But if you can't tolerate it, like me, you gradually become *dependent* on alcohol. I tell you, it was oddly cheering to know that I was merely addicted, not just an old soak."

She was lolling on the hearthrug, cuddling the sheepdog, Buster, who had been out in the rain and smelled like a damp blanket. "It's amazing that the government allows the stuff to be plugged on TV when they know that drink is the third highest *killer* in the country."

"Did anyone talk to you?"

"Nobody asked me anything, I just sat, watched and listened. One thing I learned—you just try not to drink for one day at a time." Pagan paused. For the first time she felt hopeful and not hopelessly weak-willed. "And you're never cured. Once you're an alcoholic, you're *always* an alcoholic, just as a diabetic is still a diabetic, although he controls his illness with insulin." She was high on hope.

"Pagan, you're too damn enthusiastic about it," Kate said. "It worries me. You're not to talk to Christopher until you're calm. Otherwise, he won't realize that you're serious."

But Christopher did. "Oh, I guessed just before we were married," he said. "There seemed no other reason for the reek of mouthwash on your breath every night when I came home, so I marked the bottles—not the ones in the drinks cabinet, I knew you'd be too crafty to take those—I marked the cooking stuff in the kitchen. I was waiting for you to tell me. I hoped I could help you."

When he was able to return to work, Christopher took Pagan to the laboratory to meet his associates. "I've told everyone to explain things to you in words of one syllable," he murmured, kissing Pagan on the ear just before they got out of the car.

She was shown around the lab building as if she were visiting royalty, but the scientists might as well have been speaking Swahili for all she understood of her two-hour tour. She gazed at the machines, at the computers, at the racks of glass containers where human cancer cells were growing in tissue that would be used in the preparation of the cancer vaccine. Then she asked the least unnerving of the lab technicians to lunch on the following Sunday, because she was determined to understand Christopher's work, if she could. She'd get this black-bearded Peter to explain to her.

In the car, on their way home, Christopher said, "Look, if you're really interested, Pagan, why don't you help us to raise money? I think you'd be good at it. Perhaps Kate could help you."

"Not Kate," said Pagan thoughtfully, "but Judy might."

* * *

A few months later Pagan accompanied Christopher to New York, where he was giving a lecture at the Sloan-Kettering Institute. For the first time in thirteen years she saw Judy. They rushed to hug each other in the oak-paneled gloom of the Algonquin lobby.

"But Pagan, you look exactly the same, except you don't wear glasses any more. Contacts?"

"Yes. *You* look extremely different, darling. You always looked a child, but now you look a *rich* child." Pagan eyed the blond-streaked, geometric Vidal Sassoon haircut flopping over one eye and the creamy, raw-silk safari suit, worn with vanilla suede pumps.

"This is one of my working outfits—Guy's, of course. Must look like a success if you want to be a success. Pagan, that's the first thing you've got to remember when I get around to giving you the concentrated course in public relations that you talked about on the telephone."

"I asked Kate to tell you and Maxine the truth about what had happened to me. It's all right, you don't have to order Coke just because I'm here. . . . Kate saved my life. And as soon as she told Maxine where I was, Max insisted that Christopher and I come over to stay with them. She was simply terrific. It was as if we'd last met a week ago. Now you've offered to show me how to help publicize the Research Institute. You're all being wonderful friends—I simply don't deserve it after ignoring you for all these years. It makes me feel even more ashamed."

"Listen," Judy said, "guilt is the most useless bit of baggage. You don't want to clutter your head with it. It can't do any good and it only makes you feel awful." She offered an olive to Pagan and grinned. "Real friends aren't people you joke and have a drink with. You don't need to see *real* friends, you just know that they're there when you need them. We formed our own little support system, remember, back in Gstaad? Through sick and sin, as Maxine used to say."

She firmly interlaced her fingers. "Like *that*, we're inter-linked, we're our own best safety net, so don't you forget it. Now keep your ears open and prepare for instruction."

As usual Judy was bubbling over with ideas. Pagan took notes and hoped that she'd be able to sort them out later. Her head was spinning.

Pagan went back to London and set to work. At first she was so embarrassed by the idea of telephoning strangers that she had to lock herself in her bedroom, and she blushed before dialing the numbers. But her background and fact sheets were fresh and interesting, her determination was formidable, and picking up her old network, she found that she knew a few rich people and quite a lot of influential ones. One person led to another. Pagan quickly discovered the charms and rewards of work. Every fortnight she wrote a report to Judy, who returned two closely typed pages of criticism and suggestions.

Pagan started by writing an article for her old school magazine in which she asked for money and helpers. She sweated over this for four days and worried about it for weeks afterward, but she was delighted by the positive response. She found herself with £43.20 and two part-time assistants. Since drawing attention to the Research Unit was as important as raising money for it, Pagan started a pyramid letter. "Please send me £2.00 and pass on a copy of this letter to two friends. Don't break the chain—it's a lifesaver." This brought in £4,068—far more than she had expected.

* * *

Some months later Pagan was standing in a small private room at the Savoy, hoping that her pale gray velvet suit with silver fox at the wrists wasn't too formal for the buffet luncheon she was about to give for twenty influential journalists. It was an expensive way to start, but she wanted nothing to be skimped at her first press party. She couldn't help feeling anxious. She wanted to be able to provide the right information for each journalist rather than give general information to a crowd. She had not invited medical journalists, who were informed on the subject, only mass-circulation writers. Nobody present wrote for less than a million readers.

Much to her relief the women were not particularly tough or aggressive. Most seemed to know each other and chatted quietly until Christopher started to speak. Then they jabbed at notebooks and asked questions that were ruthlessly to the point.

"My wife has specifically asked me to use simple language," Christopher began, "because when I first explained my work to her, she didn't understand a word I said. I hope that I won't oversimplify—later I shall be delighted to be as technical as you wish. First I'll give you a few facts, but I'd like to start answering questions from you as quickly as possible. I'm here to tell you about the work that we're doing at the Anglo-American Cancer Research Institute. I'm also here to ask you to help us to raise money to continue with our work. Already one in three cancer victims recovers: we want to improve that figure."

His small audience looked politely interested until, at the end of his short speech, Christopher announced, "In our South London laboratory we have produced a very crude form of vaccine, which I shall refer to as Vaccine X; I am sorry if that makes it sound a bit like a washing powder. We cannot speak with certainty until our findings have been checked, but Vaccine X seems to stimulate the body's defense forces to attack and beat off the viral invader and prevent the formation of those particular cancer cells."

Now they were sitting up and taking notice. "In a recent experiment we took two groups of mice and injected one group with Vaccine X. We then implanted tumor cells that are associated with the virus in all the mice. After two months the tumors in the treated mice had either not grown or had disappeared completely, while the untreated batch of mice all showed considerably enlarged tumors."

There was a burst of questions and a rustle of notebooks. Pagan felt she was off to a good start.

PART SIX

CHAPTER 31

LILI STARED LONGINGLY at the burning Atlanta skyline, at Vivien Leigh shooting a soldier with rape written all over his face, at Olivia de Havilland in a crinoline and at all the other color posters in front of the cinema. Although she was now thirteen, Lili had only been to the movies twice. She bit her lower lip and thrust her hands deeper into the pockets of her raincoat, wondering how she could manage to get in.

"Have you seen it?"

She turned to see a young man grinning at her. He was blondish, tall and at least twenty-four. "No, but doesn't it look wonderful? Have you seen it?"

"No," he lied. "Look, why don't we see it together? I'm all alone in Paris."

Lili hesitated. She wasn't even supposed to be on the Champs Elysées that afternoon, but Madame Sardeau was away on her annual visit to her mother in Normandy, and Lili had invented an extra math lesson for the benefit of Monsieur Sardeau, who wouldn't notice her absence anyway, since he was at his office. Monsieur Sardeau was a boring little pedagogue, but he had long ago stopped lecturing, correcting and reprimanding Lili—or, indeed, taking any notice at all of her—because the child's well-formed breasts and her gawky, sprawling legs aroused in him a physical response that at times he was afraid his wife might notice. He had once gasped Lili's name aloud as he imagined himself lying between those slim, firm thighs, when in fact he was writhing upon the bony body of his wife, clutching at the sagging breasts of Madame Sardeau. He'd managed to convince her that he hadn't said anything, that she had merely heard a voluptuous gasp of pleasure, but he couldn't risk trouble so close to home. Conscious of the danger, he prudently avoided Lili whenever possible.

Lili gazed up at the young man who had just spoken to her. He looked a bit like Leslie Howard gazing down at her from that photograph; he had the same limpid look. He sounded foreign as well.

She'd never get another chance.

"Yes, please," she said. It was as easy as that. They moved past the box office into the darkness, into the previous century and the Civil War.

When the lights went up for the entr'acte, Lili was still in a state of romantic ecstasy. "Isn't Scarlett beautiful?"

"Not more than you," the young man said.

Lili's face was no longer childish. A tangle of dark hair was held back from her face by a velvet hairband; she had huge brown eyes that seemed to radiate a very adult sensuality; but what gave her face its most arresting quality was the elegant, slightly hooked little nose above lips so voluptuously chiseled that they might have been carved by Michelangelo. At thirteen, her figure was no longer childish. Her legs were still a trifle thin, but her body had filled out and her breasts were well developed—perhaps, in fact, *too* developed. Sometimes she though that Monsieur Sardeau was furtively looking at them, and when they walked out of church on Sunday, his hand always grasped her upper arm, his knuckles quivering unnecessarily hard against her breast.

Lili's new friend bought her an ice cream, and she learned that his name was Alastair and he lived in New York. It was clear that he thought Lili older than she was, because he didn't treat her like a schoolgirl.

The lights dimmed again and Alastair reached over and took her fingertips. His hand felt warm and firm and almost unbearably thrilling, not like Monsieur Sardeau's furtive hand, which frightened her. Lili felt a shortness of breath, an eerie excitement, as if the fine down on her arms was standing on end like a cat's. She felt a dreamy yearning to have this stranger stroke more than just the inside of her palm and the back of her wrist.

As they shuffled out with the dark, swaying mob that moved toward the exit, Alastair asked, "Would you like something to eat?"

Lili tossed her hair, summoned up her courage and said yes. They splashed through the drizzle to a restaurant, and by the end of the meal Alastair knew a good deal about Lili, although she had learned nothing about him. Toward the end of the meal Lili suddenly became anxious. It was nearly eleven o'clock—she had never been out so late before, she explained.

Without argument he snapped his fingers for the check and took her home. As the taxi splashed toward home, Alastair put one finger under her chin and gently turned her eager, anxious face toward him. Then, just like Rhett Butler, he bent over and kissed her. Trembling with this new tingling feeling, thirsty for love and warmth, Lili put her arms around Alastair's neck and lifted her head. By the time the taxi splashed to a halt, she was in love.

Creeping up the staircase, she trembled for a different reason, terrified of her reception, never imagining that she might be able to reach her room without being challenged. But Monsieur Sardeau hadn't yet returned; he had no intention of staying at home on the rare occasions when his wife was absent for a fortnight.

Lili now got up at five in the morning in order to do the sewing that ought to occupy her summer afternoons, because Alastair now occupied those hours. Never again did she dare stay out so late in the evening, but his working hours seemed conveniently elastic, so at midday Lili always ran to meet him in a café for lunch and afterward, holding hands, they would wander along the trees in the Bois de Boulogne, stroll among the exquisitely dressed children in the Parc Monceau, take a *bâteau mouche* on the Seine or window-shop.

"Why don't you let me buy you a decent dress? I've only seen you in one sweater and one blouse since we met, and always that same navy skirt."

"Oh, I couldn't let you buy me anything! Madame would see it."

"Well, what about these little red suede shoes?"

"No, I couldn't hide them, they'd want to know where I got the money." But in the stone arcade of the rue de Rivoli, Alastair bought her a heart-shaped locket on a fine gold chain that she could hide under her mattress. He'd never met such a trusting, affectionate, undemanding girl; even the youngest ones were usually after something, especially once they knew who he was. Then there were always demands for jewelry, money, sometimes even marriage. Skinner, his mother's attorney, handled them if things became difficult, particularly if a father turned nasty. Lili suited him admirably, and, as yet, few people knew him in Paris.

In the taxi Lili threw her arms around him and thanked him for the locket, affectionate as a puppy. But when they got out in the shadow of the Eiffel Tower, she looked up and asked in surprise, "Where are we going?"

"To have a drink, kitten, in this hotel. I often come here."

Behind the desk, a bored, fat concierge was knitting a gray tube that might have been a sock or a sleeve. Alastair passed her a note, and she slapped down a key. "Number nineteen. First floor. You'll have to pay extra if you stay longer than two hours."

Lili followed Alastair up the stairs: he usually took her to much smarter places. "Is it a floor show? Why did you have to pay?" she asked.

her body. It happened so quickly that Lili, bewildered by her conflicting emotions, hardly even knew what was happening. She realized only that she ached again, then ached unbearably as Alastair straddled her small body, shuddered in his climax, then rolled off to lie beside her, exhausted.

Later he mumbled, "That was wonderful, kitten, let's have you in your school clothes next time." After a bit he started to stroke her pink breasts again, then the rest of her body, until it stopped shaking. Softly he spoke words of love. She wanted him to love her, didn't she? Slowly, patiently—thinking of the following afternoon—he won her confidence again, soothed her with his stroking, reassured her with words of love, hypnotized her with his self-confidence, terrified her with veiled threats of love withdrawn, of telephone calls to Madame Sardeau.

Then he relieved himself in the washbasin, dressed and left the room, while Lili washed in the bidet. She was thinking that if he loved her, he shouldn't have brought her here. But if he *didn't* love her, he wouldn't *want* to, surely? He had done it because he loved her.

After a few minutes Alastair returned and sat on the edge of the bed. He pulled her onto his lap and produced a packet of pills. "Now I want you to take one of these every day. See, the instructions are on the label."

"Why?"

"So that you don't have a baby. It's the new pill. Promise you'll take it."

"Why can't we get married and have a baby?"

"Because you're too young, that's why, kitten. Later on, if you're good, when you've passed your exams, then we'll see."

After that there were no more trips up the river, no more strolling under the trees. Almost every weekday during that hot summer, from three to five o'clock, a frightened, timid Lili met Alastair at the hotel. When Madame Sardeau returned, Lili explained that as it had been so hot she had taken her basket of sewing to the shady park every afternoon. Madame's *chemises de nuit* were exquisitely sewn and the child certainly looked as pale as milk, so perhaps the park was a good idea, provided she was back in good time to prepare the evening meal.

The early September sun crept down the opposite side of the courtyard as Lili retched for the fifth morning in succession. Panic-stricken, she crept back to her bed. She had no knowledge of gynecology, but she knew what early morning sickness meant. Too exhausted and worried to get up, let alone sew, she heard Madame Sardeau calling her. "Lili, Lili, wherever has that child got to, why isn't the coffee on? So! Still in bed at seven o'clock!" But the child didn't look well, she seemed hardly able to lift her head and the black rings around her eyes were darkening. Perhaps she'd better call the doctor, although of course he would charge for a visit. Better see if a day in bed would cure her. There was no point in paying for a doctor unless she was really ill.

The waves of nausea passed and by midday, Lili no longer felt ill. She was merely panic-stricken. After taking Alastair's pills for three days, she had stopped, because they made her feel sick. She hadn't told him this because she was afraid he'd be cross with her.

She *had* to get out of bed. Alastair would be waiting for her at the Pam-Pam Café. Luckily, it was one of Madame Sardeau's afternoons for bridge.

When she confessed her fears to Alastair, his usually languid face hardened. Suddenly he didn't look at all like Leslie Howard.

"I might have *known* it! You stupid little *bitches* are all the same! . . . Are you *sure?*"

"I haven't seen a doctor, but I've been sick all this week."

"Well, it's your own damn fault. You're not going to pin anything on me. You don't know where I'm staying, nobody's seen us together, and for all I know you're sleeping with half the men in Paris. . . . Oh, God, *don't* start crying!" He thought for a moment; it was better not to frighten her. He didn't know how old Lili was, but she was certainly under the age of consent. Skinner might not be able to swing *that* with the French police. Though the French were tolerant about these things as a rule. . . .

"Can't we go to the hotel?"

"No, we can't. For God's sake stop sniveling and let me think." Thank God she didn't know his real name. He must have been crazy, out of his mind, to pick her up! Still, it was too late now. He had to get out of this immediately before anyone could pin it on him. Of course, there was the hotel receptionist, but she'd keep her mouth shut for a few thousand francs. An idea occurred to him. He thrust his hand into his trouser pocket and pulled out fifty thousand francs, not much, about a hundred and eighty dollars, but it was all the cash he had on him.

"For Christ's sake, stop crying, Lili, or I'll walk out of this place. Look, this is what you must do. Take this money and go to a doctor to make sure that you're really pregnant—I've no idea what he'll charge, but this is bound to cover it. If you *aren't* pregnant, then there's been a lot of fuss about nothing. If you *are*, then go straight to the concierge at the hotel and she'll arrange for you to see someone who'll fix you up. I'll see that the bill is paid. Do it as fast as you can—*and don't tell anyone.*" He threw a note on the table to cover their bill and stood up.

"Don't go, Alastair, please don't leave me, when I love you so."

"If you love me, you'll do exactly as I say. You'll obey me or I'll never see you again."

"When shall I see you? When?" Now she was too frightened to cry.

"I'll see you here in two weeks." He patted her shoulder. "Cheer up! If you're a good girl and obedient, we can forget all this unpleasantness. Now do you *promise* to do as I say?"

"Oh, I promise, but you will come back again, won't you?"

"Of course, kitten," he said soothingly, and he bent to kiss her wet cheek, with no intention of ever seeing her again.

He had gone before Lili ever thought of asking which doctor she should visit. She sat staring at the pile of notes, then stuffed them in her raincoat pocket and walked to the hotel. She hung around outside, not wanting to go in, but eventually she approached the fat, knitting fingers behind the desk.

"I was told you could help me." The woman's eyes immediately dropped to Lili's stomach.

"How long?"

Lili turned red and looked hard at the brass bell on the countertop. "I don't know."

"When were you last due?"

"About three weeks ago. But I haven't seen a doctor yet."

"Just as well. Sit on that chair and wait a minute." Bare feet stuck into carpet slippers, she shuffled to the telephone booth at the back of the hall. Lili could not hear her low conversation. Then she shuffled back and said, "Did he give you any money?"

"Yes!" She pulled out the bundle of notes and put them on the counter. The woman's fat fingers flew through them, counting.

"That's not going to get you far. You need another hundred thousand francs, tell him."

"But that's all he gave me. I can't get any more. He said he'd see that the bill was paid."

"That's what they all say, but the fact is, this sort of business is strictly cash in advance. Can't your family help?" Lili's frightened face grew terrified. "Well, can't you borrow from a friend?"

None of Lili's schoolmates had ever *seen* a hundred thousand francs, let alone owned it or lent it. Slowly she shook her head.

"Tell you what," said the concierge, speculatively. "I know a photographer who might pay you to model for him. Three thousand francs an hour, less my commission, would that suit you?"

Lili nodded hopefully. She would have agreed to anything. The old woman shuffled off again to the phone box and when she returned she scribbled an address on the desk pad. "Serge will see you right away, dear. Here's the address. It's just down the street; he's in the attic."

CHAPTER 32

SERGE, ONCE A famous fashion photographer, had grown fat, bored, lazy and old, in that order. He had flourished in the traditional world of haute-couture and did not understand the unconventional, relaxed fashions of the sixties. The fashion magazines had dropped him, then his advertising accounts had dwindled, and he'd been almost totally out of work until he started selling nude photos. They were not the sort of models he was used to, of course. You'd never find Bettina or Ali or Fiona or Suzy stooping to that sort of thing. Most of the girls wouldn't so much as touch an *underwear* shot until recently, and you used to practically pay danger money to get them into a swimsuit, but these new, untidy models had no style and no shame. He'd always photographed women in the nude, of course, it was one of his pleasures, but he'd never thought of selling the photographs until one little tart stuck his close-up of her nipple into her portfolio, after which, for a while, his pictures of naked women were suddenly fashionable. You could seldom make out at first glance which part of the body it was, but the effect was original and often startlingly erotic. Anyway, they sold.

Serge's eyes narrowed speculatively as he looked at Lili, then he gave her a slow smile. "Come in," he said. "Don't mind my judo suit, I always wear it in the studio. A glass of wine? No, well—there's the changing room, get 'em off, darling."

"Get what off?"

"Your clothes, darling. What else would I pay three thousand francs an hour for? And from what I hear it won't be the first time, darling, but don't worry, there's nothing I haven't seen before. Look, there's proof."

He waved a pudgy hand toward an enormous black felt pinboard, covered with nude photographs—and very good ones, for Serge loved women and was an excellent photographer.

Lili picked her way past the ten-foot-wide rolls of pink, blue and green backdrop paper, past a vast white hanging sheet and an even bigger black one, past two groups of what looked like silver umbrellas on sticks and a forest of studio lights. She went into the small dressing room, where odd colored pots of grease, terra-cotta covered sponges, crumpled Kleenex, dusty little brushes, flimsy chiffon scarves and hair curlers stood on the makeup counter, above which blazed a row of naked light bulbs.

Lili stood there, not moving or thinking, numbed, for five minutes. "I haven't got all day, cherub." The voice outside was cheerful, but held an underlying menace. Quickly she undressed. The curtains were pulled aside and Serge looked through. "Good, you're ready. Out here, please."

He had set up the camera and lights in front of the black backdrop. "These days I don't bother with an assistant, unless I'm on an assignment. Now, just stand straight with your back to camera, cherub." Click! "Now turn sideways." Click! "Chin up a bit." Click! Click! "Now face me, that's a good girl." Click! Click! Click!

"There, that's over, wasn't too bad was it? I'll develop them now and let you know tomorrow if I can use you."

Lili was relieved. It had been about as erotic and frightening as having a passport photograph taken. Serge thought that it was a long time since he had seen such a pretty little cunt. Mind you, he told himself, she'd need a bit of work on her, but he wouldn't mind betting that she'd look even better on the contacts. In the meantime, he had no intention of frightening her. If he played his cards carefully, she was worth a fortune to him.

At her afternoon photographic sessions with Serge, Lili quickly discovered that more was expected of her than simply stripping and standing in the nude while Serge clicked his Rolleiflex. That first sitting had clearly shown him her potential. Studying the contact prints through a magnifying glass, marking with a red chinagraph the ones he wanted to enlarge, Serge had realized that the child was even better than he'd thought. She had a rare naiveté, combined with a catch-your-breath eroticism of which she seemed totally unaware. The face had a pure, hopeful quality that was impossible to simulate, yet that mouth showed more than a hint of sensuality. She was a dream girl.

Serge knew he'd have to play her carefully. Kindness was the thing; fatherly kindness would reassure the little creature, then he'd add a light touch of authority. Lead her into it very gently, give her something to do in the first shots so that she didn't have time to think. Pay her a bit in advance, get her to sign an IOU, then, if necessary, threaten her with it. He'd have to watch out for those ribs and the gawky long legs—he'd have preferred plumper thighs squeezing that dark little bush—but the breasts were perfection. She was jailbait, but she was money in the bank.

When Lili turned up for the second afternoon sitting she found Serge waiting in the traditional photographers' costume of jeans and black sweater, with a thick leather belt that more or less squeezed his stomach into place. He had bought a frosted chocolate layer cake for Lili, while he himself sipped a tumblerful of red wine and seemed in no hurry to start.

Then he picked up his camera and said, "Tell you what, cherub, I'd like to start off with some casual shots; just as you are in that cotton frock, sitting on the old velvet chair."

He'd already positioned his lights before she arrived, and now he switched on soft, enticing, rhythmic dance music.

"Now cut another piece of cake, darling, it's all for you. . . . Hold it. . . . Turn your head slowly to camera. . . . No, only your head, cherub. . . . Now smile. . . . That's *great*, kid. I can see you're going to be good. Now perhaps we'll try it with a couple of buttons undone. . . . Would you mind? . . . Terrific. . . . Keep looking to camera. . . . A couple more buttons. . . . Now lean over to the left and take a big bite."

Carefully, Lili leaned to the left, then just as she was about to bite, the piece of chocolate cake disintegrated in her hand. She burst into peals of laughter as she turned her head to Serge and . . . Click!

Serge worked with two cameras. When he'd finished both rolls he vanished into the darkroom to change the film and came out, brisk and impersonal as a dentist. "Now let's have you in a bikini. You'll find some in the top drawer of the chest in the dressing room. Pick whichever you like."

Lili had longed for a bikini and needed little prompting. She finally reappeared in a white lace one that made Serge catch his breath as he turned on his wind machine. "Now, flower, I want you to stand with your legs apart, hair streaming backward in the studio breeze, and tilt this bottle of soda to your lips, hold it and smile. . . . That's my girl, you're really catching on."

Half an hour later, Lili was no longer nervous. "Now let's try it with just the pants," Serge said casually, fiddling with his light meter. Lili looked anxious.

"Do I have to?"

"Why, yes—if you want the money, flower. And anyway, no one will know except us."

"But what are these pictures *for?* Are they for a magazine or something?"

"Now why ever should you think that? It's art. Just take your bra off, darling." Lili was dubious, but unwilling to argue about the unformed, uneasy suspicions that Serge so smoothly wiped from her subconscious. She unhooked and stood there, looking anxious, hands held over her breasts.

"That's great, flower. No, don't smile, just like that." Click! Herb Alpert continued to play cheerfully, reassuringly in the background. "Now sit on the chair hugging your knees up to your . . .

"That's *terrific*, bud. . . . And kneel with your hands clasped behind your head. Now I want you to put on a pair of stockings." He produced a pair of thick, black stockings and schoolgirl shoes. Lili didn't think they looked very artistic, but obediently she smoothed them onto her legs. Combined with the white lace panties they emphasized her frail, young vulnerability, the innocence contradicted by her heavy, grown-up pink-nippled breasts.

The following day Serge took her out on the roof and photographed her against the Parisian chimney pots in her cotton frock, until she relaxed, until she *trusted* him. He'd throw that roll away. He wouldn't even bother to develop it. Then he tossed her an exquisite peach chiffon negligee and said, "Now let's try this on."

When she reappeared he put his head to one side, gave a small, disapproving frown and said authoritatively, "Those pants ruin the mood. Just slip them off, flower, that's a good girl." He turned away and adjusted his camera settings, then looked around. "*Just slip them off*, I said." The light menace was unmistakable.

Shivering slightly in the weak September sunlight, Lili slipped them off and Serge got some wonderfully erotic shots of those big but still pubescent breasts that topped her gawky adolescent body, seen through a thin veil of peach chiffon—which sometimes gaped open without Lili realizing it—against the slate roofs, chimney pots and pigeons of the Paris skyline. Serge was pleased. "Tomorrow we'll go to a quiet little spot in the Bois de Boulogne," he said. "We'll shoot the next lot with trees and grass."

Lili didn't want to continue with the sittings. Once away from the reassuring presence of Serge, she felt ashamed. She blushed and groaned to herself as she hurried home. She wouldn't go to the studio again.

But every morning she woke, head swimming with nausea, and as she ran down the corridor to the lavatory, she knew she had to continue the sessions. Just to harden her resolve, Serge presented her with some prints of her first sitting. Lili hid them under the mattress with her gold locket. She wanted to tear them up, but she also wanted to keep them. She *did* look very pretty in the pictures.

Madame Sardeau occasionally shouted at her, "You've got to finish my winter nightgowns before the lycée starts," but she didn't pay much attention to Lili, and she had more than nightgowns on her mind. Her husband now often worked late at the office. There had been odd telephone calls, and when she answered, the line went dead. His manner was strange, and not once since she returned from Normandy had he bothered her at night. It was odd.

Lili saw no money for her work. Serge paid it directly to the concierge and to give him due credit, he didn't cheat Lili of a sou. But the concierge would not arrange the operation until Lili had all the money, so she continued to model until she was three months pregnant.

Lili sat in the small steaming café, not wanting to get up and walk again. Her legs felt weak and her body felt as raw and painful as her thoughts. Until it was time to prepare supper, the café was a halfway house of cheerful, normal life, poised between that horrible experience this afternoon and the depression which, as always, she would feel when she approached the dark Sardeau front door.

She could not forget the humiliating *pain* of the operation, on top of the painful humiliation of Alastair's disappearance. She had thought he loved her. Was it *so* dreadful not to have taken those pills? Would it have been *so* dreadful to have had a baby instead of an abortion?

She dragged herself up the stairs to the seventh floor and rang the bell—she wasn't allowed a key. The door flew open and Madame Sardeau stood there, like a black, shrieking crow. In her hand was Lili's gold locket and the contact prints that had been hidden under her mattress.

"*What's this filth?* So *this* is what you were doing when I thought you were in the park! *This* is what you get up to when my back is turned! *This* is the way you show your gratitude, you slut!"

Lili backed away, terrified, retreating backward down the stairs as the furious woman continued to shriek at her. From below a voice shouted up the dusty stairwell, "Less noise up there."

Lili stumbled backward and nearly fell, clutching the stair rail to save herself. "You filthy little bitch, it's easy to see where you come from—the gutter! Just as we thought, you lewd little whore! After all we've done for . . ."

Lili turned and fled, away from those dreadful words, back to Serge's studio, and threw herself, weeping, against his plump chest.

"Hmm, so the old trout found out, did she?" he said calmly. "Well, I'm not surprised, but it's a pity, flower."

He was not surprised because he had telephoned Madame Sardeau anonymously and suggested that she look under Lili's mattress. . . . He wasn't about to lose her now that the abortion was done. Serge wrapped Lili in a rug, laid her on the studio couch and heated some milk for her.

"It was today, wasn't it?" he asked.

Huddled in the rug, Lili sobbed and nodded.

"Well, you'd better just lie there until you feel better, then we'll decide what to do." He softly stroked her black, tangled hair until she fell asleep. From Lili's chatter, Serge now knew a lot about the Sardeaus. She wouldn't go back. He'd got her! There was no risk of losing her now, not after they'd found out so abruptly. She wouldn't be the first teenage runaway to disappear in Paris; there was unlikely to be a fuss if they couldn't find her. She could hole up with him and hide for a bit—he had no girl living with him at the moment to complicate matters. Lili was nearly fourteen; with makeup she could pass as an eighteen-year-old. Sweep the fringe away from her forehead, give her a lipstick, some new clothes and high heels, and she'd never resemble any photographs the police might be given. And if they *did* pick her up, well, he hadn't molested her, had he?

Serge had just returned from a visit to an advertising agency. His new portfolio contained only shots of Lili. Lili lying flushed and sleepy on a tousled bed, half-hidden by a lace shawl; Lili with her hair in braids, running naked through high, out-of-focus grass; Lili, in a straw hat and skimpy shorts, pushing a bicycle along a woodland path; a back view of Lili's little haunches as she twined jasmine in her hair before a bedroom mirror that reflected her voluptuous breasts.

The art editor had pushed up his heavy black-rimmed glasses, snapped out of his boredom and reached for the phone. "Sorry to disturb you, TJ," he said, "but you know that tire calendar we're considering for next Christmas? Well, I think I've got something here."

An exquisitely tailored account executive hurried in, flipped through the portfolio in silence, then looked through it again with more attention. "They're good," he said, "but these are only of one girl."

"Well, of course we'd have other girls, but the *mood* is exactly what I'm after, something *different* from the usual tits and ass stuff, that quality of innocence, that feeling of eternal summer, that nostalgia and the counterpoint of exuberant *joie de vivre.*"

"Yes, yes, they're certainly sexy. Okay, he can have a shot at the dummy. But I want it fast, and we've got to have at least two other girls. And one has to be a blonde."

Serge draped another blanket over Lili and quietly moved out of the studio into the next-door room where he lived, ate and fucked. He reached for his black address book, threw himself on the unmade bed and lifted the telephone. "That you, Teresa? Got a nice job for you, flower."

For the rest of the week, Lili stayed hidden in Serge's loft as she regained her strength and her spirits. He had gone shopping and returned with an armful of flowers, two Beatles records, a Victorian-style lace nightdress, an organdy-petal bonnet with white satin streamers, a see-through black string vest, some steak and a shopping bag crammed with bonbons and sugary food. After a day or two Lili lost her quivering fear of the Sardeaus, and Serge firmly encouraged her to regard that part of her life as over. She had run away, the sensible little creature. Now she was going to be treated as a grownup and have fun. "Next week Teresa will take you on a shopping trip and buy some pretty clothes," Serge promised.

While Lili rested he worked hard with Teresa, a twenty-year-old model who wore her hair in blonde braids and tried hard to look fourteen. During the day she posed for margarine and soup advertisements, and in the evening she liked to go to expensive restaurants with old men. Young men bored her: she liked a sugar daddy with whom she could play at being a child. Teresa was a high-class call girl.

After a trip to the Galeries Lafayette, Lili returned with a pair of Jules-et-Jim tweed knickerbockers with a matching Jackie Coogan golfing cap; a white *broderie anglaise* cape that fell from her shoulders to five inches above the knee in layer upon layer of white frills; three dresses the color of sugared almonds, each with a matching pair of high-heeled pumps; her first handbag and a coat of white rabbit fur. Her hair had been restyled and back-combed into a bouffant, Bardotlike, sexy tangle. All thought of returning to school, all thought of the Sardeaus, all thoughts of the past and the future flew from Lili's mind and she lived only in the voluptuous present. Her new friends laughed and chatted with her as she was coaxed into posing—naked—in the fur coat, then lay on the studio bed with Teresa, both wearing lace briefs and nothing else.

Sometimes they went out in the evening with Teresa's man friend, who was in the scrap metal business, and when they did, Teresa adopted a childlike voice and spoke of herself in the third person. "Teresa wants to go to Fouquet's," she pouted. "Albert is a *horrid* man if he doesn't take Teresa somewhere pretty and Teresa won't talk to him."

She always got her own way, then immediately stopped pouting and said, "Oh, Albert is so *good* to little Teresa; she's going to sit on his knee and love him all night."

"Christ, not in Fouquet's again," groaned Serge. "Don't you *ever* wear panties?"

When Teresa was working with Lili, the older girl was not petulant and childish, but friendly, shrewd and willing to pass on the wisdom of the hotel room. She gave Lili the benefit of her experience—shrewd bits of advice and sad little ways of avoiding humiliation.

"Never meet a man in a bar, Lili, always the bar of a restaurant or in a café." Obediently she sat for Serge with one leg up on a kitchen table and hitched her skirt up so that her bare ass could be seen. "Always take enough money to pay for yourself in case he doesn't turn up, then you simply order another drink or have your meal; no restaurant charges much for an omelette."

At Serge's instruction, Teresa lay back on the wooden table while Lili unbuttoned her blouse and leaned over. "This okay, Serge? If he doesn't turn up, you don't feel humiliated and if he's late, well, you're behaving as if you're used to expensive places. Ouch, Lili, that fucking hurt, keep your teeth to yourself."

Serge moved them over to a wooden kitchen chair. Teresa stood behind and

Lili knelt on it, clutching adoringly at Teresa's open kimono. She continued her advice. "Always try to go to restaurants where you've been before, so they get to know you, and always tip well in the cloakroom."

Serge didn't like the pose so they dropped it. Back to the kitchen table. One leg up again, but this time frontal. ". . . And never go out in the evening with more money than you need for one meal and your fare home, because then nobody can borrow from you."

Both girls were directed to stand facing each other. . . . Closer. . . . Closer. . . . Touching.

Lili was told to drop her kimono. "When you're in St. Tropez," Teresa continued, "never pretend you're staying at an expensive hotel, because they'll quickly find out that you aren't. Always arrange to meet at Senequier, and if anyone asks where you're staying, say it's a little hotel that's *peaceful* and cheap. Rich men always respect that, and they're not to know you're sharing one room with four other girls."

"Stop talking and let's get down to work seriously, you two. I want Lili to brush your hair from behind as you lean backward over this wicker chair, Teresa, that'll lift those old tits of yours."

When he was confident that no official search was being made for Lili, Serge briskly pursued his next step, which was to lure her into his bed.

One evening, after working late with a series of nightgown shots on the studio bed, Serge leaned over to give Lili the light, fatherly kiss on her forehead that usually meant that work was finished for the day. But this time he snuggled up beside her and muttered, "Serge wants a cuddle."

Suddenly wary, Lili stiffened. But soon she heard his heavy breathing, and finally she also drifted to sleep. Then Serge raised his head, quickly stripped and got under the sheets. In the middle of the of the night Lili woke up, drowsy, to feel a moist stroking of her clitoris in a slow, steady rhythm. Half asleep, she stretched languorously until her body quivered. Her narrow pelvis arched away from the bed and she shuddered to her first climax.

She lay panting, astonished, guilty, fearful, bewildered, as Serge heaved himself up, started to lick her eyelids, took her little hand in his and guided it firmly down his heavy hairy torso.

Docile and inexperienced, Lili had no idea how shrewdly she was being exploited.

Teresa and Serge seemed so sure of themselves, so sophisticated.

Teresa found Lili curiously appealing, she couldn't help being touched by the younger girl's awed admiration and teased her about it. "But I've never had a proper girl friend before," said Lili seriously, "not someone who really likes me. When I was at school in Switzerland the other girls called me stuck-up because I had extra lessons and their mamas wouldn't let them play with me because I had no papa. When I was at school in Neuilly, there wasn't much time to get to know girls in school, and I wasn't allowed to see anyone outside school because Madame Sardeau said it would interfere with my work. . . . No, she meant housework. . . . So you see, it's wonderful to have a real, grown-up girl friend."

Teresa felt uneasy. "You'll soon have plenty of men friends, judging by the looks you get on the street."

"I know what you mean, but I can't understand *why* they look at me like that."

"It's something in your eyes," Teresa grudgingly said. That evening Lili spent two hours locked in the bathroom, earnestly looking at her eyes in the mirror and trying to see something in them. But she just saw eyes. She was lucky about the lashes, but plenty of people had big dark eyes and long glossy lashes without inciting the extraordinary reaction that Lili got from the average man in the street. No, she didn't see *how* it could be the eyes. But she'd give it a try. So the next time she went for a walk, wearing a cherry-red velvet suit with a nipped-in waist, she looked straight at the first man she met, straight into his eyes, then blinked in a misty way and slowly gave a little smile. Immediately she saw his everyday lust turn into helpless fascination. It is the eyes, Lili thought exultantly. She didn't know why, but they worked like magic.

Serge spoiled and mesmerized Lili; he was expansive and charming when Lili was obedient, sharp and threatening if she didn't do as he said. "Do you want the police to know where you are? Do you want them to know you had an illegal operation? Want to be in prison? Do you want to go back to the Sardeaus?" he growled one spring afternoon shortly after the calendar had been completed.

"Oh no, Serge, please don't. No more."

"Then get on that bed with Teresa, dear, and let's have no more whining."

Lili no longer felt humiliated and shamed by posing naked. The other two were so matter-of-fact about it, as were the other girls who occasionally modeled for Serge. They thought no more of stripping off their clothes than they did of kicking off their shoes. And the girls *all* slept with men. Teresa said it showed you were no longer a schoolgirl.

But this was different. This was a film. There was a movie camera and there were other men in the studio, men she didn't know. Scowling, Lili shed her cherry-red cotton wrapper and jumped on the double bed that had been pulled to the center of the studio and was now banked by lights. Serge switched on beguiling music, climbed up to the overhead camera platform and started directing Lili. She was stiff and awkward. Eventually, he said, "Okay, take a break," and moved to the bed where Lili crouched, arms around her knees.

"You're too tense, flower. Tell you what, put your wrapper on again and I'll get you some warm milk with a shot of rum in it. That'll relax you, bud."

He slipped into the grubby kitchen, crushed three Mandrax sedative tablets, stirred them into hot milk and then poured rum and sugar in it. With an avuncular beam he carried it out and offered it to Lili. "And if you don't feel better after that, flower, we'll stop," he said.

After her drink, Lili felt drowsy and unresisting. "Pinch her, Teresa, don't let her go to sleep. Now let's have some action, you two. Okay, Teresa, start on her tits." Lili now sprawled limp on the bed; Teresa gently tugged at the red sash of her wrap and eased it away from her body. Then she started to stroke Lili's breasts. Dimly aware, Lili wriggled and tried to push her away, with arms that suddenly felt limp and boneless, but Teresa held Lili's hands back against the bed and bent her mouth toward Lili's left breast.

"That's great. Now you get in there, Carl." A husky man who'd been leaning against the wall took off his leather belt, then stripped off denim battle jacket and jeans and walked toward the bed. "Easy, Carl, take it easy. I want it almost as if the film's being slowed down. Just slither onto that bed behind Teresa, think dirty thoughts as fast as you can and let's see that hard-on. Okay, now you can stroke her ass."

Serge was sweating, he'd never expected to find it so exciting. Shit, if it weren't for the rest of the crew, which was costing Christ knows how much an hour, he'd be in there getting his share. "Let's have a little more action, get your mouth off Lili's bush, Teresa, and let's see Carl go down on her. No, don't stop, Teresa, your turn will come, we've got another twenty fucking minutes of film. Now you can slide around to Carl and give him head. Don't you *dare* come, Carl, recite the alphabet backward or something. Now sit up slowly. Let's have your hands on Teresa's head. That's nice, very nice, stay with it. Now pull, Teresa, we want to see what he's made of. Oh very nice, now Carl, I want you to slowly turn around, then lam it into Lili for all you're worth."

Lili shrieked, her drugged face, panic-stricken, to camera. "Nice, very nice, that'll have them creaming their jeans," Serge purred.

After that, a weary quality was noticeable in Lili's pictures, an awareness of evil, a tired acceptance of it.

After all, where else could she go? What else could she do? As Serge endlessly reminded her, she had no qualifications, she was only fit to be a hooker or a shop assistant, and she couldn't get a job because she had no previous experience. She gnawed her little finger, knowing that what Serge said was true. But when Serge wasn't making her do those humiliating things, he was kind, gave her anything she wanted—bonbons, film magazines, records, high-heeled shoes, new clothes. He took her to the cinema, to restaurants and to parties, although she didn't much care for the parties. She didn't like the interested, slightly contemptuous, sidelong looks that the men gave her; she was glad Serge never left her alone. He saw that she never left his side for a minute; he wasn't bad to her and at least she didn't have to get out of bed at five in the morning to sew someone else's nightgowns.

Lili never thought about the past, as she enjoyed the new comforts of the present—and she tried never to think about the future. Now she was glad that *vraie maman* could never find her; when she conjured up that particular daydream, or when she caught herself remembering Angelina or Felix, she had to face the fact that she was ashamed of her present life. But how else could she live?

She started to develop a protective shell, to pretend she didn't care, that she didn't mind making these disgusting, shameful movies; only thus could she bear to lie naked on satin sheets with calculating strange men and hard-faced women of assorted age and color, in front of other strangers on the periphery of the set. She seemed wearily prepared to accept any degradation, although she'd once—suddenly—become hysterical when Serge brought an Alsatian dog into the studio.

Once again, Lili remembered that cold, dim journey through the snow and slush, those dreadful growls and the one thin scream that turned into a gurgle. So Lili clung to Serge, shrieking. "No! No! Felix, Felix, help me!" Her body shook and her teeth chattered and she was no use for the rest of the day.

Regretfully, Serge decided that he couldn't introduce animals into the act after all. He had to content himself with films of Lili chained to obviously papier-mâché dungeon walls, Lili being whipped by muscular bald boxers or manacled by monocled parodies of Englishmen, Lili kneeling to lick the cock of anyone Serge chose.

He felt not one twinge of jealousy or pity for the girl. He looked upon her as he would a clever pet monkey—she did her tricks and he saw to it that she had a comfortable life. He'd got her to sign a five-year contract with Sergio Productions—not that it was legal, mind, because she was underage, but she'd never find that out. Sergio Productions charged a steep price for slick, professionally made porn films, but Lili saw none of the money. On paper she was paid 400,000 francs a year by Sergio Productions, which was about as much as a secretary earned, but Serge deducted fifteen percent as his agent's fee, thirty percent for his fee as her manager, and thirty percent for providing food, clothes and accommodation, which didn't leave much for Lili.

In the deep, dark velvet depths of a club cinema off the Champs Elysées, one man whispered to another, "Who's the dark girl? She's new, isn't she? Serge's girl? She's too good for *this* crap. She deserves *better* crap. I'll phone him tomorrow."

The following week, Serge summoned Teresa to the big basement that he now used as a studio. More care than usual had gone into the arrangement of the simple set; the focal point was a deep, old-fashioned, white enamel bathtub that stood on claw feet in the middle of a group of indoor palm trees. A hose filled the tub with warm water, which was then heavily squirted with liquid detergent, until foam hung dripping over the side in frothy stalactites. Banks of lights were switched on. "Silence," said Serge, then "Action."

Lili did what she usually did. She had developed the trick of disassociating herself from her body. She *willed* herself to feel that her skin was as irrelevant to her real self as old overalls, and therefore displaying it was no worse than displaying old overalls. The real Lili floated up and away from those grubby, alien hands that touched her flesh. She looked down on the scene from above, distant and uninvolved in the distasteful proceedings; or she dealt with the humiliation and protected her wispy sense of self-esteem by simply imagining herself elsewhere.

After such sessions Lili would be remote and silent, she would hardly speak until she had returned to the apartment and had a long soak in a warm tub of water in a darkened bathroom where slowly her body and soul were reunited. Lili always believed firmly in her future, sure of an eventual happy ending, because she had read so many of the romantic trash magazines that Madame Sardeau read every week. She therefore knew the traditional ending to these tales. She was an orphan, wasn't she? She was being exploited, wasn't she? She was going through tough times, wasn't she, like all those heroines? That meant she was currently at about the middle of chapter four of her life, and about six chapters away from the man of her dreams and eternal happiness. In the meantime, she had to put up with the standard soap opera plot.

"Action!" said Serge again, impatiently.

Slowly Lili slipped off her white rabbit fur coat, then stepped naked into the foam. Carefully she soaped her breasts, running her fingers slowly over her slippery flesh. Then Teresa stepped forward, wearing a man's shirt unbuttoned to the waist. She leaned over the back of the bath and started to soap Lili's body with long, sensuous strokes. "Right, Teresa, now sit behind her on the edge of the bath, one leg on either side of her, more in the water Lili, now *splash*, I want Teresa's shirt soaked, I want to see those nipples press against it. Now slither in behind her, Teresa. Christ, there's water all over the fucking floor. Now, you little darlings, I want the normal action, yeah, that's nice, oh, very nice. For Christ's sake, Lili, look as if you're enjoying it, you know we'll just go on shooting until you do, that's better, now move in very slowly, Ben, I want you sitting on the back of the bath, legs in the water, cock standing at attention."

Blue-black muscles shining, Ben appeared through the palms. "Get out of the bath, Teresa, I want you standing behind him. Now, Ben, lean over and grab Lili under the armpits, slowly, slowly, you're relishing the thoughts of what you're about to do, now turn her around. I want a close-up of your hands running over her ass and in the crack. Lili, could you please show a bit more interest. Let's have some sinuous writhing or you'll be fucking sorry. That's nice, *very* nice. . . . Now, Lili, kneel down in the water as Ben stands up. We're tracking into this shot. Now purse those rosebud lips, Lili, and in it goes, smoothly. For Christ's sake, you little bitch, try and look as if it's your favorite flavor lollipop, that's better. Now slowly pull her up, Ben, settle your ass on the back of the bath and use that prick with imagination, *slower*, you black bastard."

He shot the scene three times before Ben's penis went on strike. It wasn't as juicy as their usual stuff, but that was for a carefully calculated reason. Serge wanted the attention focused on Lili, rather than the action. He didn't want it too dirty, he wanted a *pretty* fuck. It was going exactly as he had hoped it would, like a routine whiskey or bathsalts commercial, but with nothing left to the imagination or subliminal interpretation.

He knew he couldn't shoot a proper film test, but he'd be willing to bet his new Mercedes this would get the big boys interested—especially after that call from Zimmer. He was after bigger game than blue movies. He wanted to make Lili a star. Vadim had done it with Bardot, so Serge was doing his fucking best to get Lili discovered. He'd already arranged for her to have a walk-on part in the Christopher Lee sci-fi that Trianon was shooting at Versailles; she'd only be an extra, a spaceship soldierette, but she'd get the feeling of a proper set, ready for the big chance if it came.

Not if, he told himself, *when*.

Shortly before her fifteenth birthday, Lili made her first legitimate appearance on celluloid under a green, greasy film of Leichner, with her hair hidden by a silver, cardboard helmet.

The bus picked her up at five A.M. It was filled with sleepy, silent figures huddled in overcoats. They drove out of Paris, through Versailles and into the forest beyond; the bus pulled off the road, jerked down a rutted track and stopped in a large clearing where several trucks and trailers were parked. The passengers climbed out of the bus and stumped off in silence toward the nearest truck. As Lili hesitated on the steps of the bus, a thin young fellow in a white yachting cap said, "Better grab your coffee while you can."

"Where does one find coffee?"

"This your first day? Come with me." He dug his hands into the pockets of his navy pea jacket, and they walked through damp grass toward the truck. Just before they reached it, the rear door flew open and a caterer started handing out coffee and croissants. "This should wake you up." He handed her a paper cup. "For some unknown reason, the coffee's always good. You an extra? One of the spaceship crew? I'm one of the gypsies that see it crash into the clearing. Got any lines?"

"No."

"I've got three. A *part!* My first, which is why I'm so cheerful." He beamed.

"Also, I like being awake when everyone's half asleep and huddled around the coffee truck, sun barely up, birds singing, nobody around."

"I *hate* getting up early. Why did we have to get up so early when shooting doesn't start until eight-thirty?"

"All motion picture people get up early; *everyone* has to be *ready* for eight-thirty and, believe it or not, it can take three hours to get them all ready."

"You don't sound French."

"I'm not. My mother was from Los Angeles, but both my parents were killed in a car crash when I was five. I was brought up by my French grandmother. I'm called Simon Pont."

"I'm Lili, and I lost my parents when I was seven."

"Tough, ain't it? Lili what?"

"Lili nothing. Just Lili." She didn't explain that after having four family names by the time she was barely seven, she had decided that in the future she would just call herself "Lili."

"But where are the stars? Where are Christopher Lee and Mademoiselle Collins?" Lili asked hopefully, as she chewed the last ragged end of her croissant and they moved over to look at the call sheet.

"The stars stay in their trailers, which are *sacred*. Positively no entry allowed, nobody ever goes into a trailer if he isn't supposed to. There are trailers for the director, wardrobe, makeup and the stars, and everyone else has to manage without one as best they can."

"Where's the director?"

"Staying in his trailer until we're ready to go. The writer, the set designer and the press agent won't turn up until around eight-thirty, lucky bastards."

"Now I know everything I need to know about a movie set."

"Everything except where the makeup truck is, which is where you should be at this moment. Look, there's your name on the call sheet—'Makeup six-thirty.' You'd better run; I tell you, makeup can be *bitches*. You don't want little piggy eyes with bags beneath them, do you?"

She saw Simon again at lunch break, when he fetched their sandwiches from the trailer. He spread his jacket on the grass and together they sat on it. He bit into the crusty roll with teeth that were unusually small, white and far apart, like a child's teeth. "Look at that idiot driving a Mercedes down the track at that speed."

"It's Serge, my manager—the man I live with."

"Oh, well, I'll be off then." He didn't seem surprised or disappointed.

The following month saw publication of the tire calendar. The calendar itself was an annual event, always expensively produced by a famous photographer and a prominent art director: the editions were collected like antiquarian books. The 1964 calendar, which starred Lili, was an overnight sensation. Every art editor and designer had to have one, every truck driver leered at Lili, every schoolboy lusted after her, and many of their fathers did as well. Within two weeks the calendar was sold out, and copies changed hands at eight times the list price. The print order for the second printing was a quarter of a million, and it disappeared as fast as the first one.

Almost overnight Lili was not only famous, but notorious. She couldn't move in Paris without being recognized.

Lili found one of the advantages of having such a low sense of self-esteem was that it wasn't difficult to ignore her growing public image as a tough, sexy, knowing little slut.

Serge taught her to tell journalists, in a whisper, that she was an orphan; orphans had good publicity value, he said. They were sad and appealing. Lili was to stop this crazy-sounding nonsense about her mysterious "Mama," because it confused his pitch and, anyway, he didn't want a hundred crazy bag ladies turning up claiming to be Lili's mother and trying to grab half her income.

Most of Lili's early pictures were resold, and her blue movies changed hands at a price that made Serge's income almost an embarrassment. He huddled with lawyers and accountants, discussing the tax advantages of Andorra, Jersey or Monaco; of being offshore in the Cayman Islands or the Bahamas; of starting a company in Panama or Mexico; of having money paid to Dutch lawyers to lodge in numbered Swiss accounts, or Swiss lawyers in a group-participation company that fronted for big movie stars.

The pros, cons and percentages of these schemes were never discussed with Lili, because she owned none of the properties. She was under contract to Sergio Productions, so Serge owned her. All that Lili got were the sly looks, the leers and the gossip. She couldn't cope with any of it, so she greeted everyone with a suspicious stare.

What else could she do?

CHAPTER 33

SHORTLY AFTER PAGAN'S third wedding anniversary, on a warm spring day in 1965, Kate and Pagan were playing a nursery card game in the garden. "Buster doesn't like being in London much," said Pagan, as she shuffled the cards. "Still misses Cornwall, poor darling. So do I, come to that." They started to play. "Did I tell you that Christopher got tough with Mama? They both sat in the library talking in quiet, polite, nasty voices—*snap!* Blast, you're fast—and the upshot was that we all trooped along to the solicitor in St. Austell—*snap!* Blast you—Christopher said he should never have allowed my guardian to lease my property to herself, although I don't suppose for one minute that was how she put it to the poor old bugger. He seemed to think that she was running the place on my behalf and he didn't even know about—*snap!* oh, you know, her will. She'd had that drawn up by some smart crook in London—blast, too fast for me!—So for ten pounds, I purchased an option to—*snap!* Oh, you cow—purchase Ma's shares in the health farm at par upon her death, and for another ten pounds—*snap!* Bugger!—I purchased an option to purchase Selma's shares in the health farm at current valuation upon her death. Missed again, dammit. Get that? What it means is that Selma—*snap! Thank* you!—can't get her claws on Trelawney if Mama kicks the bucket, and that I get it all back in—*snap!*—the end if I outlive them, plus the health farm."

"That's nice—*snap!*" shrieked Kate. "Thanks, a splendid pile of hearts and diamonds."

"Oh, you cow, you've won!" said Pagan. "Well, I hope it's put you in a good temper because I want you to help me in a delicate matter."

"What is it this time?" Kate asked.

"I've worked out two things," Pagan explained, "for both of which I need your aid. Firstly, I love Christopher more than drink, and secondly I love him so much that I couldn't bear it if he were to die. And you know that he might at any minute, and I'd be left with nothing of him. There would be nothing left of Christopher. So I want his child. Even if it kills him, I want his child."

"Can't you get . . . er . . . artificial insemination?"

"Certainly not! I can't bear the idea of anything unnatural. I want our child to be conceived as an act of love, even if it's the last one we share."

Kate was awed by the ruthlessness of Pagan's reasoning. "In spite of what the doctor said?"

"In spite of what the doctor said, darling. So I want you to help me to seduce Christopher, because I know he'll never agree." Kate was speechless with astonishment. "What I want you to do is the opposite of birth control. I want you to help me work out the dangerous time—my *unsafe* period. Then I want you to double-check with me, because my arithmetic is abysmal and I know I'm only going to get one chance."

"Suppose one chance isn't enough?"

"It was before, remember? Only once in Switzerland was enough to produce that darling little thing."

"Let's not talk about it or I'll start crying." They both sighed.

"I've been to the family planning clinic," Pagan continued "I've got a chart and a special thermometer and I'm going to take my temperature every morning, but I want *you* to keep the chart so that Christopher doesn't accidentally find it: I'd be sure to leave the damn thing on the mantelpiece one morning. When my temperature dips slightly that means it's just before ovulation. After ovulation it rises several tenths of a degree and then stays there until I get the curse. So when my temperature goes down is the time for *action!* The clinic people said that I'd better check my pattern for a couple of months before settling down to strenuous nightlife."

Though Kate was scandalized by the idea, Pagan eventually talked her into it. Each morning after Christopher had gone to the lab Pagan telephoned her temperature to Kate. For the first two months there didn't seem to be any difference, but on the third month there was no doubt—the temperature dipped.

On the propitious day of the fourth month, when the moon was in the correct quarter and the thermometer had definitely wobbled, Pagan, calculating and steady as a tiger, set about seducing her lawfully wedded husband.

The next morning she reported to Kate. "Darling, I rushed out to Fortnum's and bought some smoked salmon, a game pie, some country blackberries. I'd turned up the heating and when he got home I was sitting in that pink, gauze Arab shift with nothing on underneath. I'd already opened a bottle of Haut Brion

'59, and as soon as he sat down I handed him a huge mint julep. Neat bourbon with chopped mint, crushed in melted sugar. Oh, it smelled divine! 'Do you think it's strong enough?' I asked him. 'Because you know I can't tell.' Darling, it was six eggcupsful of neat bourbon, but you don't notice because of the minty sugar. The rest was easy. Mind you, it was too quick to be fun and I can't *tell* you how livid he was afterward, except, of course, he dared not get too angry in case his blood pressure went up."

Amazingly, she *was* pregnant. Once he'd gotten over his initial fury and was used to the idea, Christopher was hugely pleased. Pagan said that she wanted a daughter, "a dear little girl with big brown eyes," she said, nestling in his lap, though she was much too large for it. Her husband laughed.

"Well, you're not going to get one, my darling."

"Why not?"

"Because we both have blue eyes and it's genetically impossible for two perfectly blue-eyed parents to have a brown-eyed child."

"What do you mean, genetically impossible?"

He pulled her against him and started to stroke her mahogany hair. "In the nucleus of every human cell are two sets of genes—one for each parent—and in an embryo they form the blueprint that determines the inherited characteristics of the baby."

With one finger he traced her bronze, winged eyebrow. "Now when you come to the genes for eye color, you *only* get a blue-eyed child if the genes of *both* parents are for blue. The gene for blue eyes is what we call 'recessive,' which means that a person with only *one* gene for brown eyes and one gene for blue will always have brown eyes, not blue ones. And it also means that two perfectly blue-eyed parents can *only* produce a blue-eyed child. It is impossible for two perfectly blue-eyed parents to have a brown-eyed child."

"What about hazel eyes?"

"Of course, there are degrees of eye color. You can get greenish-blue or hazelish-brown, and there's a very slight possibility of a throwback to some brown-eyed ancestor, although it's very unlikely. But this *never* happens when the color is definite in both parents." He stretched over and kissed the other winged, bronzed eyebrow. "You can't expect two clearly blue-eyed individuals to produce a clearly brown-eyed offspring, because it's genetically impossible." Pagan shut her eyes and snuggled up against his chest. "So because we've *both* got blue eyes, we have only blue genes to give to our child. You're going to have a blue-eyed baby, my darling. And I hope she'll be an exact replica of you."

The child, Sophia, was born in the summer of 1966. Surprisingly, Pagan was a perfect mother. Her carelessness and untidiness vanished overnight. This amazed Kate until one day, while she watched Pagan play pussycat on the floor with Sophia, Kate realized that Pagan treated her daughter as she treated her animals—with more care than she did adult human beings.

Naturally, Kate was asked to be godmother. "Now, listen, darling," Pagan said, "this is *serious*. I don't want to have any more disasters in my life. I want you to be the sort of godmother that she can run away to. I want her always to see you as her ally, always on *her* side, whether or not she deserves it. To be frank, darling, I want what I *didn't* have when I needed it."

Kate nodded gravely.

She gave Sophia a string of iridescent baroque pearls. Predictably, Pagan said, "I'd better wear them, they'll lose the luster if they aren't worn against warm skin. No point in keeping them in the bank."

Though her alcoholic phase now seemed like an impossible dream, Pagan still went nearly every week to her AA meeting. By now she realized that they had better be part of her life forever—if she wanted to avoid yet another fatal mistake.

PART SEVEN

CHAPTER 34

IN THE SPRING of 1956, it had been four years since Kate fled from Cairo. After her return, she had spent the first week weeping, conscious of her father's tight-lipped disappointment and indignant fury. Kate felt she had to get away from home, to get away from him. She had to think of an excuse for staying in Walton Street. She didn't want to be tied down by a full-time job, so she decided to become a free-lance translator. Kate's French wasn't good enough—neither she nor Pagan nor any other pupil had learned much at l'Hirondelle—so Kate signed up for an intensive course at the Berlitz School in Oxford Street and fled from the opulent, fake Georgian bricks of Greenways back to her old apartment in the genuine little Georgian cottage in Walton Street.

She found her work easy. She was quick and accurate, and she got as many translations as she could handle from a French literary agent in Motcomb Street so she could juggle her working hours to suit her private life. Although her father gave her an allowance, within six months of starting work Kate could have managed without it.

She tried to blot Robert out of her mind. Once more she started to see old friends, and she quickly learned that, if she felt depressed, she should never stay indoors or alone. So she would go for a walk, moving around London by herself as she had never been allowed to when a child. She mingled with the crowds of young, untidy foreigners who lounged around the base of the statue in Piccadilly Circus. She liked to sit among the stone lions and fountains of Trafalgar Square, then visit the National Gallery, where she would sit for hours in the calm peace of the Monet water lily room.

Since leaving Cairo, Kate felt that some part of her had been cut off. Partly because she was an only child and partly as a result of her father's verbal violence, she had always felt timid, tentative and lonely, but now she felt an added sense of loss and didn't understand it.

What had she lost? Not her virginity; that had gone long before she met Robert—and anyway, it hadn't been the melodramatic event that it was cracked up to be. She no longer wept over Robert, although it had been painful to hear that he had married Pagan.

But that was over—long ago—and it wasn't as if there weren't other men around to distract her. Kate knew lots of nice fellows, and as a matter of fact she was never out of love—a fortnight here, half an hour there, a five-minute passion for some unknown man on the top of a bus. She knew she was sensual, knew she loved to touch a man's body, to feel a man touch *her*. She found something to hunger after in almost every man she met. What she *didn't* know, but badly wanted to know, was why the only two men she had ever really cared about had dumped her.

Why?

Kate told herself she had been obedient, faithful, loyal, trusting and truthful. Well, almost always. So what was wrong with her? *Why* had she been kicked in the teeth?

"Why?" she asked Maxine, who was on a buying trip to London. They were sitting on the purple rag rug, drinking cocoa in front of the lavender gas flames.

"Maybe you give too quickly?" Maxine suggested. "No, of course I don't mean your body, stupid. But maybe you are too eager for love—too quick to be affectionate, too clinging, too claustrophobic." She blew on the drink to cool it. "More than anyone else I know, Kate, you need love. One can see that. So when you think you have found it, you are all over the man, like a puppy." She put the tip of her tongue in her drink and quickly withdrew it. "Perhaps you should be more reticent, more elusive. Men value what is difficult to get. But with François, I remember, you threw yourself at him, threw yourself in front of him like a doormat with 'welcome' printed on it. So, as we say in France, he wiped his feet on you."

"But I was being emotionally honest," Kate said.

"And you paid heavily for this pleasant self-indulgence and lack of self-discipline," said Maxine, with Gallic cynicism. "If you are difficult to pursue, if you make a man think and worry and invest a lot of his time and effort in pursuing you, then he will—of course—justify these efforts to himself by deciding that you are unusually worthwhile and desirable."

"Deliberately playing hard to get is nasty psychological exploitation," said Kate, "*and* it's phony."

Maxine shrugged her shoulders. "Then call it something else." She blew again on the hot cocoa. "I feel you lack discrimination. I see you with some real creeps."

"That still doesn't explain why I have this sense of loss. I mean, I hardly ever think about those two bastards who dumped me. Thank heaven, I don't want either of them. But I want to identify this sense of loss. If it's not them, what is it?"

Maxine took a cautious sip. "Kate, you may laugh, but I think what you have lost is your trust. You don't really trust people anymore. No, you *do* trust me; maybe it is only *men* you don't trust?"

Kate had been conditioned to love bastards. Without knowing or realizing it, she had duplicated in adult life the pattern she had learned at her daddy's knee: Kate was hooked on rejection. When men started to criticize her, she always fell in love with them. And when she fell in love with them, she fell into bed with them. And when she went to bed with them, she never climaxed. And she never dared to tell them. So Kate faked.

But Kate was always frightened that the man would guess. She was afraid he would leave her if he thought she was frigid. As Kate was terrified of rejection, she never had an honest relationship with a lover. Untrusting and nervous in her obsessive search for Mr. Wrong, she felt so insecure that as soon as there seemed to be even a remote possibility that he might abandon her, Kate immediately left him or pushed him out of her life.

Though she was tense and defensive in her most intimate relationships, it wasn't obvious unless you were in bed with Kate. Fully clothed, her aura of intense sexuality attracted hordes of admiring men. Kate didn't see herself as attractive: since apparently she had been unattractive to the men she had loved, she became haunted by the feeling that no worthwhile man could ever really love her.

But she had to check.

The classic one-night-stand man only wants to get involved if he thinks the woman doesn't; the classic one-night-stand woman is hopefully, unsuccessfully searching for Prince Charming and feeling forever guilty about it. Many women imagine that promiscuity brings conquests and pleasures. This may be so with a man—the sort of man who wants to try every biscuit in the tin—but unlike a man, a woman is rarely promiscuous if she has a wonderful love at home. A promiscuous man is afraid he might be *missing* something. A promiscuous woman is *seeking* something and—sadly—not finding it.

So there Kate was, a classic case of potential nymphomania, until New Year's Eve at the 1956 Chelsea Arts Ball where, among the balloons and streamers, among the real and the bogus painters, Kate met her first Design Man. Toby was a twenty-eight-year-old architect who specialized in hospital design, and had just been made the youngest partner of his firm. Toby introduced Kate to the haute-Bohemian circles in which he moved, and Kate found his friends a refreshing change from officers of the Household Brigade and budding stockbrokers. In fact, she was fascinated by the Design Men. They were so world-weary, scornful of everything that wasn't perfectly proportioned or that they hadn't thought of first. They held up a cocktail and squinted at the proportions of the glass before sipping the drink, and they could only eat from plain white china.

"The first night I slept with Toby," Kate happily told Maxine (who had, of course, heard the intimate bits earlier), "he took three, black cotton cushions off the tangerine cotton mattress—which was on the black-painted floor—and put them on the black leather sling chair." Sitting in front of the fireplace, Kate pulled her knees up and put her arms around them, then said in a dreamy voice, "There was no other furniture in the room." She rested her head on her knees and continued, "Then he went behind the kitchen bar, stood on a stool, took two quilts from an overhead cupboard, bent down and pulled out two black pillows from under the sink, then threw the whole pile onto the mattress."

She heaved a long, sexy sigh. "After that he took off his jeans and lay there reading *Design* by the light of one of those chrome caterpillars that wriggle out of the wall, as if they were trying to read over your shoulder. Then he glanced up and criticized my panties."

"Super," Maxine said politely, but to herself she thought, Oh, dear, another bastard.

Kate was hopelessly dominated by Toby, who told her how to dress, look, think, feel, behave. When he criticized her in front of Maxine for being sloppy, clumsy and inefficient, Kate not only believed him, but to Maxine's surprise actually promised she'd try hard to do better.

Kate adored Toby's self-confidence and shared his high opinion of himself. She was still a happy, groveling doormat, thought Maxine, although she had to admit that Toby was quick-witted and entertaining, if not particularly handsome; he was obviously clever and passionately interested in his work; he took the trouble to explain it to Maxine as they all sat on the pale beech floor listening to the delicate, lacelike intricacy of a harpsichord toccata.

"The drawback to hospital design is that it's often very frustrating," Toby told Maxine, as he mixed a Campari in a plain glass. "You haven't got *one* client—there's a whole bunch of them. Doctors who won't bother to read plans properly, head nurses, the Regional Hospital Boards *and* the Ministry of Health."

He held the glass of red liquid to the light. Wonderful color! "The boards and the ministries are old-fashioned; they have preconceived ideas and they won't listen to new ones. They tell me to 'economize,' when they're really suggesting that I design overcrowded wards."

"It sounds extremely complex," said Maxine politely. At last a friend of Kate with some sense, thought Toby.

Kate listened adoringly. She loved to hear Toby talk about his work, loved to visit his calm, all-white office with the tilted desks and the vast blueprints. Unlike the doctors, she had quickly learned to read them.

But Kate didn't dare let Toby move into Walton Street, because her father would have exploded with rage. "Then I suppose we'll have to get married," Toby said ungraciously, and once again Kate's eyes sparkled.

Kate Harrington. Mrs. Toby Harrington. Mrs. Harrington.

This time there was no marquise diamond—in fact, Kate only just managed to get a wedding ring at all, because Toby thought they were bourgeois, if not a primitive token of possession. However, he was reluctantly persuaded to buy a secondhand gold band with a worn heart pattern winding around it. The previous owner must have been a very worried woman, because all the hearts were worn away on the right side from nervous twisting.

Toby's widowed mother came up from Essex for the wedding. Major Hartley-Harrington's widow was a big, brusque woman, with muscular legs and a nose she could look down. Although she wore navy silk, you sensed that mentally she wore tweeds and was worrying whether the dogs were all right in her absence. She said remarkably little, and during the dreary register office ceremony, she kept sniffing and hitching her fur stole up around her shoulders, obviously under no illusion that she was acquiring a daughter.

She mellowed a little over luncheon at the Connaught, but due to the wine, rather than any growing affection for her new daughter-in-law. At the end of the first course, Kate's father, who had been struggling to talk to Toby's mother for half an hour and knew a tough nut when he saw one, banged the side of his glass with his knife and said he wasn't a speechmaker, that young people's lives were their own affair, that he realized things were done differently today—which was not to say that they were done better—but that two people couldn't really live together in a dark hole, so he had bought the house in Walton Street as a wedding present.

Kate flung her arms around him and wept for joy.

After that announcement the wedding group relaxed, and happy laughter actually accompanied the bride and groom as they flew off for their honeymoon in Milan, where the Triennale Exposition was in progress. Toby could criticize any international award-winning designs that weren't quite up to his standards.

* * *

At first they were happy.

Kate's old basement apartment was gutted, painted white, covered with cork pinboard and transformed into Toby's office. It was always full of his friends; they came pouring in to be fed, often without warning, and to talk about their work before, during and after meals.

Kate loved it.

The ground floor of the little Walton Street house was also gutted. All walls, ceilings and window frames were painted dull chocolate, the floors were covered with white vinyl tiles—which showed every footprint—a rash of spotlights appeared, and the balustrades were removed from the staircase. On one side of the "living environment," a ten-foot run of kitchen units was installed, hidden by a sliding screen of louvered pine, so that you had to heave the heavy screen back ten feet if you wanted to get a teaspoon. The wall opposite the kitchen unit was hung with shelves that supported books, drinks, visually acceptable flowers (such as a bunch of daisies in a jam jar or one long-stemmed rose in a chemist's beaker) and Toby's collection of battered Victorian toys. Toby himself had designed the metal chairs. Some looked like tractor seats, and some were made of crisscrossed wire. "Ass traps," muttered Kate's father, thinking how bloody bare the place looked; when her parents visited, Kate hid the priapic African carvings and the privately printed Aubrey Beardsley engravings.

In the evenings Kate worked hard and happily as a hostess, entertaining Toby's clients, his useful contacts, architectural journalists and the other designers who were working on Toby's projects. Kate loved learning to cook for them. After a couple of standard bride's-dinner-party disasters (a casserole burned black, a salted ham she'd forgotten to soak overnight before cooking) she discovered Elizabeth David's cookbooks, and from that moment on, only the breakfast boiled eggs were served without garlic. For a Christmas present she asked Toby for a hand-operated salt grinder and a jar of *confit d'oie* from Fortnum's. She served the preserved goose to her parents on Boxing Day. It was greasy, thought her mother, but this odd food phase will pass fast enough when she has a baby.

As he kissed Kate on the doorstep, her father bravely said, "Usually I don't like mucked-up foreign food, but I must say that was *very nice*, girl."

They were the last words that Kate heard him say.

CHAPTER 35

THE NEXT DAY, Kate's father managed to give himself a mild electric shock while changing a lightbulb in the loggia, fell backward off the ladder onto the flagstone floor and broke his neck. He was dead when Kate's mother found him.

Kate cried for a week and couldn't really understand why, for she had resented his rages and his tyranny. She would never forget the quivering, nail-biting fear of her childhood.

She was silent and strained after the funeral until the end of the month when, to Toby's relief, Maxine came to stay. Kate poured herself a Campari, sat cross-legged on the green and blue, longhaired ryja rug from Finland and burst into tears.

"It was the last thing I expected, Maxie—to feel depressed when the old bugger passed away. But I feel terribly tired and completely lacking in self-confidence. It's as if I were a schoolgirl again!" She took a swig of Campari. "His death was such a horrible mixture of farce and tragedy. When I got to Greenways there he was, lying on a couch in the hall as if he were having a nap, stone-dead in his blue-striped pajamas and clutching an arum lily. Someone had put makeup on his face, his cheeks were bright peach, and they had tied a handkerchief over his head and under his chin to hold his jaws together before rigor mortis set in."

Kate took another large gulp, looked at the Campari with distaste, got up and poured herself a Scotch. She wanted "a proper drink," as her father would have said. "If he could see himself, he'd die of shame, I thought, and it was only then that I realized that he *was* dead. That was the only point at which my mother nearly broke down. Apart from that she was bloody marvelous, brisk and cheerful at the funeral, just as he would have wanted her to behave at his last appearance."

Kate now started to snivel, looking sad and stunned. "Mummy kept saying if a bomb had got him in the Blitz he would have wanted us to feel happy when we thought of him."

She sniffed again. "He obviously hadn't expected to die at fifty-five. His papers were in such a mess that it took me a whole day just to find his medical card."

"Poor baby," said Maxine, and gave her a big hug. "You'll feel better soon."

But instead, Kate had a row with her father's lawyer on the following day. "Now, remember, Mummy," Kate cautioned before they entered his office, "for heaven's sake, don't be overawed by him."

The two women were shown into a small Gray's Inn office filled with shelves of red-leatherbound legal books, and to her surprise the normally timid Kate—feeling furious on behalf of her dead father—coldly reviewed the situation.

"Last month, Mr. Stiggins, the day after my father died, you seemed to know very little about my father's assets. You told my mother then she would be unable to lay her hands on any money at all for some time."

Stiggins nodded. "Now; there is no need for you ladies to be anxious. As you have seen from the will, the late Mr. Ryan's entire estate is contained in a trust fund for his widow, which will, upon her demise, be inherited by her only issue, Mrs. Harrington. It's just a question of waiting for probate. A few months . . . Perhaps a year."

He tapped his fingertips together. "The late Mr. Ryan named me personally as one trustee. The other trustee is his former partner, Mr. Jellaby—who, as you know, has unfortunately been in the hospital for the past two months after a stroke."

Portentously he continued, "Consequently, I am currently responsible for the late Mr. Ryan's investments, and after much deliberation and discussion with this firm's stockbroker, I have decided to sell all the shares. After death-duties have been paid, the remaining money will be invested in the British Widows Fund, which is a safe unit trust company."

"What's a unit trust company?" asked Kate, aghast that apparently such financial decisions could be taken without her mother even being consulted.

"A company with expert advisers that invests its funds in the stock market. It is, I might say, a very *cautious* company. Naturally, I cannot allow risks to be taken. . . ."

Kate didn't understand much of what followed, but she was determined to inform herself about the stock market.

The first thing she discovered was that British Widows was so "safe" that it paid minimal interest.

"I can't help thinking that Stiggins must be getting a cut somewhere," Kate muttered to herself, grimly determined to keep checking on British Widows.

She bought a child's exercise book and started to take notes on the stock market.

Two months later, Kate had another interest.

She was pregnant.

She was delighted. She rushed out and bought a wicker cot, an antique brass bed, some nineteenth-century Randolph Caldecott nursery rhyme prints and a large, traditional pram, like the ones the royal nannies push. Toby loathed it, especially as it blocked their narrow hall.

Her mother returned from an expedition to Bond Street with a pile of minute lace garments that had been hand-stitched by French nuns. Mrs. Ryan was cheerfully living on a steadily increasing overdraft, for which the bank was charging her interest at two percent above the normal rate because the loan was unsecured. She had decided to sell Greenways. It was too big for her. She was going to buy a country cottage in the Cotswolds and live there with her sister.

Kate was still absorbed by Toby's work, fascinated by his theories and his missionary zeal. On her next visit, Maxine, amazed, watched Kate pounding a pestle in an ancient marble mortar as they all three lounged around the kitchen end of the living environment. That morning, for two hours after her arrival, Maxine had listened to Kate pouring out her heart, her hopes and her happiness. Kate now seemed a new person, a person in her own right, a person of some importance. She no longer looked quiet and worried. She wore a self-confident smile and a canary maternity smock made from upholstery linen that she'd bought from Harrods furniture department—although she hadn't confessed that to Toby, because Harrods was terribly unvisual.

Maxine admired every hand-smocked, lace-trimmed item in the layette and then listened to Kate's plans, as they both sat on the tangerine linoleum of the newly decorated Visual Nursery and watched the mobiles stir in a slight breeze from the window. As Kate babbled on, Maxine suddenly realized that her friend longed for a totally unworried love relationship. Maxine herself knew that the charm of having babies is that Mother is in charge: she is the boss and she calls the shots. At last.

For the following six hours Kate questioned Maxine non-stop about pregnancy, upon which, as usual, Maxine (being one step ahead) was the authority. They endlessly discussed how much it hurt, whether you called them pains or contractions, and what it *really* felt like. "Shitting a football," said Maxine in

French with unusual vulgarity but much feeling. All the other mothers she'd known when she was pregnant had soft-pedaled this aspect to Maxine and she still felt angry about it. They discussed whether Kate should attend the new natural childbirth trust classes in Seymour Street, how much bigger your breasts become, whether they sag afterward, how long it takes to get back to normal down below, whether you would still be the same circumference *there* and what you did about stretch marks.

At this point Toby came back from a visit to the Design Center and suggested that they all have a drink. As they carefully walked down the bannisterless staircase, Maxine reckoned that, more than any pregnant woman she'd ever encountered, Kate *needed* this baby. Toby didn't seem nearly as interested as Kate in the baby, and whenever Kate mentioned hospitals (she was booked into St. George's), Toby immediately started talking about cross-infection and Florence Nightingale. Toby was devoted to the theories of Florence, the famous nineteenth-century nurse: he had a daguerreotype of her hanging in his office, and he spoke as if the famous lady with the lamp were still alive.

"She talks such a lot of *sense*," said Toby, meaning that he shared her views. "*She* says that patients should be the first concern of a hospital, although the first concern of any damn hospital is their damn medical routine. They wake you up to give you a sleeping pill and put you to bed at tea time, because that's when it suits the nurses' timetable."

Toby was pouring himself a Campari, as carefully as if he were splitting the atom. "Medical men don't seem to realize that a patient isn't an experimental dummy or a corpse to be dissected. They don't seem to realize that a patient is a frightened human being."

"Watch out! He's getting on to the subject of ward sizes," said Kate. "Now where did I put the pine nuts? Oh, you're eating them. Hand them over!"

She waved her long, narrow, tapering hands at Toby. When talking, Kate used her hands a lot. She would flutter one like a fan, or bend her elbows to her waist and, with both hands, slowly make graceful, expanding motions away from her body. Now she waved the pestle in mock threat at Toby, who mock-dodged, then continued, unabashed. "Well, ward sizes are much more important to an illness than patients realize. Of course, nurses like open wards—except when they're ill themselves—because they feel they can keep an eye on everyone."

"Toby, Maxine's come for dinner, not a lecture."

Kate touched a button and the blender shrieked, drowning conversation for a few minutes. Kate tested her mixture, added more salt and pepper and said, "*Tsatsiki*, a cold Greek soup for a change. Taste it, darling."

She held out a spoonful to Toby, who waved it aside and continued to lecture Maxine, who accepted a pale-green spoonful and nodded approvingly (thinking it had too much garlic) as she listened stupefied to Toby droning on.

When Kate was seven months pregnant, her father's former partner died, so Stiggins was left the sole trustee of her father's will. Kate consulted her stock market exercise book and found that in the previous six months British Widows had fallen by eight and a half percent, more than the rest of the market, and there was a huge lawyer's bill to pay for settling her father's affairs. Kate telephoned the Law Society and found that nothing could be done to get the Ryan money out of British Widows unless Kate's mother was willing formally to accuse the trustee solicitor of gross negligence. This complaint would have to be made through another solicitor, and it might be difficult to get a solicitor to take on a case that meant suing a colleague.

"Oh, I couldn't *possibly* change my lawyer, dearest," said Kate's mother, aghast. "I could never look your father's lawyer in the face again."

That night Kate woke with bad, cramping pains and found that she was lying on a sheet that was wet and soggy with her own blood. Toby rushed her to St. George's Hospital where, four hours afterward, he was told that she had lost her baby.

Later, Toby sat by his wife's bed and comforted her, held her hand for hours as she lay weak and speechless, brought her a bowl of blue hyacinths and was quietly advised by the doctor to get her pregnant again as quickly as possible.

He did so.

Again Kate lost her baby.

Three years later, on May 6, 1960, when Anthony Armstrong-Jones married H.R.H. the Princess Margaret, Toby went to the wedding at Westminster Abbey, saw the royal bride walk gravely down the aisle in her billowing white satin Norman Hartnell gown, then saw her grave demeanor change to happy exuberance at the Buckingham Palace reception afterward.

Kate didn't go because, although she also knew Tony, she was again in the hospital, recovering from her third miscarriage.

Passing through London on her way to New York, Maxine visited her. Kate lay alone in a very small, very high green cell. A tangle of pipes wound around the walls like serpents. "Poor baby." Maxine thrust an armful of daffodils at Kate, then blushing, she realized she'd said the wrong thing. "What goes *wrong*, my darling?"

Kate sighed and nothing was heard except the grumble of water pipes. "The first two were miscarriages at the twenty-eighth and twenty-seventh week, but this one was at the thirty-second week, and it was born dead." She pulled a face. "I can't explain how tough it is, how *depressing*. You get the contractions and it hurts like hell and you feel what it's like to be in labor, and all the time you know that there's only going to be a poor little dead body at the end of it."

"But isn't there some warning? Couldn't you lie down and stop its starting?"

"The first time I started to bleed when I was asleep and *then* got pains and lost the baby. At the hospital they blithely quoted statistics as if they were batting averages. 'Cheer up, one in six pregnancies ends in a miscarriage, try again.' But I *knew* they were lying to be kind. I knew nearly all those miscarriages would have been before the fourteenth week. . . ."

She sniffed the sour, spring-scented yellow flowers. "No vases left, I'm afraid, darling. I asked this morning. There are never any bloody vases in hospitals."

"Damn, I forgot. Should have brought you a plant." Maxine put the flowers in the washbasin as Kate continued.

"The second time was worse. I didn't even have time to get to the hospital. D'you know that if you miscarry you're supposed to keep the fetus and the afterbirth and put it in a clean kitchen bowl or plastic bag and take it to the hospital so that the lab can analyze it and tell you why you miscarried? Neither did I, so it was lucky that the doctor got to me in time."

"Yes, but *why* do you miscarry?"

"Don't think I haven't asked that. The first time they said that the fetus had detached itself from the placenta, and the second time they said I had a weak cervix because it dilated too early. So I had some treatment for it. But I had exactly the same trouble again this time. Now they're going to give me a D-and-C to clean my uterus out."

There was a pause, then she added, "The doctors have quite nicely suggested that we shouldn't bother to try again."

She lay with her hands limp on top of the sheet and she sounded almost indifferent, but in fact Kate had taken the news very badly—worse than most women, said the doctors, who suggested to Toby that they consider adoption, whereupon Kate had become hysterical and said that he was *never, never, never* to suggest such a thing again.

"Don't overreact so," Toby said soothingly. "It's just because you've never *considered* adoption."

"I have, I have. Oh, God, yes, I have." Kate became even more frantic, until a nurse rustled in with a syringe and pushed Toby out.

Kate went home weak, exhausted and unutterably sad.

Toby couldn't understand why she felt such depth of loss, such misery. It wasn't as if she had even held the child that she had just lost. She couldn't talk to anyone, she wanted to be alone, but at the same time she didn't want to *be* alone, and she cried for days. Toby was comforting, but he couldn't be around much because he was finishing a big job near Swindon—ironically, a children's convalescent home.

It made Kate sad to see her breasts go back to normal size and feel her stomach grow floppy again, when only the month before it had felt hard and firm. She felt again what she had felt at her father's funeral—an odd sense of loss and bewilderment.

What had she done wrong?

She must have done *something* wrong! Why else this perpetual disappointment when she only wanted normal human happiness? Other people had it, why was *she* being punished? Why couldn't she feel, even for a brief moment, that she was a complete woman? Kate distracted herself from her sense of emptiness with a determined round of business entertaining and the more frivolous ambiance of the Chelsea set. Her little house was only five minutes' walk from the King's Road, and at least three evenings a week, Kate and Toby would drop in for a drink at the Markham Arms, the elaborate Edwardian pub that stood next to Mary Quant's little shop, Bazaar.

Bazaar was a sort of nonstop, free-drinks cocktail party, to which the prettiest girls in London dragged their husbands and their lovers. As Bazaar had only one minuscule dressing room, the girls all had to try on the clothes in the middle of the shop, where every passerby could gaze through the plate glass and enjoy the view.

Suddenly, Chelsea seemed to have sprung into fashion as Britain's San Francisco or Left Bank. As its cellars, espresso coffee bars, beat joints, clothes and "fab" girls were internationally publicized, the little London borough ceased to be a geographical location and became synonymous with a way of living and dressing. Kate loved the excitement that throbbed from the artery of the King's Road into fashion, design, and show business; she adored the new clothes and wore skimpy, high-waisted, gray flannel tunics with white knee socks over a scarlet leotard with scarlet vinyl boots. She wore plum and ginger outfits with swashbuckling black leather coats and fur hats as large as those of the sentries outside Buckingham Palace. Outwardly, she looked a Chelsea girl, a dishy bird, challenging, confident, leather-booted and black-stockinged, in the vanguard of the youthquake, which was establishing the fact that the second half of the twentieth century belonged to the young (or so they thought) as they went about the business of trend-setting.

Kate was a little in awe of Mary Quant, a small, redheaded girl who was terrifyingly silent most of the time. She and the other dishy birds, the Chelsea girls, seemed shatteringly sophisticated and *with it*. Beside them, Kate felt hopelessly unbrilliant and untalented. Oh, to have been at art school! Oh, to be able, like Mary, not only to invent but to *wear* with aplomb the Look of the Moment whether it was the Lolita Look, the Schoolgirl Look, the Leather Look or the Wet-Weather Look with yellow plastic skirt and fisherman's sou'wester.

Kate tried. She bleached her hair and had it cut in a sex-kitten tangle of curls and black-rimmed her eyes above pale-pink lipstick (worn over a white base) and she felt utterly forlorn and unbelonging. She thought of joining Chelsea Art School and learning to paint, she timidly told Toby one evening, as they hurried through a drizzle to the Markham Arms. Toby dug his hands deeper into the pockets of his hair duffle coat, which he wore over black drainpipe trousers and sweater (he dressed like Audrey Hepburn), frowned at his beige suede boots, and said, quite kindly, that he didn't really think Kate had what it *took*.

Then Kate heard that Pagan was back in England and had been for a long time. Kate and Maxine both had heard rumors that Pagan's marriage had broken up. They had both written to her in Cairo and also care of Trelawney and neither of them had received a reply. Kate had heard that Pagan was living in Beirut and vaguely imagined her in baggy pink trousers, munching Turkish delight on a pile of silken cushions. Maxine was far too absorbed in her own marriage and her business to try to track down Pagan, especially if *she* didn't want to keep in touch. If Pagan wanted to see Maxine, well, Pagan knew where she could find her.

Then, one evening, at an art gallery opening, Kate met—and instantly recognized—Phillippa, the long-nosed, ginger-frizzed bridge player, whom Kate hadn't seen since her last visit to Cairo. Phillippa was the sort of person who made a life's work of keeping up with people, never allowing them to escape her inexorable United Nations Christmas cards. She told Kate that Robert had divorced Pagan ages ago and that Pagan had returned to England and buried herself in the country. "Nobody was surprised when they split up," added Phillippa. "Robert was always impossible—that dirty trick he played on you both was absolutely standard behavior for old Robert."

"What dirty trick?" Kate was puzzled.

"But surely you know . . . ?" Kate's surprise grew into indignation, then fury, as Phillippa told her how Robert had deliberately separated Pagan and Kate so long ago—and that the whole of Cairo knew of it; you couldn't keep a secret from the servants east of Gibraltar.

Kate instantly guessed that Pagan would be at Trelawney, and suddenly she longed to see her friend again. She longed for the comfortable, noncompetitive companionship of Pagan. Perched on the plastic, inflatable, see-through armchairs that Toby had designed for the art gallery, Kate thought it was like suddenly yearning for a comfy old armchair instead of this tortured balloon she was sitting in.

She would telephone Trelawney tomorrow.

* * *

Kate returned from her visit to Pagan's cottage feeling loving and protective and with an object for her thwarted maternal instincts to focus on. She proceeded to spend a fortune on telegrams and was as anxious as any worried mother during Pagan's brief and dizzy courtship. After her marriage, when Pagan came to live in London, Kate found to her joy and relief that their friendship was still as strong as if they had never been separated by miles and years and bitterness. They immediately resumed their odd half-sentence, no-verb, one-word, shorthand conversations, unintelligible to their husbands or to anyone else who hadn't known them for twenty years.

CHAPTER 36

JUDY'S PHONE RANG at three in the morning. Sleepily she fumbled for it.

"Did I wake you up?" asked a charming, solicitous male voice.

"Yes."

"*Good!* Because you *need* to wake up. This is Tom Schwartz of Empire Studios. You've just had the nerve to make a public announcement about one of our major new film purchases for 1963 without so much as *consulting* Empire. Yes, I'm referring to the Joe Savvy deal. Didn't it occur to you that a major studio might like to handle its own news? Or were you expecting thanks for saving us the trouble? Perhaps I underestimate your influence? Does Walter Winchell always consult you first?"

"Look, buster," Judy said in a sleepy voice, "you wanna fight, that's fine with me. The most maddening way to end a fight is by slamming the phone down, which is what I'm about to do. I'll come around to your place tomorrow around ten and let you shout at me for exactly seventeen and a half minutes, because it certainly was inconsiderate of me. I'll be wearing sackcloth; you bring the ashes."

She slammed the phone down, took it off the hook and sank back to sleep.

"Would I have *intentionally* upset someone as important as you, Mr. Schwartz?"

For seventeen minutes they had screamed at each other with increasing enjoyment in Tom's elegant office.

"As I've already indicated, I don't give a shit. But if you really want to make amends, you can start by putting your glasses back on your nose so you can at least see the top of my desk. I've seen pictures of you with that little French guy and you were wearing glasses in all of them. A woman who wears glasses for a photograph can't see without 'em."

Judy fished her enormous, black-rimmed goggle glasses out of her purse, stuck them on her nose, sat up and threw him a hopeful smile. If she deliberately made herself vulnerable, people generally forgave her. But Tom was used to being wooed by ravishing starlets of both sexes. "Cut it out," he said. "Let's stop wasting time."

After they'd been working together for two months, Tom took her to lunch at Côte Basque and said, "You're good."

"I know."

"I'm good."

"I know. Together we'd make a great team."

"Then why not?" Tom leaned over the table and covered her hand with his.

"Then take your hands off me. If you're really serious, you're the one man I'll never go to bed with."

"With you a little hand goes a long way," Tom said sourly. "D'you say that to every man who asks you out to a meal?"

"Oh yes, I always make it clear that it's not because I'm ungrateful for the hamburger. I'm frank, but polite."

"Then I might as well give up and tell you what we *can* do together. I want to quit my job, work with you and expand your office into a small coast-to-coast public relations business."

"You *did* say small?"

"Yes. Headquarters in New York and tie-ups with other advertising and PR firms in every major city."

"What would *they* get out of it?"

"Money. An affiliated office in New York. I've spent the best years of my life touring temperamental film stars for Empire and I know how to do it—which means that the local office would meet interesting personalities as a change from handling detergent accounts." Tom signaled for another bottle of Perrier water. "I want to aim for one-shots as well as permanent clients. I want people to turn to us when their own publicity department is overloaded, or when a star needs special attention; Empire could certainly subcontract to us, if they don't feel too sore when I leave."

"Why should a star agree to be handled by us?"

"If you try and book a tour from New York, it's mostly wasted effort, because it's impossible for one office to keep in touch with what's happening to the media all over America. But local offices are always up-to-date. They know which guy in town has the most influence."

"Why me?" Judy asked.

"I've been looking around for someone. You can do it."

"Would I have to drop any of my present clients?"

"No. They'll be the base we build on."

"Will I have to put up any money?"

"A little, sure. We'll need money for decent offices and a staff."

"Then the answer is no, because I haven't any money."

"I could maybe guarantee a bank loan for you."

There must be something honest about my face, thought Judy. "Where would *you* get the money from?"

"I've been investing ten percent of my income in the stock market since I was nineteen years old."

"I think the answer still has to be no. I've only just gotten *out* of hock to the bank, and I kind of like sleeping at nights."

Three years of running her own business had meant three years of constant financial anxiety for Judy. Naturally, she knew how to handle publicity, but apart from doing Guy's simple bookkeeping, Judy had never had anything to do with the business world, and it had been a great shock to find that there were people in this world who didn't pay their bills—because they couldn't or wouldn't or never intended to pay in the first place. Twice, Judy had been evicted from her studio apartment for nonpayment of rent. On the first occasion the money she owed had been paid by her former boss, Pat Rogers, who had remained a firm friend. On the second occasion, Pat insisted that Judy hire a new accountant; then she guaranteed Judy a sizable bank loan and quietly slipped her a couple of minor accounts—a floor polish, and a young, aspiring singer named Joe Savvy.

"No one's going to sack me for disloyalty," Pat reassured Judy, "because I've just been offered a job writing features for *Harper's*, so I'm moving back into journalism at the speed of sound."

Remembering her struggles to repay Pat's loan, Judy shook her head and said, "No, Tom, I can't join you. I simply haven't the capital."

"Look, if you prefer, *I'll* lend you the money, Judy."

"Why should I put up half the money when I've got the clients and you haven't?" A brazen navy-blue gaze flashed at Tom. "Why can't you just buy my goodwill for, say, twenty thousand dollars?"

"You're joking, of course." He settled back. She was going to say yes.

They haggled through the vichyssoise and the grilled sole, and eventually, over the honey mousse, they agreed that Tom would buy her goodwill for seven thousand dollars and invest a further four thousand dollars in the new business.

"But we can't continue to trade under your name alone," Tom said.

"What do you want to call it?"

"How about Local American Creative Enterprise?"

"It's a bit of a mouthful. . . . "

"Not if you use the initials."

"L-A-C-E. Neat."

Even before they'd organized their national network, LACE was showing a profit. "But I can't understand *why!*" Judy complained one evening in her office, as she and Tom went over the previous month's figures. She had just returned from a thirteen-week tour of the country, during which she had finally decided on the publicity offices she wanted to work with and had come to terms with them. Now she bit her thumb thoughtfully. "I've still got the same clients and our running expenses have gone up, but suddenly it's paying off. *Why?*"

"Put it down to logic and my twelve formative, predatory years in the motion picture industry," yawned Tom. "It's nearly ten. Let's pack it in and go home."

"I hope you invested your teenage savings in Bell," said Judy, picking a telephone bill from the top of the pile and holding it at arm's length. "That would have proved logical."

Tom yawned again. "Nobody really operates on logic, especially not a woman. Logic is merely the ability to rationalize what she's going to do anyway."

"And in a man?"

"Man isn't a rational being either, he's irrationally controlled by fear."

"Is that why we're succeeding? Because you terrify people?"

"Because I'm prepared to be ruthless, sure. If people don't see you're prepared to be ruthless, they'll take advantage of you. You used to let them, I don't allow it. That's what's different."

"And your new budgeting system doesn't hurt."

Tom insisted that fees be billed in advance and paid within thirty days. They didn't lift a telephone until the contract was signed *and* the money was deposited in their account, and they never did two minutes' worth of work after a contract expired.

Tom's responsibilities were to make sure that the business paid off, to run the office and to look after their regular clients. Judy's responsibility was to bring in the business, handle the major one-shot campaigns and supervise their local agencies. Judy also handled the creative work, planning the campaigns, working with writers and designers, which was the part she liked best. Once the general campaign had been mapped out and the design work was underway, Judy sent the proposed plan to her regional directors, who executed the campaign locally. A lot of calls were needed between LACE and the RDs—a twenty-five-city tour needed six hundred phone calls before the tour was over. But the client only made one single call—to LACE.

It was a ridiculously simple idea. And because of that, it worked brilliantly.

CHAPTER 37

KATE STILL FAKED. Not always, because she could climax with very little trouble if she lay on top for long enough and wriggled herself into position, but that didn't always seem to happen and when it didn't, if Kate couldn't sleep, she would nip into the bathroom and quickly satisfy herself.

But after she and Toby had been married for six years, something horrible happened—and continued to happen for some time.

On a hot August night, Kate lay in bed reading a newspaper account of Marilyn Monroe's sad, tawdry death. "Oh, dear, she was so lovable and funny." Two teardrops of sympathy wobbled on her lashes and caught Toby's attention.

"She was beautiful, too . . . What long eyelashes you have, Kate."

"Yes Toby, but colorless. If I didn't wear mascara, you wouldn't be able to see them."

"Would *my* eyelashes be longer if *I* put mascara on them?"

"I expect so . . . darling, it says here that poor Marilyn's feet were dirty and the scarlet polish on her toes was chipped. Oh, how sad!"

Toby disappeared into the bathroom and emerged about ten minutes later. Casually, Kate looked up, then did a horrified double take. "*Toby!*" Toby was crudely and completely made-up, like a raddled old dim-eyed dowager.

Kate said, "Oh, do take it off, Toby!"

But Toby smiled oddly, looked at her steadily and said, in a disturbing, high, brittle voice (a bit like Pagan's mother), "No, I want to make love like this."

So they did.

She didn't mention it the next day, but that evening Toby, having had rather a lot of brandy after the *quiche aux épinards*, said sarcastically, "I don't think spinach tart is one of your stronger points, darling," and proceeded upstairs.

When Kate went up to bed with indefinable fear in her heart, she found him lying on their Astrid Sampe turquoise-striped bedspread simpering at the ceiling. His face was fully made-up and he was wearing her fragile, white lace nightgown.

She said, "Now come off it, Toby, I've had enough of this. Please stop it. Please cut it out."

But Toby sat up, pouted and said in an odd, little-girl voice, "*Why* can't Toby have nice things like you do?" He pulled her onto the bed beside him and murmured, "Toby *loves* looking pretty, Toby *loves* dressing up like this, but promise it's a secret between us, between two girl friends? A *very* important secret."

He didn't take long. It was all over in ten minutes, but it took Kate twenty-four hours to pull herself together again.

And then it happened again, and Kate had another twenty-four hours of the shakes. Inexorably, night after night, Toby "dressed-up," as he put it.

Within a fortnight, Kate was white and taut from lack of sleep and anxiety, but Toby was blooming. On the following Wednesday he came back from Harrods with a size 48 sheer black swans-down-trimmed negligee and matching décolleté nightgown.

"I told the assistant it was for my mother," he said, smoothing it over his lean hips. On Friday night he lashed himself into black garters and fishnet stockings and a frilly black padded bra that he'd bought on Shaftesbury Avenue. On Saturday evening he wore a red satin, wasp-waisted corselet and high-heeled pink pom-pom mules. ("They didn't have my shoe size at Harrods, so I got these backless things, but they're still too small.")

Kate found the situation as macabre and unreal as her father's funeral. The rouged cheeks, ever so carefully shaded peach, seemed to symbolize death. And once again—she was bewildered; what Kate couldn't understand was the *suddenness* of Toby's transformation. He had never given her the slightest hint, had always been so severely practical. He had never so much as worn a frilled shirt to a party, never indicated in any way that he preferred his balls veiled by lace, never by word or deed indicated that he was not a normal heterosexual. Kate had never for one moment suspected that what Toby *really* wanted in bed was this gruesome farce. One week she had had a husband and the next week she had this horror.

She could not understand what was in his mind, could not understand his odd, trancelike state when he was wearing women's clothes. What made it even more confusing was that Toby wore two sorts of female clothing, he seemed to want to pretend to be two different types of women, so poor Kate never knew from one night to the next whether she would find herself in bed with a 1930s lascivious, black-satin, sophisticated woman-of-the-world, or a demure, white-pantied, schoolgirl virgin. When Toby wore stockings and high heels his muscular, stringy calves somehow stuck out sideways below the knees, oddly bandy, not like a woman's but, yes, they *were* like one woman's legs. That night Kate had the nightmarish sensation that the person panting on top of her was her mother-in-law, Major Hartley-Harrington's widow.

Toby refused to discuss the situation, and during the day he seemed to be a different person—that is to say, his normal self. But at night he couldn't wait to get upstairs, sometimes dragging Kate by the wrists in a steel grip. His eyes glittered strangely in his masklike makeup: Kate thought he looked like a novelette villain. "You've been reading too much Barbara Cartland," she told herself. But there was no other way to describe that relentless, breathlessly excited, glassy-eyed expression on Toby's face. Kate didn't understand what was happening and she didn't know what to do.

What *had* she done wrong? Why had this terrible thing happened so suddenly? Was Toby homosexual? If so, why did he make love to *her?* Why should she be so *frightened* of him if he was turning into a homosexual? Lots of their friends were queer and they didn't terrify her as Toby now did. What was terrifying wasn't the makeup or the drag, the padded lace bras, that monstrous red satin corselet or the way he tried to strap his balls away between his legs (no wonder when he wore high heels he walked so oddly). No, what was so chilling was Toby's mincing, simpering, obviously totally sincere mimicry of what he thought a woman was—deep down—really like. It was a travesty, an insult to her sex, and that was what Kate, who had never heard the word "transvestite," found so shocking.

She forced a scene and Toby threatened to leave.

Kate gave way.

She forced another scene and Toby gently reminded her that she was a thirty-year-old barren bitch, and would she shut the fuck up. "Oh, aim so sorry, dahling, don't cray, let's kiss and make up, hmmmm? Just a teensy little *kiss*," he said. And he bent over her and lifted her chin up to his heavily lipsticked mouth. Every pore on his face seemed magnified, as Mrs. Trelawney's scalp had been magnified, as the black wiry hair had sprung from her white scalp on that horrible bathroom evening when Kate was still a schoolgirl. Now she saw in similar, horrid, clarified detail the magenta grease that smeared the fleshy cracks in Toby's mouth and clogged the shaven bristles on his upper lip. He still wasn't very good at putting on lipstick.

As her anguish and shame increased, she still hoped every evening that it wouldn't happen that night, that Toby's fixation would disappear as swiftly as it had arrived. Kate longed to confide in someone, to have Toby's behavior explained away, to be reassured, to hear that everybody did it, that such things were part of a normal phase of a man's development. But she knew they weren't, and there was nobody to whom she felt she could unburden her embarrassing story.

When she suggested talking to their doctor, Toby went white and glared at her, compressed his magenta lips, then sprang at her and twisted her arm behind her back until she feared he was going to dislocate it. Then he violently shoved her down the small flight of stairs that led off their bedroom to the bathroom. Sprawled on the floor with Toby straddled over her in his black fishnets, hands on hips and eyes blazing, Kate promised that she wouldn't tell their doctor or anyone else. Anyway, who would believe her? she wondered hopelessly as she gazed up at lust in action.

"If you *do*," said Toby coldly, in his normal, masculine voice, "I shall simply deny it. There's nothing to prove these clothes are worn by me; after all, they're in your bureau." He heaved pleasurably at the black lace of his corset. He needs a shrink, Kate thought, but she knew she would never dare suggest it.

But she also knew she couldn't stand it. She had to get away from London, away from Toby. Increasingly, Kate felt depressed by Toby's sexual behavior, which disgusted and bewildered her. She hadn't mentioned it to Pagan at the cottage because Pagan obviously had too many problems of her own to cope with, but when Pagan returned from her honeymoon with glowing descriptions of New York (despite the ordeal of Christopher's heart attack) and an invitation from Judy, Kate decided to go and spend a month there. She wanted to run away and forget her misery for a few weeks.

During the war, when Kate was seven, she had found an orange in her Christmas stocking when nobody in Britain had seen oranges for years. Her father had bought it for a vast sum from a sailor in a pub. Kate could hardly remember what an orange was; like bananas and ice cream, they no longer existed. But obviously Santa Claus did. She'd been having doubts, but the orange proved it. Carefully she sniffed the fruit, dug her nails in the skin, peeled it in one long length; then she took a whole day to eat it, sucking each segment carefully, savoring the fragrant juice that spurted into her mouth. After that she nibbled all the peel and made it last for a week.

To Kate, New York wasn't the Big Apple, it was the Wonderful Orange. She knew London, Paris and Cairo and had expected New York to be another, similar, big city. But New York was like nothing she'd ever imagined. Out of her bedroom window she blew kisses to the city like a child.

Judy made a great fuss over her, gave a party for her, spoiled her, told everybody how wonderful Kate was and suddenly she came to life again. The glittering sparkle and excitement of the city simultaneously soothed and exhilarated her. It was like that shot in the arm they'd given her in the hospital, it made her feel that she could do anything—and made her want to do *something*.

The night before Kate left for London, she decided to tell Judy about Toby's dressing-up. She told Judy the whole story, finally finishing by yelling at her, "I can't stand it much longer, so *what can I do?*"

After a moment of silence, Kate started crying.

"D'you still do that? Still cry all the time?" asked Judy absentmindedly, as she thought hard.

"It's a fu . . . fu . . . fu . . . form of self-expression. I lu . . . lu . . . *like* crying. It lets people know how I feel and it makes *me* feel better."

"Well, kiddo, get your crying finished and then concentrate. Because I think you should head straight for a psychotherapist when you get back to London."

"You think there's something wrong with me?"

"No, relax! I merely think that you should discuss the situation with someone who knows what he's talking about. Because you don't, and I don't, and it doesn't sound as if Toby does."

So when Kate returned to London she visited a psychiatrist in Harley Street. He sat with his hands on his chin in a sage velvet wing chair on one side of the fireplace, while she sat on the other, reporting to him twice a week. The doctor first established that Kate *had* clearly told Toby she hated the "dressing up," then suggested that she do so again. Once more Kate hit the bathroom floor. The doctor wrote to Toby and asked to see him about "a matter that is gravely disturbing your wife."

Toby flew into a rage as soon as he opened the letter. "You've told him our secret. I *know* you have. I thought we agreed that it was going to be a secret?"

"It's not my secret—it's your secret," Kate shouted.

Eventually, Toby agreed to visit the psychiatrist, who later reported to Kate. "Naturally," he said, "I cannot tell you what your husband and I discussed, but he's defiant; my prognosis is not optimistic, in fact, the reverse."

"What does that mean?"

"I think he will continue this pattern and that he will increasingly take risks. Soon he may wear female clothes *outside* your home. He will take his bra to the office in his briefcase and wear women's underwear under his trousers."

"What do other wives do?"

"Most don't put up with it, so their husbands visit prostitutes, taking their drag with them. That's one of the things that whores are for." Another pause, then he said very gently, "I think you may have to make a decision. Accept it or leave him."

It took Kate another month of nightly argument and nightly capitulation to the muscular, glassy-eyed virgin or the wide-shouldered, weirdly padded, sophisticated lady before she decided she couldn't stand the dressing-up for the rest of her life. Even if he didn't do it, she would know that it was what he really wanted.

So after a battle over the house—which was in Kate's name—Toby left her, taking the silver, the priapic sculpture, the wire chairs and the more valuable old brass scientific instruments. When Kate miserably visited a divorce lawyer and told him the whole embarrassing story, she was told, to her astonishment, that she'd be unlikely to get a divorce on the obvious grounds.

"You say that he hasn't paraded in these garments before anyone but you?"

"Not to my knowledge. Well, he wouldn't, would he?"

"Then, unfortunately, we have no proof of this distressing conduct. If we had, it would count as mental cruelty, but that's extremely difficult to prove. I don't advise it. I think he must be asked to provide proof of adultery."

"But I don't think he's committed it."

"These things can be arranged."

Toby agreed to provide evidence of adultery, provided that Kate would legally agree never to claim maintenance from him. "As a matter of fact, I don't think we *could* claim maintenance for you," said her solicitor and then sighed. "This is *such* a complicated case."

"What's complicated about it?"

"Well, you own the house; most women own nothing."

Telling Pagan, Kate said, "It costs seven shillings sixpence for a license to tie the knot and thousands of pounds to sever it. D'you think that marriage was invented by lawyers?"

When Kate and Toby split up, Kate suffered a violent reaction against pureness of line and the innate structure of an object. Instead, she went in for pink, frilled, gingham curtains, flowered chintz and bird prints. She reconverted the basement back into an apartment and let it at a rental that paid for all the basic overhead of the house. But she was suddenly left without an income once again, so she advertised for translating work in the *Times.*

All their visual friends were astonished that Kate and Toby should separate. Toby wasn't easy, but hell, who was? He had a perfect eye for proportion and was certainly heading for success, had just been appointed to his first committee. As she couldn't tell them what the trouble was, Kate poured her overburdened, indignant heart onto paper and posted it to Judy. From her letters, Judy sensed Kate's depression and wrote back that she was worried in case free-lance translating at home would be too lonely an occupation at the moment, when she thought Kate should be getting out of the house and meeting new people.

"Why don't you try writing in English for a change?" Judy suggested. "You've been translating books and articles for years now; you and Toby seem to know a lot of journalists, so why not ask one of them to help you? Write a couple of articles about design and designers and get somebody to look at them. Just take a deep breath and telephone all those feature editors on Fleet Street. They can't eat you, they can only say no."

So Kate telephoned, and all the feature editors said, "What ideas have you got?"

"When?"

"Now."

"Oh."

"Submit a couple of ideas in writing and we'll let you know."

So she did, but nobody seemed to want them. Then, at a party, she met the art editor of *House Beautiful* and she started to write captions for the magazine. She was paid very little but was glad of the chance to learn to write as a professional. After six months she submitted a few more ideas to Fleet Street and was commissioned to write two of them—a piece about pop art in the home and another about a new firm that had invented a way to reproduce very convincing "antique" statues in reconstituted stone, complete with lichen stains. After that she got the hang of what was news. Anything that anyone had already read wasn't, no matter how interesting. Kate then interviewed a couple of designers in their homes and again the articles were printed. So she sent in more ideas, each one just three lines on a single sheet of paper, with her name on the top.

Then, one evening, Judy telephoned and said that she had arranged for Kate to interview one of her clients, a once fairly famous ballerina, now over the hill, who was heading for London.

"*What*?" Kate squeaked with horror. "You wouldn't *dare*?"

"Why not give it a try?" New York sounded faint, a million miles away. There was a transatlantic hiss, then Judy shouted, "*I'll kill you if you don't, after I've fixed it*."

"I'll kill you if you *do*," yelled Kate, "and she'll kill both of us."

"No, she won't. Remember that Joujou knows nothing about London or anyone in it. Or anything else. And as a matter of fact she's quite fun."

"Well, what would I do? How would I go about it?"

"Just ring the Ritz and make an appointment with her secretary. I've told her you work for the *Globe*."

"*But I don't*!"

"Then avoid saying that you do. But they're expecting you to telephone and for Chrissake act cool. Don't let Joujou guess it's your first interview. She thinks you're a top magazine writer, and I've seen enough top magazine writers to know that you could be."

"*But I can't*!"

"Where are your British guts? The Dunkirk spirit? The anatomical area that we Americans label your backbone? Stop dithering and just get on with it, Kate.

What's so terrible about failing, anyway? Not that you *will*, Kate."

Judy's bark sounded faint, but Kate could hear that it would be infinitely less alarming for her to face Joujou than to face Judy if she didn't. After another expensive pause, Kate capitulated.

Wearing a pale-pink, moon-girl, thigh-length Courrèges tunic dress with shiny white vinyl boots, Kate sat on the edge of Joujou's bed, notebook open. She felt breathless, dizzy and apprehensive. Now more of a TV glamour personality than a ballerina, Joujou had beautifully streaked blonde hair and very good skin: she had looked thirty-five for twenty years. The picture of domesticity, she sat demurely in a persimmon brocade armchair, glasses at the end of her nose, delicately dipping into a little sewing kit. She was mending some love beads that had been torn off in a brawl the night before.

The bed was littered with diamonds and date-stamped photographs of jewelry. "I have to have photos because it's a rule in the States that you've got to prove you've taken them out when you bring them back," explained Joujou. She nipped into the bathroom, shed her caftan for a towel, returned, swept Kate, the diamonds and the photos off the bed and slid onto it herself. A masseuse started to attack Joujou's right calf. Without being asked, Joujou disclosed that the secret of life was not to look too thin or too young and never to nag. "Every man I meet who wants to marry me says, 'Joujou, I used to love my wife, but she nags me so, and after a day at the office I can't take it anymore.' Ze *ozzer* zing zat men love is to enjoy their meals, so they can't stand women who are dieting under their noses. And a woman can't be too thin if she wants a good face, so she has to choose. I am eating my ass off, but carefully."

Joujou recalled occasions only by the dress she had worn. What happened when she met General de Gaulle? "Oh, I wore my brown lace." How did she like to spend her day? "Shopping. Always. Me and clothes, it is a love affair. I have brought twenty-eight feet with me," she said, jumping up from the bed and shunting Kate into her dressing room. Exquisite garments hung on coat hangers from a twenty-eight-foot length of clothes rail.

"Not much when I travel. I prefer to be chic, not showy," explained Joujou, "I buy everything from Christian Dior, my favorite dressmaker. What size? I'm size eight, dahleeng. Well, maybe size nine, no, to be honest, I'm a ten." She held matchless, pale-gray chinchilla in front of her towel. "I have the most beautiful clothes in the world. That's why I work, to pay for them. But because of the work I don't have enough time to shop. I don't have time to try them on, you see." She cast a speculative look at Kate. "You should never go alone to shop, you know. They persuade you into buying things that are bad for a big ass—I have a big ass and so do you swidhart, never mind, the men love it."

Another speculative glance, then Joujou said in an offhand voice, "You are lucky, you are my size."

Kate looked surprised. "But I'm a size twelve, and only that with difficulty," she said.

Joujou looked carefully at her. "Well, try some of my clothes."

She was right. They were the same size. "Now we can buy some more clothes for me and *you* can try them on," explained Joujou. She immediately phoned the Christian Dior boutique and asked them to send around a selection of "appearance clothes." Kate struggled in and out of them in the sweltering hot bedroom, while Joujou lay back on the bed, having her cellulite massaged away, and bought the lot.

Then the phone rang again. Joujou listened and then said coldly into the mouthpiece, "I've *never* had a facelift. I started to sue that columnist Suzy for a million dollars because, of course, I've never had anything lifted, but who the hell has time for a lawsuit?" She crashed down the telephone receiver and gave a loud snort.

Kate instinctively recognized a good wrap-up time and shut her notebook. Judy had warned her not to stay too long. She waved her thanks to Joujou, dodged past two hairdressers and out into Piccadilly. The roar of London's traffic was peaceful compared to Joujou's bedroom.

CHAPTER 38

LILI LAY SLUMPED on the slimy, seaweed-covered rocks. Her legs and arms were bleeding, her wet hair was dripping over her shoulders and what remained of her pink dress concealed very little of her nubile, seventeen-year-old body. Against the blue Aegean sea she looked exhausted, but not quite exhausted enough.

"Cut," said Zimmer, "and watch that eye, Lili." Lili's left eye squinted slightly when she was tired.

"I'd like to try one more take before the sun gets too hot, please," said Zimmer. "Remember that you're nearly dead; you can hardly move, you've just survived a shipwreck."

Please. That summed up the difference between Serge and Zimmer, she thought. Zimmer didn't treat you like a lump of meat. He was always courteous, encouraging, thoughtful no matter what was going wrong on the set—and something was, of course, always going wrong. If Zimmer stopped to work out whose fault it was, the argument would be endless and they'd never get started, so he just smiled the tight, little smile that was his danger signal—a gentle nodding of the head that indicated a sort of internal prayer, "God give me strength to deal with this situation."

Zimmer's polite consideration was a carefully acquired working habit, especially useful when working with women. He knew very few men who were really kind to women unless it was part of their job. But the way to get the best performance out of a woman, whether it was in the kitchen, the bedroom or on the set, was to praise and reassure while still remaining authoritative.

It was important to remember that an actress probably had no self-confidence, however cool she looked, so her confidence had to be built up. In a word, he had to give her the maximum possible attention. The average woman needed twenty-five hours a day of it, and if she could get a bit more, she'd try for it; but in return for that you would get the average woman's maximum performance.

There was a great difference between handling men and handling women. Women tried harder. Zimmer had seen women slumped and exhausted because they'd been up since five in the morning and it was now eight in the evening and they had to come to life again in front of the camera. And they could do it every time because, though they lacked the physical stamina of men, they had terrific reserves of determination. The actresses who succeeded were the ones who had a little luck and tapped that extra determination—but they all lacked confidence, poor cows, and they all needed reassurance. Zimmer doubted whether there was one really *happy* actress in the world. The responsibility and the sheer hard physical work finished them: by the time women were starring, they were terrified of losing their looks; once they reached the top and realized the insecurity, they could never believe they had made it. They always felt—and rightly—that they were walking a tightrope.

Lili was determined, she was a worker and she was a beauty, but she'd end up like the rest of them. That much he knew.

"Cut. Okay, print it. That's all until three o'clock, kids. When you've freshened up, Lili, would you mind coming to my trailer please? I want to discuss the beach scene with you."

For nearly two weeks the cast and crew had been stationed ten kilometers outside Athens and Lili had yet to play one scene decently dressed. Still, it was a change to wear *any* clothes. Tying the sash of her blue cotton kimono, wet hair flopping down her back, Lili flung herself into a canvas chair in the shade of a silver-gray olive tree. She looked down over the little sandy beach. Aquamarine water lapped over the rocks off the cove. At the back of the beach, where sand mingled with scrub, some fifty people were gathered around cars and trailers. Carrying scripts and clipboards, wearing floppy cotton hats and sunglasses, gleaming with suntan oil, they moved slowly about their business. Lili could see Stan Valance arguing with Zimmer. The aging American actor's face was lean as a skull—she'd never come across anyone who was on so strict a diet: the man never ate anything except *biltong*—thin shreds of dried beef that he had specially imported from South Africa. He chewed it like tobacco.

He had a remote manner and didn't waste an atom of energy talking to anyone on the set except Zimmer.

At three o'clock they shot the beach scene. Lili played a rich, spoiled, turn-of-the-century cruise passenger, and Stan Valance played the stoker who had just hauled her to shore from the shipwreck.

"Take your hands off me!" she spat at him, as he painfully dragged her out of the water by her armpits. She jerked her wet arms away from Stan's lean grasp and lay, exhausted, in the foam. "I can swim perfectly well," she panted. "I could have made it on my own!"

She tried to stand, then a look of surprise came over Lili's face as she found that her trembling arms wouldn't support her body, and her head fell forward onto the wet sand. Wordless, gasping for breath, Stan grabbed her hands and tried to pull her clear of the water. With difficulty, Lili lifted her face and through gritted teeth said, "Don't you *dare* touch me!"

Her voice made it clear that Stan was a servant and a man, and that she wore only the wet, torn shreds of her nightgown. With those five words, Lili managed simultaneously to convey exhaustion, indomitable, spirited arrogance, and shocked, virginal modesty. She also looked extremely sexy.

"Cut!"

Later, in the darkness, Zimmer and Stan Valance were watching the rushes.

Suddenly Stan leaned forward and said: "Shit, the cunt can *act!*"

The following morning Valance waited until Serge was out of the way and then ambled over to Lili's chair under the olive tree. He didn't waste words. "I knew Marilyn, kid, and I've worked with them all, Joan Crawford, Vivien, Liz, you name it, and I'm telling you—don't sell yourself short. You've got what it takes . . . The way I used to."

"You really think so?" She looked up eagerly, her eyes shining.

"Sure thing. Whatever you're doing, it works. So don't let anyone change it. And don't take any shit."

He means Serge, Lili thought, as Valance sauntered away. Serge never left her for a moment when she was off the set. This was just as well, because Lili needed Serge. She needed him because of her notoriety and her own reaction to that notoriety. Success had made Lili feel that she was merely a property that anyone could exploit or sneer at; success had made Lili feel humiliated. She could no longer shelter behind anonymity; sometimes she felt that everyone had seen the famous calendar and those horrible films. People looked at her nervously—women with unconcealed envy, men with a hard appraising stare. Lili grew increasingly paranoid. She could no longer buy a bunch of flowers from a street vendor without wondering whether he'd seen that calendar, wondering whether he knew what she looked like naked, wondering whether he'd recognized her, whether she had lubricated his dreams.

Eventually, she avoided such small human contacts; she rarely walked in the streets. She ordered what she wanted by telephone or asked Serge's new secretary to get it for her. Her insolent self-assurance was merely a pose to hide her uncertainty. When she was with people she didn't know, her manner was abrupt, awkward, rude. Often she would say something foolish, immediately regret it, then, to cover her embarrassment, say something worse.

Her mistakes were gleefully repeated around Paris and printed in the gossip columns—often inaccurately—which only increased her fear of people. Time and again her trust proved mistaken; people were nice to her only because they wanted something—and suddenly so many of them wanted something! Her autograph, her photo, her telephone number, buttons from her coat, hair torn from her head, interviews. . . . Strangers whispered that they had wonderful ideas for her; well-dressed, charming women invited her to endorse sweaters or deodorants, even a vibrator. Swift-talking, plausible men tried to get her to sign papers without reading them or tried to get her into bed, certain that she would agree. ("Well, darling, what difference could just one more make?")

Serge, with his easy self-assurance, found Lili easy to exploit and naturally did whatever he could to increase her lack of identity and consequent dependence upon him.

Serge's new secretary opened Lili's mail and answered the telephone. Lili herself stayed all day in the smart white-and-glass apartment that Serge had bought in the rue François I. She stayed there alone. Serge wouldn't even allow her a kitten because of his hay fever. He now wore Cerruti suits and was always out, too busy to be with Lili, huddled with advertising men or businessmen or directors or lawyers—cold-eyed men in dark suits with briefcases who looked at Lili with tight smiles and eyes that remained carefully blank. She was not a person to them. She was a deal to be made, an asset to be handled with care, "meat on the hoof," as one agent said. Handling Lili was a major job.

Serge was no longer as indulgent with her. Lili was now safely tied up so he didn't have to bother with her needs or problems; his secretary got Lili everything she needed within a certain budget (Serge didn't want her spending a fortune on Yves Saint Laurent), and frankly, Lili bored him now. She was nearly eighteen, but an ignorant little bitch—it was lucky the school inspectors had never caught up with him—and if it weren't for the money he would have dumped her long ago. A man could get tired of even the most luscious pair of tits, especially when they belonged to an uneducated, unsophisticated little girl, who whined for attention like a kid.

Slowly, Lili felt Serge's growing lack of interest in her. She didn't understand—she didn't *want* to understand—the reasons, but it was obvious that she exasperated him and he no longer wanted her around. On the other hand he wouldn't let her set foot outside the front door without him.

Lili was puzzled and anxious. If she didn't *belong* with Serge, then she belonged nowhere, she had no place in the world. For nearly five years, Serge had told her what to do, what to say, what to wear, how to behave. Lili was terrified that he might tell her to go, as he sometimes hinted he would if she wasn't obedient.

"And just remember you were *nothing,*" Serge would snarl, snapping his fingers under her nose, "*nothing* before I found you. And without me you'd be nothing again!"

Q was premiered in Paris just before Lili's eighteenth birthday, and in spite of the fact that it was a low-budget film with a meager publicity allowance, the movie was an immediate hit. At the premiere Lili smiled triumphantly at the flashguns, her head held high as she posed in a cream silk tuxedo, matching pants and a see-through, cream voile shirt, which demonstrated her new star status while by no means hiding the reasons for it.

After fighting their way through the crowds to return to their hired limousines, the stars, the director, the producer, the backers and the show's press agent headed for Chez Lipp, where theater custom ordained that you should wait amid the engraved mirrors, the gilt and the red velvet for the next day's first editions—and the reviews.

Since the budget didn't run to the large chunk of extra money that Stan Valance demanded to attend the premiere, Lili got most of the attention. Escorted by Zimmer, still wearing his tight, grim little grin, Lili smiled, while the police formed a cordon around her until she was able to scramble into the limousine.

"You must practice getting in and out of cars slowly," Zimmer commented. "Always move *slowly* in public. If you want to be a great star, you need more than good looks and talent, you must have style and class; you should always look in public as if you were being helped out of a Rolls, not running for a bus."

As the limousine nosed out of the crowd, Zimmer turned to Lili, his face alternately shadowed and lit by street lamps. "Lili, I want to tell you two things, one of which is none of my business," he said. "I was surprised to find how good you really are. You've got a natural instinct for the camera. You respond to it as if you were in love with the damned thing. And you listen to direction, you really *listen* to what I'm saying. You don't just wait until I'm finished and then tell me what *you* feel should be done. You've got the makings of a good actress, Lili. Provided you work with good directors."

He rested his left arm along the back seat and was silent for a moment, then he continued: "I can't help wondering if poor Serge knows the difference between a good director and a second-rate one. A second-rate director will spot the obvious things about you, but he'll probably miss the wistfulness, the fragile charm, that hopeful trust that you project. But those are the magic qualities that will keep you a star, Lili."

As the limousine crossed the Pont de la Concorde Zimmer sighed. "Now we come to the part that's none of my fucking business," he said. "Christ knows why I'm telling you this, because I'm careful not to get involved in other people's lives, but do you know that we paid you a fee of twenty thousand dollars, to a Zurich bank? Of course we had to pay a lot more to get Valance, but we needed an international name. Now, I can't help wondering how much of that money you're going to see? Christ, Lili, why don't you get *away* from him? You don't *need* the bastard."

"Yes, I do," Lili said, suddenly sad. "I'm afraid without him. That's why I need him. He's the only . . . family . . . I've got."

"That's why you cling to him—for security. But you'll never get security from Serge," Zimmer said. "Look, it's only natural to be afraid. You're still in your teens. You've been through rough times. But you'll never develop into anything until you get away from him. He *wants* to keep you dependent on him. That way, you'll be frightened to leave." He patted her shoulder, and sighed again as they drew up outside the Lipp brasserie.

Outside there were more flashguns, more photographers, a little burst of spontaneous applause from the other diners as they slowly moved to their table, where champagne was waiting in a silver bucket and a huge bouquet of lilies was surrounded by telegrams.

With a bow, Zimmer handed the bouquet to Lili, saying, "From tonight, Lili, you will be famous."

"I wish I felt famous inside," she said in a perplexed voice, as she hugged the lilies. "Inside I just feel worried."

"That's understandable after the tension," Zimmer said fondly, "and you're anxious about the newspaper reviews. You'll soon get over that. Just remember, you're going to be a *star*. I don't need to see the reviews to know that. You wouldn't remember Elizabeth Berner, but she had a fragile charm with heart-rending appeal. You found yourself holding your breath as you watched this vulnerable little waif on the screen. She had the sweet sadness of a rose petal fluttering to the ground. And you have that same delicate quality, Lili."

"I'm no rose petal," Lili said.

For the past three months, Lili had listened very carefully to what Zimmer said—in fact, she'd got into the habit of trusting him. So after the party, Lili pondered his advice. Twenty thousand dollars was a fortune—it would buy her a house of her own, maybe even a little car. Then she could learn to drive. Serge wouldn't let her drive his new Mercedes.

In the chill gray dawn, as they undressed, she casually asked Serge, "How much money did they pay for me to make *Q?*"

"Jesus, what a question to ask at this hour! You're going to be the toast of Paris today after those reviews, and all you can think about is money!"

"Yes, but how much?"

"It all depends on whether you're talking net or gross, and *you* don't even know what the fucking words mean, Lili."

"What I would *like* to know is the *total* sum that Zimmer paid to you. That's gross, isn't it?"

"Christ, it's six o'clock in the morning, Lili! Don't I do enough for you? Aren't I even allowed to sleep now? *Get to bed* or I'll beat the daylights out of you. We've got to be on a plane to London tomorrow evening, and you start shooting the day after, so sleep while you can. You look after your side of the business and I'll look after mine!"

"Serge, I want to *know*. Did they pay twenty thousand dollars?"

The flat of his hand hit the side of her head. Systematically, Serge hit her so there would be no bruising, but he didn't hold back. He put all his considerable strength into each blow.

Lili fell to her knees. Seeing her on all fours, sobbing with fear and humiliation, Serge couldn't resist a kick in the ribs as he snarled, "All you got going for you, kid, is me and those boobs. You lose me, you're nobody."

When she opened her eyes it was nearly midday and she was in bed. Her head felt as if it would burst apart. Along the passage she could hear Serge chatting with his secretary. It was no use, there was nothing she could do. She was now as frightened of living with him as she was of living without him. There seemed only one way out. She staggered out of bed toward the fluttering lace curtains of the open window.

CHAPTER 39

JOUJOU WAS THE first article that Kate sold to the *Globe*. Kate's tongue-in-cheek interview was given half a page, and the *Globe* immediately asked her for more articles. Kate started to free-lance for the newspaper, aware that when Scotty, the feature editor, phoned with an assignment, she had to drop whatever she was doing and run. When Scotty asked her for ideas he expected six good ones within half an hour and if following up one of them meant sitting up all night, then that was what she did.

What Kate at first thought to be the brusque, unfriendly atmosphere of the vast, cream-painted, windowless editorial floor of the *Globe* turned out to be one of concentration against the constant noise of typewriter fire, teletype clatter, telephone chatter and the pressure of deadlines.

As Kate had no training or experience, Fleet Street life was tough for her. Everybody was working against a deadline and there was no time to explain things to a beginner; either you were right or you were out, and anyway beginners weren't supposed to start on Fleet Street. Kate learned by listening to the other desks to cultivate a good telephone voice. She learned to keep her notebook always within reach, never to alter a quotation and to check, check and check again.

Scotty was unusually kind as well as fast, funny and deadly serious. Kate was devoted to him. Once, when he found her rewriting an article for the ninth time, he patted her shoulder and said, "Nobody's piece is ever perfect. Just try to get it as good as possible under the circumstances and then sling it in. And remember it's *not* your piece—it's a team product and you're only the beginning of the chain." Again he started to chew his horribly maimed pencil.

Kate knew that she was lucky. In her first year on Fleet Street she often worked from eight in the morning until eleven at night because she hadn't yet discovered how to take shortcuts. She loved the calm, fast world of daily papers, she loved the excitement, the knife-edge deadlines, and she loved working for the engaging, humorous Scotty, who protected her, encouraged her, egged her on and ruthlessly cut her copy.

One spring morning in 1966, Kate was called to Scotty's paneled office. Against the right wall, at chest height, stood a ten-foot-long sloping shelf upon which the newspaper layouts could be spread. Scotty never sat at his impressive mahogany desk, he always lolled by the board, scribbling, or propped himself against the board as he talked. A stream of feature writers was always shuffling in and out, lining up if there were others ahead of them.

That morning the *Globe* had run Kate's interview with an Israeli tank commander, General Nakte Nir. Talking to this hero in the lounge of his modest London hotel, Kate quickly realized that someone must have put her name on the wrong press list. Nonetheless, the article had turned out well—she was coming along very fast.

"Sit down a moment, Kate," Scotty said. "The editor liked your piece this morning." He gave her an odd look. "D'you faint at the sight of blood? Have you ever slept in the open? Could you leave home for a month? D'you want a permanent job on the *Globe?* We're thinking of sending you to Sydon."

"But there's a war going on!"

"Shrewd girl, very observant. We've already got a couple of reporters there, but we want something different from the stories they're sending back. We can get all that stuff from the wire; we want a few unusual feature articles."

"But I've never . . . Yes, Scotty, of course. When?"

"There's a flight this evening. Five P.M. check-in at Heathrow. Change at Rome. Don't take too much gear, travel light, just pens and clipboard. Remember we don't want *any* woman's page stuff. We're not sending you out for the woman's angle. The editor is sending you out because we want background material from someone with a fresh eye. And don't forget to fill in your expenses properly," he said. "I'm sick of rewriting them for you."

Kate hurried to Gamage's in Holborn and bought a pair of sneakers, a groundsheet, a backpack and a water bottle that could be slung from a waist belt. There wasn't time to buy anything else, in fact, there was just enough to telephone her mother and ask her to look after the house. Then there was an exasperating wait for her visa at the Sydon consulate in South Kensington. Luckily, it was only five minutes from home, where she had ten minutes to pack before catching a cab to the airport.

The plane landed a couple of hours before dawn, then there was a six-hour drive in the battered little airport bus to Fenza, where the *Globe* had reserved a room for Kate. It was not very clean, and there was no hot water. Nevertheless, Kate fell onto the hard bed and slept until noon when, following the hall porter's directions, she headed for the press center, in the bar of the converted Majestic Hotel.

It was the first time Kate had been in a city at war, unless you counted the London blitz, and she'd never been in the center of London during a heavy raid. But Fenza, near the front line, was a city that had already had the heart torn out of it. It was almost deserted—looters were shot on sight and anyone who could flee had fled. It was impossible to drive because of the debris that blocked the streets: walking was dangerous because a wall might topple on you at any minute.

Kate hurried through the blackened, exhausted town. Defying gravity, wrecked buildings leaned drunkenly over the forlorn rubble-filled streets. A bed hung, the ludicrously striped mattress still on it, from the wrecked upper story of a house that had no front, patterned wallpaper hanging in strips from the broken walls.

Kate smelled the heavy odor of charcoal from burned wood beams and window frames as she picked her way around piles of sandbags, ragged heaps of bricks and plaster, hurried past a broken-spoked bicycle that lay in the road among fragments of smashed furniture, past a burned-out car, and finally past a gutted truck lying black belly up on the sidewalk outside the semiderelict Majestic Hotel.

The next day she was up at four o'clock because the bus left at five. To Kate's astonishment, large buses were used to take the press corps up to the front, as if they were on a church outing. Under clear blue skies, it was hot as they bumped into the beige desert. The grit quickly got everywhere. Kate could feel it in her head, in her hair and eyes, under her eyelids, down her bra and in her pubic hair; she itched everywhere.

Kate's neighbor in the cigarette-stinking, dusty bus said, "What's happening here isn't just one lot of Arabs fighting another lot of Arabs; it's really the Americans playing Sydon against the Russians playing the Saudis; all the equipment that's been captured was manufactured in Russia."

The weary-looking man in fatigues who sat on Kate's other side explained, "Sydon's only a little country, but it's got those southern oil fields and that's what everyone wants, so any excuse will do to invade the place. Officially, Moscow has refused to interfere in the battle for the oil fields, but that's mainly because the Kremlin doesn't want to provide a pretext for an American initiative in the area."

The man sitting in front of Kate clearly thought that the *Globe* was mad to send her. "I suppose they haven't sent the fashion editor or the gardening editor out with you?" He growled. "War isn't the game they seem to think it is . . . *bang, bang*, you're dead, then get up for nursery tea." He twisted around to glare at her. "It's dirty and bloody disgusting."

He gave her a cold look of disapproval and then added, "Somebody should tell your editor that the Sydonian men won't let their women go to war because of the rape and mutilation. You don't want a hand grenade stuffed up your er . . . or suddenly find that your breasts are being cut off. And if you're a correspondent, you've got no protection whatsoever. No correspondent ever carries a gun."

They jolted on in silence.

The distant thunder changed to a nonstop, ear-splitting crack as the bus bumped closer to the front line through a harsh giant wasteland of ankle-deep dust and faded, gray-green scrub. Heavy fighting had scattered the desert with damaged tanks, twisted wrecks that once were jeeps and burned-out trucks stuck headfirst in deep sand drifts. The gunfire noise was painful.

As they got out of the bus, a bomb hit a Sydonian field gun and another hit a truck that must have been carrying ammunition, for it began to explode by itself, a stream of noisy stars. Planes flashed overhead, the ground shuddered and heaved with the concussion of the blast. Under heavy shell fire, upended, sparkling orange chandeliers streaked to the ground around them.

The front line straggled, it hid, it stopped. It was a series of little, dusty, khaki groups moving forward while other little groups tried to stop them, as men crept or dashed, bent double, from bush to bush, moving forward yard by yard. Corpses dotted the sand, flung down as if they were sunbathing with their clothes on. There was a stink of rotting flesh—although the Sydonians removed their dead every evening, they left the enemy corpses where they lay.

The sharp, acrid stink of cordite hurt Kate's nostrils and her throat. The flames and hellish cries frightened her ears and eyes. It was difficult to see. Kate crawled forward on her hands and knees through a pepper-colored mist, peering through it to the thick ocher fog beyond, hazily striped by billowing plumes of black smoke from burning tanks and overturned trucks. She was terrified.

Two weeks later Kate had changed. Instead of being nervous, tense and anxious, she was simply too busy to be neurotic or afraid. She was on her own for the first time in her life. There was no one to tell her what to do, no one to criticize her, no one from whom to seek approval. Kate alone had to decide what to do and how to do it, and survival, as well as success, depended upon her decisions.

Kate found this situation curiously exhilarating. She was thirty-four years old and she felt fifty, but the concentration that was necessary to do her job blotted out all the feelings, even the constant exhaustion. Kate now easily understood how war photographers took what civilians called "crazy risks." They probably didn't notice them; there wasn't time.

The press corps weren't at all what Kate had expected. A serious, exhausted air hung over them at the Majestic bar, everyone looked under strain and nobody got drunk. There simply wasn't time. No one made passes at her; they were all too busy and too tired. Like them, Kate became wary, furtive and untrusting, guarding a possible lead as if it were a map of Treasure Island. Like theirs, her head never stopped thinking, speculating, plotting, interviewing, translating, drafting copy and sending it off. She set off at dawn, never knowing whether she would get a story, and thought herself lucky if she'd dispatched one by ten at night.

She concentrated on reporting the effects of war on human beings, perhaps in a town that was being bombarded, perhaps from the battlefield, using her interpreter—Ali, a twelve-year-old boy who had been to missionary school and pretended to be a lot older than he was and know a lot more than he did—who trotted along behind his white woman like a devoted dog.

"Where King, Ali?" she said sharply one evening, as they stood in front of the Majestic. "Much, much money for Ali if Missus see King." What Kate most wanted was an interview with Abdullah, and she didn't realize that this was impossible because nobody had told her that the King didn't give exclusive interviews, only an occasional press conference.

For two days there had been a lull in the fighting. After initially being taken by surprise, the Sydonian army had forced the Saudis back east, toward the border between their two countries. They had pulled back behind a line of low hills that lay between the front line, now thirty kilometers east of Fenza, and the border, which was another forty kilometers beyond it. For two days, nobody had known the whereabouts of King Abdullah. He had been at the front line leading his troops, but now he seemed to have vanished.

"King in the eastern hills with Hakem tribe," Ali beamed. "Now, money please, Missus."

"But the eastern hills are behind the enemy line."

"Yes, Missus, but enemy still in Sydon."

"How do you know, Ali? I'm not going to pay you until I know it's true." It was one of the rumors floating about, but Kate wasn't paying for rumors.

"I take Missus there," offered Ali.

"How can you? We haven't got a car, and we can't take a jeep farther than the front line because the Saudis would immediately fire on it!"

"Jeep to front line like last time, then hire the camel of my cousin," said Ali airily.

Camels, thought Kate! They might not fire on a woman and a boy and a couple of camels. . . . What was an expense account for, she thought, and started to argue with Ali about the cost of a jeep and two camels.

The next day it took two hours to get to the front in the fly-ridden, buzzing, shimmering, sandy heat, along a track marked by empty gas cans, past which their outrageously expensive jeep jerked, bumped, bucked and bounced. Kate hung onto the wheel with both hands, binoculars bouncing painfully against her breasts. Her stomach had been upset since the day she arrived, and now she felt as if she was going to be sick as well, as they passed burned, blackened corpses, twisted like overdone kippers. They bumped past a hut for collecting the dead, then the field hospital that lay ahead of it. At the hospital, a doctor and two orderlies were kneeling to attend to the wounded, and flies hung in a black-peppered cloud over men who lay silent, near dead, or screaming in agony. There was a sickening stench of flesh and blood as their jeep lurched past.

Finally, Ali pointed to what had once been a small hut and was now a crumbling heap of rubble with a few gaping holes. Bullet scars on the dirty white walls testified to close fighting. The green, tattered shred of the Sydonian flag still hung from one wall.

"Here?" said Kate, incredulous. "Missus see no camels here!"

"Here wait for cousin," said Ali firmly, so Kate stopped the jeep. For a moment she didn't move, so great was the relief after the shaking jeep, then she climbed down and walked toward the hut, followed by Ali. Two Sydonian soldiers smoking cigarettes leaned against the broken entrance. She waved and they all grinned at each other, then Kate climbed over the rubble and went to where she saw a third soldier lying on his stomach, keeping watch through a gaping hole in the wall of the hut.

Suddenly Kate's gut rumbled again and she shot out of the semi-ruin. Oh, the humiliation! It was the water, the other reporters said, but she couldn't clean her teeth in beer. Wet with sweat, she didn't care that Ali was trotting along behind her as she scrambled for shelter behind a little heap of rubble and squatted to relieve herself. Then, unbelieving, she saw the sand flicking up in spurts around her as hot, jagged shrapnel fragments flew through the air. A ping on her helmet made her flinch, and she wanted to fling herself down and hide. She held both hands over her helmet, crouched lower and groaned.

Suddenly the hut in front of her seemed slowly to collapse to the left. Kate yanked at her jeans and, zipping up, ran back to what was left of the hut.

The three jolly soldiers at whom she had been waving were just empty bodies. One lay spread-eagled on his back, disinterested eyes staring at her, his stomach spilling red, glistening snakes.

Frozen with horror, Kate heard noises and shouting from beyond the hut. She was terrified, but in a quick instinctive movement, she crouched and grabbed an assault rifle from the hand of one of the corpses. She had to untangle it from his limp arm. Just get the gun and then crawl up over the rubble, keeping your head down, she thought. Christ, I hope what's left of these walls isn't going to cave in. She carefully checked to see that the weapon was cocked.

She heard scrabbling sounds from the other side of the rubble and suddenly her backside felt naked and vulnerable. Oh, Christ, suppose someone came around the back and shot her up the ass.

Now she could hear heavy breathing, gasps and a grunt as someone scrambled up the rubble in front of her. Then, like a khaki egg, slowly, the rounded top of a helmet appeared. Fraction by fraction it rose, then a dirt-streaked brown forehead appeared over the broken bricks. Kate saw two young, surprised black eyes under heavy eyebrows as she gently squeezed the trigger.

The face exploded into a carmine hole, then disappeared. She heard noises on the rubble outside. Oh, God, was that more of them, she wondered, or was that the one she'd just shot? She waited, tensed and grim, ready to shoot again.

But the enemy hadn't expected to find anyone alive in the ruin, and the two remaining soldiers swiftly scrambled back toward their own line.

Kate heard nothing. She lay waiting, unable to take her eyes off the top of the rubble, oblivious to the fact that she was lying on top of the soft, warm shreds of a body. Then, from behind, she heard Ali call softly in his singsong voice, "Missus, Missus! Bad man all run away!" He stumbled toward her.

Kate was shaking. His eyes. He'd looked right into her eyes and then she'd shot him. For nine months his mother had carried him; for years she had cared for him and loved him; and now in ten seconds Kate had just destroyed somebody's son. Those surprised eyes had looked into hers and she'd just squeezed. No doubt he would have shot her first if he'd had the chance, but Kate knew she had just taken a life and found it a terrible thing to think about. She sat staring into the rubble, agonized, ashamed of what she'd done, sternly reasoning with herself (Be sensible, it was him or you), then weeping as she thought of his family and then of Nick.

Ali fidgeted behind her, not understanding why she was upset. "She one good Missus, she kill Saudi soldier!"

Two hours later, much to Kate's surprise, they saw three specks on the southern horizon that in due course turned out to be a very old man riding a mangy camel and leading two more. Much money changed hands—three hundred and twenty dinar, which was enough to buy camels, rather than hire them. More money was offered, but the old man refused to accompany them. He hissed at the camels to couch them, helped Kate onto the carpet-covered leather saddle, and hissed again for the camels to rise. Then he handed a thorn stick to Ali, nodded and remounted his own camel, which started to lurch south again.

"What did he say?" Kate asked Ali.

"He say camels back here in one day or Missus pay more money. He say Western machines no good for desert, camel still goodest. Camel eat very little, only drink once in five days, carry big loads."

"You're sure you know where you're going, Ali?"

"Yes, yes, to the hills, Missus."

They lurched off under the hot sun. At first Kate thought she was going to be seasick; she'd never be able to stand it, this awful, heaving gait, but after ten minutes she found it quite soothingly similar to a rocking chair.

It got hotter and hotter as they made their leisurely way over sand, thorn bushes and withered, gray grass, heading for the low smudge of hills now visible on the horizon.

As dusk fell they reached the lower slopes and shortly afterward found themselves lurching along the bottom of a small boulder-strewn ravine. "Now Missus in eastern hills." Ali beamed. "Now Missus find King."

"No. Ali take Missus to King," said Kate sharply.

Ali stopped beaming and looked rather frightened. "Ali know King in hills, but Ali not know where belong in hills."

"But, Ali, you said you would take me to the King's camp!"

"No, no. Ali say take Missus to eastern hills." Ali now looked sulky.

Kate was aghast. The trip had taken far longer than she had expected, it was too late to turn back, Ali obviously had no idea where he was and they were behind the enemy lines.

"Couch my camel please, Ali. We'd better stop here for the night. It's so dark I can hardly see you."

Ali hissed at Kate's camel, which took no notice of him and continued to amble along the rocky bottom of the ravine.

"Ali, stop this damn camel!"

Suddenly, there was a slither, a click, and shadowy figures sprang out of the darkness. One of them tugged the camel reins away from Kate and she found herself looking into the muzzle of a submachine gun.

Through sobs, Ali answered in Arabic the questions that were spat at him from the darkness. His hands were tied behind his back and he was roped to Kate, whose hands were also bound. There was a muttered discussion and then, still roped together, they were roughly prodded over the ravine and then along a narrow path that led upward, then downward until Kate lost all sense of direction.

Suddenly, they turned around a bend in the hillside and moved downward into a shallow, bowl-like area covered with low, black goatskin tents. After a muttered discussion outside the tents, Kate and Ali were roughly shoved inside by their captors, and Kate, to her astonishment, found herself pushed onto her knees in front of a man she knew. Although she had never seen him wearing white desert robes, Kate couldn't mistake that lean, hard face.

"Suliman Hakem!" she said, astonished.

Her first feeling was relief that they weren't in enemy hands, swiftly followed by the sharp realization that Suliman was never more than two steps away from Abdullah.

"What are you doing here?" Suliman asked sharply, in English. So he also recognized her, Kate thought.

"I'm a newspaper correspondent. I was looking for King Abdullah, because . . . I have a private message for him."

"How do we know that you are not spies?"

"If someone could untie my hands, I'll get my press pass out of my pocket."

Kate's hands were not untied, but a man emptied her pockets and Suliman Hakem studied her press pass.

"How do I know this isn't a forgery?"

"If you'd only get a copy of the *Globe*, you'd see my printed copy and by-line and my photograph," said Kate, thinking that a nearby newsstand was rather unlikely.

Suliman barked a few guttural words. Their hands were untied and they were pulled to their feet. "You'll be returned to Fenza at dawn, under escort," Suliman said shortly. "Your camels and the boy will be cared for. Think yourself lucky that the sentry didn't shoot you."

As he strode out of the tent in his flowing robes, Kate found it hard to believe that this man had attended one of the world's smartest boys' schools and that he had then been trained at Sandhurst.

A moment later Suliman swept back into the tent. "You will be guarded all the time you are in this camp. Now you will wash and eat."

By herself, Kate was led to a small tent and a guard was posted at the opening. A bowl of water and a cloth were brought to her, followed by a boy in a white robe who carried a tin jug of water and a tin tray piled with rice and chunks of roast lamb. Kate suddenly realized how hungry she was, as she sat cross-legged in the carpeted tent, eating the food with her fingers. Through the slit, Kate could see the moon casting black shadows over the silver sand, and beyond the flames of a campfire she could see the necks and swaying heads of a camel herd silhouetted against the sky.

After she had finished her food, two more guards suddenly appeared, wearing white flowing robes and red, black-banded headdress; each man carried a rifle in his hand and a curved scimitar at his side. They said nothing, but jerked their heads toward the tent slit. Kate rose and followed them into the night, past yellow circles of light around campfires that cast shadows up into the lean faces of the shaggy-haired men who surrounded them.

She was led into a tent thirty feet long. Richly patterned carpets had been laid on the desert sand and heaped with tasseled cushions upon which, alert and straightbacked, sat King Abdullah. He gestured to the guards and they withdrew, leaving Abdullah and Kate alone.

Self-assured as ever, Abdullah's watchful eyes moved warily, arrogantly. His tawny skin was stretched tight over the bone, his winged black eyebrows rose above a nose that curved like a falcon's over his wide mouth. He looked at her and said in a deep voice: "How the hell did *you* get here, Kate?"

She told him as quickly as she could, thinking that he looked older, gray and tired, which wasn't surprising.

"You're very lucky," Abdullah commented shortly, when she had finished. "And so am I, to tell you the truth. The damned Saudis haven't made a move for the past few days, so all we're doing is waiting for them, and that's a boring business. A surprise visitor is very welcome. . . . Although you're not looking quite your usual soignée self, Kate." He grinned at Kate's dirty khaki jacket and trousers, her grubby sneakers and her tousled hair.

"You realize, of course, that this is a private and personal visit," Abdullah continued. "I can't discuss the war or politics or there would be trouble from the press corps. You may describe this place vaguely and say that I am firmly confident and looking forward to victory. And we will, of course, check your copy." Then, looking out into the night, he casually asked, "How is Pagan?"

Kate told him all her news, including the fact that Pagan was expecting and that the baby was due in a few months. Abdullah gave a curiously grim smile. "Yes, I knew about that."

There was an uneasy pause. "How old are *your* children?" Kate asked.

"Mustapha is four and looks just like me. He's a naughty little devil, always up to some wicked trick—lots of guts." There was another pause. "Of course, I'm sorry I haven't more sons." He corrected himself: "*Legitimate* sons. After all, I've been married ten years. But I'm lucky to have Mustapha. My wife had a miscarriage shortly after we were married, followed by a still-born daughter the following year. Then in 1957 she had a premature son who died two weeks after he was born." He scowled.

Kate could only stare at him, remembering her own miscarriages.

"Then nothing happened for four years. In fact, I thought of taking a second wife—as a Moslem, you know, I'm allowed four wives. I realize that in the West this would be thought barbaric: your menfolk prefer several wives in succession instead of simultaneously, as we are allowed in the East. Anyway, I eventually took my wife to a clinic in Lausanne where they found she had a malfunction in the fallopian tubes. Fifteen months after the operation, she gave me a son, an heir."

Abdullah suddenly remembered that as the child was placed in his arms, it gave a lusty yell, and much to Abdullah's surprise, he felt a flood of warmth, a choking feeling in his throat. Instinctively, at that moment, he had known that he would do anything for this imperious, tiny creature. The baby's crumpled face had turned from white to pink to an odd lavender shade as it cried. Abdullah had roared with laughter, hugged the tiny creature to him, gently kissed the soft black down on the top of the fragile head, and for the first time in his life, he felt love.

"Now I pray to Allah to send me more sons," Abdullah continued. "I visit Serah's quarters regularly. She's had another checkup at the clinic and apparently there's no reason why she shouldn't have more children. But she hasn't. . . . Anyway, let's stop talking like a couple of midwives!"

So Mustapha is the only person on earth that Abdullah really loves, Kate thought.

"What exactly are you doing out here, Abdullah?" Kate asked.

"You'd better say that it's one of my routine visits to the Hakem tribe," he said. "I'm going to tell you nothing of value to the enemy. But I regularly visit the more important sheikhs. We recruit our toughest soldiers from the desert tribes, not from the cities." He gestured toward the tent opening. "Tonight those men will sleep on the sand protected only by their cloaks. Bedouins are tough, they scorn comfort, they have only contempt for the outside world and its mechanical marvels."

"Except for pistols, rifles and transistor radios," commented Kate.

"Agreed, but they like to live with the minimum of possessions. A family might have a couple of camels, perhaps a few goats, a tent, a rug, knives, leather buckets and a rope. That's all they need and all they want." He grunted. "I promise you, Kate, I often wish I could spend my whole life among tough, simple men like these, in the desert." He looked across at her and grinned. "Now you'd better get back to your tent. You know what a fearful reputation I have, and you're going to have a tough day tomorrow."

Kate didn't realize that she had achieved the impossible—which apparently included riding a camel through a minefield—until the following evening after she had been returned by jeep to Fenza. As she walked into the Majestic bar, the other journalists clapped quietly. Just as well nobody told me it was impossible, thought Kate, or I'd never have tried to do it.

She started her article "A Day of War" with a description of the battlefield after the fighting had finished. "*A sea of white papers fluttered over the ocher sand. Even before the vultures could get at them, Arab scavengers had looted the dead bodies, ripped off the watches and torn through the wallets, looking for money. Pay books and other documents had been thrown out on the sand. Love letters that yesterday were precious, photographs of girls, wives, children, parents—all smiling up at no one.*"

Scotty was delighted with her copy. "I *said* we'd get something different from her and she comes up with an exclusive on the bloody King!" He turned to his secretary. "Send her a cable straightaway. *Congratulations Abdullah Scoop Big Kiss Scotty Globe.*" He continued to read Kate's copy. "Jesus! I didn't tell her to kill anyone! Better rewrite it in the third person. Correspondents aren't supposed to carry weapons. Maybe we'd better recall her before she gets into trouble."

The article was syndicated worldwide. It told a receptive audience, quite simply, that war was about killing people.

CHAPTER 40

WHEN SHE RETURNED to England, Kate found herself something of a curiosity, if not a minor celebrity. Christ, she looks awful; she's lost a lot of weight, thought Scotty, and gave her a two-week leave. She decided to spend it in New York with Judy.

Judy had now started to publicize books and celebrities, as well as fashion, and she had obviously prospered in the past couple of years. Kate looked around the airy living room of Judy's new apartment, which hung high over East 57th Street: that Bokhara rug must have set her back about seven thousand dollars, she thought. Opposite her, Judy leaned back with her arms behind her head in a bronze upholstered chair with curving serpent arms, the wood inlaid with ivory. She said, "The next thing you've got to do, Kate, is a book. You've achieved a certain fame, but it won't last long unless you keep it going. A book is always good for prestige, if not always for the bank account. Did you keep a diary during the war? And all your notes? Well, turn it into a book—something slim—say around sixty thousand words. You stay in bed tomorrow and write the synopsis, then I can look at it when I get back in the evening . . . *Of course*, you can write a synopsis! Sit down right now and write three simple sentences saying what the book is going to be about."

After a moment's thought, Kate fished a notebook out of her cigar-brown Gucci bag, did as Judy said, then tore off the page and handed it to her.

Judy beamed. "Great. Now just expand those three sentences into a synopsis and split it up into chapters. And I'll let you practice being a famous author by taking you to supper."

Kate had the talent all right, thought Judy, but she couldn't seem to channel it by herself. She needed someone to give her that push *up* instead of the push *down* that the men in her life seemed to have given her, although Judy had to admit that Kate sat up and begged to be kicked in the teeth. Still, she seemed a lot more positive than on her previous visit.

The following evening Judy fiddled around with Kate's synopsis, altered the pagination slightly and then said, "Fine. This I can promote. We'll call it *One Woman's War.*" She pulled a little gift-wrapped parcel from her purse and tossed it to Kate. "A present." Kate caught it with one hand, opened the Tiffany box and saw a two-inch-square navy-blue leather case, inside which was a small, square, golden, navy-blue enameled alarm clock.

"That's so you can start writing the book the morning after you get back to London."

"But I don't have time," protested Kate, "and my job takes all my energy."

"Set that thing for five in the morning, fix yourself a cup of instant coffee and type for two hours before going to the office *every single day*. . . . No, not when you get back at night, because you'll be stale. . . . All right, all right, you can have Sundays off. But if you knock out a thousand words a day you'll have finished it, allowing for the rewrite, in about four months."

Starting a book wasn't easy, because upon Kate's return to Britain Scotty worked her hard. One morning she answered his summons to find him standing in front of his work shelf, scowling as he groped around with one hand for his heavy, black-framed glasses; he never wore them for reading or writing, but he couldn't think without them. In intensely cerebral moments he polished them, so when you saw Scotty whip his glasses off his nose, fish out his grubby handkerchief and start to rub his glasses, then you knew that he was about to say something that would shake you.

"I want you to stop being a bloody celebrity and get down to interview work again. I don't want you typecast in khaki battle jacket. Go and see this woman who's just been found not guilty of murdering her transvestite husband. Seven hundred words."

Aghast, Kate looked at Scotty. "I *can't*."

"Why not?" Scotty turned his attention to the page in front of him. Kate supposed that she had no real reason for not covering the story—it might even help to get it out of her system.

* * *

Kate's book was published in June 1967. There were simultaneous editions in Britain and in the United States, where Judy was going to promote it.

Kate turned up late one night at Judy's apartment in New York. She headed for the tub and disappeared in a warm fog of Chamade, snorting, "Those swine at the airport! When I told them they'd lost my special television wardrobe, they merely handed me a form to fill in and then presented me with a toothbrush and two pairs of paper panties. Not really enough for 'Today.' "

"Oh, I don't know," said Judy, pulling a notebook from the pocket of her purple Courrèges pants suit as Kate submerged completely and lewd-sounding bubbles rose from the tub. When the dripping head reappeared, Judy started to scribble a list. "While we're making life miserable for those incompetents at Kennedy, let's buy you some stuff for the road. We'll go shopping tomorrow, and remember, the less you buy the better. A couple of lightweight dresses for the South and for evenings: one good suit with at least seven blouses because you won't have time to wash one out every night. Make sure they're polyester, not silk, so you can hand-wash them in the hotel basin. And get some junk jewelry and scarves. Margot Fonteyn tours with hardly any baggage, just one black suit. In between interviews, she sits in the back of the limo, turns the collar up or down, undoes a couple of buttons, pulls some pearls or a scarf out of her tote bag and manages six entirely different looks in one day."

There was an anguished cry from the tub. "Are you trying to make me feel inferior before I start? I am not a prima ballerina. I'm here to talk about a war. People won't expect me to look like a fashion plate."

"Yes, they will," said Judy earnestly. "All those women are going to remember what you wear. If you can't get your act together, why should they listen to you?" She shook more Chamade into the tub and added, "As for feeling inferior, wait until you get out West to the body-beautiful belt—perfectly capped smiles and twenty-four-hour immaculate hairstyles. We don't want confidence to melt at that point, do we?"

Kate scowled and slicked her hair back, reaching for the shampoo. Judy squinted at her. "Hold your hair back again. At least when your hair is wet we can see what you look like. Kenneth can cut it tomorrow. Tell him to get the hair off your face so that we can see those green tiger eyes." She dodged a wet sponge. "Christ, it's just like being back at school. You should also take one comfortable pair of low pumps and a large box of Band-Aids. On tour you have to look after your feet like an infantry man."

"Anything else?"

"Vitamin pills, some eyedrops if you don't want bloodshot eyes after long flights, and a stick of men's deodorant. Those studios can get really sweaty."

"Well, you needn't bother to get my suitcase back from Mombasa or wherever it's gone," said Kate clambering out, "because there's nothing like that in it. I brought rather stately, royal-tour-type clothes. I'm glad I lost them."

"What you've got to realize," Judy said, handing her a towel, "is that you've really got to make a constant effort to look good for every goddamn minute of this tour." Kate scowled, and Judy yelled, "It costs a minimum of two hundred bucks a day to keep you on the road, so you better look like a million dollars."

On June 5 Kate left on tour. At home, Judy suddenly stopped brewing her breakfast coffee and turned up the radio. "Lightning attack by Israel caused severe Arab losses and capture of territory, mainly from Egypt and Jordan."

It was the first radio report of what turned out to be the Israeli-Egyptian Six Day War.

Judy immediately realized that *One Woman's War* was going to be a bestseller.

"Just to bring you down to earth," scowled Scotty, when Kate returned to London, "let's see how you tackle a tits-and-ass story." So Kate was sent to interview a continental teenage starlet who was making a film in Britain, an updated fairy story that was being shot in the New Forest, Hampshire.

At first light, Kate was waiting on the set in the cold, damp forest clearing, heavily wrapped up against the weather, sniffing the autumn reek of wet leaves. A yellow trailer was parked under the trees, and suddenly, in the doorway, stood the most ravishing little creature Kate had ever seen. Lili's hands were pushed deep into a dark fur coat with upturned collar, under which she wore picturesque rags that had been carefully slashed to show as much of her body as possible.

Kate caught her breath—Lili really was exquisite. She had flawless, olive skin, huge dark eyes, an almost perfect profile. Even Lili's back view was entrancing, thought Kate. When she threw off the fur coat, ready for action, a black, silk curtain of hair hung down past her ribs, stopping just above the tiny waist. Her exquisitely modeled buttocks and satin thighs were visible under those ridiculous rags as she walked toward the clearing. A fawnlike innocence emanated from her, as if she might melt at any moment into the misty forest behind her.

On the set, Kate hadn't expected to feel anything except cold, but she was awestruck by the quietly magical quality that seemed to radiate from Lili as she moved, barefoot and graceful, through the forest.

They had very nearly finished the movie, which was well over schedule and budget. Everyone except Lili seemed to be strained, bad-tempered and bitchy. The director was only speaking to the cameraman through his assistant, and most of the company were not speaking to each other at all. In between takes, wardrobe rushed forward with a bowl of hot water in which Lili put her frozen feet until the company was ready for the next take.

Later, in the trailer, Kate interviewed Lili, who spoke good English. Serge had insisted that she learn to speak fluent English and ride a horse—both important, he said, to a movie career. Lili was composed and quiet when answering questions about her acting.

"How do you start to interpret a role?" Kate began.

"Oh, I don't think of it that way, not at all. I just read the part over and over again, until I know how I would behave if I were that character. I . . . brood over it . . . until it's obvious how that character behaves, and then suddenly, I feel that I *am* that character, and the character then becomes more real to me than my real self. I've always playacted this way since I was a little girl, so it's not difficult for me."

Lili looked wary when Kate started to question her about her notoriety and asked if she enjoyed being in the limelight. "Of course not, but this thing is part of my job, so I do it," Lili said, speaking accurately but with a heavy French accent.

"I hate these unpleasant things that are printed about me. I cannot bear when the newspapers say—always I am in bed with this man or that man. They just write lies. I would never get any sleep if I slept with all the men I am supposed to."

"You mean you *don't* enjoy being a celebrity?" Kate asked. "You don't enjoy heads turning in restaurants, people recognizing you at airports, kids asking for your autograph, all that stuff?"

"If you think that is enjoyable, it is only because you have not experienced it," Lili said in an earnest voice.

She became a little agitated as Kate started to probe into her private life and ask questions about her first public appearances. Kate had taken Lili's cuttings envelope out of the *Globe* library, and finally she produced early photographs of Lili in the notorious see-through communion dress.

"You can't expect to do this sort of thing and get good publicity."

"Those photographs were taken when I was thirteen; I did as I was told. I expect *you* did, when you were thirteen."

"But why did your parents allow it?"

"I'm an orphan, I ran away from my foster parents because . . . they beat me," Lili said, as Serge had taught her. Then suddenly she added, "As a matter of fact, I was pushed into it and. . . . " And for the first time, she found herself describing that first long-ago photo session in Serge's Paris studio.

As Lili spoke, Kate saw the helpless girl-child, saw how easy it must have been to exploit her timid vulnerability. She sensed that while Lili seemed surrounded by care and attention, in fact, she was only getting it from people who were making money off her.

"But don't you have any friends?"

"Not me, I don't have time." Lili sounded resigned. "But Serge knows *lots* of people."

The last thing Kate had expected to feel for a sexpot starlet was affection and pity.

"Get cracking, I want that piece in by five o'clock," said Scotty. Kate sat down, hashed it out and handed it in with half an hour to spare. Scotty quickly scanned her copy, then gave an exasperated groan. "I can't use this in the page three slot! This hearts and flowers stuff won't sell newspapers." He read aloud: " 'Strangely insecure and unsure of herself . . . quivering like a deer ready to dart back into the forest. . . . ' For God's sake, Kate! Let's see your notes."

He looked at them and grunted. "Give this stuff to Bruce, he's just got time to do a rewrite. He can do this stuff in his sleep!"

The article started, " '*Always I am in bed with this man or that man,*' said Miss Muck, known to the porn trade as Lili." It was a scathing attack; contemptuous and—apart from the starting sentence—more or less accurate. Unfortunately, it was accidentally printed under Kate's by-line.

"Nice," said Scotty. "A real killer."

Kate hit the roof. "Why was it run under my by-line?"

Scotty shrugged his shoulders. "You know these things sometimes happen on a daily."

"See what happens if you're interviewed without me?" Serge sneered angrily. "This English cunt tied you up in knots! You can't do a goddamn thing properly by yourself, whether it's giving an interview or jumping out of the window!"

"I didn't jump!"

"No, but you were going to in Paris if I hadn't come in and grabbed you from behind."

Serge threw the newspaper to the floor of their hotel bedroom and poured himself another whiskey. "Why can't they give you a full ice bucket? Even at the goddamn Dorchester!"

He stood looking out over the treetops of Hyde Park, watching the wet traffic slowly pass in the lamplight beneath him, ghostlike in the light London fog.

"You know your problem, Lili? You're fucking stupid. You don't even know who you are unless I'm around to remind you."

"No," said Lili sadly, thinking of *vraie maman*, "I don't know who I am."

"Well, you'll never be able to stand on your own feet unless you find out, and until that day—you *need* me, baby! In the meantime, just remember that you're now a high-class act, so start behaving like one!" He picked up the crumpled copy of the *Globe*. "You *must* have said it, it *sounds* like you, 'always I am in bed with this man or that man,' Christ, you stupid bitch!"

"She's left out parts of what I said. I didn't mean it that way. We were talking for over an hour in the evening and I find it so tiring suddenly to talk English all the time."

"But all this about the see-through communion dress! You sound like something from the gutter, a crude little whore."

"Well, aren't I?" Lili was getting exasperated.

"What's the point of staying in the best places, buying you the best clothes, angling all the publicity to your acting, if you let some smart bitch of a journalist say that you're just a cheap pair of tits?"

Serge looked at her in disgust and drained his glass. "Even if it's true," he said, "it's bad for business."

By 1968 "Swinging London" was in full swing. Fashion was suddenly one vast fancy dress party. The miniskirt had given reality to lustful, commuter dreams. Women dressed as tattered gypsies, Indian squaws with leather forehead bands and frizzy hair, fantasy female cowboys with fringed buckskin hot pants, wagon-train settlers in patchwork or as flower sprigged, straw-hatted milkmaids. Laura Ashley made a fortune. Carnaby Street was fantasy land, where once-staid British businessmen now bought their tight-assed bell-bottoms, velvet three-piece suits, flowered shirts, rainbow sweaters, high-heeled boots, necklaces and even handbags.

London was a boom town and the stock market was soaring. Kate had eventually persuaded her mother's lawyer to change stockbrokers, her persuasion having consisted of a list of share comparisons over the previous ten years and a threat to take the matter to court on the grounds of gross negligence. Having had to study the figures herself, Kate finally became intrigued by them and decided that she might as well play the stock market on her own. She borrowed from her bank, using her house as collateral, took a quick, lucky plunge into the Australian nickel market with Western Mining and found that she had made more than two years' salary in one month.

After that, Kate had no time to think about anything except her work because Scotty gave her a new job. On the theory that nobody does much on Sundays and therefore there isn't always much news on Mondays—which meant a dull paper—Scotty gave Kate a new section to edit, called LIFE + STYLE. It was intended to cover the whole frenetic new scene and the people who were making it. Kate knew little about editing, but she had now been working for Scotty for five years and she took to it quickly, working far into the night, arguing with Scotty over the content, the photographs and the articles. She no longer had time to leave the office during the day. She sat in a small, windowless cubicle behind a large desk with five telephones in front of her. Her secretary and three assistants were located in further little cubicles, opening off the corridor. Kate planned, argued, listened and gave briefings. She cut copy and dealt with crises and problems.

LIFE + STYLE was a success from the first day it was published. Advertisers lined up, the section was immediately copied by all the *Globe*'s rivals and women wrote to L + S in droves.

"You've hit on a winning formula," Scotty told her one night. "It's about time you had a night on the town. Me, too." He reached into an inside pocket of his jacket. "Hunter Baggs has just bought a vast house in Campden Hill and he's giving a party tonight. I can't find it, but the invitation promised a fantastic house-warming or something like that. Why don't I take you?"

So they ate supper at San Freddiano and arrived at the party around eleven that evening. Lights beamed from uncurtained windows, cars swarmed around a pillared porch and the noise was like being on a battlefield again.

Once inside the door, Kate blinked. It wasn't a fantastic party, it was a fancy-dress party—but a bizarre one. Several showgirls wore pigtails, short gym suits, frilly panties, black stockings and garters. A nun wore a long black habit that was slit to the thigh, revealing fishnet stockings and frilly red satin garters as she danced with a youth who wore only a golden G-string and a halo around his sprayed golden curls.

A lethal champagne cocktail was being served from a big silver punch bowl by their host, who was dressed as Count Dracula, immaculate in tuxedo, red-lined cloak and vampire teeth. He said, "Hello and welcome, darlings."

"Hunter, what *is* this?" Scotty asked.

"Don't you read your invitations, darling?" asked Baggs pleasantly. "It said 'Dress as your own favorite sexual fantasy,' and as you see almost everyone has."

He waved a hand around the entrance hall.

Kate looked around. Two lady SS officers danced together wearing black peaked hats, black shirts, black tights and jackboots. There seemed to be a great many black leather garments, whips, see-through plastic macs and the odd brandished dildo. A few men wore an old gray mackintosh, sockless shoes and a furtive look. A couple of devils danced with two black bunny girls in thigh-high satin swimsuits with little white cotton tails.

"Why don't you go upstairs?" suggested Baggs. "There's a poker room, a roulette room, a blackjack game and a blue-movie room with a water bed."

A tall, familiar figure dressed as a schoolgirl whirled past Kate, and—feeling slightly sick—Kate saw that it was her former husband, Toby.

Kate said to Scotty, "I think I'll give it a miss and turn in early."

As she walked toward the entrance she almost collided with a beautiful girl in a white lace catsuit who was angrily saying to her escort, "No, sorry—I have to put up with this sort of thing in my work, but I'm damned if I see why I should do it in my free time!" She tossed her luxuriant dark hair, which fell to her waist from a demure white lace cap tied under her chin with a satin bow.

"That's Lili!" The whisper ran around the huge hall, "That's Lili, that's Lili." The girl in white walked out into the night.

PART EIGHT

CHAPTER 41

"I'M SURPRISED THAT you ever *managed* to lure a man in here," Maxine sniffed, "or that any man manages to find his way *out* of this mess. You're a closet magpie, Judy! You've never been able to throw anything away. You're a thirty-five-year-old pack rat, that's what!"

"Well, I guess that's because it was a long time before I *had* anything to throw away! And please remember that my bedroom is also my *working* area. This is where I read, brood and scheme, as well as sleep. It's where I make my money, Maxine!"

"You always realized that money was important, Judy. It took the rest of us longer to learn."

Maxine stood up and opened the doors to the two walk-in closets that separated the bedroom from the living room. One of them was entirely full of shoes and the closet looked like a jewel box.

Judy said, "Real protection isn't a man—it's money! That's what gives you the power to do good, the power to be bad, the power to stay or to leave."

Maxine peered at shoe shelves, which were lined in crimson moiré taffeta. "Most women prefer not to think about money. They think that dealing with money is tedious."

"Not so tedious as being without it, and only if you haven't been taught how to handle it," Judy replied sharply. "We should *all* have been taught how to earn it, how to make it, how to multiply it, how to *keep* it! But women are merely taught how to spend it. And when there's trouble, few women have any money, *that* I have noticed."

Maxine agreed. "When a couple split up, the woman gets possession of the children, but the man gets possession of the money. Of course that is exactly when a woman realizes the importance of the stuff."

She examined the scarlet shelves—different ones for low pumps, for high base, pumps, for delicate sandals, for low-heeled boots and for the rows of high-heeled boots in tinted suede, supple as gloves.

"Having money isn't important, but *not* having money is vital," Judy added.

"You may know a lot about money, *ma chère*, but you don't know much about the trappings of wealth." Maxine looked around the room again. Nobody was allowed in Judy's bedroom to tidy up, so it was in a permanent state of chaos. The two bedside tables were covered by stacks of magazines, yellowing newspapers, books and legal pads. All the other flat surfaces, including the window ledge, were piled high with antique tinware, souvenir ashtrays, unframed paintings, last year's New Year's cards loudly hailing 1968, and fading Mexican paper flowers.

"Most people never get beyond the living room," Judy apologized.

Maxine sniffed, picked up one of the legal pads and sat on the edge of the bed. "A little organization is needed, *ma chère*. No, I promise I won't throw anything out, but we put it all in different places. Now you don't need three guest bedrooms, do you?"

"Well, yes, I do. That's one of the reasons Tom wanted me to get a bigger apartment: this is our entertainment base; we put up a lot of people from out of town—our regional directors—and sometimes they overlap."

"Why not try having only two guest bedrooms and a study with a convertible sofa? I'll make a list now and we'll go to Bloomingdale's tomorrow before I go on tour. At least your closets are tidy and your clothes are cared for."

"Yes. Francetta doesn't care much for scrubbing floors, but she's a marvelous maid, and her husband does the heavy work on his day off."

Maxine picked up a lavender silk pump with a single feather curling across the instep. "Handmade in Florence, I see. Your business seems to be doing as well as ours. Isn't it wonderful to sleep at night? Sixty-six was an even better vintage than '64—which was the year that really put us on our feet."

"Oh, this money doesn't only come from LACE, it's the result of Tom's speculation. I have terrible anxiety attacks about it, and as a matter of fact I *can't* sleep at night. It's different for Tom—he can be objective about it, but I *can't*.

"I've tried and tried to live with it," she continued, "because Tom seems to need the thrills and suspense of speculation the way some people need to ski down mountains or climb up them. He says he needs the adrenalin charge."

"Good heavens, you mean Tom is a gambler?"

"I say he is and he says he isn't. He says that every business move is a calculated risk, but gambling is for idiots who believe in luck. Oh, no, he disapproves of gamblers."

"Then in what way does he speculate with such danger? Has he always done it?"

"No, because his wife couldn't stand it. Hell, a lot of people invest on Wall Street. Maxine, it might *not* be dangerous. I just don't know. But what he does goes against everything I've been brought up to believe in. Not being in debt, always saving a little. . . . My mother thinks the two most obscene words in the English language are 'credit card.' "

"But I couldn't move around Europe without a credit card!"

"My mother doesn't move around Europe." Judy moved to the window and looked down over the park. "To tell you the truth, it scares the hell out of me."

" . . . Remember what Edward G. Robinson's Renoirs fetched?" Tom had asked in the quiet of their office the previous night. "No, I'm not buying Impressionist paintings because it's too late for that. But the point is that if you buy the best there's always *someone* who will buy it, if you need to sell. The best is always in short supply. . . . Anyway, I hope so, because we have just acquired a T'ang horse. Yes, an eighth-century Chinese ceramic horse about eighteen inches high, sort of earth-colored. . . . No, you can't, it's in the bank vault. . . . It's acting as part collateral for the loan that helped to buy it. For God's sake, what's the difference in principle between buying that horse and the office building mortgage, or the land near Houston? Except that we can't rent a T'ang horse out for grazing?"

As Judy saw it, LACE was the puny, endangered base that all this borrowing rested upon, and however much Tom stabbed his index finger at the balance sheet, she couldn't fight her childhood indoctrination to the point of seeing their increasing wealth as reality. LACE was a real business, the rest was just figures on paper. She remembered the fight they'd had when the LACE bank loan crossed the half-million-dollar mark and Tom had merely said, "Grow up, Judy, no business or fortune can be started today without getting into debt—and it's only the first fifty thousand that's hard to borrow."

But what worried Judy most were Tom's commodity speculations. In the last few years he had staked their hard-earned profits first on cocoa, then on sugar, while Judy lay awake nights wondering whether they were going to be stuck with a warehouse full of the stuff. As a matter of fact, Tom also occasionally lay awake at night, because he'd started to buy on margin and that was very different from his more cautious stock market investments. But he was lucky and prices moved up—cocoa by twelve percent and sugar by nineteen percent—within a month of his buying. With the profit, he went short on cotton and long on cocoa again, and lost on cocoa and made a killing on cotton. By the time he plunged into soy beans, he no longer took much notice of what he called Judy's "irrational fears" and made a profit of thirteen per-cent within six weeks of his purchase. After that, he mainly speculated in cocoa and sugar, on the whole with great success.

Judy explained all this to Maxine and added, "He wasn't like that to begin with. A couple of times during our first business year we weren't able to meet the rent payments, so Tom always took his figures along to the landlord before the payment was due, and he never got thrown out, as I did. *That* I could understand, but at the end of our second year—when he bought cocoa on margin and it paid off—d'you know what he did? He bought our office building, using the cocoa profit as a down payment! From that moment I felt strangled by the debt around our necks." Judy sighed. "The worst part is that I can't talk to anyone about it. You must remember that it's a secret, Maxine."

"Once you tell a secret to another person it no longer is a secret," Maxine pointed out. "Is this apartment paid for?"

"Yes, I *insisted* on that, and to my surprise, Tom didn't make a fuss. He just sniffed and said my useless ethics were expensive. I *cannot* understand how this perfectly rational man, who is marvelously good at a job I understand, can be so insane when it comes to money. Or why he gets so exasperated when I tell him, especially when he loses on some deal and thousands of dollars disappear overnight. After our last fight I thought we'd have to stop working together."

Thoughtfully, Maxine stroked the lavender silk shoe; then she said, "You're thirty-five, you own a smart apartment and you've got a well-paid, enjoyable job. I should forget the rest and let Tom do as he wants."

So Judy shut up, but she didn't stop worrying.

* * *

Three weeks later, Maxine returned from her promotional tour across the country.

"A true friend is someone who confesses that she weighs more than you do," Judy said, watching Maxine stand on the scales in the guest bathroom.

"Especially if she doesn't," Maxine agreed. "Can it be possible that I've put on eight pounds in three weeks on tour?"

"People either gain a lot of weight or lose a lot. Now put your robe on and come into the living room. I've brought your press clippings back from the office."

They moved into the cream-walled, double-cube living room. The ornately carved, low, dark opium beds stood on three sides of a vast *sang de boeuf* marble table. Zebra skins lay on the dark hardwood floor and an antique red-and-black painted Persian screen zig-zagged across one corner. Two elaborate Louis XV gilt mirrors hung on either side of the marble fireplace and on the opposite wall was a growing collection of Steinberg drawings.

Maxine rushed to a pink file that lay on one of the opium beds, then stretched back against mauve and blue silk cushions as she skimmed through the newspaper clippings. She hadn't seen them because she had left each city before her interviews were printed.

"Not bad, not bad. This column in *Time* with the little picture is delightful. It was so good of you to telephone every night, Judy. It was always an anxious time, not knowing whether or not one was succeeding, and it was also lonely. I almost wished that I'd taken my secretary."

"When you've finished admiring your press clippings, come and see how the bedrooms have been altered while you've been away. I told the decorator to do exactly as you said."

Judy's bedroom now looked luxurious and peaceful. Wild silk drapes covered the window wall and a rich red-fox spread had been flung over the velvet brown bed. On one side of it was a control panel for TV, stereo, radio, telephones and drapes. Two large, low rosewood chests now stood on either side of Judy's bed to hold all the work clutter. There was only one picture in the room, a Manchu noble, inscrutably lifesize, in a seventeenth-century Chinese silk painting that hung opposite the vast bed. Apart from the bed, the only other piece of furniture in the room was a chaise longue up-holstered in red-tinged chintz. The same chintz had been used for the couches in the adjoining room, which was now furnished as a study. The walls had been completely covered by bookshelves and painted deep raspberry. Judy's collection of odd objects, when spaced upon the shelves, could suddenly be seen as a collection of antique toys and other esoteric memorabilia. A Victorian rolltop wooden desk stood in front of the window.

"I love this dark red," Judy said.

"I've just used it in Guy's new offices. He's got more competition now, since Saint Laurent started his own salon, hence the revamp."

The two women moved back into Judy's bedroom where she started quickly to undress and change for the evening. "Guy needn't worry about competition. Nobody can compete with his suits," Judy commented, as she unzipped her exquisitely cut, scarlet pants suit and stepped out of it. "I've practically lived in this for the past few weeks. When did you last see him?"

"Oh, I haven't seen him for months, but now seeing each other doesn't seem to alter our relationship. It's the same with Pagan and Kate, we never write, we don't see each other for months, but when we meet we just pick up where we left off."

"Friendship expands to fill the space available." Judy pulled on a flesh-colored bodystocking.

"In a way, yes. Friendship can wax and wane and disappear like the moon—then rise and wax fat again at some later date. . . . " She clasped her hands behind her head. "I mean *real* friendship."

"My idea of a real friend was your Aunt Hortense." Judy hitched up the body-stocking shoulder straps. "I can't imagine her wearing these clothes, can you?"

"On the contrary, she'd have looked wonderful in a trouser suit. Oh dear, the last time I saw her before her stroke was when she was playing under the beech tree with Alexandre—he must have been two years old that summer—and she was wearing a green chiffon blouse. He'd managed to undo a couple of buttons and was solemnly stuffing daisies down her cleavage. She looked unusually untidy and unusually happy, and that is how I like to remember her."

The two women were silent as Judy wriggled into a thigh-length, skimpy, black crochet dress.

"*Ma chère*, you look as though you're wearing nothing underneath. These new short fashions make us all look like showgirls in the miniskirt and the high boots. No wonder men love it. Is it for some special man that you want to look as if you wear no lingerie?"

"No, no special man." She clipped on a pair of sunburst diamond earrings. "We're dining with Tom and an editor from *Newsweek*. . . . You know I never seem to fall in love like other women."

"Hurry up!" Tom yelled from the living room a couple of days later. "Move it, Judy." He poked his head around the bedroom door. "You can't be late at your own reception, especially not when the Nixons are guests of honor."

"Sorry. Maxine got stuck with a late takeoff to Tokyo." Vigorously toweling her hair, Judy zipped up her black velvet dress then quickly brushed her hair.

"Why don't you ever use makeup?" He had sauntered into the bedroom, hands in pockets.

"Because I either look like a clown or a raddled twelve-year-old, even after a lesson from Way Bandy. How's that?"

"Jailbait. Incidentally, why did the cancer people choose the Carlyle?"

"They didn't, I did. The security's excellent and their staff is very tightly screened. We've lost Martin Luther King and Bobby Kennedy this year, and with Nixon coming tonight I couldn't be more nervous."

"Sure. It's a new account, as well, and your friend Pagan moved it our way. But they know you're good, honey, you don't have to worry."

But all evening, Judy felt as jumpy as a cat, especially when she realized that she was being watched by a tall, dark-haired man. He leaned against the wall with his hands in his pockets and said, "You look wicked and wonderful," as she hurried past.

"So does Mount Everest." She smiled tightly. He was definitely not Security. She ignored him for the rest of the evening, except once, when she felt his eyes upon her back, turned, and sure enough there he was, calmly gazing at her from under heavy eyelids. To Judy's amazement she started to blush; hastily she looked away from him, down at the floor. Then with an effort, because they trembled and yet felt weighted, she slowly lifted her eyelids. Steadily he looked back at her without moving and she felt as if she were naked before him. She felt helpless, her breath unsteady, her face flushed. With an almost painful effort, she turned away, furious with herself. . . . There was something familiar about his face, although she couldn't place him. That bumpy forehead with the slight frown, the wide mouth and attractive, crooked teeth, that slow smile. . . . Now he was talking to another man, making fast, impatient movements, jerking his head to flick the dark hair back out of his eyes, stabbing the air with his index finger.

Got it!

It was Griffin Lowe of Orbit Publishing. He hadn't been on the list, but someone high on it must have brought him. Briskly she moved over toward him. "It's Mr. Lowe, isn't it? Can I introduce you to anyone?"

"No, thanks. I came with the Javitses but I don't think I'm staying. It's my second day with contact lenses, and they're fighting back. Why don't we split and have dinner?"

"Because I'm working."

"No need to, if I say you're not."

"I'm sorry, but no." Judy walked away with just a hint of rudeness. She didn't need that kind of rich man's power play and didn't appreciate it one bit.

She was the last to leave. After settling the details of the bill with Luigi, she stood under the awning and was about to ask for a cab when a maroon Rolls-Royce drew up and the back door opened. "An offer you can't refuse. A lift home, with no strings. We know the address."

She laughed and climbed into the back, which was fitted out like a small living room and smelled discreetly of real leather.

She didn't ask him in and he didn't suggest it. The car simply drove off into the night and Judy headed for a hot tub, rather sorry not to have had the opportunity to turn down Griffin Lowe again. . . .

CHAPTER 42

THAT WAS THE last she heard of him for six weeks, then he telephoned at seven-thirty on a Monday morning to ask her to dinner on the evening of her choice. She said, "You must be crazy! Is this business? Because it certainly isn't pleasure."

"Look, I *know* you get up early. It's whatever you care to make it. Sure, I use PR firms."

"Okay, how about Le Chantilly at seven this evening."

She wasn't surprised to find Griffin Lowe an interesting and entertaining companion. Of course she had ordered his clippings file sent up to her office, but everyone in the media world knew about Griffin. His publishing empire included a great deal of profitable trash, but also one or two of the best magazines in America. Everyone knew that Griffin was a tough, clever bastard who didn't care what anybody thought of him, which was just as well; they knew he could bring off brilliant, surprising business coups. They knew he had his own sense of rough justice, and that he was a forty-five-year-old, well-known womanizer. Oh, yes, and they knew he was married, with three children—or was it four?

Griffin Lowe sat across the velvet banquette from Judy and they ate lobster bisque, roast lamb with watercress salad followed by caramelized, sliced oranges. Then as they sipped their coffee, Griffin gently took her hand under the table and Judy almost died of shock. Was this not 1968, when the up-to-date standard approach was "Hello, do you feel like a fuck?" And was she not a thirty-five-year-old figure of emerging womanhood, strong, direct and adult? So was she *really* experiencing that old familiar feeling in the pit of the stomach as if she were back in school again?

Yes.

They sat there for over an hour just holding hands and saying nothing. Judy didn't move out of the restaurant, she floated. After the driver had helped her into the waiting car, Griffin murmured, "You must be wondering if this is my standard approach. I just felt happy holding your hand, so I didn't want to stop. Now d'you want this to go any further or not?"

"Well, perhaps just to the elbow." He leaned over and took her in his arms. Judy suddenly felt his mouth pressed on hers, his arms crushing her body, his breath on her cheek, his fingers in her hair.

She couldn't remember getting out of the car and into her apartment. She only knew that her hands were shaking as Griffin slowly unzipped her black velvet dress and it fell to the floor of the living room. He pulled her to him and again she felt his mouth on hers, his firm square hands sliding gently down to the small of her back, pressing her body against him until her knees shook so that she could no longer stand. Then he gently pulled off her sheer black pantyhose and laid her, still trembling, on the yielding soft cushions of the couch.

Shivering with pleasure she yielded to his touch, his fingers, his mouth. Then he, too, was naked and she could smell and feel the warmth of him against her.

He lifted her in his arms. He put her down on the silk sheets of her bed, then, savoring each moment, they abandoned themselves to slow, sensual lovemaking.

He licked her secret places. He tried to lick her ear, but Judy jerked her head away—she couldn't bear that warm messy wetness. But of course sex *was* messy, so she gave in, surrendering to pleasure. He checked where else she liked to be licked, and they found it was almost everywhere. Then suddenly he grew fierce and so did she and they had a little wrestling match to see who got on top and he allowed Judy to win, but somehow they fell off the bed and onto the red-fox spread and then she felt his fingers inside her, after which he rimmed her rather noisily and she didn't mind the warm messy wetness, not one bit. Then she twisted her body until he was powerless beneath her, or so it pleased them to pretend. She moved against him, driving him to the same frenzy that he'd made her feel ten minutes before, then she pushed him back against the cinnamon silk pillows, then leaned back and grabbed his ankles. She felt his strength inside her, his hard, hairy thighs beneath her ass, his fingers driving her wild.

She woke early, happy, and calm. Suddenly remembering the night, she jerked her head around and saw his winged black eyebrows. She felt an odd, new sensation. *She didn't want him to wake up.* When he woke up, he would leave. Immediately she felt suspicious of this new vulnerability. She suddenly felt possessive. Reminding herself that her bedmate was a well-known womanizer, Judy slid out of bed, put on her dressing gown and fixed breakfast.

Griffin Lowe opened one eye, reached out one arm and tugged at her pink lace gown, then he pulled her down on the bed and murmured how he'd like to start the day, and it wasn't with breakfast. So she slid on top of him again and once more they melted into each other, her slight body on his strong, lusty one.

At last he said gently, "I told Carter to bring the car around at eight, so I'll have to go soon. But I'll be back."

Then he showered and suddenly he was gone, leaving her breathless, incapable of thought, incapable of work, incapable of doing anything except to relive in her imagination every minute since she'd met him.

Suddenly it occurred to her that this new sensation wasn't merely carnal desire or passion. For the first time, at the age of thirty-five, she correctly suspected that she was falling in love.

Unsummoned, Griffin now drifted into Judy's thoughts when she least expected it, catching her off-guard during conferences and meetings. She wasted a lot of time gazing dreamily into space, thinking of his skin, the way the back of his neck joined his broad shoulders, the soft hair on his forearms, the shape of his hands, the scar on his left hand (Why? There were so many things to ask him), the warmth of his body. Griffin even knew how to undress erotically, that slow loosening of the tie as he looked steadily at her, removing his socks before his pants to avoid that ridiculous, vaudeville view of hairy legs between shirt and socks.

In a rosewood drawer by her bed she kept a pale blue shirt that he'd worn, and when he wasn't there, she pressed it to her face and inhaled the musky odor of his body.

Griffin immediately hired LACE for one of his new companies, pointing out that it would give them a reason to be together, which it did. Judy was surprised by his relaxed business methods. He didn't waste energy looking dynamic; at times he seemed almost idle. He would sit at a meeting in a gentle, almost apologetic manner, rubbing the side of his nose with his left index finger as he questioned, commented, queried and encouraged other people, probing for every detail. Then he would sum up the entire meeting in three minutes. When Griffin Lowe went to a meeting, whether it was a formal one in his gray suede-paneled conference room or a casual discussion with feet on the desk, everyone present seemed to think fifteen percent faster and better. It was one of the things that Judy and he had in common.

He and Judy saw each other three times a week. At first they were discreet, but increasingly they became reckless. His wife must surely know, Judy reasoned, and so did Griffin. "She won't say anything, she never does," He told Judy and she winced. She hated to think of herself as one more of Griffin's affairs.

There was a long silence.

"That was a very *shitty* thing to say," she said, and she was only half-joking. She wanted to hurt him, the way those three words had just hurt and humiliated her. "*She never does.*"

They'd had lunch at her apartment—smoked trout and half of a bottle of Pouilly Fumée at the bedside—then Griffin showered, dressed and was now about to leave.

"*Very* shitty . . ." Judy repeated, turning to him with a wicked gleam in her blue eyes. "So I'm going to punish you so that you never hurt or humiliate me again."

Griffin went along with it—he could have kicked himself for saying those three words—as she led him by the hand back to the rumpled bed and shoved him down on it. With a forced laugh—he was late for his next appointment—Griffin put a lazy arm up to pull her down against his chest, but she caught his wrist and said, "I'm going to tie you to the bed; then I'm going to have my way with you. I'm going to punish you so that you will never, never be shitty and thoughtless with me again."

She bit his forefinger hard enough to make Griffin jump with pain and surprise. Then she pulled off her maroon-silk dressing gown sash and swiftly tied his right arm to the headboard.

He tried to protest in a playful voice, going along with the game. He recognized the real pain behind her teasing tone of voice, and he also recognized that he wasn't going to make his next appointment. As she reached for his other wrist and wrapped a red silk scarf around it, he said in a resigned voice, "Aren't you going to undress me first?"

"I'll take off your shoes," Judy offered, yanking off his handmade Italian loafers and then tying his ankles to the bed with his beige silk socks, so that he was spread-eagled.

"Oh, no," Griffin said in a high falsetto. "No, no, no! *Not* Gestapo-style correction, *not* . . . the whip, *not* torture, *not* the studded leather belt with the cruel brass buckle and the vicious stiletto heels and the swastika armband!" Groaning between laughs, he didn't mind playing a masochist for once.

"Worse," said Judy, disappearing into the kitchen and then appearing naked in the doorway with a pair of shears in her hand. As she headed for the bed, still with that wicked glint in her eye, Griffin nervously said, "Okay Judy, I'm *sorry*. Now let's quit fooling around. This ridiculous horseplay has gone far enough, and I'm late as it is."

"Oh, but I haven't *started*, so I'm certainly not going to stop," she said. And before Griffin realized what she was doing she'd slashed through the jacket of his handmade suit.

"*Judy!*" He tried to jerk himself upright but found, to his surprise, that he really couldn't move. She started to snip through his silk shirt, imported the previous month from Jermyn Street.

"Judy! *What* are you playing at? *You* gave me this shirt only yesterday. Remember?"

"A mistake," said Judy calmly, carefully cutting into his left trouser bottom and slicing up, roughly, toward his groin. "You really did hurt my feelings, just then, so I'm afraid I'll have to upset your life the way you're upsetting mine."

Griffin started to simmer. He wouldn't have minded if it were a Saturday, but he had a busy afternoon ahead, and after all, they'd just . . .

"You did come, didn't you?"

"Shut up. As a matter of fact, I think I'll make sure that you *can't* talk."

She put the shears down, picked up her tights, stuffed them in his mouth and gagged him with his tan silk tie. Then she carefully slashed up the other trouser leg and yanked away the debris of gray flannel. For one second Griffin worried as the shears were flourished in the air and then slashed toward his boxer shorts.

He started to give muffled yells for mercy. Whatever she was playing at, it seemed the correct way to react.

"I'm going to punish you so that you *never do it again*," Judy said softly. "I'm going to make you sorry! I'm going to make you suffer! There's a law against what I'd *really* like to do to you at this moment!" As she bent toward his cock, to his embarrassment, Griffin felt himself stiffen. She curled her tongue and flicked it at his flesh with butterfly strokes. Griffin groaned with pleasure, whereupon Judy stopped. She scrambled off the bed and again headed for the kitchen, reappearing with a bottle of olive oil. She said in a conversational voice, "You really should be more considerate, Griffin."

Kneeling on the bed beside him, she tipped the whole bottle over him, and the oil ran off his body and onto the sheets. Judy moved to the bottom of the bed and started to massage his left foot, carefully starting with the big toe and kneading hard under the instep, then going all the way up his leg with hard, oily strokes. He thought, She's going to suck me off; that's what this is leading up to. But she didn't. She stopped short of that point and started to rub his right foot, then expertly massaged his entire body until her hands were kneading the big muscles on either side of Griffin's neck. Occasionally she brushed the tips of her nipples across his chest as her thumbs pushed rhythmically toward his ears.

"*Now* you should be limp and acquiescent," she said thoughtfully. Then she crouched over Griffin's oil-slick body and with the tip of her tongue *just* licked his stiff cock with little cat-licking-the-cream sort of licks, after which she knelt astride him and carefully stroked her clitoris with his cock, taking no notice whatsoever of Griffin, in fact, treating him as a sexual object to bring herself to orgasm. Griffin was spread-eagled on the bed and she was sitting on top of him so there wasn't much that he could do about it. A muffled groan escaped his lips. By now he was slightly purple in the face and highly excited as Judy very carefully knelt astride his hips and put just the tip of his cock inside her, then quickly lifted her body so that it almost slipped out. After a few minutes of this teasing, she suddenly pushed it right in, and ground her body against his. Then, just as suddenly, she jumped off him.

There was a muffled yell of fury from Griffin.

"No! I'm going to fix myself a highball!"

She padded away, leaving Griffin jerking at his bonds, and returned with a large Scotch-on-the-rocks. She took a swig and rolled it around her tongue like mouthwash. Then she stretched out beside Griffin, took two ice cubes in her mouth and bent down again. He gave a muffled yelp, because the stinging sensation was totally different from the normal inside of somebody's mouth; instead of being warm and soft and wet it felt freezing and dangerously lumpy.

Judy sucked away until the ice in her mouth had melted and Griffin had lost his erection. Then she curled her forefinger inside him and wriggled around a bit, feeling for his prostate, and when she found it she pushed against it until Griffin quickly jerked to a climax.

She stood up and poured the rest of the highball over his head—the bed was now covered in a revolting mixture of olive oil and melting ice—then she nipped out to the icebox. Saying, "This always looks so *humorous* on film," she returned with a lemon meringue pie, which she carefully ground in Griffith's face. She pulled the tinfoil base away, stood up and surveyed the scene.

"My *God*, what a mess!" she said disapprovingly, then turned on her heel and headed for the shower.

Ten minutes later she reappeared, immaculately dressed in a buttercup, sleeveless, short linen tunic with matching pumps. "I've got an appointment, Griffin, so I have to go now," Judy said in a polite voice. Then she picked the shears off the floor and placed them on the bed, about a foot from Griffin's head. He tried to yell his indignation at her, but only muffled sounds came through the gag in his mouth as he struggled furiously.

"*You* were in the Boy Scouts, Griffin, you work it out," she said, and walked out of the apartment.

Griffin couldn't believe it. He couldn't believe that she'd really left him. He couldn't believe that he wasn't able to free himself. He jerked and struggled with his ridiculous silken bindings, gradually getting very cold on the unpleasantly sticky, damp bed, which stank of Scotch.

Eventually he found that by curling his right hand carefully around, he was able to pick at the knot of the dressing gown sash. It took him about half an hour, but then with one bound he was free—and telephoning Carter to bring around a fresh set of clothes.

Griffin was furious.

But he was also impressed. He—Griffin Lowe, the big-dealer, the lover and leaver, who kept his women neatly organized in a private emotional filing system which never overlapped with office hours or impinged on his domestic comfort—had been faced with a situation that his power, charm and savoir faire were unable to resolve. There had been real fury behind what Judy did—and she hadn't weakened. She had also demonstrated the physical power she had over Griffin. She understood his body so well that she had kept him at the point of orgasm for an hour and a half, teasing him almost beyond endurance until his nerves were raw.

He had been humbled, if not humiliated.

From that moment, the pattern of their relationship shifted, and Griffin treated Judy with a great deal more care and respect, not because he was afraid of her, but because she had done exactly what she said she would do—she had punished him!

But Griffin knew that he had to risk her pain and fury once more. He knew he had to spell their future out to her—it was only fair. One evening, a week after she'd tied him up and slashed his clothes off, they both lay naked on her bed, in the soft, final rays of the setting sun. They were both voluptuously tired after making love, and Griffin didn't really want to talk, but he knew he had to. He held her hand hard, knowing that he had to make it clear to her, knowing that it was going to hurt her. Eventually, he simply said, "Delia knows I'd never leave her or the kids, Judy. I've fought too hard for what I've got to dump my family or to hurt them." There was a long silence. He felt ill at ease and Judy looked so closed off and remote that he slid off the bed and padded, naked, to the kitchen, returning with a bottle of Dom Perignon in one hand.

"I can't think why she puts up with you," Judy said.

"Delia knows there's an odd kind of security about a man who's always falling in love."

Judy projected anger as he untwisted the wire and eased out the champagne cork with his thumbs. He had to be straight with her. "Fact one, Judy—I meet a lot of beautiful women and I enjoy them. Fact two—I also have a family. For me these are two entirely different areas of interest, and I hope you realize this."

She stretched one arm from the tousled, cinnamon silk sheets and took the glass of champagne he offered. "I mean, Judy, I'm *underlining* it. I don't want to hurt you and I don't want you to get any wrong ideas, but I want you to understand *I will never, never leave my wife*. It would hurt her too much and I could never live with myself afterward."

There was a long pause.

"That's what they all say." Judy carefully tipped her glass over his head. "And anyway, who asked you? A long time ago, I decided I was never going to marry. I didn't see the point of making unrealistic promises I wasn't sure that I or anyone else could keep."

Griffin put down the champagne bottle and headed for the bathroom. At least she hadn't smashed it over his head. And he *had*—finally and clearly—said it.

Judy continued in a dreamy voice: "I keep telling myself that I shouldn't *want* to marry you and I don't think I really do. It's just that I hate your being married to somebody *else*." She raised her voice so that, in the bathroom, he could still hear what she was saying. "I don't want to be *dependent* for my happiness on someone else, and I can't help feeling that way."

Griffin padded back, and she thought how handsome he looked as he stood in the doorway toweling his hair. He tried a tentative grin.

"Goddamn it, Griffin, *listen*, please. I've always valued my independence, but now I notice in myself a sudden painful urge to tell you *everything*, Griffin, every secret of my life."

She looked up at the ceiling. "Now I know that you don't feel that way about me, because men *don't*. And suddenly *I want to be with you all the time*. But intellectually I know I don't *want* that." She thumped the bedspread with her small fists. There was a short silence. Suddenly she sat up and he couldn't help looking at her small rosy nipples. He threw the towel on the floor, moved toward her and bent to her breasts, but she pushed him aside.

"Griffin, I want to keep my own privacy. If you laugh at this, I'll kill you, but I want to be alone, quite often."

She slid down the bed again and pulled the covers up to her neck. "Even if you *can't* keep your eyes off my tits."

He sat on the edge of the bed and said seriously, "Why? Why do you want to be alone quite often?"

"Because so many people are frightened of solitude, instead of valuing it. I was, once—and I never want to be like that again."

Slowly she pulled herself up to a sitting position against the pillows and said, "There's a world of difference between being alone and being lonely."

He looked skeptical. She hesitated, then added, "Sure, it's sometimes lonely to come home at night after a hard day's work to a dark, empty apartment. But I'd rather be down in the dumps occasionally than trapped with someone I don't really want to be with."

She scowled. "And I don't want to play that part in some man's life." She clasped her hands behind her head and her nipples again tilted upward. "Are you listening to me, Griffin? Once upon a time if a man told me he was lonely I used to melt with sympathy. But now I run a mile."

"Sounds as if you want to have your cake and eat it."

"Neatly put, for a cake."

Laughing, he lunged at her.

* * *

On her next trip to New York, Maxine was charmed by Griffin. "At last our lives seem to be sorting themselves out," she said, as she stood in Judy's kitchen, arranging an armful of arum lilies and pink roses that she'd brought in with her. "No, thank you, Francetta, I like doing the flowers. Pagan and I are happily married, with babies as well as jobs. Kate's happily divorced and a successful writer. And *at last* you've fallen in love."

Reflectively, she sniffed the rounded, pale pink tip of a rosebud. "We all hoped it would be Nick, then we all hoped it would be someone nice." She finished the vase and stood back to admire it. "And then we didn't care *who* it was, so long as he made you happy. Darling, what's all this Dom Perignon in your refrigerator? . . . Well, tell Griffin you prefer *our* champagne. And now listen, because I have a little surprise for you."

CHAPTER 43

LONDON LIFE AND the afternoon traffic were totally disrupted, and Pagan and Judy were one of the reasons for it. Outside the gates of Buckingham Palace stood a very smart line of women in large, flowered, floppy hats and men in pale gray top hats and black suits. They were the honored guests of H.M. the Queen at the annual Royal Garden Party. Pagan saw Kate, who had just been nominated woman of the year by the Association of Professional Women, so Pagan waved her invitation in the thick, cream envelope with the dark red, royal crest stamped on the back. It listed the time as four to six P.M., but you could enter through the magic gates at three-fifteen P.M. and a lot of people seemed to want to do it. Kate wore a cream Tuffin and Foale crepe suit with a flounced jacket, Pagan wore a trumpet-shaped silk dress with leg o'mutton sleeves in Jean Muir's latest pink and gray art-nouveau pattern, and Judy looked unusually demure in a lemon linen suit from Guy's summer collection, with slightly darker shoes and a big-brimmed straw hat.

The best part was walking past the scarlet-coated sentry, through the big black curlicued gates beyond the barriers that held back summer tourists. Once inside the gates the three of them walked across the gravel and under the arch of the quietly elegant, pale gray facade. Then they were in the inner courtyard and climbing the wide, red-carpeted stairs to the Queen's own doorstep.

"It certainly was a surprise, Pagan. I still can't believe I'm actually *inside* Buckingham Palace," said Judy. "And I still can't understand how you fixed it."

"Nobody can fix Buckingham Palace," said Pagan. "Christopher suggested about a year ago that you might be welcome, because of the voluntary work you'd done for cancer research."

They found Maxine, the guest of the French Ambassador, in the main drawing room, which was decorated in gold and scarlet, like the entrance hall, and lined with glass cabinets containing priceless porcelain. Looking unmistakably Parisienne in light green chiffon, Maxine winked and moved toward them. The four women greeted each other in an unusually subdued manner.

"Let's go outside in the sun," suggested Kate, so they moved onto the balustraded terrace that runs across the back of the palace. Beyond the vast lawn was a lake, and beyond the lake was a wood. It was difficult to believe this garden was hidden in the middle of London, it was like being in the country. On a circular bandstand the Band of the Royal Marines was thumping out a selection from *Oklahoma!* as they'd done for the last twenty years. On the left of the balustraded terrace was the green-and-white-striped tea tent. Waitresses in pearl-buttoned black silk dresses already bustled around small circular tables set with cakes and teacups. Over to the right of the terrace was the small red-carpeted royal tea tent, with sumptuously gilded Regency chairs and a golden tea urn on the table.

Everyone looked happy as they strolled over the lawn. It was like being at a favorite cousin's wedding, but with no drunken uncles. Half the women were dressed like the Queen and the other half were dressed like Princess Anne. One guest wore black goggle sunglasses with a topless, shocking-pink sheath; among the white kid gloves and the rose-trimmed straw hats she stood out like someone from another planet. Considering that 1969 was the year when fancy dress was fashionable, it was odd to see nobody dressed as a flower child, no wealthy gypsies, no outrageously embroidered Afghans, no buckskin-fringed Indians or other ethnic oddities, although there were quite a lot of expensive-looking milkmaids, romantically ruffled by Laura Ashley.

Toward four o'clock everyone suddenly moved toward the terrace as the band struck up the anthem, then everybody froze to attention. A small figure in turquoise stood out from the group that had appeared on the terrace, and the Beefeaters leaped into action in a surprisingly sprightly manner to clear the royal path.

The Queen wasn't in turquoise—that turned out to be a lady-in-waiting. H.M. wore a red silk dress over a cream petticoat that the wind revealed quite often. She and Pagan were the only women who wore low-heeled shoes, but then it was Her lawn. Under a big-brimmed red straw hat, Her Majesty's face was pale, neat and animated as she talked to guests whom the ushers beckoned forward at random, as she slowly moved toward her tea tent. Red-liveried footmen with white stockings served as Her Majesty chatted to the diplomatic corps.

It was a perfect Edwardian tea: white-iced layer cake, pale-orange layer cake, chocolate cake, plates of bread and butter thin as vellum, cucumber rounds covered with cream cheese and minced gherkin. No liquor was served, but there was plenty of iced coffee, tea and fresh orange juice.

"A neat place to have a reunion," said Judy from beneath the brim of her huge straw hat. "None of us expected *this* twenty years ago." She waved a hand at the resplendent scene as they sat at a table.

"We never expected *any* of the things that happened to us," said Kate, smoothing her cream lace ruffles as she sat down. "And we never got any of the things that we *did* expect, like Prince Charming."

They talked nonstop, with much infectious giggling, of children, husbands, lovers, houses, friends, enemies and all the paraphernalia of being alive. Then, more thoughtfully, they drifted into a grown-up version of the way they used to talk in the moonlight, after lights-out at school, as they discussed what they wished they'd been taught.

"To earn my own living," Pagan said firmly.

"To handle my own financial affairs," Kate said, thinking of how her father's real estate had been mismanaged.

"To realize that we were going to run into trouble," Maxine said thoughtfully. "You cannot expect to skip through life with a princess-and-the-pea attitude, hoping to find no lump under the bedclothes. The bed is always lumpy."

Judy said, "I wish we hadn't picked up the idea that you were a failure if you didn't have a man because then you would be without status and protection."

"We picked up that idea from our mothers as well as our fathers," Kate pointed out. "It was our mothers who brought us up to be dependent and lazy where it matters most—in the head."

"I suppose we can't blame our parents for not teaching us things that they didn't know themselves," Maxine argued. "They did the best they could."

Judy said, "That was the problem. Somehow you got this feeling that a dependent woman *was* feminine and an independent woman *wasn't* feminine, that it was unfeminine to be responsible for yourself."

Kate agreed. "I might have avoided a lot of the problems I ran into if only I'd had the self-confidence to think for myself instead of relying on other people's opinions." They stood up and wandered over the lawn toward the lake and the rose garden beyond as Kate continued, "From birth we were all wrapped up in warm lace shawls and it's very tempting not to struggle out of them, to stay snuggled up in the lace and let someone else run the world for you. But these shawls are spiderwebs of false security. . . ."

"Which is worse than no security," Maxine injected, "because they make you so damned vulnerable when you find that your lace shawl has been whipped away by Fate, leaving you naked and defenseless."

Judy nodded in agreement, thinking that it would be nice to pick a rose to send to her mother.

But it was a very small rose garden.

CHAPTER 44

SHORTLY AFTER JUDY returned to New York, Tom put his head around her door. "We've landed our first dirty movie. Empire Studios has bought that French film, *Q*. The title's a pun, remember? It means 'ass' in French. Lili stars, and we're going to tour her. We have to think up something special because her English isn't so great. Okay if you handle it?"

"Sure. Maybe we could tie in with the Jewelry Federation's Year of the Emerald launch. How would Lili like to tour in two million dollars' worth of emeralds? That's pretty special!"

Judy set up the tour for early January, which was always the dead season: nothing much was happening, everyone was at home in front of the TV. She decided to travel with Lili because Lili was definitely difficult and the emeralds could easily attract trouble. Anyway, it was time Judy visited the boonies.

After delays from the Legion of Decency and innumerable Bible Belt organizations, *Q* was released just before Lili's twentieth birthday, and after Christmas she flew to the States to promote it. Serge had come ahead of her. He wanted to talk to a few people on the Coast. Surprisingly, he didn't meet Lili when she flew in, but the press agent waiting at the airport told her that Serge had been feeling ill, he'd see Lili by the hotel pool. Lili let him see that she wasn't pleased. A likely story, she thought—probably a hangover. Or some girl. It was just too bad, she'd just traveled halfway around the world to meet him and he couldn't even be bothered to turn up at the airport.

She sulked until they reached Beverly Hills.

Lili found Serge lying on a yellow daybed, on the sunny side of the aquamarine rectangle. Opposite him was a row of lemon-and-white tented cabanas. A few children were jumping off the diving board at one end, but apart from that nobody seemed to be swimming—none of the women had the sort of hair that got wet, their hairstyles were all immaculate and twenty years out of date and several women even wore diamond jewelry with their swimsuits. Serge looked up at Lili and waved a languid hand. "God, I feel terrible," he moaned.

She forced herself to look concerned, solicitous, bent over to kiss his cheek. "What's wrong, Serge?"

He groaned again peevishly, scratched his hairy belly, lifted his sunglasses and said, "Liver. The hotel doctor says I need a rest. Christ, I can't tell you how terrible I feel."

"Why aren't you in bed then?" She still didn't believe him, didn't even believe he'd seen a doctor; it was simply too damn comfortable lying here in the sun, with palm trees waving beyond the high pink walls. He had some chick here, hidden away. "What's that you're drinking?"

"Fucking orange juice, with nothing in it—doctor's orders."

"May I?" She sipped his drink. It really was plain orange juice. Maybe he really *was* ill.

"You want some juice or something, Lili?"

"No, no thanks, but maybe something to eat. Has this doctor given you any medicine? How long are you likely to be ill? We're supposed to start on Thursday, you know."

"Yeah, I've been worrying about it." While Serge heaved his body off his couch and wrapped himself in a lemon toweling robe, Lili took another look around the pool. Middle-aged men in sunglasses were reading *Variety*. A couple of dark-brown old men, wearing heavy gold necklaces, were simultaneously smoking cigars, playing backgammon and talking on the telephone.

"I didn't expect Hollywood to be like this. These people look so ordinary, just like any families at a resort." What sort of hotel had Serge picked? Where were the stars? Lili was disappointed.

As Serge started to amble toward the café tables at one end of the pool, a pale, exquisite creature with waist-length golden curls appeared on the steps that led down from the hotel. She wore a burgundy one-piece swimsuit, burgundy high-heeled sandals and burgundy toenails. As gently and carefully as if she were tending a sick child, she devoted herself to rubbing oil on the chest of her escort, a tiny gnarled gnome with a head like a brown-speckled egg.

"That's not a starlet. That's a whore," Serge said, reading Lili's thoughts. "They have *wonderful* ones out here, sweetheart. She's seen more hotel rooms than a Gideon Bible distributor. Now come on, if you want lunch."

They moved up to one of the white banquettes, sat down and ordered Caesar salads. Serge picked morosely at his lunch.

"The fact is, Lili, the doctor's forbidden me to tour with you. I have to stay here, maybe move into a clinic, take tests—"

"*I don't believe you!*" Lili's fork crashed to the table and she leaned toward him, raging in a low voice, so that the waiter couldn't hear. After that *Globe* article written by Kate, Lili was terrified of seeing journalists without Serge. "I'm going to see this doctor for myself." Except that there was no point, she thought. Serge would have fixed him. She'd guessed right the first time. He'd found some bitch. Her velvet brown eyes glared. "You've got a girl here somewhere!" Her voice was low, fast, and angry. Serge knew she was building up to an explosion. "This is all I need, no protection on tour because my so-called manager is resting up in Hollywood, that well-known health resort." She glared at him. "You're pushing me off on tour so you can screw some other bitch in comfort on *my* money."

"For Christ's sake, Lili, do we have to have a scene before you've been here five minutes? Even if they don't speak French, they can hear that we're having a fight. Keep your fucking voice down and use your fucking brains."

Three young men slumped into the banquette on their other side and ordered three black coffees and a telephone. "Think about it," Serge urged. "I never allowed you to see one goddamn reporter on your own after that English bitch fouled you up, did I? So is it likely that I'd suddenly push you off on a goddamn important, expensive four-week tour all by yourself? My financial future is just as much at stake as yours is."

"That's true." But somehow it didn't feel right. "You're not telling me everything. Something's wrong. You're being evasive, I can *feel* it."

"Lili, darling, when I get you alone in our little pink bungalow, I'll knock your fucking teeth in if you don't shut up," Serge said. "I'm feeling like death; in fact, I may be dying and you have to start a scene." He was starting to feel self-righteous, because for once she was wrong. "There is *no* other chick here—and if there was I couldn't do much about it. I feel so sick I can hardly raise my goddamn head, let alone anything else." Serge pushed his salad away. "You can speak to the doctor yourself, when he calls tomorrow. Incidentally, I've also asked him to give you a quick physical—I thought it might be a good idea to check that you're really fit before you start this tour. And don't worry, you're *not* going alone. The president of the PR firm that arranged the tour is going to travel with you, and I'll telephone you every night. . . . Now could I *please* have a little sympathy?"

He certainly didn't look well. In fact, he looked terrible. Lili leaned forward, contrite, and patted his hand.

Serge *was* ill. The truth was that he had syphilis. A couple of days before, he'd noticed two swollen lumps in his groin and then he found a small blister under his foreskin. Fuck, he'd thought, and phoned the doctor, because you didn't kid around with that, it could rot your brain, paralyze you, eat your nose away, even kill you.

The doctor had given him the usual caution about warning all sexual partners (which Serge ignored), and prescribed an immediate course of penicillin injections, which is why Serge had to stay in one place and dump the one-town-a-day tour.

Thank God he hadn't touched Lili for some time, Serge thought. But the doctor said she still had to have a physical. She'd be surprised when she found that the physical included a vaginal examination, but he'd let the doctor handle that one—he was getting paid enough for being discreet.

If Lili was clean, there'd be no need to say anything to her. He didn't want to upset her before she went on tour. But Serge was worried about that. He didn't like sending his bank account off on her own.

So Lili arrived alone at Kennedy, huddled in an ankle-length black fox coat, a cloud of black hair around the pale, feline face. Tired after her night flight, she hardly spoke to Judy on the trip to the Pierre, where two bodyguards and a security man from the Jewelry Federation were waiting for her. They all moved to the manager's office, where the door was locked, then the safe was unlocked. A big, flat, dark-green leather case was brought out and put on the manager's desk, then unlocked. Everyone looked at Lili. She moved forward, slowly swung the lid back, and they all caught their breaths.

Inside, on dark-green velvet, to celebrate the Year of the Emerald, lay a magnificent bracelet of blazing emeralds encrusted with diamonds, an emerald and diamond brooch, a pair of green stud earrings, a pair of heavy, chandelier earrings and two matching finger rings—both square-cut emeralds—banded with diamonds. But the pièce de résistance was a magnificent emerald necklace.

Slowly, with both hands, Lili picked it up and held it to her white throat. Her fatigue fell away as she looked in the mirror at the green fire that flashed against her breast.

"It does tricks," said Judy, "let me show you." She picked up a silver diadem, and hooked the necklace over the top spikes, converting it into a tiara. Gently she lifted it on to Lili's head. Lili seemed to grow six inches, as regal as a Snow Queen.

"That will do nicely," said Judy. "We'll photograph you in that after you've freshened up. Sorry about the rush, but we need pictures right away for the press kits. There's a hairdresser waiting in your suite."

By five o'clock that evening, the big reception room was hazy with cigarette smoke and buzzing with journalists flipping through their dark-green press kits. They quieted down as Judy stood on the dais to introduce Lili, then looked expectantly toward the door, outside which Lili was slowly counting to ten before making her entrance.

Suddenly, she was in the room, head thrown back, chin high, in a white satin evening dress that was a perfect background for the emeralds that shone from her hair, her throat, her ears, her wrists.

She gave a slow, gentle smile, then walked over to Judy, green fire flashing, her satin dress like a moonbeam. She's got class, Judy thought with satisfaction, she looks like a princess, not the two-bit stripper they'd expected. What a contrast to those wet rags she wore in the movie! And why not, Judy thought. She'd had Guy Saint Simon design the entire tour wardrobe.

* * *

All over America, hotel detectives were waiting for them and the police had been alerted. After the "Today" show and other TV and some newspaper interviews in New York, they flew to Seattle, then down to Houston, Dallas and Atlanta, then north again to Philadelphia, Boston, Cleveland, Baltimore and Detroit, followed by Los Angeles, Cincinnati and Pittsburgh, where Lili was mobbed at the airport and they quickly decided to switch hotels. To Lili, the cities were a bewildering blur of hotel suites, heavily guarded cars, planes, tape recorders, cameras and questions. She had to concentrate to catch the often fast-spoken queries in the strange accents; sometimes her own answers exasperated her; sometimes she fumbled for words; but the press was amiable and the coverage was fantastic.

Merv Griffin was affable. Phil Donahue was lovable. Mike Douglas gave Lili an easy ride on what a poor orphan felt like when wearing two million dollars' worth of emeralds: he jokingly concluded that the emeralds were almost an inconvenience for any normal happy woman—too much trouble, too much of a responsibility. Johnny Carson took to Lili on sight and managed to cover her career truthfully, but sympathetically, without making the sordid parts sound terrible, as if they were some kind of obstacle course Lili had bravely circumvented in order to reach her true destiny—the spotlight of fame and the flashing green fire of those emeralds.

Nevertheless, Lili felt that she was repeating herself too frequently as she tried, haltingly, to give different answers to the same questions repeated over and over again by different mouths in front of different microphones. She rarely left her hotel and ate her evening meal in her suite. Sometimes she switched on the television, but she was generally asleep before the program ended.

In spite of the luxury and care that surrounded her, by Monday of the fourth week she was red-eyed, depressed, exhausted and sneezing in the biting cold January wind of Chicago.

"Cheer up, you're on your last week," consoled Judy. The kid had been no trouble up to now. Quiet, almost limp in fact, although she came to life miraculously as soon as she saw a camera. "You've done very well so far. *Everybody* is exhausted and disoriented after three weeks on the road. They've all said the same thing over and over. Tell you what, if you really feel too ill to do it, I'll cancel everything for the afternoon. The only really important spot is Soapy Finnegan this evening. After that we'll tuck you into bed and leave you alone with a couple of aspirin."

Soapy Finnegan was a smiling, self-opinionated Irishman with a double ration of blarney and a treble quota of charm that was carefully beamed at his audience of respectable, suburban matrons. Soapy knew their reaction to his every word, innuendo and gesture; he could almost see them all out there, feet up, coffee cup in hand, comfortably watching their good friend Soapy, who shared their values and their viewpoint, who wanted the same sort of things that they wanted, a quiet life with no problems, who enjoyed the same simple family pleasures that they did. They were not to know that Soapy Finnegan wore a girdle under his suit, had just had his second facelift and was obsessed by constipation remedies, especially enemas applied by young male nurses.

Waiting to be cued by the floor manager, Lili willed herself not to sit down on the offered chair. If she sat down she'd never get up. She only had to do this one little show, then she could collapse into bed and they'd get her a doctor. Her forehead was burning, her head throbbed and her ears felt muffled. Certainly, she couldn't go on tomorrow.

Later she was to wish that she had not struggled on that evening, as Soapy Finnegan mercilessly slaughtered her on the altar of respectability. He had been charmingly solicitous to her in the green room, so Lili was unprepared when he suddenly started to attack her, raised his voice in a loud, fast, judgmental monologue, hurled questions at her as if she were being cross-examined and then answered them himself, not giving Lili time to speak. After a long tirade, he suddenly switched away from the camera and turned to the bewildered Lili.

"How exactly would you describe yourself?"

"Why, as an actress."

"You wouldn't describe yourself as a *woman* who *exposed* herself when hardly out of *school* to whichever *gentleman* was willing to *pay* for this doubtful *pleasure*?" His voice became louder, faster. In the producer's box Judy sprang to her feet. She could see what was coming. The self-righteous voice continued to accuse Lili. "*Flaunting your body for a string of emeralds!*"

Judy ran along the passage that led to the studio. Lili could never handle this alone.

But she could. Bewildered by the loud stream of accusations, trying to answer, groping for the English words, stuttering, Lili was at first afraid that she was going to burst into tears. But she'd cried enough in private. So far she'd always managed to conceal her true feelings in public—that had been her only protection—and her secret pride. So why cry for this bastard? Almost without thinking, she concealed her emotion with anger and action as she sprang to her feet and tore the emeralds from her ears. "They're not my emeralds," she said in a low voice. "I've had enough of you and I've had enough of them. I *knew* they were unlucky. Emeralds are always unlucky!"

She tugged the bracelets from her wrists, then with both hands she yanked at the necklace, breaking the safety clasp and scratching the back of her neck. "*You* keep them," she cried, throwing the jewels into the plump lap of the astounded Soapy Finnegan. "*You* see what it feels like to be paraded like a circus animal." Hardly knowing what she was doing, knowing only that she had to escape, Lili ran from the cameras and past her bodyguards at the studio door and bumped into Judy, who was rushing down the passage in the opposite direction.

"Please, Lili, go back, we'll go on together. *Please, please.*"

Lili pushed her away and glared at her.

"Lili, I'm on *your* side. You can't afford to lose your temper."

Lili continued to glare.

Judy's own temper flared up. "So why should people always be nice? You should have shut up and smiled, or looked *dignified*, for Chrissake, then you might have got some audience sympathy. Now you've behaved like a stupid street brat, which is exactly how he described you. *And you called the emeralds unlucky! Twice!* That'll be all over America within hours."

She beckoned to the hovering bodyguards. "Let's get back to your dressing room, Lili. Christ, I can't decide whether to phone the Jewelry Federation and apologize or quietly slit my throat."

Or yours, she thought, as she hurried Lili down the corridor, waving people away, still muttering. "I can't *believe* you let him get to you so easily; it's so goddamn *unprofessional*, Lili. Can you imagine Jane Fonda or Liza Minnelli behaving like this? Or any reputable actress? Oh, God, where can I get a jeweler at this hour to mend that necklace before we leave tomorrow?"

"I leave now," said Lili, in an offhand voice, as they entered her dressing room. "No more tour."

"You *can't* go off in midtour," said Judy, aghast.

"Yes, yes, indeed, I *can*. Oh, I forgot these." And she tugged the rings from her fingers, carefully placed them on the makeup counter, grabbed her coat and walked out.

Back at the hotel, Lili threw a few clothes into a suitcase and put a call through to Serge. He wasn't in his bungalow.

She telephoned him again when she reached O'Hare, but there was still no reply.

So, head throbbing, she sat and waited two hours for a plane to Los Angeles and peace.

Serge was astounded to see a bedraggled Lili appear in his room in the middle of the night. He sat up in bed. He was alone. They both noticed that. "What the hell's happening? You're supposed to be on tour for another week." He squinted sleepy eyes against the sudden light. "Where's that PR woman? Stop crying, cherub, come to papa."

Lili flung herself into his arms. Serge terrified her, Serge depressed her, and Serge physically abused her, but nevertheless Lili basically felt safe with him.

"She's st . . . st . . . still at Chicago. I telephoned you from the ho . . . ho . . . hotel, then I telephoned again when I re . . . re . . . reached the airport, they paged you but y . . . y . . . you weren't there so I wai . . . wai . . . waited at O'Hare and c . . . c . . . caught the next plane to L.A." She burst into tears again.

"There, there, cherub, calm down. Whatever's happened, Serge will fix it. There, there. There." He stroked her hair until the sobs turned to sniffs, then he pulled her around and kissed her. "Now tell Serge, cherub."

There was a pause, then Lili said, "The first part was fine. The reception in New York was fine; they gave me a very easy time." She paused again. "The woman from the agency was nice and friendly. But we did so *many* shows a day and my English just wasn't up to it." She sneezed. "It's such a relief to be talking French to you again. And to talk without being guarded." She coughed hard. "And always in English, you see, and very fast. Then I caught a virus, so the hotel doctor, in Michigan I think it was, gave me pills, but they made me sleepy and stupid. My head felt like a big balloon stuffed with cotton."

Lili grabbed another tissue as she started to sneeze again. "By yesterday evening I also had a throbbing headache, so I took some different pills, otherwise I swear I don't think I could have moved."

She pulled her shoes off, then her clothes, dropping them in a heap by the side of the bed. "And after all that, this loathsome little swine said these revolting things to me in front of thousands of people—what a filthy whore I was, a shocking example to the youth of America. . . ."

Serge thought even with her nose and eyes streaming, even when she had totally lost her cool, Lili naked was nevertheless one terrific sight. And much to his surprise, he'd missed her. It was like finding that you missed a dog you were used to kicking.

"I felt as if I were being cross-examined in a murder case."

"There, there, petal," soothed Serge, one arm comfortingly around her.

Serge telephoned Judy in Chicago and sorrowfully explained that Lili had a fever, a temperature of 102 degrees and was under doctor's orders not to be disturbed. He hoped she'd be better in a couple of days. Maybe he shouldn't have let her go on tour, poor kid. She'd had a hectic year, she was really too tired, and now she'd caught the flu.

But Lili didn't recover after a couple of days. She had worked nonstop under pressure for months, she had been coaxed, wheedled and pushed beyond her powers of endurance by Serge. Two weeks later, Lili still lay in bed, listless. She didn't seem to hear Serge, she wept silent tears if anyone spoke to her, she didn't want to eat or drink or read or watch television. She just lay in bed, limp as a rag doll.

"We'd better transfer her to a private clinic," the doctor said. "She's suffering from what you could call exhaustion or a clinical depression—that's how this condition is generally described when the sufferer is a celebrity. But I'm afraid she's heading for a serious nervous breakdown."

There was a pause.

Serge looked worried.

"When will she be able to work again?" he asked.

CHAPTER 45

CAP CAMERAT IS a rocky headland on the French Riviera, half an hour's drive from St. Tropez. A white lighthouse on the tip of the cliff warns ships to keep their distance. Beyond it, clinging tenaciously to the steep mountainside, is a newly built cluster of villas constructed of naked brick, exposed concrete and unadorned wood. These dwellings are furnished in what the French call "contemporary" style, with conical wickerwork chairs that look incapable of supporting a round human bottom, tables inset with handmade ceramic tiles and messy splashes of violent color.

In the spring of 1970, Serge borrowed one of these villas from a bachelor friend so that Lili could recuperate in the warm air of the Mediterranean. He was glad to have her off his hands for a month. She seemed to have no energy, no stamina, and dissolved into tears whenever he suggested a little work.

Since her breakdown, the twenty-year-old Lili had lost her self-confidence and nerve. At the age of twenty, she was now frightened of being with strangers and terrified of being alone. Serge found her easier to manipulate when she was obedient and listless, but he also knew that she had lost the strange vitality she used to possess when facing the camera.

For the moment, Lili's magic had gone. The face was the same, the body the same, but she had no life in her. Lili had little to do with normal people; her sort of success inevitably attracted gapers, con men, and sexual exploiters. Women were always on their guard against Lili; they mistrusted her, and they were jealous of her because of the mesmeric effect she had on men. So she had no close girl friends to coax her back to vitality. Serge had tried everything. He soothed the little bitch, flattered her, fucked her silly, frightened her, even roughed her up a couple of times. Two films had been canceled—it was bloody lucky he was covered by the medical clause—and he'd lost a lucrative poster contract. She hadn't earned a penny for him in the last six months, and she was costing him a fortune in medical fees.

The doctor had recommended plenty of sun and a quiet life—no parties, no late nights, and even . . . no Serge. So he had hired a nurse to look after her. Someone he could trust. Serge promised himself he'd be on the first plane to Nice if there was the slightest sign of another man sniffing about. He'd given the nurse an immense bonus for keeping Lili under constant surveillance, and just to make sure of AC as well as DC, he'd picked the ugliest bitch on the nursing agency's books.

Lili sensed that she was being spied on, but she didn't care. She just wanted to be left alone. Nevertheless, she cheered up as soon as she and the nurse were driven beyond the palm trees of Nice airport under the Mediterranean sun.

From inside the house, the view of the sea was almost obscured by a mass of green vegetation that hung over the glass doors from the roof above: the light that filtered through was dim and green. But outside on the patio in the brilliant, Provencal sunlight, standing in a writhing, dark green jungle dotted with tenacious pink geraniums and watching little white yachts slowly move over the dark blue sea under a pale blue sky, Lili stretched her arms up to the sun. At last she felt alone, unpressured and at peace.

Few of the neighboring villas were occupied so early in the year, so Lili was able to wander about the village unrecognized. Every morning she sunbathed naked on her private beach, although the water was still too cold for swimming.

One morning, just as she was about to climb back up the winding, rock path to the house for lunch, she felt a shadow fall across her body. Opening her eyes, she was alarmed to see a black, rubber-clad figure leaning over her.

"Lili! I thought I recognized you!" said Zimmer, who had been spearfishing in the bay.

Lili was delighted to see him, and Zimmer was obviously just as pleased to see her. "I'm staying in the next bay; I shut myself up for a month to write a screenplay. You're the first woman I've seen for weeks. I leave on Monday, which means I'm not going to see much of you because I've promised to lunch with the Fouriers tomorrow." He looked at her. He'd heard she was ill and had had to cancel a couple of things, but she seemed fine now. "Their parties are always terrific. Why don't you come with me?"

"I don't want to see people."

"Wear a *yashmak* and talk to me alone," Zimmer said. "Serge can't object if you're with me."

Lili had never been anywhere so exotic as the Fourier place. Monsieur Fourier was a rich Belgian in the transport business. To offset the toughness of his work, he surrounded himself with opulent luxury, which included an art collection consisting mostly of nudes. His pornography was covered by a veil of respectability: all his art was either virtuously antique or else the product of famous sculptors and painters. The oak door was flanked by a couple of naked ladies desperately clutching their slipped marble draperies; the vast room beyond was hung with Russell Flint watercolors—gypsy women in various alluring states of undress. A maroon-leather visitors' book lay open upon the entrance table, next to which lay a plaster cast of Madame Fourier when newly married—to be exact, it was a hand-tinted replica of her buttocks, which had, at the time, been heavily smeared with Vaseline before being slathered with plaster of Paris.

Life-size stone nymphs lined the path that led through the garden to the swimming pool, at one end of which a frenzied stone orgy was in permanent progress. Beyond the pool stood three Corinthian columned Greek temples, and under the central pediment a more sedate party was in progress: turbaned Indian servants proffered drinks, including five different sorts of freshly squeezed fruits for anyone who didn't want whiskey or champagne, as well as a profusion of bite-size hot pastry shells filled with seafood.

When Lili appeared between the Greek columns, wearing a flesh-colored chiffon bikini, there was a slight but noticeable lull in the talk. She settled onto a purple, cotton-covered couch. A pink-turbaned Indian bowed as he offered her caviar from one silver salver, cold lobster and a dish of little crabs from another. Suddenly, Lili felt hungry again.

Zimmer propped himself up on one elbow. "Look who's just arrived," he murmured. "Stiarkoz with La Divina, making her usual late entrance."

All eyes flickered toward the avenue of cyprus, down which a small, silver-haired man slowly walked toward the pool. Beside him was La Divina, looking exactly as she did on all her record albums, with her magnificent head thrown back. La Divina managed to carry off a big nose, a big mouth and a big head: enormous quantities of coarse, black hair made her look a little top-heavy and her heavily made-up doe eyes glittered. She was a tough prima donna who for many years—at least four of them before his wife died—had openly been the mistress of Jo Stiarkoz.

Now, as she moved slowly forward, her quivering, upthrust breasts threatened to break loose from her low-cut gown of mantis-green gauze. She no longer sang in opera but her voice was still superb. All over the world people waited all night to get into one of her concerts, while managers shuddered at the thought of the trouble she caused. Their hostess fluttered forward to greet her latest guests, as the turbaned Indians offered platters of fresh salmon dressed with fennel.

Shortly afterward Madame Fourier clapped her hands and suggested that they all have lunch.

"I thought that *was* lunch," groaned Zimmer. "I've already eaten too much," he added. "D'you want to meet Stiarkoz? He's an incredibly rich, Greek ship-owner with a wonderful art collection, a really nice old boy."

CHAPTER 46

SWINGING IN THE hammock on the geranium-scented patio, Lili could hear the nurse arguing at the front door. Presently she appeared with a golden antique birdcage in one hand. Inside it was a white cockatoo. "I don't know where we're going to put *this*—the saints alone know what it eats!" The beautiful bird looked at Lili with bright topaz eyes. Delighted, Lili jumped off the hammock, pulling up the yellow strings of her bikini top.

"No card?"

"No. And the delivery boy didn't know who sent it."

Half an hour later, while Lili was still playing with the cockatoo, a camellia tree arrived. Hanging from one leafy branch was a small packet wrapped in pale blue silk and tied with fine gold chain.

"Feel how heavy this thin chain is," the nurse said. "D'you think it could be *real* gold?"

Inside the pale blue silk package was a white seashell in which nestled a huge, square-cut aquamarine pendant on an almost-invisible gold chain.

"It's the color of the Aegean," Lili cried, running to a mirror in the living room and clasping it around her neck. In the greenish light she saw the pale blue rays flashing from her throat.

The telephone rang. "Hello, Zimmer. Did you by any chance send me a bird in a cage or anything else this morning? . . . Hang on a minute, that's the doorbell again."

This time a pale blue beach buggy awaited her signature on the receipt. On the driver's seat lay a thick, cream envelope addressed simply to "Lili." Inside was a card across which was neatly penned, "Shall we say Senequier this evening at eight?"

Lili tore back to the telephone. "No, it's not me," Zimmer said. "It's either Fourier or Jo Stiarkoz. I'd bet on Stiarkoz. Fourier would merely have sent you a diamond brooch. Stiarkoz has more style. Now that I think about it, why *hasn't* Fourier sent you a diamond-studded something? You must be losing your touch, Lili."

"Maybe he thinks you and I are having a scene?"

Zimmer giggled. "Not me, darling, that they know. I'll drive you into St. Tropez this evening, then you can say you were with me if Serge hears about it."

Lili shivered. Serge would beat her mercilessly if he suspected she were flirting with anyone. Once he had actually cracked her rib. Particularly since her American tour, he had seen that she was never left unguarded.

That evening Zimmer drove the buggy into St. Tropez. Lili had dressed with unusual care; she wore a white silk blazer and a finely pleated skirt that matched; besides that she wore nothing, no blouse, underwear or jewelry, except for the glowing aquamarine that settled at the base of her throat.

St. Tropez looked like a lavish film set. Where trawlers and fishing smacks had once anchored, the harbor was now crowded with expensive white yachts. The quay was a solid line of smart boutiques and casual but expensive restaurants; under the famous orange awning of Senequier, the beautiful people who sipped aperitifs were better dressed than the patrons of the Ritz bar in Paris. Threading her way to the table that Zimmer had reserved, Lili reflected that the women looked straight out of the pages of last week's *Elle*; not one pair of white jeans had cost less than a thousand francs, not one of these beautifully tousled women had taken less than two hours to dress.

At exactly eight o'clock Zimmer winked at Lili. "I was right, there's Stiarkoz getting out of his Rolls-Royce. I wonder what conjuring tricks he's planning for the cocktail hour. Perhaps he'll pull a string of pearls out of his ears?"

He stood up and waved to Stiarkoz, who bowed slightly and moved to their table. He was a well-cared-for man of sixty, with thick silver eyebrows that hung over alert eyes. His lower lip protruded under his upper and curled up at the left corner, giving him a permanent look of amused belligerence. Stiarkoz was a careful man. He never signed his name to any document, whether a check or a love letter, because he did not like to commit himself. But he made up his mind fast, especially when he wanted something. And he wanted Lili.

Although Lili did not sense the seriousness of his interest, it was immediately apparent to Zimmer. Stiarkoz did not seem surprised to see Zimmer and made no effort to get rid of him; he obviously didn't want to alarm Lili. He wasn't going to make a crude grab at her. This was an exploratory meeting.

They ate a leisurely dinner by candlelight. Stiarkoz didn't ask Lili personal questions, but he sought her opinion on everything they discussed and listened carefully to her answers. As Zimmer described the making of *Q*, Lili felt less self-conscious, and she even started to laugh as he recounted an incident when a huge polystyrene rock had bounced off her head. Stiarkoz seemed pleased that both of them had so obviously enjoyed their visit to his country. "All Greeks love Greece," he said, "especially the ones who live in London, Paris, New York and Monte Carlo."

Zimmer's next film was also going to be shot outside Athens. "It's not just another sex epic," he explained, tongue-in-cheek. "It's a modern Greek tragedy played against a background of the international shipping business, a fight to the death between two shipowners who both want to marry the same beautiful girl, the daughter of a third Greek shipowner. Her father forces her to choose the richer man, rather than the handsome younger one who only owns one cargo boat."

"Brute," said Lili.

"Not at all," said Stiarkoz. "Many Greek shipping marriages are arranged. Marriage is considered too serious a family matter to be decided by love. So is money."

"Are all big shipowners Greek?" Lili asked. "It always sounds like such a clannish business." She sipped champagne as Stiarkoz took out a brown leather cigar case and selected one of the five cigars in it.

"Most of the world's commercial shipping is controlled by Greeks." He sniffed the cigar. "Out of a total dead weight tonnage of about fifty-two million, Onassis controls about four million and Niarchos about five million, apart from his shipyards." Gently he slid the band from his Monte Cristo Number 2. "Which leaves about forty-three million tons belonging to a small group of people that you never read about in the gossip columns, people like the Paterases and the Hadjipaterases, the Colocotronises, and the Lemoses; usually all intermarried."

He leaned back and took out a tiny gold cigar cutter. Lili looked at it. "Once this belonged to my great-grandfather," Stiarkoz said.

"Was he a shipowner?"

"Eventually. But he started as a barefoot sailor, trading around the Greek islands."

"A simple sailor?"

Stiarkoz smiled. "Powerful Greek shipowners are never simple. They are highly complex men with a minimum amount of sociability and a maximum of egocentricity. Other people usually can't stand them." Again he grinned at her.

Two expensively dressed girls approached their table. The redhead wore a sea-green lace see-through catsuit, her companion wore three blonde hairpieces above a red and white, diagonally striped minidress that barely covered her bottom. Stiarkoz put his cigar down, politely stood up and greeted them, but didn't introduce them to his companions. When they moved on, he again sat down. "The husband of the lady in green is an arms dealer and has the mooring next to mine in Monte Carlo. I didn't think you would have much in common."

At this moment a waiter hurried up to Stiarkoz with a telephone. He excused himself for a moment, picking up the receiver. "Well, what's the present price of bauxite? No, no, on the Chicago exchange. . . . Well find out. . . ." He called for another telephone, dialed and said, "Get Amsterdam on the telex and check the bauxite price."

"This won't take a moment, forgive me," he apologized to Lili. "Well, *make* them. . . . Well, hire another Lear jet. . . . Dammit, don't bother me with details, hire two. . . . Now, what are the bauxite figures? . . . Fine, buy six hundred and fifty thousand from Chicago."

The two telephones were removed from the table and Jo smiled at Lili.

"Finish about the shipowners," she said. "What do they do with all that money?"

He turned toward her in his chair. "If you were to ask these men *why* they are amassing all their wealth and what they're going to do with it, they simply wouldn't be able to give you an answer. You'd be surprised to see how poorly they live, particularly the women of shipowners."

"What about love?" asked Lili.

"They're interested in sex, of course, but again in their own special way. For the normal person, sex doesn't exist in a vacuum. But if a Greek shipowner meets a woman and likes her, then he wants sex with her straightaway. *Immediately*!" He shrugged his shoulders. "Just as they can't make friends, they find it difficult to approach a woman, and afterward they don't know what to do with that woman, which I think is appalling."

"They sound like lousy lovers."

"Certainly there's a lot of divorce, but a major reason for that is because the women always think they're marrying a husband and then they wake up to find they've married a business."

"Don't they ever think about anything except business?"

Stiarkoz reflected. "After their fiftieth birthday, they seem to wake up—

suddenly—and realize that there's not much time left. It's exactly at this moment that they feel panic and get into those messy situations with mistresses, divorces and remarriages. That's when they start to look pathetic. Their end is often positively tragic, because they eventually realize that business is not the only thing in life. Then they realize all they've missed."

The following day Lili lurched up and down the coastal road in the beach buggy, then played in the shade with her cockatoo. She was excited but wary, for the nurse had persistently questioned her about her anonymous gifts and was clearly suspicious about Lili's evening out with Zimmer.

After an evening swim off the rocks, Lili showered and changed into gold Grecian sandals and a white silk, ankle-length sheath under which she wore nothing.

At eight o'clock a chauffeur-driven Rolls appeared. The nurse looked surprised, then worried. "Where are you going? I *must* know where you're going!" She caught hold of Lili's fragile wrist. "You're ill, you mustn't go out alone."

Lili quickly twisted her arm away and slid into the back seat. Speeding through the fragrance of the warm pine trees, Lili felt the excitement of an obedient child who suddenly defies its nursemaid and, as the evening breeze lifted her dark hair, she started to sing the "Marseillaise."

This time Jo Stiarkoz was waiting at a discreet table in the rear of the café. She was not physically attracted to this small, quiet Greek, but she was enjoying her defiance and she felt he was no threat. He would, of course, make a pass at her, but she felt it was unlikely that he would pursue it if she made it clear that she wasn't interested.

To Lili's surprise, Stiarkoz made no attempt to touch her. He didn't try to detain her after they had finished dinner, although it was barely past eleven o'clock.

"I know you've been ill," he said, "so I don't expect you want a late night."

They drove back to Cap Camerat through a silent landscape. Stiarkoz knew that he was no longer young, and he had never been handsome. But a man who has made billions is generally an interesting man, provided he talks about subjects that interest him. Jo wanted Lili to feel at ease with him. He knew that any man who got the chance probably made a pass at Lili, so he wasn't going to try. He wanted her to wonder why he didn't.

And he wanted her to wonder what it would be like if he did.

The following morning Lili went down to the beach at ten o'clock and swam ten meters to a small speedboat that was waiting to carry her to the *Minerva*. The bay wasn't deep enough for the huge yacht to come in close to shore.

As she was helped up to the white deck, Lili suddenly felt as free as a seagull. Strength flooded back into her body. As Stiarkoz showed her over the vessel, she again found herself humming the defiant tune of the "Marseillaise," the rallying song of the French Revolution.

According to Stiarkoz, she was a small boat—no swimming pool and only one helicopter. But the *Minerva* could sail across the Atlantic, if Lili wished. She could cruise anywhere in the world.

He had ordered a cabin to be prepared for Lili's use. The rosewood-paneled stateroom was somewhat larger than Lili's bedroom at the villa; two sea-blue bathrooms led off it, both with the regulation dolphin gold-plated fittings, both stocked with expensive toilet articles, Christian Dior perfumes and a complete, unopened range of Estée Lauder makeup. The walk-in closet contained a stock of scarlet dress boxes from Joy, the most exclusive beachwear shop in Monte Carlo. Six new swimsuits, six new beach wraps and six couture evening dresses hung from a rail. On the bed lay a huge Christian Dior box, inside which was a cream silk, lace-trimmed negligee, delicate and beautiful as an antique christening robe. "In case you wished to change or rest," explained Stiarkoz with a wave of his hand.

They lay on deckbeds on the main deck sipping champagne under the blue awning. They were not entirely alone—a secretary and two aides moved discreetly in and out of the forward cabin and from behind the door Lili could hear the impersonal clatter of a telex. Two stewards attended them on deck, along with a large, silent sailor with a mole on his left cheek, who followed Stiarkoz everywhere. "Socrates, my bodyguard," Stiarkoz explained.

All day they stayed at sea, swimming from the boat or lying in the sun. Jo asked no questions about Lili's background or her work. (In fact, the evening after he met her, one of his shore secretaries had handed him a hair-raising dossier on her.) Jo skillfully chatted with Lili; he instinctively sensed her mood and tailored his conversation to suit it. She is the most sensational woman I have ever seen, he thought. She is young enough to be my granddaughter and I do not give a damn. I am about to make a public fool of myself and I do not give a damn. I am only afraid that she will make a fool of me, and if she does, then life will not be worth living. Jo knew he wasn't being prudent; he wondered why he put his private life at risk, but Lili's presence drove all prudence from his head.

In a daffodil bikini she was sitting on the edge of a chair with one foot up on the seat and her head thrown back, as she held the last spear of asparagus above her mouth and sucked at the tip. She looked as natural and unaffected as a charming little animal, totally unaware of anything except the sun, the sea and her own laughter.

Jo watched the butter sauce running down her chin. He thought, she is a beautiful, sensual, ignorant, uncultivated little savage. Why don't I just give her dinner this evening, say goodbye nicely, send her home in the Rolls and never see her again? But what he said was, "Do you want more, Lili?"

At dusk they docked in the glittering port of Monaco. The castellated towers of the royal palace topped The Rock to the left of the harbor. Beyond it rose the town, pink and white layers against the lavender mountains. As they slid into harbor, the sky turned from aquamarine to violet, to purple, then to velvet black and strings of fairy lights lit up the town.

Because of the heat, the roof was open in the grill room of the Hotel de Paris. They ate quail stuffed with white grapes, after which they strolled down the hill to the harbor, discreetly followed by the Rolls.

Jo asked if Lili would care to stay the night on board the *Minerva*.

Immediately wary, Lili explained that she had to sleep at the villa, since Serge telephoned every morning. Jo immediately said that she should be driven back at eleven that evening. He made no attempt to dissuade her.

On the darkened deck of the *Minerva* they sat listening contentedly to Strauss waltzes from the stereo. The odor of seaweed wafted from the cliffs beyond the harbor and mingled with the fragrance of Jo's cigar. Blue smoke trembled on the still night air.

Suddenly there was a scuffle at the end of the gangway. Lili heard her name yelled by a voice that she recognized only too well. Suddenly afraid, she jerked upright. Stiarkoz slowly stood up, looking neither unsettled nor surprised. He put an arm around Lili's shoulder, touching her for the first time. "There's no need to be frightened."

"Lili, Lili! I know you're there, you bitch, I can *see* you." Serge was lurching up the gangway toward her. Jo tightened his arm around her shoulder.

"Don't break his fingers, Socrates, just hold him." Socrates moved surprisingly swiftly out of the shadows of the quay and Serge's arms were jerked up behind him. Stiarkoz, moving toward him, took a puff of his cigar.

"My friend, I regret my lack of hospitality. Why are you here?"

"Because you've got my woman, you Greek bastard. When I heard she was with *you*, I caught the next plane to Nice. What do you think you're doing with that old goat, you stupid bitch?" he yelled at Lili.

Jo turned to Lili. "Are you his woman?"

"Yes. . . . No. I don't know." Lili burst into tears.

"Well, do you want to be his woman?"

"Oh no, no, no! But he protects me. I haven't anybody except Serge."

Stiarkoz put his arm around her and turned to Serge. "I'm afraid she prefers the old goat. So would you please get off my ship before I have you arrested."

He spoke softly in Greek. Socrates tightened his grip and Serge screamed. "Aaaagh! You bastard. You oily Greek bastard. Aaaaah!" Socrates had grasped Serge around the waist from the rear, lifting his feet off the ground, and was carrying him backward down the gangway.

"A perfect suplex," murmured Stiarkoz. He turned his back on the struggling man, put his hand under Lili's elbow, and guided her toward the saloon. "I think we will spend the night at sea." He reached for the ivory intercom.

Just after midnight, the *Minerva* slowly moved out of the harbor. Standing in the stern, Lili and Jo watched the golden outline of the town etched against the black sky in a billion golden pinpricks. As the town receded, Jo threw his cigar butt into the phosphorescent wake of the *Minerva*.

"You mustn't worry," he said. "You mustn't feel trapped. I don't want you to feel that you are moving out of one cage and into another. For the moment you are my guest. Later, when you feel strong enough, we can discuss your future. If you have signed any contracts, they can be renegotiated. That's what lawyers are for. You have nothing to worry about." He broke off for a moment, then continued, "You are a very lovely young woman, with your life before you. You can earn your own living, you can live alone, you can do whatever you wish. But don't think about it until the morning." Then he gently turned her chin toward him and Lili felt the firm pressure of his mouth on hers. She smelled the faint odor of starch and cigar and clean, warm flesh as she leaned against him, agreeably surprised at the strength of his arm.

Serge stormed into Senequier, drank a bottle of brandy, then drove wildly to Cap Camerat where he strangled the white cockatoo.

CHAPTER 47

*F*ROM THE JASMINE-SCENTED terrace, the view across the valley looked like a Cézanne painting. Rows of silver olive trees climbed to the blue line where the mountains met the sky of southern France. Dark cyprus trees lined the road that wound up to Vence between terracotta villas surrounded by orange and lemon trees.

"It's unlike Jo to be so late without letting us know," Lili apologized to Zimmer. "His driver usually telephones from the car. Are you *sure* he said three-thirty, Constantine?"

"Yes, I'm sure Jo said three-thirty, but really it doesn't matter. The contracts don't have to be signed today, we can backdate them." The big man smiled at her, but only with his mouth. His heavy-lidded, half-closed eyes never showed any expression. His fleshy beak of a nose hung over a luxuriant mustache and beard. Shoulder-length, silvery locks made Constantine Demetrios look oddly patriarchal, more like a Greek Orthodox priest than a lawyer.

Behind them, the villa stretched away, ornate as a wedding cake and large as a palace. The marble terrace where Lili sat was as wide as a ballroom and edged by a classical stone balustrade, upon which stood stone urns, planted with white geraniums and babies' breath.

"Well, I'll tell them to put off tea for another half an hour," Lili said. "Would either of you like to stroll around the garden?" Demetrios shook his head, but Zimmer stood up.

"It looks too perfect to be real, Lili, I'm going to check whether those yews are plastic." He pointed beyond the marble statues which surrounded the splendid baroque fountain below, to the hedged walk which led toward the thirty-meter swimming pool.

Lili tucked her arm in his and they moved away, toward the curving marble steps. "We grow our own vegetables and fruit here. Everything you ate at lunch came from the estate, it's brought in daily by the head gardener. We also produce our own chickens, turkeys, and pigs; we press our own olive oil and make our own vin rosé; unlabeled but very good."

Zimmer laughed. "You make it sound so quaintly rural, but this must be one of the most splendid estates on the French Riviera. Very different from that dank villa I found you in three years ago." As they passed one of the statues, he patted its marble fanny.

In fact, he didn't much care for the huge house, though he had to admit that the pictures were wonderful. No obligatory El Greco, no suspect Rembrandt, no second-rate Degas, no self-consciously slick Salvador Dali. With the exception of a little Constable river sketch, the pictures had mostly been painted after 1850 and had obviously been chosen by a connoisseur to please himself. Zimmer's favorite was a soft, mauve Seurat of a girl picking cabbages, but that Monet—the lily pool at Giverny—was breathtaking.

"Yes, very different from every place I've lived in," said Lili, as they reached the yew walk. "Everything about me is different from three years ago, thank God. We lead a very quiet life, and if I'm not filming I spend most of my time here." She was silent for a moment as they strolled toward the aquamarine pool. "The first thing that Jo did was to free me from my contract with Serge. Constantine handled it—he's Jo's chief lawyer and they're old friends, so we see a lot of him. If any loophole exists in an arrangement, then Con will find it. He never signs anything he can't get out of." They moved downhill to the left. In front of them, half-hidden by the trees, was a simple, white, rectangular building. The whole of the north wall was glass. "Did I tell you that I'm studying history with a retired professor in Venice?" Lili asked. "I generally paint in the afternoon. This is our studio."

She pressed a button and the wooden door swung open on a twenty-foot-high room lit by overhead skylights. The interior smelled of turpentine, linseed oil, dust and Diorissimo, that lily-of-the-valley fragrance that Lili always wore. There were four big easels, a couple of donkey stools and two old wooden tables, all spattered with paint.

"I'm not very good yet, but I love painting. I have a teacher twice a week; Jo chose a tough one because he wants me to learn about structure, not just to pat paint on."

"Jo's collection certainly is fantastic."

Lili hesitated before she responded. "It isn't *his* collection. All the pictures are mine. He gave them all to me on my last birthday."

Zimmer's mouth fell open. "*All* of them? That Van Gogh cornfield and the Matisse goldfish bowl?"

"Yes, all of them, his whole collection. You haven't seen the ones upstairs yet."

She remembered her birthday. Although it had been October, her bedroom had been filled with lilies and roses. Jo had led her to the big bay window. On a circular marble table stood a large antique box inlaid with ebony and a design of ivory cupids. She had opened the box expecting to see a piece of jewelry, but instead there had been a mass of legal documents. Jo had explained that the papers were proof of the authenticity of each painting and proof that she, Lili, was now the legal owner of each one. The gift was a relatively quick, discreet way for him to give her a fortune. The museums of the world would bid fiercely for most of these pictures. If she wanted a house in Paris or an apartment in New York, she need only sell one picture.

Zimmer whistled. "And they say that diamonds are a girl's best friend!"

"Oh, I've got diamonds as well, and ropes and ropes of baroque pearls. Jo loves to see me in diamonds and pearls. He says I look best in white, with sparkling wrists and throat and hair."

Zimmer whistled again. Stiarkoz was obviously still completely besotted. They left the studio and started back to the house up the grassy slope toward the long, low mansion.

"Is this what you want, Lili? This quiet life? Isn't it a bit staid for a girl of twenty-four?"

"What you really mean is how can I possibly be happy with a man who's nearly forty years older than me, isn't it? People are always asking me that indirectly. Of course Jo isn't *young*. He can't leap about and play tennis for hours and he'll probably die before I do. We've discussed all that. But that's his only disadvantage and it doesn't much affect me." Lili bent and tugged a sprig from a rosemary bush. "As a matter of fact *I* feel constantly at a disadvantage with him because I'm so ignorant."

"Ah, that's exciting for an older man," Zimmer said. "To open a young girl's eyes, to awe her, to be a god to her. . . . Until she meets someone who says, 'That's not a god, that's just an old man with money.' "

Lili scowled. "I find it odd that other men should assume that Jo has nothing to attract me *except* money." She pointed a rosemary branch at him accusingly. "Jo has plenty of advantages that a young man couldn't have. He's carved his own path through life, he's forged his own way; he's gutsy and that's always exciting in any man, whatever his age. Age doesn't matter so much to an intelligent man, because he doesn't rely only on his physical attributes to attract a woman." She crushed a couple of rosemary spikes between her fingers and paused to inhale the fragrance. "I love to hear Jo *talk*." She sniffed again.

"Of course I'm not denying that Jo can provide what women have traditionally *always* looked for in a man—protection and security." Lili's voice shook as she tucked the rosemary sprig down the front of her dress. Jo represented all the protective men she had lacked since losing Felix, and for that she loved Jo with passionate gratitude. "As a matter of fact, I don't even consider Jo's age to be a drawback, because without his age, he wouldn't have that wisdom of experience. A relationship that's going to last isn't based on sheer sexual madness and nonstop sexual excitement but on . . . understanding and tolerance."

"And so there is no sexual madness?"

"Jo has never left me unfulfilled, Zimmer. Not once. And that's more than I can say about most of the men in my life."

They had nearly reached the long pool, its immaculate surface unruffled by wind or leaf. "Are you two getting married?"

"What's the point? I don't particularly want to marry Jo. You see, so many women have tried to force him to do that. I don't want marriage." Zimmer turned to look at her and raised a quizzical eyebrow. "No, Zimmer, I want Jo. I do not ask for marriage. This way he knows that I'm not . . . what his children tell him I am . . . a gold digger."

They walked around the blue pool and the surface quivered in the breeze as Lili added, "Anyway, Jo's never suggested marriage, although I'm sure he's thought about it. Zimmer, haven't you noticed that these very rich old men never marry their luscious young mistresses? They're afraid of making fools of themselves, especially if the marriage doesn't work out. And they never seem to."

They moved up the worn, stone steps. A white-gloved footman was about to place a silver tea tray on a terrace table. Zimmer said, "It's none of my business, Lili, but I can't see how this is going to last. Your life is just beginning, and you're tying yourself down to a man whose life is ending. And you're still not happy—don't deny it, I *work* with you and I *know* you! You're *still* being dominated, only in a different way. Pretending to enjoy this staid, matronly life in the sun! You're a brilliant actress and you're never going to get where you should be if you're semiretired. The public forgets unless it's constantly reminded." He shrugged his shoulders. "Your own personality is being swamped. Stiarkoz has to dominate everything in sight, even *you*, so you're in danger of losing sight of yourself again. If you abandon your real identity, you're going to lose your true self. When you live by somebody else's standards, you betray your own. You're turning into Jo's echo, Lili!"

Lili looked exasperated. "I've never felt I had a real identity, so how could I lose it?"

Zimmer snatched at a honeysuckle branch as they passed it. "I can see that Stiarkoz can buy you plenty of expensive toys, but haven't you noticed, Lili, that with all his wealth he hasn't attempted to give you what you really want?"

"*Shut up*, Zimmer! You can't know what Jo gives me. He makes me feel protected, he's given me dignity, he educates me and he—demands little in return."

"But he hasn't tried to give you what you *really* want—because he knows the danger. He might be able to trace your parents for you! But if you found your true identity, he's afraid he'd lose his power over you. And he's very possessive, he likes your being dependent on him, because if you weren't—you might leave him!"

"How dare you say such things about Jo!" Lili said, glaring at him.

"Lili, I'm one of the few men who value you and don't want to possess you. I've known for years that you won't feel what you call 'real' until you feel real self-confidence. At the moment, you only have that when you can shed yourself and be an imaginary person."

In the sunlight, Lili suddenly looked exhausted and forlorn. "Zimmer, I think you'd better leave."

"Darling, I was just about to go. Tell Jo I'm sorry to have missed him."

Lili saw him to his scarlet Maserati parked halfway down the white gravel drive, then she wandered back toward the house.

Suddenly Demetrios appeared in the open front door. He came running toward her in an oddly slow way, a heavy man in a dark, expensive suit. She felt an odd foreboding.

Demetrios heaved toward her, crunching across the gravel in slow motion, his pink silk tie flapping over his jacket. It was so odd to see him running.

She knew immediately that something dreadful had happened to Jo.

CHAPTER 48

"THERE'S BEEN AN accident, a car accident," Demetrios panted. "They've taken Jo and his driver to a hospital in Nice. That was the police on the telephone. They couldn't tell me anything except that the Rolls had been traveling back from Monte Carlo when it shot off the Nice motorway aqueduct. It simply went through the wall and plunged over the side into the valley below. They've taken Jo and the driver to the Princess Grace Hospital."

He didn't tell her that the police had asked for someone to visit the hospital and identify Jo. Both he and his driver were dead—their bodies had had to be cut out of the mangled Rolls-Royce.

Cold water was trickling down her neck and back. Lili opened her eyes. She must have fainted. Her maid, silent and frightened, was kneeling by the couch and sponging her face. The footman stood a few paces behind, looking helpless and apologetic, as if he'd just dropped the silver tea tray.

Demetrios reappeared and walked across the carpet toward the little group. He leaned over the back of the couch. "Lili, my dear, don't move. The doctor is on his way."

The doctor wasn't Doctor Jamais; he was a small, sallow man with rimless glasses whom she'd never seen before. "Where's Doctor Jamais?" she murmured, but he took no notice. He merely pulled back her eyelid, felt her pulse, murmured something to the maid, and moved to a table where he undid his bag and turned his back to her. After a couple of minutes he turned toward Lili, and she saw a syringe in his hand. "What's that for?"

"Shock, madame. You are in a slight state of shock. There's nothing to worry about." He crouched by the couch and with a piece of cotton swabbed the inside of her left arm. Lili smelled hospitals. "Just a *slight* prick. There, that's over. It didn't hurt, did it?"

"I don't understand, I'm not ill, I just felt dizzy. I fainted. . . . I don't understand."

Her eyelids slowly closed and then her jaw fell.

Someone was holding her right hand. She was in bed in a small, gloomy room that she'd never seen before. Lili turned her head to the right and saw that Demetrios held her hand. She felt too weak to speak. Slow, silent tears trickled down her cheeks, her right ear felt damp. Demetrios patted her hand and replaced it gently on the blanket.

"How are you feeling, my dear?"

"Awful. I've got a splitting headache. But I've got to get to the hospital. I've got to see Jo. Where is this place?"

"It's a clinic outside Nice. Do you think you can get dressed? If so I'll call for a nurse to help you, then I can drive you to the hospital. But first there are a couple of formalities. Would you mind signing this, please."

"I can't sign anything now. Surely it can wait, Con, whatever it is?"

"I'm afraid not, my dear. It's the authority for the hospital to release the . . . er . . . Jo. Oh, my dear child, I'm so sorry that you have to suffer this, but bureaucracy is always with us, so exhausting."

Gently he pushed a pen into her hand and guided it to the page. "And here also." Shuffle of documents. "And here, and here, and this is the last. . . . Oh, no, there's one more."

He patted her shoulder, quickly took the typed documents away from her, leaned to the floor for his briefcase, snapped it open on his knees and swiftly tucked the documents into it. "Now I'll call the nurse to help you dress." He pushed the bell knob.

"But, Con, you must tell me what *happened*."

"It was the driver. He had a heart attack. Only thirty-five and looked as fit a man as ever I'd seen. The police think that he slumped over the wheel with the weight of his leg on the accelerator. The car was very heavy. It simply leaped forward and smashed through the retainer wall, then went over the side of the aqueduct."

"But Con, you must tell me what happened to Jo."

"Jo was cremated three days ago," he said quietly.

Lili gave an anguished shriek and tried to sit up. The nurse swiftly restrained her and lifted the telephone for help. "Tell the doctor that this patient needs another shot," Demetrios whispered. "She's hysterical."

When Lili regained her senses, she waited for half an hour until her head felt clearer. Then she put her legs over the side of the bed. She felt very weak and seemed about ten pounds thinner. She hobbled to the armoire in the corner, tugged open the door and found her clothes inside. She carried them to the bed, then sat on it and slowly dressed. Then she moved to the washbasin and looked in the mirror. Her eyes were sunken, her face looked thin and her hair was flat and listless. She splashed cold water on her face and looked out of the window. The sun was almost overhead.

The door to her room opened and a starched little nurse appeared.

"My goodness, you shouldn't be up and about."

Lili turned, the tooth glass in her hand, her only weapon. She was looking into the pleasant, surprised face of a girl of about her own age, who said, "I'd better call Sister."

"No, don't yet," said Lili. "How long have I been here?"

"Why, ten days."

"But *why?*"

"You were brought in unconscious, you'd had a very bad hysterical reaction to a shock and had to be treated with sedation. My, you were a difficult patient! The doctor insisted on looking after you himself."

"Well, I want to leave now. Would you please call a cab?"

"Oh, my, you can't discharge yourself like that, madame."

"Get me the doctor, please."

"He's out at the moment. Sister is in charge."

"Then get Sister, please."

Lili settled into the back seat of the cab. It had taken her twenty minutes to talk her way past the head nurse, but in the end they had asked her to sign a paper and she had left. Of course, there must be some simple reason for her stay. Jo would explain. . . . No, of course, he wouldn't, couldn't. If only she hadn't fainted when she heard that Jo was dead!

Forty minutes later they reached the iron gates of the estate, but when the cab honked no one came running to open them. She got out and walked over to the small side door which was always open. There was nobody on duty at the lodge.

Lili walked up the white gravel drive to the house and rang the doorbell. She rang it again, sharply. Twice. What on earth were they all doing?

Then she heard footsteps cross the marble, a bolt was drawn back, the great door swung open and Lili found herself looking into the mournful, creased face of Socrates, Jo's bodyguard.

"Hello, Socrates," Lili said, "where is everybody?"

The burly sailor scratched the mole on his cheek. "The whole staff was dismissed, Madame, the day after the funeral. There's only the housekeeper and me left up here now, and we have strict instructions from Mr. Demetrios not to let anyone into the grounds. Of course I know he didn't mean you, Madame, but the photographers have been a bit of a nuisance. We all thought you were very wise to stay away until it was over."

"Did Mr. Demetrios tell you that was why I stayed away?"

"Why, yes, Madame."

"D'you think you could ask the housekeeper to bring some coffee to my bedroom, please. I think I'd like to lie down a bit, but first I want to talk to her."

"But Madame, the furniture has all been moved, it's gone into a storage warehouse. The rooms are empty. Mr. Demetrios told us. We assumed you *knew* that, Madame."

Lili looked around the circular, domed hall and saw that it was indeed bare of furniture, curtains and carpets. As she climbed the circular staircase, her legs trembled. She still felt very weak, but her bedroom suite was just at the top of the stairs.

The room was empty. In fact, the only thing in it was her wall safe, which was normally covered by blue taffeta curtains. She moved closer. The door to the little gray safe was ajar.

But only she and Jo had the keys to the safe! Not that Lili's best jewelry was kept there, that was all in the bank vault.

She pulled the safe door open and peered inside. There was a small gleam of gold at the back. She fished it out with her forefinger—it was a charm from her bracelet, a miniature copy of the *Minerva*.

No, she wasn't dreaming.

Then she realized that all the pictures were missing. She looked around the room at the rectangular blank where her Rousseau bicyclist used to pedal in his red striped vest, at the pale patch where the pretty Dufy watercolor of Antibes had once hung.

She rushed into her dressing room and opened the doors. Even her clothes had disappeared. She ran to a window, threw it wide and looked out. The garden looked as usual in the low rays of the setting sun. She ran back to her bedroom, knelt by the ivory telephone on the floor and lifted the receiver. It was dead. Demetrios must have taken leave of his senses.

And then she remembered signing the papers.

For about an hour she remained motionless, kneeling by the telephone. Then she heard heavy footsteps climbing up the carpetless circular staircase and Demetrios appeared in the doorway.

"The clinic telephoned to tell me you had discharged yourself. Very foolish of you, Lili."

Demetrios still looked the same, but now, instead of being reassuringly large and dependable, he seemed large and sinister. His dark clothes looked menacing, the heavy nose seemed predatory and the dull brown eyes were hard and cold as stones.

"Where are my clothes, Con?"

"They have been packed and are waiting for your instructions."

"You got Jo's key to the safe, didn't you? Did the police just hand it over to you? Yes, I suppose they did, you're his lawyer after all. Where am I supposed to sleep tonight? I don't even have a change of underwear."

"You have over fifty-three thousand francs in your current bank account."

"How do you know what's in my bank account?"

"I know you have plenty of money, so you can stay at a hotel. And you've got your own car to drive to one."

"And my pictures, Con? Where are my pictures?"

Demetrios looked straight into Lili's angry face and slowly stroked his beard. "What pictures?" he asked softly.

Jo had been right. Con *was* fast and clever and had undoubtedly tied up every loose end, but Lili knew that Jo would have wanted her to try to regain her pictures and her jewelry, so she consulted a lawyer. He listened in silence to Lili's story, then regretfully he said that nothing could be done, and that under French law Lili had no claim to any part of the estate of Mr. Stiarkoz. There was a silence, then he added, "It sounds as if Mr. Demetrios bribed a shady doctor to keep you sedated, then he probably offered a deal to the children of Mr. Stiarkoz. Possibly he offered to get your signature on all the necessary legal documents upon payment of—oh, perhaps ten million francs or more: that's a fraction of what such paintings might be worth." It was well known that the art collection was the property of the late Mr. Stiarkoz; it was *not* known to be the property of Mademoiselle Lili and she had no documentation to support her case.

Mr. Demetrios had undoubtedly removed Mademoiselle Lili's strongbox from the bank, but he had her signed authority to do so, and nobody at the bank knew what was in the strongbox when it was removed or when it was returned. When Mademoiselle Lili eventually opened the strongbox herself, it only contained copies of Mademoiselle's old contracts and there was no jewelry and no documentation concerning the origin and authenticity of the paintings, and there was no deed of conveyance specifically assigning the ownership of each picture to Mademoiselle Lili. And as Mademoiselle did not know the whereabouts of the jewelry or of the art collection, from whom could she possibly claim them?

Lili sat silent, thinking that the jewelry and the pictures were not all that Jo had given her: he had given Lili something else of great value—her self-confidence. Instead of sheltering her completely, instead of allowing Lili to exchange one golden cage for another, Jo had encouraged her to find out what she was good at and to use her gifts. He had insisted that she make at least one film a year, so she hadn't dropped out of sight and she wasn't broke.

She would sell the Rolls-Royce Corniche and buy an apartment in an inexpensive part of Paris.

Then she would ask Zimmer to recommend an agent and get back to work as fast as possible.

PART NINE

CHAPTER 49

THROUGHOUT 1969, LIFE + STYLE, the newspaper section Kate edited, had continued to be what Kate called "froth rather than beer." After much argument, she was allowed to run a letters column and had hired a "Dear Abby" who visited their new consultant psychiatrist once a week with the readers' more difficult problems.

After Kate's thirty-seventh birthday, she started a second book, *Danger! Women at Work.* Although it was based on her vast mailbag, she also interviewed many women on the difficulties of getting work, the difficulties of not working. To launch the book, her publisher and the *Globe* jointly sent her throughout England on a promotion tour. Once outside London, Kate became even more conscious that she was no longer really interested in the empty froth of LIFE + STYLE. She was far more interested in real women, in real situations and problems. As this seemed to be what concerned the newly formed Women's Liberation Movement, Kate had looked it up. This was not easy, since no telephone number was listed and the directory personnel hadn't heard of the Women's Liberation Movement. Eventually, Kate got a telephone number that turned out to be a bookshop off Leicester Square, but the number had just been disconnected for nonpayment of account. Kate was to discover that one of the most depressing things about Women's Liberation was that everyone in it seemed to be broke.

Kate attended four meetings of the Women's Liberation group, but found them all disappointing. Every woman's experience was considered of utmost importance, however boring. There was much rapping and consciousness-raising, but not much seemed to get *done*. The sisters never seemed to talk about practical considerations; discussion was either directed to experience-sharing or else utopian theorizing. Kate was depressed by the muddled Marxist political thinking: " . . . The family is the basic unit of capitalism . . . system of oppression. . . . We must destroy it. . . . Women are slaves whose function is to service the male workers. . . . Before the Industrial Revolution the home was the center of productivity with husband and wife participating equally in work and child care. . . ."

Kate started to wonder what could be done for the women who wrote those sacks of letters to her every week. On the whole, her readers loved their men and depended on them. If they didn't have a man, they wished they did. Kate's consciousness had already been raised by the lawyers after her father's death and before her divorce. She knew society was unfair to women. However, it wasn't about to change overnight. Women would have to tackle injustice slowly, without hate or aggression, which could frighten other women away. Kate wondered what she could do to help the situation. She didn't think there was much point in attending any more meetings.

For two weeks Kate brooded over an idea before she phoned Judy. "Judy, I want to launch my own monthly magazine for the new, emerging woman. Will you help?"

"Haven't you got enough problems?" Judy's voice barked back. "*What* new woman?"

"For heaven's sake, you're one of them!" Kate exclaimed. "It's 1970 and the Sleeping Princess is waking up. She's got her own job, her own money, she can make her own rules and run her own life. At the moment she's tentatively groping her way, but she's alert at last and she's got a lot of power, because—collectively—she's first generation money."

The line buzzed and faded. Kate yelled, "I want to start a magazine that will pay special attention to the psychological needs of a woman, a magazine that will help her understand her own emotions. No magazine is doing that; there's a clear gap in the market."

"What about *Cosmo?* What about *Ms.?*"

"We don't have them yet in Britain."

"Describe your readers again."

Kate repeated her idea. "Obviously I can't give you an off-the-cuff answer," Judy said. "I'll talk to Tom about it and call you back."

"We're interested," Judy told Kate. "Why don't you fly over for a couple of days. We want you to talk to a few people over here whom you already know. Griffin Lowe, my favorite publisher, and Pat Rogers, my former boss, who's now features editor of one of our top magazines. She feels pretty much the same way as you do—fed up with the frosted pap that's being put out for women. But we're not thinking of starting in Britain. We're thinking of starting over *here*."

Kate booked a Thursday night flight and took a long weekend off. Those four days were spent in Judy's apartment with Judy and Pat, who did most of the talking, and Griffin and Tom, who didn't say much or do much except scribble the occasional note on their alligator memo pads. It was the first time that Kate had met both men. On her previous visit, Tom had been working with the LACE office on the West Coast.

Griffin grilled Pat and Kate until he knew everything about their reader except her pantyhose size. Then he and Tom sat at one end of the dining table and wore out a calculator, while the three women continued to talk, argue, guess, predict and hope.

The bulk of women's magazine advertising lies in the multibillion-dollar beauty business. After Kate had returned to London, Griffin and Judy took Mrs. Lauder out to lunch at Orsini's to see what she thought of the idea. Mrs. Lauder was small, quiet and extremely shrewd. Lunch for four cost three hundred and fifty dollars. Every dish had a special sauce, but nobody ate anything—they just pretended to.

Mrs. Lauder thought the idea sounded plausible.

After a second meeting, Mrs. Lauder agreed that *if* the magazine were to be as they described it, and *if* it hit the anticipated circulation, then she *might* take space. She agreed that there was a gap in the market. A definite maybe.

One by one they lunched the other beauty-business magnates. Eyeing the bills, Tom suggested maybe they ought to go into the restaurant business. Judy called Kate again. "We're getting a market survey, and if that looks good we'll do it."

But Judy didn't like the deal that Griffin offered. "I can't agree to seventy percent for Orbit, Griffin."

"—Judy, I have to justify this to the shareholders. Our relationship isn't the world's best-kept secret."

"—And I want the staff to have some kind of participation."

"—A nice idea, but I've never known it to work. It's an incentive that stops working as soon as they get it. Stick to bonuses based on increased profit. Don't encourage equality on the editorial floor or you'll never get anything printed."

Judy phoned Kate again.

"I'm phoning to offer you the job of joint managing editor and to say that we're willing to offer you two percent of the action if you can raise $170,000. Tom can arrange a five-year, back-to-back loan for you in some way that's legal if you can put up collateral in Britain. It'll cost you one percent extra interest, but it's the only way that you can buy in because apparently your idiotic exchange-control regulations won't let you take money out of Britain to invest elsewhere."

Kate rushed off to Barclay's Bank. If she sold all her stock she would still be about five thousand pounds short, but her mother agreed to guarantee an overdraft to cover it. So after another quick trip to New York, she told Scotty that she wanted to leave.

"Agh, you bitch," he said. "How could you do this to me after eight years together? What d'ye expect me to say? Except congratulations. Now stay out of my way for a few days, I'm too angry to talk to you."

Kate let Walton Street on a three-year lease to a General Motors executive, put her furniture in storage and flew to New York, where Tom had taken a short lease on an eleventh floor suite of offices on 53rd Street.

Countless evenings were spent in Judy's apartment, trying to decide on a name for the magazine. Eventually they decided to call it *VERVE!* with an exclamation point. It had an exultant, glad-to-be-alive feeling (which is how they wanted their readers to feel), and it was short and easy to remember.

VERVE! threw its first party at the Four Seasons.

Tom, looking like one of those suave, impeccably dressed fashion drawings in *The New Yorker*, made a brief speech of introduction. Then Judy introduced her team and stated their editorial policy. The presentation lasted almost forty minutes.

Kate felt oddly detached, as if she were watching her own performance from somewhere on the ceiling. "The key to self-expression is style, and every woman should learn how to develop her own. Every reader is important, because she is an individual and we want to encourage her individuality. But every reader also forms part of an enormously powerful economic force. Who are the enormous spenders of this country? Not Jackie, not Zsa Zsa, not Liz. The collective mass of American women probably form the biggest money-spending force in the world. *VERVE!* will not only show them *how* to spend it, we'll also show them how to make it, how to earn it and how to multiply it. It's time that women thought more about money—and had more of it for themselves. We intend to make this very clear."

Judy hoped that the magazine would give its readers the support that she had found in Kate, Maxine and Pagan. Together, the four of them had certainly brought out the best in each other. Without the other three where would they be? Kate was the only one who had real talent, but she was a quiet mouse who worried too much. Without Judy to push her, she'd probably be an unhappy divorceée, spending too much at Harrods. Without Kate, Pagan would still be a misfit brought up in a privileged world in which she never felt at home—a perplexed, hopeless drunkard. Maxine had gone a long way with her determination and hard work but she would never have been world-famous without Judy to show her to the world, and although Judy was a tough go-getter, she would never have started her own business if Maxine hadn't pushed her into it. Alone, their frailties might have overwhelmed them. Together, they had strength and speed and style—which is what *VERVE!* was going to push as hard as it could.

CHAPTER 50

"DO YOU WANT to know what a woman finds attractive in a man?" Kate asked. "I just got the survey results." She looked at the alert faces around her desk at the eleven o'clock Monday conference. It was thirteen weeks after the party at the Four Seasons, three weeks before the first issue was due to be published. "What women find attractive in a man and what men *think* women find attractive in a man turnout to be entirely different. Twenty-two percent of the males admitted that what they thought appealed most to a woman was a large, tight-trousered bulge, but only three percent of the women thought so."

They all giggled. *VERVE!* had started with a shoestring full-time staff of fourteen plus free lancers and contributing editors. Most of the journalists were always working on at least three stories at once, in different stages of progress. The fashion editor was due to join them in two weeks—in her absence they were using high-powered fashion stylists at enormous expense.

"The men didn't think that slimness was important in a man, but most of the women thought it was vital," Kate continued. "Only two percent of the men thought that the male buttocks were important, whereas this area easily was top attraction with women, at forty-two percent."

Kate had started that morning's conference by giving a rundown of the schedule for the next issue: sixteen weeks in advance of publication, they discussed the rough shape of the magazine; copy deadline day was ten weeks later, and the following six weeks to publication was a fast-moving battle between the editors, the assistants, the art department and the printers.

Life was fun, thought Kate after the conference, but it wasn't the sort of fun that their readers imagined. It wasn't a playgirl existence lived from champagne reception to dress show. *VERVE!* was absorbing work. *That* was the best possible fun. Sitting with six snarling telephones in front of her and a couple of people leaning against the wall just inside her door, Kate reflected that most of their readers would probably hate her job, but as far as she was concerned, she would gladly have paid to do it. Launching *VERVE!* was the most exciting thing she'd ever done and, however exhausted she was, she hated to stop in the evenings.

There was only one fly in the ointment. Kate didn't find Tom easy to work with. He had been brought up on the West Coast and before teaming up with Judy, he'd worked only in the motion picture industry, which inevitably colored his attitude toward women. He couldn't help categorizing women as mothers or hookers of one variety or another. Some of them were also properties, and these were liable to give trouble; you treated a property warily, as you would a baby cheetah. For Tom, Judy was a very valuable property. But Kate—well, she hadn't proved her value yet. Tom intended to produce a magazine packaged a bit like the Virginia Slims ads . . . "You've come a long way, baby. . . . " But Kate didn't fit the glossy, Virginia Slims-Lib image any more than she did the heavy *Ms.* image. Tom couldn't place her. Sure, she wrote that book, she was a minor celebrity, but that didn't mean she was going to make money for him. So Tom and Kate kept clashing until Judy took it upon herself to soothe Kate down. "Look, Kate, all backers are difficult. One of the reasons that Tom keeps our backers happy is because he thinks the same way as they do. We're taking a big, big gamble, which we certainly couldn't do without Tom. His personal disadvantages are business advantages. He can deal with all that shit and leave us to get on with the work." Judy took Kate by the shoulders. "Remember that *your* responsibility is to get the magazine out on *his* budget. It's *his* responsibility to make a profit and he's very, very good at that; but he might not be if he were the sort of liberated guy that you approve of."

As they neared publication date, Tom's growls could be heard around the office. "Do you *realize* what a bleed-off costs? . . . Does anyone in the art department realize that the little rule around the picture on page ninety-two added fourteen percent to the page cost? . . . Does anyone in the art department *care?*"

Kate had always been terrified of violence—both physical and verbal. As a child she had never dared to show her own anger and always quailed before her father's rage. As an adult, she still always caved in when voices were raised. But Kate didn't forgive and she didn't forget. She capitulated and remembered. Instead of discharging her anger in a blazing row, she stored up her resentment, which always built into a bigger and bigger head of steam until the day that Kate exploded.

A messenger hurried down the office aisle. It was ten o'clock at night and the room was silent except for the occasional machine-gun burst of a typewriter. Only three people were still at their desks. Kate and the art editor were brooding over the page proofs as the messenger came up to them and handed over a big envelope.

Inside, fresh from the printing press, was a rough-cut copy of their first issue. Blazing confidence, Lauren Hutton grinned up at them.

Kate picked it up and ran to Judy's office. "Look!" she yelled. "We're in business."

CHAPTER 51

ALL THE RIGHT people turned out for *VERVE!*'s launch party. There were plenty of celebrities, some agency heads and a lot of big advertisers—about five hundred people in all. The top columnists were there, the dailies had turned up and a couple of reporters from *Time* and *Newsweek*, as well as the trade press. There was no television coverage, but it was probably just as well—cables and lights would upset the party atmosphere, and anyway Kate and Pat had already appeared earlier on the breakfast shows.

There was a murmur of voices, a clink of glasses, cigar smoke mingled with expensive perfume and the champagne flowed. Unexpectedly, however, the party to which Kate had looked forward to for months seemed to her a depressing anticlimax. She would have preferred to see this money spent on the magazine. She looked pinched and ill, so miserable and woebegone that Tom moved over to her.

"Cheer up," he said, "*we've* just had a successful launch and *you're* having a normal, understandable reaction: you're experiencing the depression that sets in with exhaustion after some mighty exertion that results in achievement. That's how Shakespeare probably felt after he'd finished *Hamlet*."

Kate didn't laugh. "I know it all feels stale to you," Tom added. "You've been thinking about nothing else for the past three months. I know some of those guys out there looked bored, but when people are listening very carefully, their faces always look blank. It just means that they're concentrating on what's being said to them. Every single guest tonight was sounded out first, they're all good potentials and a great many of them agreed to support us. You, Kate, are now part owner of a real, live magazine."

Kate's eyes brimmed. "It's just that I'm feeling exhausted and homesick and I suddenly felt so lonely. I'm missing Walton Street and London and Scotty most of all."

"Yes, well, it's tough being a big girl. I'd better take you home."

They caught a cab back to Kate's apartment where Tom said, "Going to help myself to a real drink, can't stand that fizzy stuff. You get into bed and when you're comfortable I'll get some food sent in."

"I really couldn't eat a thing, thank you, Tom, but there's some cold stuff in the fridge."

When she was wearily propped against the pillows, Tom appeared with a tray of coffee, some stale doughnuts, a stick of limp celery and a bowl of soup. "I promise I'll do better next time," he said, sipping whiskey from the depths of the blue cotton-covered armchair. He wondered how to cheer her up as Kate picked at her food.

"Do you realize, Kate, that in the last three months we've spent more time together than the average married couple?" He leaned forward, elbows on his knees, and earnestly added, "Another thing you probably don't realize is that you've made a lot of my old ideas look pretty stale. I'm not sure that this is the right time to say it, but I want to apologize. I underestimated you—your ideas, your originality and your experience. I thought you were just Judy's British buddy and I didn't see that we needed you. But now I've seen you in action and I am impressed. I'm sorry I've been so abrupt and offhand and, well, such a tough bastard."

"I like tough bastards. That's one of my problems."

"Well, one of my problems is that I can't get results *without* being a tough bastard. Now get some sleep and see you tomorrow."

For one moment Kate had thought he was going to make a pass at her. Her love life had been nonexistent in the past few months, and it hadn't been so great before that; she'd almost given up hoping that one day she'd meet a man who would make her climax effortlessly with love and truth and abandon.

But none of them did.

The following day she woke feeling much better and was just getting out of bed when the intercom rang.

"There's a guy down here with some flowers."

"Send him up," Kate said, expecting a delivery boy. To her surprise, Tom appeared behind a foaming armful of yellow mimosa and a paper sack containing fresh coffee, bagels, lox and cream cheese.

"Hi. Breakfast. Back to bed," he said, and handed her the morning papers. All the dailies had covered their launch, including a front-page splash in *WWD*. Kate immediately felt better.

"I feel ashamed about last night. I tend to cry when I'm tired."

"Forget it," said Tom. "That's what intrigues me—you're such an odd combination of strength and vulnerability. You're tough without being masculine, you work as hard as Judy, and that's saying a lot, but you're very fragile in some areas. Although you won't admit it, you need looking after."

"I'm *being* looked after," said Kate, grinning at him. "Lucky it's Saturday."

"I'll have to go into the office pretty soon."

"Me too."

She looked pale but pleased with herself as she lay back against pink pillows in a white lace negligee. Tom, watching her against the pillows, suddenly realized that he was going to make love to her. The tray crashed to the floor and bagels flew across the room.

After one moment of astonishment, Kate was conscious of his hands on her skin, his hard mouth on hers, the smell of newly laundered cotton and a man's warm body. She didn't even have time to be self-conscious as she felt his hands exploring her body, sliding over the lace. "I don't think this is a good idea," she gasped.

"I think it's an *excellent* idea," Tom murmured into her hair.

"I thought you were against fornication among the staff. . . ."

"Yes, this is madness," Tom cheerfully agreed, as he felt for her breasts. "Now are you going to undo this or do I have to tear it off you?"

With one wriggle Kate was out of it, and then he was stroking her body with possessive tenderness. His mouth never left hers as he unbuttoned his shirt and pulled off his tie, and then she felt his hard chest against her soft breast and smelled the erotic, fresh-straw-smelling sweat of his armpits. She bent her head and nuzzled there, inhaling the soft down in the pit of his arm, the only soft hair on his body. Then they were both naked and lying together, each wondering at the warmth of the other's body, each touching and feeling, slowly exploring each bend of arm and leg.

Very slowly, Tom slid on top of her and she felt him warm inside her. He moved softly, then with more strength, his hard legs against her soft thighs, his mouth crushing hers, his broad hands cradling her breasts, feeling her small, beige nipples harden beneath his touch.

Kate felt excited and yet strangely peaceful. Of course her body had been made for Tom, this tender, tough man, her love. *Her love?*

Alarm bells rang. She gasped and suddenly stopped moving. "What's up?" murmured Tom.

"Well, I don't want to get involved."

"Of course not," he murmured and softly stroked her breasts, as she quivered under him. Slowly she let him draw her down again into the soft, warm, erotic depths. As their passion mounted, she felt Tom's warm breath in her ear, his hard, insistent body on top of hers, then she was up on the ceiling, oddly dispassionate, looking down at herself and Tom in the bed below, and for Kate the moment was lost as Tom climaxed with an animal growl.

They lay clinging to each other. A faint almond whiff of semen rose from the rumpled sheets.

"Mmmmmmmm, mmmmmm . . ." he murmured, hugging her, "but I wish you had come."

"I did."

"No, you didn't, darling. I don't mind if you don't have an orgasm, but I *do* mind if you fake. Where does it get you? What's the point?"

Gently he kissed her and stroked her shoulders. She felt his hands slowly slide over her body until, softly, he started to stroke the small, dark forest, started to feel her with a soft, steady touch, his hands moving lightly and with sensitive patience until Kate relaxed then suddenly arched toward him in ecstasy and fell back, melting into his muscular arms.

She woke to feel his lips on her small secret slit, his tongue gently caressing the pale pink seed pearl, his face against the delicate folds that surrounded it. Pink upon pink, soft, sucking flesh; swirling, exquisite oblivion, falling into a caressing sea.

"What a wonderful way to wake up," murmured Kate, going to sleep again.

Afterward they took the phone off the hook, had a shower together, started to make love under it and decided that it wasn't really all that comfortable in the slippery tub with the water raining down. They slid back into the crumpled bed. Like a bird's-eye view of the Alps, thought Kate for one moment, before all thought was wiped from her mind and sensation alone flooded her body.

Later, still naked, they pulled the bed straight, but as soon as they'd smoothed the antique patchwork spread Tom gently pushed her back on it and again reached for her breasts. Kate pulled him down, dodged his hands and instead slid down between his thighs; lying curled between his legs she stroked him, feather-soft, cupped him in her hands. He felt her warmth, the soft stroking touch of her hand on his manhood, then her lips were sucking, soft as a sea anemone, then more insistently. He felt her tongue searching, reaching, sliding, slipping, sucking until Tom could think of nothing except the scratching fingernails on his inner thighs, that sure insistent mouth, the mounting, quickening pressure of her lips upon him until, with a groan, his pent-up force was spent.

Kate, who never knew whether to swallow, spit or dribble, tasted the oddly pungent, acrid almond odor. "What do men like?" she timidly asked Tom later.

Silence, then he said, "Naturally, I can't speak for the rest of my sex, but when borne on summits of delights such as I have just experienced, I neither know nor care."

It was six o'clock in the pearly grayness of Monday morning. "You're quite something," Tom said. "I don't want anyone or anything else. But let's keep this from the office, huh?"

Naturally, that was impossible. Monday, Kate was a different, sparkling creature, thought Judy, from wan, little Friday Kate. Tom hadn't been in all weekend and she'd left plenty of messages, getting crosser and crosser with his answering service. Both of them had been unavailable. Unavailable together all weekend, concluded Judy.

Before Monday was over, Kate had casually asked Judy what Tom's wife was like. "She's just a simple all-American girl," Judy said. "Aged twenty-three, golden hair and a handspan waist, radiant as the dawn, that sort of thing. . . . No, I'm joking, she's really ninety-five and the poor woman's only got one eye, no teeth and these thirteen lovely children, all very hungry. . . . " She relented. "In fact, they split up before Tom and I joined forces. His ex is all right, there's nothing wrong with her; she's just a spoiled Jewish princess who never stops yacking—heavily into macrobiotic nutrition and meaningful encounter groups. But the two boys are really neat. Tom doesn't talk about them, but he sees them as much as he can."

When they were together, Kate felt an irresistible and seemingly irreversible love for Tom. This wasn't like her girlish wish to be married to Robert. This wasn't like the awed infatuation she'd felt for Toby, her ex-husband. This was a growing, tender lovingness. She didn't feel hemmed-in, she didn't feel humble or in any way subservient, she didn't want to get on her knees and worship and she didn't feel that she was putting on an act or altering herself to please him. Not once did she feel the urge to scribble Kate Schwartz, Mrs. Tom Schwartz or even Kate Ryan-Schwartz. She simply wanted to be with Tom, whenever she could, and to hell with the future. Suddenly Kate's neat navy suits were seen no more; instead she appeared in an amethyst linen suit from Yves Saint Laurent that she wore with no blouse underneath. This went down so well that she went back and bought another version in shocking pink. Shortly afterward she turned up at the office wearing a Spanish orange jersey jumpsuit. Nobody in the office needed to be told that Kate was in love.

Tom also had suddenly changed. He became more affable and mellow, he was seen to smile during office hours and his sharp sarcasm softened. To Kate, he was surprisingly loving, gentle and generous. Aware of his office reputation as a tightwad, he consciously tried to overcorrect, and Kate loved him for it.

But she didn't want diamonds, she didn't need emeralds—all she wanted was Tom.

The first edition of *VERVE!* had a good cover but it was not well printed. It was way over budget and the advertising was sparse. Nevertheless, they all had secret joyous moments when women on buses were seen to be reading *VERVE!* or someone was spotted actually *buying* the thing from a newsstand.

The second issue contained better text, better pictures and marvelous beauty coverage, but again, it was badly printed. Again the ads were sparse, and it was a day late on the stands.

The third issue was always the test, after initial curiosity had died down. For the third issue they had to go bigger. Pat frantically tapped her secret network of moonlighters—journalists on the staff of other publications who were prepared to make extra money by unofficially and anonymously taking on extra work. The third edition was still thin on advertising, because the agencies weren't prepared to take space in the early issues of a magazine which had now lost its novelty value but wasn't firmly established. They were sitting back and waiting to see whether *VERVE!* was going to be a fast folder.

But the third issue had an exclusive Jane Fonda cover, and a lead interview that they were able to tag "How to Enjoy Your Man in Bed" and link with their sexual pleasure survey.

The ads came in for the fourth issue and *VERVE!* took off.

Kate was frightened of her new happiness. Everything was going too well; she was frightened of allowing herself to be vulnerable again. She already knew that what triggered love for her was harsh rejection and an abject, humiliating need for approval. She knew that as soon as she fell for a man, she turned into a groveling doormat and asked to be kicked in the teeth. She knew that the last thing she needed in a permanent mate was another man who would make her feel unlovable.

So she was terrified of admitting to herself that she was in love. She hesitated to commit herself. In order to test the strength of her feelings for Tom, she started going out with other men, rather as some women flirt in front of their husbands with men who don't interest them in the slightest. It wasn't difficult for Kate to find other men, because success is a powerful aphrodisiac. Besides, at thirty-nine, Kate's invisible, sexual glow was as much in evidence as it had been when she was seventeen. For the next few months, tough Burt Reynolds look-alikes waited for Kate in the small reception area of the *VERVE!* office. Kate broke dates with Tom at the last minute, and other men's shirts and shaving gear were obtrusively obvious when he stayed overnight at Kate's apartment.

Tom scratched his head and decided to turn a blind eye to her odd behaviour. He seemed to be the first man (except maybe for Scotty) who was genuinely fond of Kate as opposed to being irresistibly attracted to her. He loved her for what she was, and he didn't demand what he realized she couldn't yet give him—her trust. So although he found it difficult, Tom ignored her exasperating behavior, ignored the muscular hulks in the lobby and her other little tedious traps to test his love. Tom understood Kate's insecurity better than she did herself, and the reason was that he had suffered similarly.

One Saturday afternoon, after she had asked some question about his family, Tom clasped his hands behind his head as Kate snuggled up to his bare chest. "To a certain extent, I can understand how you feel about your father," he said, "because what *I* resented in *my* life was my mother. She was a very domineering, typical Ukrainian boss-mother. If I asked my father for anything, he'd say, ask your mother. He was a huge, strong man—he'd been a professional fighter—so physically he would never lift a finger to his wife or to me, because he was afraid of really hurting us. And my mother knew this, so it gave her complete control of the household. *He* would decide whether Roosevelt was right to appoint Eisenhower supreme commander in Europe, but he wasn't allowed to decide whether I could have a new pair of shoes—because she made all the decisions. I resented her complete control and the way she threw it in his face. They had an argument or a fight every single day for thirty-seven years, after which she died. I still resent those arguments. I also resented the fact that she always criticized everything I did. *Nothing* was ever good enough for that woman. I felt guilty because I wasn't good enough for her and guilty because I felt resentful."

"That's how I felt, too. What did you do about it?"

"Look, I'll show you." He gently pushed her aside, jumped out of bed and padded back with his wallet in one hand. "I look at that." He pulled out a white business card upon which was scrawled in capital letters FUCK GUILT.

"I taught myself to accept guilt and then forget guilt. Sometimes I have to say I'm sorry, and sometimes I have to compensate for some revolting thing I've done. But then I simply go out and get on with my life, and somewhere up in the heavenly accounting department, I assume that an angel is adjusting my profit-and-loss sheet. I'm sure I'll end up showing a net profit."

The other side of the card said FUCK 'EM ALL.

"It helps me keep cool," Tom explained, "stops me from paying too much attention to other people's opinions instead of relying on my own."

Kate nestled closer to him.

"There's one further thing we have to discuss," Tom said quietly. "I'd appreciate it if you don't fake orgasm *ever* with me again. Keep it for these handsome hairy hulks that leave their shirts here."

There was a pause, then she said sulkily, "I don't always."

"I know," he said gently, pulling her to his chest, and stroked her hair softly, as he carefully said something that he'd been meaning to say for a long time. "Kate, darling, sex is the closest possible communication between two people and faking is lying." He gave an exasperated sigh. "I can't think why women do it."

"Out of politeness, sleepiness or feelings of inferiority," Kate said defensively. "I suppose I do it because I'm frightened that I'm not up to standard; I don't get there in ten point nine seconds or whatever the going rate is."

"What's the point? Where is it going to get you? Why don't you *help* me to make you feel wonderful? Faking isn't helping, it's sabotaging yourself and our relationship because you're sometimes too damn prim to tell me what you want, you silly little prude." Tom nibbled her left earlobe. "You have as much right as a man to an orgasm and the way you reach it is your business. *You* know what's right for you and until ESP is with us, it's up to you to show me, otherwise how the hell am I to know?"

So Kate told him a bit. Then she told him a bit more.

Then Tom swung into action and pulled out his entire repertoire. First he went down on her, and then she went down on him and then they tried it on the kitchen table and knocked the milk jug over, so they moved to the living room floor and took up sixty-nine positions on the carpet and then Tom impaled Kate and staggered around the living room thus, and all the time they asked each other all the relevant questions, such as do you like it like this, harder, softer, faster, slower, and then Tom produced a little packet and said don't for God's sake sneeze and he laid out three lines each on the low glass table in the living room and offered Kate his hollow gold telephone dialer from Tiffany and she dutifully said it was wonderful, which was nothing less than the truth . . . except that it left Kate with a slight chemical tang at the back of her throat and in her heart. Compared with the dizzy excitement that Tom aroused in her, the coke didn't quite make it. Somehow the whole scene hadn't been about loving, but about scoring.

"How was it for you this time?" asked Tom tenderly, and she started to say wonderful, but then heard herself say, " . . . Darling, if we're telling the truth . . . I thought it was strung-out and artificial."

A flash of blind panic crossed his face, followed by a defensively aggressive expression that meant he was about to hurt this person as hard as he could for attacking him when he had laid down his defenses and offered her his all. He opened his mouth and was about to tear her to pieces so that she'd never be able to put herself together again, when he paused to consider. Then an expression of relief crossed his face and he said softly, "I know what you mean."

Kate said tentatively, "I think I like you better than that."

Tom said, "I think we both like each other enough not to play games."

Suddenly Kate was no longer afraid that he might despise her or leave her if she didn't perform satisfactorily. She no longer felt that she had to impress him or seek his approval.

"It's not that I don't like conformist sex, I just don't like it according to the self-improvement books," she confessed. "I'm conformist all right, but I can't perform if some dominant person in bed is determined to make me come, or if I feel that some invisible doctor is nodding wisely as he watches my efforts from the ceiling."

She wriggled onto her bare stomach on the greengage carpet and propped her head on her hands. "What I *really* like sexually," she said thoughtfully, "is corny rubbish. Candlelight and sheer chiffon and being pressed to his manly breast by his muscular arms and feeling the seas pounding relentlessly in my ears and fierce waves surging up the unresisting beach as I sink back and he murmurs thickly in my ear, God, darling, I never knew it could be like this."

She turned to Tom, also lying naked on the green carpet, and added, "Corny rubbish is what really makes me feel sexy."

"If I suddenly started spouting purple prose, you'd only laugh," said Tom with conviction, "and what's more to the point, I'd feel like a fool. So I don't know how I'll handle the dialogue, but I promise you that next weekend is going to be in the land of corny rubbish. . . . "

" . . . By the seaside?"

"Connecticut," Tom promised. "The complete experience. Sandy beaches, pounding spray, lobster dinner and galloping white horses. And there we will play at total corniness."

The following Friday evening, they arrived at a seashore cottage that belonged to a friend of Tom. On Saturday, they ran along the beach, climbed gray rocks with the wind whipping their hair, licked the salt from each other's lips and ran along the lace-fringe of the gray ocean, barefoot, with their jeans rolled up. On Sunday Tom tried, and failed, to climb a pine tree, and then they went for a ride. (It had taken Tom over an hour on the phone from New York to arrange for the horses to be waiting for them after breakfast outside the cottage door.) Tom had been on a horse only once before, in his teens, when he'd spent a weekend on a dude ranch outside El Paso. Kate amused him with her prim English trot, and then she amazed him by making her bay hop, one foot at a time, over a fallen tree trunk. Tom couldn't get his stubborn chestnut mare to move—she took no notice of the human on her back, but kept putting her head down and cropping grass in a determined manner, as if she intended to shave the whole of Connecticut.

"Take up your reins and use your legs; squeeze firmly with your thighs," Kate advised. Tom did, whereupon the mare took off as if someone had set fire to her tail. Somehow Tom stayed on, until Kate caught up and yelled, "Sit back and gently tighten up with your hands," whereupon the chestnut suddenly stopped as if she'd been switched off, and Tom tumbled over her head.

That evening, after sipping white wine in front of the flames and eating the regulation lobster dinner, Tom carried Kate up the open redwood stairs to their bedroom. They could see through the triangular window, beyond the dark pines to the starlit sea and the lighthouse, and they could hear the wind shrieking around the house and the rain slashing against the plate glass as they snuggled under the flowered quilt. Tom started to caress her. "Too tired," murmured Kate, "too sleepy." But holding her to him and stroking her softly, he slipped into her.

And suddenly, through the mist of sleepiness, Kate realized that it was going to happen. *It* felt exactly as she had read it felt like. Soft, intense waves rather than her excitingly violent, direct clitoral orgasm. *It* was unmistakably different and *it* was undoubtedly happening. Kate felt fecund, indescribably female, an earth mother. She felt happy, she felt at last a complete woman. For a never-ending moment she gloried in it, then flung her arms around Tom and clung to him, held him tight in her arms; she was never, never going to let him go.

"I did it, I did it!" she shouted.

"No, *I* did it."

"Well, *we* did it."

Tom said, with considerable satisfaction, "I knew it would happen when you finally relaxed."

CHAPTER 52

KATE AND JUDY were waiting for Tom with growing irritation. They would now be too late for the first act of *La Bohème*, which contained most of the best arias. "Dammit, why doesn't he call? After all, this *is* supposed to be a little party for your fortieth birthday, Kate . . . and it's not as if La Scala popped over to the Met every other week," grumbled Judy.

"He was looking forward to it as much as we were, but he didn't know how long the medical conference would continue, and you know he wanted to talk to some of the doctors afterward. After all, you started this fuss, you're the one who wants him to sell the Hoffmann-La Roche shares." Kate leaned back against the suede and stared at Judy through the haze of yellow flowers that stood on a low, smoked-mirror table.

They were sitting on the beige suede couch in Kate's huge, quiet living room. Leopard-skin and tiger-skin cushions were strewn on the couch, which ran thirty feet along the depth of the room. Above them hung a collection of paintings and engravings of tigers and leopards—some were primitive oil paintings, one was a charming child's drawing. An exquisite Stubbs engraving of tigers was so ominous that the hairs almost rose on the back of your neck.

The wall opposite consisted entirely of panels of smoked-mirror glass, each concealing liquor, games, TV, stereo, projector or other valuable clutter. One complete side of the huge room was a sheet of sliding glass that led onto a leafy terrace, beyond which stretched a sumptuous treetop vista of Central Park. Opposite the vast window was a fifty-foot run of floor-to-ceiling bookshelves lacquered Chinese red. Not all the shelves contained books; Kate's collection of antique snuff boxes stood on one; another held a small collection of terra-cotta ancient Greek votive statuettes and other shelves held small, charming objects—a seventeenth-century bronze of a man wrestling with a bull by Garnier, a tiny yellow Meissen patch-box that had once belonged to Madame de Pompadour.

The lights were turned low. Instead of lamps, Kate created atmosphere with an intricate system of ceiling spotlights—just a single moonbeam if she and Tom were listening to Sibelius; a series of pencil-slim beams for parties, to spotlight their Mexican art collection.

As they sat waiting for Tom, suddenly Judy felt a sharp, nasty feeling—a sort of yellow jab in the head—that, to her surprise, she immediately recognized as jealousy. Jealousy of Kate. Judy's apartment was just as luxurious as this one, Judy was just as successful, Judy was just as attractive as Kate, in a different way, and Judy loved her man as much as Kate—and was passionately loved in return. But Kate *lived* with Tom; they went to bed together and didn't always make love, they yawned together in the morning; Kate knew what Tom was like when he had influenza, and he knew how to look after her if she had a bad period. *Judy longed to share that same intimacy with Griffin.* Kate had her man, Maxine was happily married and so was Pagan—now that the medical world had decided to encourage heart-attack patients to make love—but Judy didn't have what most women expected and took for granted, once they'd got it. Judy felt ashamed of herself for feeling this way toward Kate but couldn't stop.

"When Tom bought the Hoffmann-La Roche shares nobody realized the harm that tranquilizers could do," Kate was saying. "It seemed an ideal medicine for a world with plenty of harassment, plenty of tension, but not enough psychotherapists or mental hospitals." She picked up a small, amber-inset, eighteenth-century pillbox and carefully examined the pattern without seeing it. "You know Tom's view is there's nothing immoral about tranquilizers; his view is that they're not being prescribed or taken with enough caution." She snapped the box shut. "He bought twenty shares on fifty percent margin at $16,000 a share and they're now worth $48,000 each. He said this morning that's a gross profit of $800,000, and apparently you've also benefited from an increase in the value of the Swiss franc during 1972, which makes it almost a million-dollar profit on one deal." She looked straight at Judy. "He feels you're ungrateful to complain. After all, he isn't *always* successful with his deals and he wants to hang on."

"But it's not as though it's his *only* deal," Judy said. "We're deep into sophisticated engineering companies and computers as well as pharmaceuticals." She sighed and looked at the low cedar table beside her. She picked up an enameled Russian bear. "You have such beautiful things, such a beautiful apartment, but Tom seems to see such an ugly future. Americans besieged on the energy front, deep into military muscle and popping tranquilizers as they work out their interest rates on their little pocket calculators."

The door banged as Tom hurried in. He kissed both of them and ran for his dinner jacket. "You know how sorry I am to be late," he called. He appeared in the doorway. "Kate, could you please fix this tie. Okay, Judy, I'm selling the Hoffmann-La Roche shares, not that I've changed my opinion, but we might as well take a profit, and I think I'm going to leave it all in Swiss francs, I don't see why this upward trend should stop. Where are my cuff links, Kate? Where's Griffin?"

"He couldn't make it. His goddamn wife and her goddamn charity function." Judy longed to hear Griffin call her to fix his shirt or find his cuff links. She yearned for this hurried intimacy as Kate stood behind Tom, pecked the back of his neck and then tied his black bow.

Griffin and Judy had now been together for four years. Twice during that time they had fought bitterly and split up. The first time was after their first year, when they had a blazing fight about Griffin's possessiveness. The second time had been after two years together, when Griffin's wife, Delia, finally made a stand and demanded that he give up Judy. She hadn't minded the models too much, but she felt humiliated and embittered by her husband's open liaison with a successful, well-known woman. For the sake of his family and their years together she wanted him to attempt a full-scale reconciliation and an exclusive relationship with her again. His children had been brought into the row. His elder son had been bitter and scornful; his elder daughter had been so understanding that he had broken down and cried.

Griffin and his wife both tried hard but they both knew they were trying to rekindle cold ashes. Griffin then asked Delia for a divorce on any terms she wanted. But although she finally agreed to their living separate lives, she asked him to continue to live in their home for the sake of their children; whatever happened she wanted to keep their family together. When Griffin pointed out that their youngest son was fifteen and would soon leave home, Delia had threatened suicide and hauled in her doctor. From then on, they had lived in a sexless truce under the same roof.

Or was it sexless? Judy sometimes wondered. Men always said they never made love to their wives, but they always did. What else could they say to you?

As the theater curtain fell for the last time, Judy felt the same old sadness returning, those same pangs that she firmly called sentimentality, that longing to share Griffin's life as opposed to seeing a lot of him. As always when she was fighting misery, she turned a little truculent.

Tom was annoyed at not getting more reaction to his morning news that they were about a million dollars richer and his evening news that he'd done as Judy wanted. As they took their table in the Four Seasons, he shrugged his shoulders and said to nobody in particular, "Naturally, I didn't expect to be thanked."

"Thanks for some things and no thanks for others," said Judy, staring hard at the chain draperies that shimmered like cascades of water. She wished they'd gone somewhere gayer; she really only liked the Four Seasons for lunch. "Of course I'm glad I'm not poor anymore, but we've now been in business for nine years and you no longer have any interest in LACE or *VERVE! You're* only interested in making more money. *I'm* interested in being paid up so I can sleep at night without counting all the money we owe."

"For nine years I've been telling you that your old-fashioned virtues are a poverty trap." Tom mimicked a mindless, singsong female voice. "Save up for the purchase price before you buy something, never borrow money, don't buy real estate because it's better to rent and if you're going to save money, then stick it in government bonds. I am making you *rich*, and all you do is whine. Where are your *guts?*"

"Never mind my guts. I know where your *heart* is. In that cluster of money boxes called Wall Street."

"It's sad to see an insecure poor girl turn into an insecure rich one. Originally you aimed high, remember? Don't get frightened just because you passed your target."

They ordered baked oysters followed by roast pheasant. Tom continued in a low, angry voice. "If you really want to split, I'll sell you my shares in LACE and you can sell me your shares in *VERVE!* Or vice-versa."

"Judy doesn't want to give up anything and neither do you, Tom," Kate interjected. "Perhaps Judy would be a little happier if she were a bit less rich. And you, Tom—I love your speculative streak because I've got one myself, but you are turning into a walking, talking investment company."

She stopped talking while they were served and then continued, "You think Judy's ungrateful, but she's not, she's very grateful for what you've done for her, but there's a sort of tension that she loves and a sort of tension that she can't stand. Surely, with this latest gain you can sort out the LACE portfolio and separate the investment business from the rest of the company?" She paused and sighed, then said crossly, "I don't know what's gone wrong with this evening, but I wish you could stop arguing about money and tell Judy our news."

Tom fiddled with his wine glass, raised his eyebrows, opened his mouth, shut it again, then said, "Uh, I don't know how to put this, but Kate and I are going to be married. The full commitment."

Judy flung herself toward him and kissed his ear.

"Tom, you dear old-fashioned fellow! Why that's wonderful." She gave a Cheshire cat grin. "I know exactly what I'm going to get you for a wedding present. Kate will love it and you'll loathe it because it's a conditional gift." The happy couple both looked quizzical. "On condition that you have it standing in your living room, I'm going to give you half of the T'ang horse." Kate shrieked with surprise and joy. Tom looked uneasy.

"Well, that's wonderful, Judy, but . . ."

"We do still have that horse, don't we?"

"Yes, but it's really not feasible to have it in the apartment where it might get broken; it's a museum piece; it's too valuable to have out, Judy."

"I don't think the guy that made that horse intended it to be stabled in a bank vault. I think he'd want Kate to have it."

Tom looked at Kate's excited face. "Yes," he agreed, "I guess he would."

Over the breakfast grapefruit, one warm October morning in 1978, Griffin's wife suddenly freed her husband from the tentacles of guilt and duty that had bound him. They were eating at a walnut dining table that was big enough to seat forty, and as usual, Griffin was tearing through the morning papers as he ate.

Suddenly, triumphantly, Delia had said, "Griffin, this is the last goddamn time I have to sit here and listen to you eat grapefruit."

Griffin put down his spoon, mumbled sorry, read another inch of *The Wall Street Journal*, then did a double take and jerked his head up. "What do you mean, the *last* time?"

"I'm leaving you, that's what I mean!" She looked exultant. "That's what you *want*, isn't it? Well, that's what you're *getting* for Christmas. For two years now, Griffin, there's been another man and *you* haven't even noticed. . . ."

Quickly he did a flashback in his mind; no, he had noticed no man. . . . Except . . .

"That guy who fitted my contact lenses, Greenburg, Granheim, something like that. . . . The optician."

"Greenheimer, right. Right as usual!"

Griffin said nothing, but over the top of the *Journal*, she had his complete attention for once.

"We're going to Israel together to start a new life on a kibbutz before it's too late."

Griffen put down his paper and looked warily at his wife. He couldn't see Delia laboring in the fields and eating communal meals. He suspected a trick. "What about the kids?"

"Fred's hardly a child. When he's home from school he's practically never here as it is—he's always out with that girl. I think he's going to move in with her. He'll need a little financial help from you of course, and so shall I. But I know I can rely on you to look after me. In fact, I've already had a word with Marvin about it."

Griffin dashed down his paper, stood up and roared. "You've already been to a lawyer without so much as mentioning to your husband the fact that you're leaving him?"

"Do you think I'm a fool?"

That evening Judy opened the door of her apartment to see Griffin leaning against the living room wall, swirling his usual predinner glass of ginger ale. He looked oddly taut and gauche. As soon as she untwisted her key from the lock he strode across the room, and without pausing to kiss her, he grabbed both her wrists. As if he could no longer keep it to himself, as if he couldn't believe that it was true, he burst out with his news.

Judy's mouth fell open. "You mean *she* wants a divorce? *Really* wants one? Do you believe it? This isn't another of her cat-and-mouse games?"

"Yes, I believe it this time. She's never been like this before—gloating, exultant, almost vengeful."

"Griffin, to be honest, I don't blame her."

"None of that has anything to do with you, Judy. Delia and I had a relationship that didn't work and she didn't want a divorce. So we regrouped." Gently he shook her wrists. "Now look, I didn't come here to discuss that guilt-and-responsibility thing again. I'm here to ask you, now that it's possible—will you marry me, darling?"

To her surprise, upon hearing the words for which she had waited ten years, Judy found that she couldn't say yes.

She simply didn't know.

PART TEN

CHAPTER 53

BEYOND THE ORANGE trees and marigold beds at the end of the palace gardens, a scarlet Kiowa waited on the concrete helipad. The small, orange windsock hung limp. Two armed guards in khaki fatigues stood smartly to attention as the royal party approached.

Although in 1972, many educated Eastern women wore Western clothes in their home, Queen Serah always wore traditional robes in Sydon. Now she flicked up her long white *burka* as she was helped into the front of the helicopter. Squealing with pleasure at the prospect of the coming flight, ten-year-old Prince Mustapha and his white-uniformed servant climbed into the three back seats of the transparent bubble. A stickler for detail, Abdullah walked around the machine to see that all the doors were shut and handles latched. He completed his circuit at the right door, climbed in and settled himself in the right-hand seat of the opulent custom-built cabin. The trip from Dinada Palace to the hunting lodge in the eastern mountains, which would have taken nearly eight hours by car, was only twenty minutes in the five-seater jet turbine helicopter.

Heat shimmered on the sand as Abdullah strapped himself in. He went through the start sequence and a sudden wind whipped up the sand as the helicopter roared, shaking the bones and teeth of the passengers. Abdullah clapped on his earphones, turned on the ADF and dialed in the eastern mountains frequency; the needle on the instrument face immediately pointed in the direction that they were to take. As he rolled the twist-grip throttle away from him, the noise was deafening, as if their ears were being pierced by a pneumatic drill. The royal pilot flicked a last look at the dancing numbers on the control panel, checked that pressures and temperature were stabilized, then smoothly lifted the helicopter clear of the ground.

Once in the air, the noise wasn't bad, more like the steady throb of a submarine. Peering down from the rear window, the small boy waved goodbye to the shrinking white Dinada Palace as their magic dragonfly rose, then turned east before settling on a straight course. On the perimeter of the helipad below, a small cluster of guards and courtiers still stood at the salute and would remain so until the machine had vanished over the horizon.

A sudden gust of turbulence distracted him momentarily, so Abdullah didn't notice the needle on the oil pressure gauge shudder for a moment, then draw toward zero. At 300 meters above the desert, Abdullah leveled off. He was looking forward to a few uninterrupted days with his son.

On the previous afternoon, a mechanic had suspected that an oil line running on the outside of the engine to the front engine bearing was cracked and he had replaced it. It was almost unbearably hot in the hangar, and just as he began to tighten the front end of the line, he felt a buzzing in his ears and his knees gave way. He grasped the side of the aircraft with suddenly weak hands, slid down from the ladder and took a swig from the water bottle at his waist. When he felt better, he climbed the ladder again, checked the connections and signed off the machine as airworthy for flight. But he forgot that the oil line connection was only finger-tight.

Suddenly, sound blared from the overhead panel. Every faculty alerted, Abdullah swiftly checked the instrument panel before him. Adrenalin flooded his blood and he tensed like a runner waiting for the starting gun. It was unlikely, the odds were against it, but it was happening!

Then the engine-failure horn sounded. All three engine indicators were fast unwinding to zero; the continuous loud screaming from the low rotor speed horn meant that the blades were slowing down. To Abdullah, everything that was happening so swiftly appeared to be in slow motion, but the long hours of pilot training rendered his movements fast and automatic.

He had no time to be frightened, and there was no need for fear. In the event of engine failure a helicopter doesn't drop like a stone, it glides to the ground like a glider. Abdullah lowered the pitch control on his left, which put the helicopter into a glide, and it entered the stabilized autorotation which Abdullah knew, after hours of practice, would safely land the aircraft.

The helicopter dropped and for a moment became weightless.

As toys hit the cabin roof and a teddy bear was flung violently against the Queen's head, all passengers were thrown against their safety belts and the servant in the rear began to scream with fright.

As the helicopter dropped, the Queen instinctively grabbed the front panel and cried, "Stop playing tricks, you're frightening the child!" She turned to look at her husband. His face was tense and masklike as his hands and feet worked in perfect coordination, fighting to regain control of the aircraft.

The Queen had never seen him look like that and she panicked. "You're not to let it crash, it will frighten Mustapha!" she screamed, pulling at his shoulder. "Stop it, I say, Abdullah, stop it!"

Abdullah heard neither his wife nor the screaming servant. All his concentration and willpower were focused on the machine. He realized with relief that he had the autorotation under control, and that when he had gone into the glide, the machine had felt exactly as it had in practice long ago, when his instructor had been sitting on the seat beside him.

Confident once more, his mind ran swiftly through the emergency checklist. He could touch down almost anywhere ahead in the sand.

"Stop it! Stop this machine immediately!" the Queen shouted hysterically. It was the first time she had ever dared raise her voice to her husband. She started to pummel his left arm with her fists and then, screaming, she lunged for the black control stick between Abdullah's knees.

The helicopter shuddered and dipped.

Once more his wife lunged toward him. Abdullah hit her as hard as he could with the side of his left fist. It caught her on the cheekbone, split open the side of her mouth and knocked two teeth inward. She fell back, clapping both hands to her bleeding mouth, still screaming with fear and panic as Abdullah turned once more to the controls.

He was now down to twenty miles an hour and dropping, which was far too slow. He would have to regain a speed of at least sixty miles an hour if he was to avoid a crash. Abdullah shoved the stick forward to regain speed by diving. Suddenly he was frightened and sweat started to run into his eyes.

Again the helicopter dropped violently and correctly, but the needle didn't climb fast enough, and at fifty feet above the ground Abdullah knew that he would have to make a sloppy emergency landing. He flared the aircraft, easing the control stick back toward his body, in order to haul the machine out of the dive and bring it to a halt before touching ground.

Obediently the machine slowed up and started to sink. Abdullah realized that it would probably be a walkaway crash; it wouldn't be his first. He prepared to level the helicopter before touchdown, easing the stick forward.

It was at this moment, with touchdown imminent, that the Queen again threw herself against him, beating Abdullah's body with her fists and wildly shouting through her bleeding mouth, "My child! My child! You don't care about my child!" She lunged toward him and with both hands, she yanked the control stick toward her, bent her body over it and clung to it with surprising strength. The aircraft obediently rolled to the left.

There was an enormous, bucking jolt as the traveling blade in the back struck the ground hard and dug deep into the sand, then stopped dead.

The braces that held the blades in position snapped cleanly, but the huge and very expensive pin that held the blades to the aircraft did not snap. The tip of the 150-pound blade was still traveling counter-clockwise and near the speed of sound when it smashed into the front of the cabin and crashed downward, slicing through the overhead panel, silencing the screaming horns, and slashing the Queen's head roughly from her body.

The severed, bloody head was flung backward onto her son's lap. Little Mustapha screamed and pushed the bloody horror away from his bare knees, down among the toys on the cabin floor, as, with one last tremendous jolt, the blade finally hit the ground and the aircraft jerked to a halt.

A gush of blood spurted up from the severed lump of crushed bone and tattered flesh that had been the Queen's body. The sticky scarlet fountain drenched Abdullah, the incarnadine, inescapable spray clung to his hands and soaked his clothes, his arms, his hair and his face. He tried to wipe the blood out of his eyes, but with fingers that were red, wet and dripping.

For a few seconds he was mentally and physically paralyzed. After one look at the bloody lump of flesh on his left, Abdullah's conditioned pilot's mind registered that he wouldn't need to help her—his priority was to get the screaming servant and child out of the wreckage as soon as possible, because apart from the stench of blood and vomit from the back, he noticed two distinct smells—the burning electrical wires in the smashed overhead panel, and the fumes from the seventy gallons of volatile jet fuel that was pouring into the back of the cabin from the tank beneath the back seats.

He jerked into action, tore off his safety belt and tipped off the headphones. He levered his body upright, neck and shoulders protruding from the smashed and buckled front window. Then, less than sixty seconds after the helicopter had touched ground, there was a sudden roar. Abdullah felt as if a huge hand had picked him up and flung him through the air and across the desert sand.

He landed on his stomach, winded, gulping and gasping for breath, with his leg twisted beneath him. He felt no panic or pain, although in fact he had suffered a concussion, a compound fracture of the leg and broken several ribs. For a moment he lay dazed, then, with enormous concentration and willpower, he lifted his head.

Slowly, steadily, sickeningly, the horizon tilted forty-five degrees to the left. Trembling with the strain, Abdullah hoisted his body on his arms, the jelling blood dripping, as he faced the helicopter. The machine had turned into a roaring ball of fire. Impotent, Abdullah gazed at the flaming mass of debris. Grimly he started to drag himself forward on his hands toward the fireball before he collapsed unconscious on the sand. Apart from the searing, roaring flames, there was no sound in the impersonal silence of the desert.

It had been exactly seven minutes since takeoff.

CHAPTER 54

IN THE LATE June sunshine, Lili's scarlet Jaguar dipped along the highway, heading east of Paris. Five kilometers after Epernay, she turned off the N51 toward Le Mesnil-sur-Oger. On the right, meadows of brilliant yellow mustard flowers alternated with stretches of golden corn, sprinkled with scarlet poppies, blue cornflowers and white marguerites. On the left the dark green, seven-foot box hedge bordered the de Chazalle estate.

Lili swung the car to the left through a pair of open, black, curlicued iron gates. The hedges and trees looked unusually neat, the grass was freshly cut. Half a mile away, at the end of a straight gravel drive, was the eighteenth-century French château, a perfectly proportioned stone building, with row upon row of tall windows that glistened in the sunshine.

Zimmer was right. It was time she started to go out by herself again. She had sheltered—or rather hidden—under his wing for eight months.

For all those months Lili had lived alone with her grief for Stiarkoz, refusing to discuss him even with Zimmer, with whom Lili would only talk about her work. Then one day Zimmer had entered the dressing room where Lili sat in a mauve flowered wrapper, wiping off her makeup in front of the brilliantly lit mirror. Without asking, Zimmer shoved past her dresser and locked the door. Then he stood behind Lili with his hands on her shoulders, looking at her in the mirror, and said, "Lili, I've tried to hint, but you refuse to listen, so I'm telling you directly that to shut yourself off from the world and everyone in it is bad for your acting. My dear, Jo is dead and you are alive. You must make a conscious effort to interest yourself again in all the things that you pursued with Jo—and you must also make an effort to make new friends and have some fun. Fun is good medicine; moping is self-indulgence."

In the mirror Lili had glared at Zimmer, but she knew that isolation *was* bad for her acting. Which was why she had accepted the invitation from Madame de Chazalle.

Lili stopped the red Jaguar in front of the imposing portico, climbed out and rang the bell.

Nothing happened.

She had expected at least two liveried footmen to swoop out and pick up her luggage. She peered through the glass panels of the door and saw an enormous stone-flagged hall flanked by pillars, between which hung gold-framed portraits. Still no sound.

Puzzled, Lili rang the bell again. A masculine voice behind her said, "There must be another crisis in the kitchen. Let me carry your suitcase." She turned to see a very tall young man wearing a turtleneck navy sweater and jeans so tight that they might have been sprayed onto his long legs. Untidy, toffee-colored hair fell over hazel eyes and a thin, tanned face. His overlarge mouth slowly widened in a welcoming grin.

"No need to ask who *you* are." At the age of twenty-four, Lili was world-famous. He took her navy leather suitcases, kicked the door open, and stood aside to let Lili walk through. As they ascended the six-foot-wide, curving marble staircase, they met Maxine descending.

For ten seconds, Lili found her formidable, then Maxine smiled. "So you've already met my youngest son, Alexandre. I'm delighted to see you again. It is not often that I meet anyone so charming on a charity bazaar platform. I was really only there for publicity, so to make a friend was a bonus."

She led the way downstairs, still chattering. "As I said in my letter, this weekend we celebrate our anniversary. It's been eighteen years since the château was opened to the public."

"Where is everyone, Maman?"

"The entire staff is on the terrace preparing the fireworks display. *You* should be helping them, Alexandre." She ruffled the toffee-colored hair. But her son, who had no intention of leaving Lili, ran upstairs, dumped the suitcases at the top and then followed the two women into the salon.

Beyond the terrace was a silver rectangle of water into which fountains gently splashed. The sixty-foot-long, white-paneled room shimmered with reflected light from the lake outside and from the great antique mirrors that hung along one wall. Little glass tables held seventeenth- and eighteenth-century objects. They stood on soft lavender and gray Aubusson carpets. A sleek gray Weimaraner was trying to gnaw a hole in the arm of one of the brocade sofas.

"Sheba gives the place that lived-in look," Maxine observed. "I'm always being told that I am overneat. The whole place would look like a museum if it wasn't for my sons and my dogs."

"The whole house *is* a museum," Alexandre explained to Lili, "but it isn't dull or dusty. Maman has made it most fascinating. You'll see when you tour the public rooms. The lighting changes by remote control, the rooms are full of flowers and the room in which Diaghilev stayed is daily sprayed with Mitsouko because it was his favorite perfume."

* * *

Lili's suite overlooked the park. The bedroom walls were covered in pale yellow silk, as was the couch in front of the hand-carved, white marble fireplace. The huge bed was set back in an alcove of dark topaz velvet. On either side of it were a row of shelves, upon one of which lay a pile of the latest best-sellers and a history of the castle entitled "Château de Chazalle—A Place to Make Friends." There were also a candle in a brass holder, an ivory telephone, notebooks with little gilt pencils, a velvet box of tissues, an antique gold box containing biscuits and several little china dishes of pink sugared almonds and peppermints. A silver nightcap tray offered different sorts of expensive bottled water and cut-glass decanters of whiskey and brandy. Beside the telephone was a list of the guests, with room numbers as well as telephone extensions.

Lili picked up the thick cream card engraved in green with the de Chazalle crest—a rearing lion with a rose in its paw. Under the date—June 21, 1974—her fellow guests were listed: two ambassadors; a producer and his ballet-star wife; a Hollywood film director; a Greek shipowner whom she had met with Stiarkoz; three other very rich men; a world auto-racing champion and his beautiful wife; a redheaded, jet-setting jeans designer from New York with her sixth husband; an Italian prince; a British duke and—aha—Andi Cherno from *Paris Match*. So there was going to be photo coverage of the party. No wonder the guest list was so ostentatious. Lili mentally ran through her clothes. They had already been unpacked by the Portuguese maid and were hanging in a dressing room lined with cupboards that lit up when opened. The maid had run her bath, told Lili to ring if she wished to be helped with her dress and hair and had disappeared.

On Friday evenings Maxine served an informal buffet dinner so that guests could move around and meet each other. Although there were sufficient footmen in green and gold livery, Charles de Chazalle circulated about the silver salon carrying a bottle of the estate champagne. Monsieur le Comte hadn't his wife's ability to slide into an animated conversation for ten minutes, then extricate herself and glide gracefully toward the next cluster of guests. Charles used the champagne bottle as an entry and exit device. He would wander up to a group of guests saying, "Everybody got a drink?" and he would detach himself by saying, "Well, I'd better move on," slightly lifting the bottle in a farewell salute as he went about the duties of a host.

Very tall and thin, he stooped slightly as if a chill wind were blowing on the back of his neck. His fair hair was turning gray and had started to recede, but this only made him look more distinguished. His face reflected amiability and slight astonishment at the way his wife had altered his life. Personally, he preferred the place as it used to be, although it had been a bit shabby when he was a boy. But if it wasn't for all this razzmatazz, they wouldn't be able to live here at all, and he didn't know if he could bear that. So Charles viewed the glittering celebrity occasions, the crowds, the applause and the wall-to-wall photographers as a sort of penance that had to be endured in order that he might be able to vanish to the library.

As women always expected Lili to pounce on their husbands at parties, she always made a point of talking to the women first. Linda, the red-headed jeans designer, was surprisingly funny and charming as they talked about the universal difficulty of doing up the zip of a garment that women always bought one size too small. "But then, jeans are the modern equivalent of corsets; you squeeze into them and they mold you into a predetermined shape," the designer said. "If Scarlett O'Hara were alive today, she wouldn't be lacing up her corsets. She'd be wriggling on the floor trying to zip up her jeans."

Andi Cherno pointed his lens at them and the two women immediately stopped talking and posed as *if* they were talking. They were both used to being photographed and knew that if you really talked, then the picture would probably show you with your eyes shut and your mouth lolling open above three chins. "*Ecco belle!*" grinned Andi and asked them to stand by the window with the Hollywood director and the Greek shipowner, whose eyes brightened hopefully as Lili moved toward him.

"Hello, Steni. Last time I saw you was on the *Creole.*"

"Yes, it took two weeks for my nose to stop peeling and ten weeks for my liver to recover."

Maxine worked hard to make her parties look effortless. She had been up since six o'clock that morning, consulting her lists and ticking off items or conferring with the head gardener, her chef or her butler. She had checked the fireworks display on the far side of the lake, as well as the one on the terrace, and then inspected the food, the wine, the ballroom, the cloakroom, the first-aid room and toilet arrangements for the band and disco. At nine in the morning she had been joined by Mademoiselle Janine, who had been busy removing all small valuable objects in the public rooms.

Maxine moved around the château, working steadily until eleven, when she went to her bathroom, satisfied that her home was ready for the four hundred guests who would be at the ball that evening. Maxine hated the formality of traditional country house parties. She always offered her guests plenty of amusements, but she also made it clear that if they wished to stay in their rooms, or if they wanted to wander alone over the wooded estate, that was fine, too. Today, Maxine had organized horseback riding, a miniature-golf party, and tennis for the Americans. But the men would probably laze around the swimming pool while the women rested or had their hair done by the two hairdressers sent from Paris.

Nobody appeared until lunch time. The meal was served on small tables on the terrace. The fountains were soft silver plumes in the sunlight, ice clinked in glasses and scrunched in buckets; the tinkle of silver cutlery and laughing conversation were the only sounds to accompany the meal.

Alexandre had gotten to the terrace before anyone else and changed the place names so that he was next to Lili. He could not take his eyes off her, as his mother noticed with exasperation. She had never allowed her sons to behave with familiarity toward her guests. They were not allowed to speak to the press, or be photographed with a celebrity or ask for anyone's autograph. She would call Alexandre to her dressing room that evening and remind him of his manners and his youth.

Lili's nipples were only just hidden by the white taffeta dress that Zandra Rhodes had given her as a twenty-fourth birthday present. The enormous puffed sleeves emphasized her tiny waist, pulled in by a tight cummerbund above swirling folds of taffeta skirt. She wore a pair of blazing diamond chandelier earrings, all that remained of her Stiarkoz collection. (On the day Jo died, they were being repaired by Van Cleef in Monte Carlo.)

Lili looked like a delicate, eighteenth-century Spanish princess as she slowly moved down the marble staircase. The scent of jasmine and warm grass from the countryside outside the windows mingled with the more sophisticated fragrances that rose from soft, bare shoulders. The gentle buzz of conversation sparkled with an occasional burst of laughter, and in the long, chandelier-hung ballroom the orchestra softly played, "I'll Be Seeing You." Beyond the row of open glass doors that led to the terrace, a warm, hay-scented dusk hung over the lake.

An elegant buffet, *un repas rose*, had been laid out in a salon next to the ballroom. Everything was pink. Pink tablecloths were hung with swags of dark green laurel and crystal vases of palest pink rosebuds stood behind the food. White-hatted chefs carved slices of York ham and paper-thin slices of dark-red prosciutto. There were piles of translucent rosy prawns, silver bowls of *sauce aurore*, great, dark-red mottled lobsters, brittle crayfish, delicate, pale-pink poached salmon and seafood salad of squid and octopus. One long table was banked with salads that still smelled of early morning gardens; another pink stretch of linen held four-foot-high pyramids of rose meringues Chantilly, silver dishes of strawberries Romanoff and deep crystal bowls of raspberries and cream. And naturally there was pink champagne.

Maxine knew that Charles' sisters would think it all unspeakably vulgar, but the press would love it.

In contrast to the ballroom elegance, a couple of wine cellars on the other side of the château had been turned into a darkened, strobe-lit disco, where even the bottles at the bar pulsed to the exuberant thump, thump, thump and vibration of rock music.

Not until six in the morning did the last car vanish through the summer mist at the end of the gravel drive. Lili had been asleep for three hours. She had snuggled into her warm bed thinking that the evening could not have been more perfect. She had been on her best behavior, had danced with all the men in the house party and had posed endlessly for photographers. As usual, she had been besieged by men and had flirted with a couple of them, but she carefully did not dance with anyone in particular. She still didn't feel Jo had gone.

Not a guest was seen before Sunday lunch, which was a very quiet, sleepy meal. After Alexandre had carried coffee over to Lili, he asked if he could show her the woods and the rock pool where he and his brothers swam. He had spent the last two days planning how to get Lili away from the other guests.

Lili was not unpleased by this youthful adoration. After drinking her coffee, they strolled over the spongy lawn, sprinkled with buttercups and daisies, and into the forest.

Alexandre couldn't believe his luck. If only his classmates could see him! He felt as lighthearted as one of the Weimaraners as he bounded along the path, occasionally leaping up to grab high overhead branches. Lili felt relaxed and curiously young as she followed him. His naturalness, his directness and his exuberant boyish energy were a contrast to her sophisticated, brittle fellow-houseguests.

When the path became overgrown, Alexandre held the beech branches back so that they didn't tear Lili's white voile dress.

The pool was a shallow, pebble-floored bulge in the river, edged by tall green reeds and bulrushes. Willows leaned over to caress the water and their branches trailed soft, gray leaves dappling in the sunlight. They pulled off their shoes and dangled their legs in the river, watching the clear water shiver and distort their pale feet.

Suddenly Alexandre could bear it no longer. He had to touch her. With gauche determination, he slowly lifted Lili's hand off the grass and kissed the little finger with grave ceremony. His lips pressed her pink nail, then quivered apart, and the end of her finger slid into his mouth, up to the first little joint, then farther to the second joint, then he sucked her whole finger in his mouth, between his wide, quivering lips. Panting, he held her finger gently between his teeth, rolled his wet tongue around it, pulled softly and insistently on her flesh, tasting the soft skin.

Lili had half expected something of the sort, but she certainly hadn't expected the violence of her reaction. She had thought she would gently push him away. He was too young. But at his touch her back arched, her stomach tightened, her nipples tingled and she felt as if they were connected to her groin by two invisible, tugging threads. She gasped, and for a few moments she didn't move, but her trembling body demanded that she respond. Unable to stop herself, she pushed her trembling fingers through his thick, strawlike hair, and stroked the sunburned nape of his young neck. Neither of them spoke as he raised his eyes to hers. Her lips slowly parted as she gazed at the golden down on his cheeks, the aristocratic nose.

His hazel eyes looked oddly dazed as he lunged toward Lili; his large mouth brushed her cheek, then his lips were on hers and she felt his insistent, silky lips.

Slowly, they fell back on the grass. Alexandre lay half on top of Lili and his eyes closed languorously as he sucked her mouth into his. At each pull, Lili's stomach contracted, and her body stiffened under Alexandre's smooth hands. Suddenly she remembered that the hands of Jo Stiarkoz had felt like wrinkled walnuts. She felt a sudden stab of disloyalty as she smelled Alexandre's musky odor, the erotic odor of fresh sweat on a young body. She sniffed the sweet fragrance of his hair, mingling with the green scent of the crushed grass beneath them.

Her slim arms wrapped around his body, then slipped up inside his T-shirt. She felt the rippling muscles of his back as with his eyes shut, he edged his way further onto her body until she was firmly imprisoned beneath him. As if possessed, her hands slipped down the back of his jeans, slid under the rough, tough fabric and over his silken, hard buttocks. Oh, God, she thought, young, *firm* flesh. For a fleeting second she again remembered, with guilt and against her wish, the tortoiselike, slightly pendulous pouches of Stiarkoz, the doughlike sinking of his flesh when touched.

Clinging to Alexandre, she felt his hardness through the bulging denim. Slowly he pushed his quivering hands inside her dress, slowly undid each pearl button, his lips still sucking at her mouth. Her tingling nipples were erect and waiting for his hands. Gently he squeezed the soft whiteness and felt her hard little rosebuds under his palms. Then his hands brushed farther down her body, as his lips ran clumsily over her breasts, sucking insistently first one pink nipple and then the other. Harder and harder he sucked, and with each gentle tug Lili felt a matching, yearning tug deep in her groin. With one hand he pulled up her skirt and felt beneath the fragile fabric. Lili felt the hard warmth of his hand press against her naked stomach, then slowly slide downward beneath the scrap of white lace. Softly, hesitantly, he touched her and she arched toward him, helpless beneath his hand. With growing confidence he stroked her, laced his fingers in the dark silken hair and tugged it gently; then rhythmically, insistently, he stroked again until she arched her half-clad body to the sun and gave one sharp, high cry among the rustling trees.

For a few minutes she was oblivious as sun freckled through leaves from the blue sky beyond. Then she felt his trembling hands tearing at her belt, unhooking it. She helped him to pull her dress from her body. Together, they tugged off his jeans so that they both lay naked in the long grass. With a low moan, Alexandre flung himself on top of her, his eyes still closed. Again Lili felt that wonderful moth-mouth settling on hers, his hands on her breasts, his hardness on the naked flesh of her soft belly. Aroused again to the point of frenzy, she felt for him, and as she guided him, throbbing, into her body she could feel the heavy beating of her heart against his own. More than anything she wanted to feel him inside her, to feel joined to this wild, hard-muscled boy bucking on top of her, thrusting deep inside her body, groaning until he flung his head back to the sky, quivering as he called the name that had possessed his mind for the last three days. "Lili, Lili, Lili!"

He clung to her, his eyes still closed, his downy lashes against the tanned face, and eventually he whispered into her ear, "Was it . . . all right for you?"

Lili wrapped her slender, brown arms around him. "It was wonderful," she whispered.

So Alexandre made love to her again.

Afterward he was still unable to keep his mouth off her. Lili snuggled against the golden body, purring into his armpits, sniffing the soft down. She felt alive again, excited, exalted. She bent her head so that her cloud of dark hair hung down, and then she trailed the black silken sheet over Alexandre's body until he flung himself at her again.

He couldn't stop touching her. Every soft stroke of his hand felt as if he were holding something fragile and precious.

They slithered naked down the bank and stood, waist-high, in the water. Lili felt her toes sink voluptuously into the soft mud as Alexandre pulled her, laughing, spluttering, into the clear water of the stream. For a few minutes they struggled playfully. Then gently Alexandre lifted her dripping, satin body and laid her on the river bank where he sat and looked at her. Slyly, as if it were forbidden, his gaze traveled down her wet brown body. He exulted. He gloated. Like a young wolf, he was unstoppable. He leaned forward and ran his mouth over her breasts again, tugging harder now at the nipples. Lili shuddered in ecstasy as she felt the warm tongue move down her ribs, the wet warm tip trickle across her stomach, dip lovingly into her navel, then trace its slithery route south. She felt his hot breath in her dark hair and his tongue flicker over her quivering flesh, gently insistent that she yield totally to the pleasure he was affording her.

Afterward they waited in the wood until Alexandre reckoned that everybody was gathered in the drawing room for drinks. Quietly, they slipped from the trees at the side of the lawn to the door of the orangery. Alexandre looked like a tawny, sleepy beast. He was hugely pleased with himself and he still couldn't keep his hands off Lili, whose hair was a wild tangle and whose dress was grass-stained and ruined.

Inside the glass-walled orangery stood dark green tubs of fragrant white camellias and sour, sharp-scented scarlet geraniums. Orange and lemon trees stood between the carved stone benches that were placed every five meters.

On the end bench, sitting upright in tangerine satin, was Maxine.

Earlier that afternoon, Mademoiselle Janine had pressed her forehead to the window of the blue salon as Lili and Alexandre wandered across the lawn toward the wood. She was not the only person to have noticed their departure, but she was the only one who immediately moved over to the coffee table and murmured the news to Madame la Comtesse. Maxine was suddenly possessed by a violent jealousy that swept away all logic. Like everyone else, Maxine had noticed her son's infatuation, but she had hardly expected her star guest to take much notice of a fifteen-year-old boy, especially when there were so many more suitable men present. Try as she might, Maxine found that she couldn't ignore the situation. She was bursting with indignation and rage. She guessed that they would not be back before sunset, when (if Alexandre was anything like his brothers or his father) they would no doubt enter by the little hidden door to the orangery where the woods came nearest to the château.

As they changed for dinner, Maxine asked Charles to look after their guests for a few minutes. He gave her a swift, worried look; something was up when Maxine used that carefully casual voice, but he judged it better to say nothing and do as she wished.

Quietly the door to the orangery opened and they slipped inside. Alexandre immediately pulled Lili to him again and bent his head down to her throat, but she gently laughed. "You must *never* touch me when anyone might see."

"Then may I come to your room tonight?"

"You will go to *your* room *now*, Alexandre." It was his mother's voice. Caught off guard, the tall boy suddenly looked like a guilty six-year-old who had been caught stealing candy.

He hesitated. Lili gave him a little push toward the corridor and he fled.

Maxine looked at Lili with loathing. "Couldn't you leave my son alone? Did you *need* to seduce a fifteen-year-old boy? Can't you leave *any* man alone?"

"Don't be ridiculous. *He* seduced *me*. . . . Is he *really* only fifteen? . . . I thought eighteen . . . or maybe seventeen."

"I hate to think of his *touching* you."

"But what is so dreadful? It was obviously not the first time."

"He should love someone of his own age and his own kind."

"I'm only twenty-four."

"I don't care *how* old you are. You're no better than a whore."

Maxine had gone too far. Lili was suddenly furious. "You are *jealous* because I had him and *you* can't."

Stepping forward, Maxine slapped the face of this creature who had bewitched her youngest and favorite son.

As fast as a fighting cock, Lili flew at Maxine and her hand flashed across the older woman's face. Blood flowed in three small trickles down Maxine's face.

Crying with indignation, Lili flung herself at Maxine, pounding at the older, bigger woman, arms flailing, engrossed in her rage and her need for revenge. Aghast, Maxine flung up both arms to protect herself from her attacker and kicked Lili away with one tangerine satin toe. But Lili sprang back at her, eyes narrowed, lips drawn back.

Maxine was ashamed, mortified and alarmed. She had never hit anyone in her life, not even her sons when they were children. Yet she had now allowed herself to behave as badly as this slut. She broke away and fled to her room, her hair falling down on one side, her cheek bleeding and her dress torn.

She flung herself on the blue silk bed, grabbed the ivory house telephone and dialed the housekeeper. With difficulty she kept her voice calm. "Please pack Mademoiselle Lili's clothes straightaway, and tell Antoine to bring her car to the front door. She will be leaving immediately." Then she rang for the butler to come to her bedroom.

She changed quickly into her bathrobe, brushed and pinned her hair into place, bathed her scratched cheek, which had stopped bleeding, and dabbed Concealstik on the wounds. When the butler arrived she simply said, "There has been a slight disturbance, Lamartine. Miss Lili is leaving. I want you to see that she is out of this house within half an hour. And Lamartine—the meal had better wait until she has gone. We do not want to disturb the other guests, and we don't want a scene. Serve more champagne, please."

Lili was already flinging her clothes into her suitcases. She left the house with head held high, conscious of the expressionless, watchful Lamartine in his role of upper-class bouncer.

Shrouded in twilight, the beautiful château receded in the rearview mirror as the Jaguar sped down the drive. As soon as the car had nosed out of the gate, Lili pulled into the side of the road and collapsed in tears.

But the episode had not yet ended. In the following issue of *Paris Match* there was no photo coverage of Maxine's glamorous guests at her anniversary ball. Instead there was a single color spread under a banner heading that read "Château de Chazalle—A Place to Make Friends."

It was the first of an idyllic series of photographs of a young couple lying in a forest clearing. *There*, unmistakably, lay Lili in the long grass and it was undoubtedly Alexandre who leaned over her. *There* was a close-up of Alexandre's mouth and his hand on her breast. *There* they were clasped together and laughing as they fell through the spray of river water.

It was fairly discreet as these things go—no nipples, no pubic hair, no sex organs, no navels—but it was unmistakably erotic.

Andi Cherno's telephoto lens had snapped another scoop.

When she saw it, Maxine sat up in bed and burst into tears of mortification.

So did Lili.

So did Alexandre. He had been painfully humiliated. Lili had left without a word, and he had been ferociously punished by his parents. Nevertheless, he could feel the wordless, amazed admiration of his father and brothers and the awed respect of every single boy in his class.

But he would rather have had Lili.

CHAPTER 55

THE WINTER OF 1975 was unusually cold in Paris, and the scarlet Jaguar skidded slightly as Lili drove—rather too fast—along the cobbled streets of Paris.

"Slower," Zimmer suggested, as they slid sideways toward an ornate, dark green urinal. Lili steered into the skid, straightened and continued as fast as before. Zimmer said, "I don't know what's got into you, Lili, but I know something's wrong. *What is it?* We've made nearly a dozen movies together, and in the last year or so you've had two wonderful parts. You're only twenty-five and you've won every European acting award there is. What's eating you?"

Lili was silent. After Stiarkoz's death, she had felt like an outsider among the rich. She buried her grief in the one distraction that had never failed to absorb her—her work. She started to work with a passion and discipline, as if her life depended on it. Which it did. Even Zimmer was surprised by her fierce concentration and tenacity. He'd always known she had star quality, but it had originally been hampered by lack of ambition, lack of self-discipline, lack of direction. Now, at twenty-five, Lili seemed to know what she wanted, where she wanted to go. There was no holding her.

And Zimmer was the perfect counterbalance for their relationship. He knew, with cynical self-awareness, that he wasn't egomanic enough ever to be a *great* director, he couldn't be tough enough with himself or anyone else, but with Lili his work was outstanding and so was hers. She trusted him completely, she seemed to know instinctively what he wanted and he always drew a first-class performance from her. Until now.

"Why are you finding this part such a problem?" Zimmer sounded puzzled, although he knew the answer perfectly well. "You've got one of the best female roles ever written." He twisted around to look at Lili's profile, the little jutting chin, the slightly predatory nose. "Think of the women who have already played Sadie—Gloria Swanson, Joan Crawford, Rita Hayworth—it's a classic. But for the first time since I've worked with you, Lili—you're overacting. You're hamming it up. *What's the matter?*"

Lili snorted and drove a little faster.

"What you need is a man," said Zimmer, with irritating conviction, knowing it was a remark that always annoys a woman, especially when it's true. He wanted to get a reaction from her.

"It may be the answer for you, but it isn't for me. So stop pushing Schenk at me!"

"You're not very sophisticated in your business, Lili," Zimmer said, with a shrug. "After all, Schenk is putting up forty percent of the money for *Rain*. Why did you have to turn down such a powerful man so publicly?"

"Because he *asked* me so publicly! And he made it clear what I had to gain. Look where that sort of filth got me before I met Jo. I never want to go back to doing anything I'm ashamed of. Those pictures in *Paris Match* were bad enough!" The little red car screamed around a corner and Zimmer grabbed the dashboard.

"Oh, my dear, it's exasperatingly self-indulgent of you to ignore Schenk. You're like a self-willed little girl who's just been told not to step on a banana skin, but insists that she's got the right to break her own leg."

"Oh, God! Does the whole world revolve around sex and money?"

"Yes."

"I don't have to obey Schenk. It's not a royal command. What can he do, anyway? Ruin my career?" She snorted again.

"My dear, don't think he can't." The light from the dashboard glowed green over Zimmer's tense face. "Nobody gets a big role by screwing, but anybody can lose one by not screwing. Of course, it wouldn't be attributed directly to that, you'd be described as 'uncooperative' or 'neurotic.' " Briefly Zimmer mentioned the name of a Hollywood studio chief and a once-famous star whose career had suddenly seemed to dissolve.

"I've heard your story dozens of times," Lili said, "and each time about a different actress. It's amazing how people will believe anything if it's nasty enough. Look at the rumors that fly around about me, although I haven't slept with a man for months."

Zimmer said nothing. The humiliating episode at the Château de Chazalle had had the effect of making Lili retreat further into the shell of privacy that she had carefully constructed after the death of Stiarkoz. Now her reputation as a serious actress was suffering because those magazine pictures reminded everyone of the way in which she had originally become notorious. She slammed her foot on the accelerator and burst out, "Oh, what's the point of working so hard when my every move is misinterpreted to fit their filthy image of me so that they can feel better about themselves! You *know* how hard I try, Zimmer."

Zimmer nodded. He knew the tough, self-imposed routine she followed when not working. Exercise and dance classes, drama and voice lessons, early to bed and a careful diet.

At one point Zimmer had feared that he was in danger of becoming her substitute for Stiarkoz, but he realized quickly that Lili didn't want to lean on anybody, she wanted to stand on her own feet. She was determined to succeed, to carve her way like Jo.

Lili didn't like to think too much about Jo, for the sharp sting of her loss was still too painful. Instead, she found—just before she fell asleep—that her thoughts were turning childishly again to her unknown real mother. Increasingly, Lili saw that shadowy maternal figure as her invisible guardian angel. Yearning for such warmth, Lili had started to daydream again, to wonder who her real mother was, whether she was still alive.

The scarlet Jaguar swerved dangerously as Lili remembered that Sunday afternoon when Serge had telephoned her—speaking in his old masterful voice as if he'd last seen her only the day before. "Lili, darling, it's like trying to get the fucking President's telephone number. I've missed you, you naughty little girl, and I wondered if you felt like having dinner tonight, for old time's sake . . . ?"

Carefully, gently, Lili had placed the receiver on the table and walked away, leaving Serge talking to the air. At the memory, Lili felt so agitated that she braked too late and the Jaguar nearly hit a Renault in front of it. Impatiently, Lili waited for the light to change.

"Tell me what's wrong, Lili," Zimmer urged again. "Before you fucking kill us both." She was silent, so he thought he'd better tell *her*. "When an actor works on a part that's so close to him, he often can't see it objectively, so he feels frustrated and angry because he feels he has no control over his part. What such an actor finds difficult to realize is that what he has to do is—nothing." The Jaguar passed dangerously close to a truck, which blasted its horn. Zimmer continued gently, "You know what humiliation feels like, Lili, you know what it's like to feel worthless, *you* understand exactly how Sadie feels, so what you should do with this part is—just let it happen."

"*Shut up, Zimmer!*" There was an explosion of wrath from Lili as the little scarlet car skidded again, swerved around 180 degrees and slid sideways into an ornate lamppost. Lili and Zimmer were flung forward, then yanked backward by their safety belts as the car stopped abruptly—the right front fender crumpled like a discarded tomato can.

"Now, look what you've made me do!" cried Lili. "If you're going to analyze my acting and my character, you should have picked a better time!"

A small crowd started to gather around the sports car. Lili took no notice of them as she said angrily, "*Of course* I understand Sadie. She's basically a nice, cheerful tart who likes a good time because it makes her forget that her real life is such a mess and she hasn't enough imagination to see that things could be different. But that sanctimonious missionary rams home the fact that she's worthless until Sadie actually *believes* it. *Then* he promises her he can provide salvation, so Sadie starts to hope. . . . But *then* the dirty bastard rapes her and that . . . destroys her hope, rapes her soul."

A blue-cloaked gendarme was hurrying toward the car but still Lili took no notice. "That's not going to happen to me, Zimmer. I'm *not* Sadie—and no man is going to do that to me! I'm an actress and my imagination is my soul—what makes me an actress. I *had* to develop it to survive those dreadful years. It's all I have to show for them. That's why I can think myself into someone else's head so easily."

The gendarme had nearly reached the car. "Oh, I know I'm calm and efficient on the set. That's because I know exactly what has to be done and how to do it. But off the set I have to be *me* and I don't know how to do that, I don't know my lines, I don't understand the plot and I don't know who I *can* trust."

Zimmer nodded.

"On the set I'm a star, off the set I feel that everyone's sneering at me . . . and it's such a damn lonely feeling." She hid her face in her hands and burst into tears.

Zimmer opened the car door to the gendarme. "Officer, might I have a word with you? . . . "

As soon as Lili's name was mentioned, the officer's face lit up and the crowd doubled as if by magic. Within minutes six passersby had tugged and lifted the crumpled car away from the lamppost and Lili, now smiling like an angel, had scribbled autographs for all of them. She then drove off slowly as snow began to fall, having given the policeman an extra autograph for his mother.

"Bloody lucky that cop recognized you or we'd still be at the police station," Zimmer grumbled.

"I can live without such fame!" Lili said sourly.

The little red car limped through a pair of huge green doors and into the courtyard beyond. Zimmer and Lili dashed through the snowflakes to the door of the apartment building as lace curtains twitched at the concierge's window.

As they waited for the old-fashioned elevator cage, Lili shook the snowflakes from her silver fox cloak and Zimmer said, "Maybe you think you don't like fame but you'd miss it if it disappeared. Those people weren't threatening, they only wanted to know what you're like, Lili."

"*I* want to know what I'm like, Zimmer." Lili shrugged off her fur cape and threw it on a chair. "I want to know who I *really* am. I want to meet the real me!"

She kicked off a maroon-leather boot, hopping on one foot as she struggled with the other boot.

Zimmer chuckled. "I've had to conceal the real me for years or I'd have been arrested. We all have to come to terms with what we are, as opposed to what we *wish* we were. In the end, we all have to settle for what we've got—and you've got so much, Lili!"

"Yes, except what everyone else has—a family. I *really* don't know who I am."

"So what! Who *does* know who they are? Don't you think that perhaps you use your lack of a family as a convenient excuse for whatever's going wrong in your life?"

Lili didn't hear Zimmer's last remark as she padded on stockinged feet into the dining room, poured neat whiskey into a cut-glass tumbler and brought it out to him. Zimmer, who was throwing more logs on the blazing fire, straightened up, took his drink, turned toward the mantelpiece and blinked in astonishment. "What's *this?*"

He picked up a large white envelope covered with exotic stamps that had been propped against the gilt carriage clock. Turning it over, he peered at the ornate crest and started to laugh. "Oh, my dear, *now* how do you feel about your fame?"

He handed her the envelope. Quickly Lili tore it open, pulled out a large gilt-edged card and read, " 'I am commanded by His Majesty, King Abdullah . . .' Why, it's an invitation to Sydon, to celebrate the anniversary of his reign. But I don't *know* the man!"

"Ah, but he knows *you! That's* fame!" cried Zimmer, already planning what to tell his publicity department. "It will be wonderful publicity for you! *Now* you can't say you don't care about fame!"

Lili turned around to face him. "Do you know how much this means to me?" She waved the invitation in his face. "Nothing! One minute Serge is telling me to shake my tits in the camera, the next minute some king is inviting me halfway around the world. Who the hell do they think I am? I really would like to know. There's a part of me that's missing and I don't even know what part it is. I just know that I feel the emptiness inside me, and high-powered invitations aren't important compared to that feeling."

"High-powered invitations are always important, Lili. Especially when you stop receiving them!" Zimmer put his drink on the mantelpiece and looked amused, which further enraged Lili.

"Do you know how much this means to me?" Lili waved the card at him again, then threw it into the burning logs.

"Oh, Lili," exclaimed Zimmer, "don't you know how much you mean to me?"

He thrust his bare hand into the flames and plucked the invitation out.

CHAPTER 56

A THRILL OF trumpets rang out as the double doors at the far end of the Grand Hall were thrown open. Men bowed and women curtsied as His Majesty King Abdullah III slowly strode over the crimson carpet toward the golden throne of state, pausing en route to greet his guests. Lili thought the King looked more alive than in his official photographs, which always showed him in combat clothes or ceremonial uniforms.

Tonight, knowing that many women would be wearing formal white dresses and diamond tiaras, Lili had picked a halter-neck, backless, sea-silver-green chiffon dress embroidered with art nouveau lilies. As Abdullah reached her, Lili bent her head—a permed, gypsy-like cloud of dark curls—and sank into a curtsy. She lifted her eyes and gazed up into his, and Abdullah's sensual, heavy-lidded stare met another of equal power. He forgot his formal few words of greeting and stopped as they both stood and stared at each other in silence, both feeling an electric tension between them.

During the three years since his family had been killed, Abdullah had rarely appeared in public. Racked with grief and guilt, he had been unable to discuss his feelings with anyone. For weeks after the helicopter crash, Abdullah had spoken to no one and nobody dared speak to him. Occasionally he rode alone into the desert, where the silence of the sand soothed his grief but could not eradicate his memories. In his heart, Abdullah knew he would have other sons, but no other child would ever replace Mustapha—the only person Abdullah had ever loved.

As his royal master grew increasingly irritable and morose, Suliman racked his brains for schemes to divert Abdullah and had his head bitten off for his trouble. Abdullah seemed unable to concentrate on his hitherto cherished irrigation schemes or the desert reclamation and reforestation projects that had been his main interest before the fatal crash. A scheme to drill for underground water lay on his desk for weeks. He was listless, unable to work, without his former concentration and energy. Abruptly he canceled all plans for the 1973 festivities to celebrate the twentieth year of his reign. Instead of rising at dawn, he got up late, slumped through the day and spent his evenings watching old movies before retiring early and alone.

Then, one evening, he suddenly sat up, watched the movie with alert concentration and immediately commanded the projectionist to run it again. "I feel I already know that woman," he puzzled, "although I'm sure we haven't met and I've never seen this film. *Q*—strange!" He leaned toward Suliman. "Get her for me."

"Oh, Sire, this actress is well known in Europe. For what reason should I invite her to our country? And for how long, Sire?"

"Invite her with a small group. No, a large group. Oh, I don't know. Just get her."

Suliman saw his chance. "A reception, Sire? As we had planned for the twentieth year?"

"Oh, I suppose so. Reduce the original fortnight of events to a couple of days, but make sure this woman comes."

"It is done, Sire."

Now, as Lili sank before him in a sea-green curtsy and her black-fringed eyes stared at him, Abdullah took a deep breath and suddenly—at last—he felt alive again. He gave her a slow, unusually gentle smile and then regretfully moved on toward the next white satin curtsy.

Lili clutched her neighbor's arm. The long flight from Paris and the subsequent reception at the airport had been more tiring than she thought, and it had been followed by a motorcade to the palace on the hill. The excitement and the jet lag must have exhausted her.

Golden trumpets heralded two hundred guests into the dining room. White damask tables were set with silver and lit by candles. The meal had been supervised by a team of chefs flown from le Grand Véfour in Paris. Beluga caviar was served, then fresh sliced oranges vinaigrette, followed by roast duck stuffed with boned pigeon, stuffed with quail, stuffed with spiced rice and almonds. After salads, rose-leaf sorbets were served with pomegranates and grapes.

Abdullah, seated among the most important guests, was far from Lili. At the end of the meal he rose and made a speech of welcome, then announced that trifling mementos of their visit would now be handed to each of his honored guests. White-robed servants placed small dark wood boxes in front of each place, each exquisitely inlaid with a geometric design of mother-of-pearl. Every man received a pair of cuff links made from ancient Roman gold coins, and every woman found a pair of earrings; each was different from the next, and each had been especially designed by Andrew Grima, the jeweler most favored by the oil sheikhs. Lili's earrings were robin's-egg-size turquoises set with small diamonds and sapphires in roughly worked gold.

There was an instant buzz of delight. The speeches of extravagant congratulation from the diplomatic corps lasted until past midnight, when the guests returned to the throne room for dancing. As the band struck up "Oh What a Beautiful Morning," His Majesty offered his arm to the wife of the American Ambassador. Lili found Suliman at her elbow and together they whirled under the chandeliers. At the end of the dance Suliman immediately steered Lili up to King Abdullah, who smoothly requested the next dance.

She felt the warm palm of his hand on her naked back as, lightly, he pressed her to his white dinner jacket. She could feel Abdullah's chest rise and fall as he breathed. She raised her eyes to his. Neither of them said much as they moved together, each aware of the rhythmic breathing of the other.

As the music stopped, Abdullah murmured, "Regrettably, I must now dance with the other ladies, but I should like to talk to you later. Shall we say in half an hour's time in the jasmine garden? Colonel Hakem will escort you."

Lili felt the silky brush of his mustache on her hand, and as he moved away, she found Suliman bowing before her.

"I don't think I want to dance," Lili said, her face pink, the blood still pounding through her temples.

"Perhaps you would care to sit in the jasmine garden?" He led her through long, white marble corridors and out into the star-sprinkled night. The creamy moon floated in the sky above a small, softly lit garden. Great sprays of star-white jasmine hung from the high walls, scenting the dark air with intoxicating perfume. Colonel Hakem patted his hands twice, and white-clad servants appeared with a silver tray of coffee and sorbets.

Lili turned to the Colonel, but he had melted away and in his place stood Abdullah, fiercely handsome in the moonlight. He lifted the tips of her fingers to his lips and she felt the touch of his teeth on her nails, the soft caress of black silky hair against her hand.

"I feel that I already know you, that I've always known you," she whispered.

"That's exactly how I feel," he murmured as his lips brushed against her throat, "as if we belong together."

After that Lili remembered nothing but kaleidoscopic flashes of moonlight, the velvet night, the jasmine, the fairytale unreality of the shadowy garden, and the yielding couch beneath her, as her white arms reached up to him.

It was almost midday when Lili opened her eyes and saw the unaccustomed cerulean-domed ceiling and a brilliant blue sky beyond double-arched white windows. Abruptly she sat up in bed and pulled the soft sheets to her naked body. She was alone.

But she hadn't been alone.

Slowly she lay back on the pillows, remembering the feel of his flesh. Her visual memory was blurred. It had been dark in the garden, and later, when he had guided her back to her suite, she could only remember a dim figure. But never would she forget what had happened among the jasmine flowers, and for the rest of her life the smell of that sweet, erotic odor would magically, instantly, transport her thousands of miles back through time to the silver and black silent garden where, for the first time in her life, Lili had felt passion.

A servant slid into the room and bowed, barefoot in a long, white robe. Silently he offered a silver tray upon which was fruit, tea and the little earring box that Lili had left in the jasmine garden. Then he bowed and disappeared again. Lili glanced at her wristwatch, then reached for the thick cream official folder that contained the program of events. Thank goodness, there was still nearly an hour before the ladies' luncheon, after which the wife of the commander-in-chief was to escort the ladies on a tour of the bazaar while the gentlemen, who were lunching with His Majesty, would spend the afternoon inspecting the desert reclamation plans and models.

In the early evening the guests assembled in the outer courtyard, where a fleet of Land Rovers waited to drive them along the coast toward Dinada and into the desert for a moonlit feast. The men wore casual clothes, the women wore silk dresses, and each guest had been presented with a crimson wool *burka* in case the night turned cold.

The scarlet-robed guard presented arms; silver scimitars flashed through the air, to be held level with fierce dark eyes, as King Abdullah slowly descended the shallow, *bleu belge* marble steps of the palace. He moved slowly in public, his back ramrod-straight, his head thrown back, apart from other men, distanced from them by his rank. Never for one minute was anyone allowed to treat Abdullah as an equal in public, and very few were foolish enough to try it even in private.

Now, as his guests bowed and curtsied, Abdullah looked at Lili with no sign of recognition, but when all the guests had been ushered by the major domo into the long line of Land Rovers, she found herself seated at his side. Lili felt a touch, light as a butterfly, brush her left arm, raising the soft down, making the hairs lift on the back of her neck, taking her breath away. Apart from that, Abdullah behaved to her exactly as he did to his other guests—so much so that for one moment, she wondered whether she had imagined his hard, naked body against her soft white belly on that silken dark divan. But then her eyes caught his, that black, liquid stare met hers, lingered, and she felt a thrill of exultation, of passion and suspense.

As dusk fell, they bumped through a yellow haze and onto the rough desert track. Twenty minutes later, as they passed through a gully of blackened, blistered rocks, the moon slowly rose above the endless silver sand.

"How on earth can the driver see where he's going?" Lili exclaimed.

The King laughed. "The desert only looks the same to Westerners. A Bedouin can find his way back to the same spot again and again, with no more trouble than you'd have in getting from the Place Vendôme to the rue de Rivoli."

Suddenly, on the horizon, they saw the ancient ruins of an enormous Roman amphitheater. Three crumbling, curving, rose-brown tiers of arches were open to the sky: cunningly spotlit, from the distance, each arc of blazing light looked magically perfect, as if the amphitheater had been built yesterday. Silken rugs had been laid before the old arena, where gladiators had once fought for their lives, where runaway slaves had shivered before the glaring green eyes and open jaws of lions and leopards, where crowds had bayed for blood.

That night Lili again hurried along wide, marble corridors to the dark silent warmth of the jasmine garden. Abdullah moved forward from the leafy shadow and clasped her in his arms. She felt his lips on her dark hair, her slender neck, and then her mouth as effortlessly he swung her into his arms and strode toward the silken couches.

Before an hour had passed Lili realized that for the second time in her life she loved a man, but this time it was with a violent passion, a total abandon such as she had never experienced.

Much later she felt his velvety cheek nuzzling her. "Will you stay here?" he asked.

Lili had no means of knowing that Abdullah had never before brought a European woman into the kingdom, that he was flinging caution to the winds, that his passion for her was politically dangerous.

She hesitated. Her heart and her body told her to say yes, but her reason and her memory reminded her that she lay in the arms of an international playboy. Lili definitely didn't want to appear to the world as merely the latest in Abdullah's string of women. Since finishing *Rain* she had felt a growing sense of self-esteem. The picture hadn't yet been premiered, but everyone in the business knew that Lili's Sadie Thompson was a superb performance—and a personal victory for Lili. She was determined that *nothing* was going to rob her of what she had worked so hard to achieve—respect as a serious actress. But life was for living, and never before had Lili felt so alive and yet so at peace.

The premiere was still five weeks away.

A week or two in Sydon could hardly matter, could it?

CHAPTER 57

A *YEAR LATER,* Lili was still in Sydon. Those idyllic twelve months had seemed endless, and yet they had passed quickly. Abdullah was passionately devoted to Lili. When he was with her, his past unhappiness ceased to exist and he could think only of that moment. To her surprise, Lili found that her initial, dazzled fascination developed into an inexplicable happiness. She felt an extraordinary peace when she was with Abdullah, something that was totally different from the sedate calm that she had experienced with Stiarkoz and had thought was peace. Lili also experienced an unexpected respect for Abdullah as she saw how great his dedication was to his people, how awesome was his responsibility to them, how total was his power over them. One word from Abdullah could mean death to a man. Just a nod to Suliman and the servant who had been caught hiding in the Dinada royal garage, where he had no business to be, started to scream in horror as he realized his fate and was roughly dragged away.

"There was no proof, no poison, no bomb, no knife! That man wasn't allowed to say a word in his own defense. How can you possibly know that he wanted to kill you? How can you be so cruel?" Lili burst out, as they sat upon the terrace that overlooked the sea.

Abdullah looked thoughtfully at her. "You're wrong, I'm not cruel," he said. "Cruelty is finding pleasure in inflicting pain. I inflict pain only when it is necessary, and I don't find any pleasure in it."

He looked up at the sky and added, "However, I am certainly ruthless. If I weren't, I'd have been dead before I was sixteen. Some people find that after a shock their hair turns white overnight. After the first assassination attempt, when I was fourteen, I woke up next morning and found that I was ruthless. You see, the alternative was death."

She had come to accept the harsh reality that lay behind this life of luxury. She loved living at Dinada Palace. Poised on the outer curve of a sheltered bay, the palace was built into the low cliff and descended in a series of white, arched spans, down into the rocky waters of the sea. Each of the five levels had its own terraced garden—below her Lili could see white-turbaned gardeners bending over rosebeds as they tended the honeysuckle and white-starred jasmine that quivered against the palace walls in the light sea breeze.

Surrounded by junipers, cypresses and silver-leafed olive tress, Dinada Palace was a quiet, informal retreat compared to the ceremonial formality of the imposing old palace at Semira. Semira was where Abdullah waded through all the paper work, where he conferred with his council and his commanders, where he gave audiences to foreign diplomats and tribal sheikhs. Dinada was where they relaxed, swam in the fishscale-silver sea or in the underground, heated swimming pool which had been carved from the rock. Dinada was where they rode horseback along the white sands of the bay, water-skied, fished and sometimes entertained their friends aboard the royal motor yacht.

Zimmer had visited them twice and was due to reappear shortly for a few days before he and Lili flew back to Paris. Lili had made no films during the previous year, but Zimmer had eventually tempted her with "The Jewels," a classic story by de Maupassant. Lili was to play the modest, angelically virtuous wife of a government clerk who adores his wife, although he disapproves of her interest in the theater and her passion for imitation jewelry. "My dear, when a woman can't afford to buy real jewels," the little clerk says sternly, "she ought to appear adorned with her grace and beauty alone."

"Not that anybody can afford just to be beautiful, darling," Zimmer had murmured one evening, as he and Lili leaned over the terrace balustrade and watched the sun slowly fall into the sea. "A girl needs status, especially if she isn't married and is involved with a very powerful man. Status is what they understand and respect." He turned to look straight into Lili's eyes with a seriousness that belied his mocking voice. "Status is what gets a girl mass admiration. A girl's status can occasionally remind such a man how fortunate he is to have her—and how many other men would like to. In other words, my darling, status is what keeps him toeing the line and stops his eye from wandering when he's bored."

Lili had thrown back her head and glared at Zimmer, but he was determined to say what was on his mind. "It might be as well for you to remember, my darling, that although you are as ravishing as ever, His Majesty is not exactly famous for his fidelity."

Unwillingly, Lili thought of Zimmer's words as she moved slowly into her bedroom, a fifteen-meter-long room with three glass walls and a mirror-covered rear wall that overlooked and reflected the sea so that she felt suspended in azure space. Lili had already considered the possibility that Abdullah might tire of her, but she had shrugged it to one side. She would think about it only if it happened. In his strong brown arms, her face upturned to his kisses, entangled together in silken sheets, she could not believe that it ever *would* happen, that he would ever want such happiness to cease. But when, as now, she had been alone for several days, she sometimes felt a sudden dread, a twinge of panic.

Slowly she shrugged off the gauze gown that glimmered with gold and silver thread and was embroidered with real pearls. She wandered naked through her second bedroom, where she slept when the weather was hot. It was an arched room of similar size, painted the soft peach shade of her powder compact so that the room exactly matched her skin. This second bedroom had a three-meter-square sunken bed that was covered with cushions of apricot silk. The only other furniture in the room was a French Empire chaise longue, upholstered in Abyssinian leopard skin, and a large marble writing table with a white Saarinen swivel chair behind it.

Lili threw herself onto the bed and forced herself to assess her situation. This carefree luxury was all to easy to accept without giving a thought to the future. But she was twenty-six and *had* to think of her future.

Lili had been flung from her protected childhood to the harsh regime of the Sardeau apartment in Paris. She had survived her first lover's betrayal. She had survived the world's contempt when she was a porno star. She had even survived the shock of Jo's death and his lawyer's corruption and theft. After a struggle, Lili had started to regain her self-confidence and had worked hard at her profession, hoping for a reason to be proud of herself. She had tried to direct her own life, to follow her own path and not be dragged down somebody else's. And then she had flung all her endeavour aside for love.

She knew that Zimmer was right; she could not rashly abandon her career or her new, hard-won success. This sybaritic life of love and luxury could not continue indefinitely, and Lili wasn't even sure she *wanted* it to. Arab women couldn't understand Lili, they were as contemptuous of Lili as they were jealous of her. Their menfolk kept the women away from Lili, with her dangerous ideas of freedom. A woman's place was with the women, in the harem. Prudently, the men, too, stayed away from Lili; they wished no casual conversation with her to be misinterpreted by their King; few of them spoke good French or English. Abdullah's days were filled with official business; Lili never knew when she would see him, so although her nights were exciting, her days were lonely. She felt an itch to get back to work, to lead a life of her own rather than this soft, confined life as the mistress of the King.

The attraction that had lost none of its power to charm Lili was Abdullah. From time to time he would take her face in his hands and look into her eyes and then with one finger trace her eyebrows, her forehead, her nose, as if he were planning to sculpt her head or as if he were trying to imprint it upon his memory forever. When he did this he would smile at her gently with the same odd, infinite sweetness that she remembered from the first time she looked into his eyes. Then Lili knew without a doubt he loved her. But at other times, when he was preoccupied by some political question, he treated her as if she were a tiresome puppy that exasperated him.

He had never spoken to her of his wife or child. Realizing the terrible loss he had suffered, how deeply it still pained him, and how private and agonizing were his thoughts about the tragedy, Lili never dared refer to it. But she knew there was no possibility that Abdullah would marry *her*. She was an infidel. It was his duty to his people to choose a pure-blooded Queen who would provide acceptable heirs to the throne.

The painful part was that Lili longed to *give* him a son, she longed to feel Abdullah's child stir in her body, feel it kicking, take Abdullah's hand and proudly place it on her swelling stomach, watch her breasts grow big and heavy, ready to suckle his child. More than ever, Lili longed for permanence in her life and the things that most women seemed to achieve without difficulty—to settle down, to be married, and to have a baby upon whom she could lavish all her stored-up love.

There was another reason why Lili could never marry Abdullah. In this land, where a girl risked having her throat slit by her father if she were suspected of being alone with a man, Lili was regarded as the concubine of the King, and she could sense the polite disregard in which she was held by the Court. She was the King's whore.

And there was still another reason why Abdullah could never share his life with her—a reason that was also uncontestable proof of his love for Lili. She was a Westerner and, as such, an enemy.

The previous week, when Arab guerrillas had launched a seaborne attack on Tel Aviv, Abdullah had been sullen and preoccupied before granting an emergency audience to the American Ambassador.

After an early breakfast, Lili, wearing jodhpurs and a white shirt, was crossing the turquoise tiled courtyard of the old Semira Palace, heading for the stables, when she heard her name called and turned to see a beaming face that she recognized. "Why, Bill Sheridan, how wonderful to see you again! Is Linda with you?" she called.

The big Texas lawyer tumbled out of his official limousine, bounded over to Lili and enveloped her in a bear hug. Warmly, she kissed the old man's cheek. "Of course Linda is with me—getting used to being an ambassadress and rearranging every stick of furniture in the Embassy. We heard you were here, but I didn't expect to run into you so quickly. Now when can you come and visit? D'you remember the barbecues Linda used to fix in that place we had in the rue Monsieur? That's nothing to what she has in mind for Sydon. They're gonna see real Texas hospitality!"

He pumped her hand. "But *you* don't have to wait until we've got the carpets down! I'll bet it's been months since you had a good steak with all the trimmings! I've had them flown over from the ranch. When can I send a car over for you, honey?"

Lili considered. Abdullah was about to attend a *mansef* in southern Sydon and he'd be away for at least three days. "How about next Thursday?"

"Fine, fine, Lili, around six o'clock? We'll sure look forward to it. Now I'd better get in there with my briefcase." He nodded toward the arched main entrance of the palace and lumbered up the *bleu belge* steps, as Lili continued toward the stable.

When she returned from her ride, a white-clad servant was waiting for her. He bowed, then barked, "The King wishes you to attend him immediately."

Lili hurried into the palace, past a group of white-robed courtiers waiting outside Abdullah's chamber of state: they shot her sullen looks of hate and resentment. What had she done now? Lili wondered.

Abdullah was pacing the chamber like an enraged tiger.

"*What is this I hear about your consorting with the new American Ambassador?*"

"Why, Bill Sheridan is an old friend. I've known him and his wife for years!"

"He is an uncultured millionaire lawyer who happens to know just enough about the oil business and to have contributed enough cash to the Republicans to get this position! If he wasn't the U.S. Ambassador I wouldn't sit down to eat with him. You will most certainly *not* see him, or his wife."

"I most certainly *will* see my friends, Abdi!"

"I cannot allow you to associate freely with the Embassy, no doubt to be casually questioned over the hamburgers by that dog of a C.I.A. agent who calls himself the cultural attaché! We know you never see or hear anything of strategic importance, but *they* don't! And they all saw you being—*embraced*—by that American pig!"

Lili suddenly realized the significance of what the infuriated Abdullah had said. "You mean, *you* have me watched! You don't trust me, Abdullah?"

Abdullah turned away from her, folded his arms and glared at the orange trees outside the arched window. "You must understand my position! My advisers resent my—consorting—with a Westerner, and they cannot *afford* to regard you as trustworthy!"

Lili gave him a silent look of fury, turned on her heel, stormed out of the chamber and through the disdainful group of white-robed men gathered outside the door. *Never* had she felt so humiliated! Suddenly she wondered what she was doing in this heap of sand where she wasn't allowed to drop into the American Embassy to meet an old acquaintance.

By evening Lili had calmed down and she listened in silence to Abdullah's heated attack on American policy toward Israel as they were driving to Dinada. But at sunset, as they walked barefoot along the edge of the sea, their caftans soaked at the hem, she suddenly said, "How long is this senseless fighting going to continue? Obviously not forever. Why *can't* the Arabs make peace with Israel?"

Abdullah swiftly turned and caught her wrist. "For the last time, woman, I will tell you why war will continue in Palestine. In 1917, the infidel British decided that it would be a good idea to make Palestine a home for the Jews." He snorted. "But they didn't seem to realize that ninety-three percent of the people of Palestine were Moslem or Christian." In the dusk his face was bitter with rage as he took her by the shoulders and roughly shook her. "So those Arabs found themselves homeless, they were thrown out of their homes and their country—for the benefit of seven percent of the population and a lot of other Jews who had never *seen* Palestine, let alone lived in it."

Suddenly Abdullah saw Lili only as a Westerner, his enemy. He wanted to dominate and possess her. For a long time he had refused to admit to himself that he had fallen helplessly in love with a European woman. Abdullah could only see this as a weakness in himself and a possible breach in his defenses. He was alarmed by the intensity of his feelings and he was frightened of loving another human being as deeply as he had loved his little son, frightened that if he loved again, he might again lose that love. Exasperated by these mixed feelings, he again shook Lili's shoulders.

Sharply Lili looked at him, silhouetted against the blood-red sea. She stumbled, felt him roughly push her down, then she was lying half in shallow warm water, half upon the beach. She felt his weight pressing her into the sand as his wet hands quickly felt beneath her sodden caftan and with a grunt he thrust inside her—hard, rough, heavy, male, with not a sign of *imsak*.

Afterward, drenched and covered with grit, Lili sat up on the sand and scowled at Abdullah, who had flung off his caftan and was about to plunge into the sea. It was too much! Too much like one of those stupid films she used to make—and just as humiliating. Suddenly Lili was tired of being the wrong race, the wrong creed and on the wrong side.

"This is never going to work, is it?" she cried. "Constantly I am made aware of the reasons that I am *wrong* for you, Abdi, but do you realize that there is a major reason why *you* are wrong for me?"

She pounded the sand with her fists. "No matter how passionately our bodies are united *you cannot give me* your unreserved love." Her voice shook. "We both knew your position makes that impossible—but I'm not sure that's the only reason." She took a deep breath. "The problem is, Abdi, that you can't *trust* anybody—not even me—and you can't love someone if you don't trust her."

There was a pause. "It's difficult to trust someone," he said, his voice imperious and sulky, "when you know that however well you do your job, there are many people who want to kill you simply because you have that job."

"I could have killed you a thousand times if I'd wanted to!" Lili cried, wiping a strand of wet hair back from her face. "You withhold the important part of yourself from me and I find that unbearably painful and humiliating." Her voice trailed off, then she burst out again, "I'm ashamed of this part of you—the part that makes you deny me. I'm ashamed that I'm not good enough for you for reasons that have nothing to do with me. It makes me hurt and angry that you deliberately withhold your love from me."

"Your hurt and anger aren't because of me," Abdullah said, roughly pulling Lili to her feet and cunningly changing the point of the conversation, as men so often do when women get too close to the truth. "Your hurt and anger, Lili, are because—as you've so often told me—you don't know who you are, and you're relying on love to make your life worthwhile, to give it meaning."

She saw amused contempt in his eyes, as if he were listening to a child's outburst.

"You're right," said Lili, "I was." She was astonished to find herself using the past tense.

Abdullah was disdainful. "You Westerners, with your endless quest for identity, you never know who you are. If you really want to know, then why don't you try to find out, instead of simply talking about it?"

"All right," said Lili, "I will." She pulled her wrists from his grasp and ran away from him, along the lace-fringed, darkening sea.

PART ELEVEN

CHAPTER 58

AS SOON AS the press realized that Lili had returned to Paris, her apartment was besieged by reporters, the building opposite her bedroom sprouted telephoto lenses at every window and her telephone had to be left permanently off the hook. She lived in a state of siege, grappling once again with her misery and humiliation, but this time Lili also felt the impetus of anger and indignation.

"I know I did the right thing," she said to Zimmer, as they sat in front of a log fire and she repaired his vicuna overcoat, the lapel of which had been torn as Zimmer forced his way to Lili's front door. Lili bit the thread. "There, you'd never know it had been torn. . . . I suddenly realized the country and the people were hostile to me so that a break with Abdullah was inevitable and that the longer I stayed, the more painful the break would be." She threw back her head as she added, "And I felt that for the first time, I was deciding what was going to happen in my life. Oh, Zimmer, you can't believe what despair I felt, how miserable I was—still am—to be without Abdullah. I felt as if part of my body had been torn away, and I swear that sometimes I feel physical pain." She pressed her left hand to her breast and was silent for a moment. "But the odd thing is that I've never *once* regretted what I did. I'm proud I had the strength to do it. For once I felt really *proud* of myself. I expected to feel a sense of psychic destruction—God knows I've felt it before—but instead I felt grimly determined never to be humiliated again."

"Aren't you going to talk to the press? It's been six weeks since you left Abdullah, but they're still waiting outside—"

"—like a pack of wolves! For once, my private life is going to *stay* private—I'm not going to talk to anyone about it, Zimmer. What I want to do is get back to work as fast as possible. It's the one, never-fail anodyne for pain."

Dripping with fake diamonds, Lili shivered in the skinny clerk's arms. She was wearing a tightly laced, burgundy satin evening gown with a bustle and had just caught a cold on her way home from the opera. She was about to die of pneumonia next week. The skinny clerk's pince-nez fell off his nose, and he said, "Shit!"

"Cut!" Zimmer said, as the crew started to laugh and the skinny clerk bent to pick up his rimless eyeglasses.

"The spring needs tightening," he announced, "but I can probably fix it myself if you give me a couple of minutes and a pair of eyebrow tweezers."

The actor's pointed chin was covered by a short beard, required for his part as a Victorian government clerk, but Lili had nevertheless recognized his long, lean figure and the steel-blue flash of his eyes.

"I've met you before, haven't I?" she said when they met. "A long time ago on my first film—you explained what everyone did. You're . . . Simon . . . aren't you?"

Simon looked a little wary. "Simon Pont," he said. "I didn't think you'd remember." He'd already decided to keep his distance—to keep well away from Lili. He wanted no complications, no paparazzi, no PR-organized romance, just a nice, juicy, well-paid part in a quick film with Zimmer, and, please God, no trouble with Tiger-Lili.

However, during the next few weeks, Simon found to his surprise that Lili was not the spoiled prima donna the media said she was. She seemed surprisingly quiet, almost shy. She hardly ever ventured from her dressing room, but if the door was open she could be seen sitting behind a ridiculously large pair of tortoiseshell spectacles, reading a book and making notes as she did so. "And it isn't a pose," Zimmer told Simon over lunch in the cafeteria. "That's what Lili's really like, only I didn't bother to tell you beforehand because I knew you wouldn't believe it."

"But who's going to read her notes?"

"Oh, there's always some teacher or professor creeping in or out of her apartment," Zimmer said. He added, "You see she's relatively uneducated and very much aware of it. I think her little self-improvement program is rather touching and charming."

"She's very professional," Simon reflected, "and I haven't seen a sign of the famous temper."

"As a matter of fact, she's not short-tempered," Zimmer said. "She's medium-tempered. But she does tend to overreact if she's attacked, which happens quite often. Basically, she wants a quiet life when she isn't working. She's still unhappy about Abdullah, and she's besieged by journalists trying to find out why they split up. That's why she's a bit remote—she's wary, she knows that her most casual sentence might be misinterpreted, repeated and sold to a gossip columnist."

"What's Lili like when she's with her friends?" Simon asked.

"She doesn't have many friends," Zimmer said. He wiped his plate with a bit of bread. "Look, I didn't have lunch with you to discuss Lili. I want to go over tomorrow's scene, once more. When she's dead and you're starving and you try to sell the fake jewelry, because that's all you have left to sell, I want you to think what it means to you when the jeweler tells you that the stuff is all real. There are so many implications and I need to see them *all* on your face at that moment. . . ."

"What would hit first?" Simon asked. "Incredulity . . . hope . . . relief. . . . Then the realization that the wife he adored must have had a rich lover for years. . . . Their relationship has been destroyed. . . . But it also means that he is rich, free. . . . After all, he celebrates in a brothel, doesn't he? Do you want them to laugh or cry, Zimmer?" Simon was an established comedy actor.

"Both," said Zimmer firmly.

"Couldn't I *really* swing form a chandelier in the brothel scene?" Simon asked hopefully.

"We could give it a try."

Simon was agile and athletic and insisted on doing all his stunts himself when he was filming, which wasn't often, for he preferred the legitimate stage and the reaction of a live audience to the impersonal tedious repetition of film work.

"He's doing this film strictly for the money," Zimmer had told Lili, "lump sum alimony. He was married for years to a spoiled little bitch who's really stinging him. He's still badly bruised."

"Married for how long?"

"How should I know, Lili? Long enough to have a little girl, maybe seven years, something like that. Just avoid the subject, darling."

"Don't worry, I'll avoid *every* subject. It's not difficult. He hardly ever says a word to me off the set."

On the second week of shooting Lili caught her fragile gold link bracelet on a door handle and tore a link. "I'll fix it," Simon offered, picking it up as he pulled out his red Swiss penknife. Lili looked horrified, but five minutes later the bracelet was back on her wrist. "Faster than Cartier's," she said with approval.

"And cheaper."

Two days later Lili turned up with a bandaged thumb. "I nearly always burn the toast," she explained. "I'm a rotten cook."

The following day a huge, shiny, beribboned box was delivered to her dressing room. Digging deep beneath the tissue paper, she found a small toaster and a loaf of bread. Laughing, Lili thanked Simon. "He might not say much, but he certainly listens," she told Zimmer later. "Now, I'll have to buy a present for *him*."

So the following weekend Simon accompanied Lili to the Paris flea market, where, unobtrusive in a mackintosh with a turned-up collar and an old scarf tied under her chin, Lili liked to browse among the curiosities, hoping to pick out an antique from the junk. She chose a teak chest inlaid with an elaborate mother-of-pearl design for Simon, then she saw a group of Noah's Ark miniature wooden animal carvings—pairs of giraffes, elephants, monkeys and lions. "Oh, what a perfect present for a child," she cried. "Simon, would you prefer these? You could give them to your little girl!"

Simon scowled at her. "I haven't got a little girl," he said roughly, and turned away.

Afterward, driving Lili home in his Range Rover, Simon broke the silence. "Look, I'm sorry I was rude," he said, with visible effort. "I used to have a daughter, but she died two years ago. Meningitis. She was only four. There was no need for her to die, meningitis is rarely fatal now, they treat it with antibiotics. But we were filming in Egypt and there was a hospital fuck-up. It all happened so fast. She was so small in that hospital bed, shrieking with pain and we could do nothing about it. Jean and I just stood there, clutching each other, although we hadn't so much as held hands for years. Then they told us that she was going to recover but that night they phoned to say she'd had a relapse. We rushed around and she was lying there, very still and a horrible pale color. She died almost as soon as we arrived. She didn't move but we both *knew*. One moment she was lying there and the next moment she'd left us. . . ."

Lili leaned across and pressed his hand in silent sympathy.

* * *

Next Sunday they went to the zoo. Laughing, Lili was feeding a white goat in the children's enclosure, when suddenly she heard an unmistakable click. Simon leaped over to the two men on the edge of the animal compound and said, "Please don't photograph her. This is a private visit."

"For me, it's business," the photographer said. "Piss off."

He deliberately raised his camera at Simon. Angrily, Simon jumped forward and knocked the camera out of the man's hand, then suddenly the back of Simon's head hit the ground. "Plenty more of that if you want it," offered the second photographer, as an anxious zoo keeper hurried up.

Lili helped Simon to his feet. "Let's get out of here," she urged. "You're going to have a nasty black eye. The faster we leave, the less there is to report."

Back at Lili's apartment, she soaked a pad of cotton with witch hazel and the excess ran down his neck and soaked his shirt. "Oh, how silly of me!" Lili cried. "Look, take the shirt off, put on a bathrobe and I'll dry it and mend the tear. No, no, as a matter of fact I'm proud of my sewing—I guarantee you won't be able to spot the tear when I've finished. You're not the only one who can fix things."

The maid brought a tray of coffee to the sofa, where Lili sat in front of the log fire, carefully stitching the shirt, while Simon, wrapped in a white terrycloth bathrobe, examined the books on the antique desk. He picked up a well-thumbed *Encyclopédie Larousse.*

"Zimmer said you were studying," he said. "Do you read any philosophy?"

"Good heavens, no," Lili replied, laughing. "I'm not at all intellectual."

"Oh, philosophy isn't only for intellectuals. Philosophers want to understand why the world exists as it does and what the best way is to live in it."

"That certainly interests me." Lili bent her head and cut the thread with her small white teeth. "Here's your shirt and good as new."

"I'll bring something amusing to the studio tomorrow. You're right! I can't see where the tear was."

"I was taught to sew when I was very young," Lili said, suddenly sad.

On Monday morning, Simon told Zimmer of the incident, adding, "Who'd have thought that Tiger-Lili was a seamstress!"

Zimmer grunted. "She's always yearning for the quiet domestic life. The child in Lili wants the nursery fireside—but that's only one side of her, the underdeveloped part. Lili is a born actress and she's stuck with it. That talent demands fulfillment; talent stifled is personality stifled. She'll never be happy if she isn't working in front of a camera, however well she stitches shirts."

"She's amazing on camera," Simon agreed. "It's as if nobody else is on the set and she's having an intensely confidential relationship with the lens. I know *I* haven't got that magic."

"You don't even *like* making movies, Simon."

"Right, that's why I don't often make them. I was twenty-four years old when I had my first movie success nine years ago, but I knew there were dozens of better actors who hadn't achieved that instant fame."

"You've never wanted fame," Zimmer said. "But of course you've always wanted *success.*"

"I'd rather call it achievement. I'm still learning, but you don't learn in front of a camera, you learn in front of an audience: you learn timing and boredom-tolerance. You get instant brutal reaction to what you do, and you have to edit yourself instantly according to that reaction—and without any help. So I consciously decided that my first ambition was to be a good actor—it was more important to me than making a lot of money, and the place to learn wasn't in front of a camera, it was on the stage."

Later that day, as they ate canteen hamburgers, Simon read aloud to Lili from *An Outline of Intellectual Rubbish*. Naturally, Zimmer noticed and smiled with quiet satisfaction. Perhaps what Lili needed after two larger-than-life, powerful, destructive men was a quiet, intelligent fellow who wasn't more interested in himself than he was in Lili—someone secure enough to handle her with firm indulgence and give her the reassurance she needed. Simon wouldn't be jealous of Lili's film career, and he would understand the strains and pressures of it, he would accept that as an actress she would be demanding and fiercely so, but not in her personal relationships. He would understand that she needed more protection and attention than most men are prepared to give a woman.

Simon presented Lili with an antique orange circular tin music box. As they listened to the crystal tinkle of "*Au clair de la lune, mon ami pierrot . . .*" Simon stopped turning the handle when he noticed tears in Lili's eyes. "What's the matter, don't you like it?"

"Oh, Simon, it's a lovely gift. It's just that it reminds me . . . " She remembered Angelina rocking her to sleep as she sang the lullaby in the moonlight, while outside her little bedroom window, the pine trees rustled in the night.

Then Lili gasped with pain.

"What's the matter?" Simon asked, alarmed.

"It's nothing . . . well, I hardly slept last night, it's my back tooth. But an aspirin will fix it, it always does."

"Why don't you visit your dentist?"

"I hate dentists. It'll go away."

"No, they don't go away, they get infected." Simon picked up the telephone. "I know an excellent dentist; he's my neighbor and he won't hurt you, I promise."

It was late afternoon in the Place Saint Sulpice and the little Parisian square with its overpruned trees and the beautiful old church had the dusky purple tinge of a Monet street scene. Since the 1968 student riots, this charming, quiet little square was where the riot police parked their vans.

Astonished, Lili stood on the steps to the dentist's door. An hour beforehand the snow-covered square had been empty, but now it was a heaving mass of unruly students waving placards tacked on sticks. According to these, the students were protesting against the abrupt and forced resignation of a favorite left-wing professor, and they were all chanting, "We want Boulin!"

Nobody took the slightest notice of Lili, partly because she looked much as they did. When not in front of the camera, Lili rarely wore makeup and had the useful knack of being able to switch off her high-voltage glamour and walk down the street unrecognized, in a beige raincoat and a drab headscarf pulled well forward and knotted under her chin.

The novocaine injection from the dentist had left her face feeling swollen and numb. She felt groggy and her eyes started to water in the wind as she gingerly moved down the steps, hanging on to the rail. Suddenly she found herself pressed back against the stone building she had just left as a young man with a megaphone started shouting slogans and the students' chant swelled into a roar. Lili tried to push her way through to the street, but in the swaying crowd this was impossible and twice she was swept off her feet.

As the police started to spread out around the square, Lili pushed harder, surrounded by the student yells of "*A bas les flics! . . . enfant de putain . . . sale vache . . . salope . . . sale con.*" Lili dropped her purse and found it impossible to pick up. Helpless and suddenly frightened, she tried to push harder toward the front of the swaying, shouting crowd.

She was jabbed hard in the chest by an elbow and then unexpectedly found herself in the front of the picket line, facing a dark line of cops who were removing their capes. The capes of the Paris police force are weighted in the hem with several pounds of lead; judiciously swung, such a cape can break every bone in a man's body and yet the agent cannot be said to be carrying a weapon.

Suddenly the crowd behind Lili swayed forward then sideways, and she was thrown to the left against one of the banner poles; the rough edge of the wood caught her cheek, which started to bleed. Lili staggered and to prevent herself from falling she clutched at the banner, which read "*Reinstate Boulin!*"

It started to snow again, lightly.

The police charged.

The angry, shouting crowd fell back and Lili found herself struggling with a furious cop. She was suddenly more indignant than she was frightened. "*What* do you think you're doing? Stop hitting these kids!"

"Shut up!" said the cop, flinging Lili's banner aside as he roughly started to drag her toward one of the black windowless vans into which angry, noisy students were being pushed. Angrily, Lili fought back as a wail of sirens announced the arrival of the riot police, who tumbled out of their wired window buses wearing battledress, bullet-proof vests and gas masks. Carrying riot shields, cans of teargas and flexible rubber truncheons, they quickly formed a line and started to advance on the crowd to Lili's left as she continued to struggle with the cop. "*Vous faites une erreur,*" she gasped. "*Je ne suis pas une étudiante.*" As she flung her head back defiantly and glared at the man, her scarf fell back from her head.

"I don't care *who* you are! You're a pack of filthy scum," he yelled, as Lili kicked him on the ankle.

"Take your dirty hands off me!" she cried.

"*Merde!* You little bitch," he shouted, grabbing Lili by a handful of her thick black hair and reaching for his handcuffs.

As he unbuttoned his fur-lined overcoat, Simon watched the scuffle from the windows of his apartment. The students had deliberately provoked the police and the police had reacted in the way that French police always react. What else did the kids expect? . . . Wait a minute, he thought. . . . That woman reminded him of . . .

As she tossed her head and glared at the cop, her headscarf fell back and he realized that it was indeed Lili.

Simon ran for the door, leaped downstairs and fought his way across the square to Lili. He managed to insert himself between her twisted body and that of the cop, who still had Lili by the hair. Above the noise of the crowd, Simon shouted, "Wait . . . there's been a mistake, officer."

"*Ah, non, alors!* Fuck off or I'll take you as well!"

Simon knew that French cops are generally accommodating if you treat them tactfully and are careful not to provoke them, so he spoke to the furious policeman as politely as if they were both in a duchess's drawing room.

"I hope you realize what you're doing, officer," he said. "You do understand that this is Lili, the actress."

"Lili, my ass," grunted the cop.

"No, officer, look again," urged Simon. The cop looked sideways at Simon, calm in his fur-lined vicuna overcoat. Then he looked at Lili in her torn raincoat, her black disheveled hair, her puffy face, swollen mouth and bleeding cheek, her nose and eyes red from the wind. She looked just like the rest of them, he thought. What the hell would a famous actress be doing in this mob? Nevertheless, he paused to consider, the handcuffs dangling from his right hand. He'd better make sure before he snapped the cuffs on her, because after that he wouldn't be able to change his mind.

Simon said, "I would be happy to accompany this lady to the police station with you," and he whipped off his coat, revealing his immaculately cut, pale gray Cerutti suit. He draped the coat, mink-side outward, around Lili's shoulders. "*Smile*," he managed to whisper as he did so. Reacting as if to Zimmer's direction, Lili somehow managed to draw herself up six inches and flash a gracious smile at the officer who had been trying to put the handcuffs on her. Simon, still behaving as if all three of them were in the foyer of the Ritz, pulled out his visiting card and presented it to the officer, who looked at him again more carefully. Yes, he thought, this guy certainly *looks* like Simon Pont—he'd often seen him on television—and his clothes were unmistakably expensive. He'd better not risk it.

He took his hands off Lili and muttered, "Well, you'd better get her out of here!"

Left shoulder leading, Simon forced his way through the swaying crowd, protecting Lili with his body and leaving the puzzled-looking policeman standing with handcuffs in one hand and Simon's visiting card in the other.

Once inside his first floor apartment, Lili started to shake again from the tension. "My God, Simon, it was terrifying when they charged!" She couldn't talk properly because her mouth was still swollen.

Simon gently lifted the coat from her shoulders. "*What* were you doing down there?"

"Leaving your dentist. I was in there for over an hour. Then before I knew what was happening, I found myself in the middle of that mob and . . . I was helpless . . . I couldn't understand what was happening. Then suddenly that cop attacked me." Lili caught sight of herself in the cherub-encrusted hall mirror. "No wonder he didn't recognize me! I look terrible."

"You don't to me. To me, you look wonderful."

Lili peered at herself. "I think I've got a black eye. Zimmer will kill me on Monday . . . I don't know how you can say I look wonderful, Simon!"

He gave a Gallic shrug of the shoulders. "I like you without makeup. I like seeing the real you." He added, "You ought to have some tea; sweet tea is how to treat shock. Let's go to the kitchen."

He took her hand and led her through his apartment. She noticed the rich, dark colors, the book-lined corridors, the antique horse portraits, the cozy, luxurious warmth.

The kitchen, gleaming with copper saucepans and smelling of herbs, was a country-style kitchen exquisitely executed by John Stefanidis for a price that no peasant could ever afford. Simon pulled a walnut rocking chair forward. "Sit down and let me wash the blood off your cheek."

Lili collapsed onto the chair. "I feel awful," she snuffled. The Charvet silk handkerchief was whipped out of Simon's breast pocket. A runny nose merely made Lili look more vulnerable and appealing. He liked the idea that very few people had seen her so defenseless, he thought, as he boiled the kettle and then served tea at one end of the long, pine harvest table.

"I don't take sugar."

"You do today. Four lumps."

Reluctantly, Lili reached forward for the sugar bowl at the same time as Simon reached forward to push it toward her, and for a moment their hands met. Lili almost gasped as she felt the light touch of his warm flesh, unexpected and thrilling. Incredulous, her swollen lips slightly apart, she stared up at him. Simon stared back at her in the same way, a blank look of surprise on both their faces. Then Lili's caution about men got the better of her and she jumped to her feet. She didn't want to get involved with anyone. Clumsily, she started to button up her raincoat. "I really ought to get back home and go to . . ."

Simon walked across to the window and stared out of it with his hands in his pockets and his back to her. "Yes, of course, you must go," he said.

Lili sat down again. Then she stood up again. He turned from the window and she took a step toward him, her hand automatically outstretched to say goodbye, as is the French custom.

Simon took her hand. But he didn't let it go.

As Lili nervously tried to pull her hand away, she said jokingly, "I can't leave without my hand, Simon."

"You can leave without it or stay with it."

CHAPTER 59

FROST HAD LEFT a pattern of white lace that veiled the gray rooftops of Paris beyond the bedroom window. Snow started to fall, the scene grew paler and less distinct. Inside the bedroom Simon gently tickled Lili's toes, often a prelude to his lovemaking. For two years now they had lived together here in her flat in peace and relative quiet. Never in his life had Simon known such calm happiness. To his astonishment he found Lili undemanding. Apart from moments of sudden rage when she saw some lie printed about herself in the papers, Lili was quiet and liked a quiet life. They read a lot and listened to music, and Lili still painted on Sundays.

Simon wiggled Lili's left little toe. He started to stroke her thighs, to feel the little dark forest. On Sunday mornings he liked to wake her like that, and she loved to drift back to life, conscious of erotic sensations that slowly deepened into passion. Now, eyes still closed, she fumbled sleepily for him.

Much later he brought in a tray of coffee. Lili sat up, gazing as she did so at a small oil painting that hung between the two windows opposite the vast cream bed. It was a picture of a twisting mountain river that she had bought the week before from Paradis in the rue Jacob.

"I'm not sure I like that, hanging there," she pondered. "It's too small to see from this distance, but it's so pretty. It reminds me of the river when I was a child at home, you couldn't see it from our chalet because it was in a deep gorge and we weren't allowed to go there, but my brother Roger often took me. We used to catch trout there and splash in the shallows."

Her voice softened as, holding her bowl of coffee in both hands, she gazed at the picture opposite the bed. "There was a rickety old suspension bridge over it; the water was very deep in the middle, always ice-cold and very clear, always twisting and turning, always rushing and noisy, especially in the spring when the snow was melting on the mountains." She took a sip of the café au lait, not taking her eyes from the picture. "It was always prettiest in the early morning when the mountain slopes were covered with silver mist and the far hills just a smudge against the sky." She shut her eyes and smiled. "It used to be very quiet, except for the rushing water and the whine of the sawmill in the valley, cutting pine planks and stacking them, ready to metamorphize into another little chalet in no time at all."

"I wonder if you realize how constantly you dwell on the past," Simon said, with mild irritation. "Why aren't you thinking of building a future with *me?* We could build our own chalet in Switzerland with the planks from that sawmill. And you could start your own family, instead of always harking back to the one you lost. We've been together nearly two years now, and I'm damned if I understand why you won't marry me."

"Such an old-fashioned idea."

"And a good one. I want a commitment, Lili. It's 1978, I'm thirty-five and I want children. What puzzles me is that I know *you* do as well. Yet time and again you've wriggled out of talking about this. Is it that you don't love me? That you don't believe I love you? That you don't want to commit yourself because you're afraid that if you do, I'll dominate you like Serge and Stiarkoz and that bastard Abdullah?"

"No, it's not that." She was hesitant. "It sounds so silly. I just don't feel *settled.* You know where *you* belong, but I don't." She put the empty coffee bowl back on the tray. "Most women long to have a baby by the man they love and I'm no exception, Simon." She looked at him—a sad, long look. "A baby would be a new life, my rebirth, a wiping-out of the pain of the past, a fresh start with a family of my own. *Don't think I don't want that. I long for it.* But how can I have a baby, how can I take on such a responsibility, when I'm so unsure of myself, when I don't know who I am? I want my baby to feel rooted, settled. So I want to wait until this restlessness of mine has passed." Her voice shook, then hardened. "But it hasn't and sometimes I'm afraid it won't. I don't think it will disappear until I know who my parents are. And although I desperately long to know, at the same time I'm frightened of finding out. Because they might be—oh, unpleasant in some nasty way. After all, they abandoned me." She sighed. "Anyway, it's probably impossible to trace them. It's hopeless."

Simon said thoughtfully, "No, I'm sure I can fix it for you—or at any rate, I'll try. . . . At least if you found your real parents, you might stop looking for substitute parents in almost everyone you meet. That's why you're so vulnerable to these exploiters you inevitably attract." He drained his own bowl of coffee, put it down and said, "A man has only to say something in a reassuringly avuncular voice and you think he's Santa Claus; you'll sign any paper he puts before you. But Santa Claus doesn't exist, so stop looking for him, Lili."

"I can't help this . . . yearning." She hugged her knees tighter, laid her cheek against her knees.

"Then for heaven's sake, let's try to trace your parents instead of vaguely hoping they'll pop up out of nowhere," Simon urged. "We'll hire detectives. Your lawyer can recommend a firm. I've been thinking about it for a long time. But you must realize that you might not like what you find."

Lili moved her knees and the coffee tray lurched dangerously toward the edge of the bed. Simon stood up and stretched. "I think your mother was probably a young, unmarried girl who worked in town but who came from a country peasant family. You know how practical the Swiss are—a middle-class family would probably have tried to arrange an abortion for the girl, even though it was illegal and possibly against their religion."

He wandered over to stare at the little picture of the river. "Another thing—your father may have been married to someone else. I can't help thinking that if your mother had stayed unmarried and if she were alive, then she would have claimed you, or at least visited you. So my theory is that there was a mountain village girl who came down to the valley to earn money for her dowry, had a baby by a married man, then went back to her village and married some peasant and never dared confess about the child."

"Oh, I don't care, I just want to *know*," Lili exclaimed.

The following afternoon a detective called Sartor visited Lili in her apartment. He had thin, gray hair, parted in the middle, and wore rimless spectacles that somehow rendered the rest of his face invisible. He was neat, dapper, polite and expressionless. Her lawyer had recommended the Sartor Agency because of its international connections. He had explained that Sartor had contacts with a well-known detective agency in each of the biggest cities in the world so he could simply subcontract any work in that country to the local agency.

Sartor sat in Lili's sitting room taking notes on a pad that fitted into his left hand. No, she knew nothing about her birth except that she was supposedly born in Gstaad or Château d'Oex, Switzerland, on October 15, 1949, and that she was not the natural daughter of her foster mother. Her foster mother had at that time been Angelina, widow of Albert Dassin, a guide who lived in the village of Château d'Oex, Switzerland. No, she had no proof that Madame Dassin was not her natural mother. Yes, that was a possibility, but she would have imagined that Madame Dassin, a widow, could not have disguised her own pregnancy in that small village. Lili's real mother was definitely a mystery to the village—she had been teased at school about that. That Madame Dassin was her foster mother was generally accepted, although Lili was called Elizabeth Dassin. Yes, Madame Dassin had remarried in 1955, a Hungarian waiter, Felix Kovago. Yes, it definitely had been established by the Swiss consulate that both the Kovagos and the child, Roger Dassin, had been shot and killed by Hungarian border guards in 1956. Certainly she would like Monsieur Sartor to check that. No, she could think of nothing to add to those details, except that Madame Kovago had arranged for her to take private lessons in English and French elocution, and Lili felt that it would have been out of character for her to have done this of her own accord. No, her son, Roger Dassin, had not been given such lessons, neither had any other child in the village school. No, Madame Kovago had not given her any photographs or jewelry that might have had any bearing on her birth.

"We'll check the birth certificate straightaway," said Monsieur Sartor, pushing his tiny notebook into his inner breast pocket and standing up. Simon saw him to the front door and handed him his beige raincoat, still damp with melted snow.

Three days later he telephoned. Simon was away on a promotional tour for two weeks and Lili answered.

"Our Swiss contact has checked with the registry office. The Gstaad area is in the region of Saanen, which has a population of around 6,000. Two baby girls christened Elizabeth were born there on October 15, 1949. We have already traced and spoken to one of these young women, who is unmarried and still lives in Gerignoz with her widowed father. The other child was born in the hospital at Château d'Oex to a woman called Post—Emily Post. The Swiss birth certificate always gives the name of the obstetrician. In this case, it was Doctor Alphonse Geneste, who unfortunately for us died on November 4 last year, but our man in Switzerland has spoken on the telephone to his widow, who lives at Siedenstrasse 9, Gstaad, and they have arranged to visit her tomorrow."

"Goodness," said Lili, "Emily Post. That sounds English, doesn't it? Not Swiss-French, not German or Italian—which is what you'd expect of a woman having a baby in Switzerland."

"There is, of course, the possibility that it was a Swiss, French, German or Italian woman who assumed a false name—perhaps the name of a foreigner, perhaps the father of the child." A dry cough. "On the birth certificate the father is listed as 'unknown.' "

Another almost apologetic cough. "But if the name is genuine, then certainly the mother might be English, Scottish, Welsh or Irish. Or she could be Canadian, American, South African or Australian. Or perhaps she came from some other part of the British Commonwealth—Kenya, for instance—or even from some of the smaller English settlements—Hong Kong, perhaps. I will telephone as soon as there is further news."

"You're the policeman, aren't you?" The man nodded, untruthfully, to the shriveled old woman who had opened the door of Siedenstrasse 9, Gstaad. Her thin, bouffant hair was dyed an unnatural shade of blue. She wore blotchy makeup with blue eyelids and uneven patches of heavy rouge on each cheek. Her sagging neck was encircled by a thin, scarlet velvet ribbon and she wore a bright red jersey trouser suit. She looked terrifyingly decrepit as, with bent back, she shuffled slowly into an overheated, unfurnished living room.

"I don't know whether I can help you, young man, but from what you said on the telephone, one thing is lucky. As you know, under Swiss law, one must keep one's account books for ten years. My husband's go back to when he first started out here in his own practice in 1927. I kept the old books up in the attic and never bothered to move them." Blue eyelids blinked before him. "I was his bookkeeper, you know; that's how we met. I married the boss!" She gave a dry cackle and the agent smiled encouragingly. "I can get them down from the attic if you want, officer, although not today, it's one of my bad days today. Now you say you want to trace a missing person . . . a baby that my husband delivered. You said on October 15, 1949? A baby girl, you say, and the baby was fostered by a woman in Château d'Oex, a Madame Dassin?"

Again, the wrinkled blue eyelids were lowered, then suddenly lifted to reveal surprisingly bright black eyes. "Well, I don't need to refer to the books for that. I remember it very well because the girl was so very young—she was still at school—and because she didn't pay her bill."

"She didn't pay her bill?"

"No, the bill was paid by four other girls. I think they were all at l'Hirondelle, a school that closed about ten years ago when the headmaster died. Anyway, you'll find all those details in the documents books. I seem to remember that one of the girls paid cash. Those girls were very good to the young mother, and my husband also helped her a great deal . . . too much. But he had a kind heart and an eye for a pretty girl." She smiled. "Anyway, the payments will all have been noted in the accounts book. No, we couldn't go up there today—and tomorrow is Sunday—but Monday morning, perhaps? I'm better in the mornings."

On Monday morning the detective stood again on the snowy doorstep. The old lady let him in and, after a few moments of conversation, led him upstairs to the attic where the old records were stored in dusty piles.

At a snail's pace, the old lady moved up the stairs to the landing, where a steel ladder hung down from a ceiling trapdoor to the attic. "I can't manage that thing, young man, but you go up with the flashlight. You'll find the account books in the thirteenth file from the left, right at the back. You'll want the ledger, it's a brown cloth book and the year slip is pasted on the spine. You said 1949, didn't you? Yes, well, up you go."

Prepared for a difficult, dirty search, the agent gingerly clambered up into the cold, unheated attic and picked his way over the dust-laden ceiling beams to the back. To his surprise, he found the book he was looking for almost immediately, exactly where the old woman had said it would be. He blew the dust off the book, hopped back over the beams, carefully descended the wobbly ladder, then pushed it back to the ceiling.

The old lady turned the pages until she came to the right one. "Here we are, young man. The first entry is in mid-June, you see, under Post. That was the girl's name. And here are the payments, you see. To start there were three checks signed Trelawney and Ryan—and big checks they were—then a small cash payment from Mademoiselle Pascale."

A series of erratic payments were listed as being paid by J. Jordan, P. Trelawney, M. Pascale and K. Ryan but—according to the immaculate account book—never a sou was paid by Miss Post, the young mother.

Strange.

Madame Geneste couldn't remember what Miss Post looked like. She had never seen her.

On Tuesday the agent telephoned Monsieur Sartor in Paris, who immediately delegated to his chief assistant a search to check all Swiss finishing-school archives in the Gstaad area. He also wanted to locate the birth certificate of Maxine Pascale, probably born between 1928 and 1932, possibly in Switzerland, Belgium or France. Sartor then placed telephone calls to the detective agencies that he dealt with in London, Washington, Montreal, Canberra, Johannesburg and Auckland. That would do for a start. He wanted routine birth certificate checks on Emily Post, Pagan Trelawney, Kate or

Catherine or Kathleen Ryan, Judith Jordan—probable dates of birth between 1930 and 1935.

On Wednesday morning an overnight cable from Washington lay on Sartor's varnished desk.

JUDITH JORDAN EASY STOP BORN ROSSVILLE VIRGINIA 1933 STOP RICH NEW YORK BUSINESSWOMAN DOSSIER FOLLOWS AIRMAIL STOP EMILY POST ARE YOU KIDDING BORN BALTIMORE MARYLAND 1873 PARENTS BRUCE JOSEPHINE LEE PRICE MARRIED EDWIN POST 1892 TWO SONS DIVORCED 1906 WROTE MAGAZINE ARTICLES THEN BOOK ON ETIQUETTE PUBLISHED AUGUST 1922 IMMEDIATE BESTSELLER REPRINTED 99 TIMES IN 47 YEARS EMILY FAMOUS AMERICAN LEGEND DIED PNEUMONIA 1960 STOP PURSUING BIRTH CERTIFICATE DATES GIVEN ACES

So Mrs. Post was seventy-six years old in 1949 and unlikely to have been pregnant. But perhaps that was the first name that jumped into the mind of a frantic, pregnant girl who wished to conceal her identity? If you choose a fictitious name, you try to choose one that is in no way connected to yourself and yet is easy to remember.

By Friday, Maxine Pascale's birth certificate had been traced and by the following Tuesday he had a photocopy of her marriage certificate. Also on Tuesday afternoon, Monsieur Sartor had received a telephone call from London. Pagan Trelawney (christened Jennifer) was born at St. George's Hospital, London, in 1932. Married twice, presently Lady Swann, living in London, photocopies of birth certificate, second marriage certificate and current address upcoming. Her first marriage was thought to have been in the Middle East.

There were dozens of Catherine and Kathleen Ryans born in England and hundreds in Ireland. The agency was ploughing through them, narrowing them down by date. South Africa, Australia, New Zealand, Canada and America were also compiling great lists of baby Ryans, but Washington cabled NEW YORK JOURNALIST KATE RYAN BORN BRITISH FITS DATE NO BIRTHCERT USA SHOULD PURSUE? ACES.

On Wednesday Sartor put through another call to Washington and asked for a check on whether Jordan or Ryan had been at school in Switzerland in 1949 and if so, where? He carefully didn't suggest a possible location—that would be his check on the accuracy of the information he received.

By Friday he had further information on Emily Post. It seemed that the etiquette writer had not only been heard of, but also admired, wherever English was spoken. One had to suspect that some of the Miss Posts had been deliberately named after her. There were seventeen in the United States, one in Canada, six in Britain and two in Australia, although none had been registered during that period in New Zealand or South Africa.

On the following Monday, three weeks after he had been assigned to the case, an overnight cable from Washington awaited him. JUDY JORDAN KATE RYAN NOW WORK TOGETHER STOP BOTH GSTAAD SWITZERLAND 1949 ACES. Sartor telephoned Lili and asked to see her as soon as possible.

At six that evening, the doorbell was answered by Simon and the three of them sat around the log fire as Monsieur Sartor reported to them.

"I am of the opinion that the mother was one of the four girls we have located, and that if we are successful in tracing the Emily Posts, they will be found to have no connection with this matter."

Sartor gave his little dry cough. "But there *is* another possibility. If our Emily

Post exists, all four of the women we have tracked down will know about her. Do you wish my agents to attempt to interview them?"

"No!" Lili sprang to her feet. Her face was flushed from sitting by the flaming logs and her dark hair was disheveled.

"No!" she repeated violently. She thought of the screaming row she had had with Judy Jordan; the article that Kate Ryan had written about her; that terrible scene in the orangery with Maxine. She didn't know about this Pagan woman, but she never wanted to have anything to do with the other three.

Simon gently took her shaking hands in his. "My darling, you must realize that one of these women might be your mother."

"No!" Lili's wistful yearnings for *vraie maman*, for the quiet, kindly and gentle madonna of her dreams had, in an instant, turned to rage. It looked as if Lili had not been abandoned for pathetic and forgivable reasons by a humble peasant woman. It looked as if Lili had been *dumped* by some rich little bitch who'd been unable to get an abortion. She choked back her fury.

"I know three of these women, and if they have anything to hide, then I don't believe for one minute that they will see one of your agents. And if they do, I very much doubt that they will give away any information they don't wish to divulge." She thought for a moment. "I would like you to let me have a dossier on all four of them."

"No problem, madame. It would be easy, they'd all have C.V.'s."

"I will decide what to do after I have seen the dossiers."

Lili carefully read the dossiers that Monsieur Sartor provided on Pagan, Kate, Maxine and Judy. Her mother was almost certain to be one of those four women. She hoped it was Pagan, since she had never clashed with her. But regardless, Lili was determined to discover which one was her mother.

For some reason these four women had covered up Lili's birth, had kept it a secret. If one of them was approached, she would probably contact the others immediately and then they'd all clam up. None of them was a stupid woman; they were all brilliantly successful. Lili reasoned that the only chance she had of finding out the truth was to confront them together, to surprise or shock them into telling the truth. She would watch their faces, watch their eyes and their reactions. Surprise was her only chance of getting them to reveal something.

PART TWELVE

CHAPTER 60

OUTSIDE, THE TREES of Central Park rustled in a warm, October breeze. Inside the hushed, creamy opulence of the Pierre suite, Lili harshly repeated her question.

"*Which one of you bitches is my mother?*"

Pagan, Judy and Maxine had regained their composure after the surprise of seeing each other. Kate, however, standing just inside the door that led from the hall to the suite, was still too astonished to understand what was happening. She couldn't connect the world-famous Lili standing before her in a white silk gown to that remote incident in Switzerland or that little girl who had been killed while trying to escape from Hungary in 1956.

Lili tried again. "Which one of you bitches is *Emily Post?*"

This time Maxine flashed a quick look at Pagan. None of the three looked at Judy, Lili noticed.

"Unless you can really catch them off guard they'll either deny it completely or say it's Judy," Simon had prophesied. "She's the only one who isn't married. She's the only one who wouldn't have to explain anything to a husband. She's the only one whose life wouldn't be complicated by the sudden addition of an adult daughter who's a celebrity."

Lili took two steps toward the apricot velvet couch, clenched her fists and hissed, "Which one of you had a baby delivered by Doctor Geneste?" She spun around to Kate, still standing by the door in her smart mulberry suit. The memory of the vicious article that Kate had written about her flashed across her mind.

"Was it *you* who had the baby?"

Kate's eyes slid sideways as she looked toward the seated group. Thinking fast, she tried to counter Lili's verbal attack with an equally aggressive one. "Why have you brought us here? What are you trying to do? What's your game? What makes you think that one of us is your mother?"

"Because I *know* that one of you is my mother. I know that one of you four had a baby on October 15, 1949." Lili swiftly twisted around to Maxine. "Was it *you?* Did you have a baby in the hospital at Château d'Oex? Did *you* farm me out to Angelina Dassin?"

The coffee cup rattled slightly in Maxine's hand and a few drops spilled on her pale blue silk dress, but her face remained impassive and she said nothing. She was not going to be bulldozed into blurting out whatever Lili wanted to hear. Besides, the whole thing was impossible. That poor child had been killed. There had been official proof of it, that letter from the Swiss consulate. How dare this fornicating bitch bully them. No, this infamous gold digger, this seducer of children could not possibly be that little waif whom they had left with Angelina.

"Is Lili your real name?" Pagan suddenly asked. After all, Lili had mentioned Emily Post. How could she possibly know about Emily Post? She'd got the correct date, the correct place and the foster mother's correct name.

"No, my real name is Elizabeth, but Felix always called me Lili. Felix was married to my foster mother and it was he who saved me from the soldiers in Hungary. He threw me over the barbed-wire fence and told me to run."

"What happened to you then?" Pagan asked gently.

"I was taken to a refugee camp in Austria, then on a train to Paris where I was adopted. I don't really remember much about it, I was ill and only seven at the time."

Lili did so hope it was Pagan! She desperately didn't want to discover that her mother was Maxine, Alexandre's mother. The possibility that she had committed incest was too painful to consider.

Lili moved swiftly toward Pagan and crouched down, grasping the arm of the apricot couch as, yearning, she looked up into Pagan's face and murmured in a voice that trembled with hope, "Are *you* my real mother?"

Pagan looked desperately at the other three women in the room. Lili had a right to be told. Couldn't the others see that she probably *was* little Elizabeth? Pagan looked down into Lili's upturned face. All the sophistication and poise had vanished: Lili suddenly looked eager, trusting and very vulnerable.

Then suddenly Judy spoke. "No, Pagan isn't your mother," she said. "I am."

All heads turned toward Judy.

"I had a baby girl in Château d'Oex on that date. If you really are that baby, Lili, then I suppose—I am your mother." Judy felt confused and exhausted. She had thought her daughter dead, she had almost pushed her baby out of her mind. Yet now this notorious little prima donna was claiming to be that daughter! But it was impossible to think of Lili as the gentle little girl whom Judy had cherished in her mind and read about in Angelina's letters, which she still kept hidden away.

Upon hearing the answer to the question that had tormented her ever since she could remember, the pent-up pain and accumulated fury of twenty-nine years exploded in Lili.

"*Why didn't you keep your child?*" Lili cried. She sprang up, beating her fists against her thighs in impotent rage. "Why did you give me to somebody else? Why didn't you ever come and see me? *Why did you abandon me?*" She leaped toward Judy, and as she did so, Maxine threw down her cup and saucer and Kate ran forward with apprehension. But it was Pagan who thrust herself swiftly between Lili and Judy, who still sat slumped in her brown velvet suit on the edge of the apricot couch.

"My dear girl," said Pagan, "you *must* let us explain what happened, you mustn't jump to conclusions. We can all guess how you feel, but *please* listen to us because, you see, you were frightfully important to *all* of us. It could have happened to any of us." She paused. "Any one of us *might* have been your mother, and so we decided that we would *all* be responsible for you. In a way you had three godmothers, Kate, Maxine and me. We all wanted you, we all worried about you, we all hoped for you and we all loved you."

"And we all paid for you," said Maxine. "In every way we felt that you were our joint responsibility."

"Then why didn't you keep me with you?" Lili threw at Judy through clenched teeth.

"My dear," Pagan tried to explain, "you *can't* imagine what the moral climate was at that time. Things have changed so utterly in the last thirty years. Then, nobody *ever* even admitted that they had slept with a young man before marriage—even if they were engaged—and, in fact, very few girls did. You must realize that your mother was only fifteen years old, still a child herself. Please try to imagine how *we* felt. We were at our wits' end to know what to do. Certainly your mother couldn't take a baby back to America with her. She refused to abandon you, so we arranged for you to have a foster mother until Judy could get a home of her own for you to live in—and we all knew it would be years before she would be able to do that."

Pagan put her hand on Lili's shoulder and her voice softened. "But we didn't abandon you, we did what we thought was for the best. Don't you see, it was a frantic attempt of four schoolgirls to save one of us from disaster? We never, *never* intended to abandon you."

Gently stroking Lili's shoulder, Pagan was mildly surprised to find that she felt so maternal toward this tempestuously glamorous creature. Pagan had felt a twinge of jealousy when the newspapers had started to report Abdi's love affair with Lili, when she saw photograph after photograph of them together. She had to admit to herself that one of the reasons she had wanted to meet Lili was to get a good look at the only European woman whom Abdi had ever taken to Sydon, the only white woman with whom he had lived openly.

"The alternative would have been adoption," Kate broke in, "and Judy wouldn't hear of it. She couldn't bear to give her own child to someone else. She loved you. We all did. You *must* believe that, Lili."

Maxine said gently, "If it had happened today things would be different. Your mother would probably have an abortion at an early stage, but such an alternative was rarely possible in those days. And if your mother *had* had an abortion, *you* would never have existed. You owe your life to her, you know. She carried you in her body for nine months, and she had to work hard all that time."

Lili felt a sudden pang of guilt as she remembered that she too had been pregnant when still a child. But Lili had gone to an abortionist. The life had been scraped out of her body, and until that minute she hadn't felt a moment's guilt. In fact, what she had felt at the time was a flood of relief; Lili could still clearly remember sitting in that café, listening to the jukebox, sipping milky coffee and thinking that her troubles were over.

But Judy had not had an abortion. Judy had had a baby.

Pagan advanced her arm farther around Lili's shoulder.

"We *all* wanted you and we are all happy to meet you at last," she said, still unaware of Lili's disastrous encounters with the other three women, all of whom were remembering those unhappy clashes.

There was a moment's silence and then Kate walked up to Lili and said earnestly, "Lili, I'm really sorry I was so unkind just now. There's no excuse and I can't say anything except how deeply I regret it." She took a deep breath. "But Pagan is right, you *mustn't* condemn your mother. Couldn't you perhaps try to admire her decision, as we did? She was young and alone and we were proud of her. And we still are. She did the best she could. In fact, we all did."

"In that case, why didn't you look for me after the revolution?" cried Lili. She was still resentful and agitated, though she felt less hurt. She was starting to understand what had happened, starting to lose her resentment.

"We did," said Maxine. "Why don't you sit down again, then I'll tell you."

Lili sat with her back to the window, next to Kate, and Pagan sat beside Judy on the adjoining couch.

"Judy telephoned me as soon as she heard the news on the radio," Maxine began. "She knew you'd gone on holiday to Hungary, and she knew you should have been back at school, but she wanted to make sure. Angelina had no telephone so Judy phoned the manager of the Hotel Rosat, who told her that Felix had injured his leg in Hungary and hadn't yet returned. We were pretty sure you were on the other side of the Iron Curtain, so Judy caught the next plane to Paris and I met her at Orly. We went straight to Austria on the night train. When we eventually got to the border, we found that the situation was chaotic. Refugees were pouring out from Hungary—over a hundred and fifty thousand escaped, you know—and most of them were being sorted out in temporary camps. The weather was terrible, the camps were disorganized and everything was muddled." She shuddered. "We visited every single camp. We checked every single list, we talked to everyone we could and we checked every child we saw. But nobody had any news of Elizabeth Dassin."

Every night during their search at the Austrian border, it had been almost impossible for Maxine to drag Judy away to bed. Judy felt that if she left the frontier, she might miss some tiny clue, some pointer. Maxine remembered Judy's frenzy and self-accusation as they waited in the snow outside a hut, hoping to see yet another refugee committee official.

"If only I hadn't left her, Maxine."

"You had nowhere to take her."

"I should *never* have left her."

"*You could do nothing else, Judy*. Stop blaming yourself. What's happened is terrible, but it's not your fault."

Months afterward, Judy had received a short formal letter from the Swiss consulate in answer to hers, informing her that a family of Swiss origin called Kovago, formerly Dassin, had been shot and killed by Hungarian border police while illegally attempting to cross the border near Sopron.

Heartbroken, Judy never ceased to blame herself for Elizabeth's death. She almost managed to control her mind, but in her heart Judy had often felt the sudden, chilling pain of bereavement, a silent sense of loss, endless yearning and constant regret for what might have been.

Hesitantly, Judy tried to explain this in the unnatural quiet of that luxurious hotel suite. She found it difficult to find the right words. Her habitual self-assurance had deserted her and she was unusually deflated.

Lili listened. What was important was not that she should be placated, but that at last she should know *the truth*.

Lili knew she had to double-check the answer that Judy had given her—and she knew exactly how she was going to do it. Whomever the women now looked at would be her *true* mother.

"In that case," Lili said, "who is my *father?*"

CHAPTER 61

OUTSIDE IT WAS still snowing hard. If it didn't stop, there wouldn't be much point in going with Nick to Saanenmoser tomorrow, thought Judy. The 1949 ski trials would probably be postponed, so they might as well stay in Gstaad. Midnight had just passed; it was officially February 7, her mother's birthday. Judy had sent her a card and beautiful cream lace blouse. It must be awful to be thirty-five, she thought, thirty-five and stuck in Rossville forever! "Happy Birthday," Judy murmured as slowly she bent down outside the bedroom door, picked up a tray heaped with the debris of a meal, then hurried along the dim passage of the Hotel Imperial. In another hour and a half she could get to bed. She was almost asleep on her feet; she'd never felt so exhausted.

Eight months of too little sleep, tough physical work and the effort of concentrated study in a foreign language were starting to whittle away her youthful resilience. Longingly, she thought of her iron bed in the partitioned cubicle under the attic roof. She was lucky to have a room to herself. She drew a deep breath, puffed it out and straightened her back.

As she hurried along the corridor toward the back staircase, the metal door of the old-fashioned elevator was suddenly flung open.

Judy crashed straight into it.

Filthy half-filled ashtrays, semiempty coffee cups and sauce-smeared plates flew into the air and fell silently on the maroon carpet. Judy's elaborately embroidered blouse and scarlet skirt were splattered with dark brown stains.

"Goddammit," she said, and burst into tears.

The man who had charged out of the elevator looked uncertainly at her in the dim light. "I regret this deeply."

Sniveling with exhaustion, Judy ignored him as she wearily bent to pick up the broken china.

"It was clumsy of me. I ask your forgiveness." She turned a white, tear-streaked face toward the man and wobbled to her feet again, holding the tray.

"Don't drop it again," he said, taking the tray from her. "Let's clean you up a bit. My room is the second on the left." Balancing the tray on one hand he unlocked a door and beckoned her in. Judy followed.

This was one of their best suites, Judy thought, looking around the sitting room. He must be an important guest. Side lights were already switched on, lazy flames flickered from the log fire onto a black bearskin rug; glasses and a jug of orange juice stood on the low table.

"Sit on the couch," said the strange man. He put down the tray of shattered china and went into another room. When he returned he had a towel, a sponge and a glass of water. "I really don't know how you do such things, I thought maybe these . . ."

Dazed and exhausted, the coffee-smeared blouse sticking to her breasts, Judy drooped in front of the fire, wishing she were in bed with no problems. She took the sponge from the man, and for the first time he saw her pale and fragile face. Then she bent her head and he could only see fair hair as she started to rub at her skirt.

Judy supposed he was very good-looking, if you liked dark foreigners. Then she jumped. He had sat on the couch beside her, stretched out one hand and gently touched the base of her neck.

The stranger drew her toward him, pulled her head against his chest and slowly stroked her hair. Judy let him do so, surprised by her lack of resistance. But it was very nice. This soothing stroking could easily send her to sleep. It was *very* nice.

She caught her breath as she felt a warm mouth brush her neck. Then the tip of his tongue touched her earlobe. Slowly and surely, Judy felt her body relax. Her exhaustion fell away to be replaced by a softly erotic trance. As the dark stranger murmured softly into her ear, she felt an odd, silken sensation that she had never felt before, as if each slow movement was somehow predestined and she could only respond to it. She gave a soft sigh of satisfaction as she felt his arms shelter her in the comforting warmth of his body. She felt safe, surrounded by the silence and quiet warmth of the room, as he gently lowered her onto the rich fur rug.

She could smell the crackling pine logs, the musky harsh prick of fur against her face, the disturbing scent of this man whose cheek was rubbing hers, whose firm mouth softly pressed upon hers. Judy no longer felt in charge of her suddenly languorous body as he tugged the drawstring of her blouse, and then she felt the flesh of his warm mouth. Her body twisted as desire fought shame and apprehension, then she yielded to that mouth.

Sometime later she was naked to the waist and clinging to him, mouth to mouth. She felt as if she were swimming in warm water, in a delightful dream. Then she felt his hand cup her knee, slide snakelike up her leg until it reached the taut, black stocking top and hesitate for a moment at the black elastic garter. Roughly he thrust his hand up between the soft flesh of her thighs.

The spell broke. Judy jerked sharply back to reality. She couldn't believe this was happening to *her*. That she lay, half-naked, under a total stranger, had been eagerly responding to his hands, his mouth, his warmth as it melted into passion and passion pounded into frenzy.

She *had* to stop this. She tried to move away but his body pinned her to the fur rug. Still she struggled to push him from her body. But suddenly his breath was almost a snarl in her ear as he thrust his hand higher between her wriggling thighs, up her pantie leg. Then his thumb found the quivering point it sought, and at this new, sharp ecstasy, Judy again felt her body blot out her mind. She felt the strength of her passion crash against the barrier of her puritanical upbringing.

"Stop, stop," she panted. "Please. Please!" She struggled to get away. "No, I mean please *stop*."

He was far stronger than she and his body pinned her to the floor.

"Please, you don't know what you're doing." She started to sob but he fastened his mouth to hers. She could not jerk her head away from his.

Fiercely he yanked at her skirt and Judy heard the fabric rip. Then he was pinning the top of her body to the floor with his chest and tearing at her panties with one hand. For one moment Judy didn't want him to get off her. Except for her black laced corselet and stockings, she was now naked, and nobody had seen her naked since she was ten years old.

She had to *stop* him!

She jerked her head away and gave a wild, strangled cry, but the stranger thrust his left hand over her mouth. She couldn't cry now. She couldn't breathe. He was stifling her. He was going to smother her. Maybe he was going *to kill her*.

Judy had been alarmed when she felt her body respond to the stranger. When he thrust his hand over her mouth and nose she was frightened. But she felt claustrophobic terror as he roughly forced his way inside her body, tearing her flesh, plunging into her, gasping, thrusting. No longer able to struggle, Judy could smell his animal lust, could feel salt tears run silently down her cheeks and into her eyes. She cried with no sound, eyes open, blindly staring upward. Oh the pain, the splitting *pain!*

She felt her puny weakness, the hopelessness, the soundless panic, then desolate shame engulfed her as, with a wild cry, the dark stranger climaxed.

"Don't cry, little bird," he murmured, "why this weeping? The first time there is always pain, little bird." Like many men he didn't regard rape as rape if it didn't happen in a back alley and there weren't any bruises. He rolled over on his back, stretched luxuriantly upon the rug, and the fire's shadow blackened the lower part of his face and his crumpled clothing. Thank God for that, she thought, because she couldn't bear to see his thing.

At first unable to believe that she was free, she lay there limp, spread-eagled on the rug, then she curled her body, ashamed that he should see her nakedness, her humiliation. Then slowly she got up and staggered to the door—clutching to her body what was left of the traditional Swiss costume—grabbed the handle with a hand that trembled, flung open the door and ran along the corridor, naked except for black stockings and corselet, her only thought to get to her room at the top of the servants' staircase.

She spent the rest of the night trying to scrub him off. She was disgusted by the physical evidence of his possession, his power over her, that relentless animal lust. She was disgusted by his slime and her blood. She washed it off fiercely, hating to touch it, hating it to touch her.

Nobody must ever know. No boy ever goes with a girl that's been raped. She would only be despised. She had to suffer this misery *by herself*.

Once in bed, she couldn't sleep, she felt humiliated, embarrassed and oddly vexed. What a stinking rotten way to lose your virginity. She didn't worry about catching a sexual disease because she didn't know that they existed, and oddly enough, it never once occurred to her that she might be pregnant. Not when it had happened only once. Not when the Lord knew that she hadn't really wanted it to happen, that she had been harshly violated, taken by force.

But one thing worried her very much. Across the valley, above the dawn mist, snowcaps slowly turned pink as Judy reluctantly faced her anxiety. Had it been . . . that is, how *much* had it been . . . in what way had that incident been her own fault?

Had she led him on? And, if so, to what extent was *she* guilty?

For two days Judy refused to leave her room. Listless and pale, she pretended to be ill. Knowing that she worked zealously, nobody disbelieved her. They thought she had either overtaxed her strength or was suffering from a bout of influenza. Nick hovered anxiously at her door, brought her hot milk, homemade beef broth, glasses of fresh orange juice and aspirin.

On the third morning, Judy watched the red winter sun scatter diamonds on the snow beneath her window. I must put this behind me, she thought. I mustn't let it ruin my life.

With determination she buried her shame and mortification, lifted her chin and went out to face the world.

On the night of St. Valentine's, there was an excited bustle in the ballroom as pretty girls and muscular young men swarmed to foxtrot in aid of the Swiss ski team. Then the band slid into "Mean to Me" and more couples moved to the dance floor. Judy had just started night work again. During the holiday season you worked without query or complaint until all the work was finished, and the Chesa staff often had to help out at the Imperial on gala nights.

Suddenly the music stopped. Everyone felt that expectant hush that precedes the entrance of royalty, and the band launched into a boombadoom national anthem.

Two figures appeared in the doorway. The girl was Pagan, wearing a spangled cloud of gray tulle as she stood in the doorway, her hand on Prince Abdullah's immaculately tailored arm.

Judy almost dropped another tray.

The man with Pagan was the one who had raped Judy the previous week. Her dark stranger was the Prince of Sydon.

With a half-smile, he turned to murmur fondly into Pagan's ear, and Judy realized something else, something that upset and bewildered her. The dark stranger was obviously in love with Pagan.

Judy felt a rush of indignation and pain. Suddenly she felt again the humiliation and anxiety that she had felt on that dreadful night. She felt unable to breathe, she needed air.

Carefully she put her tray on a table, pushed through the staff swing doors, down the backstairs, out of the crowded noisy kitchen and into the starlit night. Shivering, she watched the black shadow of a dog lope along the silver walls of the street.

It didn't really matter who he was or why he had behaved as he had. If he was Pagan's man, she was going to stay silent. She wouldn't say a word and, by God, he'd better stay quiet too! Eventually, she rubbed her cold bare arms and turned back to the kitchen door.

She wasn't waiting on the top tables, and although Pagan twice winked at Judy as she passed them, Prince Abdullah never noticed her. It would not occur to him to notice the face of a waitress. He was accustomed to being surrounded by obsequious servants: they were there to give service, and he no more thought of paying attention to their feelings than he would to the feelings of a faucet or a chair.

On the evening when Abdullah had so unexpectedly bumped into Judy, he had just left Pagan, who had aroused his passion to an extent that he would never have believed possible. But she was maddeningly elusive. In spite of his rank, his royal wishes and the arts taught him by the *hakim*, she resisted him. One moment he thought that he held her, and then she would give a throaty laugh, he would hear that damned bathwater gurgle of hers, as physically and mentally she slipped away. He wanted to possess her, not only her body, but also her brain: he wanted all of Pagan with a power and an urgency that he knew he could convey to her if only she'd let him.

But he couldn't have her. She wouldn't allow it.

So he had left her, but his blood was pulsing with passion and frustrated desire as he crashed toward his rooms. Then there was a smash of china and that tiny blonde girl was weeping on the floor. What had happened afterward would be considered an honor for a serving girl in his country. Abdullah had been mildly surprised that Judy had disappeared before he could press a benefice into her hand, but apart from that he never again thought about the incident.

CHAPTER 62

BY APRIL JUDY had missed two periods and woke up retching every morning. She felt even more tired than usual, and kept rushing to the lavatory.

She knew why, of course. Her main reaction was fear—not of giving birth, but fear of her father and mother. Nothing so shameful had ever happened in her family. Whatever happened, she couldn't go back to America before it was all over.

Apart from her family's reaction, Judy also panicked at the thought of being responsible for another life. Although she rarely admitted it, Judy knew that she was still only a schoolgirl herself.

She wished she didn't feel so alone.

It was *so unfair* that she should feel guilty. But she was guilty, wasn't she? After all, she had trotted after the stranger into his suite. She simply hadn't thought about it at the time, had felt no reason for alarm. It had never entered her head. He was a guest in the hotel and she hadn't entered his bedroom. But then, before the seductive warmth of that fire, she had to admit that, at that moment, she *had* been guilty, hadn't she? Oh, dear, it had all happened so fast there had been no time to think.

Eventually Judy decided she would ask the girls to help her, but she swore to herself that she would never say anything about the person who was responsible for her condition, the man that Pagan loved. But she needed advice, she needed money, she needed moral support, and the girls seemed her only source of help.

* * *

Over the red-checked tablecloth, three pairs of eyes widened with astonishment and awe, three mouths fell open, speechless. It was what every girl dreaded.

"Who *was* he?"

"Was it Nick?"

"Look. I'm not going to tell you who he was, so please don't ask me. There's a very good reason why I'm not going to tell you, but I'm not even going to tell you what it is. All I can say is, there's no hope of any money from him or any help of any sort."

"Does Nick know?"

"No, and you're not going to tell him. In fact I'll kill you if you tell anybody."

"What are you going to do?"

"I want to get an abortion."

There was another silence. Hot bath and gin, all four of them immediately thought, but Maxine was the one who suggested it. They decided that the following Saturday afternoon, Maxine would sit by Judy as she drank a bottle of gin in the hotel bathtub.

Judy gasped and spluttered. With difficulty, she had eventually drunk the whole bottle of gin and now she was going to be sick.

"Please don't throw up," pleaded Maxine, "*please* don't. That gin was so expensive, and we'll only have to buy another bottle. Please don't waste it. *Please* try not to vomit."

Neither of them had expected Judy to throw up. Without mentioning it to each other, the girls had expected Judy suddenly to go berserk. She might start smashing things or run amok, naked, down the hotel corridor, hollering raucous soldiers' songs. It was Maxine's duty to prevent that sort of thing: in fact, she had an extra scarf in her handbag with which to gag Judy and stop the drunken singing.

Instead, Judy fell asleep in the bath. Maxine reluctantly prodded Judy's shoulder. She had never seen another woman entirely naked and certainly never touched one. This uncovered flesh was embarrassing for both of them. She prodded a bit harder, then shook the shoulder. Alarmed, she gripped both shoulders and shook hard.

Judy's head lolled sideways, she gave a little grunting snore and started to slip downward into the water. Quickly Maxine pulled out the plug and kept Judy's head above the water until it had all been swirled around and sucked down by the drain.

"Judy, get out," Maxine hissed in her ear, trying to heave the wet, floppy body out of the tub. *Mon Dieu*, how did murderers manage? She remembered that man who drowned six brides in turn, having thoughtfully insured their lives. Who would have thought little Judy could be so heavy? Maxine hoped she wouldn't have to call Nick. She'd sworn not to tell him.

Eventually Maxine removed her shoes, stockings and skirt, climbed into the tub herself, pushed Judy's head over the side, pushed each wet arm over the rim, then heaved Judy up around her middle so that her shoulders fell over the side of the tub, then heaved on her waist again until Judy slithered unconscious over the side of the bath and lay beaming on the wet green linoleum. Maxine wrapped her dressing gown around Judy's floppy body and half-carried, half-dragged her back to her room and onto the iron bedstead. Maxine covered her with a quilt, toweled her hair dry, sat with her until seven o'clock and then quietly left.

But nothing happened.

"I think there are some pills you can take," Kate said. It was the first day of May. "My cousin Tessa's a student nurse. She's a bloody smug prig and I'm not sure she'll help, but I'll write to her and say it's urgent."

She wrote off to her cousin, who immediately assumed that Kate was pregnant and airmailed her a box of Black Magic chocolates. The second layer contained a phial of little pink capsules, stilbestrol, the cousin explained in her letter. She didn't know if they would work, but one should try taking them over two days.

That's what Judy did, but nothing happened—except that she felt sick for two whole days instead of only in the morning.

Pagan had privately decided that if nothing had happened by June 1, then she would ask Paul for help. Surely he, the headmaster's driver, must have encountered this problem before? Naturally, he would think that it was *she* who had the difficulty. Pagan had the sinking feeling that if she asked Paul for a small favor, he would ask her for a big one in return. But she would try playing that card if all else failed.

In the meantime, Maxine had suggested that they simply do the obvious thing and ask a pharmacist.

As the only fluent French speaker, Maxine hung around the doorway of the pharmacy for an hour before she dared enter. She gazed with feigned absorption at the window, lined with white-china, gold-lettered apothecary jars, until the shop was empty of customers. Then she went inside and, blushing so hard that she looked as if she were suffering from a bad case of sunburn, she asked the pharmacist if he could give her some medicine to bring on a period.

How long overdue?

"Four months."

The pharmacist's face was immediately wiped of expression. It was like speaking to an automaton, thought Maxine. He said, "You mustn't consult me, you must ask a doctor. Try Doctor Geneste, he's a gynecologist. A very sympathetic man. I regret that I can sell you nothing." He wrote down an address and handed it to Maxine, who couldn't get out of the shop fast enough.

Once outside and around the corner she leaned against a stone wall until she regained her self-possession. Then she asked the way to the gynecologist.

It was an old-fashioned house in a quiet street. Maxine looked for a long time at the worn brass plate on the olive-green front door, then slowly lifted her hand to the doorbell.

A nurse with low-heeled white shoes, a white uniform and an empty face opened the door. Maxine asked to make an appointment with the doctor. "Speak up," said the nurse, "I can't hear you. What's your name?"

But Maxine found it impossible to raise her voice above a whisper. "It's not for me," she said. "It's for a friend." Hurriedly, she gave the false name that Judy had suggested.

The following Saturday Judy stood outside the olive-green door accompanied by Maxine. The girls sat silently in the reception room until they were beckoned into the consulting room by the impassive nurse. The consulting room was a cream cubicle with two metal chairs in front of a pine desk. On the desk stood a telephone, an old-fashioned brass dinner bell, a large diary, a scribbling pad and a small green-glass jar of cornflowers. In one corner of the room stood a green cotton screen, and in another was a white porcelain sink over which the doctor bent, his back to them.

The girls could smell the faint, reassuring odor of antiseptic as he turned around to face them. He wasn't a cross, fat French doctor, as they had both feared. He was tall, thin, relatively young and handsome—rather like Gary Cooper, Maxine thought.

He treated them like adults. They agreed that the weather was wonderful. Then, in a kind voice, he asked, "How long has it been since your last period?"

"I think the third week in January," said Judy. "I mean, I never took much notice."

There was a silence. "Better check whether or not there is real cause for alarm," he said. "I would like to examine you, so perhaps your friend won't mind waiting outside."

Judy took her clothes off behind the screen and stood shivering, not wanting to leave its protection. Then she put on the sleeveless gown that was folded over the screen and sat with her legs dangling over the side of the high examination couch, at the end of which were fixed two unnerving stainless-steel stirrups.

"You must remember that I am here to help you. There is no need to be frightened. I have to make an examination. But I am a doctor and you must regard me as your confidant, not as a man, and my nurse will be here. Now, have I your permission to examine you?" Judy nodded. He rang the brass bell for the nurse. "Now please just lie back and rest your legs on the stirrups." Shutting her eyes and feeling unbearably humiliated, Judy lay on her back and allowed her legs to be pulled apart and propped into the impersonal steel stirrups. She felt a probing of rubber-gloved fingers. She heard sticky, greasy sounds. Then he helped her down. The nurse left the room and Judy went behind the screen again to dress. Maxine returned.

The doctor sat behind his desk looking gravely at the girls. "Of course, I will do tests. But I don't need tests to know that this miss is almost certainly four months pregnant."

Judy felt the black despair. No hope. She was caught. Trapped. She wanted to scream and stamp. She would refuse. She would demand a replay. It could *not* happen. Not to *her*. Why, why, *why?*

The doctor said that abortions were illegal. In any case, miss might be twenty weeks pregnant, so it was too late. If they did not mind his saying so, the question was not whether miss was pregnant, not how to get rid of this baby, but rather to consider where and when it would be born. There was another silence, then casually the doctor asked if the father was likely to be supportive.

"No."

"Ah."

Another long silence. Then the doctor added that he understood Judy's situation and he would like to assure her that it was not nearly so rare as she supposed. He had attended other young ladies in similar situations and was used to exercising discretion in these matters. It would almost certainly be possible to keep the matter secret, but the problem was Judy's age, her parents would have to be told.

"That's not possible, both my parents are dead," Judy heard herself say.

The gynecologist looked skeptical. "Then who are your guardians?"

"My elder sister, who's married," she said. Then, with a flash of inspiration, "My sister, Judy—Judy Jordan." Innocent navy-blue eyes stared at him.

"Then I must write to your sister and inform her of these matters and ask her permission to care for you. There is also the matter of payment. Where you have your baby depends quite frankly on what you can afford."

"There will be no problem about payment," said Maxine swiftly. Judy opened her mouth, then shut it again. They were talking as if having a baby were no more of a problem than buying a pair of skis.

But already, sitting in this neat consulting room and talking to an adult, she felt calmer. Perhaps it wouldn't be so terrible, provided her parents never found out. Perhaps, after all, it wasn't the end of the world. And she didn't know quite how to describe the sensation, but her feelings had altered in the last month in a very strange way. It was as if the rest of the world didn't really matter. What mattered was that under her rotund little stomach (now hard as a tennis ball) she had felt a sort of flutter, a butterfly-wing touch.

In fact she thought it *might* have moved.

Suddenly she had realized that *this was a real baby*. It was *her* baby. To Judy's surprise, she had dwelt on this private thought with catlike complacency, and after those first moments of panic, when she faced the doctor, this feeling of smug unreality had returned to her.

The gynecologist was saying, "After the baby is born you will have three choices. You can keep the baby; the baby can be adopted; or it can be cared for by foster parents until your life is more settled."

He carefully rearranged the little blue flowers in the green jar. "If you have the baby adopted, then you will have to say goodbye to your child forever, but the advantage would be that you will never have to pay anything. On the other hand, if you find foster parents for the baby, then you would have to pay for its keep, because the child would still be yours."

He looked up at Judy gently and said, "Naturally, you can't decide such things immediately. You will no doubt wish to consult your sister."

"Look, I can tell you right away what I'd *like* to do," said Judy. Suddenly she felt that her baby was not rubbish to be gotten rid of, not an unwanted pet to be handed over to somebody else. Her baby was lying there under her heart, curled up in her body. Already it had a little nose and mouth and minuscule fingers. It *was* her flesh and blood. She couldn't hand that to somebody else, like a parcel over a post office counter.

Without much logical thought, but with already developed maternal instincts, Judy suddenly heard herself say, "I want to keep it. I don't want to give my baby away. I would like to find my baby foster parents until I'm old enough to have a home of my own for him."

"Well, that is something to be thought over carefully," Doctor Geneste said. "We can discuss it on your next visit."

Afterward the two girls went to a quiet tearoom. "Why did you say there would be no problem about money?" Judy wanted to know.

"Because there won't be. I'll talk to the others tonight. Between the three of us we should surely be able to raise the money for your medical bills."

* * *

It was after midnight. The white lace curtains had not been drawn back from the window. In front of the silver rectangle, three dark figures sat whispering on Maxine's bed. "Doctor Geneste said that the hospital fees would be about one thousand Swiss francs. Between us we can almost certainly raise that amount. He said that to put a child in a foster home costs five hundred francs a month. That's six thousand francs a year."

Maxine summed up the financial situation on her fingers. "That's fifteen hundred Swiss francs a year from each of us. Now the question is, can we afford it?"

"Only twice as much as stabling a horse in London," Pagan offered. They all pondered.

The girls treated Judy's pregnancy with the awed respect and horror of those who had narrowly escaped such a dreadful fate, and were therefore prepared to make a financial sacrifice of thanksgiving. They also regarded the situation as if it were a school escapade in a girl's adventure book, desperate but not immoral. They, her friends, would stand staunchly by Judy. With the cheerful idealism of girls who have never had to face a truly serious situation, they all agreed that they wanted to help support the child.

"I'll have to tell some enormous lie," said Kate thoughtfully. They all told lies and only regarded lying to each other as a sin. "I'm sure that if I can think of a real whopper, I'll get money from my father. The only problem is that he might be very inquisitive."

Maxine said, "Aunt Hortense has promised me a dress allowance when I get back to Paris. It won't be much, but I'll also have an allowance from Papa. I'm sure that somehow I can scrape up thirty Swiss francs a week."

After a great deal of arithmetical plotting, Kate wrote and asked her father if he would send a contribution to the Gstaad Athletic Fund. As Miss Gstaad, she wanted to make a truly magnificent contribution.

By return post came a letter from Kate's father saying that he'd asked the headmaster to advance her four hundred pounds, and was delighted that his girlie was featuring so prominently in local life.

The same evening Pagan clattered up the wooden stairs, burst into the bedroom and triumphantly flung a sheaf of francs onto Kate's bed. "*My* contribution! Three thousand six hundred francs."

Maxine gaped at the notes. "But how generous of your mother!"

"Oh, I didn't ask her! I wouldn't have got a sou from *her*. No, I took my pearl necklace to Cartier. . . . I've always hated the bloody thing! Every birthday I was given two extra pearls to add to it. . . . Cartier wouldn't buy it—they only buy back their own stuff—but they were terrifically kind and that little man with the pince-nez took me to another jeweler, who at first offered two thousand, but pince-nez beat him up to that." She pointed gleefully to the money on the bed. "The only other thing I had to sell was Grandfather's signet ring, and that really would have been painful, so I'm glad it wasn't necessary."

Those two sums alone would take care of the first two years. They had plenty of time later to plot where they'd get the next payments.

Maxine was only able to pay three hundred Swiss francs in cash from her allowance. She couldn't manage to squeeze another sou from her family, but she asked her papa if her stay at l'Hirondelle could be extended so that she could sit for the French Commercial Diploma in the autumn. She was taking the course anyway, and as the class proceeded at the snail's pace of the non-French-speaking girls, it would not require much work to pass the course. Thus she could stay in Gstaad until Christmas and look after Judy until the baby was born.

Judy's next visit to the gynecologist was calm and reassuring. Nothing is really important except birth and death, and the people who sat in that small consulting room only thought hopefully and happily of birth. Other problems, such as money and danger, seemed distant and unreal. What was important to them and Doctor Geneste was that nothing should upset his mothers and their babies.

By Judy's third visit, Doctor Geneste had received a letter from Miss Post's sister. She thought that under the circumstances, the doctor was doing the right thing for her sister Emily. She herself had only recently married and didn't want to take on someone else's child at the moment, but Emily could rely on them for help when she returned to the United States.

"She isn't much of a letter-writer, but I knew I could count on her," said Judy, whose parents had forwarded Doctor Geneste's letter to her. She had immediately written and thanked her mother for forwarding the letter—a dentist's bill mistakenly sent to her U.S. address instead of the hotel. She then wrote a reply from her "sister" to Doctor Geneste, addressed the envelope to Monsieur Geneste rather than Doctor, and sent it to a girlfriend in Rossville. Judy asked her to post it to Switzerland, explaining that it was a brush-off letter to a boy and Judy wanted him to think she was back in the United States.

By her fourth visit, Doctor Geneste said he had heard of a suitable woman to be a foster mother. Farther along the valley in the village of Château d'Oex was a hospital where he worked as a consultant. One of their ward maids, a young widow with a baby, had applied to be a foster mother. She was strongly recommended by the hospital as quiet and reliable. Would Miss Post care to visit her?

The following Saturday, Maxine and Judy caught the little blue bus and traveled up the valley. It was a narrow valley, with low-lying fields and a few clusters of chalets around a gray church with a very thin spire. It was midsummer and the cows had been taken up to the mountain pastures. The bus passed through fields thickly sprinkled with wild flowers under a sky that was the same color as the wild forget-me-nots at the side of the road.

Judy had felt miserable for months. She only felt calm in the doctor's consulting room. But suddenly she felt indescribably happy and contented as they bounced along that little country road. Furtively, she felt the hard curve under her coat. For the first time she longed for it to grow bigger.

Angelina Dassin was waiting for them by the fountain in the cobbled square. A young woman with dark hair drawn back in a bun, she had the rather gaunt, highly colored face that is typical of that region. She was carrying a black-eyed, solemn baby boy whom she shifted onto her left hip in order to shake hands with them.

They all walked through the village to the dark wooden chalet with the fish-scale-tiled roof. Madame Dassin had been told the situation and felt sorry for this small, forlorn blonde child. While Madame Dassin went for glasses of fresh milk, Maxine and Judy sat in the barely furnished living room and looked at the spectacular view across the valley to the snow-topped mountains.

Both Judy and Maxine thought this rustic scene ideal. The atmosphere was one of serenity, the little boy seemed a lively child and Madame Dassin seemed to live up to her hospital recommendation. So they arranged that Judy would move into the chalet for two weeks after she stopped work, before the baby was born. After the birth, she would then rest at the chalet for a month while she breast-fed the baby. Both girls earnestly stressed that, when Judy was older and had a home of her own, she would wish to take back her child. Madame Dassin nodded.

Maxine added that, at the suggestion of Doctor Geneste, Judy did not want the child told any details about Judy, other than that one day his mother would come and take him to his real home. There was to be no attempt to deceive the child by telling him that Madame Dassin was the natural mother.

Angelina Dassin agreed to this. "What do you intend to call your baby?" she asked.

Hunched in a shabby armchair, Judy looked out the window across to the sharp Alpine skyline and said, "If it's a girl it will be Elizabeth after my mother. If it's a boy it will be Nicholas."

Maxine wasn't surprised.

By the end of September, Judy's stomach seemed enormous. Her situation was apparent to the rest of the hotel staff, who sympathetically said nothing. She now walked with an odd sway, a stiff-backed lurch, and she found it hard to sleep the whole night through because of the baby's kicking. She would lie in the moonlight, thinking how wonderful it was to feel her own baby dancing under her heart.

On the seventh of October, two weeks before the baby was due, Judy said goodbye to the staff of the Imperial and caught the bus to Château d'Oex laden with gifts: a fine white knitted shawl and two boxes full of baby clothes from Maxine, Kate and Pagan, a bottle of kümmel, a jar of peaches pickled in brandy and a magnificent smoked ham from the head chef.

On the thirteenth of October Judy woke at five in the morning. "Ouch!" She caught her breath. No, it wasn't the baby kicking, it was a pain in her back.

She sat up in bed, already feeling an excited thrill of achievement. She couldn't wait to tell Angelina. She heaved her unwieldy body out of bed, wrapped the white lace shawl around her shoulders and sat in the living room, twisting the twin coral rings, one for each middle finger, that Nick had given her just before he left Switzerland.

"I know you won't accept a ring for the finger I want to put it on," he had said, as they sat among the brilliant yellow king-cups that grew in the damp soil on the river bank, "but I want to give you a ring, because somehow a ring is connected with a promise, and with this ring I promise that I'll always love you." He had slipped one rosebud on the middle finger of her right hand. Then he picked up her left hand.

"Just a minute," Judy had said, "what does *that* ring promise?"

"That I'll always be ready to help you." He had kissed the fingertip and slid the second ring on it. "You can always rely on me."

Suddenly Angelina appeared in the living room and scolded Judy. "Back to bed! You don't want a cold as well as a baby," Angelina cried. She felt a proprietary interest in the impending birth.

The flutters in Judy's abdomen continued irregularly throughout the day. Doctor Geneste had been alerted and was quietly reassuring. "Nothing is likely to happen yet," he said.

Twenty-four hours later, Judy began to experience definite strong contractions. By eight o'clock in the evening the contractions were coming at half-hour intervals and Angelina decided to take her to the hospital. They left Roger with the farmer's wife next door and two red lollipops, then together they walked down the main street in front of the arched town hall, where they waited for the bus.

Once inside the hospital, all romance was wiped from Judy's mind. Angelina was not allowed to be present. She would have to wait in the waiting room. Judy undressed, had a bath, was given an enema by an unfriendly nurse and then found herself lying in a small cubicle on an anonymous, iron-hard hospital bed, rather like her old one at the Hotel Imperial.

Nobody sat with her. Every half hour the nurse brisked in and bent to examine Judy. "Hmmm, not time yet," she always said.

At eleven o'clock, the nurse said, "Hmmm, six centimeters dilated." By then Judy's contractions were between two and five minutes apart. It was agonizing. "Stop making a fuss," warned the nurse. "There's worse to come."

Judy felt oddly irritable and sick. She felt cold, shaky, and was getting cramps in her left leg. The pain in her lower back was now severe and she felt increasing apprehension and fright. She wanted to stop this whole business. At eleven forty-five P.M. Doctor Geneste was alerted, and at fifteen minutes past midnight Judy was wheeled into the labor ward. She was propped up in a semiseated position, against a mound of pillows and under a blanket, with the soles of her feet together and her knees lolling apart. Already she felt tired and shocked. It was so much more painful than she'd expected.

Again her body stiffened and arched, but this time with a different motion—it started to writhe in a compulsive manner, similar to that involuntary, expulsive feeling that meant you were undoubtedly about to throw up. Judy felt that something inside her had to be violently, immediately expelled from her body. She began to feel slightly—then with increasing urgency—the need to push downward. The muscles of her abdomen were jerking to expel something, like machinery that hadn't been oiled or used for a long time.

Another spasm racked her body, arched it. Now her body was no longer controlled by her mind. Her gasps grew louder, then turned into screams. A second nurse appeared, held her hand encouragingly and wiped her streaming forehead. Judy started to whimper as her body went out of control again. Why hadn't anybody told her what would happen? Why hadn't anybody explained? Why hadn't they warned her?

Another great pain tore at her body.

"Don't push," commanded the first nurse, "*don't* push."

"But I want to push, I can't *not* push, my body is pushing, it's irresistible, I can't stop it, I can't control it, I'm frightened."

"Your cervix isn't completely dilated, the aperture isn't yet ten centimeters, you *mustn't* push or you might hurt your baby's head, *stop pushing.*"

"Give her gas," said the second nurse laconically, bending down to examine Judy. The first nurse wheeled over a trolley with six gas cylinders clipped on it and placed a rubber mouthpiece over Judy's nose. "When the pain gets too bad, take a deep breath, but use it as little as possible."

Judy took a great greedy gulp.

Eventually, she heard the nurse's voice again. "Try to go along with the contraction, but don't force it." It sounded as if the woman were speaking from the end of a cotton-lined tunnel. "Right, now you're ten centimeters. You can push, but only during contractions; try to relax between them. No! Take your hands off your stomach, no use pushing there. You must let the perineum stretch naturally, otherwise your flesh will tear."

By now she was very tired, and the area around her vagina felt as if someone was cauterizing it with a white-hot poker. She couldn't stand much more of this burning pain that seared her body. One nurse muttered to the other. "It's about time the doctor arrived, I think this baby's going to be born any minute."

Suddenly Judy saw Doctor Geneste's head above hers; over the surgical mask, his eyes were lined and looked exhausted. He had just come from his fourth birth of the day and hadn't had a proper meal since breakfast. Another scream was torn from Judy's mouth, but she felt a sort of weak relief. Her friend had arrived.

"Now you must be brave, because your baby's soon going to be here," he soothed, "and you're soon going to be a little mother. We're all here to help you," he added, as another agonizing contraction shook her body.

She took another gulping breath of the gas and felt the room swim slightly, mercifully. Her eyes were shut tight, her face was running with sweat, her hair was wet with sweat and behind her eyes all she could see was a mist of pain. She could hear the murmur of the doctor and the nurse at the opposite end of her body, which was being torn apart. Dear God, she had never, never thought it was going to be as awful as this.

"Steady, steady. Please try not to bear down. The baby mustn't be born too quickly."

Judy tried to control herself.

"This might be the last contraction." Somebody swabbed her forehead, someone was holding her hand. "Pant again, now slow breathing please, now pant again."

The red and green mist was turning black and she felt another searing pain as the doctor quickly bent to rotate and ease out the baby's head. The doctor and the nurse leaned over, absorbed in their task, as the little dark wet crown of the head grew larger, then the wrinkled little scarlet face slithered out. There was a pause, then Judy was told to give another gentle push as each shoulder was eased out into the rubber-gloved hands of the doctor. A perfectly formed baby slipped out of her body and, with a whimper, little Elizabeth was born.

CHAPTER 63

IN THE LUXURIOUSLY hushed hotel suite overlooking Central Park, Lili looked with less resentment at the four women. As she listened to Pagan's explanation of the events surrounding her birth, Lili had started to thaw. She began to understand what had happened almost thirty years ago to those four girls, and her resentment started to melt.

In front of her, Pagan sprawled elegantly in pink wool across an apricot couch. Judy sat on the edge of it, an anxious little figure in brown velvet. On the other apricot sofa, Kate, in her mulberry suit, sat upright and alert at Lili's side. Opposite them, in the square beige armchair, Maxine fingered her blue silk collar.

Lili had just launched her second bombshell—the other question that she'd waited a lifetime to ask.

"In that case, who is my *father?*"

Immediately three heads turned to look at Judy, and Lili thought, It's true, she really is *vraie maman. She* is my mother, *this* is the one!

Judy had never thought so fast in her life. She had not yet recovered from the shock of finding that her long-mourned daughter was still alive, and that the little girl had metamorphosed into the spectacular Tiger-Lili. It left her almost speechless and uncertain of her feelings. She, too, had seen all the photographs of Lili and Abdullah's closely documented love affair. Without meaning or wanting to, Judy couldn't help noticing what the papers said about Abdullah, couldn't help being interested in anything she read about Sydon or about Arabs. She couldn't simply forget someone who had so drastically altered the course of her life, who had caused her such physical and mental pain.

But it was incest!

The word flashed so loudly in her head that Judy was almost surprised the others couldn't hear it. She couldn't avoid Lili's question. But how could she *possibly* tell Lili who her father was?

In the last few minutes Judy had suddenly realized the secret of Lili's personality. That hot-headed, hasty, volatile temper, that proud rebelliousness, was obviously inherited from her father.

And so were her guts. In spite of her past, Lili had been an amazing success in the eyes of the world. She was undoubtedly a gutsy lady. Her natural gift for acting had reluctantly been acknowledged by the critics, and in the previous three years, Lili had steadily improved her performance. She had worked hard, she had turned down lucrative, showy parts and had accepted only those roles that would build up her reputation as a serious actress.

What effect, Judy wondered, would the truth have on Lili and her career if

Lili were told that she was the illegitimate daughter of a king who had raped her mother? And would Lili not be equally horrified when she thought what her past relationship had been with her father? What psychological damage might such knowledge inflict on her? Certainly Lili was unlikely to shrug her shoulders and accept these unpleasant revelations as another of Fate's little quirks.

As these thoughts flashed through Judy's mind, she slowly twisted the coral rosebud ring on her left hand. Nick had said that she could always count on him, that he would always help her.

Swiftly, Judy reached a decision. Her story should sound plausible—and loving.

She sat up, flicked a glance at her friends and then said slowly and carefully, "Your father's name was Nicholas Cliffe and we loved each other very much. In fact, on one occasion—too much. It was on St. Valentine's night. He wanted to get married before he did his National Service, but we couldn't because I was only fifteen and it would have been illegal, so we were going to wait. By the time I found out I was pregnant, he was with the army in Malaya, and then, just after you were born, he was killed." She paused and gave a sigh, as she remembered Nick. "But I shall never forget him," she said firmly.

Lili suddenly looked happy enough to cry. Yes, she'd swallowed it. Her voice was catching as she leaned eagerly toward Judy and said, "I have waited for this moment all my life. I have often imagined it, but now it comes to me as a complete surprise."

In the reunion scene that Lili had imagined all her life, she had always flung herself into the arms of *vraie maman*. Now slowly she stood up and took a tentative step toward Judy. Her mother wasn't what she had expected, but nevertheless, Lili had found her. And to Lili's surprise she had already warmed to Judy. Judy had carried Lili in her body for nine months, had given birth to her and had then supported her. In fact, for seven years all four of these women had supported her, and it couldn't always have been easy for them. She felt their supportive warmth, their closeness to each other, and the invisible bond that certainly existed between them. They even seemed to communicate without speaking, just by a look or a glance.

Lili didn't realize how fast and fierce were the invisible messages flashing around the room as she took another hesitant step toward Judy and said, "You know, I can't believe it's true."

The other three women looking at Judy had immediately known she was lying. Lili couldn't see the incredulity, astonishment and disbelief in their eyes because she was looking at Judy. But Judy could. She held her breath, willing the others to keep silent. Did Pagan and Kate know? Or guess? Would any of them say anything? Why the hell had she said St. Valentine's night? To make her story sound more romantic, more charming and acceptable to Lili than the ugly, brutal truth. Lili had to be protected, Judy thought, as she glared at Maxine, Pagan and Kate, whose mouth was open and whose green eyes were big with disbelief.

Kate was remembering the night of the St. Valentine Ball, that night when she had stayed with Nick, when they had clung to each other on his creaky iron bedstead. Kate had told herself there was no need to feel guilty; she reminded herself that Judy didn't *want* Nick. Nevertheless, Kate wouldn't have wanted Judy to know that she and Nick were—well, as a matter of fact they *weren't*. . . . Because try as she might, even with the most delicate strokes and kisses, with encouragement and affection, Nick was unable to make it. Embarrassed, neither of them referred to this, but there it was, limp, impossible.

Neither was it possible for Judy to have spent that night with Nick because Kate had been in his bed. So why was Judy lying? Why had she mentioned that particular date? *Could* Judy have slept with Nick on some other subsequent night?

Kate didn't think so. Although he never so much as kissed her again, although Kate guessed that Nick also felt guilty and faithless, although they neither of them ever again mentioned that night together, from then on Kate had become Nick's confidante. He poured out to her the hopes and yearnings that Judy, more sensible, refused to take seriously.

Kate had no idea who Judy's lover had been, but she was sure it wasn't Nick.

Maxine's eyes had also widened in astonishment at Judy's news. She knew Judy had just lied and couldn't understand why she should do so on a matter of such importance. Maxine was remembering that summer afternoon in the yellow nursery at the Château de Chazalle, when Nick's mother had clearly said that after contracting mumps complicated by orchitis, Nick could never have children.

Oh, no, it certainly couldn't have been Nick, thought Maxine. However, Maxine wouldn't let Judy see that she had disbelieved her story. After all, Judy had been Maxine's friend for over a quarter of a century. It had been Judy's idea to open the château, and it was she who had organized Maxine's American lecture tours. It would be indiscreet and foolish, Maxine decided, to let Judy see she knew her story was a lie.

Maxine also knew that, try as she might, she could never be fond of Lili. She would never be able to forget that horrible scene in the orangery with her adored son. But for Judy's sake she was determined that nobody should ever know her true feelings, so, lying in her teeth, Maxine turned to smile at Lili. Gently she said, "*Ma chère*, you have not only found a mother, you have found a whole family. We are, of course, surprised. But we are also very, very happy to have found you again."

Lili was also surprised. Suddenly she felt the warmth of total happiness. Amazingly, something had happened in twenty minutes that she would not have imagined could happen in twenty years. Suddenly Lili realized the deep truth of what Maxine was saying and she felt a part of this warm, tightly knit group of women. Whereas twenty minutes ago, Lili didn't have a mother, she felt now that for the first time in her life she had four firm friends.

Judy felt drained. In only twenty-four hours her life had changed dramatically. She was still finding it hard to realize that her long-mourned child was not dead, that she really had a daughter. For years, Judy had been lucky enough to have success, fame, money and love, but until today, she lacked what most women hope for, and indeed expect—a husband and a child. And now she suddenly knew that she could have it all. Griffin was free to marry her, and he *wanted* to marry her—that was what mattered to Judy. To her surprise, however, a small voice at the back of her head kept insistently whispering, "What have you to gain by marrying Griffin? Griffin consistently cheated on his wife: ignore the reasons and remember the fact; for years Griffin has followed a pattern of cheating on his wife. No matter whether he felt trapped, bored or resentful, or whether he felt he was missing something, *Griffin has developed the habit of cheating on his wife*. So why risk turning into Griffin's wife? Why not continue your present relationship, which has been rock-steady for so long?"

Yesterday Judy would perhaps have grabbed at the chance of a loving and supportive relationship that was underlined by the traditional laws of society. But today . . . and so unexpectedly . . . Judy had suddenly discovered that a firmer bond existed in her life: her child had been restored to her.

Judy stood up and moved toward her daughter, her face still tense but smiling.

"But . . . but," Pagan blurted out. "It was impossible, *impossible* . . ."

She stopped short in midsentence, as Lili looked astonished and Judy turned furious blue eyes on her. Pagan, remembering Nick's aquamarine eyes, turned her head and looked up—straight into Lili's big, slanting, velvet-brown eyes.

As she stared, Pagan was remembering what her husband had said, years ago, when she had first discovered she was pregnant. She had told Christopher she wanted a little girl with big brown eyes and her husband had said, "Well, you're not going to get one, my darling."

And then he explained that the color of a child's eyes depends on the gene-grouping of its parents. Two blue-eyed individuals could not produce a brown-eyed baby. He had been definite about it.

Pagan turned her head again and looked at Judy's navy-blue eyes and then at Lili. Why on earth was Judy lying? What *possible* reason could there be?

Pagan had only paused for two seconds as these thoughts flashed through her brain, but in that time Maxine had jerked upright and said sharply, "Sick and sin, remember, Pagan."

"But, but . . ." Pagan stuttered, realizing that she had just been reminded to support Judy now and always.

What the hell had she been saying? Oh yes.

Pagan beamed at Lili and carefully continued, " . . . It was *impossible* for anybody to forget your father, Lili."

And that at least was the truth.

EPILOGUE

L A C E : *a delicate, decorative fabric woven in an open web of different patterns and figures: a cord of string drawn through holes; to lace: to fasten: to add a dash of spirit: to interlace: to join together (fingers, patterns): to intertwine: to mingle or blend in an intricate way: to intersperse, to diversify, to change the patterns.*

LACE 2

FOR PETER
WITH LOVE

PROLOGUE

August 31, 1979

THEY ARE THE most expensive breasts in the world, thought Lili, as she soaped them. Lace rivulets of foam slipped over her rounded flesh and, as she touched one cinnamon-tinted nipple, Lili shivered with sensuous pleasure. She stretched one rose-tipped toe to push the old-fashioned, ivory-handled dial which released hot water; then she stroked her other nipple with the sea sponge, and again her body quivered in response. It was as if the tips of her breasts were part of an electrical circuit of sensation which connected directly with the sensual core of her body, Lili thought, as she watched the two cinnamon buds grow hard, then break through the carnation-scented foam.

Everything was in perfect working order; Lili's body was fully practical, as technicians said when they checked props on the set. But the satin slopes that started to swell immediately below her collarbone were considerably more than practical; Lili's breasts had been her passport, her work permit, her meal ticket, and now they were her fortune. Currently, those two impertinently rounded breasts were insured for a seven-figure sum by Omnium Pictures, which had just negotiated a record fee for Lili to play Helen of Troy.

Nowadays my breasts are worth far more to other people than they are to me, Lili reflected wistfully; but, for almost fifteen years, whatever power she had possessed over her destiny had been derived from these two pounds of flesh which, to Lili, were as familiar as her knees and hardly any more remarkable.

Lili sighed, threw the sponge aside, slowly rose from the over-full bath and carelessly splashed a lake of water over the pink marble floor. She wrapped herself in a buttercup-yellow towel and wandered into the sitting room. A bowl of figs stood on her breakfast tray, each fruit cut in quarters to expose the red flesh; Lili nibbled at a segment as she glanced at the newspaper: 1979 was not proving a good year for President Carter, she thought, as she read about the siege of the American Embassy and the hostages held in Iran. Lili knew what it felt like to be suddenly confronted by violence.

Born in Switzerland, Lili had never known her mysterious mother, but when she was six years old, she had been on holiday with her foster family in Hungary. They had been trapped by the 1956 Hungarian uprising against the Communists, and Lili had seen her beloved foster parents shot by border guards before she had managed to escape. From an Austrian refugee camp, she had been sent to Paris where she had been adopted by an aging, childless couple. By the age of seven, she had virtually become the unpaid servant of Monsieur et Madame Sardeau, a skivvy who longed for the love, peace and happiness that she had once known and still hoped for.

It had been easy for the rich American playboy to seduce Lili, and easier still for him to abandon her when she found herself pregnant. Thrown out by the Sardeaus, Lili had paid for her abortion by posing naked for a truck drivers' calendar. Overnight she became famous as a lewd, baby pinup. Terrified, helpless and dependent on her exploitative manager, Lili had eventually been rescued by Jo Stiarkoz, a Greek ship-owner who had encouraged Lili's natural acting and painting talents and who gradually changed her from a suspicious, wary child of the gutter, unable to equate sex with love, into a cultured, discerning beauty.

When Jo was killed in a car accident, Lili sought oblivion in her film career, and then had flung herself into a notorious year-long affair with Abdullah, King of Sydon, a tiny oil-rich state on the Persian Gulf. But eventually Lili could no longer tolerate her position, described by some as an unofficial concubine and others as the Western Whore. Lili then returned to her home in Paris to search once more for dignity, love, and peace. And, so far, she had not found them.

Sighing, Lili threw aside the *Herald Tribune* and slowly walked through the carved cedarwood shutters onto her balcony, which hung over the grape-green water of the Bosphorus. Around the balcony, the domes and sharp minarets of Istanbul sparkled in the hazy morning sunlight of August. The sounds of the city, muted and distorted, traveled over the waters of the Bosphorus as shouting voices, bicycle bells and the occasional goat bleat blended with the roar of the traffic. Lili hugged the golden bath sheet around her as she absorbed the sights and sounds of Turkey. There were worse places to want love, peace, and happiness.

Across the Straits, on the Asian side of the water, the sun also warmed the stubby gray barrel of a Smith & Wesson Magnum .357, a UZI 9mm, a Kalashnikov, and two hand grenades. They lay on a rickety table in a small room that smelt of stale marijuana smoke.

He hadn't been able to risk bringing the hardware through customs, but when he'd arrived in Istanbul, he'd obeyed instructions and everything had gone smoothly. He'd ordered two cups of coffee, simultaneously, in the small Bazaar café, then he'd sent them both back, complaining that the coffee wasn't strong enough. After a few minutes a dark-suited, dark-featured man had appeared before his table, and he had followed the dark stranger as they walked through a maze of narrow streets, then up a dirty staircase to a small dark room, where he had shown his passport. From the poor selection of guns that he had been offered, he'd picked three, realizing that he had very little choice in the matter.

He'd hoped for a .44 Magnum, because that stopped anyone close-up; even a big man would be thrown, dead, on his back. The UZI submachine gun was easy to get anywhere in the Near East, because it was used by Israeli infantry. It weighed seven and a half pounds and was the shortest submachine gun (twenty inches folded), which made it not impossible for you to strap it inside your trouser leg. It could fire 600 rounds a minute, as well as single shots, and used 9mm ammunition, which was easy to get hold of because it was a common size for pistols, as well as SMGs. He'd also chosen the Kalashnikov because it was handy and reliable. It was slower than the UZI but the longer barrel made it more accurate. God knows how it had ended up in Istanbul, because it was a Chinese '56 model with a wooden stock and a permanently attached folding bayonet, which might well be useful.

Beside the hardware lay an untidy heap of bullets, two ammunition clips, a coil of nylon rope, 500 milliliters of clear solution in a glass bottle, a roll of three-inch-wide white surgical tape, two maps of the city, a water pipe with a few crumbs of half-burned resin in the bowl and a copy of *People* magazine.

The man moved to the rusting, metal-framed window and swept the opposite shore with high-powered, army field glasses. He saw low hills wooded with cypresses and pines; too high, he thought, and corrected. He saw a blurry mass of buildings pierced by the decorated spires of minarets; he was still too high. Then he was focused at the correct level, but the jumbled, dirty-brown houses were confusingly similar and only the larger shapes of a mosque, shrine or palace offered directions to the watcher. Impatiently, the man picked up his tourist's map and peered at a photograph. Again, he raked the distant shore with the field glasses, this time slowly tracking along the water's edge.

At the point at which Galata bridge spanned the Golden Horn, the man fiddled with the focus until the image was so sharp that he could see the faces of the passengers on the ferry, which was pulling away from the landing. Carefully he watched the laden boat begin its journey toward him, then he swept the binoculars further to the right and saw the gleaming façade of a palace, a small park shaded by Judas trees, and the ruined shell of a fortified tower. Finally, with a grunt of satisfaction, he was focused on a large terra-cotta-colored building directly on the edge of the water. Systematically, he checked each window, beginning with the square casements of the top floor and working down to the tall French doors of the first floor, some of which opened onto small domed balconies, suspended over the water like white birdcages. While the man watched, a pair of shutters was pushed open and Lili, wearing her golden towel, walked out on the balcony.

The man dropped the field glasses and grabbed the copy of *People* magazine. Those tawny, almond-shaped eyes, the mass of black curls, the provocatively outthrust breasts were unmistakable. He had found more than he had expected.

Lili wandered back into the sitting room of her suite, squashed another fig segment into her mouth and moved into the dressing room, where she stepped into a loose white-linen shift, the only thing which offered her any hope of navigating the Grand Bazaar without being pinched black and blue by lecherous fingers. Yesterday she had spun round after a particularly insulting nip, to find that the fingers had belonged to a ten-year-old boy. Lili slipped her feet into snakeskin sandals, pinned up her mass of dark hair with antique tortoise-shell combs and applied as little makeup as possible because, thank Heaven, she wasn't the photographic target for today. Leaving clothes and cosmetics scattered all over her suite, she left it, then knocked on the next door.

"That you, Lili? Come on in, honey, I'm waiting for this to dry." The preoccupied voice held a hint of Louisiana. Sandy Bayriver (born Flanagan) was finishing a delicate job of restoration. The area on which she was working had been cleaned and rubbed down, and she was draping a minute web of strengthening gauze over the fingernail crack. In Sandy's business, a girl could not afford to be seen without a perfect set of ten matched talons.

Lili wandered around the opulent, brocade-furnished drawing room, picked up a tawdry diamanté crown slung rakishly over the marble ear of a bust of Alexander the Great and held it on her head. "How d'you keep this thing on, Sandy?"

"Bobby pins, honey. Once, when I was Lake Pontchartrain Oyster Queen, I clean forgot to pin it on and the damn thing fell off halfway across Churchill Plaza." She looked up. "It really suits you, Lili—maybe you should take over as Miss International Beauty and I'll just go shopping today."

"You won it, you wear it," Lili threw the coronet back on the statue's head. Sandy never missed an opportunity to say something sweet, the way some people never missed an opportunity to say something nasty. It was easy to forget that she was in the piranha pool of competition for these gaudy crowns, Lili thought, as Sandy wriggled her toes into scarlet sandals.

"Four-inch heels would cripple me," said Lili.

"Hell, honey, I'm used to them." Sandy tripped into the bathroom where she carefully removed the heated rollers from her wild tawny hair which curled naturally, but Sandy preferred a disciplined cascade of shiny ringlets. "Let's go find your mamma," Sandy giggled, ever conscious of the two notorious women with whom she was traveling.

At the top of the immense double staircase which swept down to the foyer of the Haroun al-Rashid Hotel, Sandy hung onto Lili's arm as, carefully, she moved sideways down the slippery marble steps. Waiting at the bottom of the ornate staircase was a small, delicately boned woman in a red silk dress.

Judy Jordan, founder of *VERVE!* magazine for working women, was not sure that she was enjoying her role as traveling companion of two of the most beautiful women in the world—one of whom happened to be her long-lost daughter.

The guide in baggy black trousers led them to the water gate of their elegant rose-washed hotel, which had once been the summer palace of a sultana, built at the water's edge for coolness.

"Where are we going today?" asked Lili, as the three women settled into the canopied private launch.

Judy pointed. "Over there. The Topkapi Palace, where the Ottoman sultans lived. That enormous pile of buildings on the hill; you're both being photographed in the Palace Harem."

"Surely not me, too?" exclaimed Lili. "I'm not made-up."

Judy looked at her, thinking now that patience was the outstanding quality required by any mother, as she said, "Lili, last night I told you that we needed shots of you, as well as Sandy. Anyway, you look fine."

Of course Lili looked fine, Lili always looked fine, thought Judy wistfully. I always looked fine when I was her age. Now, if I watch my diet and work out every day and only drink wine at Christmas, I can still look good, but not as good as I did when I was Lili's age. Judy knew that in her red Chloé dress, with its rippling bias-cut skirt, her figure was still girlishly slim; she still had the waiflike appeal of an exhausted Little Orphan Annie, in spite of her present problems. Judy thought, I wouldn't have to be involved in anything as tacky as a beauty queen competition if I wasn't so broke, and Lili hadn't been so indiscreet, and Tom hadn't taken one business risk too many.

And there was one other problem. After almost a year as Lili's mother, and a week traveling with eighteen-year-old Sandy, Judy was forced to acknowledge that she was of a different generation, and that made her feel uneasy. Not jealous, of course, just uneasy. If Jordan felt uneasy, by now she knew that millions of her women readers felt the same way about the same things. Putting her life into her magazine, and knowing when to trust her gut instincts, had made Judy her first million dollars.

She found Lili the more disturbing of her two traveling companions because elegance, to Judy, meant neat hair and formal clothes, not expensive garments that were *intended* to look crumpled and hair that had been carefully dressed to look untidy. Nevertheless, since gaining a daughter, Judy had stopped arguing with her fashion editor when spreads were proposed on street-chic or models swathed in knotted muslin.

Sitting with her back to the Bosphorus, Lili dearly wished she had not forgotten about today's photographic session. Eventually, she leaned toward her mother and said, "I'm sorry I forgot. I'm so glad you persuaded me to come on this trip, Judy."

Judy smiled politely, recognizing the peace offering. It was the politeness that came between them, thought Judy, but she didn't know how not to be polite. A real mother isn't polite; she yells at her kids, hollers when her daughter pinches her pantyhose, then goes without a new winter coat so that her daughter can have a really pretty first formal. A mother washes your clothes, and her time and her love are the ingredients that go into every stack of lunchtime sandwiches she cuts. A mother's always at you about your galoshes (putting them on, taking them off, putting them away) and you ignore her or groan theatrically, but her scolding is comforting because you know it means that she cares. Every day, between a daughter and the mother she's grown up with, there are a thousand unspoken reference points which add up to the feeling of comfortable, affectionate intimacy, the feeling that a puppy has for the blanket in its basket. Without discussion, a mother knows that you like goat's milk cheese and don't like Aunt Bertha. A mother knows your temper tantrums, and where they come from, and how to stop them before they start. Between Lili and Judy there was liking, respect, and even the start of a touching friendship, but both of them were silently aware that there should have been love, and there was no love—yet. They both pinned their hopes on that "yet."

From the other side of the boat, Lili watched her mother's short blond hair ruffle in the breeze. Lili had always expected her unknown, mysterious mother to be a quiet, kindly madonna, an apron-covered, ample figure, always stirring something delicious on an old-fashioned kitchen range. But when, almost a year ago, Lili had finally tracked down her mother, she had found this glamorous, lonely public figure instead of the comforting creature of her daydreams.

Both Lili and Judy were alone in life and they both longed not to be; so they tried to behave as they imagined a mother and her daughter should behave. They made odd little stabs at what they thought was the appropriate way to act. But, although she had made such a great effort to discover her real mother, Lili was suspicious of her own feelings. Lili was an instinctive actress; her fame was the result of having the raw talent, then slowly acquiring the craft, then polishing the talent. She had always had to play her life by ear, so her impulses were important, but she was suspicious of her facility to take on a mood when she wanted to act it. Lili did not want to act love. She wanted the real thing. She wanted what she had always felt she had been deprived of—mother love. Lili knew she was not getting the real thing, she felt it deep in her heart and her bones and her being, but she did not want to face it; so she continued hopefully to grope for it.

Lili also feared that something else might sabotage the relationship with her mother that she was trying so hard to establish. Lili knew from her acting work, and from watching other people's stage work, that when a coach or a director asks an actor to play affection, what sometimes unconsciously comes up is bitter rage, always followed by sudden tears and breakdown. This was another reason why Lili feared that she might unconsciously be acting the love for her mother that she so longed to establish with Judy. Lili did not want suddenly to cause an unforgivable showdown with Judy because of Lili's forgivable but unforgettable resentment of her mother's abandonment.

The pink fringe of the canopy swayed in the breeze as their little launch darted over the gray-green water. Lili leaned over to Judy. "After the photo session, can I go shopping? I want to buy a carpet in the Grand Bazaar."

"I'll come with you, it's better to bargain with two people, you'll get a lower price if I stand behind you looking grim. Offer one third of what they ask and settle for half."

"That's not really the way I hoped to do it. I want to buy you a present, Judy. I want to buy you the most beautiful carpet in the Bazaar."

"That's sweet of you, Lili, but you know it's not necessary."

Without realizing it, Lili had expected her real mother to be a duplicate of her beloved Swiss-peasant foster mother, Angelina, and Lili had expected her mother to be poor, like Angelina. Lili had expected to be able to show her love by helping her mother financially. She had had a little fantasy of taking her mother to the best store in town and buying her mother her first fur coat. But then her mother had turned out to be a millionaire. So Lili kept trying to buy Judy expensive presents, which embarrassed Judy. Any show of affection embarrassed Judy, especially touch. Her strict, Southern Baptist parents had never touched each other; they had not kissed or cuddled their children or each other and, consequently, there was a distance in all Judy's relationships, because, to her, touch was related to sex, not affection.

Lili sensed the loneliness that Judy would have fiercely denied. Judy had achieved everything that spells success—she was a Liz Smith regular, a Page Six standby, she had expensive designer clothes, maids, secretaries, an East Side apartment, a place on Long Island, plenty of men friends and three very special women friends. But nobody . . . close. Perhaps that stemmed from her feelings of guilt.

Judy had spent many years feeling guilty about abandoning her child, feeling responsible for her child's death, feeling guilty that her life hadn't turned out as planned, and all because she hadn't been an instant success in The Big Apple.

However much she justified her actions, however tenderly her friends reassured her, there was no getting away from the fact that she had—as Lili felt it—abandoned her own daughter when she was three months old. There had been plenty of justification. Judy had been a sixteen-year-old waitress, working her way through The Language Laboratory in Gstaad, Switzerland, when she had been raped. Judy's three rich girlfriends at the nearby finishing school had all helped to pay for Lili's birth and then for her keep. But no matter how hard Judy had tried, business success always, at first, seemed just beyond her reach, and whatever way Judy turned, she came up against an impersonal blank wall at the end of a cul-de-sac. And all the time she knew that she had to succeed as fast as possible, because—her own ambition apart—she couldn't support her baby daughter until she was successful and made money. Judy's lack of early success had made her feel helpless and unloved, as well as a failure.

With the cheery arrogance of youth, Judy had expected quick success to be the result of brains and hard work. She didn't realize that you can put all your heart and energy into your work but the opportunities you deserve just aren't offered to people who are only moderately attractive; it can make you bitter when the other, less gifted people get the opportunities that should be yours.

Sure, Lili had suffered, but nevertheless Lili had all the things that Judy had never had at her age: beauty, sexuality, money, and time. Time to play, time to go out in the evening without feeling exhausted, time for men. Judy remembered once wondering whether she would be successful while she was still attractive or whether she would ever be able to afford to wear a wonderful dress, to go to a wonderful place and perhaps meet a wonderful man there?

Perhaps it would all have been much easier if only she had been a little bit more beautiful. Judy was ashamed of the fact that she was jealous of Lili's beauty.

On the opposite side of the water, in the Asian part of the city, the man with binoculars still slung around his neck pushed his way through the boys selling chewing gum and evil-eye beads until he reached the Galata ferry. A few minutes later, the wide wake of the flat-bottomed ferry crossed the wash of the pretty little launch that carried the three famous women, as they sped toward the shore, where richly decorated palaces and mosques crowded together at the water's edge; the entire view rippled in the heat, so the buildings seemed to be part of the water itself.

"Problems, Judy, problems," warned the photographer at Topkapi Palace. "They say we can't shoot in the Harem. It's impossible."

People with longer experience of Judy Jordan never used the word "impossible." If you told Judy that something was impossible, she merely lifted her little nose an inch or so and said, "Only impossible people use the word 'impossible,' " or simply, "It *must* be done." Now Judy said, "We *must* shoot in the Harem; the copy has already been written, all the headlines are set and your film is going straight back to New York tonight to be developed and printed in time for Friday's deadline." She turned to the guide from the Turkish Tourist Board, "What's the problem?"

"The Harem Quarters are enormous, Mrs. Jordan . . . "

"Can't we use part of it for us to get a few shots? Everything was cleared with your office."

"There must have been a misunderstanding. Photography is forbidden because of the restorations."

"But isn't there even one room . . . "

"Please understand, Madame. The Topkapi Palace is a magnificent national treasure and the Government would be most unhappy if it were not seen at its best. All the most beautiful rooms are in the part of the Palace which is open to tourists. Let me show these to you."

"OK, do that," agreed Judy. She looked at her watch and thought, an hour to set up, another hour to get the shots. Yes, there would be time for a quick tour.

"Do you suppose they'll let us come back and have a proper look?" Sandy asked Lili as they hurried through a library lined with carved wooden bookshelves, inlaid with mother-of-pearl and tortoise-shell.

"No." Lili was listening to the guide's heavily accented voice, as he told a story about some favorite concubine.

"Is it always like this? Being on tour?" asked Sandy, still reluctant to learn that the glamorous life looked better than it lived.

"Yes," said Lili. "You never have enough time, except in airports; it doesn't matter where you are, all you really see is the inside of dressing rooms and studios; you can't go to the discotheques because you'll have bags under your eyes tomorrow; you can't sunbathe because you'll look browner in some pictures than others; you can't eat most of the food so you won't either get fat or sick; and everyone is always late and frantic. Isn't success wonderful?"

"Time to get ready, girls," said Judy. "We're going to shoot in the Sultan's dining room." She led them to a tiny chamber with walls and ceilings covered in gold-embellished paintings of lilies and roses, pomegranates and peaches. The photographer looked doubtfully at his light meter. "All this interflora stuff might look like psychedelic oatmeal by the time the pictures are printed."

"Then let's do a few more shots outside, by the Harem gate, where you'll get better light." Judy suggested.

After the photo session was finished and the film had been dispatched to the airport, Sandy and the photographer stayed behind for a more leisurely look at the Palace. "After all, honey," said Sandy, as they headed for the treasure chamber, "how often does a girl get a look at rubies the size of pigeon's eggs?"

Judy and Lili climbed into their limousine, kicked off their shoes and asked the driver to take them to the Grand Bazaar.

As she got out of the car, Lili's tiny snakeskin bag slipped off her shoulder and fell onto the cobbles, spilling coins, lip-gloss and letters. Quickly, Lili snatched them up, but Judy had spotted the airmail letter.

"Not fast enough, Lili." Judy couldn't stop herself saying it. "He's still writing to you, isn't he?"

Lili opened her mouth and then shut it again; after all, whatever she said would be wrong.

Still, Judy couldn't stop herself. "Do you think I don't know my lover's handwriting after all these months?"

"Judy, *I* can't stop Mark writing to me. *I* don't want anything to do with him, I never did. . . . "

"But he wants *you*, Lili, doesn't he? And he certainly doesn't want me anymore." Judy knew she was being destructive and knew that she should stop, but now that she had begun she could not stop; she had been suppressing this for weeks. "Lili, don't tell me you didn't know that Mark was falling in love with you in New York, right under my nose. You can't pretend that you don't know what effect you have on men—Lili, the world's most famous sex symbol." Judy knew Lili's most sensitive point.

"You're not being fair, Judy. What kind of a woman do you think I am?"

Suddenly, Judy's self-control snapped as jealousy, unhappiness and fear controlled her. "The kind of woman who might seduce her mother's lover. The kind of woman who could ruin her mother's business—that's the kind of woman you are!"

Lili burst into tears of rage. "You're impossible! I wish I'd never found you. I wish I'd never met you. I never want to see you again." Impulsively, she turned, plunged into the jostling crowd, and vanished. Grimly, Judy watched her go. Their raised voices, the faces twisted with anger and misery, had gone unremarked in the noisy crowd. But both women knew that their play-acting was over. Within two minutes, the fragile relationship, that both had tried so hard to establish, had been wrecked.

The man with the binoculars watched them argue, then saw Lili burst into tears and disappear under the great stone gateway of the Bazaar. Quickly he followed her, elbowing his way through the heaving mass of people, determined to keep Lili in sight.

"Where the hell can Lili be? She should never have gone off alone like that."

"Going off alone is her idea of luxury," Sandy reminded Judy as she tipped back her chair, crossed her feet on the balcony rail and watched heavy black clouds gather behind the minarets. "You know that Lili doesn't like the usual star entourage. The rest of them may not move an inch without PR people, bodyguards, a couple of studio executives, two gofers and a hairdresser, but that's exactly the part that Lili hates. Nobody can make an entrance better than Lili but, although she's not exactly Garbo, Lili doesn't care for all the fuss and glitter that I long for."

"But she knows we're supposed to meet the agency people in ten minutes."

"Maybe she doesn't want to meet the agency people. Why don't we just go ahead and eat?" Sandy stood up and pulled down the zipper of her gold lamé jumpsuit. "Lili can follow us when she turns up."

But when Judy tried to leave a message for Lili, the clerk pointed out that Lili's key was still in its pigeonhole. "Miss Lili went out many hours ago. No, not alone. With a man."

"What sort of man?"

"Not a guest. Maybe Turkish. I don't remember his clothes. A dark suit, maybe." In luxury hotels in Turkey, the clerks speak impeccable English.

"That's odd; we don't know anyone Turkish, except the agency people," Sandy said as they turned toward the dining room. Judy said nothing.

As the agency people made over-polite conversation, Judy picked her way through a series of dishes with suggestive names: Holy Man Fainted (stuffed eggplant with tomatoes, onions and garlic), Sultan's Delight (sautéed lamb with onions and tomatoes), Ladies' Navels (fried pastries with pistachio nuts and whipped cream). Then the lights dimmed and six plump girls in neon-pink gauze undulated across the dance floor. After the belly dancers came the fire-eaters, then the snake charmer. Not until two o'clock in the morning, when the last cobra had been re-coiled in its basket, could Judy stand up and leave.

Back at the hotel reception desk, her anxiety increased as she stared at Lili's key, still in its pigeonhole. "This is not the kind of town for a girl to be out with a strange man," Judy said to Sandy. "However angry Lili was, she would have sent us a message. After all, she wouldn't want the police looking for her, if she was just romancing."

Feeling increasing guilt, Judy turned to Sandy. "We'd better not call the police. We don't want to upset the local people and we don't want to look foolish if Lili, if she only . . . " she paused.

"Exactly," agreed Sandy.

As soon as Judy woke, she telephoned Lili's suite. No answer. In her red silk dressing gown, Judy hurried down to the reception desk. The clerk, a nervous new boy on the daytime shift, refused to give her the key to Lili's rooms. Judy demanded to see the hotel manager and, together, they hurried up the marble staircase. An anxious Sandy waited outside the double doors of Lili's suite.

They rushed across the empty drawing room and threw open the bedroom door. The billowing pink silk canopy of the elaborate antique bed was caught back with golden rope, but the plump velvet pillows in their lace coverings were undented and the ivory chiffon sheets were still as smooth as when the maid had turned them down the night before.

Sandy ran into the dressing room and opened the closets. "Her clothes are still here." She pulled open the bathroom door. The makeup was scattered on the marble counter, as Lili had left it.

Sandy dashed back to the sitting room, to see Judy, on her knees, tearing at a cylindrical brown-paper parcel on the floor. She pulled out an exquisite silk rug. "Lili must have bought that after she left me in the Bazaar."

"Maybe the man she went out with was a rug merchant?" suggested Sandy.

"Maybe she met someone in the Grand Bazaar?" Judy worried aloud.

Sandy always told people what they wanted to hear. "Lili might have taken up with some good-looking guy and decided to have a little fun," she soothed.

The discreet tap at the door made both women jump, then hurry toward it. Judy was the first to reach the handle. "Lili, thank God you're . . . oh!" Outside stood a hotel page boy, carrying a gigantic bouquet of red roses.

"Who would send us flowers when we're leaving tomorrow?" Sandy wondered, as she unpinned the tiny envelope and handed it to Judy. She pulled out the card, and read it, then gasped, "Oh, no!" and dropped the card.

Sandy snatched up the card and read it aloud. "Wait in your hotel suite to hear from Lili's father. He must pay the ransom." Slowly she turned to Judy. "So now we know. Lili's been kidnapped."

CHAPTER I

October 15, 1978

STANDING, DAZED, IN her hotel room, gazing at the beautiful bunch of red roses which had accompanied the kidnap letter, Judy said nothing. But she thought, this is my fault. Once again I have been responsible for a disaster in my daughter's life. Why, oh why, doesn't God stick up red flags when you accidentally do some little thing that's going to lead to calamity? *I* persuaded Lili to come with me on this tacky trip because I never had enough *time* for her back home in New York; there I told myself that it wasn't my responsibility, I hadn't been expecting a long-lost daughter to drop in on me. I had a magazine to run and a business to run and my charity commitments, and my lover to look after. But that article on Lili in *VERVE!* was my idea. I should have known that article was asking for trouble—and that we'd all get it in shovelfuls. I wish I could turn the clock back to a year ago, to that first meeting at the Pierre Hotel.

It had been a warm October evening; nevertheless, a log fire had burned softly in the quiet, cream hotel suite, with the spectacular view across the purple dusk of Central Park. Firelight had flickered across the faces of the two women as they moved toward each other. Judy had felt the strange animal magnetism that emanated from Lili. Looking at Lili's black, soft curls, falling to the folds of her white Grecian tunic, Judy felt a new appreciation of that world-famous oval face, with the high cheekbones that looked both innocent and predatory, the thickly lashed chestnut eyes that always glistened as if tears were about to fall. Judy found it hard to believe that her daughter, believed dead, was alive—let alone that she was Lili, the most famous professional waif since Marilyn Monroe. It was impossible to match this sensuous creature with the image that Judy had treasured, of a well-behaved six-year-old girl with braided hair.

Judy had always imagined that her long-lost daughter would look exactly like herself, but their only resemblance lay in the slim-boned frames of their bodies. The three other women in the room sat motionless—hypnotized by the drama of the moment—as Lili took a hesitant step toward Judy. Pagan, elegant in pink wool, suddenly noticed that Judy and Lili had the same doll-like hands. She leaned across to the green-eyed woman in the mulberry suit. "Do you think we should leave?" she whispered to Kate, who was sitting next to her on the apricot-silk sofa.

Kate Ryan shrugged her shoulders, unable to take her eyes off Lili. She found herself mentally taking notes, as if writing one of her articles, as Lili moved toward Judy, but Judy stood motionless and silent. Kate opened her mouth to say something but the third onlooker, an elegant blonde in blue silk, lifted her fingers to her lips, as all three women watched the mother and daughter hold each other in a nervous embrace. Sharing a natural impulse to dissolve the pain and embarrassment of the moment by reaching toward physical contact, they were hugging each other, but not kissing each other, Kate noticed.

As she held her daughter, Judy realized that this was the first time she had touched Lili since the sad moment when she had handed her three-month-old baby to her foster mother, that morning years ago, in the Swiss hospital where Judy's illegitimate child had been born. As she held Lili close to her heart, Judy realized that, since that day, they had shared a physical need for each other that was close to hunger; their embrace was an expression of that need, rather than of warmth, of affection, even of liking; but both women realized that this was an expression of goodwill.

This is my daughter, thought Judy, as she felt the trembling warmth of Lili's body; this voluptuous woman once came out of my body; those wild brown eyes and slanting cheekbones—once they were a part of me, I made them. She looked down at Lili's gold-skinned forearms and thought, that is flesh of my flesh.

She does not *feel* like my mother, thought Lili, hugging the slender Judy, in her brown velvet suit. A mixture of resentment and relief swirled in Lili's mind; she had built up her unknown mother's identity into a romantic mystery because the alternative was to face her mother's brusque rejection of her as a baby. When she finally met her mother, Lili had expected to feel as protected as a child, but when she looked into Judy's eyes and saw pain, fear and guilt, Lili felt unexpectedly protective toward her mother.

Oblivious of the three seated women who watched, Lili was also near to tears as she remembered her deep-rooted restlessness, the profound anxiety and uncertainty that had shadowed her adult life. Now she instinctively recognized it as a sense of loss—sad and constant—even though it was for a woman that Lili had never known, her *vraie maman*, as Lili used to think of her mother, in the little Swiss village where she had been raised by the local seamstress. "Mother?" Lili said the word softly, as if forming it for the first time, and then tried it again. "Mother."

The two women drew back, gave tearful laughs and simultaneously said, "You're not what I expected!" Then Judy added, "How did you find us?"

"It wasn't difficult," said Lili. "I hired a detective. He discovered that my mother had been one of four teen-age girlfriends who had been students in Switzerland, and then he followed the trails until he identified you." She turned to the green-eyed woman in the mulberry suit. "You were the most difficult to track down, Kate, because the world is full of Katherine Ryans. But, once he did find you, my detective couldn't discover *which* of you four was that teen-age mother, which is why I arranged this confrontation." She hesitated, and nervously bit her lower lip. "I hope you'll forgive me; I do so hope you'll understand why I had to know who my parents are, why I had to know *who I am*."

The last thing Kate had expected to feel for this sex goddess was a sudden rush of affection and pity. Gently she said, "We do so hope, Lili, that you will understand why Judy couldn't keep her baby. In 1949, a sixteen-year-old girl from a poor family, who had to earn her own living, couldn't also look after a baby."

Anxiously, Judy said, "Did you . . . were you . . . did your foster mother look after you?" She added in a rush, "I can never forgive her for taking you to Hungary, after the Russians occupied it."

Lili said, "I shall always love Angelina. She loved me and she never lied to me; she always told me that one day my *vraie maman* would come for me."

"She did come for you." The elegant blonde in the blue silk dress spoke, for the first time, in an unmistakable French accent. "We knew you were on holiday in Hungary and when we heard there'd been a revolution, Judy flew over to Europe and we went straight to the Hungarian border. The situation was chaotic: a hundred and fifty thousand Hungarian refugees were pouring over the Austrian border into camps for displaced persons. We visited every one of them. But nobody could trace you." Maxine remembered Judy's frenzy and self-accusation as they stood in the snow outside hut after hut, waiting to see yet another refugee committee official.

As Judy remembered her constant self-accusation for having abandoned Lili, for not having done enough to find her, she sat down heavily on the apricot-silk sofa and buried her face in her hands; her little gulps, splutters and sniffs were the only sounds to break the silence.

Kate picked up the ivory telephone, and said, "Champagne is what you celebrate a new baby with, isn't it? D'you think they have any Krug '49?"

"I would prefer you to order our champagne," said Maxine firmly. "Ask for a magnum of Chazalle '74."

After a great deal of emotion and champagne, Pagan suddenly said, "How is the press going to react to this news? Do you think we should keep it secret?"

"It's bound to get out somehow," said Maxine, "we're all public personalities as we all live our lives in the spotlight. Why, within a week, someone would have overheard a telephone conversation, stolen a letter, and sold the story to the *National Enquirer* for a meager fifty dollars." She turned to Kate. "You're a journalist, right?"

Judy remembered the cruel descriptions that she had quite enjoyed reading about Lili, as maliciously enjoyable as any tidbit about Elizabeth Taylor, Farrah Fawcett or Joan Collins. "We'll be able to set the record straight, Lili, we'll print your *true* life story, as told by you."

"No!" Lili looked frightened and anxious. "You know the lies, the filth that's published about me, they'll all just dredge it up from their files again."

"Don't worry, Lili," said Kate. "I'm the editor of *VERVE!* magazine, so you can control the story. We'll print whatever you want." She turned to Judy for confirmation. "If we get in first with an exclusive story and splash it big enough, we'll have scooped the rest of the world; nobody will want to run it after that."

Lili said, "It's quite a story."

As Maxine poured champagne, all four women listened to the quiet voice of Lili reciting the tale of her life since 1956, the success story of the Paris porn model who became an international movie star, the sad story of an exploited, lonely girl as incapable of controlling her own destiny as the autumn leaves that fluttered from the trees below them in darkened Central Park.

* * *

It was two o'clock in the morning before Kate let herself into her apartment. She stood in the doorway of her huge living room, rubbing her tired eyes as she looked across at the man who lay asleep on the thirty-foot-long, beige suede sofa that ran along one wall. Above the sofa hung a collection of antique paintings and engravings of tigers. On the floor below the man lay a pair of loafers, a pair of socks, a crumpled copy of the *Wall Street Journal*, and a silver salver upon which was a slice of cold, leftover pizza and a half-empty glass of beer. Tom would never be a gourmet, no matter how many elegant meals she served him, thought Kate, as she tiptoed over to her husband and gently shook him awake. "Bedtime, darling," she whispered, as he leaned against her, blinking, then suddenly hugged her in a hard grip. "How'd it go, darling? Did you reach an agreement with Tiger-Lili?"

"Tell you in the morning. Everything's fine, but right now I'm exhausted and I just want to be in bed. How I wish that someone would invent a machine with a button that you press and suddenly you find yourself undressed, showered and in bed with your teeth cleaned."

"With me."

"You'd be an optional accessory. Very expensive."

In her softly lit bathroom at the Plaza Hotel, Maxine carefully broke open three glass ampoules, mixed the clear liquids together, then patted the solution carefully around the delicate skin of her eye socket. She used a pink cream to remove her makeup, a clear solution to exfoliate her skin and a white preparation to stimulate cell renewal while she slept. Along the fine lines of her forehead, no more definite than the veins on a leaf since her face-lift, she traced a tiny paintbrush dipped in a solution of synthetic collagen. Finally, her generously rounded right buttock, smooth as a peach thanks to regular treatments to dispel la cellulite, received a slimming injection. Carefully, she hung up her blue silk dress, then Maxine wrapped herself in an oyster-silk peignoir edged with point-de-Chazalle lace. She brushed her hair with a hundred strokes, then climbed into bed, opened her maroon-leather traveling office and dictated half a dozen memos to be telexed to her secretary on the following day. Then, in her large, loopy handwriting, she thanked Judy for making her so welcome in New York and wrote an encouraging note to Lili. She always wrote her thank-you notes at night, when she was still feeling grateful, no matter how late the hour. Maxine never considered it an excuse to neglect her body, her business, or her gift for expedient politeness.

Pagan sprawled across her old-fashioned brass bed in her room at the Algonquin and again tried to direct-dial her husband.

It was two in the morning in New York, which meant seven in the morning in London, so with luck she'd catch Christopher just before breakfast, she thought, as she looked around the small pretty room. Her Jean Muir pink coat was thrown carelessly over the rose-velvet armchair and her discarded underwear was scattered over the malachite-green carpet.

"Darling, that you? How are the dogs? Is Sophia doing her homework *directly* when she comes home from school? Are you helping her with geometry? . . . Sorry, it doesn't seem like twenty-four hours, it seems weeks since I saw you last, darling. . . . Yes, I've met Lili, but I don't want to talk about it on the telephone. . . . No, we didn't discuss the possibility of a donation to your laboratory, darling, you're even more tactless than I am. . . . No, there simply wasn't a chance to discuss the importance of cancer research." She pushed her heavy, wavy mahogany hair away from her face and wriggled her long-legged, lean, naked body into a more comfortable position on the lace blanket cover. " . . . Yes, I know I forgot to pack my nightclothes, but nobody's noticed, darling, I'll hide in the loo when they bring breakfast up. . . . Oh, damn, did I really forget the grocer order again? Thank heaven for Harrods and Globe Car Service. . . . " Eventually, in a carefully casual voice, Pagan said, "How are you feeling, darling?" After his heart attack, she always worried when she was away from Christopher.

" . . . No, I hardly slept at all last night, you know I mustn't take sleeping pills or anything addictive. But tonight I'm prepared to enjoy a sleepless night. I've bought this absolutely gripping book called *Scruples*. . . . "

Judy had also spent a sleepless night. Huddled under the red-fox spread of her big, luxurious, peaceful bedroom, she restlessly gazed at the peach-colored walls and matching wild-silk curtains, at the pretty Victorian oil paintings of peaches and grapes, apples and apricots that hung from the walls. She was almost glad that Griffin wasn't here; he'd had to fly to the West Coast for a couple of days to launch a new decorating magazine, the first of his many publishing ventures to be based in San Francisco. Only the previous evening, Griffin had asked Judy the question that she'd been waiting to hear from him for ten years. Although Griffin was a major shareholder of *VERVE!* and although they'd been lovers for over ten years, there had always been a subject that she was forbidden to discuss. That subject was Griffin's home life. Everyone in the media world knew that it had been clearly established years ago, before he'd met Judy, when that tough, clever bastard, Griffin Lowe, was still being seen around town with the best-looking models and young actresses in New York, that none of them stood a chance: Griffin would never leave his wife and three children, because he'd fought too hard to climb his way up the ladder of success and he wanted all of it, the successful, respectable life that he'd established as well as his notorious, amorous adventures.

And then, a few days ago, Griffin's wife had left him for another man; they were going to Israel together, to start a new life on a kibbutz. The long-suffering Mrs. Lowe had walked out on her handsome, rich, debonair, double-crossing husband.

What was equally surprising was that Griffin had immediately asked Judy to marry him. What was even more surprising was that, after hearing the words for which she'd waited ten years, Judy found that she didn't want to marry Griffin. Griffin had developed a habit of cheating on his wife and therefore she wasn't too sure that she wanted to become his wife. Old habits die hard.

Silhouetted against the russet shade of the bedside light, the slim naked figure looked like an alabaster Praxiteles; slowly his fox-shaped face broke into an intimate smile. "No, darling, it's absolutely safe; Lili's out there playing the biggest role of her life." Softly he laughed into the ivory telephone. "I'll be back in Paris on Saturday . . . promise, darling . . . you can save it for another couple of days . . . you'd better. . . . " The man's head jerked up as the door was flung open and Lili stood there smiling. Hastily, the man said to the telephone, "Sorry, this is suite 1719. I think you've got the wrong number." He replaced the telephone and held out both his arms to Lili, who hurled herself into them. "You were right,

Simon! It worked just as you said it would!" She threw her arms round his neck and kissed him full on the lips. "At last I know who I really am, at last I know who my mother is!"

Simon Pont was an actor. A good stage actor who needed an audience to produce his best work, who hated movies and only occasionally made one, strictly for the money. He and Lili had lived together for two years and it was Simon who had originally persuaded Lili to search for her mother. A quiet, intelligent, thirty-five-year-old, he seemed secure enough to handle Lili with firm indulgence, seemed to understand that she needed more protection and attention than most men are prepared to give a woman. It was Simon who had given Lili the reassurance she had needed, and it was he who had realized that Lili needed to trace her mother in order to firmly establish her own identity. Simon had pointed out that if Lili found her real parents, then she might stop looking for substitute parents to love in almost everyone with whom she became involved—which is why she was so vulnerable to the exploiters, the con men and the con women that the rich and the famous invariably attracted.

Now Simon held Lili to his handsome naked body and licked her ear with his long, curly tongue. "Tell me who your mother is, darling. Lady Swann?"

"No, not Pagan Swann; it's Judy Jordan. She admitted it almost at once, but I remembered what you'd said—that they'd be bound to pin it on the only woman who wasn't married and didn't have to explain me to a husband!"

He pushed the white silk from her shoulder, and nipped the golden flesh with his little wide-spaced teeth. Lili wriggled. "So I suddenly asked Judy who my father was and—just as you said—the other three all snapped round to look at Judy, so I knew that she was telling the truth, that she really is my mother."

Simon pushed Lili's dress from both shoulders, and gently flicked one sandalwood nipple with his finger and thumb. Lili wriggled again, "Listen, Simon, she wasn't some rich bitch who'd just dumped me because she couldn't get an abortion." Simon tugged at Lili's white belt as she continued. "Judy was poor, from one of those grim Baptist families in West Virginia, a scholarship student in Switzerland, working her way through college by waiting on tables. And she was only sixteen when it happened."

"And who helped it to happen?" Simon's voice was gentle. "What about your father? Who's he?" He tugged again at Lili's belt, and the white Grecian tunic slithered to the floor. Simon pressed her naked body against his and stroked Lili's hair.

"That part's sad," said Lili, sorrowfully. "He's dead. He was an English student that she met in Switzerland, but he was drafted into the British army and died fighting the communists in Malaya. He never even knew she was pregnant."

"Do you believe that?" Simon put his arms round Lili and grasped her buttocks.

Lili thought for a moment. "There was something odd about the way she told me. Pagan Swann started to say something, then thought better of it."

"What about the rest of his family?"

"I haven't asked Judy yet. There was so much to talk about. It's a really strange story. Apparently all four girls paid Angelina for my keep. Judy didn't dare to tell her parents, you see. Judy intended to come to Switzerland for me as soon as she was able to support me by herself. But she was only a twenty-two-year-old secretary when I disappeared."

"I'm glad she didn't get an abortion." He rubbed himself against Lili's big soft breasts.

"She couldn't have done that in Switzerland in 1949. It was illegal and dangerous."

He trickled his finger up her spine. "So now, can we start a family of our own?"

"What, right now?"

"Right now." Gently he pushed her backwards onto the gray-silk bedcover. She always felt safe with Simon, Lili thought as he began to kiss her. She trusted him. There was no need for him to dominate her, envy her or exploit her, because he was a successful actor in his own right. And she knew that he had her interests at heart. Why else should he have encouraged her search for her mother?

After her sleepless night, Judy didn't feel tired. She felt contented and apprehensive. A fizz of anticipation colored all the chores of planning future issues of her magazine, because the future was now the future for both Judy and her daughter. She picked up the telephone. "Dick?" she said, unable to keep the excitement out of her voice as she spoke to New York's most famous portrait photographer, "I want you to take a very special picture for me. . . ."

Next, she called her florist. "Do you have tiger lilies?" she asked, her voice quivering. "Then please send every single one to Mademoiselle Lili at the Pierre, and put a card with it saying . . . "With all my love, Mother." As she hung up, she savored that word. All her life she had thought of a mother as someone like her own mother—disappointed and inwardly desperate. The picture of that ineffectual woman, setting out for Chapel every Sunday, flashed into Judy's mind. Sin and its avoidance were the only things in which her mother had seemed interested, and when Judy's father had plodded home from the grocery store to break the news that he had lost everything, all her mother had done was to kneel and pray; she had merely accepted the disaster, and hadn't tried to fight it. Motherhood, to Judy, meant drudgery, dependence and the sublimation of all the joy of living into faith in an unforgiving God. But now that Judy herself was a mother—truly a mother—with a living daughter to prove it, the notion of motherhood began to become exciting. Her morning rushed by in a froth of delight.

"D'you suppose there's a new man in Mrs. Jordan's life?" wondered the junior secretary as, one after another, the magazine's senior staff came out of the pastel-painted office looking startled, but pleased, because for once their proposals had been received with uncritical enthusiasm. "Did you know that Griffin Lowe's wife walked out on him last week?" the senior assistant whispered as she stood up to take in Judy's morning mail. "I think that's why she's lit up. When your lover's wife finally concedes after ten years, it must feel pretty good."

Every Friday, Kate the editor and Judy the publisher of *VERVE!* had a weekly editorial conference for all staff. It always took place over lunch in Judy's office. The ten men and women who created the magazine pulled up lucite chairs and hurled ideas at each other for an hour and a half over the long table, cold meats, cheese and sodas. Judy found the Friday conference an excellent way to channel the thoughts of her staff for the weekend, and Monday always produced a satisfying stack of memos which crystalized the ideas that had been thrown about during the Friday brainstorming session.

Today, Kate's green eyes flicked over her agenda, as she tried to work up the necessary enthusiasm to motivate her staff. Thank heaven, next week she'd be away from the highly polished, shallow world, where, at the end of the day, nothing could happen without the lipstick advertisements. It had been eleven years since her last best seller, eleven years since she'd done something worthwhile on her own, and now she was itching for the end of the month, when she was to start her first sabbatical—a year on her own.

Suddenly, Kate was startled to hear Judy ask, "What do we think about working mothers?" She picked up a stick of celery and nipped off the end. "I'm concerned that our feature coverage is getting too heavy on emotional and sexual issues; we didn't get two million readers by treating them as if they had nothing more important to think about than multiple orgasms. I want some solid feature ideas about the basics of our readers' lives."

The team couldn't believe it. Family life was a no-no on the magazine. Few principles were written on tablets of stone in that office, but one of the unbreakable commandments was that children should never be mentioned between those assertive, glossy covers. Both Judy and Kate were childless.

The youngest assistant editor tentatively said, "The last readership survey showed that the majority of *VERVE!* readers planned on working again after they had started their families." She picked up a celery stick with the same gesture as Judy; she was editing an article on body-language-in-the-workplace, which advised that mirroring a superior's movements was a good way to establish subliminal empathy.

"Let's have a breakdown of those figures." Judy snapped the celery stick. "I want to know everything we can find out about our readers' attitudes toward children, childcare, stepparents—that whole important area."

There was an astounded silence as Judy continued, "And I'd like to see us become a little less parochial, a little more international. How about a regular feature on successful European women? Starting, of course, with internationally known actresses."

"Our readers don't relate to these European stars." Judy's business partner, Tom Schwartz, raised his eyes from the hot dog he'd had sent up. He winked across the table at his wife, Kate, and Kate knew that the idea was about to get firmly kicked at, as Tom continued. "My instinct is that our readers are interested in the new identity that women are creating for themselves and these sexy actresses from over the ocean merely represent everything they want to reject. They aren't relevant to a girl who's focused on getting her qualifications and her business skills in shape."

Judy was about to protest when she realized she was overreacting. Twenty-four hours ago, she, too, had also considered Lili a glamorous, irrelevant, continental pain in the ass.

Kate wished that Tom hadn't taken a stand on European stars, since she was about to do as Judy asked and propose the feature on Lili, without telling the magazine staff the full significance of the story. Now she was forced to override her husband's opinion in public and, despite Tom's unsinkable self-esteem, she felt ungracious as she announced, "There's always an element of risk when we're trying a new idea. But I've decided that we're going to run a major interview with Lili in the December issue."

The production editor looked as if she'd swallowed a toad instead of a caviar canapé. "It's already too late. Unless we put it in the Hither and Yon section, it'll cost us a fortune. The printers will probably need to replate."

"It'll be the cover story, so whatever it costs we're going to do it," said Kate. "I want it run over two spreads and we're getting a special cover picture from Avedon. Tomorrow." Kate raised her eyebrows at Judy, who nodded behind her tortoise-shell spectacles. The rest of the staff, who respected Kate's sure judgment and professionalism, were irritated, but not surprised. Kate's background in newspapers had given her what the staff called a "hold-the-front-page, I'm-changing-the-comic-strip" mentality. Correctly, they felt that she rather enjoyed wrecking editorial plans at the last moment, for the sake of squeezing in the most up-to-the-minute material.

"We're going to tell Lili's story right from the beginning," Kate went on. "She's agreed to tell us everything about her early days, even that blue-movie stuff when she was thirteen. Things she's never talked about before."

"Small wonder," somebody muttered (but very quietly). "Can we dig up one of those classic tire-calendar shots of her?" the art director wondered, from the far end of the table. "Maybe that one with a sunflower in the navel?"

Judy shook her head. "No early shots. Only the Avedon portrait." Kate threw a warning glance at Judy, catching the protective, emotional tone of her voice.

"What about the men in Lili's life?" Tom reached for another prawn, wondering what his wife was up to. This morning over breakfast, Kate had been oddly reticent about her meeting with Lili.

"All of them," Kate explained, "the photographer who put her in dirty movies and ripped her off until. . ."

"Until she had a nervous breakdown on the promotional tour I managed for her first straight film. I'll never forget that." Judy found that the memory of that television tour—previously nominated as the worst fuckup of Judy's career—now seemed less painful; but she tried to sound correctly resentful in front of the staff.

"We all know about her relationships. What we're dying to know is *more* about some of them. That Greek shipping millionaire, Jo Stiarkoz and then after he died, King Abdullah. And what's it like with Simon Pont. And are they going to marry?"

Kate gave her tight smile. "If they are, she'll tell us. Lili's promised to tell us the whole truth and I think you'll find it's quite a story."

After lunch, as they all left Judy's pretty cream-and-green office, Kate felt a hand on her shoulder. "Wait a minute, Kate," said Judy, "I want a word with you. . . ."

Kate threw herself onto the cream art deco sofa. "It's no use. You can't stop me. I'm off," she said, her British accent still distinct in the clipped short "o" sound. "It's been terrific, Judy, but I feel smothered under equal opportunities programs and contraceptive sponges. I want to get back to hard news."

"Kate, for heaven's sake—the goddamn magazine was your idea in the first place."

"You can run it with Pat Rogers for a year—she should have been promoted long ago. I'm going to Chittagong."

"But Kate, who *needs* a book about settlement wars in the Hill Tracts of Chittagong. It won't sell two thousand copies."

"That's not the point. And anyway, I've a feeling that the situation's going to escalate."

"Where the hell is Chittagong anyway?" Judy's new maternal euphoria started to disperse. Sure, Judy and Kate's deputy could run the magazine while she took a sabbatical, but Judy's plans for 1979 had included launching a new magazine, aimed at the generation of readers who had grown up with *VERVE!* and now had mature lifestyles, families and spending power to match. Unless she made a last-ditch attempt to stop Kate leaving, she'd have to postpone the new magazine.

"Bangladesh, east of the Ganges delta. It hasn't changed location since I told you about it last month, Judy. The Bengalis have been fighting the hill tribes there ever since the state of Bangladesh was created seven years ago, and it virtually amounts to jungle genocide. Thousands of people have died, but because the war area is so remote, nobody knows what's going on." Kate was becoming irritated. "It's a terrific assignment, Judy. You bullied me into becoming a writer. I wouldn't have written my first book if you hadn't pushed me into it. Now be a pal and let me bug out."

After leaving Judy's office, Kate poked her head back around the door. "There's an enormous Tarzan figure out here waiting to see you. Who's he?"

"Our new exercise instructor," said Judy. "I've decided we can all work out for an hour."

Kate laughed. "It's the mean Irish in you. You don't want the staff to even leave for lunch."

Under their continental quilt, Tom's elbow gently prodded Kate. "Sure you want to go?"

"Sure. Judy won't really miss me, once I'm gone; she's more identified than I am with the magazine. That's one of the reasons I want to get out and do something on my own." Kate turned on her back and watched a little wink of light from a passing 747 travel from one corner of the window to the other. "I'll be on that shooting star next week."

"How do you know I'll be here when you come back?"

Kate gently prodded Tom. "You'd better be." The reason she hadn't gone off earlier was that she couldn't bear to leave this wonderful man, who loved her without wanting to own her, encouraged her without patronizing her, and admired her talent without exploiting it. "I'll miss you, too. Be careful."

"Come over here, woman."

"What's on your side of the bed that isn't on my side?"

"Me."

Judy handed Griffin his vodka martini with olive on-the-rocks and sat down in her living room, which had just been restyled by David Laurance in soft turquoise, an excellent background color for blondes. Judy drove her decorator crazy by decorating one room at a time instead of having the whole apartment done over.

Griffin said, "So when are we doing it?"

"I'm not sure, Griffin."

"Not sure about what?" He ate his olive. "Tell me about it while you get dressed. We're due at the Sherry Netherland in twenty-five minutes."

Judy hurried to her dressing room, not because she was late but because she wanted to put off the discussion. But, as she started to select her clothes, Griffin followed her, and leaning against the door he repeated, "Have you decided when you want to get married?"

"Not yet." She turned away from him and selected a black sequinned jacket, then thought, better get it over with and gently said, "Maybe not ever, Griffin. I don't really want to share the whole of my life with you or anyone." She carefully avoided looking at him. "I think we should face the fact that we're both independent people—and that's why I suited you as a lover. I didn't pester you to get divorced and marry me. . . ."

"But we've waited so long! I always thought. . . "

"*I've* waited so long, is what you mean, Griffin. I've waited too long. It's become a way of life with me. I've had to make too many excuses for you; I've had to spend too many Thanksgivings without you, too many Christmases, too many holidays and too many Sundays—*they're* the loneliest days of the week, Griffin."

She looked at Griffin and a hundred tall, dark, astounded Griffins looked back. The entire dressing room, including the ceiling, was covered in mirror glass. Judy could stand in the middle of the room and see herself from every angle without craning her neck. She could also, in a playful mood, give a high kick and see herself reflected to infinity, like a one-woman Busby Berkeley chorus.

"Do you really mean you *don't* want to marry me?" Didn't all women want to get married? Was she really turning down one of the most successful publishers in the country, whose empire included some of the best magazines in America? Was she turning down the maroon Rolls Royce, the money, the servants, the old-English manor house in Scarsdale, the social position, the sensational times in bed? Griffin's forehead wrinkled in perplexity. "What's got into you tonight? Is it the wrong time of the month?"

"Griffin, it isn't premenstrual tension, it's common sense." Judy thought she'd better be firm or she'd duck out. "After all, what do I really know about you except that you're in the habit of cheating on your wife? How do I know that when I'm your wife you won't want the same surreptitious excitement?"

Carefully, Griffin put his drink on one of the glass shelves that lined a complete mirror wall but did not interrupt the reflected perspective into infinity. "That's a cheap shot after all these years. You didn't complain when you were getting your share."

Judy looked at him. He thinks he's a great lover and he's right, she thought. But, for him, the satisfaction is being seen to be a great lover, not simply enjoying himself with me. His constant craving for admiration will always make him flirt with other women, because his ego is insatiable.

Griffin rubbed the scar on his left hand, a sure sign of irritation. "So where do we go from here?"

"How about the Sherry Netherland? What's wrong with business as usual, Griffin? Can't we continue as we are? You keep that mansion in Scarsdale, I'll stay here, and we'll be together three or four times a week. And maybe Sunday."

What Judy really meant to say was, "This relationship will stand or fall on how we feel for each other, moment by moment. I do not want you to take me for granted, Griffin. I do not want cozy warmth and domestic security. Or even domestic insecurity, which would be more likely." Griffin wasn't used to earning a woman's affection. He wanted his mate dependent, tied, safe and always there—waiting. Workaholic Griffin needed a steady partner because his kind of insecurity meant that he needed to know that there was always someone waiting at home for him, no matter what he did or where he went.

Suddenly, Judy realized that she didn't like having a man watch her while she got dressed. She opened the walk-in shoe closet, newly covered in jet black moiré, to match the carpet. "Griffin, I've got something really important to tell you."

She picked a pair of silver sandals. "Yesterday, my past caught up with me."

"What happened?" Was that why she was acting so strangely tonight?

"You know I was a scholarship student in Switzerland. I got pregnant while I was there. The baby was adopted."

"Well, that was a long time ago." Now that Griffin understood, he knew when to be magnanimous. "That shouldn't come between us. Don't let it upset you."

Suddenly the love affair, which had seemed overwhelmingly important to Judy for ten years, looked very insignificant beside the new fact that she had a daughter. "Griffin, will you listen? My child is alive and she's tracked me down."

"Huh?" He was suddenly all attention. "I'll get the lawyers onto it first thing tomorrow. Boy, has she picked the wrong lady to touch for a few bucks!"

"Griffin, she isn't short of a few bucks. She's Lili—the actress, *the Lili.*"

"Tiger-Lili?" That was what she was called by the press.

"Yes."

Griffin thought for a moment. "There must be a reason for it. She's after the publicity."

"Griffin, she can get all the publicity she needs by simply appearing in public."

"Don't worry, I'll fix it. She's bound to be after something."

Judy gave up.

Maxine leaned forward and sighed with pleasure, as the navy-blue Peugeot crested the gentle hill and she saw her vineyards spread below her. She always enjoyed flying Concorde on a Sunday, when it was never crowded. The car cruised quietly out of the snow-speckled forest and began the gentle descent toward the Chateau de Chazalle. Maxine's mind was already running down the list of arrangements she needed to make for the forthcoming week, when she and Charles were to meet a rider from the French Olympic equestrian team, and Maxine's first boyfriend, Pierre Boursal, now the trainer of an exciting young skier who had already won the European women's slalom. Since Maxine had decided that Chazalle was going into sponsorship, they had entertained more suitors than a fairy-tale princess, she reflected with satisfaction.

The car scattered a flock of white doves on the crescent-shaped gravel drive and the cooing birds bustled out of Maxine's way as she walked happily up the wide stone steps to the imposing doorway, where the butler waited, with a footman behind him.

Eagerly, Maxine ran upstairs to her bedroom. "Honorine, have all my bags put in the dressing room," she called over her shoulder to her maid, as she pulled off gray kid gloves. "Send the jewel box to the strong room and please run me a bath. . . ."

She was fully inside the bedroom before she realized that the room was not as it should have been. Instead of being smooth and perfectly in place, on the enormous boat-shaped Empire bed, the pale-blue silk bedcover was crumpled on the floor. On tousled sheets, her husband Charles lay naked on his back, and astride him sat a big, dark woman wearing the shreds of a green silk camisole. Charles clutched her breasts so tightly that flesh bulged between his fingers as, with one arm, the woman held up her mass of dark hair; her other hand was busy between her legs, helping herself to climax.

Like a stunned animal in an abattoir, Maxine buckled at the knees. Her first instinct was to step back and swing the doors shut, to blot out the sight of her bed, her husband and his mistress. She leaned against the wall of the wide corridor, shaking with shock, but then her tactician's mind told her what to do.

Maxine pulled on her gloves, then she flung open the double doors of her bedroom and strode furiously up to the disordered bed. She grabbed the writhing woman by the hair and pulled her away from her husband's body. "Charles, how dare you?" Maxine demanded in fury. "In *our* bed! Why couldn't you keep this whore in Paris, with all your other divertissements?"

CHAPTER 2

October 17, 1978

UNHAPPILY FOR MAXINE, the dark woman was no cheap *jupon*; after the hallucinatory flash of the first few seconds, Maxine realized that the girl making love to her husband was Simone, his impressively qualified personal assistant.

"We thought you were coming back tomorrow." His explanation was hardly an excuse, thought Charles, and his habitual expression of mild astonishment changed to frantic alarm. The girl in the shredded green slip shook herself free of Maxine, then calmly sat on the side of the bed, grabbed Charles's limp hand, and twitched the sheet over his long, thin, naked body with a gesture of possession.

"Charles has something to tell you, Madame la Comtesse." Charles's assistant looked Maxine straight in the eyes. "Go ahead, Charles, don't let your wife push you around."

For an instant, husband and wife looked silently at each other, then Charles cleared his throat and said, "Maxine, I want a divorce."

Maxine could not believe her ears. "Never," she said softly, sounding far more resolute than she felt. Then her voice rose. "Get her out of this bed! Get her out of this room! Immediately!" Maxine's legs shook and she felt as if she were running in slow motion across the treacherous surface of the moon as she ran into her bathroom and slammed the door against those two naked bodies on the wrecked bed.

By the following morning, Charles's assistant had disappeared and a frosty silence had settled on the Chateau de Chazalle. Maxine was still in a shocked trance, but she plunged into a frenzy of work to distract her mind from her grief and pain; she attacked her accumulated mail, demanded to check the china and linen lists, and sent servants scurrying on different errands all over the chateau. Maxine's secretary left her office with enough work for a month; without being told, Mademoiselle Janine, who had been with Maxine for twenty-two years, knew the reason for Maxine's frantic activity, and silently sympathized with her mistress for being faced, yet again, with one of the Count's regrettable indiscretions.

By midday, Maxine's competent mind had worked out that her charming, correct husband would never have acknowledged the existence of his mistress to her—let alone have asked for a divorce—had Maxine not surprised them together, had that bitch not forced Charles to speak. Too late, Maxine realized that the cleverest action would have been quickly to close the bedroom door and walk away, then later to have tackled Charles on his own, when, Maxine knew, he would have agreed to whatever she demanded. But now, it was too late.

It was not the first time Maxine had felt her marriage to be in danger. By tradition, aristocratic French couples often lived discreetly separate sex lives, but they never allowed anything to threaten the sanctity of their family, their home and—most important—their inheritance. But Charles was too easily seduced, and Maxine too romantic, to follow this civilized way of life, and their friends considered the mixture of Charles's déclassée mistresses and Maxine's perfect fidelity to be an immature invitation to trouble.

After Charles's first serious affair, what had brought them together again had been Judy's intervention. A little of her Yankee common sense had made Charles realize what he stood to lose. So if Maxine couldn't handle this situation by herself, she thought, she'd send an SOS to Judy in New York.

Lili yawned as she answered the telephone. "Who? Paul Kroll? For Simon?" Damned directors thought they could phone an actor at any time of the day or night. "Paul, can't it wait until tomorrow? It's eleven o'clock in New York and Simon's in the shower."

"Simon never minds what time I call him."

"Well, I mind. Are you in London or Paris? I'll get him to call you tomorrow when we wake up."

"Why not wake up now, Lili?" Paul's voice was slurred and backed by party noise.

"What do you mean? I am awake."

"No, dear, you're in Dreamland." The silky, bitter note in his voice reminded her that Kroll was gay.

"What the hell do you mean?"

"What I mean, lil ole Lili, is that you won't face what we all know." Now his words were running into each other, but there was a triumphant note in Kroll's voice.

"What *do* you mean?"

"I mean that no matter how hard Simon tries to pretend he's straight . . . he's only pretending. We've been at it together for years, darling. We all know that any actor will do anything for a good part, but Simon does it because he likes it. He *loves* it, darling. He hates to admit it, but that long tongue gets in the strangest places, don't you find? When you were shooting *Cherie*, Simon and I were in Marrakesh. When you were making *The Sun King*, Simon and I were in Tangiers. When you . . ."

Unable to speak, and unable to put down the telephone, hypnotized by Paul's disgusting, detailed story of lust and treachery, Lili listened with tears falling down her face until Simon's wet forearm reached over her shoulder and snatched the telephone from her. Without saying a word, he, too, listened. Then he shouted, "Shut up, Paul, you're drunk . . . because I can tell . . . you've wrecked everything, you stupid idiot." Simon slammed the phone down and stared defiantly at Lili. "Paul doesn't mean anything to me."

Lili knew that Simon was lying.

The massed narcissi and pink rosebuds of La Grenouille defied the November mist outside; the cheery buzz of the lunchers—mostly elegant women, was a counterpoint to the white strained face of Lili, as she leaned across the restaurant table to Pagan and said, "I never meant to tell you about Simon, but I'm so miserable that I haven't been able to think about anything else for the last few days. I didn't want to tell Judy because . . . it would just make our situation more complicated, when I want it to be simplified."

"Lili, your reactions are understandable," Pagan soothed her. "That would have been a devastating experience for anyone. It was a rotten way to learn the news, and Simon did a rotten thing in walking out on you."

"I suppose he was forced to choose. I suppose he was being honest with himself at last. We didn't have a row, you know. We both just sat on the bed crying. But after the things that Kroll had told me, I couldn't bear for Simon to touch me. And as well as his homosexuality, there's his deception; the thought that I would have been used as camouflage; that we would have had children—just to make Simon look normal. . . . "

"Be fair, Lili, he may really want children."

"I can't be fair. I feel so . . . humiliated."

There was a pause, then Pagan leaned across and pressed Lili's hand. "There *is* life after humiliation, Lili, I promise you. As you get older, you'll find out. You have to learn to overcome humiliation, to live through it. And although you never want anyone to know about it, it's always much easier for you if you tell somebody, because *everybody* has known the bitterness of humiliation at some time; everyone's experienced it, and that's why any sensitive person sympathizes with someone who's been humiliated."

"I certainly know about humiliation, but I don't believe that any of you four rich, successful women really know the meaning of the word."

After another pause, Pagan said, "Yes, I do." Even after all these years, Pagan still felt a twinge of jealousy as she remembered the nineteen-year-old Prince Abdullah and the happy intimacy they had shared, until he had contracted a political marriage at the command of his grandfather, then assumed the role of Sydon's ruler and embarked on his philandering career as the Playboy Prince of the Western World.

When his father died, Abdullah's time was fully taken up with the political problems of his country, and the gynecological problems of his wife, who had a series of miscarriages, a stillborn child and a son who died two weeks after birth. King Abdullah, as a Moslem, could have four wives. Four childless years later, he was on the point of taking a second wife to provide him with heirs, when his son Mustapha was born and, from the moment his father held the tiny body in his arms, Mustapha was the only person in the world that he loved.

In 1972, Abdullah, piloting his own helicopter, was flying his wife and ten-year-old Mustapha to their hunting lodge in the eastern mountains of Sydon. Because of faulty servicing, the engine failed, the helicopter had crashed, and the 150-pound propeller blade roughly slashed the Queen's head from her body; then the helicopter had exploded, throwing Abdullah through the air and across the desert sand, where, severely injured but not unconscious, he watched the helicopter turn into a roaring ball of fire that reduced his son, Mustapha, to a twisted black crisp.

During the following three years, Abdullah, racked by grief and guilt, had rarely appeared in public, until he met Lili. For the next year, Pagan remembered, Lili and Abdullah had been inseparable, until Lili had suddenly returned to Paris and her career.

Pagan looked across the narcissi and rosebuds on the restaurant table to Lili, the only white woman that Abdullah had ever openly taken to Sydon. Suddenly, Pagan remembered Abdullah's arrogance and the commanding voice which masked his apprehension and, sometimes, fear. Lili had had what Pagan had never been allowed—and Lili had turned it down; she had walked out on Abdullah.

Pagan couldn't resist mentioning it. She said, "If we're talking of humiliation, we must remember that you humiliated King Abdullah."

"No, I didn't," said Lili, "he didn't feel humiliated when his Western Whore went back to the West."

Again, Pagan couldn't resist asking, "Why did you leave him?"

"I was kept in a gilded cage, his courtiers spied on me, they didn't trust me. I was an infidel and there was no possibility of his marrying me, because Abdullah needs a wife—perferably a Moslem wife—to provide him with heirs, and my . . . shall we say my 'exotic' past rendered me unsuitable wife material. In a word, Pagan, I was not respectable enough for the job."

"But immediately after you left, he adopted his only blood kin, his nephew, Hassan, as his heir, so it doesn't look as if he intends to marry again. Haven't seen a word about him in the gossip columns lately."

"He's too busy with his civil war."

"No, Lili, it isn't a civil war. Abdullah's army is fighting the communist-backed guerrillas in the Eastern Hills of Sydon."

Lili gave Pagan a sharp look. "I know that, but most people don't realize how complicated the political situation is in Sydon at the moment. You seem to know a lot about Abdullah."

"We were all at school in the same little town in Switzerland. Abdullah and I used to be pretty good chums." Pagan thought she needn't tell Lili more than that.

Lili threw a quick look of reassessment at Pagan; she noticed the Englishwoman's long legs, tucked awkwardly around the table legs, the mahogany-colored hair that fell carelessly around her pale blue eyes, and the beautifully cut tweed jacket, with a man's cream-silk handkerchief flopping out of the breast pocket. Lili asked, "What happened to you after Switzerland, Pagan?"

"Something nasty happened to me. I married Mr. Wrong and then found out that he didn't really love me, he was just after me for my money. Funny thing was, I didn't have any money. I'd inherited my grandfather's estate in Cornwall, but it was mortgaged to the hilt. Robert never forgave me for not being rich. I cheered myself up with vodka, which blotted out the reality of Robert, and eventually ended up a drunk most of the time." She raised her glass of Perrier. "You see before you a card-carrying member of Alcoholics Anonymous. I can assure you that I know about humiliation, because I was responsible for my own humiliation." She took a sip of water. "Kate saved me. Kate's always been my best friend since we were at school together. She took me over and wouldn't let me give up. I'll never forget what she did for me."

Lili, who hadn't touched her avocado and salmon salad, said wistfully, "There's something about the four of you that I can't put my finger on, something warm and protective. I could almost feel it when we were in the room together."

Pagan finished her last forkful of mushrooms. "That's friendship. Since we were in Switzerland together, we've helped each other through thick and thin—or sick and sin as Maxine calls it. Like most French people, she pronounces 'th' as 's.' "

"Don't tell me that Maxine knows about sin!"

"Maxine may be a bit of a prig, but she certainly knows about sin—and humiliation. Her husband, Charles, finds other women . . . difficult to resist. Maxine felt humiliated for years until one day she couldn't take it any longer. Crunch point. Separation. Judy flew over to France and had a colossal stand-up fight with Charles, pointing out that he was going to lose if he was idiot enough to let Maxine walk out on him. Since then, he seems to have toed the line. Judy can be a fierce little thing, when she believes she's fighting for the right."

"What was my mother like when she was young?"

"Brave, like a little drummer boy marching into war. Her father had gone bust in the depression and that made her determined to be successful. She always worked very hard. Unlike the rest of us, she had an iron discipline. The poor girl never even had time to learn to ski."

"And my father? What was he like?" Lili's innocent question was the reason that she had invited Pagan to lunch. "What did he look like?"

Damn, Pagan thought, I'm hopeless at fibbing, but I must make this sound good for Judy's sake. She said, "He was—um—was very good-looking. He had black hair and aquamarine eyes, and beautiful manners. He was terribly shy, like most English boys.

"Judy met him first, because he was a waiter learning hotel management at the Imperial, where Judy worked. He was like a brother to us and we all adored him—but he had eyes for nobody but Judy." Pagan didn't add that, although Judy liked him, she simply didn't feel sexually attracted to Nick. And if a girl doesn't, she doesn't. No matter how handsome, rich and eligible a boy was, if the chemistry wasn't present, there was no use trying to force it. Poor darling Nick had been potty about Judy—when he left, he'd given her those two carved rosebud rings from Cartier, but, although Judy liked him, she had drawn away from a physical relationship.

"Judy said he was an orphan."

I'll bet she did, thought Pagan. That meant that Judy would have no further questions from Lili to answer. "He charmed us all," Pagan said. "Then he went to do his National Service as a soldier in Malaya, and the next thing we heard was that he'd been killed. We were heartbroken."

Lili did not miss the hesitancy in Pagan's description, or the overcarefulness of her speech, so unlike Pagan's normal careless frankness. So there is something more to find out, Lili thought, mechanically brushing toast crumbs off her white leather trousers. "Was Judy . . . er . . . popular with boys when she was a student?"

"Judy? She worked so hard that she hardly had time for dates. Why do you ask, Lili?" Attack is the best method of defense, Pagan thought, returning Lili's velvet-brown gaze.

She's challenged me, Lili thought, sensing the bond between the four women, so strong it was almost tangible, an invisible wall between her and the last shreds of the mystery of her identity.

"I suppose there was no doubt that Nick was my father?"

There, I've said it, Lili congratulated herself.

"I should think not." Pagan's tone was firm with a scandalized edge. Lili realized that she would get no further, as Pagan continued, "What happened to Judy could have happened to any one of us. We were all experimenting with life, we all had our first love affairs in Switzerland and we shared everything, so it seemed natural to us to share the responsibility for you, until Judy could afford to give you a home. But she was only earning a secretary's salary when you disappeared."

"How did she start her business?"

"She worked in public relations, and then Maxine pushed her into starting her own business. In fact, Chazalle was Judy's first client. It was rough for Judy with no experience, no reputation, and no money. She keeps quiet about it now, but she was twice evicted because she couldn't pay the rent. She was almost as broke as the Research Institute is today." Pagan thought she might as well do what she'd come to New York to do. "My husband was so excited when I told him you were considering a donation to the Anglo-American Cancer Research Institute. He desperately needs a new electron microscope."

Lili wriggled, feeling guilty. She had certainly lured Pagan to that meeting at the Pierre with the promise of money for cancer research. "I could ask my agent if we could open my new film with a benefit premiere in New York. Or a gala in London."

"Or both?" Pagan had come a long way since, quivering with fear and shame, she had first asked for a charity donation.

"I'll do my best," Lili said, then added, "I wish that Maxine hadn't had to return to France. I wanted so much to get to know you all properly."

"You will, in time. We don't see that much of each other these days, not that it matters."

"Why doesn't it matter?" asked Lili, as the waiter served their lobsters.

"A real friend is someone you don't have to be with. These days, a friendship between two women can last longer than their marriages." Pagan picked up her lobster crackers. "If both women accept that there will be tough times as well as good ones," she sucked the juicy flesh from the claw, "and that sometimes you'll want to strangle your friend and sometimes she'll want to strangle you. A true friendship isn't static, it comes and goes."

"Then what pulls friends back together?" Lili wondered.

"You just feel more comfortable, more at home, with certain people than with anyone else."

"But why?" Lili persisted.

"Oh—shared experience, understanding, tolerance and trust, that sort of thing." Pagan gestured with a red lobster claw. "A good friendship is like a marriage is supposed to be, but very rarely is. Today, the men seem to come and go in a woman's life, but our female friendships are often more enduring. In fact, as marriages crash and the generation gap widens, female friendship seems to be the only growth area in relationships."

"What do you mean?" Lili was fascinated.

"Lots of relationships are now being questioned and rethought, because it's clear that the old relationships aren't working as we had been led to expect, when we were young."

"So what were you led to expect?" Lili licked a scrap of pink carcass.

"We were all taught that our purpose in life was to get a man," said Pagan. "So we all hung around, waiting for Prince Charming to turn up." She separated shreds of flesh from shell. "After I married, I thought that I'd live in pink bliss forever; I never imagined that my Prince Charming husband would be unkind or unfaithful. We've turned out to be pioneers, just as much as those women in covered wagons." Pagan wiped her fingers on her pink napkin. "But we are pioneers of the emotions, and one of our problems is that we don't realize this." Lili had hardly touched her lobster, Pagan noticed as she continued. "Those pioneers knew when they were traveling through hostile territory; they could hear the war whoops, see the Indians and feel the arrows. Today, some of us are under fire, some of us are walking wounded and some of us on crutches; but our scars are invisible, and often you don't even realize that you've been in battle." Pagan paused as they ordered coffee, then continued. "The pioneers end up scalped, of course; it's the next generation that reaps the benefit, and enjoys the promised land."

"Where the hell is the promised land?" Lili demanded.

"A place where men and women can be honest with each other, and share their responsibilities, and base all relationships on truth, not inadequacies and fear."

"What do you mean by fear?"

"Most relationships are based on fear to varying degrees; fear that your mother will be cross, fear that your teacher will be angry, fear that your boyfriend will leave you, fear that your boss will fire you, or fear that the Russians will kill you."

"What do you mean by inadequacy?"

"An example of a relationship based on inadequacy is a marriage that a woman enters into because she's frightened that she's unattractive, or she's frightened that she'll never get married, or she's frightened that she can't support herself."

Slowly Lili said, "Then we are pioneers and explorers, and what we are discovering is a better way to live."

"Hopefully, yes."

Sand and rock spurted into the shell hole where the American war photographer and three Sydonite soldiers pressed themselves into the shuddering earth. Another shell burst at the far lip of the crater, half burying their legs. The next one will get us, thought Mark, his lean body cringing against the hot earth. I must not panic, I must not panic, I must not panic, he chanted silently to himself, like a mantra; if the next one does not get you, you will have to run, and if you panic, your legs will turn to water, and you'll move so slowly, you'll get hit immediately. I must not panic, I must not panic. He brushed his dirty-brown hair off his forehead and knuckled the dust from heat-sore gray eyes.

At his side, two soldiers leapt up as another shell whistled overhead; they struggled up the sliding sides of the crater, trying to run forward as the ground crumbled under their legs, and the shell ploughed into the sand behind the crater.

A burst of gunfire caught the men squarely in the neck and chest, and flung them back into the shell hole. Their blood splashed over the two remaining men crouched in the crater and Mark wiped some of the spattered drops off his camera. Mark's wide mouth was bleeding, his big lips were sun-cracked and his thin face was covered with sun blisters; his small, pugnacious nose was pink and raw because he always forgot his sunblock.

Another shell howled overhead, and bullets smacked into the sand around the crater. "No way I'm going to get killed while being unprofessional," Mark muttered as he reloaded his camera. "When they roll my carcass over, the last shot will be fit to print."

In the few seconds the distant mortar took to reload, two Sydonite soldiers and an officer hurled themselves forward into the shell hole, falling over their dead comrades. They scrambled to their feet, pushed the bleeding bodies to one side, and started to position a missile launcher.

Mark noticed that the young officer was using an infrared tracking device to aim the missiles. For once, thought Mark, King Abdullah's petrodollars have been well spent. The officer was calm and businesslike, they would have been proud of him back at Sandhurst. Did this quietly competent youth know that he was in charge of a suicide mission? Mark wondered. Major Khalid had tried to stop the photographer from coming out with this patrol. With hindsight, Mark realized that the major was *too* insistent that this was merely to be a routine reconnaissance mission, of no interest to the Western press. But, because so much desert warfare was carried on at night, when it was impossible to take photographs, Mark had argued with the Major. What the callous bastard had not chosen to spell out to Mark was that the platoon had been sent out as cannon fodder, to draw the guerrillas' fire, and the Major didn't want any half-baked heroics from an American journalist.

Again, Mark wiped the lens of his Nikon, composed the shot in his mind's eye and carefully photographed the dead men, who were huddled together in the dirt like sleeping children; both were drenched in blood and the smaller soldier had a boot print clearly stenciled in carmine across his face. Concentration steadied Mark's hands and wiped the panic from his body, as he cleared his mind to get the high definition which made his pictures look so vivid. A Mark Scott picture could be sent by wire around the world and not be reduced to a blur when it was printed.

Mark's panic surged back as soon as the shutter clicked, and he watched the other three men in the shell hole work to wipe out the enemy position, grimly aware that this was their only chance of getting out alive. One soldier loaded the first slim missile down the launcher's muzzle, and the officer watched his tracking device as it hurtled forward in a high arc.

From the hillside ahead, another shell roared over the shell hole as the angle of the missile launcher was lowered and again fired at the mortar emplacement ahead, which was tucked under a rocky overhang behind a wall of sandbags.

Mark focused carefully on the intent faces around the launcher. These men would have no chance of leaving this crater alive unless they could get a rocket into the eighteen-inch gap between the rocky overhang and the sandbags to blow out the gun and the men manning it.

Another adjustment to the weapon, another rocket down the spout, another retort as it was fired. This time, no answering shell screamed back from the hillside ahead.

The Sydonite officer ordered another round and again there was no response.

The air was harsh with heat, smoke, and the sweetly pungent stink of war. Now Mark fought relief with the same intensity that he had earlier fought panic. Cool it, cool it, for Chrissake stay cool, stay down, stay alive. Mark had often seen men jump up in elation, believing they had been snatched from the jaws of death, only to be mown down by an enemy who understood that his last chance would be the other side's carelessness.

The young officer ordered his two remaining men to crawl forward, one by one, taking advantage of every rock and every rise in the cracked earth, as they snaked forward, until they were below the rocky hill.

They started to scramble upwards. When they were closer to the enemy mortar emplacement, a grenade was thrown into the gap from which the gun barrel still projected. Caution saved them. With a howl of pain, a man's body was catapulted out by the blast. Behind the billowing pall of dust and smoke, Mark saw the machine gun whipping to and fro on its tripod.

"Better use the back door," said the officer. "Grenades may have weakened the roof of that cave."

They crawled out of the heat into another opening in the rock, part of an interconnected labyrinth across a limestone cavern, packed with stores which looked like the usual guerrillas' jumble of substandard or obsolete arms and explosives. Over a hundred crates, containing 1000-gram sticks of TNT were stacked by polyethylene bags, each containing 24 sticks of gelignite. Beyond was a box of safety fuses and a crate of No. 27 instantaneous aluminum detonators, half-hidden by a tangle of Cordtex detonating cords. Further back in the cave were a few primer sticks of TNT and two boxes of TNT flakes. The hot dessicated air of Sydon had preserved the arms from rust, but nitroglycerin had soaked through the wax coating of some of the cartridges, so the pile was liable to explode at the slightest impact.

"Why did we bother?" the young officer was cheerful as he spoke to Mark in his correct, but guttural English. "One cigarette would have done our job for us." It was a weak joke, but to the four survivors of the fourteen-man platoon which had set out that morning, it was hilarious.

Bright sunlight slid through slits in the rock and illuminated the interconnected caves as Mark wandered below the stack of old equipment. Seeing that some of the crates were marked in Cyrillic script, as well as English, Mark used his Swiss army knife, the only weapon he ever carried, to lever out the nails. The crate was full of Russian MUV igniters, for use in priming booby traps.

Further back in the cave, Mark found crates of Kalashnikov rifles, Chinese grenades, 122mm BM 21 Katyusha rockets with 20 kilo warheads and a Goryunova SG-43 machine gun. The inner cavern was a treasure trove of Soviet arms, and, unlike the elderly Western supplies near the entrance, they were clean and new.

Mark quickly moved to the devastated front of the cave, where the mortar still stood among the debris of fallen rock and torn flesh. The six bodies wore ragged U.S. army surplus battle fatigues. One man was still alive, although his chest was a gaping hole filled with blood; his lips stretched wide in agony as he tried to speak. Realizing that the man might live long enough to give them useful information, the Sydonite officer reached for his water bottle and dribbled some liquid into the cracked mouth. As the dying man mumbled a few words, Mark realized that they were not Arabic. The dying man was dark haired and olive skinned but, as Mark looked at the dirt-caked face, he realized that those features were unmistakably Latin.

"Cubanos?" Mark asked.

The man hissed his last words. "*Si. Viva . . . re . . . revolución.*"

Four of the dead men were Cubans. One of the corpses wore a neck medallion with Castro's head on it. The other two enemy corpses were unmistakable Arabs; one had a prayer written in Arabic script on a scrap of cloth tied around his right wrist. "He asked the Prophet to guide his hand," explained the officer, tossing away the rag.

"Mercenaries?" asked Mark.

"Sure," the young officer answered. "Intelligence warned us that the Fundamentalist guerrillas had Soviet equipment. It's not surprising that they also brought the men to use them."

He ordered a soldier to carry the damaged explosives down the hillside; they then threw a grenade into the lethal pile and destroyed it.

The four survivors waited until starlight before approaching the nearest village. They entered the settlement with caution and were similarly greeted, then escorted to the headman's house. A young boy in white came forward and offered a brass bowl of dates. Wearily, Mark pushed the food away.

"You will eat!" the young officer angrily told him. "While you are with my men, you are my responsibility, so you will eat and drink when I tell you."

Mark apologized. He never remembered his physical needs while he was working; his goal was first to get his pictures, then to get back alive.

"And now we sleep," the officer told him. Obediently, Mark stretched out with the three soldiers on the mud floor of the hut.

At dawn, Major Khalid drove into the village and Mark shipped out on a truck that was crammed with wounded men. This was going to be a stinking, uncomfortable ride, Mark thought. Then, to his surprise, two black-veiled peasant women also climbed onto the truck. Between them, they carried a seven-year-old girl, her abdomen greatly swollen above filthy swaddled bandages which bound her legs together like a mummy. The child was running a high fever, her eyes rolling upward and her cheeks dry and flaking, as she lay across the legs of the two peasant women.

When the truck reached the hospital, Mark helped to carry the wounded into the building. Then he heaved his kit bag on to his back and set off for the gate. He was almost out of the hospital grounds, when a male nurse ran up to him. "Come," said the male nurse, "come—take picture." Mark followed the male nurse along the hospital corridor. Outside the casualty room stood a gray-haired, tired, skinny woman, with her hands thrust into the pockets of her white coat. "You are a journalist?" she asked Mark.

"Sure."

"To whom do you sell your photographs?"

"*Time, Newsweek*, all the European magazines; my agency sells worldwide."

"Then I want you to photograph that girl. It must be done without her mother's knowledge or she will prevent it."

Mark followed the white-coated woman to a small beige room where the girl lay on a stretcher, her stomach bloated, as if she were pregnant. A female nurse was gently unwinding the bandages that held the child's legs together. Mark had asked no questions, because the urgency in the doctor's voice had told him that whatever he was going to see might be important. In silence, he prepared his cameras, while the nurse rigged a drip into the girl's thin arm; as she increased the volume of the liquid flowing into her vein, the girl slipped into unconsciousness. The smell of septicemia pervaded the small room.

As the bandages were removed, Mark saw a mass of pus and blood oozing between the little legs; her delicate young genitals were caked in a brown paste of what looked like chewed grass. As the nurse gently sponged water over the stinking mass, another nurse held the small dusty feet together, then eased the girl's thighs apart, allowing the coltish knees slowly to fall outwards.

The lips of the girl's vulva were speared by a row of long acacia thorns lashed across with black twine. As the caked paste and scabs of blood were washed away from the cat's cradle of thorns and string, Mark saw cloudy green pus trickling from a tiny opening at the bottom of the closed slit. Quickly, he photographed, as the nurse snipped the threads, picked each piece off with tweezers, then carefully, so as not to break them, pulled the thorns out, one by one. The last thing Mark saw was the child's mutilated genitals gaping bloody and rotten as the last thorn came out. Then he fainted.

Mark opened his eyes in an emergency room, reached for a kidney bowl and vomited the remains of the previous night's milk and dates into it. The woman doctor heard his retching and came over to him. Mark said, "What had they done to that girl? That's the most horrible thing I've ever seen."

"They made her into good marriage material." The doctor was unable to keep the fury out of her voice. "A virgin bride and a docile wife. They do that in most of Africa and also some of the most primitive communities in the Arab states. They circumcised her; they deliberately mutilated her genitals. First, they cut out her clitoris and all of her labia minora; a wife that cannot fully enjoy sex is less likely to stray."

"But who did it?"

"Probably the village midwife used the razor, while the girl's mother and her sisters held her down. Of course they have no anesthetics. Then, earth or ashes would have been rubbed on the wound to stop the bleeding. Then they sewed her up, as you saw, with thorns and twine. They leave a miniscule opening for urine and menstrual blood. Then they bind her legs together to immobilize them."

"Why is her stomach so swollen?"

"It is swollen with blackish, foul-smelling blood."

"But what happens after she's married?"

"What do you think? Her husband cuts her open with a dagger, then runs around the village, waving the bloodstained blade so they can all see that the bride has just been deflowered. It goes without saying that mutilated women feel severe pain during intercourse, and sometimes the husband doesn't cut enough, so when the girl has her first child, she splits open like a melon."

"Are they all . . . operated on at such a young age?"

"The earlier a child is mutilated, the greater is the damage, since infantile and adolescent masturbation teaches the orgasm."

Mark heaved a further mouthful of bile into the bowl. "What do you want me to do with the pictures?"

"Photographs may alert the Western World to what is happening here." The doctor pulled off her heavy-framed spectacles, and rubbed her tired eyes. "I was one of the doctors who gave evidence to the United Nations Commission that investigated female circumcision in the Gulf States, but their report was ignored. However, as you know, a picture is worth a thousand words. I see cases like that girl every month, some are even worse." She sighed. "But the government of Sydon, which pretends that this practice no longer exists, would be unable to ignore a photograph in an American magazine. Western pressure would force the Sydonite government to take action."

"Do you mean King Abdullah?" asked Mark.

"No, not the King. The Department of Health suppresses all information. I think they keep the facts from the King because many of his Western reforms are unpopular."

Mark felt a quick sympathy for this doctor. Pity for the wretched peoples of the earth was the driving force in his life; however many corpses he photographed, however many of his friends disappeared in combat zones, Mark's compassion was as profound as it had been ten years earlier when, an idealistic teen-ager, he had run away to his first war. He said, "Before I leave Sydon, I am to photograph King Abdullah. I will try to show him the pictures." Behind the doctor's spectacles, Mark saw gratitude and hope.

From his army helicopter, Mark saw Semira on the skyline. The political capital of Sydon rose in tiers of white fortified walls from the green plain that lay below it, on the bank of the country's only river. As the helicopter flew over the white-domed rooftops, Mark could see the Royal Standard flying from the castellated towers of the Palace that crowned the ancient town. Even though he was stuck in the desert, Major Khalid had been able to pull the necessary strings to arrange Mark's audience with King Abdullah because Major Khalid wanted full credit for the discovery of the enemy arms dump, the existence of which had been proved by Mark's photographs.

Mark was conducted by two ADCs into the King's presence. The King rose from behind his elaborate antique French desk.

"*Salaam Alaikum.*"

"*Alaikum a Salaam.*" King Abdullah preferred the simple traditional greeting of peace to the elaborate extended courtesies which were his birthright, as the fourteenth hereditary ruler of his country. "Intelligence tells me you have been in the Eastern Hills with Major Khalid, and that you are one of the survivors of the Major's assault on the guerrillas in Wadi al Hasa. Let's look at your pictures."

Mark knew better than to point out that Major Khalid had nothing to do with the success of the operation, as he opened his folder of photographs and spread the still-damp prints on a mahogany table at the side of the room. Mark handed him a magnifying glass and, carefully, the King bent over the shots. "These are really magnificent pictures of desert warfare." He peered closer at the prints. "You are obviously a brave man, Mr. Scott." He looked again at the shots of the Soviet arms cache. "As every discontented man calls himself a communist, we could not be sure of Soviet infiltration; we suspected it, but we had no proof. You have done my country a great service. Thank you."

Mark saw his moment. "Your Majesty, I have some other pictures I would like you to see."

"By all means." Swiftly Mark gathered up the pictures that proved Russian intervention in Sydon and replaced them with pictures of the circumcised child being tended by the nurses.

Abdullah looked in silence at the helpless, feverish face and mutilated young body, then softly he demanded, "Who committed this atrocity? What kinds of soldiers are guilty of this perversion?" Mark could see from the faces of the two ADCs that they knew what they were seeing, but that Abdullah's mistake was genuine.

"Your Majesty, this is not an atrocity committed by the guerrillas," Mark explained, "this is the result of an infibulation operation on a young girl. I was asked to take these pictures by a doctor at the Dinada hospital."

Abdullah's calm was chilling as he walked slowly back to his polished leather wing chair and asked Mark to sit down and tell him about this barbaric practice. He scribbled the doctor's name on his note pad and ordered one of the ADCs to summon the Minister of Health immediately. The King then fixed the other young ADC with his black glare. "Did you know of this custom?"

"Yes, Your Majesty," the ADC stood stiffly at attention. "But it is only practiced by the most primitive peasant women. . . ."

"Ninety-five percent of our people are primitive peasants." King Abdullah's voice was still quiet but his eyes were angry. "Why was I never told of this? Is there any reason for it?"

"Nothing beyond superstition, Your Majesty," the ADC answered, "but the Moslem Fundamentalists approve it. There is no reference in the Holy Koran to such a practice, but some of the great learned men of the past regarded the tradition as commendable."

"May Allah preserve us from the evil that is done in his name." Abdullah turned back to Mark. "What will you do with these pictures?"

"Offer them to *Time*," said Mark at once. "They'll certainly take the shots of the Russian armaments."

"But what about these?" Abdullah asked, indicating the pictures of the suffering child.

"I'll also offer them to *Time*, but they may not take them; they're too shocking."

Abdullah nodded, sharing Mark's opinion. "Do you appreciate my difficulty? I can give the order for this practice to cease immediately, and the women will obey me. Thirty years ago no house in Sydon could be repaired, no man could even leave his village, without permission of the King, and the simple people will still obey royal commands without question. The simple people are not the problem. The problem is that if I make a dictatorial gesture, the fanatics will use it to foment revolt. If I am to succeed in stopping this disgusting custom, it must seem as if I am bowing to the will of the people, not trying to impose my will upon them."

"So you need the Western press to shift the climate of popular opinion?"

"As well as Western politicians, scientists and diplomats. . . . Have you ever exhibited your photographs in a gallery, Mr. Scott?"

"Yes, I'm with Anstruther's in New York."

"Then please arrange a gallery exhibition of these photographs. We will pay for it, of course. Our Ambassador will see you when you get back to America."

Quietly, a side door opened six inches. King Abdullah's head jerked round. Two nervous brown eyes looked round the door, then a twelve-year-old boy entered. He was wearing an elaborate miniature white military uniform. King Abdullah thought his heir should enter the room like a prince, not peer round the door like a servant.

"I'm sorry to bother you, Uncle. I thought you'd finished." Prince Hassan had been waiting outside the door for two hours, torn between love and dread of his uncle, his guardian, and the King whose throne he would inherit.

CHAPTER 3

November 1978

"DO YOU MIND answering the door, Zimmer? That'll be the hotel maid with my dress." Lili was, as usual, in the tub.

Zimmer stuck his head round the bathroom door. He had directed Lili in most of her best movies, including the scandalous *Q*, which had made her an international star. "When you're ready, darling, a small jungle has just been delivered."

"Check there isn't a small journalist swinging from the trees." Since the news of her breakup with Simon Pont had flashed around the world, Lili had once again been besieged by photographers. Zimmer thought, thank heaven for Lili's sake that nobody had discovered the real reason for the breakup; but then, they never did.

Lili wandered out into the luxurious sitting room wearing a white bathrobe with her wet hair wrapped in a peach towel. With care, she approached the luxuriant orchid plant. From an arching spray of unnaturally perfect, succulent pale-yellow flowers dangled a small emerald-velvet pouch tied with silk cord. Lili opened the little bag and tipped out a small scarlet jeweler's box. Inside, a pair of dazzling blue-white diamond earrings sparkled in the weak November sunshine.

On the apricot couch by the fireside, Zimmer clicked his tongue approvingly. "That's the third packet this week—now you've got the complete set: Madame Pompadour's thirtieth birthday present, auctioned in Monte Carlo last month. No one can say Spyros doesn't try."

"Shut up, darling." Lili threw a kiss to the small, slender man on the couch and put the little scarlet box on the coffee table. "You know Spyros Stiarkoz is only after me because I was his brother's girlfriend; I'm just another part of the old Stiarkoz empire to be annexed." Lili tugged the white sash even more tightly round her slim waist. "And, Zimmer, I'm not letting you bully me into a high-profile, low-satisfaction relationship just to make your next movie a little bit more bankable."

"Not many women would turn down someone as rich and powerful as Spyros Stiarkoz."

"I don't care about his riches and his power. After Simon, I want a bit of peace and quiet. I want to be left alone. Don't you understand?" Lili sat on the other end of the apricot sofa and started to towel her hair. "Stiarkoz is *just another man* to me, another man chasing me because of something in his own imagination. Being pestered by Stiarkoz is just the same as being chased by photographers, or any of those sickies who write filthy letters to me. To them, I'm hardly human;

I'm some sort of fabulous sex goddess. All that's important to them is how *they* feel! They never think of *my* feelings, of what *I* want."

"Spyros knew as soon as Simon left for Paris. He's just trying his luck as fast as possible, before anyone else gets on the field."

"Exactly, Zimmer." Lili leaned forward and ruffled his graying blond curly hair. "I am the hare, I am the quarry. This is the nightmare of my life, the obverse of the cost of success."

"But basically it's flattering, Lili." Zimmer waved his small, neat hands in the air, begging her to be reasonable. "You're love-hungry, Lili, that's your problem and always has been. But you can't stand men being 'in love' with you because you're more intelligent than the *average* sex goddess; you don't want to mesmerize them, you want communication, not lust. You want loving warmth instead of the heat of passion."

"Exactly." Lili stopped toweling and flung her still wet hair backwards. "I have had it up to *here* with sex." She touched her nose. "My allure, sex appeal, whatever the hell it is, brings me nothing but trouble, Zimmer."

"At least you don't have to worry about that with me, darling."

"No, but I come up against your naked-eyed, beer-swilling MCPs every time I set foot outside the door. *You* can't imagine how it depresses me. *You* think it's a joke. But I sometimes wonder if anyone will ever love me just for myself, as Angelina did, instead of being mesmerized by the superstar, or loving because they really want something from you. There are so many star fuckers, Zimmer, who just want to bed me and run out and tell all their friends, so many people who want me to endorse some body stocking or bicycle, so many people who want me to invest my money in their sure-thing project." She turned to Zimmer and gently touched his hand, saying, "That's why it's so important for me to establish a loving relationship with my mother."

As he looked into the glowing dark eyes, although he wasn't the worrying sort, Zimmer thought, she can't really blame men for the effect she has on them.

"And that's why we can't persuade you to do this film? That's why you're wasting your career time hanging around New York, turning down all the parts that Swifty and I suggest?"

"That's why."

"I don't want to press you, Lili, but please think again. Mistinguett is such a wonderful part; she was the Marilyn Monroe of the twenties, all Paris was in love with her, she was the girl who put the Ooh-là-là into the Folies Bergère, and her legs were the toast of Europe."

And you, Lili, have the most wonderful legs, Zimmer thought but knew better than to mention it. "*The Best Legs in the Business* is going to be *the* biggest musical of the year. Glitter! Glamour! Fishnets! Showgirls! Sequins! Feathers! And we're after Richard Gere to play the young Maurice Chevalier."

"Sounds over budget before you start shooting." Briskly, Lili tossed the diamond earrings back into the scarlet box and threw it to Zimmer, who caught it with one hand. "In the hotel safe?"

"If we've now got the complete set, I'll return them to Spyros tonight."

"God, how I hate women who are too pure to accept jewelry. Why are you going out with him tonight if you want nothing to do with him?"

"I'm going to say no politely."

* * *

Lili and Stiarkoz sat stiffly in their private box, hardly speaking to each other as, on the distant stage, Prince Albrecht danced with the vengeful spirits of maidens deserted at the altar.

"Why do you have to tell me here?" Stiarkoz hissed.

"Because," Lili said steadily, "I don't want to tell you in public but in private." In fact, she wanted to be in a protective atmosphere. She didn't want to be taken out to sea, abducted by white Rolls to Greenwich, Connecticut, or flown to Spyros's private island in the Grenadines while he "reasoned" with her for five days nonstop. "Spyros, I'm flattered by your attention, but the answer is no. I'm sorry." Lili's voice sounded suitably contrite. Onstage, the white net corps de ballet moved relentlessly toward Prince Albrecht, their pink slippers dancing lightly over the hallowed areas of the misty graveyard. "You've been very generous to me, Spyros, but I cannot accept this beautiful jewelry from you."

"Don't thank me, Lili. I want to give you everything you want." He touched her soft hand with his wrinkled one, and Lili could not imagine anyone enjoying the touch of that claw.

Below them, fickle two-timer Prince Albrecht collapsed before the onslaught of ghostly brides. In the box an inch of cigar ash fell on the crimson carpet. "I am a careful man, as you know, Lili, and I consider all my decisions. Is there nothing I can give you to persuade you?"

Prince Albrecht staggered on, but as far as Lili was concerned, the scene was over, and she hoped to escape. Lili whispered fiercely, "How many times do I have to tell you, Spyros? All I want you to do is to leave me alone. So long as I'm dependent on a man, I'm frightened that I won't be able to cope on my own. That's why I want to start out again—by myself."

"What rubbish! All women like to play hard to get. If you don't want to see me, then already there must be another man."

Lili shook her head in frustration, and her pearl earrings shone as they caught the light. "You men can't believe that when a woman says no, she means no." She leaned forward, "There isn't anyone else. The only other person in my life is *me*. Can't you understand that at the moment I don't know who I am or what I want, or what I can do? I have found my mother, I have the beginning of my new identity, and I want to be left in peace to discover the rest—that's all. That's why I want to be left alone."

"Left alone? For twenty-four hours, perhaps." Angrily, he ground out his cigar in the bank of white chrysanthemums that fronted the private box.

In the Stiarkoz white Rolls Royce, Lili thought, Spyros is a greedy old reptile. How surprising that two brothers could be so similar and yet so different. Spyros had Jo's twinkling black olive eyes, and the rough, tough business acumen, but he lacked his dead brother's vitality and charm. Then, suddenly, in the hushed, padded interior of the car, Lili realized that Spyros was about to pounce, and that she was in a luxurious pale, pigskin prison. Lili panicked, as she remembered being told that when a Greek shipowner meets a woman and likes her, he wants sex with her straightaway.

Spyros was tough, coarse, and muscular. He went straight for Lili's breasts, ripping the embroidered white-chiffon gown. Seed pearls bounced over the carpet as his stubby hands reached for her. Lili cast a frantic look at the back view of the chauffeur. No hope there. She managed to shove Spyros away from her.

Spyros muttered, "I don't need to rape you, you'll find you will belong to me.

I will look after you better than Jo did. When he died, my brother left you penniless, didn't he? But I will give you everything you want, Lili. Your place is on my yacht, Persephone, without a care in the world, except to go shopping." Again, he fumbled at her breasts and, this time, Lili let him. She realized that if she continued to resist, he might rape her. No, her only thought was how to get out of the Rolls.

"Spyros, you can either force me, or you can give me time. It's not . . . the right day of the month."

His unblinking, tortoiselike stare searched her eyes. Lili held up her flowerlike face to his lips, and suffered his embrace until they arrived at the Pierre.

She was sweating with relief as she hurried down the long cream corridor, pulling her chinchilla wrap around her wrecked chiffon dress. At the elevator, she paused, then turned on her heel and approached the reception desk. She handed the night manager the scarlet jewel boxes. "Would you please have security deliver these to Lady Swann at the Algonquin."

Nothing would irritate Spyros more than giving his diamond bribes to charity.

Angrily, Lili stood naked in the mirrored bathroom and looked at her breasts, where bruises were already starting to form. She remembered how her body had ripened early, at twelve; how embarrassed she had felt as her breasts had swelled. Young girls always worried about their growing breasts; they were either too big or too small or too low; but whatever they were like, they attracted attention. Lili remembered how she had hated the new interest of the unknown men who lounged on the street corners of the shabby Paris suburb where she had grown up; even her adoptive father, Monsieur Sardeau, from behind his prim, civil-servant's pince-nez, had furtively swiveled his eyes over her body, as Lili worked her way through the household chores each day after school.

From the age of six, Lili's existence had been a vortex of catastrophe, a downward spiral of misery over which she had had no control. Lili had been one of life's victims—until she had learned how to use the power of her body, the power of those two upthrusting breasts.

Lili had once asked Jo Stiarkoz why men had this automatic, knee-jerk response. Why—even when they were talking to her—men would gaze helplessly at Lili's breasts, and not at her face; what was so compelling about those two pounds of flesh?

Jo had laughed and said, "I've never thought about it." Then he added thoughtfully, "What's so good about breasts is that they *wobble*; when they bounce and they jiggle, a man just wants to *grab* them. I can't say why, it's an instinctive reaction, it's gut lust."

"But *why*? When a woman sees a group of workmen in the distance, she knows that, when she draws close, there'll be this glazed-eyed, following-the-tennis-ball-at-Wimbledon reaction, as she passes the workmen. *Why*?"

Jo had said, "I really can't tell you. A man has no control over these feelings. But if a woman isn't wearing a bra, so that you can see her nipples and watch them bounce, or if she's wearing tight clothes that look as if her breasts are bursting to escape, then a man feels that there's a special conspiracy between himself and that woman, because he's wanting to touch them and knows that he can't, and he knows that this unknown female knows just how the man feels."

"What an impertinent assumption. So they wobble; so does Jello and men don't go glassy-eyed about that."

"To a man, a woman's breasts are something hidden, mysterious, forbidden. And that soft lilting movement is both a hint and a promise of that woman's sexuality: those breasts convey a secret, sensual message from the female to the male."

"Rubbish," said Lili. "That's the cause of all the trouble. No message is sent. When a woman's not making love, then her breasts just get in the way if she's doing anything athletic, or trying to look elegant, because clothes hang better on a flat body. *That's* what a woman thinks about her breasts; they're just *there*, like her knees. I'm not promising every man *anything*, simply by having breasts."

"You may not be, but that's how it appears to the man."

"That's just a man's excuse for bad behavior," Lili had sniffed. "*She was asking for it*, is what men say, conveniently shifting the responsibility for *their* attraction onto the woman. A woman likes to be admired by, and attracted to, men—but only the men of her choice."

It was a typical New York small gallery opening. Clutching glasses of white wine, intellectual men wore jeans, and intellectual women wore Martha Graham robes or black dresses: standing with their backs to the dramatic photographs of Sydon battlefields, they bitched about the gallery owner, the other critics, and Beverly Sills. Mark Scott said even less than usual as Anstruther led him from the *Village Voice* critic to the *New York Times* critic, then turned to a small blond woman who was actually inspecting the pictures through huge, tortoise-shell spectacles.

"These pictures of the little girl are shocking," Judy said. "I'd like to discuss what we could do about it in *VERVE!* magazine. And I like your other work. We can't use war photography, but I'd like to see your portfolio. I'd like our art editor to see your work."

Suddenly, another man was at her elbow, a tall, muscular, swarthy man with coarse features and an expression that veered from anxious to menacing. "Everything all right, Judy?"

"Yes, Tony, everything's fine. Would you mind getting my coat, please?"

Judy turned back to Mark. "Tony is just being protective, he's a little overzealous sometimes. He thinks I work too hard and I do too much and that people take advantage of me. I'm afraid he's especially protective when he sees me talking to a handsome young man."

"Then let's talk where Tony can't see us. How about dinner?"

Tony's daily aerobics class at *VERVE!* had been an instant success, and Judy fell into the habit of inviting her friends in to work out, instead of taking them out to lunch.

As Judy told Pagan about her new friend, the war photographer, Lili pulled on several pairs of dirty leg warmers, all full of holes. "Zimmer calls these my refugee rags," she laughed as she arranged the knitted layers over her black sweat trousers, then flopped over to tie her shoes with the well-trained suppleness of a Degas figure.

Pagan could admire with detachment the beauty of the slim young woman; Pagan had always been blithely unconcerned about her appearance until she met Christopher.

After forty minutes in the exercise class, Pagan's face was flushed with effort and she was gasping for air. On either side of her, Judy and Lili seemed to be barely sweating. "Thank God I'm going home at the end of the month, much more of this would kill me," Pagan panted.

Tony's glistening muscles were set off by white satin shorts and a white T-shirt with rolled sleeves. His muscles bulged, knotted, quivered, and twitched as he demonstrated the next exercise in front of a panel of mirrors that now lined one wall of the *VERVE!* boardroom.

"This exercise increases flexibility." He demonstrated. "Feet apart, pointing forward. Now bend your knees, shoulders down and relaxed—don't stick your ribcage out, Pagan. Now move your hips forward right, back, left, swing your hips in a circle. Don't move any other part of your body." Blank-faced with concentration, he rotated his pelvis.

Somebody snickered. "Go to it, Tony."

Tony stopped moving. "This isn't funny. It's a basic jazz isolation exercise, also found in many other schools of dance." He scowled. "Even classic Eastern belly dancers perform this movement . . . "

Without thinking, Pagan interrupted him. "No, they don't, Tony. Belly dancers don't bump and grind, that's far too crude a movement. They sort of . . . shimmy all over."

Tony didn't like being contradicted. "No girl gets to be the King's favorite unless she can shake her ass, and if she won't practice her exercises, she's whipped by the chief mistress of the harem."

Stubbornly, Pagan said, "I don't know where you studied your Eastern philosophy, but you've got it wrong. There's no such person as a chief mistress; a proper harem is run by the King's mother and the Chief Eunuch and no wives would ever be beaten because Royal blood must never be spilled. They used to strangle naughty wives with silken bowstrings."

Judy didn't want Pagan to tease the not-overbright exercise instructor. "Okay, everybody, that's enough," she ordered. "Let's switch to inner thigh exercises and stop this nonsense."

The girls groaned and started spreading out on the floor. As they stretched out on foam mats, Judy muttered to Pagan, "If they're not gay, they're health food nuts, or Harvard Business School robots, or Eastern philosophy freaks. I sometimes think that Mark Scott is the only normal, good looking guy in New York. And that's not saying much!"

Later, in the changing room, Judy reprimanded Pagan. "Listen, Tony hasn't had the benefit of your background and education, so it's unkind to tease him. He may be only an exercise instructor, but he's a damn good one and I don't want to lose him."

"He *used* to be only an exercise instructor." Pagan wriggled out of the black leotard which made her legs look four inches longer and her hips two inches smaller. "Do you realize, Judy, that Tony's turning into your shadow?"

"Maybe he's a little overdevoted, but it's because he's been a garbage collector, a guard in a detention center, a subway cleaner. He's merely grateful that he's now working in an attractive, clean office among a lot of attractive, clean women who all appreciate him." Judy carefully smoothed on her coffee-colored silk lace teddy. "And Tony's very useful, very strong, very willing to do odd jobs for me that don't exactly fit into anyone else's job specifications. And he's touchingly devoted to me, simply because I gave him this chance. In fact, he's almost become . . . "

" . . . Your damned personal bodyguard," snorted Pagan.

"Is that such a bad thing, considering the state of Manhattan today?" Judy checked herself in the mirror. "As a matter of fact, if he's becoming anything, he's becoming my driver. I never realized how useful a driver could be, until Tony came along."

"They're useful, but drivers can also be a royal pain in the ass," said Pagan, wriggling into her sheer black tights. "They're never there when you really want them, which is late evenings and the weekends; you always have to see they're fed, and they're often sulky. The only way to have really efficient transport is to have three drivers, each working an eight-hour shift. I must say, that would be heaven."

Pagan paused, as she remembered what her grandfather had once told her, after reluctantly dismissing his driver for theft. Her grandfather had said that passengers often forget to close the sliding glass panel between the front seat and the back and, consequently, a driver gets to know everything about his employer's life, because the people riding in the back seat forget that the driver is a person, not an anonymous, automatic robot, not a piece of impersonal mechanism like a faucet. Pagan remembered her grandfather saying that a driver carried two dangerous weapons: his ears.

"Be careful," Pagan said to Judy.

Judy looked up from her laden desk, and jumped to her feet beaming with surprise. "Mark! I wasn't expecting you until this evening. I've got a meeting in ten minutes."

He said nothing, looked at the four telephones on her desk, picked up the nearest one, and handed it to her. "The meeting can go ahead without you, surely?"

Judy hesitated as he walked behind her, then she felt his right arm in the small of her back, pressing her against his frayed khaki sweater. She took the telephone from him. "Tell Tom to start the meeting without me, Annette."

"Miss Jordan, I have Los Angeles on the line."

Judy put her hand over the mouthpiece and looked at Mark firmly. "Just give me ten minutes, okay?"

He sat down in her white leather desk chair, and Judy switched her attention to the telephone. "Swifty? Hi, how are you? About the 1979 agreement, there are a few points I want to clear up with you before we finalize." She dragged a heavy file toward her.

Exactly ten minutes later, Judy was still discussing sub-clauses, when she felt strong tapering fingers creep slowly up the inside of her thighs, stroking the petal-soft skin as the fingers moved upwards toward the neat globes of her buttocks in their covering of coffee-covered lace. Judy pressed her thighs together in discouragement. The fingers were not discouraged; instead they parted the thighs, pushing them apart so firmly that it felt almost painful; the fingers continued to stroke the pale skin, working relentlessly upward, then two hard flat palms molded themselves over Judy's rounded buttocks and squeezed gently, savoring the firmness of her flesh in silken covering.

Damn you, Mark, and damn your lovely hands, Judy cursed him to herself, as she stood over her desk and tried to absorb the complicated point which the agent was explaining over the telephone. Right now, she had serious things on her mind—and again she wondered, a little cynically, if Mark's relish for making love in her office wasn't a way of expressing his resentment against the career which, as she had explained to this unexpected, thrilling man in her life, always would be her first love.

As she leaned forward to make another note, an insinuating finger traced the crease of her buttocks, and carried the movement down between her legs, transmitting a caress through the screen of silk and lace. His light butterfly touches felt like flames licking her legs. Most of Judy's consciousness was now confined to that small part of her body which he was stroking, but she struggled to keep her mind on the representation agreement. She felt Mark's fingertips carefully push aside the gauzy fabric and intrude between her moist lips. Then he knelt down behind her and his warm, wet mouth kissed the inside of her thighs, lightly at first, and then more and more hungrily as his fingers reached deeper into her. He pushed her thighs further apart and she swayed in obedience to his touch, helpless to regain control of her trembling knees.

"Mark," she whispered angrily, her hand over the mouthpiece, "darling, this is important! I have to do it." Judy tried to concentrate on the long-distance conversation as Mark took another nip at her thigh and said, "I know you have to do it, darling Judy. You just go right ahead and do what you have to do, and I'll do what I have to do." He stood up behind her, reached his hands around her, unbuttoned her dress and slid each arm out of it. The dress fell to the floor. Then Mark pressed his body against Judy's back and she realized that he was now naked and insistent. He ran his hands quickly up under the delicate brown silk and held her small breasts, slowly slipping into her as she tried to scrawl a note on the desk pad. He pulled her body back against his, rolling her small, hard nipples in his fingertips, and with her thighs braced against her desk she was trapped against him, the telephone still explaining into her left ear as Mark began to nibble the right ear. Damn it, she needed to hear Swifty's opinion.

Mark's pile of discarded khaki clothes on the floor reeked of stale sweat and cigarette smoke, but his body smelled hot and musky, and she could feel him moving gently as his hips moved hard against her buttocks.

She could no longer concentrate and there was now an inquiring silence at the other end of the telephone line.

"Swifty, may I just look through the file again and call you back?" Judy asked weakly as Mark's left hand slid down from her breast over the small curve of her stomach to plunge between her legs once more.

"Okay, you win." She dropped the telephone, twisted round, reached up with both arms and claimed Mark's sun-blistered lips. Together they fell back into her chair. "You bastard, you'll get me fired," she giggled.

"You liar." He was still hard and insistent in her body, his right hand still closed around her breast. "The directors know you do your own research." He kissed her hungrily, sucking her pink tongue into his mouth, as he pushed a pile of papers off her desk, then the page proofs of the next issue cascaded to the floor, followed by Judy's in-tray.

Later, they shared the shower in her silver office bathroom, water sluicing down his knotted brown back and her pale body. In the outside office, the secretaries grinned at each other. After ten years of that two-timing stuffed shirt, Griffin, the boss deserved a bit of fun.

CHAPTER 4

December 2, 1978

J*UDY PINNED UP* the December cover of *VERVE!* on her office wall. The latest in a long series of glossy triumphs was the photograph of Lili and Judy. Judy wore a simple, high-necked, madonna-blue silk dress and Lili wore a crisp, white pique dress with a low, square neckline, a tight bodice, huge puffed sleeves and a full skirt. Although they were holding hands, they looked different; there was an intimacy between them that was, simultaneously, natural but apart. How can a camera pick up something between us that we, ourselves, are hardly aware of, Judy wondered, stepping back to study the hypnotic double portrait of mother and daughter. Judy thought, I feel closer, more loving, toward Lili than I ever have to any other person. She is my only living blood relation and, at the same time, she's a stranger, almost an alien.

Lili entered Judy's office, wearing the white pique dress, in which she looked like a Spanish Infanta; it was a ludicrous outfit for a Manhattan morning in late November, but one that would show up splendidly on the monochrome page prints: *newspaper print*. If you want to jump out of a newspaper page, always wear white or black or stripes, for maximum impact.

"Nervous, Lili?" Judy asked.

Lili shrugged. "What's another press conference? Whatever we say will be taken down, twisted the wrong way and used in evidence against us."

"I still think Kate's decision was correct." Judy remembered Kate stuffing her underwear into a well-traveled Vuitton suitcase and advising, "The best thing you can do, to take the heat out of the situation, is to hold a formal press conference just before the *VERVE!* December cover goes on the stands. Give the papers a fair crack at the story and they won't want to buy anything from the paparazzi, who will then leave you alone."

Lili came across the room and shyly kissed her mother on the cheek; they had never kissed on the mouth.

Judy said, "There's something I want you to have." She opened her desk drawer and produced a small, silver photograph frame; in it was a black-and-white, much-creased, blurry snapshot of a laughing young man, wearing a wool hat with a tassel, and brandishing a bamboo ski pole.

"That's Nick," said Judy, "your father." She held out her little paw-like hands to Lili. On each central finger was a thick band of gold, mounted with a tiny, coral rosebud. "Nick gave me these rings when we said good-bye, he said they were to remind me that I could always depend on him. I've worn them ever since. Now, I'd like you to have one, Lili, so that you will feel you can always depend on me."

"I already depend on you," Lili said, as Judy slipped the ring on Lili's slim finger. "Maxine was so kind to me. And Pagan and Kate were so supportive about Simon. It helped me get through the humiliation and the pain." She hesitated, then shyly said, "I've never really had a woman friend before, never felt this unconditional acceptance and silent affection."

Someone yelled in the corridor, then Pagan stormed in. "For God's sake, Judy, the security in this building is ridiculous! Some lout's just searched my purse!"

"Sit down, you stupid Limey, Lili's just telling me how warm and silent our relationship is."

Pagan flung herself onto the cream art deco sofa as Lili said, "I feel that I need female support to help me to learn to live on my own. After Simon, I've decided that I must live alone and learn to stand on my own two feet, or I'll never know what I'm capable of, I'll never get to know myself properly." She looked at the endless, anonymous rows of windows in the opposite building. "I still don't know who I really am, and I'm tired of relying on love to give my life some meaning."

Judy looked across the room. "A quest for identity is a journey that we all have to make."

"Spare me the psychobabble." Pagan propped her red leather boots on the sofa.

"Going through tough times is what forges your identity so fast that you don't have time to notice it." Judy walked to the door.

Pagan said quietly, "I don't think Lili and I would agree with you, tough times almost pushed us under. Friends are to keep you afloat."

Jostling photographers filled the *VERVE!* boardroom.

Journalists rapid-fired questions: "How does it feel to be a mother, Judy?" "Have you seen Lili's films?" "What do you think of the tire-calendar pictures?"

Suddenly, "Who was Lili's father?" the girl from the *New York Post* asked.

"Lili's father was a British student whom I met in Switzerland," said Judy smoothly.

Pagan looked carefully at the ceiling. No doubt there was an excellent reason for Judy's little fib, but this was not the right time to ask about it.

"Tits 'n' ass, that's all there is to Lili," a balding photographer brayed over his shoulder, as he jostled past Pagan on his way to the exit. "None of these junior sex symbols turns me on, give me the mother. Fifty if she's a day and she still looks terrific."

"Ms. Jordan is forty-five," the *VERVE!* publicity girl said quickly.

"Oh sure, another child bride."

Judy felt the first painful wrench of readjustment to the new status of motherhood as the press turned away from her and clustered around Lili. "Is it really all over between you and Simon Pont?" "Are you marrying Spyros Stiarkoz?" "Is this true about Senator Ruskington?" "Is it true that you're pregnant?" "Is it true that you're dying of cancer of the breast?"

Lili smiled, looked somber, turned left, turned right, crossed and uncrossed her legs because, after a basic clinch picture with Judy, each photographer wanted an exclusive shot of Lili.

"Can't think why I came," Pagan laughed at Tom. "Nobody's interested in me or the benefit for the Institute that Lili's promised."

As Judy listened to them, she suddenly caught sight of her reflection in the ornate mirror. Fifty if I'm a day, she thought bleakly. So that's it, is it? You become a mother and next thing you know your life is over—bang—just like that. Tomorrow, I'll give away this boring dress; no one's gong to write me off just because I've got a beautiful daughter.

The December issue of *VERVE!* was a sellout.

The day after publication, Tom Schwartz, Judy, and the magazine's lawyer met in Griffin's gray, suede-paneled conference room.

Griffin rubbed the side of his nose with his left index finger. "Is this true or not?" He tossed the writ back to the lawyer.

"Doesn't matter," said the lawyer. "Truth is no defense in a case like this. Senator Ruskington claims malicious libel."

Judy leaned back in her gray-suede swivel chair. "Personally, I don't think we should lose sleep over this. We've had writs like this before. It happens all the time."

Griffin looked over at the lawyer. "What's the substance of the allegation?"

"In Lili's life story as carried in *VERVE!*, Lili states that Senator Ruskington tried to rape her when they were both staying in Spain at the seashore mansion of the Duchess of Santigosta."

Griffin looked puzzled. Tom leaned towards him. "Lili is quoted as saying that he looked like an ugly old tortoise and behaved like a billy goat on LSD."

Judy grinned. "He *does* look like a tortoise and every Washington call girl knows he's an old goat. Our readers love it when these sanctimonious jerks get their comeuppance."

Griffin said, "Aren't we covered by the first amendment?"

The lawyer cleared his throat. "Not in this case, because the Senator claims malice on the part of Miss Jordan. In essence, he's saying that *VERVE!* magazine is repeatedly attacking him because he opposed Equal Rights legislation in his state."

"He did," said Judy, "and certainly we wrote about it, and we have repeatedly criticized Senator Ruskington, with good cause."

Griffin asked, "How much is he claiming?"

Tom said, "Sixty million bucks, which means about five, but that's enough to put the magazine out of business, at this moment in time. Unfortunately, we're financially vulnerable right now."

Griffin pulled out his alligator note pad and scribbled on it.

Judy burst out, "I can't believe that a lecherous old senator can send us sliding into bankruptcy when *we're* telling the truth, just because *he* has a smart lawyer!"

"Judy, you know perfectly well that the law isn't about truth or justice." Griffin was irritated by her naivete. "The law is about obeying a certain set of rules."

Tom said, "Maybe if we call his bluff, we won't hear about it any more."

"Senator Ruskington has been my good friend in Washington," Griffin said slowly. "I assume that Lili will back her story?"

Judy looked at the serious faces around her. "Of course she will!" But suddenly she wasn't sure.

* * *

Two days later, Judy walked briskly up Fifty-Seventh Street toward Griffin's office. It was odd that he wanted another office meeting, when they would be having dinner together that evening. But Griffin's recent behavior had been strange. Or had Griffin always been odd, but she'd viewed him through rose-colored glasses, she wondered, as she waited for the lights to change at Madison. Or was his behavior simply a masculine reaction to rejection? After ten years of explaining to her—at least once a month—why he wouldn't marry her, Griffin had been amazed, angry, then sulky, when Judy had carefully explained why she didn't want to marry him.

From that moment, Griffin had acted strangely, particularly about Lili, whose name he never mentioned, but to whom he always referred, with sarcasm, as "your daughter," as in "I see that your daughter's faggot boyfriend has left town."

If it hadn't been for the new, and so far secret, excitement in her life, Judy realized that Griffin would have had her running in circles as usual, wondering what she'd done wrong. Instead of which, every time Mark suggested a date, she minded less if Griffin broke one at the last minute; every time Mark laughed, Judy minded less when Griffin evaded giving an opinion; Judy sometimes wondered whether Griffin would commit himself to anything, even agreeing on the date, let alone promising to love and honor her for life. The only thing both men had in common was their concentration on their work, but, whereas Griffin never forgot his, Mark seemed willing, if not eager, when they were together, to concentrate on Judy. And what Judy most enjoyed was her increasing feeling of freedom, now that she wasn't bound to Griffin's routine of adulterous deception. So Judy didn't feel a bit guilty about these wonderful weeks with Mark. Well, not very guilty. Well, not guilty enough to stop seeing Mark, and feeling Mark, and feeling Mark feel her. Judy hugged her Burberry around her; the weather was almost cold enough for her new lynx, she thought, as she sniffed the tang of smoke from the hot-chestnut vendor's stand on the corner of Fifth.

To Judy's surprise, there were two lawyers in Griffin's office.

After a long preamble about the corporate image of his publishing empire, and the editorial policy of *VERVE!*, Griffin avoided Judy's eye as one of the lawyers leaned toward her. "Therefore, Judy, you will appreciate our reluctance for these two concerns to be further associated, and in view of Orbit Publishing's long-standing relationship with Senator Ruskington. . . ."

"What long-standing relationship?" exploded Judy.

"Naturally, we do not care to publicize our Washington connections, but you should have known that the Senator is aware of our position on the quotas related to imported wood pulp."

Judy realized that, indeed, she should have made the connection, and she also realized that it would not have damaged the story's impact, had she dropped those fatal paragraphs about Senator Ruskington.

"In view of Orbit's wish to distance itself from this issue, it has been decided to sell Orbit's 50 percent shareholding to Creative Magazines."

"At what price?" There was a steely glint behind Judy's tortoise-shell spectacles, as she realized that this was Griffin's uptown, gray-suede, bum's rush.

"Two ten. Ten above market price."

"We might offer you two twenty." Judy and Tom both held 24 percent of the *VERVE!* shares, Kate held the remaining two percent.

* * *

"Judy, two thirty is a crazy price." Tom was an experienced stock-market speculator. "Don't make a fool of yourself for that rat fink's benefit." Tom leaned back in his office chair. "God, I wish Kate were here, she'd talk some sense into you. Sure, we made a wonderful profit last year, but it's not in a heap in a wheelbarrow. It's all tied up, and we're going to need all our cash to fight that scumbag, Ruskington."

Judy had never seen Tom look so worried, and she also felt that he was holding something back; gradually she realized what it was. "I know what you're thinking, Tom. You're thinking that if it hadn't been for my asterisk-asterisk daughter, Lili, we wouldn't be in this mess."

Tom said nothing. Judy added gloomily, "I suppose I think that as well. But I also suppose there's no parent alive who hasn't thought that at some time or other."

Tom said, "Kids! You hope that when they grow up the problems will stop . . . but that's when the big ones start."

Tom leaned over and patted Judy's shoulder. "It's pointless to worry about what's happened or whose fault it is. We should be concentrating our energy on how to get out of this mess. But this time, I don't think we can, Judy. I don't think even you can wriggle out of this one."

Judy thought, it's one of those rare occasions when we both need moral support from each other, and neither of us is strong enough to give it. She tried to sound cheerful as she said, "Miracles sometimes happen."

"Such as?"

"Oh, I don't know, Tom. Give me time to think. How about you kidnapping Lili for ten million dollars, then handing the money over to me?"

Tom laughed. "Sorry, I wouldn't know how to *start* to kidnap someone."

"Weakling! If I can't rely on you, who *can* I rely on?"

As she lifted the telephone, Tom asked, "Who're you calling?"

"Curtis Halifax."

"I could never understand why Curtis backed us in the first place. I know he's your old beau, but you can't expect the poor sap to be a perennial Santa Claus."

Judy leaned back in her leather chair, grinned at Tom and lifted the telephone.

"Get out of here!" Tony slammed his black-booted foot into the photographer's stomach to keep him out of the limousine. The man fell into the road, yelling obscenities at the back of the departing Rolls as it sped away from the airport. "Those guys sure are persistent," Tony said in amazement, as the limousine cruised back to the *VERVE!* office.

Lili ignored him, grabbed the radiophone and called the *VERVE!* office. "Judy, it's impossible," she shouted. Limo telephones always sounded as if you were calling from outer space. "We just couldn't move—if Tony hadn't been there, I'd have been torn to pieces. I had to lock myself in the cloakroom and climb out of the window to get away."

"Did Pagan get off all right?"

"Yes. You were right, it was crazy of me to see her off. These photographers really frighten me. I think I'll have to go back to Europe."

"Don't worry, Lili." Judy's voice crackled soothingly. "I've arranged for you to hide out until this fuss dies down. You can stay at Mark's apartment in the Village for a couple of days. I'll send someone to the Pierre to get your things. Tony will see you safely into the apartment and I'll come down later."

* * *

Mark's white loft in Greenwich Village had been transformed by Judy's staff with a speed and care which Lili found touching, as she noticed huge vases of white lilies, the freshly made bed with lace-edged linen sheets, ample supplies of essences and scents in the bare little bathroom beside a complete range of cosmetics, courtesy of the *VERVE!* beauty editor.

Tony ostentatiously checked the bedroom windows, enjoying his role as temporary bodyguard to an international celebrity. Logs of juniper wood blazed in the fireplace, and a light but steady fall of December snow began to drift against the wall of glass that overlooked the roof garden; the faint sounds of the city were blotted out. Lili felt that she was in a warm white nest, thousands of feet removed from any danger.

Snow swirled in spirals between the high buildings, as if a giant pillow had burst outside the glass wall. Lili felt safe. Fresh from a warm bath, wearing a white lace-trimmed vest and shorts, she lay curled in front of the glowing fire, blinking into the heat like a comatose cat. For the first time in twenty-four hours, her mind was blissfully relaxed, so she was nearly asleep, and she didn't hear the multiple soft clicks and rattles as the door locks slowly slid back.

Mark stopped abruptly in the doorway. His face was mottled with cold, and melted snow was trickling down his neck. He could see the living room reflected in the wall of bronze mirror which ran from the front to the back of his loft, linking the different rooms and levels. In front of his fire, he saw a topaz-tinted picture of some mythical creature—half woman and half cat, basking in the warmth. Then he realized that this must be Judy's daughter, his temporary houseguest—the notorious Lili.

For a few moments, he was stunned by the force of his own appetite, as he watched her. As Lili heard him dump his camera cases on the floor, she jumped up with fear, then smiled. "I hope you're Mark." Mark felt as if his stomach had just dropped from the fifth floor to the basement.

"Is there anything to drink?" Abruptly, he headed for the kitchen, to get away from this exotic vision before he jumped on her. Judy's staff had filled the refrigerator with fruit, salad, cheese, and several bottles of de Chazalle champagne.

"Here," Mark turned to Lili, who had hastily pulled on a sweater and jeans, and offered her a tumbler of champagne.

Lili smiled as she raised her glass. "You've got ice on your eyelashes."

Mark put a half-pound of Beluga and a loaf of rye bread on a tray, then carried it to the fireside.

"How did you meet my mother?" Lili wrenched off a caviar-laden corner of bread with her pointed little teeth. She liked the possessive ring of "my mother."

"It's hard for me to believe that I only met her a few weeks ago. I've never met anyone like her. I fell for her on the spot," said Mark. "We met when Judy came to an exhibition of my Sydon pictures. She looked like a fierce, inquisitive little terrier, dashing from one picture to the other, with her eyes shining, while all the rest of the crowd was just drinking and yakking. I loved her enthusiasm. She's using some of my pictures for a feature on women as leaders."

During the time it took to empty the caviar tin, Mark talked increasingly about Judy and, if the conversation turned toward some other subject, Mark firmly steered it back to Lili's mother and the problems that might affect their relationship because of Mark's assignments in warring foreign countries.

"But maybe it'll be easier than if I was always around," he said as he finished the caviar. "It's lucky for me that Judy doesn't want the demands of a full-time relationship any more than I do; I'm pretty impossible when I'm not working; being inactive tends to make me edgy."

"Why are you a war photographer?"

"Because I'm not a soldier," he grinned at her in the firelight. "I come from an army family, my father was an infantry colonel, and that's what they wanted me to be."

"Then why aren't you in the army?" Lili poured herself another tumbler of champagne.

"If you'd grown up with my Dad, you would have thought twice about the army as a profession. He was in Korea from the beginning, lost two toes on one of his feet from frostbite, but he was lucky—that was his only wound—until they were pulling out. Then a junior officer went crazy in the mess and shot seven people, including my Dad. He came out of the coma with brain damage and, since then, he's been like a five-year-old child; I hardly remember him any other way." Mark thought of the tall, stooped figure that floated like a ghost around the airy house in San Francisco, always shadowed by his mother's unspoken disappointment. "The army ruined my father, and I disapprove of war. That's why I'm not in the army."

"But surely what you're doing makes war glamorous?"

"No. There's nothing glamorous about killing people. I hope that my pictures show the horror of war."

Silently, they stared into the fire. "I suppose this must be what it feels like to have a brother," said Lili. "Let's drink to brotherly love."

Lili realized that, for the first time in her life, she had just enjoyed a couple of hours alone with an attractive man without feeling threatened by the man's sexual interest. But, as the snow piled higher and higher on the roof outside, the normally silent Mark found himself talking about anything to fill the silence, which would otherwise have been flooded with his growing carnal desire for Lili.

CHAPTER 5

December 1978

TOM PUT HIS head round the door of Judy's office. "First letter from Kate!" He waved the airmail flimsy. "She says its like the West Bank of Jordan, it's a forced settlement operation. It's a way of invading without invading. Thousands of hill tribe people have been murdered, detained without trial or tortured. And Kate's got dysentery."

Judy looked up and said, "Just the holiday she needed," then continued her telephone conversation. "Maxine, of course I'll come. Invent an excuse for inviting me, let the situation cool for a few weeks and I'll fly over for a weekend in the New Year. Through thick and thin, remember?"

"You're crazy, Judy." Tom looked disbelieving as she put the telephone down. "You can't go to France now—we're up to our eyebrows in problems."

Judy said, "I'll only be gone over a weekend. Now, what do we have to tell the brilliant attorney who's going to wrestle Senator Ruskington to his knees?"

"Judy, I wish you wouldn't joke about this." Tom was exasperated. "The fees are piling up; you'd think those guys wrote to each other on solid gold notepaper. Financially, we're on the limit of our contingency fund, and if this should ever come to court—which I pray to God it won't—and Ruskington wins, we'll be completely ruined."

"When that day comes, promise you'll hold my hand as we take a dive together from the fiftieth floor." Judy briskly opened the file.

"Okay, you've got a date!" Tom put his hand on her shoulder. "Look, I want you to know that if this turns out to be real trouble, we'll be in it together. I'll be with you right to the end."

"Thanks, Tom. Now, what do the lawyers need?"

"We have to demonstrate that you, personally, have no malicious intentions toward the Senator. We have to show that you are not prejudiced against him in any way. It's a tough one, Judy, because the old bird is a Bible-thumping Baptist, the biggest chauvinist pig in the pen, and your daughter claims that he tried to rape her. So he's pretty much everything you hate in a human being."

"If the Senator is a bigot and a rapist, surely hating him is a reasonable attitude?" Judy argued. "He'll never take this to court, Tom. A scandal like this would finish him in Washington."

"What's he got to lose? The scandal's blown up already and he wants whitewash. We're the ones who'll be in trouble, Judy—a mess like this won't do our circulation figures any good."

Judy stood up, determined to rid Tom of his doubts and boost his confidence. "What's got into you, Tom?" she asked, "this loser talk isn't like you at all—you know that all publicity is good publicity. We won't lose any readers by fighting this case—they'll all be rooting for us."

Tom left Judy's pastel office feeling that nothing would make her realize how serious the situation was. More anxious than when he entered, he took away the audited circulation figures for the past quarter, without showing them to Judy, because they registered a definite fall. Could Judy's judgment—for years as deadly, fast and accurate as a Cruise missile—be faltering at last? he wondered. As Tom passed the boardroom, he noticed a few assistant editors limbering up for the daily exercise session. Judy had never been interested in sports, unwilling to walk if she could ride, and now the spectacle of her gallantly sweating through Tony's workout, whenever her schedule allowed, was surprising. Maybe Judy was starting to feel her age, at last.

An hour later, Judy put her head around Lili's bathroom door. "I thought I'd find you here. Do you mind if I come in?"

Lili was up to her nose in pink bubbles. When Lili craved comfort and security, she always headed for a warm tub.

"The whole world has already seen me in the tub, I don't see why my mother shouldn't," said Lili. "How are things with you?"

"The Senator is really putting on the pressure." Judy wondered if she should tell Lili the full scale of the battle that threatened *VERVE!* magazine after her fatal interview.

Lili looked over the rim of the bath at her mother. "I've been waiting for a good moment to say this, but I don't suppose there'll ever be one."

"Say what?"

"I'm sorry that his lawsuit is all my fault."

"You told the truth, Lili. We took the risk. Your life story in *VERVE!* boosted the circulation. We miscalculated the Senator's reaction and that's all there is to it. We're still hoping that the Senator will settle out of court."

"Oh, him. . . " Lili sniffed. "He won't be any problem to you, Judy. I told you I'll stand by what I've said and what you printed. He won't want to face me in court," Lili reached for the shampoo, "because he won't want his voters to discover that the man they sent to Washington is a dirty old goat." She submerged her head in the carnation-scented water and came up dripping, big-eyed and sleek-headed as a seal.

Judy hesitated, then asked, "Was he really as unpleasant as you made him sound?"

Slowly Lili said, "It depends on what you mean by unpleasant." She remembered how, a few months after Jo's death, she had been a guest of the Duchess of Santigosta at her palatial Spanish beach house on the Malaga coast. Lili had still felt her loss after Jo Stiarkoz' death, but Zimmer had suggested that she try to get more fun out of life and accept a few of the stream of invitations that any celebrity receives.

The first two days had been delightful. The twenty-two other guests were mainly European business acquaintances of the Duke, who was no longer rich and supplemented his income by acting as an entrepreneur, a go-between, for his business partners, when they wanted to establish contact with, and impress, someone with whom they hoped, later, to set up a deal.

They swam, they water-skied, and everyone else in the party water-parachuted, including the Italian jeweler's wife who was a grandmother and trying it for the first time. It was easy, she saw; so, obediently, Lili had been strapped into her parachute harness, taken a run off the end of the jetty, then found herself jerked into midair, fifty feet above the little speedboat that was towing her. Lili looked down, her stomach turned over, and she thought for one moment that she was going to be sick. She knew that she suffered from vertigo, so she never stood near the edge of balconies or bridges, but she had never felt vertiginous in an airplane, so it hadn't occurred to her that she would do so now. The ten-minute ride was purgatorial, but eventually the speedboat stopped back near the jetty and Lili floated down toward the blue waters of the Mediterranean where her harness was quickly unstrapped by the boatman's assistant, who then started to gather up the parachute that was drifting in the sea water. Gratefully, Lili floated on the water with her arms apart, feeling too ill to strike out for shore. It was at this moment that a nearby swimmer, a balding American Senator with whom Lili had hardly spoken, swam up to her. "Great sensation, isn't it?" he asked, then he noticed Lili's dazed expression. "Are you all right, my dear?"

"Yes . . . no . . . I don't know . . . please," a wave broke over Lili's head and she accidentally swallowed a lot of sea water. "Please, could you h-h-h-help me back to the beach?"

"Put your arms around me, my dear." Lili did so and felt her body drift against his, then the man was lying on top of her in the water as, dimly, Lili thought, surely this isn't the way that lifesavers do it? After what seemed an eternity, the man panted, "I think we'll make better progress if you let go, my dear, and I hold you from behind."

A lifesaver swims backward, kicking only with his feet, as both arms are needed—the left arm holds the drowning victim across the collarbone and the right hand cups the victim's chin above water. But this was not Senator Ruskington's lifesaving procedure. He had, indeed, swum backward toward shore, kicking only with his feet, but he held Lili's body on top of his with both his hands firmly on her breasts.

Once ashore, Lili had lain in the shade and, within an hour, she had recovered, had thanked Senator Ruskington for helping her, and had decided to go to bed early. And that, Lili thought, was the end of the incident.

Lili was awakened by a strange sensation. She opened her eyes and from her four-poster bed she could see the silver moonlight striping the room. Still half asleep, Lili shivered, then realized that the covers had been drawn back from her bed. Sleepily, she felt a flood of warmth in her body that she hadn't experienced since Jo's death, then slowly she awakened, realizing one thing at a time. Her nightgown no longer covered the lower part of her body. Between her legs she felt a warm, heavy, rough sensation, like having your hand licked by a calf. Lili realized that a man was crouched by her bed, parting her lower lips with his hands and steadily licking her clitoris. As she realized what was happening, a hand slid up her body and felt underneath the nightgown for the nipple of her breast, upthrusting and hardening in automatic response to this dark stranger's stimulation.

Lili gasped in horror and tried to sit up, but the hand that was on her breast pushed her hard, back against the pillows, and suddenly the man was on top of her. He was naked, she realized with growing horror as she felt his hardness against her. She screamed, then his mouth was on hers.

I can't believe this . . . it's a nightmare . . . no, it isn't . . . he must be a burglar . . . And then he'd taken his mouth away from hers and, in the moonlight, she had recognized his face as he arched his back and tried to thrust into her, as painfully he held her by her breasts against the pillows.

"You liked me touching you in the water, didn't you?" the man panted. "You didn't stop me, you led me on, you little bitch." It was that balding American Senator who had helped her swim to shore that afternoon.

Lili screamed again and simultaneously reached down the bed and grasped for the balls behind his groping cock and twisted them as hard as she could. The man grunted, gasped, doubled up in pain and Lili felt thankful that she had remembered this old tart's trick from her past.

Lili managed to wriggle from beneath the gasping fat body, then she shot across the floor to the door, flung it open and ran along the wide, silent corridors until she reached the servants' backstairs. She ran down three flights and threw open the door at the bottom. She found herself in the imposing entrance hall, silvered by moonlight. Lili raced for the guest bathroom and sat shivering on the cold seat for the rest of the night, until she heard the bustle of servants starting to clean. Then Lili crept back to her bedroom.

It was hard to believe that horrible scene had really happened. The bed was in disarray but there was nothing to indicate . . . Lili ran forward as she saw a navy, red-dotted piece of silk protruding from beneath the bed. It was the tie of a man's dressing gown. Lili bolted the door and reached for the ivory bedside telephone and demanded to speak to the Duchess . . . well, as soon as Her Grace was awake, in that case. It was an urgent matter.

Two hours later, the plump Duchess floated into Lili's bedroom wearing an embroidered pale-gray crepe de Chine peignoir that must have taken months to stitch.

Lili poured out her story, showed the dressing gown tie, and looked into the chubby face for sympathy. The Duchess took the dressing gown cord and held it in her hands. Then she said, "My dear, Senator Ruskington is a very influential man with whom my husband hopes to arrange . . . certain matters. This entire house party is being given to entertain him. I think perhaps you had a bad dream. And if you didn't my dear, well, nothing has happened to you that hasn't happened to you before. A gentleman was *bouleversé* by your beauty; he had perhaps had a little too much to drink. I doubt if this morning he will remember what you say has happened. So any unpleasantness would be reduced to his word against yours. Or he might even say that you had invited him to your bedroom, in which case, what does a dressing gown tie prove?" The Duchess stood up and, in a polite but distant voice, she said to an angry Lili, who could hardly believe what she heard, "I feel it might be best for all of us, my dear, if you left immediately."

Judy said, "Rape is never pleasant." She held out a terrycloth robe for Lili as she stepped out of the bath, "Especially if anyone suggests you were asking for it."

Nearly five and a half miles, thought Debra Halifax, relentlessly pedaling on. Although she was in her late thirties, her silhouette was that of girl of twelve. Each rib was visible through the candy-pink leotard, as she gazed with determination at the illuminated screen built into the bicycle's handlebar. The preprogrammed rides could be dialed on the control panel; they could increase the machine's resistance from an easy, five-minute trip to the toughest half-hour program which, her husband complained, was like cycling over the Rocky Mountains.

Although the clock in her private gymnasium showed 8:30 A.M., Debra was halfway through the program for the second time that day when her husband, Curtis, appeared at the door of the gym. He wore a handmade gray suit, a white silk shirt, and carried a well-polished black briefcase. There is something obscene about a woman who deliberately starves herself, Curtis thought, as he saw bands of sweat spreading across the pink leotard below the areas where his wife's breasts used to be. Debra's whole appearance had become a macabre caricature of the delicate little sprite he had married; there was now a monkeylike appearance to her head, her face was deeply lined, and the outline of the skull was prominent at the temples. Curtis looked down at the bicycle dial and realized that she was pedaling the Rocky Mountain program for the second time. "Debra, please. . . ."

"Don't say another word, I won't listen."

"But you'll kill yourself."

"I will do no such thing. I am promoting my health."

"Surely it isn't necessary. . . ."

"You know the way my metabolism is. I only have to look at a lettuce leaf to put on weight."

Curtis gave up.

"I'll see you at the Peabodys' tonight, dear." He said good-bye with a dry kiss on the top of her head. She did not stop pedaling.

In his car, Curtis leaned back and wondered what he could do to add some meaning to his wife's life. He reached for the window control, then remembered with irritation that he must always keep the windows closed. Each day Curtis left Chestnut Hill for the bank at a different hour. Hawkins, his driver, brought the car round to the front of the house only when the butler called him on the house telephone, and both Curtis and Hawkins wore coats with a layer of ballisticproof wadding in the lining—the least conspicuous substitute for a bulletproof vest. His staff was even more exasperated than Curtis by the new security procedures. He had been obliged to call them together and explain that the insurance people now insisted on a full executive-protection program against kidnap or assassination, and that it was his responsibility, as the bank's chairman, to follow their request.

When he arrived at the bank, Curtis, who was no longer allowed to take the mahogany-paneled private elevator to his suite, joined his employees in one of the regular cars. Alighting at the forty-eighth floor, he walked down the long corridor between two rows of early American primitive paintings to his office, where Curtis's large antique desk stood below portraits of his father and grandfather, so that anyone standing opposite Curtis looked at three generations of Halifaxes.

"Good morning, Miss Brady." Curtis's secretary handed him the card on which she had listed his day's appointments. "The usual reservation at the Philadelphia Club at twelve, but make it for two people, please. And no calls for an hour."

In these impressive surroundings, Curtis had very little work to do. No matter what kind of idiot Curtis Halifax III turned out to be, the basis of the family's wealth would always remain stable. The senior managers were all clever men, from old, Anglo-Saxon, East Coast families. Their loyalty was to everything the Halifax family stood for—the best, historic traditions of American life: self-reliance, thrift, hard work, and Republicanism.

Curtis's grandfather had been determined that the Halifax family would, one day, provide a President for America, a wise, dignified, cautious man who would lead the country back to the old-fashioned virtues and rigorous standards of their caste. He had married both his sons into similarly minded families, and had been disappointed that his two healthy boys, between them, had managed to produce only one son—Curtis, the sole heir to his grandfather's ambitions. Grandfather Halifax had insisted that Curtis's bride should also be chosen from an ideal background, and when she was nine years old, he had selected Debra for his grandson to marry. She had been born into one of the wealthiest Philadelphia families; her pedigree, her bloodline, her studbook entry were impeccable—in fact, too much so. Curtis had grown to suspect that Debra's inherent instability stemmed from overbreeding, and, ironically, this would frustrate the ambition of Grandfather Halifax.

Curtis sighed as he settled into his leather wing chair, beneath the portraits; he knew he had disappointed them. He had failed to fulfill his family's political hopes and, because of Debra, he was becoming more of a liability than an asset to his political party. He settled his feet on the green leather-topped desk and picked up his appointment card for the day. The only name on it was Ms. Judy Jordan.

* * *

Tony drove Judy to Philadelphia in her cream Mercedes 350SL convertible. He was a fast, neat driver and Judy always felt safe when he was at the wheel. During the entire two-hour journey, Judy scribbled memos. She was only going to be in France over the weekend, but she wanted to leave nothing unfinished before she left. Tony never interrupted her train of thought. He now recognized Judy's moods, knew when she was feeling ebullient, knew when she wanted to work out an idea aloud, knew when she needed soothing, and he also recognized the rare occasions when she was thinking hard and didn't want to be interrupted.

When the Mercedes slid to a stop outside the Patriots Halifax Bank, Tony jumped out of his seat and opened the door for Judy. Although her face looked strained, Judy was very appealing in a violet suede Calvin Klein coat and dark-violet suede boots.

But her pretty appearance made no difference to her reception. After arguing, in the most charming way, for over an hour, Curtis Halifax leaned toward her over his huge, antique mahogany desk and clasped his narrow, nervous hands. Judy looked at the tall, well-built, fair-haired man and thought he'd probably never worn a store-bought suit in his entire life. "I know we're . . . old friends . . . and because of our . . . special . . . relationship, I've done as much as I could for you in the past, but this time I just can't swing it. The Board won't wear it."

"You might at least try once more." With an effort, Judy kept calm reasonableness in her voice. "If we show our projection figures for next year, your Board will see that we only have a temporary problem."

"Judy, don't be unreasonable. Last month, I went to the limit for you, so that you could buy Griffin out, and now you're asking for more." Curtis looked uncomfortable as he fiddled with the new, automatic gold Cartier calendar. He continued. "No banker in his right mind would invest money in the outcome of a lawsuit. And, as I've already explained, my personal funds are committed, long term. This time the answer really has to be no, Judy."

"No is not my favorite word, Curtis," said Judy, a shimmer of a smile touching her lips as her dark blue eyes looked into his pale blue ones.

Curtis responded with a flash of exasperation. "That's a low blow, Judy, and you know it. Stop trying to make me feel guilty."

"I'm sorry Curtis, but *VERVE!* is my whole life and I'm desperately worried. Don't you know anyone in Washington who could lean on Senator Ruskington?"

"I'm afraid not." Curtis started to feel resentful. "I haven't got that sort of clout." The door suddenly opened and Curtis and Judy looked up in surprise, to see a fine-boned blond woman, with a beautiful but gaunt face, wearing a dark mink coat with a bunch of violets pinned to it. She said, "Surprise, Curtis darling!" Then she realized that he was not alone and added, "Oh, I hope I'm not interrupting anything important."

Curtis stood up automatically. "No, Debra. Of course not. I don't believe you know Judy Jordan. My wife, Debra Halifax."

"So glad to meet you." Debra flashed a faint smile at Judy, then ignored her. "Curtis darling, I'm on my way to lunch with Aunt Emily, but I just dropped by to tell you that I've changed my mind. I don't want the emeralds tonight, after all, red looks better with white crepe. So tell Perkins to get the rubies out of the vault, will you?" She blew a little-girl kiss toward her husband. "Must go." She flashed another brilliant smile at Judy and she left the room. "Bye-bye then."

There was a short silence, then Judy said enviously, "You can always tell old money. It must be wonderful to have nothing to worry about."

"Debra doesn't have such a carefree life as people think, and you know it, Judy."

"What a pity that your folks were so wrong about her. Given a clever wife, you might be President by now."

"Don't say that, Judy. Can't you ever forgive me? Can't you ever forget the past? You wouldn't really want to be in Debra's place."

"Oh, wouldn't I?" Judy's light tone conveyed that she still felt rejected by this impeccable man with his duties, responsibilities, obligations—and money. "I wouldn't mind Debra's wonderful clothes, Debra's marvelous parties, and Debra's ability to wave a wand and have anything she likes. Just because she happened to have inherited a fortune. After that, the rest just followed naturally—including you, Curtis."

"Judy, don't be bitter. I really wish that I could help you, and you know that I would if I could. And money isn't everything; Debra has her own problems, as you know."

His telephone buzzed. His car was waiting to take them to lunch. Curtis rose. "Let's forget money and Debra for an hour, Judy," he pleaded. "We've got so many more important things to discuss, haven't we?"

Judy gave him her most bewitching smile.

It was after midnight, and the servants had gone to bed, when Judy arrived at the Chateau de Chazalle. Maxine, wearing a lace-edged gray-silk peignoir, kissed her warmly, then said, "Let's go down to the kitchen and make a cup of hot chocolate, like we did when we were schoolgirls."

In the cavernous kitchen of the castle, Maxine selected a small, spotless copper pan, then pushed back the sleeves of her peignoir. She laughed. "That reminds me of the evening before my wedding, when my mother gave me some advice." She poured milk from an enameled jug. "She told me that if I cooked chocolate late at night after a party, I should always remove my fur coat, because otherwise I would singe the cuffs." Maxine whisked the foaming chocolate, then poured it into porcelain cups. "That was the only advice she gave me about married life—not much use, in these circumstances." Suddenly, Maxine put her head in her hands and her heavy blond hair tumbled around her face as she began to cry. Judy put an arm round her heaving shoulders and waited for the shuddering sobs to stop.

"What am I going to do, Judy?" Maxine sobbed in despair. "Charles has moved into his dressing room. He won't look at me and he doesn't speak to me. I feel so humiliated, so rejected."

"What is she like?" Judy asked, "Blond? Beautiful? Slim?"

"No, no. She has no style, no delicacy. She's the sort of woman who wears a black bra under a white blouse," Maxine sniffled.

"She must have something that Charles wants. And she sounds determined to have him, doesn't she?"

Maxine sat up and looked indignant. Good, thought Judy, she won't be able to cope with the situation from a position of complete despair—she needs to be a little angry.

Maxine said, "I'm sure that bitch deliberately staged the whole thing. I sent a telex from the Plaza, giving Charles my flight time. She should have known that

I was coming. I'm sure she never showed it to him. Charles can't stand rows, and he's always been absolutely discreet. I can't think how she managed to get him into bed in our home."

"Maybe she bullied him into it," Judy said softly. "It's the classic mistress's move. Maybe Charles likes being bullied a bit?"

"But why would Charles. . . " Maxine began to protest, then she saw what Judy meant. Perhaps this awful woman appealed to Charles precisely because she was so domineering. She remembered that olive body writhing furiously on top of her husband, but Maxine could not recall the last time that she had climbed on top of Charles when they made love. She felt horribly exposed in such a position, slowing the beginnings of a little double chin, looking fatter than she was, to Charles below. Placid and easily contented, Maxine suddenly realized that she had lazily allowed Charles to assume all the responsibility for whatever had happened under the blue silk canopy; it was years since he had tumbled her wickedly in any other environment, as he had loved to do before they were married.

She pushed away her cup. "I can't believe that he really wants to marry her—he can't possibly, she would destroy the business within a year. Please help me, Judy."

"Maybe it's Charles who needs help," said Judy, "help to get out of a situation that he never wanted to be in. I've dealt with predatory women before." She sipped her chocolate. "Why on earth did you hire her?"

"We'd been asked to advise the Chinese government on the development of their own champagne industry—that bitch had a degree in Oriental studies."

Maxine sat at her gold-columned dressing table, which had once belonged to the Empress Josephine. The light of the raw February morning, intensified by the crisp crust of snow on the gray parapet of the chateau, was harsh on her drawn face. The antique mirror reflected, with a dead-gray radiance, the face of an opulently beautiful, but very anxious woman. She thought, I used to be a decorator, why ever did I design a gray bedroom? Why did I let good taste take the place of sensuality? What did my Aunt Hortense say? That no woman over thirty should wear gray.

A cheap office duplicate book was always near Maxine, so that she could immediately make notes and distribute them to her staff through Mademoiselle Janine, her secretary. Now she pulled a book from the dressing-table drawer and, by the time her maid came in, she had completed a new decoration scheme for the bedroom.

"Not sables this morning, Honorine, they're so heavy and dark," she said as the elderly woman in black moved toward the fur closet. "It's a long time since I wore the red fox. And for this evening, please lay out my pink St. Laurent with the red petticoat."

With only ten guests to consider, Maxine had organized a simple program; partridge shooting on the estate, riding through the vineyards, cards and conversation for those who preferred to stay warm indoors and on Sunday, a stag hunt on the neighboring estate.

Charles was the first down to breakfast in the yellow Chinese morning room.

Diffident and modest, Charles was attractive in his sheer helplessness; it was the sweet, absent-minded Cary Grant bit that the girls fell for, Maxine had explained to Judy. Now, looking guilty, he stood in his favorite position, feet astride, back to the crackling logs in the fireplace.

Next to enter was Guy St. Simon, yawning in his navy foulard dressing gown. "The Louis Quinze bed needs a new mattress, Maxine."

Guy was getting chubby, Maxine thought, and his hemp-colored hair was starting to recede from his forehead, but the slightly hooked Roman nose and the wide sensual mouth were unchanged. She was still amazed that her childhood friend had metamorphosed into one of the top fashion designers of France, with his own chain of boutiques, "Limited Editions."

Guy pulled his square-framed black spectacles out of his breast pocket, stuck them on his nose and picked up *Le Monde*. Slowly, all Maxine's guests entered, chose their food from the heated silver chafing dishes on the mahogany sideboard, and sat down at the breakfast table.

A tall man beamed good morning at Maxine as he sat down next to her. "Maxine, you defy time."

"So do you, Pierre," Maxine replied, thinking that it was indeed almost true. Living in the fierce Alpine climate had tanned her first lover's face a deep, leathery brown; the etched straight lines around his eyes were white against the tan, but his tightly curled blond hair was as thick as ever and his body looked hard and strong.

Judy was the last to appear in the morning room. Her first reaction upon waking had been to telephone an old friend, now the head of *Time*'s Paris Bureau. "I can't tell you why I'm asking," she began confidently, "but I need to find a job for a girl with a degree in Oriental studies—something that involves a lot of travel, or even a posting abroad."

That afternoon, while the other guests were shooting, Judy won four hands of piquet from Guy before he threw the cards at her, yelling, "You haven't changed a bit in twenty years. A game is never a game with you. You Americans are obsessed by winning. You always want to be first. Here in France, we know it's much more important to be first class." In spite of his careless pose of witty decadence, Judy knew that the secret of Guy's success was an obsession with quality and the ability to work like a dog.

Judy picked up a purple paperweight and pretended to throw it at Guy, who laughingly held his hand up to ward it off, saying, "I know you won't throw that hunk of amethyst at me. Kate gave it to Maxine as a wedding present." Suddenly he stopped laughing. "It was such a pretty wedding. I can't bear to see Maxine looking so unhappy today. I always know when Charles is fooling around because Maxine dresses so badly. Lugubrious colors and no jewelry. She really ought to give Charles a dose of his own medicine, instead of letting him walk all over her."

The butler appeared. "A telephone call for Mademoiselle Jordan in the library." Judy followed him to the paneled library where, in the rich atmosphere of hush, dust and old leather she learned that Montpellier University had just acquired an important bequest of ancient Chinese jade and ceramics and was searching for a properly qualified curator to identify and catalogue the pieces, working in liaison with the People's Museum in Peking. Back home, a good networker can get to anyone in three moves, thought Judy, and asked Maxine if she knew anyone who knew anyone at Montpellier University. After a few minutes spent with her nose stuck in her maroon address book, Maxine said, "The best I can do is Ghislaine, my cousin, who is married to the Rector of Grenoble."

It took four more contacts, six telephone calls and the rest of the afternoon to discover that Montpellier University had unsuccessfully advertised the curator's post for three months and were delighted by Maxine's recommendation.

At dinner, Judy caught Maxine's eye between the silver trumpets of the flower-laden epergnes. Unobtrusively, she gave the thumbs-up sign.

"I can't thank you enough," said Maxine later, as she slipped off her coral velvet dinner dress and reached into one of her closets for a pale-turquoise satin peignoir.

"Other people's problems are always easier to solve than your own," Judy grinned at Maxine in the mirror. "Especially their amorous problems. And we all have them."

"Do you have them with this new young man of yours? Twenty-nine years old, isn't he?" Maxine tied her sash and looked up under her lashes. "What is love like, Judy, with a much younger man?"

"Maxine, you sound like a soap opera. There *is* a difference and it *is* important, but not in the way you think. What's important isn't that women are starting to go to bed with younger men; what's important is that age no longer smacks of terror to a woman. Women often fail to develop a strong sense of personal identity until they're into their thirties or forties; it's then that they start to find out who they really are and what sort of man they really want." There was a thoughtful pause, then Judy added, "Anyhow, age doesn't come into our relationship; Mark and I suit each other because we're both independent and we respect each other's freedom. What he gets is a woman who admires his talent, respects his commitment, and doesn't want to cling to him for status or affection. And what I get out of it is a wonderful lover who doesn't demand hot dinners every night."

"As I never cook, that would be no advantage."

"A younger man's demands and expectations are different from those of men who can remember the second World War, as well as the sexual revolution."

"In what way?" Maxine fluffed up her maribou collar.

"Older men don't like a woman to spread her wings, in case that might get in the way of their wings. But a younger man is adventurous, and interested in having a woman who isn't only going to boost his ego but develop her own personality; that's what they like in an older woman and that's what they respect."

"But aren't you afraid of the future, Judy, of looking an old hag, of being abandoned, of being humiliated?"

"There's the possibility of that at any age. With any relationship, you can expect suffering when it ends, plus a kick in the pants to your pride."

Maxine said, "Men can get away with so much more than a woman."

"The world has always known that a man can be fascinating at any age. Now we're finding out that a woman can be as well. Women have always been exterior-oriented, but we all know beautiful women who are dull. Fascination has nothing to do with the tortoise-like state of your neck, but the unwrinkled state of your mind."

Maxine rushed to the mirror. "You think my neck is like a tortoise's?"

Judy grinned. "Maxine, I'm never sure whether you're into vanity or self-improvement."

* * *

"Take care of Lili for me, Mark," were Judy's parting words to her lover before she left New York. He had been dismayed. While Judy was present in his life and his bed, Mark could control the way that he was growing to feel about Lili but, without Judy, he was alone and at the mercy of the violent desire that Lili aroused in him. Hating to be out of control of himself, Mark found himself transferring the dislike of his own weakness on to the cause of it. Irritably, he complained to Lili that she was making his apartment untidy, and pointed to the makeup and magazines that were scattered over the living room floor in front of the fire.

"I can't help it," Lili looked surprised. "I'm *stuck* here all day. I can't go outside, because of the photographers."

"Oh, don't be so dramatic, there's no reason not to go out. If you avoid the smart parts of town and stick to the places where nobody would expect to see a film star, you won't have any trouble."

Lili looked sulkily defiant.

"Come on," said Mark, "I'll show you."

He took her for lunch on Saturday to a tiny Oriental restaurant and listened patiently while Lili talked about the Mistinguett part that she had been offered. "I'm not sure that I want to do it. I may be an international star hut I think the part needs a brilliant dancer. There's more singing and dancing than I've ever done before, and I'm not sure I'm good enough. I'm afraid of making a fool of myself. Do you think I should do it?"

"I'm not the right person to ask, Lili. Surely your agent knows if you can do it, why not talk to him?" As Mark passed Lili a bamboo steamer, he thought that Judy never asked him to make her business decisions. He was desperately looking for traits to criticize in Lili and praise in Judy.

Later Mark took her to see the Rembrandts in the Metropolitan Museum and afterward they walked through the dirty slush of Central Park. The snow howled down again in the evening, so they struggled no further than the Italian restaurant on the corner.

"Do you know," Mark asked, "how to get a free bottle of wine in an Italian restaurant? No? I thought not." So he told the waiter that it was Lili's birthday, whereupon the rotund padrone rushed out of the kitchen, kissed her wetly on both cheeks and presented them with a bottle of Italian sparkling wine—on the house.

"Have you ever tried that with Judy?" Lili asked.

"No, I haven't done it since I was a kid." Mark poured the wine. "Don't worry. I'll pay for it in with the tip. Happy Birthday! Judy doesn't like Italian restaurants. She says the food's too tempting. She's very disciplined, as you know. It's one of the things I admire about her."

"What are the others?" Lili crunched a slice of fennel.

"Lots of things, not just a couple. Apart from the fact that Judy's clever and fun, I like her professionalism and her energy, her poise and her experience. . . ."

"And her status, her position and her influential, interesting friends?" asked Lili cynically.

"Of course, why not? Like I said, lots of things. Some of the things I like about her are things that other people might not like. She can be sharp and tart. But that's part of being a straight-shooter. Women never understand that a man doesn't fall for this or that in a woman. He doesn't like the breasts but not the hips, like the eyes but not the nose. He doesn't like the wit but not the criticism. A man falls for the whole package, whatever it is. But women don't seem to view themselves that way. They're always worrying about the few things in themselves that they wish were different. But Judy doesn't waste time that way. And I like the way she's prepared to help me."

"How?" Lili was astonished.

"She made me feel self-confident. A long time before I met Judy, I lived with a model, but eventually I got tired of feeling like somebody else's supporting cast." He refilled Lili's glass. "However self-confident a young guy looks, he's probably uncertain of what he can do. It's good to get reassurance from someone whose opinion and experience he can respect—and who isn't his mother. He knows his mother thinks he's wonderful." He laughed. "Judy used to worry because she thought she had some sort of maternal attraction for me, but it isn't a bit like that. I already have a wonderful mother, so I don't need another one."

"Isn't she lonely, though, when you're away?" Lili asked.

"I don't know." It had never occurred to him that shiny, confident, poised Judy might ever feel lonely. In spite of himself, he again compared the two women. Lili ate lustily, Judy picked at food. Lili bored him with her indecision over the Mistinguett film, Judy never talked about her business when she was with him.

On Sunday morning Mark taught Lili to make popcorn, but it worried Mark to stand in the tiny kitchen right up against Lili and her animal magnetism. On Sunday afternoon they went to a scruffy little Chinese puppet theater off Lower Broadway. The narrow benches were filled with noisy families. The owner welcomed Mark to his own bench and sat them between a moon-faced baby and his grandmother. In such surroundings, free from her crushing public image, Lili's natural grace flowered. Mark watched her take the baby on her knee, to look at the dragons and the gods fight it out for the lily-footed maidens. The rest of the family chattered, smiled and nodded their approval, as the baby threw handfuls of cookie crumbs on Lili's pink suede suit and tugged her hair over her face. So much, thought Mark, for the world's best known sex symbol.

Maxine shivered on the high seat, as the antique racing carriage followed the stag hunt through the forest. Cheeks stung scarlet with the bracing cold, she was feeling a little apprehensive. Shortly after they entered the humid forest, three heavy lumbering red deer had splashed across the muddy track ahead of the hunt. The tufters immediately leaped forward, baying with excitement. The mounted huntsmen, resplendent in gold-collared jackets, tore after the shaggy deerhounds, and the musical calls of their antique brass horns echoed plaintively through the forest.

Pierre, who was gently holding in the eager horses, turned to Maxine. As the high bench seat bounced on its curved black springs, Maxine felt the stealthy pressure of his thigh against hers, underneath the thick fur rug which was tucked around their knees.

"Is there a short cut? We don't want to get bogged down on this wet track." Again Pierre pressed his hard thigh firmly against Maxine's soft leg. Message received and understood, thought Maxine, as she pointed. "If you take that track through the beeches, we can meet up with them at the bottom of the hill."

The horses trotted swiftly as Pierre leaned closer to Maxine, and then suddenly turned and quickly brushed his lips against hers. Equally suddenly, Maxine thought, why *not*? He's been flirting with me for the whole weekend and I love it. It's especially flattering when your first lover makes it clear that he still wants to go to bed with you. I have been faithful to Charles for twenty years, and my reward was that bitch in my bed.

Maxine felt flattered, excited, and a little nervous, which is the essence of flirtation. "There's a barn a bit further on," she suggested as they bounced past tall trees hung with tattered brown leaves.

"Perfect," said Pierre. They both knew that an invitation had been issued and accepted.

Outside the high timbered barn, Maxine now shivered with anticipation as Pierre put blankets on both horses and looped the long reins over the carriage hook. "It's a hay barn," said Maxine, so he brought out half a bale, grunting, "this should keep them happy for hours."

Then he turned and looked at her for a moment. As they faced each other, he cupped her chin in his hands and quickly and firmly kissed her chilled lips. "Let's climb to the top where it's warm."

He caught her hand and they scrambled up the prickly steps of hay to the top. Pierre threw the fur carriage rug on the sweet-smelling hay, then leaned toward Maxine. At first she was taut and trembled, but then her tension dissolved and she felt soft and boneless as a pillow. He took her in his arms and as he pressed her to his body, Maxine felt a long-forgotten lurch of pleasure. Warm, melting desire was heightened by the fact it was forbidden. She whispered, "I can't stand up, my knees are shaking."

"So are mine."

Together, they fell against the tightly baled hay. His fingers felt under the glossy red fox of her coat; her trembling fingers undid the fasteners, then he was pulling up her russet sweater and pulling down the lace cups of her bra. "Maxine, your breasts haven't changed." He teased her nipple with his tongue, then started to move from one breast to the other, nipping the little peaks with his teeth. Maxine purred with sensual pleasure, thinking that there must be a bit of inner, magic elastic tugging from the nipples to the groin.

This is it, Maxine told herself, this is the moment when all you want is to lie back and let this easy pleasure wash over you. But perhaps that had been what had gone wrong between her and Charles. She had always expected him to do it to her; she had always been passive and timid in a way that people who knew Maxine out of bed would never have believed possible. If only she hadn't been plump, if only she had been the perfect shape, then she wouldn't have been so shy and self-conscious, wouldn't have minded bouncing around erotically all over the bed. But she was, so she didn't.

Pierre pressed her breasts together and ran his tongue down her cleavage. How can I do things to him while he's doing things to me? thought Maxine. I can't concentrate on two things at once; when he's kissing my breasts and driving me out of my skull with excitement, I can't think, I can't do, I can only feel.

"My turn now," said Pierre, as if mind reading. He rolled over on his side and unclasped the buckle of his belt, then Maxine reached for his hard solid body.

Later, Pierre gently pushed her head downward and Maxine licked the pink tip of his penis, which swayed as she took it between her lips. She steadied it with her cold hand, hoping that she wouldn't shrivel him. She was terrified of biting him by accident. She tucked her lips over her teeth, making a hollow monkey mouth which slid easily over the penis. No way could she get all of this in her mouth, she worried.

Pierre wriggled. "Move your hand and mouth up and down together at the same time with the same rhythm." Sprawled happily on the fur rug, Pierre made small involuntary movements with his hips toward her mouth. I seem to be doing it right, thought Maxine. She could feel a bump under the ridge of his penis, so she swirled her tongue round it experimentally. Pierre whinnied with delight, and his hips jumped eagerly toward her mouth. Maxine lost the rhythm, panicked, and thought she was going to choke; then she felt Pierre's hands on her head, gently guiding her. Suddenly, she felt quite powerful and very pleased with herself.

Later, Pierre pulled the red fox fur tenderly over her plump, white body then nuzzled underneath, into her softness. "I have dreamed of your breasts for twenty years. Did you ever think of me?"

Maxine thought this must be standard, French post-coital dialogue, so she did her best to reply in the same vein of syrup. "Of course. Doesn't every woman always remember her first lover?" He raised the glossy fur and dropped a kiss of homage on her soft honey-colored pubic hair.

"What about your wife, Pierre?" she said curiously.

"Obviously, you're not used to committing adultery, Maxine. Rule one is never to mention the wife but, since you ask, she is obsessed by the children and we do our duty every Saturday."

Maxine thought, that sounds like Charles and me.

"You're not just after our sponsorship for your skier, are you?" Maxine asked, immediately wishing that she hadn't been so insensitive.

"No, I am after *you*. Seriously." He kissed her. "You can always find a sponsor if you're the best—and I think my pupil will prove to be the best. But I hope we sign up with Chazalle, because then it will be necessary to meet two or three times a year—at least."

"At least," agreed Maxine, carefully picking a wisp of dried grass from his hair.

"We wondered if you'd turned over," called the huntsman, as the antique racing carriage bounced across the glade.

"Took a short cut and got lost," Pierre called back to him, his round blue eyes expressionless.

How can Maxine get lost on her own estate? wondered Judy and looked at Charles, scowling astride his slush-spattered gray, as he wondered the same thing. In the circumstances, he can hardly play the jealous husband to Maxine, Judy realized. But why did Maxine have to be so stupid and choose exactly the wrong moment to screw up Judy's pitch to Charles? If Judy ever got to make her pitch to Charles; in spite of her determined efforts to catch him alone, it was obvious to Judy that Charles had been avoiding her with equal determination.

So Judy was surprised when he offered to drive her to the airport, to catch her Concorde flight. As they set off down the kilometer-long, gravel drive, Charles surprised Judy by saying, "I thought I might as well give you the opportunity to reason with me again, which is obviously why you hopped over the Atlantic for the weekend. How I hate women's plots!" He suddenly accelerated violently, tires squealing round a corner, and Judy remembered what a bad driver Charles was, as he continued, "I fail to understand why Maxine expects me to behave with decorum, when she fools around with her old boyfriend under my nose, as everybody saw yesterday."

Maybe Maxine hadn't been so stupid to flirt openly with Pierre, thought Judy, as she said, "I'm sure Maxine wouldn't have looked at him twice, Charles, if you hadn't hurt her so. Why do you do it? Have you reached the age where you need to prove your virility?"

"You make adultery sound like arthritis. Why don't you mind your own business, Judy?"

"Maxine *is* my business, and she's your business as well, Charles. Surely you can see that this assistant of yours hasn't the sophistication or the style or the background to run the castle and handle all the business entertaining? The public associates Maxine's glamour with your champagne. She's starred in your TV commercials all over the world. You'll find you can't switch images as easily as you can switch wives."

Charles turned onto the highway and increased speed. "It's not that easy to switch wives, the lawyers have already made that clear. You needn't worry, Maxine will have plenty of money."

"That's not what she wants. She wants you."

"You expect me to believe that, after seeing her today with that attentive oaf?"

"I don't know anyone else who's been faithful to her husband for so long. But you know that Maxine loves you. And you love her. She makes you laugh. You've gotten used to her, like a baby to its blanket, and she's the mother of your children. Nobody's going to spell it out to you if I don't."

They drove in silence, through the sleet. Judy thought, I've got to give it one more try, and said softly, "I think your hand was forced. I think that what you really want, Charles, is to have the clock put back a month."

Another silence.

"So how would I get out of it?" Charles addressed the windscreen, as they turned into the airport.

"You'll have to take a deep breath and tell this woman that you have no intention of altering your life. Maybe you'll have to pay her—call it severance, of course. A year's salary should do it. And fix a better job for her, with more prestige. Make it clear that she has a choice of the cash and the job—or nothing."

"You American women are so tough."

"Tough means being sensible and firm, refusing to be exploited. I hope you're tough, Charles."

That evening, Judy heard the whine of a police car hurtling down Fifth Avenue, far below. "It seemed a long weekend without you," Judy murmured sleepily as Mark snaked his arm around her thin waist and pulled her close to him, under the cinnamon silk sheets. "What did you get up to, Mark?"

"Nothing much, the weather was foul. Took Lili to a couple of restaurants."

"Sounds a drag." Judy wriggled hopefully against him.

"Yes." Mark suddenly realized that those two days had been wonderful; that after spending forty-eight hours with Lili, his first reaction of purely physical lust had changed. He remembered her eagerness, her ebullience, her rages, her depression, and her pathos. All now seemed violently appealing to him.

Mark felt the tip of Judy's tongue, and automatically slid his hand between her thighs. He remembered hearing her once say that when men feel guilty, they make love with especial care, because they don't want their women to guess what's happened, and because they want to reassure themselves that it really doesn't make any difference. Expertly, Mark began to caress Judy, determined that she should not realize that, instead of her neat firm buttocks he wanted Lili's ripe, rounded ass, and instead of Judy's little pink-nippled breasts he wanted Lili's golden, dark-tipped flesh, and instead of Judy's charming, button-nosed face, he wanted Lili's dark eyes, misty with ecstasy and her full lips whispering his name as he thrust inside her.

CHAPTER 6

March 1979

PAGAN LAY AWAKE listening to the early morning sounds of home: the click-whirr-click of a London milk cart, the chink of bottles, a blackbird piping with indignation in the mischievous March wind, a heavy thud on the doormat as the *Times* came through the letterbox, a lighter thud as the British Medical Journal hit the doormat, soft swishes as the mail was pushed through the brass door flap. Downstairs, her old sheepdog, Buster II, gave a token growl at each invasion of his territory by Fritz, the dachsund.

Sophia must be awake, thought Pagan, as she listened to her daughter's rock music drift up from the basement. Seven o'clock in the morning and she's playing the drums already. Pagan then heard the noises she had been unconsciously waiting for, the sounds of her husband getting up. She heard footsteps on the polished boards of his dressing room, snatches of Mozart, whistled while he shaved, then stairs creaking as he thumped down to the kitchen.

With much whirring of weights and rattling of ancient brass chains, the grandfather clock struck seven. Then there was silence until Pagan again heard Christopher's feet on the stairs, then the rattle of her bedroom door-handle—and there he was, gray hair still damp from the shower, deftly balancing her breakfast tray. "We seem to have run out of marmalade."

"Christopher darling, I'll never make a housewife, you must have noticed by now." He rearranged the antique lace pillows behind her head, then took the *Times* from her tray and sat on the end of her bed, saying, "I thought the lack of marmalade was part of a plot to force me to divorce you."

Pagan began to pour their tea. "Grabbing the newspaper first—*always*—is practically grounds for divorce in Britain." Her primrose cotton nightdress slipped off her shoulder and her mahogany hair fell into her eyes as she leaned forward and handed him his cup.

"I once thought you might run off with a gigolo." Christopher bit into his butterless toast. "When the cardiologist said it might kill me to make love to you again, my first thought was, how long will Pagan stand it?"

"Thank Heavens that medical opinion eventually changed its mind," growled Pagan. "But I've always loved you for your brilliant conversation." She never told Christopher how much she loved him. She was superstitiously afraid of doing so.

Christopher was the mainspring of her life, the focus of her days, the theme of her thoughts. Only her husband's care had transformed Pagan from a self-destructive, insecure, upper-class failure into a society figure famous for her outrageous glamour. Ironically, when Lady Swann, in some dazzling dress, swept into the room on the arm of her older, quieter husband, people naturally assumed that it was she who dominated the partnership, but the foundation of Pagan's cheerful flamboyance was Christopher's emotional stability.

For the first few weeks of their marriage, Pagan and Christopher had continued their rich and, for Pagan, revelatory sex life. When his first heart attack had ended that phase of their relationship, Pagan had been far more concerned about losing her husband than losing their good times in bed. "Sex is like opera, darling," she used to tell Christopher. "Something that other people find fabulous, but which simply doesn't thrill me." She hadn't really missed it that much.

"Are you ready for your joke of the day?" Christopher asked. Pagan crunched her toast and nodded.

"If you believe in the Virgin Mary's immaculate conception, then Jesus Christ must have been a woman, because the Virgin's baby could only have had X chromosomes!" He roared with laughter.

Pagan looked blank. "Don't you remember my little lesson in genetics? Women have only X chromosomes, men have both X and Y. You can't give birth to a boy without Y chromosomes. You can't have Y chromosomes without spermatozoa. You can't have spermatozoa without a man."

Pagan still looked blank. "I can see you'll never win the Nobel Prize for genetics, darling. Don't you remember that I was able to predict when you were pregnant that Sophia's eyes would not be brown, because the color of a child's eyes depends on the genes of its parents. Two clearly blue-eyed parents can't produce a brown-eyed child. More toast?"

"Tomorrow morning, darling, I'd like a joke that I can understand without a Ph.D."

Pagan leaned back in bed, sipped her tea, then reached for her letters. She grabbed the one with the New York postmark and read it. "Half a million dollars!" She sat upright, waved the letter at her husband, then threw it to him. "See for yourself. That's from Stash, Lili's agent. That's the profit they expect from the premiere and it's all for the Foundation, as well as the money we'll get from Spyros's jewelry."

"Tiger-Lili certainly wants to try out for the team."

"I think she does; it's rather sweet. She seems to have had such a rotten life, in spite of all the fame." Pagan leaned back against the lace pillows. "She's always on her guard, always wary, very conscious that people try to use her—which they do all the time. It's perfectly disgusting. Lili can be a bit imperious but, basically, she's a perfect pet."

"She's certainly a generous friend." Christopher kissed the top of Pagan's head. "I'm off. Cross your fingers for the new strain of hepatitis-B. It should either do the trick, or give us an epidemic."

As he eased his elderly Rover into the flow of traffic heading south, Sir Christopher reflected that Pagan was probably the only woman he knew who would automatically feel nothing but sympathy for a voluptuous star like Lili. Perhaps Pagan understood her because both of them were a mixture of surface shockingness and underlying insecurity, he reflected, as he waited in traffic between two container trucks.

A bread van cut into the line of vehicles ahead, then swerved violently out again. Sir Christopher checked a rush of anger. Traffic snarls were a classic stress-inducer; no sense in shortening his life over someone else's bad driving.

Morning mists lay in ethereal slabs over the gray river as the line of traffic started to move along the Thames embankment, then picked up speed down the clearway. He wouldn't be late, after all, thought Sir Christopher, still in convoy between the two massive trucks.

He never saw the bakery van shoot the lights, make an unsignaled right turn, then crash head-on into one of the graceful spherical street lights that stand on the stone balustrade of the River Thames.

But Sir Christopher heard the crump of metal, the thin crash of glass, then the louder impact as an oncoming automobile piled into the back of the bakery van. He slammed on his brakes at the same time as the orange truck ahead of him, which stopped abruptly, air hissing from the pneumatic breaking system.

The worn disc brakes of Sir Christopher's car were not so effective, and he realized that he would not be able to avoid hitting the lurid orange truck ahead.

The driver of the green truck behind him reacted more slowly, and crashed into the back of Sir Christopher's old Rover. The momentum slammed the Rover into the truck ahead. As if made of paper, the Rover crumpled into the back of the truck. The steering column slammed against Sir Christopher's chest like a mallet hitting steak, smashing his ribs and heart to pulp.

He was rushed to St. Stephen's Hospital and hurried into the intensive care unit.

Twenty minutes later, Pagan, in her primrose nightdress, held her husband's limp hand.

"I'm afraid it's hopeless, Lady Swann." The doctor felt that he could talk bluntly to a fellow doctor's wife. "Even if we obtained a replacement organ, there's nothing left to attach it to—the thorax has been completely destroyed."

In a daze, Pagan signed one form giving consent for the life-support system to be switched off, another giving permission for Christopher's remains to be used for medical purposes, and a third, authorizing the undertakers to proceed. She felt very cold and, to her horror, very angry. "How could he do it?" she thought. "How dare he leave me now?" Then she thought, "How can I even think such a dreadful thing?"

"A mother-and-daughter conspiracy suit? What the hell is that?" Judy demanded, in the *VERVE!* office, wondering if she had correctly heard what Tom had said.

"Just what it sounds like," he told her. "They allege that you and Lili hatched a malicious plot to ruin Senator Ruskington's political career."

"But that's ridiculous," Judy protested, her heels angrily kicking up the apricot kelim rug as she paced her office.

"Of course it is." Tom was being patient. "But conspiracy is a bitch, Judy. It's the vaguest, stickiest area in the whole legal code. Just talking to someone, even on the telephone, can amount to a legal conspiracy, if the circumstantial evidence stands up. The fact that Lili has now moved in with you could be disastrous if the judge decides that it's significant. Frankly, it's a pity that you've asked her to stay in your apartment."

"Lili and I have a lot of catching up to do. God! This is all so stupid," Judy raged. "When Lili did this interview I hardly knew her."

"Can you prove it?" Tom asked patiently. "You'll have to go through all your papers tonight to see if there's anything that we can produce at the hearing on Friday which will substantiate what you say!"

So Judy cancelled her entire afternoon's program, then read through an 18-inch-high pile of legal documents. After that, she turned out her filing system, her desk drawers, her purse, and her briefcase in search of anything at all to prove her point. She finished at eight that evening, exhausted by the effort of concentration. "Damn that hypocritical old buzzard," she said to Tom, as she shrugged on her lynx jacket. "Senator Ruskington has now lost me almost a day's work on top of every spare cent we have."

Tom nodded. "This case is wrecking our budget, Judy. We'll have to make fast compensation cuts, as many as possible, no matter how small."

"What do you mean by small?"

"Do we really need an exercise instructor? Couldn't we let Tony go?"

"If we have to cut down, let's switch to a cheaper printer; that would be the easiest, quickest saving."

"And cut the quality? You're only saying that because you're angry, Judy."

"But it would be a really big economy and I would watch the quality like a hawk. We could make the contract conditional on quality. And what we pay Tony is a drop in the ocean compared to what we're paying the lawyers." She jammed on her lynx hat. "The exercise class is good for morale, and it means that I'm too tired to lie awake at night, worrying about that damned Senator."

"*You?* Lie awake?" he queried. "What's happened to the unstoppable Judy Jordan self-confidence?"

"It was always more fragile than you thought." Judy's voice was unusually low. For the first time, Tom realized the depth of her anxiety, and immediately switched into reassurance. Playfully, he ruffled her hair. "We've been in jams before, Judy, and you're still top of the heap."

"So there's farther to fall. And you get no sympathy. You're supposed to be invulnerable. Did Henry Kissinger stay awake at night, crying?"

"At least you've got Mark," he comforted her. "I'm finding it tough without Kate."

"I don't want to burden Mark with the troubles in my life."

"Do you mean you're frightened of doing so? Frightened that he only loves the glamorous Judy Jordan that the world sees, not the real woman that I know?"

"Mark's a lot bigger on moral issues than he is on practical ones. I can't talk to him about business because he doesn't understand it. And he doesn't understand that a lawsuit is about a set of rules, not about justice."

Fondly, Tom put an arm around her fluffy fur shoulders. "We'll struggle through somehow."

"Talking of struggling, how's Kate?"

"She says the problem is much bigger than she had thought. It's not just a tribal war, it seems to be systematic genocide. The Bangladesh government has tried to settle the Chittagong hills with their own citizens, and drive out the peaceful Buddhist peasants who live there. They're trying to take away Kate's visa."

"And to think I didn't even know where Chittagong was before Kate left."

Judy said good night to Tom, then walked slowly down the dark corridor. She noticed a light shining under the boardroom door and opened it. Inside was Tony, sweating in his shorts and vest as he went through a sequence of fast turns and kicks in front of the mirror.

"Still here, Tony!"

"Yeah! Working out the new routine for tomorrow." He leaped across the floor. "D'ya think the girls will go for it? I think they're ready for this. I think they'll manage. What d'ya think?"

Anyone who put in longer hours than she did gained Judy's instant admiration. "Hiring you was the best decision I ever made, Tony," she called as he whirled past her, spinning drops of sweat from his forehead each time he turned. He finished in a dramatic pose, kneeling on the floor with arms outstretched, then slowly stood up, panting. "Getting hired by you was the smartest thing I ever did. Did ya see my picture in *New York* magazine? My Mom's shown it to everyone on the block."

"That's great, Tony. I know they'll love it. And the girls all really appreciate the trouble you take."

Tony began to towel his dripping face. "Do you mean it? They really dig the routines?"

"Of course. And you, too, Tony. Why's that surprising?"

"All this female attention. Goes to a guy's head."

"Oh, come on," Judy laughed. "With that body, you must have had hundreds of girls after you."

"No, I was the original Charles Atlas weakling, that's why I started working out in the first place."

"You've made up for it since, Tony." Judy turned to leave the room. "Don't work too late."

"No chance, I'm taking my Mom out tonight," he answered.

"What a lovely thought, Tony. Enjoy yourselves."

"Can't we turn the volume down?" Tony's mother scowled. Carefully dressed diners were shrieking with laughter, calling greetings and gossip from table to table, while waiters clattered with laden trays across the white tiled floor.

"The fashion crowd comes here, Momma." Tony hoped she wasn't going to make a scene. "I wanted to take you somewhere real nice."

"Nice! This old-fashioned stuff!" A scornful laugh indicated her opinion of the fawn leather and chromium interior, all of which had been salvaged from the liner *Mauretania*, that floating objet d'art of the thirties.

"So now you've got a job, you got money to burn!" Tony's mother picked up the elegant menu. "I could cook this stuff for a tenth of the price! Papa and I never wasted a penny. Now, there was a careful man."

Tony didn't remember his father as being careful; his earliest memories were of his father fighting with his mother, while Tony cowered beneath the cracked, checked oilcloth that covered the kitchen table.

"What'll you have, Momma? I'm gonna try the crab salad."

"Crab salad! What nourishment is that? You like chicken, Tony, remember?"

Tony remembered the different grease stains on the kitchen wallpaper, each of which marked a spot where his father had hurled a meal against it. Roast chicken had been the easiest dish to pick off the floor. Tony hated roast chicken. "Okay, I'll have the chicken, Momma. Now, what'll you have?"

Small black eyes peered at the menu, reading with difficulty. "I'll have the hamburger. Why couldn't you let me fix something in your smart new apartment, Tony?"

She'd never stopped criticizing his apartment. Quickly he said, "It's being decorated. Wet paint everywhere." Tony wasn't clever enough to wonder why this small, scowling woman, who was in her forties but who looked twenty years older, should turn every pleasure offered by her son into an excuse to criticize him.

"Why aren't *you* doing the decorating?" She waved the menu at his face. Tony raised one arm and ducked as if to ward off a blow, then she continued. "So now you're too high and mighty to paint your own apartment! You always were lazy; you always lay around doing nothing."

They fell silent until their food was served, then Tony's mother suspiciously prodded her hamburger with her fork. "This meat is raw!"

"It's continental style, Momma, underdone." Tony felt an almost uncontrollable urge in his gut as his mother criticized on, on, on, and raised her voice until the other diners turned to look at her. This, too, had been the pattern of his childhood meals. She'd complain because Poppa was always late and, in return, he'd criticize the food. Then they were off, bickering about nothing. Voices would rise, fists would be raised, shouting would escalate into screaming, and then the food would hit the wall. Mealtimes were the only times that his family couldn't avoid being together, and they used these occasions to attack, undermine, and casually wound, using their intimate knowledge of each other to destroy with the accuracy of heat-seeking missiles.

"Please keep your voice down, Momma," Tony pleaded.

"That's a fine way to talk to your mother!"

"Momma, I'm only trying to give you a good time." Once again, Tony wondered whether he would ever earn adult status.

"Don't interrupt me, or I'll make you wish you'd never been born!" Tony felt sick. Inside his magnificently developed body, he felt again like a small boy, a small boy terrified of his mother's unpredictable, sadistic rages, a small boy overpowered by the unreasoned guilt of childhood. Every day, the small Tony had heard that savage voice and moved about the apartment in terror, lest she should pick on some trifling fault—a peanut-butter stain on his shirt, unfinished schoolwork, chores skimped—as an excuse for a beating.

Tony unlocked his front door and crushed his mother's bag of homemade cookies into the overflowing garbage bag. Another treat for the roaches. He fed a tape of *Captain Blood* into the video, threw himself on the permanently converted, never-made Murphy bed and turned to the night table, upon which stood a signed photograph of Judy in a silver frame. "I don't take her out, I'm neglecting her; I do take her out, I'm wasting money!"

"Isn't Spyros ever going to give up?" Lili picked the plain diamond bracelet from the newly delivered basket of butterfly orchids and tossed it on Judy's blue and mauve silk sofa. "If I had kept his bracelets, I'd have enough to reach my elbows."

"Lucky girl, isn't she, Mark?" Judy picked up the brilliant stream of jewels and admired it over the back of her brown hand.

Mark shrugged his shoulders and gazed at the smoldering log fire. "That bracelet would feed an African village for years."

"Don't be so smug!" Lili reached forward, grabbed the diamond bracelet and flung it at Mark. "*Give* it to the Africans, then," she said. "I don't want it, because I know it isn't a gift, it's a bribe." Lili snorted. "When one of Spyros's little gifts appears in a basket of flowers, you're supposed to roll over on your back, and be grateful. He orders these diamond bracelets, a dozen at a time, from Cartier. To him, they're trading stock."

"Like beads and mirrors?" Judy suggested. "As used by the Conquistadores to buy Aztec gold?"

"Exactly." Lili's expression was offset by her bizarre makeup; she had spent the afternoon trying to copy Mistinguett's makeup; her guide photograph lay among scattered cosmetics on the low, red marble table.

"You'd better get that stuff off your face or you'll be late for the concert." Judy picked up the brass poker and prodded a falling log back into place.

"True." Lili stood up, stretched and headed for the bathroom. "Won't you need this makeup?" Judy called after her, meaning get this mess out of my sitting room.

Mark said, "She likes being untidy, you should see the state she left my place in."

"So what does a little mess matter? The reason Lili wanted to move in with me was so that our relationship could develop." Softly, she touched Mark's long, tapering, brown fingers. Gently, Mark pulled his hand away.

"Tom told me that having Lili living here with you, Judy, could be playing with fire; it might prejudice the lawsuit."

Judy neatly replaced the poker on the poker stand. "We're never going to get to know each other properly over restaurant tables and in hotels." She turned as Lili appeared, glorious in dark-green shot silk and opal earrings. "I'm off."

Lili's carnation scent lingered in the sitting room as the front door slammed. Mark wished that he, too, could leave. It's a classic double bind, he thought miserably: if I leave, then Judy will take it as rejection, and if I stay, the whole thing will shortly explode in our faces. Here we sit, sipping Perrier on top of an emotional time bomb. Surreptitiously, he sniffed the carnations and couldn't help imagining Lili's gold-skinned body as she emerged from the tub.

Lili let herself into the apartment and unclasped her green velvet cloak. They hadn't gone to bed yet, she could hear Judy's earnest voice saying, ". . . But why, Mark? Why have you tried for four hours, in various indirect ways, to get me to ask my daughter to leave this apartment?"

"For Chrissake, don't you understand, Judy?" Unseen, Lili heard Mark's weary pleading, and her hands halted on the gold clasp.

And, suddenly, Judy did understand. "Of course! I must have been blind! You're in love with her, aren't you, Mark?" Her voice was hard. "I must have been blind!"

"I don't want to hurt you, Judy."

"Too bad, sweetheart, you just did," she flashed back at him. "Men always say they don't want to hurt you, when they've just dealt some woman a death blow."

"I don't want to hurt Lili, either. She trusts me. I don't want to upset her life, or your life, or your life with Lili, or my life." Mark tried not to raise his voice. "To Lili, I'm the only man she knows who isn't trying to get into her pants."

"Except that's what you want to do, isn't it?" Judy demanded.

There was a pause, then Mark said in a low voice. "If you want the truth, I don't think any man could resist Lili's extraordinary sexuality."

Lili caught sight of her reflection in the dim silver depths of an elaborate Louis XV mirror. What is it, she thought, what is it that I have in me that casts this spell, this curse, on almost every man I meet? What is it? I can't see it. Why can't I switch it off?

As if echoing her thoughts, in the living room Judy shouted, "I can't see it, and neither can any other woman. That's why it's so maddening to see you men all making fools of yourselves over Lili."

Gazing at her reflection, Lili realized that she was tired of being a sex object, tired of being considered a male plaything, tired of being idolized by both sexes—unknown men because they desired her and unknown women because they desired to be like her. Lili realized that her fatal attraction was, above all, fatal to herself.

"Does Lili know you feel this way about her?" Judy was trying to control her voice, because she had to know the answer to her question.

"No," Mark answered, "and I don't want her to know."

"What does she feel about you?"

"I think she trusts me." He paused. "I think she sees me as a brother."

"Are you and I living in the same century?" Judy suddenly yelled, "Brother, indeed!"

"I'm not going to threaten the only shred of family security that Lili's ever had."

Judy interrupted him bitterly. "Well, that just makes it perfect." Her voice was vicious. "I'm losing my magazine, my money, my job; then you try to fix things so that I'll lose my daughter and my lover into the bargain. And to top it all, you're full of sympathy for *her*, not me."

Mark shouted back, "Look, I don't want Lili. I want you. But I want you like you used to be."

Judy heard the pain behind his words and realized that Mark was telling the truth when he said that his passion for Lili was something that he didn't want.

"You're difficult to sympathize with, Judy." Mark finally found an exterior focus for his anger. "You've changed since I met you. You were such fun. Ambitious, hardworking, successful, and tough—sure. But fun. You were kind to people and strong. You gave me support and self-confidence."

"Now, I'm the one who needs support," Judy wailed, suddenly out of control and frightened.

Suddenly, Mark was able to crystalize his feelings and put them into words. "You seem to have lost your own self-confidence."

"What do you mean?"

"I don't recognize you any more. You taught me that real self-confidence isn't put on every morning like a silk shirt, to impress the outside world. Self-confidence is something that's built on knowing what you can do and what you can't do. Now, you seem to have forgotten that. What's got into you?"

"What's got into me?" Judy was suddenly quiet. "I'm terrified that I'll end up like my mother, feeding the cat and watching the neighbors and waiting. I don't want to be powerless like she was, just sitting helplessly in the middle of her own life, waiting for it to end."

"There's a lot to be said for that sort of life." Now Mark was angry. "At least that sort of woman isn't jealous of her own daughter." He was unable to resist the urge to hurt the suddenly vulnerable Judy. "You used to say that jealousy was the penalty of thinking only about externals. You used to say that there would always be younger, more beautiful women in the world. You used to say that jealousy never troubled a self-confident woman."

"So now I know I was wrong!" Judy shouted. "Do *you* want to know how it feels to become a mother when you're my age and then suddenly find that your baby is one of the most beautiful women in the world?"

In the hall, Lili didn't want to hear any more but she didn't want to leave. Mesmerized, like a frog in car headlights, she felt unable to move.

"Do you *really* want to know what it feels like to be Lili's mother?" Judy continued. "It feels as if I'm slowly becoming nobody! It feels as if I'm becoming the Invisible Woman! Little by little, I'm losing my identity! Very quickly, I'm losing the business that I spent twenty years building up. So I'm losing my job, my status, my money. I'm facing financial and professional disaster and disgrace. And I'm desperately afraid of failure—all because I'm Lili's mother." Her voice cracked. "Everything's slipping away and I'm frightened, Mark." Too late, she was finally telling her lover what was on her mind.

Lili stood up and tiptoed to her room, tears running down her face. She didn't want to listen any longer, as the two people she cared for tore their relationship to pieces—because of her.

Judy perched in front of her breakfast counter sipping her high-energy drink—the juice of an orange, a teaspoonful of honey and a whole, raw egg; it was blended every morning for her breakfast, and tasted nicer then it sounded. Force of habit had compelled her to get up at her usual six o'clock, but this morning there had been no reason to linger because Mark had moved out the night before, with his clothes stuffed into a khaki duffel bag. He had been exhausted and angry because Judy couldn't understand his predicament. As Mark saw it, he was being falsely accused of disloyalty, when he had tried to be truthful and faithful.

Gallant, confident Judy, the brave little drummer boy, had suddenly crumpled into a clutching, distraught female, and Mark simply didn't know how to cope with her; he wished he could help her but he couldn't. He could see that his presence upset her. So he had left. It seemed better than having an all-night row, which is what they had been obviously heading for. He had said, "Take care of yourself, Judy," then walked out of the door, leaving Judy bitterly to wonder why people always say, "Take care of yourself," when they meant that *they* don't intend to take care of you. She'd never needed a man in her life so badly before, and now, when she needed Mark, he was leaving her. He thought he'd be able to get an assignment in Nicaragua. It might as well be the moon.

As Judy finished her drink, Tom called from the *VERVE!* office. "Not good news, Judy," he warned.

"Hit me, I can take it," she replied, dully, their joke formula for riding a crisis.

"Judy, I can't keep up this juggling act much longer. I've held the creditors off for as long as I can, but they won't take our-check-is-in-the-mail any longer. This is now more than a cash problem. We'll have to pull something out of the hat, fast, Judy."

There's nothing left in the hat, Judy thought to herself, as the other phone rang and she picked it up. It was Lili's agent, Stash. A phone clasped to either ear, Judy said, "Morning, Stash, d'you want Lili? I think she's still asleep."

"No, I want you." His silky voice held a trace of middle Europe. Judy turned to the left telephone and said, "I'll call you back, Tom," then turned to the right and said, "Why, Stash?"

"Would *VERVE!* magazine like to be one of the sponsors of the International Beauty Pageant this year?" the world-weary voice inquired.

"Sounds interesting." Judy's voice was guarded. "What does it involve?"

"They want you to be one of the judges in Miami, and then you would chaperone the winner to Istanbul and Egypt, on the start of her world tour."

"Our policy on *Verve!* is to soft-pedal the beauty contests. We like to think that our readers have more on their minds than lipstick." Judy's response was automatic. "In any case, our sponsorship program is allocated for this year." Years of experience had taught Judy never to say no outright, even when people approached her for money.

"This isn't the normal deal; you won't have to put in a cent. They're offering you a big slice of equity in return for coverage in the magazine and identification with yourself. They want to reposition the beauty contests so that no woman would feel them degrading."

"I appreciate your offer, Stash, but I couldn't leave New York."

Stash said, "These days, New York is only twelve hours away from anywhere, and your magazine works on a six-week schedule; it's not as if you were running a daily newspaper."

Judy paused. Stash mentioned the money involved. Judy gasped. Carefully backpedaling, she said, "We've always made a point of staying in touch with the average American woman and her ambitions; and there's no doubt that the beauty queen is one of the most fascinating figures of our age. Providing the terms are right, I think it would be in all our interests, but I may have to fly back if there are any . . . business problems."

After discussing further details with Stash, Judy exuberantly called Tom. "Hi, this time we really *are* about to mail the check."

"She bought it right away, just like you said." Wearing his usual vicuna coat and black leather gloves, Stash walked into Lili's bedroom without knocking. Judy had long since left her apartment and gone to the office. Stash knew that there was no chance of being overheard.

Lili gasped rhythmically as the Japanese masseur made delicate crisscross movements up and down her spine with his thumbs. "Are the International Beauty people happy?" she asked, as she was rolled over.

Stash's glance at her flesh was that of professional appraisal. Knowing how much Lili could eat, he vigilantly checked her weight and, when he did so, he also made a covert inspection for needle tracks in her arms, crepe skin that would indicate diuretic abuse, puffiness that might be due to drink. That was part of an agent's job. As usual, Lili was amused by the lizardlike, quick appraisal.

Stash said, "Frankly, they took a lot of persuading. They said they didn't need a woman's magazine."

Lili yawned, "If they want me as a judge, then they've got to have *VERVE!* as a sponsor." The Japanese masseur started to attack Lili's left thigh as she continued. "Oh, Stash, I've decided to do the Mistinguett film after all."

Stash was surprised. "I thought wild horses couldn't drag you away from your mother at the moment!" He looked serious. "It's about time you got back to work again, Lili. We both know that I get no percentage if you don't work for six months. But you can't afford to be out of view for that long. *You* know how fast they forget, and how fickle the public can be."

"Yes, but I thought that learning to love my mother was more important than money or fame; now I now that the best thing I can do for my mother is leave town."

"Okay, I'll set up meetings with Omnium." He was delighted. Not only was it a great dramatic part, but it was the best vehicle yet for Lili's considerable singing and dancing talents. She'd have to get fit fast, but that was the only problem.

Lili sat up on the massage table and pulled out the tortoise-shell pin which held her silky hair clear of the massage oil. "It'll be fun to spend the summer in Britain," she said, without much conviction. "Though I can't understand why they want to make a film about a French vaudeville star in Britain."

Stash shrugged. "Maybe they got a tax situation; maybe Omnium has some money blocked somewhere; maybe a reciprocal deal . . ."

CHAPTER 7

March 1979

S*IR CHRISTOPHER'S COFFIN* was carried out of the chapel at Trelawney; on top of it was a single red rose from Pagan and a nosegay of white daisies from their fifteen-year-old daughter, Sophia.

In spite of the dreadful weather, Pagan had insisted that the funeral party walk to the private chapel from the stone manor house. A fierce Cornish wind blew from the cliffs, thrashing the blooming thickets of rhododendrons, whipping at Pagan's black veil and threatening to blow the sodden, black umbrellas inside out.

Pagan had insisted on an old-fashioned burial, and there had been an explosive family row when Selma, her mother's partner, had remarked that, as most of Sir Christopher's organs were now in the deep freeze waiting to be dissected by medical students, it hardly seemed worthwhile to bury what was left.

Pagan knew what had prompted her vicious remark. Selma had helped Pagan's mother to convert the debt-ridden manor house into a profitable health farm. Selma had almost succeeded in cheating Pagan of her inheritance, and Selma could never forgive the younger woman for the fact that one day the entire estate and the entire business would belong to Pagan.

"Darlings, don't come, I want to be alone," Pagan had firmly told Judy and Maxine. So now Pagan stood alone at her husband's graveside, and the rain beat down on the big black umbrellas, as the box that contained Christopher was lowered into the rich red Cornish earth.

Pagan still couldn't believe that Christopher was gone and that, after her sixteen years of care because of his serious heart condition, her husband could have been wiped out by one careless driver's one careless moment. After long years of cancer research, Christopher's team had been on the verge of a triumphant breakthrough, but now success had been snatched from him, and he had been snatched from her.

Pagan felt far away, as if she were watching the entire scene from the top of the tiny seventeenth-century church. Everyone present, including herself, seemed doll-sized, as they huddled in the graveyard. As the priest intoned "ashes to ashes, dust to dust" in the teeth of the gale, Pagan wondered if there was a sinister reason why the grass in graveyards was always so thick and green; she could hardly see the little yellow aconites which studded the turf.

Beside her, young Sophia cried silently into one of her father's enormous handkerchiefs. "I'm sorry, Mummy, I can't stop crying."

"It doesn't matter, my darling. Daddy won't mind you howling your eyes out."

Why aren't I crying? Pagan wondered. She blinked her eyes to try to make tears come, but nothing happened. I *should* be crying, Pagan told herself, I've lost the only man who ever loved me. She tried thinking of all the tenderest moments that she had shared with Christopher, but still no tears came. Mortally wounded men on the battlefield often cannot feel pain. Similarly, some widows cannot cry, and although they often seem to be amazingly collected (almost unfeeling), they are anesthetized by shock.

Suddenly, a blast of wind blew her umbrella inside out and tore off Pagan's black velvet hat and veil. Blast God, she thought, for taking Christopher before his work was finished. How dare God do this to me! How *can* He? I did all I could. It's not fair. I can't be expected to put up with this. Why should I? I've done so much good. (Well, I haven't done much bad . . . Well, I've done less bad than most people.) What *more* does *He* want? Why did *He* have to pick on me?

After the mourners had left, Pagan walked to her favorite cliff-top.

Her old sheepdog, Buster II, wheezed at her side through the dead bracken. Pagan sat on the weather-beaten wooden bench and recalled Christopher's black figure sitting here, hunched against the gray sky, when first they had met. Suddenly, Pagan no longer felt sheltered, like a big baby. She felt nothing: no misery, no pain, no grief. Her body felt numb. Inside her head, there was chaos but no feeling; her thoughts bolted crazily in all directions, like a herd of panic-stricken animals. Unwelcome pictures slid into her mind, and she remembered, with distance, her husband's knobby feet, the way his bald head freckled in the sun, and his irritating habit of loudly crunching peppermints. Pagan thought, how dare Christopher leave me alone? She felt bewildered, disoriented, and frightened by her own feelings. She felt as if she were in a never-ending black tunnel—the Valley of Despair.

During the following three weeks, Pagan was unexpectedly calm, as she held meetings with lawyers, trustees, and accountants. Then she began to forget things. Christopher's secretary quietly took over the organization of his memorial service at St. Bartholomew's Church in Smithfield, after she discovered that Pagan had forgotten to invite most of her husband's closest friends.

Every morning Pagan heard the newspaper thump through the letterbox and waited hopefully. She always thought, it isn't true, it hasn't happened. God wouldn't let it happen to me. I haven't done anything to deserve it. It must have been a bad dream and Christopher is really shaving in the bathroom at this very minute.

"I wish that I wasn't so terribly tired all the time," Pagan complained to Sophia, "and I wish it wasn't so cold in this house." She sat, swaddled in her old Persian lamb cloak, in front of a roaring log fire, and added, "Christopher was so mean about the heating installation." Sophia decided not to mention that, while the rest of London enjoyed an unusually balmy spring, Pagan's sitting room thermostat registered 78.

Two days later, Sophia came home from St. Paul's school to find her mother pale but dry eyed, briskly digging a hole at the bottom of the garden. Buster's dead body lay under the plane tree. "I forgot his lead, and the stupid dog ran off after a cat—straight under a motorbike. God knows what we've done to deserve two road deaths in one month. But Buster's time was up, he was almost twenty." To Pagan, life was unreal. It was a nightmare from which she hoped, shortly, to wake up. Actions were meaningless. People were meaningless. Nothing in life made sense. What *was* the point of life?

The following day, Pagan's old MGB was stopped by the police, doing almost 100 mph down the crowded streets of Ladbroke Grove, and she could not remember the registration number of her car. "I have all these huge, black holes in my memory, officer," she explained, but he didn't seem to understand. Bloody man.

"I do think, darling," Pagan told Sophia that night, "that your father might have picked a better time to leave us. I've no idea how he wanted to allocate the money from the premiere, and there's nothing in any of his papers to tell us whom to appoint as the new director of the Foundation. Why on earth should I be expected to put up with all this? Just what am I supposed to do now?" She prowled around the pink, hydrangea-patterned drawing room, thinking, who can I talk to now? Who can I do things with? Who can I share things with? Who knows my past, my jokes, my fears? Who am I supposed to spend Christmas with? Aloud, she said, "Just what am I supposed to do now?"

"You sound like Grandma," said Sophia bluntly, hoping that this unforgivable insult would shock Pagan into becoming, once again, her erratically adoring mother instead of this whining automaton. Pagan took no notice. She switched on the television, picked up a box of chocolates and watched a raucous game show until Sophia burst into tears and rushed out of the room. Then a black pool of cold panic started to rise in Pagan's body, as she heard that Mona, from Chipping Norton, had won a hostess trolley, a facial sauna and a giant Donald Duck. What's happening to me, Pagan wondered, why can't I control what I'm thinking? As she watched Mona scream with unbelievable joy and hug her husband, Pagan thought, why can't I behave as I want to? Why can't I remember things? As Mona, who couldn't think of the name of a peanut farmer who lived in a white house, was ignominiously bundled off the stage, Pagan thought, perhaps I'm going mad. Perhaps I'll go to the doctor tomorrow. She did not know that she was suffering from the classic symptoms of bereavement, that she was groping her way through the tunnel of death.

But the next day she looked around her kitchen and decided not to visit the doctor. There's no point in saving a worthless person like me, thought Pagan, swinging from shock to depression. Doctors are for people who are really sick, not women who haven't enough self-discipline to pull themselves together. She looked around the cozy kitchen at the bunches of rosemary and thyme from Trelawney which hung from the ceiling, the well-used pans, the hand-thrown terra-cotta pots, the baskets of brown Cornish eggs and fresh vegetables. The delicate pink-rimmed Minton dinner service she had inherited on her marriage was ranged along the ashwood shelves of the country dresser. Whatever is the point of trying to make a kitchen attractive? she wondered. It's just a food-processing plant, dolled up by pretty china. Plates always break in the end, however much you like them. Everything breaks in the end. Pagan took one of the Minton tea plates off the dresser, opened the window, threw the plate out and watched it smash in the basement area. That's what happened to me, she thought. My life is smashed like broken china.

Half an hour later, Sophia stood in the kitchen looking at the empty shelves of the dresser. She had already noticed the pile of smashed china, when she opened the front door. "Mother, I'm going to stay in Tuscany with Jane for the holidays." Defiantly she flicked spikes of auburn hair back from her face, silently daring her mother to care for her, daring her mother to say, "Oh, no, you won't! You'll stay here with me."

"Whatever you like, darling," Pagan replied, absentmindedly.

"Mummy, I can't stand seeing you like this anymore. I'm leaving now," Sophia shouted. Pagan took no notice as Sophia ran to her bedroom, stuffed two shirts and her tape player into a tote bag, then rushed out, slamming the door.

Suddenly, the house seemed quiet and empty. Pagan picked up the bottle of cooking brandy from the kitchen shelf, and put it to her lips. She felt an emptiness within her. I am worth nothing, nobody cares about me, and nobody ever will again. I don't want to live. Life is my enemy and death is my friend. The future is black and pointless and threatening.

By midnight, she had also drained the gin, whisky, and vermouth in the drinks cabinet, followed by the Drambuie. She threw up in the kitchen sink.

Then she thought, I'm not going to let it happen to me again, and telephoned Alcoholics Anonymous, to find out the date of the next meeting in the crypt of the church at Trafalgar Square.

"Now the openings—push against me, harder . . . harder . . . goddammit, will you take that away?" He poked a finger into Lili's stomach.

Lili shut her eyes and clenched her abdominal muscles with all her strength to pull her belly concave. "It won't go any flatter," she gasped between clenched teeth.

"Too much tension in your neck, relax." Again, the Pilates trainer folded Lili's knees against her chest and leaned on them with all his weight. "You'll have a back like Makarova by the time I'm finished with you. Okay, that's enough, now the weights."

Lili moved across the studio to the fixed bed. Outside the rain lashed against the skylight; God, she was sick of this New York winter.

"Are you doing better in class, yet?"

"My ballet teacher's using me to demonstrate." Lili strapped the black-leather weight belts around her ankles.

The trainer believed her. Lili had been badly out of shape a month ago, and he had been surprised by her fierce concentration and tenacity. Accustomed to training professional dancers, he had seldom met with such a capacity for discipline in an actress. He knew that he could be tough with her, because she would fight back and try harder, whereas most actresses would burst into tears and he'd never see them again.

"You're not Folies Bergère standard yet, Lili." He pushed her onto the exercise bed, where she lay on her right side, bending her right leg and extending her left leg straight in front of her.

"Okay, up and down fifty times," said the trainer. "You still need more strength in that left leg." He corrected her pelvis position and watched carefully as Lili slowly grunted to the fiftieth lift.

"Look—you're changing," he pulled her upright, and in the mirror he pointed out to Lili the sleek, long muscles that were appearing on her thighs, the hollows in her buttocks, the flat, taut area below her breasts, where her stomach muscles were developing. It was okay. By May Lili would be in shape for *The Best Legs in the Business.*

The old London cinema had been especially decorated for the rock concert. It now looked like a giant scarlet parcel topped with a silver-ribbon bow. The red plastic wrapping bellied in the wind, straining dangerously at the nylon ropes that held it together. Each time the wind gusted, the ropes slapped loudly against the giant yellow sign which announced: ANGELFACE HARRIS: GIFTWRAPPED. BRITISH TOUR BEGINS TONITE. APRIL 5 SOLD OUT.

Eddie thought life had been a lot easier for a publicity agent back in the good old days of punk, when everybody was broke, but they believed in what they were doing and all you had to organize, publicity-wise, was getting one of the band arrested at the start of the tour, then the ballyhoo took care of itself.

As he approached the star's dressing room, the door was flung open and a girl was thrown out into the corridor, blood streaming down her lower face.

"You fucking cow," she yelled, shoving tufts of black hair back from her pallid face. She struggled upright against the grimy wall, pulling the black-leather miniskirt over her chicken-skinny thighs. "You fucking fat London tart!" One hand checked the silver chain that pierced her left nostril, looped across her left cheek and hung from her ear. "Who the fuck d'you think you are?"

A cheap orange-plastic toolbox was flung out of the dressing room. As it crashed to the floor, the box burst open, spilling greasepaint, wads of dirty cotton, glittering powders, and gels in a dozen crude colors.

"I'm his wife, darling, and nobody better forget it!" A tiny woman, wearing a white fox, floorlength coat, appeared in the doorway. "Now get your skinny arse out of here before I do you an injury."

"Now would that be this week's wife or the one before?" spat back the girl in the miniskirt. "Or is this one of Angelface's special relationships and you're going for a whole month of wedded bliss? Someone ought to organize a grand reunion for Angelface's old ladies—at Wembley Stadium."

There was a moment of electric silence and then Maggie, the fourth Mrs. Angelface Harris, stepped forward on her six-inch high-heeled silver cowboy boots, and raised her tiny hand to the other girl's face. But instead of slapping her, Maggie hooked two fingers through the silver chain that ran from ear to nose and yanked it hard. The girl screamed, as blood spurted from her nose and streamed down the length of her body, like rain down a windowpane.

Eddie, the publicity man, muttering "For Chrissake" as he ran forward, pushed Maggie aside, then hurried the bleeding, screaming girl upstairs to the boxlike room behind the stage where the two Red Cross volunteers were reading paperbacks.

Eddie reached for the radio in the back pocket of his jeans. "Kev—the makeup girl's had an accident. Get a car round to the stage door and take her to the hospital. And there's a bit of a mess outside Angelface's dressing room. Get someone to clear it up."

He walked into the dressing room and waved at Angelface Harris, who was standing at the counter, finishing his makeup. He wore only a dancer's support, the small black-elastic pouch kept in place around his genitals by a G string running between his hollow-cheeked buttocks.

"Everything under control?" Angelface raised his cherubic eyebrows, widened his innocent blue eyes and put down the *Daily Mail*. Even with red greasepaint streaked down his cheeks, his face had an appealing urchin impertinence. Eddie looked at the white, sinewy body and wondered what was the secret of Angelface's legendary, evergreen youthfulness. Whatever he's on, I'd like some, too, Eddie thought to himself, as Angelface squirmed into a red-and-silver striped leotard and then clipped on a massive, winged silver collar, studded with rhinestones, which swept out beyond his narrow shoulders. Angelface now had a V-shaped silhouette of a body builder.

Of course, Angelface's musical secret was that he had always stuck, leechlike, to the spirit of rock'n'roll, which was a mix of black American blues and American country music. Angelface had been one of the original rockers of the fifties; then in the sixties he'd reinvented himself, with a band, as a lead singer of the Dark Angels. Every time rock'n'roll rushed up a blind alley, Angelface's career had wobbled. In 1967, he had been buried by psychedelic rock but, by 1977, Angelface was top of the heap again, and *Rolling Stone* magazine was wondering how many times this lovable old strummer could be recreated, as Angelface relaunched himself in black leather and studs on the crest of the punk-rock wave.

It was simple, really, Eddie thought. Every time a new generation of fans rediscovered rock'n'roll, they also discovered Angelface; two years older than Mick Jagger, he still looked as cute and skinny as the day he first stepped into the spotlight.

Maggie buttoned rhinestone-covered silver gauntlets around her husband's wrists, then fitted silver wings around her husband's Flash Gordon boots. Angelface peered into the dressing-room mirror and made a few, tentative passes at his eyebrows with the black greasepaint.

"I hate doing me own makeup, Maggie," the singer grumbled to the bundle of white fox that covered his sulking wife. "I wish to God you'd kept your hands off the makeup girl until she'd finished my face. You know I'd never touch a nasty scrubber like that."

"Filthy bitch bled on me," muttered his wife, sponging a spot of blood from the white fox. "Right, I'm off to get me hair done for tonight."

After she left, Angelface sucked in his small beginnings of a belly and leaned toward the mirror again. Sometimes he wondered if Maggie wasn't a bit of a nutter. Chicks always got uptight when they thought it was expected of them, but Maggie sometimes went over the top with jealousy. Last week she'd set fire to that chick's hair, just because he'd touched her bum as he came off-stage; one click of Maggie's cigarette lighter and the girl was a hospital case. This week she tears the makeup girl's nose in half. What the hell was he in for next, Angelface wondered, as he picked up the telephone and dialed a New York number. "Judy? Yes, it's me again. Gotcha at last. Listen, don't hang up on me or I'll reach for me lawyer . . . I'll *tell* you why I'm phoning. Says in the *Daily Mail* that Lili's due to film in Britain next month . . . I've told you before, I don't believe you . . . You know bloody well that the reason I couldn't help you when the baby was born was because I was as broke as you were, but that ain't the case today, Judy. Today I'm worth eleven big M's and I want to get to know me daughter. I want to meet Lili . . . what d'ya mean, I *can't*. I'm entitled to . . . don't you tell me I'm entitled to nothing . . . it's a bit late to tell me that I'm not her father, and I don't bloody well believe you, Judy . . . don't give me that line again about being irregular and getting your dates wrong. I gotta *memory*, Judy, and I remember you was crazy about me . . . Judy, I'd hoped that you'd be nice about this, but since you aren't, I'm *telling* you. First, I know I'm her father. She gets her looks from me, don't she? Second, I'm gonna meet her without telling her . . . because I'm gonna make sure she likes me for meself, before springing the big surprise. And you can't stop me, Judy, so don't bitch it up from your end, or you'll be sorry. That's what I wanted to tell you!" Angelface slammed the phone back in its cradle.

In Manhattan, Judy slammed the phone back in its cradle.

And somebody in the adjoining room, quietly, carefully, replaced the extension telephone.

May 1979

Lili stalked furiously across the café, ripped the lighted cigarette out of the man's mouth and slapped him across the face. Energized with fury at her insolence, he grabbed the cigarette back from her pouting lips. Again, Lili snatched it from his mouth, so he flung her to the floor by the old, upright piano, then spat insults at her, as she scrambled to her feet. Then he grabbed her arm and savagely whirled Lili into Mistinguett's famous apache routine. Lili kicked the man and he dealt her a brutal blow to the head. She fell to the floor again, and again he dragged her upright. She spat in his face as he ripped her skirt off, and so they danced on, portraying a lover's quarrel, at the end of which Lili groveled at the man's feet in an ecstasy of masochistic passion.

"Cut!" Zimmer shouted. The technicians and the watching dancers softly applauded. Lili's magnetic animal sensuality effortlessly supplied the passion that was needed for the apache number.

"Zimmer!" Lili called, still on the floor of the French café set. "Do I really have to hit him so hard?"

"But of course," Zimmer shouted back, "the apache number has to be savage and sadistic. It's about the eternal battle for supremacy between a man and a woman. You *must* hit him hard; you are hitting back for all the oppressed women of the world, remember! That's it for today, everyone."

Zimmer nodded. "Action!" The clapboard snapped.

Thirty-six showgirls in flesh-colored fishnet tights, holding up their ten-foot-long white ostrich-feather trains, paraded down the glittering staircase, their tall feather headdresses nodding as they walked.

At the top of the staircase, Lili stepped forward. She was wearing a few square inches of spangled gauze, a spangled chastity belt and a huge, blue peacock tail.

"CUT!" bellowed Zimmer. "What is this on your legs?"

"Tights," Lili shouted back into the dark emptiness beyond the pool of bright light.

"Get them off—I want shiny legs!" the director hollered. "Take five, everybody!"

Back in her dressing room, Lili peeled off the fishnet tights and said, "I should have listened to you, Guy." Guy St. Simon was Lili's personal wardrobe designer for *The Best Legs.*

"He's edgy because he's so anxious," Guy explained. "This is the biggest budget picture that Zimmer's ever made. He merely wants your legs to have that smooth, shiny, twenties look. Let's get you into the silk tights."

Carefully, they eased three pairs of silk tights over Lili's legs. Lili replaced her spangled chastity belt, the designer fixed the huge blue peacock tail behind her, and they looked in the mirror. Lili wailed. "My legs look like sausages!"

Guy nodded sorrowfully. "Mistinguett must have had legs like sticks, to get away with three pairs."

Lili started down the staircase again.

"CUT!" yelled Zimmer. "Your legs look like *saucissons.*"

"You wanted Mistinguett's authentic costume," Lili shouted back. The technicians let out a mass sigh of ennui as another break was called. Lili released her cumbersome feather tail and ran down to the footlights, her breasts bouncing under their crust of glass jewels. "Where are you, Guy?" She searched the darkness for the designer. "Quick, I've had an idea." The footlights flung dramatic black shadows over Lili's face and silken legs as she leaned over and peered into the dim stalls.

"Doesn't she look like an early Toulouse Lautrec?" murmured Zimmer, who collected French music hall paintings, to his visitor.

"Yeah," said Angelface Harris, "that dwarf painter."

Angelface had dropped his well-brought-up English accent. He no longer spoke correctly and enunciated clearly. Like so many pop stars, he dropped his h's and adopted a pseudo-working-class accent with a mid-Atlantic twang.

Angelface sat, unusually still and silent, as Lili pushed back her cloud of hair and called again for her costume designer. She was the most beautiful, amazing chick he'd ever laid eyes on. And she was the sexiest chick he'd ever seen, he thought, as he watched it all spill out of the spangles.

"Anyone screwing her?" Angelface asked suddenly.

He can't wait to get in there, thought Zimmer, as he shrugged his shoulders. "No idea. You can't meet her today. She's not to be distracted."

But Angelface had not felt lust; he had suddenly felt a burning desire to flatten whoever was screwing his daughter.

Twenty minutes later, plumes once more in place, Lili again started down the staircase, her legs gleaming under a thick application of oil.

"Perfect," said Zimmer as Lili reached the front of the stage, the microphone swung over her head and she began to sing. "*C'est Paris . . .*" Lili's confident, throaty voice rang through the empty theater as the chandelier twirled and the thirty-six showgirls twitched their feather tails and stepped forward.

"She can *sing.*" Angelface sat up in surprise. "Her phrasing is great. She's got a sort of harsh quality in her voice that chicks can't usually get. It's a strong voice and a sexy voice, but not a sweet voice." Angelface hadn't expected Lili to be able to sing. But he knew who she got her voice from.

"CUT!" Zimmer yelled. "Mike in shot."

And so it went on. Unlike the rest of the cast, Lili was in almost every scene and, when shooting finished at nine o'clock that night, she was too exhausted to absorb further criticism and her left eye had started to squint slightly, as it always did when she was tired. Nevertheless, Zimmer appeared in her dressing room with a sheaf of notes. "About your singing, Lili."

"I'm sorry I missed that top G," she said quickly. "I lose my range when I'm tired."

"*All* your singing is wrong. Mistinguett, she had a voice like a cement mixer, you are singing too *well*. I want you to *rasp!*"

Three months with the Met's voice coach. Why did I bother? Lili snapped, "If you want me to sing like Louis Armstrong, why not dub my voice with a cement mixer?"

A month later they were shooting in the countryside and Lili no longer had to try to roughen her voice because it was hoarse with overuse. A scarf was wound around her neck to protect it against the damp air of the May evening as Lili strolled by herself through the field.

Her calf muscles ached and her battered joints protested as she climbed over a five-barrel gate.

Physically, Lili was exhausted, but mentally she was content. Halfway through the shooting, Mistinguett looked very promising, although Lili knew that you couldn't consider a film successful until you saw the final print. A film could be spoiled in the editing, badly dubbed or lost in a film industry vendetta, never to be screened. But the dailies were good and so was the atmosphere on set. There was a hopeful buzz about the whole production. Zimmer was no longer tense and had even grunted, "*Pas mal*," today. He was rapidly turning back into the charming, supportive colleague who had been the first person to treat Lili as a serious actress, and who could coax a better performance from her than any other director.

Swallows cruised against the iridescent pink of the evening sky as Lili sauntered into a muddy lane. On either side of the road, rainwater chuckled down the ditches, bluebells gleamed in the hedgebanks and raindrops dripped softly from fern fronds. England was very pretty, when it stopped raining, Lili thought, as she paused in the middle of the lane to re-tie her headscarf. Listening to the faint call of the swallows, Lili was hardly aware of a thin, insectlike whine in the distance, until suddenly the whine became a roar and a black shape leaped from the corner in front of her, mud and water spewing from under its wheels. Lili shrieked as she threw herself against the hedgebank.

The car howled past her, then screeched to a halt, further up the lane. A man in dirty mechanic's overalls flung himself out of the car and raced back toward Lili, calling, "Are you okay?"

"Of course not!" yelled Lili angrily, as the man reached her. This reckless fool could have killed her.

"I'm most awfully sorry." He helped her to stand upright. She winced with pain and started to pull the brambles from her hair, as he continued, "I never expected anyone on this road, because it's private. And this part of the country is always deserted in May—even in the holiday season it's only used by ramblers. Are you on holiday?"

"No, I'm working and I can't afford a broken leg. Why don't you look where you're going?" Lili took a few steps and winced again as pain shot through her left knee. She took another step, felt sick with pain and staggered. The man in dirty overalls steadied her arm. "I'd better give you a lift back," he offered.

"No, thanks, I can manage." Lili set off, limping, down the road, hoping that this idiot hadn't blown the film for her.

He caught up with her, running his fingers through his sandy hair, streaking more grease on his already dirty face. "I'm so very sorry. I promise you, I'm a safe driver. I was just seeing how fast I could corner her, because she still needs a couple of adjustments to the gears."

He'd be quite good-looking if he washed, Lili thought, in spite of her pain. In fact, he might be *very* good-looking if he cleaned the grease and mud off his face.

"Please let me drive you home—it's the least I can do." Nice gray eyes, long straight fair lashes, big freckled nose . . . Lili agreed. The low cockpit of the beetle-black car was little more than a shell of raw metal with taped wires in different directions across the interior.

He drove very fast. "Doesn't this car do less than 70 mph?" Why had she agreed to be driven by this lunatic? Omnium's insurers would probably cancel on the spot, if they could see her.

"She's not very good in the lower gears yet," the gawky, good-looking Englishman apologized. "This is the prototype. We're still working on it, and I shouldn't have taken it out of the garage. Would you mind not mentioning to anyone that you've seen it?"

As the car stopped in front of Lili's hotel (a famous eighteenth-century coaching inn), her driver asked, "How long are you staying at the Rose and Crown?"

"Another four weeks. I've got a part in the film they're shooting at the manor house. What's your name?"

"Gregg Templeton. What's yours?"

"Um . . . Elizabeth Jordan."

He made no move to help her out, and Lili made no move to open the door. It was that awkward moment when two people, who have only just met, are both reluctant to make the first move and invite rejection. Eventually, Gregg offered, "So shall I see you again, Elizabeth?"

"It's difficult, we never get any time off," she said truthfully. "Why not give me your number and I'll phone you when I'm next free. What garage do you work for, Gregg?"

"Eagle Motors in Whitechurch. I'll give you the workshop number." He scribbled it on the back of an envelope, then helped her out of the car. She winced again. "You need a shoehorn to get out of that thing."

"Please forget you ever saw me in it."

"Okay, your boss will never know."

Gregg looked faintly surprised, then grinned.

On Sunday afternoon, Gregg collected Lili in a beat-up Jaguar XK 150 drophead coupe, which was as grubby as if chickens were kept in the back. After another fast drive, they swept over the brow of a hill and saw Lyme Regis lying below them, the distant cliffs glowing gold and white, the pretty circular harbor cluttered with fishing boats.

"Can we go out to sea?" Lili pointed to the small fleet of clinker-built craft at one end of the ancient, stone harbor wall.

"Why not? We'll take a motor boat."

After an hour ker-chugging over sparkling water, they walked back to the town and, in a bow-windowed Regency tearoom, ate fresh-baked scones with strawberry jam and clotted cream. When Gregg passed his cup to Lili for a refill, he noticed her noticing his grimy fingernails. "My mother's always complaining," he grinned. "Drink up, time to take you home."

And to Lili's disappointment, he drove her back to her hotel, then waved a cheery good-bye without making another date.

Lili gazed around the cream, oval reception room at the London Ritz. Elegant women drifted across the pink carpet, greeting each other among the small tables and large palm trees. Behind them, a fountain trickled over a naked golden giantess with a strangely prim expression.

"I'm almost enjoying my Merry Widow act, now that I've started the good works part." Pagan's cheerfulness was brittle, Lili thought, as the Englishwoman rattled on. "Organizing your Gala keeps me busy and stops me brooding. We can have Drury Lane Theater on the last Sunday in July, if that suits you, Lili?"

"I'll have to check with Stash, my agent. He's coordinating with the choreographer, who's directing the show, and they'll check the date with the singers, the dancers and the musicians." Lili poured out more tea; this weird British custom was habit-forming. "Remember, Pagan, that we split up at the end of filming *The Best Legs in the Business*, and it's a complicated job to get everyone together again, just for a one-night live show for charity."

"I've got a terrific committee together to organize the evening," Pagan enthused, thinking that Lili looked preoccupied. Again Pagan felt that pain in her chest. The doctor had said that it was merely another manifestation of grief; he had reassured Pagan that her depression, memory loss, and strange behavior were not unusual after a bereavement. He'd also hinted at another delicate matter and asked her if she'd been, as he phrased it, "missing her husband at night."

"If you can't sleep," he suggested tactfully, "tune your radio to the BBC World Service."

He thinks nice women don't wank, Pagan had thought. But the following night at 3 A.M., she had remembered his advice, twiddled the radio dial, found some pleasant Mozart, then settled back and let black night wash velvet over her. Suddenly, a cheery, dynamic voice had urged her to buy tickets for a rock concert in Croydon. Crossly, Pagan had twiddled the dial, got what sounded like some soothing Sibelius, and recomposed herself just in time to hear the news in Dutch. As dawn blocked in the shape of her bedroom windows, feeling depressed and unsexy but wanting to sleep, Pagan had reached for Sheila Kitzinger's book on female sexuality, which fell open at the masturbation chapter.

In the Ritz tearoom, Lili fidgeted in her gilt chair. "What am I going to do about it?"

Pagan blinked. "But we've already decided what you're going to do for the Gala—a show based on some of the numbers in your Mistinguett film."

"No, I don't mean that," Lili waved aside the Gala with one hand. "I mean, what am I going to do about Gregg? Do you think I shouldn't have noticed his filthy hands? Do you think I embarrassed him? Do you think I came on too strong, Pagan? Do you think that tomorrow is too soon to telephone him?"

"Lili, you can't start an affair with some village mechanic, just because he's the only man you've met in the last five years who isn't dying to make love to you." Pagan sipped her Earl Grey. "Don't you think that perhaps you want this man so much, simply because he doesn't want you?"

"I'm not sure what to think." Lili sounded wistful. "Except that Gregg behaves as if I'm normal."

Pagan raised her mahogany eyebrows. "Were you wearing that kit when you met him?" If so, Pagan couldn't imagine any man *not* wanting Lili, who was swathed in layers of pink-and-white knitting. All Lili's clothes seemed to be made in Paris by Japanese men, who had never heard of skirts, blouses, or frocks.

"No, I wasn't wearing this." Lili was defensive. "I was walking through the mud in an old raincoat without any makeup and with a scarf around my hair. . . . Pagan, *how* can I see him again?"

"You have his number—telephone him."

"Oh, I couldn't do that! I don't want to look too . . ."

If you don't care about someone, Pagan thought, it is perfectly easy to pick up the phone and dial his number; but if you care, then all you can do is sit and watch the telephone and silently *will* it to ring.

"If he's a mechanic, why don't you get yourself the sort of car that demands attention?" Pagan suggested.

"You mean something like a Porsche?"

"No, not at all like a Porsche."

"Naturally, you can't expect everything that you would get in a new model, but our own guarantee accompanies every car we sell," said the fat salesman in ginger tweed. "How about this MGB GT—a collector's item now, Madam."

"No," said Lili, looking around the showroom at the array of battered agricultural vehicles, decrepit sports cars and ancient saloon cars that had been carefully maintained by old ladies. "I want the cheapest car you've got."

"That would be the Riley, then." Just another lady customer, they never laid out on a car. "Totally reliable model, this one, Madam."

Lili shook her head.

"We're expecting a very fine Ford Granada in tomorrow." The salesman sucked on his pipe, to imply trustworthiness.

"No, this is my only morning off." Lili's makeup call was at 5 A.M. "How about that?" She pointed to a tiny Morris painted with pink and orange flowers, cabalistic signs and the words "love" and "peace," none of which disguised the rust on the doors.

"Frankly, Madam, you would be taking your life in your hands. That's a trade-in we accepted from the hippy commune in Uttoxeter and it's only fit for scrap." No profit on that one, the salesman thought, he'd better scare her. "We could not give it our guarantee Madam."

"Perfect," said Lili. "I'll take it."

Ten miles out of town, the little Morris gave a despairing clank, shuddered and stopped. Delighted, Lili walked another mile to the nearest telephone booth.

Within an hour, Gregg was fiddling under the battered hood. "We'd better give it a run." He pulled a dirty rag out of his pocket and wiped his hands. "But I don't think this clutch will last much longer."

They jerked in silence along wet country lanes until Lili saw a painted sign swinging in the breeze at the roadside beside a white-thatched building. "The Magpie and Stump! We don't have pubs in France." Dropping a hint was a new experience for Lili.

Picking up a hint was a new experience for Gregg. "Want to go on Sunday?"

Next Sunday, after visiting the pub, they sat in the tin-roofed country cinema and watched *Spartacus.* It was raining and there was nowhere else to go. On the following Sunday, Gregg hired a fishing boat and they caught two evil-looking black lobsters. "Let's take them back to my hotel and have them cooked for dinner," said Lili. She found it uphill work. At this rate they would not be holding hands before Christmas. But she sensed that, surprisingly, this gawky Englishman did not know how to make the next move.

"Your leg okay now?" Gregg asked, as they drove past high, honeysuckle-entwined hedges.

Lili pulled up her chamois skirt and thoughtfully felt her thigh. "Almost."

"Good." He did not take his eyes off the road.

They crossed the hotel lawn and approached the kitchen door. As they reached it, a shower of pink-tipped white petals fell around them. Lili stopped and looked up into the lichen-covered branches of the apple tree.

"Oh, the poor thing—it's trapped!" She pointed up to a terrified ginger kitten stuck on the tip of a fragile branch.

"Stupid moggy. Shouldn't have climbed up there in the first place." Gregg, like most country people, was not sentimental about animals. "Can we get into that room?" He pointed up at the mullioned window close to the struggling kitten.

"Yes, it's the staircase window. I pass it every morning," said Lili.

They clattered up the uncarpeted oak staircase and Lili opened the window. but Gregg could not quite reach the kitten. Every time he leaned out the window a little more, the kitten retreated a little further back on the branch, then mewed more loudly. "Cats always back off if you grab at them." Gregg thought he was damned if he was going to risk his neck for such a dumb animal.

Slowly, he twiddled his fingers as he withdrew his hand from the branch.

Slowly, the kitten followed the fingers.

Then Gregg grabbed.

"There, there, kitty, panic's over." Holding it by the scruff of the neck, he handed the ginger scrap to Lili, who plonked down the eerily-moving bag of lobsters on the staircase and cuddled the kitten to her breasts, where it promptly hooked its claws into her white cotton sweater.

"Stroke it," she said, pulling Gregg's hand to the kitten. His hand was much bigger than the little animal. Lili stood on tiptoe, shut her eyes, and kissed him full on the lips.

After a bit, she said in a wobbly voice, "My suite is just along the corridor."

Lili's bedroom had an oak-beamed ceiling which sloped down toward the diamond panes of two small, stone-framed windows. The chintz curtains matched the yellow-flowered rug on the dark, polished floorboards; a copper warming pan hung on one side of the stone chimneypiece, while a row of hunting prints hung on the other. All this tourist-trap, Manderley kitsch was spoiled by the cheaply made, flimsy, standard British hotel bed, covered by a slippery, green satin quilt.

Gregg pushed Lili's lips apart with his tongue and explored her mouth. She felt the muscles move in his back as she slowly slid her hands down his spine and an ache of desire tugged between her legs. Gregg's soft dry lips brushed her throat, then Lili heard him murmur her name as his lips moved downward.

Once in bed, Lili noticed, Gregg lost his awkwardness, but he wasn't very experienced, she thought, gasping as he nibbled a little too hard. I mustn't come on too strong, she thought. She felt the tremor in his fingers as he parted her pearl-pink lips and moved his fingers softly, cautiously inside her.

Ought I to be doing this with firm thrusts, or three fingers? Am I going to hurt her? Gregg wondered, as with small purrs she moved slowly against his hand. Where the hell is it? wondered Gregg, groping hopefully for the tiny seed-pearl lump. The tips of his fingers found a firm tip, like the point of a pencil under the soft, slippery skin. Lili arched like a leaping trout as he touched it. Got it, he thought with relief, no need to ask for directions.

After a bit, Lili gasped, "Now, now," and he rolled carefully on top of her. With a sigh of joy, Lili welcomed him into her body and he began moving with slow, deep thrusts. The bed swayed and creaked with every thrust, releasing little clouds of dust from its chintz flounces.

Lili felt as if she were floating, falling, slipping unconsciously into a new incarnation, as Gregg thrust steadily, his lips brushing the pale blue veins of her neck. The erotic smell of his fresh sweat grew stronger as Lili pulled him into her at every stroke, clenching her muscles around his shaft to suck him into her body. The gasps and groans and odd little birdlike cries grew louder in the quiet room.

Then suddenly Gregg arched his back and shouted. "That bloody cat!" he roared.

The frightened kitten had first hidden under the bed, then adventurously it had jumped onto the night table, where it had purred like a little sewing machine. Then, with bared claws, it had dived onto Gregg's naked back.

Gregg swatted at the kitten and half fell off the bed. The green satin quilt slid to the floor, and the kitten skittered under the carved oak linen press.

Lili sat up and licked the tiny spots of blood on Gregg's back. "Forget Ginger," she murmured. Sensuous and eager, their bodies joined again. "Lili, Lili, oh, Lili," Gregg breathed as the rhythm of his body became urgent and inexorable. Lili realized that he was gone, he could not stop, he could not hear her, he was unaware of everything except that he was cresting that wave which . . .

With a crash, the bed fell apart.

"I think the earth just moved," said Gregg from among the wreckage.

The sea was gunmetal, the sky was purple-gray, and black clouds collided overhead as they battled through the rain toward the end of the jetty. "No chance of taking a boat out today," shouted Gregg, through the lashing rain and sea spray.

"Why is it that all the things Englishmen like to do, make you cold and wet?" Lili yelled above the gale.

"Be fair, there are some things I'd rather do in the warm." Gregg hugged her and their raincoat buttons tangled as he kissed her salty, wet lips.

"Okay, I can take a hint. Let's get back."

They turned and, heads down, battled against the shrieking wind toward the rocky beach.

There was a curse as the photographer slipped on the seaweed-covered rocks. "Over here, Gregg," he shouted. "Just one shot—who's your ladyfriend?"

CHAPTER 8

Early June 1979

LILI'S FACE TENSED as she looked at the photographer, but Gregg calmly turned to pose, his arm still around Lili's shoulders. "Better make it just one shot, Eric," he said pleasantly, "I'm off duty today. This is Elizabeth Jordan."

"How's the Spear coming along, Gregg?" The man reached inside his grubby duffel bag for an even grubbier notebook.

"Pretty good, we'll be racing at Silverstone next week."

"I expect Sir Malcolm's over the moon, then. Are you going to run at Le Mans?"

"He's very pleased, yes," said Gregg. "But whether we qualify for Le Mans depends on how we run at Silverstone."

To Lili's amazement, the man picked up his camera case, stowed his notebook, and floundered back up the beach as Gregg said, "Sorry, darling, I'm afraid I'm the only celebrity in town most of the time. That photographer was from the Dorset *Echo*."

Then Lili remembered that on the hotel bed he had called her Lili.

"Gregg, you recognized me!" she said accusingly, her secure happiness starting to crumble, like a child's sand castle, washed by the sea. He had been lying to her.

"Of course, Lili. You're a household face. Anyone would recognize you, in spite of the headscarf."

Lili sighed. "I thought we might have more chance of a relationship if you didn't know who I am. Any nice guy runs for cover when he sees me coming, and the creeps come out of the woodwork."

"I guessed it was something like that, because in a minor way I have the same problem myself." Gregg helped her scramble back to the beach over the slippery, seaweed-draped rocks. "I lied to you as well, for the same reason. My name is really Eagleton, not Templeton."

"Oh," said Lili. "So you own the garage?"

"Yes."

"What did he mean by the Spear?"

"I nearly ran you over in it. I'm a racing driver and I also design cars." They tramped up the pale, pebble-covered beach to the car park, where he helped her into his battered black XK 150. "I took over Eagle Motors last year, when my father retired. The firm was headed sharply downhill, but we're managing to turn it around." He drove out of the rain-gray town and headed into the open country. "The Spear's the first new car that we've launched for a long time. We're producing a racing model first, in order to attract the maximum publicity. Then we'll go ahead with the road version; that was the car with which I nearly ran you over."

"But that was just a tin can on wheels!" Lili remembered her first, bone-shattering ride with Gregg. A look of annoyance flashed over his face, as hastily she continued, "What's it going to be like when it's finished?"

"That 'tin can' will perform better than a Porsche and have more prestige than a Mercedes." They were driving through a gloomy, dripping beech wood. "She's basically a four-liter, V8, turbo-charged engine which can produce 800 horsepower with four-wheel drive. She'll do about 210 mph."

There was a pause. "What color is it going to be?" asked Lili.

"Black, because the sponsors like it." Gregg swerved to overtake a cattle truck. "When I appear on the track, I'm just a human advertising board. Sponsorship finances our entire operation."

The car darted through heather-covered countryside. "In the fifties, Eagle Motors was one of the leading European specialist manufacturers." They swooped round the bottom of a sugar-loaf hill. "My dad was once the European Sports Car Champion, but you can't eat fame, Lili. I must have been about three years old when Pa went bankrupt. My first memory is of the bailiffs taking my tricycle away from me; they took everything we had." Gregg slowed down behind a hay truck, then added, "I'm determined to take us to the top again—only this time the accounting system will be as up-to-date as the maintenance log."

They shot ahead of the hay truck. "Once I've reestablished our name on the racetrack, I'm going to launch our new sports car on the market. It looks as if we can get financial backing from the government. But first I've got to prove that I can deliver the goods." The rain stopped as they turned into a gravel drive that wound between tall elms.

"Where are we going?"

"My home," said Gregg. "I live over the shop."

The Eagle development workshop was a converted stable block at the rear of a large, ugly Edwardian house built of red brick. Inside the spacious workshop, a number of black sports racing cars, in various stages of assembly, were lined up against the whitewashed brick walls. With careless pride, Gregg waved a hand toward a wedge-fronted, sinister machine. "This one was sprayed yesterday."

"It looks far more glamorous than the one you nearly killed me in," said Lili, as he opened the door of the glossy, panther-black car.

"It has a very special feature." He patted the hood. "It can maneuver sideways, crab-wise, for parking in town." He ran his fingers lovingly over the black gloss gull-wing door and opened it for Lili. As she lowered herself into it, Lili thought, cars are really sexy for men. Women don't understand this, because cars aren't sexy for women, they're just conveyors or status symbols.

"Not bad, is it?"

Lili recognized the Englishman's understatement. She also realized that she was falling in love with a man who was in love with a car.

They spent the next ten minutes growling round the laurel-edged drive and parking the Spear sideways. The car had a hydraulically-operated fifth wheel and computer-controlled four-wheel drive. Gregg was as proud as a new father.

"Would you like a quick spin? We've got a practice track." Like a big black panther, the car swooped, swerved and slid around the small circuit, spurting gravel and rainwater under the wheels. Eventually, Gregg pulled the Spear up, neatly, in front of the workshop door.

Lili's knees were trembling, and again she felt sick as Gregg helped her out and said as if to himself, "The big question is, will the Spear be ready for the Silverstone Five Hundred Kilometer Race? If she performs well at Silverstone, it's been secretly agreed that we'll be allowed to race her at Le Mans next month. So keep your fingers crossed."

"Why is Le Mans so important?" asked Lili, stretching her bruised legs.

"Because it is one of the toughest possible tests of a car. Le Mans is a twenty-four-hour endurance race, it goes on day and night. We'll need at least twelve pit stops to refuel and make minor adjustments," Gregg explained. "I have two co-drivers and we take turns at the wheel. The car hardly ever stops for more than two minutes and it's put under a fantastic strain. So you see," he flicked a wisp of grass from the wing, "if the Spear finishes well at Le Mans, it will immediately be taken seriously by the racing world—and by the government."

Back in the workshop, mechanics in grubby, once-white overalls were crawling around and under half-completed cars. Lili shook rain from her headscarf. "Why are you working on Sunday?"

"They'll work around the clock if they have to, we're in this business to win," Gregg said as they passed a mechanic who was bolting a power tool to a work-bench. "When I'm on the grid at Le Mans in the Spear, fifty people will have put us there, a lot of them volunteers." They stepped over a pair of overalled legs sticking out from under a chassis. "The support team does everything, from hand-making the parts here to buying my sandwiches at the track." They passed a third pair of dirty overalls, bent over an engine. "The team will drive through the night to get us to the race. There's never enough time, but they'll even work on the dockside at Boulogne, if necessary." Gregg stopped at the end of the workshop and looked fondly at a pimply lad in spectacles, who was filing down a bolt. "And most of them do it for love, because I can't afford to pay them. Because they want to see Eagle on top again, just as it was when Pa was champion." Gregg gently kicked a pair of overalled legs that stuck out from under yet another black chassis.

From beneath the chassis a voice said, "Psychologically, the first race is the hardest, Gregg." The legs wriggled out. They belonged to a small, stout man with an amiable red face and a beaklike, Mr. Punch, nose. "Gad, it's chilly under here, my feet are freezing. Let's go up to the house for a glass of sherry, and you can introduce me to this charming young lady." Sir Malcolm held out his blackened hand to Lili.

Inside, the mansion was almost colder and clammier than outside, thought Lili, as she reluctantly took off her white raincoat and enviously eyed the thick, shape-less, mauve knitted jacket worn by Gregg's mother. As they sipped sherry, con-versation centered around the Silverstone race circuit. There were constant telephone interruptions from drivers, sponsors, volunteers and, finally, a London newspaper that wanted a quick quote for the diary page on what Gregg wore in bed. Lady Eagleton's serene gray eyes, a faded copy of her son's, did not register annoyance. "In thirty years of marriage, I've learned never to come between a man and his car," Lady Eagleton said to Lili as Gregg was called back to the workshop, his father again called to the telephone. "It's a pleasure to meet you, my dear. Gregg seemed to be keener on engines than girls. I sometimes think that motor racing is a disease, not a sport."

"Don't you worry about him?" Lili tried to stop her teeth from chattering with cold. As it was June, the British considered it to be summer, no matter what the thermometer read.

"You learn to live with the worry. Eventually. My husband lived through a 180-mph crash." Lady Eagleton shrugged. "Gregg's chances of dying on the circuit are one in seven. But they improve each year. I simply don't allow myself to think about it."

"WHAT DID YOU SAY?" Silverstone was the noisiest place ever, Lili thought, as Gregg, in baggy white fireproof suit, climbed into the driving seat of the Spear. The Silverstone circuit looked like a cross between a filling station and a supermarket, set in a dusty, urban park. Behind the teeming crowds that streamed on both sides of the wide tarmac track, the dazzling billboards howled their messages, like bright washing-powder packets. Every racing car, every racer, every mechanic, every ice cream van was also plastered with advertising.

Lili could not imagine a more total assault on her senses than this riot of noise, color, and stink, as Gregg shouted, "I'LL SEE YOU IN THREE HOURS." His lips poked through the balaclava which protected his face from fire. Then Gregg turned to his crew and Lili knew she was forgotten.

Two minutes later, Gregg settled his helmet over his head, and the white overalled team pushed the Spear toward the starting grid.

The Spear, with most of the cars, roared off behind the pace car, then belched flame at a corner. "IS THAT NORMAL, JOHN?" Lili asked Gregg's psychological advisor, a lean, bearded man with a mid-Atlantic accent.

"YES. DON'T WORRY, IT'S GOING GREAT, EVEN BETTER THAN AT LAST WEEK'S TESTING." He led her up to a glass box above the pits, where the noise level was lower. "We shouldn't have any trouble this time."

Lili did not understand why the car had previously given trouble. After all, it was an expensive car and, for the past few weeks, sixteen mechanics had crawled all over it, testing every nut and bolt, nurturing the car in every way short of breast-feeding it. She had not wanted to ask stupid questions of Gregg, but she didn't mind looking dumb in front of this kindly, ginger-headed viking. So Lili asked, "Why do so many things go wrong with these cars?"

John tried to explain in words of one syllable, such as could be understood even by a woman. "A racing car is a sophisticated, complex mechanism. It always performs at the absolute limit of its capability. A lot of our problems are due to things like stress, high temperatures, and fuel management microprocessors. Any human error is on top of that." He turned, as a Lancia limped into the pit next door with a plume of acrid, black smoke rising from its exhaust pipe. The mechanics scrambled to their posts like fighter pilots. John nodded. "That Lancia went out on the track as perfect and precisely assembled as the team could manage, but it is being driven at speeds up to two hundred miles an hour for hundreds, perhaps thousands, of miles nonstop. Like a racehorse, the entire machine is designed for performance and nothing else. In order to get the speed that's necessary to win, the car has to be constantly pushed to its limit. So, inevitably, you get trouble."

As the lead car passed the pits in a blur of green and orange, Lili asked the last of the questions that she'd been dying to ask for weeks. "What makes a good driver, John?"

He wiped his hands on a rag. "Hair-trigger reactions, concentration and control. It's a young man's game; a driver starts to slow down when he's about thirty, but you also need an older man's mature judgment and steady nerves. While those guys are burning around the track, their minds are running like computers, and their bodies are sensing feedback through the car's level of performance and its speed. And of course, they're violently competitive blokes, so they're always revising their own tactics to beat the rest of the field."

"And does the biggest daredevil win?"

"There aren't any daredevils on that track. A good driver never takes an unnecessary risk. They aren't foolhardy boy-racers, they're cool professionals with a deep respect for danger; they don't fool around." He handed Lili a pair of black ear-protectors and they turned back to the pit where Lili sat for two and a half hours, deafened by the snapping exhaust roars as she inhaled the stink of hot rubber and fuel fumes. The howl of engines drowned the loudspeaker commentary as the cars spread out round the circuit. The noise was all-enveloping, relentless, and extremely exhausting like a discotheque under gunfire.

"Gregg's just made the fastest lap speed ever recorded by a trial car in its first big race." John yelled in Lili's ear, "ONLY ANOTHER TEN LAPS TO GO." Lili felt her headache lessen, as the cars snarled into the last half-hour of the race.

Suddenly, Gregg's team grabbed their tools and looked expectantly to the left.

The Spear appeared, cruised silently down the pit lane, then stopped.

Mechanics crowded round the back of the car as Gregg climbed out of the gull-wing door.

Ten minutes later Gregg noticed Lili. He stomped over to her, resigned exasperation on his face. "Bloody gearbox blew up," he yelled. Then Jack, the mechanic, who was doing calculations on a clipboard, held his thumb up. Slowly, Gregg grinned, as a TV sports reporter shoved a microphone under his nose. "So it's Le Mans next stop, Gregg, for the twenty-four-hour endurance race?"

"Yes, that's always been my ambition."

"Are you going to celebrate this evening? Lili's giving a surprise party for you, isn't she?"

"If so, you've just spoiled the surprise, mate."

"I don't understand why we had to come, Angelface, especially when no one invited us." Maggie Harris looked round at the noisy party. The fresh-faced young racing crowd all wore Armani jeans and Cerruti silk shirts, with acquiescent Farrah Fawcett Majors clones hanging on their arms. Nothing to worry about there, Maggie thought, as she dismissed her opposition with one flick of her eyelashes and glanced down at her white satin jumpsuit. From armpit to ankles, on either side, the suit had a two-inch gap, crisscrossed by white leather thongs over her naked flesh.

Maggie stamped one of her silver cowboy boots. "I don't know any of these boy racers, Angelface, and neither do you." She turned on her silver heels. "Let's go. I feel uncomfortable. It's not as if you were singing."

As she started to elbow her way through the ebullient crowd, Angelface grabbed her by the shoulder. "Oh, no, you don't! I expect my old lady to stick beside me, even when I'm gatecrashing." His face had the taut, sunken-cheek look of a sixties-generation rock star. Angelface Harris was tough, as only twenty years of rock'n'roll tours can toughen you, thought Maggie, as the famous blue eyes glared from the halo of wild black hair. His voice was a deceptively mild, throaty growl as he said, "Shut up, darling, and have fun."

"Take your hands off me!" Maggie gave a quick look around the room and decided not to cause a scene; it was too early and too crowded. Besides, even if he was a promiscuous bastard, even if he was getting a bit over the hill, Angelface was still the best-looking man in the room, and if she stormed out . . . well, she wouldn't want him to stay behind, not with all this spare talent, fresh from the hairdresser, and him in his best leathers. Angelface's studded black leather suit was molded to his body and wrinkled around the joints like an iguana skin.

"You stay here and behave yourself," Angelface growled to Maggie, "I'll get us a couple of drinks."

He plunged into the crowd toward the bar, where Lili was greeting her guests. Angelface shoved his way past everyone until he stood in front of Lili.

He adopted his standard, lights-up pose—legs straddled, head on one side, hands clutching the neck of his leather jacket, which was unzipped to the waist. Lili blinked, with the usual puzzled look of a hostess who can't recognize her friends when they're cleaned up. "Er, hello."

Angelface continued to give her the old, jean-creaming, lovable, lopsided grin, the look that had launched forty albums.

"Why are you staring at me?" Lili stepped back, and her pink taffeta dress rustled. "Did my teeth just fall out? What's wrong with my face?"

"Abs . . . olute . . . ly nothing." Angelface pitched his sixties cockney-sparrow charm, then started to croon softly, in a camped-up voice. "You must have been a beautiful baby . . . "

Everyone stopped pretending that they were not looking, and the party turned into an audience. Again Angelface pitched the crooked smile at Lili.

"When you were only startin'
to go to kindergarten,
I bet you drove the little boys wild . . . "

He put his arms around Lili's shoulders, crushing her taffeta ruffles, and together they faced the crowd, moving rhythmically together, Lili smiling, but still puzzled. She hadn't realized that Gregg knew this famous rock star.

At this point, Maggie started to shove through the crowd, muttering, "So that's the reason we came, he's got the hots for that stuck-up bitch."

She reached her husband as Angelface finished the song to a spattering of laughter and applause. Angelface introduced her to Lili in a silky, amiable voice which Maggie correctly interpreted as a threat.

"Pleased to meet you, I'm sure, Lili." She smiled brightly, then whispered in Angelface's ear. "Let's get out of here—and I mean it. Now."

Angelface ostentatiously kissed Lili good-bye and swaggered down the staircase, his tiny, blond wife hanging grimly on to his black leather arm.

"If my wife acted like that, I'd send her back to the works for modifications," Gregg whispered to Lili. "If looks could kill, you'd be six feet under by now." Lili shrugged her golden shoulders, and turned back to her guests.

* * *

"You're obviously doing well, Teresa." Lili leaned across the Parisian restaurant table and flicked the pleated chiffon collar of the other woman's purple St. Laurent suit.

"Not too bad," Teresa agreed complacently, "and the work isn't as draughty as making porn movies used to be. D'you remember how cold it was in Serge's studio, Lili?"

"He did it on purpose, to make our nipples stand out."

"Sssh!" The waiter served two silver plates of ice-bedded oysters to the glossy-haired, immaculately groomed women. Lili leaned forward conspiratorially.

"What's it really like, working for Madame George? Do you still go for the old guys, Teresa?" Lili was dying to catch up with the only female acquaintance she'd had in her youth. Teresa had been kind to Lili, and had taught her the rough, street wisdom of a high-class call girl.

Teresa said, "It's a pity you can't stay overnight, Lili, and have a look at the office. *Très chic, alors*, to fly to Paris just for lunch." She slid an oyster down her throat with a flourish. "Working for Madame George is like working in a well-organized model agency. There are six girls in the office; they sit at desks, taking telephone appointments. We wait behind the office, in the pink salon, chatting, playing backgammon or watching television until we're booked out." Another oyster vanished between her glossy lips. "Madame George's drivers are all built like tanks, so you never get any trouble, and the accounts are computerized, so we always get paid on the seventeenth of the month. There's a fixed-fee scale for our services, and the girls are graded in categories." Teresa carefully dripped Tabasco on the next oyster. "Ever since that business with the Minister, they all ask for me, so I'm in Category A—own chauffeur, own apartment, own maid and a Saint Laurent credit card."

"What are the men like?" She was genuinely curious.

Teresa gulped her last oyster, checked her lip-gloss, grinned and called for a second dozen. "Madame George is a French institution, like the Louvre or the Crillon. Any cultivated man knows about Madame George, whether he's a film star, a politician, a general, or a nuclear physicist. We see them all."

"But are they any different from the johns off the street?"

"A john is a john. Some are clean, some are dirty, some are trouble, some are not, some are fast, some are slow." Teresa shrugged. "So long as they have the cash, they all get the same treatment—the best, and the most discreet—from Madame George's girls."

"You weren't very discreet when the Minister snuffed it. What exactly were you doing to him, you naughty girl?"

"Poor Maurice always needed a little . . . assistance." Teresa gave an explicit gesture and Lili choked with unexpected laughter. "Madame George said it served him right, he always paid late. If we hadn't all been at a hotel, she could have hushed it up. However, every cloud has a silver lining. Did you see my picture in *Le Figaro?*"

"Yes." Lili leaned over the bowl of cream roses and lowered her voice. "That was why I wanted to see you."

Lili couldn't think why she had ever been frightened on the small Eagleton practice track, as Gregg drove round and round it in the commercial prototype Spear, muttering to himself nonstop. "Bit of understeer there . . . still running a bit lumpy at 7300 on the straight . . . don't like the sound of third gear . . . " The high-pitched scream of the engine hurt Lili's ears, the oily stink of fumes clung to her hair and clothes and the bucket seat gave her cramp. Lili did not care for the life of a racing groupie and could not understand why Gregg seemed to prefer driving round and round this track to being in bed with her. There was always some excuse. He wouldn't do it for two days before a race, he was too exhausted the. night after, and he seemed to spend every second night in the workshop, bent over some greasy hunk of malfunctioning machinery.

"Why can't I drive it?" Lili suddenly suggested.

Gregg laughed.

"No, I'm serious, Gregg. I can drive sports cars. I've got a Porsche in Paris." She leaned across and lightly raked her fingernails down his inner thigh. "I'll tickle you to death if you don't let me."

Gregg wriggled and grinned. Lili added, "After all, the commercial Spear is supposed to be driven by ordinary drivers like me!"

Eventually, Gregg agreed. "Go easy on the gas, the acceleration's pretty fierce." He demonstrated the controls and then they changed seats. Gingerly, Lili put the car in first gear. The machine leaped forward like a hunting leopard, then bounded down the drive and swooped into the green-fringed lane. At first, Lili felt as if the machine were a savage, living thing that was running away with her, but once she became used to the power beneath her foot, she felt exhilarated by the sense of danger and mastery that it gave her, as they hurtled between the pink-campion-sprinkled hedgebanks and wind tore through the prototype's glassless side windows. Ostentatiously, Lili double-declutched as they plummeted down the sugar-loaf hill.

Gregg yelled, "Go easy, this is a blind corner!" They were on it and round it before he had finished speaking; then, simultaneously, they saw that the road ahead was blocked with languid black and white cows.

Lili swung the wheel over and boldly headed for the open gateway through which the cows had just passed. She hit the brakes too hard. The car skidded on the muddy road surface, hit the bank with a sickening crunch, turned on its back, skidded along the slippery road, then slowed to a halt within inches of the terrified, stampeding cattle.

"Are you all right, Lili?" Gregg yelled as they hung upside down from their safety belts in the crumpled wreck of the Spear.

"Lili, you can't be serious!" Maxine protested. "My butler tells me that you need another bedroom. Don't you and Gregg . . . er . . . I mean, aren't you . . . "

"Not for two days before a race." Lili pulled a face, picked up a silver hairbrush and turned to the mirror. "And as it's in Le Mans, I'm to live like a nun all week. I had to promise not to seduce him, otherwise he seriously told me that he was going to share a trailer with the Spear team." Gregg was affectionate, passionate, considerate, and inexhaustible—but he spent almost every waking moment in that damn garage, passionately absorbed by those damn cars.

Men! thought Maxine, oddly comforted as she looked at Lili's beautiful, resigned face. Charles was just as bad. It had been weeks since that bitch Simone had left, but Maxine's husband still slept in his dressing room. Her bedroom had been redecorated in voluptuous shades of claret and a group of disheveled Fragonard beauties hung provocatively on one wall. But Charles had not yet seen them, and Maxine did not know what to do next; she and her husband were on speaking terms—overpolite, in fact—but the air was still unfriendly.

"It's because of the Spear that I met him and because of the Spear that I hardly see him," Lili gloomed. "I just happened to turn up at the wrong moment in his life. Right now he needs every ounce of energy and concentration and effort for my rival, the Spear. And he's still got the big excuse." Lili slowly started to brush her black hair. "He's still bruised from our car crash, and he's supposed to rest his ankle. As the whole thing was my fault, I can hardly kick up a fuss, not when his whole future depends on this race at Le Mans."

A distant engine snarled over gravel; from the terrace below rose a cloud of agitated doves. Lili jumped up and dropped her hairbrush. "That must be Gregg!"

"What's their verdict on the fuel, Jack?" Gregg asked anxiously. Bleary-eyed from lack of sleep, the chief mechanic had just returned to the trailer after presenting the Spear in Le Mans town square for scrutinizing. He had been there for eight hours.

"Last thing they worried about, but there was a long wrangle over the driver's footwell measurements; bloody Frogs spent an hour crawling over her, taking measurements. In the end it came down to an interpretation of how the measurements were taken."

"They're bastards about the regulations. Did you send in Johnnie Walker?" They didn't want to be disqualified on a technicality before the race started.

"Two cases. It did the trick." Jack slapped him on the shoulder. The Eagle team's equipment included three crates of Scotch whisky, with which to smooth the Spear's path through the maze of pettily enforced French regulations.

"Better not risk disqualification," Gregg decided. "We can reshape the footwell overnight."

Lili drove back to the Chateau de Chazalle alone and Gregg worked through Wednesday night with his mechanics. By the following morning, the Spear's wheel bearings and gearbox had been stripped down, checked and reassembled.

On Thursday, panic threatened after lunch, when the clutch was discovered to be a millimeter off-center, which was enough to lock the system. The men worked fast, but not fast enough. At dusk they wheeled the car out. "Nothing to be done about it." Gregg's freckled skin was pale. "We'll have to do the qualifying laps as she is, then work on the clutch overnight."

Lili managed to persuade Gregg that another broken night in the trailer with his team would leave him unfit to race, and reluctantly he agreed. So Maxine's chauffeur delivered him, white and tired, to the Chateau steps, just before midnight Friday.

"We did it!" Gregg called triumphantly, plodding up the staircase toward Lili. "Whatever happens now will be a bonus—we've qualified the Spear, we're in the race, and that's the main thing."

"What did you do about the clutch?" Lili asked as they both sat in the small yellow morning room. Gregg fell on the little pot of hot beef casserole and crusty French bread.

"Jack realigned it," he said, between mouthfuls. "He's a rare bird, works for sheer love of precision engineering. So much garage work nowadays is being a fitter, not a mechanic. They don't *make* anything and no real skill is needed. If something is wrong with a car, they simply take off one unit and put on another. But every nut and bolt on the Spear must be tightened to exactly the right torque. Do you know, I can take my hands off the steering wheel on the Muslanne Straight at two hundred miles an hour and hardly feel it?"

Lili picked up one of his big, grease-stained hands and kissed it. "Why would anyone want to take his hands off the steering wheel anywhere at two hundred miles an hour?"

The moon cast black, calm shadows over the undulating silver sand. Beyond the flames that leaped from the huge campfire, King Abdullah could see the necks and swaying, supercilious heads of the camel herd, silhouetted against the sky. They had been couched for the night and their knees had been tied to prevent them straying. In spite of jeeps, helicopters, and light planes, the most reliable desert transport was still the camel, Abdullah reflected. A camel ate very little, only needed a drink every five days, could survive twenty waterless days if it found grazing, and could carry six hundred pounds of freight strapped to its back.

The Hakem tribe had spent much of the day racing camels in the desert and Abdullah had won the main race. The King's camel race win was now being celebrated by the poet of the tribe, a graybeard in black robes, who invented the verses as he declaimed them, around the leaping yellow flames of dried camel dung and dead wood. Whenever Abdullah's name was mentioned, the men yelled and fired their rifles into the air in salute.

Opposite the King, the firelight shone on the excited little face of twelve-year-old Prince Hassan, the King's nephew and his heir. Abdullah had brought Hassan to the Hakem mansef, to present the boy to the tribe over whom, one day, he would rule. It was the fourteenth mansef that Prince Hassan had attended this month. Abdullah made these formal visits to only the most important sheiks in his domain and it was upon these trips that he recruited his soldiers. The freedom of his country depended on the loyalty of the army. Fighting was the price one had to pay for being a small, backward, oil-rich country that was strategically important to the Western powers.

The poet finished and harsh, guttural voices barked loudly in the night, as the warriors started to reminisce of past fights, past camels, past hunts. The yellow flames cast shadows up into the men's lean faces, long shaggy black hair and black eyes that glittered like the star-spattered, black sky overhead. Tonight they would sleep on the sand around the campfire, protected only by their black cloaks from the chill night. Bedouins such as the Hakem tribe scorned comfort.

Thinking of his normal routine, the paperwork, the meetings with ambassadors, ministers, department heads and commanders, Abdullah felt a deep satisfaction at being among these tough, simple, courageous men who lived in the satisfying emptiness of the desert, where one day was pretty much the same as the next, and where time was not the master of men.

The feast was announced and the desert warriors followed their Sovereign into the thirty-meter-long, black goatskin tent. At the entrance, Prince Hassan stumbled and nearly fell. Abdullah glanced at the tired child as a white-robed bodyguard helped him to regain his balance. Inside the luxuriously carpeted tent, young boys bowed and offered dishes of sticky dates and speckled figs. Bitter, black coffee, flavored with cardamom seed, was poured from intricately worked brass pots into miniature cups with no handles. Gravely, King Abdullah allowed his cup to be refilled thrice, as was customary, and then they brought him the ceremonial bowl of camel milk, still warm from the udder and tasting slightly salty. When Abdullah had drained it, the Sheikh of the Hakem tribe sprang to his feet and launched into the traditional welcome speech, spattered with overstated compliments, honey-flowered flattery and showy superlatives. He thanked Allah for the mighty Slave of God, which was the Arabic meaning of Abdullah, he praised all his deeds and wished him everlasting life. This took some time.

King Abdullah looked across the tent at Prince Hassan. The boy never complained and obediently performed all his royal duties, but obedience was not a useful virtue in a future King. Will Hassan have the spirit to control men such as these? Abdullah wondered, as he glanced around him at the fierce desert-hardened tribesmen.

Abdullah did not love his nephew. Since the death of his beloved son, Abdullah had loved no one and trusted no one. Abdullah had committed himself to no one and nothing except his country, the cause of his people, and his army. Abdullah's mother had died when he was born; he felt her death as a wistful lack. The murder of Abdullah's father provoked in his son only ice-cold anger. The knowledge that his own life was in constant danger left Abdullah feeling that deep involvement with any living person would render him too vulnerable to assassination.

Inside the tent, richly-patterned carpets had been laid on the desert sand and heaped with tasseled cushions. Abdullah's watchful eyes moved warily from side to side, although he held his head still; arrogantly self-assured, with tawny skin stretched tight over the bone, his winged black eyebrows met above a nose that curved like a falcon over the wide mouth.

Boys in white robes carried huge silver trays into the tent, each one piled with a bed of rice, surrounding a whole lamb which had been roasted over a wood fire and stuffed with a mixture of cinnamon rice, plump raisins, pine nuts, and almonds. Eight men sat cross-legged around each tray, pulling off bits of lamb and dipping them in the silver bowls of yogurt, rolling the rice into small balls with their fingers, always using only the right hand, because the left hand was used for sanitary purposes.

The boys served silver trays of kanafa, sweet cakes filled with white goat's cheese and served with hot syrup. The harsh wail of a primitive clarinet, the pipe of flutes, the insistent rhythm of the drums started; it was a prelude to the dancing and singing of traditional songs that were quavering ululations with no pauses, no rhythmic or harmonic variations, only repetitions of the wailing tune pattern.

Across the tent, General Suliman Hakem caught Abdullah's eye, nodded and quietly moved behind Prince Hassan, ready to escort him forward for the presentation to the Hakem tribe. Gazing at Suliman's lean, hard face, Abdullah suddenly realized how extraordinary it was that Sheikh Hakem's son had accompanied Abdullah to the Royal Military Academy at Sandhurst. Together, he and Suliman had sat at those long, highly-polished mahogany tables, sparkling with crystal, silver and candelabra, with everybody togged out in full mess kit and the strings of the regimental band sawing through a selection from *Oklahoma!* Suddenly Abdullah was sharply aware of the dichotomy between his Eastern life and his Western life as he remembered bicycling with Suliman from one classroom to the next and drilling endlessly on the parade ground in heavy, black boots. Together, he and Suliman had learned how to handle an infantry platoon. Fully dressed in combat clothes, they had together jumped into rivers, bumped in Land Rovers over mountains at night and hurled themselves out of airplanes by day. Together, they had been acknowledged the best horsemen and the best shots at Sandhurst, which was hardly surprising, as they had both been riding and hunting in the desert for as long as they could remember. Both, at full gallop, could shoot a partridge on the wing, as could most warriors sitting tonight in this sumptuous tent.

The music stopped abruptly when Abdullah stood up and made the ritual speech that asked the Hakem tribe to pledge their lifelong loyalty to his house and his heir. Abdullah then motioned Hassan to stand. As the boy got up, his eyes lost their focus and he tumbled forward onto the antique carpet.

There was an instant cry of alarm. General Suliman pulled the boy upright, but Prince Hassan lolled against him, unconscious and moon-pale. Abdullah's face was expressionless as he ordered General Suliman to accompany the Prince to the women's tent.

Sheikh Hakem flung himself at the feet of Abdullah to protest his loyalty.

Nobody moved in the tent for ten minutes, until General Suliman hurried back to the King's side and whispered reassuring news in his ear. Prince Hassan had merely fainted, worn out by the incessant traveling and ceremony of the past month.

There was an immediate hubbub of relief.

As Abdullah washed his hands in the proffered silver bowl, none of the tribesmen around him could have guessed how profoundly anxious the King felt. Prince Hassan had been constantly ill at Port Regis, his English school. Either the child was the victim of slow poisoning or else he was unfit to be a future King.

It was a blazing hot June day and the sun beat down on the concrete grandstand at Le Mans, as gendarmes made periodic sweeps to control the crowds of hangers-on who swarmed over the track. The roars and snarls of the finely tuned engines could be heard far away, in the flat forests beyond the circuit, as the cars took their places on the grid. In the noisy, crowded grandstand, an exuberant group waved Union Jacks and the black Eagle flag.

"Where's Gregg?" Maxine strained her eyes in the bright smoke-tinged air, but couldn't see the Spear in the line-up.

Lili wriggled out of the spectators' box and ran to the pit, where mechanics worked fast and silently on the Spear.

"Throttle's jammed. It's this bloody heat," Gregg shouted over the roar of starting cars. "We're going to lose a lap."

Lili watched as the cars tore off, hugging the ground in formation behind the pace car for the pre-start lap. Then, with a howling crescendo, they began the race. Before the end of the first lap, the Spear slipped onto the track.

By the end of the second hour, the Spear was lying in tenth position. Triumphantly, Gregg jumped out of the car, shouting, "God, that car's so beautiful!"

"Who's leading?" Lili yelled, as Gregg's co-driver shot off in the Spear. The confusion of heat, the fumes, the cheering crowds and the distant cacophony on the fairgrounds made it impossible for her to keep track of the race.

"Nannini in the Lancia; he's really giving it stick," Gregg bellowed, as the Spear slip-streamed past the green BMW Sauber C7 and gradually nosed up to overtake it.

Five minutes later, the Canon Porsche spun out of control, hitting Jacky Ickx's Rothman Porsche, which spun briefly on the grass, then rejoined the race, having lost a place.

By the end of the fourth hour, the Spear was lying sixth. Lili watched the car shudder into the pit with damaged balance weights on the front right wheel; the mechanics worked frantically to replace the whole wheel in twenty-five seconds. "See why we need so many spares?" Gregg prepared to take over from his co-driver. "This race really puts a car through it."

And it puts the drivers through it, thought Lili, as for the first time, she found herself desperately anxious about someone else's safety. Suddenly, the race was not dull, it was not exciting, it was frightening. Lili felt only cold terror for Gregg as she saw a Mazda 717 briefly balk the Spear, then both cars veered apart as they tore under the Dunlop Bridge.

At the end of the fifth hour, a doube pileup on the Mulsanne Straight took both Aston Martin Nimrods out of the race and left Gregg lying second, behind the leading Porsche.

In the grandstand, Lili heard the name Eagle Spear in the crackle of noise that was issuing from the commentary loudspeakers. "WHAT'S HAPPENING?" she screamed to Charles.

"HE'S IN THE LEAD," Charles yelled back excitedly. "THE PORSCHE HAS GONE!"

Gregg knew that eight more Porsche 956s were snarling up behind him. Porsche always dominated all the endurance races, thanks to the excellent German engineering. At Le Mans, a car could self-destruct under its driver; metal would shear, rubber would wear away, plastic would melt; in twenty-four hours' hard driving, a car could simply fall apart, around and beneath its driver. Only the toughest survived Le Mans.

The third gear felt ominously sticky, as Gregg changed down, anticipating the slow right-hand turn at the Tertre Rouge. Andretti, in the Kremer Porsche, was closing up behind him. Gregg's left ankle started to throb and, suddenly, he found it difficult to concentrate all his energy on the corner.

Then Gregg felt a stab of white pain, he heard a gnashing, mashing of metal, saw the world spin in front of him and fir trees rush toward him, as the Spear shot off the road.

"Luck of the devil!" Charles threw his long, thin body into a velvet armchair. "He crashes at two hundred and fifty kilometers and all he suffers is a sprained ankle."

Outside the French windows of the chateau, the bubbling song of a nightingale and the tart scent of lime trees drifted into the library. Exhausted by the emotion, the excitement, and the anxiety, Maxine shrugged off her voile jacket and collapsed onto the blue brocade sofa. "Ouf, it's a hot night!"

They were silent for a moment. The servants had gone to bed and the library was dark except for a dim, brass reading lamp. Maxine sighed. "Charles, I'm exhausted. D'you mind waiting up until Lili gets back from the hospital? She was making a lot of fuss, but her concern was genuine. I'm getting fond of her. Maybe she really will settle down with Gregg."

"He seems like a nice enough fellow."

"And very suitable for Lili." Maxine yawned. "If he becomes the European Sports Car Champion, he'll have nothing to gain from Lili's success. He doesn't need to hitch onto her fame and, as he's not in the same business, their ambitions won't clash."

Charles nodded. "He won't feel threatened by her." Slowly, he stretched his arms and legs.

"I can never understand why men find a successful woman a threat." Maxine eased off her white sandals. "Women don't find a successful man a threat." She lifted her toes and wriggled them. "Women think success is sexy."

Maxine stretched her tired legs out and rotated her ankles. Even after twenty years of marriage, Charles couldn't take his eyes off Maxine's long, pale, rounded legs. Maxine knew this perfectly well, and so continued to twirl them slowly in the dim, amber light.

Eternally pragmatic, Maxine realized that seeing someone you know nearly die really sorts out your priorities fast. Charles had been nicer to her than he had been for months, as they drove back from the hospital where Gregg had been taken. Delicately, Maxine massaged her left calf, thinking, our situation won't be resolved until he says he's sorry, and he's never going to say he's sorry. But Charles will always *show* that he's sorry, if I give him the chance and don't rub his nose in it. She pulled back her voile skirt and started to massage her left knee. Softly she said, "Charles, I'm sorry." It was better to put yourself in the wrong and get your own way, than to stubbornly insist on being right and continue to be miserable.

"What are you sorry for, Maxine?"

"Everything."

Charles pounced.

"Successful women are always overdressed," he whispered in her ear as she squirmed happily beneath him. Charles plunged his hands inside the filmy fabric of Maxine's dress, ripped off her peach satin camisole, and started to flick his tongue, lizardlike, over his wife's creamy body.

CHAPTER 9

Mid-June 1979

OUTSIDE THE SYDONITE Embassy, the June sun sparkled on the distant Potomac. A picket line of dejected feminists in jumpsuits carried placards that read "Arabs oppress women." "Islam equals mutilation," and "CUT IT OUT!"

Wearily, the cops cleared a path for King Abdullah, who flashed out of the maroon Rolls and through the imposing front door, followed by General Suliman.

"Mark Scott's exhibition is a great success." His Majesty peeled off white gloves and thwacked them onto the silver salver proffered by a robed servant. "And that leader in the *Washington Post* about the circumcised child was exactly what I'd hoped for."

"If the World Health Organization really got behind us, such atrocities would be forgotten in ten years," said General Suliman. "Tomorrow, Your Majesty will meet the Coptic woman doctor who led the campaign against female circumcision in Egypt. I have put the United Nations report on your desk."

"What's the summary?"

"Only the Sydonite women themselves can stop this practice. A man may agree that a virgin bride need not be proven so by mutilation but the women do not believe that, when it comes to the point, a man will accept such a girl. Because of their fear, no progress can be made."

Abdullah sighed, then asked, "What's next?"

"The child specialist is waiting in the audience chamber, Your Majesty; then this evening you will preside at a banquet which is being held here, in the Embassy." The General stood aside as Abdullah strode into the audience chamber. Two neat, gray-suited men were waiting for him. Abdullah looked surprised. "I was expecting you alone, Doctor."

"My colleague, Doctor Margolies, specializes in the psychiatric problems of adolescents."

The King raised his eyebrows. The doctor elaborated. "After examining Prince Hassan, I find that there is nothing physically wrong with him, Your Majesty. He is a healthy boy."

"Then why is he constantly ill at school? He's missed so many lessons that the headmaster's warned me that my nephew may not be accepted for Eton. Yet two years ago, he was a perfect student."

"Perhaps too perfect, Your Majesty," the psychiatrist suggested. "Prince Hassan seems to be a quiet, well-behaved and studious boy, but he is abnormally docile for a twelve-year-old, and shows little sign of aggression or curiosity. He is exhibiting the classic behavior of a child reared in an overly authoritarian home environment."

"What has that to do with his illness?"

"Prince Hassan seems to . . . prefer being ill to being healthy."

"If my nephew is malingering because of idleness, then he must be disciplined."

For nine months of the year, Prince Hassan attended Port Regis, a British boys' boarding school in Dorset. During the holidays, Prince Hassan was tutored in twentieth century history, military strategy, tactics, and modern statecraft. For one hour a day he was permitted to play. This meant training his falcons, with the keeper of the Royal Mews. Prince Hassan was not encouraged to play with children of his own age, because it was thought that this would make him vulnerable to kidnap and assassination attempts.

Doctor Margolies said, "Prince Hassan is not malingering, Your Majesty. His bronchitis and sinus problems are genuine, the physical symptoms are unmistakable."

"Then I don't understand what you're telling me. Is my nephew ill or is he not ill?"

"Psychosomatic illness is a physical illness in every respect, but the underlying cause is not physical. In Prince Hassan's case, his lengthy periods of sickness meant that he was confined to the school sanatorium, where he was cared for by the matron, who seems an exceptionally gentle, affectionate woman." His Majesty looked perplexed, as the psychiatrist continued, "We suspect that your nephew's illnesses are merely nature's way of ensuring that he gets something he lacks, but which is vital to the well-being of a twelve-year-old. That is, the love and care of a woman."

"Naturally, my nephew misses his mother." Abdullah was puzzled. "Sadly, my sister died five years ago, but there are women in the prince's household."

"I don't mean female servants, Your Majesty," Doctor Margolies explained. "Prince Hassan is lonely, and he is at the threshold of puberty. Normally, a mother encourages and supports her son, as he grows to manhood. Ideally, an adolescent boy makes his first, inevitable mistakes in a nonjudgmental environment of encouragement and shelter. Without this, a lonely child might well lack the urge toward curiosity and aggression, two qualities that are necessary to any adult male."

And especially so to a King, thought Abdullah. No Bedouin tribe would be ruled by a weakling.

At midnight, a depressed Abdullah, followed by General Suliman, strode from the banquet hall, through beautifully carpeted corridors, toward his bedroom. He had not been able to secure the help he needed to defeat the Fundamentalist guerrillas, who now controlled one quarter of Sydon. American diplomats were being held hostage in Iran, and the United States did not want another overt involvement in Middle Eastern politics at such a sensitive time.

This evening's banquet, designed to smooth the negotiations, had been a disaster. The old Ambassador must be retired. Immediately. Clearly the wine had been ill-chosen, because the American guests had barely touched it, neither had they eaten the overelaborate nomad feast. In fact, Abdullah had heard one guest remark to another, "Greasy rice and tough mutton is bad enough, but, by the end of those damn speeches, it was cold as well."

The three American women guests had looked ill at ease among the many silent Sydonites, who were not used to making conversation with women. The atmosphere had not been one of all-male joviality, neither had it been one of graceful hospitality. Abdullah resolved that his next Ambassador to Washington would have a cultivated, intelligent wife who could properly organize, entertain, and administer the social side of his Embassy, like the wives of the Western diplomats. He had heard that the wives of German diplomats received salaries for supporting their husband's work, and, after this evening, Abdullah understood why.

Earlier in the week, Sheikh Yamani of Saudi Arabia had given a banquet in honor of King Abdullah. Yamani's chef had been flown in from the Paris Crillon, the white truffles came from Italy, and the string quartet from Vienna. Tonight, by comparison, the Sydonites had looked like prehistoric savages. Without being told, Suliman knew how Abdullah felt; he was the only person who understood why the carefree, promiscuous Abdullah had turned into this grim-faced ascetic. After years of bravery and patience, struggling to preserve his country from Communist infiltrators, after years of attempting to drag his reluctant subjects into the twentieth century, Abdullah was, quite simply, tired. He was also lonely and isolated, he trusted no men and most women bored him.

Abdullah said good night to General Suliman, then lifted the red scrambler telephone. After arranging to replace his ambassador in Washington, he opened the day's box of State Papers and began to work through them. At the bottom of the pile, he found an engraved invitation with, attached to it, a three-line file update from Intelligence on Pagan, Lady Swann. Abdullah's black brows compressed in a puzzled frown as he recognized the handwriting on the invitation.

* * *

Behind her untidy desk, piled with brochures, gala programs, opened envelopes, silver-framed pictures of her family, a moth-eaten rabbit's foot and old copies of *Horse and Hound*, Pagan looked puzzled as she worked her way through the morning mail. Again, she read the thick cream page, embossed with a crimson crest.

"His Majesty, King Abdullah of Sydon, has asked me to reply to your invitation to the Royal Gala in aid of the Anglo-American Cancer Research Foundation on July 31. His Majesty regrets that he is unable to be in Great Britain on that date, and will therefore be unable to attend.

"His Majesty has further asked me to request the pleasure of your company at Ascot Racecourse on Ladies Day, to watch his filly, Reh al Leil, run in the Chesham Stakes." It was signed with a squiggle, by an equerry.

But I didn't invite Abdullah to the Gala, Pagan thought, checking the guest list again, as the telephone rang. "Yes, this is Lady Swann speaking . . . Oh, does he? . . . Hello? . . . Of course I'm surprised to hear from you . . . yes, I've just received it." She turned over the letter. "Of course I'd love to see you again, Your Majesty, but I'm afraid it's not possible. . . . No, I'm no longer in mourning, but I can't go racing next week." Pagan's automatic response to every invitation since Christopher's death had been to refuse it. " . . . not at all. I'm very busy, organizing a charity gala. . . . A widow's life isn't as empty as you seem to think . . . it's just . . . it's just . . . " Flustered, she offered a final, weak excuse. "Well, I haven't got the right clothes. You know how everyone dresses up for Royal Ascot. . . . Oh, all right, Abdullah, I'd love to come."

Pagan put down the telephone thinking, that's the first time I've called myself a widow. It didn't sound so bad. She stood up and peered into the mirror over the mantelpiece. Anxiously, Pagan counted her laugh lines.

Ever since she and Abdullah had first met, when they had been students in Switzerland, Pagan had possessed an almost magic power to make him discard his wary, formal attitude. Pagan could make Abdullah relax and laugh. In an odd way, he had always regarded Pagan as a woman who belonged to him. She had been his first love and he had been her first love. He had never stopped trying to seduce her, even throughout her marriage to Sir Christopher, and Pagan had never stopped refusing him; although the relationship was only a friendship, Pagan never told her husband when she was meeting Abdullah; although it was only a friendship, she always dressed with uncharacteristic care before racing off to the Dorchester; although it was only a friendship, Pagan knew that Abdullah could only think of a woman in sexual terms, so their friendly meetings wafted along on an undercurrent of unmentioned eroticism.

As she stared at her reflection in the mirror, Pagan felt hopeful, flattered, and afraid.

An hour later, the doorbell rang, and outside stood a messenger from Fortnum and Mason, carrying a tower of dress boxes. Beside him stood the deputy fashion buyer, ready to bring a further selection if nothing was to Lady Swann's liking.

Pagan dithered between a green-and-white flowered chiffon dress and a pale-primrose silk suit. Then the deputy fashion buyer opened the hatboxes. Secretly, Pagan thought that she looked wonderfully romantic when she wore a hat but, invariably, as soon as she found herself wearing one on the street, she felt overdramatic or silly. So she picked the smallest hat. The buyer looked doubtful. Pagan snatched off the little white sailor beret. The buyer confidently handed her a large-brimmed floppy straw, which folded back like a fisherman's sou'wester. The rich ocher straw framed Pagan's pale skin and mahogany-colored hair. The buyer nodded. Every woman looked good in the straw sou'wester.

"Isn't she getting overexcited?" Pagan asked Abdullah as Reh al Leil curvetted sideways round the paddock, her chestnut neck stained with sweat.

"Isn't it natural for a girl to get excited on her first outing?" Abdullah smiled. "I seem to remember that when you were a debutante, you were sometimes quite hard to handle."

Pagan laughed, then again looked doubtfully at the filly. "Look at her—she's running the race in the paddock." The filly was dancing in circles around her groom, a telltale white lather of perspiration building up around her girth.

"Aren't you going to bet on her?"

"Not if she carries on like that. She'll be exhausted before the race begins." Pagan teased him. "Young horses are pretty much the same over a short distance, so I always bet on the jockey, like the rest of the bettors. I'm putting my fiver on Lester Piggot, on number seven."

"Golden Gondola." Abdullah checked the race program. "The favorite. So you want to play it safe, Pagan?" She became aware of his soft black stare and the warmth of his hand on her arm.

"You know I've always been a coward, Abdullah."

He smiled at her and clicked his fingers. An equerry stepped forward. "Lady Swann wishes to place a five-pound bet each way on the favorite."

"Abdullah, don't be silly. I was only teasing. Of course I'll put my money on your horse."

As soon as he had mounted, Reh al Leil pitched her jockey onto the velvet turf, and the odds lengthened to 100–7.

As the other horses cantered sedately down the course to the start, Reh al Leil tore off at a gallop, her once-glossy flanks thickly plastered with white foam and her nostrils gaping wide and red.

She reared in terror at the starting stalls, again unseated her jockey, and delayed the race a further ten minutes.

When the starting gate finally flew open, Reh al Leil was twenty feet behind the other horses and heading in the opposite direction to the race.

"Wherever did you find that filly?" Pagan asked Abdi, as Golden Gondola set a businesslike pace in the lead.

"Kentucky," he said pleasantly. At the first furlong, Reh al Leil was the last horse in the race.

At the third furlong post, she was halfway up the field of eight young horses, and showing extraordinary speed.

By the last furlong, Golden Gondola had dropped back to third place and Reh al Leil, cheered on by the roar of the packed grandstands, was out in front, then triumphantly won by a neck.

"I'm glad I didn't bet on the favorite, she's lost a lot of money today," laughed Pagan, as they made their way to the winner's enclosure. "She couldn't have gone slower if she'd been a real golden gondola."

"Most modern gondolas are motorized."

"How unromantic. Were there ever golden gondolas in Venice?" Pagan asked

Abdullah, as they watched Reh al Leil, draped in sweat rugs, being walked steadily up and down.

"Yes. In fact, there still are, Pagan. Haven't you ever been to Venice?"

"No," said Pagan. "What's your tip for the next race? Oh, watch out, here's the Queen Mother." With difficulty, Pagan curtsied in her tight primrose silk skirt.

Afterward, Abdullah and Pagan walked slowly past the paddock to the sun-dappled half-circle of white rails at the end of the racecourse grounds. "This is my favorite part of Ascot," Pagan said dreamily, as she watched the horses being prepared for the journey home. The farrier removed the light racing plates from Reh al Leil's oiled hooves, and Abdullah rewarded the horse with a couple of peeled, scrubbed carrots.

"His Majesty is upstairs," the ancient doorman told Pagan the next day, after directing her to the back staircase. Women—or lady guests, as they were known at Black's—could only enter certain parts of the club and they were forbidden to use the main staircase.

In the shabby dining room, the walls were covered by gold-framed pictures of bloodstock. Elderly waitresses moved slowly from table to table. "I see nothing's changed," Pagan said to Abdullah.

"Nothing has changed." Abdullah smiled back at her. "The food is as bad as ever." He nodded amiably at the Minister of Defense, as he passed their table. The part of Abdullah that had been educated at Eton and Sandhurst, the lover of field sports and a respecter of tradition, was extremely comfortable at Black's. The part of Abdullah that was proudly Arab detested the claustrophobic atmosphere of privilege and prejudice in the dim-paneled rooms, where judges, politicians, churchmen, and diplomats drank fine champagne from silver tankards, snoozed in old leather chairs and, although polite, really wanted nothing to do with dirty wogs.

In the early days of their friendship, when lunch at Black's had been a frequent event, Pagan and Abdullah had realized that the only way to eat well in the club was to order food that had been purchased from the members' own estates, which meant river fish, game, and esoteric vegetables such as salsify and samphire.

Abdullah watched Pagan as she dipped slim green asparagus spikes in melted butter, then ate plain salmon trout with new potatoes, fresh peas, and cucumber salad.

When the raspberries arrived, Abdullah ate them with his fingers, picking up each small red fruit, one at a time. Why should such a harsh man have such a soft mouth, Pagan wondered, watching him; his lips look as soft as Reh al Leil's nose. Pagan felt the elation of flirtation. She realized that not once, since they had sat down, had Abdullah taken his dark eyes from her face.

When the waitress removed the silver raspberry dishes, their hands were half an inch apart on the white damask tablecloth. Abdullah slowly stretched his fingers and Pagan felt the warmth of his fingertips.

Speaking very slowly and pinching her fingertips very lightly between his, he said, "I don't want to play games with you, Pagan, and I don't want us to mess it up this time. I want you. I want a real relationship."

"I didn't realize that you have real relationships in Sydon," Pagan babbled, speaking too fast in her nervousness. "I thought you had political marriages." She immediately regretted her words.

"Darling Pagan," Abdullah said, thinking he'd like to thump her, "we are not in Sydon now."

"Will you be having coffee, sir?" the waitress interrupted.

"Why not have coffee in my suite at the Dorchester?" Abdullah suggested.

Pagan sat silent for a full thirty seconds, her lips parted, her legs trembling, and her mind frozen with alarm.

Abdullah said a word he very rarely uttered, and he said it quickly, with force. "Please, Pagan."

"Why not?" Pagan heard herself agree.

What on earth am I doing? she asked herself as she glided down the back staircase, listening to the fears in her head. "I'm a widow. I haven't made love for ages. I'm only used to Christopher. I must be out of my mind. I'm no longer the girl he remembers. He won't want me once he sees me with my clothes off. Arabs treat women like donkeys, and Abdullah's hurt me so much already. He's dangerous for me. If I get involved with him again, he'll hurt me again." All her old feelings rushed back to frighten Pagan, the fear of private humiliation or, even worse, of public humiliation.

Internal red lights and warning sirens continued to blare at the back of Pagan's head as she reached the bottom of the threadbare staircase. Abdullah stepped forward, caught her in his arms, and pulled her out of sight behind a pillar. "Don't you dare change your mind, you little coward," he breathed, brushing her lips with his. She felt the tip of his tongue touch her lips, erotic and inviting. She melted, then clung to him. Abdullah said, "Let's get out of here."

At the doorway of the club, they were stopped by a policeman. "Sorry, sir, we can't let anyone leave the club. Another bomb scare. Please return indoors, and keep the lady as far as possible from the windows."

Outside, they could see that the road was crisscrossed by white tape; a police transporter was slowly towing away all cars except for a blue Ford on the right-hand side of the road. At the end of the empty street, a small group of police chatted beside an ambulance, its door ominously open.

"What are we going to do?" Pagan asked Abdullah, almost crying with disappointment, but at the same time relieved. A group of club members, noisy with drink, was turned back at the door. Led by a rubicund bishop, they clattered up the staircase, back to the bar.

Abdullah led Pagan away from the door. He took her hand, quickly pressed the narrow pale palm to his cheek, then kissed it and licked each finger with his warm tongue. "I've wanted you for years, and I'm not going to be stopped by an IRA bomb."

"Abdi, stop starting, when we haven't anywhere to go. A bomb scare could trap us here for hours, you know."

He kissed her palm harder, crushing his lips against it. "Run up the ladies' staircase," he whispered. "I'll meet you on the top floor, in the billiard room."

The billiard room on the top floor of Black's was as quiet as a cathedral. The windows were permanently covered by green velvet, so only a few motes of dust floated in the occasional ray of sunlight. In the green gloom stood two billiard tables. Larger than pool tables, they were made of smooth, heavy slate, covered by green cloth. Pagan eyed the polished boards of the floor, the narrow black leather bench that surrounded the room, and then the tables. "Abdi," she whispered, "we can't! Not on the table!"

"We can," he said, as he locked the door in the half-darkness and pulled her toward him. He kissed her slowly and gently. Then he crushed Pagan's body against his, and she felt the side of the billiard table press against the back of her thighs.

Slowly, Abdullah took off the green-and-white dress, kissing each exposed area of flesh as he did so. He looked at Pagan in her plain, white satin slip, picked her up in his arms and laid her long white-satin-wrapped body on the green baize table. The slate felt hard and cold, beneath the cloth. Soft, slow kisses traced Pagan's collarbone, then she felt his lips on the delicate skin below, where the faint shadowy outlines of her ribs appeared. As his warm lips touched her skin, she thought dreamily, I'm lighting up, like the sun rising over the Swiss Alps, when the mountain peaks get that living pink glow that spreads slowly down to the valleys. Suddenly, she realized that it had been years since her body had felt so alive.

Pagan's slip slithered off the table as Abdullah started to kiss her breasts, then moved downward, beyond her ribs, his warm breath clinging like mist to the rise of her belly. Pagan suddenly thought of the dark velvet of a horse's nose, and the potential power of that animal's strength for danger and destruction. The tip of Abdullah's tongue traced round her navel and slowly trickled over her lower abdomen. Then, maddeningly, his lips returned to kiss her on the mouth, and Pagan felt the harsh fabric of his uniform, the hard metal of brass buttons against her bare flesh.

"But suppose we spoil the table?"

"Then the table will be spoiled." He unbuckled his belt.

"Abdi—please! What if somebody comes up?"

"They will find the door locked, that's all." Slowly he undressed, and Pagan thought, why, he's treating me like a young horse. Act confident, make no sudden movements, and never let them know you're scared. Having shed his clothes, Abdullah leaned over the table and kissed her body again until Pagan quivered, moaned, and forgot about the table and the bishops and discovery, as a warm brown arm encircled her long white waist. Abdullah's velvet brown eyes looked into Pagan's pale blue eyes, then his full lips moved forward as he bent to kiss her again. Then he pulled back, lips smiling, eyes dancing. Pagan tried to kiss him, but he ducked his head. Giggling, they struck at each other like snakes, then finally surrendered in a long erotic embrace as they both felt the strange hard chill of the slate that lay below the bright green baize covering the table.

As she became increasingly conscious of the lazy warmth and sympathy of their entwined bodies, Pagan felt her self-consciousness evaporate. The comfortable friendship, which had endured since they were teen-agers, now wrapped them in cozy intimacy as Abdullah's fingers slowly caressed her body as softly as his lips had done before. He kissed the arch of her mahogany eyebrows, the fine bridge of her nose, the long line of her jaw. He began to kiss her breasts, nuzzling her right nipple with his lips, sucking, first gently, then more insistently. He's taking the whole afternoon to get to know my body, thought Pagan, tingling with ardor.

As Abdullah slipped his hand inside the back of her white cotton panties, Pagan wished with all her heart that they were apricot satin and lace from Keturah Brown, and didn't have a safety pin on the side. She felt another flash of vulnerability as light warm kisses fell on her soft mound, and the the hot tip of his tongue wriggled into the opening under the curls. Then she felt nothing but yearning, crushing pleasure as his hands slid under her buttocks and pulled her to him, so that he drank from her, like a cat lapping cream.

Repeatedly, Abdullah swept Pagan to the edge of orgasm, then moved up to kiss her mouth again. Then, slowly, he mounted her and began to enter her quivering flesh, pushing inside her a millimeter at a time. This deliberate, careful slowness made Pagan feel as if she were moving in a dream. When they had first met, Pagan had imagined what it would be like, to let Abdullah make love to her. After her teen-age decision not to let him, Pagan had never allowed herself to regret it, or even to admit that there was anything to regret.

But she'd never imagined anything like this.

"Open your eyes, Pagan," he breathed. As she looked at him, inhaling her own musky odor on his mouth, he pushed slowly on and Pagan felt as if she was being swept away on a foaming Hokusai wave. She gave a weak cry as her climax gathered, then broke over her. Abdullah held her body tightly to him, cherishing the communion of their flesh.

She did not cry, as he had expected, but lay quietly in his arms, mouthing gentle kisses with her narrow lips. Abdullah considered taking her again to climax, but decided to wait until he knew the long, pale body better, as gently he returned her light kisses and began to satisfy himself. He knew that he could sensually dominate the timid Pagan, but he wanted her to love him and to come to his arms with confidence. Later, he would show her how to caress him, teaching her, as he had been taught, the art of love.

Afterward, they lay together in the green quietness of the billiard room, her long pale body and his brown one, side by side. Faint bursts of tipsy laughter wafted up from the bar on the floor below, where the bishop and his friends still quaffed champagne from silver tankards.

With his lips against the mahogany hair that spread over the green baize, Abdullah whispered, "When I first met you, I tried to imagine you naked, but I never could. I think that's when I discovered that, for me, you were different from other women, because I couldn't do what I wanted with you. I couldn't even undress you in my own imagination."

Pagan pulled him toward her and felt the room recede, together with her sadness and confusion and timidity, as she felt the flesh upon flesh of their lips.

Then the bomb went off.

The explosion shook the entire building, including the heavy slate-bedded table on which they lay.

There was an instant of silence. It seemed to last forever. Then, glass began to fall in deadly waterfalls from the windows.

Snake swift, Abdullah scooped up Pagan and pulled her naked body beneath the billiard table. A cacophony of voices rose from below them. "We should perhaps get dressed," Abdullah suggested.

The telephone call from a call box in Kilburn to the *Daily Mail* news desk was semicoherent. A voice announced that the bomb had been planted outside Black's Club, and that they hoped the Minister of Defense had enjoyed his last lunch.

When the antiterrorist squad discovered King Abdullah playing billiards with Lady Swann, they realized how much more serious the terrorist attack might have been. This time, instead of the senseless, pulped-flesh carnage of the usual IRA bomb attack, there had been no casualties, except for a superficial cut on the cheekbone of the uniformed doorman, who was reluctantly escorted to St. Thomas's casualty ward, muttering that he didn't know what London was coming to, what with the Irish killing old women and children, the Iranians holding

Americans hostage in their own Embassy, the Lebanese machine-gunning each other, the Syrians hijacking airplanes, and the Nigerians kidnapping their diplomats and crating them up for export. Sometimes he wished he was back in the trenches, he grumbled to the paramedic; at least on the Somme, you knew who your enemy was and where Fritz was hiding.

Abdullah turned to Pagan, who was huddled in the corner of his Rolls. "Next time we must go somewhere quieter," he suggested.

"Abdi, your driver will hear."

"No, he won't. That's a permanent, bulletproof, glass partition." He noticed that, for the first time, she had called him by his old pet name of Abdi.

"Will you spend the weekend with me? We could go where nobody knows you." Abdullah's hand was insistent on her thigh.

Pagan gabbled, "I couldn't do that. People would talk. It's only been five months since Christopher died and I was very fond of him, you know."

"That is exactly why you need a few days away from life. A weekend in Venice. We could be there and back before anyone noticed."

Pagan hesitated. "What do you mean by a weekend?"

She felt his forefinger trace her calf, then her knee, then her thigh again. Pagan wished that she wasn't wearing chainstore pantyhose. She wished that she was wearing black sheer silk stockings with black satin garters and lots and lots of lace. She'd better nip round to Keturah Brown before this trip to Venice.

Pagan walked slowly up the stairs. It seemed a very long climb to her bedroom. Once inside, the drawers of the Queen Anne tallboy were difficult to open. Where did I put my bathing suit? she wondered. Aimlessly she began to pull out clothes and throw them on the floor. Suddenly she felt something hard and knobby in her hand. She looked at it for a few moments before realizing what it was. The old red dog collar was worn and curled at the end; a few of Buster's coarse hairs were still caught beneath the metal studs.

Suddenly, Pagan saw Buster lying dead on the road, then this was replaced by a different mental picture. Pagan saw the hospital sheet draped over her husband's mangled body. She felt her mouth open in a distorted scream. At last, she felt tears in her eyes. "Christopher!" she shouted to the empty room, as sobs tore at her chest. Why am I crying? she asked herself. I shouldn't be crying. Christopher died months ago. This is ridiculous. I must stop it.

One of Mark Scott's war photographs flashed into Pagan's mind. She saw a bombed building, exposed like an open doll's house to the outside elements. The flowered wallpaper was hanging in strips from the walls, the pictures were crooked, a chair and a smashed television set were piled on top of the rubble. Coats still hung from the hooks in the hall, but the end of the hall was missing. It wasn't meant to be like this, the building mutely said. That was how Pagan felt about herself and her altered life. One minute it was there, whole and complete, and the next minute it had been smashed. Half of her life was missing, like half of that building was missing.

Suddenly, Pagan was able to accept that the life she had known was a thing of the past. It was gone forever. She was able to accept that her situation had changed, that she had to make her own way in the world. She realized that she was not alone in the world, that she had known good times and bad times before Christopher died, and she would do so again. Life would never be the same again, but she would make a different life. Life would go on, and so would she.

Pagan could not stop crying. When Sophia returned home from school, she found her mother curled up on the bedroom carpet, still clutching Buster's collar in her hand, and sobbing noisily.

"Mummy, what is it? Why are you crying?" Sophia stroked Pagan's head and wondered what to do, who to call.

"I don't know," Pagan howled, "but I can't s-s-s-s-stop."

Sophia sat down beside her and also started to bawl.

At last, together, they were able to share their grief.

CHAPTER 10

Late June 1979

"THEY'LL JUST HAVE to wait for their money, my blood isn't bankable." Judy wearily shoved a pile of bills off her knees; they slid down the fox-fur spread of her brown velvet bed with a menacing little shoosh to Tom, who was seated on the end of the bed. "At least switching the printers paid off. We've saved a slice of this month's budget." Noisily, she blew her nose; her bout of summer flu just made everything that much worse.

Tom shook his head. "I didn't want to discuss it until you were back in the office, but the color reproduction of our July issue is way below standard."

"The printers swear that they'll do a better job next month. Teething troubles, they said."

Again, Tom shook his head. "Next month is too late. Lady Mirabelle Cosmetics has withdrawn the new fall campaign because they say our color reproduction is no longer good enough."

Judy's already pale face went white. "When did that happen?"

"This afternoon. That's why I had to talk to you. A lot of advertisers have been griping; we've already lost a few of the smaller ones, but Lady Mirabelle's a body-blow." Judy knew perfectly well that the Lady Mirabelle Christmas Gift campaign accounted for a big chunk of their revenue, from September to Christmas. "We can't replace that money," Tom emphasized.

"Does anyone else know?" asked Judy.

"No."

"Are you sure no one knows?" she persisted.

"No." Tom gave a short laugh. "Not even Tony knows about the Lady Mirabelle problem."

Judy flopped back wearily on her cream silk pillows. Tom looked at her and thought, it's not like Judy to act so spoiled and sound so sorry for herself. And she hasn't got that much to be sorry about. Just because you were born poor doesn't mean that the world owes you a living at some later date. Parts of Judy's life had been hard, but they'd nearly all been interesting, and she'd had some really lucky breaks on her way to the top. Maybe she'd become overambitious, maybe they both had. Tom knew that was Kate's opinion. Trouble was, Judy wasn't used to losing. And they were both under great strain. Tom said, "Judy, we took a gamble on the printing and we lost the gamble. But winners always take risks and sometimes they lose. Failing sometimes is a part of long-term winning. You can see their point, Judy. They aren't going to spend millions developing plum colors, then run ads for them in a magazine that prints them light purple. Switching printers was a false economy." Tom's usually cheerful face was strained. "And there's another thing that you may have forgotten. All our business loans are guaranteed against each other. The PR company is still doing fine, and so is the property company, but they guarantee the magazine, which, in turn guarantees our stock market investments . . ."

"Losses, you mean!" snorted Judy.

" . . . which means that we can't liquidate one part of our business without the domino effect. They'll all start crashing."

"Tom, this is like a nightmare. A crash is what I've always dreaded, and you've always told me my attitude was overcautious. You always said that we were borrowing in order not to miss business opportunities. Why, only nine months ago, you told me that we were worth two million dollars *more* this year. What about the Hoffmann-La Roche profits that you stuck in Swiss francs?"

"That was before our copper futures problem." Tom looked uncomfortable. Judy had always hated him playing the futures market.

Judy said, "I wish we'd sorted out the *VERVE!* portfolio and separated the investment business from the rest of the company, as Kate suggested."

"We just never got around to it. I wish you'd never run that interview with Lili! Let's both stop wishing and think positive!" He handed her the box of Kleenex. "Our financial situation is a house of cards; we've borrowed from Peter to pay Paul for months now and we can't go on much longer."

"Sometimes," Judy's voice was flat, "I'd just like to take a plane and leave it all behind me." She looked at the space on the wall where her treasured silk painting of a Manchu noble had hung until it had followed the jade collection to Sotheby's a few weeks earlier. Despite the warmth of her apartment and the thick fur spread, Judy felt cold and bone-tired. Why hadn't the *VERVE!* lawyers picked up the danger in that fatal interview with Lili? Why didn't the First Amendment apply to magazines as it did to newspapers? How could one lousy paragraph of print have sabotaged her entire life's achievement? If I could wipe out five minutes of my life, Judy thought, I'd choose the time it took for Lili to tell me about Senator Ruskington.

Tom stood up, then picked up the heavy file box that contained their depositions for the hearing on the following day. "I want you to read your statement once again, before you sign it, Judy," he said gently. "We've got to get this absolutely right."

Judy sighed, took the document from him and began to read it. "At least after we win this hearing, we'll wring a few thousand in damages out of the Senator when we counter-sue for libel."

"Nobody wins a lawsuit, Judy, you know that, Even if we win, we'll still be thousands of dollars in hock."

"Not 'if' Tom, 'when,' " Judy stressed, with weary stubborness. She hadn't achieved what she had by giving up easily. Tom said nothing and looked at his scuffed Gucci loafers. To change the subject, he asked, "Want to hear what's happened to Kate?"

"Of course." Judy brightened, as Tom pulled from his pocket an airmail envelope covered with neat, small handwriting, with no loops or flourishes.

" 'The hill tribe guerrillas are getting stronger,' she says. They've raided banks, attacked the Bengali settlements and the army garrison and she thinks they're secretly planning an assault on the oil companies. That will be Shell, I suppose. Her typewriter's been stolen, but she hopes to buy a new one on the black market, and she says she'll sleep with it chained to her wrist."

"You don't seem very worried about her, Tom."

"You know Kate. She hates a dull life, so I go along with what makes her happy. Of course I'm worried about her."

"Hasn't anyone got any good news to cheer me up?" Judy picked up a second legal document from the pile.

"No news of Mark?"

"I've already told you, that's over. Mark and I were finished months ago." She buried her head in her hands. "I can't take it any more," she whispered. "Why is it that the minute you're off balance, the vultures close in, trying to bring you down? Mark's in Nicaragua, and he's in Nicaragua because he doesn't care to be around unsuccessful, old me."

Tom silently offered her another tissue from the box on the rosewood table beside her bed. "Judy, I can't imagine that anyone would leave you just because you're vulnerable or depressed or not sixteen any more. You're a complete woman, Judy, and an honest woman. I think you're the most honest woman I've ever met, and any man could love you for that alone."

She shook her head and slowly wiped her reddened eyes. "All that Mark really liked about me was the fact that I *didn't* need him. As soon as I needed him, *really* needed him, he ran away in the most destructive possible way." Again, the tears started trickling from the sides of her eyes. "The crisp executive in me was irresistible so long as she was giving her attention to Mark's brilliant career and his home comforts. He was very pleased to live off my emotional strength when I had enough for two, but when I needed someone to take care of *me* for a change, he couldn't take it." Judy's voice crackled with misery and she sobbed silently behind her hands.

Tom said, "It's normal to suffer when a relationship ends. You get a few kicks in your pride, your dignity gets a bit dented, it's a diminishing experience for everybody," he soothed. "But Judy, you've only got to compare the divorce rate and the marriage statistics to know that people can split or hitch up any time, at any age. You're still attractive. . . . "

"That's great, Tom, just great—that makes me feel like Methuselah's mother. 'You're still attractive' means that when people look at me they can see the day coming when I won't be attractive anymore. It means that time's running out." She blew her nose again. "This isn't the way I want to end up, Tom, alone in bed with my work. This wasn't the rosy vision I had in front of me when I first ran away from Rossville, to make my fortune." She scraped her face with a tissue, leaving red weals on her cheeks.

"Don't be too hard on Mark," Tom pleaded. "I don't suppose either of us is the easiest person in the world to be with, when we're under this sort of strain."

"That's not it." Judy pushed her fingers through her hair with a gesture of anguish. "I'm not easy to be with, because everybody's got the wrong idea about me. Mark's no different from any other man. To him, a woman in a top job is tough, self-possessed, independent—all the things he has to be to stay at the top of his profession. What he doesn't understand is that, just because I am those things at work, it doesn't follow that I want to be the same way at home. Like all you men, Mark thinks a successful career woman isn't interested in kindness, or caring and sharing, and he thinks I don't need it. But I *do*. I'm just as thirsty for love as any housewife running a couple of kids and a recipe club; the only difference is that I run a corporation."

"Finish these papers, Judy, and then I'll take them all away," Tom coaxed her. "Crying won't get us out of the hole we're in."

As Judy dried her tears and finished reading her statement, Tom turned on the TV in time to catch the late news. As he had anticipated, Senator Ruskington was interviewed with his loyal wife at his side. Her face was serious and indignant. The Senator answered the interviewer, "This is indeed a most unpleasant case, which is why my wife and I feel that it is my duty to the public to expose this situation for what it is." Expertly, Ruskington turned to face the camera head-on. "An unpleasant attempt to sell an unpleasant magazine through salacious innuendo and un-Christian lies. Any money which comes to us through this lawsuit will be donated to a charity which will be chosen by my wife." The Senator was glibly pious.

"But you are claiming ten million dollars in damages," the reporter reminded him.

"Whatever the court sees fit to award us will all be given to charity," the Senator confirmed. "My wife and I wish it to be known that there is not a shred of evidence to support the vile accusations printed in *VERVE!* magazine. We feel it is appropriate that the people who publish this dishonest magazine should see the rewards of their evildoing."

Judy shook her fist at the TV screen and gathered up the scattered papers on her bed. "I'm going to go through these once again, Tom," she said.

The woman TV reporter suggested, "Some people find it hard to understand why you are pushing this case against *VERVE!* magazine with so much vigor."

"Attagirl!" Judy cried, sitting up in bed. "I bet she reads *VERVE!*"

On-screen, the Senator again turned to the camera. "My wife and I feel that until some person in our situation makes a stand, any so-called actress can draw attention to herself by linking her name with that of a prominent public citizen." The Senator paused for breath. "I want everyone to know that our family is united in fighting this attempt to blacken our good name and to brand me as a fornicator and an adulterer."

"But Senator, isn't this also an attempt on your part to obtain a great deal of money?" the reporter prodded him.

"My personal reputation is worth more to me than any sum of money," said the Senator. The interview ended and Tom switched off the TV.

Tom left her apartment shortly after midnight, saying, "Take care of yourself, Judy."

That's what I've been trying to do for the last thirty years, she thought.

Judy remembered how depressed she'd felt in Switzerland, where she'd worked all day at the language laboratory and every evening and weekend as a waitress at the Chesa. She'd never learned to ski, she'd never gone to dances, and she'd never had pretty clothes like Maxine and Kate. She still remembered her sudden bitterness when the young Pagan had, without thinking twice, returned the diamond necklace that Prince Abdullah had tried to give her; that necklace would have paid for Judy's entire year in Europe.

Judy never permitted herself to remember what it felt like to be really poor, because she panicked when she recalled what it felt like to have only one pair of shoes and one repeatedly patched dress. But when she remembered her mother's hopeless face and the strained, tense atmosphere in their home, for the two years during which her father was out of work, then Judy felt grim determination to succeed—at no matter what cost to herself.

Tom told me to take care of myself, she thought bitterly, picking up her ebony bedside mirror and looking at her face, which reflected the tension of the past few months.

Judy worked through the night on her deposition and finally finished it at six in the morning. She heard the maid's key in the lock, and called, "Forget about breakfast, Francetta, and call me at eight o'clock. I'm off to Philadelphia again." Then she drifted off to sleep.

"What time will you be home, Curtis?" Debra Halifax asked her husband.

He walked to the sideboard and lifted the silver entree dish for a second helping of scrambled eggs. "Usual time, I expect." He wondered how it was possible to feel so worn and jaded at the beginning of a new day. "What are you planning to do today, Debra?"

"I'm not planning to do anything." Debra managed to make the statement sound like an accusation. At least, thought Curtis, she was eating again, although she did not seem to be gaining any weight. Doctor Joseph thought that her infertility had been linked to her anorexia.

"Don't forget what Doctor Joseph said. If you want to make a full recovery, you must start leading your own life and you begin by structuring your day. Why don't you go shopping with Jane?"

"You don't get over a nervous breakdown by going shopping. That's all I've ever done with my entire life. That's the trouble!"

"Now, Debra, Dr. Joseph explained that it wasn't exactly a nervous . . . "

"Oh, yes it was!"

She's almost proud of it, Curtis thought wearily; it's her one achievement in life, the only thing she ever managed to do entirely on her own—have a nervous breakdown.

"Doctor Joseph also said that what I needed was the love and support of my husband."

"I do love you, Debra, and I try to support you." Curtis said once again.

"Then why don't you spend more time with me?" she demanded. "If you're not at the bank, you're at the Philadelphia Club or off playing golf or fishing with your friends."

"Now that's not so. I spend a lot of time with you, Debra."

"Not alone." Her voice was vinegar. "We give parties, and we go to parties; we meet the same people over and over."

"But they're our friends," Curtis protested.

"Would you say we have friends, Curtis? I wouldn't. We have your business people and your political people and our families, but we don't have any real friends, do we? And I never have a spare minute, but I lead an empty life." Again, her accusatory tone flicked at her husband as Debra started her weekly moan.

Curtis never knew what to say or what to do or what to suggest. "Look, I've got to leave, I'm late. Why not take Jane to a museum?"

"You know very well that museums depress me. A museum wouldn't solve *my* problem. Not now that I know what my problem is." Debra's voice trembled. "There's someone else, isn't there? You're in love with someone else, aren't you, Curtis? That woman I saw in your office. I know she lunched with you yesterday, I saw it in your appointment book. She's always coming down to see you. You're having an affair with the famous Judy Jordan, aren't you, Curtis?"

"No. I see her on business!" Curtis felt exhausted, as his wife's persistent questions continued. Debra had started to stage jealous rages over his imagined infidelity almost immediately after they married. Doctor Joseph had explained Debra's jealousy was the classic result of paranoid delusions. Curtis had bowed his head under the onslaught of accusation. After all, he had a reason to feel guilty, although he was pretty sure that Debra didn't know about it.

Gradually, Curtis recognized that Debra said little which was founded on reason, and then, slowly, he had come to realize that his wife was not entirely . . . well. Doctor Joseph used the phrase "borderline psychotic." After twenty years of marriage, Curtis Halifax knew that his wife's grasp on sanity was easily loosened; her family had always known of this and now the Halifax family knew of it. but the subject was never discussed. Debra was nervous, that was all.

Now she said, "If Judy Jordan was only in your office to discuss business, then why was she crying?"

"I don't recall that she was crying."

"Yes, she was. Or she had been. I saw her eyes."

"I simply haven't got time to rerun this scene today. I promise you, there's nothing personal between us." Curtis rose from the damask-covered breakfast table, gave his wife a quick, impersonal kiss on the forehead and left, late for his meeting.

Once her husband had left, Debra Halifax went up to her pink bedroom where, leaning over the hand basin painted with apple blossoms, she stuck two fingers down her throat and vomited up her breakfast. To disguise the telltale odor of her stomach juices on her breath, she swilled eau de cologne around her mouth, then spat it out; the repellent taste was a punishment for having eaten two pieces of toast at breakfast. No wonder Curtis no longer loved her, she thought as she pinched her thigh, I'm fat, I'm self-indulgent, I've got no self-control.

Every time Debra looked up at her reflection in the mirror she really believed that she saw a lumpish, frowsy, fat woman, instead of a small skeletal figure. She panted through her morning session on the exercise bicycle, dragging her body through the Rocky Mountain program twice, then worked out with weights to punish what she believed were her too-plump thighs and well-cushioned stomach.

Afterward, aimlessly, Debra wandered through the quiet house. A lot of her day was passed in an uncoordinated mental state, in which she was never fully aware of the time, of where she was, or what she was doing. She flicked through magazines, read a few sentences and left them. She picked up a piece of petit point which had lain on her worktable uncompleted for several months, sewed a few stitches and abandoned it. She watered a handsome Clivia plant, which the gardener watered each week in any case. Debra's luxuriant house plants often died because of their owner's erratic attentions.

For the fourth time that morning, she picked up the telephone to call Jane, but the effort of talking was too much for her. Besides, Jane only liked being with her because Jane had no money. Perhaps Jane had her eye on Curtis. That would make sense from Jane's point of view. But Jane was a Catholic and she was married with two children. Always running through Debra's head, like the sound of a distant river, was the idea that Curtis was unfaithful to her with some woman. By midday, when the maid brought her lunch on a tray, Debra had formed the image of a faceless seductress who was stealing her husband away from her. By the middle of the afternoon, when the shadow of the magnolia tree was lengthening across the lawn outside, she hated this anonymous woman with murderous ferocity.

It was too hot in the garden. Debra drifted into the library and sat in her husband's chair behind the green leather-topped partner's desk. She imagined Curtis on the telephone to his faceless mistress, while she, Debra, slept innocently upstairs. She imagined her husband whispering hot words of love and saw his features soften with affection and sensuality, as she remembered them during the first few weeks of their marriage. By the end of the afternoon, the vision of her husband's infidelity was far more real to Debra than any real experience she had encountered that day.

One by one, she opened the drawers of the desk and rifled through the papers she found in them. There must be love letters, but where were they? Sure enough, the small top drawer was locked. Debra scattered the pens from the pen tray, found the silver paperknife and forced the little lock.

Inside the drawer were some black and white photographs of a small girl, a pile of press clippings, and a curl of dark hair tied with a white ribbon. Debra's claw-thin hand pulled out a few recent clippings and turned them over. "Lili to star as Mistinguett," she read. So Curtis was fooling around with an actress. Debra shivered with rage. You may be young, beautiful and famous, Lili, but let's see if money can hurt you.

The Spear flashed by, unmistakably black among the white, green, and orange bodywork of the other competitors at Brand's Hatch. Inside the hot cockpit, Gregg sat in a pool of sweat; a driver could lose over five pounds in a long race. Ahead of Gregg, a white BMW went into Stirling's Bend too fast, lost adhesion, ploughed straight on to hit the bend hard and, as Gregg passed it, burst into flames.

Gregg suppressed the vision of his own body enveloped in flame, as the Spear streaked past the grandstand for the fifth time. He listened to the high-pitched whine of the engine as he dropped two gears to set the car up for Druid's, the hairpin bend. Coming out of the bend, he saw the Dinetti-Mazda not far ahead. He's in trouble, I'll pass him on the Cooper Straight, Gregg thought.

By the end of the first hour of the thousand-kilometer race, Gregg was lying seventh, but the gaps were small and that meant nothing at this stage; a bit of bad luck could knock you right out of the race in a second.

He rounded Stirling's bend, and accelerated away down to Clearways. He projected his mind ahead to Clark Curve, which always looked deceptively gentle, but which demanded extra concentration for a car with the power of the Spear. Gregg was now close enough to take the Aston Martin Nimrod on the top straight. He blinked sweat from his eyes as, three cars ahead of him, the green-and-white Jaguar shed a rear wheel with no warning, swerved into the barrier, then shot backwards onto the track amid a shower of sparks.

The Porsche behind it pulled out fast; the two cars touched but the Porsche managed to straighten up and hurtle on. The Nimrod driver miscalculated the Jaguar's continuing path across the track, and crashed into the spinning Jaguar. The two cars twisted together with a sickening crunch of metal, then the force of the impact hurled them both off the track, two seconds before Gregg would have hit them.

Now bathed in cold sweat, Gregg's legs involuntarily shook, and it took a fierce effort to turn his mind to the road ahead and away from the burning destruction behind him—of which he had so nearly been a part. Suddenly Gregg felt a thread of pain shoot up his left leg and his foot jumped on to the clutch. Must be that ankle. Thank God he got off the throttle in time. He'd hand over at the next pit stop.

Four hours later, Gregg was lying close behind the leading Porsche, a position that, for the previous twenty-seven laps, he had grimly clung to, but had been unable to improve. Then the gap between the Spear and the car ahead began slowly to close, as Gregg, sandwiched between two Porsches, crept closer to the lead car, and they braked for Paddock Bend.

Just ahead, Gregg calculated, a group of slower cars were bunched together. Gregg decided to make an immediate bid for the lead on the inside of Druid's, beyond which they would catch two of the slower cars. On Hailwood Hill, he pulled out and left his braking to the last moment. The Spear shot past the Porsche as they entered the corner.

Gregg held the tight inside line, but slid out wide on the exit. The Porsche stayed behind, this was no place to retake. Then Gregg was weaving between the back markers in front of the South Bank stands, aware of a crescendo of spectator cheering as he roared past with sixteen laps to go.

His ankle ached but the pain was easily bearable. It was really just a bloody nuisance. Inside the noisy cockpit, Gregg could not hear the mounting excitement of the PA commentator. ". . . and with three laps to go, it looks as if Gregg Eagleton in the Eagle Spear is increasing the lead over the Porsche . . . ."

As he hurtled into Dingle Dell Corner for the hundred and fiftieth time that day, Gregg struggled to keep his eyes on the track. The pain in his left leg was increasing. Suddenly, his sight became misty and he thought, dear God, stop me blacking out before the race is over.

The turbo-charged engine belched flames as Gregg missed a gear before the grandstands. Suddenly, each movement of his injured foot produced an excruciating wrench of agony. He heard the voice from the Eagle pit over the radio link that was built into his helmet. "Stick with it, Gregg, you're well in the lead now."

"How much lead have I got?" Gregg's stomach was beginning to churn with pain.

"Fourteen seconds."

No chance of pulling into the pit and handing over to his co-driver for the last few laps. Nothing for it, he was in this race to the end.

The next time he left Paddock Bend, Gregg again fumbled the gear change. His injured foot was now so swollen that he could barely move it.

"Porsche is creeping up, Gregg," the voice warned in his ear.

The Spear flew on.

As he pushed the Spear out of Hawthorn Bend, his left foot had only just enough pressure for the clutch pedal, and Gregg felt vomit in his mouth. For a moment, he lost his concentration.

Passing the Aston Martin Nimrod, the Spear swerved frighteningly close to the other car, and got off line.

The Porsche slipped through at Dingle Dell.

Through a rising mist of pain, Gregg registered the delighted howl of the crowd, then the Eagle flag, to signify the last lap, was flourished at the side of the track.

Another mouthful of bile and Gregg lost concentration for another fatal second. The radio voice registered no emotion. "Stephenson in the BMW is creeping up as well. Will the foot hold out?"

"Yes." Gregg's voice cracked with the effort of controlling the pain in his body. For the last time, and in a maze of pain, he took the car around the tree-lined circuit; he could feel an internal grating pain in his ankle at every movement. He barely noticed the BMW pass him.

"Yes, the Spear is definitely in trouble. This is going to be a great disappointment to the Eagle team," gabbled the commentator as they turned into the Brabham Straight. "And, as the flag drops, it's first place to Werner Hentzen in the Porsche," announced the PA, "followed by Stephenson in the BMW and Eagleton just manages to scrape third place in the Spear from Dinetti with . . . and something is happening to the Spear! . . ."

From the viewing area above the pits, Lili saw Gregg flash past in third place, then the Spear lost speed dangerously fast and began to weave toward the side of the track. The drivers crossing the line swerved to avoid the black Spear. One did not.

Lili screamed in terror as the white and orange Lancia obliquely hit the back of the Spear. Both cars spun off the track and the Spear slammed into a barrier. Ignoring Jack's shout of warning, Lili set off, running behind the pit area toward the twisted wreckage of the Spear, from which a column of smoke was now billowing upward.

"Get back, get back, you stupid bitch—she could blow at any second." A paramedic picked Lili up and half-threw her behind the barrier.

The other paramedic yanked open the door of the Spear and pulled out Gregg's inert body. Within minutes, the medical helicopter, with Gregg aboard, lifted toward Sidcup and St. Mary's Hospital.

The PA blared, "Eagleton is definitely injured . . ."

"A stress fracture in these bones, that's the cause of the trouble." The doctor waved his pen over the X-ray plate. "As your first accident was several weeks ago, and the injury wasn't diagnosed at the time, I'm afraid it's possible that the associated swelling and distortion may have affected the other joints."

"So how long before I can drive again?" Gregg's face was bleached and strained.

"Difficult to say. We'll give you painkillers of course and a series of injections to reduce the swelling, but healing the fracture itself is something that we can't do much about. Only time will put it right."

"But how *much* time? I've got to race in France again in three weeks."

"The best advice I can give you is to forget all about racing for at least two months." The doctor slipped the X-ray back in the buff file. "Complete bed rest for a minimum of six weeks, and no hard exercise of any kind until you are one hundred percent fit. With this kind of injury, nature must take its course."

After the doctor had left, Gregg began to work through his letters with his secretary until Jack arrived with a detailed report on the Spear's condition. "She's looking good, Gregg—the fuel pump was as clean as a whistle this time. What about you? Shall we get Pete to stand by for Richard?"

Lili waited patiently at the end of the line of visitors. Then, as she bent to kiss Gregg, a young blond nurse popped her head around the door to say, "Time's up for today, everyone. Doctor's orders. Mr. Eagleton has to rest!"

As the others moved toward the door, Lili said sadly, "I've hardly had a chance to talk to you, Gregg."

"Sorry, darling, but I'm trying to run my business from a hospital bed. I've got to see Jack, my secretary, the sponsors, and Dad as well as you, and I'm only allowed visitors for an hour a day. I know you haven't seen much of me since you met me, but I don't want you to get the wrong idea. You've met the team, Lili, and you know what my responsibilities are."

Lili looked down and sighed as Gregg said, "I'm not in business on my own, darling. Everyone in Eagle Motors depends on me and I depend on them. I have to meet a pretty large payroll every month, to feed families. There are men in the Eagle team working for me, for my father, and for the idea of a British privateer outfit in salon racing, who put in twenty-four-hour days on their vacations. I can't let them down, Lili." He reached for her hand and pulled her to his side. "I can't do what I want, or go where I want when I please, or step into that car at less than my best. It would be unfair and irresponsible. You've got to understand that the business comes first in my life, and I can't let anything divert me from it, not even you, darling."

Silently, Lili bent and kissed him. "I can wait."

Debra Halifax leaned back against white broderie-anglaise pillows and aimlessly turned the newspaper pages until she reached Liz Smith's column. Suddenly an item caught her attention and she read it aloud. "Lili to star in charity benefit. . . ." Debra looked up, instantly alive, and said softly, "This is what I've been waiting for."

CHAPTER 11

Early July 1979

THE PINK-HYDRANGEA wallpaper matched the heavy, chintz curtains, which were swagged back by tasseled gold ropes. A maple-framed portrait of Lord Byron hung above Pagan's desk. The back of the high satinwood desk was lined with tiny drawers and cupboards; silver-framed photographs, small bowls of potpourri, an antique silver calendar, jostled for space with a pile of letters that were weighed down by her long-dead grandfather's lucky hare's foot. It looked like a Royal desk, the sort of desk upon which there was no space to work.

"Any other business?" Pagan looked around her drawing room at the eleven other members of the fund-raising committee that was planning Lili's Gala for the Anglo-American Cancer Research Institute. They had discussed the rehearsal costs and the extra time demanded by the stagehands' union for working on Sunday; they had approved the program design and the seating arrangements for the Royal Box. Pagan had joyfully announced that the theater was sold out, and now her chewed yellow pencil was poised above the last item on the agenda.

"One final matter." The organizing secretary passed her a letter on the blue writing paper of the Grosvenor House Hotel. "Someone has offered to give a pretheater party for us."

"How very thoughtful. Who is it?"

"Another anonymous benefactor, Lady Swann."

Pagan skimmed the letter quickly, "A champagne reception for two thousand guests! That's wonderful news."

"Someone must think a lot of the Foundation."

"Or of Christopher," said Pagan, momentarily sad.

"Or of Lili?" the wife of the chainstore millionaire suggested. "Perhaps it's one of her admirers?"

"He must have a bob or two, to lay on champagne for two thousand people," said the gray-haired merchant banker, who was smoking a cigar.

"We'll send the invitation out with the tickets." Pagan leafed through her file.

"But is there time to print invitations?" The Scottish Duchess looked anxious.

"Yes," said the secretary. "I've already checked with the printers."

Pagan, notorious for the tight financial control with which she organized her fund raising events, flipped through her file. "Have we got the check?"

"The Grosvenor House Hotel has been paid direct, by banker's draft."

"How *very* thoughtful," Pagan said. She stood up and opened a window, because she hated a room to smell of cigar smoke and it took at least two weeks to get rid of the smell. She walked back and leaned against the rather ugly black marble fireplace, which was covered by a jumble of blue chinoiserie plates, a ginger jar, a Regency biscuit box, and a small blue-enamel clock with a diamanté-encircled face, that had been given to her grandmother by Queen Alexandra.

Pagan smiled at her committee. "I'm sorry we've run a little over time, today, but this unexpectedly generous offer had to be discussed. Now, if you'll excuse me, I must dash or I'll miss my flight to Venice."

The wind whipped at Pagan's hair as the high-powered speedboat raced across the lagoon toward Venice. In the distance, she could see the gray domes of the Cathedral, the ornate bell tower in St. Mark's Square, the candy-striped mooring poles sticking at crazy angles out of the water, and clouds of pigeons fluttering in the hazy blue sky.

Abdullah's private jet had flown them to Marco Polo airport, and they were now heading for the Cipriani Hotel. In the launch behind them traveled Abdullah's four bodyguards and a great deal of luggage, most of which belonged to Abdullah.

Pagan looked at the enticing city rising straight out of the water. She was excited. "Oh, Abdi, it's so beautiful. It's floating in the sea like a shimmering, gold mirage!"

"Don't expect too much romance," Abdullah warned her. "A lot of people loathe Venice."

"Why, for Heaven's sake?"

"The smells, the crowds, the claustrophobia and that dreadful, vulgar glassware."

Pagan laughed. "In that case," she said, "I won't expect any golden gondolas!"

"The golden gondolas only come out once a year, for the gondoliers' festival races."

The battered, green crocodile suitcase, that had once belonged to Pagan's grandmother, was deposited on the pale-coral carpet of the suite. The walls looked hand painted with an airy green forest, which blended with the green sofas and the green and silver Fortuny curtains. Pagan rushed through glass doors that led onto a terrace lined with miniature cyprus trees; it overlooked the orange trees that surrounded the hotel swimming pool, and beyond that, the entire panorama of Venice.

"Do you like it?" She heard Abdullah's voice behind her.

Pagan looked embarrassed and uncomfortable. She didn't know whether Abdullah was planning to share her suite.

Abdullah grinned. "I shall be in the next suite . . . if you need me. Sadly, there is no billiard room in this hotel. Space is at a premium in Venice."

The following morning, as Pagan waited by the two black-and-white-striped mooring poles of the Cipriani jetty, she clutched at Abdullah's arm. "Look! You were wrong!" A golden gondola bobbed toward them, over the scummy green water.

Abdullah said, "As a matter of fact, it's yours. I hope it's not too ostentatious for you."

Under the golden, arched canopy, sitting on the faded, purple cushions, Pagan gazed up at the naked, golden back-side of Neptune, as he wielded his trident over the poop of the boat. To her disappointment, this glorious vessel was motorized, with a spluttering engine more appropriate to a fishing smack than a ceremonial barge.

The gondola chugged down the Grand Canal between boats delivering coal, Coca-Cola, Japanese tourists, and gangs of workmen to their appropriate destinations. They passed pink-and-ocher baroque palaces, tidemarked by water, with ferns twisting their bricks apart, and cobwebs veiling their patchy, peeling plaster.

"Don't ask the gondolier to sing Santa Lucia," murmured Abdullah, "because it is a Neapolitan song and he will grind his teeth."

Pagan sniffed happily, "I love everything about this place, even the smell."

"The smell is decay and water rot, which smells fascinating so long as it is not in your home."

Later they landed and explored a little of the town on foot, but as soon as they left the large, crowded streets for the narrow, winding alleys behind them, Pagan looked puzzled and stopped. "All these alleys look the same. I'm confused." One of the bodyguards stepped forward and muttered a few guttural words to His Majesty. They followed the man until they again found themselves at the small wrought-iron bridge where the golden gondola awaited them. Abdullah said, "Although Venice is such a small town, it's very easy to get lost here. It's a well-known hazard. All the bridges and buildings look different according to whether the tide is in or not. The streets are a twisting maze, so you can't look back and get a sense of direction."

Abdullah then insisted that Pagan do some shopping in the shops round St. Mark's Square. She was measured for a pair of silver snakeskin shoes and then chose a classic shoe in red. Abdullah said, "They're very elegant. Order them in every color they have." He waved his hand at the excited young shoemaker and strolled out of the shop, as Pagan mused, "What on earth will I do with twenty-seven pairs of pumps?"

By the time they were drinking their lunchtime Bellinis (the mixture of champagne and peach juice that was invented in Venice), the bodyguards were also guarding a second launch, laden with a complete set of calf luggage, with golden clasps, twenty meters of handmade lace, which Pagan planned to keep for Sophia's wedding dress, and more clothes than Pagan had ever possessed in her life, including three antique Fortuny dresses, in coral, brown, and dark green, and an opera cloak in canary yellow silk.

They spent an unforgettable afternoon in bed.

"Your Majesty, this is the Sala del Maggior Consiglio, the very cradle of Western democracy, where the Great Council of Venice met to elect representatives to the governing committees." Pagan and Abdullah obediently followed the curator's finger with their eyes, as he pointed up to the painted ceiling, where the nacreous light from the lagoon outside played on the rich colors of the panels. "Notice the frieze of the seventy-six Doges, the painting of Paradise by Tintoretto, and here the Apotheosis of Venice, by Veronese."

"Cradle of democracy!" muttered Abdullah, amused. "How can they make such a claim when Renaissance Venice was a corrupt state, run by spies and assassins, with dungeons, daggers, and poison." He and Pagan were both tired, after hours of pacing through the richly ornamented palace, followed at a respectful distance by Abdullah's two bodyguards. Pagan's neck ached from looking at the sumptuous stuccoed ceilings and her feet were sore from the hard marble floors.

"At least only the Venetians elected their rulers," Pagan argued.

"They elected them from the aristocratic elite. That is not a free election in the democratic sense," Abdullah corrected her.

Stung by his patronizing tone of voice, Pagan retorted, "Five hundred years ago, Venice was still more democratic than Sydon is today. Your Council of Five isn't elected by a free ballot of all your citizens."

"Pagan, don't be stupid. Democracy can only operate in a country with literacy, a good standard of living and no endemic corruption. The average citizen of my country would vote for anyone who promised him two goats and a bracelet for his wife."

"Then why don't you do something about it?"

"You know that I'm trying." Abdullah's voice was frosty.

"I think you're happy as a benevolent despot," Pagan snorted.

"Democracy doesn't insure a healthy state. Good government does that."

"In a democracy, wealth isn't in the hands of a few tribal clans as it is in Sydon."

"That is a foolish remark."

"Oh, don't be so bloody pompous!" Pagan snapped, turning crossly on her heel. She strode through a doorway into yet another immense room. Hearing footsteps behind her, she turned to see that one of the Royal bodyguards was following her, while Abdullah, as if nothing had happened, was talking to the guide. Being a Royal tourist was worse than being a schoolgirl, Pagan thought irritably, you were never allowed to walk alone. After only one day, she found it oppressive. She started to walk faster. She was damned if she was going to be nannied.

As the Doge's Palace had been closed for their visit, Pagan moved with increasing speed through the empty rooms to the staircase which led down to the courtyard. But, as she dashed under the triumphal arch of the Palace and out into the crowded Piazza San Marco, she could hear the bodyguard clattering down the steps behind her.

Damned if I'm going to let Abdullah's bloody sheepdog round me up, she thought angrily, darting through a small herd of German tourists.

Seeing the restaurant where, that morning, they had drunk Bellinis, she ran blindly into the back and opened the washroom door. But it turned out to be the kitchen door. Pagan hurried past astonished waiters and cooks, past crates of fruit and vegetables, to the exit at the end of the room. Outside, she found herself in a small, smelly alleyway where the rosy evening sunlight reached only the highest balconies that overhung the dustbins of the restaurant.

Pagan darted into a doorway and peered round it at the restaurant kitchen door until she was sure that the bodyguard had not followed her. Then, jauntily, she set off down the alley, intending to go back to their hotel.

But, although they had explored the city by gondola that morning, Pagan suddenly realized that she had no idea where she was or the address of her hotel. No problem. Venice is a small town. When she found a canal, she could walk until she saw a water-taxi, then ask him to take her to the Cipriani.

Getting lost had never worried Pagan. However far she wandered as a child, she had always been able to find her way across the Cornish moorland, back to Trelawney. In fact, she rather liked not knowing where she was, Pagan thought, as she turned into another alleyway; life seemed full of delicious, unexpected possibilities when she was lost. I wonder why I like surprises and hate routine, Pagan mused, as she considered whether to cross a carved stone bridge to her left or to plunge into the maze of alleys on her right.

At the top of the arched bridge, Pagan stopped and watched the dirty gray canal below, crowded with boats of every kind. She could also see the landing place, where the little launches—taxis of the town—were taking on passengers. She moved toward it, but when she had nearly reached the landing, Pagan changed her mind. An hour of freedom in Venice was not something to be squandered, just because your feet hurt. She turned and strolled in the opposite direction.

Seeing an enormous wooden door ajar, Pagan walked inside, and found herself in an incense-scented church. Unlike the magnificent churches that she had visited with Abdullah, which were more like picture galleries than places of worship, this was a working church. Dressed in black, several old women were praying; the statue of the Saint, Anthony of Padua, was encircled by half-burned votive candles. An array of gold and silver tinfoil images were pinned to the wall, messages of thanks to the saint who had granted the prayers of worshippers. The tinfoil hands, feet, arms and legs, were for healed injuries; tinfoil babies were from once-childless couples; tinfoil hearts with crowns, roses, or ribbons around them were from newlyweds. These people don't hide what they want, thought Pagan. That's one of the differences between the English and the Italians.

The huge door creaked as she squeezed through it, into fading daylight. As Pagan turned around the corner, she heard the door behind her creak again, then light footsteps on the steps. Pagan suddenly realized that those steps had been much too quick for the arthritic old ladies in the church. The pearly light of the Venice evening was fading fast, as Pagan hurried back toward the canal. Only she hadn't been walking toward the canal, she discovered. She stood in front of a narrow waterway with houses rising straight out of the dark water. Suddenly, she recognized a fall of asparagus fern from a first-floor balcony down the path on her left. Aha, she'd noticed that this morning; she was on the correct route.

Again she set off, confidently. Again she heard the light, stealthy footsteps behind her.

She stopped and looked over her shoulder, her heart starting to thump, as she realized that it was some time since she had passed anyone in these narrow alleys.

The footsteps also stopped. Pagan started to hurry between the high, crumbling walls.

She stopped again and listened. The light pitter-patter of footsteps behind her stopped again.

Pagan spun round. The road curved behind her and she could see no one, but she was certain that someone was following her and, suddenly, Pagan was frightened.

Darkness was falling and, as she began to run, Pagan thought, it's not Abdi's bodyguard, I'm sure I lost him. Perhaps it's a mugger? I'll go back to the church and ask one of the old women to help me. No one will mug me in a church. She ran faster.

As she scuttled down empty lane after empty lane, blindly turning corners at any faintly familiar sight, Pagan realized that she had no idea where she was. And as she ran along the crisscrossing labyrinth of dank alleys, the footsteps behind her grew louder and closer. Pagan stopped helplessly at yet another crossroads.

Suddenly, a powerful hand grabbed her by the shoulder and spun her around.

It was Abdullah.

With relief, she threw her arms around him. "I thought you'd never catch up!"

"Why were you running?"

"I thought someone was following me," she said, unwilling to admit that she had been frightened.

"Do you know where you are?"

"No. Where are we?"

"I haven't the faintest idea." He put his arm around her. "You know you're in the most confusing city in the world."

"I think we're near the fish market." Pagan wrinkled her nose.

"The whole of Venice smells of that watery, rotting smell," Abdullah dismissed her suggestion.

Around the corner, they found themselves in the deserted fish market.

"At least we know where we are." Triumphantly, Pagan pointed. "There's the canal! Now, all we have to do is find a water-taxi!"

Abdullah looked at her tired face, drew her to him and kissed her.

"I've been hoping you would do that all day." Pagan wound her arms around his lean body. "It's so nice to be without your bodyguard chaperones."

"You should be used to them by now." Abdullah brushed her eyebrows with his lips.

"I don't think I'll ever get used to them; they make me feel claustrophobic. I'm so glad I managed to throw them off."

Abdullah pulled back, alarmed. "I sincerely hope you have not thrown them off." He quickly looked around. "If they aren't behind us, then we must return to the hotel immediately."

They hurried on. As they crossed the wet market cobbles, Pagan heard the stealthy noise of following feet. Again, she felt a twinge of panic. "Abdi, I think someone is following us. Maybe the bodyguards are catching up, after all?"

"Nonsense, Pagan, it's just the echo of our own footsteps. You always hear that in Venice, the sound ricochets around all the little alleyways."

"Yes, of course," Pagan's voice was doubtful. There were footsteps behind them, coming from the deserted market buildings.

Pagan and Abdullah had almost reached the canalside, when, from a side street, two young men stepped out and blocked their path.

Abdullah pushed Pagan into a doorway with one hand and, with the other hand, he seized one of the men around the neck, grappling for the pressure point, through which he could make the man unconscious.

There was a dull glint of metal as the second youth opened a switchblade and circled the two struggling men, looking for his chance to attack.

"Run, Pagan! They've got knives!"

Abdullah slipped on the slimy stones and fell, losing his grip on his opponent, who fell with him.

Pagan was no longer frightened. She felt calm and almost elated, as she whipped off her high-heeled shoes and flew at the attacker on the ground, when he tried to get up. With her metal-tipped stilettos, Pagan lashed at his head. As the second man lunged forward, Abdullah seized his knife hand, and then, with an agile heave, he threw both the attacker and the weapon into the canal.

As Abdullah whirled to help Pagan, the second youth managed to dodge her blows and started to run along the canalside, chased by Abdullah. The mugger ran fast, but he was unlucky. As he rounded the next corner, he blundered straight against the broad chests of Abdullah's bodyguards.

"You're carrying a knife as well!" Pagan gasped to Abdullah. "Goodness, you fight dirty." She pushed her hair out of her eyes.

"All Kings fight dirty," Abdullah panted. "When you are a King," he added, adjusting his tie, "you must always fight to win."

That evening, they had dinner on the terrace of their suite, looking at the blazing lights of the Piazza San Marco across the lagoon. Abdullah waited until the silver tray of coffee had been removed, then he leaned forward to Pagan, who was wearing her dark green Fortuny.

Abdullah said, "Shut your eyes."

She heard his chair scrape against the stone flags as he rose, then she sensed that he was standing behind her. She felt his hands lift the hair from the back of her neck and place something warm and heavy on her collarbone, as Abdullah murmured, "I hope that by now you're old enough to accept a necklace from me."

Pagan rushed to the huge Venetian glass mirror in the salon. A necklace of platinum links, scattered with emeralds, lay against her pale, freckled chest.

In the mirror, she saw Abdullah approach and hold her shoulders. He started, "We worked well as a team this afternoon. . . ."

"You're not just a pretty face," Pagan allowed.

"You aren't as tough as you think you are," Abdullah grinned.

"You really were protective."

"You really were aggressive," Abdullah said. "Can't we be together for longer than two days?"

Pagan suddenly felt nervous. "I don't know."

"Would you spend the rest of the summer at my place in Cannes?"

"I don't know," she stalled.

"If I invited Maxine and Charles, would you come?"

"I've never thought of Maxine as a chaperone before." Abdullah's insistent black gaze made Pagan feel as if her guts were dissolving. "I think that would be . . ." She had intended to say impossible, but heard herself say, "Wonderful!" As she said it, bursts of falling green and pink stars were reflected in the water from a fireworks display on the other side of the lagoon.

Abdullah held Pagan's bare shoulders and turned her toward him. She closed her eyes and turned her face up to him, expecting a kiss, but instead, Abdullah said earnestly, "Listen to me, Pagan. I have to explain to you about Sydon. The Fundamentalists are getting help from the Communist bloc, and if I can't defeat their guerrillas soon, I'll have a full-scale war on my hands. I can't defeat them without American arms and aid, and at the moment I can't get help from the Americans."

Pagan hadn't expected a political lecture. "I know that modernization has brought you problems," she said, hiding her disappointment.

"Another of my problems is the women of my country."

"In what way?" Pagan asked, without much interest at that moment, in the problems of other women.

"In every way. It has been far harder for the women, than for the men, of my country to become part of the modern world. In the old days, when they lived behind the veil, they were completely dependent on their men, but also completely protected. Independence frightens them, but they cannot cling to the old ways forever." A burst of golden sparks cascaded across the sky, as he added, "They pity Western women, struggling along without male protection. . . ."

"But they don't!" exclaimed Pagan.

"Under Koranic law, a man is obliged to support all the women of his household. A Western man can discard his wife, with very little responsibility. So a Western woman does not always have the absolute security that she thinks she does."

Thinking of her divorce from her first husband, Pagan could only nod, as Abdullah continued, "Nevertheless the younger women of my country are starting to question some of our traditional ways."

"Such as?"

"As you know, female infibulation is still practiced. And a woman's body belongs to her father or her husband, like their goats."

"I know all that, Abdi, you've told me over and over again. Why are we discussing it now?" Pagan was puzzled.

"Because unless women play an active part in my country, we can never be part of the modern world." A screaming green rocket flared briefly and fell into the sea. "I need an experienced, diplomatic, sophisticated woman with organizational ability at my side. That is what my country needs."

"You sound as if you're drafting a want ad," Pagan told him, "gynecological experience an advantage."

Abdullah released her shoulders and walked across the terrace to the balustrade, then turned to face her. "I need someone who understands Western ways, and Western women, and the need for our women to assert themselves."

"Why not propose to Gloria Steinem?"

Abdullah's mouth twitched with anger. "I swore to myself that I would not lose my temper. Pagan, I will *not* allow you to misunderstand me again." He shook her by the shoulders. "I realize that you're headstrong, impulsive and . . ."

"Self-conscious?" Pagan interrupted him. "Mustn't forget that. That's why we used to have so many rows when we were young. You were nervous and pompous and I was just nervous."

Behind Abdullah's back the white filigree facade of the Doge's Palace gleamed in the floodlights at the far side of the lagoon. Abdullah said, "We are no longer young."

Pagan laughed. "You're so tactful. But, Abdi, I still feel young and nervous and uncertain when I'm with you."

"You would get used to me."

Suddenly, Pagan realized the reason for the political lecture.

Abdullah said, "Yes, I want you to marry me!" Earnestly, he said, "Let's not mess it up again, Pagan."

"I can't believe it."

"I knew you'd say that." He rose again and strode away to the edge of the terrace again, silhouetted against the gold flares of the fireworks as they whistled over the sea.

Pagan rustled across the terrace and laid her hand on his arm. "You don't understand . . . " she began.

Abdullah interrupted her. "Yes, I do understand, Pagan. You're afraid of being humiliated again, you're afraid that I'll reject you again, as I did when I was nineteen." He sighed. "Please remember that was a bloody long time ago!"

Pagan said, "It's true, I don't want the pain of hoping again, Abdi. I don't want the uncertainty and then possibly . . . the realization that, at my age, I've allowed myself to hope for too much, that I've made a fool of myself again—but this time with the whole world watching."

Abdullah took both her hands in his. "But I *really* need you. *Especially* you, Pagan, because you have also been hurled from a life of ancient tradition into the modern world, so you will understand my people."

Pagan still felt as if she were being recruited for a particularly unpopular diplomatic post, rather than being courted by a man who wanted to marry her. She thought, here we are in this beautiful romantic place, the moonlight is trembling on the waves and the gondoliers are poling around down there, singing love songs, and Abdi's talking to me as if he were hiring a Middle-East liaison executive.

"I can see why you need a Kinga," said Pagan, "but I'm not sure I understand why you need a wife."

There was a pause. "For the usual reasons." He looked away from her.

"Abdi, in the center of her heart, every woman is always seventeen, and this seventeen-year-old wants to hear it." I'll make him say it, if it kills him, Pagan promised herself. Every woman wants to hear it, and men never understand why.

Finally, Abdullah looked at the floor and muttered, "I love you."

Gently, Pagan said, "And I love you."

"Can I assume then that your answer is yes?"

Again, Pagan caught the odd, brisk note in his voice. Was this the notorious lover? The romantic playboy, the man who had spent a fortune on red roses? She said, "There are a couple of subclauses that we really should discuss."

Nuzzling her neck, he said, "I don't want to hear that you're not young enough or unsuitable in any way. Let's brush these insecurities aside."

"No, let's pull them all out in the open, *now*, Abdi. First of all, I think I'm too old for you."

"Kindly let me be the judge of that."

Pagan touched the green ribbon of the order of Semira, which hung over Abdullah's white dinner jacket. "I know this isn't the traditional moment to bring this up, but it's very important to me. I must know. Do you intend to be a faithful husband, Abdullah?"

"Why must you Westerners confuse sex and love? Sexual fidelity has little to do with marriage."

"*Do you intend to be faithful to me*?" Pagan felt as if she were walking on eggshells, but she was determined that Abdullah should answer her question. "After all, in the East, sexual fidelity has a lot to do with marriage—for the wife. Adulterous women are still occasionally beheaded, aren't they? So what are your intentions, Abdullah?"

"When one knows that one can have any number of nubile young women by snapping one's fingers, one feels less inclined to snap them."

"Abdi, don't evade my question. Will you be faithful to me?"

"I cannot say."

"We're being honest," she reminded him.

He paused. "Then I doubt it."

"You might feel inclined to snap the fingers?"

"We're being honest."

Pagan felt a dull ache. "Then my answer must be no," she said with dignity, as her ache turned to pain. She pulled away from him, disappointed and angry. "Why are you so impossibly arrogant?"

"You asked me to be truthful. But once again you put your pride before reality." He looked at her, trying to control his anger. "I swore that I wouldn't let you lose my temper again."

"Me—lose *your* temper!" Pagan shouted.

Abdullah grabbed her hand. "We must stop this, Pagan." He controlled himself with difficulty. "We're having a quarrel about something that happened thirty years ago."

"Something that didn't happen, you mean." Pagan's tone was bitter.

"Something that could happen now," he insisted gently, pulling her toward the couch.

Pagan thought, he's just demonstrated the perfect way not to propose to a woman. She said, sadly, "Abdullah, I don't think such a marriage would ever work."

The last of the fireworks spluttered out and the sea seemed darker than before. Abdullah accepted temporary defeat. "But you will still come to Cannes?" he asked quietly.

"Are you sure you want me to come?"

"I think we should both consider what we may be missing."

Does he mean it or doesn't he? Pagan wondered. It was like listening to those pursuing feet earlier and trying to work out where the sound was coming from; every indication seemed deceptive.

But I'll never know if I don't dare to find out.

"I'll come to Cannes," she promised him. "After my Drury Lane Gala."

CHAPTER 12

July 1979

"W*E'VE MADE A* lot of extra money on the drinks, party and the raffle." The Scottish Duchess looked around the ballroom. Bare-shouldered women in bright taffeta gowns talked to men with pearl-studded shirt fronts, on their best behavior.

Pagan, whose face ached with smiling at her guests, was hardly listening as she anxiously wondered whether the hotel had allocated enough waiters.

"It's a long time since I've seen so many real tiaras," said the Duchess. "Hardly anyone wears their real jewels today. Nicole Birmingham said that the last time she wore her aquamarines, it cost five thousand dollars for the insurance and the bodyguards, so the next morning she went straight round to Kenneth Lane."

Pagan anxiously eyed the clock set in the wedding-cake plaster molding above the door. Another five minutes and she'd have to make her speech, then marshall the two thousand guests to the Theater Royal, Drury Lane.

Suddenly the banquet manager was at Pagan's side. "May I have a word with you, milady?"

"What's wrong, Mr. Gates?"

"I've just spoken to Mr. Zimmer, who telephoned from the theater. He told me to tell you that they've had a slight technical problem, something to do with the fire curtain. So Mr. Zimmer asked if you would announce that the Gala will take place an hour later than scheduled, at eight-thirty. He told me to tell you not to worry, everything is under control, the engineer just needs time."

"What a nuisance, Mr. Gates," said Pagan, thinking *bloody* fire curtain, "I'd better tell everyone straight-away."

She made her way to the podium, climbed up the steps and took the microphone. "My lords, ladies and gentlemen . . ."

"The curtain should have gone up ten minutes ago, but there isn't one person out front." There were tears in Lili's eyes as she peeped through the red velvet stage curtains. Beyond it were two thousand empty theater seats.

The stage manager, his bow tie askew, nodded tensely. "There's still no sign of anyone in the theater. Not one person."

Beyond her heavy stage makeup, Lili's eyes looked scared. Nervously, she pulled up the long black glove which covered her right arm. "I can't believe it." She shook her head, scattering spangles from the three white Prince-of-Wales ostrich feathers that hung from her skullcap. "What the hell has happened?" She bit her bottom lip to control her agitation, then nervously smoothed the skintight black velvet dress which left one shoulder and one leg bare.

"I don't know." The stage manager ran his hands through his greased blond hair. "They should have poured through the doors at least half an hour ago. The theater is absolutely empty."

Lili tapped her silver shoe, her leg, elegant and taut as that of a polo pony, in her gleaming silver tights. "Please check the tickets again. Please check that they printed the correct date!"

"We've already checked. There's nothing wrong with the invitations." The stage manager looked helpless. Charity benefits—run by amateurs—were always a nightmare.

Zimmer put his arm around Lili. "Don't cry, darling, or you'll have to redo your makeup. Best thing is to get back to your dressing room, like everyone else. Stash will find out what the hell's happening."

Lili's agent nodded, patted her spangled shoulder, then hurried to the stage-door telephone.

Zimmer knew that this was not a run-of-the-mill theatrical disaster; there must have been some colossal street accident near the hotel, maybe a 707 had crashed in Piccadilly, but his job was to calm the leading lady, so he said, "Toughen up, Lili. You're a professional, remember? Worse things have happened in the theater. Nobody's dropped dead on stage. Abraham Lincoln hasn't been assassinated out front. The Phantom of the Opera is still in Paris."

Lili gave him a weak smile. Zimmer was at his best when things were going wrong; the worse the crisis, the calmer he became.

Stash reappeared in Lili's dressing room. "Mystery solved," he said. "They're all still at Grosvenor House because someone announced that we had backstage problems, and that the opening had been postponed for an hour. I managed to speak to Lady Swann and she's going to get everyone here within fifteen minutes. They're radioing for every cab in London."

Zimmer said, "It'll take fifteen minutes to seat everyone. So, Lili, you've got half an hour to calm down, to think yourself into your role and keep your legs warm."

He was right. Lili reached for her grubby purple leg-warmers.

"And check your makeup, darling," said Zimmer. Tears had smudged her thick black eyeliner. "Then concentrate on your part, Lili. Forget everything else. Leave it to me."

Zimmer knew that any actor is in a fragile state of mind before going on-stage. Often the half hour before curtain-up is spent quietly sitting in a chair and thinking himself into his part, concentrating only upon what lies ahead and blocking out any extraneous thoughts. During that time an actor hates to be spoken to, or interrupted. A good actor produces his performance from inside himself, which is an unconscious process; he's learned his lines, he's studied, he's rehearsed with the rest of the cast, and before curtain-up time is when the part takes over the actor. The conscious mind is suspended as the subconscious takes over, transferring all rehearsed input into a living performance.

Twenty minutes later, there was a tap on the dressing room door and a distraught Pagan appeared in a tulip-skirted cream satin dress, and Abdullah's emerald collar.

"I don't know what's happened, Lili, but I know that someone's tried to ruin our benefit and *we're not going to let them.* You'll have a full house in fifteen minutes."

"It's all very well for you, Pagan," said Lili, sounding exhausted. "You don't have to go out there and smile and knock 'em dead, as if nothing had happened."

"Lili needs to be alone, now," Zimmer said firmly. He led Pagan out of the dingy dressing room and up to the backstage area, where the crowd of dancers were sweating in the hot July night. Zimmer tiptoed across the stage, peeped through the spyhole in the center of the curtain, then tiptoed back to Pagan.

"They're coming!" he confirmed, then turned to the theater manager. "Please get your security men to search the entire theater. Tip up every seat, check the flies and the scenery storeroom, empty the lavatory cisterns, clear the street outside."

"We can't possibly do that, it'll delay the performance even longer!" The house manager promised himself that he'd never let the theater owner give another charity event, so long as he still worked at that theater.

"We know that someone out there doesn't like Lili," Zimmer said. "So we must insist on a full security check." He turned back to Pagan. "This is a terrible thing to happen to a performer, the opening is going to be very tough for Lili."

"I know. That's why my opening speech is going to be different from what I'd planned."

Pagan found that her legs were shaking, as she walked out to the center of the stage. A stagehand pulled the red velvet curtain aside for her. She took a deep breath and stepped through the opening. The spotlight temporarily blinded her. She held up her hand for silence and saw the upturned faces in the front row seats. Beyond them was blackness, although Pagan knew that they had a full house, as she beamed at her audience and started.

"Many things can disturb a star's self-confidence, but the one nightmare that every performer knows about is that no one will come to watch the show. Because without an audience, there can be no performance." Pagan was aware of the hush in the theater, as she went on. "Tonight, for almost an hour, it seemed as if that nightmare had become a reality, for Lili, our star. . . ."

After Pagan ended her speech, a few scattered handclaps quickly grew into a roar of applause. Pagan hurried into the wings as the curtains drew back and the lights dimmed, leaving the stage black. Then a single spotlight picked out the silhouette of Lili's small, silver-spangled figure at the top of the elaborate staircase.

The applause became a standing ovation, as the audience clapped, and shouted their approval, for a full five minutes before Lili could start to sing. "*C'est Paris. . . .*"

" '. . . can only praise her jaunty courage,' that's the *Mail.*" Lili's agent tossed the newspapers onto Lili's bed, pulled off his black leather gloves and unbuttoned his vicuna coat. "The *Times* says you're the natural successor to Piaf and Garland, and the *Sun*'s given you the front page—'Sex Goddess Lili Drama.' They've all run it as a news story. You've got great coverage."

"And you still have no idea who planned this horrible joke."

"All we know about him is that he must have plenty of money. It was an expensive operation."

"Talking of expenses, did you send the money to Teresa?"

On the nightstand lay a delicate pair of gold handcuffs from Van Cleef in Cannes. An empty bottle of Bollinger, and a lipstick-smeared champagne glass stood beside a plastic bag of cotton balls and a small pharmacist's box of amyl nitrate capsules. The other glass lay smashed on the floor, beside a purple satin, black-fringed negligee.

Teresa was wearing an elaborate, black leather Barbarella costume with four-inch spike heels on her black leather thigh boots. She was lovingly cooing scatological insults into the ear of the stout man who lay on the bed beside her.

"Please stop," he begged. "Don't be so cruel, I didn't mean it."

"You mean you lie to me as well." She shoved him away from her and he fell over the side of the bed to the floor, yelping as his body hit the broken champagne glass.

He crawled away from the bed on his hands and knees. Nimbly, Teresa jumped off the bed, kicked his wobbling, hairy backside with her high heels, then, with a practiced hand, she flourished her thin black whip over her head, just missing the plastic chandelier.

He whimpered, "Don't kick me, don't kick me, please."

"These boots are filthy," she snarled, "you haven't cleaned them properly!" She took another neat jab at his rear, thinking, I'd better be careful, I don't want to mark him.

As expertly as a rodeo cowboy, she lighted flicked his ear with the whip. "Turn around," she commanded, thinking she'd better get this over fast, she didn't want to be late for her tennis coach this afternoon at Washington's prestigious Potomac Club. She jabbed at the fat man's pendulous stomach. "Now, lick my boots!"

As the man did so, Teresa could see that at last his claret-colored private parts were responding. Thoughtfully, she tickled his spine with her whip, then threw it on the bed and leaned backward toward the cotton balls and the capsules.

She kept up the litany of abuse and, from time to time, she gave him an encouraging whack with her hairbrush, as she deftly wrapped the capsules in cotton, then twisted them in a handkerchief.

"Ah . . . ah . . . ah," he groaned in ecstasy. Teresa looked down. The john was nearly ready for her. He wasn't a bad old boy and he was generous. She'd give him an extra kick or two, on the house. After all, she *was* getting paid twice over.

"You'll never learn to do it properly, you filthy pig." She pulled her feet away from his tongue and reached for the whip. Briskly, she kicked him flat, turned him over with an economical jab of her toe, and straddled the whimpering plump body. With her left hand she reached for his penis. Her right hand grabbed the empty champagne bottle, smashed it against the lumpy handkerchief, and then briskly held it under the fat man's nose. A purplish-red flush suffused his face and neck; Teresa heard inarticulate noises, gurgles, and groans as he turned purple and his pop-eyes looked up at her in ecstasy.

How much more can this old bastard take? wondered Teresa. By the time she got back to Paris, her backhand would be invincible.

* * *

"Would you please stick this in a red file before you leave for the night?" said Judy. In her personal office, all productive work which had an end aim—and a deadline date—was put in a red, transparent plastic envelope. These red files had their own "in," "pending," and "fallow" tray. All "in" red file work was always done first thing in the morning, before any other work was discussed, even before the telephone was lifted. This meant that priorities were painlessly sorted out and the achievement work was dealt with before the routine work.

The secretary left the office and Judy picked up the projected advertising figures for August. Next month looked as if it was going to be even more depressing than July; summer was always a thin period for advertising revenue.

There was a knock and Tony entered. "You left this file in the car, Judy. Gee, I'm sorry we've lost Lady Mirabelle." Judy looked up in surprise. Tom had said that nobody knew they'd lost that account. As Tony left the office, he almost collided with Tom, who was entering. Tom waited until the door had closed, then he said, "Okay, Judy, we're ready to go belly up, if it has to be. I've prepared for everything except hocking our watches."

Night after night, after the staff had gone home, Tom had secretly worked to prepare *VERVE!* magazine for closure. Bit by bit, Tom had transferred every asset owned by *VERVE!* magazine into the names of two holding companies which had been set up for the purpose. Now, everything tangible, from the office lease to the messenger-boy's motor-bike, might be saved from the wreck so that they might start again. Tom had checked through all the staff contracts and, without Judy's knowledge, quietly negotiated for two of the longest-employed editors to be offered good jobs on rival magazines, thus saving their compensation payments from his company. He had set these strategic savings against the disastrous projected loss. He no longer felt any regret for the years of business triumph, only the calm determination of self-preservation. Tom's clear head and inventive business brain would, he hoped, save the roof over both his families; Kate didn't know of the impending crisis, but now she owned their apartment and their country house. His ex-wife and two sons had a trust fund that could be touched by no one. Tom had always been more realistic than Judy. Although he took high risks in business, they were always carefully calculated. A good gambler always knows bad luck when he meets her, knows that when he's on a losing streak, he has to toss the cards on the table, stand up and say good-bye.

"I'm afraid they'll have to be shot, Suliman, as quickly as possible. Give the orders at once." General Suliman saluted and left the room. Abdullah leaned back and allowed his eyes to close for a few moments. He pinched the bridge of his sharp aquiline nose, where a knot of tension had formed between the winged black eyebrows. Then he rose, walked slowly to his London Embassy, over the green grass of St. James's park and looked up the Mall, toward the severe gray stone of Buckingham Palace. He'd returned from Venice the day before, to find a crisis waiting on his desk, of course.

His ancestors had not known the comfort or the complications of civilization. Their life was simple because there was very little to clutter it up: neither possessions nor sentimental attachments; but what his Bedouin ancestors possessed was the ultimate luxury of freedom; their lives were circumscribed by the cruel physical environment and pitiless discipline of the desert, but their spirit was free. Suddenly, Abdullah felt the old, familiar urge for the harsh peace of the desert. He sighed and moved toward the drawing room.

"Well?" Pagan pushed her heavy mahogany hair back and looked at Abdullah with concern. He seemed to have grown ten years older in the two days that he'd spent anxiously considering the fate of those three terrorists.

"Execution." Abdullah took the chair next to her, his somber face and khaki uniform contrasting with the blue silk cushions. "My father was right. Forget the smell of mercy when dealing with your enemy."

You don't have to teach a cat to sit by the fire, Pagan thought, and you don't have to teach a Bedouin to be cruel. The desert is cruel, and so is anyone who survives in it. Desert life is so harsh, that punishment has to be even harsher. Pagan could understand Abdullah's Bedouin nature, but she wondered if she could ever get used to it. "Your father never had to deal with the Moslem Fundamentalists," she said doubtfully, privately thinking that the old bugger had only had to deal with the traditional gang of power-crazed second cousins trying to stab each other in the back.

"No, but he had his own fanatics to put down," said Abdullah.

"Will the priests find out?" Pagan knew that if the terrorists were executed, Abdullah risked making them martyrs.

"Not immediately. When they get no news of their men in prison, then they'll know, but too late. It's hard to make martyrs months after the event. And if these men had been popular in their own village, there would have been a greater outcry when they were arrested. The priests were unable to whip up much of a demonstration. I think their power is weakening, at last. The priests exploit the ignorance of the people. In Sydon, we've had to achieve centuries of development in thirty years. It's the same for every nation on the Gulf; I don't want my country to go the way of Iran. I will not see Sydon hurled back into ignorance and superstition. My job is to guide my people into the twentieth century."

He jumped up and prowled around the room, remembering his dusty country, neatly wedged between Oman and the United Arab Emirates on the Persian Gulf. He thought of the camels and Cadillacs side by side on the desert roads, the extremes of feudal poverty and half-assimilated modern sophistication.

"I've disposed of eleven revolutionary groups since I became King." His voice was somber. "Each one of them was led by one of my own blood relations, and they were all executed."

Pagan thought, no wonder Abdi has only one heir.

"They all want the same thing—power. The priests are no different, except that they use the sacred name of the Prophet to justify their betrayal. They confuse and frighten my people, who, like all people, hate change. It's difficult for them to change from our traditional ways to the modern way of life that's been developed in the West. They prefer to rush back to the Middle Ages."

"It's the same choice for you, isn't it?" ventured Pagan.

"What do you mean?" Abdullah looked at her in surprise.

"You're also stuck between two worlds, aren't you? You can't be an absolute ruler like your father . . ."

Born in the East, Abdullah had been deliberately educated in the West so that he would be capable of dealing with the rulers of the West. Through his Western ego, he had learned to criticize his own people; he had dropped one culture and not been accepted by another. So he felt an isolation in his life and Pagan had spotted this long ago.

Abdullah perched on the arm of Pagan's chair and kissed the tip of her freckled nose. "My father's problem," he said, "was persuading the nomad to build a house. Then his problem was persuading the nomad to build a lavatory in the house. After that, when I became King, the problem was to teach the nomad to stand in front of the lavatory instead of climbing on the bowl. Now, if the priests are not controlled, the nomads will convert their cisterns into camel-troughs because the priests tell them it is not the way of Allah to piss indoors."

Where other women felt an urge to rearrange the furniture, Maxine rearranged the now priceless treasures of the de Chazalle family. Years ago, she had saved them from mildew and moth when she had saved the chateau by opening it to the public, as a beautifully presented, historic showcase which also promoted the family champagne business.

When Pagan arrived at the Chateau de Chazalle, she was shown to the wide, Chinese-yellow picture gallery on the first floor, known to the public as the History Walk, although the family called it Ancestor Alley.

Maxine, in her stockinged feet, was standing on a chair and hacking at a gold picture frame with a kitchen knife.

"Whatever are you doing, Maxi?" Pagan blew her a kiss. "Why are you ruining that picture frame?"

"I'm not ruining it, I'm distressing it," Maxine smiled down at her. "I'm making it look old and worn, as if it has been hanging here for at least one hundred years, instead of three days."

"What's the point of that?"

Maxine jumped off the chair and kissed Pagan on the cheek. "It's the essence of shabby chic, the way that aristocratic houses should look. Anyone with money can have everything new, but it's far more difficult to achieve this slightly worn, not-perfectly-matched, artlessly charming look of a room in which a priceless painting hangs next to a watercolor of Sorrento by your grandmother."

"But what's chic about having a chipped picture frame?"

"Anyone with money can buy that glossy magazine look. You need generations of family history to feel comfortable with an Aubusson carpet that's worn on one corner, chintz curtains that are faded because they've been hanging at the same windows for over one hundred years and Chinese hand-painted wallpaper that is, perhaps, a little dim because it was painted in the eighteenth century by Chinese artists whom your ancestors imported from China to do the job."

"But what's the point?"

"Snobbery, darling Pagan. It's the new decorator look. The point of shabby chic is that you can't achieve it unless it is authentic, or unless you have a very clever decorator."

"Don't you ever stop working, Maxi?"

"If I enjoy work more than pleasure, then is it work or pleasure?"

"Crumbs, don't ask me. I hate decorating. If the shops have what I want in the right color, then it's the wrong size. Always. Sophia wants her bedroom redone for her birthday, and I really can't face it. She wants stripped pine furniture and a Victorian brass bed."

"I'll do it for you, if you like," Maxine offered, "but not in stripped pine and brass, that's too passe." She took Pagan's arm. "Now let me show you to your room, and then you can tell me why you have to see me so suddenly. What's so important that you can't talk about it on the telephone? What is it that can't wait until our holiday in Cannes?"

"I want to ask your advice. But first I want to talk to Charles."
"Charles! What on earth do you want to discuss with Charles?"
"Politics. Eastern politics."

After dinner, Pagan steered Charles to a green leather sofa in the library. She knew that Charles had Middle East associates, and he had known Abdullah as an acquaintance since he had married Maxine.

"Charles, I want to talk about Abdullah," she started, then felt embarrassed. "You know—Abdi, playboy of the Western world."

Charles twirled the brandy in his glass. "It's only in the West that people regard him as a playboy, Pagan. In his own country, and among the Gulf states, he's considered a brave, devoted leader." He sniffed his brandy. "Abdi is the most skillful of all the Gulf rulers at dragging his country into the twentieth century, although he's in such serious trouble at the moment."

"What do you mean?" Pagan, accustomed to listening with only half an ear while Abdullah talked of his state affairs, suddenly wanted Charles to tell her more. Now that Abdullah and she were apart, Pagan managed to drag his name into every conversation, no matter how odd the context.

"Like every other oil-boom people, the Sydonites are bewildered by the modern world, and confused about their national identity." Charles took a sip of his Napoleon brandy. "You really want to know more?"

Pagan nodded.

"The Fundamentalist guerrilla army is getting help from the Communists, Pagan. If Abdullah can't handle that situation, not only will he lose his country, but the red flag will shortly be flying over one of the most strategic positions on the coast."

"I had no idea . . . I didn't realize . . . "

"Combine that with the Iranian situation and the Ayatollah on the other side of the Persian Gulf and you might end up with Muslim fanatics controlling eighty percent of the world's oil—and taking their orders from Moscow."

"No wonder Abdullah's so grim about it all," Pagan murmured.

"Sydon is a grim place and it's a crazy place. In fact, the whole Gulf area is crazy. I've done business with Saudi Princes who wear silk shirts, drink whisky and speak better English than I do. But at their homes, their mothers and wives wear long black traditional robes. Then, underneath the robes they wear the latest Paris fashions, and the most wonderful jewelry, Christian Dior and Cartier. The women are never seen in public and only wear these beautiful clothes to drink tea with each other. And that's about all they're good for."

"What do you mean?" Pagan asked, intrigued.

"Because they've always been excluded from public affairs, most Arab princesses have no sense of social responsibility. They don't do a thing to help the poor of their country."

"How do *you* think a Gulf Princess should behave?" Pagan tried to sound casual.

Aha, thought Charles, so that's it.

"She shouldn't be spending her time watching video tapes, gossiping, and eating cakes. She should organize help for the young, the old, and the poor. She should do the sort of work you do for the Research Institute, Pagan."

"Do you think so?" Pagan didn't sound as casual as she had intended. She jumped up and fidgeted with a bowl of pink peonies. The library was filled with peonies and pink hydrangeas in blue chinoiserie bowls.

The following morning, Maxine suggested a walk in the park. "I want to get you on your own, Pagan," she said, as they strolled over the grass behind the bounding, pink-gray Weimaraners. "Now, what's up?"

Pagan burst out, "Maxine, why do men find it so difficult to say 'I love you'?"

"Ma chère, they say it, but not in those words. They say, 'I wouldn't be here if I didn't, would I?' or 'But I married you, didn't I?' "

Pagan stomped across the grass in silence.

"Words don't matter," Maxine encouraged. "It's the actions that count. Any Latin con-man can say 'I love you.' You must judge men by what they do, not what they say."

Pagan was silent until they reached a little arbor. They sat down under the lichen-covered statue of Apollo. Pagan said, in an off-hand voice, "What do you think the world would say if I married Abdi?"

Maxine jerked her head around so suddenly that her sunglasses almost fell off. So Charles was right. "You mean he's asked you, Pagan?"

"Yes, but I haven't said yes. That's why I wanted to talk to you. You remember how he behaved . . . when we were young. That's why I haven't said yes."

"Why not?" Maxine couldn't believe her ears.

"Because, if I married Abdullah I'd also be marrying his country, his people, his oil fields, his seat at OPEC, his Communist guerrillas, his backward people, and his oppressed women." Pagan bit her bottom lip. "I can't *cope* with all that, it scares me to death."

"Rubbish! You coped with that audience at the Theater Royal all right. You coped with Christopher's illness, you've raised thousands of dollars for the cancer institute. You have a positive genius for coping—except when you're in love." Maxine took off her sunglasses and stared at Pagan's worried face.

"But suppose he dumps me, like he did before?"

"So few women realize that there *is* life after humiliation. And why should he dump you?"

Pagan jumped up nervously. "Let's keep walking."

They sauntered in silence along the seven-foot-high box hedge that bordered the estate. Eventually, Pagan burst out, "I asked him if he intended to be faithful. The rotter said . . . well, he indicated . . . Maxi, the silly bugger said, 'I cannot promise you fidelity because I do not know if it is possible, I simply don't know.' "

Maxine laughed at Pagan's imitation of Abdullah's most pompous manner. "But that's very sensible of him. It doesn't mean that he's going to dump you. It means just the reverse. He's being very honest."

Pagan looked anxiously at Maxine, as if asking a fortuneteller to read the future. "But I don't think my pride would let me turn a blind eye to a crowd of young blondes with big tits. In theory, perhaps, but in fact, I'm pretty sure I couldn't."

"Pride has always come between you and Abdullah. Abdullah's fierce pride and your stubborn pride. You'll learn that one of the good things about getting older is that one learns to compromise, to give and take."

"So I've noticed with you and Charles. You give and Charles takes."

Reaching the curlicued, wrought-iron gates, they turned to walk back on the grass at the side of the drive. "Charles is very careful of my dignity," Maxine said, with dignity. "Well, nearly always. He has his little affairs, but he is very discreet, he never humiliates me. Well, hardly ever."

"That's what *you* settle for—your dignity and a quiet life. What is the difference between your dignity and my pride, Maxine?"

"I have decided to settle for ninety percent of the cake instead of fifty percent of the alimony." Maxine crossly removed her sunglasses.

"You see, here we are talking about divorce and I haven't even got married yet," giggled Pagan. Maxine began to understand how Abdullah might sometimes be exasperated by Pagan's flippant charm.

"Oh, Pagan," she sighed. "Abdullah is what you've always wanted. I can't understand why you don't jump at the chance of marrying Abdi, when you've been in love with him for years."

"Being in love is different from loving!" Pagan said. "I can't imagine loving Abdi in the way I loved Christopher. Christopher really cared about all of me; we trusted each other, so we could expose our vulnerability. I wouldn't like to risk exposing my vulnerability to Abdi. And he'll never trust anyone."

In the distance, the eighteenth century turrets of the chateau shone purple in the sun.

"But what about all the wonderful things that the hakim taught him when he was sixteen?" Maxine reminded Pagan.

Pagan hesitated. "When we're in bed, it's physically wonderful, but Abdi's not emotionally involved. That love doctor in Cairo taught him everything about eroticism and nothing about love. I don't want only a sexual relationship. I want warm intimacy and mutual concern."

"Perhaps you can change him?" Maxine made the female's fatal error of believing this to be possible.

"At least I'm not stupid enough to think that!"

"But if he's asked you to marry him and you're not certain, why not ask for a six-month engagement, a secret engagement that the world will never know about, to give you time to get used to the idea? You have nothing to lose with a secret engagement."

On the distant stone building, row upon row of windows glistened in the sunshine. Pagan turned the idea over in her mind. The most attractive aspect of Maxine's suggestion was that Pagan would now be able to put off her decision.

"Maxine, I think you've solved the problem," she said, looking at the row of fountains in front of the chateau terrace, where the July sun formed rainbows in the dancing water.

CHAPTER 13

August 1979

LAYER UPON LAYER of swan-white lace swayed softly as Sandy moved her hips, and the half-hidden diamanté brilliants twinkled like the stars in a Walt Disney sky. Sandy crossed her wrists in front of her, which pushed her breasts together and upward. The flounces helped as well, she thought, but she sure wished her tits were bigger.

"How much is it, Ken?"

The dress manufacturer's plump pink hand carefully smoothed the satin petals of the ice-pink rosebud between her breasts. "Let's not talk about the price, Sandy, just tell me what you think of it."

Sandy knew that when a man said "let's not talk about the price," the deal was going to be very expensive. However, the circuit gossip was that Ken liked it straight and came fast.

"Why it's just beautiful, Ken," she cooed, right into her Southern belle act. No girl got to be a beauty contest finalist in a dress run up by her mother, in spite of the rule that no evening gown could cost more than two hundred dollars. Which is why Ken Sherman loaned his dresses for publicity value, if he thought a girl had a good chance of winning the beauty pageant. And, of course, a girl had to be nice to Ken.

"I could not imagine a finer antebellum gown in the whole world," Sandy smiled her gleaming, wholesome smile. In the gloom of the deserted showroom, Ken twitched the pink satin sash into place, stood back from the spotlight and slowly nodded. No girl could lose in that dress. "Right," he said briskly. "Care for a cocktail at my place?"

"Why Ken, I would be honored," Sandy breathed. The bullshit level had to be higher, the closer you got to the top.

The bedroom floor and walls were covered by white fur. The lamps were Lalique crystal seashells and the circular bed was covered with a white leather spread, upon which lay Ken with his legs apart while Sandy cheerfully sucked his stiff little cock. The girls were right about Ken, this was the cheapest dress she'd ever acquired. But Sandy was merely making her down payment; Ken wanted more for his money, and he knew that he wouldn't have another chance after tomorrow's contest.

"Let's take a look at you." Ken pushed a white fur bolster behind her head and spreading out her waterfall of pale blond curls, he felt for the zipper of her silver lamé boiler suit and yanked at it. "Listen, baby, you got nothing to worry about, tomorrow." He took a look and thought they'd hardly make a 34B, as he ripped off the silver lamé. "Like some music?" He pushed a couple of buttons on the bedhead console that looked capable of flying a 747. Dolly Parton started to wail "Stand By Your Man" and, overhead, the remote control videocamera started to roll as Ken purred, "Why, you're as bald as a baby down there," and pushed Sandy onto her back.

Who did he think he was fooling with that mirrored ceiling, thought Sandy, as Ken squeezed gobs of her body lotion over her breasts. Obediently, she massaged the translucent white goo over her breasts; no wonder the bedcover was easy-wipe white leather. "Honey, you are amazing," she breathed as she thrust one immaculately manicured finger inside her pink gauze panties, then stuck her rump in the air and pulled at the bows which held the pink gauze in place.

Half an hour later, Sandy had been squeezed and shoved and pulled, pushed and arranged in a hundred different poses. She realized that the videotape must be running out, because Ken squeezed her breasts together, felt around her clitoris for a few moments, missed it, poured body lotion on his penis, shoved it inside her, gave ten very careful thrusts, gasped, rolled off, felt around for his cigarettes, and said, "What happened to the thatch, honey?"

"Electrolysis. Hurt like hell. Worse than having the teeth capped. They should give you an anesthetic."

Ken dragged on his cigarette. "So do we have a deal?"

"What sort of deal?"

"If you win the Miss International Beauty Pageant tomorrow, you'll need more gowns, at three thousand dollars a throw." He pushed his cigarette end into a built-in ashtray on the bedhead. "You get the gowns from me for ten percent of the prize money. And don't try to bargain, that's the going rate."

"Why, honey, whatever you say. I have no head for business."

Ken leered at Sandy. "You don't need a head in this business."

Sandy slid off the bed and smiled. "Honey, I've got to take a shower and get home for my beauty sleep." In the shower, she ran through her plans. When Ken showered, she'd jump on that bed and push at the mirrored tiles until she found the one that concealed the camera. You certainly *did* need a head in this business: only last year, the California Citrus Princess had been forced to resign, when a boyfriend published split-beaver pictures of her in a stud magazine.

By the third day of the Miss International Beauty Pageant, the Clarence Plaza Hotel in Miami overflowed with females of every age and shape. Like grown-up children playing with their Barbie dolls, pudgy professional mothers, often obese, chaperoned their still-slim, professional-virgin daughters. Looking as wholesome as strawberry yogurt, these girls had learned to be as tough as infantry boots, but the rules insisted on one chaperone per entrant, and a mother added greatly to the clean-living, all-American apple-pie atmosphere. The unspoken, uncodified, and unstated agreement was that this Image should be preserved, unsullied. This was why, however jealous, desperate, cynical, or vicious a competitor felt, she never let it show. The currency of conversation was always candy-coated The myth was that all the girls were loving friends.

Sandy's mother, wearing a peach polyester pants suit, sat on the terrace overlooking the swimming pool. Ostentatiously, she stitched the ice-pink rose on the front of Ken Sherman's extravagant gown; you scored extra points if your gown was homemade. Lying beside her, Sandy sunbathed in a swimsuit that was carefully cut to match her competition costume, so that her tan marks would match up. Sandy was certain of being one of the three finalists, and knew that she had a good chance of winning the title.

So did the other contestants. On the next lounger, Miss Canada propped herself up on one elbow and asked, with honeyed friendliness, "Are we going to see you use those wrenches today, Sandy?"

Sandy immediately dived into her tote bag and produced a pair of nickle-plated plumber's wrenches. "Why, honey, I never go *anywhere* without them. Good conversation point. Good defense weapon. And you'll see me use them in the talent section."

"How did you figure out your neat act?" marveled Miss Canada, who was sick of seeing Sandy giving her frank, freckle-nosed virginal grin, as she brandished her gleaming wrenches in contest after contest, to the delighted surprise of the crowds. Sandy allowed herself a moment of complacency. "It's easy if you've got personality." She put the wrenches back in her tote bag and reached for the suntan oil. They both knew that personality was the winning trick. It was what the judges were looking for, because they needed a girl who could speak up on a talk show or at an opening ceremony. Personality meant the ability to define your own chosen character in three words, and in Sandy's case it was SOUTHERN PLUMBER'S DAUGHTER.

"Sandy's always had personality." Her mother bit off the cotton thread and held up the seafroth-white gown for inspection. "Just as well, because she cracks the windows if she tries to sing, she can't dance worth a dime, and the only thing she was ever any good at was baton." Proudly she stroked the satin rose again. "Sandy, honey, your dress is all finished."

"That is the most adorable dress I have ever seen," Miss Canada said, sitting up and curiously looking at the delicate lace. "I can hardly believe it only cost two hundred dollars honey."

Sandy sauntered on stage in overlarge denim coveralls, with a red and white spotted handkerchief in the pocket, plumber's wrenches in each hand; she looked refreshingly wholesome. She began to twirl the wrenches as if they were batons, whirling them up in the air, then catching them with panache. As the banjo music slowed, Sandy mopped her forehead with the red handkerchief, gave it a flourish and pulled a bunch of flowers from it. After her little conjuring trick, the tempo of the music quickened, as Sandy produced three giant metal washers from the back pocket of her faded blue coveralls and deftly juggled the metal circles to a crescendo of applause. Sandy thought, fuck you, Miss Canada.

On the following evening, Sandy dripped blue drops into her eyes to make them sparkle; she cleaned her teeth with red toothpaste to make them extra white; she checked the thick tan makeup on her shoulders; she looked at herself in the mirror.

Perfect.

Then she squeezed into the tight white-satin corselette and hooped petticoat which went under Ken Sherman's gown. "Hook me up, honey," she murmured to Miss Canada, who was sticking on her left eyelashes. Carefully, Sandy stepped into the middle of Ken's white-lace masterpiece. Miss Canada felt for Sandy's zipper, then paused. "Hey, Sandy, something's wrong with this zipper."

Sandy instantly sensed disaster. She grabbed a hand mirror from the makeup counter, spun around and examined the rear view in the mirror. The zipper down the back of the gown had been slashed in a dozen places and, as she touched it, the zipper fell away from the dress.

What Sandy wanted to say was "holy fucking shit." What she automatically said was "Jeepers creepers." Using unladylike language was a sure way to get thrown out of a beauty pageant on the spot.

Goddammit, I told Mama not to let the dress out of her sight, Sandy thought, as she shrieked for the pageant supervisor. It was not abnormal for the best dress in the pageant to be sabotaged with a razor blade. It only took thirty seconds.

"Okay, you're on last," said the pageant supervisor, taking in the situation at a glance.

"Mama, go get the hotel maintenance man here with his toolbox," Sandy ordered.

When the bemused janitor arrived outside the dressing room door, Sandy dived into the toolbox for the roll of waterproof adhesive used to make temporary repairs in cracked water pipes. It was wide and strong and sticky on both sides. Swiftly Sandy cut twenty inches of the tape and ordered her mother to stick it down her back. Without a word, Sandy's mother spread a dust sheet on the floor, then held the dress as Sandy stepped into it. Clutching the white flounces to her breast, Sandy carefully lowered herself onto the dust sheet, face down. Then, while her mother held the edges of the dress in place, Miss Canada walked daintily on Sandy's spine, her bare feet pressing the dress firmly onto the double-sided strapping. Then both of them helped Sandy to stand up. She thought, thank Christ I really am a plumber's daughter, as she said, "Thanks. Guess I mustn't breathe too deeply, but I reckon every cloud has a silver living, because now I've got the last number." The last girl in the parade had the best chance of making a strong impression on the judges.

Sitting at the judges' table, Judy and Lili watched the endless stream of girls, glassy-eyed and stiff, walk down the catwalk towards the cameras, the host, and microphone. Their smiles were peppermint-fresh, their faces were peach-perfect and their flesh was the color of peanut butter.

"Can't think why they chose Miami in August," muttered Lili to Judy.

"Politics, politics," Judy murmured back to Lili, who had flown over from Europe for the judging. Both women had agreed not to stay in Miami for one minute longer than was necessary. The humid, tropical heat blasted them every time they left the over-elaborate lobby of their gaudy hotel, and within minutes their clothes would be soaked with perspiration, and the energy drained from their bodies.

The final parade, in formal gowns, was the first time that the audience had heard the girls speak. Each girl was interviewed to determine whether or not she had personality. Translated, that meant whether she would be able to stand up for herself on talk shows in the appropriately charming, self-deprecatory manner.

Suddenly, the hot, tired women in the theater gasped as Sandy glided down the wide staircase. Sandy looked as if she had been sprayed with lace foam that was slowly slipping down from her shoulders and about to reveal her body.

"Tell us about yourself, Sandy," encouraged the white-suited host as he handed the microphone to Sandy.

Sandy gave the judges her most brilliant smile. "I am majoring in social science and then I plan to be a teacher because I just love children." Pause at that point, thought Sandy.

"This is a beautiful dress you have on," the host prompted, holding the microphone under the tip of her nose.

"I usually make all my own clothes," Sandy confided, thinking, keeping the answers short, "but my Mama helped me with this." She blew a kiss to her mother in the audience.

"And what do you do in your spare time, Sandy?"

"I like to water ski, I go dancing and I'm taking an evening course in domestic engineering."

"*Domestic engineering?*" The host glanced briefly at his prompt card. "What is that, Sandy?"

"I guess it's just a fancy name for plumbing," Sandy repeated her confident laugh. "My Daddy's a plumber and he taught me all I know. When I get married I'll be able to fix the washing machine." Roars of applause.

"May I ask if you are courting at this time?"

"Do you mean, do I have a boyfriend?" Sandy moved closer to the microphone so that her voice sounded breathy. "Well no, I do not. Right now my life is just so full of opportunities that I want to get on and enjoy it to the full."

"And now, Sandy, for the final question," the host finished. "Tell us why you are proud of your country."

The beauty queens had all rehearsed their answers, but Sandy's reply sounded enthusiastically impromptu. "Because America really *is* beautiful, American really is friendly, and America really *is* free! I believe that America is the land of opportunity and I am the living proof of that. My Mama was a dancer from Sweden and my father came over from Ireland, when he was just a kid. Why, if it hadn't been for America they would never have met up." Sandy deliberately turned away from the host and waved to the close-up camera. "Hi, Mama and Daddy, I am so glad *you chose America!*"

The theater erupted in a storm of cheering and clapping. Many in the audience dabbed their eyes or wiped away tears as they stood and applauded. Sandy mentally evaluated her chances. Sudan was statuesque, almond-eyed, and the Third World girls always got sympathy votes. Sri Lanka might be an added threat, because she had been a stunning sight in her national costume, ultramarine silk, with tinkling bracelets on her tiny, high-arched feet.

As the ten nervous girls clattered up the backstage stairs, Sandy wondered why, for Chrissake, Canada had been selected. According to Sandy's research, Canada and the United States were never chosen together, since it was considered undiplomatic to pick neighboring countries. Maybe Canada has something going for her that we don't know about, maybe someone down here owes someone up there one big favor, Sandy decided as, carefully, she pulled her full skirt clear of her high heels, and walked across the dirty backstage floor, crisscrossed with electrical leads.

While the audience was entertained by a team of dancers in azure chiffon and sequins, the judges withdrew to a side room and considered their decision. Judy unpinned the lurid purple orchid from her cream silk lapel and pondered the three nordic, three hispanic, three black, and one oriental finalist; she realized that the color mix for the final line-up was as predictable as the colors in an ice-cream sundae.

The international photographer offered first opinion. "I want Sudan," he said firmly. "She's marvelously photogenic; she's got terrific presence, and she's unattached."

The Mirabelle man interrupted quickly. "Sudan would be of limited value to us." He meant that the Mirabelle range was not designed for a black skin. "Our vote goes to United States, her microphone manner was professional."

Lili asked, "What about Sri Lanka?"

Several judges shook their heads. "She'll never make it on talk shows."

"My vote goes to Italy," said the Hollywood agent.

"Italy is just a little bit adult for us." The Mirabelle man meant that, at the age of twenty-three, Miss Italy's skin had already lost the childlike smoothness that made mass-produced cosmetics look good in a high-definition color photograph. He added, "and United States has the look that Mirabelle will promote next year."

After another twenty minutes of argument, the judges marked their prepared ballots and tossed them into the wire basket held by the organizer, who announced with satisfaction, "United States it is, with Sudan second and Italy third."

When the prerecorded trumpet fanfare blasted and the host announced that Miss International Beauty of 1979 was Miss United States, Miss Sandy Bayriver from Louisiana, Sandy looked suitably astonished and elated, then wiped an imaginary teardrop from the corner of her eye, and allowed the host to lead her to the winner's throne. Gotcha, she thought, as yet another diamanté crown was placed upon her head.

Judy signed the hotel bill for two glasses of freshly squeezed lemon juice and turned over on her yellow sunbed, to let the Florida sun toast her back. Lili sat up and poured both packets of sugar into her glass. Lili's sweet tooth and Judy's taste for bitter drinks were both satisfied if they ordered two freshly squeezed lemon juices and Lili used all the sugar before adding water to both glasses. In ten months, this was the nearest they had come to a family custom.

Lili wriggled on her sunbed. "This heat! I'm going for another swim." She jumped up and ran toward the blue sea.

After a bit, Judy noticed that Lili's small red snakeskin purse lay between their two yellow sunbeds. The catch wasn't closed and the contents were spilling over the sand. Judy leaned forward and carefully shook sand from the lip gloss, the tissue and the unwritten postcards. Then she picked up the airmail envelope and froze as she noticed the Nicaragua stamp, Mark's familiar handwriting and his name on the back.

The envelope was still sealed, but it was badly sealed and only stuck down at the tip of the flap. Furtively, Judy started to raise the side of the envelope. She couldn't help herself. Peering into the envelope, she could just make out the words "love" and "helpless," then she heard Lili's voice behind her. Quickly she stuffed the letter back in the purse.

"It's no use. You'd think they'd leave me alone when the place is stuffed with beauty queens. I'm going inside to the air conditioning." Lili picked up the red snakeskin purse, stuck her sunglasses on, and walked toward the hotel.

Judy turned on her stomach and buried her face in her beach towel, to hide the tears which prickled her eyelids. Thank God Lili was flying back to Europe tomorrow.

Thank God this race was only five hundred kilometers, thought Lili, as the Riviera sun blazed down upon the raw, white-painted concrete of the pits, and hurt Lili's eyes with its savage glare.

This sun was almost as fierce as Miami's had been, last week. The only difference between the Paul Ricard circuit and the British tracks seemed to be that the grandstands were flanked with dusty tubs of oleanders, the French spectators were not quite so badly dressed as the British ones, and the car park was littered with empty wine bottles, rather than empty lager cans. Apart from these points, the tawdry souvenir booths sold the same tasteless BMW baseball caps, Ferrari bomber jackets and Lancia T-shirts as they did in Britain; the competitors were the same, they drove the same cars, the noise and the smell were exactly the same. Only the wording on the billboards was different—Michelin instead of Dunlop and Elf instead of Mobil.

Wistfully, Lili looked at the purple smudged hills in the distance and longed to be in the dappled shade of the pine forests instead of by this stinking, sunbaked racing circuit.

The low black Spear snarled past, hugging the ground like a sinister giant insect. Lili checked her stopwatch. Two seconds faster than his best practice time. With any luck, they'd be back in time to have a swim before dinner.

The PA droned on. "And halfway through this 400 km race, it's Werner Hentzen's Porsche in the lead, followed by the Dinetti, then Gautier in the Lancia . . . and the Spear has just overtaken the Lancia and it's pulling ahead. . . ."

Lili yawned, stuck her ear protectors back on and pulled the script for her next movie out of her leather hunting bag. It had arrived that morning, from Omnium Pictures. She would have some terrific outfits as Helen of Troy and, after the Mistinguett role, she was in good shape for another musical.

A blue airmail letter fell from the leather hunting bag. Lili sighed. She'd stuffed it in there this morning before Gregg saw it. Mark knew and used the secret code that was used to bypass Lili's fan mail, so she always received his letters. And she always tore them up, unread. It was the least she could do, she thought sadly, as she tore the pale blue envelope into strips, and threw it away. Then she turned her attention to the script.

By the time King Agamemnon had pitched his tent in sight of the walls of Troy, the Spear was challenging the Porsche for the lead, as the PA shrieked ". . . and with only three laps to go, the Spear is lying behind the Porsche and Werner Hentzen is fighting off the challenge. . . ."

By the time Paris wished that he had listened to Cassandra's prophecies, the PA was ecstatically screaming, "and now the Spear is neck and neck with the Porsche . . . and Eagleton has passed the Porsche! With only one lap to go, the Spear is in the lead. . . ."

Insulated from the noise by her earmuffs, Lili did not know that Gregg had gained the lead. Neither did she know, as the triumphant Hector wearily unstrapped his gleaming breastplate, that Gregg had lost the lead and fallen back behind the Porsche.

But after the giant wooden horse, its belly full of soldiers, had crossed over the plain toward the walls of Troy, the other spectators started to jump up and down and this distracted Lili from the script.

Lili pulled off her ear protectors, to hear the PA gabble ". . . and the Spear has taken the Porsche on the inside . . . now they're coming down the final straight toward the flag and it looks as if . . . yes . . . IT'S THE SPEAR . . . with the first win for Gregg Eagleton!"

Gregg was hauled out of the car, weighed down with a laurel wreath, soaked in champagne, kissed by half-a-dozen girls promoting a new cocktail mix, carried shoulder high to the grandstand, awarded a silver rose bowl, then more champagne, then photographed with his arm round Lili in a crush of champagne-drenched admirers.

Gregg posed for one last picture, then they stumbled away to the trailer park. The Spear, its wings coated with red dust, was being wheeled into its trailer by two mechanics. Gregg climbed into the driver's cab to change and shower in the tiny compartment behind the seat. The mechanics walked back to the pit to pack up their tools. Lili sat on the edge of the transporter, swinging her legs and waiting for Gregg.

Five minutes later, he climbed into the back of the trailer, his hair still damp from the shower.

"Give her a rest, darling!" Lili jumped up and picked her way into the dark, petrol-smelling interior, knowing that Gregg could not pass the Spear without wanting to lift the engine housing and fiddle with something. She didn't notice the elated gleam in his eyes and the urgency in his manner, as he pulled the lever that closed the back doors of the trailer.

"Gregg. Stop playing around! It's dark in here." Lili crossly felt her way forward in the dim, hot trailer and blundered into his arms. He kissed her hard, then pulled her up the ladder, to the driver's bunk above the seats.

"Stop it, Gregg. And it's as hot as hell in here!"

"Can't stop, I want you now." He kissed her harder, as he pulled off Lili's white linen shift, under which Lili was naked. The stink of oil and petrol normally made Lili feel faintly sick, but now it seemed erotic. Sweat poured from Gregg's body, as their flesh met and Lili felt a hot rush of warm pleasure.

"What's got into you?" murmured Lili.

Gregg said, "Winning. That's the real turn-on."

"This is such a wonderful view!" Pagan jumped onto the parapet of Abdullah's turreted chateau, and waved her arm at the lavender hills of the French Riviera. Her loose red cotton dress blew behind her like a flag in the breeze, as she turned to Maxine and said, "Aren't you glad you came? Who'd have thought all those years ago in Gstaad, that we'd still be friends today."

Maxine shrugged. "Perhaps we wouldn't be such friends if we all lived next door in each other's pockets. As it is, we're not round each other enough to demand more closeness or support than we're able, or want, to give."

"Maybe the secret of friendship is not being too friendly."

They left the roof and started to walk down the elaborate wide staircase of the sumptuous chateau, passing richly colored tapestries, suits of moorish armor and crimson-brocade curtains. What a pity, Maxine thought. The tapestries were nineteenth century fakes, lacking the delicate color, the rat-nibbled charm of the real thing.

Pagan wondered what the servants would think if she slid down the banister, then said, "It was easy to be friends at school, when all our lives were pretty similar but, later on, friends travel down different roads, and some of them are marked 'No Entry.' " She lifted the elaborate metal visor of a medieval helmet, and said, "Boo!"

"I don't know where Abdi got the decorator," said Maxine, "but he's gilded everything from the light switches to the banisters. All the furniture legs have claws, and look as if they're about to stagger across the floor."

"I knew you'd hate it," said Pagan, as they passed a green-malachite table edged with ormolu and supported by two overweight gold cherubs. "It gets worse."

For once, Maxine was speechless, as they walked through the salon and out onto the terrace.

Abdullah waved from the side of the pool. How much older Abdullah looks, Maxine thought, noticing the frosting of gray hairs among his strong black curls, and the deeply etched lines of his forehead.

That evening, in the darkness, on the terrace, Abdullah pulled Pagan to him and kissed her. She could smell the vanilla-scented bougainvillea bushes and the old-fashioned cologne Abdullah wore and the faint odor of his Turkish cigarettes and the starch of his shirt.

"Have you decided, Pagan?"

Nervously, she said, "I need time to get used to the idea. I'm worried because it could be so difficult, not only for you and me, but for your country—if it didn't work out. I wondered, that is . . . would you mind if . . . we have a six-month secret engagement?"

He released her so abruptly that she almost fell over the parapet. "Secret! Are you ashamed of me?"

Pagan's mellow happiness dissolved, leaving her with a stomachful of anxiety. "No, I'm afraid of the future, Abdi."

"You can't be ruled by fear in life. Who doesn't dare, doesn't win." Abdullah was an angry silhouette against the blue-black sky. "I'm sorry, Pagan, but you can't have me on approval."

"But I want to be certain." Pagan thumped her knee with her fist.

"Oh, Pagan, you can never be certain." Abdullah sounded exasperated and sad. "Life is a series of risks, Pagan. You either open the door marked 'risk' or you stay in the cabbage patch forever."

"But, Abdi, you're asking for a lot. You're asking for my whole life."

"Yes, Pagan, I am asking a lot. I am also offering a lot. I am sorry that you can't accept it." He strode away, leaving Pagan alone on the empty terrace.

CHAPTER 14

September 1, 1979

I*N HIS PHILADELPHIA* office, Curtis Halifax watched his family attorney read the telegram. Telling Harry hadn't been as hard as he'd expected, in fact Harry hadn't batted an eyelash as, haltingly, Curtis had told him of the long-kept secret; but attorneys were accustomed to hauling family skeletons out of the closet. Curtis leaned back in his leather wing desk chair, feeling relieved. At last he had told somebody.

"Dear Daddy, unless you pay them ten million dollars within fifteen days, they will kill me. Stand by for payment in Istanbul. Directions will be sent to Mommy at the hotel. Love—Lili," Harry read and then raised his eyebrows. "Curtis, this telegram reads like something from an Andy Hardy movie." He read the telegram aloud. "Are you sure this isn't some crazy joke?"

"No, I've already spoken to her mother."

"And this Lili is the *movie star*?"

Curtis nodded.

"You're *sure* . . . that is . . . there's no doubt in your mind that you are the father?"

"No doubt at all, Harry." Curtis shook his head. "I've known about the child since she was born. She lived with foster parents in Switzerland, and her mother and I were told that she'd died at the age of six."

Slowly Harry sipped his highball. It wasn't unlikely that a childless man of Curtis's age should be proud of fathering an illegitimate child, but the Halifaxes were an illustrious Philadelphia family and everyone knew what Debra was like; a scandal like this might push her over the edge.

"Curtis, are you sure you want to go to these lengths? You're really prepared to fly to Istanbul? How are you going to explain that to Debra?"

"No problem. I fly to Europe on business quite often. Debra won't mind, unless I'm not back in time for Ceezee's Thanksgiving party."

Harry glanced up at the portraits of Curtis's father and grandfather hanging against the paneled walls. "My advice would be to consider that other issues might come to light, as well as your paternity of an illegitimate child."

Curtis knew that his attorney was hinting at the long series of loans the bank had made to Judy Jordan's group of companies, as Harry continued. "Curtis, it all happened a long time ago. Why not just forget it?"

"It may have been a long time ago, Harry, but I've always regretted the way I treated her mother." Curtis reached across his desk and held out his hand for the telegram. "It's simple. My family raised me to be responsible, and I'm going to be responsible for my daughter, who's in danger."

"But you say you've never even met this woman!"

"I wanted to meet Lili." Curtis remembered the previous October and his meeting with Judy in the dim, discreet, New York restaurant. Angrily, he had brandished a copy of the *New York Times* and pointed at the story of Lili's search for her mother. Wrathfully, Curtis had asked Judy why she had invented the story that Lili's father was a dead soldier when he, Curtis Halifax, was the father of Lili. Reproachfully, Judy whispered that she had lied to protect Curtis's marriage. How would Debra feel, if told that Curtis had an illegitimate child? How would an ex-porn star fit into Debra's social life in Philadelphia? How would such a beautiful stepdaughter affect Debra's anxiety about her external appearance; if she didn't starve herself to death, Debra would be in constant surgery having her body and face restructured and lifted.

"You must protect Debra." As usual, Judy had gently played on his guilt. "Leave Lili alone."

Curtis had hesitated. "But she's my . . . "

Judy had interrupted. "After all, you once left me alone, didn't you? You made *your* choice twenty years ago. You didn't know that you were choosing loneliness when you married Debra, but I knew that loneliness was what you were choosing for *me*."

Curtis's attorney looked at the silver-framed photograph on the banker's mahogany desk and, as if reading his client's thoughts, he said, "Well, you know what'll happen to Debra, if any of this leaks out."

"Look, Harry, I asked you to drop by to check my legal position, not to hand out marriage guidance." Suddenly Curtis looked like the portrait of his grandfather.

"Curtis, if you admit paternity of this child, you could lay yourself open to . . ."

Curtis impatiently cut him short. "Harry, I hear what you're saying, but I've made my decision. Now, can we get on with the logistics? How can I raise the money?"

"Even if we could raise that much fast, Curtis, there's no way you could pay kidnap ransom, because it is against government policy to pay kidnap ransom. So, for a start, remember that you'll be up against the law, if you transfer the money out of the country."

Again, Curtis showed his grandfather's drive. "What about our Bahamas operation, Harry, what can we raise there? And we've got the properties in Rio, as well as the Tokyo development. There's enough security there. You're not going to tell me that we can't raise a lousy ten million bucks outside the country!"

Harry looked doubtful. "My advice is to play this one for time. Both Lili and her mother are influential people with influential friends. By the time you get to Istanbul, you may find that the Turkish police have already found her."

Curtis propped his neatly groomed gray head on one hand. "I hope you're right, Harry, but in case you're wrong, I want you to raise as much as you can on those Brazilian leases and transfer it to Istanbul. Nothing you say is going to stop me from flying out there tonight. I feel so fucking powerless, sitting behind this fucking desk when my daughter is in danger."

In twenty years, Harry had never heard Curtis swear. "Okay, Curtis." The attorney stood up. "But try to stay within the law. I don't want to be part of your defense team."

September 2, 1979

"Stop throwing plates, Maggie, I'll explain!" Angelface Harris ducked behind the closet door of the all-black kitchen, as his wife hurled another handful of expensive, handmade pottery at him.

"I've had enough of your bloody lies," Maggie screamed, as she grabbed a yellow Italian soup tureen from the black worktop and threw it at her husband. A pile of ceramic shards was building up in front of his hiding place, and the gleaming black kitchen shelves were almost bare. "You've lied to me every day of our marriage, why should I believe you now?" A scarlet meat plate followed the yellow tureen.

"It serves you bloody right for going through my pockets!"

"I was only looking for grass. And if I hadn't been, I wouldn't have found that telegram." Maggie flung a Carol McNicholl teapot. "Dear Daddy, unless you pay them ten million fucking dollars within fifteen days, they'll kill me." Maggie picked up the food processor, then changed her mind and went for the coffeemaker. "You ain't going to Istanbul, Angelface, and you ain't sending any money to that fucking porn queen."

"Maggie, I told you, I've no idea what this is about."

"I never knew you *had* ten million dollars," Maggie shrieked, "or I'd never had signed the fucking premarital agreement." Maggie had now thrown everything she could lift and the kitchen shelves were almost bare.

"Maggie, be reasonable!" Angelface looked round the closet door. "Of course I don't have ten million dollars! What's more, I intend to hang onto every penny I got."

With difficulty, Maggie picked up the food processor and pitched it. The machine hit the door, scraped the paint off and flew apart as it hit the floor.

Angelface knew that Maggie had no ammunition left. Warily, he stepped out. "I got no intention of paying ransom for Lili *or* going to Turkey *or* getting involved with the fucking Turkish police." He picked his way across the seventh set of crockery to be broken since their marriage. "Now, will you swear not to tell about that telegram?"

Maggie scowled at him. "I might and I might not."

"You better not, you stupid bitch." Angelface looked down at her and glared. She reached up and slapped his face. He grabbed her hand and pushed her back against the black worktop. Maggie was not intimidated, she was gasping with excitement, and Angelface's eyes were glittering as he tore her shirt open and lunged at her breasts. "I'll teach you a lesson," he panted, feeling his cock start to harden. Maggie tried to knee Angelface in the crotch, flailed frantically at him with her free hand, then she pulled a heavy cast-iron saucepan from the sink and smashed her husband over the head with it.

With a roar of rage, Angelface smacked her face.

Maggie's head cracked against the wall, and she collapsed into a screaming heap on the floor.

Angelface jumped to the far side of the black table, as if he wanted a solid barrier between himself and his wife.

"You shouldn't have bopped me with that iron pot, that wasn't playful," he muttered.

Maggie continued to weep, blood streaming from her split lip.

"It wasn't funny, Mags."

Piteously, Maggie looked up; mascara, blood, and lipstick streaked her face.

"Oh, shut yer face and come 'ere," Angelface ordered, out of the side of his mouth. He wasn't going to pick her up.

Maggie picked herself up and tottered toward his grudgingly opened arms. Angelface licked the blood from her split lip and whispered hoarsely, "I'm sorry, baby, but you shouldn't provoke me that way." He gently pulled off what remained of Maggie's silk shirt and used it to wipe the tears from her red-and-black streaked face. Cheekily, he pinched one of her nipples and she gave a mollified sniff.

"For all I know, Maggie, I might have hundreds of kids around the world," said Angelface, reproachfully, "but I'd be daft to own up to any of 'em." He thought, I am tickled fucking pink to think that my kid's turned out to be one of the most beautiful chicks in the world, but I'd better not tell Maggie, or she might really try to hurt me.

Slowly, Angelface pulled down the zipper of her jeans. "You know how the chicks come after me, Maggie. Knickers off and legs up in rows outside me dressing room door. It was before you come along, darling." He slid his hands inside her jeans and comfortingly squeezed her ass. Maggie was so tiny that one of her buns was hardly a handful. "You know I got me appetites, Maggie." He grabbed her hand and thrust it down his pants, where she could feel his growing affection. "And you know you love it, baby."

Entwined, they tottered upstairs to the bedroom, then hurled themselves at each other, on the unmade, blacksheeted bed.

Two hours later, when their Filipino houseman had cleaned up the kitchen and Angelface had locked himself in the recording studio with his band, Maggie leaned back against the black sheets, lit a joint, reached for the Mickey Mouse telephone and called her best friend. "I dunno what I'm going to do, Joanie," she moaned, with no preamble. "He busted me lip again and I'm sure he's broken me wrist. D'you think I should leave him this time?"

Joanie asked what had started it, after which, they discussed the ongoing tragedy, and the proper etiquette for an upgraded groupie when faced with an illegitimate stepdaughter who was far more beautiful than Maggie, and famous.

By eight o'clock the next morning, when Angelface crashed on his bed, reeking of brandy, and Maggie was deep in barbiturate-assisted sleep, Joanie had called the rock column of London's evening newspaper. By eleven in the morning, the editor had decided to splash the story and, by one o'clock, billboards all over the city screamed: LILI—KIDNAP SENSATION.

La Divina stretched her ripe, red mouth as wide as if she were projecting a perfect high C to the dome of La Scala, then firmly clamped her lips around the penis. Slowly, she pushed her mouth over the smooth flesh. With satisfaction, La Divina thought that no younger woman, however beautiful, could do this as well as she. Twenty years of practice kept the rhythm steady and helped her to sense if she was going too slow, too fast, or too gently (the most frequent male complaint) as Spyros rubbed against the roof of her mouth. Oops! Spyros twitched and La Divina nearly gagged, as her uvula made an involuntary movement. That's what happened if you lost your concentration. It should feel, to the man, as sensuously satisfying as having a hand sucked by a newborn calf.

Suddenly the thought of calves and kittens and puppies came into her mind, and La Divina seemed to see a view of herself on the bed from a corner of the ceiling. Oh, Heavens, why was she doing this? It really wasn't an act of love, mouthing this bratwurst with such care. It was a well-practiced, pathetic act of desperation, a sensual bribe, her last resort, inspired by despair at the thought of losing Spyros and all that he stood for. Her love was no longer love, it was fear; the fear of being abandoned, of public humiliation, of being alone. La Divina sucked harder. How much longer was he going to take? She would start counting the thrusts. Ten . . . twenty . . . forty . . . She started to get a cramp in her jaw.

The fey young men who had formed La Divina's entourage when she was the world's most adored diva now sniggered that her mellifluous voice had failed because of the damage done to laryngeal tissues by her bedroom practices. But La Divina no longer cared about the gossip, which rustled through the opera houses of the world, about her affairs with the Stiarkoz brothers. She was deathly tired of that demanding circus, the adoring audiences who would shout for blood as readily as for the thirtieth curtain call. Buenos Aires had been a nightmare. She had adequately performed the first half of the recital, then halfway through the aria from *Norma* she had failed to reach high C and an almost crowlike harshness had crept into her lower notes.

There had been catcalls, jeers and howls of laughter. On the following day, when she read her notices, La Divina had cancelled the rest of her tour and fled back to Europe and the sanctuary of the yacht Persephone which was cruising the Greek Islands. Last night, she had been reunited with Spyros. Now, all that she cared about was hiding from the world with this man in one of their private places—on his island or his yacht. She wanted to forget that she had ever been a *prima donna*, to forget the anxiety, the responsibility, as well as the honeyed applause. She wanted only to pass her days in sensual reverie and her evening hours feeling him move into her hungry body, thrusting a reason for living back into her immaculately maintained shell.

"I had forgotten how good it feels to be with you." Spyros slowly drew his blunt fingertips down the fullness of her left breast until he reached the hard dark peak.

But I have forgotten nothing, thought La Divina. She remembered living in a mist of unhappiness after Jo Stiarkoz, as if hypnotized, had abandoned her for that bitch, Lili. It had happened overnight, and La Divina had at first felt numb with misery, then suspended in a miasma of pain and loss. For weeks that grew into months, La Divina lived in a trance of shock, sorrow, and humiliation. Finally, she became apathetic; she couldn't be bothered to get out of bed, to get dressed, to go out, or to see anyone. When Jo Stiarkoz had been killed in a car crash, La Divina did not (as everyone expected) become hysterical upon hearing the news, because she had been mourning Jo for years.

And then, one day, shortly after Jo's death, her maid had brought to her bedroom a willow basket planted with spring flowers. Twisted between the miniature cyclamen and wood anemones La Divina had found a delicate eighteenth-century diamond collar of rose-cut stones linked by fine bows of smaller brilliants. The card read "Spyros Stiarkoz." She smiled. This would only be the beginning, she knew. He would not expect her to thank him, but to wait for his next move.

The next morning she had unwrapped the warm croissant on her breakfast tray and a pair of matching diamond earrings fell from the pink napkin. As she held one, dangling to the light, her bedside telephone rang. "I've just finished my calls to Hong Kong—may I see you?" asked Spyros Stiarkoz, without introducing himself. La Divina guessed what Spyros meant, because his older brother, Jo, had always preferred to make love in the early morning, after the Hong Kong trading had finished or late at night, after the American markets had closed.

Two hours after receiving the earrings, La Divina had been standing on the deck of the Persephone. The tang of the sea had mingled with Spyros' faint odor of starch, cigar smoke and clean, warm flesh. That night, before she had a chance to undress, he had quietly appeared in her stateroom. Without a word, he had moved forward and silently held her against him, for a long time.

Then, with care, he had softly pulled at the shoulder of her topaz satin gown. She had not moved as he pulled the dress down to her waist, then bent his lips to her large, dark nipples and kissed them lightly, feeling the buds grow hard. Then he had sucked hard at them, and fierce stabs of pleasure had shot, almost painfully, between her legs as he held the tips of her breasts softly between his teeth, then teased them with his tongue, and La Divina had shuddered as life washed into her body once more. Although she had scarcely begun to moisten, she had pulled Spyros close to her, hungering for his vital hardness, feeling the warmth of his erection through the thin silk of his navy dressing gown.

They had fallen back on the bed and she had felt his hand softly, slowly, stroking her inner thighs, higher and higher. Still, he made no sound but, as he reached her mound of Venus and started to softly stroke it, she rose eagerly against the rhythm of his hand, feeling no anxiety, no necessity to hurry, just the certainty of her eventual orgasm. When she climaxed, her whole body arched in ecstasy, then she felt for the head of his penis and guided it into her; their mouths were together and their fingers entwined.

Later, she had sobbed with gratitude as Spyros held her to his hairy damp chest.

Slowly, La Divina's confidence, career, and greedy appetite for life had revived and now, six years later, she knew the responses of Spyros Stiarkoz's body better than the power of her capricious voice.

Yes, I have forgotten nothing, La Divina thought, as she lay against the body of Spyros Stiarkoz. She would always remember what he had done for her. Why, when she had telephoned two days ago from Buenos Aires, after cancelling her tour, he had comforted her and told her to fly straight back to Athens.

She had only arrived this morning but his helicopter had been waiting to carry her to the Persephone, which was anchored off Aegina.

That afternoon, they had made love for over an hour, until both were exhausted and sweating, but Spyros had been unable to have an erection. Afterward, La Divina had, silently, considered all the possible reasons. Of course, Spyros would never see sixty again. Perhaps he had a health problem; ten different sorts of tablets and capsules stood on the tray beside the gold dolphin faucets in his bathroom.

This evening La Divina was determined to arouse him. Now, as her throat accepted the flesh she loved so much, she ran her fingers lightly up his thighs, softly raked his buttocks with her fuchsia nails, then plunged her fingers into his dense pubic hair. But, as she massaged the sensitive area behind the base of his testicles, she felt his balls begin to slacken away from his body and realized that she was not getting the usual response.

La Divina hollowed her cheeks and sucked harder. But it was no good. Spyros's erection had faded.

Finally she pulled away, and looked at him, her eyes filling with anxious tears. Spyros seemed completely unconcerned as he said, "It will be fine later, darling, I promise you."

"No, no!" She broke into noisy sobs. "It's different, isn't it? What have you done with that creature, that now you can't make love to *me*?"

Spyros did not reply, because there was no point in saying anything to her when she was determined to make a scene. And, in fact, he was extremely worried about his lack of response. Nothing like this had happened since he had started taking the serum.

"It's not enough for you to have Zeus Air! It's not enough for you to have more tankers and bigger tankers than Jo had in his fleet!"

La Divina started hitting the cream linen sheets with her clenched fists, and crying louder. "It's not enough that the Persephone is ten meters longer than Jo's yacht! It's not enough that you have *me!*"

Spyros sighed. The first tantrum after twenty-four hours of peace. Ashtrays would be flying within five minutes.

"It's not enough that I love you, Spyros, more than I ever loved your brother! Don't you realize that *nothing* will ever be enough to make you feel you've beaten Jo?" La Divina started to hit his hard, gray-haired chest with her clenched fists. "But now I know what you want. I didn't think it was true, but it is. *You want*

Lili as well. Don't try to deny it. I saw that photograph of you two in the *New York Post*, last November, at the opera. *Dozens* of kind friends sent me the clipping. You remember, I was singing in Sydney. The press was on my neck the next day. Had I any comment, they wanted to know? I had to smile pleasantly, say no, no comment, *and then step out on that stage!*"

So she *had* known about Lili. And for ten months she had not mentioned it. Such emotional self-control was rare in La Divina.

"I promise you, darling, I haven't spoken to Lili for months." No, Spyros thought, but Lili had been on his mind every day since he had touched her. La Divina's instinct was uncanny.

Spyros had wanted Lili's succulent body for added reasons that he did not care to acknowledge. Certainly, Lili had rejected him, but Spyros never gave up. When anyone opposed him in business, Spyros single-mindedly concentrated on destroying that person. When Spyros wanted something for his collection of Greek antiquities, he was prepared to wait for it—sometimes for years—and he was prepared to pay far, far above the market value for something he really desired. He was very rich, and because he was growing old, there was very little in life that he wanted.

But he wanted Lili.

Now, he briefly kissed the hand of La Divina and returned to his cabin, pausing to admire the purple silhouette of Aegina against the darkening Greek sky.

Back in his own suite, Spyros telephoned for the ship's doctor and then showered. Afterward, one milliliter of serum was injected into his muscular left buttock, which was then respectfully swabbed. The serum was provided by the Swiss clinic that Spyros attended every winter for a week. The precious drug was cultured from the gonadal tissue of embryo pigs; within an hour it would make the sixty-eight-year-old as virile as a fifteen-year-old, Spyros hoped as he dressed. By midnight, La Divina would have dried her tears; she would be exhausted and contented and, he hoped, as his valet fastened his platinum cufflinks, she would also be quiet. Thank God she didn't know about the telegram, which had arrived that morning.

There was a knock at the door and a white uniformed aide entered, holding a paper. "Just came over the radio, sir. They've located Judy Jordan's hotel in Istanbul. Mr. Menecik at the Turkish Foreign Ministry has radioed back to you, offering his services and Mr. Vlassos of Interpol will be available in twenty minutes."

September 3, 1979

Across the road from the Sydonite Embassy, the ducks sailed serenely on the pond in St. James's Park. Abdullah stared at them, then looked up in surprise as Pagan, wearing a blue Japanese kimono and no makeup, burst into his library, brandishing the *Daily Mail*.

"Abdi, this is terrible!"

Abdullah, who had already signed a thick folder of decrees and state instruments, used the peaceful morning hours to read his most important reports. Now, he put down the précis of his Intelligence Department's Washington report.

"Look what it says in the *Daily Mail!*" Pagan read aloud, " 'Angelface Harris and Lili, Kidnap drama.' " She looked up at Abdullah. "Lili's been snatched in

Istanbul! Judy's still there. I must telephone her straightaway."

Abdullah waved his bodyguard out of the room. "Does anyone know the identity of the kidnappers or what they want?"

"No idea who they are, but it says here that they've demanded ten million dollars from Angelface Harris. Judy will be frantic!" Pagan loped around the large library, her untidy hair unbrushed, her kimono flying out behind her. As she passed Abdullah's desk, she caught her kimono sleeve on a silver tray and impatiently tugged at it. The filing tray fell to the floor, scattering a pile of papers and a telegram. Adbullah jumped up, picked up the telegram and stuffed it in his pocket, then started to shove the papers back onto the silver tray. Pagan was so distraught that she did not notice this strange action. Normally, Abdullah would have pressed a button on the floor beneath his desk, whereupon a black-robed secretary would have entered and picked up the papers.

"I'll get home and pack my bags straightaway, Abdi. I'll have to go to Istanbul as soon as I can get on a plane. Judy will need friends around her at a time like this." She flung a Burberry raincoat over her kimono, as Abdi rang for the car.

An hour later, Abdullah appeared at Pagan's front door. She had just hurled open a newly packed suitcase, hunting for her passport.

"I don't like the idea of your going to Istanbul alone," Abdullah said. "I think I'd better go with you. My people have never trusted the Turks so we have a good intelligence system there. So we might be able to help in some way. We have a very pleasant little palace in the diplomatic quarter. My dispatch boxes can be sent there. Suliman has arranged everything, our plane will leave in two hours."

Pagan jumped up and kissed him. "Darling Abdi, you *are* so kind!" It did not occur to Pagan to wonder why Abdullah should be so willing to make this uncharacteristic gesture of support. "Now, where the hell is my passport?"

Patiently, Abdullah said, "Your passport is of no consequence when you are traveling with me. I suggest, however, that you ask your maid to find you something more suitable to wear." Pagan looked down and realized that she had been about to depart in her blue kimono.

"Miss Jordan is expecting me," Pagan explained to the desk clerk for the fourth time, demonstrating the universal habit of raising the voice to uncomprehending foreigners. The next moment, she was almost knocked off her feet, as the plump and sweaty manager of the Haroun al-Rashid bustled forward with two assistants and bowed to the thin man in uniform, who was standing behind Pagan.

The marble lobby of the hotel was alive with journalists of every nationality. Television cables crisscrossed the rich rugs on the floor, tripping the flustered bellhops as they carried messages. The telephone switchboard was lit up like Las Vegas, and one of the operators was quietly weeping. Everyone was sweating, shouting to make themselves heard, and confused by the hysterical rumors which swept through the press corps every half hour or so. Photographers jockeyed for position at the entrance on the side street; one intrepid lensman had climbed onto the roof of the hotel annex and was hopefully fitting telephoto lenses to his cameras in order to pry inside Judy's suite.

Finally, Pagan threw up her arms in despair and, having been told that Judy was on the first floor, she bolted up the staircase to the first floor, shouting, "Judy, it's Pagan, tell them to let me through!"

Judy heard her, flung open the heavy cedar doors of her suite, and Pagan tumbled into the room, and the two friends hugged each other.

"It's like World War Three out there," Pagan gasped when she got her breath.

"We're waiting for the police chief," Judy explained. "I hope he's got some news." There was a knock at the door and she whirled toward it. "That'll be him now!" But, Gregg Eagleton, looking pale and crumpled, stood in the doorway. "I couldn't get an earlier flight, Judy. What the hell is happening?"

Ten minutes later, the hotel manager escorted into the room a small group of Turkish policemen, headed by the tall thin man who Pagan had seen in the lobby.

Colonel Aziz had round, heavy-lidded eyes and a melancholy expression. He wore the beige uniform of the Turkish police but spoke perfect English, with a slight American accent, having done his basic training in Miami. He reassured Judy that everything possible was being done to find her daughter. "We have involved Interpol, the Sûreté in Paris, and the FBI; we have never had a case such as this. You, Miss Jordan, have informed the police of three ransom demands that sound like jokes, all beginning "Dear Daddy," sent to a Greek shipping magnate, an American banker, and a pop singer. But I understand from Miss Jordan," he inclined his head to Judy, "that Mademoiselle Lili's father died before she was born." He spread his long, narrow hands in a gesture of surprise.

He thinks this is a publicity stunt, Judy realized, as she handed over the telegram that Curtis had given her that morning, before disappearing to sleep off his journey. The British police had already sent out Angelface's telegram. And Stiarkoz, when he spoke to Judy via the ship's radio, had promised to deliver his cablegram when the Persephone docked in Istanbul.

Colonel Aziz examined the three pieces of paper. "There is little we can discover from these, other than that the messages are identical. We found no sign of force or struggle in Mademoiselle Lili's suite, and our informants in the Grand Bazaar report no unusual disturbance yesterday."

What would he describe as an unusual disturbance, Judy wondered, gazing up at the dusty chandelier, as she remembered the noisy, sweaty crowds that jostled in the smelly booths of the Bazaar: you could have garroted twenty people in that chaotic place and nobody would have noticed.

"So we are left with the possibility that whoever has abducted Mademoiselle Lili may be someone whom she knew, someone whom she would trust not to harm her." The Colonel sat back in his green velvet armchair and looked from one strained face to another in turn. Gently he asked, "Who does Mademoiselle Lili know in Istanbul?"

"No one, as far as we know. She's never been here before." Judy took off her tortoise-shell glasses and rubbed her tired eyes. "Miss Bayriver, the Beauty Queen winner, and I are the only people that Lili knows in Turkey, apart from the hotel staff, our driver, and the guides. I can't imagine any friend of Lili's being capable of this."

Gregg was slouched in a corner of the sofa, one ankle resting casually on the other knee. "Surely this is either a straightforward criminal case or a terrorist kidnapping?" Gregg had only ever before felt this anxiety fill his chest when his father was racing. He wished to God he hadn't treated Lili as an ordinary woman: that was what she wanted, so he had tried to hide his bedazzlement behind a façade of unconcern. But she couldn't be treated as an ordinary woman, because she wasn't one. If only he'd looked after her more carefully. He wanted to accompany her on this trip, but Lili had insisted that she wanted to travel in the smallest possible group in order to get to know her mother. Gregg couldn't stop accusing himself of neglecting Lili. If only, if only, if only, he thought.

"I'm inclined to rule out terrorism," said Colonel Aziz. "Certainly, in Turkey, we have our fair share of these groups—AMLA, the PLO, some Kurdish separatists. What modern capital city is free of these parasites?" Colonel Aziz shrugged. "But when terrorists kidnap a person, they have two aims. They want a substantial sum of money to buy arms to use against people such as myself," Colonel Aziz gave a tight smile, "and they want the maximum publicity for their cause." He coughed. "Kidnapping an international celebrity is a highly effective way of insuring worldwide maximum press coverage, but it's unusual for the terrorist group not to make themselves known immediately. Anonymous kidnapping is not terrorist style."

Gregg said, "Are there any other alternatives?"

"Regrettably, yes." The Colonel hesitated, looked at Judy, then continued. "We cannot rule out the possibility that this is an elaborately disguised murder. It's not unknown for a murderer to lay a false trail, and the peculiar nature of the ransom notes suggests that this is not an authentic kidnap. Do you know whether Mademoiselle Lili had any enemies?"

"Why, I've just remembered something!" Pagan jumped up and knocked an engraved brass tray off its stand. "Lili's just done a charity benefit in London and the performance was almost sabotaged. The man who did that is undoubtedly an enemy of Lili!"

Colonel Aziz made a note on his pad. "Did you make any inquiries at the time?"

"Yes, of course. Someone threw a big party for the entire theater audience at a smart hotel. That party was an expensive, well-planned, weird operation, like this kidnap."

"Who paid for the party, Lady Swann?"

"The hotel staff was far too discreet to tell us who paid their bill. As nothing illegal had been done, they had to respect their client's wish to remain anonymous."

"We have no proof that whoever paid for the party made the hoax telephone call," Gregg reminded Pagan.

"Now that something illegal *has* been done, the hotel will have to tell us all they know, and so will the bank which paid the draft." The Colonel tore off a sheet of note pad and handed it to one of his assistants.

"I think it was a nutter," said Gregg. "Just another sicko, with a bit more loot than most of Lili's crazy fans. Lili gets a regular stack of hate mail. Any one of those creeps might have flipped his lid and decided to grab her."

"I doubt that the person behind this operation is the sort of person who pesters film stars." Colonel Aziz looked from one face to another. "The obsessive fan is usually an inadequate, pathetic personality who can't form relationships with real people, and so lives in a fantasy world. Any reality usually defeats such people."

"But they still manage to assassinate the occasional rock star or head of state," Judy observed, sourly. Having seen Lili besieged by obsessive male admirers, none of whom appeared inadequate or pathetic, she was exasperated by the Colonel's bland psychological explanation.

"Such acts are generally accidents, rather than carefully planned crimes." The Colonel dismissed Judy's point. "But we are treating this as a carefully planned, clever crime. Whoever has kidnapped Mademoiselle Lili took great care to investigate your background, Miss Jordan. And he knew that Mademoiselle Lili would be in Turkey at this time."

Gregg jumped up angrily, and started to pace around the room. "Anyone who can read a newspaper knows that Lili was on tour in Istanbul with Miss International Beauty."

Colonel Aziz ignored him. "An obsessive man might want to possess Mademoiselle Lili as an art collector desires a painting."

Gregg stood still. "Do you mean that the point of kidnapping Lili might not be to get money, but to get Lili herself?"

Simultaneously, Judy and Pagan thought of the same man.

Slowly, the yacht Persephone sailed past the Leander Tower Lighthouse, then the vast white craft anchored in the middle of the shallow bay. Within a few minutes, the Haroun al-Rashid private launch, with one solitary passenger, was gliding across the blue-green water toward the yacht.

From the white linen cushions of the aft salon, Spyros Stiarkoz rose to greet Judy. No wonder this man frightens Lili, she thought, as she looked at the blunt hands, massive shoulders, and acquisitive, Levantine eyes of her host.

"My lawyer says that it's unwise for me to be here." Spyros waved Judy toward a white couch, and she sat down. A white-uniformed steward brought a brass pot of sweet Greek coffee, as Spyros handed Judy the much-fingered sheet of buff paper. "Here's the telegram." Judy twisted her hands together in her lap, then pressed them against her thighs to steady the trembling. Wordlessly, her face asked Spyros a question.

Spyros shook his head, "I will not pay the ransom."

"Then why invite me on your yacht?" Judy tried not to sound as hostile as she felt.

"Naturally, I'm concerned for Lili's safety or I wouldn't have sailed here. But my advisors have made it clear that if I accede to one single kidnap demand, I will be paving the way for every member of my family and every employee of my organization to be kidnapped. I cannot afford to be as soft as Getty, and see my grandchildren threatened by kidnappers forever."

Judy jumped to her feet. "Then what exactly does your concern for Lili amount to, Spyros?" Her voice shook. "Floating around on the Bosphorus, wishing us well, while these bandits start cutting off Lili's fingers in order to motivate us?"

"I'm here to make sure that this affair is properly handled." Spyros sipped his syrupy black coffee. "Police are the same all over the world—incompetent, mediocre bureaucrats."

"But. . ." Judy stopped as Spyros held his hand up.

"I wonder if you are aware, Miss Jordan, how easily a situation such as this can be mishandled?" He stressed the "Miss" lightly, but with contempt. "If the kidnappers' hiding place is found, the local police might be trigger happy and attempt to storm the building." He put his cup down and motioned to the steward to refill it. "If so, they would probably kill half the bandits, get killed themselves, and perhaps be responsible for the death of innocent onlookers. And by the time they found Lili, she would also be dead."

Judy hated him for being right. "Do you think the kidnappers are bandits?"

"Perhaps. My people are making inquiries, but we haven't had any firm news yet. It could be the Kemaiat—like your Mafia—or it might be AMLA, which is, as you know, a group called the Asia Minor Liberation Army. So far they've funded their activities only by robbing small-town banks and by hijacking lorries, but perhaps they're getting more ambitious."

Half an hour later, Judy had repeatedly, unsuccessfully, pleaded and begged Spyros to pay the ransom. She stood up, intending to leave, because there seemed no point in staying.

"I'd like to make it clear, Spyros, that I think the most useful thing you can do is pay the money. Somehow, between us, Lili and I will be able to pay you back."

This damned yacht had cost far more than ten million dollars. The Persephone, for all its glittering white luxury, seemed sinister and claustrophobic to her, and Judy was afraid that if she stayed any longer, listening to Spyros's patronizing refusals, she might lose her temper and alienate a very powerful man. Judy was also afraid because Spyros Stiarkoz was a rich man, a careful, clever man, an obsessive art collector, and he was besotted by Lili. His other passion, as every gossip writer knew, was to acquire whatever and whoever had belonged to his dead brother.

Certainly, Stiarkoz had received a ransom demand, but wouldn't it be the move of a clever man to send one to himself, in order to throw the police off the scent? With a heavy heart, Judy realized that if Stiarkoz had abducted Lili, then his presence there could only be for one of two reasons. Either he had the gall to openly check on police progress, or else he had arrived to gloat at their unsuccessful efforts to find Lili. Either possibility would mean that Stiarkoz could not be entirely sane. And either possibility meant that Judy was unlikely to see her daughter again.

Later that night, before dinner, Judy and Sandy waited for Pagan in the comforting darkness of the domed, carved balcony that hung over the Bosphorus like an enormous birdcage.

"That Colonel Aziz shouldn't have questioned you for hours." Sandy's voice was sympathetic, but she couldn't help wondering what was going to happen to Miss International Beauty's world tour. After all, they were now supposed to be in Egypt, but the Turkish police wouldn't allow Sandy to leave.

"He was only doing his job," said Judy, "and in very difficult circumstances." The world's press had descended upon the hotel and Sandy's picture had been flashed around the world. The press couldn't believe their luck: one international beauty kidnapped, and another one available for photographs.

Sandy and Judy were now virtual prisoners in their hotel suite. All day, one or the other of them had been barked at by the police and eventually, the telephone had been disconnected, because the Turkish operator could so easily be fooled by lying journalists, who assured her that they were returning Judy's calls.

"I could have spat in the eye and stamped on the foot of that Colonel," said Sandy. "In fact, when I think of what he put you through, I feel like kicking him in the balls."

Judy was astonished to hear Sandy drop her genteel speech. "Why, Sandy, that's the only criticism I've ever heard you make." Judy was eager to divert her mind by talking about anything rather than the kidnap.

"Honey, in my business, a girl learns to watch her mouth," said Sandy.

Judy looked at Sandy; she was pretty, bright, shrewd, and deftly practical, but all that cleverness and capacity for calculation was carefully used to give the impression that she was foolish and incompetent.

"Sandy, what made you decide to be a beauty queen?"

"Honey, that's only the first step up my ladder. In a few years, I aim to be hostessing my own TV show."

"But why start on the glamour circuit? No one will take you seriously after that."

"What about Bess Myerson? She was Miss America and now she's in consumer affairs. Anyway, being a pretty girl is the only start you can get in a place like Baton Rouge."

"Pretty is OK, Sandy, but what about your Southern belle act? Sure, the guys love it, especially the old ones, but you'll have to stop being . . . acquiescent . . . if you want to host a talk show."

"Honey, I guess I was brought up to be agreeable."

"Sandy, it won't work when you get older, and it won't work when the going gets tough. There's nothing more gruesome than an aging Blanche Dubois, simpering with girlish charm."

Sandy was suddenly stung by the comparison to a Tennessee Williams version of a washed-up, neurotic Southern belle.

Boldly, she said what she'd been dying to say for days. "Judy, what I can't understand is how Lili's father can pay the ransom, when Lili told me that her father died long ago?"

"I have no idea, Sandy, how this kidnapper could be so crazy or so cruel."

Sandy remembered the ransom note that had been delivered in the bunch of red roses. It read: "Wait in your hotel suite to hear from Lili's father. He must pay the ransom."

Sandy said, "I wonder how much longer we'll have to wait?"

Judy's nerves snapped. "For Heaven's sake, can't we talk about something else?"

Sandy said, "Why, yes, Judy, there is something else I have been *longin'* to talk to you about, something I really want to ask you, Judy." Sandy took a deep breath, then burst out, "Just which one of those bastards is Lili's father?"

CHAPTER 15

September 3, 1979

"IT'S NONE OF YOUR BUSINESS!" Judy's voice echoed across the dark water and rang around the still room behind them. "How dare you ask a question like that!"

"Honey, I'm not the only one who's asking," said Sandy. "Colonel Aziz gave me a really hard time in his office for two hours. After all, you told the world that Lili's father was dead, then suddenly all these guys got telegrams."

"For all we know, Sandy, ten other rich men may have received that telegram. Next week, the lunatic who's writing them is probably going to send one to John Travolta and President Carter!"

Sandy persisted. "Who was it, Judy?"

"Lili's father was a British soldier who was killed by the Communists in Malaya."

Sandy said, "They'll check."

Judy jumped up from her seat and leaned over the balcony, with her back to the other woman. Sandy added, "Colonel Aziz said they'd do blood tests. He's spoken to Lili's doctor in Paris and he's getting Lili's medical records. A modern blood test can really narrow down the field, it's not like one of those old maybe-he-is tests." Sandy's voice was soft but warning. "They're going to find out, Judy."

Judy turned around to face Sandy. Beyond the darkened balcony, just inside the sitting room, moths were dancing around the fringed, pink-silk shade of a table lamp. As Judy watched, one of them swooped too close to the hot light bulb and fell, fluttering in agony, on the tabletop.

Sandy stood up and put an arm around Judy's shoulder. "Honey, *I'm* rooting for you. We've got a lot in common, after all. *I'm* a small town girl. *I* know what it's like to be no one from nowhere, and how tough it is to get started. I'm sure that there was a good reason for whatever you did or said." She patted Judy's shoulder comfortingly. "But I'm a card-carrying twister of the truth, and it takes one to know one. I'm sure it wasn't pleasant to hear Colonel Aziz ask if you'd slept with all these guys. But watch what you're saying, because I can see that the Colonel doesn't believe *anything* you're telling him."

In the cool, soothing darkness, only the lapping of water under the elaborate balcony could be heard. Since Lili disappeared, Judy had been in a state of almost unbearable tension, she hadn't slept for two nights and, even before that, she had been exhausted by months of anxiety, due to her multiple business problems.

Suddenly, Judy cracked under the strain, buried her face in her hands and started to cry.

Sandy stroked Judy's hair and softly reassured her. "Don't fret, honey, you're not the first girl to screw more than one guy in a month."

Through her sobs, Judy snuffled. "It wasn't the way you make it sound, Sandy. They weren't all in one month and besides, I've never been regular." She gulped, snuffled again, and blew her nose. "The whole trouble started when I was a fifteen-year-old student in Switzerland and working as a waitress. For the first six months, I had to work too hard to have any fun. One of the waiters, Nick, had a crush on me but, physically, the chemistry just wasn't there, for me. Then, one night, I was raped. It was on my mother's birthday, February the 7th. It's silly, the things you remember. He was one of the guests at the hotel."

"Poor baby. What a stinking, rotten way to lose your virginity."

"When I saw the bastard in the hotel afterward, he didn't even recognize me. I meant nothing to him, but that experience changed my life. It made me feel degraded. So I never told anyone what had happened. It was my dirty secret." She blew her nose again. "Then I met Curtis Halifax, and he made me feel clean again."

Like people who confide their secrets to a complete stranger on a train, because of the unbearable urge to unburden themselves to someone, and because they feel that never again will they meet that stranger, the overwrought, despairing

Judy told Sandy the story that she had never told anyone, the secret that only one person had guessed, the tale that had started so long ago in the small, Swiss luxury resort of Gstaad.

February 14, 1949

Judy remembered the stars on the ballroom ceiling, as the Swiss accordion band played "*La Vie en Rose*," at the St. Valentine's Day Ball. She had just carried a heavy tray of glasses at top speed up from the kitchens. Without a word, a hard-pressed barman grabbed the tray from her thin, childish hands, and crashed it on to a bench. "*Aidez-moi, paresseuse!*" he snapped.

Judy picked up two of the still-wet glasses. The barman quickly loaded glasses from the tray onto the rack above his head. "*Vite, vite!*" he shouted again. Judy stood on tiptoe, as she tried to push the glasses onto the high wooden rack, but she couldn't reach it.

"*Mademoiselle n'est pas assez grande*." It was the worst French accent Judy had ever heard. From the customer-side of the bar, a bow-tied American boy smiled at her.

Judy grinned. "That sounds like an East Coast accent."

"Philadelphia. I'm Curtis Halifax. Listen, I'm tall enough to put those glasses away for you, if you'll pour me a bourbon?"

Periwinkle-blue eyes crinkled, a bright, frank smile dimpled his cheeks. He looked the sort of tall, clean cut, wholesome guy you saw on Coca-Cola ads, thought Judy, as she swiftly stacked the dirty glasses.

From their little table by the dance floor, Kate in cream moire and Maxine in pale-blue silk waved at Judy, who explained to Curtis, "They're my friends." Curtis turned and looked at them, gave a brief glance to the other rich, pretty girls sitting round the dance floor, then firmly turned his back on them, clearly fascinated by the tiny blond American waitress behind the bar.

There was a sudden roll of drums. All heads turned to the glass ballroom doors, where the guest of honor, Prince Abdullah of Sydon, stood stiffly by the side of Pagan, in a sparkling gray-tulle ballgown. Curtis gave them a brief glance, then turned back to Judy. "Do they ever let you out from behind that bar? How about skating on Sunday?"

Judy didn't have time to reply, as a waiter dashed forward with an order for the royal lemon juice.

"Nick, I can't read your bar slips," Judy called. "The head barman will have your head on a platter if you don't write more clearly, sweetheart."

Curtis looked worried as Nick dashed off with his tray of *citrons pressés*. "Sweetheart?"

"A figure of speech. We're just good friends."

Curtis was no better at skating than he was at speaking French. While Judy whizzed around the crowded rink, Curtis struggled to stand upright but, every time he let go of the barrier, his long thin legs went gliding out from under him. Eventually, he gave up, and sat with Judy on the terrace, sipping hot spiced punch. Curtis said, "Rumor has it that you have a fiance back in West Virginia."

Judy wasn't sure that she wanted Curtis to know about her nonexistent fiancé:

she had invented Jim as a smoke screen, behind which she could escape from involvements she didn't want. Judy's goal was to learn fluent French and German in a year, then head for Paris to make her fortune. Her days were spent in the language laboratory and her evenings as a waitress at the Imperial Hotel, in order to pay for her year in Switzerland. There was no place in Judy's schedule for a man.

But Curtis took no notice of Judy's good resolutions. Every day, as soon as the sun left the valley and the shadows lengthened across the narrow, snow-packed streets, Curtis appeared in the hotel coffee-bar. Once, when her supervisor started to give Judy sharp looks because of the time she wasted talking to Curtis, he apologized to the man with Ivy-League charm, then tucked a big tip into the beer stein by the till, where the staff tips were pooled.

The following day, as Curtis slid into his usual seat, with a bright-eyed smile that was simultaneously knowing and innocent, the supervisor winked at Judy and jerked his head. "Here's your rich boyfriend again."

Judy was thoroughly charmed. The boys she had known back home in Rossville were awkward and gauche; they preferred beer, football, and fishing to girls. But Curtis had beautiful manners, which is why Judy felt completely at ease with him. Curtis treated Judy like a lady, and, shell-shocked by the peculiar, alien atmosphere of Europe, she enjoyed being with a fellow American, who was as homesick as she was. They told each other what they missed about America: Hershey bars, thick milk shakes, steaks that were not leathery flat slices of *bifteck* which stuck in your teeth. "And what I wouldn't give to go to an undubbed American movie," said Curtis wistfully. "I can't understand films in French."

Curtis first kissed her after they'd been moonlight skating, and were watching a torchlit display on the ice. As Judy felt the rough, male touch of Curtis' fur-lined, camel-hair coat, she no longer felt homesick, but safe, warm, and happy in his arms. She also felt a delicious melting-inside sensation. "It's too cold to kiss outside," said Curtis. "Let's go to my place."

Three weeks later, Curtis sat on the edge of her bed, pulling on his white socks. "Of course I love you, Judy. Ever since St. Valentine's Day, remember?"

Judy sat up in bed, pulling the quilt round her shoulders. "Then why are you going back to Philadelphia to marry someone else?"

"I've explained it over and over. This was all planned a long time ago. Debra and I were pinned on her seventeenth birthday and everyone expects us to get married, especially Debra. My father, and my grandfather before him, built up the business with the aim that one day a Halifax would become President of the United States. That's what they both live for, and I'm the only heir, so I have to try for them. It's my responsibility."

And I'm not your responsibility, thought Judy sadly, as Curtis earnestly continued. "To get a crack at the presidency, I need money; politics is an expensive business. And I need the right wife." Curtis looked uncomfortable as he reached for his snowboots.

"You mean a rich wife."

"I've grown up with Debra. I'm very fond of her and I couldn't possibly hurt her. The whole of Philadelphia has known for a year that we planned to marry at the end of her debutante season."

"But why didn't you tell me?"

"When I first saw you, being bullied by that Swiss barman, something happened to me. I just wanted to put my arms around you, take you away, and look after you forever." Curtis couldn't look her in the eye, but he was trying to be honest. "I can't figure out how a guy can love two women at once, but one minute I was drinking bourbon and the next minute I couldn't think about anything but you. You're so different from the girls I know back home, you've got so much pep and go, you're so full of life. I guess I just fell for you."

"But how can you love me and marry someone else?" Judy scrubbed away her tears with the corner of the quilt.

"I can because I must," Curtis said miserably. "Anyway, you're going to marry that guy in Rossville."

Judy said nothing. Once again, she wished that she hadn't invented that goddamn Jim in West Virginia.

The little scarlet cable car swung in eerie silence, suspended from one taut metal rope, high above the sparkling white valley. Doll-sized skiers swooped soundlessly over the ski *piste* below as Maxine listened to her Aunt Hortense's scurrilous Paris gossip and hoped that the two smart Italian women and the boy in the black ski suit couldn't understand English. The two Italian women were middle-aged, pear-shaped, and wore mink-lined parkas. They were immaculately made-up and coiffured and, despite their pristine pairs of Head skis, they obviously had no intention of skiing when they arrived at the top of the mountain.

In her gravelly voice, Aunt Hortense confided to Judy, "Of course, everybody likes to think that Roland is *tapette* and so when Zizi found him in the. . ." She stopped abruptly as the cable car gave a frightening lurch, halted, then started shaking from side to side, as the couplings up above ground noisily.

There was a moment's sickening silence. Judy felt helpless and trapped, as if the walls of the car were closing in on her and growing smaller; she wondered how long the air supply would last, and whether they'd freeze to death before help arrived, as claustrophobia started to set in.

"*Dio mio!*" cried one of the Italian women, and she lunged to the end of the car. Her shifting weight made the cable car bounce, as if it were about to uncouple itself from the cable and plunge onto the rocks far below.

"Don't move!" Aunt Hortense said sharply, in Italian, but the woman ran back to her original place.

"*Santa Mamma Mia!*" Pink-mink parka started to beat her breasts. "My children! My husband! What will they do?" She threw herself into the arms of her friend. The cable car, which was the size of a small elevator, lurched under the sudden movement, then swayed sickeningly.

Aunt Hortense's craggy face looked mildly regretful as she briskly cracked the back of her ski mitt across the woman's face. "Your husband and children would not want you to get hysterical, Signora." Aunt Hortense's wide purple mouth softened. "There's no danger, so long as we don't move. We should all sit down on the floor very carefully. Down there, they know what's happened to us, and the mechanics are working on it. What we must do is think about something else. I suggest a game of poker."

Mauve parka whispered to pink parka, who was blazing with rage as she watched Aunt Hortense flip up the back of her white fox coat, then carefully arrange herself, cross-legged, on the floor of the cable car. She opened her large, crocodile Gladstone bag, groped inside and produced a silver hip flask of cherry brandy, which she handed round to the five other passengers as they carefully sat on the floor.

"I know there's a pack of cards in here somewhere." Aunt Hortense searched in her bag. Her emerald eye shadow matched her Pucci après-ski outfit, and in spite of her shaggy white-fox hat, her beaky nose was red with cold, as she searched for the cards. She pulled out a Swiss army penknife ("So useful for the corkscrew"), a menu from Maxim's ("Bébé Bérard drew this picture of me the night before I left Paris"), and a battered hand-rolled cigarette, which she hastily put back; then she discovered the cards and turned her wide, enchanting smile on the boy in the black ski suit, as he held out his hand to take the cards and shuffle them; obviously, he was the only other person present who could play poker.

Half an hour later, by the time the cable car shuddered into life again, the cherry brandy flask was empty, the Italians had lost all their money, and Aunt Hortense was kicking herself for not having called this English boy, Bobby Harris, on a pair of twos.

The restaurant was perched on top of the mountain. Maxine bit into a méringue as she leaned over the wooden rail of the sundeck and looked around at the shadowed peaks, jagged against the sapphire sky. "Maman wrote that you've chosen me some lovely summer clothes from Christian Dior," she said. Aunt Hortense blotted her purple lipstick and smiled indulgently. "What are godmothers for?"

Judy felt angry and rejected, humiliated and crushed, as she looked at Maxine. Thank heaven she'd never told the others just how involved she had been with Curtis. Curtis would never have dared dump a girl like Maxine, Judy thought. Dumb girls from poor families in small towns are always going to get screwed by hypocritical rich bastards with fancy manners, because they had all the power and all the know-how, they could use plain folks like Kleenex, then throw them away when they'd served their purpose. Feeling like a depressed sparrow, huddled in her old navy pea jacket, Judy momentarily envied Maxine more than her wealth and social position; unlike her, Maxine was happily in love and the sight of her complacent, sensual satisfaction made Judy feel that twinge of envy. "That's your third méringue, Maxine," she said. "Pierre won't love you if you get fat."

"But I'm still starving," Maxine objected. For a moment, Judy felt violent resentment. Judy's reluctant memory of the painful poverty that she had endured as a child was triggered when she heard anyone cheerfully say, "I'm starving!" Suddenly, Judy's knees would tremble, her guts would shrivel, and she would feel as if she wanted to pee.

She felt a gust of rage as she thought, Maxine has no idea what she's talking about. Until she left home, at the age of fifteen, Judy had been gnawed by hunger almost every day. Her family in West Virginia had been painfully poor, and the shame had been almost worse than the hunger. Judy remembered the sniggers of the kids at school, because they knew that she would be forced to refuse anything that cost money; Judy also remembered the giggles as she appeared in the same threadbare winter coat, year after year. At first the kids sniggered because her brown coat was far too large for her, an obvious hand-me-down; eventually they sniggered because, when she outgrew the coat, her mother had sewn on cuffs and a false hem, cut from an old gray blanket. "Listen to Judy's coat!" the kids would shriek with the cruelty of youth; her coat rustled because her mother had sewn newspapers behind the lining, to make the threadbare coat warmer for winter.

What Judy most remembered about poverty was the humiliation.

"And how do you intend to avoid starving? Or do you intend to play poker as a profession?" Aunt Hortense waved her gold bracelets toward Bobby, who was standing next to Maxine and shading his big blue eyes from the sun.

"My father wants me to be a stockbroker and join his firm." Something in Bobby's voice made it sound unlikely. "That's why I'm a student at the business school."

"But what do you really want to do?"

"I want to be a singer." He gave Aunt Hortense a crooked grin.

"A singer? Like Frank Sinatra?" asked Aunt Hortense as Maxine licked her fingertips, stretched her arms to the glittering sun and then unzipped her jacket, thinking that nice boys from good families do not go into show business.

"Not like Frank Sinatra, not like anybody you know!" Bobby threw her an impertinent, urchin grin.

"Then do you play the piano, like Cole Porter?" Aunt Hortense persisted.

Bobby gave Aunt Hortense a cherubic smile. "I play the piano, but not like Cole Porter." Still modest at eighteen, Bobby could also play the guitar, the flute and the organ; if they intended to take music scholarships to Oxford or Cambridge, the most gifted music students at Westminster school were allowed to practice on the massive, seven-keyboarded organ in Westminster Abbey. Bobby Harris's stockbroker father had firmly told him that any kind of career in music was out of the question, but Bobby wouldn't and couldn't stop playing, any more than he could stop breathing.

"Where do you sing, Bobby?" Aunt Hortense demanded.

"I don't sing in public, I just sing." Bobby scratched his curly dark hair and felt uncomfortable; he didn't want to make polite conversation about music to someone's aunt.

"So what are you going to do about your future?"

"I don't know."

Aunt Hortense had no children, but was still, at heart, a child herself. She enjoyed doing whatever it was that young people were doing that week and (unlike them) she had all the adult goodies—the cars, the cash, the credit cards, and the credibility—to make fact of the fantasies of the young. Now, Aunt Hortense leaned forward and said, "No one will throw you into jail if you don't become a stockbroker, Bobby. And if you don't like it, you'll probably be a bad stockbroker. People generally perform best at what they like doing best. So what do you like doing?"

"I write songs. I play a bit." Bobby shrugged and lifted his high-arched eyebrows even higher.

"So why don't we go this evening to a nightclub, and ask the band if you can sing with them for a few numbers?"

"*We* can't," said Maxine, crossly, "because Monsieur Chardin, the headmaster, would never allow us out of school for the evening."

"I can't." Bobby was obviously embarrassed. "Because my allowance has run out, and I've just paid for our lunch with my poker winnings."

"Aunts are for when your allowance has run out. Would you like another méringue, Maxine?" Aunt Hortense waved her purple-nailed hand at a waiter. "Myself, I have not much money, but I have enough for serious frivolity. I will ask Monsieur Chardin to make an exception for you tonight, Maxine, and I will beg your supervisor to free you for one evening, Judy. Then we will all dance all night together."

"She will, too, she's as strong as an ox," Maxine said to Bobby.

Unfortunately, Bobby did not sing the kind of songs that provided good rhythm for dancing, and he was embarrassed by Aunt Hortense's insistence that he perform in the small, dark, pine-paneled nightclub. Reluctantly, he went into a huddle with the band—four middle-aged men, wearing lederhosen and green felt jackets. There was much head scratching and explaining, then Bobby said, "Forget it, fellows, just forget it. Give me the guitar and I'll get this over with." He dragged a stool up to the microphone and started to play.

Judy was surprised to hear this diffident English boy open his mouth and holler two blues numbers as, under his agile, skinny fingers, the tired old dance-band guitar produced tortured wails and hot rhythms. Then Bobby jumped off the stool and replaced the guitar on its stand as the audience, sitting at candle-lit tables, gave a cheerful round of applause. But Aunt Hortense sent him back to the microphone saying, "The band has taken a half-hour break, so it's your job to entertain us."

Judy soon found out that Bobby only liked black American music. Under the bed in his chilly, bed-sitting-room, he kept a heavy portable record player and a suitcase full of American records. All the records seemed to be by blues singers with three names: Blind Lemon Jefferson, T-Bone Walker, Sunny Boy Williamson. Bobby treated his 78s as if they were made of spun glass; he dusted the records every time he played them, and he changed the steel needles in his record player, almost every day, to make sure that the discs weren't damaged.

"I suppose you couldn't write home to one of your friends, Judy, to get me some records?" Bobby threw her his angelic smile. "It's terribly difficult to get blues records, even in London, and it's downright impossible in Switzerland."

So that's why he's being so cute, thought Judy, who now found it hard to believe that any boy could be nice to her, simply because he liked her. But Judy soon found out that she was wrong about Bobby Harris. He genuinely liked Judy because she was nothing like the twinset-and-pearls, protected, fluttery girls of whom his parents approved. Bobby liked Judy because she was brash, independent and—above all—because she was American. Anything American was magic to Bobby. Little blond Judy, in her pedal pushers and navy pea jacket, seemed as glamorous and alluring as his new pinup, Marilyn Monroe.

Judy liked Bobby because he made her laugh, and because she was flattered by Bobby's comparing her to the blonde in the potato sack, who was pinned up on his wall. Bobby's friendly attention helped to rebuild Judy's demolished self-esteem and, with the puppylike resilience of youth, she quickly started again to look forward, hopefully, instead of backward, regretfully.

Bobby's courtship strategy was to play his most sexy, suggestive songs late into the night. However late Judy finished work at the Chesa, Bobby would always be awake and waiting for her, ready to throw open the big, double windows of his room and help her scramble up from the street below. His fat, sulky landlady would not have allowed it but, luckily, she was a sound sleeper. One night, as Bobby played to her, Judy went to sleep, sitting on the floor with her back against the wall, and didn't wake up until morning. Soon, Judy couldn't see the point of crunching back to the Imperial through the starlit streets at four in the morning, when she would have to be up again at six. Somehow, she managed to survive on hardly any sleep, muttering that if Napoleon only needed two hours a night, then she had better cultivate his habit.

One evening, when Judy was sitting cross-legged on the threadbare rug in Bobby's room, she said, "Maxine's boyfriend, Pierre, says you're going to get thrown out of the business school, Bobby, unless you start working. He says you're rude to the lecturers and never write any essays."

"At least I'm not so dumb as that ski-bum, Pierre." Bobby fixed a capo on the neck of his guitar to alter the pitch. "The Head had me in for a wigging, but as a matter of fact, I hope that they do chuck me out." He readjusted the capo. "Anyway, if I get expelled, I'll be unemployable, and then I'll be *free*!"

"But you'll never get a good job," Judy worried. "You can't waste all your time playing these songs. You ought to be studying in the evenings."

"I wish you'd stop telling me what to do." Bobby was annoyed.

"It's for your own good, Bobby. I'm only thinking of you."

"I wish you wouldn't."

"What do you mean?" Judy thought, not another one, getting ready to walk out on me. She said anxiously, "Why shouldn't I think of you? You love me . . . don't you? You've told me so, often enough."

Bobby said nothing.

"Telephone, Monsieur Harris, from Paris!" He could hear the disapproval in his landlady's voice as she shrieked up the stairs after breakfast.

It was Aunt Hortense, with a surprising suggestion.

"You're a frivolous, irresponsible old woman," he happily shouted into the black receiver.

"And I miss you, too," Aunt Hortense's mellifluous voice floated out of the trumpet-shaped ear-piece.

"You have told them I like to sing the blues, not le hot jazz?" Anxiously, Bobby raised his high-arched eyebrows even higher. This was too good to be true.

"They are delighted, delighted. It's a very *louche* little club, they love the idea. And, when they see that angel face of yours, they'll love you on sight."

Bobby scrawled Judy a note, then caught the next train to Paris.

"Two men in two months—that doesn't make you a fallen woman," said Maxine, comfortingly. "It's not your fault." She passed Judy her handkerchief, looked around Judy's narrow servant's bedroom and thought, growing up seemed to need a lot of handkerchiefs. Again Maxine read Bobby's crumpled note: " ' . . . I didn't tell you I was going because I knew we'd have a row . . . know you don't really like my songs or my music, but I'm determined to give myself a chance . . . hope you'll understand . . . hope you'll come and see me at the Hep Cat Club when you come to Paris. Don't be mad. Lots of love. Take care of yourself. Bobby.' "

"But what did I do wrong?" Judy threw herself on her bed, lay on her stomach and buried her face in the big square pillow. Her muffled voice demanded, "Why do they all leave me, Maxine?"

"Maybe you're a bit too . . . bossy?" Maxine suggested. She was not sorry to see the collapse of this unsuitable liaison, but she was sad to see Judy's misery. "A boy does not like to be told what to do, he gets all that from his mother."

"I'm not bossy, I'm decisive," wailed Judy. "Why can't I be how I am? All I want is a direct, honest relationship with a boy. I want to be loved and trusted. I want to be his friend as well as his girlfriend. I can't be a flattering, calculating, clinging vine."

"Then you're in for a hard time, Judy, because most boys do not want an independent girl." Maxine shrugged. "Why not be clever, Judy, and pretend to be a little helpless sometimes?"

"I don't think it's possible for me to play a part. I want to be an honest person." Judy sat up. "But if that's how things are between men and women, I guess I'll just have to try being devious."

In the darkness, Sandy was only a curly haired shape against the Istanbul skyline, but Judy could hear the warm sympathy in her voice, as she said, "So that's why you never knew which one was the father of your baby."

"Bobby left for Paris in early April. By the end of April I thought I might have missed two periods, but then I've never been regular, so I didn't worry much. And somehow, I never thought that God would let it happen to me. After that, I wasn't really interested in men for years."

"Why didn't you get an abortion?"

"You're young, Sandy, you've no idea what it was like for a woman, only a few years ago. We were only schoolgirls, we had no idea how to get an illegal abortion, and the doctor was Catholic, in Switzerland."

"Did any of those guys help you, when the baby was born?" Sandy would never have gotten pregnant in the first place and, had she done so, she would have gotten rid of it, in the second place. And, on the way, she would have milked any man for any money she could derive from the situation.

Reluctantly, Judy said, "At first, I didn't want to ask either of them, but then I remembered what Maxine had said. Why didn't I try a little female manipulation? Kate, Pagan, and Maxine had been so supportive—they had each agreed to help pay for the baby—but I was the only one who couldn't manage to scrape the money together—although Lili was *my* baby."

The Turkish balcony lit up briefly as the beam of the Leander Tower Lighthouse swept over it. Judy added, "It was easy for Maxine, because she had an allowance from Aunt Hortense. It was easy for Pagan, because she had an allowance from a family trust fund. It was easy for Kate, because her father was rich, but I was a fifteen-year-old waitress." Judy remembered that long-ago day, when Dr. Geneste, her gynecologist, had let her use his telephone to place the international call. She remembered Curtis's reaction. Even at that distance, his voice had sounded frightened as he said, "But, Judy, why didn't you tell me earlier?"

"How could I?" she had hollered down the receiver. "You'd just been married, Curtis. You were somewhere in the Virgin Islands, on a yacht."

There was a pause. "Don't worry, Judy. Let me have the details and I'll send you money for the baby's care. But promise me that Debra will never know about this."

"Of course," Judy shouted gratefully. "I promise that she'll never find out."

In the empty Hep Cat Club, just off the Champs Elysées, the silver-foil fringe around the stage looked tawdry with the lights up. The smell of cigarette smoke and old cooking fat lingered in the air as Judy said, "Look, Bobby, do you want to see your daughter?" She looked straight into his innocent blue eyes as she handed him the photographs. Bobby flipped through them once, then more slowly, then he stopped at the close-up of the pudgy little face with black-currant eyes. Slowly, Angelface grinned. "Yeah, she looks like me! Cute smile, isn't it?" He pulled out his notecase and carefully tucked the photographs away. "Just one thing, Judy, we must keep quiet about this, and there's no question of marriage, understand? There never was, and I told you that all along. So let's keep this just between you and me, and I'll let you have as much cash as I can."

Judy felt weak with relief. She didn't care who was the father or how she got the money, so long as her baby was properly looked after. It looked as if things were fine for the moment, but you never knew what would happen next. She'd save any extra money for a rainy day, in case the baby was ill or something. She felt guilty because she hadn't told Curtis about Bobby, or Bobby about Curtis, but then, had she done so, probably they would both have refused to help her.

The moon came out from behind a cloud and lit up the distant domes of the Topkapi Palace. On the balcony, Sandy turned to Judy and said, "You did the right thing, honey. Life is tough for a small-town girl, once she's left home. We have to do whatever we can, to get wherever we can."

Judy decided not to continue. Even Sandy might not understand the full story.

CHAPTER 16

September 4, 1979

THE BUILDING WHICH Abdullah had described to Pagan as "a pleasant little palace," was an eighteenth-century, imposing pale building with an Arab garden, through which Pagan and Abdullah were walking in the early morning sunlight, along an avenue of lofty palms, toward an elaborate fountain. The palace gardens, scented with rosemary, roses, and jasmine, were purple with falls of bougainvillea. The soft splashing of water came from the interlinked streams, fountains and pools among the verdant foliage and bright flowers.

At the end of the avenue was an octagonal, white-marble pool with fountains jetting into it. Pagan sat on the edge of the pool and trailed her hand in the water.

Abdullah sat beside her and gently caught her hand underwater. He said, "Pagan, I know I'm a difficult man and I have a difficult job to do. I have been involved with many women but you were my first love, and it seems that you have always stayed in my heart." He looked at her, in her lavender-gauze, loose, long robe, with her hair streaming down her back. "Let's not waste any more of our lives, Pagan. I love you and I need you, and I'm only going to ask you once, and I must request a positive answer. Will you marry me?"

Pagan looked at him and, slowly, she nodded. Abdullah took her in his arms and held her against his heart. Together, they laughed with relief.

They felt that they shared a secret that the world did not yet know. Abdullah seemed to drop his worries, and, gleeful as a schoolboy, excitedly started to plan their future.

Much, much later, Pagan said, "We can't announce it now. We'll have to wait until this business of Lili is . . . resolved." She added, "I can't bear to see Judy so distraught." Hesitantly, she looked at Abdullah. "Are you sure that it's not possible to help her raise the money, Abdi?" Privately, Pagan was thinking that ten million dollars wouldn't amount to more than one day's output from Sydon's oil fields.

Pagan, sitting on the low surround of the marble fountain, said, "Couldn't you possibly . . . help Judy directly, Abdullah?"

Abdullah thought, I shouldn't have come here. When first he had read that weird telegram, he had thought it some drunkard's joke. He had once loved Lili, but she had walked out on him and it was no affair of his. He had intended to stay uninvolved, to ignore the telegram. Then Pagan had read the newspaper report, and Abdullah realized that Lili's disappearance was genuine. They had arrived in Istanbul to discover that identical telegrams had been sent to other rich men in Lili's life. Abdullah had decided to keep silent about his telegram, rather than attract undesirable publicity. That wouldn't help the situation.

Pagan trailed her hand in the fountain pool. "*Please* help, Abdi."

"Pagan, I've already explained that one should never give in to kidnappers; many more lives might be in danger if ransom is paid to terrorists, because they'd use the money to kill innocent people."

He seems so detached, thought Pagan. She was uneasy about the objectivity with which Arabs view women, particularly Western women. Suppose I had been kidnapped, Pagan wondered. Would Abdi talk like this? Maybe women are expendable to him.

Abdullah added, "Paying the money wouldn't guarantee Lili's safe return. Once she'd served her purpose, as soon as they got their money, the kidnappers might kill her; it would be safer for them."

A red uniformed servant approached the fountain to announce Abdullah's next appointment, so Pagan went into the conservatory. Pagan had always loved conservatories. Waiting among the scented orange trees and the dripping fern fronds calmed her anxiety. She was feeling her usual optimistic self by the time she saw the gray Mercedes slowly drive from the Palace entrance and pass the conservatory. In the back of the limousine was a small, slim figure who seemed familiar but, although Pagan strained her shortsighted eyes in the bright sunlight, she could not see the face of the passenger.

Mark Scott, wearing his usual crumpled khaki shirt and trousers, carried his battered silver camera case into the lobby of the Haroun al-Rashid and asked for Miss Jordan. The clerk at the check-in desk was unhelpful; Miss Jordan and her party had left the hotel. Mark asked for a room, and was told the hotel was full.

Mark tucked a fifty dollar bill in his passport, handed it to the desk clerk, said he was sure that there was a free closet somewhere and which suite did Miss Jordan occupy? The clerk said he would try to find a room, kept the money, handed back the passport and delicately rested his hand on the pigeonhole numbered 104. Mark dumped his bags and ran up the marble staircase to the first floor.

Somehow, Mark had expected to find Judy alone, not sitting with a group of people that included Gregg, Sandy, and two policemen. His rehearsal speech forgotten, he simply looked at Judy and said, "I came as soon as I could." Judy seemed smaller, sadder, and older than he had ever seen her look, thought Mark, longing to take her in his arms. "Can I help in any way?" Mark asked.

"No, there's nothing you can do, Mark," Judy said quietly, "the police are handling the problem. Would you please go."

Mark looked at the group. "Judy, can't we speak alone? I want to tell you why I've come here."

She longed to touch him, to smell him, to hold him. But she knew that she dared not invite humiliation. "Mark, I know why you've come, but I want you to go. Please."

Mark said, "In case you change your mind, I'll let you know where I'm staying, as soon as I know."

Back in the lobby, Mark sat down and checked his cameras. After thirty minutes, the desk clerk discovered that two German tourists were leaving, because they couldn't stand the pandemonium of police and photographers. So Mark had a room. Again, he climbed up the marble staircase (no elevator), but Gregg, who had been watching him from the floor above, stepped out and barred his way. "No you don't, chum. Find somewhere else to stay. Judy doesn't want you here."

Angrily, Mark shoved Gregg aside, saying, "What's it to you?"

Gregg shoved Mark. Mark lost his footing and grabbed Gregg's arm, then slipped on the smooth marble staircase. Together, the two men tumbled down the stairs, shouting accusations as they fell, and then continued their fight in the hotel lobby. As Mark struggled to rise, Gregg grabbed Mark's foot, and again he lost his balance.

The two men were strangers. Gregg only knew from Lili that Mark fancied her. Mark didn't know who the hell Gregg was, but knew that he was frustrating Mark's attempts to see Judy. Had it not been for the tension they both felt because of the kidnapping, they would not have been fighting, but the fight enabled them to externalize their feelings.

As the two men kicked and punched, grappled and yelled, the pressmen who were hanging around the lobby formed a noisy circle, then started taking pictures, shouting, cheering on their buddy, Mark, and betting on the result of the fight.

Suddenly, there was silence as Colonel Aziz and his escort entered the lobby.

"Who is Mr. Eagleton fighting?" the police chief demanded of the nearest cameraman.

"Mark Scott—a freelancer who works mostly for *Time* magazine," the man replied. Colonel Aziz immediately remembered that Mark's name had been included in the long list of men who were, according to Judy, obsessed by Lili.

Colonel Aziz pointed to Mark. "Get that man off the floor and arrest him," he ordered his men.

Accustomed to being jailed by hostile police officials, Mark knew that he had only to bide his time until his fellow journalists, who had seen the arrest, were able to telephone his editor at *Time* magazine. His editor would then telephone their man in Washington, who would have a word with the appropriate government department on Capitol Hill; he would send a note, via the U.S. Ambassador in Turkey, to the Turkish Foreign Ministry, and at that point, some Turkish civil servant would lean on the Police Department and secure Mark's release. It would take less than twenty-four hours, in a trivial case such as this.

Mark still thought he had been arrested for brawling, and not as a kidnapping suspect.

At about 3 A.M., Colonel Aziz decided to interrogate Mark. He was brought from his cell and told to sit in front of the police chief's table.

Colonel Aziz said, "You have been arrested for causing a disturbance at the Haroun al-Rashid Hotel, and I am holding you to help us with our inquiries into the kidnapping of the French actress, Lili. Tomorrow a lawyer will be appointed for you by the court. You are not obliged to say anything but I strongly advise you to cooperate."

"How long am I being held here?" asked the astonished Mark. "I want to telephone my embassy. You have my passport, you can see that I only entered the country yesterday. Surely that's enough evidence? I can hardly have arranged a kidnap from Nicaragua."

"Passports can be falsified. Nobody has accused you of being a kidnapper, but it's interesting that you should jump to that conclusion. How long have you known Mademoiselle Lili?"

"None of your business."

"Oh, but it is. Be careful, Mr. Scott. You are perfectly qualified to have committed this crime. You are accustomed to procuring illegal services in foreign countries, and you are accustomed to conducting clever, lengthy research investigations. And I am informed by Miss Jordan that you were involved with the victim."

"And I'm probably the only suspect you've got?"

"Be careful. You are a long way from home, Mr. Scott. You are clearly capable of being involved with this crime, and you have a motive."

"A motive? Why would I do it?" Mark laughed and put his hands behind his head.

A policeman stepped forward and prodded Mark painfully in the ribs with a truncheon. Sharply, Mark brought his arms down.

"Your motive might be vengeance. You might have kidnapped Mademoiselle Lili because she would have nothing to do with you."

"What a crazy idea! There was never anything between us." Mark wasn't worried, but he was irritated and knew he had to hide his irritation. The best thing to do was not to refuse to talk to Old Bootface here, but to say as little as possible, and just put up with the situation for a couple of days.

"But perhaps you *wish* there was something between you, Mr. Scott. You are under suspicion because you know Mademoiselle Lili. We have reason to believe that she was abducted by someone she knew. If you had told her a plausible story, she might have left the hotel, accompanied by you, without struggle."

"If you look at my passport, Colonel, you'll see it would be very difficult to fake." Mark looked at his thick, much-stamped, many-visaed, often-confiscated, dog-eared passport, which was now laying on the Colonel's table. "You'll soon receive news of me from your superiors, Colonel. As you also confiscated my accreditation, you're aware of my connections."

Colonel Aziz jerked his head and said to the policeman standing behind Mark. "Take him back to his cell."

The next morning, Mark was released and his property was returned. With resignation, he signed for it, knowing in advance that it was unlikely to include most of his cash and his most expensive camera.

* * *

In a small park by the edge of the Bosphorus, Curtis Halifax was walking with Judy, who wore large dark glasses. Judy said, "So now you know as much as I do about these weird telegrams, and I've told you as much as I'm prepared to tell you about my affair with Angelface Harris, but remember that I only became involved with Angelface because you left me."

After so many years of guilt, believing Judy's child to be his, Curtis had been stunned by the news of Angelface's ransom telegram, which he had read about in the *International Herald Tribune* as soon as he stepped into the Istanbul Hilton.

Honest himself, Curtis found Judy's deception difficult to understand. Now he said, "But you let me think that Lili was my daughter. You asked me to pay for her care as a child."

"Curtis, I'm sorry. I can't bear to hear myself say this but at the time I didn't know which of you was Lili's father. You paid 25 percent of the cost of her care, and there was more than a 25 percent possibility that Lili was your child."

"She still might be my child."

"No," Judy was sorrowful but firm. "The grown-up Lili resembles her father, in temperament more than looks. I'm truly sorry that I involved you, but at the time I thought I was doing the best thing for my daughter. You and Angelface both helped to pay for her care, until she was six, when I was told she was dead. There was some surplus money, but not by the time I'd finished searching for Lili in the refugee camps. That trip cost a small fortune and left me in debt."

"Nevertheless, I've paid for someone else's child. And why did you lie on TV? Why did you say that Lili's father was a British soldier?"

Judy spun round and faced the angry Curtis. "Just be grateful that I didn't say it was you, Curtis." Suddenly Judy was equally angry as she demanded, "Do you understand what desperation is, Curtis? You've never been poor, you've never been desperate. You've never been tempted, you've never had to survive by yourself!"

Judy remembered that bleak winter day in 1956, after the Hungarian uprising, when she had returned to New York from Europe after her unsuccessful search for Lili in those chaotic refugee camps on the Austrian border.

Returning after a fourteen-hour, overnight flight, Judy had staggered into the hallway of her apartment house on East Eleventh and dumped her shabby suitcase in the hall. She felt desolate and alone. After Lili's birth, after breast-feeding her for three months, Judy had been forced by poverty to hand her baby daughter to somebody else, and Judy had never seen her again. Now her daughter was dead; Judy would never know her. Judy felt as if the world had turned against her. Everything seemed pointless. She would never achieve anything. Life was going to be one endless struggle, and there was no reason to continue it. Everyone wanted to take, take, take. No matter what talent she had, however hard she worked, Judy was never going to get her head above water in this tough jungle called New York City.

She checked her mailbox. Bills, bills, bills. And on top of those, she owed Pat Rogers the plane fare. Pat Rogers was the department head of Judy's office. Pat knew that Judy hated to borrow money, because it made her feel humiliated, but Pat also understood that Judy couldn't exist in New York City on only stamina, ambition and one hot-dog a day, cut into three pieces.

Standing beside the dark waters of the Bosphorus, Judy could still remember what it felt like to be hungry, not to be able to afford bus fare, not to be able to afford shoe repairs. Even though she lived and worked in luxury, Judy would always be that young girl who had lived on a hot-dog a day and, at heart, her sympathies would always lie with hopeful young girls who had not yet been kicked in the teeth by fate, or dumped by rich boys with no problems.

Judy looked at Curtis and suddenly didn't mind giving him her next bit of information. She said, "I think I ought to warn you that the Turkish police think that your wife may be involved with this kidnapping."

Curtis stood still and gaped at Judy. "Debra?"

Judy nodded. "You know that party I told you about, before Lili's gala in London. It turns out the anonymous benefactor was Debra. We were only told this morning."

Curtis's neat-featured face seldom registered emotion, but now he looked horrified. Somehow he knew that this time Judy was telling the truth. She said, "The Turkish police got Scotland Yard onto the London hotel; they opened up their books and found that the money for the party had been anonymously paid, but it was traced through the paying bank. It came from Debra's account in Philadelphia."

"My God!" Not for the first time in his life, Curtis wished that he had stayed in Switzerland with Judy, instead of bowing to the family ambition and marrying that bundle of trouble. He said, "But Debra doesn't need ten million dollars! She's worth far more."

"The Turkish police think that Debra might have arranged to have Lili killed, and that all these mad ransom notes are just a cover-up for the murder." Judy's voice cracked, "I've already been told that if Lili's body is found, Debra will be a murder suspect. I'm sorry to distress you, Curtis. It's obviously untrue and I don't believe it. Only a crazy person would do a thing like that."

Curtis said, "I'll have to get back home immediately." He thought, I'll telephone Harry and Dr. Joseph from the Hilton before I catch the plane. He dared not think further than that.

"Kidnapping insurance?" Hopeful ecstasy was on Judy's face. "You mean, Omnium took out kidnapping insurance? The insurance company can pay the ransom? Wonderful!" She beamed at the three men who had been waiting for her when she returned from her meeting with Curtis.

Oscar Sholto was head of the legal department at Omnium Pictures. He was accompanied by a chubby man called Steve Wood, who was from Special Risk, Inc., Omnium's Paris-based insurance consultants. A weary, pale Colonel Aziz had joined the group and now they sat around the table in a private dining room, which Colonel Aziz had commandeered for his investigations. Around the room, spindly gilt chairs were stacked in fours. The bedraggled decorations from a party were fading and curling.

Oscar Sholto had been darkly handsome, but it had all dropped a little. He cleared his throat. "As you know, Miss Jordan, it's not unusual for the star of a major picture to be insured by the backers. Omnium has millions tied up in Helen of Troy."

Smiling, Judy sat back in her chair. "I'm thrilled to hear this! I know it's tough for the insurers but if I get my daughter back. . ."

"I must warn you, Miss Jordan," said Oscar, "that Omnium cannot act in any way against Turkish police policy. And the police don't want the ransom paid, because it's against their national policy. No payment for kidnapping, because it only encourages other kidnappers. The main aim of the police is to *find* the kidnappers, and that will probably take time." He folded his plump hands on the dust sheet which covered the round table and said, "But the Turkish Police have to decide between two alternatives. They don't want an international kidnapping to take place in their country, but neither do they want to transgress their own laws by turning a blind eye to ransom payment."

"Of course they've got to allow payment!" Judy's smile had disappeared.

Oscar said, "What we're telling you is that the Turkish government may not allow us to pay the ransom *here*."

Judy broke in, "What are you going to do, as it's illegal to pay ransom in Turkey?"

"We have to work out how to get around the law. Maybe pay it over at sea, outside territorial waters," said Oscar.

"All we can do for the moment," said Steve, the insurer, "is to wait for contact. The kidnappers will probably ask us to set up a safe, untapped telephone, so we can talk to them. Just give us time."

"Time!" exclaimed Judy. "How much time? Months? Years?"

"Two weeks," said Oscar. "Special Risk also covers Omnium for any other delay in shooting Helen of Troy. We're due to start shooting in a couple of weeks."

"That should be ample time," Steve confirmed. "But, as you know, we first have to establish contact with the kidnappers, then establish that they really are holding Lili, then establish how we're going to get her back, then establish the price, then. . ."

"But we know the price!" Judy interrupted. "They've already asked for ten million dollars."

"At Special Risk, we always try to bargain down," Steve said evenly. "If we draw out negotiations, it gives the police more time to discover where the kidnappers are holding their victim."

"And your company saves their cash, of course. So what happens after that?" July had heard enough tactfully understated explanation; she wanted the bottom line on getting her daughter back. She had worked out the insurance company's old, familiar angle, which was always the same whether you'd had your bicycle or your Lear Jet stolen. Steve was only offering advance justifications for not paying the insurance in full. Judy was unimpressed; she'd used more ingenuity to string along the landlord of her East Eleventh Street studio, in the bad old days when she was starting out in business.

Smoothly, Steve said, "As soon as we are in communication with the kidnappers, we start stalling. We'll say that the payment has to be okayed by a lot of people in America, and then paid over discreetly, so we'll ask for five days' extension. Then we'll go back to them and say that we can only raise five million in cash, so we ask for more time. When they see five big ones within their greedy grasp, they'll give us more time. And then, in the end, we settle for six million." Steve looked around the table, then added, "And we take as long as we can over the whole business, so that the police and our special contacts can try to find Lili and perhaps obviate the necessity. . ."

"Of paying over your money," Judy angrily interrupted. She turned to Oscar Sholto. "Lili's made a fortune for Omnium. She won't be able to make any more money for you if she's dead, will she?"

"Miss Jordan, both you and Omnium want the ransom paid fast," said Oscar.

"That's why Omnium paid enormous insurance premiums to Special Risk."

Steve said, "I'm here to pay the ransom to the right people, provided we get the right results. Of course, we'll do everything we can to get Lili released as fast as possible." He saw the panic on Judy's face. He had encountered parent hostility before, so he emphasized, "Remember, Miss Jordan, as soon as we start to bargain with the kidnappers, Lili's life is much safer."

Judy threw him a flinty stare. "I'm Lili's mother and the way I see it is that the longer we wait, the more dangerous it is for Lili. I can't bear to think of her in the hands of those thugs."

"They won't be thugs if this is a terrorist operation." Steve tried to smooth out the hostile atmosphere. "If we're dealing with terrorists, they're not likely to be disadvantaged peasants striking back at society, they're far more likely to be clever, well-educated, middle-class idealists, and they won't treat your daughter badly, Miss Jordan. They'll be in the whole business as much for the sake of their public image as for the money."

Colonel Aziz said, "Whoever they are, I don't understand why the kidnappers haven't yet been in touch, to instruct us where to pay the money."

"The delay makes me think it's likely that the kidnappers *are* terrorists," offered Steve, "because terrorists don't always want the money, they want the maximum publicity over the maximum time. Terrorists fight dirty because there aren't many of them, and they haven't got the money to run the sort of war they want. A kidnap is sometimes a really cheap publicity stunt. You don't need many people, or much equipment, and you get a nice financial bonus at the end. Their weapon is intimidation—kill one and frighten a million."

"This is terrifying." Judy looked at Oscar and Steve who had started to put their files back in their briefcases.

Oscar got up and extended a hand to Judy. "Try not to worry, Miss Jordan. Lili will be in less danger as soon as we are communicating with the terrorists, and they see they're getting newspaper space for their message. It just takes time to set up the communication."

Steve added, "We're also concerned about your safety, Miss Jordan. We'd like to fly you out of here. There'll shortly be dozens of people coming forward, with reports and information. All of it will be false, and every time another witness comes forward with another story, your hopes will be raised and then dashed to the ground." For several reasons, Steve always tried to remove close relations of the victim. First, if any real communication was conveyed, then a distraught relative had only to tell *one* friend (and they always did), and the secret was general news within twenty-four hours. Second, you never knew what distraught relatives might do. They might refuse to cooperate with the police, or agree to cooperate with the police and then change their mind without informing anyone, thus screwing up a carefully prepared police ambush.

"I'm not going anywhere!" Judy almost shouted at Steve. "I've a right to be here! I'm not leaving my daughter and you've no right to make me leave. I also have the right to know everything that's going on—and I insist that you tell me everything!"

As he and Oscar climbed back in their car, Steve muttered, "Tough lady."

"Are we going to keep her informed?" Oscar asked.

Steve looked at the rabble of photographers who still kept a disorderly vigil at the hotel. "Of course not. We'd be crazy to pass on any information. She's emotional, and she might become hysterical, so she's a bad security risk. We're going to tell Miss Jordan as little as possible."

Half an hour later, Judy and Pagan sat together in Judy's hotel sitting room. In silence, they sipped iced water. Judy had just finished telling Pagan of the conference with the Omnium lawyer and his security consultants.

Judy said, "I can't stand this inaction. Just sitting around and talking is driving me crazy."

Hoping to distract her thoughts, Pagan said, "By the way, I got a letter from Kate today, sent on from London. She's bought a typewriter, a 1952 Remington which cost seven hundred dollars. The secondhand ribbon was fifty dollars extra. She says that the major powers—China, as well as Russia and America—are getting involved in Chittagong and it isn't just the little jungle war that it appears to be. It could be as expensive and senseless and unwinnable as Viet Nam, she reckons."

"Any more good news?"

Pagan turned over the crumpled blue paper. "They interrogated Kate for two hours, and she's afraid that the Bengalis are going to throw her out. Apart from that, she's well and happy. Isn't it odd that Kate's never happy unless she's uncomfortable?"

Judy didn't answer.

The only sounds in the room were the faint roar of the city and the insistent lapping of the water below.

A knock at the door brought Judy to her feet. Pagan watched expectantly as she opened the double doors; beyond them, a page boy held a cellophane-wrapped bouquet of roses, identical to the one that had concealed the original kidnap note. Judy snatched the flowers and ripped open the plastic to get at the envelope that accompanied them. "Thank God they've made contact at last!"

Pagan peered over Judy's shoulder as she ripped open the miniature envelope and pulled out a garish florist's card.

Judy gave a moan and dropped the card as if it had burned her, then fell into a brocade armchair and began sobbing. Pagan picked up the florist's pink and yellow card. Below the good-luck messages printed in Turkish were a few typewritten lines. "Put one million ten-dollar bills into a briefcase. At six o'clock tomorrow evening, let a man with a red armband take it on the Guzelhisar ferry that crosses the Bosphorus. Further instructions will follow. Tell no one. Lili will be strangled with silken cords unless I am obeyed."

It was almost midnight and Abdullah was working at his desk in a soft green study, scattered with rich rugs and hung with cream-gauze curtains.

As the breathless Pagan burst in, he looked up and his frown of concentration changed to a smile, as he grabbed a newspaper and said, "Look what's in the *Tribune*." He gestured to a two-inch front-page story which announced the death of Senator Ruskington in the Washington apartment of a French call girl. "So now, Pagan, Lili is vindicated, and it looks as if Judy's money problems can be resolved."

Pagan paused for breath after running along three corridors and up a flight of stairs. "That's wonderful news, darling. I mean, I'm sorry he died, but the old bugger was asking for trouble."

"Why are you out of breath, Pagan? What's happened?"

Pagan held out a bit of paper. "I wanted you to see this as fast as possible. Judy's received a second note from the kidnappers. Here's a copy."

Abdullah skimmed it. "I still can't decide whether these people are cunning or crazy. This sounds like an eighteenth-century sultan's threat. If they wanted to get rid of one of the royal concubines at Topkapi Palace, the woman was strangled with a silken cord." He paused, then added, "Common concubines were sewn up in sacks, weighted with rocks and thrown into the Bosphorus. One sultan got rid of two hundred eighty concubines like that. A few years later, a diver found all those ghastly sacks, still upright on the sea bed, swaying in the invisible current, as if they were dancing to music."

"I know, darling, you've told me before. A long time ago. But what do you make of the rest of the note?"

"Obviously, the police will lay an ambush on the ferry and at both landings, but often, with bandits, the first rendezvous is never kept, it's merely a test to check police reaction. However, this last sentence is strange. Why not just say that Lili will be killed?"

Pagan burst into tears. "I can't bear to think of it."

"My darling, it's late and we're both tired. Let's go to bed and I'll see what my people can deduce from this note tomorrow morning."

CHAPTER 17

September 5, 1979

BUT PAGAN COULD not sleep and turned restlessly on her bed in the hot night. Eventually, at three o'clock in the morning, she decided to take a soothing walk in the moonlit garden. It would be perfectly safe, because the grounds were guarded by sentries and also an electrical alarm system.

Pagan knew that someone would be watching her, as she walked between the low clipped hedges of rosemary to the circular pool, where a family of terrapins was kept. It was impossible to be truly alone wherever Abdullah slept. His bodyguards kept an endless watch outside his room, and in the corridors there were always silent servants waiting for commands or simply sleeping in corners.

As Pagan sat on the stone coping around the pool, she disturbed a skinny gray cat, which spat at her as it ran away in the half-darkness. Something in her head was prompting her; she felt that something important was laying half-hidden at the back of her mind, like an unanswered letter on her desk.

Suddenly Pagan jumped up, and nearly fell into the terrace pool. As the moonlight painted the beautiful garden in strange shades of gray, she abruptly remembered the exercise class in the *VERVE!* office, when that exercise instructor had started to make strange jokes about his harem; that is, his grave remarks had been interpreted by the class as jokes, but Tony had obviously been nettled when the girls had laughed at him. And Pagan had told Tony that royal concubines were strangled with silken cords. It could not be a coincidence. Tony must be the person whom Lili knew and trusted, the person who had been able to lure her away from the hotel. Tony must be one of the kidnappers!

Pagan hurried back to the palace, losing a slipper as she ran along the tiled pathway, still slippery with dew. The palm trees stood out as dark silhouettes against the predawn sky, as Pagan ordered a limousine from the sleepy-eyed attendant at the main door, after failing to get Judy on the telephone. The switchboard staff of her hotel were obviously still asleep.

Speeding through the pale gray streets, Pagan sniffed the spray of jasmine that she'd pulled from the garden's ancient, high walls, and thought how cruel this twice-over loss of her daughter was for Judy. Pagan remembered the *VERVE!* cover photograph of Judy and Lili, and the way it highlighted their similarities: the tiny, doll-like build and the little, paw-like hands—as well as the differences between mother and daughter. Judy looked so blond, blue-eyed and Nordic whereas Lili was so dark and exotic. The cover photograph had also emphasized their odd apartness. However hard they tried, and however much they longed for intimacy, Pagan didn't reckon they'd achieve it; their relationship seemed almost a casual juxtaposition of two completely un-alike people. There was so much they had shared, but so much they couldn't seem to share. However much a mother might want closeness, however much a daughter might want closeness, often it isn't truthfully possible because they have so little in common; hence those dutiful birthday cards, Pinteresque monosyllabic Christmas dinners, and uneasy outings to the theater or the movies: anywhere where they could avoid conversation.

Pagan thought of the intimacy that Judy and Lili had struggled to achieve, the intimacy of love. I wonder if it will be like that with Abdi and me, Pagan mused. Sometimes, when they made love, Pagan looked at her pale English skin next to his tawny flesh and felt curiously apart from Abdullah, no matter how sensitive his caresses, or how strongly her body responded.

In some ways, I suppose Lili's like Abdullah, thought Pagan, as she crushed the sprig of jasmine and sniffed the cloying perfume of the dying sprig. Lili and Abdullah are both aggressively defensive; they both have that quick temper; they both have that greedy, sweet tooth. And sometimes, when Lili throws back her head and glares, she has that same angry-falcon look as Abdullah.

Abruptly, the kaleidoscopic jumble of Pagan's random thoughts fell into a sinister shape. Then, reluctantly, the corroborating evidence flooded into Pagan's mind. At first, the conclusion that she reached was so unpleasant that she tried to push the whole idea out of her head and look out of the window at the leaden waters of the Bosphorus, but the unwelcome notion pushed back into her mind with a force of its own. Could Judy have slept with Abdullah? Could he be Lili's father? Pagan remembered Judy's expedient lies, from the desperate deceptions of her early, poverty-stricken years to that odd white lie she had told Lili about her father. Why she'd even repeated on television that Lili's father was poor Nick, who'd been shot in a jungle war, when Judy's friends knew that although Nick had had a crush on Judy, she would have nothing to do with him. So certainly Nick could not have fathered Judy's child. Then Pagan remembered her dead husband Christopher's last joke. He had said that two clearly blue-eyed parents could not produce a brown-eyed baby; he had been definite about it. Curtis and Angelface both had blue eyes. Spyros Stiarkoz wasn't around when they were all in Gstaad, so it couldn't have been him. Maybe I won't win the Nobel prize for genetics, Pagan told herself bleakly, as the car drew up in front of Judy's hotel, but I can't ignore the facts.

"I'll bet Tony wrote that ransom note," Pagan insisted to a puffy-eyed Judy, who was sitting up in bed. "Don't you remember that silly argument about harems we had in the exercise class in New York?"

"I vaguely remember."

"But you were present when I told Tony about strangling disobedient concubines with silken cords," Pagan insisted. "The second ransom note is too much of a coincidence."

"I should imagine that half of Istanbul knows that tourist-guide story. Pagan, are you telling me that some guy who's only capable of pumping iron on Fifth Avenue could fix a kidnapping in Turkey?" Judy was still only half-awake.

"No, I don't believe that dumb ox could work this out by himself," said Pagan. "He must be working with somebody else."

"That's certainly a possibility!" Judy jumped out of bed and pulled on an ivory-cream negligee. "But that still doesn't tell us where Lili's being held."

"I'm not so sure." Pagan walked to the window and looked out. In spite of her tenseness, she appreciated the glittering sweep of water on which the Sancta Sophia Mosque and the Blue Mosque seemed to float. She said, "The link between Tony and the second ransom note is the royal concubines. Where were they kept?"

Pagan looked at the rounded domes and soaring minarets of the Topkapi Palace and, suddenly, she had an idea where Tony might hide out. A place that would never be searched, because it was guarded: a place that nobody was allowed to enter.

Together Pagan and Judy tumbled into their limousine. As it drew away from the curb, another battered Mercedes pulled out from the side street and followed them.

In the limousine, a reluctant Judy finally admitted to Pagan that Abdullah was Lili's father. So then she had to explain to Pagan how the conception occurred. In the nasty silence that followed, a grim Pagan finally asked, "But why didn't you tell me at the time?"

"How could I?" pleaded Judy. "You were my friend and you were in love with him. How could I tell you that your beau had raped me? And what good would it have done? I know that it probably didn't seem a rape to Abdullah. To him, it was merely a prince having his way with a servant. I'm sure he doesn't remember it, and I'm sure he wouldn't do it now. All our values have changed so much in the years since we were sixteen."

Pagan was silent. Judy put her hands on her shoulders and turned Pagan to face her. Earnestly, Judy said, "Please don't wreck *your* future because of something horrible that happened years ago in *my* past."

Pagan looked mutinous. Judy said, "And you mustn't say anything to Abdullah about it, for the same reason I can't tell Lili who her real father is. Because the whole world knew that they had a passionate affair. Because, unknowingly, they committed incest. Why lay that burden of guilt on two human beings we care about, when it's unnecessary and will achieve nothing?"

Eventually Pagan asked, "Does anyone else know about it?"

"Only one person. Maxine guessed, as soon as she saw Lili at the Pierre. She didn't say anything at the time, but she asked about it later, one Sunday when Tony was driving us up to Westchester to have lunch with Griffin. Maxine said that the resemblance isn't so strong today, but that as soon as she saw Lili she was reminded of Abdullah as a youth. Lili had his coloring, his features, his mannerisms . . . and his abrupt temper."

Judy remembered that she didn't even have to admit it. Maxine had seen from her face that she'd guessed correctly. What's more, Maxine had immediately understood why Judy had found it difficult to establish a warm, loving relationship with Lili. Because Lili's beauty had come from a man who had raped Judy. She had always tried to push the thought to the back of her mind, but Judy couldn't help feeling forlorn because Lili was not a child of love. Lili didn't know it but she was a child born from violence and hatred.

"We'd like to go into the other part of the Harem Quarters, the part that isn't normally shown to tourists." Pagan folded a five-hundred-lira note and tried to tuck it into the shirt pocket of one of the Palace guides. Accustomed to curious tourists with more money than sense, the guide said, "I'm sorry, it is forbidden. There is nothing I can do." He swept Pagan and Judy out of the entrance.

"Damn." In the bright morning sun, Pagan stamped on the ancient stone courtyard. "I suppose I should have offered him more."

Judy wasn't listening because she was peering across the courtyard. She jammed her tortoise-shell glasses on her nose, and again stared at the colonnade across the courtyard. "Pagan, I know this sounds crazy," she said, "but I think I just saw Mark."

Slowly they walked down the path to the entrance gate, then Judy spun around, almost tripping up two German tourists behind them. "It is him! I'm sure I saw him. Mark! Mark!"

She ran toward the colonnade, still calling Mark's name, and the familiar khaki-clad figure appeared between two columns. Judy, breathless, stopped in front of him. "What are you doing here, Mark? We thought you were in jail, number one suspect."

"They let me out when my editor pulled rank, long distance, on Colonel Aziz. I've been following you, on the fire engine principle—follow the fire engine and you'll find a story at the end of it. So where's the fire engine, Judy? Why are you rushing off on this mad sightseeing tour with Pagan?"

Slowly, Judy smiled. "We think we've found out where the kidnappers have hidden Lili." Judy wasn't ready to confess to Mark, but she needed help to get into the Harem. "We think they're in the old part of the Palace Harem, but we can't get in because it's closed. D'you think you can help us to get in?"

Mark said, "Should be easy. Come on, let's fall in with the next guided tour. It starts at ten o'clock." He thought, first chance I get I'm going to grab her. I'm no good at explaining how I feel with words.

Again, Judy and Pagan, now joined by Mark, were conducted through the labyrinthine Palace. They inspected the Armory, the Treasury, and the Sultan's Robes. Some of the rooms were carved, some were gilded, some were tiled, and some were elaborately painted. They peered through pierced screens at the Valide Sultan's apartments, and shuffled with the other tourists along the pillared façade of the Black Eunuchs' barracks.

The self-important guide reformed his group near the Harem entrance and, as he launched into another singsong speech, Pagan nipped to the far side of the group.

Suddenly, Pagan clutched at the shoulder of a Japanese tourist, who buckled under her weight. Groaning, Pagan slid to the floor. The tourist party crowded around her lanky, prostrate body. The guide said, "Get back, get back, everybody!"

As soon as Pagan's prearranged diversion had attracted the attention of the group, Mark and Judy slid unnoticed into the wide, dark doorway to the Harem. Above one of the doorways they had noticed a decorated grille. Between the top of the grill and the bottom of the stone arch of the gateway was a very small gap. Judy pulled off her shoes and climbed on Mark's shoulders. She could just reach the grill.

Quickly, she scrambled up to the gap and wriggled through, then dropped into the open alley on the other side.

Mark followed her. They landed on a pile of builder's rubble and trash, and lay quiet, listening, as Pagan was carried to the first-aid room. In the hot sun, Mark and Judy lay on the stinking heap of rubble until the noisy band of tourists had moved on, behind the guide.

Then Mark took Judy in his arms and held her tightly against him, as slowly he kissed her mouth with his sun-blistered lips. And, lying on the rubble, Judy felt that, for the time being, nothing else mattered.

Eventually, Mark said, "Do I make myself clear? It's you I love, not Lili. It's you I want and nobody else. On a scale of one to a hundred, I shall probably feel something for every beautiful woman I see. So would any other man. But you're the woman I want to spend my life with."

A bit later he said, "Why didn't you ever write back?"

"I never opened your letters. It would have hurt too much."

"That's what I guessed. That's why I wrote to Lili. I asked her to explain things to you, I asked her to tell you how I felt about you. But she never once replied."

"I expect your letters met with the same fate as the rest of her fan mail, darling. We can find out later. But right now, we should be looking for Lili."

Judy opened her purse and pulled out her expensive guidebook, which included a map of the Palace. Mark took it from her and pulled out a pen. "This place is on a hill. We won't get lost, so long as we remember which way is up."

"Famous last words. There are supposed to be over three hundred rooms in this place." Cautiously, Judy set off down a dirty, stone-flagged corridor, dimly lit by an overhead skylight. Rusting iron bars braced apart the crumbling walls of the passage.

Gloomy corridors twisted through a maze of small rooms, linked by staircases and dark passages and tiny courtyards, where the sun scarcely fell. Sometimes a wall shone with blue or sea-green tiles, patterned with flowers. Through barred windows, Judy noticed dusty unlit lanterns hanging over the tiny rooms of long-dead concubines. She peered into the ornate, gilt, crumbling mirrors that still hung on the walls, dimly visible streaks of silver against the gray gloom. In some of the rooms they explored, the shutters of the windows were falling off, in others there were cobwebs, rotting sheets of rose velvet, and tattered canopies.

As they peered into each debris-strewn room, Mark methodically crossed it off their plan, but after half an hour, he slowly realized that the tourist plan wasn't accurate. He checked his bearings, the corridor they were in, the rooms leading off it. Then he rechecked, and after that he was certain the map was inaccurate. But he didn't tell Judy that the map was wrong. He merely walked beside her in silence, noticing the frantic, mounting anxiety with which she searched each room.

Some corridors led down half-broken flights of steps to yet more rooms on lower levels of the Palace. Some rooms smelled damp, others of urine or rotting hangings. One room was alive with rats, which swarmed over the carcass of a dead cat.

As the sunlight turned golden in the late morning, Judy said, puzzled, "I'm sure we've searched this room before. I remember those tiles with cypress trees on them."

They were standing in the middle of a small, open courtyard. On all four sides, the walls were pierced by small, screened windows. Below the windows were two iron-studded closed doors, and two doors that gaped open.

Mark said, "I'm sorry Judy, but the map's inaccurate. I hoped we might stumble on a way out, before I had to tell you. We're going to have a problem getting back, Judy. And we've nearly run out of matches."

"Mark, this is hopeless, we'll never find her."

"Yes, we will." Mark took her in his arms and pressed her trembling body against his. She felt protected and consoled. Then, suddenly, she sniffed a scent that was familiar. There was nothing stale, moldy, or rotten about it; it was a fresh, rich, delicious smell; it was Lili's carnation bath oil.

Judy pulled away from Mark, then raised her hand and put a finger to his lips. She sniffed, then so did he. He nodded, understanding. They looked around them. Nothing moved in the silence. Mark shook his head, they must have imagined it.

Then, suddenly, they smelled carnations again.

Outside, Pagan waited anxiously in the shade of the courtyard. Judy and Mark had been gone for ages. Pagan had just telephoned Colonel Aziz about her suspicions, but, as Judy had said, the Colonel obviously regarded them as a pair of interfering, "hysterical" women. Judy had been right to try to get proof, before speaking to Aziz.

Pagan decided that she'd try to get inside the Harem to look for Judy. She'd just look around for ten minutes and, if she found nothing, then she'd come outside again and telephone Abdullah. He would fix Colonel Aziz.

She'd had a brilliant idea for gaining entrance to the Harem. The official tour of the Palace included a brief visit to the roof. She'd wait for the start of the next tour and then hide on the roof. Then, when the rest of the party had gone on, she'd find her way across the roof to the Harem quarters, and try to gain access from above.

Making sure that it was a different guide from the one she'd fainted in front of, Pagan carried out her plan and, when the party was shown that part of the upper Palace which overlooked The Divan Council Chamber of the Imperial Ministers, Pagan hid in an adjoining room until the party had moved on, then she climbed out of the window and onto the wide parapet.

The roof of the Topkapi Palace, a forest of little gold-topped turrets and rounded domes, looks like a small, enchanted, deserted city. Pagan was easily able to get her bearings because she could see landmarks that she recognized, in the city and the water around the Palace.

Without much difficulty, Pagan picked her way around the domes and turrets until she judged that she was above the Harem quarters. This part of the building had been uninhabited since 1909. Some of the windows that led onto the roof were rotting, some were only just hanging on their hinges.

Pagan picked the most decrepit window she could find, smashed the glass with the heel of her shoe, then carefully put her arm through the smashed pane, undid the latch, and pushed the window open.

It led onto a small staircase. Pagan followed it down until it ended in a foul-smelling, dusty passage, littered with mice droppings. Pagan picked her way along it, and turned the corner.

From behind, an iron grip grabbed her arms and pulled her to a panting male body.

Pagan screamed. Her arms were mercilessly twisted.

Half an hour later, Mark and Judy had still seen no trace of Lili. "Let's just look in that last passage, then we'll give up and grope our way to the entrance," Judy suggested.

"It's no use, Judy," Mark said reluctantly. "We've run out of matches, and we may have a problem just getting back. Let's concentrate on that, huh?"

As they moved on, at the foot of the passage that Judy had wanted to explore, a heavy iron door opened a crack, and a dark eye looked out at the departing couple.

"Thank God he's taken our gags off," Pagan hissed to Lili. Both women were lying on a dirty, green-striped mattress in the corner of a bare room. Light came from two window apertures on the far wall; the window frames had long since rotted away.

"He knows no one could hear us, even if we yelled for help," Lili whispered back. "Any idea where we are?"

"In the Harem quarters of the Topkapi Palace." Pagan wriggled into a new position. Her hands and feet were tightly bound with rope; Lili's wrists were handcuffed and her feet were also tied. The room was filled with rotting furniture that stank of cats' piss, rat-nibbled brocade bolsters, stained mattresses, and semidecayed hangings which had been arranged in a bizarre, conversational group around a brass table-tray.

Lili listened for sounds of Tony's return. In her four days of captivity, she had grown acutely aware of his whereabouts, and since he had left the room five minutes ago, she had tracked him mentally, listening to his fading footsteps. Now she could hear nothing.

"Lili, how did he get hold of you?" Pagan wriggled until she was sitting more or less comfortably against the cobweb-covered wall.

"It was ridiculously easy. I went to the Bazaar, bought a carpet, then took a cab back to the hotel. Tony was waiting in the vestibule. He carried my carpet up to my suite. He said that Judy had sent for him to look after the baggage. I wasn't surprised, because it had already been lost twice. Then Tony said Judy had asked him to tell me that she wanted me to meet her at the Saguchi Tea Room. He said she was seeing a diamond merchant there. He said she wanted to buy me a present. As we'd had that row, I thought Judy was trying to say that she was sorry." Lili gave an exasperated sigh. "I'm so used to Tony acting as Judy's hired muscle I never suspected there was anything wrong, until he laid me out in the taxi. With chloroform, I think. Anyway, some chemical on a pad that he shoved over my nose. And I woke up here." She shivered. "He's got guns, hand grenades, and God knows what in the next room. So, act obedient, Pagan, don't give him anything to worry about. Who knows, maybe he'll untie us."

Suddenly, Lili jerked her head up and listened. She could hear Tony's footsteps in the corridor outside. "I think something's gone wrong with his plan, because he seems to be panicking and he's reacting aggressively, like a cornered man."

The rusting, iron-bound door crashed open and Tony glared at them. Gently, Lili smiled at him, in a way that she hoped was friendly without being seductive. "Won't you please free our feet, Tony. I can't feel my toes, the circulation has gone."

"Maybe I'll untie you later." Tony walked toward the window, turning golden rose in the late afternoon sun. As soon as it was dark, they'd have to leave this place.

Pagan tried her luck. "Could we please have water, Tony?"

Tony grabbed a brass jug from the tray-table and walked over to Pagan. He drank from the jug himself, then held it roughly to her mouth and carelessly jerked her head back, as if she were a rag doll. Pagan spluttered as the water ran down her face and stained her now grubby, black-and-white striped, suit.

"Maybe you want something to eat, as well, Lady Know-It-All Swann?"

Tony moved to the low circular brass table, where a box of Turkish delight lay unopened. He ripped off the wrapper and took a piece of green, sugar-covered jelly out, walked back to Pagan and held it out.

Pagan said, "But I hate Turkish delight, Tony."

"Open your mouth!"

"No, Tony, it's okay, Pagan doesn't want any. . . ."

"I said, open your mouth, Pagan."

Reluctantly, Pagan parted her lips and Tony jammed a piece of candy into her mouth. Before she had time to chew and swallow the sickly sweetmeat, Tony rammed another piece into her mouth, then another, then another. Pagan gagged but he roughly held her mouth shut until she swallowed the Turkish delight.

"And now, some pastry." Tony picked up a honey-soaked baklava cake off the dirty brass tray-table and stuffed it whole into Pagan's mouth. She widened her eyes in helpless terror as he stuffed it down her throat, leaving her face smeared with honey and covered with flakes of pastry. Tears of anger began to dribble out of Pagan's blue eyes.

Suddenly, Tony jumped up and listened. He grabbed the submachine gun from the corner of the room and ran to the glassless window.

As Mark and Judy dejectedly left the Topkapi Palace, they saw Gregg, Colonel Aziz and four minibuses packed with Turkish police, followed by armored cars.

"Thank God Pagan has called the police," said Mark as they moved forward to meet Colonel Aziz.

Colonel Aziz clearly believed himself to be on a wild goose chase but, as he had been summoned by the friend of the King of Sydon, he knew he would have to give a perfunctory search.

The small group marched briskly through the gardens surrounding the Palace buildings, until Mark pointed to the corner of the building behind which, according to their map, the courtyard lay.

"I thought we'd never get out of there alive," Judy muttered to Mark as she looked up at the ancient stone walls. Above, she could see the amazing roof of the Palace: dozens of breast-shaped domes were crowned by gilt spires, while, between them, needlelike red and white turrets stabbed the sky. As she looked up, for one instant, Judy saw a face she recognized. "There he is! Look! Tony's at that window!"

CHAPTER 18

September 5, 1979

"I CAN'T SEE anyone." Using a pair of police binoculars, Mark scanned the windows, one by one. Judy followed his line of vision. "Look to your left."

"My God! Yes! That does look like Tony."

With the binoculars, there could be no doubt. Colonel Aziz snatched up his own pair, then turned and issued a stream of commands into his hand-held radio.

Unaware that he had been seen, Tony spied on the small group in the tree-dotted park below. Aware that his attention had been distracted, Lili leaned over, and with her sharp little teeth, tugged at the ropes around Pagan's wrists. The thin nylon cord was harsh and slippery, but once Lili had succeeded in getting a grip on it, she pulled with all her strength, and the slippery knot unraveled with surprising ease. Pagan kept an anxious eye on the bulky back of her captor, who was trying to peer out of the window without being seen. With quiet, stealthy movements, Pagan freed her hands; then, with cramped and shaking fingers, she picked at the ropes around her feet, all the time aware that Tony might turn around at any moment.

Quickly, Pagan wriggled down the bed and untied the knot that bound Lili's feet, but she could do nothing about Lili's handcuffs. Holding her breath, Pagan slid soundlessly off the bed. Barefoot, she tiptoed to the iron-studded door and gently touched the rusty bolt. Carefully, she drew back the ancient catch, but a faint scrape of metal alerted her captor.

Tony whipped round, shouted, and bounded across the room, forgetting the central low brass tray-table, which tripped him. As he crashed to the floor, Pagan slammed back the bolt, and fled from the room before he could reach her.

Outside the door was the square courtyard, overlooked by high barred windows, where, unknown to the captives, Mark and Judy had so recently searched for them. Wildly, Pagan ran across the courtyard, hesitated, then bolted at top speed under the nearest arch. She found herself running along a dark corridor, with a massive green-tiled fireplace at the end of it. Ahead and to her left, a narrow spiral staircase of stone wound upward.

She heard the sounds of Tony thumping across the courtyard in pursuit as she started to scramble up the spiral staircase.

Tony sprinted along the dim corridor, then he stopped, uncertain of the direction that Pagan had taken. He ran to the fireplace that blocked the end of the corridor and looked up the chimney; he saw a magpie nest and the soot of centuries, but no Pagan. Then, from behind him to his left, he heard her scrambling up the spiral stone staircase.

Tony spun around, dashed back, then leaped in pursuit up the narrow stone steps. As he charged upward, he nearly tripped over his Uzi machine gun. Cursing, he propped it carefully in an alcove, then once more bounded upward.

The staircase gave on to the leaded roof of the Palace. As Pagan scrambled out of the opening at the top of the staircase, she found herself in a shimmering hot landscape of ten-foot-diameter domes, and small towers with catwalks between them. As she heard Tony's angry shout, the panic-stricken Pagan tore along a catwalk between two rows of gold-spiked domes until, breathless and sobbing, she reached a parapet, beyond which was a sheer drop.

In desperation, Pagan jumped onto the parapet and ran along the narrow wall. At the corner, she stopped and turned. Tony was nowhere to be seen. Pagan realized that she was an easy target and made a split-second decision to hide in the deep shadow behind one of the red towers. Quickly, she fled to the nearest small tower and dashed behind it—straight into the arms of Tony.

Triumphantly, Tony grabbed her, but Pagan ducked and managed to evade his grip. Terrified, she jumped back onto the parapet and ran from Tony along the narrow edge. Tony's long athletic strides quickly lessened the distance between them, which grew shorter and shorter until Pagan could hear his rasping breath behind her. Sensing that he could almost touch her, Pagan panicked, screamed, and almost lost her balance on the parapet.

Suddenly, down below, among the trees, Mark heard the scream, looked up, caught sight of the chase along the parapet, and started to run forward.

Again, Pagan screamed in terror, her arms flailing wildly as she tried to regain her balance. Somehow she succeeded and took a breathless step backward to safety, but the enraged Tony was right behind her and, with one hand, he shoved her forward, off the roof and into the sheer drop below the parapet.

Screaming, Pagan managed to spin round and clutch at Tony, her weight pulling him toward the vertical drop. For a moment, they swayed together on the parapet, and it looked as if both of the figures, silhouetted against the blazing late afternoon sky, were going to plummet to the ground.

Then Tony managed to shake himself free of Pagan and violently shoved her forward. Screaming, she fell over the parapet and plunged toward the earth below.

Transfixed with horror, Judy watched Tony recover his balance, scramble off the parapet, and disappear from sight.

Down below, among the dusty foliage, police paramedics ran toward the copse of small trees where Pagan had fallen. A whistle blew and orders were barked. Colonel Aziz's men immediately scattered around the Harem area of the Palace and, as Judy watched, police marksmen appeared on the domed roof and took up their positions behind the slender turrets.

Tony had again disappeared into the depths of the Harem.

Still handcuffed, her feet numb, Lili stumbled along yet another dark corridor. Her heart was pumping wildly and she was panting with fear but as she half-ran over the uneven stones of the passage, her fright was nothing compared to the terror she had previously felt, lying handcuffed and helpless, as again and again

Tony had loaded and unloaded his machine gun, taken random aim at the wine jug, the window, or the woman tied on the bed, then pretended to squeeze the trigger.

Suddenly, Lili saw a faint glimmer of light and, hopefully, started to run toward it. Dimly, she could make out a wide stone doorway.

Thankfully, she reached it, then stopped in surprise. Beyond the doorway, brilliant sunlight shone down like spotlights from the high arched windows of a big room; the far half was covered by a low platform surrounded by a golden balustrade. The ceiling was fretted and latticed in gold and the walls were edged with elaborate scrolls of gilt leaves and ribbons. The entire, sumptuous golden room was spotted with mold, and hung with cobwebs. Tiny, even rows of claw-marks on the floor showed where birds had hopped in the thick carpet of dust.

Opposite Lili, at the far end of the gorgeous room, was another elaborate doorway. Joyfully, Lili dashed toward it, to find herself in another equally sumptuous, sunlit room with high, unreachable windows, and another elaborate doorway facing her. Each room led into another room and, as if in an eerie nightmare, Lili ran through salon after overdecorated salon, each one smothered with dusty, golden swags of fruit, and *trompe l'oeil* paintings of formal gardens that seemed to offer fresh air and freedom, but then cruelly denied it.

Finally, Lili reached the end room. It was a square, tiled chamber with no windows and no further door. The walls were covered in an ogee medallion pattern of neat blue flowers, and eight feet above the floor was a gilt frieze of inlaid Arabic script.

Frantic, Lili looked about her for a way out of this lavish, silent, cul-de-sac. But there was no way out, she realized. Despondently, she started to stumble back along the way she had come, through all the golden rooms, following her own bare footsteps in the dust.

When she reached the last golden room, the dark corridor lay in front of her. Regretfully, she turned her back on the treacherous sunlight. In the distance, echoing and distorted through the many passages, Lili could hear Tony's faraway voice, although at first she couldn't hear what he was yelling. Then, faintly, she heard him cry, "I know you're there, Lili! I'm not going to let you get away!"

Lili firmly told herself that there was no need to be frightened. All she had to do was to hide in a dark place until she heard the sound of a search party. Lili's heart thumped with fear as she plunged again into the gloomy labyrinth before her, looking for somewhere to hide. As she half-stumbled, half-ran, along, she noticed, in an alcove, a horseshoe-shaped trap door, raised and lying at a drunken angle against the wall. Below it gaped an opening, down which led stone steps, hollowed by the passage of many feet. Lili hesitated, then she heard a door crash open near at hand, and Tony's voice again threatened. Quickly, Lili lowered herself into the darkness, taking care to make no sound.

Once below the level of the floor, Lili's eyes quickly adjusted to the darkness. At the bottom of the stone steps an underground passage beckoned and, in the faint light, Lili could see a low, half-open door to her left. She would hide behind that door, she decided, and pushed it.

The door was stuck. Lili leaned against it and shoved as hard as she could. As the door flew open, Lili felt a rush of unearthly, fast, frightening terror. She seemed to be surrounded by flying demons, as, with a flapping of leathery wings, she felt sharp little claws, furry talons, skinny limbs, and blinding little creatures beat against her head and body.

In the darkness, Lili screamed and screamed and screamed.

She heard Tony cursing as he crashed down the steps behind her and grabbed her by the hair.

"Is Pagan dead?" Judy anxiously asked Mark, as he crouched down beside her in the juniper brush.

"No, but she's badly hurt. It looks like two broken ribs, and a broken leg, shock, and concussion. Luckily, the trees broke her fall. They've taken her to the French Hospital behind the Divan Hotel. I saw her into the ambulance, then came back here to look after you. Colonel Aziz is informing the King."

"Nothing's happened here for the last thirty minutes," said Judy. They were both silent for a moment, listening to the interminable police megaphone as it ordered Tony to come out with his hands up.

"The police always string out a siege as long as they can," Mark comforted Judy. "The longer it goes on, the jumpier the kidnapper gets, and the more likely he is to make a mistake, or lose his nerve and surrender."

A burst of machine-gun fire came from the window overhead, as Tony opened fire on the policemen below. Everyone scattered to take cover.

Mark pulled Judy behind some juniper bushes, out of the line of fire, then he snaked forward toward the shooting.

Judy jumped as she felt a hand on her shoulder. It was Gregg, who had crawled up behind her, through the juniper bushes.

"How did you get here, Gregg?"

"Came up with the *Tribune* reporter. The hotel bar emptied as soon as they heard about this siege. Is Lili still in there?"

"Yes, Pagan said he'd got her handcuffed in one of those rooms. Then Pagan passed out, so that's all we know." Judy nodded upward. "He's up there, where the shots are coming from."

There was a burst of fire from Tony's Kalashnikov. Again, Colonel Aziz turned on his megaphone and ordered Tony to surrender. Crouching low, a junior police officer ran up to the juniper thicket and ordered the three Europeans to vacate their inadequate cover and get behind one of the armored cars, positioned below the Palace walls.

As they cowered behind the hot metal vehicle, Judy, her face sunken and pale, leaned against Mark's chest for comfort. "Mark, what's going to happen?"

"I don't know." He stroked her fine blond hair. "I've seen gunman behave this way before. They get carried away by the excitement of it all, and by what appears to be their power. Then, as soon as they've fired the first shot, it's too late for them to get out, so, whether they know it or not, they're in it to the death."

"And Lili's up there with that lunatic?" Gregg anxiously watched the window where Tony had appeared. "Are the police inside as well?"

"Crawling all over the Harem by now, but there's not much they can do while he has Lili as a hostage!"

On either side of them, young, eager Turkish policemen crouched with their weapons. Judy remembered Spyros Stiarkoz's warning about trigger-happy police. She said, "Colonel Aziz won't let us go into the building. But I'm terrified that if the police storm that room from the outside, someone will accidentally shoot Lili."

"Judy's right. These boy cops are longing for a shoot-out; look at their faces!" said Gregg, picking up Mark's binoculars and scanning the Palace walls. "There are a lot of handholds on that building; it shouldn't be difficult to climb down it, from the roof, by rope."

"What would be the point of that?" Mark asked.

"If somebody distracted Tony, at one window, I could toss a smoke bomb in the second window and then jump in after it."

"Smoke bomb?" queried Judy. "Where do we get a smoke bomb?"

Gregg said, "The police are sure to have some. If not, they'll have tear gas, which will be nastier, but even more effective."

Mark said, "I suppose you want me to steal a smoke bomb."

"I'll offer the guard a cigarette while you sneak into the minibus."

Ten minutes later, Mark had a rope, and two smoke flares, an axe, and a distress rocket. Twenty minutes later, he and Gregg were among the breast-shaped cupolas of the Harem roof.

Leaning over the parapet, Gregg pointed with one finger as he sketched his idea to Mark. "This wall is at right angles to the wall with the windows in it. If you let me down on the rope, to the little ledge, I can shuffle along it, swing round the corner, get my foot on the ledge again, edge along until I reach the window, toss the smoke bomb through, swing in after it, and grab Tony from the rear."

"Why not drop down from the parapet, straight above the window?" Mark asked.

"Because my legs would appear in the window; there'd be no element of surprise. And I wouldn't be able to maneuver into the window with the correct momentum. I'm going to have to dive into that window."

Mark thought, the guy's got guts. "Okay, let's go. Tell me what you want me to do."

Gregg showed Mark how to slip the rope around the nearest turret and take the strain, as Gregg tied the other end of the rope around his waist, then threw a leg over the parapet.

Hanging onto the rope, Gregg planted his sneakers on the ancient stone wall, leaned out and started to walk down. As he descended, Mark played out the rope. Gregg could not be seen by Tony because the corner of the building lay between them.

Gregg passed two ornamental ledges, then stopped at the third one. Inch by inch, with arms outstretched, Gregg slowly shuffled sideways along the ornamental ledge, toward the corner on his right. Trying to feel as if the wall were sucking him into it, he clutched at handholds in the rough stonework, until his right fingertips eventually touched the corner.

Gregg silently looked up at Mark and nodded, then swiftly he pushed the upper part of his body out from the wall and swung himself around the corner, feeling with his right foot for the continuation of the ledge he was standing on. He had checked from below, before he started, that the ornamental ledge continued round the building.

Gregg was sweating as he put his right foot round the corner. This was partly because of the blazing heat and partly because he knew that, as soon as he turned the corner, he would be within gunshot range of Tony. Dangling from the rope, Gregg felt naked and vulnerable. Firmly, he told himself that Tony couldn't see him, and wouldn't see him, because Tony wouldn't risk putting his head out of the window, or the Turkish police would shoot it off.

Then, to his horror, Gregg realized that the continuation of the ledge on the far side of the corner was not the same depth as the ledge upon which he had been standing. It had not been possible to see this, either from below the Palace or from the roof.

Gregg kept feeling for the ledge with his right toe, but the ledge was only about an inch wide—too narrow to stand on—and as soon as Gregg put any weight on it, his foot slipped off.

He tried again, but the ledge crumbled, and again his foot slipped as soon as he put his weight on it.

Gregg turned his sweaty face up to Mark and shook his head. Slowly, he began to inch back along the ledge. He was almost directly below Mark when his left handhold, a piece of decorative leadwork, came away from the wall. Gregg stumbled, swayed, then fell off the ledge, dangling on the end of the rope, like a spider on the end of a string.

Mark braced his feet against the parapet and took the strain.

Very slowly, Gregg swung his legs, searching with his sneakered toes for a foothold on the pitted wall. Eventually, one groping toe found the ledge. Gregg leaned out, pulled on the rope, and began to slowly climb to the top of the parapet.

"Shit!" he grunted, as he swung himself over and onto the roof.

Mark nodded.

Once again inside that gruesome room, her feet tied more tightly than before, Lili lay on the green-striped mattress, quivering with terror. "Tony, for God's sake, let's give ourselves up!" she begged. "Otherwise the police are going to kill us both."

Sheltering behind the window embrasure, Tony said nothing, but fired a burst of machine-gun fire into the dusk.

Lili closed her eyes and linked her handcuffed fingers in an unconscious gesture of supplication. As she did so, she felt—on her center finger—the coral rosebud of the ring that her mother had given her. It comforted Lili.

"I'm pretty certain that if he lets me in, I can talk him out." Judy stood in front of Colonel Aziz, a resolute expression on her face. "He knows me, he trusts me and, when he's in his right mind, he's devoted to me. If anyone can get through to Tony, I can."

Covered with gray dust, Gregg added, "There's only one guy in there; I don't see what we have to lose."

Eventually, Colonel Aziz said, "As you say, it is worth a try. Very well. You will go in with six of my men. You will try to persuade him to open the door. You will stand aside as six of my men throw themselves into the room. If two men take the gunman, two throw themselves to the left, and two to the right, and shoot, we will have the best chance of getting Mademoiselle Lili out alive."

"No!" Judy spoke quietly and firmly. "I want to go in and persuade Tony to come out. I know exactly how to do it. If I fail, you can storm the room with smoke bombs, tear gas and bullets. But I won't have such unnecessary risks taken with my daughter's life, until I've tried to get Tony to come out peacefully."

Outside the studded wooden door, Judy shouted "Tony! Thank God I've found you. I'm alone. Please let me in."

"What do you want?"

"To get you out of this alive. Please let me in."

There was a long, nerve-racking pause.

"No."

"Tony, I don't want you to come out, *I* want to come *in*." Judy pleaded, "I'm your friend, Tony. This is *Judy* out here."

"Things ain't goin' as I hoped, Judy."

"That's why I'm here, Tony, so that together we can work out what to do next."

Nothing happened.

"You're sure you're alone, Judy?"

"I'm alone."

Another long pause.

"Okay, I'll undo the bolt and cover the door," shouted Tony. "Come in, then bolt the door behind you. If there's anyone behind you, I'll shoot."

They heard the sound of the bolt slowly being pulled back.

Judy gestured frantically, and the men behind her took cover in the doorways. Judy stepped forward and pushed the massive door open.

"Bolt the door," said Tony. "Gee, I'm glad to see you, Judy."

"Judy!" gasped Lili, struggling on the green-striped mattress. Judy looked at her with dismay, but fought back her natural inclination to run to her daughter. She ignored Lili and beamed at Tony.

"I've missed you, Tony." Judy tried to behave as if they were still in the *VERVE!* office. "And I sure could do with a workout. I'm out of shape."

"Yeah, well. . ."

"May I sit down, Tony?" Judy knew that she should move slowly and deliberately and, at any cost, avoid startling the gunman.

"Sure, go ahead."

Judy sat on a stained rose-brocade mattress. "May I eat a peach, Tony?"

"Sure, go ahead."

From the central, low brass circular table, Judy picked up a half-rotten peach, around which a few flies had been hopefully buzzing. She knew that the table was really a brass tray on a plinth, and she considered flinging it at Tony, then leaping to unbolt the door. But not yet. She was supposed to try to get him out peacefully.

Outside there was total silence.

Inside, Tony stood, submachine gun in his hand, with his back to the wall by the window. Lili lay on the green-striped mattress, not moving.

"What was the plan, Tony?" Judy asked.

"I never meant it to get outta hand like this, Judy. I only wanted to help you."

"You've always been wonderful to me, Tony. But why did you think I needed help?"

"I knew that the magazine was gonna fold. I heard Tom talking to the Lady

Mirabelle people. Then, late one night, when I was waiting to take you home, I heard you tell Tom that you wanted someone to kidnap Lili."

"*What*?"

"It was after Tom had said something about kids giving you more trouble when they was grown up than when they was small." Tony shifted his weight from one foot to the other. "Judy, you said you wanted a miracle to happen. You asked Tom to kidnap Lili for a ten-million dollar ransom, then give the money to you. But the putz said he didn't know how to handle a kidnapping. You called him a weakling, Judy. You said you couldn't rely on him."

"But I *can* rely on you, Tony," beamed Judy, as, with horror, she vaguely recalled her joking conversation with Tom. She took another bite of the disgusting peach and leaned back against the pink brocade.

"Yeah, so I thought, I'll do Judy a favor and make a bit for myself as well, then hide out in Europe, change my appearance a bit, that stuff. I never had such a great life in the States until you appeared, Judy, and I knew that if the magazine closed, I'd lose my glamour job. But, like it says in the *VERVE!* self-help articles, nobody has to put up with what they think they're stuck with."

"The clever thing," said Judy, hoping that she wouldn't retch, "was those ransom telegrams. They got *front page coverage*, Tony! How did you think of that?"

Tony looked pleased. "The Greek guy was easy. He wanted to be Lili's sugar daddy. That's what gave me the idea. Originally, that is. I sorta kept this idea hangin' in my mind, then bits got added."

"Like?"

"Like I hear the pop star yellin' at you on the phone. I think the guy's got no manners, the guy's rich, and the guy seems to think he's Lili's father."

"Then?"

"Then I'm waitin' for you outside Mr. Halifax's office and the door's open a crack . . . I can hear you cryin' . . . well, I guess I opened the door. His secretary's got her own office, so she doesn't sit outside the boss's door. I reckon that's a big mistake. So, anyway, I hear that Mr. Halifax has got the same idea as the pop star and I think, little Miss Jordan, she sure kept them guessin', even when she was a kid."

"But how did you get here, Tony?"

"Simple. I flew to Britain, caught a ferry across the Channel, then got here by train and bus. Don't worry, Judy, I didn't leave a clear trail."

"Then what did you do?"

"I had a copy of your travel itinerary, the one you left for the office. So I knew where you'd be staying, and I knew you'd have one of the fancy suites, facing the water, so I rented a room on the Asian side of the Bosphorus and bought some hardware in the Bazaar. I followed you pretty well as soon as you arrived. I know Lili likes to go around by herself sometimes, so I just waited for a chance. It came sooner than I expected."

"And what did you plan to do after you'd got the money?"

"My contact at the Bazaar, the guy I'd bought the guns from, put me in touch with a seaman who was going to hire a speedboat. After the man with the red armband got onto the Guzelhisar ferry, I was goin' to wait until the boat was in the middle of the water, then grab the suitcase from him and jump over the side. Then the speedboat was going to pick me up."

"But wouldn't that have been very risky, Tony?"

"Judy, you know I'm a first-rate swimmer, and the whole thing took less than thirty seconds in our trial. You see, the ferry can't stop suddenly. I knew there would be police on board, but they probably wouldn't be able to shoot straight, not from a moving boat on choppy water, at a speedboat on an erratic course."

Judy thought with horror, I wonder if he realizes that kidnapping is a crime punishable by death in some American states. Gently she asked, "And then what were you going to do?"

"I was going to send another bunch of roses to tell you where to find Lili."

"Such a *clever idea*, Tony."

"Yeah, then I was going to fly to Egypt, meet you there, and give you half the cash." He frowned. "Maybe *lend* you half the cash. Until your business was straightened out." Suddenly he raised his machine gun as something outside the window distracted his attention.

But it was only a bird.

Neither Judy nor Lili moved. They were both terrified. Suddenly, Tony relaxed and grinned. "I also reckoned you musta bin quite a goer, when you was a girl, Miss Jordan."

Judy gave a tight smile as Tony continued. "Then the fourth telegram I sent to your friend, the King, after I heard you and Maxine talkin', on your way up to Westchester last fall. She said she guessed. . . "

Judy looked astonished when Tony mentioned the fourth telegram, then she quickly interrupted him. "Maxine was right, Tony, and so were you, to send those telegrams to men with plenty of money. But what we have to do now is figure out how to get out of here."

"Yeah. I could do with a few ideas on that subject. Like I said, it ain't worked out as I intended."

"How to get out of here *fast*, Tony. I've got a limo outside with smoked-glass windows. If we can make it into that, we've got a chance."

"What about *her*?" Tony jerked his head to Lili, who was lying gagged and handcuffed on the green-striped mattress.

"What matters is *you* and *me*, Tony. All they want is her, so they can have her," said Judy in a firm, reasonable voice. "But you and I have to get to the limo."

"How about we distract their attention by droppin' Lili outta the window?"

Judy's stomach turned over. She'd hoped to get Tony out and leave Lili in the room. "Better if we use her as a hostage. Take her with us."

Tony looked at her with an unnerving, cunning expression. "How do I know there ain't an ambush out there?"

Judy swallowed hard. Dammit, she'd gone too far too fast, as usual. In a quiet, soothing voice, she reassured him. "I'll walk in front and you follow, with the gun." In a reasonable voice, she added, "I'd hardly be likely to put myself right in the line of fire, would I? Anyway, the police don't know I'm in here."

"You were in here before. With that guy."

"Well, then you know I wasn't with the police. And I've shaken off Mark. You know, I haven't wanted anything to do with him for months, after I caught him in bed with *her!*" She threw a contemptuous glance at Lili.

Tony thought about this for a few moments, then grunted in agreement.

"So how do you want this played, Tony?"

Tony thought again. "Untie her legs."

Judy slowly got up, walked over to the green-striped mattress and, without looking at Lili, she untied the nylon rope around her ankles, then helped Lili stand up.

Lili felt painful pins and needles in her legs, because the rope had been tight around her ankles. She looked at the floor, avoiding eye contact with Tony.

"Now what, Tony?" Judy asked, then realized that she had made another mistake, as Tony looked harassed. He had no idea what to do.

Judy said, "Would you like me to unbolt the door? Then you can follow me, with the gun, and that troublemaking little bitch can walk behind you, until we're safe. Then we can dump her."

Tony moved away from the window to the wall behind the door. "Okay, Judy, open it."

Slowly, Judy opened the door and walked out. As she appeared, Colonel Aziz's marksmen drew back into the shadowed doorways of the courtyard, out of sight. They couldn't jump Tony because he had his gun in Judy's back. If anyone shot Tony, Tony would probably shoot Judy as he died.

Judy stumbled along the corridor. Although fully dressed, she felt so naked and exposed, totally vulnerable as they moved into the courtyard. Tony walked behind her. His right hand held his SMG trained on her back and, with his left hand, he dragged Lili by her handcuffs.

They reached the courtyard beyond the room. Judy thought fast. She screamed, "My God, Tony, the police are on the roof!"

Tony looked up.

Judy threw herself to the ground, covering her face with her arms. Lili twisted herself from Tony's grasp and flung herself to the ground. Tony was momentarily thrown off balance, and staggered.

There was a burst of gunfire, bullets ricocheted around the small stone-enclosed space, and then there was silence.

Judy uncovered her head and slowly looked up. First, she saw a pair of large, cheap black boots that belonged to a police gunman. Beyond them, she saw a rivulet of blood trickling into the center of the courtyard.

Tony lay dead on the stained stone flags in front of her. Suddenly, the courtyard was full of activity.

Judy picked herself up and ran to Lili. "Are you all right? Are you hurt?"

Lili shook her head. Crying, Judy beckoned to a policeman, who produced a knife and cut off Lili's gag.

"Where are the keys to your handcuffs?"

"In Tony's shirt pocket."

Judy ran to the slumped figure of Tony and, with shaking hands, felt in his shirt pocket. She returned to Lili with the key, but her hands were shaking too severely to unlock the handcuffs. Colonel Aziz stepped forward, took the key from Judy and unlocked the handcuffs.

As soon as Lili's hands were free, she flung her arms around Judy. "You did come for me," Lili said, as she fought back tears of relief and happiness. "My real mother did come for me, in the end."

CRIMSON

For my very dear friend
Jennifer d'Abo

What women want in life is love and what
men want is power—and men want power
as much as women want love:
women think that they don't understand what
power is, but in the nursery, power is
called getting your own way.

From *A Burning Heart* by Elinor Dove

BOOK ONE

CHAPTER I

Monday, 5 July 1965

W*ITHIN THE CHÂTEAU* de Saracen, cream blinds had been lowered in the main bedroom, but the glare of the July sun reflected from the Mediterranean Sea below could still be felt by the gaunt, white-clad nurse as she rustled from the bathroom with a small tray. She had a sallow face; beneath her sunken eyes were dark, liverish pouches.

As the church clock struck the noon hour, the nurse checked her watch; with an angular, careful walk on legs as thin as breadsticks, she approached the bed. The magnificent eight-foot-wide four-poster had once been the property of a Spanish princess; the high canopy was surmounted by ostrich feathers made of beaten silver; the hangings were stiff with cream brocade; and the interior of the curtains was heavily embroidered in gold, with a design of lilies. This ornate silver pile only escaped vulgarity because the other furniture in the room was simple and sparse.

They'll probably be squabbling over that bed by tomorrow, thought the nurse, although it's beginning to look as if the old girl might last another few days. So far, her three granddaughters had only been anxious and concerned about her, but once they knew that she was going, then the fun would start! Confusion always built up as the end approached. The cross-currents of emotion and the momentary paralysis of shock were followed by the whispered anxieties and accusations; then came the little plots; and after that, the squabbles and the mighty, roaring rows.

Yes, thought the nurse, when it came to money, blood was thinner than water. Her experience had been that every family was a seething caldron of violent feelings: beneath the surface of the stew simmered expectations and demands, disappointment and suspicion, evasion of responsibility, greed and fear. And a deathbed was frequently the setting in which this stew of potential violence came to an explosive boil.

An unusual amount of money, such as this old girl clearly had, was especially tempting—and therefore especially destructive in its volatile ability to draw bad or weak family characteristics to the surface.

The nurse carefully placed her tray on the bedside table and picked up the syringe. As always, she wondered what people might be tempted to do for a fortune. *Anything*, provided they weren't discovered, she decided as she flicked the syringe to expel air, preparatory to injecting the medicine into the thin arm of the feeble figure that lay in the bed.

The nurse spoke a little English but could not follow these foreigners when they talked among themselves. She didn't need to, however; she knew with certainty what had drawn them here: they had sniffed money and followed the scent of the sous here to her part of France. Now that they *were* here, she knew they would return. For once they have heard it, the siren call of the south of France will always beckon visitors back to the timeless, sensuous landscape; back to the sun, to the sharp, exhilarating intensity of the light; to the sea and the pine-scented air; to the delicious food, the delicate, seductive wine.

Luckily, the foreign tourists of July and August were usually seen only in the well-publicized resorts and rarely found the tiny, quiet villages along that sun-drenched coastal strip known as the Côte d'Azur. Saracen was exactly such a place: built on a hilltop that plunged three hundred feet to the sea on the southern side, the medieval, tan-roofed village was dominated by this eleventh-century stone chateau, firmly perched on its truncated summit.

The nurse picked up her tray and returned it to the bathroom. She lingered at the window, looking out at the spectacular view. On both sides of Saracen, cedar- and pine-covered mountains descended directly to the deep aquamarine sea. As she leaned out, the nurse could also see behind the village, to the north, the perpetually green forest of the hinterland, which still provided shelter for wild boar, rabbits, and birds.

Down below the castle, the stone arches and narrow roads shimmered in the heat; leaves drooped from plane trees and dogs panted beneath them. Windows were shuttered against the burning glare of the midday sun, which sapped all energy from the day and everyone in it. Not a single villager would be visible until four o'clock. The voluptuous summer heat of the Riviera was enjoyable only if you did not need to work in it, so by tradition, nobody did.

The nurse yawned, and wished that she, too, could take a siesta. She knew that during this long, somnolent afternoon, most inhabitants of Saracen would stay indoors in shuttered shade to doze, to make love, or simply to enjoy their temporary, midday withdrawal from real life. It was a tempting prospect. Then, when the church clock chimed four, the villagers would open their shutters, stretch their arms, call greetings to one another from their black, curlicued wrought-iron balconies, and generally behave as if, like Sleeping Beauty, they had just awakened from a slumber that had lasted one hundred years.

The nurse yawned again. Unfortunately, she could not sleep now. She had to sit with the old woman; that was what she was paid to do. She walked toward the still figure in the ornate bed.

Abruptly the nurse stopped, startled, as her patient stirred slightly, then moaned.

Lying in her silver bed, Elinor O'Dare surged in and out of consciousness, suspended in a sea of incoherence.

For what seemed a long time, a black void of fear and pain had been Elinor's only reality. Disoriented, she no longer knew in which direction the sky lay. She now felt sick and giddy, as if she were seasick, as if she were being tossed around by a monstrous wave. Elinor sensed that should she move, the steel band around her head would tighten like a tourniquet, increasing the ruthless pain.

Long ago, during the First World War, when Elinor had nursed dying men, she had at first been terrified by the noise of their pain, by the ululating groans and sharp screams that rose from their blood-soaked stretchers and their sweat-drenched beds. Even now she could recall the sweet, putrid smell of death; she also remembered the fear that had blanketed those wards, and now felt it herself, as pain wrapped her body in a formless black haze.

Was she dying? The thought was light as an autumn leaf, floating in her mind. Vaguely Elinor reasoned that if that were so, then the pain would cease and nothing else really mattered. Gradually, however, the waves of pain seemed to lessen, to lose their anger. She sensed a coming calm. Dare she hope that the pain was receding, or would that tempt the dark gods to increase it? No, there was no longer any doubt. The pain was slowly but definitely withdrawing from her body.

Eventually Elinor knew the almost forgotten luxury of *no pain*. Little by little her body relaxed, but still she dared not move, for fear of again inviting those searing stabs of agony. Elinor, who felt as if she had been holding her breath for hours, tentatively tried to take a deep breath.

Immediately a thousand needles jabbed her ribs. Her instinct was to scream, but she was unable to make even a sound. Something hard and smooth was clamped over her face, she realized with a shock, and her head was constricted by a contraption she could not see.

Though Elinor did not yet try to move, she could listen and she could smell. Concentrating, she could make out the faint, steady lapping of the sea against the rocks below her window; intuitively she sensed the sun's warmth and smelled the Provençal scent of summer.

Suddenly she knew where she was!

She was in her own bed at Saracen, on a warm summer's day. She could smell the soft breeze that blew off the hinterland, wafting rosemary, thyme, and the hot-baked-earth smell of the mountains.

Lying in her bed, Elinor decided that she must have had a nightmare, one of those terrible visions with the lingering power to convince, even after she had awakened. Better open her eyes *now* and ring for breakfast, she thought. Her bowl of milky coffee, her croissants and fruit, with the morning papers and mail would put her world in order again.

At first her eyelids seemed too heavy to lift; but slowly and with great effort, Elinor opened them a little, gradually registering the soft golden glow of filtered sunlight.

Yes. Everything was as usual. Before her, above the fireplace, hung a large, elaborately framed picture, which had been painted eight years ago, in 1957. In the life-size portrait, three girls dressed in white ball gowns sat on a misty blue brocade sofa in a shadowy drawing room. You did not have to be told that these girls were sisters: they shared a happy complicity, and although their coloring differed, they all had the same small, neat nose and large, slanting aquamarine eyes.

From the left, eighteen-year-old Clare, dark and tiny, leaned forward with a serious expression, offering a rose to tawny-haired Annabel, unquestionably the family beauty. Miranda (sixteen, skinny, still at school) perched like a bird on the back of the sofa; her face was pale and she hadn't yet dyed her beige hair that odd marmalade color. She appeared slightly withdrawn but as charming as the other two, and as heedlessly ready to fly into life.

Only Annabel could be called a beauty, for Clare's expression was too anxious and Miranda's features were a little too sharp. All three, however, reflected the charisma of breeding and privilege. More significant in Elinor's eyes, all three reminded her of her dear Billy.

The portrait always comforted Elinor. She remembered satisfying moments when the girls were small and she had taken a day off work and was about to take them out to tea or on a shopping trip: all three children would be clean and neat—socks still pulled up, hair ribbons tied—and almost quivering with eager anticipation.

Such moments of true happiness had been rare in Elinor's life and they had never come when expected but blossomed quickly, at surprising moments. She had long ago decided that you couldn't plan happiness, but you *could* plan achievement; and she had planned well, for she had succeeded beyond all reasonable expectations. In spite of all the early setbacks, the treachery, disappointments, and sheer drudgery, her success had been considerable: her twenty-two novels had been published in some forty countries; her fan mail arrived weekly by the sackful; and she received from everyone the respect that was her due. The legendary Elinor O'Dare was famous, successful, and very, very rich.

The legendary Elinor winced abruptly. The burning pain had started again, and it was *within her body*. Lying inert in the heat of her shaded bedroom, she realized that she could not move her limbs. There seemed to be no strength in her arms or legs: she willed her arms to lift, and they did not do so. She was paralyzed. She was *not* dreaming. *She could not move!*

She tried to speak, then to scream—but she couldn't. Nor could she open her mouth. Her head felt woolly and muddled. The thought slowly registered—she must have had a stroke. No! It couldn't be! She didn't want it! She hadn't yet finished living!

The effort of her anguished thinking exhausted her. Her eyelids fluttered shut, and black oblivion slowly drew over her. She willed her mind to go blank, yet somewhere outside her mental enclosure, she heard a sound. It was the well-remembered rustle of a nurse's starched apron. She smelled the hospital smell of ether and the sour whiff of medicine.

"Am I dying?" Elinor whispered in French, finally willing her frozen mouth to move awkwardly.

"No. Do not upset yourself." The nurse's voice was calm, flat, and disinterested. Elinor knew she was lying. Her first reaction was one of indignation. She was used to being in command of her life, used to writing the plot herself—as she did those of her best-selling novels. But now she was rendered impotent by her helplessness—at the mercy of this mean-voiced nurse. An invisible, inexorable pen was scribbling "The End" before Elinor had finished her story—and this time there would be no happy ending.

For years Elinor had successfully avoided thinking about death. Like many strong-minded and successful people, she had not wanted to face the fact that, one day, she would die. She had not bothered to make a will, for that would mean having to make unpleasant decisions, decisions dealing with her own mortality. So she had put it off, resisting her lawyer's gentle, persistent urging, preferring to ignore the subject, to think of herself only as enduring, invincible.

But today, lying in this shuttered room, she knew that the invincible had met the inevitable. She could only hope that she might have some time to get things in order. And she had better make her decisions quickly—or she might lose the chance to do so.

Elinor felt the uncomfortable contraption being tugged from her face. She felt too tired to move, to think, or to complain; she felt helpless and at the mercy of this impersonal stranger. Obviously, death was going to be a humiliating business, and she knew that helplessness was only the start.

Hearing the sharp, efficient moves of the nurse around her bed, Elinor fleetingly remembered daydreams from many years ago—from 1917, after she had left the small family farm near Excelsior, Minnesota, to train as an auxiliary nursing aide. She was only seventeen, still idealistic and romantic enough to envision herself as a calm, reassuring angel of mercy. World War I had inspired many young women to volunteer for auxiliary service of some kind; for most, it was a first step away from home. For most, it was also an abrupt end to innocence.

Elinor remembered her own reaction when she first arrived at the casualty clearing station in northern France to which she had been posted. She had expected the quiet orderly calm of the wards at her training hospital, not that shocking, awful noise in Ward C: the animal-like whimpers, sobs, sharp shrieks of agony, men crying in loose-mouthed delirium, while a phonograph played a Bing Boys' tune to comfort those who knew they were about to die.

Now, almost half a century later, realizing what little time remained to her, Elinor's patience vanished as instantaneously as had her innocence. Lying there, trapped in her bed, she found to her surprise, however, that it wasn't the physical act of dying that she minded, or leaving what she had fought so hard to achieve. But the girls still needed her; they needed her strength, her advice, her emotional and moral support: despite the fact that two of them were married women and the third had already established a thriving business, Elinor was convinced that the girls could not yet survive without her. Her fortune, of course, would ensure their comfort and their social prestige, but who would be there to advise and protect them?

Elinor had been able to give her granddaughters what she had not had, and what she had been unable to give her only son, Edward: a life virtually free from care; a life in which there was the time and opportunity to look for happiness and, should they find it, simply to enjoy it; a life untroubled by the financial anxiety with which Elinor had lived for the first forty-five years of her life. It was an anxiety that had faded only when—thanks to her darling Billy—she had been able to grasp success and to savor its rewards.

At the thought of Billy, Elinor's eyelids slowly lifted. In the dim light, she could just make out the small group of silver-framed photographs on her bedside table. Once again Elinor gazed into the smiling, confident eyes of the fair-haired young man she had loved so much. There he stood, flying goggles pushed back on his head, hands thrust in the bottom pockets of a battered tunic; his plane, a primitive machine made of canvas and struts, was behind him.

Billy O'Dare had been one of the few men to survive Ward C. His navigator had pulled him, unconscious, from his shot-down plane before it burst into flames. Billy had suffered a concussion, a slight cut on his head, and a bullet through his left foot that fractured the calcaneum.

Nearly fifty years later, Elinor still happily remembered the evening she fell in love with Billy O'Dare. The ward was relatively quiet when, shortly after midnight, she heard choking cries from bed 17. Grabbing the lantern, she hurried to find out what was wrong. Gently she shook the young man awake—he'd had a bad dream, that was all. Flight Commander O'Dare continued to sob, however, now clinging to Elinor's hand. His face was partly covered by a turbanlike bandage, but her lantern shone into his eyes, reducing the pupils to pinpoints of black against irises of an unusual, dazzling shade of aquamarine. Elinor thought she had never seen anything so beautiful.

"Sorry to make such an ass of myself," she mumbled.

"Don't worry. Plenty of patients have nightmares," Elinor comforted, trying to ease her hand away. She could smell, against the harsh wool of his blanket and the antiseptic whiff of bandages, the pungent male perfume of his body. He was no longer sobbing now, and she knew she should move away. Still, she could not stop staring into his eyes.

Patient 17 raised Elinor's hand to his lips and she felt the tickle of his blond mustache against her thumb. For a moment, she thought he was going to kiss her hand, but instead, he turned it over and pressed her palm to his mouth. As Elinor felt the caress of his warm breath, Billy O'Dare gently licked her hand. She felt his moist tongue run slowly over her flesh and knew again that she should move away; her feet, however, seemed glued to the floorboards. She felt a blush rise from her breast and held her breath as he continued to stroke her hand with his warm, catlike tongue. Her trancelike state was broken only when another patient suddenly screamed.

By morning, Nurse Elinor Dove knew patient 17's medical notes by heart. She also knew that Flight Commander William Montmorency O'Dare of the British Royal Air Force was twenty-five years old.

By some odd form of osmosis, the entire ward seemed to know immediately that Nurse Dove had tumbled in love with O'Dare. Beneath Elinor's nunlike white headdress, her grape-green eyes glistened, and her cheeks were even pinker than usual. There was a lively spring in her step, and Sister had to admonish her for singing to herself.

On a visit to Ward C, Billy's former navigator, Joe Grant, immediately spotted the romance. He told Billy he was a lucky dog, that Nurse Dove was special, different from the rest. When Billy repeated this observation to Elinor, she sniffed, "That's what you men say to *all* us girls. What's so different about *me?*"

Billy looked at her thoughtfully, then said, "The girls at home are pale imitations of life compared to you. You have such vitality, such get-up-and-go! You have energy. It's positively infectious!" He hesitated. "It is so American, it seems. I've seen these qualities in your soldiers as well; it's something you don't see in the Frenchies or Tommies. Whatever it is, you really *are* very special."

Looking up from his pillow, Billy O'Dare hunched his right shoulder and slightly bent his bandaged head toward it as he smiled gently at Nurse Dove. From that moment on, she was forever in his control. Long after they were married, when Elinor knew fully the true cost of love, the slow grin that so clearly showed Billy's impudent Irish charm—that complex combination of innocence and artfulness—would always wipe away her anger in an instant.

All these years after their meeting, Elinor recalled that irresistible grin; it was how she liked to remember Billy. In fact, it had become the only way she allowed herself to remember Billy—as the smiling, dashing young war hero who became her romantic bridegroom. Any subsequent unpleasant memories had been hidden in some dusty corner of her mind.

It was a pity that color photography hadn't been invented then, she thought as she stared at the silver-framed, sepia photograph. All three sisters had inherited Billy's aquamarine eyes, although only Miranda had inherited the beguiling grin. From Elinor they had inherited . . .

Elinor was suddenly reminded again that she hadn't made a will. Their inheritance: yes, there was that to deal with. She closed her eyes, then, with an effort of will, opened them again. Slowly the room settled into focus.

The nurse leaned over her patient. "Can you open your mouth, madame? . . . A little more . . ." From a spouted cup, she dribbled a few drops of water into Elinor's mouth; then she carefully rubbed ointment over the dry lips.

Painfully, Elinor whispered, "Where . . . are . . . my granddaughters?" She couldn't move the right side of her face, so she spoke slowly and awkwardly, slurring her words as if tipsy. She could move her right fingers and toes, but she could not feel those on her left side.

Feeling panic start to rise, Elinor remembered that when she was very young and woke at night, she used to clutch her rosary to keep the devil at bay; now she groped for something similarly comforting to reassure her. More urgently she croaked, "*Where are my granddaughters?*"

"I believe the ladies are on the terrace. I will call them."

The nurse went to the window and pulled back the shutters. Yes, there they were, typically heedless of the afternoon sun. She called down.

From her bed, Elinor could hear excited voices, then the sound of metal chairs scraping against earthenware tiles. Tremulously she smiled, struggling to adjust her eyes to the sudden infusion of light.

A few minutes later, her bedroom door was flung open. Elinor first saw Clare's animated, pale face, framed by long, straight dark hair.

"Darling, we've been so worried." Clare's voice was high and soft. She rushed to the bedside, knelt down and kissed her grandmother's face, then the thin, blue-veined hands.

"Don't overexcite her," warned the nurse.

"My turn," said Annabel, whose long, honey-colored hair was wet and tangled after swimming. For the past seven years, Annabel's lovely face had gazed, wide-eyed, from every Avanti cosmetics advertisement around the world. When Elinor looked at her, she thought of white Persian kittens, feather beds and pale pink peonies: Annabel was soft, voluptuous, and feminine. Gently Annabel stroked her grandmother's long, fair hair, now white at the roots, as it spread, fanlike, upon the pillow. She kissed the sunken cheeks and whispered, "Oh, Gran, we thought we'd lost you."

Both sisters were close to tears as they gazed lovingly at their grandmother. Only Clare had even the slightest memory of their parents (killed in 1941 in a German bombing raid on London), and Elinor had always been the center of their world. They couldn't imagine life without her. She had always seemed a combination of Isadora Duncan and Elinor Glyn—a bold, dramatic, and immortal figure.

"Where's Miranda?" Elinor whispered.

"She had tc return to London for the day—a business meeting," Clare said softly. "We've all been here for the last two weeks. Annabel flew from New York as soon as we heard you were ill, but it took me a bit longer to get organized in Los Angeles. Miranda's flying back tonight, by helicopter."

"And where is Buzz?" Buzz was Elinor's lifelong friend, now her secretary.

"Gone to Nice to get your medicine. After that, she's calling at the airport, to see if Annabel's luggage has turned up. Buzz never gives up hope!"

"We don't want to overexcite Madame before the doctor sees her." The nurse firmly held open the bedroom door. "You must go now, and I will call him."

Annabel turned rebelliously toward the nurse, clearly prepared to ignore the edict.

Clare, however, immediately became the anxious and responsible elder sister. "Don't be difficult, Frog," she coaxed, using the childhood nickname that referred to Annabel's large and sensuous mouth. "We'll be back as soon as they let us."

Clare gently pushed her sister out of the bedroom. Elinor turned imploring eyes toward the nurse. Silently they said, *Please get a move on. I have so much to do*. Elinor's indomitable spirit was reasserting itself.

Clare, wearing a white bikini, lay on a beach mattress by the pool. She was small and skinny, but managed to look slim and fragile; she had a fey, elusive charm: you felt that she might slip between your fingers, like clear water from a mountain stream.

Lying on the next beach mattress, Annabel wore a claret-colored silk dressing gown that belonged to her husband. She always carried this item and a set of spare underwear in her hand luggage, for the rest of her baggage seemed invariably to travel on without her. This trip had proved no exception.

When the poolside telephone rang, Annabel grabbed the ivory receiver. "Maybe it's about my luggage. If it's gone on a trip to eternity, the airway will have to pay for all those new clothes." She looked at the buttons on the telephone, which also served as an intercom, and frowned. "I'll never get the hang of this thing." She pressed a button. The line went dead. "Hell, I'm hopeless with machinery." Annabel noticed that Clare looked anxious. "Sorry, Clare. Are you expecting a call?"

"Not really. Well, perhaps . . . I thought that . . . " Clare pushed dark strands of hair from her forehead. She suddenly burst into tears, covering her face with her hands.

Annabel scrambled from her mattress and ran to her sister, embracing her, pulling her close. "What's up, darling? I *knew* something was wrong! Otherwise you wouldn't have lugged Josh and his nanny all the way from California. Tell me. Why hasn't he telephoned?"

Gradually Clare's sobbing subsided. In a tone filled with angry indignation, unlike her normal soft voice, she told Annabel of the row. Clare had gone to the beach for the day, accompanied by Josh and his nanny. She returned early because of period cramps, and in her bedroom, she found a thin, tanned woman lying naked beside her husband. A bitter scene ensued. Clare stormed to her dressing room and started to pack. She heard his car spray gravel outside her window as it took off, too fast. Kneeling by her suitcase, Clare wept until another car arrived and Josh and his nanny clattered, laughing, into the house. At that moment, Annabel had telephoned from New York.

"Then you told me about Gran's stroke," snuffled Clare.

"Poor darling," Annabel murmured, stroking Clare's long, dark hair.

"He's so clever at sidetracking. He makes *me* look like an overemotional idiot, when all the time *he's* in the wrong." With the back of her hand, Clare wiped tears away. She had always told herself that despite his casual promiscuity, her husband loved her in a *special* way, that he would never abandon their *real* love or jeopardize their son's happiness. She told herself he was only asserting his male prowess with those other women, and he wouldn't *ever* take one of them seriously. But then, that day, Clare had suddenly found that she could bear no more humiliation. So she had left him.

In the late-afternoon Provençal sunshine, Annabel silently hugged Clare and waited.

Eventually Clare continued, "I didn't want the usual reconciliation scene, the usual flowers, the usual promises—and then the usual pain next time. Suddenly I simply didn't care what happened to him." She hugged her sister. "Oh Annabel, you won't tell anyone, will you?"

"Have I ever told your secrets? But if you've really walked out for good, everyone will have to know *sometime*. Are you sure you're going to . . ."

"Get a divorce? Yes. Absolutely. I don't want Josh growing up to be like his father."

"Well, don't let Gran know, at least not yet. You know it'll upset her. In fact, don't tell *anyone* until you're sure you're sure."

As Annabel comforted her sister, a maid approached. Speaking in French, she said, "The pool telephone malfunctions. New York awaits Miss Annabel."

"I'll take it in my bedroom," Annabel said, jumping up with almost childish enthusiasm. She ran upstairs to her pale pink apartment, which overlooked the cobbled entrance courtyard and the church beyond it.

"Darling? At last! What's your news?" Annabel could hear background sounds from the New York TV station for which her husband was a news anchorman. He was one of eleven reporters, only three of whom appeared as on-air newscasters.

"Local or national, angel? It's eleven in the morning and sticky hot in New York. Yesterday Martin Luther King called for an end to the Vietnam War, but it looks as if Johnson will order more troops in. My lead story for this evening? Kennedy's original view of Vietnam as a quick in-and-out operation might end in world war." Annabel could imagine his teasing smile. "I hope your news is less alarming."

Annabel told her husband about Elinor's return to consciousness.

"That's wonderful, angel. When are you coming back?"

"I don't know. When Gran's better. Does it matter?"

Her husband hesitated. "Sidney wants to talk to us."

"Why?" Sidney was their accountant, and the sound of his name instantly set off alarm bells.

"I've decided to go after a better job."

Annabel could hear the lack of self-confidence in her husband's voice. She said, "But you love your—"

"It's a little earlier than I planned to make my move, but that's not so terrible. We're sinking deeper into debt each day, and we have to find some way to shore up our finances."

Annabel said miserably, "Oh darling, I'm *so* sorry. *I* was the one who insisted on the new duplex. It never crossed my mind that Avanti might not renew my contract." She gave a shaky laugh. "I know I'm twenty-five, but that's not *old*. Not in the normal world. Only for a model."

"Avanti still might renew your contract. We don't know."

"I wish they'd make their damned minds up," Annabel said. "I could *kick* myself for buying that apartment! I can't *think* why I was so extravagant."

"You bought it to give me the right background. You said, 'A good picture needs a good frame,' " he reminded her. "You said in order to get into the Mike Wallace league, I have to look as if I am already in it."

"Absolutely. And you will be." Annabel cheered up. Her husband had the same quick, hard intelligence as Mike Wallace: he could be just as probing and provoking when interviewing. He could also produce the sort of insistent question that turned a news interview into a psychodrama. *And* he had the voice.

"Darling," she went on, "you're one of the best newsmen on television. And remember, you're only twenty-nine years old. Mike Wallace was thirty-eight before he got his break on *Night Beat*. Plus I love you."

"And I love you. In the meantime, angel, don't take all the blame for the apartment. Remember, New York is a town about showing you can make it, making it, and then showing you've made it. Who knows, the apartment *may* help land my new job."

Annabel laughed. "Well, if you don't get your job and I don't get mine, we'll just have to the sell the place and rent, like the rest of New York. It really doesn't matter where we live. We'll still have each other."

Strapped into the noisy helicopter, Miranda tucked an unruly strand of marmalade-colored hair behind her intercom headset as she looked out at the sullen, gray English Channel below. "We left London at two-thirty, so we'll get to Saracen by seven—in good time for dinner." Miranda kept her voice as low as possible, her tone steady and deliberate; she spoke that way because she found that it commanded attention. She pressed her face against the tough plastic bubble that enveloped them. "I do *so* wish that Gran would let me learn to fly. Couldn't you persuade her?"

Miranda then remembered that this might not be necessary. It was so hard to reconcile herself to the reality of her grandmother's illness. She bit her lip and willed the tears away.

Sitting next to her, Adam Grant shook his head. He was tall, dark, and brown-eyed, with firm-hewn features and a cynical air of assurance. Miranda thought he looked like one of those almost perfect men drawn in magazine advertisements for cashmere sweaters, or that he might have fallen from the pages of one of Gran's romantic novels.

Adam's father, Joe Grant, had been Elinor's longtime legal adviser and close friend. After his death, five years before, Elinor's business affairs had gradually been passed to Adam, who also worked for the family legal firm of Swithin, Timmins and Grant.

Adam had asked Miranda for a lift in the Bell because this was one of the rare occasions when all three sisters would be at Saracen. Having them together like this would provide him with the opportunity to discuss, gently but firmly and as unemotionally as possible, what would happen should Elinor die intestate. Despite her dual U.S. and British citizenship, Elinor was resident in France, and the French tax authorities considered theirs to be the controlling law for her entire estate. Once again Adam regretted that he had been unable to persuade Elinor to make a will, because there were always complications when anyone died intestate. Perhaps he should have been more insistent, but Adam valued their longstanding relationship, and he had not wanted to upset Elinor, who clearly hated the thought of discussing her own death.

It was Elinor who had asked Adam to guide Miranda's steps into the business world, and in the three years since Miranda had opened her first small makeup shop, her business had spread—albeit sparsely—all over Britain. Last year, Adam, her unofficial adviser, had become a part-time director. He had just restructured the balance sheet for their next leap ahead.

"You know I wouldn't persuade Elinor to do anything she didn't want to do," Adam said gently. He found it interesting that this twenty-four-year-old red-haired baby tycoon who wanted to fly should still submit to Elinor's wishes. Generally Miranda made her own rules and ignored what other people thought of her.

Looking at Miranda, Adam once again found himself thinking that if all women were basically beautiful, their bodies would probably resemble Miranda's. Her slim figure wasn't voluptuous, but it was perfect: her breasts were small, high, and rounded; her waist was neat, her stomach flat. And when she walked, her long, slim legs moved in a graceful stalk. In addition, Miranda was always appropriately dressed for the occasion: that gray silk suit, simple but feminine, had been perfect for this morning's monthly office meeting.

Miranda shrugged her shoulders and decided to change the subject. She switched off the intercom to the pilot so that he couldn't hear what she was saying. "Adam, I'm not entirely happy about Ned Sinclair."

"I think he's settled down very fast." Adam had poached their new financial director from a rival cosmetics manufacturer.

"He asked me one or two unnecessary questions about our future plans. It bothers me, although perhaps I've become oversensitive since Mary Quant started her beauty business."

"Quant doesn't own a chain of retail shops." Adam's hand flipped his hair back as if to brush away an irritation. His dark hair was still cut as it had been when he was at school; parted on the right, it flopped over his left temple and gave his face an endearing, seemingly innocent charm.

"She's my direct competition because we think along similar lines. I bet she'll be international before I am. I shouldn't be surprised to hear that Ned has approached her."

Once again it occurred to Adam that Miranda had inherited many of Elinor's characteristics: her intuition and the ability to act on it, her stubborn determination, and her guts.

He smiled. "I'll run a check on Ned. *You* could be international—if only you would agree to franchise."

"I won't franchise because I don't want to lose control of my business! However tight the contracts are, you lose control once you do. Others might not want to work as hard as we do, and they may not have such high standards of presentation. So please forget it."

"If you won't franchise, then you'll have to put up with being short of money," Adam said firmly, looking at her from large-lidded dark eyes. "What *would* you do for a lot of money, Miranda?"

"What *wouldn't* I do for a lot of money!" Miranda laughed.

"I wonder," Adam said thoughtfully.

"Oh, you're so resolute, so determined." Miranda smiled. "I can't think *why* we seem to be on an endless financial tightrope."

"Because you want to expand faster than we can afford." Adam spoke laconically. He shrugged his shoulders. "But who knows what lies ahead . . ."

How *dare* he! "I *know* what you're thinking. You're thinking that if Gran dies . . ." Miranda burst into tears.

Adam was astonished, partly because she had correctly guessed his thoughts. Also he had never before seen Miranda cry. She rarely showed her emotions.

He pulled a Paisley silk handkerchief from his navy blazer and silently handed it to her.

"Damn, I've lost a contact lens," Miranda gulped. "Can you see it on my skirt? Or has it fallen to the floor?"

"Keep still. I can see it on your lap."

As Adam leaned over her, Miranda inhaled his faint musky scent. Adam moved in a miasma of sexuality, which he seemed not to notice although it was as definite as warm breath. She thought he smelled a bit like a well-groomed horse. Close up, his odor reminded her of expensive leather. This subtle erotic scent contradicted Adam's careful lawyer's demeanor, his understated Savile Row suits and shirts, his horn-rimmed glasses.

Miranda knew that Adam had a devastating effect on women. She had first observed it on a shared family holiday in St.-Tropez, twelve years ago. Miranda, only twelve at the time, had noticed that even the grumpy old French housekeeper happily danced attendance on twenty-three-year-old Adam.

Miranda knew why Adam had never made a serious pass at her or her sisters. To have done so would have been unprofessional and might have adversely affected his job. Additionally, all three sisters, while acknowledging his attractiveness, had grown up thinking of Adam as a young uncle. He in turn had always regarded them as children, much to their indignation at the time.

Now, as Adam carefully placed the contact lens in the palm of Miranda's hand, she reminded herself that he was *not* her uncle. Then she pushed this thought to the back of her head and told herself jokingly to keep her hands off the staff. Turning away from Adam to reinsert her lens, Miranda also reminded herself that at the moment, she hadn't time for a lover. In this respect she was unusual; the Pill was now readily available and every liberated girl was on it, whether or not her mother knew. Increasingly a woman was expected to jump into bed after the first date—something that didn't suit Miranda, who felt only anxiety when in bed with a man whom she didn't know well and therefore didn't trust. At this point in her young life, there had been only one man who made her feel secure.

Adam said, "Even if it distresses you, there's something I feel we should discuss before reaching Saracen; it's your grandmother's will. She hasn't yet made one, but we have discussed the matter."

Clearly worried, Adam was silent for a moment, then continued in a low voice: "For me, this is a difficult dilemma: Do I stick to my standards of professional discretion, or do I break my client's confidence in order to do what's best for her and those she loves? Does the end justify the means? Would Elinor—my client, my friend and benefactor—allow it? That's what I can't decide. Because I know that Elinor would want whatever is most advantageous to all her granddaughters."

"I'd advise you not to break your client's confidence," Miranda said, "but be sensible and tell me what the hell this is about."

"Without breaking Elinor's confidence, I can tell you that although she intends to leave the bulk of her fortune to you three sisters, various methods of controlling the money have been considered."

"What do you mean, Adam, *controlling the money?*" Whenever it came to finances, Miranda was instinctively suspicious.

"She's anxious that the money not be . . . frittered away. There are various possible ways of protecting it. She doesn't like the French legal requirement to share the property equally among all descendants. As you know, Elinor lost touch with her family many years ago, and she doesn't want her brother's children—if he ever had any—to suddenly appear, claim money, make trouble. But as Elinor is a resident of France, this *will* happen unless she makes . . . alternative arrangements."

"What sort of arrangements?" Miranda demanded.

"She's had a few rather . . . dramatic ideas, as you would expect. She doesn't like the British system, where the eldest inherits everything on the understanding that the inheritor cares for the rest of the family."

"I should think not!" Miranda was the youngest of the three sisters. For her, primogeniture would be disastrous. "Gran saw what happened to her own husband!"

Billy's grandmother, a considerable heiress, had left all her money to her elder son, an impulsive weakling, who lost nearly all of it in an Edwardian stock exchange swindle. When he died, Billy's elder brother inherited what was left of the family estate; Billy inherited nothing.

"Elinor seems to think the Greek system is the most sensible," Adam said.

"What's that?"

"A wealthy Greek father often leaves all the family money to the child most capable of looking after it, on the understanding that the inheritor looks after the immediate family."

"The most financially capable sister is me," Miranda stated.

"In financial matters, certainly. But Clare has always been very conscientious and responsible; she was like a mother hen toward you and Annabel when you were little girls."

Miranda sat up sharply. "All my life I've had Clare shoved down my throat!" Clare was the eldest, the responsible sister, whose duty it was to look after the little ones. She could be relied upon because she was steady and practical. Conscientious Clare would never tell a lie—not even a white one—and could be relied upon always to be fair, as Clare herself never stopped reminding people.

It was Clare's much vaunted sense of justice that made her feel responsible for the whole damn world, particularly every underprivileged person in it, Miranda knew. If Clare grabbed the purse strings, then they would not be opened for Miranda, who was not Clare's idea of a needy person. Miranda would be pushed back to the position of baby sister.

"Unfortunately, Elinor thinks you . . . Would *you* say you were steadier than Clare?" Adam asked.

"You mean Gran thinks I'm too . . . rash?"

"I wouldn't say that, *exactly*," Adam said reflectively, "although perhaps Elinor does think you take too many risks. She sees you as the daring young girl on the flying trapeze of business. But of course, Elinor doesn't understand that in business, it's necessary to take risks. I see your adventurous streak as a business asset."

"It's not *fair!*" Miranda retorted bitterly, remembering how often she had said that as a child.

Eventually she asked, "What will happen if Gran dies without making a will?"

"There may be a nasty legal mess that might take years to disentangle," Adam said. "And that's something I don't intend to allow. As soon as Elinor is well enough to do so, I will insist she make her decisions." He paused, then added: "There *is* an alternative to the Greek system that would safeguard the money and yet be fair."

"What's that?" Miranda quickly looked at Adam.

"It would mean that you would be certain to get your fair share."

"*What is it, Adam?*"

"I wondered whether Elinor would respond favorably to the idea of setting up a family trust," Adam mused. "What do you think? If you think not, then I don't want to distract her by the idea." Adam knew that, as the shrewdest and most forceful of the sisters, Miranda would be a formidable opponent should she object to his suggestion.

"What would be the point of setting up a trust?" Miranda asked cautiously.

"Making a trust is a bit like making a will, except that you put it into practice before you die," Adam explained. "If Elinor were to set up a trust, naming her granddaughters and their descendants as beneficiaries, then the money would be protected as Elinor wishes, because there's no risk that one heir can squander it all. The trustees wouldn't allow it: their job is to guard the trust, not slavishly obey the whims of the beneficiaries."

Miranda ran her hand through wild red hair. "You mean Clare couldn't sit on the money and refuse to share it, and she couldn't give it away to charity? And Annabel couldn't buy a couple of yachts?"

"Exactly. The advantage of a trust is that there would be a permanent cautionary control over the capital," Adam said. "I suspect that *you* would have nothing to lose, Miranda, were a trust to be established—and you might possibly have a great deal to gain. Trustees do not like frivolous expenditure; they might, shall we say, guard your sisters from themselves."

Miranda said firmly, "Then I vote for a trust."

"And what do you think Annabel will want?" Adam asked. "Perhaps it would be best if *you* discussed this with her, rather than me." Such a matter was always difficult to bring up with a close relative at such a time: that was why he had discussed it with Miranda before their arrival at Saracen. Adam added apologetically, "You know better than I do how to handle Annabel so that such a discussion won't upset her. I'm afraid she'd turn on me, perhaps think I'm being cold-blooded."

"I don't see why she should," Miranda said. "But I think *you* should talk to her because you can answer her questions, if she has any; I know nothing about the legal ramifications. Don't worry, Adam. Of course, Annabel *is* ridiculously sentimental, but after all, *you* have nothing to gain—you're only trying to prevent trouble for us. Basically, I'm confident that Annabel won't want Clare holding the purse strings, back in a position to boss us around. Stress *that* to Annabel and she won't be sentimental."

The apricot flush of the evening sky paled beyond the balustrade of the terrace, and the quivering reflections of the sea faded on Elinor's bedroom ceiling. She had been drifting in and out of sleep; the churning noise of the helicopter rotors finally awakened her. After the noise ceased, Elinor heard shrieked greetings and laughter from the far terrace. Only a few moments later, her bedroom door burst open.

"Darling Gran, this is wonderful!" Miranda ran to the bedside and kissed her grandmother. "Welcome back!"

* * *

Outside on the terrace, while Clare put two-year-old Josh to bed, Adam sipped champagne and chatted with Annabel. As he had done to Miranda, he mentioned the possibility of a trust as an alternative to Clare's being left in charge of the family fortune.

Annabel reacted with surprise, followed by irritation. "I had quite enough of being pushed about by Clare when we were children. Tell me more about this trust idea."

After dinner, Adam suggested to Clare that they take a walk. He wanted to be sure there would be no time-wasting opposition or bickering among the sisters when Elinor had so little strength left.

"Do we really have to talk about this now, Adam?" Clare was in no mood for financial discussion as they sauntered downhill, through winding narrow streets lined by bougainvillea and dimly lit by old-fashioned lampposts.

"I hoped that I could rely on you to be sensible, not sentimental," Adam said firmly. He added, "I'm only trying to arrange what Elinor would want and what is best for all of you. That's my duty as Elinor's adviser."

Clare thought how pompous Adam sounded. Why did Gran always have to have some man around to tell her what to do? When Daddy Billy was alive, his word had always been final. Then Gran's lawyer—Joe Grant—had become the great male authority figure in their lives, and now his son, Adam, had inherited the mantle of wisdom.

"I don't see what's wrong with just sharing it out," Clare said. "In case you haven't noticed, old friend, we aren't babies any longer. I'm a grown-up married woman."

Hesitantly Adam said, "Miranda and Annabel like the concept of a trust."

Clare spoke tartly. "Of course Annabel will agree—without thinking—to whatever Miranda suggests, because that's what she's always done. But *I* don't see why a trust is necessary. In fact, it seems an unnecessarily complicated idea."

She was as stubborn as her grandmother, Adam thought regretfully as he tried a new tack.

Clare listened, then shook her head lightly and said, "It won't work anymore with me, Adam. I've heard it too often."

"Heard what?"

"The adult equivalent of 'Daddy knows best.' "

CHAPTER 2

Tuesday, 6 July 1965

DR. MONTAND STEPPED from the glare of the morning sun into the chateau's shaded interior. The entrance hall was scented by roses in a blue jug on a dark antique chest. He was greeted in atrocious French by an angular woman with carelessly dyed jet-black hair; as they walked to the elevator, the doctor spoke in fluent English; so many Riviera residents spoke only English that an ambitious practitioner needed to be bilingual.

The woman was Buzz, Elinor's oldest friend. In 1947, after Billy's death, Buzz had traveled to Elinor's house in the Wiltshire countryside and had simply never left it; she saw that the house ran smoothly, supervised the three little girls and their nanny, paid the bills, did the bookkeeping, and relieved Elinor of all small distracting tasks, so that she could concentrate on writing novels.

Buzz came from a working-class background and had a harsh South London accent; her frequent cockney modification of the Queen's English made it easier for the Riviera natives to understand her French than her English. Because her manner was blunt and matter-of-fact, outsiders tended to underestimate Buzz, even to ignore her. She simply ignored them in return. She watched and listened and made up her own mind about everything. But no matter what, Buzz always protected her friend Elinor—sometimes from herself.

The elevator jerked to a halt at the bedroom floor, where a maid folded sheets into a cherrywood armoire: each pile of antique, lace-trimmed linen was tied with butter-colored silk ribbon.

The family bedrooms led off this hall. On the floor above were six suites for guests, each with its own bedroom, bathroom, and small kitchen. The entire chateau had been planned so that, should Elinor ever again find herself short of cash—an unlikely event but her constant back-of-the-mind anxiety—she could easily turn the Château de Saracen into a luxury hotel. The owners of the two hotels in the village, uneasily aware of this, were almost as delighted as Elinor when each of her romantic novels leapt straight onto the world's best-seller lists.

Before opening Elinor's door, Buzz turned abruptly to the doctor and said, "You'll tell *me* the truth, won't you? I can take it, but them girls can't."

"I have told you all I know," said Dr. Montand, "Madame O'Dare has had a partial stroke—a cerebral vascular accident, as we call it." The doctor patiently repeated what he had said the previous evening. "Her left arm and leg are paralyzed and so is the left side of her face. Later, she will need further investigation: an arterial brain scan, X rays, and electroencephalography. At the moment, there's no point in taking her to a hospital in Nice: anything that can be done there can be done with nursing help here, in her home."

Buzz nodded. "A better idea. No risk of cross-infection. Hits one in four patients in Western hospitals."

"I see that you keep up to date," the doctor said, assuming that this tall, graceless woman in the unfashionable navy dress had once been a nurse. He sensed that unspoken complicity between nurses and doctors, an absence of the frightened trust that most relatives exhibited.

Buzz's shrewd eyes had asked the question before her mouth: "Will she make a complete recovery?"

Dr. Montand shrugged. "She's not overweight. You say she doesn't smoke or drink heavily. She isn't diabetic, and her blood pressure is almost normal for her age." The patient was sixty-five years old, and no civilized doctor would suggest that she go on a diet, cut out drink entirely, or take up exercise. He would counsel them to let her enjoy her remaining life—should she recover.

Buzz pushed an unnaturally black wisp of hair behind her ear. "You ain't answered my question."

"It's too early to tell," the doctor said. "It takes time to recover. A patient often has impaired mentality—but not always. I really cannot say. Now you should get some rest, madame, after sitting up with her all night." She hadn't said so, but this woman was the sort that didn't trust a night nurse.

After the doctor had finished his daily poking and probing of Elinor, Buzz returned to the bedside. Elinor lay in a cream lace nightdress against silk pillows.

"He says you'll soon be as fit as a fiddle," Buzz said. "I'm getting a physiotherapist so you'll get proper exercise."

"But I'm too weak. And I can't move or talk properly," Elinor protested, her voice still slurred.

"A physio will soon get you on your feet, Nell . . . "

"But will I ever talk properly again? My left cheek feels frozen, as if I've had a dentist's injection."

"You'll talk properly soon enough—then the Lord help us."

Elinor's anxiety dissolved, and she relaxed. Buzz was so reassuring, so comforting. The two women had shared some tough times when they were young. Buzz knew Elinor's faults and didn't care; Buzz would never reveal her secrets.

"What exactly does Buzz *do?*" people sometimes asked. Supposedly a secretary, Buzz never typed if she could avoid it, and whatever shorthand she may have known was long forgotten.

"She protects me," Elinor would say with a little laugh.

"But why do you let a secretary speak to you in that offhand way? Why do you let her criticize you? Why do you put up with her?"

Elinor would firmly close the subject by answering, "We've been together a long time. You wouldn't understand."

Although outsiders never understood their relationship, it was clear enough to the two women: Elinor was Buzz's friend and her boss; Buzz was Elinor's secretary but not her slave. Elinor was glad to have forgotten what life was like without Buzz, this odd woman who had become a vital part of her existence.

They had met long ago, during the First World War, on a drizzling autumn day in 1918. That day was to have terrible consequences for Buzz, although to eighteen-year-old Elinor it had been just another of those endless, stinking, exhausting everyday scenes in a casualty clearing station near the front line.

On that November evening, an ambulance convoy had just arrived at casualty reception. Gray-blanketed stretchers were everywhere, many on the floor. The filthy, exhausted men on the stretchers wore muddy, torn khaki; their bandages were dirty and bloodstained.

"Hey, Nurse!" Hearing the high-pitched nasal voice, Elinor turned. She realized, to her surprise, that the lanky ambulance driver with dark cropped hair was a woman.

"I've just driven in a diphtheria case," the driver said. "He's in a bad way. Should be seen immediately. He's also got a smashed left patella and a fracture of the left tibia. Get a surgeon, will you?"

A tired young surgeon took one look at the ginger-haired soldier struggling to breathe and said, "Tracheotomy. Get him on the table fast, Nurse. No time to scrub up." He gestured to the small side room, which contained an emergency operating table.

Lying on the table, the young patient gasped for breath as the membrane in his throat started to strangle him.

The surgeon nodded at Elinor. "You—take his head!" Then he turned to the ambulance driver. "Do you think you can hold him down?"

She nodded.

As Elinor held the injured man's head firmly to the sandbag pillow, the weary surgeon lifted a sharp scalpel from the tray on the trolley. Elinor saw his hand shake.

The surgeon glanced at Elinor and hesitated. If he accidentally slit the jugular vein, the patient would die.

Elinor prayed silently. "Please God, let him get it right."

The doctor still hesitated, his shaking right hand revealing his exhaustion.

The patient's gasps changed to a gurgle. Elinor thought, if he doesn't cut now, this lad is going to die anyway.

The surgeon leaned over the ginger head and with the scalpel made a swift incision.

Immediately a crimson stream flowed from the patient's neck.

Elinor kept her eyes on the dying man because she did not want to look at the surgeon. Wearily he said, "Clean up, Nurse, and move him out of here. I'd better get back."

After the surgeon had left, Elinor looked at the lanky girl; her face was white as her dark eyes stared down at the young man who had just died.

"Did you know him?" Elinor asked gently.

Slowly, with chattering teeth, the girl said, "We was going to be married, Ginger and me."

Later, in Elinor's Nissen hut, the women shared a tin mug of milkless cocoa. Elinor knew that the white-faced girl, who had not yet shed a tear, must be suffering from shock: she was moving in a daze but chattering as though nothing out of the ordinary had happened.

"Poor Ginger was one of my stretcher-bearers. They'll let his mother think he died a hero's death for King and country, not that he tripped over someone's boot in a trench, fell off the duckboard, was accidentally shot in the knee by some trigger-happy idiot, then left out in the open too long, and afterward killed by a mistake."

"The surgeon's only human. We all make mistakes," Elinor said wearily. "I know I do."

The girl sighed. "This whole ruddy war's a mistake."

"What's your name?" Elinor asked.

"Buzz Mann."

"That sounds more American than English."

"You're right. I was christened Doris. Some doughboys gave me the nickname 'cause I always seem to be the first one in the know. Simply a matter of keeping your ears open and talking to the walking wounded before they're handed over to you nurses to sort out the mess. Cor, what a rotten job you nurses have!"

"Your job doesn't look so hot to me."

"I was ruddy lucky to get accepted as an ambulance driver," Buzz said. "Generally, the War Office don't take working-class girls from Tooting; they take nice gels with private means, because we're all volunteers and practically unpaid."

"Then how did you wangle it?" Elinor asked.

"I was working as a housemaid in Wimbledon—nice family, indoor staff of nine—and our Miss Ruth was determined to volunteer. So the mistress made me go along as well. I was supposed to look after Miss Ruth. There wasn't half a bit of string-pulling, I can tell you! Of course, I had to say I was twenty-three, not eighteen. Miss Ruth wasn't a bad sort but she wasn't used to this sort of life. Before we'd been here three weeks, she got pneumonia with complications, nearly died, and had to be sent back to Blighty. The commandant puts up with my lack of breeding—as I heard her call it—because I understand how an engine works, and there ain't many ladies as does."

After that, the two young women met often in Elinor's hut. Elinor was intrigued by Buzz's brusque attitude, her lack of concern over what other people thought of her, her contempt for anyone in command—and her carefully hidden warmth and kindness.

Just as she had comforted Buzz when Ginger died, Elinor was comforted, two months later, by Buzz, who found her crying quietly on her narrow, hard bed in the Nissen hut.

"What's up?" Buzz asked.

Without a word, Elinor handed her the letter.

"Dear Nell," Buzz read. "This is a hard thing to tell you but your dear mother passed away. She been ill six month with tuberculosis but would not let me write you. Last Sunday about five she quietly slipt away and we buried her Wednesday. I nursed her well as I could. She had Doc Mackenzie and drugs but it was too late. On Saturday she says to me, Listen Marius, I feel better. It does not matter I am thin. You can fatten me like a Christmas goose now I am healthy again. She had a decent buriel, with Casket, Hurse and Grave at St Mary to the far left of the porch. My poor girl was in her wedding dress she was all skin and bone. She was very dear to me although I did not tell her often. Your grieving father Marius F Dove."

Eventually Elinor gulped, "At least this means I'll never have to see *him* again."

Buzz and Elinor had now been close friends for forty-seven years, and so far as Elinor was concerned, Buzz had only one failing: she had never liked Billy.

Once again Elinor turned her head to look at the photograph of Billy beside her bed. She thought back to the humiliation she had suffered from his relatives' disdain, though in the end it had been she who restored the fortune of Billy's family. Elinor was now the *star*—more socially acceptable than they had ever been. And she certainly wouldn't make the same financial mistake that *they* had.

Now, in the warmth of the Riviera, within the splendor of her castle, Elinor looked up at Buzz and said in a faint but determined voice, "I *must* be sure that those girls are safe for life. . . . I want them to have a happy life, with no burdens. . . . I want them to have what you and I missed: more time—time to enjoy life, time to think. More time for their children than I had for Edward."

Buzz said soothingly, "You did the best you could at the time, Nell, and that's as much as any person can be expected to do. Maybe it was lucky you only had one kid." Buzz knew better than to express her opinion on why this was so.

Elinor whispered. "I want to see Adam *now*."

"I'll not have you talk business when you're barely able to talk at all," Buzz said. "We'll wait till you beat me at Scrabble." Before Elinor's stroke, they had played one game a day, always at five o'clock. At the end of the previous year, the score had been Elinor 36 games, Buzz 329.

"Buzz, this is urgent. I haven't made a will."

Buzz turned to the bed. "That's not *urgent*, you old fool. Important, but not urgent. You'll just have to wait! I'm not letting that Adam in before the doctor okays it, and that's flat! I'm off to make you a dish of mashed bananas and cream. You can eat it with a teaspoon. *I* know what you like, Nell."

Elinor smiled. She had spent her life looking after other people and now it felt strange, but pleasant, to lie with her eyes closed while other people glided around her, murmuring and making the decisions for her.

Monday, 19 July 1965

Two weeks later, seated on one of the silver-gray sofas in front of Elinor's bedroom fireplace, Adam quickly sorted out his papers, then placed them on the low table before him. Buzz had warned him that he had only a few minutes.

Elinor's voice was still weak and she remained able to talk only out of the right side of her mouth. "I'm sorry I didn't do this earlier, Adam," she said.

"There's no hurry." The lawyer had been well briefed by Buzz. "We might as well settle it now, though, if you feel up to it."

With difficulty, Elinor lifted her head. "Put those papers down, Adam. Come and sit by me."

As Adam moved to the bedside, he glanced toward the photographs clustered on Elinor's table. One was a group photo of World War I pilots, their faces flushed with victory. He found it sad that one of those jaunty, carefree young men had turned into his careful, punctual father—a pillar of the local community, respected in the legal world; a man who had never been allowed by his wife to forget that he had married the boss's daughter and had better live up to it. He had done so, concealing his feelings, hiding them behind a carefully organized life in a comfortable country mansion not far from London.

The sight of frail Elinor, so recently close to death, nearly caused Adam to momentarily lose his composure. Her fragility, her pale face, the smell of the sick room, stirred his sense of loss. His father had died, very slowly, from lung cancer. What Adam most regretted losing was what he had never had: the father-and-son companionship that other chaps casually enjoyed. Of course, there had been little chance of spending time with his old man when Adam was a child and confined to the nursery by a mother who had preferred bridge to motherhood. Adam also wished that when he was growing up, he'd been more understanding of his father's behavior. The old man hadn't really been as harsh and demanding as he seemed. Adam grew to understand that he'd only wanted his elder son to get the best out of life. And when Adam was articled to the family law firm, he knew, Dad had been careful to have nothing to do with him in the office because he hadn't wanted to appear to favor him over the other clerks. Adam had always known that was the reason, but it had hurt at the time.

Elinor noticed Adam's glance at the photograph and whispered, "I still miss your dear father. Joe looked after my affairs so well, especially after Billy died."

Adam smiled reassuringly. "I'm here to help you, just as Father would have done. Simply tell me what you want and I'll arrange it. I have a list of your assets here. Perhaps you would like to tell me which people you might . . . want to have something . . . at some time in the future, and then I'll draw up a . . . document for you to consider."

Noting Elinor's silence, Adam wondered if her mind worked more slowly now. He said, "Do you want to leave any money to your family in America?"

She reflected briefly on her brother, and again considered whether he might still be alive, with children of his own. She remembered the jealousy she had felt at her father's obvious love for Paul, and her pain because of his lack of interest in her. She had always felt guilty for being a girl and therefore not strong enough to carry out the perennial chores on the farm in Minnesota. Her childhood had been spent in terror of her father's rages and his ability to reduce her to a cowering, bewildered creature. How she had dreaded his anger, which always seemed to be directed at her. How she had hoped for—just once—some sign that he loved her; instead, the only love she ever felt came from her mother, a sad, broken creature. Elinor remembered her relief at finally breaking away from her family and their hold on her.

She shook her head slowly. "No. They never did anything for me. And I haven't heard from them since 1932, when my brother had to sell the farm. I inherited nothing and I owe him nothing. So I think the simplest thing would be to divide everything between the three girls and Buzz . . . "

Adam looked worried. "The simplest thing is not always the wisest," he said gently. "The girls must be protected from possible exploitation, embezzlement, and theft. You've always protected those three lucky sisters from harsh reality, from the jungle of life." He hesitated. "Perhaps they should now also be protected from . . . themselves . . . unless you truly believe that they will always look after the money carefully and prudently, taking no risks and resisting the temptation of extravagance."

Elinor considered Adam's words of caution. She didn't care to think of her girls as wasteful, but there were warning signs. Fleetingly she thought back to Annabel's eighteenth birthday, when, exuberantly, the girl had jumped into the terrace fountain and ruined her pink Hartnell ball gown. Miranda clearly took dangerous risks in an already high-risk business, and she seemed to think nothing of hiring a helicopter, at heaven knows what cost, simply to travel to London for a few hours. Why did Miranda waste money in this way?

Adam said, "Of course I know that Clare, as the eldest, has always been very responsible, but I am concerned lest she be persuaded to be, shall we say, over charitable? Clare seems to think that it's her responsibility to look after the entire world."

Elinor understood that Adam was warning her that her hard-earned fortune might well go down the drain with amazing speed.

"The girls must be prepared," Adam went on, "to spend a considerable amount of time doing their financial homework and discussing their business affairs with stockbrokers, accountants, lawyers, and other professional advisers."

Elinor considered what he had said. "Well, you already look after Miranda's affairs, don't you, Adam? And the other two have husbands to handle that sort of thing."

Adam looked slightly embarrassed. "I feel I should perhaps play devil's advocate and point out—do forgive me—that Clare's husband is a film producer: some of his films have been successful—but not all of them. I'm sure that, should he persuade Clare to invest your money in his movies, he would *expect* them to be successful . . . but such risky investment can be hugely expensive, as well as dangerous."

Inwardly Elinor shuddered though her rigid body stayed still.

Adam continued, "And there is one other thing: the divorce rate is rapidly increasing. There now is one divorce to every three marriages in Britain, and I believe the rate is even higher in America. Of course, we all hope that they will both stay happily married, but Clare's husband has been married twice before, and as a lawyer, I can tell you that it is a rare husband who will put his wife's financial interests before his own in the event of . . . such a sad event." He paused briefly to let Elinor consider.

"Clare and Annabel are both charming and delightful young women, but are you completely confident that they have the financial acumen to handle a fortune—especially as they have no training or experience in such matters? In particular, do you think that Annabel would be willing . . . or capable?" Annabel was everybody's favorite sister, but she was also known as the family scatter-brain—a not-too-bright beauty with a sunny temperament.

After a few moments of silence, Adam added, "And I can't help wondering, should Annabel ever be on her own, whether she would not be easy prey for fraudsters or . . . the sort of men who, frankly, *stalk* women with money."

Elinor spoke in a whisper. "Please tell me what to do, Adam. You always know best."

So Adam explained the advantages of setting up a family trust, concluding, "Of course, a main advantage would be that the trustees—men of impeccable reputation—would relieve the girls of all responsibility, make all business decisions, and operate the trust smoothly, to your satisfaction, before . . . during your lifetime."

After a thoughtful silence, Elinor whispered, "A *very* sensible idea. The Dove Trust. Why didn't you suggest it before now, Adam?"

"You preferred me not to discuss your . . . these matters," Adam reminded her.

"Whom would you appoint as trustees?" Elinor asked.

Briskly Adam replied, "I do *not* advise a bank, no matter how respectable. They are in business to make money for themselves." He knew that the aim of a bank would be to get as much money as was possible and legal out of the trust account. This might well erode the money—a small percentage here, another there—by as much as five percent a year; if so, within twenty years, Elinor's fortune would belong to the bank. Adam cautioned especially against Swiss banks. "They are the best publicists and the worst extortionists. That's why they put up such an impressive facade of you-can-trust-us reassurance, with expensive writing paper and old-fashioned business offices meant to look as if they have been doing respectable and reliable business for hundreds of years."

"Then whom *do* you advise?"

"You need reliable, responsible professionals whom you can confidently expect to keep a careful eye on all the affairs of the Dove Trust. The trust will hold all your major assets, although, of course, you will also need to make a will for minor things, such as the disposal of personal effects.

"The trust will then administer the estate," Adam went on, "and annually consider whether to apportion any of the trust income to the beneficiaries named by you, and if so, how much."

"How much does a trust cost to run?" Elinor whispered. Adam's well-intentioned warnings had enervated her.

"The cost of setting it up would be about a thousand pounds, perhaps a little more, if property, such as the chateau, is involved. The yearly charge might be half a percent of the trust value. The trustees could continue to work with your present bank, stockbroker, and other advisers."

"Would STG continue to be my lawyers?"

"Of course. In fact, should you wish, our firm could act as trustees."

Buzz's head appeared around the door. "Two minutes more, Adam." Then she saw Elinor's pale face and said, "No, you'd better leave *now*."

"Two more minutes." Adam smiled gravely at Buzz, who hesitated, nodded, then shut the door.

Adam looked at Elinor thoughtfully over the top of his horn-rimmed spectacles. "That reminds me. In my judgment, it would be best not to include Buzz in the trust. She can be looked after by them—exactly as you wish, in the same way as the girls—but for many reasons, in our experience—the experience of Swithin, Timmins and Grant—it is simplest to confine a family trust to family members only. And there are other legal reasons that I won't bother you with."

"Are you *sure* Buzz will be properly looked after?" Elinor inquired anxiously.

"I'm absolutely certain of that." Adam shuffled his papers into order and stood up.

"How long does it take to set up?"

Immediately Adam understood the implications of Elinor's question. He said reassuringly, "It could be done in two weeks, but in an emergency—overnight."

"Better do it as fast as possible," Elinor murmured, adding, "I'd like you to explain everything to Buzz and the girls as soon as possible."

"I'm here to do whatever you wish," Adam reassured her. "I'm happy to explain your wishes to Buzz and the girls . . . but only when your doctor allows such a meeting. We mustn't tire you, Elinor."

That afternoon, all of them sitting on prim Directoire chairs arranged around Elinor's sumptuous bed, Adam could see that the girls felt uneasy, as if they had suddenly realized that this was a formal occasion; something important was about to happen.

Buzz clucked a bit to ease the atmosphere. "Them shorts you're wearing don't leave much to the imagination," she said to Clare, who wore white tennis clothes. "Why didn't you put on something pretty for your gran, like Annabel?" Annabel had changed from her swimsuit into a bluebell silk dress.

"Don't nag, Buzz." Miranda, in pink slacks and matching blouse, knew that she had passed the decency test. "Let's start this meeting, Adam."

Gravely Adam said, "Your grandmother has decided to establish a family trust, for the benefit of you, her granddaughters." In a carefully neutral voice, he then explained Elinor's plan and stated the amount of money involved.

"Just under nine million pounds!" Miranda gasped.

Annabel's mouth stayed half open. "Heavens, that's . . . that's about twenty-seven million dollars!"

Clare spoke hesitantly. "That's much too much money for just one person . . . or one family." Detecting a certain frostiness from her grandmother's direction, she added, "I mean *nobody* should have such a huge sum when half the world is starving."

Adam saw that Clare was behaving exactly as he had expected: ever the romantic idealist and liberal. Priding herself on her honesty, she would end up a loser. Starting now.

"How does a trust work?" Buzz asked warily.

"It's a bit like setting up a company, but one run by trustees instead of directors," Adam explained. "To check that the trustees do their job properly, a trust protector is appointed, to act as a sort of policeman. The trust is funded by the person who sets it up—in this case, Elinor—and will be run for the benefit of the beneficiaries named by Elinor—in this case, her descendants. In case," Adam added, "at some future point, there should be no descendants, a final beneficiary should be named, although that might not be relevant for a couple of hundred years."

Elinor liked the idea of her trust continuing for hundreds of years, producing yearly dividends.

"But if Elinor isn't a beneficiary, will she have any future control over the trust possessions?" Clare asked.

"What about Buzz? *She* isn't a descendant of Elinor O'Dare," Annabel said.

Adam ignored that for the moment and said, "The trust will always consider Elinor's wishes in every respect. She can put *all* her requests in writing to the trust."

"And must the trustees obey her?" Miranda asked.

"The trustees use their own judgment, as do a board of directors, and should always act in the best interest of the beneficiaries."

"Sounds a bit complicated—a bit unusual—ain't it?" Buzz said suspiciously.

"A trust situation is not unusual among the wealthy," Adam explained. "To avoid death duties and bad money management, Lord X makes over his fortune to his children, on the understanding that they will provide for him until he dies."

"What if the kids don't see it that way?" Buzz asked. "What if the kids change their minds, after Lord X has signed over all his worldly wealth?"

"If the children aren't trustworthy, then of course you wouldn't consider such a trust." Adam's voice was carefully civil.

Buzz said, "If Elinor gives everything she owns to this here trust, then what does *she* live on?"

"The trust can provide Elinor with a salary for the work she does, which will provide ample money, after tax, for her to live on."

Miranda concealed her exasperation. Couldn't Buzz see that the reason for a trust was that Elinor was almost certainly dying?

"And who will these all-powerful trustees be?" Clare asked.

"Elinor's lawyers have been asked to provide trustees," Adam said. "Elinor knows that STG are capable and reliable, and she doesn't want to deal with people she doesn't know. So I propose to ask our Bermuda office to set it up. Offshore trusts are not liable to alteration by changing laws."

"You mentioned a protector. Who will that be?" Miranda inquired.

"Probably Paul Littlejohn, who now works in our Bermuda office. He is familiar with Elinor's affairs."

Buzz frowned, looked at Elinor's white face, bit her lip, started to speak, then clearly thought better of it and stayed silent.

Relieved that the meeting seemed to be finished, Elinor asked in a shaky voice, "So it's settled then?"

Clare said uncertainly, "Can we talk a little more? Because I don't *like* this idea. If Gran wants to leave us some money, why can't she just do that? Why complicate the situation?"

"Adam knows best," Elinor told her firmly. "Don't be difficult, Clare."

"I think I'm old enough to be in charge of my own financial affairs," Clare protested.

"There's no proof of that," Miranda said sharply. "You've never had *any* business experience."

"I'm confident that I can manage my own." Clare was indignant now. "I'm a married woman with a child. Surely that's proof of my responsibility. Why do I need to be nannied by lawyers?"

Elinor said faintly, "Adam has gone to a great deal of trouble to organize this, and Adam knows what's best for us, darling."

"*Why* does Adam know what's best for me?" Clare asked in an exasperated tone.

"Because Adam's a professional man," Elinor whispered. "He's a qualified lawyer with years of legal experience. That's why."

"Gran, all my life you've told me that some man in a dark suit knows best," Clare said. "It started when we were little girls, with Daddy Billy. 'Daddy knows best' was what you always said. But we all knew—even then—that he didn't. I don't want to find myself in *another* nursery situation, being told that Daddy knows best—only this time Daddy is some lawyer that I've never met, some faceless man who's sitting in the middle of the Atlantic."

"Now, Clare, no criticism of Daddy Billy," Buzz warned. She hated this name Billy O'Dare had given himself, she suspected because he couldn't bear to think of himself as old enough to be a grandfather.

"Sorry. I didn't mean to criticize Daddy Billy," Clare said quickly, but she knew that this was an important conversation with her grandmother, so she leaned toward Elinor and said, "I'm only trying to be truthful, Gran. *I don't like this idea!*"

"Adam's gone to all this trouble . . . " Elinor repeated faintly.

"But why didn't you discuss the idea with us beforehand, if we're to be the beneficiaries?" Clare protested.

"I told you. Because Adam knows best, dear. He's an expert. I pay him to think about these things carefully and decide, and it would be foolish not to take his advice."

"Miranda doesn't treat Adam with such deference," Clare pointed out. She couldn't understand why her grandmother had never had confidence in her own decision making, had never trusted her own instincts and judgment.

"Clare," Elinor said, "please show a little more respect for Adam! I am *so* sorry, Adam."

"I wish you'd stop treating us like children," Clare cried. "You sound just like you did when we were little. Whenever we questioned some decision, you always said, 'Because Daddy knows best'! It wasn't a logical answer then, and it still isn't. Can't you see that, Gran? *Why* do you always say, 'Because Adam knows best'?"

"Because he does," Elinor said firmly.

"You've always taken some man's advice, and you've always managed to produce some good reason for doing so." Clare wondered whether this was her grandmother's way of trying to avoid final responsibility for her actions.

"Now, now, Clare," Buzz said reprovingly. "You ain't writing *Wuthering Heights*." This was a gentle family joke, used when Elinor became overdramatic.

Equally anxious to defuse the situation, Annabel—the family peacemaker—spoke up. "I'd also like to ask a question. Could this trust set up awards, bursaries, things like that?" Annabel, who remembered Elinor's beaming pride when the University of Minneapolis asked her to donate her manuscripts to their library, continued. "For instance, could the trust use some of this money to set up an annual Elinor Dove prize—a literary award on a popular level—a really big award that couldn't be ignored by reviewers who sneer at popular fiction? And how about an Elinor Dove traveling scholarship for the most promising first novel of the year, and a few more similar things that would impress the literary world?"

Clare burst out, "You *can't* be serious, Annabel! Anything like that would make the literary world see Gran as an even bigger—"

Buzz stood up. "That's enough, Clare! If you can't behave, you'd better leave."

"Am I being told to leave the room like a disobedient child?" Clare retorted.

"That's about it," Buzz said levelly. Clare's the one that's most like Elinor, she thought to herself. Got that same passionate, extra stubborn, extra strong, and willful nature.

Nobody spoke. Everyone watched Elinor.

In the stormy silence, Elinor croaked, "If you are so dismissive of my work, my money, my advisers and their plan for the future, then perhaps you would prefer not to participate in it, Clare. You need not be named as a trust beneficiary."

"That's okay by me!" Clare's lips trembled. She was damned if she was going to be manipulated like this. And she certainly wasn't going to cry in front of Adam.

Adam said reprovingly, "I think you had better apologize to your grandmother, Clare."

Clare stood up and silently left the room.

Adam coughed. "Elinor, do you wish Clare included in the trust?"

"Of course," both sisters said in unison.

Elinor said crossly, "*I* don't want Clare put in the trust as a beneficiary until she has apologized to me." Her voice was clear and firm.

"You *can't* leave Clare out!" Annabel protested.

"You *must* put her in!" insisted Miranda.

Adam looked embarrassed. "I suppose, formally, I . . . er . . . ought to protest on my client's behalf at this attempt at coercion," he said lamely.

"Oh, shut up, Adam," Buzz said.

Everyone present knew that Elinor was generous and indulgent, except when she thought she was being taken for granted or taken for a ride. Then she could be as tough as nails. At that point, if criticized or made in any way to feel guilty or vulnerable, Elinor became incredibly stubborn.

Buzz said, "Elinor, I'm sure it bothers you that Clare would prefer you wrote that kitchen sink stuff about poor people with miserable lives. I know she criticized your books. But you don't want to hurt Clare in this way." Buzz's last sentence was almost an order.

"Clare hurt *me*," Elinor responded stubbornly, a theatrical note in her shaky voice. Another page from *Wuthering Heights*, they all noticed.

Sourly Buzz said, "I suppose you'd like the butler to hand Clare a tourist-class ticket back to Los Angeles."

"That's enough, Buzz." Elinor leaned back limply against the pile of pillows.

"Elinor, you're just being stubborn." Buzz spoke crossly now. "What you don't like in Clare is what she's inherited from you!" The kitchen timer in Buzz's pocket blared, and she stood up. "Time's up," she said. "Outside, the lot of you! In double-quick time!"

"I have just one further thing to say, to Adam—alone." Elinor's voice was faint.

After the door closed and Adam and Elinor were alone, she said slowly, "You'd better get this trust set up as fast as possible, dear boy. A little later, we can add Clare's name to the beneficiaries."

"No," Adam said, "the trust would be irrevocable in that respect."

"Well, go down to the pool and ask Clare to apologize." Elinor's voice trembled with exhaustion now. "Ask her nicely. Come straight back and tell me what she says. I hope I've already made it clear that I won't be intimidated and I won't be bullied. I'm sure she'll be a sensible girl. And then everything will be neatly settled." She gave a deep sigh of relief. "Hurry," she whispered.

Adam sauntered to the swimming pool and squatted on his haunches by the pool. "Your grandmother wants an unconditional apology from you for what you said about her books, her money, and her advisers. She wants it immediately, and I think you should know that she intends to punish you severely should you not do this."

Clare looked up, astonished. She stood in the water and smoothed back her wet hair. "I'm a married woman, Adam, not a child who can be stood in the corner until it gives in. I won't respond to threats. I believe that what I said was true and I see no reason to retract any of it."

"So you won't apologize?"

"Certainly not."

Elinor looked up, cheerfully expectant, as Adam entered her bedroom. Her expression changed when she saw his perplexed face.

"I'm sorry," Adam said, "but Clare refuses to apologize. I put the matter to her fairly forcibly, knowing . . . the possible consequences."

Elinor sighed. "What exactly did Clare say?"

"She said, 'Certainly not.' "

Adam broke the silence that had fallen between them. "Do you wish Clare to . . . er . . . be included in the trust?"

Elinor's voice sounded very weary. "Of *course* I want Clare included in the trust. But please don't tell her—not until she has come around. You would think she could put aside her stubbornness at a time like this."

Adam glanced warily at Elinor and said nothing.

* * *

Through the window of her ground-floor office, Buzz could clearly hear angry voices at the swimming pool, where Miranda and Annabel had joined their sister.

Sadly Buzz thought, Hardly a cross word among them since they were children—and now listen! And when their grandmother is on her deathbed! She knew that because the sisters were so close, they knew exactly where to jab at each other's sensitive spots. They're exactly the same as they were eighteen years ago, she thought, when she first went to live with Elinor. But now, instead of cheerfully bickering over hair ribbons or stolen pencils, they were quarreling over a fortune.

At the side of the pool, Clare said crossly, "Of all the unctuous, hypocritical little creeps, you two are the worst! I never *realized* that your devotion to literature was so great, Annabel. Scholarships, prizes, and bursaries to perpetuate her life's work, indeed!"

"Well, why not!" Annabel cried. "It's *her* money! I wanted to cheer her up, after you'd been such a bitch."

"Well, why *not?*" Clare yelled. "Because Gran's life's work has probably done more damage than she will *ever* realize!"

Her sisters groaned theatrically: together, they mimicked Clare's high, soft voice: "Those sentimental novels give women readers a romantic, unrealistic, and dangerous view of life."

"Well, they do," Clare said defensively. "All those women readers have been taught to believe in happy endings. If they're going through a tough period of life, they simply tell themselves that they're in the middle of chapter five, but the hero will be waiting, to put things right, in chapter seven. They've been indoctrinated to be passive, to put up with their lives, not to try and change them."

"What's so terrible about escapist literature?" Annabel demanded. "Most women read it—and why not? *I* do."

"Gran's books sell by the million," Miranda said, "so obviously a great many people enjoy them."

"Clare, why not check out your own reality," Annabel suggested, "and stop yelling at *us* because of *your* domestic problems."

"That's probably why she's in such a foul mood," Miranda continued. "I bet they've had a falling out, and she's temporarily disenchanted. No longer believes in romance or true love."

"True love died out with pterodactyls," Clare said curtly.

"No it didn't. But I'd like to know where to find it," Miranda mused.

"That wonderful vibration between the two of you," Annabel said dreamily. "That stars-in-your-heart feeling, when you don't need words to communicate . . ."

"I've never met a man who knew what I was thinking," said Miranda, "and if there's no need to communicate, how come you telephone New York so often? At Gran's expense."

Exasperated, Clare said, "I really don't understand how you two can chat so flippantly about any form of love or communication after that hypocritical scene you just played. I was disgusted by your calculating flattery!"

"And I was disgusted by your squeaky self-righteousness!" Miranda snapped.

"At least I didn't suddenly turn into a lover of literature, like Annabel!"

"I simply wanted to make her *happy!*" Annabel shouted. "After *you* had upset her."

"You know I can't stand her Daddy-knows-best line," Clare said.

"Who cares what *you* think, when she's dying, you self-righteous little prig!" Miranda said angrily.

Clare burst into tears and ran indoors. Stumbling to her bedroom, she wondered, as she had so many times, how Miranda could, with so few words, goad her to feel such violence and passion. Once again Miranda had reduced her to a point where she felt as though she were naked and vulnerable, being mercilessly poked by an electric cattle prod.

The pool area was silent.

Buzz sighed. She left her office and returned to Elinor's bedroom: Buzz liked to appear there unexpectedly, to make sure that when her back was turned, the nurse wasn't slack.

White and exhausted, Elinor lay against the pillows; one thin hand upon the sheet clutched the silver-framed photograph of Billy as a young flier. She looked up at Buzz, and her face was frightened as she whispered, "I'll soon see him again."

"Rubbish. I'll have you back on your feet in no time," Buzz said firmly.

"You don't understand about Billy, Buzz. You never understood."

"I understand that Billy owed everything to you."

"Oh no, Buzz, I owed everything to Billy," Elinor whispered dreamily. "He was the only man for me—right from the beginning . . . "

CHAPTER 3

Tuesday, 15 October 1918

ON NIGHT DUTY in the casualty clearing station at La Chapelle in northern France, eighteen-year-old Nurse Elinor Dove was in love and that, for the moment, was all that truly mattered. It was the first time she had experienced the intoxicating effect.

After that first night, when Billy had kissed her hand, Elinor blushed whenever she had to go near bed 17; if he called for her, she tried to avoid touching him. Her nervousness seemed to amuse him, and the rest of the ward.

One morning, just before she went off duty, Nurse Dove, exhausted, was wearily scrubbing up the carnage from the previous day's many operations. Alone in the sink room, she suddenly heard a tapping sound approaching from behind. She turned to see Flight Commander O'Dare, on rubber-tipped crutches, swing himself through the door. Under his aquamarine gaze, Elinor felt an all-too-familiar blush. Why didn't this fellow get back into his bed if he felt ill? Why did he look at her so steadily, with that hint of a smile? Why did he make her feel so warm and embarrassed and vulnerable? And why did she feel guilty?

He *knew* he was making her blush.

"Why are you out of bed?" she asked, feigning irritation.

He grinned. "You know I might be transferred soon," he said as he moved toward her. Suddenly one of his crutches slipped on the wet tiles and he lost his balance, crashing to the floor.

Nurse Dove dashed to her patient. "*Don't move!* Let me help you!"

Carefully she turned him on his back, then gently felt his neck. "Can you move your head to the left? . . . Now to the right . . . That's fine."

Billy O'Dare opened his aquamarine eyes, and in them, Nurse Dove saw not pain but determination. Without speaking, he gripped her upper arms, pulling her down on his chest. For a moment, he stared into her eyes, mesmerizing her. Then silently he pulled her closer and fastened his warm mouth upon hers. Once again she was overwhelmed by the seductive, forbidden smell of him.

Lying on top of him, feeling his body beneath her, Elinor started to tremble: an odd, compulsively strong urge seemed to knock all the sense from her head. Her eyes were closed. She felt as if she were pleasantly drowning in warm water. Then she felt the tip of his tongue part her lips and gently explore her unresisting mouth as his hand reached beneath her nurse's headdress to the thick fair hair coiled in a bun at the nape of her neck. Billy gently stroked the back of her neck, and every time he did so, a shiver ran down her spine. Through her navy serge uniform, she felt his knowing hand on her breast, his gentle touch warming her heart.

Elinor was oblivious of the ward noises around her. As if of its own volition, her body arched against Billy O'Dare. His arms enfolded and imprisoned her. He kissed her harshly, bruising her lips against his. His hand slid downward to press her buttocks against him, and she felt his hard body against hers.

She stiffened in alarm.

Between kisses, Billy murmured soothing words: ". . . lovely creature . . . wanted you the moment I saw you . . . lovely eyes . . . love . . . love . . . *love.*" As he kissed her, one calculating hand slowly raised her skirt and groped beneath it.

Nurse Dove sharply returned to reality. Frantically she fought against his insistent strong hands. All the sensuous excitement evaporated, turned off as if by a switch. She knew what happened to girls who let a fellow go too far, and it wasn't going to happen to her.

Billy lay on the floor looking up at her, his eyes imploring. "I'm sorry! But you're so lovely, so special," he whispered.

Elinor scowled at him again, her pale green eyes flashing with indignation.

"You don't understand how a fellow feels," Billy said reproachfully. "Besides, Nurse Dove, I really *do* love you."

Two weeks later, somewhat to his surprise, Flight Commander William O'Dare asked Nurse Elinor Dove to marry him.

To Elinor's dismay, Buzz did not share her joy at Billy's proposal.

Sitting on Elinor's bed in the Nissen hut, Buzz eventually said, "*You* know the dangers of wartime marriages, Nell. There are so few women out here . . . their attractions are magnified . . . and all the men fall for them. Even my boot-faced commandant has a string of beaux. Things get out of perspective—on both sides." She inhaled cigarette smoke. "I admit Billy's a good looker. Them blue eyes and that tangle of fair hair. I agree he's got plenty of lanky, twinkle-eyed Irish charm. But what do you *know* about him, Nell? You know nothing, except he's six foot tall, good-looking and could charm the bloomers off practically anyone. Why get married so fast? They say the war's nearly over, so Billy's unlikely to get killed. There's no hurry—or so you tell me!"

"What a wet blanket *you* are!" Elinor said crossly.

"What a romantic, headstrong idiot *you* are," Buzz retorted. "You know *nothing* about his family. What's Billy going to do in peacetime? What will you live on? Suppose he turns out to be a lazy layabout or a rotter? What if he turns out to be tricking you?"

"Tricking me?" Elinor exclaimed indignantly. "Why would Billy want to trick me? I haven't got a bean!"

"I don't *know*," Buzz worried. "I just think he's too good to be true. If he's such a good bet, then why not wait until you've met his family?"

"I've had enough of death and depression, and so has he! I want some *life*, and he's offering it to me."

Eighteen-year-old Elinor and her twenty-five-year-old bridegroom were married by a French Catholic priest in a church (most of which was still standing) five miles from the hospital at La Chapelle. Elinor wore her best cream silk blouse and a borrowed burgundy wool skirt. The marriage witnesses were Billy's observer, Joe Grant, and Buzz, who wore a pink blouse and an air of suspicion.

The newlyweds were given official permission to spend three nights in the *estaminet* at La Chapelle. After a wedding meal of red wine, rabbit casserole, and a blackberry tart that cost Billy a fortune in cigarettes, he led Elinor upstairs.

The bedroom, papered in bronze chrysanthemums, contained only a few sticks of furniture; by the light of a flickering candle, Elinor saw a large feather bed. She looked away from it, partly out of embarrassment, partly out of fear, and stood in the middle of the room, still, stiff, and silent.

Billy grinned at his bride, opened a second bottle of wine, and unbuttoned his tunic.

Elinor was hypnotically aware of Billy's musky smell and the light blue flash of his eyes as he lifted her in his arms. Without speaking, he carried her to the bed and laid her on the quilt. He pushed her skirts up, then slowly slipped off her shoes. Next he removed her blue satin garters and peeled silk stockings from her pale legs.

He kissed her bare feet, sliding his tongue between her toes, and licked them. His kisses crept up her plump thighs.

Elinor lay rigid with embarrassment.

Billy untied the drawstring of her bloomers and felt below; softly he stroked her navel, then moved downward. Slowly he pulled down the bloomers, until Elinor's white belly and blond hair were revealed to him.

Impeded above her waist by a wrinkled mess of clothing, Elinor felt trapped and alarmed. She clamped her eyes shut as her entire body blushed with shame. Even though Billy was moving slowly, it all seemed to be happening so fast.

Carefully, caressingly, Billy unbuttoned her blouse, then unbuckled the belt from her narrow waist and removed her skirt. He pulled the string of her underskirt and lifted off her chemise. When, finally she was completely undressed. Billy paused to touch her breasts and lightly pinch her nipples, just enough to excite her.

Still Elinor kept her eyes shut. Had they been open, she would have seen Billy undress like an eight-armed Indian god, hurling his clothes to the floor.

Billy was fascinated by the whiteness of Elinor's skin as she lay naked in the soft, golden candlelight. He was enchanted by her heavy, beige-tipped breasts and the slender waist below it, which then swelled again to a rounded belly, above pale thighs.

In the quiet candlelit room, there was no sound, not even of breathing. Elinor was so tense she could not draw a breath.

Billy laughed and whispered, "You are a beautiful and voluptuous woman. I'm going to make you realize that—and enjoy it—before the night is over."

Again he began to caress her slowly, his eyes open to watch her reactions: the soft, fleshy mysteries of a woman's sensuality were no secret to Billy.

Elinor shrank from her bridegroom, squirming slightly beneath his touch. Her head tried to pretend that it didn't know what was happening to her body.

He tickled her stomach with his mustache and slipped his tongue into her navel and then licked upward until she felt his breath—scented by her own body—against her lips; to her, it tasted scandalous.

Gently he breathed into her ears and her mouth. His lips sucked at her eyelids, her cheeks, her chin, and her lips; his tongue tickled her white throat. Softly he bit at her breasts, then her buttocks. Inch by inch, his hands and his mouth discovered her body, leaving no secret place unfound. Subordinating his pleasure to hers, Billy slowly led her into a new and thrilling but frightening world.

She felt his fingers traveling delicately over all of her body . . . touching, probing, sliding into every shadowed crevice, until his hand finally moved toward the division of her thighs. At the bottom of her triangle of blond hair, his index finger located the little bump no bigger than a pea and he started, gently and rhythmically, to rub it.

Slowly Elinor relaxed. Her body surrendered to the pleasure of Billy's touch; it seemed to melt, no longer controlled by her, and then it lifted, taut as a bow beneath his fingers, and her spirit soared.

Panting, bewildered, she opened her eyes. Above her, in the candlelight, she saw Billy's smiling, triumphant face.

"That's only the beginning," he promised. "Now let's have a look at you." He bent his head toward her belly, and his fingers slipped between her legs.

"Open your legs," he whispered.

Elinor stiffened at this command, so totally contrary to her strict upbringing.

"Please," Billy insisted.

His strength demanded her submission. She must surrender this, and with it her moral responsibility. Had she not just promised to love, honor, and *obey* him?

Quivering as she moved her legs slightly apart, Elinor felt timid and guilty; her heart pounded with anxiety. She felt unbearably vulnerable.

Slowly she parted her legs.

Billy's interest seemed curiously objective, and his eyes narrowed at the corners, as if he were a connoisseur examining a hothouse orchid, an exotic flower surrounded by pale pink, fleshy leaves and nestled in a soft blond bird's nest.

Carefully he pushed her lips apart and continued his clinical exploration. He lowered his head and licked her, until once again Elinor's body ignored her mind and ecstasy triumphed over shame.

Billy raised his head and looked up at her. "Now admit that it isn't so bad," he muttered as he slipped his hand between her thighs.

By the time his hand reached its goal, Elinor was once more quivering with fear. Billy's fingers softly probed her moist warmth until his middle finger met less resistance. Insistent, he pushed. Eventually his finger found the small opening and worked its way inside, enlarging it, with minimal pain to his bride. Elinor whimpered as he won his gentle battle.

At first she felt panic as he entered her. With his body stretched upon her, Billy lay still and reassured her with gentle kisses until she relaxed.

"Like this," he whispered, and his hands twisted her hips in a circular motion. Slowly her body took up the motion.

In silence, Billy controlled each movement, each twist. Limbs entangled, they writhed in a leisurely, horizontal dance as they explored each other. Through the night, they slid from one side of the feather bed to the other, sometimes moving slowly, sometimes lunging swiftly, as their hunger for each other mounted and then was satisfied, only to grow again.

At times, he crouched above her like some great triumphant beast, looking down on his conquest spread out below him.

She felt that the entire world existed only as a vague two-dimensional blur. Only their crumpled nest of pillows and sheets, and the pungent male body on top of her—sliding, slipping, thrusting inside her—were sharply in focus, three-dimensional, and real. She could not think beyond this erotic joining of their flesh in the dimly shadowed, voluptuous bed, perfumed by their bodies.

Sometimes he lay beneath her, cradling her breasts in his hands, feeling her soft flesh quiver against his lips, and she sat panting upon his stomach as his strong hands held and rotated her hips. He gripped her to control her movements, so she could not move as she wished, could not move except as *he* wished.

At first she had demurely crossed her arms to hide her breasts, but eventually, flinging her arms high in abandon, she rode him like a plunging dolphin, until she fell forward, exhausted, and her breasts rubbed against the damp hair of his chest.

By morning, her flesh was bruised in places, like an overripe pear, and these pale contusions marked her as the property of Billy as surely as a cattle brand.

She was besotted, enchanted, in love, completely in Billy's thrall. Like lightning, he excited, frightened, and fascinated her.

That morning, momentarily disoriented, Elinor sleepily lifted her head from the pillow. Then she remembered the night, and she buried her face in the bedclothes. Her face grew hot as she recalled how Billy had manipulated her senses and rendered her boneless and helpless beneath his touch.

Then she realized that, in the billowing warmth of the feather bed, she could feel no body next to hers.

She sat up.

Billy—*her husband*—was leaning out of the open window. He was stark naked. For a moment, Elinor looked through lowered eyelashes at his cropped fair hair, his strong neck, his long back; she gazed admiringly at his long, lean legs—the left foot still bandaged—and his muscular buttocks, so different from her soft, pliable flesh. Throughout her life, this private peek at Billy's body was frozen in her mind, and at the memory, Elinor would melt, and forgive him anything.

During the first weeks of her marriage, Elinor slid slowly, agreeably, voluptuously into sensuality.

What had originally attracted Billy to Elinor as much as her beauty and exuberant energy was the innocence that she had protected so firmly, and to which

Billy had responded with classic male determination.

Having destroyed that innocence, Billy now sought to artificially rebuild it, for the pleasure of again breaching it. At first Elinor refused to reenact her timid virginity so that Billy could then pretend to break her in as he had on their wedding night.

"Why can't we undress before we go to bed, as usual? I don't understand why you want me to playact," she protested. But then she grew to enjoy his little fantasy.

Dexterously, swiftly, Billy turned his bride into a slave of her own eroticism. She could think about nothing else. She was still at heart a farm girl, and in bed, Billy encouraged her impudent flirtatiousness, her adolescent awkwardness, clumsiness, blushing and innocent corruptibility. To Billy's young and unsophisticated bride, this physical passion—her adoring proof of love and devotion to her husband—came as an undreamed-of surprise. In bed with Billy, Elinor shook and trembled and sobbed until she was exhausted, until she felt overwhelmed and ecstatically weary.

Every time Billy touched her, Elinor felt herself fall, spinning dizzily into a void. When he raised his eyelids and the intense blue light of his eyes flashed straight at her, Elinor always caught her breath. When Billy spoke to her as a prelude to love, his voice would deepen, holding a silken note of promise—and of threat. His voice alone could make Elinor's legs tremble. And when, in this voice that reminded her of dark honey, he called her name, she felt his mouth caress her without touching her. So vivid was the sensation that she was astonished that other people in the room did not notice it, especially when the newlyweds visited his family.

Without being told, Elinor knew that, for her, sex alone could never be fulfilling. The abandonment of her body had to be combined with the passion in her heart and the devotion in her soul. For her, such a feeling of complete, abandoned love was possible with no man except Billy. Only he knew when to coax, when to tempt, when to insist. He was the only man to whom she could trust her body. She knew instinctively that there would never be another man for her.

After being shown by a maid to an impressively large bedroom, Elinor turned, grinning, to her husband and asked, "Why didn't you *tell* me?"

Billy took her into his arms, tilted her chin up, and kissed her tenderly. "It would only have made you nervous. Better you see for yourself what my family are like."

"But why didn't you *say* your folks were rich?" Elinor asked.

"Because they aren't!" Billy laughed. "Look how threadbare this carpet is. See how shabby the curtains are. You'll soon feel the darns in the sheets. And wait until you taste the sherry!"

"Then how come they live as if they are rich? And what about the silver and the servants?"

"My father lost most of his inheritance through unwise investments, the silver's only plate, and there aren't really as many servants as there used to be; the ones that remain aren't paid much and they eat food grown here on the estate."

Elinor shook her head. She was truly in a foreign land. It defied all logic. Here was a penniless family, living in a house stuffed with servants, in which elaborate meals were served and all the women wore pearl necklaces. Yet, as Billy explained, it was impossible to find a stamp, or anything else that had to be paid for with cash.

"And why did the man in black call your mother 'milady'?" Elinor asked.

"Because my father is a baronet."

"You mean he's a *lord?*"

"Nothing so grand. I'll explain the English class system to you someday when I have the strength and the time. Believe me, it truly isn't important to us. For now, let's forget it. Besides, we mustn't be late for dinner. It's the one thing my mother never forgives."

That night, after dinner, a maid helped the embarrassed Elinor to undress. Lying in a four-poster bed with blue brocade curtains, Elinor watched her bedside candle's hypnotic flicker. As she waited for Billy to appear, she mentally reviewed the events of the long day.

As nervous as any bride about to meet her mother-in-law for the first time, Elinor had been tense with apprehension as the pony and trap trotted from the station through a marzipan-colored, curving land of brown and green. Suddenly, across open parkland, she had seen what looked like a gray Greek temple nestled in trees, and Billy had said in an offhand voice, "That's Larkwood." Already overawed, Elinor had followed the butler into the drawing room, where a group of tweed-suited, staring people were gathered around a fireplace at the far end of the dark room. Even at a distance, Elinor realized that she was about to undergo some sort of test; she was so nervous that she was unable to link names with relationships until much later—except for Billy's mother, a faded version of Billy, who brushed Elinor's cheek with a hint of a kiss.

Later at dinner, there was a lot of political talk that Elinor didn't understand. She sat next to Billy's father, and followed his example when picking up the silver cutlery that surrounded her plate; it was the first time she had eaten a pear with a knife and fork.

Now, lying in bed, Elinor longed for Billy to appear and reassure her of his love, because clearly his family felt none for her.

Where was Billy?

Elinor slipped from her bed and quietly opened the door. Then she froze as she heard her name.

Outside, on the landing, she heard Billy's mother speak angrily of her new daughter-in-law with words that hurt and angered Elinor.

"It's perfectly clear why you married her, darling. She is a *very* good-looking girl, and luckily, she has that charming American accent. But perhaps you might tell her—in the most *tactful* way, of course—that she really cannot sit at my dinner table and say nothing: she must learn to talk, to listen, to *sparkle.*"

"She sparkles enough when she's feeling confident," Billy said. "I think you might *all* be a little more patient and generous-spirited. Whether you like it or not, Elinor is now part of this family."

"Ah! That's the *point*. This is some sort of punishment for me, isn't it? Heaven knows what I have done to deserve it—except not give birth to you first! Don't you think it's a *little* unkind to have married someone out of your own class, Billy?"

"I'm penniless, I have no prospects, I'm slightly disabled, and I can't get a job, Mother. What sort of class does that put me in?"

"You know you can always live here."

"And watch Marjorie count each mouthful of her husband's inheritance that we consume? No thank you!"

With that, Billy turned and entered the bedroom. He found Elinor staring tearfully at her reflection in the cheval mirror.

"Oh, Billy, I feel so sad. . . . I so much wanted your family to like me."

"Don't be silly. The family thinks you're a corker." He stood behind her and pulled her body against him, his arms encircling her, his hands caressing the thin fabric that covered her breasts.

Elinor knew, however, that she had not misinterpreted what she overheard. She felt hurt, inadequate, and inferior in this nest of effortless superiority. And for the first time in a very long while, Elinor was aware of just how far away from home she was.

Billy slipped her nightgown from her shoulders, but for once Elinor did not immediately respond to his lovemaking. She was overcome by indignation. She was an American who had just survived a war, and she had earned her place in the world. She was not about to be put down by these out-of-date, supercilious, upper-class Britishers of unearned privilege. They regarded her as inferior because she came of humble folk who worked with their hands. Well, she would show them.

But Elinor was unaware of the degree to which her bullying father had conditioned her, and how this would adversely affect her future, and her ability to show them.

Even after they were comfortably settled in their own flat, Billy visited his home as often as possible. For him, it was a place of security, a refuge from a world that made demands he was not yet ready to face. Nonetheless, he obviously felt himself to be anybody's equal; Elinor wished she could be as comfortable and secure as he seemed, in the presence of the O'Dare family.

"I feel I'm not as good as them," she confided to Billy as, on a subsequent visit to Larkwood, they lay in bed, "and sometimes I suspect they *want* me to feel like this."

"They don't mean to embarrass you, old girl," Billy comforted her as he stroked her body. "You just aren't used to our offhand English ways."

"But I only feel this way with them," Elinor puzzled. "I feel comfortable and equal to anyone at school." Elinor now attended evening classes at the Polytechnic, hoping that an improved education would enable her to hold her own more easily against Billy's standoffish family.

"And so you are," Billy murmured, caressing her pale flesh.

"You don't understand," Elinor sighed. "Because *you* can hold your own anywhere."

But Elinor was wrong. True, Billy was an educated, well-mannered gentleman, handsome, sensual, and possessed of animal grace. He had experienced life's abundance and assumed it would continue, for he knew that he was intelligent and clever. What he did not know, or could never admit, was how very lazy he was.

Indeed, to all appearances, Billy was a sophisticated man-about-town who knew the ways of the world. Before the war, he had already made an impression in the drawing rooms and ballrooms of London as a charming young fellow and a polished conversationalist.

In the masculine world of London's clubs, however, Billy had projected a different image. There it was recognized that the sexes had clearly defined and different purposes: Men shared sport and danger; they gambled and provided each other with companionship and conversation. Women provided sexual pleasure, children, and home comfort. In these clubs, Billy had not been considered the equal of his respected father and elder brother; rather, he was rumored to be unreliable and unscrupulous—dangerously close to a cad—with perhaps too practiced an eye for a pretty ankle. Jealous men referred to him as a "ladies' man."

For his part, Billy remained impervious to their remarks; he seemed to feel it was his duty in life to charm *all* women, debutantes and married women alike. His self-confidence appeared unassailable.

In prewar London's plush bordellos, Billy's careless generosity, his atypical concern for the sexual fulfillment of his partner, his voluptuous exploits, and his sometimes delicate, sometimes harsh exploration of human flesh had also made him a favorite of expensive whores. For Billy, sexual pleasure consisted not only of lust but of frivolity, licentious play, and a perverse, detached curiosity. He was as inventive and imaginative as he was unscrupulous, as adventurous as he was amoral. He was almost irresistible in bed.

Postwar London, however, was different, especially for a penniless married man.

At first Billy had no anxiety about his future. His wonderful, get-rich-quick schemes were put to Elinor with such confidence that, for a short time, she believed in them. Gradually, though, she realized that the mercurial Billy—incautious and impractical, feckless and immature—was not the stuff from which successful self-employed businessmen were fashioned. Finally he tried to find a job, but could not get one.

Still, they had to have a home, and in Earls Court Square, Billy found a cheap, shabby two-room apartment with one communal bathroom. "It will do for a few weeks," he said. Elinor, with a newlywed's enthusiasm, tried to make the depressing flat into a comfortable home. She seemed to be able to do little, however, to improve the increasingly depressed spirits of her husband or to shore up his rapidly eroding self-confidence.

One morning, six months after the war had ended, Elinor, still in her teens and now pregnant, lay in bed and watched as Billy shaved. She was bewildered and distressed by the transformation of the assertive, devil-may-care air ace she had married into a man who grew more and more bitter and morose, who seemed mired in apathy, frozen in a state of anxious despair. She wanted to reach out and comfort him, to try to reassure him, but she knew she dared not.

"You might stop looking at me so reproachfully!" Billy said, catching Elinor's eye in his shaving mirror.

"Honey, I'm only a little concerned. You seem so tired." Already she had learned not to say more.

What Elinor wanted to say to Billy was, "We are alive, aren't we? We aren't about to be blown to bits at any moment. And we surely won't starve so long as there's food to feed the family servants at Larkwood!" And they had each other, didn't they? Surely she and Billy could enjoy being together, able to comfort each other and cheer each other's spirits when life was tough. Wasn't that the whole point of being married—being loving and protective and struggling together through the hard times? That was a lot more important than sailing through the sunny days.

Elinor still failed to understand that Billy, the golden boy, so brave and dauntless as a sky fighter, was uniquely unprepared for life's real and continuing battles. There he proved himself to be not only a dispirited and disheartened combatant but a bad loser as well.

Billy looked into his own eyes, reflected in the shaving mirror. In that same mirror, he had watched his face develop from a handsome lad's into that of a self-confident man. Gradually, however, since the war, since he had married Elinor, that splendid male arrogance had been replaced by anxiety, soon followed by desperation, as Billy searched unsuccessfully for his place in the postwar world. His failure left him feeling ashamed, emasculated, bereft of self-respect. What had gone wrong? He really had been a golden boy, and he still couldn't quite believe that he had been abandoned by the gods. They had smiled upon him so indulgently for the early part of his life, given him his privileged background, his good looks and fine body. Surely they had guided and protected him as an air ace? He had not only survived, he had been called a hero.

But now the gods seemed indifferent, abandoning him to this postwar purgatory, where heroes were two a penny and there were no jobs.

Billy had originally tried to get a job that involved airplanes—but so had every other ex-flier, and many did not have the disadvantage of an injury. It was ironic that so few flying jobs should be available, when Billy was certain that aviation—to carry mail and even, perhaps, passengers—was one of the few industries that could be expected to expand rapidly.

But there were just no jobs for him, and Billy found it humiliating. How was it that he couldn't manage what was surely the basic requirement of a man—to care for his wife and family?

Observing the frustration reflected in Billy's face, Elinor considered how fortunate it was that she knew one surefire way to bolster his self-confidence.

In bed, Billy was in charge of their world. There, he regained, if only fleetingly, a sense of potency—something that seemed to be inexorably dissolving from the rest of his life. Making love, he felt the power that he knew was his due.

As Billy stropped his razor, Elinor lay back in the bed and stretched languorously. She smiled at her husband. "I've never seen anyone with eyes like yours; they're the color of sea water over white sand; they shine with secrets. No wonder all the nurses fell for you. But I was the lucky one."

In the shaving mirror, his eyes met Elinor's and he smiled. Billy recognized her invitation. He wiped the lather from his cheeks and turned toward the bed.

With each month of Elinor's pregnancy, Billy's disposition worsened. She, of course, worried that her husband's changed attitude was due to her increasing inability to provide the full sexual involvement he needed. In truth, Elinor could never provide what Billy needed, which was self-respect.

At first Billy seemed merely sullen. Gradually he became volatile, short-tempered, sarcastic, and deliberately unkind. Elinor became more and more disconcerted, eventually immobilized by her own confusion. What had become of the man who had made love so real, indeed almost tangible? The loss of his affection so depressed her that it became an effort to do anything. A year earlier, she would not have put up with such behavior, but rebellion was now the last thing on her mind because, quite simply, Billy and pregnancy had knocked it out of her. Little by little, Elinor's vivacity, bounce, and drive were submerged, buried in despair.

Almost childlike in his determined self-absorption, Billy became Elinor's master. If he wanted her to do something, she knew she was expected to drop whatever she was doing and turn her attention to him; otherwise he sulked. Billy also attempted to overcome his insecurity by subtly reminding Elinor that *he* had the education, the worldly experience and knowledge that she, as a woman, lacked. He attacked her humble background, and once introduced her to a male friend as his "American bumpkin." Billy enjoyed her helplessness and her inability to stand up to his glib, facile verbal cruelty.

Elinor watched Billy struggle with his demons as, bewildered and frustrated, he increasingly sought oblivion in drink. And whenever he drank, the dashing, popular charmer became aggressive and maudlin, occasionally even abusing her verbally. On the day after a drinking bout, however, Billy would always be childlike in his remorse, relentless in his contrition, and he was always both hurt and astonished if Elinor did not forgive him immediately.

By being wistfully contrite and then making her laugh, Billy could coax and wheedle his wife into doing anything he wanted. On the rare occasion when that ploy didn't work, Billy would withdraw in sullen temper: immediately anxious, Elinor always crumpled before his projected disapproval. Sometimes Billy would become exasperated by her timidity; sometimes he found it erotic. Invariably these episodes ended the same way, for he was always forgiven in bed.

But in the long run, nothing really worked because nothing fully erased Billy's sense of failure and of despair.

Feeling powerless outside his home, Billy compensated by being dictatorial within it. Like the chairman who snarls at his secretary, like the secretary who snaps at the office boy, who then kicks the cat, Billy externalized his anxiety upon the only person willing to put up with his bullying—his wife. He was contemptuous of her meek acceptance of his bad behavior.

But Elinor had learned from her mother, who had humbly accepted her husband's tyranny, that authority was a masculine concept. Vaguely she understood that a bearded God possessed ultimate power in the universe, before which everyone bowed down; the equivalent domestic power was a husband. From her mother, Elinor had learned that every woman needed a man and a shouting bully was better than no man at all. At least, Elinor comforted herself, Billy never walloped her, as her father had done; at least life could never be as terrifying as it had been when she was young.

Then one Sunday, Billy didn't turn up for the major meal of the week until midafternoon—after the pubs had closed. Elinor took the dried-out leg of lamb from the oven and placed it on the table. *"That's* not fit to eat," Billy said. He grabbed the joint of meat and threw it at the wall.

As Elinor stared at the greasy, dark stains and the gravy dripping down, she remembered another time. She had been helping her ma to prepare their Thanksgiving dinner. Eleven-year-old Nell had slapped her small brother's fingers away from the cranberry sauce and Paul had yelled in protest as their father came in from the barn.

Seeing his son's tears, Marius jumped forward and boxed young Elinor's ears. As he turned to comfort Paul, Nell crept toward the door. Marius yanked her back. "And where do you think *you're* going?" he roared, then pulled off his leather belt, sat down, shoved Nell over his knee, and roughly pulled down her drawers.

"It wasn't Nell's fault! Don't spoil our Thanksgiving!" her ma cried, but he took no notice. As always when he strapped her, Nell howled with pain. Her ma burst into tears and ran from the kitchen.

"There, see what you've done!" Marius shouted at Nell. "Now you've spoiled our Thanksgiving!" From the kitchen table, he picked up the platter of turkey and hurled it at the dresser. Quivering with fear, Nell watched the grease and gravy drip down and form a puddle on the floor. . . .

Now, Elinor found herself quivering with the same fear as she watched the gravy dribbling down the wall. In silent apprehension, she heard Billy slam the front door. She refused to admit to herself that she had chained herself to another bully, but Billy's behavior made Elinor feel as hopeless and inadequate as her father's had when she was a girl. Increasingly she dreaded Billy's disapproval, his growing coldness and contempt, and his lacerating sarcasm. And her dread merely seemed to make him feel the more superior.

So Elinor remembered how to be stoical. When nervous and timid, she reapplied her childhood techniques of willing herself to be inconspicuous, fading into the background; anesthetizing her mind to the brutality of her father; her anxious passivity made her an easy victim.

Gradually all Elinor's frightened responses resurfaced, having lain dormant during the war, when courage and determination had overridden her other characteristics.

Just as Elinor's father had dominated her childhood with his violent and unquestioned parental authority, so when Billy demanded obedience, she almost always did as he told her without resistance.

Billy especially enjoyed his ability to dominate Elinor sexually. He used sex to thrill, to control, and to comfort her—although never to reassure her, because Billy knew that an uncertain woman is always obedient, whereas a self-confident woman might want her own way. After their son was born, Billy expanded his powers of sexual mastery: he enjoyed seeing how quickly—or how excruciatingly slowly—he could produce her climax. His rampant masculinity was reinforced by the knowledge that whenever he pleased, he could, sometimes with careful cruelty or unexpected kindness, reduce Elinor to a trembling, acquiescent creature at the mercy of her own flesh.

Although she did not realize it, Elinor enjoyed this abnegation of all responsibility, sexual and otherwise, to her domineering, overpowering, excitingly threatening husband. For her, Billy held the dangerous, sensual excitement of a wild animal that had been domesticated yet never tamed. There was a threat in everything he did, and she never sensed it more than when they made love. Even when their financial situation began to improve, his sexual hold on her did not change.

Eventually, in 1921, through the influence of a family friend, Billy was hired as a society gossip writer on the *Daily Globe,* a London newspaper. It was a job that suited him perfectly, for Billy's Irish gift of gab meant that he could talk to anyone about anything; his outward cheerful ebullience put everyone at ease, and his charm and sympathetic demeanor—those journalist's weapons—lowered all social drawbridges. But, although Billy attended all the smart parties, he knew (as did the other guests) that between him and them lay a line which could not be crossed, for Billy was present as a paid servant, a hired hack.

Elinor, of course, never accompanied Billy to these functions, and in truth, she did not want to: that was his world, not hers. To her, the only real drawback to Billy's new job was that he was never at home in the evenings, except on Sunday. Also, one of the side effects of his employment seemed to be a permanent hangover, but nevertheless, Elinor was certain this situation had to be a better one for Billy; she did not realize the sense of humiliation he felt at being an outsider in the world to which he had been born. She only sensed the relief that he was now working, and that it was no longer necessary to borrow money from his old friend, Joe Grant, now an articled clerk to a firm of London solicitors.

Elinor suspected that Billy—who never wrote anything longer than a frivolous paragraph if he could avoid it—actually could write serious articles if he wanted to do so. One of his colleagues also told her that Billy had the makings of a good theater critic, but he did not care to subject himself to the concentration necessary to write the review in his head as he watched a play. Billy, who did not like hard work, preferred to amuse himself at the theater, and afterward in restaurants, at fashionable dinner parties, or at the daring new nightclubs.

Once, Billy had been a man with high expectations and high ambition, known by everyone; now, although he *knew* everyone, he seemed to be nobody's friend. It was clear to him that he was going nowhere. As a result, his smiles and his charm were reserved almost exclusively for the people he saw when he was on the town. At home, he wore his depression like a cloak and only rarely allowed any warmth or humor to show through.

In spite of all this, Elinor managed to be happy. She loved living in a big city with all of its conveniences. She cleaned and cooked, she cuddled her baby son, Edward, and she borrowed romantic novels from the local penny library: these books (in which the heroines never wore secondhand clothes, and the heroes were as considerate as they were handsome) had provided her with precious hours of escape from the anxieties of life she had known when pregnant, with Billy out of work. Now Elinor read romantic fiction while waiting for Billy to come home, because she could never get to sleep until he lay safe beside her.

On one occasion, when he slammed the door of their bedroom at four o'clock in the morning, Elinor whispered, "Don't make a noise! You'll wake the baby! Where have you been?"

"Stop nagging," Billy yawned as he removed the studs from his evening shirt.

"What do you mean, nagging?" Elinor whispered indignantly.

"I mean your constant criticism, your silent hurt looks of reproach, your unreasonable demands," Billy said, pulling off his socks. "This sock needs mending." He peered at it somewhat drunkenly.

For once, Elinor decided to give full vent to her true feelings. She hopped out of bed and stood angrily in front of Billy, her legs apart, her hands on her hips, her body hardly hidden by a flimsy peach-colored nightgown and robe.

"How can you be so unfair?" she asked in a low voice. "Wouldn't *you* want to know where *I* had been if I went out and left you at home every night?"

Billy turned slowly and looked intently at his wife. He stared at her shadowed breasts, glanced at his watch, grinned, and moved toward her.

As his right hand slid beneath the peach chiffon, Elinor felt her nipples harden; immediately her body betrayed her and her anger melted away. As his lips caressed her ear, her neck, her senses swirled; their argument was forgotten.

Billy murmured, "Have you got it in?" Shortly after Edward's birth, he had sent Elinor to the shop in Holloway where Dr. Marie Stopes gave free advice and cheap contraception to women.

"Yes." Now he'd know that she had been hoping.

With one hand, Billy pushed his discarded clothes from the bed and with the other, he pulled Elinor's body to his. Her kimono fell from her shoulders to the floor, and she felt his warmth and strength against her.

As he lowered her to the bed, she pushed down the thin straps of her nightgown. "No, don't take it off," he murmured, and touched her breasts with the tip of his tongue.

His right hand stroked her thighs, then felt beneath the taut peach gauze . . . Where *was* the damn thing? He located her tiny clitoris, felt it harden beneath his thumb.

"Lie on top of me," he ordered. "Now spread your legs, wide." That way she climaxed so much quicker.

Elinor could not bear her husband's displeasure. One Sunday evening, after Billy had complained that she didn't iron his shirts well enough, she cooked his favorite dish for dinner. Afterward, her finger traced his cheek, her usual delicate signal to him.

Billy frowned slightly and jerked his head away. At first, instinctively, Elinor wondered what she had done wrong. Then she wondered why she should feel guilty. There were, of course, no answers. Whatever the cause, his rejection of her timid sexual advance made her feel ashamed of being so forward.

Billy grinned to himself. His disapproval always bewildered Elinor—and always brought her quickly to heel.

Some days later, when Elinor had had time to reflect on the incident, she decided to try the same thing with him. When Billy touched her breast, she flinched slightly; she wanted to see if his reactions were the same as hers.

Billy laughed at her refusal. He lifted her into his arms and carried her to the bed. Silently and deliberately he undressed her, button by button.

Resolutely determined to resist him, Elinor would not be wooed. When he laid her on the sheet, she did not move, willing herself to lie passively still.

Kneeling, Billy slowly pushed his knee between her legs and forced them apart. He felt her, quivering and moist, beneath him.

"You see, it's no use," he said. "I *know* when you want me."

He took her especially harshly that time, and when she whimpered, the face above her smiled.

"You've got to learn who's boss," Billy said softly, pinching her nipples a little too hard.

Although their erotic life was still one of intense passion, some of Billy's requirements puzzled Elinor. In bed, Billy preferred a half-dressed woman to a naked one, and he liked her to wear thick black stockings—like those of a schoolgirl—rather than her best silk pair.

One summer evening, Billy returned home with a gift box for Elinor. Inside, she found a white smock and a plain pinafore.

"Oh, Billy!" she cried in confused disappointment. "Surely you don't expect *me* to wear this! It's the sort of thing I wore when I was a little girl and wore my hair in braids."

"Then braid your hair," Billy said evenly.

"But—"

"That's enough! If you want to please me—braid your hair."

"No, I *won't."*

"Then I shall go to someone who will." Billy left the room, whistling.

He returned at six o'clock the next morning, his step unsteady, his speech slurred, his clothes reeking of the sour, sharp smell of whiskey and stale tobacco. On his skin, Elinor detected the strong scent of perfume. Her eyes registered a look of hurt and bewilderment.

Billy laughed. "Well, *you* didn't want me."

All day, Elinor hugged her baby to her and wept with shame and grief.

Billy did not touch her for a month.

During that month, Elinor's nipples ached to feel him; her belly longed to feel his fingernails scrape lightly across it, before his hand slipped knowingly between her thighs. Alone, restless, and unable to sleep, she tossed in their big brass marital bed; she banged pillows into shape, tortured by mental pictures of Billy doing all those private things to someone else.

On the fourth Sunday evening of her enforced celibacy, Elinor timidly entered the living room and stood before Billy. She was dressed in the white smock, the pinafore, and the thick black stockings; her hair was in braids.

"Do you like it?" she asked him shyly.

Later, she remembered her surprise at the passion unleashed by that pinafore as, on their bed, his hand groped beneath the tangle of her childish clothes.

This seduction of innocence—or the pretense of it—seemed to be the core of Billy's sexual pleasure, providing the energy that fired his loins with greatest power. Gradually their relationship grew from that of a man and a woman to that of a calculating seducer with a trusting child, for Elinor was now also expected to behave like a submissive child bride outside the bedroom. In public, Billy now liked her to appear submissive and deferential; dutifully passive, with head bowed, she looked meek and acquiescent, but both she and Billy knew the secret passion that lay behind her lowered eyes.

Only once more did Elinor protest at being dressed as a child. Standing ready for bed, wearing only a white frilled pinafore and long black stockings, she said hesitantly, "Billy, I don't mind dressing like this *sometimes,* but must I do it always? We never seem to do anything else!"

"And why not?" Billy lay on his back, both arms behind his head. Elinor looked at the blond hair glinting in his pale armpits and on his upper chest; below the nipples, his body was hidden by rumpled sheets.

"Because . . . because . . . I feel you're behaving like a strict father with his little daughter . . . and that would be wrong, wouldn't it Billy?"

"It would certainly be incestuous." Billy stretched his arms in a yawn. "But what does a little more corruption matter?"

"Corruption?" Elinor stared.

"Certainly," Billy said. "The delights of the flesh to which you are so addicted are viewed by the world as corrupt behavior. Ask any decent woman."

"What do you mean? Surely what we do is normal between a man and his wife?"

"Normal? You know perfectly well, Elinor, that *ladies* find the sexual act distasteful. The things that you and I get up to are considered unspeakably degrading, and would shock any decent woman." He laughed. "No respectable woman enjoys the sexual act—only whores."

"But . . . but . . . *you* showed me all those things."

"Because you clearly enjoyed them, my dear. You *always* wanted what I offered. I did *nothing* against your will. You clearly have the heart of a whore. You enjoyed every perversion that I offered you. You positively shook every time I touched you. You *love* it all."

"But . . . what *are* these perversions?"

Slowly and deliberately Billy listed the acts of eroticism in which he had encouraged his wife to participate, clearly enjoying her confusion.

He smiled again. "Don't worry, Elinor. *I* enjoy your depravity. But we'd better keep it a secret, hadn't we?"

"Depravity?" Elinor stammered.

He laughed. "I think you're more depraved than I am, darling. But if you don't agree, then why don't we ask other people for their opinions."

Her frightened expression aroused him so much that he carefully repeated his accusation. Observing Elinor's guilty, crimson face, Billy suspected that in the future, he would be able to manipulate his wife in any way he wished, and get her to agree to do anything he requested, simply by hurling this suggestion at her.

Elinor was simply unable to resist the temptations offered by Billy. And of course, she did not dare resist, although she now felt bitterly ashamed of the physical desires of her body and her willing capitulation to Billy's domination. With some success, she made excuses to herself: I didn't want to do it, but Billy *made* me do it, and he's my husband, and *I must obey him*.

Torn between her pleasure and the resultant shame, Elinor felt her guilt steadily grow. And increasingly Billy manipulated, dominated, and exploited her.

Hidden beneath his apparent sophistication lurked the little boy who enjoyed pulling the wings from moths. At bottom, Billy was still a bully who found pleasure in domination.

Sometimes in the street Billy asked Elinor if she had noticed some young girl's fine eyes or long legs. Aloud he wondered what it would be like to caress her. He enjoyed seeing Elinor's jealousy, which she thought she hid so well, as he developed these erotic daydreams.

What he said he would like to do to the girl, Billy later did to Elinor, whispering further erotic details as he touched her. He told Elinor that both men and women fantasized in this way. "Stop being a stupid farm girl, and acquire a little more sophistication in these matters," he ordered.

And Elinor acquiesced. Against her will, she became fascinated by his erotic fantasies, and eventually she willingly collaborated in this sensual playacting. Then she looked forward to it, as an alcoholic looks forward to feeling his senses swim when his brain abdicates after the first few drinks.

Billy continued to be openly flirtatious and did little to conceal his occasional infidelities from Elinor; the worse he behaved, the more submissive she became, for she was now so completely insecure that she was terrified of losing him. Whatever was wrong was her fault; whatever was wrong she must make right. Obsessed by Billy, she had become addicted to his love.

Also obsessed by jealousy, Elinor wanted to know nothing of Billy's amorous sorties, and yet perversely she longed to know every detail of them. She knew that Billy would obligingly provide these details, that he would both torture her and satisfy her craving—but he always made her ask for them. Always, in the end, she did.

It became a game—a game that Billy obviously enjoyed. He would ask her what she thought had taken place between himself and the lady in question. He would have Elinor state her anxieties in specific detail, occasionally interrupting her jealous visions by murmuring remarks such as "You mean you suspect I did this to her." And then he would touch Elinor's body in the way she had described.

Eventually the game itself became a passion for Elinor, the passion an obsession. There lurked behind the game, however, the secret fear that—one day—one of Billy's street girls, or one of the schoolgirls, or one of the society beauties he met, would unexpectedly gain as slavish a hold over him as he had over Elinor.

In fact, Billy's passing physical thirsts were quickly slaked and as quickly forgotten, but he took care that Elinor should not realize this. Slowly she built up in her imagination the figure of her husband as an irresistibly attractive, potent, and all-powerful man.

Billy would now rarely tell Elinor that he loved her. He liked to keep her in a permanent state of anxiety and jealousy, so that he could make her do anything he wished. Elinor longed for the words that she now seldom heard. It was essential that Billy love her. And of course, it was essential that she love Billy, because this assuaged her feelings of guilt about enjoying sex.

Elinor was also terrified of losing Billy because, like so many women of her generation, she felt inadequate, unable to face life without a man, no matter how badly he behaved. She had no money of her own and would be unlikely to get even domestic work, accompanied by a small baby. Like most other women, she was totally dependent upon her man, and so never allowed herself the luxury of reacting with anger to his bad behavior.

But one morning, as Elinor did the dishes after breakfast, she suddenly found herself shaking Billy's breakfast mug in a fury. The previous night, Billy had stumbled home, late and drunk. While undressing, he had knocked a photograph frame to the floor and then accidentally stood upon it; this had smashed the glass and torn the only picture of her mother that Elinor possessed.

As, enraged, Elinor shook the mug, she suddenly realized, with cold horror, that Billy could make her feel as anxious and muddled, as miserable and worthless as she used to feel after a strapping from her father.

But Billy was not the inescapable tyrant of her childhood! Billy was Elinor's husband, chosen by her. He was her beloved . . . wasn't he?

Bewildered by the sudden violence of her emotion, Elinor made herself a cup of tea and sat at the kitchen table. For almost an hour, she stayed there without moving as the cup of tea cooled before her. For once, she considered Billy's behavior toward her without rationalizing it. She did not mentally suppress his cat-and-mouse cruelty and remember only the charm he had shown during courtship. Instead, she asked herself why both Billy and her father could make her feel the same dragging unhappiness.

Suddenly Elinor could no longer refuse to admit that she had indeed chained herself to another bully—one who would darken the rest of her life. Her savior had become her tormentor. And with that realization came tears that burned with pain. Elinor put her head on the scrubbed wooden table and sobbed until she was breathless and her eyes were so swollen that she could hardly see.

Lifting her head, she pulled herself together. Billy was her husband, and Edward was her son, and this was her life. She had no choice but to go on.

She turned her face away from the reality that she couldn't bear to the romantic vision of Billy with which she had fallen in love. Last night's drunken oaf was not the man she had married. The *real* Billy was the handsome, charming hero in the photograph at her bedside. He was having a difficult time at the moment because he had been forced to take a job that wasn't good enough for him. Of course he had reason to be upset. She would push all unpleasant thoughts out of her mind and focus only on helping Billy. Surely, in time, things would get better, life would improve. Of course it would.

CHAPTER 4

THE NEXT TEN years were difficult for Elinor, as she saw less and less of "the real Billy," and her husband's drinking increased.

More and more, she found it necessary to justify and to compromise. Bewildered, she found it hard to understand what was happening to her life. She wondered miserably whether she was doing all she might to help Billy, because everything would be all right and their life would be happy—if only Billy didn't drink.

Sometimes Elinor also wondered whether, as Billy often said, his drinking was in any way her fault. If so, how had she disappointed him, as he repeatedly accused her of doing? And she wondered too why she could never stick to her ultimatums. Why did she always believe that Billy would change simply because he always promised to do so? He never did.

Elinor never knew when he would be home for meals, or whether he would be home at all. Eventually she learned not to count on Billy for anything, neither his presence nor his absence. If, thinking Billy safely out of the way, she invited a friend from her Polytechnic class to her home, Billy invariably staggered in and insulted the friend. Elinor, who didn't like to embarrass people, gradually stopped inviting anyone home, except Buzz, who was impervious to Billy's bad behavior. On the few occasions when Billy not only was sober but did not have a hangover, he was so defensive that Elinor was rarely able to discuss his drinking.

Edward, a pale, quiet child, kept out of his father's way as much as possible. He was a self-contained boy, who seemed able to communicate almost wordlessly with his mother, much to the irritation of his father. He had a gentle and sensitive nature, although he had inherited his father's impressive, wide-shouldered physique and was clearly going to be tall and strong. He also had his father's untidy strawlike hair and neat features, though after Edward's nose was broken in a football game, Billy wouldn't allow the boy to have it reset, because it made him look tougher: Billy was exasperated by his son's lack of obvious manly qualities and his preference for nature study to sports.

Some aspects of their life together remained normal. Billy still saw Joe Grant, who had married his boss's daughter early in 1929. Elinor still saw Buzz regularly. Buzz never said, "I told you so."

But one summer Sunday evening, after Billy had been particularly abusive to Elinor in front of Buzz, the two women went to the cinema. As they reached the Kensington Odeon, Buzz quietly asked, "How much longer are you going to put up with Billy's rotten behavior? For the rest of your life?"

"Don't tell me I ought to leave him. It'll spoil our outing."

"But why? You've got the guts and the gumption—we all saw that in the war—but where's your backbone gone? I've *never* understood why you don't just get up and leave Billy."

"It's not that simple." Elinor shook her head.

"Don't say that! Why don't you stop inventing obstacles? Why don't you decide that next time he's a bastard, you'll just walk out of that front door! Nell, you ain't got a hero to save you. No woman has. *You got to save yourself.*"

"I know you mean well," Elinor said as they entered the Egyptian magnificence of the theater foyer. The fantastic architecture reminded her of her childhood daydreams of being a changeling, when she hoped that one day she would be swept off to become an adored princess. Now her forlorn hope was that one day her fairy prince would turn back into a fairy prince, that one day Billy would see how destructive his behavior was; this pathetic hope enabled her to live with him, as did her equally pathetic insistence on seeing Billy through rose-colored glasses.

As they entered the darkness of the auditorium, Buzz added, "You used to have a mind of your own before you married Billy, but now you can't seem to make any decision for yourself."

"Do we have to discuss that again?"

"At least you used to know when Billy treated you like a doormat. Now when he treads on you—you don't even *notice!* You almost apologized to *him* this afternoon when he'd finished criticizing the meal."

"Be fair, Buzz. Billy isn't violent; plenty of husbands are; but Billy's never lifted a finger against me . . ."

"No, only his tongue: he's beaten you black and blue with that."

Elinor said, "I know I'm short on self-confidence, but Billy means well."

"*I* don't think Billy means well," Buzz said. "I've watched him *smash* your self-confidence. That's not a well-meaning thing to do."

"Billy only criticizes me to be helpful. He means to be kind."

"There ain't no such thing as being cruel to be kind! People like Billy are cruel to be cruel! Don't mistake *that* for loving kindness." Buzz lit a cigarette. "I can't think why you don't leave him."

"Because he loves me—he does really!"

Buzz snorted. "A funny sort of love! I can see that you love *him*—you make endless sacrifices for that rotter. And like all doormats, you do it because you secretly wish that's what he'd do for you! Nell, I know you fell in love with Billy. I was there, remember? He was a charmer—a girl would've had to be made of stone not to take a shine to him. We all watched him when he turned his charms on you, and we was all a little jealous. So I know, Nell. I know why you fell for him, and I know how. What I don't know, and what I don't understand, is why you can't see that the Billy O'Dare we met and fancied then is not the same man you've got to go home to tonight."

"But Buzz, he loves me. I know he does."

Buzz paused. "Maybe he does, Nell, I can't speak for him," she said slowly. "But I can say that his love ain't enough anymore. Not the way he treats you. And don't you deny it. Yes, maybe in his own twisted way he does love you, but again, Nell, *it ain't enough!* What's gone, and what you'll never get back, is the romance he used to win you over, and that's what a woman needs. It's an important part of a woman's life, and men just don't understand it, or respect it, for that matter. They think it's silly. But it ain't, and when it's gone, it leaves a void. I know."

Buzz realized suddenly that she'd allowed her voice to rise enough to attract the attention of others in the cinema. Besides, they were still standing in the darkened aisle, both a little startled by the passion in Buzz's plea.

Self-consciously they sat in the nearest empty seats. Mellifluous, soothing music rose from the cinema organ, a warning that the movie would soon be starting. Struggling to lean forward from the depths of the crimson plush seat, Buzz couldn't resist raising one other important point. "And just how long do you think you can stand Billy's boozing?"

"I can't stop him. I can't do anything about it," Elinor said miserably. "But Billy's always sorry in the morning. He always promises he'll change. I'm sure that one day he'll really mean it." Often a repentant or badly frightened Billy had promised that he would stop drinking. The sad thing was that several times he *had* seriously tried to stop.

"One day pigs'll fly," retorted Buzz, who knew that hope can be destructive where, in reality, there is no hope.

"You know I couldn't leave him! Where would I go? And what would Edward and I live on?"

"You *could* leave him," Buzz said quietly. "You could get some sort of a job; you could be a waitress or a shop assistant. After all, Edward isn't a baby now—he's nine years old, and at school all day. You could both sleep in our front parlor until you got yourself sorted out. Ma wouldn't mind."

Elinor shook her head. "No, I could never leave Billy. He needs me." She could not imagine life without him. "Look, this is my night out. Please don't let's talk about this anymore."

It was still light when Elinor hurried home. As she put her key in the front door, she hesitated. It sounded as if Billy had company.

In the living room, she found nine-year-old Edward, naked and with his head hidden under a black top hat, sitting on a table. He was gurgling with laughter. In his hand, he held a tumbler containing an inch of green liquid.

His father was sprawled in the chintz armchair, a drink in his hand, a bleary smile on his face.

Elinor dashed forward. In one movement, she swept the hat from Edward's head and grabbed his tumbler. She sniffed it: crème de menthe.

Edward gave his mother a slack, happy smile. He swayed and nearly fell from the table.

Elinor caught him. Her son's body was cold. She tried to control her voice. "Time for bed, Edward."

A silly smile spread over Billy's face. "It's a father's job to teach a chap to drink," he said.

White-faced, Elinor snapped, "How dare you!"

She dressed the swaying Edward, then went to the kitchen. From her best teapot, she took the two bank notes that she kept hidden for emergencies. Without saying a word, she took Edward and left the apartment.

On the following day, Buzz visited some friends, two doors down, who were looking for a lodger. For an extra ten shillings a week, they were persuaded to take both mother and son.

On Monday, at midday, when Elinor knew that Billy would be at work, she returned to Earls Court Square to pack.

As she entered the dark entrance hall, a woman looked out of the ground-floor flat. "I thought it was you, Mrs. O'Dare," she said lugubriously. "I knew someone would have told you about the accident. The police want to see you, dear."

Forty-five minutes later, Elinor was sitting beside Billy's hospital bed. His bandaged leg was raised in traction, and one arm was in a plaster cast. His head was also bandaged, and the left side of his face was badly grazed.

"I ran after you." Billy sounded sheepish. "But the curb seemed to move, and a lorry got me from behind. Bloody stupid thing to do."

"Poor, poor Billy!" Elinor said as she tenderly kissed him. "Don't you worry about a thing, darling." For only a fleeting moment, she feared the wrath of Buzz.

But it was Edward who objected. Still suffering from a hangover, he looked at his mother and said in a voice of hopeless misery, "I didn't think you'd make me go back. Oh, *why* can't you leave him, Mummy?"

"Things are going to be different," Elinor promised, but as she saw disbelief in Edward's face, she suddenly wondered how *she* could have stubbornly held on to that belief for so long. She remembered hoping that things would change when her baby was born. As long ago as that! Then she hoped that things would change when the baby stopped crying, then when the baby stopped teething. She had always managed to find an excuse for Billy's bad behavior; she had always managed to produce an apparently rational reason—however tortured her rationalization—for his hurtful words and actions.

"Darling," Elinor said sadly, "what would Daddy do without me? And what would everyone say?"

"It won't matter what people say—we won't be there to hear them. And what happens to Daddy will be *his* problem, not ours." Edward grasped her hands and pleaded. "You know as well as I do that Daddy's a drunk and a bully and a rotter. *Please* let's not go back."

"Oh Edward, you don't understand," Elinor said miserably. "You see, I love him."

Elinor could not explain—because she did not herself understand—her love for Billy. She simply knew in her heart that Billy was her man, and she would love him to distraction and destruction until death parted them. Elinor longed for and believed in hope and in love, with the firm confidence of one who never dared to doubt it for a moment.

Edward said, "Mummy, you don't understand how *different* you are when Daddy isn't around. When you're with Daddy, you let him kick you around. I hate to see it."

Elinor remembered that Buzz had accused her of being a doormat. Sadly she said, "I can't help it, Edward. That's the way I was brought up. We're going home now."

* * *

Friday, 7 August 1936

Every month or so, Billy took his family to Larkwood, which continued to crumble into decay. His parents were now quite frail and seemed to spend their time huddled like sparrows in bad weather on either side of the drawing room fire. Elinor occasionally wondered why she had been frightened of them.

Elinor spent her visits to Larkwood either going for long vigorous walks in the park or reading in the library, a dark room that smelled sourly of old books and ghostly cigar smoke; it contained no books of value but the complete works of many popular nineteenth-century novelists, outdated atlases, musty reference books, and many boxes of family papers.

One threatening afternoon in early August, when the sky was slate purple and the air ominously still, Elinor opened a dusty box of old household books: the earliest account book was dated 1712. The weekly household accounts had been analyzed in thirteen columns, and so had annual general expenditure. The menu books—written in careful copper-plate—showed exactly what had been ordered from the cook on each day. The wages book recorded amounts paid long ago to staff, under the headings "House," "Laundry," "Stables," "Kennels," "Gamekeepers," and "Gardeners." The cellar book noted what wines had been bought and when they were drunk. Fascinated, Elinor started to read.

Later, she looked up as her mother-in-law entered the library. "Look what I've found!" Elinor held up a small chunky book bound in green leather so dark it was almost black, except on the corners, which had worn away.

"Oh, that's Rachel O'Dare's diary. One of our family treasures. She lived in the reign of Queen Elizabeth. There are some interesting recipes in it—you purchased one recipe at a time in those days, and they were expensive. I seem to remember that Rachel paid a guinea for a dish of peas with bacon and chopped onion. Of course, she also had her own family recipe book: they were copied out by a clerk for each daughter, upon her marriage."

Elinor leafed through the thin, brittle pages. "Here's a recipe for candied flowers!"

"We still use that for crystallizing violets, primroses, and rose petals. Rachel also had some pretty ideas for using flowers in salads."

Elinor said, "I think I'd like to try some of these. Could I take the book to my room and copy some of the recipes?"

"By all means."

More than three hundred years after they happened, Elinor shared Lady Rachel's adventures. In the blue bedroom, as Elinor carefully turned the pages, she learned about Rachel's life. In her diary, Rachel had recorded every detail of her country day, every domestic squabble and reconciliation, every wager her husband lost, every gown he bought her, every game she played with her children, every problem she had with her servants, every time she felt depressed and was "loste yn melencholy." Rachel noted in detail what happened at the local fairs, on the holy days, on Christmas and other feast days. Once, she was presented to the Queen, when Her Majesty paid a visit to a neighbor, the cost of which nearly bankrupted him.

Before dressing for dinner, Elinor started to decipher the crabbed hand and odd spelling of Rachel O'Dare's candied flower recipe.

"Thinking of starting a sweetshop, Elinor?" Billy was looking over her shoulder.

"No. I'm copying a recipe from an old diary."

Billy's arm reached around and slowly turned the pages of the worn green book.

Busy scribbling, Elinor murmured, "She has such a wry sense of humor. I feel I know her. In fact, that diary seems like reading a letter from an old friend. I know all Rachel's friends. I know she didn't like her father-in-law."

"He wasn't a very likable man." Billy yawned. "He had to get out of the west of Ireland pretty quickly, after leaking information to the English. He was a sort of collaborator—a fearful swine, by all accounts." Again he peered over Elinor's shoulder at the little diary. "It's damned difficult to read, isn't it! Spidery handwriting and crazy spelling."

"You need patience." Elinor slowly read: " 'Today I walked the orchard with Parson, and we did talk upon Joanna's wedding, which now grows near. As we did turn beneath green leaves, Parson did eye the fat, black cherries, until I promise him a basket. He spoke then of the feasting here. Again I see his eye right hungry, when I do promise 'twill be mighty. "What manner of dishes?" asks he. "Five spits of roasting meat are set up in the kitchen," say I. "We also shall feast on roasted swan, boiled fowls, and many little birds. Also much pike and salmon, with mighty, hot meat pies, and a cold one with live larks—to set the ladies skipping and shrieking." ' "

Billy said, "Don't stop." He was listening carefully.

"I'm glad you like it too. I'll go on with the greedy parson." Elinor read, absorbed: " ' "And sweetmeats?" asked Parson. "Such as never have here been tasted," promised I, "following my mother's receipt book for creams and syllabubs, jellies and puddings. Also my own spiced fruit cake." "And drink?" asks Parson, so I poured for him from my mouth a stream of claret wines from France, with sack, mead, cordials, and liquors, such as is meet for this marriage feast. Then doth he lick his lips, whether at the sound of this banquet or thinking upon the swiving that would follow, I know not.' "

"What does 'swiving' mean?" Billy asked.

"Making love, I guess."

"*Don't* say 'I guess.' "

"Sorry, Billy," Elinor responded mechanically. Although she didn't attempt to alter her midwestern accent, she tried not to use American expressions, because Billy didn't like her to and the British didn't understand them.

"Better stop that and dress for dinner. You know how testy Mother gets if we aren't down before the gong stops ringing."

Tuesday, 11 August 1936

When they returned to Earls Court from Larkwood, Billy was in a bad temper. A visit to his family home always reminded him that his elder brother would inherit the estate in its entirety. Edward, now sixteen, disappeared to the bedroom they rented for him on the floor above their apartment.

Elinor opened the sitting room window and leaned on the sill, looking down on the square. The soft summer breeze smelled of dust, roses, warm grass, and horses' droppings.

Billy poured himself half a tumbler of whiskey, sat down in the sagging chintz armchair, and said wearily, "I suppose I'll have to tell you sometime. I've been fired." His nonchalant air did not disguise his pain.

Elinor turned from the window. "Billy! *Why?*"

"First thing a journalist must remember when he's fired is that the reason probably hasn't a bloody thing to do with his work. The *Globe*'s getting a new editor, and he wants to bring in his own gang." Billy added casually, "I don't think I'll look for another newspaper job."

Elinor realized that he meant no other newspaper wanted to hire him.

The following morning at seven o'clock, Elinor carried a cup of tea to Billy. Sitting on the edge of his bed, she said, "Why don't you see what other sort of work is available? Perhaps you could apply for this job?" She handed him the newspaper: she had ringed one entry in red pencil.

Reacting slowly and reluctantly, Billy read, " 'Needed at once, for large manufacturing chemists, live-wire men qualified to call upon doctors and chemists. Splendid prospects for sound men.' " He looked up at Elinor. " 'Sound men.' That means no war veterans need apply."

"I know that your limp is painful, Billy, but a limp doesn't make people feel uneasy—like a missing arm or leg," Elinor said persuasively.

"You needn't think I'm going to turn into a commercial traveler," Billy snarled.

"What *are* you going to turn into, Billy?" Her clear green eyes carefully studied him. Although he took little exercise, Billy's body was still tall, lean, and firm. But today he had a hangdog air and his shoulders sagged—familiar signs of a hangover. Elinor looked at the leathery pouches under his eyes and his gray cheeks covered by silver stubble.

She could not think why she loved him.

Billy gave her a sly smile. "It so happens I have a better idea for making money."

He threw back the bedclothes and walked naked to the chest of drawers. He pulled open a top drawer, then turned to face her. In his hand he held a small dark green leather object.

"Why, that's Rachel O'Dare's diary! Does your mother know you have it?"

"No, she doesn't. She'll never notice it's gone. Don't worry, I'm not going to sell it. I've only borrowed it, and I'll return it."

"*When* are you going to return it?" Elinor was shocked that he had so casually removed something valuable.

"When you've written a book called *Diary of an Elizabethan Housewife*," Billy said triumphantly. "I know just the right publisher for it!"

For a moment, Elinor wondered if he was still drunk after his bout of the previous evening. She studied Billy's face: if he was drunk, his facial muscles slackened, giving him a vacant look. But that telltale sign wasn't there this morning.

Quietly she said, "Billy, I'm not a professional writer. I love scribbling letters and I once won an essay prize in school, but I don't know how to *begin* to write a book."

"You've got the beginning here." Billy waved the little green diary at her. "Simply translate it into modern English. Add explanatory paragraphs, where necessary, to expand what Rachel is saying, or what's going on in the rest of the sixteenth-century world—print those bits in bold type instead of footnotes: you don't want the thing to look scholarly."

"Where would *I* find out what was going on in the rest of the sixteenth-century world?"

"What's the British Museum for? Ask the librarian to guide your research."

"But I don't know *how* to do research!"

"Ask Edward to show you." Edward was studying history, hoping for a scholarship to Oxford. Billy added with airy truth, "Research just means finding out things."

Elinor and Billy planned the book together; he advised her to stick as closely as possible to the original text, as that would be the easiest way to operate. Billy drew up a list of work deadlines for each item so that he would know immediately if Elinor was falling behind schedule. Edward showed his mother how to handle her research in an orderly way: plywood orange boxes were piled against one wall of the living room, and at Christmas, Billy gave Elinor a second-hand filing cabinet.

By the end of March 1937, Elinor had finished *Diary of an Elizabethan Housewife*. The book was to be published in November by Stansfield and Hart.

Just before publication, Billy hurled himself into a flurry of activity. He wrote press releases; he persuaded every suede-shod gossip writer he knew to mention the book, in return for various favors. Billy also carefully chose Elinor's outfit for the book launch party, to be held at the Russell Hotel in Bloomsbury.

Elinor did not care for his choice. Standing in a changing room at Fortnum and Mason, she exclaimed, "What's gotten into you, Billy? I can't wear a bright pink moiré cocktail frock at three o'clock in the afternoon! Your mother would say it was dead common. And we can't afford it!"

"Joe Grant's paying for it," Billy said, and turned to the saleswoman. "The hat will be very important for the photographs. Let's try that white silk turban with the pink ostrich feathers."

"*What* photographs?" Elinor asked, bewildered.

Billy looked carefully at his wife; she was nearly thirty-seven now. Elinor's face was thinner, but her pink, white, and golden coloring was still striking. "Pity they won't be in color," Billy said. "I've booked a sitting after lunch with Angus McBean—he's the best theatrical photographer. You're going to be launched like a leading lady!"

And Billy saw to it that everything went according to his plan. He supervised the press coverage, the interviews on the wireless, and the trips to bookshops for autograph sessions, to which Elinor traveled, at Billy's insistence, in a hired white Rolls-Royce—paid for by Elinor's astonished publishers, who had never before done anything to attract publicity beyond sending review copies to a few literary editors.

To the surprise of everyone except Billy, *Diary of an Elizabethan Housewife* by Elinor Dove was an immediate success. The illustrations were copious and charming; the book was historically correct yet didn't read like a dull history book, for Elinor had re-created Lady Rachel's life so vividly that readers felt they could lean out and touch her. As Billy kept telling the press, almost anyone would find the book an acceptable Christmas gift, and many did.

Edward, who had won a senior exhibition and was now reading history at

Merton, was as delighted by his mother's success as he was by his new freedom. He loved Oxford—all the more so as he had just acquired his first girlfriend. Her name was Jane, and she, too, was a first-year history student.

Saturday, 1 January 1938

Elinor leaned back against her pillows and stretched luxuriously in the weak warmth of the winter sun, marveling at how her life had recently improved. This was the first time since she'd known him that Billy hadn't had a hangover on New Year's Day! He had started to cut back his drinking after a painful illness, when his doctor warned that his body wouldn't stand up to such punishment. He hadn't minced words, and Billy had been frightened by the verbal sketch of cirrhosis of the liver.

Lying naked beside her, Billy yawned and stroked his mustache. "I've got a present for you, darling. A new contract for the next book."

"Oh, good. The Elizabethan cookery book?"

"Not exactly," Billy said. "They want a novel."

In the crimson and gilt splendor of the Café Royal, Billy had lunched with the publisher and his senior editor. They both thought that Elinor had a natural talent for writing. Her work showed a rare observance, fresh directness, and an eye for the unexpected. Her characters were not two-dimensional stereotypes but real people who leapt right off the page, prepared to talk or argue with the reader.

Billy had sat back, immediately thinking: international best-seller . . . first novel . . . Margaret Mitchell . . . *Gone with the Wind* . . . Hollywood . . . movie rights. He said, "I have to tell you that we have already been approached by Billy Collins . . ."

The advance was agreed by the end of the meal.

Billy now saw a new life stretching before him, and it was very like his old life before the war. It was clearly in his interest to develop Elinor's ability as a novelist because if Elinor could earn good money, then Billy—as her manager—would never need another job.

As he sketched Elinor's new career to her, she sat up in bed and blinked. "But, Billy, I've never written a novel!" She was bewildered. "I couldn't do it—I wouldn't know how to start!"

"I'll teach you. It's simple."

Elinor knew immediately that Billy was serious, and that it would be useless to argue. She realized that her day would be wasted trying to change his mind. "I'll get breakfast," she said, shifting to get out of bed.

"No," Billy said, restraining her, "I'll get breakfast."

Ten minutes later, Elinor stared at a worn, flower-patterned tray upon which stood a jug of milk, an apple, several slices of buttered bread, and a red exercise book.

Billy said, "That's all you're getting until you fill ten pages—to my satisfaction."

"But what shall I write about? What do *I* know about? Life on a farm? The horror of a French hospital in the war? Trying to survive after it? People don't want to read depressing stuff like that—they know too much about it!"

"Write what other people don't know about," Billy suggested. "Then they can't check on you. Write a historical novel. Start with a rape."

"But I've never . . . I don't know what—"

"Then I'll show you." As Billy hurled himself upon her, the milk jug crashed to the floor.

Later, Billy murmured, "You have talent, but that is only the beginning. The first thing a writer has to learn is discipline."

To teach her this, Billy locked Elinor in the bedroom.

Her first reactions to imprisonment were defiance and revolt. She did not touch the red exercise book.

"What an ungrateful bitch you are!" growled Billy at midday, when he brought her bread and milk. "If it wasn't for me, you wouldn't have *had* this success that's so clearly gone to your head!"

Elinor, of course, knew that this was true, because Billy had said it to her so many times.

After a day of boredom, with no one to talk to and nothing to read, Elinor capitulated. At teatime, she dipped her pen into the bottle of Steven's blue-black ink and started to write.

Billy made it clear that he was not satisfied with her efforts. "You're not trying hard enough!" he exclaimed with a frown as he read what she had written.

"*You'd* think that Scott of the Antarctic wasn't trying hard enough!" Elinor said, showing a flash of her old spirit.

He gave her a slim book on punctuation. "Learn this by heart. I'll test you on a chapter every evening, before supper. If you don't know it, you get no supper."

When Elinor flubbed the third chapter, Billy locked her in the bedroom again, as if she were still a schoolgirl who hadn't learned her lesson. Then he left the flat and stayed out all night.

He returned at eight o'clock the following morning, disheveled and tired. He smiled at Elinor as he stood in the bedroom doorway. "Can you now tell me the difference between a colon and a semicolon?"

In a frenzy of jealousy, anxiety, and fear, Elinor quickly recited the carefully memorized lesson, moving all the while across the floor toward Billy.

Her heart pounded when he bent to kiss her; she lifted her face toward his, as a prisoner toward the light. She felt his hand grasp her breast with rough passion; then, without a word, he swept her into his arms and carried her to their bed.

She felt the erotic, harsh scraping of his mustache against her soft hair, and the light scratch of the stubble on his unshaven face. Her anxiety was replaced by the tension of passion.

Eventually Elinor produced a story synopsis that Billy found satisfactory. Together, they visited the London Library and left with fifteen research books.

Elinor felt a little more cheerful. "I suppose I must remember that everyone has at least *one* book in them," she said.

"That's a lie, as any publisher will tell you," Billy grunted. "Some people haven't got so much as a paragraph of a pamphlet in them."

Billy proved to be an unsympathetic, tough, but ultimately excellent critic, who repeatedly urged Elinor to concentrate on plot, pace, and action scenes. "Cut scenic descriptions to a maximum of two lines," he told her. "If your readers wanted to read about birds, trees, and sunsets, they'd buy a nature book."

Elinor wept when she didn't understand what Billy wanted her to write, or felt that she couldn't do it. "Why? *Why* do I have to rewrite it *again?*" she complained one evening. "I can't see what's *wrong* with what I've written!"

"Then listen to me more carefully," Billy said in a soft voice that raised the hairs on Elinor's spine. "As you write, you must think yourself *into* each of your characters. Be an actress! I want to know what Lydia *feels* when her sister's husband kisses her!"

"But I've told you—"

"Don't *tell* me what's happened—*show* me what's happening! I want to experience it!" Billy roared. "This dull rubbish sounds like a newspaper report. Get some life in it! Remember that you are the eyes, the ears, the nose, and the heart of your reader. Always remember that. I want to feel that I'm *there*, hidden in the cold shadow behind the hedge, as Cynthia watches her husband kiss Lydia. I want to see them embrace in the garden, and I want to shiver in the moonlight as I bite my lip to stop myself from crying or cursing at them!"

Elinor stared at Billy with surprise. He had just sketched what it felt like to experience jealousy. He must therefore understand the pain that he had made her suffer.

The following evening, she cried tearfully, "Yesterday you told me that I need more emotion in my work, that I must feel the passion that my characters feel—and today you hand me this dusty little book on grammar. How *can* I feel passion when I have to think about grammar?"

"Try," Billy advised grimly, "*and never forget that I know what's best for you.*"

Often, in despair, she flung herself upon the bed and wept, but tears did no good. Paradoxically, the only thing that made her forget her helplessness, her bewilderment, her anxiety, her indignation, and her despair was scribbling in the red exercise books.

Every morning, Elinor hurriedly threw on a bathrobe and ate the meager breakfast Billy fixed for her. He then locked her in the bedroom, and did not unlock the door until she banged on it at midday and then pushed ten pages of scribbled manuscript under it. If her pages were good enough, Billy carried a tray of fruit and coffee to the little desk at the bedroom window, where Elinor worked. If the pages were not good enough, he simply tore them up and threw the pieces out of the window, to flutter slowly down to Earls Court Square.

When Elinor finished her frugal luncheon (Billy feared a large meal might make her sleepy), she hurriedly washed and dressed while mentally preparing the next ten pages. After a further ten pages (a total of five thousand words a day), she was released from the bedroom to prepare the evening meal.

While Elinor cooked supper, Billy scribbled his transitional suggestions in the margins of her work; he corrected her grammar, her punctuation, and her abysmal spelling. After supper, Elinor rewrote her work; Billy stood over her, urging her to cut this or emphasize that.

When her writing was finished to Billy's satisfaction, he would pick up Elinor in his arms and carry her to bed.

There he would caress her exhausted body until it wearily responded to his touch, with increasing willingness, and finally with a passionate abandon she had not thought possible, spent as she was from writing.

After a few weeks, Elinor no longer resented the sound of the key turning in the lock of the bedroom door after breakfast. Instead, she trembled with carefully concealed excitement as she waited for the little click of the lock, which now transported her into the mysterious and limitless world of her imagination.

But by the end of the day, Elinor was not only exhausted but anxious; she worried whether her work was good enough. Only Billy could lull this anxiety; only Billy could reassure her that her work reached his high standards; only Billy could then caressingly transport her to a world of passion in which description and narrative thread were forgotten.

In Billy's arms, Elinor felt successful, sensuous, desired, protected, happy—and safe. She did not see herself as a bird imprisoned in a cage, for no cage was needed. Elinor was bound to Billy by the invisible, secret silken cords of a voluptuousness of which she was ashamed but to which she was addicted. She was both captivated and motivated by Billy, who, having made her totally dependent upon him both mentally and physically, kept her firmly under his thumb.

Elinor was bullied, cheated, rejected, and treated with amused and open contempt, but she was Billy's victim, his invisibly-shackled slave: she was helplessly, hopelessly enthralled by him. Billy's mesmeric gaze could still make Elinor feel worthy or unworthy, anxious or confident. And sometimes he permitted her to be happy.

One of these occasions was in June 1938, when Elinor's work was interrupted by the marriage of their son, Edward, to Jane, the girl he had fallen in love with at Oxford. The ceremony took place in St. Bartholomew's, a small Norman church north of Oxford that had not been much altered in the past nine hundred years. Elinor helped with the decorations and, in the process, got to know more of her daughter-in-law, a young woman she found both intelligent and endearing. Elinor liked Jane's quiet tenacity and her earnest but forceful speech. In truth, she wished that Edward had not insisted on rushing into marriage, but if he must (and he had hinted that it was necessary), then he could not have chosen a more appropriate bride.

Eventually, after much effort, anxiety, and pain, Elinor produced a well-constructed novel with well-developed scenes and believable characters; she finished it in early January of 1939, two days before Jane produced her and Billy's first grandchild.

As she sat by Jane's hospital bedside and held baby Clare in her arms, Elinor was astonished to find herself a grandmother, for, at the age of thirty-nine, she still felt seventeen inside.

Again she examined the tiny, perfect toes as they curled and uncurled. She lightly stroked the miniature, Nefertiti-like head, marveling at the still-visible skull joins beneath the dark fuzz. With joy, she gazed into the old, wise eyes of this poised newborn baby.

"She has Edward's eyes," Jane said proudly.

"Apart from that, she's the image of you." Jane was small and thin, pale and dark.

Although they were so young, Jane seemed perfect for Edward. They lived in a big house in North Oxford with Jane's father, a widowed history professor, who didn't seem to notice. He didn't care what happened, provided nothing upset his routine.

* * *

To Billy's disappointment, Elinor's Elizabethan romance, *Rebellious Princess*, did not achieve the same level of success as the diary. No messenger appeared from Paramount or MGM, and although Billy personally delivered a copy of the book to Vivien Leigh's London home, he never received an acknowledgment.

The publishers were more pragmatic. "You can hardly expect her to pull off a winner with her first nonfiction book *and* her first novel," Mr. Stansfield said, over oysters at Wheelers. "The book is selling well for a first novel, and we're pleased with her progress." Stansfield and Hart had purchased an option on Elinor's next five novels. "I'm only sorry that your wife couldn't spare the time to have lunch, for I could then reassure her in person."

"She hates to break up the day—finds it stops her momentum," Billy murmured, having neglected to tell Elinor of the invitation. "She's already started on the next novel—kept to the same period, as you suggested, which cuts down her research. She's settling down in that period nicely. Shouldn't be surprised if she started to wear padded sleeves and a farthingale."

Billy now spent his mornings reading the newspapers, and behaved as if Mr. Chamberlain relied on his advice—which was to kick those German bastards out of Austria and back into their own country, before the British found themselves in another war. But Mr. Chamberlain didn't listen, and by September, when baby Clare was nine months old, Britain and France declared war on Germany.

Jane was again pregnant. "Just as well her mother left her a bit of money," Billy said sourly. Elinor said nothing, although she secretly agreed with him. Edward had done the right thing when Jane first became pregnant, but they should both have been more responsible and taken precautions after Clare's birth: two children were too much of a load for two kids of nineteen—especially now, when Britain was at war.

"Appeasement," Billy said, on the morning before Christmas. "We should have been tougher with the bastards earlier. We were too aggressive the first time, and not aggressive enough this time. We should have rubbed their Nazi noses in it, like puppies, when they made their first little mess and marched into Austria."

That evening, Billy returned home late, only mildly drunk and very happy because of his new job; he was to work in an administrative capacity at the War Office, liaising with the R.A.F.

As he was telling Elinor about it, the telephone on the hall table rang. Billy picked it up, listened, and said in his new, clipped voice, "Well done, m'boy. I expect you'll want to tell your mother. . . . Edward and Jeremy, that friend of his, have joined up. They've been drafted into the intelligence service."

On the afternoon of Monday, 11 March 1940, Edward telephoned his mother to tell her that Jane's second baby, Annabel, had just been born, two weeks early.

Elinor was unable to reach Billy, as he was not in his office, so she had to contain her excitement until that evening, when they had planned a rare night out to see Greta Garbo and Melvyn Douglas in *Ninotchka*.

Outside Billy's favorite pub, the Star and Garter at the top of Whitehall, people slowly groped their way through the black-out. As Elinor walked into the bar, a blast of light and noise greeted her. A piano pounding "Roll Out the Barrel" was surrounded by a singing khaki-clad crowd, their fists wrapped around tankards of beer. Elsewhere a group of sailors gathered round an accordionist were bawling, "All the nice girls love a sailor." The place smelled of stale cigarettes, stale hops, and stale sweat, but nobody cared, and the atmosphere was one of cheerful euphoria. Elinor struggled through the crowd to a small corner table where she had spotted a couple of unoccupied seats.

When Billy appeared in the doorway, she stood up and waved until he saw her, then cradled an imaginary baby and gave him the thumbs-up sign.

"Boy?" he mouthed questioningly.

Elinor shook her head.

Billy shrugged, smiled, then fought his way to the counter to buy drinks.

As he carried them from the bar, Elinor saw a young girl, hatless and slim as a bulrush in a dark brown coat, dash forward and tug at Billy's sleeve; her face was anxious as she spoke to him.

Billy looked exasperated as the girl clung to his sleeve. With a sudden movement, she laid her head against his shoulder.

Billy angrily jerked his head toward Elinor.

The girl looked her way and Elinor saw a freckled, oval face with short brown hair and large, tearful dark eyes.

Billy yanked his sleeve free, then continued to battle through the crowd toward Elinor.

"Who was that?" Elinor asked him when he reached her.

"Oh, just a girl from the newspaper office. One of the secretaries."

"What's her name?"

"I forget, actually."

"If you don't tell me, I'm going to ask her."

"For Christ's sake, Elinor, can't we *just once* have a night out without your jealous imagination taking off like a Spitfire? I think she's called Pat Kettle."

"Why is she crying? And why did she ask you to help her?" That had been obvious.

"Some trouble at the office. Some documents are missing. She's under suspicion. *I* can't do anything about it, as I told her."

"She's in love with you—I can see it."

Standing by the bar, the girl still gazed sadly at Billy; she wore an expression that Elinor knew well, the expression of a puppy that has just been kicked by its master.

"I can't help that," Billy said tersely. "Drink up, or we'll be late."

"For heaven's sake, Billy, she's only a child," Elinor said angrily. "Couldn't you have left her alone?" She watched as Miss Kettle turned despondently away, toward the door, and disappeared in the crowd.

"Be reasonable, old girl. Can I help it if some woman takes a shine to me?"

"Yes, you *can* help it," Elinor replied bitterly. She put her untouched drink on the table. "We've been married for twenty-two years and you're nearly fifty, for heaven's sake. How old is she? Nineteen? A young girl doesn't fall for a man of your age unless she's pursued and courted. I can just about remember your romantic approach, Billy. It was very effective."

Billy laughed this off. "No, darling—*you* were always the romantic. Now tell me about my new granddaughter. And drink up. We're already late for the cinema."

CHAPTER 5

Saturday, 8 March 1941

ALMOST THREE YEARS after they were married, Edward and Jane were celebrating Jane's birthday at the Café de Paris in London, when two fifty-kilo German bombs fell down an air shaft of the nightclub, straight onto the dance floor. Edward and Jane were killed instantly, their bodies charred almost beyond recognition.

Billy, silent and regretful, was kinder to Elinor than he had been since their marriage. Elinor, in a state of shock from which she felt she would never recover, took charge of the orphaned children and had to adapt quickly to the demands of a young family.

A few months after this tragedy, at closing time at the Star and Garter, Billy fell in the blackout, with a resultant compound fracture of his left fibula, which was slow to heal. He now found it difficult to walk and was unable to continue with his job. Eventually he joined Elinor in the country with the three little girls; everybody said how sad it was that Miranda had been born only a month before Jane and Edward were killed. The near-derelict cottage was on the Larkwood estate; there was no space at the big house, which now served as an officers' convalescent home.

Their new circumstances required new literary discipline. Billy now made Elinor get up in the dark, at five A.M., to write until nine A.M., seven days a week. But those few hours a day belonged only to Elinor, and during that time, she forgot the cold, discomfort, and deprivation of war; she even forgot the loss of Edward, which otherwise was constantly present in her waking time, sapping the strength and hope from her body. As her pen detailed the rich clothes, splendid jewelry, and sybaritic banquets of delicious food with delicate wine, Elinor escaped back to the leisurely, bountiful, lyrical life of Elizabethan England.

The rest of her day was spent looking after the three baby girls, struggling to shop and cook for all of them, and coping with life without electricity, running water, or inside sanitation: there was a wooden shed at the end of the garden, and water was pumped from a well in the courtyard. Elinor ignored this lack of comfort. She was determined to see only the romantic charm of the cottage, which stood on the southern slope of a wooded hill, with a view of undulating fields beyond the small garden where Billy raised neat rows of vegetables. Elinor enjoyed the peace of the country, especially in winter on cold, clear snowy days, and in summer when the wind rippled through the field of ripe wheat; then, she was always reminded of her childhood, although British wheat fields were tiny compared to those of Minnesota.

And Elinor quickly became a doting grandmother. Everybody said what pretty little girls they were: all three had Billy's mesmeric aquamarine eyes, solemn and staring. Clare, the eldest, was dark and frail, a quiet child as her father had been. Annabel looked like Elinor as a child; she was a rosy-cheeked, chubby little thing, with thick fair hair and an unusually pretty face. Miranda, the youngest, had a pale, freckled face; she was skinny and small for her age.

"Yes, we're very lucky," Elinor would smile when anybody complimented her on the three sisters. But no number of adorable grandchildren could replace Edward. Like most mothers, she had thought of her own child as still flesh of her flesh and blood of her blood, still a part of her own body, joined by an invisible umbilical cord that could never be cut; and so now she felt bereft, as if a part of her had been amputated.

Every time Elinor saw aquamarine eyes staring up at her, in her mind's eye again she saw Edward as a child and felt poignant, wistful regret. She wished that she had not been so careless of those ordinary hours when he had been in the room while she ironed, or darned, or listened to the radio. Every time she remembered her beloved only son, Elinor's heart seemed to shrivel and she felt a physical pain in her breast. Rather than give in and break down in tears before the frightened little girls, she would make an effort of will and turn her mind to her plot problems with her book, a diversion that was always successful.

Sunday, 5 August 1945

Nearly two years after starting it, Elinor finished her fourth novel. She had enjoyed almost every moment of it; she had even persuaded herself that getting up in the dark was exciting, although the past winter had been so cold that she wore her coat at her desk, draped blankets around her legs, and propped her feet on a hot-water bottle.

Elinor worked all day on the novel. Billy, knowing that the rhythm and crescendo of the ending should be uninterrupted, saw that she was undisturbed. He brought fresh cups of tea and soup to her desk and took away the cold, untouched ones as she scribbled, oblivious to his presence.

Just after eleven o'clock that night, Elinor put down her pen, removed her spectacles, rubbed her eyes, stretched, and like any novelist, started to have doubts.

Perhaps it should not be called *Deadly Fortune* but *Fatal Fortune*. Elinor didn't want it to sound like a detective story, although that was exactly what the novel was—a series of murders in one Elizabethan family, in order to gain control of an estate.

Elinor stretched again. She felt as if she needed a walk. She felt as if she wanted a drink. She felt hungry. She felt wide awake. She felt light-headed.

A bottle of cider stood on the kitchen dresser, a lamb chop lay in the metal-mesh meat safe that hung outside the kitchen door; she cooked the chop and drank the cider. For the moment, she felt completely alone in the world, and comfortable. She picked up the *Daily Telegraph* from the kitchen table, folded it at the crossword, then decided not to do it, because she could never finish the thing and it made her feel inadequate. She looked at the headlines once again: nothing much was happening.

Far away on the other side of the world, where it was early morning, a small parachute was floating down from a B-29 bomber. At 8:15 A.M., a nuclear chain reaction in the bomb built up a temperature of several million degrees centigrade, which created a fireball that seemed brighter than the sun. This fireball expanded to measure two hundred and fifty yards in diameter. One second after it had been detonated over Hiroshima, the world's first atomic bomb signaled the end of the war.

Tuesday, 9 July 1946

Joe Grant's office in Carey Street, immediately behind the assizes court, was almost a replica of his study in the country, with its dark green leather appointments. Joe looked older than fifty-one, Elinor thought as she sat in a wing chair by the side of the empty fireplace. She suspected that he carefully cultivated his Pickwickian traditional-lawyer look.

Joe smiled and said, "You haven't changed at all, Elinor. A touch older, as we all are, but you haven't changed." He basked in her wide, delighted smile.

"What flattery," said Elinor, now forty-six. "How's your family, Joe?"

"Ethel has a touch of arthritis, but the boys are fine. Michael has finally settled down at Eton—it helps if your elder brother is already there."

Elinor briefly reflected that, while Joe's children had benefited from their mother's money, she was glad Edward had not been brought up as strictly as Adam and Michael Grant. Their mother—five years older than Joe—had been forty years old in 1930, when Adam was born. After the difficult birth, she had suffered badly from what was not then recognized as postpartum depression, and seemed never to have forgiven Adam for her misery; Ethel was more lenient with Michael, who was born two years later, although she had not welcomed either pregnancy. Elinor had never seen Ethel Grant kiss her children; even at bedtime, she merely offered a cool cheek to be kissed by them. They had been restricted to the nursery by a severe and strict nanny and had been expected to behave as little adults rather than as children. At least in Edward's too short life, he had known the warmth of a mother's love.

Joe looked over his neat desk. "Why did you want to see me, Elinor?" Billy made all her business arrangements and had signed all the contracts prepared by Joe for the thirty-seven publishers around the world who had purchased *Deadly Fortune*.

When Paramount Pictures bought the film rights to *Deadly Fortune*, which had been an instant best-seller, and Vivien Leigh agreed to star in it, Billy had bought a vintage Lagonda, and Elinor had once again made a secret visit to an empty house about twenty miles distant from the cottage, a dilapidated estate called Starlings. The house was too big to run comfortably in wartime but not big enough to be useful to the forces, so shortly after war was declared, the entire estate had been turned into carrot fields; after the war, when the boisterous land girls and Italian prisoners of war who raised the carrots happily abandoned them, the land was left neglected. Now the place had fallen into disrepair, its earth knee high in coarse grass.

In Joe's dark office, Elinor outlined her plan with barely contained excitement. She wanted to surprise Billy by buying him his own country place!

"It's not as grand as Larkwood, but it's just as pretty!" Elinor said. "It's outside a little village called Maiden Bradley, near Warminster. I'd like you to handle the purchase, Joe." The folder she gave him included snapshots of a decrepit but beautiful small stone Elizabethan manor house, with a cherry orchard to one side of it. "Don't you think, Joe, that if Billy lived in the way he was brought up, he would . . . settle down, and relax, and be happy?"

Poor Elinor was still hoping that she could tame the old rascal, Joe thought. Aloud he said, "It's beautiful, Elinor, but . . . how can you afford this house?"

"It's a bargain—five thousand pounds!" Elinor exclaimed. "Paramount paid forty thousand dollars for *Deadly Fortune*. There *must* be enough money somewhere, even after tax."

Joe said uncomfortably, "All the money was paid to Billy, as your manager." There was a note of sorrow in his voice.

Elinor looked sharply at him. Slowly she said, "You mean . . . he's spent it *all?*"

Joe hesitated. "I believe that Billy may have made some unwise investments on the stock exchange." He realized that Elinor, who could rationalize and excuse her husband's drunken bullying and lechery, was now faced with undodgeable evidence that Billy was a liar, a cheat, and—some might say—a thief. Joe added, "To be fair, Elinor, Billy insisted on repaying every penny I've ever lent him."

Elinor's eyes filled with tears. *Nothing* in her hand, for all that work.

Up to now Elinor had willingly believed Billy's plausible explanations of his lying, cheating, and other petty dishonesty: he had done it to help someone out; he hadn't realized what he was getting into; he had been lied to; he had been let down. But nothing could explain away this betrayal.

"I might be able to raise a loan for you," Joe said, "or a further book option—of course, I couldn't go directly to your publisher behind Billy's back . . . "

Which meant that he would, Elinor reckoned.

"I'm confident," he went on, "that Stansfield and Hart would be open to some agreement so that you could purchase this house. After all, you will probably be happier and write better in more congenial surroundings."

Fighting back tears, Elinor said, "Please speak to Mr. Stansfield as soon as possible." She looked hard at Joe, who knew that she was also saying, *I'm trusting you to do this in some way that won't humiliate Billy, because otherwise my life will be intolerable, and I shall have to live with the real Billy instead of my romantic view of him, which is the only thing that makes the reality bearable for me.*

Mentally replacing her rose-colored spectacles, Elinor said firmly, "Without Billy to make me work, and to sell my work, I would have achieved *nothing.* So I suppose it *is* really his money. . . . Because truly I owe my career to Billy." She had once argued that the talent was hers, but Billy had quickly pointed out that the talent had been trained and disciplined by him, and so her success was due to him. Billy repeatedly told her, "You owe *everything* to me. Without me, you would be *nothing!* Without me, you would never be able to write. And without me, you would *certainly* never be published. *I* am the one who persuaded publishers to risk their money on your work."

Elinor had to admit there was some truth in what he said. Before Billy's schooling, she had known nothing of the craft of writing, and she had had no idea how to discipline herself.

Joe looked at Elinor. There were things he would have liked to say to her, but it wouldn't be correct to do so. Besides, Billy was indisputably the man in Elinor's life, and Joe did not intend to interfere in their marriage.

Sunday, 13 July 1947

One year later, after her brisk midday walk, Elinor strolled up the winding drive of her new home, between rhododendron bushes that formed great banks of shiny, dark leaves splashed with mauve and white blossoms. This floral guard of honor meandered half a mile, from the house to the hedged boundaries of nineteen acres of garden and parkland.

After she rounded the final bend and could see Starlings in front of her, Elinor paused to admire it once again. The long, low, beautifully proportioned Elizabethan house, with its front of mellow brick, stone mullions, and tall chimneys, now looked as well kept as it probably had been four hundred years earlier.

Briefly Elinor remembered their Earls Court home: the entire apartment would have fitted into the oak-paneled entrance hall of Starlings. Edward had been raised in that cramped flat in sooty London, but his daughters were now able to enjoy a gracious life in the country, thanks to their gran's busy brain and ever-scribbling right hand.

As she inhaled the honey-tinged air, Elinor wished that her mother could know about her success, could see her lovely house, as romantic as if it had sprung up from a child's book. How strange it was, she thought, that her mother's idea of bettering herself had been to get away from the grinding, incessant toil of life on the land. But now that Elinor could do as she pleased—after midday—what she most loved was to work in the soil. Gardening gave her great satisfaction; it also gave her time to think of new plots for books, to dream up new schemes, imagine new characters.

Sometimes, of course, her mind wandered to real matters, some of them quite disturbing. One memory she couldn't seem to escape was the day they had moved into Starlings, when she had accidentally uncovered a batch of battered photographs in Billy's den. They were black-and-white studio pictures of what looked like a ten-year-old girl, shot from the waist downward. Her slim, coltish legs were sprawled across a bed; Elinor recognized the dragon-patterned blue bedspread that she had scrapped when they left Earls Court. The child wore short white socks and black, Shirley Temple, ankle-strap shoes, and that was all. In some pictures, she lay on her back; in some, she was on her stomach, one leg languidly kicking back, bent at the knee.

When, with shaking hands, Elinor showed these pictures to Billy, he shrugged his shoulders and agreed that the photographs were obscene. He said he thought he had destroyed them: they had been taken years ago by a photographer who had been bombed out of his studio, when Billy had put him up for a few days. Elinor had been in the country, preparing the cottage for their occupation.

Elinor wanted to believe him.

With stubborn determination, she focused on the many pleasant things in her life and shut her eyes to Billy's increasingly unpleasant behavior which was, Elinor told herself, only due to the fact that once again he was drinking far more than was good for him.

Billy's three granddaughters, now six, seven, and eight years old, were embarrassed and bewildered when "Daddy Billy smelled funny," which invariably meant he would "act funny" as well, frequently teasing them in a rough way, sometimes even scaring them.

Annabel and Miranda ran off and hid whenever they heard the front door slam followed by Billy's heavy, uncertain tread upon the stairs. But Clare reacted differently. Perhaps it was because he was irritated by Clare's anxiously self-righteous air—the air of an elder sister who felt she was supposed to look after the little ones—that Billy picked on Clare more than on the other two.

But of course, Billy treated Clare with cruelty only when there was nobody around to see him do it: when Elinor was visiting her publisher in London, or when it was the nanny's day off. Clare, whose instinct was to smooth, not ruffle troubled waters, never mentioned her grandfather's harsh treatment, and indeed she would have found it difficult to describe what she was complaining about. Few children feel that they have the power to complain about an adult; and every child in Clare's class at school talked of being slapped occasionally, or beaten if the crime was serious.

As a result of his mistreatment of her, Clare avoided Billy whenever possible. When she returned from school, she always asked, "Is Daddy Billy at home?" And if the answer was yes, no matter how cold the weather, Clare would immediately ask if she could play in the garden or go for a walk in the woods.

Poor Clare. As the eldest, she was the only sister with vague memories of her dead parents, and she had a forlorn air, as if she were a lost child, forgotten on some railway station platform. She survived Billy's cruel attacks in the only ways that a vulnerable young child could: by mentally withdrawing from any painful scene and by hopefully using magical means. Hidden behind the rhododendron bushes, she would mix potions of berries and grass and daydream, as she willed Daddy Billy to die.

Other minor superstitions also helped Clare: *if* she could count up to seventy-five while holding her breath; *if* she put her knickers on in the morning, left foot first; *if* there was an even number of letters in the advertisement on the side of the school bus—then *he* wouldn't be at home when she returned from school. Sometimes these spells worked.

As Clare grew more apprehensive and frightened (reported as "highly strung" by her school), Elinor saw that, like her father, she was developing into a quiet, nervous child. Elinor tried to blank out these comparisons because they conjured up guilt when she recalled unpleasant memories of Edward's childhood: his father's bewildering behavior and humiliating, drunken cruelty had wrecked Edward's self-confidence—until he grew bigger and stronger than his father; then, when Edward was at home, Billy curbed his bullying.

Instead, Elinor reminded herself how well Billy treated Annabel. Golden-haired and pretty, she was Billy's favorite grandchild; she would jump on his knee, put her little arms around him, and lean her silken head against his shirt. Billy was flattered by her flirtatious manipulation and responded with generosity. When Annabel had made Billy smile, she would quickly ask him for what she wanted.

Shrewd little Annabel.

Billy couldn't be bothered to torment Miranda. "Dull little thing," he said. "Nothing to say for herself. No fun."

Clever little Miranda.

Unfortunately, Billy's increasingly bad behavior no longer caused only local scandal. He had given several regrettable interviews to London newspapers; Elinor's publisher had pointed out to her the folly of such actions. Her public wished to think of her as a romantic creature draped upon a chaise lounge in a negligee, who wrote with quill pen on crackling parchment to a background accompaniment of gentle Scarlatti. They should not hear that Elinor was a half-witted puppet who could not have written her books without her husband's Svengali-like direction and inspiration. There had also been strong rumors (also, unfortunately, started by Billy) that he had actually *written* Elinor's books.

"But surely nobody believes that?" Elinor had protested. "*You* have all my manuscripts, written in longhand, in my handwriting."

"Plenty of hacks will print a malicious story without bothering to check that it's true," Mr. Stansfield had said. "Malicious gossip sells newspapers, which makes money for newspaper proprietors."

"Why tell *me?* Why don't you talk to Billy?" the wretched Elinor asked.

"I *have* talked to your husband, but unfortunately, it hasn't stopped him. I hope you can make him see how damaging such publicity is—for all of us."

As Elinor stared now at her beautiful house, she couldn't help recalling that depressing luncheon with her publisher. She felt vexed with herself. Why did such unpleasant thoughts not stay hidden at the back of her mind? Particularly today, when she should be looking forward to her hour of triumph in her new home. She should be checking that the Georgian mahogany table had been properly laid and the wine decanted, and that the food preparation was proceeding smoothly for her luncheon party. Because, for the first time, Elinor was about to meet her sister-in-law as an equal.

Behind her, a horn hooted. She turned to see Marjorie waving from a battered prewar Armstrong Siddley. Drat! They had arrived early. Elinor steeled herself to assume her normal air of optimistic happiness as she prepared to show her romantic home to her sister-in-law.

Marjorie's admiration for Starlings somehow left Elinor feeling depressed. "*Such* a lovely old house—have you had it checked for woodworm?" Marjorie trilled as she ate her rabbit pie. "And subsidence? The Crawleys lived in a house *very* similar to this. Had to be pulled down before it fell on them. . . . *Delicious* carrots, although I find a knob of butter helps the flavor. . . . What an original idea to spread a *lace* tablecloth on a luncheon table . . . "

After their guests had departed, Billy returned to the dining room to help himself to another glass of port. "You'll never get it right, old girl," he grinned at Elinor. "Marjorie will *never* let you forget that, to her, you're a jumped-up farm laborer, and whatever you do, she's never going to change her view. I can't understand why you bother with the old bitch, but then whatever you hold against me, no one can say I'm a snob."

"No, you're not a snob," Elinor said, trembling with fury, "but you do love using me to tease your family. You were teasing them when you first took me to Larkwood. You were showing your brother, who was going to inherit all the family wealth and power, that you had it in your power to humble your family by introducing me into it." She paused as an idea struck her. "No, it's not teasing—what you really enjoy, Billy, is *tormenting* people! I bet that when you were little, you pulled wings off butterflies, and legs off wasps, and . . . and . . . "

"Steady on, old girl. Save the drama for your plots." Billy refilled his glass.

Elinor stormed out. In the entrance hall, Betty, the nanny, stood at the bottom of the stairs. "Might I have a word with you, madam?" she asked. Betty's normally plum-colored cheeks had flushed almost to purple.

"Certainly, Betty. What's upset you? Has one of the girls been naughty?"

"It's not the little girls, madam," Betty said hesitantly. "Perhaps you'd best come to the nursery and see for yourself, madam. Now that they dress themselves, I wouldn't have noticed until bathtime tonight, but Miranda pushed Clare in the lily pond, so I had to change her clothes."

In the sunny day nursery, Betty exhibited eight-year-old Clare, wearing white vest and navy knickers; Elinor could see the bruises on her upper arms.

"Maybe you could have a word with him. He doesn't know his own strength, madam," Betty said coldly. She pulled Clare's hands forward; the nails were bitten to the quick, and the surrounding skin was ragged from nervous picking.

The befuddled Billy had rarely seen Elinor so angry as when she confronted him in his study about Clare's bruises.

Elinor concluded, "If it happens *once more*, then you leave this house! You are never again to hurt *any* of them! I *won't have it*."

Billy, for once, was horrified by what he had done: "I'd no idea that I was holding Clare so hard. I'd had a few and didn't realize . . . "

"What do you think Edward would do to you if he could see Clare's arms?" Elinor cried. "You couldn't bully *him* after he was big enough to lick you!"

"Elinor, I'm truly sorry. What can I do to convince you? How do you suppose *I* feel?" Billy pleaded.

"I don't *care* how you feel! Just make sure I never see a bruise on that child again!"

For once, Billy could not coax Elinor into forgiveness.

On the following morning, after a sleepless night, Elinor almost canceled her business trip to London, but she knew that her publisher had taken a great deal of trouble to arrange two press interviews and lunch at the Savoy with the W. H. Smith fiction buyer.

As Elinor was driven to the station, she waved to the three little girls, but they did not notice. They sat in a circle under a magnolia tree: they had removed their sandals and socks, and each child was bending her head down to her foot. Elinor smiled. It was their latest craze, a competition to see who could first get her toe in her mouth. Elinor found this sight reassuring.

Elinor caught the last train from London and returned home at about ten o'clock. She found the house in darkness except for the lights in the hall. Her depression returned as she slowly mounted the polished stairs to her bedroom, where she quickly undressed and washed, wearily pulled on a peach chiffon nightgown, and fell into her bed.

At seven o'clock the next morning, Mabel burst into Elinor's bedroom. "Oh madam, something awful . . . "

Elinor sat up abruptly. "What's happened?"

"He's in the hall, madam. . . . He's . . . lying there!"

Elinor jumped out of bed and ran down the stairs. On the Oriental carpet at the foot of the stairs, Billy, fully dressed, lay in a pool of vomit. An empty bottle of brandy lay near him. Billy's eyes were open; they stared at the ceiling, the aquamarine now faded, the whites yellowing, bloodshot, and glazed.

Elinor knelt by Billy and felt his cheek, which was cold. There was dried blood on his left temple. He smelled of stale drink.

"Telephone the doctor," Elinor told the maid. "And keep the children upstairs."

Kneeling by her husband, she grasped his hand and stroked it. She remembered his face as she had first seen it. How she had loved that smiling young man she had met so long ago. But where had he gone?

Softly she began to cry, her body racked with pain for Billy, for herself, for what might have been.

BOOK TWO

CHAPTER 6

Sunday, 17 July 1949

"*WHO DO THEM* scissors belong to?" Buzz asked, producing them from her pocket at the breakfast table. "Come on! Own up!"

Annabel and Miranda looked at each other and kept silent.

Ten-year-old Clare, spooning yogurt, casually said, "They're from the nursery sewing box."

"Colonel Bromley found them scissors in his greenhouse," Buzz said tartly. "He said someone—someone not very tall—had stolen his grapes."

"*Sneak!*" Annabel spat at Clare.

"Shut *up*, Annabel," hissed Miranda, too late.

Buzz knew that further questioning was pointless because freckle-faced Miranda would never sneak on her sister, the two were inseparable, but although Miranda was the younger, it was always she who thought up the devilry and led the way, while Annabel trotted after her. Buzz said firmly, "You two young'uns go round and apologize to Colonel Bromley, and ask if you can do any odd jobs in his garden this morning."

"Sneak," Annabel hissed again at Clare.

Buzz looked crossly at Clare. "You should have stopped them."

Clare ran a hand through her short, dark hair. "But I didn't know . . ." As the eldest, Clare was often unfairly blamed for their naughtiness.

"That's what you always say," Buzz scolded. "If you didn't, you should'a done, so you must share their punishment."

"It's not fair!" howled Clare. "They're *always* getting me into trouble! And Annabel *always* gets off lightest!"

Buzz knew that this was true and she knew why. Buzz, an inconspicuous and plain child, had seen early in life that pretty, self-confident little girls like Annabel, with charming, flirty ways, could wriggle their way out of trouble.

"Life is unfair, Clare," Buzz said, "and the sooner you find out, the better."

Clare scowled. Buzz had lived with them long enough for Clare to know that she never changed her mind or relented, as Gran did.

After Billy's death two years earlier, Buzz had immediately gone down to Starlings, intending to stay with Elinor for a week. She never returned to her hated stenographic job in the City of London. Buzz now handled Elinor's secretarial work, ran the household, and organized the details of Elinor's life for a considerably larger salary than she had been paid by the grocery-chain head office. Furthermore, she was no longer lonely, no longer hungry for affection.

Buzz was meticulously efficient and irritatingly critical, and a constant but amicable battle was waged between Elinor and Buzz, the only person who dared criticize Elinor, and who wasn't particularly tactful about doing so. To each of the women, these minor arguments were proof of affection. Their friendship could withstand the squalls.

Buzz protected Elinor from outsiders with common sense and bulldog ferocity. Immediately after Billy's death, such protection had been necessary to deal with the bureaucratic requirements; the extravagantly vulpine suggestions of the undertaker, who naturally wanted as expensive a funeral as possible; and the crowd of reporters that had appeared.

In due course, the coroner concluded that, while intoxicated, Mr. William O'Dare had fractured his neck in a fall from a staircase, vomited while unconscious, and been asphyxiated by his vomit. The verdict was death by misadventure.

Elinor had appeared to be dazed after Billy's death. In public, she did not shed one tear: she stared into space and asked to be left alone. Buzz knew why; she had seen mortally wounded men, fresh from the battlefield, who could not feel pain because they had been anesthetized by shock. The young local doctor had confirmed Buzz's diagnosis to her as she showed him to the front door.

"It's often the case with widows," he said. "They literally *cannot* feel anything until they can accept the death, which may be long after the loss of the husband."

"I'd have called it good riddance," Buzz muttered.

The doctor decided to ignore this. "You can expect Mrs. O'Dare to be totally unlike her normal self: she may be bewildered, disoriented, and frightened by her own feelings. If she had recently quarreled with her husband, she might even feel guilty, because now they can never kiss and make up."

Looking at Buzz's face and remembering stories he had heard about Billy, the doctor added, "Especially if she . . . er . . . felt resentment toward Mr. O'Dare or had . . . hmm . . . sometimes wished him dead. . . . I hear he was a difficult man." He paused. "On the other hand, don't be surprised if Mrs. O'Dare's mind now blanks out all bad memories of her husband, exaggerates the good ones, and starts to view him as a wonderful person, in which case it is kindest not to contradict her."

"She's been doing *that* for years," Buzz said sourly.

In the days that followed the funeral, Elinor felt numb and cold, permanently weary: her movements slowed down, as if she were sleepwalking, and any movement seemed to take a lot of effort. She felt wizened, as if the juice had been squeezed from her body. For the first time in her life, she felt old.

After a few such days, Buzz shooed Elinor to her desk. Thanks to this, and to her own imagination, Elinor was able to escape from her misery: it was difficult to think about anything else when writing the first draft of a novel.

Elinor's romances were never out-and-out bodice rippers: each sexual chase was described in detail, but once the heroine was in the hero's arms, only a row of dots followed. Although breasts heaved frequently and there was a great deal of panting, the heroine always—even if only by a hairbreadth—went a virgin to the marriage bed (never described) that she was about to share with the dark, winged-eyebrowed, aristocratic gentleman on the book jacket, who was called Peregrine or Torquil and lived on some vast country estate: Elinor's heroines never married mechanics.

Now Elinor chose Paris as the glamorous setting for her next novel—Paris in the year 1870, when the city was besieged by the German army. Happily she turned to planning the romantic situation, the problems that would confront the lovers, and the solutions. Always, in Elinor's novels, it appeared that the heroine would be forced to choose between two ghastly alternatives; always the plot twisted ingeniously at this point, to provide the heroine with a third alternative and eventual, eternal happiness. In Paris with her heroine, Elinor would once again forget the misery of reality.

Immediately after their grandfather's death, the three small sisters howled for days. Clare wept from guilt as much as sorrow, blaming herself for her grandfather's death. It must have been that last spell—the mixture of primrose, violet roots, and sheep droppings. She must have wished too hard.

Miranda bellowed in sympathy, and then asked for the recipe.

Long after her sisters had dried their tears, Annabel continued to sob; she was afraid to go to bed in the dark and woke screaming every night.

"She's the softy of those three," Nanny explained to Buzz.

Buzz knew that Annabel wasn't the only inhabitant of Starlings who had a soft heart. The former ambulance driver did not find it difficult to be firm: she dealt briskly with truculent plumbers, lazy domestic staff, and insolent girls behind shop counters—who never ignored her. Buzz dealt with life's small exasperations as she dealt with buzzing gnats: she swatted at them, then dismissed them.

But after Billy died, like a punch-drunk boxer, Elinor found it difficult to stand up for herself. Her timid and unaggressive behavior and her obvious wish to avoid an argument (let alone a row) left her vulnerable.

"Nell, you shouldn't let people walk all over you," Buzz scolded one morning as they stood in the hall. "You're a ruddy sight too generous and helpful." She gazed through the window at a purple figure disappearing down the drive. "You've just given your new coat to Doreen, haven't you?"

"I know she stole the spoons, but she said she was sorry," Elinor said defensively. "And it's such a cold morning for July. She was wearing only a flimsy cardigan."

"She's ruddy lucky not to be in prison. And she could have worn the green coat you gave her last year. You're a mug, Nell."

Elinor scowled; she preferred to see herself as warmhearted.

"And while we're on the subject, why the hell did you bail out Stinker Baldwin?" Buzz asked, referring to the village drunk.

"His wife came to see me, with three of the children. She said it was his birthday next week."

Buzz threw her a look of scorn. "A ruddy good reason for getting drunk and beating her up again. Stinker should *always* be in prison on his birthday. Did you give her money?"

Elinor hesitated. "Just a little."

"There you go again! And I'll bet you thought of some *good* reason to do such a daft thing."

"Is it so wrong to give the poor woman a little money?"

"Yes. Because she'll drink it—just like Stinker! You'd have done better to give her food in a basket."

"It would have humiliated her," Elinor said, rationalizing her impulsive action.

"Rubbish! She'll soon be back for more cash!" Buzz knew how easily Elinor was able to identify with the wretched, and how quickly the wretched realized it.

"Well, I can afford to give it," Elinor said.

"Not at the rate you're going, my girl! I've just balanced your checkbook! We send a check off to every blinking begging letter that drops on the mat! You haven't enough money—or time—to solve all the problems of the world—and it ain't your job."

"I only try to help people."

"Charity begins at home, Lady Bountiful. You're a soft touch, Nell. The girls can twist you round their little finger. I punish 'em for stealing grapes, so they run off to you and you dry their tears, cancel the punishment, and give 'em chocolates. You're far too lenient with 'em, Nell—they're getting spoilt rotten."

"You see, I can't help remembering . . . that the poor little things have no parents."

"Poor they ain't!" Buzz scoffed. "You should put a stop to their weaknesses, not encourage 'em."

The following morning, Buzz came into the breakfast room, shuffling envelopes. "Only one for you today, Nell. And I've had a long letter from Bertha Higby." Buzz still corresponded with the mother of her dead fiancé, Ginger Higby; in 1922, the family had emigrated to Cleveland, Ohio, where eventually Mr. Higby opened a hardware store.

Reading excerpts from Bertha Higby's letter, Buzz did not notice Elinor's face until the door burst open and the three girls bounced into the breakfast room.

"Look what we've got for you!" Miranda thrust a wilting bunch of wildflowers into her grandmother's hands.

"What's wrong?" Clare asked, looking at her grandmother's face, at her untouched breakfast, and at the crumpled handkerchief in her hand.

"It's nothing . . ."

"Yes it is—we can see you've been crying," Annabel said.

"Well, that was silly of me. I thought I might win a prize—the International Romance Writers Award, but they gave it to Daphne Du Maurier."

"Well, *they're* silly!" Miranda shouted. The three girls flung themselves upon their grandmother and hugged her.

"We think *you're* the best at *everything*," Annabel said loyally.

"We'll make you your favorite chocolate cake," Miranda promised, "and we'll write 'Number One Gran Award' on top."

Smiling at this display of loyalty, Buzz knew that Elinor would forget her disappointment by teatime. Elinor had long ago acquired the knack of instantly dismissing or forgetting anything that made her unhappy. Buzz supposed that this was how she had managed to survive life with Billy. For a moment, Buzz remembered Billy's drunken, angry, bloodshot, half-closed eyes, yet she knew Nell remembered only the clear, sea-blue flashes that had originally entranced her. Over and over Nell astounded her as she told some journalist that the reason she had not remarried was that she knew she'd *never* find anyone to replace her darling husband.

Whether or not Nell had brainwashed herself into believing that, Buzz knew the truth of the matter. Elinor, now freed to fly high in the sky, was afraid of finding herself chained to another bully.

Saturday, 24 March 1951

"What's that noise?" Twelve-year-old Clare, in a ginger tweed coat and black gum boots, ran to the bottom of the orchard, followed by her sisters. Beyond the boundary hedge was a rough meadow above which rooks swirled in a light blue sky. Elinor's overgrown woods lay to the left. From the hill on the right came the faint sound of horses' hooves.

Again the melancholy sound of a horn hung mournfully in the air.

"It's the hunt!" Clare climbed the five-barred wooden gate and sat upon it. Her sisters joined her, and they watched a wisp of russet streak down the hill to their right.

Hard-hatted black heads appeared above the hill, followed by shoulders of scarlet or black; then the heads of horses, followed by their graceful bodies and long, delicate legs: the hunt looked an unstoppable mass as it rushed toward the hedgerow at the base of the hill, and even from a distance, the girls could sense the exuberance of the Warmingford Hunt in full cry on a fresh, damp day.

The hounds were gaining on the exhausted fox: streaks of black and tan, they bayed with the excitement of the chase.

Some four hundred yards behind the hounds, a bunch of about thirty horses and ponies now thundered down the hill. Straggling behind were a group of children from the Pony Club mounted on shaggy, dark ponies; their hooves threw up clods of earth as they leapt the hedge in pursuit of the fox.

The desperate vixen was clever: several times she had thrown the hunt off the scent by running through streams, past manure heaps, and once through a flock of sheep. But after being hunted for four hours, she was bedraggled and exhausted.

"It's the vixen who lives in our woods!" Annabel exclaimed. Only the previous week, the vixen had broken into the O'Dares' chicken house again, gnawing through the planking to steal a couple of birds. "Can't we hide her? She's *our* fox; she lives in *our* woods." Annabel jumped down on the far side of the gate and started running toward the frightened animal.

"Come back! The hounds'll knock you down!" Clare shouted after her sister, jumping down to run after her, followed closely by Miranda.

The fox was a pathetic sight; her eyes were glazed, her tongue hung out of her mouth as she panted, and her breath came in heavy gasps. She slowed her pace, then staggered and swayed, unable to go farther.

When Annabel was about ten yards away, the hounds caught up with the vixen, who had no chance. Weakly she turned her head and bared her teeth at her tormentors; then the leading hounds flung themselves at the fox's body, each seizing whatever part of her flesh it could reach. The rest of the pack piled on top of the exhausted animal, like a rugger scrum upon the ball.

As the hunt cantered down the hill toward the kill, Clare recognized a couple of local farmers, the vet, and Colonel Bromley on a well-groomed bay.

"You girls! Keep out of the way!" shouted the Master of the Hunt. Mounted on a gray, he was a splendid sight in scarlet coat, white breeches, and black boots with tanned tops.

"You damn, damn, damn bastards!" screamed Miranda, using forbidden swear words.

"You damn, damn murderers!" yelled Annabel.

Colonel Bromley, in black bowler and beige raincoat, moved toward the girls. "Don't be sentimental," he said. "Foxes kill my lambs, my pheasants, and your chickens. You mustn't cry over a fox. Hunting keeps the foxes down, and it isn't as cruel as other killing methods."

Clare sobbed, "Why can't you kill the foxes some other way? With traps or with poison?"

"Farmers can't put down poison, in case their working dogs eat it. And if an animal is trapped, it might be held in fearful pain for days."

"Well, shoot them! That's fast and not so cruel," Annabel shouted.

"Farmers can't sit up all night waiting to shoot foxes."

"I'm glad I'm not the sort of person who hounds an animal to death for fun," Annabel shrieked, "and then watches while other animals tear it to pieces!"

"Keep your voice down," Colonel Bromley said. "Your grandmother will not be pleased if you upset the Master."

"We don't *care*, you bloodthirsty old pig!" Annabel shouted.

Colonel Bromley looked at them in silence, and kept his horse between the girls and the rest of the hunt until it had moved off.

Two hours later, when Elinor and Buzz returned from a shopping trip, the sisters were in the orchard burying what was left of the fox.

Having heard the car come up the drive, the girls hurled themselves at the returning travelers before they had time to unbutton their coats.

When Elinor disentangled their story, she said indignantly, "I'd like to see the Master after *he'd* been hunted for four hours by huge bloodthirsty, baying creatures—I bet that'd change his point of view! Expensive dressing up can't disguise barbarity."

Later, Elinor skimmed the hand-delivered letter from Colonel Bromley: " . . . undisciplined . . . worse than hooligans . . . no more disturbance . . . police . . . their headmistress . . . "

"Around here you can't upset the hunt without running into trouble," Buzz said. "And the Master of the Hunt has complained to the police. You'd better lay on the charm, old girl."

Elinor looked worried. She had now been accepted by local society, but she knew that, should she argue against the hunt, she would be . . . well, not exactly ostracized but . . .

"The girls were absolutely right to behave as they did," Elinor said firmly.

Nevertheless, hoping to circumvent any further complaint from the Master of the Hunt, Elinor saw Sergeant Brown, who was well aware of her generous annual check for the police widows and orphans fund. Elinor also visited the headmistress of the local school.

"Frankly, I'm not surprised to hear of this behavior from Annabel," said Miss Pryor. "She behaves as if she were an only child." Spoiled, selfish, imperious, was what she didn't say.

"Annabel is overshadowed by her sisters," Elinor rationalized, "because Clare is clever and Miranda has a very strong character."

"Annabel is certainly *jealous* of her sisters," Miss Pryor said firmly.

Overprivileged little tyrant, she thought. "Had you considered sending them to boarding school? Not Benenden or Heathfield—somewhere where they'd learn to fend for themselves."

After a long pause, Elinor said, "I'll think about it."

She went home and telephoned Joe Grant.

Tuesday, 27 March 1951

On the back lawn, swaying golden stretches of daffodils bent before a wind that swept scudding clouds from the sky; they looked like fat cupids being shooed off to bed by Nanny, Elinor thought. She pulled her coat collar up and turned to Joe. After a delicious meal of grouse and an excellent claret, he was dutifully admiring the daffodils: they ran down to a stream that wandered along the back of the garden, under pale green fronds of weeping willows.

Elinor laughed with excitement as the trees rustled before the frisky March wind. Her blond hair whipped around her cheeks. "I feel as if my face has been dipped in a snowdrift, Joe. Isn't it *exhilarating?*"

"It's damned cold." Joe left *his* garden to the gardener and only enjoyed looking at it from behind snugly closed, draft-proofed windows. "I don't know why you want my advice," he added. "You're perfectly capable of making up your own mind."

"A woman needs a man to guide her." Elinor smiled at him. "I know how lucky I am to be guided by you. Thank you for that income forecast, by the way."

"You could do that sort of forecast much more cheaply from *here* if you had a bookkeeper in once a month."

Elinor looked up at Joe with gratitude. "You see? Bookkeeping is the sort of thing that I simply don't know about—so it would never have occurred to me to do that forecast. Remember that the girls of my generation had *no* business training."

"Business training is useful but not all-important," Joe said. "Common sense and hard work are just as important. What a business boils down to is having a product, or a service, and selling it, and that applies whether your product is a book or a bulldozer. You increase your income in two ways: by decreasing costs and by increasing prices, or production."

"But that doesn't apply to an author."

"Oh yes it does. I think you should try to dictate your books. You'd double your output. Incidentally, I've arranged for that history professor to correct your manuscript; he'll pass it on to an English professor, to check the grammar and spelling."

"Of course I learned Yankee spelling," Elinor said, "but then I ended up over here, and now I can't spell in either language. But I didn't ask you here today to talk business."

In answer to Joe's raised eyebrows, she added, "I want you to advise me about the girls."

Joe laughed. "You've always said that Ethel and I are too harsh with our boys. But boys need discipline—and so do girls. I've always told you that you should send those girls to boarding school when they're old enough. It's not fair to keep them at the village school so you can have them at home with you. They'll suffer for it later. Quite frankly, it's your duty to send them somewhere where they'll get an excellent education and be among the sort of girls that they'll mix with socially when they grow up."

"I want . . ." Elinor paused. "I never want them to feel the sort of amused and supercilious contempt that I ran up against when I met Billy's family. I don't want them ever to know that sort of anxiety and humiliation. I want those girls to be the social equal of *anybody*."

"You are the equal of anyone," Joe said angrily, "and you always were! Billy was lucky to have you." He remembered Elinor's vitality, her cheerfulness and popularity in that Frenchie hospital where he had visited Billy so long ago. He remembered her wedding day, when Elinor carried a bouquet of white chrysanthemums, which Joe personally had liberated from what was left of somebody's garden.

"We were all a bit in love with you, Elinor—with your vitality and warmth—but Billy made sure that nobody else got a chance to get near you." Fiercely Joe added, "Billy married you because you were the prettiest girl he'd ever seen, and he wasn't the only one who thought *that!*" He smiled at her. "And now you're a beautiful woman. But I don't suppose I'm the only man to tell you so."

Elinor looked delighted. "Nobody's told me for a long time, Joe."

Joe glanced lovingly at her. "The only possible reason is that you don't allow a man to get close enough to say so. But you need a man in your life, Elinor. You're still young enough to enjoy . . . male companionship."

"Men want more than companionship. I don't want to lead a man on and then refuse him," Elinor said. "Because I shall never remarry. Nobody could ever replace Billy in . . . in certain ways." She looked Joe straight in the eye and softly added, "And as I'm sure you realize, I would never have an affair, Joe."

Well, Joe thought, he'd hinted and she'd given him her reply. He smiled again and put his arm affectionately around Elinor's shoulder.

"About the girls," she said. "As you know, I want them to have the best I can give them, Joe. A proper society debut. And I want you to tell me how to arrange it."

Joe understood at once what she meant. He had come a long way himself and knew that Elinor wanted her family to go a lot farther. He looked at the little girls playing on the front lawn. "If that's what you want, I can certainly help you," he said. "But remember that too much privilege can be a disaster." Briefly he thought of one or two of Adam's arrogant friends at Eton.

Elinor nodded. "That's what I want."

Joe said, "You start by getting a better car."

"But it's almost impossible to get *any* car! The dealers' waiting lists are *years* long!"

"I think I could get you a prewar white Rolls. Chap I know wants to get rid of his."

"But *I* can't drive a Rolls-Royce! It's far too heavy."

"No," Joe agreed, "you'll need a chauffeur. And the first place he should drive you to is Norman Hartnell."

"*I* can't afford the Queen's dressmaker!"

"Hartnell is the best designer of appearance clothes, and that's why the Queen goes to him. And you *can* afford it if you produce more books. You must dress the part before you play the part." He added, "As you no doubt know, you can only be presented at Court by a lady who has herself been presented. I'll arrange for someone to present you next year and give you a season in London. I happen to know that Sonia Rushleigh came out of her divorce badly, and she needs money."

"But how can I spare the time for a London season, Joe, if I'm writing books to pay for it?"

"Get up earlier."

"That's what Billy always told me."

Hastily Joe said, "About the girls. Finishing school in Switzerland or Paris, where they'll acquire all the social graces. They must all be able to—"

"Sparkle?" Elinor suggested, tongue in cheek. When Joe nodded, she said, "They *already* sparkle. What else do they need to know?"

"Only seven things." Joe ticked them off on brown-leather-gloved fingers. "*One*, never criticize the royal family, blood sports, or newspaper owners, because they gang up to protect each other. *Two*, don't get any publicity in the cheaper papers during the Season. *Three*, pick a newsworthy charity to support, preferably connected with dogs or children. *Four*, support your local community and make sure you're seen doing it. Open the vicarage fete, and when you do it, publicly present a check for the church roof—that sort of thing." As they drew near the front door, he shivered. "Dear Elinor, I think I've had enough nature for one day. Can we please, please get back to that log fire in your study?"

Elinor laughed. "Not 'til you've finished."

Joe wrapped his arms across his chest to keep warm. "*Five*, show an interest in one of the arts, but nothing too avant-garde—ballet or the opera is fine." He quickened his step as they arrived at the front door. "*Six*, buy some place that people long to be invited to—somewhere like Somerset Maugham's villa on Cap Ferrat. There's a place called St.-Tropez that's getting popular."

"And the seventh commandment?" Elinor asked.

"Always write thank-you letters immediately and post them within three days." Joe grinned.

Elinor looked guilty. She hated writing letters, especially letters of thanks; instead of dashing them off while she still felt grateful, she delayed until the last minute before she risked offending people. At that point, she would contritely write several pages, invent some reason to explain why she hadn't written before, feel guilty about her lie, and send flowers.

Elinor pushed open the ancient oak front door. "But all that you've just suggested will cost a fortune!"

"Then make one, Elinor."

Buzz looked dubious when she heard about Elinor's plans for the girls' future, starting with boarding school. "Don't you think you're being a bit old-fashioned, Nell?" she said. "I know you want them girls to have what you didn't, but you ain't realized that by protecting a woman, you leave her unprotected if she's ever left on her own."

Fleetingly Buzz remembered what it had felt like, after her home had been bombed in the Second World War, suddenly to be without a family, without anyone.

When Miranda heard that her two sisters were going to be sent away to school in the autumn but that she wasn't old enough, she raged, proclaiming she was *sick* of being the littlest, because she was always left out. Eventually Elinor yielded; Miranda could accompany her sisters.

Saturday, 29 September 1951

Hazlehurst Park Manor School was only thirty miles away from Warminster—a minor reason for Elinor's choice. It was a nineteenth-century reconstruction of an eighteenth-century reconstruction of a Gothic priory. All the teachers were clearly ladies who had known better times in better years; they seemed amiable and well-meaning, but were by no means intellectuals.

On their first Saturday afternoon away from home, the three sisters—who were not allowed in each other's dormitories—felt lonely and homesick. Together, they walked down the school's drive, heading for the nearest sweet shop.

"I can't think why Gran sent us to this *prison!*" Annabel grumbled.

"Because she wants us to be ladies," Clare said gloomily.

Miranda added, "Because she was put through hell by all the ladies when she was a young bride."

"They don't like us here," Annabel kicked at the bracken by the side of the road.

"They don't know us yet," Clare pointed out.

"How will we know when they like us?" Miranda asked, darting forward to pick up a spiked greenish ball that enclosed a shining conker.

"When they share their secrets with us," Clare said.

Soon, of course, secrets were exchanged. All three girls quickly learned that the period after lights-out was a time when the girls of Hazlehurst Park, amid steady giggles, shared their common fascination with boys and sex.

These inaccurate accounts of the strange things that adults did to each other in bed in order to achieve ecstasy, combined with the behavior of the demurely romantic but firmly virginal heroines of Elinor's novels, gave the sisters an odd picture of adult coupling: This involved a wildly romantic waltz into the future, wearing a low-necked dress as if you didn't realize that your top was showing. After your wedding, you had to allow your husband to see you naked without being embarrassed, and let him kiss you hard, an action which fused true twin souls together, to think as one, after which no verbal communication was needed. Your true love, now your husband, would read your thoughts, enjoy everything you liked to do, and give you everything you wanted, including spotless babies; that was his function in life.

A few months into the girls' first term, in February—Joe said it was the best time to buy and the worst time to sell property in Europe—Elinor and Buzz flew to France for a week, during which Elinor purchased a small but pretty villa on the outskirts of St.-Tropez; the sea could be seen beyond the pink oleander bushes at the end of the small garden. Sufficient funds for the purchase were obtained by Joe Grant, who had Elinor's French publisher make the financial arrangements.

Monday, 6 July 1953

By early July of the following year, Elinor's villa had been redecorated, furnished with simple Provençal furniture, and curtained with intricately patterned, bright traditional country fabrics. She invited Joe Grant and his family to be her first guests. It was arranged that his son Adam should fly to Nice in advance of the rest of the family, who were to drive through France.

Before the visit, the two Grant sons were much discussed by the O'Dare sisters, who had not seen the boys for several years. On the day of Adam's arrival, the girls took three hours to dress in cinch-waisted, flowery dresses that were both too tight for the temperature and too elaborate for the occasion; they then sat on the patio for nearly two hours, none admitting that she was waiting for Adam.

At last, as late-afternoon shadows crept across the patio, Adam, in naval blazer and open-necked white shirt, sauntered through the living room. As he did so, he again wondered whether his father was having—or had ever had—an affair with Elinor O'Dare. They seemed unusually close for friends of the opposite sex, and Adam had noticed his mother's almost imperceptible withdrawal when in the same room as Elinor: it was something that Adam had noticed in rival cats.

Adam, now twenty-three years old, had spent his two years of national service in the navy, where he obtained a commission; he had decided to be a lawyer, and in due course became articled to the family firm of Swithin, Timmins and Grant, this being the simplest way to obtain his legal qualifications.

When he wasn't studying, Adam acted as his father's assistant and was also loaned to any of the firm's other lawyers who needed a spare pair of hands to prepare a case: while the senior lawyer conducted the main interviews, Adam ran around, acquiring the evidence and bringing it into the office, where he checked it and then sorted it into appropriate files. He now looked forward to a luxurious holiday in the sun, during which he would not be treated like the messenger boy.

On the wide steps that led from Elinor's living room down to the patio, Adam paused, grinned, and said, "Why, it's the three Graces!"

This was the first time that the sisters heard the tag line destined to be pinned on them; they were flattered and dazzled by a compliment from this tall, tanned young man with dark hair and big brown eyes. All three immediately fell in love with him.

That evening, before going down to dinner, fourteen-year-old Clare stuffed socks in the sides of her bra, which pushed her small breasts together. She had heard about this trick at Hazlehurst, though it didn't quite accomplish the look she was striving for.

Annabel sneaked Gran's new camera and flash so that she could take photographs of everyone, and made sure that she took more of Adam than anyone else.

That night, Miranda hugged her pillow and daydreamed about being with Adam in his private plane: "Oh my God, Miranda, I feel a touch of my old malaria coming on . . . Do you think you can manage to land her?" Wearing a glamorous white flying suit and leather helmet, Miranda said, "Of course, Adam, simply tell me what to do." Adam gasped out the instructions before losing consciousness. . . .

When the girls came down for breakfast the following morning, they found that Adam had already left to charter a speedboat. He did not return for lunch.

That afternoon, Clare was lying on the beach, sleepy as a cat in the sun, when she felt a shadow fall across her face. She opened her eyes and knew instantly that the young man standing before her in scarlet swim trunks was Adam's brother; they had the same flyaway dark eyebrows that almost met in the middle. But Adam's face was leaner, his mouth tauter, his eyebrows drawn closer to each other. Adam's finely cut features looked—Clare now had to admit—just a little bit twitchy, like Gregory Peck when worried about what the villain was going to do next.

The young man stared at her navy-blue school swimsuit. "Are you Clare? I'm Mike." Mike's clear gray eyes, set wide apart, gave him an air of transparent honesty that he found very useful in getting out of trouble at school. He added, "I've been sent to find you. Adam hired a motorboat and we're taking it to the islands. Like to come along?"

Mike looked less cynically amused and more approachable than Adam, although there was something violent about his stillness, as if his body wanted to leap forward. Mike had even longer legs and wider shoulders than Adam; dark hair curled crisply on his chest and descended in a faint line to below his navel.

Clare almost fell out of love with Adam.

Later, as the motorboat cleaved the water, trailing churning foam in its wake, each sister felt similar turmoil beneath her breastbone. they all returned to the villa dazed by a love far more exhausting than that which Clare had felt for the tow-haired games mistress, Annabel for Robin, her pony, and Miranda for the milkman.

The next day, the five of them drove to the long sandy crescent of Tahiti Beach; here each sister, for the first time, felt the painful and humiliating sorrow of rejection.

Adam and Michael took one look at the lithe, suntanned young Frenchmen flirting with feline French girls in sexy bikinis and made no attempt to hide the fact that this was their idea of paradise. The two Englishmen immediately lost interest in the three young sisters.

That evening, none of the sisters came down to supper. Buzz found them, still wearing swimsuits, in Clare's bedroom. Clare was crying, facedown on the bed. Also sobbing, Annabel was spread-eagled, facedown, on the floor. A scowling Miranda leaned against the wall with legs crossed and arms folded.

"What are you all moaning about?"

"Go away, Buzz—it's none of your business," Clare hiccuped.

"I'll never, never love anyone again," Annabel sobbed.

"They're both *beasts*," growled Miranda. "And we must all buy bikinis as fast as possible."

"Don't be silly little geese," Buzz chided. "Adam's twenty-three years old and Mike's twenty-one! Of *course* they like the look of them curvy, pretty French ladies!"

"But Mike was *charming* to Clare before he saw those girls on the beach," Annabel gulped.

"Adam showed Miranda how to water-ski before he saw those old bags, but after that, he *ignored* her!" cried Clare.

"Frog is just as pretty as those beastly tarts on the sand," Miranda said, scowling again.

"Don't use that nasty word, or I'll give you what for," Buzz corrected automatically. "Of course the lads were polite to you—because they're nice lads." She hesitated and then said firmly. "To them lads, you're still only kiddies. Now have a wash and come downstairs—there's chocolate meringues for supper. And no more of this nonsense about bikinis. What would Annabel and Miranda put in the top bit—tennis balls?"

CHAPTER 7

Tuesday, 21 July 1953

AT THE CROSSROADS, Adam pulled the wheel of the family Humber to the left: in the moonlight, the silver road ahead disappeared between dark conifers.

"Hey, Adam, you've gone the wrong way," Michael said, waking from his reverie. "You've taken the road to Nice."

Adam turned left again onto the coast road; below them lay the dark glitter of the sea. "We're not going to Nice, we're going to Cannes—to the casino."

Mike laughed. "I suppose that's why you offered to drive old Maclean back to his villa." Mike knew that his brother was an opportunist.

"*And* why I asked you to come along. It was pretty early for old Maclean to leave Elinor's dinner party, pleading a headache. I reckon he's jumping into bed with something juicy at this very moment."

"Dad'll kill us if he finds out we've been gambling," Mike said.

Adam laughed and pressed the accelerator. "Dad's determined that we're not going to take after *his* dad." Joe Grant's father had been a racecourse bookie, a fact that his wife tried to hide.

"Granddad Grant *never* gambled—he took the money *from* gamblers. He always said that gambling was a mug's game."

"Look, Mike, do you want a night out or not? If so, stop being so bloody pious." Adam's persuasive nature and elder brother's self-assurance overshadowed his brother, who quickly gave up arguing.

"Sorry. It's a great idea," Mike said hastily. "After all, we can't gamble at home." Gambling was illegal in Britain, supposedly because of its bad effect on public morality. "But what'll we do for money?"

"I've got four weeks' wages," Adam said. Through the open car windows, he could now feel salt air on his face and smell the beguiling aroma of pine.

"Surely forty quid won't get us far in the Cannes casino?"

"It'll get us *in*. We have a drink at the bar, we look at the glitterati, we have a mild flutter. That's all. Easy."

But Mike knew that behind Adam's supercilious sophistication and condescending facade, his brother was unsure of himself. Talking down to Mike always subdued Adam's own anxiety. Mike made Adam feel equal to anything or anyone, because Mike always assumed that his elder brother would be successful in everything he did, and Adam assumed that Mike would always fetch and carry, jump to obey him, and protect his secrets.

Adam could confide anything to Mike and Mike wouldn't raise an eyebrow—

or tell anyone: Mike had worshiped Adam through their lonely childhood, in which neither brother had ever felt close to their rather cold parents who seemed to love neither their children or each other. The boys had spent their early years with a rota of swiftly changing nannies, who never seemed able to reach Mrs. Grant's imperiously high standards. Adam and Mike had shared an expensively efficient, forlorn, and loveless life in the nursery, devoid of any tenderness except that which they had shown to each other. Now each knew that he could depend on the other, and neither really trusted anyone else.

As Adam drove the Humber a little too fast toward the casino, Mike sighed. It was such a beautiful night. Perfect for a bike ride. Wistfully he remembered his first night rides on the Norton Dominator with the feather-bed frame—his first brand-new bike. Motorbikes were Mike's passion. When he was fourteen, he had acquired his first bike, a secondhand army surplus BSA M20; it was a messenger bike with a bouncy saddle and no suspension. Mike had concealed the bike in an unused potting shed, where it was later joined by an equally ancient Triumph Speed Twin 500, which had a lot of poke for its size. None of his subsequent smarter bikes had given him as much pleasure as those two.

At the Palm Beach Casino—considered more chic than the Casino Municipal—the brothers produced their passports and purchased chips with which to gamble: to avoid theft, cash bets weren't allowed at the table.

Waiters glided around the gaming room; cigarette girls proffered their tray. A couple of security men in dark uniforms stood, immobile, although their eyes never stopped moving.

"They're shills," Adam murmured as he stared at the glamorously dressed women who sat on revolving stools before the long bar, their sophisticated faces reflected in the mirrored rear wall. "Their job is to get the punters to play the tables."

At the bar, Adam and Mike ordered whiskey sodas, sniffing the agreeable odor of good food and expensive perfume; they swiveled their stools around to watch the gambling.

An effervescent excitement hovered above the sixteen tables. People stood around them, the men in dinner jackets and the women wearing long strapless dresses cut to display décolletage. A few elderly ladies sat, firmly clutching their purses, their wrinkled bosoms bulging over strapless net bodices. The gamblers seemed to be mostly French, German, or Greek, although Mike heard a couple of Englishmen playing at a nearby table while their noisily disapproving wives worried about British currency restrictions.

"Well, how do we start?" Michael asked. "You'd better tell me what the form is. I was never asked to any of the smart games at Eton." The Grant brothers were not nearly so rich or aristocratic as most of their schoolfellows.

"I haven't the slightest idea," Adam was obliged to admit.

"I'll show you if you like," offered a pale, angular Englishman who sat next to Adam. "The name's Giles Milroy-Browne. You should start on roulette—most beginners do, because you need no knowledge to start playing."

The three men drifted to the nearest roulette table and stood behind the players. Here the atmosphere was tense, the anxiety level high, and the action very fast. The three croupiers—handsome, clean-cut young men in immaculate dinner jackets—moved with great speed as they called out the winning numbers or paid winnings.

"The easiest way to bet is simply to gamble that the ball will fall in a red or a black slot," Mr. Milroy-Browne explained to Adam. "There are thirty-six slots and the odds are even, which means that if you put two thousand francs on, you win two thousand. If you 'play the dozens,' you gamble on which of three sequences of twelve numbers the ball will fall in—and that pays two to one. But the most exciting and dangerous way to play is to bet the numbers. Actually pick one number because the casino pays out thirty-five to one. So, if you put a thousand francs down, you get thirty-five thousand back."

Carefully Adam bet, on red, a chip that cost the equivalent of one pound. He felt a rush of anxiety as the ball clattered around the wheel, slower . . . and slower . . . It settled in a red slot, number 3. Adam had won!

He lost his winnings on the next throw, but told himself that it didn't matter because, overall, he'd lost nothing. Still, he trembled as he laid the equivalent of ten pounds—a week's pay—on red. but suddenly Adam no longer felt self-conscious and anxious; he felt sophisticated and excited. And although determined to play modestly with small stakes, he nevertheless felt a weird new impulse: a need to challenge fate.

Again red won! Adam felt his fingers and toes tingle. Then, as if it didn't belong to him, he watched his right hand carefully place twenty pounds on red. It would hurt if he lost, but the pain would feel exquisite. . . . Again the ball fell into a red slot! Clearly, he had been right to bet on red. It was as though he were guided in his choice by some invisible, benevolent force. He felt as if he were breathing rare air, and a tremendous sense of well-being flooded his body.

Adam did not always win, but he lost very little.

Playing roulette seemed a beguilingly easy way of getting rich in a couple of hours, without doing any work. It was as if money grew on trees and Adam merely had to stretch out his hand to pluck bank notes. Each time he won, he felt release, and relief, as with a sexual encounter. Winning made him feel more manly, more virile. It also made him feel different from the other people gathered around the table: Adam had the golden touch; he was favored by the gods.

Two hours later, when Adam had won a total of one hundred pounds—the equivalent of ten weeks' salary—Michael whispered in his ear, "Stop now, Adam, while you're ahead, you silly ass. You *know* it's a mug's game. You *know* that the only people who win are the organizers, the casinos, the bookies."

"Shut up and let me concentrate." Adam shook off the restraining arm, but he knew that Michael was right. Adam looked at his pile of winnings; he should take them *now* and leave. Leave! *Leave!*

But he couldn't.

Just one more bet—then he would go.

But Adam could no more stop himself than an alcoholic could stop himself from picking up an open bottle of whiskey.

His earlier tentativeness had vanished and he now looked around the table with increasing confidence; no longer was he merely a junior articled clerk. As he had always subconsciously suspected, Adam was one of God's chosen. He began to experience a feeling of power: if he concentrated, then that little white ball would obediently fall where he wished it to.

The exhilaration of winning made Adam feel a little high and a lot larger than life. His heart pounded, adrenaline coursing through his blood. He was almost ill with excitement, this dark joy that spread throughout his body, making him feel aglow, as if his veins were red neon tubes.

Michael, who had not bet at all, returned to Adam's side at two o'clock in the morning and suggested once again that they leave.

"No, not yet." Adam looked at his pile of winnings, which totaled a hundred and eighty pounds. "Okay," he relented. "Just let me have one more bet." Half expecting to lose, he put his original ten-pound stake on a number—36.

The ball rolled into slot 36.

Adam had just won thirty-five times his stake! The croupier paid him three hundred and fifty pounds—almost a year's pay!

Inside his head, Adam shrieked with joy, for he knew that his winnings were not due to blind chance. He felt as if he were smelling the hair of the most beautiful woman on earth and inhaling the perfume of her skin: Lady Luck was at his side.

After that first casino visit, Mike refused to accompany his brother. Their father, who believed that Adam had found a girlfriend, winked as, each night, he handed over the car keys.

Sometimes Adam won and sometimes he lost. After ten days, he had won a total of more than two years' salary, and in a manner far more exciting than doing the donkey work for some lawyer.

On the tenth evening, Adam started to lose steadily. At first he didn't worry because he knew he'd win it all back on the next throw.

But by two o'clock in the morning, when Adam usually left the casino, he had lost over six hundred pounds and could hardly believe it. He felt the desolate despair of a man who discovers his loved one in bed with somebody else. He felt guilty and ashamed. How *could* he stupidly have lost so much money so fast? It had taken him two weeks to win six hundred pounds—and then he had lost it in less than an hour. *Why* hadn't he stuck to his system?

Adam had abandoned the system he had decided upon, because at times, in order to follow it, he had to stop gambling—and he was now unable to do this: he felt *so strongly* that his luck would return on the next throw . . . in a few minutes . . . within an hour.

Adam slowly left the casino and, in a daze, drove home. His clothes felt crumpled and grubby, and as he slumped in the driving seat, he felt depressed, as if he were about to catch influenza.

"Adam seems down in the dumps," Mrs. Grant said to her husband the next day at sundown, as she tucked the Ambre Solaire bottle into her beach bag. "He turned down that invitation to visit the Boccasso yacht, and he's spoken to nobody all day. He ignored that nice girl he water-skied with yesterday."

Adam's father could not keep back a grin. "I think he's got a woman tucked away," he said in a man-of-the-world voice. "He's clearly had a row with her."

"But why hasn't he brought her to the beach?" A new thought struck Mrs. Grant. "Joe, do you think she's a . . . shopgirl type?"

"She's more likely to be one of the married women on the beach with young children. Nothing to do after the little 'uns have been put to bed . . . husband slaving away somewhere . . . No, Ethel, you're to say *nothing* to Adam. He's twenty-three, he's spent two years in the navy, and he won't thank a mother who tries to interfere in his love life."

* * *

On the following day, Adam found it hard to get out of bed. He only did so eventually because he knew that if he didn't, his mother would call a doctor, and then maybe he wouldn't be able to get to the casino that evening.

All day, Adam baked his body on the beach as feelings of apathy and lethargy swaddled him like a wet, dark fog. He couldn't eat or drink. He could only wonder if his luck would turn tonight at the casino.

One of the great failings of gamblers is to follow their losses. Adam did this, returning each evening to lose. He kept hoping that the next throw would cancel out those losses. It never did.

He borrowed thirty pounds from Giles Milroy-Browne (who by now knew quite a lot about Adam's background), but he didn't win it back.

Two days before he was due to return to London, Adam sold his gold wristwatch (a twenty-first birthday present) but when he attempted to repay his borrowing, Milroy-Browne refused to accept the money, saying that the debt could wait.

By midnight, Adam had lost the proceeds from the sale of his watch.

Giles lent him a further fifty pounds, which Adam also lost.

Adam left the south of France deeply grateful—and three hundred pounds in debt—to the obliging Mr. Milroy-Browne, who said there was no hurry, Adam could repay it when convenient. Adam agreed to pay one percent interest per month on this debt.

Adam was not unduly worried. When he returned to London, where gambling was illegal, he'd go to a private gambling party and make it back.

He was simply, temporarily, on a losing streak.

CHAPTER 8

Saturday, 15 December 1956

"DO YOU THINK IT will stop snowing before lunch? It's so boring indoors, with nothing to do." Kneeling on a window seat, sixteen-year-old Annabel twisted her blond ponytail with one finger as she pressed her nose to the diamond-leaded panes of the drawing room window. Seen through flickering snowflakes, the garden that encircled Starlings was a lumpy white blanket; beyond it, the bony branches of the orchard were weighed down by snow.

Annabel turned to look at her two sisters: Miranda was waltzing around the piano, tartan skirt aswirl. Clare, in a black batwing sweater and black stretch pants, lay on the carpet in front of the fire, reading a book.

Two years before, Clare had left her smart boarding school for an equally smart finishing school in Lausanne. No dreary secretarial school threatened the three sisters; neither Elinor nor Buzz considered it necessary: of course, the girls were destined for marriage.

At the finishing school, Clare had not learned to speak French, cook, sew, or write business letters; she had learned to jitterbug, to apply makeup, and not much else, except to glide downstairs gracefully.

By the time Clare returned from her year in Switzerland, Elinor had planned her eldest granddaughter's social debut with the painstaking thoroughness that she reserved for her book launches. So Clare was photographed regularly at chic events for the newspaper gossip columns or for *Tatler*, high society's picture magazine. Lady Rushleigh presented her to the Queen at Buckingham Palace. Clare wore a slim, white satin dress that looked like an upended arum lily; she hated it because it was so different from the white net crinolines of the other debutantes, which is why Elinor had chosen it.

Clare then devoted herself to the exhausting life of pleasure that constituted a London season, during which a girl was introduced, at great expense, to society. Clare, like all the other girls, was conscious of the unspoken hope that she might "meet someone nice"—by which all the mothers of the debutantes meant someone wellborn and rich.

She went to debutante lunches, at which girls became acquainted, and then she was made to rest at home during the afternoon, in order to save her strength for the cocktail parties, dinners, dances, or balls of the evening. She cheered loudly at the Oxford and Cambridge boat race, clapped sedately during cricket at Lord's, clamped binoculars to her eyes at Ascot, ate strawberries and cream between tennis matches at Wimbledon, held her breath with excitement at the clash of polo sticks at Cowdray Park and Cirencester, appreciatively sniffed the Chelsea Flower Show, and admired the mediocre pictures at the Royal Academy summer opening: at the previous year's exhibition, Pietro Annigoni's romantic portrait of the Queen (looking remarkably like Ingrid Bergman) had drawn unprecedented crowds, but this year there was no showstopper.

Finally, having sent thick, properly engraved invitation cards from Smythsons, Clare appeared at her own coming-out ball, which was held at the Orangery in Holland Park. A new young designer, David Hicks, had turned the place into a white net, candlelit fairyland.

During Clare's debut, inevitably Elinor also attracted a lot of publicity. By now Elinor Dove had become a legendary figure, beloved by thousands of hopeful girls and women whose dreams were disappointed but not yet dashed. Briskly recirculated stories of the former farm girl's struggles against adversity, her growing fortune, and what she spent it on were tangible proof to Elinor's readers that fairy stories *could* come true. As charmingly professional to photographers as H.M. the Queen Mother, Elinor was constantly photographed: descending from her white Rolls-Royce in glittering ball gowns, beaming in white fox furs, cuddling photogenic white Pekingese, or smiling from beneath one of her elaborate apricot hats—she had decided that apricot was "her color."

Two steps behind her, Clare sometimes felt as if she were one of her grandmother's accessories—something more important than Elinor's handbag but less important than her five-strand pearl necklace: merely a part of the glamorous picture that she so carefully presented to her public.

By the end of the season, Clare felt that she never wanted to shake another hand or clap her white gloves just hard enough to sound enthusiastic but softly enough to be polite. She had acquired a lot of dancing partners, about five regular escorts, and plenty of girlfriends with whom to giggle about them. Clare knew that she was a lucky, lucky girl, and she hoped that she would never have to make the debutante round again: a life of pleasure left her feeling exhausted and curiously empty.

Although she dared not say so, Clare thought she had wasted the year. She tried to explain this to Annabel, who would shortly be exposed to the same blaze of pleasure and publicity, but Annabel did not understand her sister's warning. Annabel, after her first term at a Swiss finishing school, *longed* for the boys, the balls, and the ball gowns; she longed to be photographed for society magazines and couldn't wait to dance until dawn in the arms of a man—preferably an older one.

But that was later. Right now Annabel was stuck with her sisters, snowbound at Starlings, which was not her idea of fun. She jumped down from the drawing room window seat. "Clare, let's have another bridge lesson."

Clare looked up and yawned. "Not enough time before lunch."

When the telephone rang, like a black cat Clare flung herself toward it. "Hello?" she cried hopefully, then, disappointment in her voice, said, "Sorry, Buzz, but I'm expecting an important call." She crashed the phone back on its cradle.

"I bet it's Henry," teased Miranda.

"It can't be Henry." Annabel returned to the window seat. "Henry's regiment's just been posted to Suez."

"Shut up, both of you!" Clare snapped.

Again the telephone rang. Clare leapt from the sofa, but Miranda had snatched up the receiver. "Who's speaking? . . . C.N.D.? What's that? The Campaign for Nuclear Disarmament . . . I think you have the wrong number."

"It's for me!" Clare blushed violently, grabbed the telephone, made an appointment to meet someone in London, and replaced the receiver.

"Who was *that?*" Annabel asked.

"What was that *about?*" Miranda chimed in.

"None of your business," growled Clare.

"Gran won't like any ban-the-Bomb movement," Miranda said. "She'll say the atom bomb won the war for us in ten minutes. . . . The Prime Minister doesn't need to be told how to run the country by ignorant ungrateful rabble-rousers. . . . *You* know what Gran will say, Clare."

"C.N.D. is perfectly respectable," Clare said defensively. "Bertrand Russell and six other Nobel Prize winners support banning the atomic bomb, and Albert Einstein did too. In any future war, nuclear weapons might wipe out this whole planet."

"Gran still won't like it," Miranda warned.

"I cannot stand deceit!" Elinor croaked as she waved a letter at Clare the following morning; she lay in the sunny opulence of her bedroom, nursing an attack of bronchitis.

To avoid her grandmother's eye, Clare looked around the pretty room. The walls were cream, the curtains buttercup, to match the brocade hangings of the four-poster bed. Upon the faded yellows of the Bessarabian rug stood a Regency sofa with tiger-skin cushions. Piles of books and fragrant pots of narcissi filled the room.

"Kindly look at me, Clare." Elinor sneezed. "I'm waiting to hear what you have to say for yourself," she added crossly as she gazed at Clare, who stood before her in a pink sweater and tweed skirt, a furtive expression on her face.

Again Elinor wondered anxiously whether Clare had a lover: this was what all the mothers worried about, although none of the debutantes (more innocent than their mothers realized) ever knew it. She wondered if the man was married, if he made some business excuse to his wife on Tuesday and Thursday evenings, when Clare was clearly not doing what she said she was doing.

I'll have to lie again, Clare thought miserably. She remembered being puzzled as a child because grown-ups taught children not to lie, but then they looked you in the eye and lied about where babies came from. So from adults, Clare learned to tell "fibs" to avoid hurting people's feelings, to protect somebody else, or to avoid adult wrath.

"I'm waiting," wheezed Elinor, furious. She sneezed again, and one of her letters slid to the floor. Clare could see the Swithin, Timmins and Grant address flowing across the top of the page.

Looking away again, Clare said without thinking, "I was with Adam Grant."

"Twice a week? And always home by ten? Exactly *what* were you doing with Adam?"

"He was teaching me to play bridge. I want to be really good."

"Well, that's easy enough to check." Elinor reached for the cream telephone.

Clare, never a facile liar, felt helpless.

"Good morning, Adam? Have you seen Clare recently?"

Clare's heart sank. She had hoped that Adam might not be in his office.

"I fail to understand why you can't give me a straight answer," Elinor said, "but you may talk to her if you wish." She motioned to Clare to pick up the telephone.

Adam's voice in Clare's ear said: "Listen, Clare, I can't lie to my client. If you're in trouble, I'll try to help you, but tell me the truth or I can't help. . . . Are you seeing some man secretly? . . . No? Good! Are you doing anything illegal? . . . No? *Then tell Elinor where you've been!* Tell her straightaway. Whatever you've been concealing from her can't be nearly as bad as her fears, so you *may* be forgiven immediately. And next week, I *will* take you out to dinner—so that will be something to look forward to."

Clare replaced the receiver and, in a low voice, said to Elinor, "I go to night school."

"*Night school!* But that's for people who haven't . . . " Elinor, remembering the impoverished students at her Polytechnic classes, was puzzled. She said, "You've had a *good* education, Clare."

"I don't think so. I didn't learn much at Hazlehurst Park. I only got two O levels before you whisked me off to that stupid finishing school."

"What ingratitude! No man wants a bluestocking for a wife—a man wants someone who will grace his drawing room, in a ladylike manner."

"I don't intend to sit in a drawing room for the rest of my life! We're living in the twentieth century, not in the old days at Larkwood!" All three sisters knew that Elinor still smarted from the hurt feelings of inferiority inflicted upon her by Billy's family. Clare added, "I want to do something useful with my life!"

"Aren't wives useful? Aren't mothers useful?"

"There can be more to life than being a wife and mother!"

"Well, what exactly are you studying to make you more useful?"

"Sociology," Clare said defiantly.

Elinor looked astonished and alarmed. "My dear child, surely you're not going to be a *social worker?*"

"I don't see why I shouldn't be," Clare replied defensively. "It's a very useful job."

"Of course it is. That's all very well for other people. But not *you*, Clare. Not traipsing around slums."

"*Why not?* Gran, what have you got *against* sociology?"

Elinor sighed. "What exactly *is* sociology?"

"It tells you how society developed and how it functions—or doesn't function sometimes," Clare said.

"But, darling, your studies at school never reached the level required for these subjects, so . . ."

"*Exactly!* I'll also be studying anthropology, psychology, and philosophy."

"Surely not in only two evenings a week?"

"Since you now know about it, I'd like to be a full-time student. If I have enough basic qualifications. And if not, I'd like to get them."

"To what *purpose*, dear child? Nice men don't want to marry a sociologist or a philosopher. Why can't you study something less highbrow and a bit more useful? How about a cookery course at the Cordon Bleu school? It's always an asset to know how to plan menus."

"Gran, can't you understand that I'm interested in the world beyond my kitchen?" Clare spluttered angrily.

"Of course you are. You're an intelligent young woman and you must follow what the men are talking about."

"*I* want the men to follow what *I'm* talking about—which will *never again* be cocktail party chitchat!" Clare shouted.

"*How can you say that to me?*"

"Gran, I don't understand why I *can't!* Why do I have to be furtive? Why don't you understand what I want to do, and why?"

"But sociology . . . how will that help you?"

"Gran, I'm interested in helping other people. Everywhere I look, I see inequality."

"But philosophy . . . isn't that flying a bit high? And what has philosophy got to do with slum children?"

"Philosophy is concerned with ideas, and ideas are what democracy is based on," Clare said, exasperated. "I don't understand how the world got into this state, but I'm going to try to find out—and then do something about it."

"One young woman can't do anything to right the wrongs of the world," Elinor said, equally exasperated.

"I'll never do anything if I don't try." Clare was wearing her stubborn look.

"Why can't you leave such things to politicians, who've been trained to do their job?" Elinor cried.

"Your generation is going to be the last one to have blind faith in politicians!"

"My generation seemed to manage without *your* intellectual pretensions," Elinor said acidly.

"*Your* generation was the one that got us into the Second World War!"

Tuesday, 18 December 1956

As she handed her green satin cloak to the butler, Clare once again felt the butterflies rise in her stomach—the wish-I-could-turn-around-and-run-out-of-here feeling that she always experienced when she arrived at a party. Everyone else seemed so self-assured. When she knew nobody, Clare liked to slink to the cloakroom as fast as possible and stay there as long as possible, before facing a throng of people who all seemed to know each other.

Tonight Clare felt doubly nervous, because Adam had taken her, for the first time, to one of the illegal gambling games that were fast becoming fashionable in London. These parties were always held after dinner, from ten o'clock to dawn; no charge was made for the abundant and delicious food and drink, or the traditional English breakfast of bacon and eggs, sausages, kidneys, and kedgeree that was served from two A.M.

Clare knew that tonight's party had been organized by Michael Grant. Good-looking, presentable, an old Etonian and ex-Guards officer (although only national service), he was the perfect sort of person to organize a chic but illegal game.

All invitations were issued on the telephone—nothing was ever put on paper—to people who had plenty of money and enjoyed a little naughty excitement and glamour. It was reminiscent of Americans during Prohibition.

Merely to know the venue meant one was chic; no one considered the danger. Michael Grant's guests had been brought up to consider the police as people who got you out of trouble, not into trouble. Besides, the possibility of a police raid added to the thrill, and to be caught on such a raid was considered proof of sophistication and daring.

For the fashionable young people who flocked to the gambling parties, there was also the added thrill of rubbing shoulders with genuine criminals, whom they were unlikely to encounter in any other way. Tough bouncers were hired to protect the organizer; they saw that no drunk tore the place apart, and that losers paid up promptly. The protective services were paid for with a cut of the house take, and one of the mob was always present in order to check on it. Thus, rich young society gamblers were now on first-name terms with some of the toughest hoods in London's East End; this, too, was considered chic.

As Clare and Adam walked into a well-furnished Belgravia drawing room, Michael Grant stepped forward. "Here you are at last! We've got an interesting crowd tonight—nearly all the Eton gambling mafia's here. . . ." Michael looked at Clare as her eyes played around the roomful of people in evening dress talking quietly over drinks. "*This* is Clare O'Dare?"

It had been almost four years since their holiday in St.-Tropez. No longer small and skinny, Clare was now gracefully slim, pale, and elusive, with the flashing blue-eyed stare and enigmatic allure of a mermaid. Tonight her fey quality was emphasized by a blue-green chiffon gown.

Clare said shyly, "You look exactly the same, Mike—but you seem somehow . . . different." She sensed recklessness in this wide-shouldered, well-groomed man in the beautifully cut dinner jacket; and Mike's slow smile did not contradict a feeling of menace. Clare felt uneasy with him, whereas she felt completely safe with Adam.

Adam murmured something to his brother that Clare couldn't hear; they seemed to be very close, she thought as they laughed together. Adam looked around the room and laughed again. "It looks as if you've lived here for years, Mike!"

In order to avoid the police, these illegal games took place at a different address each night. Mike persuaded socially acceptable people, for a huge fee, to rent out their London home for twenty-four hours; sometimes this was done by a son or daughter while the unknowing parents were abroad or in the country. On the morning following a party, the furniture removal van that Mike kept permanently employed would arrive to shift the furniture, china, linen, and cutlery to the next house. Mike always used the same firm of first-class, professional caterers, the normal servants of the house not being considered trustworthy on these occasions.

"Let's get some champagne and go into the back rooms, where they're playing roulette and chemmy," suggested Adam, not present for pleasure only.

Mike had asked Adam to look around, because Mike's game was straight and he wanted to keep it so. A few games had been quietly taken over by their "protectors," after which the games were crooked. East End thugs were astonished at the idea of running a straight game. Of course you let the punter win a bit at first, in order to encourage him, but after that—naturally, the house won. You were in business to make money. And if, by chance, a punter had a big win, he was generally relieved of his winnings on the way to his car, and nobody could prove that the mugging was connected. However, this was rarely necessary, since the punter usually lost—it was the law of nature.

Mike reckoned that, should anyone try to put pressure on him, Adam would know someone to apply a little firm counterpressure.

Adam now worked full-time for the family firm; he had taken his solicitors' finals the previous year and was now fully conversant with trust accounts and bookkeeping, papers and property law, conveyancing and the law of contracts. At night, whenever possible, he gambled.

By one o'clock in the morning, Clare was tired and ready to go home but Adam was still playing roulette. Again he offered Clare fifty pounds with which to gamble but she shook her head. "Take money from a man? Gran would throw me into the snow and cut me off without a shilling."

"Rubbish. She's mad about all of you. *You'll* never be cut off without a shilling. She may lose her temper from time to time, but Elinor's bark is far worse than her bite. Look how your row ended—she's agreed that you can go to a crammer and study."

"I won't be able to study anything tomorrow unless you get me home soon."

"Just one more throw," Adam promised.

Clare yawned as she watched Adam swiftly place his stake. She felt too tired and shy to speak to anyone else, and anyway, the people in this quiet room were intent only on gambling.

Above the rattling clunk of the ball, Clare heard a faint commotion from the hall.

Adam's head jerked up. Ignoring his winnings, he took Clare by the arm in a grip that was hard enough to bruise. "That sounds like a police raid. Follow me quickly."

"But, Adam . . . my cloak . . . "

Adam had hustled Clare out the rear door while other guests were still looking puzzled.

"Ow, Adam, you're hurting me," Clare cried, but Adam took no notice. He opened a door at the back of the hall and pushed her down the stone stairs to the basement. She nearly collided with a waiter, who was carrying champagne up from the kitchen below.

Once at the bottom of the stairs, Clare could hear hammering against the front basement door, around which scared kitchen staff had gathered.

"Better let 'em in, Ernie," she heard someone say as Adam dragged her out the back door and into the dark garden.

"There should be a ladder to your right," Adam whispered. "Get up it and wait on top of the garden wall."

"But I can't . . . my *dress!*"

In the dark, Adam grabbed Clare's chiffon skirts, pulled them up to her waist, and threw them over her shoulders. "The ladder's right in front of you, Clare! *Climb it!*"

Clare pulled off her silver slipper—she'd lost the other on the stairs—and slowly climbed the workman's ladder, which wobbled each time she cautiously moved her foot up a rung into the darkness.

"Get a move on!" Adam whispered urgently. "I can hear the police in the kitchen!"

Tentatively Clare groped with her left hand, feeling for the wall, but pawed only air.

"*Hurry!*"

She moved up two more rungs and again stretched her hand upward, but still felt nothing. This wall was as high as the Great Wall of China!

Again Clare reached out her hand, and this time touched the damp, uneven, unyielding bricks. Below her, she felt the ladder tremble as Adam started to climb. Clare thought she preferred to be caught by the police, rather than break her neck falling from a ladder in the dark.

After she climbed the next rung, Clare's hands groped forward, but she grasped empty air. Clearly she was now at the top of the wall and would have to get off the ladder.

As she crouched atop the wall, she heard windows thrown open with a crash. Someone shouted, "Send two men into the garden!"

Adam nimbly scrambled up beside her.

No time to pull the ladder up so we can climb down the other side, Adam thought, and pushed the ladder backward. Before it hit the ground, he had jumped into the dark safety of the neighboring garden.

"I'm in a flower bed," he whispered up to Clare. "You'll have to risk it. I can't see to catch you. For God's sake, *jump!*"

Clare clung to the top of the wall, too frightened to jump. "What about Mike?" she whispered anxiously.

Adam hesitated a moment, as he thought of the many occasions when Mike had loyally shouldered the blame for his adored elder brother. Adam fleetingly remembered the bi-weekly ceremony of stealing chocolate from the local sweet-shop counter, where, eventually, the police had been brought in by the irate shopkeeper and were waiting for the two schoolboy thieves; Mike confessed (although Adam had been the ringleader) and Mike refused to name the other schoolboy conspirator, for which bravery he was soundly whipped by his father. Adam also remembered the ringing-doorbells-and-running-away episodes when Adam, the ringleader and the faster runner, had always managed to hide in someone's garden or up an alley, where he listened—heart pounding—to Mike's capture, knowing that a thundering row with their father would follow, and that Mike, after loyally swearing that Adam had nothing to do with it, would be beaten and punished.

Through childhood and adolescence, there had been many similar instances and never once had Adam confessed to having taken part in them. He had become used to this useful, fraternal hero worship. So now, in the earthy, damp darkness, he shrugged his shoulders and whispered to Clare, "Mike won't mind, he never does. Now, for God's sake—*jump!*"

The back door behind Clare opened with a crash.

She jumped downward, into the dark, into Adam's arms.

Before she had caught her breath, he grabbed her right wrist. "Let's get to the back door. It should be open."

As quickly as he could, Adam groped his way along the garden wall toward the silent house, shoving shrubs aside as he did so.

Eventually the garden wall ended and his fingertips moved to the left: they touched . . . a window . . . more brick wall . . . and then a paneled door. He felt for the handle, gently turned it to the left, and pushed.

The door opened.

Adam yanked Clare into the house; then slowly and very quietly he shut the door. His fingertips found the key in the lock, and he turned it carefully to the right. Swiftly he pushed upward, until he found the bolt and rammed it home.

"Adam, we've just broken into someone's house!" Clare whispered.

"Mike always plans an escape route for himself."

"But you pushed the ladder away, so Mike couldn't use it!"

"Your grandmother wouldn't like anything to happen to you."

"What do we do now?"

"We sit here until morning. Then we'll borrow a couple of coats and simply walk out of the front door—and pass the police."

Adam draped his jacket around Clare's shoulders. They both sat on the stone-paved floor of what seemed to be an old scullery, leading off a kitchen.

In the dark, Clare shivered as much from excitement as from cold. The voluptuous gambling party represented the kind of decadence that she had always considered waste, but it had been exciting to feel decadent, and wickedly sophisticated, just for a few hours.

After that evening, Clare always felt protected when she was with Adam. It never occurred to her that, had Adam not taken her to an illegal game, there would have been no need to rescue her from it.

CHAPTER 9

Thursday, 17 April 1958

"I *DON'T SUPPOSE YOU* deserve breakfast in bed," Buzz said as she carried a tray into Annabel's frilled pink bedroom. "How many hearts did you break last night?"

"Ow! Buzz, darling Buzz, please don't pull back the curtains. Ow! That sunshine is *blinding*."

"It's nearly midday." Buzz cruelly drew the curtains farther apart, and looked down to see Elinor picking anemones beneath the white and pink blossoming trees of the orchard.

Eighteen-year-old Annabel sat up and stretched. She looked older than her age, Buzz thought. Beneath that tangle of tawny hair, Annabel was the sister who most resembled the young Elinor; she had the same steady gaze and full, moist mouth with a natural curve, so that she seemed always to be smiling slightly, even when asleep.

The difference between Annabel's debut and Clare's had been that Annabel loved every minute of it. Lady Rushleigh had again been very helpful, and Elinor not only had paid her expenses for the London season but also had given her a sunburst diamond brooch she had admired when Elinor wore it.

Lady Rushleigh's protégée had met with great success. Beautiful, indolent Annabel was always surrounded by men; flirtation seemed natural to her, and she was as gently provocative to the postman and the butcher's boy on his bicycle as she was to the more eligible young men with whom she danced. Lighthearted, gay, and frivolous, Annabel did not restrict her encounters with these gentlemen to the dance floor: there had been much furtive groping on ballroom balconies, in taxis, and, early in the morning, in the cold and darkened drawing room of Elinor's London flat.

Annabel was wildly excited by the eroticism of the forbidden as well as by the turbulent hormones that coursed through her body. No matter how tired she felt when she left a party, she was always reenergized by the feel of a man's arm around her waist, a man's hard, warm palm on her naked shoulder as he pushed straps aside and explored the soft flesh of her breasts: Annabel felt a swooning, delirious tug from the bottom of her stomach as she murmured, "You mustn't . . . you really *mustn't* . . ."

Trembling from these touches, Annabel would sometimes allow what, earlier in the evening, she had decided on no account to permit; and a man's hand would slide beneath the net or taffeta skirt to her smooth, nylon-covered knee, eventually to move stealthily over the stocking top, over a taut satin suspender, and slip inward over Annabel's soft, quivering thigh. The young man was then pushed off into the night, tumescent, throbbing, painfully frustrated.

"Time you was up and packing," Buzz said, turning again to the window.

Elinor, in the orchard, looked up, saw Buzz at Annabel's window, and waved. In her gardening clothes, she did not look the glittering, glamorous legend that she had become since Billy's death. Buzz had been astonished by the change in her personality: Nell had blossomed; she had clearly become a person in her own right as well as a soaring success in the world.

Her American publisher now wished her to meet her readers on the other side of the Atlantic, so Elinor, accompanied by Annabel, was about to fly to New York, the first city on her U.S. tour.

Annabel yawned. "Buzz, has anyone taken breakfast to Harry?"

Buzz sniffed, placed the tray before Annabel, and chopped off the top of Annabel's boiled egg with an unnecessary violence that clearly showed her opinion of Harry.

"You don't want to bother too much about *him*," Buzz said. "There'll be tears before bedtime over that young masher."

"I don't understand why you dislike him, Buzz. You've hardly met him,"

Annabel protested. Buzz had lectured her incessantly about the pitfalls of love.

Buzz poured herself a cup of coffee and sat on the end of the bed. "Seen his type before: Don Juan." Buzz pronounced the *j*, as in *jab*. "Harry don't love you, my girl—Harry don't love *anyone*. Pays the girls a lot of attention, o'course, but so does a hunter stalking deer. I bet Harry rushes from one girl to the next, just to show himself he can." She wrinkled her forehead. "I ain't never fathomed why a man who gets through a lot of women is reckoned to be some sort of hero, while a woman who has a lot of fellas is called a nymphomaniac."

Annabel said, "And how do *you* know so much about men, Buzz?"

Buzz hesitated. She still felt mild astonishment that Ginger Higby had, long ago, so clearly preferred her to all other women. She still kept all his letters, and his mother—showing great kindness—had given her two photographs of Ginger as a child. Buzz was comforted by the big buff envelope that contained these remnants of all the sexual love she would ever know.

The feelings that Ginger's body had aroused in her had, after his death, led Buzz to touch herself experimentally, hoping to remember those past moments of thwarted passion. To her astonishment, she discovered the erotic climax, which should have been the culmination of her always abruptly severed lovemaking with Ginger. Because she alone was responsible for her pleasure, Buzz felt guilty, felt disloyal to Ginger. She knew instinctively that this was a forbidden game. But why, she asked herself defensively, should she not experience those physical feelings she had been denied by some unknown soldier who would never know—if he still existed—that an accidental squeeze of his finger had caused an eternal void in Buzz's life, which had not seemed empty before she met Ginger.

Looking at beautiful Annabel, able to have any fellow she fancied, Buzz sighed and said, "I know about rascals like Harry because I've got eyes, miss, and I've been using them for years. The Harrys don't bother about an old stick like me—they don't notice I'm watching 'em." Harry reminded Buzz of Billy.

The door was flung open and seventeen-year-old Miranda made her entrance; she wore Stuart tartan slacks and a black sweater; her thick, shoulder-length hair was the brilliant orange of marmalade.

"Like it?" As Miranda twisted her head from side to side, the flaming hair swung outward. "John French. Cost a fortune—four guineas."

Annabel was impressed. "Gran'll *kill* you."

"Theatrical," Buzz sniffed. "You'd better wash it off before she sees you."

"Can't. It's dyed." Miranda was triumphant.

"She'll definitely kill you," Annabel said respectfully. "Dyed hair is unladylike."

Miranda was defiant. "Gran's fifty-eight years old, hasn't got a single gray hair, and is as blond as Marilyn Monroe. Gran goes to John French."

Clare pushed open the door. "So this is where everyone is. What are you talking about?"

"Love." Annabel stretched happily. "Love that makes you feel as if you're high in the clouds, with masses of energy and no need for sleep."

Remembering, Buzz nodded. "No wonder women long for it. Gives 'em something exciting to think about while they're doing the dull things that women do—which is where your gran comes in."

"*Gran!*" Annabel exclaimed through a mouthful of buttered toast. "How?"

"When a woman reads about some exciting man in a novel, she forgets she ain't got a man, or she ain't got the right sort of man. She falls a little bit in love with the hero, and although he don't exist, her feelings about him exist, all right. She *really* feels a bit excited."

"That's the whole point of escapist literature," Clare said tartly. "You can pretend you're really living it."

Buzz nodded again. "Some women get hooked, like a drug, on romance and they'd rather have it out of a book than not at all . . . the sort of woman that feels hopeful before a party, wonders if her Prince Charming will appear, is disappointed when he don't, and goes home feeling a failure."

"I don't want to marry Prince Charming," Clare said firmly. "Just an honest . . . trustworthy . . . supportive . . . sensitive . . . man."

"*That* doesn't sound very exciting." Annabel licked her buttery fingers. "I want one that's strong . . . fascinating . . . dynamic and a bit mysterious."

"I want a man of action," Miranda said. "A romantic-looking leader of men, like Rupert of the Rhine."

"Titled? Rich? Powerful?" Buzz queried. "Good-looking, tall, blue-eyed?"

"Blue eyes aren't absolutely necessary," Annabel conceded.

Buzz said sourly, "And this almost perfect man that you all want—*if* he exists—what exactly are you each offering him? Similar perfection?"

"Oh Buzz, we were having a nice sexy talk and you've turned it into a lecture again." Annabel yawned.

"I'm trying to knock a bit of sense into your head before exciting Mr. Heartbreaker Harry wakes up." Buzz reached for the tray. "There ain't no perfect men, and exciting men make women miserable." Again she thought of Billy.

Monday, 21 April 1958

In spite of the air freshener, the windowless greenroom of the New York TV news station still smelled of dead cigarettes and stale coffee.

A girl dressed casually with an oversized man's shirt over her skirt opened the door and beckoned to Elinor, who stood up feeling terrified but looking calm and self-possessed. She wore a Christian Dior apricot silk dress and duster coat, suitable for any formal day or evening occasion that didn't call for an ankle-length dress. Her blond hair was in a chignon. Careful dieting had kept her weight what it had been when she was seventeen; neat cosmetic surgery around her eyelids and chin had left only a few, faint lines at the sides of her mouth to indicate her age.

"Good luck," whispered the publisher's press agent.

"Knock 'em dead," encouraged Annabel, who wore heavy makeup and a silver, sleeveless sheath from Bazaar.

In the studio, the charismatic fair-haired young interviewer introduced Elinor as this year's winner of the International Romance Writers Award and then, predictably, asked the secret of her success.

Elinor beamed. "The secret of writing good romantic fiction is to *feel* romantic, *look* romantic, and *be* romantic."

"Some people describe your books as trash. What do you feel about that?"

The publisher's press agent had warned Elinor that Scott Svenson would listen to her every word, remember her every word, and not hesitate to use it against her; he never gave anyone an easy ride, but he was the station's best interviewer.

Elinor continued to beam. "Millions of my readers wouldn't agree. Today's classics were sometimes described in the past as trash—Charles Dickens's books were serialized in popular magazines, and Thomas Hardy's work was called pulp fiction. Even Shakespeare—a very commercial writer—was accused by his contemporaries of writing potboilers."

"And what is *your* formula for a potboiler?"

"The ingredients of a good novel are as basic and simple as the ingredients of a soufflé," Elinor said with a smile. "Good characterization, a believable, well-constructed plot, detailed research, and dialogue that's easy to read. I keep to the point, write short paragraphs, ration my adjectives, and try never to use superfluous words."

"Your sex scenes have been described as 'limp.' Would you agree?"

"My books contain love scenes, but *never* a sex scene. I see no need to follow my heroines to the marriage bed: we all know what happens there."

"You have been accused of lack of realism in this respect."

"Realism is the last thing my readers want: they get enough of that at home. My books provide a holiday from reality. . . ."

She was a tough old bird, Scott thought. How could he shake that smile? He tried again. "Although you live in a world of romance, you have never remarried. Why is there no man in your life?"

Elinor still smiled. "There will be a man in my life when I choose to have a man in my life," she said, "just as the heroine of my new novel, *Heartbreak in Jamaica* . . . " After all, the point of being on this show was to publicize her book.

Annabel and her grandmother came out of the greenroom just as the interviewer was exiting the stage door.

Scott stopped. "Hi." He threw them the careless, boyish smile that made thousands of women stop their husband from switching channels.

"I'd like to say how great you were, Miss Dove," Scott said respectfully. "Is this your daughter?" Maybe he was piling it on too thick? "I wondered if . . . The Plaza's just around the corner, if you'd care for a drink?"

"Thank you, but we are tired after our trip." Elinor swept out. She had felt under slight but unyielding pressure during the entire interview.

Annabel lingered, unwilling to be dragged to bed on her first night in New York. "Why don't you come to our suite for a drink?" she suggested. They were, in fact, staying at the Plaza.

By the time they reached her hotel suite, Elinor had heard that she possessed a natural screen presence, although Scott would like to suggest one or two little professional tricks. He added, "As a matter of fact, I could tell you were from the Midwest. It wasn't only your accent, it was your forthright, no-nonsense attitude."

Elinor gave a genuine smile. "I could tell straightaway that *you* were. I knew I couldn't pull the wool over your eyes."

By the time the champagne bottle was empty, Elinor had thoroughly interviewed Scott, to his amusement.

Scott came from Cleveland, Ohio, where he'd started to write for his high school paper in his senior year, then studied communications at college. He worked as a junior assistant on a local Cleveland paper—no, unfortunately, not the *Plain Dealer*—and eventually slid into the foreign editor's office as a freelance researcher. At that point, a locally owned and operated TV station wanted a cheap, fast, noncomplaining researcher-writer, and as the job paid twice as much as the newspaper, Scott took it. Gradually he was allowed to cover minor stories.

Scott did not mention that his boyish good looks and engaging smile had earned him the malicious nickname of "Pretty Boy."

He had been lucky that he first appeared on the box when stations were out to woo the youth audience and all newscasters over the age of thirty-five were secretly having their eye bags removed. With just enough training and experience, Scott had turned up at the right time, but not quite in the right place. A year later, he applied for the job of news reporter on a local TV station in New York City. Once hired, he surprised the director of news by his hard-nosed, carefully researched stories and hard-hitting interviews: recently he had been allowed to appear as a relief newscaster and interviewer.

By midnight, Elinor was asleep in her bed, but Scott and Annabel (having promised not to return too late) were drinking more champagne at "21."

An hour later, they creaked around Central Park in one of the romantic horse-drawn black cabs that wait dolefully outside the Plaza. Scott gently kissed Annabel's nose and tried to think of ways to keep her in New York.

Then the obvious idea hit him. "Why don't you try modeling?" he murmured in her ear. "I can fix you an interview with the best agent in town."

"*All* the girls I know want to be air hostesses or models," Annabel said. "But I'm not sure Gran would let me."

"Then don't ask her."

On the following morning, Annabel sat opposite a well-groomed blonde, aged forty plus, in a beige gabardine suit. The wall behind her desk was covered by citations. Scott had briefed her on Bates Model Agency—run by a husband-and-wife team, Moses and Jenny Bates. Ten years before, they had borrowed a thousand dollars to set up their company; within three years, they had a stable of thirty-nine models and total billings of $300,000. Mrs. Bates chose and supervised the models; her husband was responsible for their bookings. They discovered that marketing the most beautiful women in the world was not very difficult, but finding them was a problem.

Each year, the Bateses saw and rejected about five thousand applicants; they held talent contests all over America and also overseas—for blond models were the most popular, and the best were to be found in Germany and Scandinavia. The cosmetics industry was especially willing to pay very high fees for an exquisite new face; while complaining about the Bateses' high charges, cosmetics companies continued to pay them because there was no cheaper way to find girls of the high standard of beauty, charm, grooming, and professional behavior (punctuality, patience, and amiability) so carefully set by the Bateses.

"Don't pluck her eyebrows yet, just tidy them up—we'll see how they photograph," ordered Mrs. Bates. She tapped her pencil against her teeth and scrutinized Annabel's face once more. "Go and wash your face in the dressing room. I need to see you without makeup."

When Annabel returned, Mrs. Bates squinted at her, then nodded briefly. "We'll fix a few test shots. Janey here will arrange them for this afternoon."

When she saw Annabel's test shots, Mrs. Bates smiled and called her for a second interview.

* * *

Jenny Bates leaned forward across her white desk. "Don't think a model's job is easy or glamorous. Less than one percent of beginner models are immediately successful, and when they are, it's rarely because of their beauty but because—for some odd reason—they catch the eye of an advertising agency as being 'different' and 'right for now.' " As with newscasters, a girl who was the toast of the town for one period would—automatically—not look right for the next.

"And if she's to stand out from the rest," Mrs. Bates added, "a girl needs some extra, unique quality that the other models don't possess." The model's face also needed enough sensual appeal to attract a man, but not so much that it would make a woman feel threatened.

"Have you heard of Suzy Parker?" Mrs. Bates asked.

Annabel nodded. Who had not? Redheaded Suzy Parker and her brunette sister, Dorian Leigh, had been the top models of the fifties: they both possessed classic beauty, an exquisite sophistication, and dazzling "glamour"—the cosmetics industry's euphemism for sex appeal. Now they were past their professional peak; in a blaze of publicity, Dorian had opened a model agency in Paris and Suzy had signed a film contract. The top seats were vacant.

Jenny Bates, looking over the flowers on her desk, wondered whether Annabel might fill that vacancy. She had beauty, feminine charm, and that unmistakable, uncopyable old-money look; her sleepy aquamarine eyes were most unusual, as was the large mouth that should have looked too big for her tiny face but didn't. While kitten faces were currently fashionable (Leslie Caron, Audrey Hepburn, Brigitte Bardot), Annabel's face was more like that of a wild mountain cat.

"Stand up once more, and walk to the door, please," ordered Mrs. Bates. She watched Annabel closely. This girl was not glamorous, groomed, or sophisticated; she didn't even shave her legs. She must be tidied up immediately, but without losing that just-tumbled-out-of-bed look.

And then she *might* prove right for Avanti. Avanti was looking for a face to work exclusively for them; they were also willing to pay the face to do nothing when they didn't need her, rather than be used by a rival. Avanti had asked for a classic Scandinavian blonde because all cosmetics companies believed that a blonde could sell anything to anyone. Annabel was not such a blonde, but golden highlights would probably do the trick.

Avanti had pulled itself into a position where it almost rivaled Revlon: they hoped that their next, ambitious promotion would rival Revlon's "Fire and Ice" campaign of 1952, regarded by the trade as unbeatable. Featuring Dorian Leigh in a tight-fitting sheath of silver sequins and a flowing crimson cape, it had combined elegance, class, and sensuality; it suggested that beneath the ordinary woman lay another woman—a smoldering temptress.

Avanti's shorthand specification for the girl they were seeking to rival the Fire and Ice girl was "a class act and a tiger in the sack." The creative director had specified: "young—but not too young, a graceful and sophisticated international woman," lively but not noisy, glamorous but approachable, sporty but not sweaty, and equally at home in town and country.

And the final requisite would be no problem, for Annabel clearly came from a respectable background: The morality clause included in her contract would stipulate that, should she be (or have been) involved in a scandal, which might adversely affect the Avanti promotion, the contract would immediately be terminated.

Annabel had better spend tomorrow at the hairdresser, Mrs. Bates decided, first for highlights, then to try different hairstyles. For her interviews, Annabel would need more sophisticated clothes than this butter-colored shirtwaister. After the hairdresser, she'd better take her to Bergdorf.

Jenny Bates, wondering whether, at last, she had found a contender for the number one slot, said, "Do you really have to leave for Chicago tomorrow?"

Wednesday, 23 April 1958

"It must have been something I ate last night—maybe those oysters," groaned Annabel, who had carefully chosen oysters. She knew that only a supervised and not-too-serious illness would persuade Elinor, who could not easily cancel her tour, to leave her granddaughter alone in New York.

The hotel doctor was puzzled. "I can't find anything wrong with her, but you say she vomited and suffered from diarrhea during the night, so she's clearly not well," he said. "She shouldn't travel yet. Better leave her here under observation—she'll be perfectly safe at the Plaza. I'll visit her every day and keep you informed of her condition."

The publisher's press agent shot him a look of gratitude and relief. She didn't want Elinor to miss the Chicago plane.

"But I can't leave a child alone in New York!" Elinor said, "*especially* if she's ill." Nevertheless, she hesitated, knowing how carefully her publisher had planned this expensive tour, and how long it had taken to organize.

"There's clearly nothing seriously wrong with your granddaughter," the hotel doctor reassured her. "It'll probably clear up in a couple of days."

"No, I can't leave Annabel alone," Elinor decided.

"But all the dinners, and the signings . . . You can't disappoint all those people who are looking forward to meeting you," the publisher's agent pleaded.

Elinor shook her head. "I'm sorry."

"Couldn't you ask Buzz to fly over?" Annabel asked. "Although I'll probably have joined you in Chicago by the time she arrives."

Elinor considered. "That *might* be the answer. . . ." She went to the phone.

A startled Buzz agreed to get to New York as fast as possible, and then insisted on speaking to Annabel about her symptoms. "A touch of colic," she decided. "Now you be a good girl and stay in bed with a hot-water bottle until I get there."

"Oh, I will," Annabel promised, feeling increasingly guilty.

Annabel stayed in bed until after the plane's departure. Then she threw back her bedclothes, tore off her nightgown, and danced like a whirling dervish in the middle of the room. She was free! She was alone in New York! Alone at the Plaza!

She rushed to the window and looked down on the green treetops of Central Park; to her right, beyond the line of listless horse cabs, a fountain sparkled in the sun. Behind it lay the excitement of Fifth Avenue, and somewhere behind that was the Bates Model Agency, where her future—her life perhaps—would be decided. . . .

Jenny Bates had no idea that Annabel had faked illness to stay in New York. She knew that Annabel had no cash, although she could order anything she wanted at the Plaza; it was the same with all the British, who had to budget on a ludicrously low, government-regulated travel allowance and rely on friends to finance them.

Later that morning, Mrs. Bates took Annabel across the street from the Plaza to Bergdorf Goodman: Bates Model Agency paid for her new clothes, in advance of fees due.

At lunchtime, Annabel telephoned Buzz, hoping it wasn't too late to tell her not to buy her ticket to New York yet: Annabel's "colic" was much better and tomorrow she might be well enough to join Elinor in Chicago.

"Thank heaven for that," said Buzz. "You haven't *half* given us a fright. I wasn't able to get a seat until the morning. . . . Keep well wrapped up, and do as the doctor tells you."

"I will," Annabel promised her, and skipped off to Saks.

On the following morning, after another glorious shopping spree, Annabel walked in spring sunshine down Fifth Avenue to the crimson door of Elizabeth Arden, where a grooming session had been booked for her. Five hours later, a perfectly groomed Annabel emerged with a personalized makeup chart, false eyelashes, and false nails. Her hair had been trimmed, streaked blond, and restyled. Roberto had designed a wig and two hairpieces for her (one a chignon), but these would take three weeks to complete.

She rushed back to the Plaza to telephone Buzz before her bedtime, and reported that she now felt fit enough to join Elinor.

"That's good news," said Buzz. "Wish I could speak to Nell myself, but it takes hours to get through. The Warminster telephone operator makes enough fuss about booking a call to London, let alone New York!"

"I'll give Gran your love," Annabel told her, and dashed off to Bloomingdale's.

That evening, Annabel also used maybe-tomorrow tactics when Elinor telephoned. Considering that mothers have been daughters, Annabel thought as she waited for Scott to finish his broadcast, it's surprisingly easy for a young girl to deceive them.

Early the next day, Annabel returned to Elizabeth Arden's pink gymnasium for a personal head-to-toe reshaping course, during which her exercise expert found body exercises for muscles that Annabel never knew she had. She also had her posture corrected; she was taught to lift her rib cage and "box" her stomach and rear with her hands, as ballet dancers do before dancing, and also to walk as if she were lightly holding a coin between her buttocks.

"I never realized that being beautiful is a full-time business," Annabel told Scott that evening as they sipped martinis in the Plaza bar.

Scott looked at her with bemused surprise: in four days, Annabel seemed to have changed into a taller, paradoxically wilder but sleeker version of herself. She now projected a feline delicacy, a demure but concentrated look, as if deciding whether to pounce.

This air of being totally in command of herself was what Jenny Bates hoped Annabel would project on film; this was the quality that distinguished her from the other models in the Bates stable. It was, Mrs. Bates hoped, the look that matched the female mood of the moment—the look of the approaching sixties.

Mrs. Bates decided that before she was presented to Avanti, Annabel needed to lose her self-consciousness and gain modeling experience before the camera, or she would photograph at only twenty percent of her potential. As she was inspecting Annabel's composite sheet of photographs, a frantic photographer telephoned the agency. A model had been taken ill at his studio and he needed an immediate replacement; the client had specified a blonde.

"Would you try a very promising beginner?" Mrs. Bates asked.

"Send her around fast."

On her first assignment, Annabel was stiff and nervous. She felt like an artist's clay figure: it seemed to take a conscious effort to move her limbs.

"You need to, like, loosen up," said the photographer, who had been suggesting this for thirty years. "Forget everything except the camera. Ignore everyone else in the studio. Look, talk, smile to the camera, as if you were in love with it." He knew he was lucky to save his session, but he also knew that the shots wouldn't be very good. Beginners had a lot to learn.

Beginner models were easy to exploit too, as Scott told Annabel that evening, over fettuccine Alfredo at the Café des Artistes. "Young models are notorious prey for lecherous photographers," he warned, "especially the older ones. Don't be fooled by their masterful act; don't let them mesmerize you with their charisma of authority or their Daddy-will-look-after-you pitch. These guys like to be seen all over town with the face of the moment; they're often domineering and frequently abusive, to keep the girls under their control."

"Then you'd better keep an eye on me," Annabel said.

"I'm going to be guiding you every step of the way," Scott assured her.

"Lucky me," Annabel breathed demurely, batting her eyelashes and ignoring Scott's warning. *She* had never had any trouble with older men. She could twist them around her little finger as easily as she could younger men; what intrigued her about Scott was his refusal to be thus manipulated. He was also refreshingly nonjudgmental, the first man she could talk to as openly as to her sisters, and the two of them laughed a lot. Besides, Scott was even better-looking in real life than he was on a TV screen.

On her way to appointments, Annabel would peer from yellow cabs at the city. Her favorite sight was the silver, spiked top of the Chrysler Building, which might have been built by the Wizard of Oz; that apart, clearly the only bit of Manhattan featured in movies was the relatively small area of glittering glass and steel skyscrapers around Central Park South. Although other parts of the city were endearingly eccentric—apartment buildings were topped by ancient Egyptian temples, Gothic towers, or Moorish arches—most of Manhattan was unglamorous, noisy, crowded, and dirty. But Annabel gazed with excitement at the hectic, nonstop life of the street, where fire sirens wailed constantly and steam mysteriously billowed up from manholes, as if direct from hell. The polyglot mix of nationalities, colors and religions seemed to tolerate any behavior: it was clear that you could do exactly as you pleased in New York City.

After his fifth "house" call, the weasel-sized hotel doctor looked over his spectacles at Annabel and said rather coldly that in spite of her symptoms, he could find nothing medically wrong with her and would inform her grandmother accordingly.

"You'll have difficulty getting in touch with her," Annabel warned. "Gran is in Chicago; then she's going to Los Angeles. All day she gives lectures and autographs books, and then in the evening she has literary dinners; she says she's kept very busy." On her telephone calls to Annabel, Elinor had sounded weary, and her American accent had become more pronounced, as always happened when she was tired.

When Elinor next called, Annabel announced her recovery and said she'd really like to stay in New York. There was so much to do there; the Metropolitan was about to start a series of lectures on the Impressionists, and at tea in the Palm Court, she'd met a nice girl who was studying history at Sarah Lawrence. Couldn't Elinor ask her publisher to introduce Annabel to one or two more nice girls?

After a certain amount of argument, Elinor admitted, "I'm certainly not having much fun—it's all too tiring."

"So you see, Gran, why drag me along?"

"Perhaps it's best that you're in New York. . . . I'm glad you aren't lonely, darling. Incidentally, have you heard from that charming TV interviewer?"

"Had lunch with him yesterday," Annabel said as nonchalantly as possible. "He showed me around the TV station."

"You sound a little feverish," Elinor said anxiously. "Are you *sure* you've recovered?"

"Oh yes," Annabel said. "I've started to go on long walks. Get plenty of exercise. There's a lot to see." Now *shut up*, she told herself. Miranda said that she always knew when Annabel was fibbing, because she said too much, too fast.

In fact, Annabel wasn't seeing as much of Scott as she had hoped. He seemed to work nonstop from ten in the morning until eleven o'clock at night, when the news broadcast ended. During these hours, their meetings were brief, but after the broadcast, Scott took Annabel to dark bars where tinkling pianos played brittle 1930s Gershwin, or to dimly lit, smoke-filled jazz clubs, or to parties given by avant-garde painters in the lofts or converted warehouses of SoHo. Scott seemed to find it amusing that bohemian artists now lived where once the city's vegetables had been stored.

By the beginning of her second week in Manhattan, Annabel had learned to relax in front of the camera. She preferred studio shots to location shots, where there always seemed to be lighting problems and something vital was always forgotten.

To Annabel's surprise, she found that it was very exhausting work to dress and undress all day long. And at the end of the day, when everyone was exhausted, she must not let tiredness show on her face; grimly she learned to dredge up vitality on demand.

Annabel also found it surprising that the models were treated as if they were wooden cigar store Indians, with no brains or feelings; nobody paid the slightest attention to them—they were the meat—until the girl was needed before the camera . . . when she was cooed at, encouraged, and flattered.

By her third week, Annabel's feet ached permanently, but now, immaculately groomed, she felt her self-confidence increase with each assignment and harden with each rejection. No matter how experienced or famous, a model always had to audition for the next job, and if ten girls were interviewed, then nine were rejected. Often this was not because of any lack of beauty but because one was too tall, one was too short, another was in some other way not "right" for what the creative director had in mind. Young models were philosophical about this, but tension and anxiety were visible on the faces of those who were approaching their twenty-fifth birthday; after that day, the skin started to lose its bloom.

Saturday, 10 May 1958

On the day before Elinor was due to return to New York, Annabel was called for her preliminary audition for Avanti.

In a big attic studio on Forty-sixth and Fifth, colored background papers fell from overhead rollers, lights stood in groups, and black cables snaked on the black linoleum floor, a hazard even when you knew they were there. A group of horn-rimmed male executives from the cosmetics firm and BBSQ, the advertising agency, were seated in a corner on dark slab chairs; this part of the room was dimly lit.

The batteries of harsh lights in the studio were focused on a black backdrop, in front of which each model had to walk, stand, turn, and hold her smile.

The door of the models' dressing room opened. "Annabel O'Dare," an assistant's voice called.

Annabel, who had refused a seat in order to avoid crumpling her white piqué dress, stepped out and into a blaze of light.

Late that evening, in a dimly lit nightclub, Scott murmured, "Of course you'll get the job." He eased Annabel's collar away from the back of her neck and blew gently down her dress. She quivered as she felt his warm breath lift the hairs of her spine: she could not have stood up at that moment. A hopeful trance of lust enveloped her body, but Scott made no further move. He guessed that a gaggle of lovelorn young men danced attendance on Annabel, so he had decided not to pounce until a disappointed Annabel was wondering why he hadn't. He knew that she saw other men during the day, but as she had a standing date with Scott at eleven P.M., he also knew that these men were not a serious threat to his intention, which was that Annabel should fall in love with him so thoroughly that *she* would pursue *him*.

Again Scott breathed lightly down the back of her dress.

"Where do you learn these things?" Annabel whispered.

"In the brothels of Hong Kong," Scott breathed.

"I don't believe you."

"It's true. I managed to wangle my way out there for a couple of months, when I was working for the foreign desk in Cleveland."

"You . . . er . . . actually met Chinese prostitutes?" Annabel was both intrigued and repelled.

"I did indeed. I learned a lot."

Annabel longed to know what but didn't like to ask.

In her private sitting room at the Plaza the next day, Elinor stared again at Annabel. Not only did she look completely different—and about ten years older—but she behaved with a new self-assurance. How could her darling have changed so in three weeks?

"What do you *mean* you aren't going back to England with me, Annabel? *Of course* you're leaving with me tomorrow, and I don't want to discuss this again."

"I know you're tired, Gran, but if I don't tell you now, you'll say I've been deceitful. I'm staying in Manhattan."

"*No you are not!* Anyway, you only have a four-week visitor's visa! You'll be *forced* to leave!" Elinor's brain tried to grapple with Annabel's defiance. Had Miranda behaved like this, she would not have been surprised. But Annabel was so gentle and easygoing.

Suddenly Elinor realized. "It's that young man, isn't it? The TV interviewer." She did a double take. "*What did you mean when you said that if you don't tell me now, I'll say you've been deceitful?* Have you been . . . Have you let him . . ." Blushing, Elinor said, "I mean . . . *Have you been to bed with this young man?*"

"No, Gran," said Annabel, truthfully. It had happened not on the bed but on a rug in Scott's apartment.

"Then *why* do you want to stay here?"

"Gran, I have a chance at a big modeling job."

"If you want to be a model, you can be one in London, where you won't be lonely and don't need a permit. I can keep an eye on you in London. Manhattan is no place for a young girl!"

"Gran, Mrs. Bates's lawyer says that there will be no problem about the work permit . . ."

"*Who* is Mrs. Bates, pray?"

"You'd better meet her."

Over lunch, Elinor was slowly reassured. Mrs. Bates was elegant, well-spoken, and well-mannered. Mr. Bates, a Harvard man, projected authority and reliability; he made it clear that he understood and shared Elinor's concern for Annabel's safety.

"We pride ourselves on looking after our models as if they were our daughters," Mr. Bates promised her, "and every one of those girls understands that *her* reputation is *our* reputation."

Elinor looked at Annabel's imploring face, then back to the reassuring bulk of Mr. Bates. "Very well," she said reluctantly. "Annabel can stay for another month, provided she stays in this residential hotel for young women that you recommend."

Tuesday, 13 May 1958

When Elinor returned to Starlings, Buzz—forewarned by telephone—looked at her exhausted, miserable face and said, "No need to look so low—Annabel ain't *dead*. You can call New York any time you please. It only takes an hour or two to get through."

Slowly Elinor removed her coat. "Where are Clare and Miranda?"

"Shopping in Warminster. We wasn't expecting you for another couple of hours. What you need, Nell, is a nice hot bath."

Elinor had a long soak and wondered whether her aching bones were due to old age or that bumpy twelve-hour flight on the Britannia. She then put on her garden coat and gum boots and stumped out for a comforting chat with Mr. Jeffreys, the head gardener, who was planting sweet corn and French beans. After that, she wandered around the garden, hungry to see what had happened in her absence. As she admired the wisteria that fell from the wall above the kitchen, Buzz joined her. They walked in silence, enjoying the weak spring sunshine.

"You can't keep 'em with you forever," Buzz said eventually.

Elinor said sadly, "I never realized until now that, one day, all three of them will leave, with never a backward glance or thought for us."

"It's only natural. You wouldn't want it any other way."

Elinor was not consoled. Of course she wanted her girls to marry and have children, and obviously, in order to do that, they had to leave home. But Annabel hadn't left home with a husband, she had left to get a *job*—although heaven knew why the child should want one.

As they scrunched along the gravel drive back toward the house, Buzz said, "Clare's got another bit of news for you. It ain't exactly bad, but you ain't going to like it. No, it's her business to tell you. I'm just warning you—so you don't get in a temper and say something you'll later regret. Remember that Clare can be as stubborn as you are." Buzz dug in her pocket. "I almost forgot! I've got a letter here that might cheer you up. The rest of your post can wait till tomorrow."

Elinor held out her hand for the opened cream envelope with the O'Dare crest on the flap. Quickly she read the short letter from Marjorie, her sister-in-law. ". . . Since John's death . . . Of course, my daughter-in-law is very capable . . . To be blunt, I feel unwanted here . . . hope you will let bygones be bygones . . . would like to come and stay with you . . . seems such a long time . . . frankly lonely . . ."

Elinor stared at the letter. For years, she had suffered Marjorie's spiteful arrows. Now it looked as if the time had come for retaliation. Perhaps she should invite Marjorie to Starlings to subtly hurl her success in her face. Or write back a barbed letter, reminding Marjorie of the many occasions on which she had been willfully cruel to Elinor.

She reread the letter which in the past would have brought her such reassurance. Now that revenge was within her grasp, Elinor found it worthless, pointless, demeaning.

Slowly she tore the letter into small pieces. "No reply," she said, and tossed the pieces to the breeze.

From her bedroom, Elinor heard Clare's Triumph two-seater slide on the gravel. She heard shrieks of laughter, the barking of the Labradors, the bang of the front door.

Clare, in dark gray sweater and slacks, and seventeen-year-old Miranda, in her lumpy green school uniform, tumbled through the bedroom door and flung themselves upon Elinor.

"Darling Gran, we've missed you so."

After Elinor had presented the girls with gifts (suits and shoulder bags from Bloomingdale's), and had filled them in on the news of Annabel's stab at modeling and her American boyfriend, she said half playfully, "What's this nasty surprise you have for me, Clare?"

Clare was standing in front of the mirror, holding her raspberry linen suit before her. She took a deep breath and said, "I've started to do voluntary work in London."

"But I think that's a very *good* idea. The Red Cross?"

"No," Clare said. "C.N.D. Ban the Bomb. When you thought I was staying with the Bedfords last month, I was actually on the Aldermaston protest march, with twelve thousand other people." Clare looked pleadingly at Elinor. "Oh Gran, if you could have seen all those people—especially the mothers with young children, who don't want them blown to bits. . . . Anyway, while you were away, I agreed to work in their London office."

"And what about your sociology course?" Elinor asked.

"That can wait. This can't. No use having a sociology degree if the world is blown to bits."

Elinor was grateful for Buzz's warning. She had just said goodbye to one granddaughter; she didn't want to drive another one away. Biting back her consternation, she said, "I'm proud of you, Clare. I want to hear *all* about it—and I'd like to help. Now, where have I put my checkbook?"

Saturday, 24 May 1958

Scott's studio apartment on East Eleventh Street seemed simultaneously bare and covered by paper: newspapers, letters, and files were heaped on tables, chairs, and the floor.

The afternoon was an advance warning of the muggy heat of summer, and Scott wore only blue jeans. He leaned back in a big black leather swivel chair, took a sip of white wine, switched on the record player, and said, "Okay, I'm ready."

A sensual rhythm with a steady tempo started.

Annabel slid out of the kitchen, wearing her severe, sophisticated black linen suit from Bergdorf. She looked self-conscious and very embarrassed.

"Not too many clothes with not too many buttons, or I'll go to sleep," Scott warned.

Annabel untwisted her golden chignon and hair fell upon her shoulders. Moving slowly and stiffly to the rhythm of the music, she unzipped her skirt and stepped out of it, which left her wearing a waisted jacket, black French knickers, garter-belt stockings, and four-inch heels with ankle straps.

"Even slower," Scott said, "and look proud. This is a therapeutic exercise to overcome your physical shyness, so that I can turn a light on now and again."

"This jacket has only two buttons and I've still not taken it off. Can't be much slower than that."

"Don't take your shoes off," Scott reminded.

"How can I take my stockings off if I don't take my shoes off?"

As Annabel spoke, the telephone rang. She froze, her eyes fixed upon it.

"Should have left it off the hook," Scott said. "Ignore it."

"Darling, I can't. I gave the agency your number. They said they might know early this evening." Annabel flung herself at the telephone. "Hi! Yes. . . . I *have?* Oh, that's wonderful news!" She turned from the telephone. "*I got it, Scott!*"

"Congratulations," Scott said in a voice that didn't sound very enthusiastic. He knew that from now on, Annabel would be a pampered, glamorous figure constantly in the limelight. By later this evening, she would be the talk of New York, and a clutch of handsome young men on the make would telephone her, send her flowers, and ask her out to dinner.

Annabel whirled around excitedly with her arms in the air. "How shall we celebrate, Scott?"

Scott said firmly, "Let's get married."

Astonished, Annabel stopped dancing. "You really mean it?"

"Let me prove it."

Some time later, Scott's tousled head looked up from the crumpled sheets. He said, "I cannot go to the altar with a lie upon my lips."

"What do you mean?"

"I've never been to Hong Kong."

"You *invented* that sexy rubbish?"

"Not quite. . . . Ow! Ow! My brother works for a toy importer and they sent him to Hong Kong for six months. He came back with these strange stories. Ow!"

CHAPTER 10

Tuesday, 27 May 1958

CLARE, WHO HAD always longed to see how a movie was made, wangled an invitation to the set of *Grain Race* from a quiet, stout young man with black curls, tight as a sheep's. She had met him on the Aldermaston march; Steve, a graphic designer, was working on the titles sequence for the movie, which was based on a nineteenth-century seafaring story.

Clare shivered on Cargill's Wharf, a disused area of the London docks just below Tower Bridge on the river Thames; it was a cold, bright day—more like March than May, Clare thought, wishing she'd worn a scarf. Wearing a Burberry mackintosh over her green tweed suit, she had been introduced as a free-lance journalist and was doing her best to make herself invisible on the set, standing in front of a pile of barrels, well back from the scene, at the rear of the cobbled wharf, where actors in nineteenth-century clothes were waiting to be shot as extras.

During the previous week, the interior scenes had been finished at Pinewood Studios, and now they were shooting the final exterior shots. Some of these were supposedly set in the Port of Liverpool, but the old Liverpool docks were silted up and couldn't be used, so the scenes were being shot at Cargill's Wharf, away from the portion of the dock still in use.

Grain Race was the story of two competing brothers: the elder one was an adventurous buccaneer, the younger a charming, deceptively mild, devious man. After inheriting a three-masted trading schooner, the brothers, with a combination of ruthlessness and good luck, built a shipping empire, from which the younger gradually ousted the elder. Their final confrontation came when each brother, in a different ship of their fleet, competed in a grain race around Cape Horn; they also competed for the wife of the skipper of a third ship.

The actors, wearing seafaring clothes, sat talking with the director, a lean and anguished-looking man who wore expensive jeans. Clare could just hear William Holden, who was playing the elder brother. Justin Watton, a thin, supple man with red-gold hair who was only just getting good parts, played the less important part of the younger brother. Simone Signoret also sat with them; she played the third skipper's wife.

Holden was arguing over the emotions in one scene. "*Anyone* who spots the way Simone looks at me would know she's crazy about me."

Heedless of the cold, Clare watched in fascination as the three actors walked through the scene, rehearsed it twice, and made minor adjustments.

The director opened his mouth to say "Action!" Then he paused. "I want more barrels—a bigger stack. I can see a modern window in that far building. We need to block it out."

A group of assistants moved toward Clare, who was still standing in front of the stacked-up spare barrels. She dodged out of the way, then crept back to her previous position.

The clapper board, now reading "Take 2," was held in front of the camera. The director called "Action!"

Clare screamed.

From behind, a man had pushed her, which sent her flying violently forward. She landed on her face with a strange, heavy body on top of her, pinning her to the ground. Barrels bounced around them, rolling over the cobblestones.

"What the hell do you think you're doing?" the deep voice above Clare roared. "Those barrels weren't properly stacked. If I hadn't pushed this girl out of the way, they would have fallen on her—she might have been injured."

The man scrambled off Clare's back and helped her to her feet. He was built like a bear, with a well-worn, tanned face, merry black eyes, and abundant black hair: his wrists were hairy, and so was the top of his chest, which showed above his unbuttoned collar. He looked carefully at Clare's skinned hands, her dirty face and clothes. "Come to the dressing rooms and we'll call a doctor." His accent was clearly American.

"Oh, don't bother with a doctor. I just need cleaning up."

"Call a doctor!" the man ordered. He wanted to establish that there was no serious injury, in case of a phony insurance claim later. When he smiled at her, Clare noticed he had slightly crooked teeth—obviously because he couldn't be bothered to get them fixed: all the other Americans on the set had expensively perfect, gleaming choppers.

An hour later, Clare was back on the set—but this time she was sitting on a canvas director's chair. The bearlike man—the producer, Sam Shapiro—was sitting beside her. In contrast to the somewhat tense atmosphere on the set, he projected a careless bonhomie that was very appealing. Clare, who decided he must be around forty years old, noticed how he dominated the set, with both his big physical presence and his strong animal vigor.

"Lucky I came along today," Sam said. "I'm not usually on the set during productions."

"Then how do you know what's happening?"

"I see the dailies every evening, when we pick out the best shots."

"Then why were you here today?" Clare asked.

The man shrugged. "Shooting's always a tense time, but especially in the last week, so the director likes a little backup when everyone's exhausted. Tempers explode, tears flow. My role tends to change from producer to diplomat. I keep everybody off each other's throats. It's a tough time for everyone because any extra shots have to be squeezed into the schedule, which drives everyone crazy. In fact, we're doing a couple of scenes here tonight after dark. I have to see a guy for dinner, then I'll be back. D'you feel like dinner?"

"I'm not dressed for dinner."

"Who cares? I promise they won't throw you out."

During the lunch break, when the cast and crew ate in the private room of a nearby pub, Sam Shapiro solved everyone's problems with his cheerful bonhomie. He clearly loved action, excitement, and to be surrounded by people, all working on his project. Clare noticed that he was warm and generous with praise; his laughter was a roar; his ebullient, quicksilver charm was hard to resist. Behind this front of camaraderie, Sam Shapiro was shrewdly persuasive; he marshaled his arguments logically, presented them skillfully, and seemed able to rationalize any situation to suit himself, while persuading everyone else that he was acting for the general good. Clare had never met anyone with such vitality and authority.

In spite of his agreeable persuasiveness, Clare could see that Sam had an explosive temper. When the second male lead complained of a headache and asked if he might have the afternoon off, Sam's tightly controlled patience suddenly evaporated. He thumped the cherry plastic tabletop with his hairy fist and growled, "*No*. I'm not going to pay for your hangovers, Justin." The chilling tone of voice revealed the potential violence behind Sam's affability, which was clearly what helped to preserve discipline on the set.

Clare managed to rush back to Elinor's flat in Chester Terrace, where she dived into her best Belinda Belville black taffeta and telephoned the C.N.D. office to say that she couldn't manage this evening.

Instead, she dined with Sam Shapiro in the crimson plush and gilt splendor of Les Ambassadeurs Club. Clare, who had never been asked out by an older man, and who barely remembered her father, was fascinated by the strength and power that Sam projected. She felt safe and protected. As he entered the restaurant, people sat up and whispered to each other.

Clare sat on the plush banquette next to Sam's other dinner companion—a small, weary-looking, neat-mustached banker, whose business proposals were constantly interrupted by people who came to say hello to Sam Shapiro.

Sam whispered to Clare, "I've known this guy for years; he represents Paramount. I work pretty closely with their business and creative staff—been under contract for the past ten years, on a per-picture basis."

"How many films do you make a year?" Clare asked.

"One picture every two years. That's fairly slow, but I'm a working producer. I tend to get obsessively involved in every detail. It isn't the most productive way to work, but it's the only way for me."

"Are you only in England for this film?"

Sam shook his head. "Last year I moved my base to London. Right now, Europe—especially Italy and England—are the cheapest, most efficient places to make movies."

"Say! Sam Shapiro!" Another beaming dinner jacket thumped Sam on the back and looked down at the empty gilt chair. "May I?"

Paramount's banker sighed, reached across the table, and returned the sheet of figures to Sam. "I think we'd better discuss this some other time." He smiled at Clare, to whom he had hardly spoken. He could see what Sam Shapiro liked about her: the pastel, ladylike look, her evanescent charm—a class act, very different from what was available in L.A.

* * *

As Sam's navy Rolls-Royce stopped at Cargill's Wharf, the director jumped inside. "That bastard Justin's drunk again."

"He clearly had a hell of a hangover at midday," Sam growled. "I thought you'd have had the sense to stick close until we're through with him."

"I'm not his fucking nursemaid, Sam. I've been going over a scene with Bill and Simone—I'd like you to see it, by the way. Next thing, Justin's lying in his dressing room surrounded by empty vodka bottles, dead to the world."

"Has he been stomach-pumped?"

"Of course. The doctor's still with him, but he's not fit to work."

"Get his agent. Check his contract. First thing tomorrow, I want details of the time he's cost us." Sam jumped out of the Rolls and walked fast toward the trailer dressing rooms.

Just before he reached Justin Watton's trailer, the door was flung open: silhouetted against a yellow rectangle of light was the thin figure of the actor. He saw Sam and staggered toward him. "Fucking big shot! Fucking stupid script! Fucking lousy money. Fucking waste of my time."

Sam did not move out of his way. "You're the one who's wasting time, you stupid bastard."

Justin pulled back his right fist and punched at Sam. For a heavy man, Sam dodged nimbly. He grabbed the actor by the collar and called to the director, "For Chrissake, don't let anyone hit him! If his face is marked, it'll cost us more lost time. Get the handcuffs and hose him down until he's fit to work."

"Okay, okay."

"No, wait!" Sam shouted. "I've got a better idea!" With one swift move, he pinned the drunken actor's arms behind his back, then frog-marched him to the edge of the wharf and shoved him into the cold black water.

Then Sam said, "Someone dive in and haul him out. If he drowns, we'll be even more over budget."

By one o'clock in the morning, the scheduled scenes were, miraculously, in the can, and Sam remembered Clare. He walked over to the edge of the set, where she sat, wrapped in a topaz velvet cloak.

"I'm sorry. This wasn't the sort of evening I had in mind, Clare. But we're finished here now, so what would you like to do? Dancing? The Orchid Room? The Four Hundred?"

Clare, who wanted to seem like a sophisticated woman of twenty-six, said, "How about a gambling game?"

"Whatever you want. Where?"

Clare swiftly telephoned the only other older man she knew: Adam agreed to take Clare and her chap to Mike's gambling game, one of the most popular in London. It had been over a year since a court had ruled in favor of a man who had been charged for keeping a common gambling house at a London flat. Since then, the police had turned a blind eye to smart gambling parties, which, it was thought, would shortly be legalized.

Sam, who enjoyed an occasional gamble, took some time to lose a hundred pounds at chemin de fer, at which point he stopped playing. He and Clare wandered to the roulette table.

Adam looked up. "I don't know what's got into this wheel tonight. I've lost a packet. I'd better see Mike."

Mike reluctantly agreed to a further loan. "But watch it, Adam," he warned.

"You're near your credit limit and they won't extend it."

"Rubbish! They know I bring well-heeled punters to their parties. And they're making a fortune from me!" As Adam lost larger sums, the interest on the money he borrowed had been increased to one percent a week.

Mike didn't hide his worried look. "Don't say I didn't warn you."

"I hear you've been to see Dad," Adam said.

Mike followed his train of thought. "Yes, yesterday. But he's not going to kick the bucket yet." The previous month, Joe Grant, now over sixty, had fractured his breastbone when his Mercedes rammed a bus. The fracture was relatively unimportant, but, beneath it, the damage to heart and lungs was serious.

"I'm going home again this weekend. Like to come?" Mike offered. "I'm trying out a new bike." Mike still kept every bike he had ever owned. No longer housed in a potting shed, the elderly bikes were sumptuously stabled in an immaculate garage at the end of Eaton Terrace, alongside Mike's Manx Norton single-cylinder racer; his Norton Inter, with its high-torque overhead cam engine; and the quick but noisy BSA Gold Star, Mike's cross-country bike, used for weekend scrambling with the boys.

"You and your bikes," Adam said, half indulgent, half contemptuous. He was more impressed by Mike's success than he cared to admit. Adam felt astonished, irritated, and humiliated by his younger brother's prosperity and his house in Eaton Terrace. At the age of twenty-eight, Adam still earned a pittance as a lawyer's clerk in a dark and stuffy office, where he was only just being trusted to handle important clients. In contrast, Mike effortlessly earned a fortune, and seemed to live at a permanent luxurious party, surrounded by beautiful people.

"How was Mother when you were home?" Adam changed the subject.

"She hasn't missed one bridge game since Dad's accident," Mike said. "She's reached the Surrey County semifinal."

Sam and Clare approached to say goodnight. After they left, Mike commented, "He seems a bit old for Clare."

"She's unlikely to meet a teenage film producer," Adam said. "Shapiro produced *Windjammer* and *Whaler*."

"Those Humphrey Bogart films?" Mike was intrigued.

Sam was not so intrigued by the two brothers.

Clare was disappointed. "I could see you didn't like them. But why not?" she asked, settling into the soft pigskin comfort of the Rolls.

"Adam seems too terribly, terribly British to be true," Sam said.

Clare laughed. "You mean too handsome!" Men were frequently jealous of Adam's lean good looks, his big dark eyes and almost blue-black hair that still flopped boyishly over his forehead.

Sam shook his head. "Good-looking guys are a dime a dozen in L.A.," he said. "There's something odd about Adam. And his brother. Mike's the type who gets a charge from taking risks." In the shadowy privacy of the limousine, he put his arm firmly around Clare's topaz velvet shoulders.

"No, it's Adam who takes risks. Mike never gambles," Clare said.

"I didn't mean that sort of risk." Gently he tilted Clare's chin up toward his mouth.

Friday, 30 May 1958

"I'd like to come home for tea—just once—and not find the house full of strangers!" Miranda fumed, after the departure of Elinor's last guest.

"I only have tea parties on weekdays."

"Gran, you have tea parties *every* weekday!"

Elinor shut the heavy front door and turned to look at Miranda, who stood, scowling, beneath the portrait of the three sisters painted the year before by Pietro Annigoni. Elinor wished that Miranda more resembled her demure painted likeness.

Elinor turned away from the triple portrait and smiled at Miranda. "Surely I can invite my friends to my own home? Be reasonable. They only come for an hour or two."

"Friends? Publishers, journalists, fans, strangers!" Miranda said crossly. "Sometimes I can't decide whether I'm living in *my* home or *your* publicity center."

"My visitors sell and buy my books, so they help pay for *your* home," Elinor reproved. "And it doesn't take up much time."

Elinor entertained from four o'clock to half past five: this did not interfere with her writing and was a relatively inexpensive way to play hostess to many people every year.

Delighted visitors were met at the station by a chauffeur in a claret-colored uniform at the wheel of her white Rolls. Over tea (served in the old-fashioned way, on a big mahogany table in the dining room), Elinor effortlessly kept in touch with her publishers, most of whom were now accustomed to making this pilgrimage to Wiltshire whenever business took them to Britain. She listened carefully to their opinions because she knew that to achieve the star status of a best-seller writer, it took the right book published by the right publisher, at the right price, at the right time—and the right, expensive promotion: Elinor's contractual conditions had taken years to establish, and now before she signed their contracts, her publishers were requested to outline their promotional plans over the tea table.

Elinor's tea parties also provided her with useful feedback. She particularly liked to check the response of her visitors to the jacket design of her next book. Elinor had spent a lot of time observing bookshop customers, trying to learn what attracted them to a book—and the jacket was crucial.

So, no matter how it bothered Miranda, Elinor couldn't give up her tea parties. Looking at her granddaughter now, she said without conviction, "You *know* you love parties, Miranda. All girls do!"

"Not me!" Miranda shook her head. "You'd like to think that, Gran, but I *hate* your literary tea parties almost as much as I *hate* the smart London ones. As a matter of fact, I *hate* being a deb!"

"How can you say that, you ungrateful child? The Season's only just started!"

"I've had enough of it to know that I'm bored by an endless round of parties at which the same people say the same things."

"Most girls—" Elinor began.

"Would give the eyes out of their head for a chance to be a debutante! I know, I know! But not me!" Miranda preferred to sneak off to the jazz club at 100

Oxford Street, or the socially unacceptable and totally forbidden Hammersmith Palais, where she could dance to rock and roll.

"After all the trouble I've taken . . . " Elinor fumed.

"And all the money you've spent!" Miranda nodded. "I don't want you to waste any *more* time or money on me, Gran."

"You haven't been a debutante long enough to decide whether you like it or not! Once you get to know the people better . . . "

"I'll be yawning more!" Miranda said firmly. "If I asked one of those deb's delights what he thought of Harold Pinter's dialogue, or how much MJQ was influenced by Bach, he'd look at me as if I'd tried to bite him!"

Equally firmly Elinor said, "You've got to learn the social graces, and I don't want to hear another word about it, Miranda! You can't always do as you please."

"I've been doing what pleases *you* for seventeen years!" Miranda retorted. "Why can't I stay in London? Why do *I* have to come down here for weekends? You let *Clare* stay in London by herself."

"Clare has work to do. You're not old enough to stay alone in London without a chaperon, and that's final!"

Glaring, Miranda stormed off to her bedroom. She knew why Clare stayed in London at the weekend, and it wasn't extra work for C.N.D., as Elinor thought: Clare was—at last—in love with an older man who was—what sophistication!—*divorced*. Miranda, of course, could be relied upon to tell nobody, and Clare had decided that, for the time being, it was prudent to keep this a secret. In Britain in 1958, the subject of divorce was for other people's families perhaps but not for one's own, never mind allowing such a person into the family. Clare did not want to risk upsetting her grandmother unnecessarily, should her romance not end in marriage.

Just then Buzz bounced into the hall from the kitchen. "All the guests gone?"

"Did you hear what Miranda said?" Elinor exclaimed. She knew Buzz had been listening.

"A bit of it," Buzz admitted.

"And that girl has had *all* the advantages we never had!"

"She's at the rebellious age," Buzz reminded Elinor. "She's a teenager." The teenager was a recent phenomenon: For the first time in British history, young people were earning good money, so after years spent obeying their parents, they could now do as they pleased. They spent their paychecks on clothes and cosmetics, music and dancing. "Wasting it," their fathers grumbled, but their mothers, who knew what lay ahead for them in life, said, "They're only young once."

Christened "the Youthquake," this new market force had invaded the media, music, fashion, and photography; the boys modeled themselves on James Dean; the girls wore black jeans and sweaters, long shaggy hair, and no makeup except for their Cleopatra eyes.

Buzz knew that, by nature, Miranda did not feel at home in the soft, predictable world of the debutante. With her marmalade ponytail and pale pink lipstick, Miranda, a natural rebel, belonged with the Youthquake.

Elinor gazed up at the triple portrait. "None of those girls have any respect or gratitude! Sometimes I feel as if my heart is broken."

Firmly Buzz said, "Save that overdramatic, sentimental rubbish for your next novel! *The girls are growing up!* You should stop thinking of them as children and treat them as young women. Remember what we was doing at their age—fighting a war! *You've got to let them go*, Nell! Then they'll come back to you.

But if you try to stop 'em, they'll only resent you: then a visit to you will be a duty and they'll only come when they can't put it off any longer."

Elinor glared at Buzz. Eventually she said, "Of course, you're right, as usual. But I *do* remember the tough times we had. I want to protect them from that . . . from danger and poverty, give them all the things that poor Billy tried so hard to provide for Edward . . ."

"Hey, wait a minute, Nell. This is Buzz you're talking to . . . remember? We've been through this before, and I ain't buying it. Usually I'd hold me tongue, but you'd better remember that the real Billy isn't the Prince Charming you talk about at tea parties. It's about time, Nell, that you started to live life as it really is."

CHAPTER 11

Tuesday, 3 June 1958

ON THE TUESDAY following Clare's first meeting with Sam, *Grain Race* finished shooting. Clare attended the wrap party, at which almost everybody quickly became drunk, due to the release of so much nervous tension. The film crew was friendly but cautious and overpolite to Clare: they had known before she did that Sam Shapiro had his eye on her.

After the party, Sam fished a black bow tie from his pocket and took Clare to the Four Hundred. Women in frivolous cocktail hats and taffeta dresses energetically danced the samba under the benign eye and baton of Edmundo Ross. Sam suddenly felt very tired.

"Let's get the hell out of here, Clare," he said. "I want to talk to you."

During the limousine's short journey to Sam's flat in Hill Street, he sat with his eyes shut, his head thrown back. Clare, sensing his weariness, said nothing.

Once, Sam turned his head to look at Clare, pretty in lime taffeta. He patted her hand.

Later, in his comfortably impersonal beige sitting room, Sam put his arm around Clare in a paternal rather than loverlike gesture and said, "There's no nice way of saying this, but I think we should stop seeing each other."

Clare felt as if her stomach had gone into free-fall. "Why? What have I done wrong?" She was hurt, astonished.

"There's only one reason, but it's insurmountable. I'm twenty years older than you."

"That's not a good reason to stop seeing me!" Clare said fiercely. With sudden insight, she realized that Sam's suggestion must mean that his feelings were engaged, that he cared for her, that he preferred *her* to those confident, beautifully groomed actresses who had tonight changed from their drab nineteenth-century outdoor costumes into clinging silks and satins.

Sam looked down at Clare. "I'm too fond of you to hurt you." He had reluctantly decided that she was too young to bed without a lot of postcoital trouble.

Clare twisted away from him. She couldn't think properly—couldn't think at all—with Sam holding her gingerly, the way some uncle might do. She threw herself into one of the elephantine leather armchairs. Sam had practically said that he loved her. There was no reason why he shouldn't have an affair with a much younger girl . . . unless he cared a lot for her . . . enough to marry.

Like a candle, hope lit Clare's small, pale face; she glowed with radiance and sat up. She wanted to rush back into Sam's muscular arms, smell his curly hair, feel his bristly square jaw against her own. But not in the frustrating grab-and-tussle embraces they had shared before.

She said, as seriously as she could, "I think your age is irrelevant. I love you. I want to marry you."

Sam had heard many a veiled proposal—usually from beneath tousled sheets—but never had he had such a direct one. He felt spellbound by Clare's aquamarine eyes. "What will your folks say?"

"I don't care what they say!" Clare rushed into Sam's arms, and he wrapped his hard body around her until she felt that her legs could no longer support her. "*Do it*," Clare said.

Sam picked Clare up and, still kissing her, carried his lime-taffeta bundle toward the bedroom door. Moonlight fell through the ugly steel-framed windows. Without speaking, he laid her upon his bed, and gently slipped her lime satin shoes from her feet, as if even her feet were precious to him. Then slowly he undid the long row of tiny taffeta buttons that reached from her breasts to her knees. He gazed at her body with anticipation and frustration: a white lace, boned corselette stretched impenetrably from bosom to midthigh.

Clare trembled with passion and fear, eyes shut, waiting. She knew that this was *the moment*. She was glad that it was about to happen with someone mature, experienced—not with a fumbling, clumsy youth.

Sam slid off her pale stockings, stroking her thighs, then felt the dark, damp area that lay between them. Smoothly he unhooked her lace corselette, with nimble expertise.

Clare, who neither moved nor spoke, felt eroticism surround her like a cloud. She thought that she would swoon from pleasure. As Sam started to caress her breasts, her excitation built gradually toward its peak. He felt for her hymen with his middle finger, which he gently and slowly inserted into her delicate little body. It hurt her, a bit.

Without speaking, Sam stood up and stripped, fast as a Buster Keaton sequence.

Clare was glad that he hadn't switched on the light, so she didn't have to look. But she felt it, firm against her thighs, before Sam gently pried them apart and slid into her. She felt his body on hers, and smelled his odor; his scent reminded her of a sweaty horse, tired after a good gallop; she loved it. She felt his heavy masculine body ride her. Sam grabbed her buttocks with both hands and pulled them up to meet his thrusts: as the tempo of his drive speeded up, he gasped faster and faster.

Suddenly his body shot forward, then relaxed upon her, as if boneless.

Sometime later, Sam murmured sleepily, "Darling, you were wonderful."

Clare did not dare move. She felt sticky liquid trickle down her inner thighs, then a sticky tongue of flesh fall between them.

Sam shifted his body and lay beside Clare. He put his hand on her breast and whispered, "Happy, baby?" In a moment, he was asleep.

Clare lay rigid in the moonlight. She felt breathless, as if she needed more oxygen in her lungs. There was a turgid ache in her lower back. She wished Sam would wake up and kiss her; she longed to feel again his mouth tugging at her nipples.

An hour later, Clare still lay wide awake. She felt unhappy, disappointed, and resentful—not of Sam but of something. She didn't know what.

Perhaps love was addictive, like caviar; perhaps you had to practice it and get used to it. Clare wished she could talk to Annabel, in case she was doing something wrong.

Two hours later, Clare wriggled away from Sam, moving one limb at a time in order not to awaken him. She groped her way to the bathroom. Closing the door slowly to avoid any noise, she groped around the unfamiliar space until she found a light. She allowed herself only a glimpse of the disheveled person she saw in the mirror, quickly turning on the basin tap to disguise the tinkling sound as she peed. She then washed her hands—something she normally never bothered to do, except in a cloakroom where someone was watching her. Subconsciously Clare hoped that the righteous and justifiable noise of the tap would wake Sam up, but it didn't.

Toward dawn, Clare cried quietly into her hands, then fell asleep.

Shortly after sunrise, Sam woke and again made love to Clare. Afterward, he felt refreshed and vigorous: he whistled in the shower.

At eleven o'clock, breakfast for two was sent up from the restaurant on the ground floor. A subdued Clare ordered only hot milk and toast; Sam ordered a full English breakfast.

As they ate breakfast in the beige satin bed, leaning against the art deco headboard, Clare felt an urgent need to know further details of Sam's divorce. Feeling immodest because she was bare-breasted while eating marmalade and toast, she wondered how to tactfully approach the subject.

He had already told her about his parents, Russian immigrants who had lived in New York and worked on Seventh Avenue: his father had been a tailor, his mother a presser. Sam was their only son.

"I suppose everyone asks how you got into show business?" Clare ventured.

"No. Nobody except you has shown a burning desire to know anything about me. It was through my first wife." Sam poured his second cup of coffee.

"*First* wife!"

"We met when I was on leave." Clare knew he had been a naval supply officer during the war. "I would go to L.A.," Sam said. San Diego was a staid, naval town: the women were in Los Angeles. "After I left the navy, we got married. It was 1945. The only job I could get was in a supermarket. Sheila was assistant to a story editor at MGM. I read for her when she had too many scripts. She said I summarized well: the navy taught me that."

Timidly Clare asked, "When did you break up?"

"We only lived together for a few months. Then she ran off to Toronto with another guy, but found she was three months pregnant by me, after which the other guy ran off. I haven't seen her since she left me. The baby died at birth."

"I'm sorry." But Clare felt relieved. No threat, no passion, no rivalry there. "So how did you become a producer?"

Sam said, "I went to night school to study screenwriting, then took a folder of my MGM summaries to the chief story editor at Paramount. Some months later, there was a vacancy. I was taken on as the story editor's assistant." No need to tell Clare of his passionate affair with Rhona, the chief story editor.

"And then?" Clare prompted.

"In 1948, I gave an NDG assessment to a sea story script called *A Life on the Ocean Wave.*"

"NDG?"

"No Damn Good. After we turned it down, I met the screenwriter." Sam had telephoned him, pitching himself as an independent producer with special naval history expertise: they arranged to meet for dinner at Chasens. Over the meal, he persuaded the writer to agree to a contract that gave Sam exclusive rights to the rewritten script for three years and allowed him fifteen percent of the sale price, should Sam manage to sell it. The writer also agreed to equal billing. He figured, What did he have to lose? The script had been turned down all over town. Even his agent stood to gain if Sam sold the script.

Sam added, "After we'd rewritten the script for costume and called it 'Windjammer,' I persuaded a . . . friend of mine to get her boss to read it. He liked the script and wanted to buy it, but I said I wanted to produce it. The studio refused, but they'd shown the script to Bogart. He liked it, so Paramount eventually agreed to my terms, I agreed to their money, they gave me a good line producer, and *Windjammer* was a success. Then Bogey and I did *Whaler*, and after that, *they* rang *me*. Anything else?"

In a low voice, Clare asked, "Any other wives?"

Sam laughed and planted a kiss on her forehead. "So *that's* what you really wanted to know about. Yes, I've been married twice—a very low average for L.A. Louise and I split up three years ago, after five years together, no kids."

"No more?"

"No, I swear."

Clare said, "I don't know how I'll tell Gran."

"Is there any need to tell her anything yet?"

Grain Race moved into postproduction, which took over three months of barely controlled frenzy as everyone worked against the clock to release the film in time for the Christmas holiday season.

Sam flew to L.A., first to negotiate terms and play dates with release theaters and then to schedule the previews, at which he and the director sat among the audiences to check reaction: by torchlight, they scribbled notes about timing mistakes, any unscheduled mirth, or, worse, comedy that didn't make people laugh.

When Sam was in London, Clare was caught up in the excitement for *Grain Race:* she was whirled into the kaleidoscope of action and drama in which Sam seemed to move. But when he left for Los Angeles, she felt deflated: every morning, she battled against inertia in order to get out of bed. During this period, it dawned on Clare that her passion for Sam was matched by his passion for making movies: more demanding than most careers, producing dominated his life and thoughts. At times, Clare felt a little jealous.

The month before the release date, Sam flew to Los Angeles to plan the publicity campaign and link the trailer, the TV ads, the print and PR campaign. As usual Clare accompanied him to the airport. Seeing her sad little face as yet again she waved him off, Sam turned back and leaned over the barrier.

"Anything to see you smile," he said. "I'll break our news to your grandmother after the British premiere."

Monday, 3 November 1958

Like most men, Sam looked his best in a dinner jacket, so he was at his most charismatic when he arrived at Elinor's Chester Terrace flat to take the O'Dares to the Odeon, Leicester Square. Sam's blue eyes sparkled with anticipation of the movie's success: word of mouth was good, so were bookings, and the advance publicity for *Grain Race* had been a rising wave of adulation.

In her bedroom before leaving for the theater, Elinor slipped a crimson evening wrap over her black lace gown and murmured to Buzz, "Of course, he's too old for Clare, but he's *very* good-looking."

Buzz said, "I can see why Clare might like a mature man. She's never known one." Two hours earlier, Clare had confided in Buzz, who realized that twice-divorced Sam wasn't the dashing young earl for whom Elinor had hoped. Buzz had promised to soften up her old friend, but there was undoubtedly going to be a big row—because Clare was almost as stubborn as Elinor.

After the premiere, Sam was greeted by applause from the theater supper crowd as he and his large party entered the Ivy. Now he could relax. He would wait up all night to read the reviews in the morning papers, but the tense silence during *Grain Race* and the loud clapping at the end had foretold a hit.

Two hours later, Sam insisted on interrupting his party to escort Elinor and Buzz back to Chester Terrace; there he spoke alone to Elinor and told her that Clare and he were to be married.

Elinor was speechless, even though Buzz had warned her ahead of time—dating him was one thing, but marrying him quite another. "But you're too . . . But *Clare's far too young!*" she gasped.

"Clare doesn't think so," Sam said gently. "She'll be twenty soon. How old were you when you married?"

"That's got nothing to do with it," Elinor said, a hundred questions whirling through her mind. "I suppose you *can* look after Clare . . . financially?"

"Very well," Sam promised cheerfully. He was established and respected in a way that few young men could match.

"It's too late tonight for me to think clearly," Elinor said, suddenly feeling exhausted. "I'll talk to Clare in the morning."

Five minutes later, she shook Buzz awake. "You can't imagine what that man's just told me!"

Buzz mumbled, "He wants to marry Clare."

"So she told *you!*"

"Yes, because she was frightened to tell you. Don't worry too much, Elinor. We'll talk about it in the morning."

Elinor shook Buzz again. "I won't sleep a wink! I *must* talk about it now. It's so unexpected! What does she *know* about this man? Where are his family? What is she walking into?"

Buzz sat up. "I seem to remember that *I* said that to you before you married Billy. And did you take any notice? *No!* Clare's just as stubborn as you are, so you'd better not ask those questions if you don't want to see them marry. Because he's a real charmer."

"Yes," Elinor said, "but what does *he* see in Clare? She's not the glamorous type, not sophisticated. Sam clearly isn't interested in improving the world for a future generation; he isn't the bookish type, like Clare. I can't help wondering how long it will last. These Hollywood types seem to get married again and again. I don't want that for Clare."

Firmly Buzz said, "Why not try looking on the bright side, and just be glad that Clare is happy? If you object, you'll lose her even faster."

The following morning, Elinor knocked on Clare's door. As there was no reply, she entered, and saw that the bed had not been slept in.

Just before lunch, white-faced from lack of sleep, Clare quietly pushed open the front door and started to tiptoe across the hall.

"Is that you, darling?" Elinor called from her study. "Would you come here, Clare?"

Clare blushed as she entered the room; she still wore the hyacinth chiffon gown, now very crumpled, that she had worn the previous evening.

"Sit down, darling." Elinor cheerfully patted the place beside her on the sofa. "I want to tell you how much I like Sam: such drive, such force, such self-assurance and authority. I'm so glad you've chosen someone older who clearly knows his way around the world and can protect you from it."

Clare's eyes shone with astonishment and pleasure. "I'm so glad you can see why I think he's wonderful! I feel so . . . safe and happy when I'm with him."

"I hope and pray that you always will, darling. Now run along and change."

Saturday, 28 February 1959

"It's beautiful," sighed Miranda. She wore dead-white makeup, ghostly pearlized lips, black-outlined eyes; her orange hair was plaited into a coronet.

"I wish *I'd* had a proper wedding gown!" Annabel cried, having forgone a formal marriage ceremony in her rush to marry Scott.

In Clare's bedroom at the Chester Terrace apartment, the two sisters gazed at the bride: she wore a high-collared, tight-waisted, full-skirted, calf-length dress of cream satin by Norman Hartnell; her hair was dressed in a Grecian knot, cross-bound with cream satin ribbon.

"I feel wobbly," said Clare. "I think I'm going to cry . . . "

"Not on your wedding day!" Annabel pleaded. Although Clare looked lovely, she was almost outshone by Annabel, who wore a crimson silk suit and an air of triumph. Avanti's campaign "Do you dare to wear Avanti?" had not been as successful as Revlon's Fire and Ice campaign, but it had been successful enough to shoot Annabel into the headlines. American women had been surprised that an English girl (traditionally mouseburger material) should project such sensuality. Annabel seemed to epitomize the surprising emergence of London, as that once stodgy city metamorphosed into the fashion leader of pop culture.

Miranda looked at her sisters and gave a mock scowl. "How do you suppose *I* feel? You've both gone and left me without a backward look! Off you dash with your glamorous husbands—I'm the one who should be crying!"

Nevertheless, it was tough to look forlorn in the pale pink satin-bound tweed coat dress by Sybil Connolly.

"Nobody's going to cry," Annabel said firmly. "We're still sisters, and when we meet, we'll still feel the same way and do the same things."

"What sort of things?" Clare's voice wobbled.

"Everything from a night at the opera to toe-in-mouth competitions," Annabel said cheerfully.

Miranda jeered. "You two old married ladies couldn't get your toes in your mouths now."

"Bet I can," said Annabel, sitting on the carpet. "Bet you two *can't*," she added as she pulled off her crimson slippers.

Miranda immediately kicked off her shoes, sat on the floor, grabbed her big toe, and guided it toward her mouth, but couldn't get it closer than six inches from her lips. She giggled. "I'm a bit stiff."

Clare started to laugh. "You both look idiotic!" Removing one slipper and carefully smoothing her dress beneath her, Clare sat on the carpet and took hold of her big toe.

"I've nearly done it!" Miranda gasped.

Annabel mumbled, "*I've done it!*"

As he opened the bedroom door, Sam said, "Honey, I know I'm not supposed to see you yet, but is there any chance of a Bloody Mary? . . . What the *hell* is going on in here?"

The three sisters collapsed on the floor, shrieking with laughter.

Before the reception at Claridge's, the small wedding group posed on the steps of Caxton Hall Registry office for photographers. Besides being twice divorced, Sam was Jewish and thus not eligible for an Anglican church wedding. The photographers were unable to persuade Clare to smile; having been very disappointed by the brisk civil ceremony, which had about as much romance as a buff envelope, she now felt even more wobbly and close to tears.

Saturday, 23 May 1959

"She won't allow me to do anything that's fun!" Miranda complained to Buzz.

"If you mean flying lessons," Buzz said, "you'll never convince her that it ain't dangerous. She'll never allow it."

"I'm sick, sick, sick of being treated like a baby! I'm more likely to hurt myself skiing than flying."

"You ain't likely to *kill* yourself skiing."

"Other grandmothers don't *hover* like she does!"

Elinor, severely depressed by the suddenness with which she had been deprived of Annabel and then Clare, now lavished affection on Miranda, to whom it was a claustrophobic burden.

"I feel guilty if I'm not with her," Miranda added, "and guilty when I am—because I long to get away. She doesn't really like the sort of things I like, she only pretends. I can tell because she gets the names wrong—Pelvis the Elvis and Buddy Holiday indeed!"

They sat in Miranda's bedroom at Starlings listening to the thumping rhythm pumped out by Miranda's new stereophonic speakers, surrounded by wall posters of rock heroes (Buddy Holly swathed in black net) and the better-looking revolutionary leaders.

Hopefully Miranda asked, "Do you think Gran might ever get married again? That would take her mind off me!"

Buzz shook her head. "She falls in love with her heroes, and they ruin ordinary men for her."

"I don't mean *that* sort of love!" Miranda said, confident that passion could not be felt by those over thirty.. "I mean . . . companionship."

"A husband likes a lot of attention," Buzz said. "And when would Nell find time for that? She's writing in the morning, and still has her head in the clouds when she gardens in the afternoon. Then there are the tea parties, and if she ain't going out in the evening, she's doing research in the library or going to bed early with a pile of galleys. That's the life she likes, and what husband would put up with it?"

"Another writer?"

"He'd expect to be pampered. And what man would put up with the fuss Nell makes over you and your sisters? Annabel lifts her little finger and your Gran pops across the Atlantic to visit, pretending she's off to see her American publisher. And since Clare got back from the West Indies, Nell drives to London every week to help her buy things for that little house. If she had a husband, your Gran wouldn't be able to drop everything when you three call her. Men are used to ruling the roost. Nell would never knuckle under again."

In a wheedling voice, Miranda said, " Then, Buzz, darling Buzz, will you help me do something? *Just* this once?"

Buzz knew that this always meant, "Will you gently break my news to Gran, and be on my side?"

"What is it this time, Miranda?"

"I want to be trained as a beautician," Miranda said excitedly. "It's a one-year course in London, and it starts next month. I've already put my name down, but now they want a deposit. I thought of flogging my pearls, but what's the point? I'll have to tell her sometime."

"You mean a *manicurist*, a massoower? She ain't going to like that one bit—she likes to think of her girls being on the receiving end of all that!"

"I suppose I'll have that lady rubbish flung at me again." Miranda bit her lower lip. "I've told her I hate those parties."

"You met that nice Angus at a deb dance," Buzz reminded. "*And* he's on the List." The List was prepared by an aging, sycophantic gossip columnist and circulated among ambitious mothers with eligible daughters: it listed young men whose birth, wealth, and position made them suitable escorts or husbands.

Miranda blushed; then, from beneath heavily mascaraed eyelashes, a lopsided smile slowly spread across her face. She said, "Angus would *never* waste his time at deb dances, but he had to turn up at that one: it was his sister's coming-out ball."

She had met him shortly after Clare's wedding. Miranda, who longed to leave the overheated ballroom, had refused another dance, yawned, looked at her wristwatch, and reckoned she could leave in half an hour. *If* she stayed awake that long! She had opened the French windows and slipped onto the terrace for a little fresh air.

After the smoky fug of the ballroom, the dark night was quiet, crisp, and refreshingly cold. Before her, Miranda could dimly see the brown lace outline of the huge chestnut trees lining Rotten Row. From behind her came a scent that reminded her of Lifebuoy soap and flannel pajamas.

Miranda turned sharply. "Who are you?"

"I'm Fiona's brother, Angus."

As Miranda's eyes adjusted to the dark, she saw a large man in a dinner jacket leaning against the wall, in the shadows, smoking a cigar. He said, "I was about to leave. Got to get to work in the morning. Here, take my jacket or you'll die of pneumonia before I get a chance to know you." His laconic speech sounded like a paratroop commander sending his troops into battle.

When they went back to the ballroom, Miranda turned to look at Angus Maclayne; he returned her glance with an ice-blue stare from a face that appeared to have been rough-hewn from rock, although his hair was Viking gold and his mustache was ginger.

As soon as Fiona had recovered from her hangover, Miranda hauled her out to lunch. She discovered that Angus had been the Captain of Boats and had ended his school career as the Captain of the Oppidans. He had also edited the Eton College *Chronicle*; at Oxford, where he had been a rowing blue, he read politics, philosophy, and economics, after which he worked for two years in New York as a trainee banker. Angus had then gone to Paris for a year, as a trader on the Credit Suisse foreign exchange desk, after which he spent a year in Hong Kong, and then a further year in New York before returning to London, where he worked for Chase Manhattan. He liked salmon fishing and playing poker, and it was difficult to make him lose his temper.

"Honestly, there's nothing else to tell you," Fiona said when pressed for further information. "Nobody knows much about their own brothers. Angus is . . . all right. If you want to know him better, why not come up to Scotland for a weekend at Easter?"

"Thanks, but I can't manage it at the moment," said Miranda; she didn't want Fiona to think she was that keen on her brother; Miranda preferred to wait until the invitation came from Angus.

Angus now frequently took Miranda to an evening at the cinema or theater, after which they ate at Wiltons, Rules, or other London hotels that provided (at great expense) the food of Angus's youth: sausages and mashed potatoes, toad-in-the-hole, milk puddings, steamed puddings, treacle pudding, or jam roll.

In case something drastic happened to the dollar, Angus could never be far from a telephone until late evening, which was late-afternoon closing time for the American market. He never took Miranda to a nightclub because he was always at his desk by seven in the morning, for the Hong Kong closing prices.

Unlike other fledgling bankers Miranda knew, Angus wasn't stuffy and didn't shoot his shirt cuffs or keep tightening the knot of his tie. Although his suits fitted well around the shoulders, not even the best Savile Row tailor could produce a suit for Angus that didn't look as if it had been made for somebody else: his craggy Scots frame looked ill at ease in anything other than a heavy jersey and kilt, or baggy trousers tucked into Wellington boots.

Because Angus was unexpectedly posted back to New York for nine months, Miranda had to wait over a year for her invitation to Scotland. As she had been forbidden by Elinor to go to New York ("Look what happened to Annabel!"), Miranda ran up enormous telephone bills, finished her beauty course, and (edged in by a friend of Elinor's) started work behind Elizabeth Arden's crimson-doored salon in Bond Street as a trainee beautician.

Saturday, 6 August 1960

Just before the shooting season started, Miranda took the overnight train to Inverness to join Angus, on holiday with his family at Maclayne. The sleeping-car attendant locked her into a single compartment, which contained a let-down bed and a piece of linen called a drugget, upon which to stand while she undressed. She had difficulty in locating the sanitary arrangements, but eventually discovered a cracked white chamber pot concealed in a cupboard beneath the washbasin.

Maclayne Castle was a large, ugly, late-nineteenth-century building with fairy-tale turrets. Along its long, dark corridors dashed what seemed like many children in well-darned blue jerseys and tartan kilts; these clothes were also worn by the adults of the family and all their friends. Even in August, howling winds blew along the corridors, the longest of which was from kitchen to dining room: this had been deliberately planned, in order to prevent the odor of food from permeating the place. Unfortunately, it meant the meals were always lukewarm when served.

The castle walls were hung indiscriminately with paintings: on one side of a Lawrence portrait was a watercolor of Venice done by some Maclayne great-aunt, while on the other side hung photographs of long-dead hunting dogs. Also suspended upon the walls were many ancient relics of the British empire: assegais from Boer War campaigns, ceremonial flyswatters from the Sudan, moth-eaten stuffed heads of dead animals, and the occasional oar, lettered to indicate in which university boat race it had been pulled.

Miranda decided that the castle sanitary arrangements were little better than those provided by the railway: raised bathtubs with ineradicable greenish-brown marks on their enamel, caused by years of leaking taps; lavatories, encased in mahogany boxes, operated by stiff hanging chains.

When Angus was not out shooting or fishing, he took Miranda sightseeing, either in an estate car with a wired rear compartment to keep the dogs from licking his ears, or in an arthritic Daimler, the back seats of which were flecked by straw and smelled of chickens. Angus would stop this car at the base of some heather-clad craig, and he and Miranda would scramble to the top of it, to gaze over other heather-covered hills, all the color of Angus's ginger tweed jacket.

At the knobbly summit of one of these hills, as the sun was setting in a particularly lurid salmon-pink sky, Angus took the hand of a breathless and puffing Miranda and asked her to marry him. Miranda, who had been hoping for this for months, was taken by surprise.

After she had puffed her acceptance, Angus briskly burrowed beneath the heather and pulled out a ginger wicker basket; this contained a tartan rug, a thermos flask of ice, a bottle of Veuve Clicquot, and two glasses.

At Miranda's look of astonishment, he grinned and said, "Never accuse me of being unromantic. I heaved this up here before breakfast."

That night, Angus crept along a long, dark corridor to Miranda's room, and was allowed to enter.

* * *

Elinor, depressed at losing Miranda but delighted to lose her to the brother of an earl, was determined that one of the O'Dare girls should have a traditional white wedding; it was planned for Monday, 3 April 1961, at St. Margaret's, Westminster, the reception afterward to be held at the Savoy Hotel.

After her beauty classes, Miranda often drove her new purple, custom-painted Mini to Clare's smart little terrace house in Poulton Square. The visits continued even after she had started to work, and here in Chelsea, as autumn leaves drifted from the trees in the square, the sisters pondered over Miranda's many lists. There were lists of guests, of hoped-for presents, of seemingly endless suppliers of seemingly essential nuptial purchases: all details of these purchases were of vital importance, from the correct source of invitation envelopes (Smythsons of Bond Street) to the specific red-coated major domo who would announce the guests (Mr. Pecksniff).

Monday, 14 November 1960

"Why do I need fish forks? Why does *anyone?*" Miranda asked. Clare's pert, careless, nineteen-year-old French au pair (only two years younger than her mistress) was serving them tea from an elaborate silver tray before the fire in the drawing room.

Clare, no longer a bride but a housewife, checked that everything necessary was on the tray: tea, cake, plum jam from Starlings, and a pile of muffins to toast. Both sisters had kicked off their uncomfortable stiletto-heeled, sharp-pointed shoes. Clare wore a primrose linen suit with a short, tight skirt, Miranda a spinach-green tweed tube with an enormous black knitted collar.

"Fortnum's chocolate Sacher torte!" Miranda cried. "When I'm married, I shall have it every day!"

Clare laughed and said, "Please put towels in the pink spare bedroom, Marie-France. My sister is staying the night." Sam was away, on business.

At two o'clock in the morning, Clare was shaken awake. Alarmed, she quickly sat up and saw Miranda's face, weakly spotlit by a silver shaft of moonlight that fell over the dark trees of the square.

"Listen, Clare," Miranda whispered, "I *must* talk to you. At teatime, I was too . . . Hell, I was embarrassed." She climbed on the bottom of Clare's bed, where she sat cross-legged, her face again in the shadow.

Clare rubbed her knuckles into her eyes and reached for the bedside light. "Can't it wait until morning?"

"Don't turn the light on," Miranda urged. "It's easier to talk in the dark. I can't . . . I've never been able to talk to anyone but you and Frog about sex, and I can't discuss it over the telephone, with New York operators listening . . . "

"What's wrong, Miranda?"

"Do you know about *Lady Chatterley's Lover*?"

"Of course, everyone does," Clare said, puzzled. A few weeks before, Penguin Books had been acquitted of a charge of obscenity for publishing this book after the Public Prosecutor had asked the jury, "Is this a book you would wish your wife or servants to read?" The question had become a public joke.

"When Angus and I are in bed together," Miranda went on, "it doesn't feel for me like it did for Lady Chatterley. No peaks of ecstasy."

Silvered by moonlight, Clare pulled her knees up and clasped them. "Me neither, as a matter of fact."

Both sisters were silent, until Miranda said, "I can't understand why I find it so difficult to talk to you about sex now, when at school we used to discuss nothing else."

Clare pushed her hair behind her ears and said sadly, "Do you remember how we all used to wonder what a good lover does? And how one could be better than the other?"

Miranda nodded.

"Well, I *still* don't know," Clare said. "Sam seems to think that being a good lover is doing it in a hundred acrobatic positions. Sometimes I feel I'm back in the school gym."

"Angus seems to think it means banging away until I'm sore and exhausted and sort of embarrassed for him because I know it won't work. He doesn't seem to notice that I have a problem—since he's clearly satisfied, I expect he thinks I am, too."

"Sam says I'm frigid . . . although it often feels as if something is *about* to happen to me, but then at the last moment—it doesn't."

"I know the feeling."

Hesitantly Clare added, "Before we married, Sam said it was probably because I was afraid I'd get pregnant. He said I'd relax after we married, and then everything would be okay."

"But it wasn't?"

"No. Now after we've made love, I get back pains that last for hours, and I can't get to sleep because I feel so churned up I want to cry."

"I want to shake Angus awake and kick him *hard*."

After another long silence, Clare said, "Who would have thought it would be so disappointing? I never expected to feel frustrated; I expected to feel a oneness with Sam that I'd never experienced before, as if we both floated on the same warm cloud. I expected ecstasy."

"That's what Gran's heroines always get," Miranda replied mournfully. "Endless bliss in his strong arms. How did Gran manage to convey the idea that a virile, masterful lover was the ideal lover—without describing what he did?"

"By endlessly repeating that he was virile and masterful, as if that was all that mattered," Clare said tartly.

"But where did she pick up that idea? I wouldn't describe Daddy Billy that way." Miranda looked thoughtful. "In fact, I can't imagine them ever doing it!"

"Those two certainly had *something* going," Clare said. "You could sense the electricity, even when Daddy Billy was quite old."

"Perfect lust and mutual climaxes like Lady Chatterley and her gamekeeper?"

"D'you suppose that's really possible?" Clare asked.

"I've no idea," Miranda said, "What *is* good sex supposed to be like?"

"I suspect that D. H. Lawrence's sex was as idealized, in a masculine way, as Gran's romantic, no-knickers-off sex in her silly novels."

"So how can we learn what we're missing?"

"I don't know," Clare said helplessly. "I thought of talking to Annabel about it: she *said* she doesn't have a problem."

"Lucky bitch!"

After a few minutes, Clare said gloomily, "I must be doing *something* wrong."

Miranda retorted crossly, "You're taking the blame, as usual: that's the difference between you and me. I think that *Angus* is doing something wrong. Or perhaps . . . perhaps Angus is the wrong man for me. Perhaps I'm too small for him." She sighed. "If I didn't love Angus so much . . . But I'm not sure I'll be able to live like this forever . . . On the other hand, perhaps we just need more practice . . . perhaps things will improve."

"They didn't for me," Clare said morosely.

Miranda looked worried and depressed. The room darkened again as the moon disappeared behind a cloud.

Thursday, 17 November 1960

In the dimly lit living room of his chambers in Albany, Angus crumpled up another sheet of paper and hurled it into the cozy glow of the fire. At least Miranda hadn't sent him a letter to tell him. Yesterday she had told him, face-to-face, in this very room—not that this had helped Angus to understand her reasons for calling off their wedding.

Miranda had dodged the issue; she said she thought that, at nineteen, she was too young to marry, she wanted to see a bit of life before settling down, she hoped to have her own business one day and she'd never get around to it if she was married. She swore there wasn't another man, which was the first thing that had occurred to Angus.

Too young? Angus pointed out that Miranda's mother had already given birth to two children by the time she was nineteen.

Miranda burst into tears.

Okay, so he was tactless, but Angus had merely meant to point out that life might be short, and it was crazy to put happiness on hold if it wasn't necessary.

After she stopped crying, he had pointed out that, as the wife of an international banker, Miranda could expect to travel a lot and so see plenty of life *after* settling down; he added that he was happy to set her up in a little business, should she want some distraction from domestic life.

Miranda had abruptly stopped looking evasive and apologetic; instead, Vesuvian rage erupted as she repeatedly accused him of masculine complacence. After she stamped out, banging the mahogany door behind her, Angus immediately telephoned Elinor, who already knew.

"Perhaps the best course of action would be to ignore her for a few days," Elinor suggested. "Give her a little time to calm down; the poor darling is clearly experiencing wedding nerves *well* in advance of the ceremony, instead of the night before it."

"What was odd," Angus said, "was that Miranda wouldn't say that she didn't love me. I kept asking her, but I couldn't pin her down." He added sadly, "But neither would she say she loved me."

"Do you love *her*, Angus?" Elinor asked. She seemed a trifle nervous.

"Good Lord, *yes!* I've never before asked anybody to marry me. Of *course* I love Miranda!"

He agreed with Elinor that the best plan was to keep calm, do nothing, and give Miranda a chance. She was certain to reconsider her hasty action.

However, the following morning, Angus opened the *Times* to read that the wedding of the Hon. Angus Maclayne to Miss Miranda Patricia O'Dare would not take place. Only Miranda could have inserted the announcement.

After the sixth call of commiseration, Angus angrily took his telephone off the hook.

Now he started another letter to Miranda, but again threw it in the dying embers of the fire. He could not put what he felt into words. His instinct told him that he hadn't heard all of Miranda's story; he felt also he would have a better chance of getting what he wanted if he kept quiet, refused to discuss the matter, and let everyone think it was over between them. Angus was determined to marry Miranda.

CHAPTER 12

Tuesday, 20 December 1960

THE WEEK BEFORE Christmas, Adam drove to Starlings in a maroon Rolls-Royce Phantom V: this Christmas present to himself had just cost him nearly nine thousand pounds. He whistled cheerfully as he turned off the main road down the bumpy country lane that led to Elinor's home.

On a winning streak, Adam had recently paid off all his debts. Strangely, this did not bring him relief but a feeling of unease. He worried that if he wasn't using all his available credit, then he wasn't deploying all his available assets. And if he didn't use all his assets, he would never be able to afford a house like Mike's in Eaton Terrace. And Adam was determined that when he could afford it, he would purchase an even grander house than his brother's: a reassuring facade was just as important to his business as it was to a bank.

If he didn't make the money by gambling, he might well do so from insurance, for Adam had just become an external member of two insurance syndicates at Lloyds of London. Each big risk at Lloyds was generally shared among a number of syndicates, in order to reduce any individual loss. It was a pity that Adam could afford to belong to only two, because the risk would have been better spread had he belonged to, say, twenty of the four hundred syndicates.

Each syndicate member of Lloyds had to meet the necessary financial requirements, which included showing assets of £75,000, part of which had to be kept in interest-bearing deposit at Lloyds. Although Adam did not possess £75,000, he had enough cash to lodge the deposit, and he had been able to borrow the remainder, temporarily, in order to pull the wool over the eyes of the council of Lloyds, which regulated the business ethics and standards of its market and everyone in it.

Beside Adam, on the seat of the maroon Rolls, lay his briefcase containing a Lloyds prospectus and also a list of Elinor's investments, together with their total current worth and reasoned suggestions as to which should be sold. The briefcase also contained several contracts that required Elinor's signature. After his father's death the previous January, Adam had checked years of back correspondence to familiarize himself with Elinor's business affairs, and now she gratefully turned to him to advise her on all decisions; in fact, Adam had almost reached the point where he would describe himself as her business manager as well as her lawyer.

As the butler took Adam's coat, they both heard angry voices coming from behind the door of Elinor's study.

"Perhaps you would care to wait in the drawing room, sir?" said the butler, serene as a Buddha. "Shall I bring you sherry or tea, sir?"

"No, I'll wait here in the hall. Whiskey and soda, please." Adam sat on a sofa, vexed that Miranda clearly hadn't informed Elinor on the day before his appointment, as he'd asked her to do.

As he sipped his drink, he could clearly hear what was being said next door.

In the oak-paneled study, Elinor, in electric blue, faced a scowling Miranda.

"I don't understand what's gotten into you this year," stormed Elinor. "First, you broke your engagement . . ."

"Angus and I would never have lasted," Miranda said firmly, not liking to acknowledge to herself that she still missed their comfortable intimacy. "He'll be much happier with a traditional Kensington deb. He's the only twenty-nine-year-old man I know who wants to get married and settle down."

"That's not something to hold against him!" Elinor said vehemently. "Then you badgered me for dangerous flying lessons—and now you want to open a shop! My granddaughter is *not* going to be a shop-girl!" Biting her lip to stop tears of anger and disappointment, Elinor turned away from Miranda and looked out past the garden, now having its winter rest; the two flame-shaped holly trees on either side of the gate to the orchard never failed to provide red berries for Christmas.

"And you know *nothing* about commerce!" Elinor added.

"Neither did you when you started work." Miranda, in a purple jumpsuit, stood her ground, arms akimbo, before the slowly burning applewood fire.

"You would be fighting against huge competition. Arden, Rubenstein, Revlon . . ."

"Gran, I work at Elizabeth Arden. I know what kind of fortune a woman spends on her face once she walks through that red door."

"Exactly! You wouldn't stand a chance!" Elinor turned, triumphant, to face Miranda.

"*Yes I would!* Because Arden isn't interested in someone with only a few shillings to spend! *But I am!* Think of the millions of Youthquake girls who can only buy old-fashioned, masklike, heavy makeup in middle-aged colors. . . . Sure, they can go to Woolworth's—but is Woolworth's trendy?"

"*You* know how much money the big firms spend on development. Miranda, if there were a gap in the market, as you claim, they would have spotted it!"

"There *is* a gap!" Miranda insisted. "And they aren't interested in spotting it. That sort of firm simply doesn't understand what young girls want, and they don't understand what a lot of money these girls can collectively spend." Her voice rose in exasperation. "I want to sell to the other girls I see dancing at Humph's—we're forced to paint our faces from a child's paint box. Ask Annabel about it. She knows I'm right."

From Annabel, Miranda had learned the makeup techniques used by American models. Annabel had ransacked Concorde, the dimly lit chemist on Madison Avenue that seemed to contain every cosmetic in the world, to send samples to her sister.

"*Why* must you be so difficult, Miranda?"

"*Why* must you be so unhelpful? Didn't anyone help *you* get started when you were young?"

"No!"

"All the more reason why you should help me," Miranda retorted.

"I'm not going to throw thousands of pounds away on a risky, foolish venture that has little chance of success . . . "

"Although you were willing to spend thousands of pounds on my wedding, which I think had *no* chance of success."

"Let's not harp back to *that* again! That poor young man!"

Miranda changed her tactics. She jumped to the fire, took up the poker, and prodded the smoldering wood until it flared. Then she lowered her voice and spoke winningly. "Gran, I can *prove* that you wouldn't be throwing money away—if only you'd pay for a bit of research. Cosmetic profit margins are huge! Sixty percent of the retail price goes to the manufacturer, and only *eight percent* of that is spent on raw materials."

"I don't want to hear any more of this nonsense! It costs *millions* to launch a cosmetics company—"

"Rubbish!" Miranda leapt to the sofa table, thumbed through a copy of *Vogue*, and stabbed her finger at it. "There! You only have to look at the small ads in the glossies to see that there are plenty of small companies—but those ads have no style. *I have!*"

"You're too young, Miranda, and that's final!"

"Annabel says there's a girl in New Jersey—Adrien Arpel—who started in 1959, when she was only eighteen. Her *father* gave her four hundred dollars to start, and now she's thriving! What would *my* father want you to do?"

Elinor had been halted.

After a few moments, she said in a quieter voice, "As a matter of fact, my mind is not as closed as you think, Miranda. I spoke to my stockbroker. He said that getting a line of cosmetic products into the stores against the competition of the big companies is *almost impossible*."

"A fat lot that bald old Billy Bunter knows about it! There's still room for starting up in your own salon!" Miranda cried. "And what does *he* know about the sort of lipsticks girls want? Look at my face!"

Elinor looked, and managed not to shudder.

"You can't get *any* of these colors in London," Miranda rushed on. "And Annabel says you can't get them in New York either! To get a light, shiny pink lipstick, I have to use theatrical whitener under light pink Caran d'Ache crayons, then top it with Vaseline. *I want to do it all with one product!* And I'm sure there are *plenty* of girls like me! And I can sell to them from my own little shops, instead of going the expensive route in the big stores: I'm *never* going to waste time flattering the buyers, or jostling for cover space, or waiting months for late payment that'll upset my cash flow!" Miranda continued, seeming not to pause for breath. "Oh Gran, won't you even let me have a market survey done—to prove what I say? Annie Trehearne says—"

"Your new friend, Miss Trehearne, is a fashion editor, not a fortune-teller!"

Ebullient, blond Annie Trehearne was known for her outrageous ideas and her uncannily accurate fashion predictions.

"Exactly! She's fashion editor of *Queen*. Her business is spotting trends. *That's* why she understands what I want to do! *She* can see the gap! The young want something different, and Annie senses that!"

"A pity you didn't just quietly paint her nails. Do you tell *all* your customers of your hare-brained schemes?"

"Gran darling, Annie *specializes* in hare-brained schemes! Come off it—you know you like her, really." Miranda added, "And Annie's wheedled an advertising agency into doing a cut-price market survey. She told them she wants it for a story, and she's offered to splash me when I launch. And Adam has got a financial projection."

"How *dare* you go behind my back to my lawyer!"

"Gran, I've known Adam since I was a little girl," Miranda pleaded. "He's *my* friend as well as *your* lawyer. And he didn't have to pay for the financial projection. The merchant bank prepared it."

"*What merchant bank?*"

Miranda moved to the mantelpiece, picked up a little globe, and started to spin it as she spoke. "When I go into business, Gran, I'm going to need a merchant bank, aren't I? Won't you *please* look at Adam's figures? . . . I have them here."

Elinor looked less sure of herself. "Why didn't you say that you had consulted Adam? If Adam thinks there's a possibility . . . I suppose there's no harm in looking at the figures."

In the hall, Adam stood, picked up his briefcase, and knocked on the door of the study.

Three hours later, Elinor had agreed that for Miranda's twenty-first birthday present, she would buy her a little beauty shop and provide enough money for a secretary and two shop assistants for three years, plus sufficient working capital to cover other overheads and products to stock the shop.

Adam was to be Miranda's business adviser, and Miranda had agreed that for the first three years, she would not take any action that was contrary to his advice.

In return for all this, Miranda agreed not to take flying lessons. Adam noticed that Miranda did not say that she would *never* take flying lessons.

Miranda decided to call her business KITS. She spent the spring of 1961 in a whirl of work, not all of which she enjoyed.

Rather than sell the overpriced, branded products produced by other firms, Miranda wanted to package and retail her own cosmetics; then, she knew, she would have direct control over quality, packaging, and pricing, which would also help to sharpen the identity of KITS.

She knew exactly what this all-important image of KITS should be: bold and young, visually sophisticated but inexpensive. It would project excitement, and it would also be practical. In the KITS store, a customer could buy a set of empty bottles and boxes and then select her colors to fill them: this meant that instead of a collection of gaudy, ill-matched bottles and boxes in her bathroom, she would have only one well-designed, matching set—stamped with the KITS logo, of course.

Miranda also knew that, where two products were indistinguishable, a shopper tended to buy the one with the clearer public image; dull packaging, and subsequent lack of image, was the reason for the failure of many private-label, inexpensive cosmetics. And she knew that inexpensive cosmetics need not mean inferior ones; the same products from one factory were frequently sold at different prices: a face cream might cost a pound in one pack but five pounds in another pack with a more expensive name.

Having targeted her market, Miranda now had to locate suppliers, choose or design her makeup and her skin-care range, write her sales literature, acquire a shop, and hire staff.

After deciding on a final list of basic cosmetics, Miranda developed them in Elinor's kitchen at Chester Terrace, much to the indignation of the housekeeper, who hated the pungent smells. Miranda was less confident about her skin-care products: although she had learned basic formulas during her training, she planned to discuss this line with a qualified cosmetics chemist. So Miranda telephoned four cosmetics manufacturers: Three refused to see her, brusquely explaining that her order would be too small to bother about. The fourth was Ladyface.

Friday, 31 March 1961

Sitting in the Ladyface reception area, Miranda fidgeted; her appointment had been for eleven o'clock—it was now forty minutes past. Was this an example of Ladyface reliability?

"Hello, I'm Cherry Dawson, the publicity officer." A charming blonde in her late twenties stood smiling in the flimsy doorway. Her job was to deal with timewasters like Miranda and save her charm to entertain the press and the groups of American executives who flew in regularly from the New York office. Miss Dawson smiled regretfully. "I'm afraid we have no vacancies of any sort at the moment."

"I don't want a job, I'm a potential customer," Miranda said firmly.

When Miranda proved persistent, Miss Dawson (growing less charming by the minute) said that clients were not her department and escorted her to the office of Miss Scotson, a brand manager known for her ability to get rid of anyone, with speed. While Miranda was describing her plans to Miss Scotson—a suspicious and dismissive woman in her mid-thirties—the brand manager was abruptly summoned by her boss.

Waiting yet again, Miranda looked gloomily around Miss Scotson's office, a tidy white shoe box covered with notice boards. She wondered how it was possible to become so deeply depressed in only twenty minutes. She stood up, stretched, and examined the schedules on the notice boards, none of which she understood. She then glanced at the pile of letters on the manager's desk: the topmost letter was headed "Arthur Bell Cosmetic Products Ltd., Birmingham." The letter started: "We much regret the late delivery of the EPO2 range for Nigeria . . ."

Miss Scotson suddenly materialized. "So good of you to let me know your plans, but we can't help you, especially in view of your . . . unusual . . . testing requirements." Miranda wanted no animal testing involved in her product development.

"Perhaps I can help *you*," Miranda said pleasantly. She pointed to a dummy advertisement pinned on the wall. It read, "Let your skin feel Ladyface sink into it . . ."

"The skin is an excretory organ," Miranda said. "You can't shove things into it, any more than you can into any of your other excretory organs, and any cosmetic claims to do so are ludicrous."

She stalked out.

The following Monday, Miranda's taxi drew into a grimy, dark red brick Birmingham back street, at the end of which "Arthur Bell Cosmetic Products Ltd." was painted on a large pair of gray gates.

Kenneth Bell, a cadaverous-faced man with a sallow complexion and wearing a brown leather jacket, treated Miranda as a lark, an unexpectedly interesting happening in the dull routine of his life. He asked Miranda out to her first business luncheon: they sat on cane furniture in Birmingham's first and only coffee bar, among a jungle of rubber plants, listening to the squawks of an indignant caged macaw.

"You can get all the cosmetics you want from us, except the lipsticks," Ken said, spooning up runny chili con carne. "For them, you want to visit Shama Cosmetics—in Manchester, they are."

"Can you help me with the skin-care products, Ken? I won't feel confident unless they've been properly tested."

"Can do, Miranda, can do." Ken blew the froth from his cappuccino. "A pal of mine's a dispensing chemist in Wimpole Street—he'll work on the formulas with you. He works for them smart dermatologists in Harley Street; you'll be safe with him."

From that day, Ken Bell acted as Miranda's supplier, industrial spy, and adviser, and he oversaw her ambitious efforts with fatherly concern and pride.

Wednesday, 7 February 1962

Another important factor in Miranda's business had been choosing the right property, for she would at first rely on sales from passing trade. Looking for the best and busiest street location that she could afford, she searched for a property as near as possible to an underground railway station, a main bus stop, or a street crossing. Eventually she chose a small shop and overhead flat on the corner of Oxford Street and Tottenham Court Road.

Once Miranda had signed her expensive lease, she had to move fast because from that point, she was spending money: rent, local taxes, utilities, insurance, lighting, heating, and refurbishment all had to be paid, yet the shop would generate no income until KITS opened its door.

Before sunrise on her twenty-first birthday, Miranda was ensconced in her own shop window, watching the half-awake working crowd shuffle past her store.

For her opening party that evening, Miranda needed a striking window display. She had sprayed a window dresser's model with silver paint and dressed her in a wild silver wig with a few wisps of pale gray net. The model stood with her legs apart, toes turning in, and arms outspread, seemingly to catch a shower of crimson KITS boxes and containers, suspended from the ceiling by invisible nylon cord. Miranda had chosen white and crimson as her house colors, when she hired a designer to project the KITS image: she had noticed that at Christmas, people always opened the red packages first.

Miranda couldn't afford a publicist, but not to worry, said her friend Annie Trehearne. Annie advised her to promote herself. After all, Miranda had seen her grandmother entertain journalists, keeping them informed about her books, so why shouldn't Miranda do the same thing to publicize her makeup?

Just before the opening of the shop, leaflets and price lists were printed entitling customers to a "buy one, get one free" makeup sample. Miranda and her new assistant, Linda Grey, spent the morning distributing these leaflets to the many nearby university and college buildings. This saved further money on publicity.

On the afternoon of the KITS opening, Elinor appeared in the shop to find chaos: carpenters hammered, electricians swore, and painters dripped silver paint.

Miranda, in jeans, stood in the middle of the confusion. "Put those boxes on the upper shelves, please. . . . Careful, Jim, I don't want another spot of paint on the floor tiles. . . . Did you get those blue spotlights? . . . Gran, darling! What a surprise!"

"I can see that you're busy, dear girl," Elinor said. "I just thought I'd call to wish you good luck and to say . . . to say that I'm sorry I doubted your business ability, but I'm right behind you now. Whatever happens, you can depend on me."

"Whatever happens?" Miranda grinned.

"Until the right man comes along, of course."

At six o'clock, Miranda opened her door to the public for the first time.

KITS looked vaguely like a smart photographer's studio: it had black floor tiles and matte black walls; chrome theatrical spotlights shone on the merchandise. The sales staff wore crimson jumpsuits. From the moment the door opened, KITS was jammed by students, passersby, journalists, and many friends of Elinor's: she had sent a crimson invitation to every person in her address book, and had also insisted that Miranda invite Angus. Miranda, who had already invited Angus, crossly told her grandmother to stop hoping.

Miranda was vexed with Elinor because she didn't like to admit to herself that she still missed Angus far more than she'd ever thought possible. But she couldn't again risk making fools of both of them by suggesting a replay. And she certainly wasn't going to be miserable in bed for the rest of her life. She had suspended her search for a suitably sized Prince Charming until she was less busy at the office; at any rate, that was her excuse. It was a pity that Angus had this one great drawback, because he was so perfect in every other way, which was why she missed him so much—more than he missed her, Miranda suspected. Because Angus now made it clear that he thought of her only as a friend—although, of course, they weren't yet comfortably friendly: maybe later, she wouldn't feel so stiff and uncomfortable whenever she saw him.

In the excited atmosphere of the crowded shop, Elinor waved as she saw Angus trying to push through the crowd toward the corner she shared with Buzz.

"Angus is the only man here who doesn't look as if he's escaped from the zoo," Elinor said approvingly to Buzz. "I'm so glad he's turned up. *I* know that Angus won't take no for an answer, not with that square jaw: the dear boy is just biding his time. Miranda is riding on the crest of a wave at the moment, but the time will come when there are difficulties, and then she'll need a strong man. *That's* when Angus will make his move."

"Romantic codswallop, Nell," Buzz growled, then added, "Funny sort of cigarettes they're smoking. No wonder you're coughing, Nell. We don't want another bronchitis attack. You've only been out of bed for a week!" She fanned her invitation. "Cor! What a noise! And what a crowd! And what *weird* clothes!"

But the headiest substance to get high on was not the pot, it was the optimism and euphoria that hung above the chic crowd, which so clearly demonstrated that fashion was no longer reserved for the daughters, wives, and mistresses of the rich. Annie Trehearne had persuaded all the big names to turn up. Models talked to photographers and trendy hairdressers; pretty girls talked to advertising men in dark glasses; debs chatted to Bow Group young Tories; truculent left-wing journalists argued with art directors in black turtleneck sweaters. Cockney and Liverpudlian accents mingled with upper class accents: "Isn't it groovy?" . . . "So switched on" . . . "super birds" . . . "fab shop" . . . "smashing" . . . "totally with it." The evening was clearly a right rave-up.

"Annabel's late again!" Elinor worried to Buzz.

But Annabel wasn't late; she was peering at the party through the two-way mirror that Miranda had installed behind the back wall to watch KITS customers and see which items they first picked up.

Miranda had insisted that Annabel (who had flown over from New York especially for the opening) should not appear until the party had been running for two hours; both sisters feared that Annabel's now famous face would steal Miranda's limelight. So Annabel would not enter until all the photographers had left. Until then, she contented herself with her surreptitious view, and wished that Miranda would fall for one of those very attractive men at the party instead of talking to Angus.

Finally Miranda flung open the door. "Okay, Annabel, you're allowed in now. Everyone please meet my beautiful sister!"

Ten minutes after Annabel joined the party, she felt a tug at her shoulder. It was Clare, who looked white and ill. She said, "Please get me out of here fast, darling. I think I'm going to faint. Don't spoil Gran's fun. Just get me home."

Annabel drove Clare's little scarlet car back to Poulton Square, where she helped her sister up the stairs, tucked her into bed, and brought her a glass of brandy.

"No, darling, I don't want a drink." Leaning back against her pillows, Clare still looked haggard. "Don't look so worried, Annabel, it's not serious. I've had tests, and I'm not pregnant—although my gyno took me off the Pill a couple of months ago, to make sure that wasn't the cause of my problem: so I'm back with the messy Dutch cap—whenever Sam gives me time to get it in."

"But what's *wrong*, darling?"

"Awful back pains. I feel as if I have a permanent, bad period."

"Where's Sam?"

"He left for Paris at dawn this morning. He'll be back tomorrow evening," Clare said shortly.

Annabel asked tentatively, "Are things okay between you and Sam?"

"Yes, of course," Clare said. She burst into tears.

Annabel hugged her sister, reached for the box of tissues, silently handed it to Clare, and waited until her snuffling stopped.

"Now tell me what's happened," Annabel said gently.

Clare started to speak, stopped, stuttered, stopped again, then burst out, "My gyno thinks my backache is because I get physically excited when we're making love but I don't climax—so there's no relief. He said a man feels the same way if he doesn't climax after having an erection." After renewed sobs, Clare wailed, "But Sam thinks I'm frigid."

"Can you masturbate?" Annabel asked.

Speechless, Clare blushed and nodded.

Annabel said briskly, "If you can masturbate to orgasm, then you *aren't* frigid and you *are* orgasmic. There's no great mystery about it."

"Then why does Sam think I'm frigid?"

" 'Frigid' is a man's word for a woman who can't have an orgasm in two minutes with the kind of stimulation that works for him."

Clare laughed bitterly.

Annabel said, "Why don't you . . . do it yourself if your back pains are so bad?"

"What's the point of being married unless we do it with each other?" Clare added resentfully, "If Sam really loves me, he should know what I need in bed."

"How? By divine guidance? ESP?" Annabel asked. "Sam isn't a mind reader: you have to *tell* him what you like—or take him by the hand and *show* him. Of *course* Sam loves you, or he wouldn't have married you, but when you're making love, you mustn't be shy about telling him what turns you on. Simply establish two things: what you like and what he likes."

"You make it sound so *easy*."

"So it should be. But there's only one person who can teach a woman to be a good lover, and that's her man. And there's only one person who can teach a man to be a good lover, and that's his woman."

"What did you tell Scott?"

"That I like to be on top, then I can control the rhythm and pressure. We . . . sort of rub rather than bounce . . . as in rock and roll."

Clare said, "Sam doesn't like to talk when he's making love. Suppose he won't listen?"

Annabel shrugged. "You can tell some men something until you're blue in the face, but if they don't want to hear it—you might as well save your breath. In that case, maybe you should go with Sam to a marriage counselor."

"I keep hoping things will get better . . . "

"You've been married three years! How much longer are you going to wait?"

"Don't rush me," Clare said crossly. "And how come *you're* such an expert, Annabel?"

"Scott taught me. And sex is practically the *only* thing that models talk about in the changing rooms. In New York, everyone talks openly about things that the British would blush to even think about: they're accustomed to discussing these things with their psychiatrists."

Clare gave a wobbly laugh. "If you told a man from Mars that the sex act was a human being's ultimate pleasure and then described it, he'd laugh until he burst into green fragments."

In the end, Clare found that the best way to talk to Sam was simply, casually, to repeat her conversation with Annabel.

Sam said, "Why the fuck do you have to discuss our private life with your sister? Don't worry. Lots of women can't climax."

"But I can when I . . . when I . . . do it myself."

"Look, Clare, nobody ever complained to me before. Everything is functioning perfectly, thank you." He lay back, bare-chested against blue-striped pillows, and clasped his hands behind his head. "Come here and I'll prove it."

Before entering Clare, Sam thrust two fingers up her; he twisted his wrist and wriggled his fingers around, harder and harder. Having entered her, he thrust longer and harder than usual, as if trying to reach some not-quite-attainable spot, like a plumber desperately trying to reach whatever is blocking the sink.

From underneath, Clare tried to do the rock-and-roll wriggle, but Sam's hands reached down and guided her hips to his movement.

Afterward, Clare, who had not climaxed, sensed Sam's silent exasperation. Eventually he gingerly felt for her clitoris. Four minutes later, she climaxed.

A few weeks later, Clare reported progress to Annabel, now back in New York.

"So everything's fine now?" Annabel asked.

Clare hesitated. "Not altogether. I can sense . . . there's still something wrong. . . . Sam's trying very hard," she said. "In every possible position. But it . . . doesn't feel loving or caring. Now I feel as if we're a couple of acrobats, performing."

"To be blunt," Annabel said, "efficient fucking isn't necessarily an act of love."

"The most depressing thing is . . . Sam won't acknowledge that the way my body works is *normal*, so that makes me resentful, when Sam clearly thinks I should be grateful."

After a long silence, Annabel said, "Maybe you should lighten things up a little. You might try a little playful fantasy."

"What *do* you mean?"

"Erotic fantasy. Next time you're in bed with Sam, use your fantasies. Say, 'A picture just came into my mind of you unhooking my black satin corselette . . . ' "

Clare looked doubtful.

Friday, 2 March 1962

Nevertheless, the next day, Clare told the au pair that she would be out all day, then took a taxi to the Matelot restaurant, where she was to meet Lizzie Bromley for lunch. There the headwaiter handed her a note saying that Lizzie couldn't make it because she had a toothache. As Clare didn't feel hungry, she took another taxi to Fenwick's.

An hour later, clutching two large green boxes of frivolous underwear, Clare returned home, planning to spend the afternoon trying out a few fantasies. She ran upstairs to her bedroom, opened the door . . . and froze.

She stared at Sam's bum moving up and down, and beyond it, the startled face of Marie-France.

Clare's first sensations were of pain and rage, followed almost immediately by sexual self-doubt: Just what did that French au pair have that she didn't? It wasn't *fair!* She was making such an effort to improve things, and had just spent a fortune at Fenwick's!

When she could speak, Clare yelled, "Get out of my bed and out of this house. *Now!*"

She dumped the green boxes on the floor, tore one of them open, dipped into it, and started to pelt the speechless Sam with black lace garter belts, fishnet stockings, half-cut satin bras, black chiffon French camiknickers, a pair of long black satin gloves trimmed with ostrich feathers, and a pair of ridiculously high-heeled scarlet patent ankle-strap shoes.

Leaving the front door open, she then ran out of the house, toward the Kings Road, where she hailed a cab and directed it to Elinor's flat.

Elinor had decided to sell the flat, for it seemed silly to keep it for just the occasional use of one person. She rarely stayed overnight in London and could stay at Claridge's if she did.

When Clare banged on the door, Elinor and Buzz were there, making lists of furniture: what to send to Starlings, what to store, what to sell, and what to give to Oxfam.

"My dear child, what *has* happened?" Elinor held out her arms, and Clare flew into them.

"I've come home," Clare snuffled against the shoulder of Elinor's gray flannel Digby Morton suit. "I never want to see him again! I fu-fu-fu-fu found him in bu-bu-bu bed with the au pair!"

Elinor tried to soothe and comfort her: "Oh my dear, you mustn't take these things so much to heart. I know you haven't been married that long, but men are all the same: they have . . . lusty appetites. You must learn when to turn a blind eye."

"Your generation might have settled for that, but *I* won't put up with it! I'm never going back to Sam!"

While soothing and sympathizing with Clare, over her head Elinor mouthed to Buzz, "Cancel the estate agent."

Sam didn't think it mattered if he cheated on his wife, provided she never found out: he'd been unlucky. Okay, he was sorry. He grew increasingly irritated as he realized how stubborn Clare could be; no persuasion would mollify her fury.

For over three months, Sam tried to persuade Clare to return.

Eventually his barrage of telephone calls slowed down, then stopped. He figured Clare would either return or not. Time would tell.

In mid-June, three prisoners, using teaspoons, gouged an escape route from Alcatraz. Reading about this in Elinor's *Daily Telegraph*, Clare felt similarly trapped, but without a teaspoon. She had just received the results of her test. She was pregnant. Abortions were illegal. No escape for Clare. Back to Sam.

Tuesday, 18 December 1962

Shortly before Christmas, Adam and Mike escorted Elinor and Buzz to the theater. The two ladies, so handsomely escorted, felt as glamorous as Adam intended they should. Heads turned toward them as they took their places in the royal box, to watch Peter Brook's production of *King Lear* for the Royal Shakespeare Company.

Afterward, over supper at the Savoy, Adam said, "I didn't much care for that. It was too bleak and contemporary for me." Again he wondered whether he should have taken the two old dears to see Agatha Christie's *The Mousetrap.*

"Paul Scofield acted very well as Lear," Elinor pointed out, careful to be positive about an evening that somebody else was paying for. "But anyone could have told the conceited old idiot what would happen."

Buzz said, "It ain't always easy to see what's happening, while it's happening to you."

"Very true," Elinor said.

"Take that bookkeeper we just fired," Buzz went on. "Fancy having to go to court for a minor gas bill!"

"An unwise choice. I should never have trusted somebody else's judgment," Adam said, annoyed by Buzz's tactlessness. The incompetent bookkeeper had led to nonpayment by Elinor of a heap of small bills, which in turn led to a bunch of complicated small lawsuits, which need never have taken place.

"Paul Littlejohn handled the lawsuit very well," Elinor said hastily, referring to a junior partner at STG.

Buzz had complained several times that there were never any problems when Joe Grant handled Elinor's legal business; he had simplified her affairs and Buzz had always understood them, whereas in less than a year, Adam seemed to have made things more difficult.

Elinor reproved Buzz and reminded her that her writing business had become more complicated since Adam restructured it into a group of companies.

Buzz retorted that she didn't understand the reasons for the restructuring, any more than Elinor did. "But you never question Adam's decisions. You just do as he says, and in my opinion, a lot of what he says is what the army calls—"

"That's quite enough," Elinor had said crisply, unwilling to consider that Adam was unreliable. What other man could she turn to? What other man could advise her what to do? Adam was understanding and sympathetic; he lifted all the cares from her shoulders, which enabled her to get on with her work: she would be lost without him.

As Adam consulted the Savoy wine list, a waiter approached the table with a silver salver upon which lay a note for Mike.

Mike quickly read it, then twisted around in his chair; he nodded briefly and respectfully toward a group of men in dinner jackets dining at the best table in the room.

After the meal, when Elinor and Buzz had retired to "powder their noses," Adam asked Mike, "What was that note about?"

Mike looked at his brother with a mixture of affection, exasperation, anxiety, and pity. "I wasn't going to tell you until tomorrow. I'd no idea that the brothers would be here tonight. I'm sorry, but they won't give you another extension. You've got to pay them back within ten days."

"Have I *ever* not paid my gambling debts?" Adam demanded angrily.

"No, but they can't afford to let other people see that you don't pay when you're supposed to pay. Suppose all their debtors behaved like you do?"

"All debtors don't provide them with the legal services that I do. I've managed to ease them out of some pretty unpleasant situations."

"Then do the same for yourself." Mike called for the bill.

Elinor and Buzz returned to the flat in Chester Terrace to find a message from Sam pinned beneath the door knocker: upon a hastily torn-out page of his diary, he had written, "Clare's gone into labor early. I've taken her to hospital."

Thirty-two hours later, after a difficult labor, Clare gave birth to an eight-pound boy.

As Elinor reverently held Joshua, not yet an hour old, in her arms, she could see the almost imperceptible ridge of his skull join from ear to ear and the slight dip of the fontanelle on top of his downy head. Eyes shut and sleepy, he looked small and fragile, quiet and long-suffering.

Gently Elinor pried open one tiny fist and put her forefinger into it. The sleeping baby grasped it firmly. She marveled at the tiny fingers and fingernails.

"I hope he'll wake up soon," Elinor whispered from beneath her face mask to Buzz. "In the first couple of days, before the face has fattened, you can see what the baby will look like when he's grown up."

Suddenly the baby opened his eyes and seemed to look up at Elinor.

She almost gasped, for the eyes that looked straight up at her were the aquamarine eyes of Billy.

Elinor was not to enjoy her first great-grandson for long. On New Year's Day, Sam broke the news to Clare that he wanted to return to live in Los Angeles.

Sam hadn't had a hit since *Grain Race*, released three years earlier. He didn't think he'd lost his touch, but he had realized that being out of the movie mainstream was being *out*. Working for the motion picture market requires the producer's presence in the marketplace, in the town where the movie action is; the town where each inhabitant, even a waitress or gas pump attendant, has an agent and at least one lawyer; the town where everyone lives, breathes, eats, talks, and definitely sleeps movies: Los Angeles.

Sam was to find that it was easier to leave than to return.

CHAPTER 13

Wednesday, 30 January 1963

AFTER FOUR DAYS in Los Angeles, Clare still felt euphoric, as if she'd stepped off the plane and traded her brain in for a driver's license. Nobody could get around L.A. without a car—in some places there weren't even any sidewalks. But she loved wearing shorts in January and sauntering by the ocean in midwinter. She also loved listening to the way everyone talked; she was fascinated by the quick, flip repartee of Sam's friends, the languid, spaced-out chat in the restaurants near the beach, the omnivorous movie gossip: by the end of her first week, she was reading the trades over breakfast.

Clare quickly found and furnished a sprawling, split-level, glass-and-timber ranch house, with pool and patio, in Brentwood. Accustomed to pleasant surroundings, she was determined to make their home a comfortable, quiet retreat from the dazzling, dizzy, absurd, totally unpredictable, and delightfully startling life of Southern California, which fascinated her but also left her breathless.

Josh was far more tiring than L.A. Clare had no idea that one small baby could be so exhausting; he was noisy, restless, demanding—and seemed to sleep only three minutes a night.

The day he found her sunburned after she fell asleep by the pool, Sam took pity on her. Putting his arm around Clare's blistered shoulders he said, "Get a nanny. No more argument about it."

To Sam's surprise and the astonishment of his friends, he doted on the baby. When Josh was one month old, Sam was certain that the baby could focus clearly on him, although Clare told him that it wasn't possible. At two months, Sam knew that those were real smiles, not wind. At three months, there was real laughing and excited waving of fists whenever Sam appeared, and Josh clearly recognized his father.

Sam's problems always vanished when he lowered the naked, wriggling Josh into his bath, or made silly goo-goo noises at the pram, or crawled on the terrace like a bear, or tried unsuccessfully to coax the four-month-old Josh to say "Dad."

Elinor hired a young English nanny who reminded Clare of a small, bright-eyed blackbird. In the way that people tend to gravitate toward each other when feeling slightly homesick, they quickly became friends, and from the day Kathy arrived in L.A., Josh metamorphosed into a quiet baby; he lay in his pram or crib or rug, blew bubbles, gurgled, burped upon demand, and gave no trouble: Clare thought it most unfair but was delighted, and so was Sam.

After Kathy's arrival, Clare started to entertain. In L.A., this was serious business, nothing like having your friends over for supper. Sam needed backup, and Clare was determined to help her husband as much as she could: she remembered the success of Elinor's daily tea parties, and methodically applied her considerable organizational ability to throwing lavish soirées. Clare was not needed at Sam's business breakfasts in the El Padrino Room of the Beverly Wilshire or lunches at the Brown Derby or Scandia on Sunset Boulevard, but she presided over all evening entertaining, whether at home, in the leafy courtyard of the Bel Air Hotel, or at Romanoff's. Sam's oldest friends were particularly impressed by his classy English wife, granddaughter of an internationally famous, best-selling author; not only was she pretty and young, Clare was an effortless and charming hostess—which is more than anyone could say for either of Sam's previous wives.

Sam had to work hard to reinstate himself, and the first order of business was to locate the right script. He spent his time searching for material, while trying to ignore the cold claw that gripped his stomach—and pocketbook—as he realized the world's indifference to Sam Shapiro. Sam had reached the time of life when it wasn't so easy anymore: he was still in the game—but only by the skin of his teeth, and he knew it. So did everyone of consequence in L.A., except Clare. Sam was still welcomed with a flourish by the maître d's. Cary Grant and Frank Sinatra still nodded to him. But there were little things, like being demoted from Swifty Lazar's "A" list to the agent's "B" list: these things reminded everyone that Sam hadn't had a hit since *Grain Race*.

Clare had known before she came to L.A. that being married to a movie producer wasn't as glamorous as she (and her envious and astonished girlfriends in England) had once thought. She learned quickly that the annual seasons were no longer spring, summer, autumn, winter, but research and development, preproduction, production, postproduction and marketing. But Clare did not know that Sam's money was running out: the income from the big hits had gone in taxes, alimony, and surprisingly high overhead.

Not realizing that Sam couldn't afford it, Clare continued to entertain lavishly.

One evening in late April, she telephoned Annabel in New York and reported, "We're having seventy-five to supper this evening. I've had such a pretty, yellow-striped marquee set up beyond the pool."

"I don't get time to entertain formally at home," said Annabel. "So if it's business, we take them to '21,' and if it's friends, I invite them for brunch on Sunday."

Clare giggled. "That wouldn't do in L.A. Sunday brunches are considered tacky. So are beach picnics or any casual get-together. Here the entertaining is rather old-fashioned and formal. I give big parties and dinners for up to sixteen at home—the caterers are wonderful, by the way—and anything in between takes place in some smart hotel."

"And are these parties filled with beautiful actresses and sexy starlets?"

Clare giggled again. "Never. The important people are family men, so there are never any beautiful starlets at the best parties, in case they make the wives feel insecure. A lot of sensational-looking women wander in and out of the hotels and restaurants—but you'll never find them at the best parties. And you never invite unimportant actors, in case they might pester someone for a part. No, the whole point of these parties is to do deals, to put all the right people together so that the next picture gets made."

None of Clare's entertaining showed the returns for which Sam hoped, however.

Because of his anxiety over his career and his failure to reinstate himself, Sam had neither surplus energy nor libido. He and Clare made love regularly, and Sam dutifully gave orgasms to Clare, who (although she didn't say so) still felt that something was missing. There was no spontaneous excitement, no loving warmth; she was not swept to the stars in his arms. Crossly Clare told herself that her expectations had been as stupidly unrealistic as one of her grandmother's breathlessly ecstatic heroines.

One afternoon, when Annabel phoned, Clare found herself asking, "How's your love life, darling?"

After a pause, Annabel said, "Mechanical."

"Yours too?"

"I always know when Scott's got something big going on at the station, because his head is someplace else when he's with me."

"I don't believe it! After you had me believing that Scott was God's gift to women?"

"He seems to be taking a sabbatical," Annabel said curtly, and changed the subject.

Clare had noticed that Sam's libido perked up when young actresses clustered around him at poolside bars and in smart hotel lounges; for them, a producer was a producer, and Sam still had his reputation. Sam clearly felt soothed by this flattering attention, but Clare felt sad, and a little jealous. She wished she had what those women obviously thought she had, which was what she herself had expected: a powerful, all protecting, sexy husband. Perhaps if the two of them could get away alone to some perfect place . . .

When Sam asked Clare the day after her big party if she'd like to accompany him to the Cannes International Film Festival, he was surprised that she decided to leave Josh alone with Kathy for ten days: but Clare looked forward to a carefree second honeymoon.

Unfortunately, at the last minute, Sam—unaware of Clare's romantic plans—

invited Elinor, who was recovering from another bad bout of bronchitis; he thought she would be company for Clare, who would then not mope around alone all day while he—he hoped—put deals together. Sam decided to stay at the Carlton rather than Elinor's villa in St.-Tropez, which was too small and too far from the action.

Monday, 6 May 1963

One week later, Clare, Sam, Elinor, and Buzz sat on the terrace of the Carlton Hotel under a dazzling sun. White yachts flitted across the bay; crowds on the beach peered at starlets; photographers snapped girls in spangled bikinis, mink bikinis, and flower-covered bikinis. Clare could spot no stars: Sam said they generally stayed in the hills behind Cannes in luxurious rented villas, descending only for their own screenings when the publicity machine had been organized to receive them.

Clare and Sam smiled at each other across the table. She was happy to be here watching the cinematic rites of spring.

Elinor noticed the exchange and felt relieved. A baby often reunited a couple who had been having problems. She hoped that little episode was far behind them.

One week later, cigar smoke wafted from the windows of the Carlton and the Negresco as negotiations became serious and deals firmed up, but Sam seemed to have no part in them. Clare learned not to ask, "But was anything *definite* agreed?" after he returned weary but still hopeful from lunch with some big player at the Hotel du Cap or the Eden Roc at Antibes. Sam's wonderful aura of assurance, which had originally captured Clare's heart, was visibly wilting.

Then one evening, Sam and Clare dined at the Majestic with a distributor who had clinched deals in seven major territories, was clear to closing another nine, was working at his negotiating strategy for the remaining twenty-one major territories, and just hoped he could pack it all into the remaining week of the festival. Watching Sam's face, Clare wondered if her husband's desperation was as clear to other people as it was to her.

After dinner, she suggested a stroll along La Croisette, the palm-tree-lined promenade: she hoped that the two of them might walk in the dark beneath the stars and forget the feverish atmosphere of the festival.

On the darkened beach, small groups of young people drank, smoked, talked, laughed.

"Who are they all?" Clare asked.

"Young movie hopefuls and out-of-work actors—you've already seen most of them; they prowl around in hotel and restaurant lobbies, deeply disappointed to find they're talking to each other and not Dino De Laurentiis or Franco Zeffirelli," Sam said. "They're all impoverished dreamers, would-be screenwriters, directors, and producers. They turn up from all over the world, carrying cans of film, files of projects, ideas, treatments, scripts . . . Most of them will have sold nothing by the time they fly back to reality."

"But what are they all doing on the beach?"

"If they can't find a cheap pension outside town, they sleep here."

Clare could not feel sorry for these healthy young hopefuls necking in the moonlight on a Riviera beach. But she felt increasingly sorry for Sam. Lack of success seemed to make it necessary for him to talk a little louder, tip a little too much, flirt a little more with would-be starlets, who didn't realize they were wasting their time.

As they reached the deserted end of the beach, Clare nudged Sam. "Let's go down on the sand," she suggested, taking his hand.

Where the sand ran into the dark sea, Clare kicked her shoes off, turned to Sam, and put her arms around his neck. "Let's forget everything for a few minutes," she whispered. "Let's forget movies and money and deals and doubts. Let's enjoy the soft sound of the sea on the sand. Let's enjoy each other."

Sam pulled her close and said helplessly, "I can't figure out what I'm doing wrong . . . I'm sorry, Clare."

"It doesn't matter. Forget it for a few minutes." She took his face in her hands and kissed his mouth hard. "Nobody can see us."

They kissed with passion, holding each other tightly. For once, Sam allowed Clare to share his human vulnerability. For the first time, he felt her strength and reassurance. For the first time, he shared, in whispers, his doubts, fears, regrets.

Clare pulled his head down and kissed away his words. "It doesn't matter, Sam. I swear it doesn't matter. Forget all that. Just remember that we're together—*and I love you.*"

Sam crushed her against him, and Clare could feel his need for her. And there on the damp, cold sand, Clare finally felt what she had always yearned for, the release she had searched for: to her surprise, she recognized Elinor's ecstatic descriptions of twin souls uniting. Finally Clare's hoped-for moment came, as she and Sam shared joy.

Tuesday, 14 May 1963

On the eighth morning of the festival, Elinor gazed around the lobby of the Carlton, lined with film posters for *Cleopatra* and *Tom Jones.*

Beside her, Buzz sniffed, "Bloody circus. Crowds everywhere. Waiters rushed off their feet. Can't get a decent cup of tea."

Behind her, Elinor heard drifts of conversation.

"When does your plane leave?"

"Why, whenever I'm ready, of course."

" . . . I can't get decent vegetable gardeners."

"I have a couple of Filipinos. Costs forty dollars a carrot, of course, but at least I know they're fresh . . . "

"Richard Burton isn't going to buy that chateau at Saracen after all. Sounds like alimony . . . "

"Did you hear that, Buzz?" Elinor said. "Do you suppose that chateau really is for sale? Why don't we drive there and see?" She knew that Saracen, one of the few unspoiled medieval French villages, had been deemed a national treasure: no new building was allowed.

Buzz grunted, "Anything to get away from this lot."

So they picked their way past the Afghan hounds, disdainful borzois, and exquisitely groomed Pekingese, whose owners sat in the sun drinking champagne or expensive bottled water. Elinor obliged two Scandinavian backpackers, who asked for her autograph. Eventually they found Sam's air-conditioned limousine and drove east.

In contrast to the noise, heat, and dust of Cannes, the surrounding countryside looked eager, freshly washed, and pretty as a girl before a dance. To their right was the sparkling azure sea; to their left were lavender fields and dark green forests, behind which mountains rose, to fade in soft lines of mauve back to the white horizon.

None of Saracen's labyrinth of winding streets were wide enough for a car, so the air of the village was fresh and clear. Some of the streets opened into small, unexpected squares, each shaded by lime trees around an old stone fountain. The narrow houses had mysterious porches and bridges that crossed from one building to another; on many a worn wooden door hung the iron hand of Fatima, to ward off evil spirits.

The high ironwork gate of the chateau creaked open at Elinor's tentative touch. She and Buzz walked into a cobbled courtyard choked by weeds. Against the castle walls grew white oleander and rosemary bushes, and trees that drooped beneath strange pale yellow blossoms: the branches were so low that the two women had to stoop beneath a ragged arch of green and yellow to reach the front door—an ancient slab of oak studded with ironwork of different periods.

They rang the bell and waited. Elinor looked up to see, high above her, a row of narrow slits. She imagined the castle defenders hiding behind, shooting arrows at invaders.

Just as Elinor decided that the building was deserted, the front door was slowly opened by an unsmiling gray-haired woman who wore a cotton overall and a pair of sneakers, cut to allow her bunions to protrude. This caretaker confirmed that the chateau was for sale, but she knew nothing of price or availability; it was for the agent to occupy himself with such matters.

Eventually Elinor persuaded this harpy to telephone for the agent, a thin, dismissive young man who clearly didn't take these Englishwomen seriously. Everyone knew that the English no longer had money. At breakneck speed, he showed them around the chateau.

The building was not in a good state of repair: The interior was damp, and the plaster was peeling. Some of the shutters were hanging off the windows, some were missing, and none had been painted for years. The two upper floors were a dusty, shuttered warren of bedrooms. The only bathroom had been installed before the First World War, and there was no central heating or air-conditioning. The agent assured the women, somewhat unconvincingly, that the chateau was kept warm in winter and cool in summer by the six-foot-thick walls. Their tour ended where it had started, on the south terrace overlooking the sea.

Elinor sauntered to the ivy-covered balustrade. To her right, in the distance, the Bay of Nice curved like a Dufy painting, edged with tall palm trees and pretty villas. Below her, rough-hewn gray rock fell abruptly to a sandy crescent of beach, where the sea was aquamarine shot with silver; beyond the bay, the water spread, deep blue, to the horizon; the color changed to indigo as it met an azure sky, across which clouds sailed, fat as cupids, in the brilliant, dazzling, inimitable light of the French Riviera.

"And the price?" Elinor slowly turned to the dismissive agent.

Buzz suddenly realized that this was no casual spring afternoon excursion.

"What would *we* do with a place this size? Just look at the mess it's in! Ain't been cleaned since it was built, if you ask me." She snorted. "You're a romantic idiot, Nell!"

Both women knew that Elinor would buy the chateau.

Later, as they walked downhill in silence, Elinor noticed that a surprising number of trees grew in the narrow streets and little squares: weeping willows, olive and apricot trees. They drank coffee at the only café, in a street studded by tubs of pink geraniums; pigeons swooped to pick up the cake crumbs that Buzz threw. Then they wandered past the dark green, studded door of the *syndicat d'initiative* and the lavender shutters of the local cooperative to the pale-blue-painted *mairie* that stood next to the blue and green pharmacy. Opposite the ancient Church of St. Peter was the village shop; in the window, plastic champagne glasses stood next to a jumble of red flyswatters, bottling jars, dusty casseroles, insecticides, local eau de cologne, honey, and herbs.

"It's almost too charming," said Elinor. These quiet sunny streets had altered little over seven hundred years. She and Buzz had driven only a short distance, but they might have been a thousand kilometers from the hustling streets of Cannes.

"It's a rash, impulsive move," Buzz grumbled on the return journey.

Elinor laughed. Having unexpectedly and romantically been tempted by fate to leave Britain, she could see only the advantages: no more fog, no more bronchitis. Instead, sunshine, warm sea, delicious food and wine.

"Won't you miss Starlings?" Buzz couldn't believe that Elinor would leave her beloved garden.

Elinor suddenly became serious, "Starlings isn't the same since the girls left." The silent void that Starlings had become made Elinor miserably conscious that the girls no longer lived there. Everywhere she looked, something reminded her of them and made her long to relive the past. In her own home, Elinor felt homesick. Perhaps at Saracen, she would find a new way of life; perhaps there she could again look forward, instead of being constantly and painfully tugged back by memories.

On the following morning, Paul Littlejohn, now a junior partner of Swithin, Timmins and Grant, flew from London to Nice. Funded by money earned outside Britain and not subject to exchange controls, Elinor eventually found herself mistress of the ancient French chateau. Although this was a relatively simple arrangement, Paul Littlejohn managed to make it sound as complicated as the division of Berlin between the Allies, and charged accordingly.

Buzz urged Elinor to query the bill. Elinor said that she had Adam's assurance that the charge was normal for such a transaction.

"It ain't *normal* to buy an eleventh-century castle," Buzz retorted. "And why does that Mr. Littlejohn always write 'done under request' in his letters to you?"

"I request it and he's confirming it. What's wrong with that?" Elinor asked irritably. "I expect the wording covers some legal point, or has something to do with exchange regulations. Besides, it's not something for us to worry about. Adam and Mr. Littlejohn know what's best for me, and I trust them. Now where *is* that decorator?"

CHAPTER 14

Thursday, 12 September 1963

ADAM SAUNTERED UP the marble steps of the Clanrickard Club. Two years before, the law had been changed to allow gambling in Britain; since then London had become one of the world's gambling centers. The grandest London clubs were Crockfords in Carlton House Terrace; John Aspinall's Clermont Club in Berkeley Square, which attracted the richest and most daring gamblers; Les Ambassadeurs, where you dined, danced, and then went upstairs to play chemmy; and the Clanrickard Club, run by Mike Grant.

As Adam reached the door, the owner, Toby Sutch, hurried out. Adam hadn't expected him to be there so early in the evening.

Toby Sutch paused. "I expect you've come to settle your account, Grant, without any trouble."

"That's what I'm seeing Mike about," Adam parried, realizing what Toby meant by "trouble." An immaculately dressed Old Harrovian, Toby Sutch was a tough bully, accustomed to being obeyed. His powerful self-confidence attracted people who couldn't control their gambling, and who often became dependent upon him. He introduced such people to moneylenders who provided six-month loans for four percent monthly interest. Should there be a repayment problem, toughs visited the borrowers and persuaded them to pay up.

Adam entered Mike's office without knocking. "You're late again, Adam," Mike said from behind his rosewood desk. "You'd better make this quick, because I'm meeting Miranda to show her a shop I've found in Pimlico."

"Miranda can wait." Adam sat in a leather chair and propped his feet up on the desk. "I want a whiskey and soda and a quick word with you, about Miranda's business."

"She's expanding at the speed of light," Mike said. Miranda had acquired seven shops in eighteen months, two of which had been found by Mike, who had property connections, a good nose for a bargain, and plenty of free time during the day.

Using her first shop as collateral, Miranda had borrowed from the bank to buy the lease of a second shop, near Holborn. Using the second lease as collateral, she had then similarly purchased the lease of a third shop. As she had launched her business just before a small London property boom, Miranda found that her collateral value seemed to increase weekly with no effort on her part: the steadily rising KITS profit figures reassured the bank of her ability to leverage property in this way.

Adam said, "She's spending too much of her time on property deals when she should be running the business. She's got an eye for good property, but she's not adept at dealing with the people who sell it: estate agents have little respect for a woman, particularly, it seems, if she's young and pretty. But *you*, little brother, have a flair for real estate, *and* you know how to handle the agents: you can wine and dine them here, introduce them to some nice girls, drop the occasional envelope of cash, and learn to lose at golf. Then you'll get first pick of properties for sale. It won't take up much of your time. You'll get two percent commission."

As he poured Adam's drink, Mike's clear gray eyes looked worried. He knew the hidden drawback to this reasonable-sounding deal: if he accepted it from Adam, Mike would be expected to persuade Toby Sutch to extend Adam's credit. But Mike did not want to ask any favors, especially not from Toby.

"Two percent," Adam said firmly.

Reluctantly Mike nodded.

Adam stood up. "What Miranda needs is to get her operation under one roof. So look for a large industrial building, somewhere outside London, in central England where rents are lower. That way we can locate the factory, warehouse, garages, and offices in the same place."

"Why not build?" Mike suggested.

"No time." Adam downed his drink and left.

Friday, 24 April 1964

"I love it, Buzz," Elinor said as she waited on the south terrace for her guests to arrive: the traditional finishing feast for the builders was about to start. Saracen would be ready just in time for the film festival. This year, Sam would have one of the most impressive backgrounds on the Riviera to conduct his business.

The stonemasons' wives had baked pizzas and prepared huge bowls of chopped tomatoes, olives, and onion, marinated cucumber, walnuts, and lamb's-foot lettuce—all tossed in the local salad dressing that used sesame oil instead of olive. Champagne and Provençal *vin rosé* had been opened, and the homemade lemonade was pressed from local lemons.

Elinor had enjoyed every minute of the restoration. Her French architect had strengthened the structure and roof beams, then renewed the tiles on roof and terrace. He tore out the foul-smelling bathroom and the kitchen, which consisted only of a sink with a cold tap, and installed a new kitchen and many bathrooms. All peeling wallpaper was scraped off, and the walls and ceilings were plastered creamy-white magnolia. Windows were replaced, woodwork painted, and floors polished. The new electrical system provided indirect lighting, so the walls and ceilings glowed.

While this work was in progress, Elinor and Buzz visited the auction houses of Nice, Toulon, and Draguignan. They also frequented antique shops off the beaten track, in the hills, where they purchased splendid beds, fruitwood tables, armoires, and charming antique chairs; modern sofas were ordered from Nice. The village dressmaker, Madame Annette, sewed all the curtains, made of cream linen, after Elinor purchased four bales at a Toulon auction.

During the restoration work, Elinor and Buzz stayed alternately at the Hotel de Provence and the Fountain Hotel; fierce rivals, they faced each other across the Place de la République. The Provence was run by a matriarch of ninety-three, Madame Sartour, and her enormous family. The Fountain was run by a male couple, Americans, known as *les pédés*. When the Fountain hired a chic Paris decorator to install soft lighting and cover the walls in *toiles de Jouy*, the Provence didn't bother to change its unflattering fluorescent lighting but installed a swimming pool. The Fountain retaliated by moving four-poster beds into all the best suites, whereupon the Provence announced Saturday evening barbecues . . .

Now, content with the results of her building upheaval, Elinor leaned against the terrace balustrade and looked up at the chateau. The newly painted white shutters were faintly tinged with pink, a blush applied by the still-golden evening sky.

Seeing her pleased expression, Buzz asked, "What do you like best about it, Nell?"

To Buzz's surprise, Elinor did not pick the spectacular view, or the silver four-poster bed that had once belonged to a Spanish princess, or the elevator that plunged three hundred feet down to the beach.

Elinor slowly smiled. "I like to think that Billy would be proud of me."

Buzz stared at Elinor; she knew that look on her friend's face. Elinor was playing one of her own heroines. This place was like one of the stately homes in her novels; here in Saracen, Elinor could live in the sort of imaginary world she created for her readers—a world she had actually come to believe in, where she no longer separated reality from fantasy, fact from fiction. Part of Elinor's fantasy was the myth of Billy O'Dare, the perfect romantic lover; in her mind, she had re-created him as a strong, dependable hero, forgetting his weaknesses, his excesses, and his ill-treatment of her.

Buzz turned for a moment and looked at her friend. They had known each other so long, and still Elinor amazed her. Billy! How she clung to his memory, reinventing him still, after all these years. Buzz knew there was no point in once again trying to remind Nell of the true nature behind Billy O'Dare's easy and intoxicating charm. He had been the one man she truly loved, and there would never be another.

"I wonder . . . I wonder what he would say if he knew I had bought a castle for myself," Elinor said.

Buzz suspected that Billy would laugh and say, "You could buy Buckingham Palace, old girl, but you won't change Marjorie's opinion of you."

Buzz said, "I'm sure Billy would be proud of you, Nell."

Monday, 12 October 1964

Miranda, her long flaming hair pulled behind a navy Alice band, wore a navy dress with a white organdy Pierrot collar for the first executive meeting in her new sales office—a converted warehouse off Oxford Street, found by Mike. Sitting at the head of her egg-shaped, white plastic boardroom table, she was surrounded by her male executives. Adam sat on Miranda's right; she had recently persuaded him to join her board as a part-time director.

Adam had appeared reluctant to accept this appointment and had pleaded other commitments, but he had finally capitulated after Miranda agreed that, should KITS ever go public, she would sell Adam fifteen percent of the total issued shares, at a nominal sale price of £15,000. Miranda considered this share option a minor concession compared to the advantage of having the experienced Adam on a board composed of people who were young, enthusiastic, and talented but had never before been directors of a company. Adam made Miranda feel safe.

For a brief moment, Miranda wished that her two sisters could see her, sitting at the head of her boardroom table while everyone listened to her and took notes of what she said. No longer was she the littlest sister, to whom no one paid any attention. She was an emerging star of the business world.

Miranda said, "The first item on our agenda is the acquisition of Framwells." This was an ailing chain of small London tobacconist shops, which had not yet been put on the market. KITS financial resources, already stretched to their limit, would be subjected to even greater strain should KITS acquire Framwells. But they could not risk this unique chain falling into the hands of a rival. So the board voted to buy Framwells. It would be expensive, but worth it.

All further items on the agenda were briskly agreed upon, until the final item, a hosiery manufacturer's offer of a licensing deal, which caused argument.

Adam spoke persuasively in favor of the deal. "We would get an assured income for lending the KITS name and logo and publicly endorsing the product. All *you* have to do, Miranda, is make a few public appearances wearing their tights: *they* then have a public image, while *we* have a decent profit margin without working for it."

Linda Grey nodded; she was no longer Miranda's assistant, but publicity manager. "We've built up a very clear image of a young, smart, intelligent woman who wants sophisticated merchandise at reasonable prices, and we project that image through Miranda herself. Customers buy her products because they see her on TV and read about her in the papers. They see Miranda as glamorous, fashionable, and giving good value. We have a high-profile managing director who projects a household name."

"Yes, that's our asset, and we're not fully exploiting it," Adam said.

Miranda wrinkled her forehead. "You said the same sort of thing about franchising. I know this *sounds* like money for nothing, but that's what's worrying me."

Linda said, "If anything's wrong with the product, the manufacturer won't get blamed by the customer—KITS will."

"And that dissatisfied customer won't only stop buying the tights—she'll also stop buying KITS cosmetics," Miranda said. She added, firmly, "We can *never* be sure that goods sold under our name are up to standard if they're manufactured by somebody else—because we don't control the quality."

Adam smiled. "Would you agree, theoretically, that it *is* a good idea to use our name to sell other goods if we *can* control the quality of those goods?"

Looking puzzled, Miranda nodded.

"We employ full-time marketing experts because that's cheaper than using consultants, and it gives us more control," Adam said. "So we have a first-class, underemployed marketing division."

"That's unavoidable, until we can afford to expand," Miranda said defensively.

Adam smiled again. "Then why don't we set up an acquisitions office, to buy old-fashioned firms that are solidly established but getting nowhere because they have no clear marketing image, so nobody wants to buy their products? Instead of licensing tights, why don't we buy some ailing stocking firm—such as Daintyfeet—and put our name on them?"

The financial director, Ned Sinclair, threw up his thin hands in protest. "You're suggesting that we turn KITS into a holding company!"

"Why not?" Adam said.

"We'd be running before we can walk!" Ned objected.

"But it's boom time," Linda said slowly. "And very few manufacturers understand what's happening in fashion right now."

Adam nodded. "Exactly. The Youthquake."

Everyone started to talk at once.

Two weeks later, the board of KITS decided that the holding company project would be pursued, provided adequate financing could be arranged. The new company would be called SUPPLYKITS, to avoid confusion with KITS.

Adam's responsibility as commercial director would be the development of SUPPLYKITS. He would seek small companies with a weak image, which needed design, publicity, and marketing services but had good management staff. There was one essential ingredient to every potential company: it had to generate cash, in order to provide SUPPLYKITS with a steady income, with which to repay the bank loan necessary for its acquisition.

"Adam, d'you think you'll be able to do all this while working part-time?" Miranda asked worriedly as the two of them sat in the boardroom after the office had closed.

"I don't see why not," Adam said, pouring Dom Perignon for both of them. "Mike finds the companies and Ned produces the figures I need from their own accounts."

"Mike's last bill was pretty high."

"The contract I drew up specifies that Mike gets two percent, but it doesn't specify *when*."

"You mean . . . "

"Legally, we could wait a thousand years before paying it."

Miranda said sharply, "If I buy somebody's services, I want to pay for them."

"Business is business," Adam said. "My little brother should have checked out his contract with a lawyer." He topped up her glass. "Relax, Miranda. Business isn't a life-or-death matter—it's a sort of game, a huge gamble; it's exciting, and that's something you seem to have forgotten lately."

"I worry that the stakes are getting so high, so fast."

"That's what's exciting!" Adam said, his eyes shining.

"Perhaps it's getting *too* exciting for me," Miranda suggested. She noticed that Adam had relaxed the careful reserve with which he normally treated her.

"There's no such thing as too much excitement." Adam grinned. "Especially not when you're around, Miranda. You create it, you know."

Surprised, Miranda looked at Adam's handsome face. Was he really flirting with her? Was she reading an invitation in those dancing brown eyes? Did she want to?

Miranda remembered the painful calf love she had felt for Adam long ago in St.-Tropez, when she was a vulnerable, flat-chested schoolgirl. She remembered Adam's perfunctory politeness, and her misery.

"You didn't always think that," she said.

"I do now." Adam leaned toward her.

Swiftly Miranda told herself that she couldn't afford to get emotionally involved with Adam: he was too important to her business. Suppose they had an affair and then broke up—perhaps he would want to leave the business. She couldn't yet manage without Adam's calm reassurance, Adam's authoritative decisions, his brushing aside of anxiety, his strength of purpose. She could only just manage *with* him.

Miranda stood up. She wasn't going to mess up her new career.

Friday, 25 December 1964

By Christmas, Elinor and Buzz had settled down in Saracen. The only major change in Elinor's work routine had been that she now flew to London to do her research instead of traveling by train from Wiltshire. Buzz supervised three bilingual secretaries, who came daily from Nice to deal with correspondence, clean-type Elinor's manuscripts, send them to relevant experts for checking, then dispatch them to the dynamic American agent who had sold Elinor's work around the world since Joe Grant's death.

Early on Christmas morning, Elinor's bedroom door burst open. As always, Elinor's heart looped the loop as two-year-old Josh appeared in Donald Duck pajamas. The child's eager blue eyes reminded her so of Billy.

Frantic with excitement, Josh showed Elinor the contents of the knobbly red stocking that he dragged behind him.

Sitting up in bed, wearing a purple paper crown and pulling a cracker with Josh, Elinor felt happy and replete. She wanted nothing more from life: all the people she loved were gathered today under this ancient roof. Sam, Clare, and Josh had flown from California, Annabel and Scott from New York, Miranda and the Grant boys from London.

Later, wearing dressing gowns, everyone ate a champagne breakfast in the cream-tented pavilion by the swimming pool, which was used as an outdoor dining room. Josh ate seven tangerines and raced around the terraces on his new French tricycle—a present from Father Christmas.

Sam gave Clare a gold neck chain; she gave him a primitive Greek painting of a fishing boat. Annabel gave Scott a set of Mark Cross luggage; he gave her a green leather Gucci jewel case. Miranda watched her two sisters hug their husbands and suddenly wished again that she hadn't broken up with Angus. But it wouldn't have worked.

Elinor murmured to Buzz, "It's wonderful to see the girls together again, so loving, so loyal, so happy and secure!"

Buzz smiled. "They're making as much noise as ever they did. You'd think they was teenagers again." Since the arrival of the sisters, their conversation, which consisted of half-sentences and puzzling allusions, had been constantly interrupted by giggles and shrieks of laughter.

"And the men seem to like each other." Elinor nodded with satisfaction. "*Everything* is going well!"

Standing beside Miranda at the buffet table, Adam whispered, "Annabel's put on weight, hasn't she?"

"I always thought she was too thin," Miranda said without conviction.

"Well, she isn't now."

Annabel, who was sitting with Clare by the pool, was aware of her weight problem. When her bookings started to slide, Mrs. Bates had crisply told her to lose twenty pounds and given her the telephone number of New York's smartest slimming doctor. With great effort, Annabel had shed three pounds.

"I love your jewel box," Clare said cheerfully.

"I chose it myself. If I hadn't, Scott would have sent a secretary out to buy something for me."

Surprised, Clare said, "Scott must be . . . very busy."

"Nobody need be too busy to buy his wife a Christmas present. Scott isn't interested in me anymore."

"Don't be silly, Annabel. He's here with you, isn't he?" Clare laughed. "After six years, you can't expect the same nonstop attention that you had as a bride—even though you're supposed to be one of the world's most beautiful women."

"I get *no* attention!"

"Rubbish. Men fall at your feet and you flirt with everyone in sight—even Adam."

"I mean that Scott ignores me—not here, of course, in front of you all. If I flirt, it's only to reassure myself that *other* men still find me attractive."

"Cool it," Clare said curtly. "Remember, it's Christmas." She didn't want to think about marital flirtation. Sam had resumed his disguise of masculine invulnerability as soon as they returned to L.A. two summers ago, and Clare never again penetrated his armor or shared the loving warmth they had experienced when their minds, as well as their bodies, were joined on the darkened sands of Cannes.

Clare had started to suspect that Sam was a compulsive womanizer; she noticed the too-casual way certain women spoke to him at parties and the way his black eyes twinkled when they did so. She told herself that Sam's affairs were probably not much more than one-night stands, and that adultery was almost unavoidable in his business, but such rationalization did not assuage her sadness.

Beyond the pool, Mike strolled to the terrace balustrade, against which Adam leaned to watch a speedboat skip across the blue water. "Shall we take a boat out after lunch? Just you and me? Get away from Elinor's family set piece?"

Adam said cheerfully, "If you've got a message for me, Mike, tell me now. No need to go miles out to sea for privacy."

Mike hesitated. "You're in trouble if you can't pay back your debts by the end of the year." He paused again. "You know what I mean by trouble. This time I can't do anything."

"You can make sure Miranda doesn't hear about it," Adam said crisply. "And don't worry. I'll fix it. I always do, don't I?"

"They all say that. Until the day they *can't* fix it."

"Ease up, Mike. Remember, we're here to have fun. Okay, this afternoon we'll sneak away on the speedboat, escape from Elinor's brood."

"Nothing wrong with the O'Dares," Mike said, "except they pick god-awful men."

Adam nodded. "I don't mind Sam, but Scott is unbelievably vapid—only interested in his job." Scott seemed incapable even of playing Monopoly without being interrupted by calls from his New York office.

Mike said, "I prefer Scott to Mr. High-Powered Hollywood. Can't think what Clare sees in him."

"Maybe the father she never had. She fell for his air of assurance," Adam said.

Standing together at the far side of the pool, Scott and Sam, both in bathing shorts, watched the Grant brothers.

Scott said, "I can't think what these women see in that insufferable couple of snobs. And they both talk like faggots."

"Nah, they're just British," Sam said. "Stand up when a woman walks in, leap around to pull chairs out—they all behave like footmen in a costume picture. I don't mind Mike, but Adam's a royal pain, and he behaves as if he owns everything in sight."

Later, as they dressed for lunch in their bedroom, Sam looked at the maroon Cartier traveling clock that Adam had given Clare for Christmas and said, "Why's he so generous to you?"

Clare laughed. "Surely you're not jealous of Adam? Can you hook my back up, please?"

"Of course I'm not jealous of that pompous legal asshole. But I can't think why Elinor invited him for Christmas."

"Because Adam is almost family, and his parents are both dead. And Gran would be lost without Adam—she's got into the habit of relying on him."

Sam shrugged his shoulders. "Some lawyers can be a very expensive habit."

In the late afternoon, after a traditional English Christmas dinner had been served in the dining room, Elinor listened happily to the shrieks of laughter around the table. She gazed with satisfaction across the oak refectory table to Buzz, with whom she had shared so many Christmases; what a pity it was that Joe couldn't see his sons, so handsome in their light suits and Christmas-gift ties. How wonderful it was to see them and her girls together again—still happy, still friends after all these years, and all reunited under one roof.

She was pleased that the girls had bothered to dress up, although their clothes were a little startling. Miranda wore a cream lace trouser suit over a nude body stocking; Annabel wore a white minidress and a bonnet of daisies tied with satin ribbons beneath her chin; Clare wore a sleeveless jumpsuit of scarlet linen edged with mustard. Buzz wore a Pucci blouse-and-pants outfit in turquoise silk, which is what she had worn every Christmas Day for the past seven years, after inheriting it from Elinor, for whom the outfit had been a little too tight.

How lucky she was, Elinor thought, gazing around at all the beloved faces. Her heart felt settled when they were all together, in a way that it had not done since her last granddaughter left home. She decided to make a little speech and tapped the table. Slowly the happy chatter subsided.

Elinor lifted her glass of champagne, but found herself unable to speak as happiness welled up from her heart. She smiled and said, "To our happy family."

Her words were echoed around the table as everyone raised a glass.

BOOK THREE

CHAPTER 15

Monday, 19 July 1965

F*ROM HER OFFICE WINDOW,* in the west corner of the chateau, Buzz could see what was happening anywhere on the two main terraces. Now, she stared out only at empty space shadowed by the late afternoon sun. Soon, thank God, things would return to normal. Elinor would be sitting out there again, and they'd be having their usual glass of champagne before lunch. The days of anxiety and concern were almost over; Elinor's recovery would, of course, be slow, but that didn't matter. Buzz had warned Clare that there were to be no more arguments, and now all Elinor had to do was get well.

Buzz's office was briskly efficient; she did not care to spend one second more than necessary in it, and nothing was superfluous in the sparsely furnished room. It held filing cabinets, bookshelves, and a desk upon which an unused I.B.M. typewriter crouched like a gray electronic cat. Behind the desk stood a sturdy swivel chair. In front of it were two nineteenth-century metal conservatory chairs for visitors; they were not very comfortable: Buzz didn't like people to stay too long.

Buzz looked at her watch. If Adam didn't arrive soon, he'd be late for the telephone calls he had booked. She opened the door and gazed down a splendid vista of reception rooms that opened out one into the next, which Buzz had learned was typical of grand French houses. Adam appeared in the distance; he hurried through the bar, the summer salon, and the television room before he finally reached the privacy of Buzz's office, which contained the only telephone that did not have extensions all over the chateau. Buzz left the room.

An aggressive French operator informed Adam that his first call had been delayed; as he waited impatiently, he glanced at the bookcases, which held first editions of all Elinor's books. Adam swiftly read the titles, most of which contained romantic words like "love," "heart," "arrow," "passionate," "fire," "dream," "kiss," and "enchanted." *Dream of the Heart, Passionate Fire*, and *Fire of the Heart* in particular caught his eye.

Unlike many men, Adam did not regard Elinor's books as a subject for jokes. He remembered a conversation he'd once had with his brother, who had teased him about his interest in the works of Elinor Dove. With an earnestness that had surprised Mike, Adam had responded forcefully. "You're wrong Mike. Leave it to the intellectuals to deride romance novels. Men like you and I can learn from them. They are our guidebooks to what women want. Often a woman reads them because they supply what's lacking in her relationship; she doesn't yearn just for sex, or even for love—she also needs romance. And so does a man, or at least he does when he first falls in love, when he's too caught up to pay any attention to what other fellows think. Then gradually, when reality starts to intrude again, he gets embarrassed about the sensitivity he's shown, and so he gradually pushes it away, to deny it's even part of his nature. It's a trap we all fall into, something I don't see changing soon. And until it does, Mike, until men and women are equal partners in romance, men who understand how women—particularly married women—feel about romance will always be able to twist them around their little fingers."

Adam could truthfully tell Elinor that he read every word she wrote and found her books absorbing. This was because he used them as guidebooks. He coldly worked out what each of his women wanted, and then coldly gave it to her. And it worked. Given this level of knowledge, almost any man could become successful at seduction.

Adam answered the telephone on the first ring. "Mike? Great to hear from you. How's the new bike? . . . How do I know? Because you *always* have a new bike."

In London, Mike laughed. "It's a rather nifty Ducati. Three fifty with single, overhead cam. Handles very well, but a bit unreliable. I've had trouble twice and she's only three weeks old." His voice became serious. "How's Elinor?"

"Much better. No more talk about scattering her ashes over the Mediterranean by moonlight. She'll soon be well enough to make her will."

"Does that matter now?"

"Not now, but it will someday, and I'm not risking this scene again."

"I'm so glad she's better," Mike said. "D'you remember how great she was to us when we were kids? She lent me the money to get my second bike—that Triumph Speed Twin: it had a lot of poke for the size. When I went to repay Elinor, she wouldn't accept the money."

"Is that why you wanted to speak to me urgently? To discuss Elinor's health?"

"Unfortunately not," Mike said. "I called to tell you that you have to pay Toby Sutch, and fast."

After a pause, Adam said. "I'll talk to Giles."

"*He* can't lend you money. As of last Wednesday, Giles Milroy-Browne is doing seven years in an open prison, for embezzlement."

"Toby's waited longer than this before."

"Exactly. He's running short of patience. I can't fix it, Adam. Remember, Toby has already paid your *French* gambling debts." Mike wished to God that when Adam went to the south of France, he would stay on the beach like everyone else.

"I don't know what I'd do without you, Mike," Adam said winningly. "Just keep Toby off my back for a few more days. Let him think that Elinor may go at any minute. Imply that I might soon have funds."

"I can't do that. . . . I don't know how you're going to get it, but you know how deep the shit will be if you don't produce at least a hundred thousand pounds . . ."

After replacing the receiver, Adam stared through the French windows to the terrace, drumming his fingers on the desk. He tugged his hair over his left eye, then jerked his head to flip it back: a gesture that revealed his anxiety. He smoked a cigarette, sucking hard at it. Finally he called Johnny Briar, a member of his insurance syndicate at Lloyds.

"What's the news? It can't get much worse, old boy," Johnny said. "We've had unbelievable bad luck. We seem to be the only syndicate that's involved in all three natural disasters. American Insurance Services have just released final estimates on the Chile earthquake. Of course, we reinsured for a cut of the premiums, but we'll still stand to lose well over sixteen million dollars. No final figures yet on the American tornado."

"And the tidal wave in Pakistan?"

"They reckon it killed sixteen thousand people."

Eventually Adam asked, "How soon will we know our final losses?"

"It looks like an open year. No money will be paid to members for three years," Johnny said, "and probably a further call after that. Frankly, this'll clean me out. I'll have to sell the house."

Adam cursed. The famous Lloyds unlimited liability probably meant that Adam would also be declared bankrupt. "How long will they wait for payment?"

"You know Lloyds don't wait, old boy. It's cash on the nail as soon as the arbitrators reach a settlement—the Lloyds reputation stands on that." Johnny added, "It's not worth messing with Lloyds, Adam, you know it isn't: no one would ever touch you again—Lloyds would see to that."

Adam's next call was to Ned Sinclair, financial director of SUPPLYKITS. With an effort, Adam steadied his voice. "Ned? I want you to take another look at that new Carefree proposal—the duty-free airport shops. I know they're asking more than we want to pay, but if we can assemble a package of cash, stock options, and newly issued shares as a good inducement, I think we'll convince the key manager and he'll persuade the others to sell. So talk to him, see what he wants, then stitch something together for next week."

"I'm already working on it," Sinclair said cheerfully.

Adam sighed as he replaced the telephone receiver. Again he ran his left hand through his hair, but this time he felt a tingle of anticipation. There *was* always something around the corner if you didn't lose your head. He had a definite feeling of success about the Carefree deal. And there were plenty more deals.

And perhaps it was time to play the trump card up his sleeve. He'd never be in a better position to do it. Perhaps it was time for a little more reinsurance.

Annabel's call from Scott came through to Saracen just as dinner was announced. She raced upstairs to her apartment and threw herself on the bedcover, a Welsh patchwork quilt in a soft pattern of cream and pink.

Waiting for Scott to pick up the telephone, Annabel could visualize the scene at the TV station. She could clearly remember the first day that Scott had shown her around, could remember being impressed by the overwhelming glamour of it all. From that day, Annabel had worshiped him. She sometimes felt that were Scott not sitting at the studio news desk, face made up and hair sprayed, ready to roll and clearly in control—why, then the news might never happen.

Eventually Scott's voice came through faintly on the line. "Angel, you aren't going to like this one bit, but you asked the agency to call me as soon as Avanti decided. They don't want to renew your contract."

Annabel suddenly felt that her mind was spiraling out of control. Her forehead felt clammy and her hands began to shake. She found it difficult to swallow. Her heart was thumping so loudly that she wondered for a fleeting second whether Scott could hear it. Her rib cage seemed too small and she panted for air. She also felt a sudden, massive drop in the pit of her stomach, the place where her self-confidence dwelled.

"Annabel? Are you still there?" Thousands of miles away, Scott heard a gulp. He said reassuringly, "Angel, it isn't the end of the world."

"It is for me," Annabel said.

Exhausted by anxiety and emotion, Clare had decided to go to bed early. In the thirty-foot-long, dark-paneled bedroom, she lay upon the Jacobean four-poster bed and gazed up at the crimson brocade canopy. Stripped down to her petticoat, she felt too tired to undress further. She wished that someone would invent a button that you pressed, and *shazam!*—you were tucked in bed, washed and with your teeth brushed. Languidly she turned her head to the west-facing windows, staring out at the neighboring mountain high above the hill upon which Saracen was built.

Again Clare wondered if she had gone a bit too far, speaking so negatively about Gran's novels, and being so emphatically against the trust.

Hearing a knock, she called, "Come in."

Slowly the door opened.

In the doorway was the craggy outline of her husband. Sam looked sheepish and apologetic.

For one glad moment, Clare wanted to rush to him, put her head against his big chest, feel his strong hands stroking her back, and let Sam do all the worrying for her. But she remembered the sight of him in bed with that would-be starlet and fought the impulse, staring angrily at him instead. "What are *you* doing here?"

"I came as soon as I heard that Elinor was . . . ill. It was in the *Tribune* a couple of days ago. I came to see if you needed me. And if Elinor is going, I want to say goodbye."

"Very touching, but Gran is getting better. You needn't have come."

"I know. Adam already told me. He was about as welcoming as you are. Why's he here if she's recovering?"

"Adam has every right to be here," Clare said pointedly. "He's been our family lawyer for years."

"I'm not the only one who doesn't trust the devious bastard. Buzz doesn't like him," Sam said, "and she is a lady with a very reliable built-in shit detector."

"Adam isn't Gran's only lawyer," Clare retorted. "There's another chap, Paul Littlejohn."

"From the same firm? Then he's probably under Adam's thumb."

Suddenly Clare realized why Sam had come, and cried scornfully, "*You* can't criticize Adam for being devious! I suppose *you* are straightforward? You've just hurtled halfway round the world *only* to say goodbye to your estranged wife's grandmother! How touching!"

Sam nodded. "Of course, I'd also like to see Josh."

"Not now. He's asleep!"

"I know. I was told by a French sourpuss nurse in the hall; she's clearly had charisma bypass surgery."

"You should see the day nurses!" Then Clare was vexed that he'd almost made her laugh. She stiffened as Sam shut the door and took two steps toward her.

Hopefully Sam said, "I also want to see *you*." He advanced, a dark, disturbing masculine presence. Each time Sam took a step forward, Clare took a step backward, toward the windows.

"You're seeing me now!" she said. "I haven't changed much in four weeks."

"I have." Sam took another step.

"That contrite line won't work anymore, Sam." Clare's voice was cold. Retreating until she bumped into a Spanish walnut table that stood before a window, she put her arms back to lean on the table, then decided that her position might look inviting, folded her arms, and scowled at Sam. "I have enough to worry about," she said crossly. "Please *leave*, Sam! You can come back and see Josh in the morning—but don't think you can march in here and wheedle your way back into my heart in half an hour—not this time!"

"Of course I know I can't change things in half an hour. I've had four weeks to realize what a stupid bastard I've been," Sam said.

Clare cried, "You don't want a real relationship, you only want ego-boosting, pseudo relationships!"

"I admit that's what it has been like in the past."

"I've had *enough!*" Clare stormed. "*You* think that if I don't know about your affairs, it can't disturb our relationship. That it doesn't matter if you cheat on your wife, so long as she doesn't find out. But it *does* matter because our relationship becomes dishonest. Even if *I* don't know it, *you* do, and that changes *your* attitude to me."

"What the hell do you mean by that?" Sam seemed genuinely perplexed.

"You invent, or goad me into, some failing to give *you* cause for complaint, so that you can then screw around with a clear conscience. Well, I've had enough of being the wife who doesn't understand you! Now I *do* understand you. And I can't stand your treachery and deceit! I can't stand that parody of a happy life in that parody of a place."

"No more affairs, I promise."

"*It's no use*, Sam. We both know that history will only repeat itself. You want to nibble every biscuit in the tin, and nothing will ever change you! I'm *never* going to forget what I saw—or stop wondering whether it's happening again."

Sam's mind quickly returned to the last time he had seen Clare, when she had returned early from the beach to find Sam in their bed, and not alone. Clare had recognized the girl—the would-be actress daughter of a neighbor who had been kind to Clare when the Shapiros first moved in.

Under Clare's glare, the frightened girl had shrunk against the headboard, her knees drawn up to hide her slim, naked body. Clare continued to stare until the girl scuttled from the bedroom to the patio; there, she hesitated, remembering her nakedness. Desperate, she cast one backward glance at Clare, then fled.

Hairy and naked, Sam had crouched on the bed feeling exposed and helpless. Then Sam had thrown her a pleading look, like a naughty little boy caught with his finger in the jam pot.

Finally Clare had screamed, "I've had enough of these scenes." Without being told, Sam knew at that moment that Clare would leave him. This time she would fling no bitter accusations or black lingerie at him. As he stared at the torment, fury, and despair in her face, he knew that Clare would not forgive him. He also knew that this disastrous episode was entirely his own fault and could easily have been avoided. After all, he could have taken the girl someplace else.

Now Sam looked at his wife as she stood at the end of the long, dark paneled bedroom, her back to the window, beyond which olive trees rustled in a hot breeze. Leaning against the walnut table, Clare felt her face tighten as she, too, relived that painful scene. Slowly she said, "I hate to admit this, but what hurt as much as the treachery was the humiliation. My self-esteem disappeared and I felt worthless, although I told myself that I was still an attractive woman, that there was no need to feel sexually inadequate."

"So it's the sex thing again!" Sam said with exasperation. "I thought we'd settled that!"

"It's not sex that's the problem, it's what you demonstrate during sex!" Clare's cry was from the heart. "A sexual relationship isn't separated from the rest of reality, Sam. It never once occurred to you that *you* might be an ignorant, selfish, lousy lover. It was arrogant of you to assume that *I* was inadequate! Deep down, you *still* don't think I'm a normal woman! You're *still* afraid of any attack on your divine male right to know everything there is to know about sex."

Sam realized that, for the first time, Clare was yelling at him instead of building up a silent volcano of resentment. He wasn't sure what to do: He didn't want to go over all that again. On the other hand, Clare was finally able to express her anger clearly to the person who had caused it.

Sam knew better than to interrupt her flow.

" . . . And while we're talking about the man's divine right to know, little babies are *born* knowing all they need to know about love: they're unself-conscious, they can communicate, and their first experience—sucking—is a sensual one! But by the time a baby boy grows up, his head has been stuffed with myths and taboos, and the idea that in sexual matters, *the man always knows best!*"

Sam looked suitably unsure.

Clare paused, then shook her head wearily. "There's no point in this, Sam. You've never listened to the things I say, and even when something is an obvious fact, you never quite seem to believe me, or to trust me. You're too trapped in your own ego to be able to hear or to understand."

"They should teach a guy these things at school," Sam said lamely, as he was clearly expected to make some response. "Please believe me, Clare, I'll do anything to get you back."

"Exactly *what* do you want to get back?" Clare asked.

"My wife and my son," Sam said firmly.

"And of course, your career?"

"Yes." Sam's last movie, *Mainsail*, had performed unimpressively.

"So at *last* we have the truth!" Clare shouted. "You turned up here because you thought I was about to inherit enough money to stage your movie comeback!"

"That isn't fair, Clare. Sure, I could use any investment that's floating around. Who can't? I've got an option on a terrific screenplay. It's called 'Voyage to the Moon.' It's about—"

"*Get out!*"

Sam did not retreat. "You say that you want total honesty from me, and then you throw me out when you get it! You know movies always came first in my life until I met you. Now they come second, but I'll admit it's a close second."

Clare wondered why she felt so hurt, when she'd always known the truth. Sam was a movie creature, first and foremost. He might say now that he put his wife and child first; he might even think it. But the fact was that ninety-nine percent of his energy, his concentration, his time, and his money was devoted to his business. His family got what was left.

Sam looked again at the dark smudges of exhaustion under Clare's eyes. He saw how thin she'd become in only four weeks. He longed to take her in his arms, but she swiftly dodged around the table to the window so that the Spanish table was a barrier between them.

"Get out," Clare said again.

The next morning, Buzz sat on a pale blue chair before the window in Elinor's bedroom. "Only one visitor at a time, the doctor said," Buzz reminded her firmly. "And keep it short. Remember, you didn't feel too good yesterday. Ten minutes each girl and not a second more! You'll see Miranda first, then Annabel."

"And Clare?" Elinor asked.

"Clare's seeing Sam and Josh off for a day on the speedboat. She'll be along later."

The day nurse pulled down the cream window blinds against the morning sun as Miranda entered.

Elinor smiled as she said, "Hello, darling." She had trouble pronouncing the words. She asked anxiously, "Can you hear me properly, Miranda?"

"Of course she can," Buzz said. "You sound as if you've got a bit of a toothache, that's all."

After ten minutes of understandably strained, cheerful chat, Buzz jerked her head toward the door and Miranda quietly disappeared. She was replaced by Annabel, who had clearly been crying.

As she talked, Annabel picked up a little box from the bedside table; it was an antique ebony snuffbox, the lid inlaid with a geometric pattern of tortoiseshell and ivory.

"That was the first antique I ever bought," Elinor said. "Cost tuppence from a junk barrow in Earls Court Road. Take it now, dear child, as a gift."

Buzz said sharply, "Annabel! Put that back! You ain't dying, Nell, and I won't have you behaving as if you was."

Annabel jumped and replaced the little box. "Sorry. I was only fiddling with it." She had wanted to disguise her trembling hands: she was not about to explain to her sick grandmother the reason for her fright, for the panic that rose within her chest.

After Annabel left, Elinor whispered to Buzz, "I want to see Clare *alone*."

"Not on your life," said Buzz. "I'm sticking to you, close as a limpet. You ain't going to overdo it today, my girl. *Nobody* is going to see you alone."

"Please, Buzz," Elinor pleaded. "I want to ask her to go back to Sam."

Buzz hesitated, knowing that Clare would never discuss this in her presence. Reluctantly she nodded. "Don't forget, I'll be sitting next door in the library with my stopwatch."

She marched past Elinor's bed into the library; in front of the large window that overlooked the sea was the wooden kitchen table upon which Elinor had written *Deadly Fortune* and her every book since.

From the window, Buzz could see Clare sunning herself on the terrace below. "Okay, Clare, you can come up now," she yelled.

Two minutes later, Clare stood at her grandmother's bedside; after a sleepless night, she looked almost as pale and exhausted as Elinor.

Elinor said, "I saw Sam for a few minutes, darling. He told me you'd had a serious tiff, but he hopes to persuade you to return to L.A."

Clare looked carefully at Elinor. "Sam only tells people what suits him, Gran."

"He's apparently just flown halfway round the world to tell you he loves you."

"Sam can certainly *act* the devoted husband," Clare said sourly. "But if he's flown halfway round the world to tell me he loves me, then why *didn't* he tell me he loves me?"

"Any Don Juan can *say* he loves you." Elinor attempted a smile as she quoted what Buzz had so often told the girls in years past. "You have to watch what Sam does, not what he says. If he gets up in the middle of the night to fetch you a glass of water, then he loves you."

"A Busby Berkeley lineup in front of his bed couldn't wake Sam in the middle of the night," Clare said. "Gran, I didn't want to tell you, especially now, but you must understand. He . . . was with somebody else. That's why I left."

"She probably threw herself at him. A little tart. Dearest girl, I've told you before, you mustn't let a little bit of fluff spoil your marriage."

"You know, she was only *one* of them," Clare said, vexed. It was typical of Sam's chutzpah to get his story in first, to gain sympathy and support, to get Gran on his team.

Reluctantly Elinor said, "I had the same problem with Daddy Billy, but in my day, wives had to put up with that sort of thing. Please be patient, darling, for Josh's sake as well as your own. Don't throw away your marriage because Sam is giving you trouble. *All* men give trouble."

Clare said indignantly, "I really don't want to discuss it, Gran, but I don't see why I should put up with my husband's adulteries just because you did—so please don't try to force me!"

"After six years of marriage, Clare, you can't expect the same relationship as on your wedding day."

"Of course I don't expect the same relationship! " Clare exclaimed. What she *had* expected was a loving and trusting relationship based on a realistic assessment of each other's virtues and faults.

"Being in love . . . " Elinor dreamily remembered what it was like to feel that your lover possessed all the wonderful qualities you wanted, before you realized that he didn't possess them, and that perhaps you had forced those qualities on him in the first place. She shook her head sadly. "Being in love isn't being married."

"Is that why you never write about marriage?" Clare inquired bitterly. "Only being in love?"

"There's no need for that tone of voice," Elinor said, clearly hurt.

"*Being in love isn't a solution to every female problem!*" Clare cried. "I've never seen *that* spelled out in a women's magazine story, or a film, or . . . a novel."

Clare was prepared to do without the ups of being in love in return for never experiencing the downs. She never again wanted to experience the feeling of being out of control and dependent on someone else's approval, at someone else's mercy. She never again wanted to feel that someone else could send her to heaven or to hell. She never again wanted to experience that feeling which led women to do too much for, and demand too much from, a partner.

"Understandably, you're feeling cynical because of Sam's naughtiness. . . . "

"Gran, he's not some mischievous schoolboy." Last night, Sam had tried to manipulate Clare, and now her grandmother was trying to do the same thing on his behalf.

For the second time in twenty-four hours, Clare's indignation overcame her caution. Having come to terms with the failure of her marriage, she was trying to pick up the broken bits of her pride, glue them together, and get on with her life. She wished that people would not interfere, would leave her alone, especially people who didn't know all the facts.

"Why not try to look upon whatever happened as a little misdemeanor," Elinor persisted. "Sam *loves* you. You know he does. And love is important because you can't live without it, dear child: without love, you only exist."

"I'm not sure that *I* love Sam. And I *can* live without love! Lots of people do—nuns and lighthousemen, for a start." Clare raged. "*You* taught me that without a man, a woman's life is bleak, empty, and dangerous; *you* taught me that a woman isn't complete without a man. But I wonder if that's so. *I* felt inadequate *because* I was living with a man."

Elinor whispered, "Don't throw away your marriage, Clare. No woman wants to live without love and romance—that's what makes a woman feel transformed . . . excited . . . attractive . . . alive. That's what I've always tried to convey in my writing."

"Romance has a bad influence on reality," Clare said. "You encourage your readers to believe that one day their prince will come."

"What's wrong with that?"

"*What's wrong is that he won't!* He will only ever be a paper prince on a paper page! You should have shown your readers that there *isn't* a Prince Charming, so they won't feel disappointed and cheated if their prince turns into a frog, like mine did. The story Sam tells about the frog is sad because it's *true. . . .* "

"The story about the frog?"

"It's not as silly as it sounds. A frog asked a princess to take him to bed with her so that he could turn into a fairy prince. But when she woke up in the morning, the frog was *still* a frog. He croaked, 'Sorry to disappoint you, but princesses always fall for that line.' "

Elinor was silent as she allowed herself to see, for once, the soft and gentle cobweb of romance she had carefully woven around her life with Billy. Quietly she asked, "Is it so terrible to let an unhappy or humiliated woman forget, for a few hours, the problems that she will probably have to put up with for her whole life?" Elinor believed that her novels provided her readers with excitement, helped them to escape from insecurity and anxiety, frustration and drudgery, misery and sorrow, and of course, the boring daily routine of a life in which nothing was likely to change.

Clare sighed. "You shouldn't encourage your readers to think that their lives might turn out like your novels. You encourage them to turn to romance rather than face reality. And then they're at a disadvantage when they have to deal with real life problems." Her voice rose.

"Clare, you're getting overexcited." Elinor's own voice had weakened to a whisper. Clare suddenly noticed that Elinor's hands were gripping the bedclothes, betraying the emotion hidden by her quiet words. In trying to articulate what she felt so strongly, Clare had forgotten that she was talking to a very sick woman.

"I'm sorry, Gran. I hadn't planed to talk about this today. But you know it's what I've always thought. And it doesn't mean that I don't love you."

Elinor was not mollified. She said sharply, "My romantic novels enabled you girls to have a carefree life, the sort of life I wish I'd been able to give your father." Elinor waited for the apology she felt was due from Clare. After a few moments of uncomfortable silence, she said stubbornly, "If you denigrate my life's work, you shall not profit by it—unless you apologize to me, Clare."

With an effort, Clare spoke softly. "Gran, I don't want to denigrate your life's work. And I don't want to talk about money. That's not important, Gran—"

"Are you going to apologize to me or not?" Elinor demanded in a shaking voice. She thought that Clare was being contemptuous of all she had done for her. In fact, Clare had been going to say that Elinor's health was what was important at the moment.

Buzz strode in from the library. "Your ten minutes was up half an hour ago, Clare. And if I'd known there would be raised voices, I wouldn't have let you in here." Clare's visit with Elinor was abruptly terminated.

Furious at the angry words, Clare telephoned Thomas Cook in Nice for tickets to London. She wasn't going back to L.A., and she wasn't staying *here*. She would take Josh and Kathy, go to cozy, comfortable London, where she knew so many people, and there she would sort out her life.

Miranda, wearing a green bikini, sunned herself on the south terrace. As she listened to the faint smack of the sea on the rocks below, she thought again, regretfully, of Angus. She had to face the fact that she still missed him.

Although she'd seen a couple of nice men recently, when it came to the heavy breathing, Miranda found that she didn't want to be touched intimately by anyone she didn't know well. She didn't feel comfortable and safe with anybody but Angus: *he* hadn't tried to push her into bed at the first opportunity.

Three weeks earlier, her secretary had unexpectedly announced Mr. Angus Maclayne on line three. Miranda's heart had looped the loop as she happily accepted an invitation to lunch at Rules, his favorite restaurant. She hoped Angus wanted to rekindle their love affair, as she did.

Rules was decorated like a Victorian library; it smelled of superior malt whiskeys and very old leather. Miranda and Angus sat in a velvet-lined, crimson booth that reminded her of an old-fashioned first-class railway carriage. The Dickensian waiter flapped his napkin and advised with more truth than tact, "Shouldn't have turbot today, sir, although the salmon's passable." They ordered vichyssoise, followed by sea bass with fresh peas, and iced apricot soufflé afterward.

There had been no expression of undying love on the angular face she had come to love. Instead, Angus treated Miranda with distant respect, twitching his sandy eyebrows and speaking of inconsequential things—just as though she were his aunt . . . or maybe his stockbroker.

Once during lunch, she thought for a moment her hopes would be realized. Over the sea bass, Angus leaned across the white linen tablecloth, his lips close to her ear. "Miranda, I've been thinking a lot about you."

Miranda smiled encouragingly. She longed to hear him say, "god, how I've missed you! Let's get out of here, darling! I want to be alone with you!"

Angus said, "I'm worried that you're expanding too fast. You seem to be financing yourself by borrowing against your leases—leveraging in an expanding property market while interest rates are low."

Miranda felt her heart crash to the bottom of her rib cage. "What's wrong with that?" she muttered.

Angus carefully dissected his fish. "If this property boom suddenly collapses, or if the government decides to jack up the bank rate to curb consumer spending, then you might find your loans withdrawn, in which case you'd have a serious cash-flow problem on your hands."

"I appreciate your concern," Miranda said crossly.

"Higher bank interest may also mean a property slump," Angus added, "And then you'd have another big problem: the leases that act as your collateral would sink in value, so the banks would run scared and ask for fast repayment." Angus sipped his hock reflectively. "That sort of situation has been known to end in . . . bankruptcy."

"Thanks for warning me, but I have no intention of going bankrupt," Miranda replied coldly; she was too disappointed to enjoy the apricot soufflé. For the remainder of the meal, they chatted politely about business and exchanged city gossip. Afterward, they parted awkwardly on the pavement, each refusing the other's offer of a lift. Neither suggested a further meeting.

Angus, who admired guts and gumption, had missed the adventurous and spirited Miranda even more than he expected. He asked her out to lunch because he hoped that she had missed him. He had kept a discreet close watch on Miranda, who, he knew, had not been seriously involved with any other man since she broke off their engagement. Angus reckoned that fast business expansion was absorbing all her time and energy, which was why he had decided to take things one step at a time and discuss only business over luncheon; a business chat would avoid putting either of them in a rejecting position.

Sadly, Miranda, too, had clearly wished to discuss only business.

However, Angus did not intend to give up his pursuit of her; she fascinated him as no other woman had. Sometimes she was fiery, or she could be ice cool: qualities that intrigued the male in Angus, although they disturbed the businessman.

CHAPTER 16

Tuesday, 20 July 1965

M*IRANDA LAY HALF* asleep on a sofa in front of her sitting room window, which looked down on the Place de la République; from there, the road led to the distant perfume factory which Miranda wanted to buy. It had been built in the depression of 1870—when most villagers were out of work—by the Countess of Saracen, whose birthday was still celebrated, and a mass said for her soul in the local Church of St. Peter.

Miranda was startled by a knock on the door. She called, "*Entrez,*" and then said, "Oh, it's you, Adam."

"May I come in?"

"Sure. I've finished my siesta." Miranda yawned, stretched, and wriggled her bare, brown toes. She was wearing an emerald silk shirt and bikini.

"I see an old friend." Adam pointed to a framed cartoon, which he had given her the previous Christmas: a startled businessman gazed at a ghost; rising from his desk drawer, it said, "I am the spirit of old notes to yourself."

"You hit home with that one." Miranda yawned again. "What do you want?" She rubbed her stiff neck. "Big mistake to go to sleep on the couch."

"I can fix a stiff neck in no time," Adam offered. "I learned massage at the gym. Lie flat on the floor."

"Okay." Another yawn. "Shirt on or off?"

"Oh, keep it on."

Miranda lay on her stomach on the kilim rug; it was patterned in ocher and the same faded blue as Adam's flared jeans and shirt.

Adam knelt behind her head and started to massage her shoulders. After ten minutes, Miranda's neckache had vanished: she lay on the rug, her eyes shut; she felt boneless and sleepy.

Adam's voice was quiet and firm. "Your body is getting lighter and lighter. . . . You feel light enough to float on a cloud. . . . When I count to ten, you will relax . . ."

Miranda thought, Why, he's hypnotizing me, and then floated to sleep.

She woke to see Adam lying with his legs up, on the sofa, reading *Paris Match*. Miranda looked at her watch. "I've been asleep almost an hour. You did a great job. I feel as boneless as a squid."

"You were very tired," Adam said, "and we've all been worried about Elinor."

"Yes." Miranda's face crumpled and she started to weep. She rubbed both eyes, then winced as, too late, she remembered her contact lenses. She edged them out and scrambled to her feet. "I can't think why I'm crying."

"A natural reaction, after this strain and anxiety," Adam said reassuringly. He watched her, his head to one side, as if undecided. He stood up. He moved toward her. "Don't worry. I'm in control of everything. You can relax now."

Miranda sniffled. She felt the flimsy cotton of Adam's shirt against her as muscular arms wrapped around her. Her body relaxed and she leaned her head against his strong chest. She felt his hand beneath her shirt; his thumb pressed along her naked backbone all the way to the nape of her neck.

Each time Adam gently pressed against a vertebra, Miranda was pushed against his body. She could feel his flat, muscular strength: she could also feel his arousal as Adam kissed her firmly on the mouth.

Long ago, Miranda had realized that sexual involvement with Adam could only complicate her life, but she had been only half awake and off guard when he made his move. Rebelliously she thought, What the hell. Why shouldn't I forget business—just for once? And why shouldn't I do as I please with my own body?

In silence, Adam lifted her into his arms and carried her (five feet nine and no lightweight) onto the bed. Miranda's hair flamed against the pillow as she lay back with her eyes closed, thinking, Too late to stop him now. And I don't want to.

Almost motionless, she lay in a trance of sensuality, Adam's mouth against the soft skin of her breasts. He whispered, "Keep your eyes closed. You're not to *move*. Here, I'm in charge."

"But don't you want me to—"

"I want you to lie still and let me . . . love you."

Miranda felt a melting and tickling inside her stomach as if someone were stroking it with a feather. Her body relaxed in Adam's strong and clearly skilled hands as he stroked her bare, smooth belly, and a warm glow spread from her navel over her entire body. His mouth warmed her as his lips traveled slowly downward from her breasts.

Some time later, Miranda said, "But *you* haven't."

"There's plenty of time," Adam said. "*I* like to do things to a woman. I get my pleasure from seeing you climax." She had thrashed around like a freshly caught trout on a grassy bank. "I told you, you're not to *move*." Adam firmly replaced her arm on the pillow.

"And what if I do?"

"I'll tie you to the bed."

Miranda opened her eyes. "Bondage? How sleazy."

"Not if it's playful," Adam promised. "I'd blindfold you with a silken scarf and tie your wrists and ankles to the bedpost with silken ribbons."

"I'd bite them off!"

"I was only joking," Adam murmured, feeling again for her breasts.

An hour later, Miranda, lying on top of Adam's suntanned, naked body, said sleepily, "that was a big surprise."

"I've been wanting to do it for years."

"Why did you wait so long?"

"The same reason as you. Prudence. But nobody could feel platonic about you, Miranda."

Miranda remembered howling as a twelve-year-old because Adam treated her as a child. Briefly she wished that child could have looked into this future. She said, "I think . . . I think I've always wanted . . . this."

"I know I have." Adam again bent his lips to her breast.

Miranda said sleepily, "I've never had an orgasm during sex like that. Sometimes I've been on the verge, but then the feeling vanished."

"I have to confess, you're not the first woman I've made love to."

Miranda inhaled the earthy smell of the bed, propped herself on one elbow, and started gently to scratch Adam's arm with her fingernails, stroking the sensitive inner flesh, from wrist to elbow.

He shivered with pleasure. "No woman has ever aroused me as you have."

"You too?"

"I've never felt like this before, Miranda. I feel that we're equals, that you'll never allow me to dominate you. I suspect you'll always keep me guessing, keep me on my toes." Roughly he pulled her to him.

His kiss was deep and passionate. Miranda fleetingly wondered how she could ever have thought that Adam had a withholding, guarded nature. And then she was drawn again into his spell and she stopped thinking altogether.

Later, Adam lazily stared past Miranda to the windows—twin rectangles of blue sky, between which hung an old mirror in an elaborately carved mahogany frame. The silvered glass was faintly green in places and speckled black where the silver had flaked off the back. Beneath this mirror stood Miranda's surprisingly feminine dressing table, skirted in spotted white muslin frills.

Adam said, "I'm surprised to find your dressing table looks like Scarlett O'Hara's underdrawers."

"Sometimes a frill is just a frill." Miranda shrugged.

"My clever darling," Adam murmured.

Miranda stretched voluptuously. "Annabel and Clare are going to get the surprise of their lives when we tell them about *us!*"

"I'd prefer to keep our secret to ourselves for a bit," Adam said firmly. "I have to settle Elinor's affairs. I don't want anyone to suspect that I favor you over your sisters, which is something they already fear because of our business connection."

He did not mention his other reason for secrecy, although they both knew it.

Everyone close to her knew that Elinor's unspoken dream was that Miranda—her only remaining unmarried granddaughter—should marry into the British aristocracy. While Elinor lived, Adam dared not risk flinging a monkey wrench into that dream.

At eleven o'clock the following morning, Buzz sat down on the blue chair by Elinor's bedroom window, pulled the kitchen timer from the pocket of her navy cotton dress, and set it to twenty minutes: the mechanism began to tick in an irritating way.

Elinor, in a cream silk bed jacket, was propped up by a stack of frilly pillows; she looked old and frail.

Elinor's cat, Fudge, now allowed back into the bedroom, padded to the gray sofa in front of the fireplace, where Adam sat, and rubbed against his jeans.

"Cats always like me." Adam leaned down and stroked the pale ginger fur; the cat curled up against his feet and went to sleep. From the briefcase that lay open at his side, Adam extracted a document. He spoke briskly. "Before I return to London, I'd like to propose a strategy, should Elinor ever again be ill, to prevent the problems that Buzz has experienced during the past few weeks." Because nobody had been empowered to sign checks on Elinor's behalf, no household bills or salaries could be paid: for three weeks, the servants' wages had been paid by Buzz from her own bank account.

"If, for any reason, Elinor can't sign checks, then I suggest I sign them for her," Adam said.

Buzz looked up sharply.

Adam continued, "But I would be empowered to draw *only* on Elinor's housekeeping account in Nice. The power of attorney would specifically state that no checks could be made out to me or the firm. We would wait for any payment until Elinor was well again."

"Why not have two signatures required?" Buzz suggested. "One of the other STG partners, perhaps?"

"Certainly." Adam nodded, then turned to Elinor. "And the STG professional insurance would automatically cover malpractice."

Elinor looked at Buzz. "That okay with you? Yes. Then please do it, Adam dear." Her voice was feeble.

After Elinor signed and the document was witnessed, Adam produced a second sheet of paper. He said, "In order to prevent literary contracts being held up, I also suggest that a general power of attorney be given to me—again only in a limited area and only to be used if Elinor is indisposed."

Buzz asked, "Is that also covered by the malpractice insurance?"

"Yes," Adam said. "Incidentally, if I deliberately breached a power of attorney and exploited it for my own benefit—although I can't think how that would be possible—I would be struck off the Roll of Solicitors by the Law Society."

"That all right with you, Buzz?" Elinor asked faintly.

"Do you have any specific objections, Buzz?" Adam inquired politely.

After a moment, Buzz shook her head. These powers of attorney were only for day-to-day transactions. If Buzz protested without cause, it might even sound fishy—as if she wanted to control Nell's money.

"Then I also agree to that," Elinor said.

Wednesday, 21 July 1965

At five P.M., Scott finished his coverage of the anti-Vietnam War demonstrators. In the newsroom, reporters hung around drinking coffee as they read or talked. Desks were littered with yards of wire stories, celebrity bulletins, picture handouts, telephone messages, and empty coffee cups. In the background, teletype machines clacked, and a bank of television monitors showed different pictures, some of which were material being fed through to the station. Somebody wailed, "You mean after *two* lawyers passed this, I *still* can't run it?"

In the news editor's office, an assistant was reading the list of stories from her scratch pad, "Report from Washington on the senator bribe story. The mayor of New York and the antiwar demonstrations. We have the mayor bugging out on this, Scott."

A head poked around the door. "Call to Europe in your office, Scott."

"Sorry, you guys." Scott hurried to his office and carefully closed the door. "Annabel? What's happened, darling?"

"Scott . . . *I miss you!*"

"I miss you too, angel."

"*I need you here.*"

Scott was sensitive to the pressure his wife had been under for the past month. First she'd learned that her grandmother, whom she adored, was dangerously ill, and had been at her bedside ever since. Then her contract had not been renewed. This was a double-barrel blow for both of them in terms of loss of money and prestige. The humiliation was worse because it was so public, and it was a good thing that Annabel had not been in New York when the news broke, when gloating gossip writers had jammed Scott and Annabel's home phones with their venomous questions.

Scott knew that Annabel was now facing the worst moment any model can face: she was officially over the hill, gaining weight, losing her looks and on the downward path to wrinkles and sag. No reassurances from Scott had been able to lull his twenty-five-year-old wife's anxiety about her fading beauty. It was ludicrous to be so young and yet a has-been.

Scott tried to handle her diplomatically. "Angel, I wish I could be with you, but we both know I can't. We've talked about this so often: you know I want to be supportive, but I also have to do my job properly. We're short-staffed here—the summer holiday period's started and everyone's stretched. I can't just walk out. If I'd come when you first asked me, I might have been in Saracen for an entire month: I'd probably have no job to come back to." Gently he added, "And what use would I have been, angel?"

Once again Scott felt that she was asking for something unreasonable, something a child might ask of a parent. He wished Annabel were not so insecure and dependent upon him; for the past few months, as she waited for Avanti to make up its mind, she had needed constant emotional support and reassurance from Scott, who had felt her clinging to him, almost like a physical weight on his back.

"I wanted you with me," Annabel wept. She had forgotten that she telephoned to tell Scott the news of the trust.

"My job means having to give up a lot of things that everyone else takes for granted in their life, and you've always known that, Annabel," Scott again reminded her.

"Your job seems to suck up your entire life," Annabel sobbed reproachfully.

"Yes, that's why I married you. Because I love you, and I want what little private life I have to be steady and permanent," Scott said.

"You're so involved with your precious career that you put it before your private life," Annabel retorted. "You put *us* on the back burner—you'll deal with it next week, next month—you'll do that until you *retire!*"

"My career *is* precious to me—and you knew that when you married me. It's not as if I worked for a large network news show. You know that *everyone* here does the job of at least two people. How would it look if I suddenly disappeared for weeks—leaving a gap that other people would have to fill—because my wife's grandmother is ill on the other side of the world?"

"*Please* come, Scott."

"It's not necessary. I can't walk out on everyone here. Please try to understand that, angel."

"Scott, I want to hold you . . . It's been months since we were in bed together. Don't you remember how good it used to be?"

"*Nobody* gets the honeymoon treatment forever, angel. That sort of twenty-four-hours-in-bed passion changes into a different sort of comfortable, caring love."

Annabel wailed, "You mean I don't attract you anymore? You don't love me?"

Exasperated, Scott said, "You've become spoiled, neurotic, overanxious, and self-absorbed. What's so lovable about that, Annabel?"

Scott's office door burst open. "You're wanted in the cutting room."

"Thanks, I'll be right along!" To Annabel, Scott said carefully, "You just have to tough it out, angel. These situations sometimes happen in life."

"That's not all." Annabel gulped, then managed to say, "I think I'm having a heart attack."

"*What!*"

After he calmed down, Scott reasoned that if Annabel were having a heart attack, she wouldn't be able to talk on the telephone. Cautiously he said, "Why do you think that, angel?"

"My heart is thumping! I can't breathe properly—I'm gasping for air!"

"It might be another anxiety attack," Scott suggested gently.

Annabel said in an agitated voice, "I feel as if my mind is whirling madly, like a hurricane. I can't control it. I feel taut and tense. I'm literally *shaking!*"

"Are you sweating? Are your hands clammy? Is your stomach knotted?"

"*Yes,*" Annabel wept.

It was another panic attack. Scott said, "Is Adam still around? Get him to the phone, darling."

Another head appeared around Scott's door. "They can't cut until you're on the spot, Scott."

Scott nearly said, "My wife is ill," but he had cried wolf too often: other people's wives didn't telephone the station as relentlessly as Annabel.

Eventually Scott heard Adam's faint but reassuringly calm voice. "Anything I can do to help, Scott? Annabel seems upset. We thought she'd gone to bed. It's nearly midnight here."

"Annabel thinks she's having a heart attack," Scott told him.

"I don't think so," Adam said firmly. "I'll take her to Elinor's night nurse immediately—I expect she'll give Annabel something to calm her down. The situation here has been very tense. It's understandable that Annabel is a little . . . overwrought."

Scott thought, He's telling me that she's hysterical. He said, "Tell me straight, Adam. Just answer yes or no. Does Annabel look ill to you?"

"No."

"I'm between a rock and a hard place. Of course I'll fly over straightaway if Elinor . . ."

"There is no necessity to do so." Adam spoke firmly again. "Elinor is progressing well, and I have everything under control here."

"I'm sure you have," Scott said with great relief.

Wednesday, 28 July 1965

A week later, just before her luncheon was served, Adam took the trust documentation to Elinor's bedroom to be signed.

As he laid the twenty-four-page Declaration of Trust before her, Adam said, "There are no changes, but one alteration. As Paul is to be the protector, the STG partners think it best to have trustees outside the firm, so we'll arrange that through the group of accountants we deal with in Bermuda."

"Did you ask Clare once more?" Elinor, looking frail, was not interested in the fine points of the trust.

"Yes. I'm afraid she's still adamant."

Elinor thought for a minute. With an effort, she lifted her head. "Remember that I don't want Clare to know she's included in the trust *until she apologizes!* She is *not* to think she can get away with behaving hurtfully. Now, where do I sign this thing? You'd better call Buzz and that sour-looking nurse to witness it."

At 7:20 that same morning, Scott had been at the site of an unusual hit-and-run story: two older men had been killed and another injured by a police patrol car. At midday, Scott returned to the studio with twenty minutes of film footage, which would be edited to two minutes plus. It looked as if it would end up their lead story.

The news editor suggested, "Let's team it with this other hit-and-run story that's just come in: two black kids, in a car out of control, ran over four children, who were hurt but not badly. The black kids have been paraded in handcuffs to the press."

Scott was interested. "The cops suspected of killing the two old guys have been suspended but not arrested, even though I'm told there's a suspicion that murder is involved. But the DA's office says they can't pin it on them yet. So let's run the story 'Why the delay at the DA's office?' "

The door opened. "Call from Europe for you, Scott."

Scott said nothing. What could he say? The entire station knew about his spoiled child bride. He hurried to his office. Once again he listened calmly to her tearful pleas, and once again Scott refused to walk out on the station and join Annabel.

That evening, Scott took his place at the news desk and ran an eye over his script. Just before airtime, a story had come in on a drug bust: space was hastily made for this.

At one minute to air, Scott grinned across to the other newscaster, looked up at the control room, and nodded.

The stress level in the newsroom was high. There was no noise whatsoever. control said, "Roll feed one . . . " The floor manager pointed at camera two and counted down: "Four, three, two, one. Cue Scott." A red light flicked on camera two as the floor manager silently pointed to it.

"Good evening. I'm Scott Svenson with tonight's news."

Even while the show was going out, work continued in the newsroom. Reporters handed their just completed text to the news editor, who edited the stories and telephoned any alterations in the program to the newscaster. "Scott, kill story four from Moscow—something better's come in, so we aren't going to run it." . . . "Scott, hold item seven, medical malpractice, for later in the show. The guy's just died, so we must update it."

As the camera pulled back on the last shot and credits were shown on the screen, the tension in the studio relaxed, replaced by an exultant mood. The interrupter-feedback button in Scott's ear said, "Nice work, Scott. Now beat it to your office. Long-distance call from Europe."

Scott tore off his mike, thinking, It must be five in the morning in France.

He ran to his office and lifted the phone. "Annabel? What's happened?"

Annabel could hardly speak through her tears. "Gran had a relapse four hours ago. Adam is here to speak with you if you don't believe me. They say there's no point in moving her to a hospital. Now you've *got* to come, Scott."

CHAPTER 17

Monday, 11 October 1965

TEN WEEKS LATER, the ambulance team that had driven Elinor from the Nice hospital carried her into the chateau and up to her bedroom.

Elinor, her arms draped around the necks of two paramedics, said, "You can take that thing right away!" She meant the wheelchair waiting in her bedroom.

"Please," Buzz pleaded. "You gotta be careful for a bit, Elinor. You gave us such a fright. We thought you was a goner."

"Well, I feel fine now," Elinor said. "Where's that bottle of champagne you promised me?"

The specialists had said that if she was careful, she could live a long time. Her doctor had told her that she had completely recovered. He saw no reason to add that from now on, her body would break down: she would gradually become slower in her movements, she would tire more easily and lack stamina, and she would probably have another stroke in seven years' time—at the latest.

Tuesday, 12 October 1965

In the gray morning light, Clare, still in her nightgown, stooped to pick up the little bottle of sleeping pills from the floor. She shook it. Empty. Better get another prescription. Careful not to wake Josh in the back room, Clare pulled on her dressing gown.

Josh was still bewildered by the sudden change in living standard from California sun and the constant care of cheerful Kathy (now working for another family in nearby Markham Square) to the stuffy flat in Pimlico where his babysitter, Mrs. Gooden, a retired cook, watched over Josh and her other six little charges, one of whom always seemed to be bare-bottomed and on the potty.

Clare hurried to the kitchenette to make Josh's breakfast. Their basement apartment cost more than she could afford, but at least she felt at home in Chelsea.

Once again she wished she understood what had happened to her in the last three months. She had such a strong sense of being in the right, of having behaved in a morally correct manner. Why then had she ended up in such a mess?

After Clare's sudden departure from Saracen, Miranda had immediately located her through friends, then telephoned and urged her sister to be sensible and apologize to Elinor, "because we all know you really love Gran."

"Of course I do, Miranda," Clare had said. "But that's beside the point." She was determined to allow nobody to treat her as a child in the future—not Sam, not Adam, not Elinor, not Buzz, and certainly not Miranda.

"This tiff is escalating to a ridiculous degree!" Miranda exploded. "Adam says the trust is going to be *irrevocable,* so for heaven's sake, think ahead, for when Joshua goes to Eton—"

"I don't think I'm being ridiculous. I hope Josh *never* goes to Eton, or any other privileged school where he's kept away from reality," Clare said stiffly. Correctly feeling that Miranda thought she was being tiresome, she added, "What counts in this tiff—as you call it—is the principle of the thing."

Miranda said, "People only say that when they can't think of any other reason for doing something damned stupid."

Clare was impatient to hang up. Enraged, Miranda said, "Okay, I can take a hint." She promised herself she wouldn't approach Clare again.

At first Clare kept in touch with Annabel after her sister returned to New York, but as her own life became increasingly difficult, she found herself unable to write the sort of letter that would prop up Annabel's crumbling self-esteem.

Via his lawyer, Sam refused to give Clare money because he didn't want a divorce. He wanted his wife and child back, and he reckoned he could tough it out longer than she could.

Clare's solicitor explained to her that men often forced their wives to return by refusing to grant a divorce and making it difficult for them to obtain money—even when it was awarded by a court. He said that returning to Sam might be best for her and her child. Clare wondered whose side her lawyer was on. She was clearly and legally in the right; she wasn't going to be manipulated and brought to heel by lack of funds.

"I'm damned if I'm going to let him bully me with money!" Clare cried. "I'll earn my own money!"

She soon found out how difficult this was.

Clare fell into the poverty trap experienced in the sixties by many single mothers. Because she had no man, she had no income beyond what she could earn. And because she had no training, she had no salable skills. She could only get a poorly paid job as a sales assistant in a Kings Road shoe boutique.

Because she had no man, Clare also suddenly found she had no public identity and was not likely to get asked to dinner parties, for society seemed to move only in couples. A full-time job, a small child, and no home help left her little energy for dinner parties anyway. And she was too proud to accept hospitality when she couldn't afford to return it. She, who had always helped lame dogs, now refused the many helping hands that were held out to her, because they only hauled her back, temporarily, into a life of comfort from which she would later have to return to reality. She became abrupt and ill at ease with her friends, who sensed this. Eventually they stopped trying.

Clare was surprised to find how much money it cost to lead what she considered a normal life. She earned eighteen pounds a week after tax. Her rent was ten pounds a week, and the babysitter cost a pound a day, which left three pounds to live on—just enough to pay her grocery bill. She didn't know how to budget or how to keep track of her expenditures, and she cried every time she opened her bank statement.

Apart from basic necessities, any other purchase was clearly now an extravagance for Clare. Her wages only just paid for her expenses: now a taxi was a memory.

Bewildered, Clare did not understand why she couldn't manage. What was she doing wrong? The other assistants in the shoe shop seemed to manage on their wages. Of course, none of them was supporting a child, and the male assistant got sixty percent more than the women. And she was living in an area of London that was relatively expensive, while her new peers lived in Battersea and Wandsworth.

But Clare was not yet accustomed to a life in which ice cream, sherry, and a telephone were luxuries. So she economized by drinking cheap cooking sherry. She felt humiliated by her poverty, especially when the telephone was cut off for nonpayment and she had to confess this to Gilda, the senior assistant in the shoe shop.

"Poor? *You* ain't poor, Clare," scoffed Gilda during their tea break. She lit up a Woodbine and puffed on it serenely. "Poor people don't have bank accounts and refrigerators and money for the launderette."

"I'm starting to realize that," Clare said humbly. "But I still need more money than I'm earning, to look after Josh."

Clare had not wanted to leave Josh (who would be three in December) with a babysitter, but she found that none of the local nursery schools, public or private, had an available slot.

When she tried to get Josh into a free day nursery, she discovered that the local authority did not regard her situation as difficult. "Difficult" seemed to mean that your pimp had beaten you up and thrown you out, and you had no money for a fix and couldn't stand up until you'd had one. In the Chelsea library, Clare read the 1944 Education Act, Section 8(2) (6). It said that a local education authority "shall, in particular, have regard to the need for securing that provision is made for pupils who have not attained the age of five years by the provision of nursery school."

So—where were the nursery schools? Clare felt protest rise within her. She was determined not to be bludgeoned into submission by lack of money and a system that seemed not to care for mothers and children.

On the following weekend, Clare sold all her jewelry except her engagement and wedding rings. She accepted the first price offered by the first jeweler, not realizing that she could probably have raised fifty percent more money by bargaining or trying other shops.

That night, as often when she put Josh to bed, Clare held the most precious thing in her world close to her heart and felt guilty and ashamed that she wasn't providing him with the things she thought she should. She lived with guilt even as she fiercely told herself that it wasn't fair that her life now should be so miserable and exhausting.

Josh had to be squeezed into Clare's tight weekday schedule: After taking him to the babysitter in Pimlico, she caught another bus to the shoe shop where she worked. Lunch hour meant a hurried visit to a launderette or one of the new supermarkets. At six o'clock, Clare again caught the bus to Pimlico, took Josh back to her basement, cooked his supper, cooked her supper (increasingly, the same nursery food sufficed for both), put Josh to bed, had a drink, looked over any paperwork required by her solicitor, crawled into bed with a book, fell asleep after reading a page, and woke two hours later, unable to get back to sleep. Insomnia plagued her and sapped her strength. Exhausted and without much hope for the future, she gradually slipped into a permanent state of depression, which made life even more difficult for Josh, although neither of them realized this.

Thankfully, on weekends, Clare felt almost normal again. On Saturdays, she stayed in bed late—although as Josh bounced up and down beside her, it wasn't a very restful experience. But she didn't mind as she cuddled his warm little body next to hers, played hide-and-seek under the bedclothes, or read aloud to him. Later, soaping her son's slippery body in the bath as he wriggled from her grasp and splashed water up at his mother, Clare would again feel happy.

On Saturday afternoons, Clare pushed Josh's collapsible canvas pram up Sloane Street toward Kensington Gardens, where she mixed happily with other children and working mothers. They were all sniffed at by the uniformed nannies, who wheeled old-fashioned perambulators rather than the canvas collapsibles.

On Sunday mornings, Clare and Josh went to Mrs. Gooden's. Here Clare (who could cook a hamburger but not much else) learned to prepare a traditional British lunch of roast meat and vegetables, followed by a fruit pie or tart.

"You've got light fingers," Mrs. Gooden said approvingly one Sunday as she watched Clare, with the tips of her fingers, mix flour and lard in the big yellow mixing bowl. "We'll make a baker of you yet."

Shortly after this, Clare started to swap babysitting evenings with Stephanie, a mother who also took her small son to Mrs. Gooden. This arrangement ensured that, once a week, both women had an evening and a night off, followed by a leisurely rise the next morning.

On Clare's first such evening off, she went to a dinner party given by an old school friend who persisted in keeping in touch. Clare's partner was a just-divorced man who talked endlessly about "that bitch who needn't think she has a free meal ticket for life," then took Clare to dance at Annabel's, London's most expensive new nightclub. He tore her dress on the taxi journey back to her flat, and after a tussle, finally, standing on the pavement at three A.M. he realized that she really wouldn't allow him in. The following morning, Clare arrived late for work.

When Gilda heard what happened, she said, "A man who's just staggered out of a nasty relationship wants a bloody nursemaid at first, and then he wants to play the field for a bit. But what he *really* wants is another relationship."

Clare said, "*I* don't want another relationship until I've struggled free of this one."

"Maybe you ought to play the field a bit," Gilda suggested.

"That's what my solicitor's afraid of," Clare said. "He says it would ruin my case. He'd like to shut me up in a box for the next two years. But Sam can apparently do what the hell he likes, with as many women as he pleases!"

On her next evening out, Clare remembered Gilda's advice. Feeling self-conscious at entering a pub by herself, she slunk into the Markham Arms, a glamorous tavern in the Kings Road where men-about-Chelsea relaxed in the evening.

Sitting on the next barstool was an antiques dealer called James; he discussed his feelings with Clare for the next two hours and then took her to dinner at the Ox on the Roof, where she chose the most filling dishes. Eating spaghetti, Clare began to suspect that James would rather talk about a relationship than have one; wolfing boeuf bourguignon, she wondered whether James was flaunting his insecurities in order to attract the maternal feelings he clearly believed nestled within every woman's breast—and from which Clare was trying to escape for the evening.

By the time the crème brûlée was served, she realized that James wasn't the gentle, sensitive, vulnerable charmer that she had first imagined but a crashing bore.

Nevertheless, having had far too much to drink, Clare woke up the next morning in James's bed, saw that it was nearly nine o'clock, fled to work in her crumpled clothes—but arrived late again. Gilda winked.

The following week, Clare avoided the Markham Arms and went instead to the Bunch of Grapes in Knightsbridge. There she met Ian, a fruit exporter. Ian was boyish, athletic, charming, and, Clare suspected, terrified of his fortieth birthday: there had been a bit of the Peter Pan in Sam, and Clare recognized the symptoms.

During dinner at the Pheasantry, Ian clearly expected Clare to be frivolously entertaining. He belittled any attempt at serious conversation with phrases such as, "Well, you're quite a bluestocking," or, "Actually, I didn't come out to discuss politics."

The next morning, Ian woke her up with a cup of tea, said he was sorry about last night, he'd had a bit too much to drink. Again Clare was late to work.

"Of *course* they both seemed nice guys," Gilda commiserated. "But they was fake nice guys, *pretending* to be nice guys. If you're going to get picked up in bars and hand it out free on the first date, you'd better check in regular at St. Stephen's."

"Is that a church?"

"No, the local clap clinic."

Always, when Clare's hangover subsided, she wondered why she did it. She found no sexual pleasure in going to bed with strangers, but, in contrast with the rest of her week, she was comforted by the feeling of being thought desirable, of having someone's arms around her, of warm cuddling beneath the quilt.

One morning, Clare found herself in a rumpled bed in a strange bedroom with only sixpence in her purse—not enough to get to work. If she was late for work one more time, she knew, she would be fired. Clare panicked and telephoned Miranda.

Wondering whether the prim Miss Goody-Goody of a few months ago had really metamorphosed into this forlorn and wanton creature, Miranda said, "I'll send a car for you, straightaway." She hesitated. "Couldn't we meet, Clare? . . . Won't you let me give you some money—just to tide you over?"

"No," Clare lied. "I have plenty of money at home."

"Gran's worried about you. We all are."

"How is she?" Clare asked wistfully. In the past, when she felt depressed, she knew that she could always rely on her grandmother to lift her spirits.

"Gran would feel a lot happier if you paid her a visit. Couldn't you fly to the south of France, just for a week?"

"No," Clare said, feeling rage rise. "I can't take time off."

"How about a better job?" Miranda suggested. "You've had experience as a shop assistant, so you could work in one of our shops. You'll probably be better paid, and have a better time of it."

"No. I want to learn to manage by myself. Don't worry. I'll survive."

"But what about Josh?"

"Josh will have to put up with the life that his mother can afford to lead."

Clare was fired for turning up late after she had to wait for a doctor because Josh had a temperature. As the shop manager pointed out, it was the third time that month she'd been late for work, and if they hadn't needed her to turn up on time, they wouldn't have hired her in the first place.

Having decided to start her own nursery playgroup, Clare sold her engagement ring, a flashy marquise diamond, in order to buy the lease of the first floor of a big Edwardian house in Pimlico: it contained a ballroom, a small rear room, and a bathroom. Clare's assistants were two other single mothers whose children were also cared for by Mrs. Gooden.

Mrs. Gooden lost three kiddies and three pounds a day but, instead, found herself cooking lunch for thirty-four, a far more lucrative occupation. At midday, Mr. Gooden cycled round to the playgroup with lunch hauled behind on a trailer. He also did Clare's bookkeeping. Clare doubled her income overnight, and felt that she was doing a useful job.

In contrast to Clare, her sister Miranda was leading the fast and frivolous life of the exciting sixties as Britain launched into the first real business boom since Hitler's war. A rush of stock exchange takeover bids coined money for shareholders, and Britain imported more French champagne than any other country, although one in three families still couldn't afford a TV.

The former aristocratic standards of who and what was acceptable were now dumped; everyone wanted to belong to the new meritocracy, based not on birth but on talent, achievement, and the resultant financial reward—the with-it people, as opposed to the dull, unwith-its.

Annabel was painted by David Hockney, and Miranda's portrait—a gloomy study in grays by Brian Kneale—was exhibited in the National Portrait Gallery. They both wished that Gran would hide her triple portrait: Annigoni was definitely *not* with it.

Fashion was madly exciting: Grannies happily wore mini-skirts and platform thigh boots, while young girls wore button-up granny boots and Victorian-style, flower-printed dresses. Females under thirty tried to look like thumb-sucking little girls; with turned-in toes, they skipped around in buttock-skimming shifts over pale tights. All females in their thirties dressed like chic astronauts; all women over forty wore jaunty, flared trouser suits.

Makeup manufacturers made a fortune.

Tuesday, 11 January 1966

Snow lay on the park outside as Miranda showed her new house in Cumberland Terrace to fashion editor Annie Trehearne. Since the heating wasn't yet working, the two young women stamped around in winter coats and boots, dodged whistling workmen, who no longer wore baggy dungarees but tight jeans as they carried planks from one room to another.

Annie looked down from the first-floor drawing room windows to the gaunt trees of Regent's Park and said, "It's simply super. Fab. Smashing. Let's face it, Miranda, not many people of your age can afford to buy a house like this. KITS must be doing frightfully well."

Miranda nodded. "But KITS has expanded so fast we're permanently short of capital. The money for this place came from a family trust."

"Everyone should have a grandmother like yours. How is she?"

"The doctors say she's responding very well to the new treatment, and *she* expects to live for another hundred years."

"Glad to hear it."

"Now, I want to know what you think of my new skin-care range," Miranda said. "It's targeted at the young twenties and I'm calling it Image. What do you think of launching it with pictures of Deneuve?"

"Pix by Bailey then. Expensive," Annie said. Photographer David Bailey had recently married French film star Catherine Deneuve, with Mick Jagger as best man.

"Of course." Miranda nodded again.

"By the way, how's Annabel enjoying her retirement?"

"Off the record? Relieved, I think," Miranda reported. "She's neatly switched to the life of a successful New York hostess—she's on every charity committee in town."

Miranda was not going to let anyone know that Annabel's self-confidence had been shattered. It had been painful to watch her struggle for her self-respect, but she had managed to ward off the threatened nervous breakdown. Endless reassurance had been necessary—not of her beauty, for nothing could persuade Annabel that it had not vanished, but of her value to them all, and of her family's affection.

Airily Miranda continued, "Annabel's just bought a new apartment. You really ought to hop over for a weekend and see it, Annie. It's a penthouse in a high rise on the Upper East Side, with a spectacular three-sided view over the city and across the river. It's simply stunning. Someone else had practically bought the place, so Annabel was lucky to get it."

"How did she manage it?"

"Simply offered more money. Adam fixed it."

"That family trust again? What lucky girls you are! What news of Clare?"

"I don't see much of Clare these days," Miranda said. "She's very busy, now that she's running a nursery playgroup." She looked out over the smudged white landscape of Regent's Park, then peered at the road below. "Hell, I've just got another parking fine. Those stupid new meters! It's getting really difficult to drive in London."

"Or out of it," said Annie.

"Yes. I was pinched for dangerous driving last month, in a radar trap. Luckily, Adam fixed it."

Wednesday, 12 January 1966

Clare still swapped one night a week off with Stephanie and reported subsequent events to Gilda, who now managed the shoe shop: occasionally she visited Clare for an evening meal.

As Clare poured sherry, Gilda asked, "So how was the BOAC pilot?"

"Tony was the worst yet." Clare never felt embarrassed discussing sex with Gilda, who could talk about little else. "He'd read all the sex manuals ever printed. Whipped a porn magazine out of his flight case after the first gin and tonic. He was coldly determined to be a good lover. For me, that was a total turnoff."

"Porn pictures are a turnoff to most women. Women like words, not pictures," Gilda said as she sipped her drink. "But I'm starting to think that everything's a turnoff for you, doll. You clearly can't have sex with fellas you ain't fond of. I expect you need a chap you know well, someone you feel comfortable with, not these one-nighters." She swallowed half the glass. "Now me, I'm the reverse. If I don't give a damn about 'em, I ain't anxious, and if I ain't anxious, then I come easy." She drained her glass.

"When Tony couldn't get me to climax, he wanted to ask another girl over," Clare said. "He automatically assumed that I was a lesbian."

"*That's* not what he meant," Gilda said. "Lots of guys find it a turn-on to watch two women making love."

"How very odd. Can you imagine a woman trying to get two men into bed so *she* could watch them?"

"Forget this guy," said Gilda. "I know what *you* need, Clare: someone you know and trust, someone who won't make you feel anxious. Then you'll relax and it'll happen—then you'll stop being one of them miserable nymphos who hop from man to man, hoping for Mr. Right, the man who can satisfy her." As Gilda held out her glass to be refilled, she added reflectively, "Although you seem more lonely than horny. Are you looking for sex, or just someone to talk to? You ain't likely to pick up Prince Charming in a bar."

Clare said, "I'm not looking for Prince Charming. I don't want the disorder, the pain, the mess, or the misery of being in love. I just want a short-term relationship, without responsibility."

Gilda laughed. "So do these fellas you pick up. But I'm not convinced that's right for you. *You* need a secure situation with someone you can trust, who you know will stick around because he loves you. I'll tell you who you ought to fall in love with, Clare."

"Who?"

"Yourself. You clearly think that you're a piece of worthless rubbish, and if *I* pick up those vibes, then so do the blokes. Why not give sex a rest for a bit, and pay a bit of attention to yourself? You never want to make a man the center of your existence. That place is for *you,* Clare."

"I am the center of my existence," Clare sang, as if chanting a psalm, pitching her voice an octave lower, as she pushed Josh to her playgroup the next morning.

A man stood on the porch, his hands in the pockets of his beige mackintosh.

"Good morning. Are you a prospective parent?" Clare asked. She felt in her pocket for the key.

"No," said the man. "I'm an inspector for the local education authority."

After examining the bathroom, the inspector pointed out that legally one toilet was required for every seven kiddies.

Clare said, "But if each child goes there every two and a half hours, one lavatory is adequate. There is a potty for emergencies. We have never had a problem."

The inspector was not listening. He was making notes on other violations.

Half an hour after the inspector left, as if to prove his point, the lavatory refused to flush.

The following morning, Clare's playgroup was ordered to close.

Two days later, Clare's mind was unexpectedly diverted from her personal problems—no job, no man—when the C.N.D. office telephoned to ask her for voluntary evening help: they were organizing another protest after a nuclear accident. Over Spain, an American B-52 bomber carrying an H-bomb had collided in midair with another aircraft. The H-bomb, with an explosive capacity of more than a million tons of TNT, had fallen into the Atlantic Ocean off southern Spain.

Clare felt cheered to be back among like-minded people, doing something worthwhile.

Monday, 14 February 1966

Valentine's Day brought two happy events. The radio reported that the missing H-bomb had been located on the Atlantic seabed. And to Clare's delight, she sold the lease of the apartment in which she ran her playgroup—for a profit of twenty-three percent.

Clare felt as if she had won a sweepstake. On the following morning, she bought a portable TV, a warm winter coat for herself, and new clothes for Josh. She didn't buy any toys for Josh because she had decided to open a toy shop.

Two weeks later, Clare bought the short lease of a small shop in the Pimlico Road, close to Mrs. Gooden's home. Though there was a lot to do, Clare, busy redecorating the shop and visiting wholesalers to buy stock, still managed to work one evening a week for the Movement.

In mid-April, just before her toy shop opened, Clare's weary, amiable National

Health doctor looked up from his desk and said, "About your vaginal symptoms, Mrs. Shapiro. You'd better go to St. Stephen's for tests: they're properly equipped to handle this sort of thing." He seemed uneasy.

"What sort of thing? . . . Not . . . cancer?"

"No, gonorrhea," the doctor said apologetically.

Clare almost fainted from surprise and anxiety, horror and shame. Then she wept.

The doctor refused to give her more sleeping tablets but scribbled a prescription for tranquilizers, which were increasingly prescribed for women like Clare, with symptoms of anxiety in stressful situations such as poverty, divorce, or bereavement; women with marital problems and women who were out of work also found them helpful, although the pills did nothing to resolve the problem responsible for the initial anxiety.

Clare, who blushed with shame whenever she thought about it, waited anxiously for the result of her tests at St. Stephen's Hospital.

The tests were negative.

But within a month, she couldn't get through the day without tranquilizers; she felt less anxious, calmer.

Clare managed to open the Red Rocking Horse by mid-May. At the opening party, an excited three-and-a-half-year-old Josh rode the pretty antique red rocking horse in the shop window.

Monday, 15 August 1966

Standing by the swimming pool at Saracen, Miranda beckoned to Adam, who was floating on the water in a transparent blow-up plastic armchair.

In a voice of soft persuasion, she said, "Will you do something for me, Adam? I'm going to learn to fly. I want you to break the news gently to Gran."

"But you promised your grandmother *not* to learn to fly," Adam objected. "It was a condition of her gift to you—the ten thousand pounds' capital to start KITS."

"I didn't say forever. I'll pay the money back to her." Miranda was defiant. "I've always wanted to fly. I won't be held by a promise that was unfairly extracted from me before I legally became an adult. And I get bored with nothing to do on holiday but lie in the sun."

"When are you starting?" Adam asked, resigned.

"This morning, at the Cannes flying school. They have English instructors. Four hours of instruction a day for two weeks. And of course, this time of year, it's perfect flying weather!" Miranda was triumphant now. "I've already passed the two written exams. Did law and meteorology last Easter, and now I've finished navigation, radiotelephony, and technical—that was the toughest."

"So that's why you're so pale."

Three hours later, two thousand feet above the Mediterranean, Miranda, alert and exultant, sat next to her instructor at the controls of a trainer plane, an ugly little single-engine Rallye which her instructor described as efficient and forgiving: you could do something wrong in a Rallye without getting immediately punished for it.

Flying was even better than she had hoped: better than skiing, better than driving a sports car. As the Rallye droned toward the lighthouse on the tip of Cap Camerat, Miranda had felt as if she were breathing the air of the gods. Gently they swooped, turned, and climbed in the azure sky.

After they reached two thousand feet, the instructor showed her how to fly level; he then encouraged her to experiment with the stick, maneuvering the plane in every direction. Miranda felt that the aircraft was an extension of her arms and her fingertips, outspread in flight.

Heading west on the return flight path, the instructor said, "This is the first time I've flown with a pupil and haven't once needed to touch the controls."

Miranda pushed home this advantage. "Then can I land?"

The instructor hesitated, then said, "Why not?" The girl was clearly a natural flyer.

After being given clearance to land, Miranda, following her instructor's directions, started her approach; she throttled back to reduce speed and control her descent as she flew toward the threshold—the point just before she intended to touch down. The plane was now moving at not much above stalling speed. As the Rallye dropped to about thirty feet above the runway, Miranda throttled back completely and held the stick back.

The plane seemed to glide forward and land itself.

The undemonstrative Miranda flung her arms around the instructor. "Oh, thank you! Thank you! . . ."

"Quite a smooth landing," the instructor said approvingly. He hesitated, then warned, "Next time be careful not to land too fast or you'll run out of runway." This woman was adventurous and ambitious: such pilots did not live long. He added, "*Careful* pilots are the ones that survive. A good pilot never takes a risk."

"The opposite of a good businessman," Miranda said, still on a high. "A businessman has to take risks constantly—and win sixty percent of the time."

"In the air, that risk factor would kill you."

Nine hundred years earlier, the great hall had been the hub of castle life: wolfhounds ate on floors strewn with rushes; servants slept on straw pallets thrown on the floor. Then, the winter salon did not smell of lilies and expensive leather but of stale, fat, stinking human bodies and animal ordure. Elinor sometimes thought of all the love and the hatred, the treachery and the killing that this hall had undoubtedly seen, when strong men fought hand-to-hand to the death, to protect their women and children.

Now the winter salon at Saracen, where Elinor waited for Adam, was not only the coolest but the most impressive room in the chateau. High arched walls of pale, honey-colored stone were hung with bluish-green tapestries; around the big stone fireplace, where logs burned in winter, stood sofas covered in the blues and greens of the tapestries; here and there were lamps, flowers, books, and piles of parlor games.

"What's keeping Adam?" Elinor asked Buzz, who was adding up the Scrabble score.

"You said three o'clock. It's only two-thirty," Buzz said. "Ninety-three for you, two hundred and sixty-four for me. That's not a bad score for you, Nell." Buzz never cheated to let Elinor win: she knew that Elinor would immediately sense this and feel humiliated.

After an intensive rehabilitation program of physiotherapy and speech therapy,

Elinor appeared to have completely recovered from her stroke, although she could no longer think of three things at once, which Buzz said was a mercy for the people who had to live with her.

Elinor was sometimes at a loss for the right word, or name, and then became impatient with herself; she was often frustrated because she couldn't move as swiftly as she did before. At times, she was downhearted and wondered whether she would ever write another book. "When you want to write, you'll write," Buzz would tell her then.

Now Buzz grunted, "Look what I tore out of the *Daily Mail.*" She dug into her pocket, unfolded a bit of newspaper, and read, " 'Sportsman Jim Clark today opened a splendidly equipped physical training college at Larkwood in Wiltshire, formerly the family home of the O'Dare family. Lady O'Dare commented, "I wish them well." ' "

"I doubt that." Elinor peered at the photograph of the new owner, a motor-racing hero, standing with her sister-in-law, Marjorie.

The doorbell sounded. "I'll go," Buzz said. "It's either Adam or the postman."

Buzz returned reading a postcard. "It's for you, from Sonia Rushleigh . . . Whoops, I mean Bromley. Who'd have thought them two would marry? She says the Colonel's taken up petit point, and Miss Hawkins is teaching him. Remember her, the schoolmistress?"

"I do indeed," said Elinor. "Frumpy sourpuss! Who's the letter from?"

"Clare." Buzz held the envelope out to Elinor.

Elinor shook her head. "You open it."

"It's marked personal."

"I don't want to read it, unless she apologizes."

Buzz opened the letter and read it. She shook her head. "It's just a friendly letter, asking how you are. But reading between the lines, I think Clare needs money."

"If she took her poor child back to his father and gave her husband a second chance, she wouldn't need money."

"How about a bit of generosity?" Buzz said. "You're a silly, stubborn old woman. And Clare's just as stubborn and just as silly. It wouldn't have hurt her to say she was sorry."

Elinor looked anxious. "Do you really think she's short of money, Buzz? I wouldn't want her to have a rough time."

This remark was overheard by Adam as, in pale blue shirt and jeans, he sauntered through the door. He said, "Elinor, you allowed ample provision in the trust for helping Clare—if the trustees consider that help is needed. I'll check on Clare when I get back to London." He put a pile of papers on a side table. "There's rather a lot of paperwork here, things that you should be aware of."

"We've had more paperwork, not less, since the trust took over," Buzz said tartly. "And I tell you frankly that I can't follow it, Adam. I thought the trustees were going to manage the business. Elinor shouldn't be made to wade through pages of paragraphs with no commas in 'em."

"Of course the trustees manage the business, and they do it very well," Adam said. "And there's no reason for Elinor to see any of this if it tires her. In fact, I'm about to suggest something that would simplify matters."

"What's that?" Buzz asked.

"I'd like to substitute Paul Littlejohn for myself in the power of attorney that

I hold on your behalf, Elinor. I'm trying to reduce the number of business administrators: the fewer there are, the simpler the system and the cheaper it will be."

"Does that mean that Paul will be legally responsible for Elinor's affairs instead of you, Adam?"

"Yes, but that's only a technicality. Paul will do as I say. And I'd also like you to sign this document," Adam added, "which absolves me and STG from any further responsibility once Paul Littlejohn has been substituted."

Buzz said, "But surely . . . "

Smoothly Adam explained, "The responsibility must clearly rest in only one area. It's in your interests to clarify the situation. It's customary."

"If you think that's best, Adam dear." Elinor frowned slightly at Buzz.

Adam decided to hold back Miranda's bombshell until later, after Elinor drank her evening glass of champagne.

Just before five o'clock, when the business session had ended and the afternoon was still hot, quiet, and heavy with languor, Buzz left to get some tea.

Adam escorted Elinor to the elevator; after taking her to her bedroom, he intended to go to the beach for a swim.

In the high-ceilinged kitchen, surrounded by the smells of mint and basil, Buzz whistled "Roses of Picardy" with much dramatic warbling as she prepared Elinor's tea. Leaves and yellow blossoms obscured the top of the window, while the bottom was covered by aggressive pink hollyhocks, seemingly determined to fight their way inside.

Sylvie, the cook, sat at the big kitchen table by the window, writing a list and shooing pigeons away. The bane of Sylvie's life was the pigeon droppings that littered the windowsill and had to be cleaned up daily.

With a shudder, Sylvie refused a cup of tea. Still whistling, Buzz laid the tray.

The soporific calm of the drowsy afternoon was shattered by the bell indicator above the kitchen door.

Someone was jabbing the bell—nonstop—in Elinor's bedroom.

Knowing that Adam was probably in the elevator on his way to the beach, Buzz hurled herself out of the kitchen and ran upstairs.

Frantically she tore open the door to Elinor's apartment. In the passage, she stumbled and almost fell, then flung back the door to the bedroom.

To her relief, Elinor was not slumped on the floor; deathly white, she clung for support to the silver brocade hangings of her bed. Wordlessly, she pointed above the fireplace.

Buzz turned her head to the left, where the portrait of the three sisters hung.

At first Buzz saw nothing, but then she gasped in horror.

Each of the three long, creamy necks had been cut horizontally: a small triangle of canvas hung downward from each slashed throat.

CHAPTER 18

Wednesday, 17 August 1966

IN THE FOYER of the Clanrickard Club, Mike Grant leaned against the wall at the bottom of a double-sided curving staircase. With his hands in the pockets of his dinner jacket, he surveyed the room. It was going to be a good night, in spite of the fact that it was August and a Wednesday. Making sure to appear casual, he carefully watched the men in dinner jackets and the women in full-length décolleté dresses move slowly over the red carpet toward the restaurant at the rear, or climb the staircase to the gaming rooms.

Mike noticed a group of heavy gamblers, most of them Greek, move toward the baccarat room, where the Sultan of Rupolei had been losing for the last hour. His attention was also caught by a woman dressed in midnight-blue satin and diamonds; the sister of a Mideastern ruler, she was known as an audacious gambler. He stiffened as he recognized a man move upstairs with a distinctive, boneless saunter: he had better send someone up to check the backgammon room. The club owners, the casinos, and the multinational bookmakers knew which professional gamblers successfully played games that contained an element of skill—such as backgammon and poker—and they preferred to have nothing to do with them; ideally, the house welcomed inexperienced, rich idiots.

"This is certainly a good night to play the odds." Mike heard a sarcastic voice from behind him.

He turned and smiled at Adam. "Come into my office for a drink. What's up?"

In Mike's office, furnished with heavily varnished Victorian club furniture, Adam shook his head curtly at the offer of a chair. "I'm not staying," he said. "I merely wanted to tell you that you've scared the hell out of everyone at Saracen—except me. So kindly curb your theatrical, James Bond streak. I knew immediately what your message meant: 'If you don't pay up, one slash is all it takes.' " He glared at his brother. "I thought you were fond of Elinor. I seem to recall that Elinor helped you to buy your first good bike. Why drag her into my problems? You might have given her another stroke."

"I don't know what the hell you're talking about, and I can't comment until I do." Mike, his face alert and wary, lit a cigarette.

Adam briefly described how the triple portrait had been slashed and added, "D'you really expect me to believe that you had nothing to do with it? *Someone* told some cat burglar where to find that picture!"

Mike stared at his brother, then slowly said, "Not me. I agree, it's clearly a warning to pay, but I swear I know nothing about it. It couldn't have been the brothers—they'd be even less subtle . . . " He inhaled deeply. "Who else do you owe money, Adam, you stupid bastard?"

"No one who'd do anything so bloody childish! How do I stop this bloody nonsense?"

"How many times must I tell you that if you let things go too far, nobody can stop what will undoubtedly happen? Adam," Mike went on quietly, "you've always taken full advantage of anyone who's fond of you. You think you can push me around because you've been doing that since we were in the nursery. You also grew up watching Grandfather's clients literally get away with murder." He sucked on his cigarette, furiously threw it into the fireplace, shoved his hands in his pockets, and glared at Adam. "Do you *want* to be found washed up on the seashore with a few vital bits missing? Are you so anxious to know what it feels like to have both eyeballs gouged out, one at a time? Do you *want* to be slowly battered to death, before dying in agony?"

"Of course not, you bastard," Adam said. "I only want to know who slashed that picture if you didn't."

"Whoever they are—and only you know that—these people are serious. Punters often try to avoid paying. Examples often have to be made. You know that." Mike started to stride up and down the room. "Take that fucking urbane look off your face and face reality, Adam. If you lose money, that's tough. But if you don't pay up, that's insanity."

"I've had enough of your melodrama," Adam snarled.

Mike glared at his brother again. "I'm not exaggerating. Remember that incident when the Sultan's sister had her Rolls stopped, at two in the morning on the Grande Corniche, after leaving the casino? They blew away the chauffeur's head with a machine gun. *She* wasn't touched. She paid all her gambling debts the very next day. And when the story was carefully leaked to the newspapers, quite a lot of other debts were suddenly settled in full."

"I'm not some goddamned sultan's sister."

"No, but you also like playing with fire. You never believe that the gods will really let it burn *you*. You think you're omnipotent—but you aren't."

"Keep your voice down," Adam growled.

"I'll do what I bloody well like in my own office," Mike said. "Don't you understand? I'm on your side, Adam. You're the only brother I have." His voice deepened. "I'm probably more worried about this than you are. If anything happened to you . . . I'd be left without you. So for God's sake, pay up, you stupid shit! Don't think you can get away with it just because you've always got away with everything, since you set that nursemaid's apron alight."

"I thought you were too young to remember that," Adam said uneasily. He added, "She shouldn't have left the matches within reach of a child."

"She was in hospital for six weeks, and I was the only one who knew it wasn't an accident. I knew you wanted to see *how far you could go*."

"Let's not argue about something that happened over thirty years ago," Adam said finally. "Can you raise money to help me fend them off? I promise you, within six months I *know* I'll have no more money problems. Never again."

"You'll have money problems as long as you gamble, Adam."

Annabel was determined to get a grip on herself and do as Scott advised: remember 1965 as the year she stopped having to go to auditions and 1966 as the year in which she blossomed into a successful young New York hostess as she met Andy Warhol, Lenny Bernstein, Baby Jane Holzer, and all the other gossip columnist fodder. By July, Annabel was a Junior Friend of the Metropolitan

Museum, a Friend of the Museum of Modern Art, and a patron of the Bronx Zoo. She also allayed her insecurity with a massive spending spree: each charity dinner required a new ballgown, and each new glittering friend—contacts for Scott—required a glittering party. So the year thus far was a busy one.

Friday, 19 August 1966

On the hottest morning of the year, Scott's news editor asked him to step into his office.

From behind the untidy piles on his desk, the news editor said, "Shut the door and prepare to listen to some good advice, Scott. I know you went after an anchor job last year and didn't get it. I know you're now up for another anchor job. I know you're going to be interviewed and I know which network it is, so don't deny a thing." He shoved a paper cup of lukewarm coffee across the desk to Scott. "I'd rather you went after it with my support than behind my back. At least if a guy from a local station gets a prominent network job, it reflects well on that station." He picked up his cup, took a whiff of it, and put it down again. "In order to get that job, Scott, you have to clarify one thing in your mind—a picture of what they're looking for as an anchorman."

Scott said nothing.

"Forget the crusading-journalist approach, Scott. Or the hard-nosed, insistent, tough approach. That's what *everyone* applying for that job will pitch. The network is looking for something extra. They want someone who looks as if he's been shot at, wounded, and spent the day crawling through minefields to deliver the dispatches. So don't go looking too neat. On the other hand, don't go looking *too* battered: they aren't looking for Walter Huston, they're looking for a younger, well-scrubbed, cheerfully confident Robert Mitchum."

"I don't think they're looking for a battered glamour boy," Scott said. "They're looking for a first-class professional journalist."

The news editor looked cynical. "Viewers don't switch channels for a good professional journalist; what prompts that switch is something less tangible."

"And they also want something else," Scott went on quietly. "A quality that you and I share."

"What's that?"

"Devotion. We love this business. You'd rather be doing your job than anything else in the world. You feel guilty about enjoying it so much. The real reason you often put in fourteen hours seven days a week is because you think it's important that people know what's happening in their world."

Jake laughed. "You can buy me a drink after you land the job."

One week after Scott's interview with the network, Jake arrived at his office to find a bottle of pure malt Highland whisky standing on top of the papers on his desk.

Friday, 26 August 1966

The feather—an ordinary pale gray pigeon's feather—softly traced Miranda's thighs. She sighed sleepily. They'd had a wonderful afternoon.

The secret of Adam's sexual success with women was simple: he took plenty of time to stroke or massage, to make sure that his partner was completely relaxed before they made love. Then he always made sure that she climaxed before he entered her. Gradually Adam would discover where and how each woman liked to be touched, and he would change his techniques to suit her, then moving on to something that she wasn't expecting or had never experienced.

Adam blew the feather into the air and let it drift to the floor. He stretched. "Looks as if we're in for a storm."

Miranda slipped from her bed and wandered to a window; leaning out, she smelled rosemary and eucalyptus as she watched the summer storm approach from the distant cobalt-blue mountains. The bright light of Provence changed theatrically as the sky darkened to gray, then turned slate purple.

After an ominous moment of silence, when not a leaf fluttered, two incandescent white worms of lightning flashed across the sky. A mighty clash of thunder followed, after which heavy rain fell. Below Miranda, the dusty terra-cotta tiles of the medieval roofs were slicked and sharpened to glistening ocher, tangerine, and brown. Then it was as if a gray curtain fell in front of the window, blotting out all color.

Miranda frowned at the rain; her visitors would shortly be arriving at the village hotels, for she had decided to hold the KITS annual sales conference weekend at Saracen.

The sales conference, held just before the all-important Christmas run-up began, was meant to psych up the sales force for the new line. Miranda loved everything about the sales conference except making her speech. She really ought to rehearse that presentation again, she thought. She drew in her head, shut the windows, pulled the heavy cream linen curtains, and switched on the lamps; they glowed cheerfully over the primrose chair covers and the yellow silk bed quilt, upon which Adam lay naked.

"I'd better creep off," Adam said. "It's nearly five o'clock. This place will be humming with staff in a few minutes."

Miranda, sounding slightly mutinous, said, "I don't see why we can't sleep together openly."

"Because we're not married," Adam said, "because I'm not an earl."

"I don't intend to marry to please my grandmother."

"Soon," Adam said firmly, "but not yet. I'm too busy with SUPPLYKITS. But there's something else I must discuss with you before I leave."

Miranda, not wishing to quarrel with Adam, did not pursue her argument.

SUPPLYKITS was negotiating for three businesses, and Adam was handling all three deals: a direct-mail business, a premium-gift business, and a public-relations business. Should all the deals be successful, SUPPLYKITS would then own five subsidiary businesses, including KITS.

A director from each of the new companies would acquire shares and sit on the SUPPLYKITS board; as Miranda owned the entire company, these inducement shares would reduce her holding, but Adam had convinced a reluctant Miranda that by relinquishing fifteen percent of her shares, she was exchanging a hundred percent of a small orange for eighty-five percent of a crateful.

Adam turned onto his back, his hands behind his head, and looked at the ceiling. "It's about time we considered going public."

Astonished, Miranda sat down on the edge of the bed. "So soon? Why?"

"We can't do it until next March, when we'll have five years' trading figures to show," Adam said. "But such a move would provide more cash for acquisitions. We can't go on leveraging forever."

"No," said Miranda, remembering that Angus had warned her about this. "But won't it be expensive to go public?"

"Very expensive," Adam said. "But you want more outlets for KITS and you want them in the best and most expensive locations."

"So the reason to go public is to finance expansion?"

"Not only that. We'll also be more respectable and credit-worthy."

"What about control?" Miranda worried. "I don't want to lose control of my business."

"You won't lose control so long as you retain over fifty percent of the shares," Adam reassured her. "But *nobody* should have all their capital invested in one sector of the market, as you have. You should sell some shares for cash and invest that money in other areas. Arrange a nice, well-spread portfolio for yourself. It's about time you saw some financial reward for your work and responsibility."

"How many SUPPLYKITS shares would I have to sell?"

"Legally, twenty-five percent of the shares have to be made available to the public. The new directors will probably be pleased to sell their incentive shares for such a quick profit, so you should only lose ten percent of your present holding. If we issue new shares, you'll end up with seventy-five percent of the business *and* a large sum of cash."

"I'd like the staff to be able to have shares," Miranda said, "to benefit from the success of the business."

"We can certainly arrange that, should SUPPLYKITS go public."

"I'll think about it."

Adam said, "It will take at least six months to organize, so think fast."

Friday, 9 September 1966

Four months after Clare opened her toy shop, her bank manager advised her to close it as quickly as possible, because she was losing money at a steady and frightening pace. He advised her to sell the shop and deposit the money in the bank. She had better not invest it in the stock market, because she couldn't afford to lose a penny and there was no such thing as a safe share.

Over supper at the basement flat, Clare discussed her woes with Kathy, her former nanny.

"It was apparently doomed from the start," Clare explained sadly, over the baked beans. "The sort of people who can afford handcrafted learning toys don't shop at the wrong end of the Pimlico Road." She scraped out the dish. "I concentrated on toys for preschool children because I thought I knew about them. But those children didn't want well-made, tasteful, pale wood Swedish toys. What they wanted was cheap, bright, plastic toys from Hong Kong, and I didn't stock those."

"Couldn't you sell Lego and stuff like that?"

"I had plenty of Lego, but what they really wanted were the expensive toys they saw advertised on children's TV."

"Well, couldn't you have sold a few of those?"

"By the time I realized that, I had no spare cash," Clare explained. "And that wasn't my only problem. The importers weren't reliable, and neither were the craftsmen, especially those who persuaded me to pay them in advance. Then I got in a financial muddle because I didn't keep my bookkeeping up-to-date."

"It sounds like a nightmare," Kathy said.

Clare shuddered. "The worst problem was theft." Her entire gross profit for the first four months had been negated by shoplifting tots. The first time Clare caught a little girl hiding a rag doll up her knickers, she angrily threatened to call a policeman. The child burst into tears. Clare, contrite, gave her the doll as a gift.

At the beginning of October, Kathy, who had again been invited for supper, arrived at Clare's apartment to find that nothing had been cooked. Clare, wearing a dirty dressing gown, was sitting on her unmade bed, staring into space.

"Where's Josh?" Kathy asked.

"I put him to bed early. It's good for him."

Kathy made two cups of tea and said firmly, "You aren't yourself, Clare, and you haven't been for months."

"I'm still depressed about the Red Rocking Horse," Clare replied vaguely.

"This started before that toy shop closed," Kathy said. "I think it's those pills you take. Why not stop them?"

"Don't be silly—my doctor prescribed those tranquilizers," Clare said. "He's a qualified doctor and you aren't, Kathy."

"But I *know* you better than he does! You aren't the same person since you started taking those things, Clare. You don't listen to what I'm saying. You don't play with Josh like you used to—you just sit! You've even stopped working for C.N.D."

"I could easily do without the pills," Clare said crossly. "But not just yet." She started to weep drearily. "I don't seem to be successful at *anything*. I used to be such a smug little prig. I was so sure I knew what was right, so critical of other people. Now I've found out how hopeless I am on my own. . . ."

"You'd be a lot less hopeless if you were thinking straight," Kathy advised. "Why don't you get away from Chelsea, move to the country? You're always saying you wished you still lived in the country. And you *could* live in the country on what you're wasting in rent for this dump!" She looked around the room with distaste. "Go to that place where you grew up and tell a local estate agent you want the cheapest thing he's got. Try to get it before Christmas, because I've got a bit of time off then, and I'll help you settle in."

Mrs. Gooden agreed to let Josh stay with her until Clare sorted out her problems and found somewhere to live.

The day he left, Kathy said to Clare, "I'll come round every evening and you can phone me anytime—I've asked my boss." To Clare's horror, Kathy then flushed the pills down the sink drain. "Now you know you'll have to manage without 'em," she said firmly.

During the first day without her pills, Clare grew increasingly depressed and agitated. By the evening, her mouth was dry, her hands had started to shake, and she felt dizzy. She didn't sleep at all that night. Her hands trembled too badly to cook and she sweated as if in the tropics. Frightened by these bodily reactions, she collapsed on the sofa and cried.

The following evening, when Kathy came to check on her, it was obvious that Clare blamed her for the shape she was in.

"If you go back to the doctor for another prescription," Kathy told her, "we'll only have to go through this again later. Now eat this stew I've brought."

By the fifth morning, Clare's hands no longer trembled.

On the eighth day, she felt her normal, clearheaded self again. Deeply grateful to Kathy, she said, "Tomorrow I'm going to pick up Josh, take the train to Warminster, and look for a place where we can start all over again."

Applebank Cottage, made of local soft Bath stone, was damp and cold, but as the agent pointed out, what did Clare expect for two pounds per week? All it needed was some heat.

From the garden gate to the front door, a herringbone brick path divided a neglected vegetable garden. Apple trees grew on either side of the double-sided small house, and behind it, the land rose smoothly to a small wood that followed the ridge of a hill.

Clare moved in just before Christmas, with a minimum of furniture, bought secondhand at an auction in Warminster. She hoped that Kathy was right, and that once away from the city, with enough money for her simple everyday needs, she would gradually find herself able to cope again.

Sunday, 25 December 1966

Neither Annabel (the hostess at a big charity children's skating party at Rockefeller Center) nor Clare (not invited) was present at Elinor's 1966 Christmas Day luncheon at Saracen, but Miranda and Adam were there; both arriving with bulging briefcases of work papers.

After the traditional turkey and Christmas pudding (made by Buzz, for Sylvie thought the recipe ludicrous), everyone left the table for a siesta. A few minutes later, Miranda sneaked to Adam's bedroom.

After they made love, Adam lay naked on the bed, staring contentedly at the ceiling. Beside him, Miranda felt too tired to think, too tired to move. She wondered how long she would be able to continue at her present pace.

Adam picked up a yellow legal pad and scribbled on it. He murmured, "Can you manage that dinner at the Mansion House next Thursday?"

"If you insist," Miranda yawned. Miranda was the prominently displayed figurehead of the SUPPLYKITS flotation, planned for three months ahead: she had become the living corporate identity of the company; her face, clothes, and style had become the visual embodiment of her business. Miranda was publicly perceived as an intelligent, modern woman on the move—the new sixties woman, not content to sit at home and wait for things to happen to her.

Because of this, Miranda, who hated being photographed or interviewed, had been obliged to entertain important people: pension fund managers, stockbrokers, bankers, and financial journalists. These business obligations made her feel impatient and frustrated: she would have preferred to spend her time working in her cosmetics business. KITS needed much more of her attention that it had been getting recently, and was now in a disturbing financial position; it didn't look as if the company would make a profit in 1966.

Although Adam pointed out that a profit was projected for the whole group, and that the group expansion had been phenomenal, Miranda felt a wistful longing for the old, less comfortable days—not so very long ago—when KITS had been her brilliant baby.

Now Adam interrupted Miranda's reverie by saying, "By the way, Paul Littlejohn says that the trustees regretfully must turn down your request for funds to redecorate your house. Apparently there have been big extra bills for Saracen this year; this place costs a fortune to run."

"Blast," Miranda mumbled into her pillow.

"The trustees are only doing their job," Adam soothed. "After all, you can't expect them to go on saying yes forever." He turned away from her as the telephone rang. "Hello? Mike? Had a good Christmas? So it arrived on time. . . . A Harley-Davidson Sportster was exactly what you wanted. . . . Of course I can afford it. . . . No, the panic's over. . . . Happy New Year, little brother. . . . I *know* you're thirty-four years old. . . . Then I won't in future. . . . We're coming back tomorrow, in Miranda's plane. . . . *Ciao*."

The day after Christmas, at six A.M., when it was still dark outside, Elinor stood in the entrance hall waiting to say goodbye to Miranda and Adam. Buzz, only half awake, wore an old Jaeger dressing gown that now looked like something from a dog basket.

"Buzz, please go and hurry Miranda!" Elinor said, smiling apologetically at Adam.

"It's been a wonderful Christmas," Adam said to Elinor as soon as Buzz disappeared. "I've used this peaceful break to consider something very important to me, and last night I reached my decision. I am going to leave STG and start my own practice."

Elinor stared, astonished. "But *why*, Adam? It's your family firm . . ."

"Quite frankly, Elinor—and in confidence—STG has been handling too many criminal cases for my liking. I don't think a respectable firm should take such a direction, however lucrative. I'm certain my father would never have allowed it. I'm not letting down STG—there are now seventeen senior partners and I'm only one of them. And since my speciality is international tax law, I feel . . . somewhat regretfully . . ."

"How will your decision affect my business?" Elinor asked sharply.

"It's up to you, Elinor. You will have to choose between STG and me. . . . I shall carry the same professional insurance as STG, by the way."

"I wish we could have talked about this when we had more time, Adam." Elinor was vexed.

"Until last night, I was undecided. *You* are the first person I have told, Elinor. I only wish that my father could know that I'm at last setting up on my own. . . . If you want to stay with STG, I'll be happy to arrange to have your work handled by one of the other partners—although it may take him a little time to be able to handle your affairs completely on his own without asking you a lot of questions."

Elinor said, "I don't want to deal with some new lawyer. I'm far too old to change. I want my affairs handled properly *without* a lot of questions. And if you're setting up your own firm, I'm sure your dear father would want me to help you start. So please arrange it."

"The simplest thing would be for you to write to STG and say you no longer wish them to represent you. Ask them to submit their bill to date—I'll check it, of course—and hand all your papers to me. No need to type the letter—in fact, a handwritten note would perhaps be best." Adam's brown eyes looked sincere. "I can't tell you how much I appreciate this, Elinor. I only wish that Dad could know of your loyalty."

CHAPTER 19

Monday, 26 December 1966

O*N THE MORNING* after Christmas, peaceful demonstrations organized by the C.N.D. took place all over Britain.

In Bath, the march started from the courtyard of Bath Abbey, which demonstrators had been forbidden to enter; the beautifully carved golden stone entrance to the abbey was protected by police horses. They stamped impatiently, legs shifting and snorting breath visible on the crisp, thin air.

Clare, wearing an old red ski suit, stood in a crowd of about three hundred people. She had left Josh with Kathy, who was spending Christmas at Applebank Cottage. Clare's banner, made from an old sheet kept taut by two broom handles, was painted with the red words BAN THE BOMB.

At eleven o'clock, the demonstrators formed a line in front of the abbey and prepared to parade slowly through the streets of the historic Georgian city. They were watched by a straggle of housewives and schoolchildren, and a photographer from the local paper.

Clare took up her position on the abbey side of the line. Just as the column began to move, a schoolgirl, pushing a baby in a pram, accidentally backed into a police horse. The horse, trained to keep calm, hardly moved, but the schoolgirl shrieked in terror and let go of her pram, which ran into the column of marchers; it hit the man standing next to Clare, who stumbled heavily against her, knocking her sideways.

As Clare staggered, her arms dropped and her banner wrapped around her head: she could not see where she was going. She tottered to her right, bumped into a police horse's hindquarters, stumbled against the horse, then screamed as she was pulled violently backward by strong arms.

Someone helped her to struggle free from her banner. Clare looked up and saw the tallest man she had ever seen; he had curly black hair and black-lashed, dark brown eyes, now filled with worry.

The man half carried, half pulled her into a nearby pub, where he propped her in a Windsor chair and went to fetch water from the bar. Clare, who felt dizzy and tearful, wondered whether she would ever again be able to move her jaw, which had received a painful blow, probably from the broomstick of her own banner. She looked across the bar to the back view of her rescuer: he wore jeans and an old maroon suede jacket buckled around lean hips; his boots were muddy.

As the man returned with a glass of water, Clare stared at his short, straight nose, above a mouth to write poems about: it was full-lipped, finely chiseled, subtly curved. Michelangelo's David come to life, Clare thought. She wished she had worn some makeup, then chastised herself for such a feeble thought.

Her rescuer said impatiently, "Sorry I took so long. It's almost impossible to get water in a bar since they don't make any money out of it." He poured water on his handkerchief, then gently dabbed at Clare's chin. "You'll have a huge bruise . . . Is there anyone with you?"

Clare shook her head.

"You shouldn't drive, or ride a bicycle, after a wallop like that. I'll take you home."

Clare mumbled with difficulty, "No, I'm okay. I'll get a lift home after the demo. I've just moved into a cottage on the edge of Warminster."

He drove her back in a battered silver sports car.

To Clare, his milky warm smell was like that of a newborn baby. She sternly reminded herself that she wasn't going to fall in love with the wrong man again just because she was sexually attracted to him, and she was *never* going to get married again. Having decided not to marry him, Clare directed her rescuer, David Arrowsmith, to Applebank Cottage.

In the kitchen, Kathy's look of incredulous congratulation was followed by concern when she noticed Clare's battered chin.

Abruptly Clare said to David, "Thank you for bringing me back. I'll be perfectly fine now. Kathy will look after me."

Clare knew that women often made up their minds very quickly, and without enough information, about other people, particularly those who were physically attractive: she had just seen Kathy do so. She also knew that, generally speaking, good, worthy men did not look flashy and glamorous, let alone theatrical; on the other hand, many rats were as good-looking as they were confident. Clare wouldn't put it past Sam to use a rat to lay a trap for her. Like many divorcées, she now viewed the man she had married as a monster of depravity, as capable as Richard III of any dirty deed. Clare's divorce petition would not be heard until July; she had been warned by her solicitor not to be seen alone with a man right now, or it might affect her petition and the custody of her son. She couldn't afford to run any risks, and there was certainly something mysterious about David Arrowsmith, something she couldn't identify for the moment: so she didn't trust him.

The following morning, after breakfast, a bruised Clare cut a photograph of herself from the local newspaper; luckily, her face was totally obscured by the banner, which had wrapped itself around her like a winding sheet. She looked like an Egyptian mummy in boots, but it was a good picture of her rescuer. She slipped the newspaper cutting into the top drawer of her bedside chest, then took the opportunity to go for a walk by herself, without Josh.

Once past her garden, Clare turned off the narrow lane onto a path hedged high with hawthorn, which led up the gently rising hill behind the cottage to the wood.

The wood was disturbingly still and silent; the twisted trunks and naked branches of the trees looked lonely and forlorn. Not a leaf moved, except for the dead leaves that Clare trod on. When she stepped on a stick and snapped it, the sudden noise caused a rook to rise from its nest with a startled beating of wings.

She looked up at the rook's nest and the gray sky beyond, then bent to pick up a clump of white winter aconites to take home to Josh. As she did so, a rusty trap sprang shut, clamping her left foot.

Clare yelled in pain as she fell on scratchy, frosted bracken. Luckily, she was wearing tough boots, so the trap had not torn her leg. She felt little pain unless she moved, which she tried not to do as she struggled to pull apart the serrated jaws of the trap. It was attached to a rusty chain hidden in the bracken. Clare could see more rusty chain around the slender, peeling, silver trunk of a nearby birch tree. She would only be able to move within the circumference of that tree. She was truly trapped.

The air didn't feel sharply cold enough for snow, and Clare hoped it wouldn't rain; she peered upward at the dull, gray sky.

She wondered how long it would be before Kathy grew alarmed. If Clare wasn't home and hadn't telephoned by two o'clock—or three at the latest—she reckoned that Kathy might phone the police, who would surely find her before long.

Unfortunately, Clare lay off the path in a place where the ground dipped, so she could not be seen. With difficulty, she rolled her body into a more comfortable position, pulled up the collar of her cherry wool coat, twisted her scarf around her head, and heaped bracken to form a pillow; with her head upon it, she stared crossly at the now leaden sky overhead. She pushed her hands deeper in her pockets and wished she had worn heavier gloves. She wondered if fate had just punished her for picking wildflowers.

Just before midday, Clare heard a noise behind her. Abruptly she sat up, winced at the pain this produced, then listened as the sound grew nearer: somebody was whistling "Lillibullero" with warbles and elaborate trills, off key, but with clear enjoyment.

Clare yelled, "Help!" several times, then stopped. She could hear nothing. Again she yelled.

This time a man's voice shouted, "Keep calling."

Eventually Clare heard a distant crackle. As it grew louder, she twisted around to face the sound.

"Oh!" she said. "It's you!"

"And vice versa," said David Arrowsmith as he scrambled toward her.

He towered above Clare, his hands tucked in the front pockets of the suede jacket. "I called to see how you were. Your nanny told me you'd gone for a walk. She saw you come up here." He squatted beside her. "Hey, not much of a country girl, are you?" He examined the trap.

"As a matter of fact, I am," Clare said. " We used to live near here. But as this is hunting country, I didn't expect a trap in the woods. And Kathy isn't my nanny. I can't afford a nanny. She's been staying with us over the Christmas holiday."

David tried without success to release Clare. Eventually he said, "This is a very old, heavy trap, and I don't think I can force the thing apart. I'd better phone the police—they'll know who owns this wood, and get him to free you. Take my gloves, and try not to get into any more trouble while I'm gone." He added ruefully, "I know I should tear that trap apart with my bare hands, but I'm not as tough as I look."

An hour later, the trap was pried apart by two mechanics from the local garage using steel bars. Teeth chattering, Clare limped back to Applebank Cottage with David, telling herself not to make a fuss.

After she had a hot rum toddy in a steaming, warm tub and showed Josh the trap marks on her leg, they all sat around the wooden kitchen table to eat vegetable soup, local Stilton cheese, and a salad of walnuts and chicory, followed by gingerbread that Clare had made with Mrs. Gooden's special recipe.

Then Josh had his nap and Kathy took Clare's bicycle to explore the country.

"You must be an Escoffier when you're in full possession of your faculties," David said. "May I have another slice of that delicious gingerbread?"

"It's a bit overdone. I've only just started to cook in a convection oven," Clare said apologetically. "And it's a bit difficult to manage with no fridge—just that metal meat safe hanging outside the back door. When I get a job, I'll get a fridge."

David, who had been briefly told about the flight from Sam, joked, "You might try selling gingerbread. I'd be your first customer."

Clare laughed. "What do *you* do for a living?"

"I'm an architect. I work in Bath. Mainly house renovations. I add an extension, convert a barn, chop off a couple of wings to make a house a manageable size—that sort of work. It's always a headache, but you have to take anything you can get when you're newly qualified."

"I thought of converting the attic," Clare said. "Making a room for Josh to sleep and play in, with bunks for visiting children. This house has only two bedrooms, which isn't ideal."

"I'll have a look at the attic, if you like."

"Well . . . I can't afford anything yet."

"But you might like to know what's possible, and how much it would cost?"

"Very much."

In the attic, David said thoughtfully, "As there's a window, you only need to lead the electrical supply upstairs, lay a soundproof floor covering—cork—and insulate the roof."

"It'll have to wait until I have some money."

After Josh had gone to bed, the three adults spent the evening roasting chestnuts before the living room fire.

At ten o'clock, David said, "I must go. But I'll be back."

At the front door, he kissed Clare on the tip of her nose, then left.

Saturday, 31 December 1966

Just after Kathy left for London, David arrived with a bottle of champagne to spend the day and celebrate New Year's Eve. Clare wondered suspiciously why this sensationally good-looking man seemed not to have any New Year's plans.

At lunch, Josh misbehaved. He pushed his food off the table and refused to eat even the cheesecake.

Clare was mortified. She had so hoped that Josh would like David. "He's tired," she apologized, and took Josh off for his afternoon nap. He kicked and screamed, furious that his mother's attention was being distracted from himself.

Darkness fell early, and it started to snow. After tea, Clare pulled the sitting room curtains together but didn't switch on the light: she preferred to watch the firelight flick shadows over the walls. In the embers of the fire, David again roasted chestnuts for the now sunny-tempered Josh, until his bedtime.

When Clare returned from putting Josh to bed, David wordlessly took her in his arms; they sat on the floor, leaning against the broken-backed armchair, and necked like teenagers.

As David's nose nuzzled the back of her neck, Clare had an overwhelming need to be even closer to him. She felt as if she were lying naked on a hot rock, stretching languorously toward the sun.

As the light of the friendly flames played over their faces, Clare felt she was in a dream world where time was suspended. She felt a physical longing too strong to resist; she breathed fast and grew a bit light-headed; she could smell the soft, milky smell of David's body and the warm wool odor of his sweater; she felt a frenzied yearning.

At midnight, David kissed her gently and left shortly afterward, saying he hoped that snow hadn't blocked the roads.

Disappointed, Clare wondered what had gone wrong. After all, he needn't have visited her. Why hadn't he wanted to stay?

Of course, she wouldn't have let him.

Wednesday, 11 January 1967

"What's so urgent and private that you couldn't discuss it over the telephone?" In his study, Adam, wearing a dinner jacket, poured whiskey into a cut-glass tumbler and confronted his brother.

Mike wore black leather biking trousers and a heavy seaman's turtleneck sweater. He said, "I've now been waiting two bloody years for my commission on the Framwell deal."

Mike's agreed commission was two percent of the purchase price of any property that Miranda acquired, either directly or indirectly, through him. The commission had been correctly paid on all the relevant purchases except that of Framwells—the chain of tobacconist shops—which was easily the biggest deal Mike had handled.

"You'll get your money," Adam said. "But Framwells was a self-financing deal. Frankly, the interest we've had to pay on the loan is very high."

"Fuck that. It isn't my problem."

"With the greatest respect"—Mike knew this phrase meant Adam was annoyed—"it *is* your problem, Mike, because no date of payment for commission was written into your contract. Legally, I could keep you waiting a hundred years for the money."

"We didn't have a contract. You wrote the arrangement on a sheet of paper over dinner, and we both signed it. Here it is!" Mike pulled a paper from his pocket and looked at it. No period of payment was mentioned.

"If you're going to be difficult," Adam said, "I suggest that either you wait for a hundred years or agree to reduce the amount payable, by half."

Mike looked at Adam in astonishment. "You're my *brother*, you bastard! Brothers aren't supposed to fuck each other over! You use me when it suits you, you get me to fix your dirty work—"

"If you didn't do it, there are plenty of others who would."

"You ruthless, evil bastard."

Mike, furious, could see that Adam clearly felt he had nothing to fear from his little brother. Adam stopped now to light a cigarette, contemptuously confident of his ability to maneuver and control.

"Kindly remember that I provide the legal know-how to protect you and your—friends," Adam said calmly. "I'll speak to Miranda about your payment. I'll see if I can hurry it."

"I'll damn well speak to Miranda myself," Mike growled.

Adam looked up sharply from his cigarette. "No. Don't do that. It isn't necessary!"

Mike suddenly realized what had happened.

"Miranda thinks she settled this bill months ago, doesn't she?" he yelled. "*What did you do?* Forge my name on the back of the check and endorse it to yourself?"

Mike saw a fleeting guilty look in Adam's eyes before his lids were lowered and his attention seemingly focused again on his gold lighter.

"No doubt you told yourself that you were only *borrowing* my money to pay your bloody gambling debts, but I call that *theft!*" Mike thundered.

Coolly Adam ground out his cigarette on the hearth.

Adam's apparent lack of concern enraged Mike, as hurt by his brother's treachery as he was by the theft. He wanted to *hurt* Adam. He wanted to feel his fist bruise flesh, smash bone, draw blood.

His fist shot out.

Adam stumbled backward, tripped over the steel fireplace screen, then lost his balance and crashed to the floor.

As Adam fell, Mike heard the sound of his head hitting the elaborate steel fender. It happened so fast that Mike was left with his arm still outstretched, toward the dinner-jacketed body of his brother.

Immediately contrite, Mike crouched by Adam and lifted his head: it lolled sideways. Mike's face was very pale.

Christ, thought Mike, I *can't* have killed him, not just with one lousy punch . . . could I? He knew that only a very good fighter—a much better fighter than he was—could knock a man unconscious with one punch to the jaw.

Hastily Mike pulled at Adam, until he lay full length on the rug. He tore Adam's tie loose, undid his shirt and collar, and stuck his finger in Adam's mouth to check that his tongue was free. He grabbed the telephone and dialed 999. He knew that the housekeeper wasn't in, because Adam had opened the front door.

After the fourth ring, the emergency operator answered: "Police, fire or ambulance?"

"Ambulance! Fast!" After giving full address details, Mike ran to the kitchen for water and a towel. How could he have hit his brother, the only person in the world with whom he felt fully relaxed, happy, and at home?

As he swabbed his brother's temples with cold water, Mike muttered, "I'm *sorry.* I can't tell you how sorry I am, Adam. My bloody temper again! Look, forget the money. Just, for God's sake, open your eyes. *Please.*"

Adam's eyelids moved slightly. Mike carefully wiped his face.

Adam looked up and said weakly, "God, my head's splitting. What happened?" He tried to lift his head, but the room tilted. Giddy, he fell back on the rug. With eyelids still closed, he murmured anxiously, "Where's my watch?"

"It's still on your wrist, old boy," said Mike, dabbing with the towel at his brother's face. "An ambulance is on its way—should be here any minute."

Adam slowly lifted his left wrist and looked at it.

Puzzled, Mike wondered what was so special about that ordinary-looking Omega watch.

Adam said weakly, "I don't need an ambulance. . . . You hit me, that's all. You're not Superman. . . . I'll be okay in the morning."

Friday, 20 January 1967

Just after six o'clock, Clare heard the squeak of the garden gate hinge. Her heart jumped. She caught her breath, dropped her oven gloves to the floor, and leapt to the window. David was walking up the garden path, half an hour earlier than expected.

As he came through the kitchen door, he said, "I'll oil that gate for you tomorrow when we clear the garden . . . Mmm, what's that delicious smell?" He took her in his arms.

"Leek-and-potato stew." Clare's newfound, short-term leisure meant that she now enjoyed cooking, instead of seeing it as an added, rushed three-times-a-day chore to fit in around earning her living. She mumbled against David's tweed jacket, "We're having chicory-and-orange salad with vinaigrette sauce, followed by mushroom croustade with a hazelnut topping, then Stilton and homemade oatmeal biscuits."

"Sounds delicious." He kissed the top of her head. "By the way, are you a vegetarian?"

"Only since last week. I decided I don't like eating dead bodies—not after being caught in a trap. I know most people think it's cranky."

Clare served supper early so that four-year-old Josh could stay up late and eat with them. She would have preferred a romantic candlelit dinner for two, but even more, she wanted Josh to see David as one of life's pluses and not as an interloper.

After Josh had gone to bed, they again sat on a rug before the fire with their backs to the broken-backed armchair, holding hands as they listened to a radio concert.

Clare murmured, "There's something I have to tell you."

She had carefully thought out what she was going to say, but when, in the firelight, she looked into his dark-fringed eyes, she forgot her rehearsed words. She sighed and said regretfully, "You're so good-looking."

"I know what you mean. I hate it. It's embarrassing. And believe me, it's a drawback. Women are distracted and men don't trust me because of my looks," David said. "But there's nothing I can do about it. I wear my hair long and I comb it forward to hide as much as possible of my face. I used to wear clear glass spectacles, although I didn't need them." He added, "But there is one great advantage: nobody wants to fight me. Sometimes if I'm sitting in a bar, I'm teased by strangers, who think I'm a homosexual. Then I slowly stand up, and they see the length of me and back away. They're not to know I'd never fight." He laughed apologetically. "I also have some cranky principles."

Clare didn't laugh. Instead, she said what she had to say, knowing that this was the time to get it out. "David, I find you almost unbearably attractive. I love feeling close to you. *But I don't want to go to bed with you.* I want to make that clear!"

"Why not?" David settled his arm more comfortably around her.

Clare lost her nerve. She had intended to say, "Because I went through a promiscuous period after I left Sam, and it was a hateful, shameful, humiliating time, and I'll never let it happen again." She also feared that early sexual disaster in this relationship would doom it.

But Clare forgot her lines; instead, she burst into tears. "Because my love life has been such a mess!"

"Well, that's in the past," David murmured as he cuddled her. "But what happened?"

Clare snuffled a bit. "Sex isn't what I was led to expect."

David said, "Sex without a close emotional relationship doesn't work for me either. I can't separate sex from old-fashioned feelings like love and affection."

"But that's what *women* usually say!"

"You know, Clare, what I like about you is your innocence. Maybe what I'm saying is the only sure-fire, tried and tested way to get a girl's knickers off in thirty seconds—which, by the way, it is. But what I said *is* the way I feel."

"I know why you're so easy to talk to," Clare said. "You don't bother to try and prove yourself. You really *listen* to what I say—and you respond to it. My husband didn't take me seriously."

"And you haven't had another relationship since?"

Clare hesitated, then took the plunge. "I had a ghastly series of one-nighters. Usually they hopped on and pumped away and suddenly it was over. I never climaxed and I was too shy and too timid to ask for what I wanted, so afterward I'd be resentful . . . "

"But if you never told them what turned you on, how could you expect—"

"I agree, it seems crazy. I wasn't too shy to leap into bed with them, but I was too shy to tell them what I needed."

"How you feel is how you feel and how you climax is how you climax, and so long as you let a man know those things, there shouldn't be a problem," David said. They settled down to some serious kissing.

Friday, 27 January 1967

The following Friday evening, after spinach soufflé, baked potatoes with sour cream, and rather a lot of excellent claret, Clare found herself sitting naked to the waist in the firelight. "Let's go to bed," she whispered.

"Promise you won't anticipate?"

"*What?*"

"No anxious thoughts."

"Such as?"

"I hope I'm going to come. . . . I hope my body's as good as his other girls' . . . . I hope I don't take much longer. . . . "

Shyly Clare added, "I hope he isn't bored or tired. . . . he'll be disappointed if I don't come. . . . "

"Hell, it's all too much trouble. I'm not going to come. I'll fake it."

Clare nodded.

David stood up and pulled her to her feet. Hand in hand, they moved upstairs to bed.

CHAPTER 20

Monday, 19 March 1967

"O*H MY GOD, DARLING,* I'd forgotten I'd ever signed that!" Miranda looked with dismay at the document that Adam had just placed on her white horseshoe-shaped desk. She suddenly felt as cold as the raw wind of March that swept the streets of London outside her office window.

Adam stared thoughtfully at Miranda; he leaned across her desk. "I've spent a long, long time thinking about this. Of course, I know you won't like giving up fifteen percent of the total equity of SUPPLYKITS—nobody would. On the other hand, it was on this condition that I joined your company: you agreed that should your business ever go public, I would have fifteen percent of the equity for the nominal sum of fifteen thousand pounds. I would like to hold you to your bargain, Miranda."

"But I thought that only referred to KITS!" Miranda said, dismayed.

"The wording of the document clearly states, 'and/or any other businesses that arise from this company.' That means fifteen percent of SUPPLYKITS, Miranda. Surely you read the document before signing it?"

"But, darling . . ." Miranda looked pleading.

Regretfully Adam shook his head. "This is not a personal matter, it's a matter that concerns your business integrity. What made me finally decide to insist on this was when I realized that had you been a man, Miranda, or had I not been personally involved with you, I wouldn't have *hesitated* to ask for these shares."

From opposite sides of the desk, they stared at each other impersonally. It was as if a glass wall had gone up between them. Miranda said quietly, "In that case, Adam, I'd like to get a second legal opinion."

"Of course. But you'd better inform Freddy Swanson immediately that there is a problem. After all, it's only two days to the flotation."

"Why the hell didn't you bring this up before now?" Miranda fumed.

"I've only just reached my decision," Adam said softly. He hadn't intended to give her time to try a countermove.

Miranda telephoned her lawyer. Having ascertained that she would, indeed, be forced to sell fifteen percent of SUPPLYKITS to Adam for a token amount, she added, "In that case, please rewrite my will and delete all reference to Adam Grant. Instead, reapportion those shares to my staff. . . . No, I've had a better idea! Add Adam Grant's bequest to that of Buzz—I mean, Miss Doris Mann."

Miranda replaced the receiver and called for her secretary. "June, please cancel all today's appointments. Ask Mr. Swanson if he would be kind enough to see me here, as soon as possible. I mean within the hour."

* * *

Miranda's ten-man board of directors had recently been expanded to include a new chairman, the Earl of Brighton, and Frederick Swanson of Seligman Swanson, the merchant bank chosen to handle the SUPPLYKITS flotation. The bank had organized everything concerning the various consultants, the share price, and the prospectus, a forty-page, glossy volume about the company's structure, trading situation, and future plans. As was customary in Britain, existing contractual obligations had been included; as was also customary, two weeks before the flotation, the essential details of this prospectus had been published in national newspapers.

Mr. Swanson arrived at the reception area and was shown to the private lift that went straight to Miranda's office on the top floor.

When he stepped out, he was astonished by his first view of the place. The entire sixty-foot room was white, including the marble floor. The furniture was white and chrome, and even the many vases of spring flowers were white. The space looked clean, glamorous, and exciting. At the far end of the room, spotlights shone on white tables, upon which cosmetics, in various stages of testing, were spread. Overriding the scent of flowers was the faint suggestion of a peculiar smell, slightly reminiscent of a school science lab, but fruitier.

Miranda walked forward to welcome her visitor. "Good morning, Freddy."

"What's happened?" Freddy Swanson asked. He was pleased by the progress of the flotation: SUPPLYKITS was thriving; KITS had sacrificed its 1966 profit only to facilitate the other company's expansion.

Swiftly Miranda outlined her problem, grateful for once that her personal involvement with Adam was a secret.

"*Why did Adam wait until so late?*" Freddy thundered. "An undisclosed stock option worth three hundred thousand pounds throws out all your figures! That means our brochure and advertisements are inaccurate."

"Originally he decided not to take up the option because he thought it would upset me," Miranda said lamely. "But Adam eventually decided that he couldn't afford such sentimental generosity."

"Which, of course, *did* upset you."

"To be frank, Freddy, he's earned it. I doubt SUPPLYKITS would be going public without him."

"Nevertheless, Adam's a qualified lawyer," Freddy said, "yet he put his name to a prospectus which says that all material information has been disclosed—but does not mention a fifteen percent stock option that I wasn't told about." He sat down on a white, tulip-shaped chair. "I'll calculate the exact figures," he murmured, "Adam has acquired one hundred and ninety-two thousand thirty-shilling shares worth two hundred and eighty-eight thousand pounds for fifteen thousand pounds, which leaves you, Miranda, holding sixty percent of the shares." Slowly he looked up from his calculations. "I suppose we can't do anything about it at this stage. All the expensive consultants' work has been done, all the donkey work is over, everyone is exhausted, and some of the public have already applied for the shares, so *very reluctantly* I will take no action. Those shares mustn't be sold to Adam until after the flotation."

Everyone in the office noticed the new, impeccably polite coldness between Miranda and Adam. Nobody guessed the reason. But Miranda felt exposed and lonely.

Early on the following Thursday morning, she grabbed the pale pink copy of the *Financial Times* from her breakfast tray. SUPPLYKITS was now on the London Stock Exchange: the share price had risen to thirty-three shillings. As Miranda poured her coffee, she realized that checking the share price would now be her first priority every morning. She was no longer the proprietor of SUPPLYKITS but the managing director and major shareholder of a public company.

For a moment, Miranda's eyes sparkled: the little sister—number three in the nursery—to whom no one had paid much attention, was now, at the age of twenty-six, clearly a number one in the business world! She was one of the few self-made women in Britain. *In the world!* She remembered her early unsuccessful struggles for equal treatment and wondered what her sisters would think of this news. To hell with equality now.

She wished she could share her glee with Adam. Miranda hated the coldness between them. Perhaps she should not have been so aggressive. After all, she *had* agreed to the option when she wanted Adam to join the company: he was only taking what he was entitled to.

Hearing a knock, Miranda turned her head to the door as the housekeeper entered; she carried a Victorian brass birdcage, in which was a dove. Attached to the ring at the top of the cage was an olive branch with silvery-gray leaves.

She tore open the card. Adam's angular black handwriting read: "Can I tell you tonight how sorry I am?"

Miranda threw back her sheets and took the cage to the window. She laughed as she watched the dove soar above the chestnut trees, which were already showing the first flecks of green.

That evening Miranda ran down the stairs to her drawing room; her heart was beating hard and she was short of breath.

Adam, in white dinner jacket, turned from the window and stared. "Darling, are you dressed or undressed? One never knows these days." Miranda wore a sheer cream chiffon Grecian gown with thonged gold sandals that crisscrossed to her knees.

"Definitely dressed. It's Zandra Rhodes."

"That dress was designed to be taken off." Adam held her by the shoulders; through the gauze, he could feel her warm flesh. As he pulled her against his body, she breathed in his body scent and felt his excitement. "How I've missed you," he murmured as his hands slowly moved down her back and then traced the swell of her buttocks.

Hungrily Miranda groped for his body; her knees shook and, together, they fell upon the thick cream carpet, where, wordlessly, they came together again.

Toward dawn, Miranda no longer knew whether or not she was dreaming, as she felt Adam's flesh against hers and inhaled the pungent almond smell of love; by the dying embers of the drawing room fire, she could just see his face.

Sleepily Adam whispered, "I find it an extraordinarily erotic idea."

"What?"

"To be in bed with a self-made millionairess."

"But we aren't in bed, darling."

"Let's get there quickly. There are things I must do to you."

Saturday, 19 August 1967

Outside, the sun beat down on the red baked earth of Provence, but the summer salon was cool. A Scrabble board lay on the floor, a reminder that so far this year, Buzz was beating Elinor by 147 to 17. Miranda, in black linen shorts and halter top, lay with her feet up on the terra-cotta-colored sofa, enjoying her idleness. She yawned and stretched; she wished her siesta could have lasted until the following morning—no, the following week.

The SUPPLYKITS interim dividend had been seven percent—an excellent figure—but in spite of this satisfying result, Miranda still fretted about her neglect of KITS. After the SUPPLYKITS flotation, the analysts, investors, and competitors had taken a much closer look at the company. An exhausted Miranda found that instead of having more time, she had almost a full-time job keeping present and future shareholders informed and happy: she prepared official reports, gave institutional and pension fund presentations, attended City lunches, and made time in her overfilled schedule for the financial press. Overworked and depressed, she felt as if she were being turned into a glamorous business machine.

Miranda sniffed the heavy scent of the lilies; in the flower room beyond the bar, she could hear Elinor and Buzz talking as they made their way slowly into the summer salon. A maid arrived with the tea tray as soon as they sat down.

"Cucumber sandwiches." Buzz nodded approvingly, "*And* chocolate éclairs."

Miranda yawned again. "Buzz, I can't understand how you can eat *anything* after these huge, delicious French lunches. The others are still working it off on the tennis court."

"Not me." Adam sauntered into the room.

The maid put down the tea tray and fished in the pocket of her dress. "*Une lettre par courier pour Mademoiselle Mann.*"

"For *me?*" Buzz was puzzled. "Nobody sends *me* letters by courier. An American stamp . . . " As she turned the letter over, her face became eager and younger. "It's Bertha Higby!"

Since the death of her fiancé nearly fifty years ago, Buzz had continued to correspond with his mother. Every year, Ginger's parents traveled to France to visit his grave, sometimes accompanied by Buzz. Now eighty-seven years old and recently widowed, Mrs. Higby remained in Cleveland.

Buzz read the short letter. "*Oh!* . . . Oh . . . But I couldn't . . . "

"What is it?" Elinor asked, teapot suspended.

"Eric left a bigger windfall than Bertha expected. She says at her age, she might not have long to enjoy it. She says she's spent her life living modestly, as Eric wanted, but now she wants to blow a bit of it on some fun. . . . Strewth! She wants to take a luxury winter cruise . . . next January. . . . Six weeks on the *Stella Polaris.* Round the Caribbean islands and South America, until the end of February . . . *and she wants me to be her guest!*"

"Why did she send it by courier?" Miranda asked.

"She wants a quick reply, to book our passages."

"Then why didn't she telephone?"

"Such extravagance! Eric would turn in his urn. Anyway, it's out of the question. I couldn't leave Elinor on her own."

"I don't need a chaperon, you old fool." Elinor handed Buzz a cup of strong

Indian tea. "I can do without you for six weeks, Buzz. Perhaps I'll get a bit of peace, for a change."

"No. Six weeks is too long to be away," Buzz said, blowing on her tea to cool it.

Adam said, "Elinor has five servants here, three secretaries, and a doctor almost within shouting distance. Perhaps it's time you had a real rest, Buzz."

"I agree," said Miranda.

"I don't *need* a rest." Buzz was affronted.

"Of course you don't," Adam soothed. "But I expect Elinor feels that as your friend is eighty-seven, she probably shouldn't be traveling alone."

"That's for sure," Elinor said seriously. "And I *do* think you need a rest from me, Buzz. It's two years since my . . . er . . . incident and you've hardly had a day off ever since—you've fussed around me like a mother hen. How long is it since you've seen Bertha?"

"Four years," Buzz said. "They came for a weekend just before we left Starlings."

"We could easily arrange for a nurse to be here during your absence," Adam suggested.

"Fiddlesticks! I don't need a nurse!" Elinor said.

"You need *somebody*," Buzz said firmly. "And she'll have to sleep in my bedroom because it's nearest to yours."

Elinor smiled at Adam. "Tell the trustees that Buzz must have a bonus, Adam. She'll need to keep her end up on a luxury cruise."

Adam pulled a notebook from his trouser pocket. As he scribbled, he said, "By the way, Elinor, Paul Littlejohn has decided to leave STG, Bermuda. He's setting up his own firm there."

"What a nuisance!" Elinor said. "Why does he want to do that?"

"For much the same reason as I did. I'm afraid that STG is no longer as reliable as it was in my grandfather's day. I've never regretted leaving. In fact, it was a great relief."

"But who will superintend *my* work in future?" Elinor asked.

"That *is* a problem," Adam admitted, "although, of course, we could transfer our affairs to Paul's new firm. We know that he can handle everything."

Buzz looked disapproving.

"Why not?" Adam said casually. "He could avoid mistakes and the need to brief someone else. But there's no need to make a decision yet. Paul has to give six months' notice to STG, so he won't be leaving until well after Christmas—probably in February."

"Plenty of time to think about it carefully," Elinor said. "Another cup of tea, Buzz? Tell us more about this cruise."

Saturday, 3 February 1968

A week after the affairs of the Dove Trust had been transferred to Littlejohn and Partners (Bermuda), Adam surprised Elinor with a trip to Saracen for the weekend. Every time his plane touched down at Nice airport and he saw palm trees and tanned porters in white, short-sleeved shirts, Adam enjoyed afresh the glamour of a life where one stepped onto a plane in bleak winter weather and shortly afterward stepped off in warm sunshine.

That evening, he and Elinor drank aperitifs in the summer salon.

Adam pointed to a pair of elaborately carved chairs in cinnamon-colored wood, inset with ivory. "Are those new?"

"Yes. Found them at my pet antiques dealer in Cannes. Eighteenth century, from Goa, made for some rich Portuguese trader. I also snapped up those two new chairs in the hall—the ones with angels' faces carved on the back: really too good for family use, but I couldn't resist them."

"What did they cost?"

"Too much to tell you, dear boy," said Elinor gaily.

As Adam refilled his glass, Elinor said, "I never realized how much I'd miss Buzz. How she'll crow when I tell her! She's obviously having a wonderful time. Every day, I get a postcard from some tropical place called Brown Sugar Island or Crab Cove. She says there are no men on board—the ship is full of hopeful widows—but the crew are wonderful and she's friendly with the purser, who dances a mean Charleston."

Adam sipped his drink. "As well as a winter break, there's another reason for my visit, Elinor, but I didn't want to alarm you unnecessarily by discussing it over the telephone."

Elinor sensed trouble.

"It's the new book contract," Adam went on. "The publishers would feel . . . happier . . . if they had a medical all-clear before signing. They know it's been over two years since your illness, but they'd appreciate reassurance. They're all overjoyed about it, but before they make their plans and get the sales force excited, they want to be . . . quite sure . . . that you are . . . completely fit."

"It's not as though I were writing a new book," Elinor said crossly "The boxed set is a reissue."

"Yes, but you've agreed to promote it," Adam said patiently. "And before they spend vast sums on the publicity launch, they'd like to know that it won't be too much for you."

"I feel fit as a fiddle," Elinor protested.

"Elinor, this is a reasonable business precaution to take," Adam persisted. "Film stars, sports stars—everyone in businesses where heavy investment depends on the health of one person—know that a regular medical check is considered a reasonable—and *professional*—precaution." Adam knew that Elinor would go to great lengths to avoid being called unprofessional.

"Oh, well, if it's only a medical check, I can go to that American nursing home at Cannes."

"They'd prefer British medical reports."

"Oh dear. How long will it take?"

"Perhaps four days."

"A pity Buzz isn't here. Although she'd only fuss if she were. She doesn't like the London Clinic. Noisy place, she thinks."

"You can be there and back before Buzz returns," Adam said. "And you needn't go to the London Clinic. I'll arrange for the best possible care. As you say, you aren't ill—so your friends will be able to visit you. Life will be one long party, with a matron to shoo people away, should you get tired or bored. And the night you leave, I'll take you to the theater."

"You make it sound quite fun, dear boy. Could you see that there are a few crates of champagne—those half-bottles, so convenient for visitors."

"I'll arrange everything," Adam promised.

Saturday, 10 February 1968

One week later, as the plane took off from Nice for London airport, Adam outlined his arrangements to Elinor.

"*Eastbourne!*" she exclaimed. "Why *Eastbourne?*"

"Elinor, you sound like Dame Edith Evans saying, '*A handbag?*' in *The Importance of Being Earnest.* Eastbourne isn't the Gorbals," Adam said easily. "Eastbourne has the highest sunshine rate in Britain."

"I can get plenty of sunshine at Saracen. And I'm not on my last legs yet, *thank* you very much! Eastbourne is filled with nursing homes in Victorian mansions with names like 'The Gables.' "

"And that is why the best specialists for this sort of medical checkup are in Eastbourne," Adam said persuasively. "It's only for a few days, Elinor, and it's just an hour and a half away from London. There will be plenty of flowers and books, delicious food, TV and a telephone . . . "

Elinor pursed her lips. "You should *not* have made these arrangements without my approval, Adam!"

Adam looked contrite. He said, "I can, of course, cancel them should you wish, but Sir George is undoubtedly the best-qualified heart specialist in the country. And he *himself* told me that the Lord Willington Nursing Home is the most *professional* of the local nursing homes. Dr. Craig-Dunlop, who owns it, prides himself on having all the latest equipment."

"Oh well, I suppose it won't hurt me for a couple of days. Stop fretting, dear boy."

With the South Downs behind it and the turbulent gray English Channel in front, the Lord Willington Nursing Home looked like a country mansion. As she stepped from her Rolls, Elinor shivered in the unaccustomed raw air of February.

Inside, a faint whiff of disinfectant was almost overpowered by the heavy scent emanating from the bowls of blue hyacinths. A smiling receptionist apologized for the matron's absence.

After Elinor had signed her voluntary consent form, she and Adam were taken to her suite of rooms. But for the mechanical hospital bed, she might have been in a first-class hotel: the sitting room was agreeably furnished in *eau de Nil*, the bedroom in old rose; the interconnecting rooms faced the sea over lawns and flower beds, though they were bleak at this time of the year.

Elinor read the cards from two identical large vases of lilies which took up all the space on the dressing table. She laughed. "One is from Miranda, one from Annabel. They both know I love lilies."

Adam smiled. "Miranda wanted to be with you today, but Dr. Craig-Dunlop wants you to settle in quickly, with no excitement. Your tests start tomorrow. Miranda wants to know as soon as you're allowed visitors. Annabel has already telephoned three times, but I've asked her not to call again, in case she disturbs a treatment. It's best if you call her."

Coffee was served in the sitting room right after their arrival. Then a smiling procession of medical staff presented themselves, each of whom told Elinor that if there was anything she wanted, she had only to ask. Finally she was given an enormous burgundy leatherbound folder that looked like some medieval city charter: it was the menu.

"Don't worry, dear boy," Elinor said over a glass of champagne poured from one of the little bottles. "I can see they're going to look after me really well."

"I'm sure of it." Adam smiled as he lifted his glass in a toast.

On the following day, Elinor's door was thrown open by a nurse who then stood to attention as, smiling benignly, Matron Ivy Braddock appeared in the doorway.

Elinor's first astonished impression was that Matron Braddock looked like a female impersonator—a sergeant major in drag: she couldn't wait to describe her to Buzz. The matron was one of the biggest women Elinor had ever seen; her neck seemed sunk between strong shoulders, and her red hands hung from beefy arms. Her face looked rough-hewn, as if carved from a cliff. Her yellow hair was cut very short, and on it, like a cake frill, perched a nurse's cap, tied beneath the square jaw. The matron moved toward Elinor's bed on legs that seemed to be joined to her feet without ankles: she did not walk so much as stomp.

"We're going to do *everything* we *can*, Mrs. O'Dare, to make you comfortable." Matron Braddock's voice was surprisingly light and pleasant.

First, blood and urine samples were taken; then Elinor was X-rayed, after which she spent the rest of the day being wired up to various machines for tests. That evening, Dr. Cyril Craig-Dunlop stopped in just to visit. He was a small, mild-mannered man with surprisingly beautiful, black-fringed gray eyes.

The next morning, the heart specialist, Sir George, was ushered into Elinor's bedroom by Matron Braddock. Elinor hated to be interrupted: she was reading Truman Capote's *In Cold Blood.*

Other specialists followed.

On the third morning, Dr. Craig-Dunlop again visited Elinor. "I've had the results of nearly all the tests," he said, "which are more or less what we expected. However, as you know, you must be very, very careful with the few years that remain to you."

In Cold Blood fell to the floor.

Elinor sat upright. "What do you mean? I have recovered completely! That's what I was told!"

Dr. Craig-Dunlop stammered, clearly confused, "I—I'm so sorry, Mrs. O'Dare. I assumed you were the type of patient who would have been told . . . "

"Told *what?*"

"The truth about your condition," Dr. Craig-Dunlop said apologetically.

"*The few years that remain to me?* Are you sure?" Elinor blanched, her pallor more obvious against her peach chiffon robe. "I'd like a second opinion."

Dr. Craig-Dunlop coughed. "Your three specialists are all of the same opinion."

Elinor stared bleakly out the window, beyond the sloping lawn to where the sludge-colored sea met with the gray sky. There was no sound in the room.

Eventually she said, "I don't want my granddaughters to know. They would worry, you see."

Shortly after the doctor left, a smiling nurse, smart in a lavender-and-white-striped uniform, entered; she carried two pills in a small vial.

"This will make you feel better." She watched to make sure that Elinor swallowed the medication. The nurses were well trained in dealing with rich patients who were used to doing as they pleased and often disliked accepting the discipline of routine; they knew that the very old, the alcoholics, and the more than slightly batty patients (called "eccentric") had to be carefully supervised. This old dear, who was to be kept under heavy sedation, clearly didn't know that she was a long-term patient, being treated for depression.

During the next two days, Elinor slept a lot, which Dr. Craig-Dunlop said might be because she wished to evade reality. But the reason was simply that Elinor was very sensitive to medicine; for her, a normal dose of sedative was an overdose.

In a moment of clarity, just before her eleven A.M. medication on Friday, a bewildered Elinor threatened to leave and was told by a nurse that this was not possible without the prior permission of the matron.

Elinor, used to prompt obedience to her wishes, flew into a rage, of which the nurse took not the slightest notice. An injection was swiftly administered, and Sister correctly reported that the patient had become uncontrollable and needed sedation.

"Paranoia," Dr. Craig-Dunlop said quietly to Matron upon reading this report.

Matron Braddock nodded. She knew that a classic symptom of paranoia was the suspicion that those who were caring for you were trying to harm you.

Saturday, 17 February 1968

After Elinor had spent a week in the nursing home, Annabel and Miranda were allowed to visit. On the way, sitting in the back of the Bentley that drove them from London, the two worried sisters spoke little. Finally, Miranda inquired after Scott.

Annabel snapped, "Don't ask *me* how Scott is! I hardly ever see him—I don't even suppose he's noticed that I'm not there this week!"

"What do you mean?" Miranda was surprised.

"Oh, he's too wrapped up in his work to bother about his wife. He even forgot our tenth anniversary!"

"That doesn't sound like Scott."

"Well, he *would* have forgotten," Annabel amended, "but I reminded him."

Annabel and Miranda were shocked by their grandmother's appearance: her golden hair was lifeless, her eyes were dull, her speech was thick and slurred, she seemed inert and limp. Forewarned by the matron to treat her normally and to ignore anything eccentric that she did or said, the two sisters immediately wrapped Elinor in an invisible cloud of affection.

Afterward, in the matron's office, where Adam and Dr. Craig-Dunlop were waiting for them, Annabel burst into tears. "I can't understand why *I* couldn't see that she was ill."

Miranda put her arms around her sister. "Don't cry, Frog. I had no idea either. It's lucky she's being properly looked after."

"Oh, what bad luck that Buzz was away!" Annabel sobbed. "She could have been here with Gran."

"What exactly *is* paranoia?" Miranda impatiently asked the doctor.

"We prefer to describe it as a personality disorder," he said. "A chronic, slowly progressive mental disorder. In this case, I fear that there will be delusions of persecution."

"What treatment is she having?" Miranda asked while Annabel wept.

"She is being given a drug called Mellaril. And sedatives as necessary."

"How long will she be ill?"

There was a short, ominous silence.

"How long?" Miranda repeated shrilly.

"I cannot say. Not yet. We'll have to see how she responds to treatment, but it may take quite a long time."

"How many weeks?"

"Perhaps you should think in terms of months," Dr. Craig-Dunlop said gently. He added, "But I must emphasize that at this stage, we simply cannot tell. She is an elderly lady, she has had one stroke, and she has a personality disorder. We simply cannot say what will happen."

"How *can* she have deteriorated so seriously in such a short time, when she only came here for a checkup?" Miranda persisted.

"It was *extremely fortunate* that she came here when she did," said the doctor gravely, "or her situation might have been much more serious."

Over a depressing hotel lunch of beige roast beef and sour cabbage, Miranda asked, "Why didn't you tell us, Adam?"

"I didn't want to cause you unnecessary anxiety until Dr. Craig-Dunlop and the specialist consultants had reached a definite conclusion." In front of Annabel, Adam was careful to speak to Miranda formally and without endearment. Although many people suspected them to be lovers, Adam still insisted on secrecy.

"But we can't leave Gran in that place," Miranda said. "She must come to London—where we can get the best medical advice, and I can look after her."

"She seems to be getting very good care where she is. The sea air is bracing, and you won't find a London nursing home in acres of garden, like this one," Adam said. "But if you want further opinions, we can go to any London consultant you choose."

"Why can't Gran go back to Saracen when Buzz returns and be nursed there?" Annabel pushed aside her untouched plate. "She loves Saracen."

"That might be a bit too heavy a load for Buzz," Adam suggested. "Remember how she knocked herself out after Elinor had her stroke? Round-the-clock nursing, such as Elinor is getting here, would mean overseeing four nurses, organizing their schedules, plus providing meals, transport and the rest of it."

"We don't want Buzz ill as well," Miranda agreed.

"I've telephoned Dr. Montand at Saracen," Adam continued. "He agrees that the best place for Elinor is an English nursing home where she can get round-the-clock medical care if necessary. In any case, Dr. Craig-Dunlop is adamant that, for the moment, she must be under proper medical supervision for twenty-four hours a day, in case her condition deteriorates rapidly."

Both sisters looked alarmed at the thought of possible further deterioration. Both were glad of Adam's presence. He was always so comforting in times of trouble.

"If you're sure this is the best place . . . " Annabel said hesitantly.

Miranda said, "Firstly, I'd like to be sure that a nursing home is the best place for her, rather than a hospital. Secondly, if she's likely to . . . be like this for some time, that the Lord Whatsit is the best nursing home available."

Annabel nodded in agreement.

From his briefcase, Adam produced a sheaf of colored brochures for nursing homes. Silently he handed them to the two sisters.

Miranda looked at the imposing exteriors and the bleak interiors of the nursing and residential homes. "These reception rooms look like pub lounges. Gran wouldn't put a maid in one of these bedrooms! I'm sure they're comfortable—but they look so deeply unattractive."

Annabel read aloud, " 'Each bedroom has a fitted handbasin.' *Big deal.* No private bathrooms."

"Elinor has her own bathroom at the Lord Willington," Adam pointed out. "But these other places have a certain number of amenities—physiotherapist, chiropodist, hairdresser."

" 'Singsongs and sideshows'!" Annabel read. " '*Bingo*'!"

"I brought only the most attractive brochures," Adam said.

"I hate to think what the others are like," Annabel said. "But *look* at the prices they charge!"

"Gran could practically live at the Ritz for what the Lord Whatsit is costing," Miranda pointed out.

Adam said in a stiff voice, "I went to considerable trouble to choose the best place, so naturally it isn't cheap. But you're welcome to move her if you wish."

The sisters looked at each other and shook their heads.

"It's not the nursing home we hate," Annabel acknowledged. "It's what's happened to Gran that we can't bear."

"We must find Clare and tell her straightaway." Miranda did not look forward to this.

Adam coughed. "I must warn you that any mention of Clare agitates your grandmother. I really feel that her wishes *must* be respected. Elinor *clearly* doesn't wish to see Clare."

Sunday, 18 February 1968

Standing barefoot in her pink-sprigged Laura Ashley nightgown, Clare looked from her bedroom window at the quietly falling snow. The moon dimly lit the woods, faintly etched against the hill behind Applebank Cottage.

She shivered, jumped back into bed, and snuggled lower under the patchwork quilt. In half an hour it would be time to take her loaves out of the oven: the only drawback to her new business was that it meant getting up early every single morning of the year. Because her business had long outgrown the kitchen, David had drawn plans to convert the outhouse into a proper bakery.

Clare had accidentally metamorphosed into a baker ten months before, when David took some of her homebaked bread to friends who lived nearby: they asked if they could buy bread regularly from her. Why not? she thought, and packed a sample treacle cake and some shortbread with her first order.

One month later, Clare had tacked a plastic-covered price list to her back door and another to the garden gate. She now baked rye bread, whole-grain bread, soda bread, and date bread; pasties, rich chocolate cake, rum-flavored fruitcake, brandy snaps, and shortbread. She cooked fruit flans when fruit was in season. Clare baked nothing that could be found at the local baker and charged what she considered exorbitant prices, which people seemed happy to pay in cash.

The main reason Clare did not allow credit was because it complicated her bookkeeping. Having experienced that particular chaos, she was careful to keep her books up-to-date, a simple matter of filling in two columns each day, "Purchases made" and "Total cash takings."

Under the patchwork quilt, David turned over and sleepily pulled Clare toward him. Her nightgown had ridden up around her waist, and she enjoyed feeling his hard, muscular legs entwined around hers. Still half asleep, he kissed her cheek and fumbled beneath her gown, seeking her breasts.

With a loud crash, the door burst open, and Josh, in yellow Donald Duck pajamas, leapt upon the bed. "Ith thnowing! Ith thnowing! David, can I have a thledge? I'm old enough now. *Oh, pleathe.*"

David sat up, turned on the light, yawned, and scratched his hairy chest.

"You can take a tea tray up to the wood and slide down to the back garden. But not now. It's the middle of the night. After breakfast." He turned and smiled at Clare. "*You* are going to have breakfast in bed. . . . No, not a word! Josh and I planned it yesterday evening, didn't we, Josh? After you've taken your loaves out, you're coming back to bed. Isn't she, Josh?"

Josh nodded happily.

"There must be a catch," Clare said. "You're *too* perfect!"

"Yes, there's a catch," David said quietly as he made room for Josh in the bed.

Later, David pulled on Clare's toweling bathrobe and led Josh down to the kitchen.

After twenty minutes, her breakfast tray arrived; upon it was boiling red soup, chocolate ice cream, and a fizzy orange drink.

David winked over Josh's head. "Josh chose the menu."

"Delicious," Clare said feebly as she looked into the smiling face and aquamarine eyes of her son. She looked down at the tray on her lap. "That's too much tomato soup just for me. Perhaps you could help me eat it, Josh?"

Suddenly Clare's baby was wearing jeans and a navy nylon anorak, and howling for tough boots like the village boys'. Now five years old, he went to school in Warminster and was trying hard to adopt a Dorset accent, having been teased about the snob way he talked. Josh liked reading comics, watching TV (especially *Dr. Who*), and peeing in his bath when his mother was looking the other way. He loved soccer and couldn't remember baseball; neither could he remember California, except for a vague recollection of sunshine and a white house and what seemed an enormous swimming pool, although Clare laughed and told him it had really been quite small—for L.A.

When Josh had scraped the plates and gone to "tea-tray" down the hill, David produced another tray with coffee, Clare's own homemade croissants, and strawberry jam.

After that, huddled under the patchwork quilt, they made love in a lazy, unhurried way. This morning Clare felt tender and loving; she wanted to be close to him. But sometimes after they made love, she felt wide awake and energetic, beautiful and happy, strong enough to lift the stove.

"It's a pity more men aren't like you," Clare murmured. "You're so sensual. You enjoy physical intimacy and affectionate contact as much as women do. I wish *all* men enjoyed their whole bodies, rather than just a little, wobbly bit of it."

"I've always thought the most important sex organ is between the ears," David said, kissing hers.

CHAPTER 21

Thursday, 29 February 1968

O*N THE LAST DAY* of February, a suntanned Buzz flew into London airport, wearing Bertha's farewell gift—a snappy white Capri pants suit. She felt energetic, almost girlish as she left the plane.

To her surprise, a ground hostess met her and took her to a VIP lounge, where Adam was waiting.

"Something's happened to Elinor?" Buzz turned white.

Gently Adam told her what had happened.

Buzz was out of the car almost before it rolled to a halt on the gravel forecourt. It was an unusually sunny day for the end of February, and cheerful nurses in scarlet cloaks wheeled or walked their patients slowly around the garden.

One nurse moved a wheelchair toward her, and Buzz suddenly realized with a shock that the cocooned creature within it was Elinor. She looked small, frail, and feeble; her face was dazed and vacant, as if she'd just been woken up and couldn't quite remember where she was.

Buzz said, "Hello, Nell."

Elinor did not look up.

In silence, Buzz listened to the nurse's nonstop starling twitter. "We've had a *good* morning, *haven't* we, Mrs. O'Dare? . . . We watched the birds at the bird-bath and we *fed crumbs* to them, *didn't* we? . . . Lean forward a bit, dear—you've pushed your cushion down again. There, that's better, isn't it? . . . Then we had a chokky bikky and the usual little argument about our nap. Then we listened to a *nice* concert on the radio, didn't we?"

Slowly Elinor looked up and glared.

Buzz felt tremulous hope. She said, "You seem a bit under the weather, Nell. Don't worry, I'll have you out of here in no time."

In Elinor's overwarm bedroom, Buzz peered at the temperature chart and medical instructions clipped to the foot of the metal bed. She frowned when she saw five different tranquilizers and sedatives listed: no wonder Nell looked bewildered and depressed. Buzz recalled Elinor's swift rage and felt another glimmer of hope, but a thought occurred to her: If they insisted on treating Nell like a crazy person, she might actually end up like one.

Peering again at the list of medications, she started to say something to Elinor, then stopped short, remembering that Adam was in the room.

Buzz turned to him. "I've a present for Elinor in my hand luggage. It's in a red box. Would you mind getting it from the car?" She turned back to Elinor and said in the rather loud, slow, and contrived voice that people use for the deaf, "I've brought you a *surprise*, Nell."

As soon as the door closed behind Adam, she whispered, "What have they *done* to you, my girl?"

Lying back on her pillows, Elinor slowly shook her head from side to side but said nothing.

"I'll be back tomorrow," Buzz told her. "I'll just turn up, without warning. Until then—don't swallow them pills. Do you hear me, Nell?" She leaned forward and shook Elinor's shoulders. "*Don't swallow them dratted pills!* Hold 'em under your tongue and play possum. Then spit 'em into a handkerchief and hide it under the pillow."

The door opened and Adam came in. "Just straightening Nell's pillows," Buzz said airily.

As she and Adam left, Buzz turned back to see Elinor silently looking at the ceiling.

Buzz's gift, a nacre box, lay ignored upon the bedside table; but even in the dull afternoon light, the shell surface gleamed.

As their hired limousine purred back to Heathrow Airport, Buzz asked, "Why didn't you let me know she was ill? They had a radiotelephone thing on the *Stella Polaris*."

"Had you been present, Buzz, there was nothing you could have done, so it was thought best not to disrupt your holiday," Adam explained. Buzz noticed he didn't say who had "thought it best." He added sadly, "It's not yet certain that Elinor will ever again be well enough to live without nursing support."

"Just as well I know a lot more about nursing than some of these young Australian madams," Buzz sniffed.

Then Adam quietly explained that she no longer had a job.

Tight-lipped and pale, Buzz listened in silence and near disbelief. *Nobody* had ever sacked *her!* Even after she had been caught in that ruined church with Ginger Higby, that old bitch of a commandant in the women's ambulance service hadn't wanted to lose her.

Eventually she asked, "Does Elinor know about this?"

"Of course not," Adam said. "As you saw, she's in no condition to discuss anything. But the trustees have considered the matter most carefully."

"Them trustees are sitting miles away in their offices in Bermuda!" Buzz snorted. "*I* know Nell better than they do! *And* better than *you* do, you young whippersnapper!"

"Of course you do," Adam said soothingly. "But in fact, it is Elinor's doctors and consultants who feel that she will no longer need you. I thought I had made that plain."

Shocked and incredulous, Buzz could say nothing more, but as the limousine glided on, she remembered a great deal: the teashop outings in Earls Court when Edward was little, comforting Nell, time after time, when Billy had had a few and behaved badly. She remembered the difficulties they'd had repairing Starlings after the war, when you couldn't get a brick or a plank of wood, not even if you was royalty; and she remembered comforting Nell as each granddaughter left home.

Now they were kicking her out! And the worst part was that she couldn't talk to Elinor about it.

Finally, Buzz stifled her feelings enough to ask calmly, "Do the girls know about this?"

"They asked me to tell you," Adam lied. "We all have to face the fact that Elinor's life has suddenly changed and she will probably continue to deteriorate."

"And they didn't mind me going?" Buzz asked painfully.

"Of course they mind—they're very, *very* fond of you," Adam said. As soon as he'd seen Buzz safely on the plane to Nice, he planned to drive back to London, where he would telephone Annabel in New York before seeing Miranda. The sisters would be told that Buzz had agreed it was best for her to leave.

"Of course them girls are fond of me!" Buzz bit back further words. She'd wiped their tears, she'd wiped their botties, and she'd loved them as if they were her own.

Adam shrugged his shoulders and said nothing.

Buzz growled, "Where am I supposed to go?" She refused to accept this mortifying disgrace. Who did this little twerp think he was? Too big for his boots, as she'd always said. Slowly her face reddened as she fought to control her anger and her tears. Eventually her voice grated, "*You* can't kick me out like this. Not after all these years."

"Of *course* we're not kicking you out." Adam spoke soothingly, but Buzz sensed a hint of contempt—or was it triumph?

"Then what exactly *are* you doing?"

"I am not doing anything. I have been asked to see that you are properly looked after in your retirement."

"*Retirement?*"

"You are eight years over the legal age of retirement," Adam reminded Buzz. "The trust has approved a generous pension; it will be paid to you monthly wherever you wish—anywhere in the world." He waved his hand expansively.

"You make it sound as if I've won a sweepstake!" she said bitterly, still fighting to control her feelings. What was that favorite saying of Elinor's? Buzz could almost hear her voice: "Stupidity is the operation of intelligence hampered by emotion."

Buzz sensed that she had to be careful, she had to box clever, she had to let Adam think she had accepted what he said and would go quietly. Seething with indignation and fury, she told herself that this was the best way to catch Adam off guard and discover what was going on.

Thoughtfully Adam said, "It was, perhaps, a pity that you were unable to stay on with your friend Mrs. Higby."

Once again Buzz noticed that Adam didn't speak like other people: he always gave himself an out. Adam couldn't say, "The cat is black." He would say, "To the best of my knowledge, the cat appears to be black."

You've got to have the sense to hold your tongue, my girl, Buzz told herself. Play along with him. Let him think that he's able to plant these ideas in your head. Let him think that he's getting away with it. She said, "I suppose I *could* always go and live with Bertha, if Nell really doesn't need me."

"Living with Mrs. Higby might be an excellent idea," Adam approved, "particularly as—eventually—it might be necessary to sell Saracen."

"*Sell Saracen!* Elinor would never allow it."

"Saracen now belongs to the trust," Adam said firmly. "If Elinor is unable to live in Saracen, the trustees might consider it an unjustifiable expense: apart from the income that might be generated by the capital that's tied up in the place, keeping five full-time domestic staff members and three secretaries would no longer be viable. Have you any idea of the cost of running that place, compared to the cost of a couple of rooms in a nursing home?"

"No idea," Buzz said, "but I'm sure you know what's best for Nell."

Buzz waited in the departure lounge. When the flight to Nice was called, she informed a brisk blue-uniformed redhead that she was feeling ill and thought she'd better cancel her ticket. He took her to the airport nurse, who could find nothing wrong with her but agreed that she might be suffering from jet lag and needed only to rest.

An hour later, Buzz hailed a taxi and returned to Eastbourne, where she booked into a modest residential hotel recommended by the taxi driver.

Buzz did not feel like sitting in the small lounge at the Eastbourne hotel, which contained a great many genteel, inquisitive, elderly ladies, all of whom seemed to be knitting. She would have liked to go for a long walk past the charming wedding-cake buildings that lined the promenade, but although it was only teatime, it was already too dark to see anything. Instead, she wandered into town, where she bought a bag of chips, well soused in vinegar and wrapped in newspaper; she took the bag to her room, where she sat on the edge of the single bed, slowly eating chips in the dark and thinking.

Buzz decided that her first priority was to see Elinor again. She would then telephone Miranda, the most decisive of the three sisters.

She did not blame herself for going on the cruise, although she sensed that Adam, always an opportunist, had taken advantage of her absence. Buzz had read newspaper accounts of old people who had been forcibly removed from their homes and admitted to nursing homes; such people had been robbed by the very guardians who were legally supposed to care for them.

She had also read about old people's homes that ruthlessly exploited their pensioners: unscrupulous proprietors grabbed all they could squeeze from the social services but gave little back to the residents; they cut corners on staff, food, laundry, and amenities and added to their profits by pocketing the difference between their sparse expenditures and the sums they actually received. If such moneygrubbing goings-on could happen in cheap nursing homes that were checked by the authorities, Buzz wondered what might occur in expensive ones, where there was a greater possibility for profit? The Lord Willington looked the sort of place into which dishonest rascals might put their inconvenient relations in order to get them out of the way: uncles with the D. T.'s, incontinent aunts, senile granddads, and cousins who'd been odd since they was born. Buzz remembered Nurse Evans, who'd been with Nell in Ward C at La Chapelle; after the war, Evans had worked in one of those rich bins before she'd married a Lutheran minister and gone to live in Scotland. Evans had relayed some hair-raising stories about the exploitation of her rich patients.

Because for what reason, other than profit, would a nursing home prescribe so many drugs for Nell?

Did Adam know what was going on? Buzz didn't know what was going on, but she certainly smelled dishonesty: it probably involved fraud, and it probably involved Adam.

Having finished her bag of chips, Buzz licked her fingers, switched the light on, and prepared for bed. She had not felt this alone and lonely since she first set out for the French battlefields over fifty years ago.

On the following morning, Elinor lay with her eyes closed, apparently sleeping. For the past twenty-four hours, she had swallowed none of her medication, although she had been unable to refuse an injection. She trusted Buzz. She knew instinctively that Buzz would reappear to get her out of this place and help her to recover.

While she lay waiting, Elinor fought back the fears underscored by the hospital bed and the smell of antiseptic. Her foremost fear was that she might lose her mind, for trying to think made her feel as if her head were filled with cotton wool. She felt muddled . . . couldn't keep track of one thought for long. She wasn't ill when she came in here . . . yes, she was sure of that . . . but she was ill now. How could that have happened . . . unless they were making her ill? . . . How could they do that? . . . Easy . . . with medication. She feared that decisions were being made behind her back, and that she was not being told the truth by that apologetic mouse of a doctor. Was she really more ill than she'd been led to suppose? If so, why hadn't she felt ill? Or was she not ill at all? And if not, then why was she imprisoned here?

It was too difficult. She would wait for Buzz.

But as she lay there, demons slid possible visions of the future into her mind: Suppose she lost the use of her body? She dreaded being immobile and physically dependent, and she certainly felt as if heavy weights were attached to her feet and her legs; she felt as helpless as if she were buried to her neck in quicksand.

Another vision slid before her, of a half-wit locked in a cell. Perhaps she would never again be able to function normally. She saw herself wheeled along white corridors, wired up to huge machines that clicked, whirred, and flashed lights: this was her greatest fear, that she might be kept alive artificially by machinery, a mumbling vegetable, after her natural time to die had arrived.

She felt isolated in this comfortable place, but paradoxically, she also wished that these young women, with their bright faces and inane chatter, would go away and leave her in peace.

The next day, the taxi arrived at the nursing home as the clock above the entrance portico struck ten. Buzz carefully counted out coins for the taxi driver, who said, "That ain't much of a tip, lady."

"It's exactly ten percent," Buzz retorted. "And what have you done to deserve a tip? You didn't help me out of the cab."

"Well, it's snowing."

"Exactly."

Before entering the nursing home, Buzz stood under the imposing portico and carefully stamped the snow from her shoes. She settled the squirrel evening cape that had belonged to her mother on top of her light summer coat, then walked in and asked to see Mrs. O'Dare.

The smiling receptionist disappeared.

Smiling Matron Braddock appeared in her place. The stocky woman looked intently at Buzz with raised eyebrows. "Is Mr. Grant with you?" Her voice was light and charming, but her eyes were hard. "He usually accompanies visitors. We don't want Mrs. O'Dare disturbed by people she would rather not see."

"I came with Mr. Grant yesterday," Buzz reminded the matron. "And I'm going back to the south of France tomorrow. I wanted to see Mrs. O'Dare once more before I go."

As Buzz entered her room, Elinor's eyelids slowly opened. "Hello, Buzz," she whispered, feeling warm relief flood her body. Now she could stop worrying. Buzz would take care of everything.

Buzz settled herself on the upright chair by Elinor's bed, firmly clasping her old-fashioned handbag on her lap. The nurse left the room.

"Can you walk, Nell?" Buzz whispered back. "Do you go to the lav by yourself?"

"Yes," Elinor said weakly. "They're not going to lay me out yet, you know."

Buzz said, "Soon as my back's turned, look what happens! That stuff they're giving you would kill a dozen cats. But once you're out of here, I'll have you well in no time. And I ain't *never* going away again."

"Dear, dear Buzz. But they'll never let me leave. Not without a fuss. I signed something."

"I expect you signed in as a voluntary patient; then they're covered, Evans said. Course they don't want you to leave. They won't get paid if you leave—I bet this costs a pretty penny." Buzz looked around the room. "But I ain't scared of that great ox of a matron, even if she does remind me of my old commandant. And I ain't scared of Adam."

Elinor's eyes filled with tears. "Do you really think that Adam . . . "

"Adam brought you here in the *first* place, my lamb."

"Why did the girls allow it?" Elinor asked sadly. She could vaguely remember Annabel and Miranda's visit, but Clare hadn't come. On the plane to London, Adam had said that Clare still refused to see her; he had hinted that she expected an apology. What sad stupidity. How silly they had both been. Of course she would apologize to Clare.

Buzz said, "The girls trust Adam, but he's getting too big for his boots—ordering everyone around. Adam even says Saracen costs too much to run. He says them trustees are going to sell it and keep you here because it'll be cheaper."

"Sell Saracen! Never! Why should Adam bother to do that? *He* doesn't benefit from the trust. . . . "

"Adam's up to no good," Buzz said firmly. "But we won't worry about that now. What's important is to get you out of here. And this is how we'll do it!"

Elinor listened carefully as Buzz leaned close to her ear and outlined her plan.

"I'll go straight back to Eastbourne. I'll buy two identical coats and hats in some bright color. Tomorrow I'll turn up here again at ten and tell the taxi to wait. I'll ask him to move along a bit, so he ain't blocking the entrance. I want him waiting by this corner. Then I come in with my suitcase, and Matron thinks I'm on my way to the airport. *She's* not to know I was supposed to catch yesterday's plane."

"Thank God you didn't."

"In that suitcase, Nell, will be a coat and hat—same as mine—for you to wear. I get you dressed. I open them glass doors to the garden. You walk out *slowly*, with your head turned away from the house, to my taxi. You get in the taxi. I wait for you to do that; then I simply walk through the main hall, my empty suitcase in my hand. Then we drive hell-for-leather to the airport and catch the next plane to Nice."

"Buzz, darling Buzz, that's a brilliant escape plan." Elinor's face crumpled and she started to cry.

The door of the bedroom flew open to reveal the huge, forbidding presence of the matron. Firmly she said, "We don't want to overtire Mrs. O'Dare."

Buzz stood up. "I was about to go. I'll pop in tomorrow to say goodbye on my way to the airport." She wagged a finger at Elinor. "Now be a good girl and do as you're told."

In the cab on the way back to her Eastbourne hotel, Buzz checked her plan; she was determined to look upon this as a lark, as she and Nell had regarded some of their dangerous escapades in the Great War. Buzz spent the cab ride reminiscing about those times, some grim and some sad, but all of which made her smile.

In the darkening afternoon, the taxi pulled up to her hotel. She paid the driver, and as she turned to enter, she felt a snap. Buzz found herself lying face up in the snow, in great pain, unable to move: as helpless as a black beetle flipped onto its back.

Immediately Buzz knew she'd broken her hip. It irritated her to think that she hadn't been doing anything reckless like running to catch a bus; but she had a private theory that an old person didn't break a hip because she fell, but fell because her hip snapped, after gradual erosion.

The taxi driver jumped from his cab and hurried to her side. "Lucky thing I saw you in the rear mirror just as I was driving off!"

As he ran to the hotel for help, Buzz realized that Elinor's escape would have to be postponed. She must let Elinor know this. She would telephone Miranda.

The following day, Elinor again hid her medication under her tongue, slipped it into her handkerchief, and later flushed it down the lavatory. With carefully suppressed excitement, she waited for Buzz to arrive.

But Buzz did not come.

After a few days, having received no telephone call, letter, or message of any kind from Buzz, Elinor started to lose hope. The medical staff had realized that she wasn't swallowing her medication, and it was now dissolved before being administered. In her occasional lucid moments, Elinor again wondered if she was losing her sanity.

CHAPTER 22

Monday, 4 March 1968

"M*R. GRANT? TELL* him to come straight in." As she replaced the telephone, Miranda, prim in a high-necked gray flannel suit, checked the Cartier traveling clock on her white desk. She had to finish reading the pile of reports in front of her—and make the necessary decisions—before tomorrow's management meeting.

Adam sauntered in, his hands in the pockets of his dark city suit. He looked at Miranda's white, exhausted face and said, "I thought you might like to knock off early and go to *Hair*."

Hair, the psychedelic tribal-love-rock American musical that celebrated hippie values, free love, hash, and hatred of the Vietnam War, had opened the day after stage censorship by the lord chamberlain had been abolished.

"I'd love to, but . . . " Miranda pointed to the piles of papers. "*And* I have to find time tomorrow to visit Buzz." Buzz was still in an Eastbourne hospital.

"Forget everything else, just for one evening. We've got something to celebrate. In our first year as a public company, our pretax profits have increased by twenty percent."

"But KITS showed a loss of thirteen thousand pounds," Miranda reminded Adam.

He shrugged his shoulders. "That's understandable. KITS paid the expenses of SUPPLYKITS during its first year of trading—including those huge consultants' fees and all bank interest. It's not really a loss if you look at the overall company situation."

"It's not only the loss that's worrying me," Miranda said. "KITS now has weak middle management and poor internal communication; that's causing us big problems. And we need better distribution, but can't afford it."

"So long as you know what's wrong, you can fix it."

"Sure—if I had the time." Wearily Miranda put down her pen. "I wish I could turn the clock back two years, when my time was spent running KITS. It depresses me to waste time being photographed and hyped."

"Your real problem is that you've become very successful, very quickly, Miranda. Some people would like your problem."

"Every morning when I wake up, I ask myself, If I'm so damned successful, why do I feel tired and miserable?"

"You just need a couple of days off," Adam soothed. "Why not fly to St.-Moritz for a long, lazy weekend? Get a little snow and sunshine." Hands in pockets, he moved into the horseshoe of her desk.

Miranda swiveled her white leather chair around to face him. She laughed.

"That's unlike you, Adam. What do you want?"

He leaned forward and quickly unbuttoned the top of Miranda's prim suit. "I want you," he said firmly, and slid his hand beneath the gray flannel.

Adam had never touched her in the office, and she was not expecting it. Miranda felt the immediate and powerful reaction of her body to this forbidden sensuality. Trembling, she reached backward for the telephone. "June? No more calls, please." Her voice was slightly overcontrolled.

Adam pulled her from her chair, undid two more buttons, quickly unzipped her skirt: Miranda was left standing in a daffodil-yellow camisole and black high-heeled boots. Adam gently slid the daffodil straps from her shoulders.

Miranda gasped, "We always said . . . never in the office . . . "

"I don't remember." Adam picked her up in his arms and laid her on her desk: reports slithered off it and the Cartier clock crashed to the floor.

"We'll leave the boots on," Adam said.

"Adam, I simply can't risk it. If June came in, this would be round the entire company within seconds. And I can't lock the door. Let's go back to my place and—"

What Adam said then was the last thing that Miranda expected. He looked down at her flaming hair and beige, naked body and whispered, "I love you."

That left Miranda speechless.

Adam started to stroke her body. He murmured, "I love your boobs, and I love your ass. And I love you because you're so exciting. And I love the way you love it."

"Only with you," Miranda whispered.

Adam reached to a shelf behind Miranda's desk and picked up a case of cosmetic samples. He flicked it open, picked a magenta lipstick, and scrawled across her breasts, GREAT BOOBS.

Gently he turned her body over. He picked up a pot of turquoise eyeshadow, dipped his forefinger in it, and scrawled across her buttocks, GREAT ASS.

Then he turned her once more, gently, and pried her thighs apart; in violet eyebrow pencil, he drew an arrow up each white thigh. At the head of each arrow, he scrawled further appreciation.

With a lipstick pencil, he drew bracelets of crimson hearts around her wrists; with green eyeliner, he encircled her ankles with bracelets of kisses. He covered her body with colorful graffiti.

Adam then selected a very expensive makeup brush, intended to apply blusher, and started carefully to brush Miranda's tuft in a circular motion.

Later, on their way to the theater, Miranda snuggled happily against Adam in the back of the chauffeur-driven Mercedes.

"By the way," he said, as if he had almost forgotten to mention it. "Remember you said you wanted a better distribution system for KITS?"

Miranda nodded.

"And you'd like to expand into other countries, where the KITS system is already being copied? . . . "

Miranda nodded again.

"It so happens that SUPPLYKITS also needs more cash. It looks as if we'll be able to buy the Stiebel-Stein mail-order business, so I've been working on ways to raise the money. As a matter of fact, that's what I came into your office to discuss, you gorgeous mantrap."

"Explain," Miranda said sleepily, wondering if she'd be able to stay awake until the end of the show.

"We'll have a rights issue."

Miranda sat up abruptly. She knew that if a company issued extra shares to raise more money, the value of the existing shares was diluted. "I don't like the idea of further diluting my shareholding," she said.

Adam ignored her objection. "To raise sufficient capital, we'll probably need a one-for-three issue."

"That'll mean issuing one extra share for every three existing shares. You're telling me that instead of owning all of three oranges, I'll own three quarters of four oranges."

"Exactly. You'll still be worth exactly the same amount, but the company will have more working capital."

In a worried voice, Miranda asked, "Won't a rights issue make SUPPLYKITS more vulnerable to a takeover?"

"Theoretically, yes, but that's unlikely to happen so long as the company is successful and the shareholders approve of the way it's run." Adam patted her knee. Miranda instinctively pulled away from him.

"You should remember that very few chief executives of public companies own a controlling interest in them," Adam said patiently. "There's no need for you to worry. Your shareholders have complete confidence in you. And let's not forget, you're all-important to the company in other ways: you're the chief shareholder and the public image of the firm."

Miranda sighed. "Adam, I do wish you wouldn't spring these things on me when I'm not expecting them."

"I'm sorry, darling. I thought you'd be as excited as I am by the idea." He should have stuck to his usual tactics. When Adam had a document for Miranda to sign that he thought she might argue about, he always included it in a sheaf of other papers he handed to her at the end of the day, when she was exhausted. He always said that these documents needed immediate decisions. While she examined the papers, he would distract her attention by asking questions about other matters. If she queried anything, he blasted her with expertise. Because she trusted Adam, Miranda allowed herself to be convinced.

On the following afternoon, Miranda went to Eastbourne. As always, she was depressed by the sight of her grandmother: Elinor lay inert, neatly tucked into her bed, white, frail, and exhausted.

And as always, although she clearly recognized Miranda, Elinor seemed almost too tired to speak. "How's Buzz?"

"She's fine, absolutely fine," Miranda said. She hadn't told her grandmother about Buzz's accident; she did not want to further distress Elinor.

"Then why doesn't she visit me?" Elinor asked.

"She's . . . back at Saracen," Miranda lied.

"I wish they'd let me have my telephone," Elinor whispered.

"No, darling, not while you're on medication," Miranda said sadly.

She then drove to Eastbourne General Hospital. Buzz lay on a high, black-barred hospital bed, in a pale green room as small as a shoe box. Pale green pipes writhed around the top and bottom of the walls and in a complicated pattern over the ceiling.

Buzz took off her radio earphones. "You're a good girl, coming to visit your old Buzz. I been looking forward to this all day. A pink azalea! Wicked extravagance, you naughty girl!"

"And I've brought this bed jacket from Annabel."

"Pink marabou! I'll feel like a blooming film star!"

"Can't they give you a prettier room?" Miranda asked as she contrasted Elinor's luxury to this austere little cubicle, the best that Eastbourne General could offer.

"Now don't you make a fuss, Miranda," Buzz admonished. She added carefully, "Have you visited your gran? Why can't I phone her?"

"They still want her to rest. They took away the telephone after Gran tried to telephone Buckingham Palace to complain to the Queen."

"They're pumping so much rubbish into her! Half the time, Nell don't know what she's doing! You should take her away from that place, my girl! Get her to the London Clinic and see what another doctor says."

Miranda looked away. If she mentioned paranoia, Buzz would insist that Elinor was the victim of a lot of quacks. Buzz's views on psychiatry were well known: psychiatrists were "trick-cyclists," not to be taken seriously, people who said that grown men were in love with their mothers: disgusting.

Gently Miranda said, "I'm sure Gran's in the best place, for the time being. We mustn't interfere with her treatment."

"Treatment!" Buzz snorted. She wondered why strong-willed Miranda was going along with what Adam wanted. Because she was, Buzz couldn't confide in her. So she couldn't rescue Elinor until she left Eastbourne General. She couldn't even write to her, lest her letters be opened by that two-faced ugly bitch of a matron.

In the thirties-style luxury of the Savoy Grill, Adam chose expensive wines to accompany the meal—Colchester oysters, foie gras, and porterhouse steak—chosen by his guest, Alistair Stacey-Cripps, a former school friend, now a stockbroker.

When the wine steward left, Adam's guest continued, "At midday, the share price was forty-six shillings, which makes the value of SUPPLYKITS three million pounds."

Adam nodded. "We're offering the new one-for-threes to existing shareholders at a discount of eight percent."

"You're *sure* that Miranda won't want to take up her rights issue?"

"Positive." Recently the trust had refused Miranda's request for a new plane and an extension to her house. Thinking of that, Adam added, "In fact, she'll be delighted to sell them."

"And you're *sure* that this Bermuda company controlled by you will lend me the half-million pounds in cash to buy these shares, at no interest?"

"Absolutely certain. Later, you'll sell them to me—at sixpence profit to yourself."

"After you've notified," Alistair reminded Adam. Although not a legal obligation, the director of a public company was supposed to notify the chairman before he dealt in company shares. "I must get this absolutely clear," he went on. "Miranda currently holds sixty percent of the shares, you hold fifteen percent, and twenty-five percent are held by the public. But if we go ahead as planned, then Miranda will own forty-five percent—a minority holding—and after acquiring her shares, and taking up your rights issue, *you* will own thirty percent."

Adam tasted the wine and nodded. The waiter carefully poured the '45 Château Margaux.

Alistair said, "And then you want me quickly to buy as many publicly held shares as possible."

Adam nodded again. "Funds will be made available as you require them."

"By this same Bermuda company?" Alistair asked.

Adam nodded a third time.

"You realize, Adam, that I'm legally obliged to inform SUPPLYKITS of my acquired shareholding?"

"If anyone asks at some later date, you can claim some oversight in your office administration. If you produce a copy letter from your files, then it will look as if you *did* inform the company. Letters are often lost in the post."

"A wonderful claret," Alistair said. He lifted his glass. "Here's to your controlling interest."

Tuesday, 7 May 1968

In the library of his apartment, Adam sipped a pure Highland malt whiskey as he waited.

Eventually Alistair telephoned. "I've bought a further sixteen percent of SUPPLYKITS. So you now control forty-six percent, which is one percent more than Miranda holds. I couldn't buy more because the price is shooting up—too much buying. Closing price was sixty shillings, which values the company at five point one million pounds."

"Good. How much did the shares cost?"

"One million four hundred and sixty-one thousand one hundred and fifty pounds."

"Then you made a decent profit, Alistair," Adam reminded him.

Alistair couldn't resist asking, "Didn't Miranda smell a rat?"

"Alistair, Miranda is extremely happy: her shares have shot up in value and are now worth well over two million pounds."

In fact, that afternoon, Miranda had been worried by the swift rise in share price; she had asked Adam whether he thought anyone might be buying with a view to a takeover bid.

Adam had laughed and told her not to be dramatic. They could expect takeover bids when the company was more firmly established, but not when it was still learning to walk.

As Adam replaced the telephone, his guest was announced—a small, mild-looking, bald man who looked at least fifteen years older than his actual age of thirty-five.

"Hello, Paul," Adam said. "Have a good trip?"

"Not bad. Weak whiskey, please." Paul Littlejohn settled himself carefully onto the sofa. "How is Mrs. O'Dare?"

"I'm sorry to say she's still alive," Adam said. "But not for much longer. I've made it clear to Craig-Dunlop that the family doesn't want her life prolonged, for religious reasons. He got the message: an enormous bonus when she dies, removal to some other nursing home if she doesn't."

"Her death no longer matters. I'm virtually in control of the trust now. You're legally responsible for nothing, Adam." Littlejohn shrugged his shoulders. "And our actions can't be legally queried under Bermuda law, British law, or any other law."

Adam smiled. "What's the income situation?"

"All book royalties have been received; two percent has been deducted by my firm—the agreed management fee. The remainder was immediately sent on to the appropriate numbered Swiss account."

"And the transfer of the capital—how's that proceeding?" The capital was the bulk of the fortune.

"Ah, that has to be done more slowly, and cautiously." Paul Littlejohn sipped his whiskey. "The shares have all been sold and cash lodged in various banks, according to your instructions. However, I can't just ship it all—in one huge transfer—to Switzerland. If I did that, there would be nasty questions from the Bermuda authorities when the sisters discover that the money's gone."

"Leave the authorities to me."

Littlejohn lifted a hand of caution. "As *I'm* going to be blamed, I must be cautious."

"You're being paid a bloody fortune for being blamed. Is everything else going according to plan?"

Littlejohn nodded. "The funds are currently being invested in our bogus companies; their value will fall dramatically over the next six months."

"Good!"

"But I'm warning you, Adam, I'll have to leave something in the Dove Trust—a bit over fifteen percent—or I can't justify what I've done."

"I don't see why you can't empty the account."

"There's nothing wrong with choosing the wrong investments," said Paul Littlejohn carefully. "Nobody can see into the future, and all stock exchange investment is a gamble. But if we don't leave something in the till, it will be spotted as a cheeky scam, and bribery or not, I won't get away with it."

Adam thought briefly. "If they're going to keep fifteen percent, then I'm going to stop showering money on those bitches—in fact, I've already started to cut back. And I'll sell that bloody great chateau as fast as possible."

"Don't be too greedy," Littlejohn cautioned. "We can't afford an official inquiry during the next year. It's the only thing that worries me. During that time, we just can't risk having our moves queried. You will have to keep the sisters quiet—I don't care how you do it."

"Leave them to me too," Adam said confidently. "I'll keep them quiet. *You* move the money into those Swiss accounts—the faster, the better!"

Paul Littlejohn nodded. Without being told, he knew that as fast as the payments were made into the five Swiss bank accounts, the money was transferred into five different accounts—the numbers of which were known only to Adam.

Thursday, 23 May 1968

Adam sat at his usual lunchtime table in the Savoy Grill—the one discreetly opposite the main entrance, so that without seeming to do so, he saw everyone who entered the restaurant. Eating quail's eggs, he frowned as he reread the letter from Lloyds: it warned him of the amount that he would shortly be expected to produce in settlement.

He looked up as the lean figure of his guest approached. Then he shoved the letter in his jacket pocket and stood. "Good to see you, Scott."

Scott Svenson wore blue jeans and jacket over a navy T-shirt and a wide, striped kipper tie, which looked ridiculous. The tie had been loaned by the headwaiter; unless male guests wore a tie, they were not allowed in the Grill.

Scott sat down. "Hi, Adam!" He noticed that Adam's appearance was unchanged. While all around him, men wore their hair at shoulder length and sported gold chain necklaces, frilled pink shirts, flared-leg hipster trousers, and colored boots with platform soles, Adam had remained carefully traditional. Scott would bet that he had never worn the snakeskin overcoat Annabel had given him the Christmas before.

Spurning the menu, Scott said, "I'll eat whatever you're eating, Adam, plus a glass of milk. I've a heavy afternoon ahead, and I'm off to Paris tomorrow—by parachute if they can't get me in by any other method. I'm covering the riots."

"You lead a more exciting life than I, I'm glad to say."

"It isn't so easy." Scott's network job was taking up more time and concentration than he'd expected.

"Nothing ever is."

"I really wanted to see you on behalf of Annabel," Scott said.

"Has something come up? I saw her briefly only two weeks ago. She was on her way to visit Buzz."

Just before Buzz was due to leave the hospital, the pin in her hip had worked loose, and a total hip replacement had been necessary.

Scott's speckled green and gold eyes looked speculatively at Adam. He said, "Annabel doesn't understand why the trustees originally allowed her large sums of money but are now refusing relatively small sums."

Adam sipped his wine. "Initially the money on deposit was distributed between Annabel and Miranda. Having emptied the honeypot, I understand that the trustees are now allowing the income to build up again before further distributions." As steak-and-kidney pie was placed before them, Adam added, "In addition, the trust has to pay Elinor's very heavy medical expenses." He sniffed the dish of peas. "Good, cooked in fresh mint. As you know, Scott, I don't control the Dove Trust, but if Annabel needs extra funds, then I would be happy to suggest further payments."

"Annabel would prefer a modest regular income to occasional lump sums," Scott said. "And if you don't control the trust, Adam, then it's time we knew who does. We want to know everything about the Dove Trust and its officers. We want to understand the structure, the aims, the obligations. We want to know precisely what funds the trust handles, where those funds are, and what regular income might be expected from the capital sum."

Adam helped himself to peas. "I thought Annabel already had that information—although, of course, there's no legal reason why she should. The trust is run like any other business, with annual accounts prepared by qualified accountants—although, again, that isn't legally necessary. I understand the final accounts for 1967 were signed last week. I'll see that a copy is sent to Annabel."

"Are accounts produced only once a year?"

"That's the usual procedure." Adam decided to stall for time. He didn't want this newsman poking his nose into the trust. "If you like, Scott, I could suggest quarterly accounts, although that's an expensive business."

"That's what I intended to ask you."

"Then I shall arrange it," said Adam, who had no intention of producing quarterly accounts for this inquisitive journalist. He decided to arrange that a large monthly income be paid to Annabel until next May: that should shut her up. Similar sums would also have to be paid to Miranda, blast it, for very quickly she would learn of Annabel's new income. Still, lose a lure to catch a mackerel—or, in this case, a whale. But Scott could stir up a lot of trouble before next May. Something would have to be done about Scott.

That evening, having explained that the best place to enjoy a peach was in the bath, Adam fed one slowly to Miranda.

The mirrored walls and ceiling of her large bathroom reflected the room to infinity. In spite of a complicated lighting system, only one candle flickered in an antique silver candlestick.

In the warm water of the square, sunken marble tub, Adam lay beside Miranda; he soaped her body as though she were a royal baby. Dreamy and passive, she lay in the scented water and gave in to Adam's sensual massage. They listened to the Beatles on Miranda's new stereo; the magical mystery of "Strawberry Fields Forever" reminded her of her grandmother, so lonely, isolated, and unreachable in the prison of her own head. Sharply Miranda diverted her thoughts: she did not want to plunge again into pointless depression.

"Where did Scott take you to dinner?" Adam asked.

"That new Italian place in the King's Road," Miranda murmured. "Why is it that pansies seem to run the best restaurants?"

"The queers are all coming out of the closet after last year's legislation," Adam said. Homosexual acts between adult men were now legal in Britain. "What was the restaurant like?"

"The usual Italian thing. Vaulted ceilings, everything white, one perfect flower spotlit in the center of each table, impeccable fettuccine primavera."

"Did Scott have anything interesting to say?"

"He was a bit too earnest to be amusing." Miranda gently splashed scented water at Adam. "As a matter of fact, Scott spent most of the first course warning me against you. He wants me to visit STG and find out more about the trust."

"The trust no longer has anything to do with STG," Adam said, hiding his annoyance as he soaped Miranda's soft right underarm. "And you saw the trust accounts for last year, remember?"

Adam turned his attention to Miranda's other tender places and casually added, "Perhaps you'd better give Annabel a call, to reassure her that you're keeping a watchful eye on the accounts. Explain again that trustees are very careful with somebody else's money. . . . That reminds me, did I tell you that the trustees have turned down a request from Annabel?"

"No," Miranda said. "What for?"

"She wanted a large sum of money to fund some project at the Bronx Zoo. Unfortunately, this request didn't come within the trust beneficiary limits. I expect that's what's behind Scott's concern."

"The trust was absolutely correct to say no," Miranda agreed. Then she added, carefully casual: "What I'd really like to talk to Annabel about is *us*. I'm sure everyone in the office guesses."

"Our relationship isn't *your* secret, it's *our* secret, and I want it *kept* secret," Adam murmured, his voice smooth but determined.

"I've never understood *why* you want to keep it a secret—I wish I did,"

Miranda said, returning to their perennial source of disagreement. A year ago—and again at Christmas—she had proposed, playfully. On both occasions, he had laughed the idea off as a charming joke.

Miranda was puzzled and humiliated by Adam's rejection. He had now been her lover for nearly three years: the physical side of their relationship seemed to be perfect. Miranda, while not vain, did not suffer from false modesty. She knew that she was beautiful, although her looks were not as sensational as Annabel's. She was a perfect size ten: at five nine, perhaps a little too tall, but Adam was well over six feet. Rich and famous, Miranda knew she was also an interesting companion.

Besides, Adam said that he loved her.

At the back of her mind, Miranda heard the ghostly voice of Buzz say, "Any Latin lover can say 'I love you,' " but she pushed the thought away, just as she had pushed away other silly possibilities. Perhaps Adam sought a bride with better status. If so, Miranda thought sarcastically, Princess Anne would soon be old enough for him.

The only other reason Miranda could think of for her failure to get Adam to the altar was her success; she knew that while many women were attracted to a man by his status, many men saw a successful businesswoman as a direct competitor. An insecure man, she knew, might not want to be married to someone more powerful than himself.

But Adam was extremely successful in his own right. *So why wouldn't he marry her?*

Knowing that Adam always liked to keep his options open, Miranda was forced to the lonely conclusion that he didn't love her enough to commit himself to her for life. As is always the case when a person wants something and can't have it, her frustration merely increased her desire.

As he soaped Miranda's back, Adam knew perfectly well that she was about to propose to him again. But if he tied himself to Miranda, he would have less influence over Annabel, who would then have legitimate reasons to doubt his objectivity. However, Miranda, who couldn't stand indecision, wasn't the sort of woman to be fobbed off for much longer. Until he controlled all the money, Adam couldn't risk either sister querying his moves: he needed to placate and control both of them.

So Adam intended, when Miranda asked him, to reassure her by promising to marry her *one day*. In fact, if she got too insistent, he might agree to an engagement on . . . say, February seventh, Miranda's twenty-eighth birthday. With any luck, the trust funds should be in his hands shortly after that date, at which point he would say goodbye to Britain forever.

Adam's wet arm lazily reached for another peach. He said, "I can tell you're thinking about something."

"You know what I'm thinking about," Miranda replied sadly.

"Well, stop it, or I'll tie you to the bedposts with silk ribbons and do wicked things to you, so you won't be able to think of anything else."

He slid his hands beneath Miranda's soapy body. As he caressed the two pale curves of flesh that rose above the water, he decided what to do about Scott.

Tuesday, 22 August 1968

Adam drove his DB4 Aston Martin rather too fast through the peaceful country lanes of Sussex. He was taking Annabel to see the latest production of *Figaro* at the Glyndebourne Festival, both of them wearing full evening dress. Some people might consider it surreal, even ludicrous, to set off for a country outing in mid-afternoon in full evening dress, but this eccentricity is part of the Glyndebourne Opera tradition, which began in 1934 when John Christie gave his opera singer wife a wedding present—her own little opera house, set in the sylvan parks of a stately house in Sussex. Now few musical occasions are more beautiful, more typically British, more exquisitely performed, and more elitist than an evening at Glyndebourne.

As usual, the seats were all occupied: part of what made the little theater so special was the fact that tickets were almost impossible to obtain. The London Philharmonic started the overture, and the audience settled back to enjoy itself as the opening bars predicted the lighthearted frivolity and charm of Mozart's enchanted eighteenth-century world.

Adam, who was not musical, found it difficult to accept the elaborate plot, with its disguises and unlikely mistaken identities, its concealments in closets and too-coincidental overheard assignations, as Figaro, the valet, fought his master, the Count, for the favors of the chambermaid Susanna. But Adam had not come here for pleasure, he reminded himself as the lights went up for the intermission.

During this especially long interval, the audience either ate a three-course dinner in the manor house or took champagne picnics onto the lawns, enhanced by the Sussex Downs in the background.

"Before the war, people used to bring their own butlers to serve their picnics in those woods." Adam pointed to the spot. "Let's have our dinner there," he suggested as he helped Annabel maneuver across a grassy ditch in her silver-beaded gray chiffon Jean Muir dress. Black-faced sheep viewed their efforts with mild surprise.

Adam carried the wickerwork picnic hamper over the grass to the trees; they walked beside a chain of woodland pools which followed the course of a stream and led to a small clearing carpeted by wildflowers.

"This might have been painted by Botticelli!" Annabel kicked off her shoes and sat down on Adam's rug. Green leaves rustled slightly on the soft breeze, and she heard the faint hum of a bee.

Adam took off his jacket, spread a white linen cloth on the grass by a still, clear pool, then poured champagne into Annabel's glass, and looked in the hamper. "We have quail's eggs, chicken in curry-flavored mayonnaise, cucumber salad, and strawberries Romanoff."

In the twilight, they ate and talked, Annabel looking like a wood sprite in her will-o'-the-wisp gray chiffon. Through the trees, in the distance, they could see the manor against the sky, decked out in lights. Annabel said, "What a delightful way to end my British visit."

"I'm sorry it's been such a sad trip for you." Adam helped himself to some quail's eggs.

Annabel had arrived in England two weeks earlier, intending to take Buzz back to Saracen to complete her recovery. But when Annabel collected her, Buzz had asked to stay the night at a posh hotel in Eastbourne. Puzzled, Annabel agreed.

Shortly afterward, when Buzz was supposedly resting, she had appeared, wearing a bright mustard coat, at the Lord Willington Nursing Home, where she asked to see Elinor. As she insisted upon carrying a suitcase into Elinor's bedroom, rather than leave it at the reception desk, the receptionist feared that Buzz was perhaps smuggling alcohol to an alcoholic patient; she immediately informed the matron.

Matron Braddock hurried to the bedroom, to find a vacant-looking Elinor being helped by Buzz into an identical mustard coat.

When the furious matron asked Buzz to leave, she refused. The matron called two male nurses, who firmly escorted Buzz to her waiting taxi. Matron Braddock later telephoned Adam, and he readily agreed that Buzz should be banned.

The following day, Buzz tried to enter the nursing home by the side gate but was spotted by a gardener. The matron had threatened to call the police if she tried again.

"What was sad," Annabel said, "was seeing poor Buzz refuse to believe that Gran was . . . how she is. Poor darling, she really isn't with us anymore, but Buzz won't accept that, as we all must. She seems to think we're part of some conspiracy to imprison Elinor. She's refused to stay with Miranda, and she's very cross with me."

"It must be hard for Buzz to accept the fact that she's also . . . deteriorating," Adam said sympathetically.

"She's taken a room in a boardinghouse in Earls Court, full of noisy Australian students. She says that once Gran used to live in the next square."

"I don't want you or Miranda to worry about Buzz," Adam said firmly as he refilled Annabel's glass. "You've helped Buzz as much as she wants to be helped." He smiled at Annabel's worried face. "I'll make a few quiet investigations. The trust will pay her rent, as well as her pension, and also any special medical care she might need. I expect she'll soon calm down and see reason."

He poured more champagne for himself. "Oh, by the way—there's something I want to discuss before you leave. Scott says that you want the trustees to provide quarterly accounts, and they're a bit mystified as to why because, as you know, Miranda keeps a close eye on the accounts. The trustees wondered if there was any particular item that *you* wanted to query in the 1967 accounts."

Somewhat confused and not wishing to seem impolite, Annabel said, "Oh no . . . nothing particular." She laughed apologetically. "I know Miranda has the business brains of the family. It just seemed odd that when I asked for a relatively small sum . . . " Her voice trailed away as she carefully examined her forkful of chicken.

"My dear Annabel, the job of the trustees is to *protect the capital*," Adam said gravely. "They can't whittle away the capital without risking serious legal charges. They are legally obliged to act for the benefit of the beneficiaries, whether or not you all agree to their actions: that is the whole point of a trust." He refilled her glass again and said reassuringly, "When enough income has accumulated, then, in addition to your present allowance, you'll probably get the same large lump sum that you had last year—especially if Saracen is sold."

"Miranda told me the trust might sell Saracen. We both hate to think of it!"

"Now that de Gaulle's had his landslide victory—with the Communist seats halved—it seems a prudent time to sell. Sadly, Elinor may never leave the nursing home. Should she do so, she could no longer manage to run the chateau, and neither, I suspect, can poor old Buzz."

Annabel put down her glass and looked about to cry.

Adam leaned over and patted her hand. "You must let the trustees make these worrying decisions. That's why your grandmother set up the trust in the first place. She wanted you to have no worries."

"She's always been so caring."

"Of course." Adam patted her hand again. "If you'd like to go over all the legal paperwork with me again—in detail—I'd be happy to do it. Can you spare, say, three hours at my office tomorrow?"

Suspecting that she might be even more confused after three hours of perusing legal documents, Annabel hastily said, "It isn't really necessary. Scott's a little overprotective. I'm sure Miranda's capable of checking these things."

"Miranda's special gift is for business." Adam nodded. "Your gifts are quite different, Annabel, and . . . very rare."

"I'd like to think I've got *something* going for me. I'd like to think I was good for something other than smiling at the camera."

"Of course you are, Annabel. I've just told you so."

"Now," Annabel said sadly, "when people say nice things about me, I can't believe them. When you're a model, the praise and flattery is endless and addictive. But as soon as your bookings start to slide, the flatterers just . . . melt away. That's when you know you're a has-been."

"What a sad little speech," Adam said gently. Annabel's beautiful face was not only her strength but also her weakness. She was afraid of getting ugly, fat, old. Her dreaded thirtieth birthday came nearer every day. "*I* think your looks have *improved* since you stopped modeling," he continued. "Since your face filled out, it's lost that worried, anxious look. You now have a delicious, serene quality."

"Do I *really?*"

"Yes, really," Adam said, looking into Annabel's astonishingly beautiful eyes. "You're really an old-fashioned girl, Annabel, with charming, traditional feminine qualities. You're so much softer and more gentle than . . . your sisters."

"Oh! Do you *really* think so?"

"Miranda's obviously the new sort of woman who's trying to take a man's place in a man's world, but when things get tough, she still dodges final responsibility and turns to a man—me," Adam explained. "Clare's another type of new woman: she also tries to take on a man's responsibility, but she won't do things in the traditional way. So she makes a mess of it, can't manage on her own and can't understand why—and when she's bewildered she becomes aggressive."

"She certainly does," Annabel said with feeling. "She was unspeakably rude when I telephoned."

"Your generation of women wasn't brought up to handle ultimate responsibility." To Annabel, at that moment Adam looked ready to shoulder the world. "Traditionally, men have always done that, and *they* know how tough it is." He smiled gently. "But *you*, Annabel, don't need or want to prove anything. *You're* happy to be looked after and to enjoy life! You're the only O'Dare sister who's a realist."

Even as he spoke, Adam couldn't believe that Annabel was swallowing this rubbish. But she was still an underdeveloped child, easily led, dependent, and naive. No wonder she had no children. Annabel was still a child herself. She wanted to be taken care of. She didn't want to grow up and grapple with responsibilities and problems.

Smiling, Adam offered the silver pudding dish, but Annabel shook her head. "I have to be careful."

"What rubbish!" Adam laughed, looking Annabel's figure over appreciatively. "I agree that you no longer look like a starved greyhound, but you *must* know that you are a sensuous and beautiful woman."

Annabel's basic amiability and good nature made her instinctively a flatterer: she always wanted to make people feel happy. Because of this, she did not recognize flattery when it was used as a weapon against her, to breach her defenses and melt her resistance.

Adam saw that, as with most women, praise would turn Annabel's head; careful flattery would counteract her insecurity, for which she would unknowingly feel grateful—and the rest would be easy.

He leaned toward her and stroked her pale, chiffon shoulder. "You look like a charming wood nymph in that gauze thing."

Through the flimsy material, Annabel felt the heat of Adam's palm against her skin. He was close enough for her to feel his warm breath and smell his erotic odor. She shifted slightly away from him.

Adam said, "Your beautiful mouth has a crumb on it." He leaned closer. Before Annabel realized his intention, he licked the side of her mouth with a fast, serpentine flick of his tongue.

His movement took her completely by surprise—and so did her own bodily reaction when he pressed his mouth on hers. Annabel felt his hands against her breasts. She felt a melting warmth spread quickly through her body.

After what they both recognized as token resistance, she slowly fell back upon the grass, feeling that happy warmth down to the tingling tips of her fingers.

Annabel was bewitched by Adam, overwhelmed by the feel of his body crushing hers. Unable to move, she felt the satin-slippery texture of his lips and his slow, hungry kisses.

As Adam tore the gray chiffon from her breasts, Annabel felt her reason drift away, replaced by a passionate longing for the continued hard strength of his body. She wanted him not only to cover her but to envelop her; she wanted to efface herself and melt into him, lose herself in the ecstasy of fusion. Adam lowered his now naked body upon hers and Annabel at last felt his flesh upon her flesh, hard and warm. She smelled the sharp scent of crushed wild thyme beneath her head as he started to move slowly, steadily, and rhythmically.

Afterward, they bathed, silent and naked, in the pool, and then—still naked—they walked, barefoot and hand in hand, through the woods. Often they stopped to kiss and touch, regardless of who might see them, and neither said a word.

Daylight had faded into dusk when they returned to their picnic site. The overturned dish of chicken and the untouched strawberries were now abuzz with wasps.

Annabel never saw the end of *Figaro*.

CHAPTER 23

Saturday, 7 September 1968

CLARE STOOD AT the front door, feeling the sun warm her brown arms. The cream climbing rose—appropriately named the New Dawn—which she had planted by the door was in full bloom. A sweetbrier hedge enclosed the garden, and before it grew fragrant, white tobacco flowers, delicate sprays of gypsophila, and very pale pink hydrangeas.

She looked down the herringbone-patterned brick garden path that her visitors were about to tread; the path was edged by herbs: behind the mint were rosemary, thyme, and tarragon (sadly, not doing very well). Then came rows of vegetables, as satisfyingly neat as a sampler, in lines of different-colored greens: cabbages and cauliflowers, lettuces, onions, and carrot tops.

Summer had spilled over into early September. It was so golden a day that Clare had almost decided to hold David's birthday luncheon in the garden, but the buffet meal looked very pretty in the kitchen—a bit like a harvest festival; she had decorated the pink-walled room with branches of elderberry and hawthorn, red berries, and sprays of blackberried brambles. Flat loaves shaped like stooks of wheat had been painted with egg yolk before Clare baked them, so that now they shone; her showpieces were the open tarts: apricot and chestnut, plum and raspberry, peach and pear, and shiny black cherry.

Clare decided to serve drinks before lunch—her homemade lemonade and elderflower wine—under the apple trees. Behind her, she heard David clumping down the uncarpeted wooden staircase and turned to face him. He looked so handsome in the cream silk shirt that was Clare's birthday gift.

In a low voice, he said, "I'm sorry. I'm leaving. Now."

"*You can't leave!* The guests are due, and they're nearly all *your* friends!"

"They know me. They'll understand. I'm sorry. I'm off."

When David was in one of his moods, he would withdraw and treat Clare almost as if she were a stranger. He was always very polite but distant.

These moods differed from David's habitual absentmindedness, which made him unreliable and unpredictable: sometimes he was so absorbed by what he was doing that he lost track of time and forgot to eat or to go to bed—only looking up from his work or his book as dawn filtered through the windows, when he would suddenly realize that he was ravenously hungry and had forgotten to phone Clare.

But when David was in a depression, he would be unable to sit still, impatient, and moody. He would stride restlessly around the kitchen or open the front door. Clare would run to a window and see his long legs hurrying down the brick path to the garden gate, which he sometimes vaulted—in his haste to get away from her, she thought bitterly.

If she tried to stop him from leaving, he became irritable. And if he agreed to stay, he would sit, immobile, in front of the fire for hours, in blank resignation. At some point, he would get up abruptly and leave without a word. When he was like this, it was impossible to persuade David to do something, for no effort seemed worthwhile to him: he was incapable of reading, of listening to the music he loved, even of eating. He wanted only to be left alone.

At such times, Clare's self-esteem would start to crumble. Her still-fragile new-found self-confidence had been built up by her growing pleasure in her successful bakery but also by David's loving encouragement.

Clare had never probed for further explanation of his moods, but now, as she stood waiting for David's birthday guests, she cried, "This time you *must* tell me! *What do I do wrong?*"

"I've told you before, it's nothing to do with you, Clare. Please let me go. I can't explain at the moment."

Behind them, Josh, in a new pair of jeans, clattered downstairs. He looked from Clare to David and said sharply, "Whatzoop?"

"Nothing, Josh," Clare said. "We're just talking." Josh ran off to climb his favorite apple tree. David fled down the garden path.

Clare's friends were surprised and sorry to hear that David had suddenly developed a migraine.

David's friends—some of whom Clare had never met before—made no comment, but exchanged swift understanding glances and enthusiastically praised Clare's homemade wine.

The following evening, after Clare had put Josh to bed, she heard the front door bang and knew that it was David.

She stayed in the kitchen, her elbows on the pine table and her chin in her hands. "David, I'd give anything to understand your black moods and be able to help."

"I'm sorry. I can't see anyone when I feel like that. I can't work, I can't talk to people. I don't even turn up for business appointments."

"*Why?* What's wrong with you?" Clare asked. Again she felt the bewilderment she had experienced when she first saw her lighthearted, friendly lover—so intuitive and gentle, so naturally in touch with his feelings—change to a morose lump, a heavy, difficult weight that Clare sometimes felt she bore upon her shoulders. Sometimes David's fits of depression lasted several days, and on the rare occasions when he stayed with her, Clare felt mentally drained and physically exhausted once he'd left.

"I've told you before. I get depressions. I feel hemmed in."

"But surely that's when you need a loving friend to cheer you up? To pour you a drink, put on a record, and cook your favorite meal?"

"That sort of loving concern only makes me feel worse. If I see that you're making an effort to cheer me up, it sends me sliding down into the black pit even faster because then I also feel guilty."

Clare said, "Have you thought of seeing a doctor about it?"

"Our family doctor said that I simply needed to snap out of my self-absorption and self-pity. But when I'm depressed"—David shrugged his shoulders in a helpless gesture—"all people, all interests, and all activities tend to shrink and dwindle until they . . . disappear. I can't think or talk or concentrate—or move, sometimes—and I feel as if I'm in a black vacuum. It takes an enormous effort to say 'Yes' or 'No' to anyone. I feel useless, unwanted, and frightened. I expect it sounds melodramatic, but I feel trapped and without hope. When that happens, it feels as if I've been in that state nearly all my life, and that *this* time I won't come out of it."

"But surely *something* must help you when you feel like that?"

"The only thing that helps is time. I just want to be alone, with no one making any demands on me, however slight, while I pray that it will pass. You must understand that *you can't help me*. Nobody can. I only bring other people down with me. I've learned that it's best if I just disappear and sit it out."

"Do the people in your office know?" Clare asked as she struggled to understand what seemed to her a change in character as abrupt, unlikely, and terrifying as that of Mr. Hyde into Dr. Jekyll.

"It's always posed a problem at work. Last time I was fired, I asked my uncle for help." David's uncle had realized that persistence, tenacity, and the medical profession seemed useless in helping David, and so he had helped him to establish a small private country practice, where the pressure was not so great as in London and David could work at his own pace. "My colleagues are understanding and tactfully ignore my symptoms," he went on. "It's the best thing to do."

"Then I will, if that's really what you want," Clare said.

After that talk, she realized that she mustn't try to get too close to David. She sensed that if she wanted him to stay with her, she had to let him feel free to leave. She must learn to trust his love for her and not to question his absences or his sudden departures.

In return, because he was neither possessive nor jealous, David was careful to give Clare the same freedom and privacy she gave him, not realizing that it was the last thing she wanted.

Saturday, 21 September 1968

In David's bedroom, Clare knelt on the window seat, from which she could look down upon a spectacular bird's-eye view of Bath. Below her, the city of golden stone spread like a beautiful, fragile toy replica of classical Greek temples, set in squares and crescents of greenery.

David's house—which he was buying on a mortgage—perched on the rim of the green basin in which Bath nestled. It was bare yet calm and wonderfully comfortable: it was a house in which you could curl up for the winter and almost regret the coming of summer. It was a home.

Beneath David's bedroom, the sitting room contained great quantities of books, piled on the floor as well as stacked on the shelves; these piles overflowed through the door and onto the staircase.

Underneath the sitting room was a large topaz-painted kitchen with a splendid view at either end. Since the terraced house was built on the side of a hill, one entered from the street directly into the kitchen. The walls were covered with pictures: architectural prints hung next to children's paintings; antique views of Bath were beside snapshots of friends; postcards were taped to the walls, as were posters by Matisse and Hockney.

David's offices were on the two lower floors. Beyond the tree-shaded narrow garden, black-and-white Friesian cows grazed in a field. When he was depressed, David often sat at the end of the garden; hunched up, he would stare for hours at the cows.

Hearing David clatter up the stairs, Clare crossed her fingers and hoped he would stay in a good mood for this afternoon's concert at the Assembly Rooms.

David burst into the bedroom. "Time we left!" he said. "You'd better wear a sweater. These late-September days can suddenly turn cold." He opened a drawer, pulled out a green sweater, and threw it to her.

"I think that Bath is the loveliest city in the world," Clare said dreamily as she shut the window.

"Small thanks to the city fathers. When John Wood drew up his scheme for rebuilding the city, the Bath Corporation didn't like it, so poor Mr. Wood was forced to build it bit by bit, starting with Queen Square." David was one of the architects involved in the rebuilding and cleaning of the city, which was slow work: a lot of the old stone was still stained black with the soot from Victorian chimneys and the early railway; there were still bomb sites from the German air raids in 1942. David asserted that even more damage had been done after the war, by the shortsighted city planners who demolished the Georgian and Victorian workmen's cottages and replaced them with ugly apartment blocks.

They walked downhill past a classic semicircle of small, elegant houses with pillared entrances. Clare paused on a stone sidewalk to peer into a bow front shop. Inside were charming children's clothes.

David gently pulled at her hand. "Come on! You know Josh would hate those rich-kid clothes."

"I wish we'd brought him with us."

"Stop feeling guilty about leaving him for once. He's much better off at the cottage making gingerbread men with Betsy." Betsy, Clare's assistant baker, was staying overnight.

"I can't help feeling guilty about depriving Josh of a lot of things, especially as Christmas approaches."

"I'm going to take you both skiing," David reminded her.

"True. You're wonderful with Josh. But I now realize that no one—however wonderful—can replace a child's own father."

"Divorce is one of the facts of life for modern children."

Clare laughed angrily. "I wish I *could* get a divorce."

Sam would not admit his adultery and refused to divorce Clare for desertion, which he was now able to do because three years had passed since Clare left him. Unless Sam changed his mind, under British law Clare would remain married to him forever: because she had deserted him, she was the guilty party.

David said, "I don't understand why you *can't*."

"No grounds. If you rule out adultery, there's only cruelty—difficult to prove in British courts—or unsound mind. Sam hasn't been continuously in a loony bin for five years, and he hasn't committed rape, sodomy, or bestiality, so—no divorce!"

"Who cares whether you're married or not?" David shrugged his shoulders. "You'd do better to ignore this legal game. Josh is happy enough. You're making enough money from the bakery. You're developing your own ideas and independence."

"Encouraged by you." Clare threw him a grateful smile. David had always helped her—sometimes by kicking her—to think for herself as she built up her bakery business. He had comforted her when she became enmeshed in bureaucratic regulations. He always said that success was built on failure, as any tycoon could tell her. "I wish I didn't need your support so much," Clare said. "I wish I could stand on my own feet."

"You're learning fast. And I need *your* support, perhaps more than you realize." Although he laughed, David was serious. He needed Clare's tenacity and stability to balance his up-in-the-air exultation and down-in-the-dumps gloom. "My passive side likes your passionate, determined, stubborn side," he added. "I like a clear, sharp-witted woman."

"But when I was married to Sam," Clare said, "I ended up a meek doormat. That was why he was so surprised when I got up and walked away."

"*That* showed your guts," David said.

Sunday, 22 September 1968

Standing next to Annabel at the Nice airport carousel, a drab young woman was identifying luggage to the porter. While she waited for her suitcases, Annabel glanced at the neighboring pile. Twelve navy leather suitcases with maroon bindings had the initials S. K. stamped on them in gold. There were also three Louis Vuittons, one black leather hatbox, a green tapestry carpetbag, eighteen cheap suitcases in different colors, one green plastic garbage bin, one enormous cardboard box held together by string, one child's folding stroller, and two brown trunks—*trunks* on a commercial flight! Each item bore the name Khashoggi daubed in pink nail varnish.

Annabel was grateful for this momentary distraction from her passionate longing for Adam. She felt a wrenching of her gut, a tightening, lurching feeling at the thought of seeing him, or—she dared not think about it—of not seeing him.

For the first time, it occurred to her that Adam might not meet her flight, which was very late. She caught her breath and crossed her fingers. Of *course* Adam would meet her! Although, naturally, they were both cautious: if somebody spotted them together, their secret would slip into the gossip columns.

Annabel no longer cared about Scott's feelings, but Adam had made it clear that, were it publicly known he had seduced the wife of a client, his professional reputation would suffer. Adam had also made it clear that if *that* happened, he would immediately leave Annabel; for the only thing worse than seducing a client's wife was marrying her.

A bitterly disappointed Annabel had protested that Scott *wasn't* Adam's client, but Adam said that this was how it would be perceived. Should Scott sue him for alienation of affections, Adam might as well say goodbye to his business, which was based on a client's trust of his lawyer.

Annabel again felt relieved that she hadn't blurted out her secret to Scott the previous evening, when he appeared with a martini jug in her dressing room.

She had been astonished when Scott poured himself a second martini and then, surprisingly, grumbled about Annabel's departure.

"I've had a tough time at work this week," he said reluctantly, "and I'd like to talk to you about it on the weekend. I need a little reassurance and sympathy."

"Are you complaining?" Annabel asked. "You've no time for *me* these days. Your brilliant career is all that matters."

"Not to you," Scott said. "I feel you don't give a damn about me now. Of course you must visit Elinor, but on the rare occasions when you're actually in this apartment, you always seem too busy with your friends to have any time for me."

Annabel, flustered, snapped, "*I'm* not responsible for Gran's illness!"

"But your trip tomorrow *isn't* to visit Elinor," Scott pointed out. "Why can't Miranda spare the time to superintend this furniture sale at the chateau? Why should *you* be dragged from another continent to do it? I've half a mind to telephone her . . ."

Annabel hurriedly explained that Miranda was holding a seminar—arranged long before Elinor's illness.

When Scott was not mollified, Annabel looked at him from under her eyelashes, pouted charmingly, and said, "Angel will be back in no time."

Scott glared at her. "Cut out that childish, cute behavior—it doesn't work with me anymore. And while we're on the subject, you can also quit crying. Your tears don't make me feel strong and protective; they make me exasperated, annoyed, and resentful." He finished his drink in one gulp. "I'm tired of having a child bride. You no longer seem interested in having a thoughtful conversation, producing a decent meal, or accepting any responsibility. If I say anything that sounds critical, you start crying, as if I'm the world's biggest brute. You are twenty-eight years old, Annabel, and *I* now feel the need to be taken care of, looked after, and loved—for a change."

"Don't blame *me* for your career problems," Annabel had sobbed.

Her reverie was interrupted by the arrival of her suitcases.

Although he knew that Annabel expected to be met, Adam did not go to Nice airport. Instead, after switching on the water and heating in the now deserted chateau, he went for a newly fashionable jog in the countryside around Saracen.

Intent on counting his paces and checking his rhythm and breathing, Adam did not notice how the light altered in September so that the far mountains were the same soft mauve as the lavender fields. As he panted along, he did not see the wild figs hanging above hedgerows thick with ripe blackberries. As he checked his pulse rate, Adam failed to smell the delicate scent of conifers and coconut-scented gorse and the acrid, sour, mysterious odor of the ditch. He might as well have been running around a cinder track or pounding lengths in a gym.

Feeling pleasantly exhilarated by his exercise, Adam showered in Elinor's bathroom—something that he'd always wanted to do. He liked to feel really, really, really rich.

He whistled as he toweled himself, then sprinkled half a bottle of invigorating cologne over his body. Through the open window, he saw the sky darken to gray, then slate purple. He had timed his jog nicely.

After an ominous moment of near silence, when only the soft rustling of the ivy on the terrace could be heard, lightning split the sky with sharp brilliance, followed by a mighty clash of thunder.

As rain slashed the chateau, Adam closed the window. He felt snug and safe as he tightened his dressing gown cord. He decided to get some champagne.

Without flowers, noise, or movement, the empty building seemed lifeless. As Adam walked through the entrance hall, his feet echoed on marble from which the antique rugs had been removed for auction. At the end of this week, the furniture would also be taken to Sotheby's. The appraiser was upstairs now, estimating the auction reserve prices.

The drinks cupboard in the beige marble bar was empty, as was the refrigerator, which had been turned off. Adam walked to the kitchen, which still smelled faintly of stale bread; he opened the door to the slate-shelved larder, normally a treasure-house, with gargantuan sausages and smoked hams hung from hooks in the ceiling too high for the cat to reach. There was still a faint smell of bacon, and a lingering peachy odor of summer, but the shelves were empty.

Adam slammed the door and opened the one beyond it, which led to the old dungeon where Elinor kept her wine. In the bulb-lit cellar, the wine racks stood empty.

Eventually Adam found a forgotten bottle of brandy in the television room. As he sipped his drink, he heard a scratching on the glass doors to the terrace. Outside the French windows, a sodden ginger cat was asking to be let in. Supposedly, Fudge had been adopted by Sylvie the cook, who reckoned that otherwise he wouldn't last long among the village toughs of the stray cat pack.

Happy to be home, Fudge curled up on the sofa beside Adam, who flipped through an old magazine, irritated that Annabel was late. How prudent it had been of him not to meet her! It would do Annabel good to feel a little dejected, a little cast down, a little forlorn.

Adam smiled. He supplied Annabel with reassurance. But in order for it to work its magic, she first had to feel unsure of herself.

He could just remember Annabel's childish flirtations with her grandfather, but how she lapsed into terrified submission if Billy slightly raised his voice. *That* was the way to handle her.

Adam liked to get tough with Annabel. When she sensed his disapproval, her lips would tremble with apprehension. Despotic benevolence in his voice, he would then reassure her ("You're so *special*, Annabel"), knowing he could get her to do almost anything for him, if she thought he really believed *that*.

With her, he was truly applying the lessons he had learned from reading Elinor's novels. For Adam knew that Annabel's head was filled with girlish hopes of romance; he knew that she was besotted by him, hungry for him. He guessed that her life now revolved around their clandestine relationship: secretly telephoning him or writing to him, their secret meetings. Adam was almost certain that Annabel longed to marry him—if only he would ask her.

Adam felt a carefully hidden contempt for the emotional dependence of such women, who needed his approval. Miranda was one of the few women he had met who didn't want to experience life parasitically, through some man.

His present situation—two sisters eating out of the palm of his hand and the other one no longer in the running—although somewhat taxing, was only for five more months: Paul Littlejohn needed a little more time than he had originally planned, but by the end of February, Adam would be in Rio.

Had the sisters not fallen so easily into his hands, he suspected he would have had a far harder job persuading them that Saracen should be sold—though if they had not agreed to the sale, it could easily have been proved that selling was to their advantage: when the cash from the sale of the chateau and its contents was invested, the resultant income would increase the trust substantially.

But the sale of Saracen was a clear indication that Elinor would never leave the nursing home, and had the sisters not both been emotionally involved with Adam, the decision to sell it might once again have raised the question of whether the nursing home was the best place for her.

Adam had pointed out to Miranda that it was no longer in their power to remove Elinor. If such a patient wished to be discharged (or should the relatives wish it against medical advice), the Mental Hospital Act provided for compulsory detention of up to twenty-eight days. That would undoubtedly attract the unpleasant attention of the press and gain nothing. A nursing home was not always the best choice for everyone, but in Elinor's case, it provided the finest care possible.

Reluctantly Miranda had agreed that Elinor was being well cared for in luxurious surroundings.

As suddenly as it had started, the rain stopped, and weak sunshine lightened the chateau terrace. In the television room, Adam's thoughts were cut short by footsteps. He looked up at the approach of Mr. Simpson, the furniture appraiser who had been sent from London.

"Excuse me, sir," Mr. Simpson said. "I've found something in Mrs. O'Dare's private library that isn't on the inventory. It's a strongbox—too large and heavy for me to carry."

Adam followed the thin, black-suited figure upstairs and through Elinor's bedroom, where the bed had been stripped and all the furniture labeled.

In the library beyond the bedroom, the bookshelves contained old children's books, tattered paperbacks, and six thousand reference books. On the cheap wooden table before the window stood a battered black tin strongbox.

"It's locked, sir," Mr. Simpson said, "but none of the housekeeper's keys fit."

"Then please break it open," Adam told him. "I should imagine there's a crowbar in the toolbox. Look in the kitchen."

Mr. Simpson hesitated, then firmly said, "I would prefer not to do that, sir, without the written permission of the owner."

Adam, somewhat irritated, went downstairs to call the caretaker, who would have no such scruples.

Ten minutes later, the black lid of the box creaked open.

Adam dismissed the caretaker and Mr. Simpson.

As soon as the door closed behind them, he bent eagerly over the box. But to his exasperation, it appeared to contain only old photographs and childish memorabilia.

Adam rifled through children's paintings and letters; he threw aside faded snapshots, with torn or curling edges, of smiling children in sunbonnets waving spades upon a beach or seated on the backs of fat ponies. At the bottom of the box were bundles of letters in envelopes with an Oxford postmark; they were tied with narrow ivory satin ribbon.

Severely disappointed, Adam was about to bang the lid down and leave the room, when he had a second thought. If Elinor had locked that box and kept the key apart from the normal household keys, then there must be a reason for it. He had better carefully check the contents, item by item.

Swiftly but carefully he sorted out the contents of the box on the wooden tabletop. After about ten minutes, he pounced on an ordinary foolscap envelope, which was sealed. Adam tore it open and pulled out two crumpled sheets of paper.

As he read them, a triumphant smile spread across his face.

CHAPTER 24

Tuesday, 31 December 1968

M*IRANDA'S NEW YEAR'S EVE* ball was, as usual, a great success. Just before midnight, she looked around the scarlet-and-blue-striped tent with satisfaction. Her vision was limited because her face was covered by a golden lion's mask that looked as if it might have been dug from an Inca burial ground; she wore a golden leotard and matching high-heeled sandals; her hair, including a luxurious fall, spread around her head like a flaming lion's mane.

This year's fancy-dress theme was a Fellini circus, and the tent covered Miranda's back garden; inside it, the lighting was low and mysterious; at foot level, swirls of theatrical mist were being pumped upward. Grouped around a revolving central circus ring were two smaller circular tents and three raised platforms, each the size of a small sitting room. The two smaller tents were striped in pale blue and silver; rising from the romantic mist, they looked as if they had last been used at Agincourt. One contained a Gypsy fortune-teller, the other a champagne bar.

A band played on the raised black platform, where three beautiful singers, wearing what looked like silver underwear and Carmen Miranda turbans, gasped the latest Dusty Springfield number. Two other pale-gray-carpeted platforms had been scattered with Louis XVI-style chairs upholstered in pale gray moiré: here guests sat to watch those dancing in the revolving center ring.

Strongmen carrying papier-mâché dumbbells danced with tightrope-walking ballerinas in pastel tutus; skimpily dressed bearded ladies, giants, and dwarfs jounced and bounced, shook, bumped, and twisted. A fairground barker danced with a monkey trainer, whose (real) monkey mournfully sat on her elegant red satin shoulder. An elephant did the twist with a lion tamer. A tiger gyrated with a Nubian slave, naked to the waist in harem trousers and a jeweled turban. The bareback rider in pink had turned up on a gray horse, which had then been led away by her groom.

The women with the best figures wore leotards, tights, and high-heels: an acrobat in silver, a performing panther in black, a contortionist in crimson, a tattooed lady in a white leotard covered with painted tattoos.

Because it was so hot in the tent, the two-headed man had removed his second head: Miranda recognized the Scandinavian prince who had purchased Saracen. Smiling, she moved back to check the midnight-supper buffet.

Inside the house, sackfuls of autumn leaves (which had been sitting in the cellars since October) had been lavishly scattered over the floor, to lend a Sleeping Beauty look to the rooms. Here, too, artificial mist rose from the floor. The furniture of the double drawing room had been replaced by circular tables set with lavender cloths and *eau de Nil* linen napkins. The only light sources were candles in silver candelabras on every table, each draped with fine silk threads shaped like cobwebs.

On her way back to the garden tents, Miranda spotted a bare-chested, turbaned snake charmer in spangled turquoise harem trousers, talking to Mike Grant in the hall.

"Scott!" she cried. "I'm so glad you were able to fly over. Pity you couldn't have been with us for Christmas. . . . It *is* Scott, isn't it? I don't recognize half my guests in their glamorous outfits."

The snake charmer kissed Miranda on the cheek. "Sure it's me. I wouldn't miss this. Where's Annabel?"

"Dancing, I think. Easy to see that you two came as a couple!" Miranda had already admired Annabel's costume: her sister was dressed as a snake. A stuffed emerald satin serpent entwined her green-sequined leotard and tights from her neck to her left ankle. She wore Alan Jones-style, scarlet, four-inch heels.

"What are *you* supposed to be, Mike?" Miranda puzzled. Although the name of an excellent theatrical costumer had been slipped in with the invitations, Mike was wearing black leather motorcycle gear; he carried a bucket.

"I feed the animals," he explained sheepishly.

"No marks for effort," Miranda said tartly. "Look how hard everyone else has tried." She wagged a finger, only half in jest. "If you can't manage something better than that, you won't get asked next year."

Scott said, "Miranda, I'm sure Annabel isn't on the dance floor. I've been looking for her for nearly an hour. Where the hell could she have gone?"

"Perhaps she's down at the swimming pool," Mike suggested.

"No, she won't be there," Miranda said. "I'm not allowing anyone in my new pool this evening. Drunken revelers may jump in and out of the fountains at Trafalgar Square, but I don't want them dripping over my newly decorated house."

As she left for the circus tent, she called over her shoulder.

"You're bound to spot Annabel at midnight—we're all going to sing 'Auld Lang Syne' in the circus tent before supper starts—foie gras, wild duck, and quinces baked in a crust!"

"You really should see Miranda's pool," Mike said. "She's turned the entire basement into a Roman bath. Not a new one—one that looks as if it had been built two thousand years ago and has just been excavated and restored. I bet you've never seen anything like it."

"Okay, show me," Scott said.

The two men, drinks in hand, sauntered to the elevator.

"Here for long?" Mike asked.

"No, just to see the New Year in."

Scott also intended to see Adam; he refused to be put off any longer by Adam's excuses. The bottom line was that the guy had promised quarterly accounting—and it wasn't happening. Finally Scott had made it clear to Adam that he was coming to London to pick up those quarterly reports personally—or find out why.

Mike stepped from the elevator and felt to the left for the switch that would light the pool with a dim, eerie radiance. "Hey, the lights are already on! I thought Miranda said that nobody was allowed down here tonight."

Puzzled, he pushed open the cream doors, and Scott saw the beautiful dark green pool. The stone columns were chipped, the vaulted ceiling was crumbling, and the walls looked as if they had been hacked out of rock. What looked like a natural spring trickled down into the far end of the pool. In front of it, before a semicircle of stone pillars, were mattresses covered by cream toweling; on one of these lay a whip and a ringmaster's top hat; on another lay a small pile of green clothing. On an adjoining mattress, a man and woman were passionately locked in a naked embrace.

Mike's clear, gray, wide-set eyes stared. As Mike saw who the man was, he felt disgust rise like bile to his mouth.

And as Scott realized who the woman was, he charged toward the naked couple, yelling, "*You bitch!*"

Mike ran after Scott and grabbed his arm, trying to restrain him. Scott tried to shake Mike off. The two men grappled, until Scott threw a hard punch at Mike, glad of an excuse to hit out, to unleash his violence.

Mike hit Scott hard: as hard as he wanted to hit Adam. How could Adam do such a bloody cruel thing? How could he have taken such a bloody *stupid* risk—Adam, who had never been seriously involved with a woman?

Scott, clumsy in his harem trousers, grappled again with Mike. They scuffled, grunting, gasping, and swearing, until one of them slipped on a wet stone. Scott's jeweled turban flew off his head and into the pool. Both men followed it.

As Annabel and Adam scrambled to their feet, Annabel grabbed a towel. She was frightened. But she also felt a frisson of excitement. Because now, at least, Scott knew—but Adam would be unable to say that Annabel had told him of their secret. And it had not been her idea to make love by the pool. She and Adam had been dancing on the revolving floor, listening to soft, beguiling music in that dim light. She had felt his warm breath on her ear as she listened to his whispered erotic fantasies. . . . It had been at Adam's suggestion that they came to the pool. No, Adam could *not* blame her for this.

Annabel grabbed her leotard and her scarlet shoes; abandoning her stuffed snake, she fled toward the elevator. She was closely followed by Adam, who didn't bother about a towel.

By the time a furious Scott pulled himself from the pool, the two naked lovers had disappeared. In his dripping harem trousers, Scott ran after them to the elevator.

Mike's leather gear was too waterlogged to allow him to vault from the pool, so he swam clumsily toward the stone steps; as he climbed up, water streamed down his body. Violently he shook water from his hair, and it streamed down his leather back.

He unzipped his jacket, threw it on the floor, and shed the rest of his clothes. Scott had landed a couple of good punches: Mike's ribs felt sore. As he wrapped himself in a towel, another thought occurred to him. If Adam—always so careful—had been caught in a compromising situation with a woman, then Mike knew that must have been what his calculating brother intended. That scene must have been carefully staged. Adam had *planned* to be caught fucking Annabel.

Why?

Toweling his hair, Mike considered. Suppose that Adam had intended Scott to discover his wife's infidelity. How could he have planned for that? Simple! Scott—arriving straight from the plane—would naturally have looked for his wife at once.

All Adam needed to do was calculate the earliest time that Scott could arrive from the airport and then, ten minutes before, start fucking Annabel's brains out until they were discovered.

If Scott did not find his wife—then Miranda always had a big 'Auld Lang Syne' singsong at her New Year's Eve party. At five minutes to midnight, at the latest, Miranda would expect Annabel to turn up in the tent; should her sister be absent, Miranda would send servants all over the house to find her.

Mike wrapped himself in a cream bath towel and headed for the elevator to get his coat. Why would Adam want to cause trouble between Annabel and her husband? he wondered. There had to be some reason. It was inconceivable that Adam was in love with Annabel, and he was too smart to fuck her for no reason. If he was cited in a divorce, he risked being landed with a woman he didn't want, so there must be a lot at stake. Of course, Annabel was an heiress, but so was Miranda. Why not pick the unattached sister if he was after the money?

No. It had to be some other reason. But what?

Fifteen minutes before midnight, as Miranda was about to send a footman to find Annabel, a maid approached and whispered a message in her ear. Miranda followed her upstairs to a guest bedroom and knocked on the door. "Scott? I hear you fell in the pool!" She laughed.

As he opened the door, Scott growled, "Come inside and lock the door."

"What's happened?" Miranda could see that Scott, who was wearing a bathrobe, was furious. She could also see that he was sober.

"Did you know what was going on, Miranda? Were you in on this? Were you helping them?"

"I don't understand what the hell you're talking about. *What's* going on?"

"I just—Mike and I—just saw Adam with Annabel."

"Oh, I was wondering where she'd got to," Miranda said. "Where was she?"

"They were making love!" Scott shouted. "Adam and Annabel! By your fucking swimming pool!"

Miranda stepped back from his furious face. "There must be . . . You *must* have made a mistake!"

"Ask Mike!" Scott roared. "*He* saw the whole fucking thing as well!"

Miranda made a noise that was half gasp, half groan. She tore off the golden lion's mask that covered her face. She felt as if icy fingers were clawing at her flesh, trying to reach her heart. She seemed to be outside her own body, watching it from a height and a distance: the true Miranda was suspended somewhere near the ceiling, silently howling with pain and rage at this double betrayal. That golden body below her moved, spoke, behaved almost normally, but it felt like a cold, dead thing.

"Where are they?" Miranda made a great effort to appear natural. Scott must on no account guess her pain, her vulnerability, her stupidity. Neither Scott nor anyone else must *ever* guess that she had allowed Adam to creep inside her soul and erode it from within. No one must ever guess her shame.

"They've both left," Scott said, tight-lipped. "One of the security men on the door said that two people wrapped in bathrobes had run out into a waiting Rolls. Couldn't be anyone else. They must have gone to his place. My bitch of a wife wouldn't *dare* take that bastard to our suite at the Ritz."

"Are . . . are you *sure*, Scott?"

"Ask Mike if you don't believe me!" Scott wanted Miranda's comfort, reassurance, and advice—not to be doubted and cross-examined.

Miranda slowly moved to the bedside telephone. There had to be an explanation. Annabel must have thrown herself at Adam. She must have taken him by surprise. He must have been drunk. It must have been a mad, lusty, sexual impulse.

But she could not recall ever having seen Adam drunk.

Miranda dialed an outside number and let it ring for five minutes. "They're not at Adam's house," she said, "or else he isn't answering."

In the silence, both of them imagined what Annabel and Adam might be doing.

Violently angry and hurt, Scott said, "I *never* thought that Annabel . . . She said these trips to England were to see Elinor! . . . *Shit!* What a fool I've been! . . . I wonder how many *others* there have been. She's probably been making a fool of me for years." He shook his head in disbelief. "I would *never* have suspected Annabel of cheating on me!"

Miranda said in a cold voice, "Annabel is governed entirely by self-interest."

Scott spoke wearily. "I'm going back to the Ritz, to try to get some sleep." He wanted to be alone, to curse in a frenzy of impotence, to hammer walls with his fists.

"If Annabel turns up," Miranda said, suddenly anxious, "*don't* do anything rash, Scott. Don't say anything stupid. Let *me* talk to her first. Let me try and find out why this is going on—and how long it's been going on." Her voice was hard.

"Don't worry, I don't want to hit that bitch! I *don't want to touch her!*" Scott said. "And I doubt she'll dare turn up tonight. She'll obviously stay with that bastard." He rubbed his eyes tiredly. "I'll phone you in the morning. As soon as I get hold of Annabel, we're going straight back to New York."

"There are a couple of gossip writers downstairs. I don't want people to start wondering what's happened to me. I'd better go down and attend to my party." Miranda was glad to have some mechanical role to perform; she would smile brightly, move around, check that everyone was happily occupied, sing "Auld Lang Syne."

Usually the last guests lingered until around five in the morning, and usually Miranda longed for that moment, but tonight she dreaded it. Because afterward, she would not be able to avoid thinking. Firmly she pushed away memories of Adam's touch, Adam's smell, Adam's whispered erotic suggestions and the faintly detached way in which he put them into practice.

Thursday, 2 January 1969

Scott telephoned Miranda to tell her that Annabel, after a thirty-six-hour absence, had turned up at the Ritz in a white fox coat and not much else. If Miranda wanted to knock some sense into her sister's head, she'd better get around fast because Annabel was packing. *He* was heading for the bar.

"What are *you* doing here?" Annabel yelled when Miranda walked into her bedroom. She hurled a pile of peach lace into the already crowded suitcase that lay on the bed. "You might as well get out of here, if you think I'm going to listen to one of your lectures!"

"Don't you dare tell me what to do!" Miranda barked.

"I'll do as I please."

"*How long has it pleased you to screw Adam?*"

"None of your business!"

"Yes it is," Miranda hissed. "*Adam and I have been lovers for over three years.*"

"*I don't believe you!*" Annabel shrieked. She faced her sister.

"The last time we made love was three nights ago."

"I don't believe he loves you! He *couldn't* love you!" Annabel's certainty returned as she fleetingly remembered the last blissful thirty-six hours, most of which had been spent in Adam's bed.

"I don't believe he loves *you!*" Miranda shouted. "If anything, you're a one-night stand for Adam. Has he given you all the trimmings?"

"What the hell do you mean by *that?*"

Miranda looked coldly at her sister. "Does he tickle your nipples with a feather? Does he slowly lick between your toes? Does he run his lips over your entire body, so lightly that there seems to be only a warm space between your skin and his mouth? Does he—"

"Shut up! Shut up! Shut up! *I don't want to hear any more!*" But Annabel longed to know more as uncertainty swept over her again. She stood staring at Miranda.

"Don't you *dare* start crying," Miranda said coldly. "There's *no* reason why Adam and I shouldn't have an affair. But you've deceived your husband—*as well as your sister!*"

"Scott had it coming to him! And I never meant to deceive you. I never *knew* about you!"

"Well, now you do. So take your clammy hands off my man!"

"But he's *not* your man!" Annabel wailed. "If Adam *really* loved you, would he make love to me?" Triumphantly she added, "If he really loves you, then why have you both kept it a secret?"

"None of your damned business," Miranda said with frost in her heart. What a fool she had been to think that Adam loved her enough to marry her: he hadn't even loved her enough to be faithful.

"Yes it is! Adam loves *me!* We're going to be *married!*"

"Has he actually *asked* you to marry him?" Miranda spat.

Annabel hesitated, then spoke the lie with conviction. "Yes."

"*Then why doesn't Adam tell me?*"

"He said the sensible thing was to wait for the fuss to die down."

Icily Miranda said, "Perhaps we should *both* see Adam together and let him clarify his intentions. Where is he?"

"None of your damned business."

"Oh, *do* stop saying that! If Scott finds Adam—and it shouldn't be difficult—he'll tear him apart."

"Scott won't find Adam," Annabel said. "Scott has to catch the New York plane tonight if he doesn't want to miss a broadcast."

"If Adam is hiding from Scott—which I doubt, by the way—then let's *both* see Adam tomorrow." Miranda looked more casual than she felt. "Where is he?" she asked again.

"I honestly don't know," Annabel lied with equal casualness. "Perhaps he's still at the Savoy. That's where we've been staying."

At the back of Miranda's analytical mind, a half-formed thought almost surfaced: Adam would have had to book well in advance to get a room for New Year's Eve at the Savoy.

But instead of pursuing this logical thought, she let her attention be distracted by the violent passion she felt. Within the past half hour, her love for her sister had turned to jealous hatred. Because Miranda knew that Annabel was right about one thing: If he really loved Miranda, Adam would not have made love to Annabel.

Suddenly Miranda could understand the feelings of someone who kills the person he loves. She certainly wanted to kill Adam—not anonymously with poison, not suddenly with a gun, but by some slow and painful method. She wanted Adam to know that she was responsible for his death. She wanted him to suffer the torment that she felt and would continue to feel.

"I'll find Adam—he won't be able to hide forever." Miranda threw a look of hatred at Annabel, then stormed out of the room.

When Scott returned later, Annabel was sitting on a suitcase that refused to close.

She looked up to find Scott standing just inside the door, looking so furious and so forlorn she wished she could tell him she was sorry she'd hurt him—because she truly was. But because of her guilt, she could not be kind to him.

"Miranda told me her side of the story," Scott growled. "I'd no idea that you could be such an unscrupulous, treacherous *bitch!*"

Coldly Annabel said, "Will you shut this damned thing, or do I have to ring for a porter?"

"Ring, dammit," said Scott. His hurt pride battled with anger and humiliation. "How could you do it to me? How could you do it to your sister?"

"I never knew that Miranda had this . . . this crush on Adam." Annabel glared at Scott and thumbed the bell.

"What the hell has this man *done* to you both?" Scott asked. "Hypnotized you?"

"Adam doesn't put his damned career before everything else! Before his life! Before his wife!"

Scott was suddenly deflated. "Believe me, Annabel, I regret it."

"*Adam doesn't take me for granted!*"

"So that's how he got to you," Scott said quietly. Adam had given Annabel the attention that Scott had provided when they first met. Scott had underestimated Annabel's loss of self-confidence when her career crumbled. He had briskly attempted to minimize the importance of what had happened to her. But Adam had consoled her with flattery. He had zeroed in on her insecurity, and his honeyed reassurance had clearly repaired the rift in her self-esteem. Scott took two steps toward Annabel. "I never realized I was neglecting you, angel."

"If you knew how I *hate* being called 'angel'!"

"Then why didn't you say so?" Scott yelled. "What does that bastard Adam call you?"

Scott couldn't believe his sense of grief, of loss, almost of mourning. He remembered feeling like this only once before—at his mother's funeral, when much too late he finally realized he had lost something irreplaceable, something that he had never known he valued so much.

Remembering his pain, Scott said, "I can't bear to lose you, Annabel."

"You can't expect *me* to feel the same way." Annabel glared at him again.

"I can't believe that this is happening to *us!*" Scott was usually so astute and observant, yet his wife had been cheating on him for months and he hadn't noticed.

"Why not?" Annabel glared.

"It would have been easy for *me* to screw around at the station. You may laugh, but I believed in absolute commitment. For me, love wasn't just fucking."

"There hasn't been much of *that* lately." Annabel stared impatiently out the window. She couldn't wait to get away.

"It takes two," Scott said. "Remember how often you visited poor Elinor?" He added quietly, "We're both going back to New York together as planned, and we're both going to forget that this ever happened."

Annabel laughed.

Scott's calm shattered. He said sharply, "If you don't, I'll divorce you."

"Go ahead." Annabel laughed again. No more lies. No more cover-ups. No more alibis. No more guilt. She would be free to marry Adam. And if that was the case, she was convinced he would marry her.

Adam wasn't at the Savoy and of course he wouldn't stay in his own home, where she and Scott could badger him, Miranda thought.

Where could that bastard hide, an unexpected guest, for an indefinite period over the holiday season in quiet and comfortable anonymity?

Suddenly she knew where he was hiding. There was one person who would always protect Adam, no matter what he had done.

Twenty minutes later, Miranda rang the bell of the dignified cream house in Eaton Terrace.

When Mike's butler answered the door, she said quietly, "Please tell Mr. Adam Grant that Miss O'Dare is a little early for her appointment."

Once inside the house, instead of waiting in the hall, Miranda silently followed the manservant up the carpeted stairs to the second floor.

The butler paused at a bedroom door. Before he could knock, she had twisted the brass handle, ducked under his arm, and burst into the room.

Seated before the mustard brocade curtains of the bedroom window, Adam was studying a page of figures.

He looked up in surprise. "What are *you* doing here, Miranda?" As he spoke, Adam slipped the sheet of paper between the cushion and the side of the chair so that it was hidden.

"I might ask the same of you!" Miranda said hotly.

"Thank you, Forbes." Adam waited until the door had closed. Then, with apparent sincerity, he said, "I'm sorry you had to find out this way, Miranda. I'm truly sorry I've made such a mess of things for you."

As painfully as if she had just stepped barefoot on a hedgehog, Miranda again felt the destructive spikes of jealousy. Tormented and miserable to the point of frenzy, she burst out, "*Why* did you do it this way, Adam? *That's* what I don't understand. *Do you love Annabel?*"

"I am not going to discuss my feelings for Annabel with you or anyone else," Adam said. He stood up and looked coldly at Miranda.

Her jealousy flared. She flew across the room and lashed out at him with her fists.

Adam easily caught her wrists. Miranda found herself powerless to shake them free. She kicked at his ankle and hit his shinbone. When he winced from the pain, she tried to bite his hands. Adam swiftly shifted his grip so that he held Miranda's face against his chest while firmly grasping her wrists behind her.

She found it difficult to move. Her cheek was pressed against him. Hatred, burning rage, and pain consumed her. "Let me *go*, you bastard!" She twisted upward and managed to clamp her teeth on his chin.

Adam jerked his head back. With satisfaction, Miranda saw blood run from his chin.

Barely concealing the fury in his voice, Adam said, "I'll let you go when I feel like it. You're about to find out who's in control, you careless, stupid little bitch."

"I'd remind you that I'm in control of the company! I'm your boss!"

"I shouldn't be too sure," Adam spat. "Why should you have so large a part of the company that I've done so much to build up!"

"You got a quarter of a million pounds' worth of shares for that! *And* you get a damned good salary! Let me *go!*"

Adam tightened his grip. "I'm sorry to tell you that I not only wished to have *more* of the business but I also wished you to have *less.*"

"*Let me go!*" Miranda desperately tried to pull free of him: her wrists were burning now and tears of pain sprang to her eyes. "By God, I'll fire you, Adam!"

"No. *You can't fire me, Miranda.*"

"I don't know what the hell you mean, Adam, but as soon as I get out of here, I'm going to telephone my solicitors and find out just how quickly I can terminate your contract."

"In that case, Miranda, please remember to tell your solicitors that you no longer have a controlling interest in the company."

"What the hell do you mean?"

"Remembering your extensive knowledge of company law, I'm sure you know that the biggest shareholder virtually controls a company."

"Yes, and that's me."

"You are mistaken, Miranda. *I* now control the biggest shareholding in SUPPLYKITS. Forty-six percent! *And you can't do a thing about it!* You have a choice, of course: you can either leave the company or you can work your ass off to provide me with a splendid income for the rest of my life." In fact, Adam now planned to sell all his shares before leaving for Rio.

"You must be mad," Miranda gasped, still trying to free herself from Adam's grip. She managed to kick him again, and he winced.

"No," he said between gritted teeth, "I'm telling you the truth, my darling. You and your bloody family are about to be wiped out."

Adam quickly twisted Miranda so that her back was against his chest. He then moved backward, toward the door of the room, dragging her with him. She fought wildly against his grip and heard her coat rip as they struggled.

Miranda panted, "*You* can't do anything to my family." She wished she'd thought of kneeing Adam in the groin while she was facing him. She waited until he had to use one hand to open the door, then gave a vicious kick backward and once more hit his leg bone. He grunted with pain—but did not release her.

"You'll find I *can* do something to your family," Adam said, gritting his teeth again as he tightened his hold on Miranda.

"*What do you mean?*"

But Adam had already said more than he intended. Still gripping Miranda's wrists painfully, he frog-marched her down the wide, maroon-carpeted stairway.

The butler appeared in the hall. He quickly concealed his astonishment and, at Adam's curt request, politely opened the door.

Adam shoved Miranda out, between the elegant Doric columns that guarded the steps to the street.

The front door slammed behind her.

As she clutched a column to steady herself and hailed an approaching taxi, Miranda remembered Adam's parting words.

Exactly *what* could Adam do to her family? She felt a lurch in her stomach, a feeling she had often experienced when he took her in his arms—but this time it was a lurch of fear.

Miranda suddenly remembered that Adam had made the arrangements to set up the Dove Trust. Suppose Buzz was right and Elinor was being deliberately kept in a drug-induced stupor so that Adam could do as he pleased with her money.

"You all right, love?" asked the taxi driver as he stopped at the curb.

Miranda, angry and worried, telephoned for an emergency appointment with Mr. Worthington, senior partner of Swithin, Timmins and Grant.

In his sunny, dusty office, Mr. Worthington reminded her that STG had relinquished control of the Dove Trust, at her grandmother's specific request.

"I appreciate that," Miranda said, "but I've come to ask you to find out what's happening to the trust *now*."

Mr. Worthington said politely, "Regrettably, STG cannot be involved because there's a conflict of interest between the parties concerned—even though Adam Grant and Paul Littlejohn are no longer connected with STG."

"But couldn't you tell me what you *think* might have happened? Off the record?"

Mr. Worthington hesitated. "*Strictly* off the record . . . after what you've told me . . . there *might* be a possibility of embezzlement, arranged so that it is not illegal."

Bitterly, Miranda said, "I expect that two international lawyers, who've worked together for years, wouldn't find it difficult to legally defraud a client who trusted them. But can't a trust be broken?"

"Often the reason for setting up a trust is specifically so that it *cannot* be broken," Mr. Worthington said. "Of course, when the trust deeds were originally drawn up, it would have been possible to insert special trust-breaking clauses. But had Adam Grant intended, at that stage, to defraud the beneficiaries, then he would have been careful to insert no such clauses. If I were you, I would immediately get a good lawyer to check the trust deeds."

BOOK FOUR

CHAPTER 25

Friday, 3 January 1969

"W*HAT DO YOU* want to see me about, Miranda?" As Miranda entered his office, the Earl of Brighton rose from behind a black leather desk. A thin, stooped figure, he unhooked his gold-rimmed half-spectacles from rather large ears and moved forward with a tentative, shambling walk; he looked far more amiable and far less intelligent than he was.

Briefly Miranda told Lord Brighton what Adam had said to her about SUPPLYKITS. She tried to sound calm, reasonable, and businesslike, explaining that she was there for one purpose only—to see that Adam did not control the company.

"What's his shareholding?" Lord Brighton asked.

"I went to the registrar myself, James, to check the shareholders. Adam holds only fifteen percent of the shares—the fifteen percent that he bought from me on option and the shares he was entitled to buy at the one-for-three rights issue."

"But Adam might control some of the other shareholders—if he's promised a few big shareholders some special inducement provided they vote with him."

"The biggest single holding belongs to a firm called Highland Croft Holdings. Have you ever heard of them? My broker hasn't."

"No. It's certainly not a publicly quoted company," Lord Brighton said, "but even if Adam *does* control forty-six percent of the shares, as he claims, if there's a real showdown he won't control the company because he needs over fifty percent to do that."

"What can I do? How can I stop Adam controlling the other four or five percent?"

"We need more information," Lord Brighton said.

Miranda hesitated. "Perhaps I should also now tell you, in confidence, that I don't particularly want to control SUPPLYKITS. I'm not interested in acquiring businesses. I'm really interested in only *one* business—KITS." She spoke with determination: "I don't want to be the figurehead of a public company. I want to be the *real* head of my *own* company! Ideally, I'd like to own one hundred percent of the KITS shares."

"So you want to purchase KITS from SUPPLYKITS."

Miranda nodded. "If KITS again became a private company, I could develop the business as *I* wish. I could make long-term plans without constant pressure to provide quick profits. And I wouldn't find my hands tied by some overcautious director who's terrific at pushing figures around on paper but doesn't understand the cosmetics business."

Lord Brighton said, "As chairman, I don't feel that SUPPLYKITS should let you go at this stage."

Miranda played what she hoped was her trump card. "I would only be prepared to stay on as managing director provided I could buy back KITS."

Lord Brighton leaned back in his chair and stared through the window at the river traffic silently drifting on the ocher water of the Thames. Reflectively he said, "We've just had that valuation of KITS."

Miranda smiled. "Leases and stock, less debts, are valued at fourteen thousand pounds."

"That's a very low figure. What about the value of the goodwill?"

Miranda said firmly, "The goodwill of KITS is so bound up with my public image that it'd be difficult for the accountants to put a price on the goodwill if I'm not there. If SUPPLYKITS *dares* to ask me to pay a premium for KITS, then I will immediately resign from SUPPLYKITS."

"Which, as I've said, SUPPLYKITS can't afford at the moment," Lord Brighton said. "As the face of the firm, you are publicly perceived to be responsible for the success of SUPPLYKITS. If you went, the share price would undoubtedly fall. SUPPLYKITS can't afford to lose you or have any rival company acquire your services."

"Exactly, James. But I want to make it clear to *you* that I intend to withdraw gradually from SUPPLYKITS. The company is now established, and my deputy, Alex Stanton, can take over as MD."

"Then I assume you'd like SUPPLYKITS to call an EGM?" An extraordinary general meeting was the only way that such a matter could be decided.

"As fast as possible, please."

"We need to give three weeks' notice of an EGM. Let's hold it on Friday, thirty-first January, which gives us a week extra."

Miranda nodded. Official approval to sell KITS back to her must come from bank, stockbroker, and stock exchange, after which the circular had to be printed and posted to all shareholders.

As he escorted Miranda to the door, Lord Brighton added: "By the way, Adam Grant should be informed as fast as possible. We'll then know his reaction well in advance."

"Could you telephone him, James?"

Lord Brighton nodded. "I could also tactfully bring up that other matter of who holds the controlling interest claimed by Grant. He'll have to give me a truthful answer, evade the question, or lie: any of those possibilities will be interesting."

"If he doesn't control those shares, I can fire him." Miranda was no longer able to maintain her carefully businesslike facade; her voice shook.

"You can't fire Grant just because you feel like doing so," Lord Brighton warned. "He's a director of a public company. Officially, you haven't complained about him—and I'm not sure that you even have the *right* to complain about his behavior: Grant has been very successful at his job, and he's entitled to acquire as many shares as he can—like any other member of the public. Be careful,

Miranda, to keep your feelings under control."

"I can still dream," Miranda said. "If you need me for anything, I'll be in Paris early next week for the Cosmetics Safety Conference. At the Ritz, as usual."

When Lord Brighton telephoned, Adam listened in silence as he was told of the purpose of the EGM. Reminded of the book valuation of KITS, he said angrily, "With the greatest respect, that's giving KITS away. The reason KITS is currently worth so little on paper is because it's been our cash cow—we've milked it to finance our expansion in other areas."

"I believe that's one of the things Miranda objects to."

Adam snapped, "What Miranda forgets—or maybe she doesn't—is that in a couple of years, KITS will once again be worth a fortune! So whatever Miranda O'Dare offers for KITS—I'll offer ten percent more."

Lord Brighton telephoned Miranda with this news. He added, "Of course, I'll have to include Grant's counterbid in my letter to the shareholders, but in view of the other considerations, I shall still recommend acceptance of your offer, Miranda. However, the decision doesn't depend on my views—it depends on the votes. And, as interested parties, neither you nor Adam will be allowed to vote, nor will shareholders controlled by either of you."

"Does that mean—assuming Adam's telling the truth about controlling forty-six percent—that the decision will be made by *only the nine percent of outside shareholders?*"

"It does."

"Are Adam and I allowed to lobby the shareholders?"

"Be careful," Lord Brighton warned again. "You don't want to overexcite the press. The share price might drop if it looked as though the directors were squabbling among themselves instead of efficiently running the company."

"Don't worry," Miranda said grimly. "I'll be careful."

"By the way, I checked on Highland Croft Holdings. The company is apparently owned by an offshore holding company, so we can't trace it further. They own four point eight percent of SUPPLYKITS, and there's no way of telling whether those shares are among the percentage that Grant claims to control."

Saturday, 4 January 1969

Although it was past midday, the only light in the room entered through a chink in the mustard brocade curtains.

They lay silent once more, enjoying closeness. Adam felt that he knew the body beside him almost as well as he knew his own feelings, reactions, and needs. And his partner knew precisely what aroused the force of Adam's passion. Slowly each in turn, with the utmost tenderness, softly kissed the other's body and face . . . lips, nose, eyelids . . . and each trembled beneath the other's touch.

Afterward, as they lay side by side and mouth to mouth, their bodies still intertwined, Adam cherished the closeness and subtle tenderness that made him feel the two of them had just fused into one person. For him, it had been an all-encompassing, overwhelming experience of soaring rapture, total understanding, and bliss, emotional as well as physical.

Adam sometimes wondered whether—as he had many times been told—he had lost the capacity to feel, whether it had really been cauterized away before he was old enough to realize it. But he never had such misgivings when he lay enfolded in these arms: here he was always totally involved; he never felt as if, from above, he were dispassionately watching himself manipulate his partner toward spasm.

In these arms, Adam felt as if he were—at last—truly in touch and at peace with himself as he both gave and received. He felt loving and trusting as, in turn, he was loved and trusted. Adam knew this to be true intimacy.

His arms tightened around the smooth shoulders. In the clear, gray, wide-set eyes, so close to his, Adam could see not only his reflection: he could see that this was the person with whom he belonged, the only person with whom he felt at peace, without pretense, and free. He felt tremendous joy.

Sunday, 5 January 1969

After seeing Lord Brighton, Miranda spent two sleepless nights thinking about Adam's triple treachery and worrying about the future of SUPPLYKITS and the Dove Trust. She couldn't cancel her trip to Paris, but luckily, she was only billed to make the opening speech at the conference, and for those two days she was determined to forget her problems, and be professional.

On Sunday morning, the sky was cloudy. Gatwick Airport informed Miranda that the cloud base on her route would be around fifteen hundred feet, with a risk of icing at that level. On a more cheerful note, the operator added that there might be a layer of clear sky between three thousand and four thousand feet. Luckily, Miranda had recently acquired her pilot's instrument rating, which permitted her to climb through cloud in weather such as this.

At ten A.M., Miranda's new plane, a pale blue Beechcraft Bonanza, took off from Redhill for Lydd, where she would clear customs.

But the higher the Bonanza climbed, the worse the weather became. That layer of clear sky must be a lot higher than forecasted, Miranda thought crossly, realizing that, as she couldn't see through the cloud that now surrounded the plane, she was committed to an instrument flight.

Unfortunately, Gatwick Met had been right about the ice. At four thousand feet, Miranda couldn't raise the tower, or any other airport, because ice had built up on the forward cabin, and when it separated, it damaged the communications radio aerial: the Bonanza had no contact with ground control. Miranda, who had been relying on air traffic control for navigation, could no longer receive instructions from the controller.

The Bonanza's air speed indicator, compass, and all instruments that didn't rely on radio were working. However, Miranda was now flying a very basically equipped airplane in some trouble. In an emergency situation, she would have to continue to follow her last instruction from ground control. She cheered herself up by thinking that ground control could still see her on their radar—and they would know she had a problem, because she wasn't answering them.

Although Miranda knew exactly in which direction she was flying, she did not know her precise position, although she reckoned she was somewhere over the South Downs. So there was no question of putting the plane down, for she risked hitting high ground. She had better stay at four thousand feet and hope for a clear patch of sky below her, which would allow her to see the ground and check her bearings.

Miranda's plan was to descend, slowly and carefully, over the sea near Lydd airport. She hoped that there was no low cloud there, because she then risked hitting the water. A crash landing, in January, in the English Channel would be fatal: she was unlikely to be rescued and wouldn't last twenty minutes in such cold water.

As she flew on in thick, oppressive cloud, Miranda felt increasingly lonely. She cursed herself for having climbed above fifteen hundred feet instead of flying below the cloud base: she should have been more cautious.

After flying for about twenty minutes, she calculated that Lydd lay directly ahead. Firmly pushing anxiety out of her mind, she started a slow decent to three thousand feet . . . two thousand . . . nine hundred . . . Still the Bonanza remained enveloped by white cloud.

Nervously Miranda took the plane down to seven hundred feet . . . then to five hundred: white silence still enshrouded it.

As she peered ahead, straining to see, one of her contact lenses started to irritate her eye. She blinked repeatedly as she went down to four hundred feet . . . then three hundred. Even at this low level, the light was dull and the cloud persisted.

Miranda screwed her eyes up and again peered downward, unsuccessfully searching the opaque cloud below.

At just above two hundred feet, she saw a change in the color of cloud. Yes, it was definitely darker.

Then she saw . . . *the tops of trees*. Although visibility, bad when Miranda had started her journey, had since deteriorated, at least she could see where she was going as the Bonanza slowly flew lower.

Now, where was Lydd? Miranda peered at the ground below, hoping to see a town or a road that she could pinpoint on the map that lay on her lap.

She stared, and then blinked. She couldn't believe what she saw. It wasn't possible to be so lucky!

Dead ahead of the Bonanza—just visible in the distance—an airport runway bisected the dirty green ground. Miranda felt a wave of relief run, like electricity, through her entire body and out to her fingertips, which started to tingle as her adrenaline level decreased.

She knew exactly where she was! She was approaching the far boundary of the hedged field that lay about a quarter of a mile east of Lydd airport. *She was going to make it!* Her face relaxed a little as she put down her landing gear at just over two hundred feet.

As Miranda adjusted from blind flying on instruments to visual flight, her contact lens again started to irritate her eye. She approached the runway. Her height was now one hundred feet . . . fifty feet, she reckoned.

But because her eye was watering, Miranda miscalculated: she was flying much lower than she thought. Just short of the runway, the Bonanza's landing gear hit the top of the hedge on the airport boundary.

As the nose of the plane jerked abruptly downward, Miranda instinctively corrected by pulling the stick back fast. With crumpled landing gear, the plane skimmed over the ground and leaned to the left; the wing touched ground, and the plane slewed around in a half-circle.

As the left wing buckled, Miranda, who hadn't pulled her seat belt quite tight enough, was thrown forward. Her head hit the top of the instrument panel.

Saturday, 25 January 1969

The thin woman in the violet coat planted a farewell kiss on Adam's cheek and moved away from the restaurant table.

Annabel smiled. "Don't tell me *that* was one of your clients." She leaned across and, with her handkerchief, scrubbed the blackberry lipstick from his cheek.

"No, she's a lingerie buyer for Harvey Nichols. Do you remember Johnny Briar?"

"That man at Lloyds? Your friend who went bankrupt?"

"Yes. He and Nora were divorcing, but she took him back when Johnny had his nervous breakdown." Adam stood up. "I'd better not be late."

"You work too hard," Annabel said seriously. "Who is this client who needs you on Saturday afternoon?"

"An important Jap." Adam blew her a kiss.

Annabel watched him pause for a few words at almost all the pale-yellow-spotlit tables as he worked his way toward the entrance of the fashionable Arethusa Club.

As Annabel ordered more coffee, a man approached her table.

"Roger! How nice to see you. Coffee?" He was an acquaintance from her debutante days, tall but no longer slim, with thinning fair hair. He wore the fashionable art director's uniform: black turtleneck sweater, hipster trousers, and a leather, brass-buckled belt that might have been taken from a cart horse.

"I was sorry to read about Miranda's accident. How is she?" Roger sat down and removed his heavy, horn-rimmed spectacles.

"She's slowly recovering," Annabel said, fighting back tears. She tried not to think about Miranda.

Roger said, "You girls were great fun, and you were all very nice to me."

"*You* were always great fun. And so was Lady Rushleigh, I mean Mrs. Bromley."

"I think Aunt Sonia hoped I'd marry an heiress. But I didn't. I hadn't yet found that I didn't belong in that world, although plenty of people made it plain enough." He smiled ruefully. "Wasn't that Adam Grant who just left?"

"Yes." Annabel brightened at the mention of her beloved's name.

"What's one of my favorite girls doing with a man like that? I know it's none of my business, but, for old time's sake, be careful."

"Be careful of *what*, Roger?"

"Perhaps you don't know Adam as well as I do," Roger said carefully. "We were at prep school together, and schoolboys rarely change. They may turn into art directors and lawyers, but behind the grown-up disguises, basic character doesn't much alter. Did you ever meet Adam's mother, by the way?"

"Yes, although I don't remember her well. She was very severe, very formal, not easy to know; a bit chilling—like the Duchess of Windsor."

"A tough old bird." Roger nodded. "She held the reins in that family. *Her* father was the boss of the business, and she never let anyone forget that. I've always wondered whether Adam inherited his impersonal attitude from her—or whether he had to develop a shell to protect himself from her coldness."

"I've never noticed it." Annabel smiled.

"Surely you've noticed that, like the Ice Queen, Adam's heart is frozen and he cannot feel?"

Annabel said cheerfully, "I think Adam and his heart are wonderful!"

"But unfeeling," Roger repeated earnestly. "Adam doesn't want to feel and he despises anyone who does. He knows that to have feelings would make him vulnerable. *Any* warm impulse of his heart alarms him."

"What are you getting at?" Annabel was puzzled.

Roger started to speak faster: "The nearest Adam gets to feeling *anything* is the pursuit of power. *That's* what excites him. Adam loves money because it brings power. He can rely on money—that's why he can never get enough of it!"

"Does Adam owe you money?" Annabel asked, bewildered and a bit cross.

"Of *course* Adam owes me money—or rather my agency. Adam owes money to everyone," Roger said. "He collected a debt for us from a defaulting client, then invoiced us for rather more than he collected." He gave an unfriendly laugh. "But *that* sort of behavior doesn't worry Adam. After all, he grew up seeing that a shrewd lawyer can get away with anything."

"I don't have anything to do with Adam's business," Annabel said coldly. She stood up to leave.

Roger jumped up and caught hold of her wrist. "I shouldn't be too sure. Adam doesn't touch anything that *isn't* business."

"Let go of my wrist!"

"If you listen to me. I've heard you're very fond of Adam."

"Yes." Annabel's voice was curt.

"Be careful, Annabel. I'd hate to see you hurt. Remember how secretive Adam is. There's a reason for that."

Annabel hesitated. She felt she shouldn't listen to this man abuse Adam, but she also felt an irresistible urge, like Pandora with the box, to hear what he had to say.

"Plenty of people are secretive," she said. "Especially lawyers."

"Adam isn't secretive because he's a cautious lawyer"—Roger shook his head—"but because he's basically selfish. Adam doesn't want to share anything with anyone."

"Why are you telling *me* this?" Annabel asked again, trying to tug her wrist away.

"Because I like you. Because I don't like Adam, and I've good reason for that."

"What makes *you* such an expert on Adam?"

"You should ask him," Roger advised. "And you should remember that Adam has a nasty habit of dumping people when he has no further use for them."

Annabel said, "Perhaps you don't know that Adam and I . . . "

"Of course I know! That's why I'm telling you this. I also know about his affair with Miranda."

That was enough! She was leaving. Annabel again twisted to free herself from his grasp.

"Look, Annabel, I don't want you to be hurt." As Roger released her wrist, he looked at her sadly. "Open those beautiful eyes," he said calmly. "Please! Look at how he's using you, manipulating you. This is not something new; he's always done it—to both women and men. Believe me . . . I know."

In spite of Annabel's fury, she paused. Roger's quiet, consoling voice had the chilling ring of truth.

"I don't believe he's ever really loved anyone," Roger said. "Maybe Miranda, for a while. She's the only woman who *almost* got under Adam's guard. I suspect that was why she lasted so long. Generally Adam likes to make a woman dependent upon him, then dump her straightaway. He uses much the same technique with men."

"With men?" Annabel asked, confusion and indignation in her voice. "What do you mean?"

"Annabel, Adam is bisexual. He likes women *and* men—or maybe, more to the point, he dislikes them both equally. Either way, he seems to be masterly at sex with both. As I said, Annabel, I know."

"Surely you don't mean . . . ? Why, that's preposterous!" Annabel seemed dazed, caught between anger and shock. She stared at Roger and saw long-forgotten pain and rejection in his eyes. Desperately she turned toward the door. How *dare* Roger suggest that Adam and he . . .

Roger hurried behind her. "If you want proof, Adam has one night a week he tries to save for the boys," he said. "He usually goes to the Hilbury Arms—a pub in St. Martin's Lane—on Saturday evenings. That's the big night. And if you decide to go don't bother to show up before nine o'clock—that's when the action starts."

CHAPTER 26

Saturday, 25 January 1969

ANNABEL SPENT AN agonized afternoon racked by indecision. She was torn between her need to check on Roger's story and the need to ignore the painful seed of suspicion that he had sown. Finally, at eight o'clock that evening, the need to know won out and she took a cab to St. Martin's Lane.

In a navy mackintosh and with a navy scarf pulled down around her face, Annabel stood on the dark, rain-splashed pavement, which was almost deserted: the theater crowds were now inside, watching the plays.

Annabel looked across the road. The exterior of the Hilbury Arms was dark green; the name was painted on the facade in elaborate gold carnival lettering; the brightly lit, frosted windows looked inviting.

Hands in pockets, feet gradually growing numb from cold, Annabel stood there for over half an hour. She was frightened of her own feelings. Sexual rage and jealousy had swept over her in a violent, scarcely controllable flood of emotion that threatened to engulf her: she felt as crazy and unbalanced as when she first fell in love with Adam. Why on earth was she standing here? This was ridiculous. She kept telling herself that nothing had happened to make her doubt Adam, who was dining with a client. How could she not trust the man she loved? Why did she feel so jealous, after listening to a malicious troublemaker's spiteful gossip?

She should have refused to listen. She should go back to Adam's flat *now*.

But Annabel had to know.

The idea of never knowing the truth was worse than her jealousy. This thought propelled her across the road and through the revolving doors of the Hilbury Arms.

Someone behind Annabel said, "Excuse me," and she was pushed farther inside the pub. Nearly everybody was clustered around the long, curved mahogany bar, although there was plenty of room elsewhere. A pall of cigarette smoke almost blotted out the bitter smell of stale hops. Brass lamps with malachite glass shades hung from a ceiling gingered by smoke. A Billie Holiday recording floated words of sadness and need above the steady babble of voices.

Annabel stared about her. A group of young men in the back corner looked like any suburban boys waiting outside a cinema for their girlfriends. Some of the young men at the far end of the bar looked like art students, in black jeans and turtle sweaters; some wore black paramilitary clothes or black leather jackets; a cluster of good-looking, well-groomed men sitting on barstools might have been actors. One, a Cliff Richard look-alike with a scornful expression, snapped at anyone who drifted up to him. Annabel did not spot any other women.

She sat down shakily just inside the door. Wishing she could be invisible, she listened to the snatches of conversation. "Not much in 'ere tonight, Georgie, let's go to the Coleherne . . ." "I wouldn't mind *that* down the lockup . . . " "Eyes off, sonny, this one's mine." "Fancy a spot of . . . " "I think perhaps you're a little bit interested in my friend George. Right, squire?"

As Billie Holliday's voice continued to moan of love and irony, Adam walked in, passing Annabel without seeing her as she hid in the corner shadows. He bounded toward the bar. The boy who looked like Cliff Richard stared disdainfully at him. Adam eagerly pushed through the crowd to the boy's side. He kissed him on the lips, held him in a long caress.

On trembling legs, Annabel jumped up from her seat and dashed through the door, back into the night. Her hands shook and she felt sick. "*Bastard! Bastard! Bastard!*" she screamed as she ran along the wet pavements and the rain slashed down on her.

Sunday, 26 January 1969

Miranda slowly put her hand to her head, and felt bandages. She opened her eyes, just a crack, and saw a small, cream-colored hospital room filled with flowers.

"My headache seems to have gone," Miranda murmured to the nurse who checked her pulse. When she first recovered consciousness, the worst pain she ever felt had sizzled through her head.

Now Miranda's head seemed filled with clear, pure air. "When can I leave this place?" she whispered.

"Not yet," the nurse said firmly. "You've made good progress in the past two days, but you've had a severe concussion—and it's only been twenty-one days since your accident—"

"*Twenty-one days!*"

"Keep calm—you mustn't get excited. The doctor's instructions were to keep you sedated. You've had ten milligrams of Valium every four hours, which is why you had those swimmy daydreams as you came round, but we've been cutting it down for the last two days. That's why you're more alert this morning."

"Does my office know I'm here?"

The nurse laughed. "Your telephone calls keep our switchboard permanently occupied. Your secretary's staying at the Grand Hotel. She's posted a bodyguard outside this door, to stop the press harassing you. I'm afraid there have been a few silly stories in the tabloids."

"Damn!"

"Your sister Annabel has visited several times and telephones at least twice a day."

"I don't want to see her! Please see she isn't let in!"

"Don't get excited. You needn't see anyone you don't want to see."

"What happened to my plane? Did it catch fire? How did I get out?"

"Your plane didn't catch fire, and it's being repaired. The airport fire-and-rescue team pulled you out: they said you were lucky the door didn't stick. Your secretary has all the newspaper clippings."

"I need a telephone straightaway."

"I'm sorry, not until tomorrow. Doctor's orders."

"If you don't bring me a phone, I'm going to call the bodyguard and have him carry me to one," Miranda said. "I *must* make just a couple of calls."

After further argument, in order to calm the patient's growing agitation, the staff sister agreed that Miranda could have the telephone trolley—for fifteen minutes.

Her secretary wasn't at her hotel, so Miranda dialed Lord Brighton's number.

"Hello . . . no, James, I'm fine. Pay no attention to newspaper stories. I want to know what's happening about the EGM. What's the proxy situation?"

"The proxy votes have started to arrive, but we haven't received as many as I expected. Perhaps the shareholders are going to turn up at the EGM. . . . No, we haven't had proxies from Highland Croft Holdings, but don't let it worry you."

"How can I help worrying, James! Highland Croft Holdings will decide the vote! Their four point eight percent leaves only four point two of other voting shareholders—as Adam and I can't vote the shares we control."

"Perhaps they plan to send a representative to the meeting."

"Or perhaps they're waiting until the last minute, when they'll auction those shares—between me and Adam—for an enormous premium, on condition that Highland Croft votes for the agreed purchaser—who will, of course, not buy until after the EGM."

"That's right. If either you or Adam buys those shares *before* the meeting, then, as interested parties, you won't be able to use the votes."

Grimly Miranda said, "If Adam gets control of that block of shares, then I can kiss KITS goodbye. So *I'll* be forced to buy them, no matter what the price. I'll borrow against my existing shareholding to raise the cash."

"You're clearly recovering," Lord Brighton said. "I made sure no one would trace my query to you, but Highland Croft is *not* prepared to sell."

"They're saying that to drive the price up!"

"There's nothing to be gained by worrying. Don't forget that without you, KITS, wouldn't be nearly such an interesting proposition. Adam can't see that because he isn't objective at the moment. I assume he's so used to getting his own way that he's forgotten how to handle himself when he can't."

As Miranda replaced the telephone, a nurse entered. "You have a visitor. She's telephoned every day. A Miss Buzz."

"*Buzz! How wonderful!*"

"Only ten minutes, mind," the nurse said.

Miranda looked up at the angular figure and burst into tears.

"A fine mess *you're* in!" Buzz took Miranda's hand. "My poor girlie. Ain't seen you cry since you was six years old, when you fell out of the beech tree, remember? There, there . . . tell old Buzz about it."

"Oh, Buzz, everything is such a mess. I thought I was so clever, but I've been so stupid. I've only just realized . . ."

"Don't fret, my girlie. There's nothing that can't wait—"

"No, Buzz! *This can't wait!* . . . I should've listened to you. I think Adam *is* keeping Gran in that place—and he's stealing her money." Briefly Miranda outlined her suspicions.

"So *that's* what he's been up to with all them fancy schemes," Buzz said sourly. "Nell should have put her money in the Woolwich—that's where my salary goes: safely tucked away in a building society. . . . What are we to do, my girl?"

"Can't you get her out of there, Buzz? I don't think we should wait until I'm fit enough, and I don't trust anyone else."

Buzz brightened. "We mustn't let them have any warning. That matron could arrange a compulsory detention order, which'd keep Nell there for another month—while the nursing home tidies up its records, of course."

"Can't you sneak in and get her out somehow?"

"Not me. That matron wouldn't let *me* in again!"

Miranda stopped snuffling as a thought occurred to her. "What's the time? . . . If it's eight in the morning here, then it's late last night in Los Angeles. I'm going to phone Sam—and find out where Clare is."

Instead of the usual operator's delay, within a few minutes Miranda was connected to Sam, to whom she quickly told her story.

Sam said, "I never trusted that bastard Adam. Too smooth and agreeable. That persuasive, masterful air, that total assurance of his—all the things you women liked about him were the things that made me distrust him."

"Maybe you've had more experience with con men."

"Yeah, they're a dime a dozen on the West Coast."

"Do you know where I can find Clare?"

"Sure. I make a point of knowing what she's up to. She's gone skiing with Josh. Klosters, I think. But Clare can't handle this! She's no match for a crooked lawyer."

"Sam, you're so strong, so capable, so experienced, such a know-it-all . . ."

"Let me think. . . . Luckily, we've just finished postproduction work. I can catch a plane tomorrow. First we rescue Elinor, then we go for Adam. I'll be happy to help you do both."

Tuesday, 28 January 1969

Still wearing her yellow ski outfit and suede-soled orange socks, Clare looked around her new bakery with satisfaction. David had designed the extension, built onto the side of the kitchen. Next to the two professional ovens were slatted cooling shelves.

A month of Swiss sunshine had tanned Clare's skin, and her aquamarine eyes sparkled. She glowed with health after her first proper holiday in four years; she had enjoyed every minute of it.

Clare returned to the kitchen, pulled a cheese tart from the refrigerator, and put it in the oven to warm for lunch. Through the back window, she could see the new toboggan that David had bought in Klosters. After school, Josh and his gang would take it up on the snow-covered hill behind the cottage.

Clare now had a luxurious, five-hour period before she started to prepare for that night's baking. She wandered into the sitting room and put a record on the stereo David had given her for her thirtieth birthday. Somewhat guiltily, she enjoyed the peaceful feeling of being alone in the cottage. She sat down and put her feet up on the brass fender before the log fire. As she dreamily watched the crackling flames, she listened to the music and thought—not for the first time—how much luckier she was than Louis XIV. Louis may have been the Sun King and all France may have trembled at his frown, but he couldn't listen to Maria Callas in his bath. Nor could he survey the world from fourteen thousand feet up in the air. And Louis XIV had never had the chance to ski. . . .

The doorbell shrilled.

Clare stood up, thinking, if it's a Jehovah's Witness, I'll scream. She opened the door.

"*Sam! What the hell d'you think you're doing here?*"

"Let me inside and I'll tell you." Sam was shivering. "Miranda called me from the hospital."

"*What's wrong with Miranda?*"

"Everything's okay, but she crashed her plane."

"Was she badly hurt? Where is she? Who's looking after her?"

"Look, could I *please* come inside?" Sam shivered again. "She'll be out of the hospital soon. I spoke to her this morning. You can call her yourself this afternoon. I'm surprised you haven't heard about the crash—it even made the L.A. *Times*."

After a battery of anxious questions about her sister, Clare explained, "I haven't seen a newspaper for nearly a month. We got back yesterday evening—two days late because of an airport strike. I haven't even read my mail yet."

Clare stood aside ungraciously as Sam stepped into the house; then she led the way to her living room.

"Where's Josh?" Sam asked.

"You can't see him this evening," Clare said curtly. "He's going to tea with a friend and then it's Cubs night."

"I can wait," Sam said, determined to be pleasant. "You look terrific."

Coldly antagonistic, Clare glared at the man who had cheated on her, and who, for almost four years, had refused her a divorce, all the while providing no child support.

"How about some coffee?" Sam suggested, warming his hands at the fire.

"No coffee," Clare said. She wondered what Sam had done to himself: he looked years younger than the last time she'd seen him.

Noticing her surreptitious look, Sam grinned. "Yes, I've taken myself in hand. For my no-flour diet, deduct two years; for no-more-vodka resolution, deduct four years; for exercise bicycle, deduct four years; for new teeth, deduct two years; for smart haircut, deduct one year; for well-cut pants and shirt, deduct two years."

"I'm not interested," Clare said acidly. "Say what you've come to say, and then get out."

Sam said, "You *will* be interested." Briefly he outlined Adam's treachery, Elinor's plight, and the trust problem.

"*Are you telling me that Gran has been in a nursing home for nearly a year and my sisters didn't let me know?*"

"Don't take it out on me, Clare. I'm the one that's just flown halfway around the world to do something about it."

"*Where's Gran? I must see her.*"

"There's a limo and a driver waiting outside to take you wherever you want to go, but first I have to talk to you. How long is it since you saw Elinor?"

Clare said brusquely, "July 1965, at Saracen."

"You mean you haven't seen Elinor for almost four years?" Sam was astonished.

"I tried," Clare said uneasily. "I wrote to Gran several times, but my letters were always answered by Adam. He said he was sorry to write formally but he had been instructed by his client that she wished no communication to take place . . . that sort of thing."

"I bet Elinor asked Adam to check you were okay. I bet she wanted a reunion. And I bet Adam covered his ass nicely."

"His letters put my back up."

"They were meant to," Sam said. "But how come Buzz didn't get in touch with you, behind Elinor's back—or in front of it?"

Clare, ashamed, said, "Buzz did try. I don't know how she found out where I was, but she turned up one evening, just after I'd moved into my basement flat. I'd had a tough day at the shoe shop—one woman took three hours to buy one pair of shoes. Buzz started telling me to be a good girl and apologize to Gran. I'm afraid I yelled at her and told her fairly forcibly to go. Then she tried to give me money she hid in an envelope—and that convinced me she was really coming from Gran."

"And Buzz never tried to contact you again?" Sam asked.

Clare answered reluctantly: "Yes. . . . She telephoned several times. I'm afraid that I . . . I thought she was Gran's spy, you see? Every time she spoke to me, Buzz said I should think of Josh and not cut off my nose to spite my face and . . . I was determined not to slink back to you with my tail between my legs, as you all thought I would. I was determined to show I could stand on my own feet and live my own life. I wasn't a little girl to be pushed around." She glared at Sam.

He sighed. "Buzz always said you were as stubborn as Elinor . . . "

"If you've come here to—"

Hastily Sam said, "Sorry! But didn't Miranda or Annabel contact you then?"

Clare hesitated, then admitted, "Yes, they did—but with amazing lack of tact! Annabel was feeling sorry for herself on the other side of the Atlantic. And Miranda's face seemed to grin out of every paper I picked up—and everything she was doing was *exactly* what I was trying *not* to do!" Again she glared at Sam. "I don't think you have *any idea* how difficult it was for me—with no employable skills—to earn my own living and look after Josh."

"I promise we'll talk about that after I tell you why I'm here." Sam then outlined Miranda's plan to remove Elinor from the nursing home. Persuasively he ended, "The nursing staff have never seen you, Clare, and they've never seen me, and they can't refuse to let us in if we turn up on the doorstep—on an unexpected business trip to England—with our passports to prove who we are. We're Elinor's blood relatives."

Clare said hesitantly, "Of course I want to see Gran as fast as possible, and I'll do anything to make her happy. But . . . have you any proof of this wild story? You said that Miranda has a concussion. Are you sure she wasn't a bit delirious when she told you this?"

"Don't forget Buzz," Sam reminded her. "She was the first person to become suspicious of Adam *and* of the nursing home, but nobody listened to her. Call Buzz if you like—she's with Miranda."

After she telephoned Buzz, Clare's reticence immediately disappeared. She said, "Eastbourne isn't far from here. Buzz says the best time to remove Gran is probably in the early afternoon, when there are visitors around and the staff won't want to make a fuss. Let's leave now."

CHAPTER 27

Tuesday, 28 January 1969

"I'M STILL WORRIED . . ." Clare said, seated in the back of Sam's swiftly moving rented Bentley. She had changed from her ski clothes to a respectable navy suit.

"I don't want to push you. The final decision is yours—and so is the responsibility," Sam said firmly. "She isn't *my* grandmother. I know nothing about British medical law, but I *do* know that possession is nine tenths of the law."

Clare stared out at the snow-covered landscape. "I never thought I'd miss her so much. Before her illness, Gran was the rock of our family; she seemed so strong and permanent—always there to look after us. After our . . . disagreement . . . there was a hole in my life. And it will never be filled. I just know it."

Sam said, "Will you stop talking as if Elinor's dead? Now it's *your* turn to look after her. That's all."

Eventually the Bentley turned off the road and passed between snow-encrusted, elaborate back gates and up a curving drive.

Sam glanced at the white columns of the mansion before him. With a note of doubt in his voice, he said, "This place doesn't look like a prison." The mansion looked as immaculately cared for as a rich child's dollhouse. On either side of the building stood snow-capped yew hedges; icicles dripped from the branches of old cedar trees; beyond them, white lawns sloped toward a dismal gray smudge, the English Channel.

In the warm, walnut-paneled entrance hall, Sam felt increasingly uneasy; he and Clare sat on a burgundy brocade sofa while the sandy-haired receptionist went to fetch Matron Braddock.

Matron Braddock entered, wrapped in a navy uniform that made her appear that much more formidable. She did not mention that she had just tried unsuccessfully to contact Mr. Grant by telephone, but instead politely asked Sam for proof of identity. In her charming voice, she explained, "We have to be careful. Many journalists have tried to see Mrs. O'Dare. You'd never believe the lies."

"Yes I would," Sam said, "I work in Hollywood." He produced two passports from his pocket. "We're glad the old lady is being well protected."

Having checked the passports, the matron briefly informed the Shapiros of Elinor's condition, but would give no prognosis or details of her treatment: that could only be discussed with Mrs. O'Dare's doctors.

Clare gasped when she saw her grandmother's gaunt, pale face; white-haired, with eyes closed, Elinor lay motionless on the metal hospital bed.

Clare ran forward and knelt by the bedside. "Gran, Gran darling . . . Can she hear me?" She looked up at the matron.

"She's sleeping," Matron Braddock said. "Her after-lunch nap."

"We'll wait until she wakes up," Clare said decisively. "She looks so frail," she added, fighting tears as she noticed, on the bedside table, silver-framed photographs of Billy, Edward, and the three sisters in their best party dresses at Starlings.

She turned to Sam. "I expect you'll be more comfortable in Gran's sitting room next door, darling, but I want to sit quietly with her."

"Can I offer you afternoon tea?" the matron asked pleasantly.

"Do you have any coffee?" Sam asked equally pleasantly, as he moved toward the interconnecting door. "And can someone ask my driver to bring my briefcase?" He wanted Steve, the driver-cum-bodyguard, to see the layout of the nursing home.

"Mrs. O'Dare might be asleep for quite a long time," the matron warned Clare.

"I don't mind a long wait," Clare said sweetly as she settled in the chair opposite Elinor's bed; behind Clare, the locked glass doors of the French window faced the snowy garden.

Just before four o'clock, Matron Braddock returned.

"I do hope Gran wakes soon," Clare said, "because we'll have to leave shortly. Sam has to get back to our hotel to take his L.A. business calls."

"I don't like to disturb Mrs. O'Dare if it isn't necessary."

"Of course not," Clare reassured her. "We can visit her again before we leave England."

When the coffee tray was removed, Clare rapped on the connecting door, her signal to Sam. He hurried to stand guard in the corridor, ready to loudly ask his way to the john should anyone appear.

Clare gently tried to shake Elinor awake.

She did not respond.

Clare shook harder.

Elinor made no movement.

Clare tried to pull her upright into a sitting position. Elinor's head flopped back, and her arms dangled like a rag doll's.

Quickly Clare rearranged her grandmother, smoothed the bedclothes, and went into the corridor. "Gran's certainly not asleep," she whispered to Sam. "She must be drugged."

"I told Steve to stretch his legs—take a walk around the grounds while it's still light enough to see," Sam said. He looked at his watch. "We'd better start before it gets dark." He joined Clare in the bedroom and pressed Elinor's bedside bell.

When Matron Braddock reappeared, Clare bent over her silent grandmother and kissed her forehead. She and Sam then followed the matron from the room.

As they moved slowly along the corridor toward the entrance hall, the matron looked at Sam. "You've forgotten your briefcase, haven't you? I'll get it for you."

"So I have! Stupid of me. No trouble." Sam turned and moved swiftly back along the corridor.

He snatched up his briefcase and quickly locked both doors leading from Elinor's suite to the corridor, shoving the keys in his pocket. He grabbed some pink blankets from the bureau in the bedroom, pulled aside the high invalid's table on casters that stretched across the end of Elinor's bed, then yanked back the brocade curtains.

Steve's pale face and pale blue eyes appeared outside.

Sam nodded.

Steve pulled up his coat collar, checked his leather driving gloves, walked back ten paces, then charged the window, turning his left shoulder toward it as he reached it.

With loud cracks like pistol shots, the doors caved inward. Glass flew everywhere, and a blast of icy air swept into the bedroom. Steve backed through the shattered doors into the room.

Sam heaved a pink armchair in front of the connecting door the to the sitting room and yanked the bedclothes from Elinor's bed.

Steve wrapped Elinor in a pink blanket, threw her over his shoulder in a fireman's lift, and disappeared through the smashed doors into the darkness. He was followed closely by Sam, who couldn't see a thing and didn't know where Steve had parked the car.

Panting, the two men ran through the snow. Steve, the first to reach the Bentley, yanked the back door open and, propping the pink bundle on the back seat, jumped in the driving seat and switched on the ignition and lights. Then he hit the horn three times in fast succession.

Sam threw himself into the back of the car and fell on top of the pink bundle. He leaned across and flung open the far door. Clare should have been running toward it.

But Clare was nowhere to be seen.

Sam panted, "If we're held up, Steve, you take off." He ran through the snow to the front steps of the nursing home, then slowed down to walk calmly through the entrance doors.

In the middle of the hall, Clare was struggling with Matron Braddock. Sam dodged past them, grabbed the screaming receptionist, and flung her at a white-coated male orderly who was running toward the matron. The orderly tried to dodge the outflung arms of the receptionist, lost his footing on the highly polished parquet, and fell to the floor.

Sam threw his right arm around the matron's neck and yanked it backward to pull her away from Clare. The matron gasped and tried to twist her body from Sam's grasp, but she did not let go of Clare.

The orderly scrambled to his feet, leapt forward, and kicked Sam in the kidneys. Sam jerked violently back, pulling the matron with him. As she fell, she released her grip on Clare.

"Get out fast, Clare!" Sam roared.

As Clare scrambled up and ran in stockinged feet toward the glass front door, the orderly raced after her, but she managed to escape. Outside, however, Clare stumbled in the darkness and fell down the stone steps beyond the front door. The man caught up and threw himself upon her.

In the hall, Matron Braddock had twisted so that she was on top of Sam, who was now lying on his back. Fighting like a man, she did her best to gouge his eyes out. Sam managed to pull his right fist back and smash it upward. He felt it strike bone, heard a grunt, and was suddenly able to see again. Half crouched in pain, he staggered toward the front door.

Just beyond the stone steps, the man in the white coat was grappling with Clare. Sam jumped to the bottom of the steps, drew his foot back, and kicked. The man grunted and fell sideways on the snow.

"Get to the car!" Sam yelled, thrusting his hand out to help her.

Together, they ran to the already moving Bentley. Sam shoved Clare into the back, then threw himself on top of her. As they sorted themselves out, the Bentley turned out of the main gates and picked up speed.

"Darling Sam!" Clare flung her arms around him.

The secretary of the Lord Willington Nursing Home did not know how to contact someone on a cruise liner in the Caribbean. She telephoned the travel agent who had arranged Dr. Craig-Dunlop's trip. He advised her to call the cruise liner's London office.

The agitated deputy matron fluttered around the telephone. She said again, "Tell them it's urgent!"

The secretary put her hand over the mouthpiece. "It's not that easy, Sister Parks. We have to contact the *Antigone* through some radio station in Somerset—the main shore-to-ship station. They say it'll take at least a few hours to reach the doctor."

"A few hours!" Nurse Parks twittered.

The secretary explained, "The radio station has to request an emergency appointment with the doctor, giving the callback frequency. Once that's been done, the doctor can speak to you from the ship's radio room. You'll just have to wait, Sister Parks."

In the casualty department of the King Edward VII Hospital, Eastbourne, Matron Braddock sat waiting for treatment. Her left arm had been put in a sling to relieve the pressure; it was painful and swelling fast; she couldn't move her fingers. The break was just above the wrist.

The matron's arm throbbed badly, but she decided not to ask for painkillers. She could take more pain than most people, and at the moment, she needed a clear head. As she waited for her arm to be X-rayed, Ivy Braddock carefully considered her position—and her options.

What did she have to lose? A great deal.

Mrs. O'Dare had been removed from the nursing home in what was clearly a carefully planned operation. Mr. Shapiro did not seem the sort of man to let the matter rest, especially since she had hit him: Matron Braddock remembered blood streaming from his mouth.

If the police were called in, she might be arrested. She might even stand trial.

Whether or not she was convicted of helping to restrain a patient for illegal purposes, after the resultant publicity she would certainly never again be able to get another good nursing job in Britain.

The only thing that frightened the matron more than the prospect of discussing

Mrs. O'Dare with the police was discussing her with Mr. Grant. Matron Braddock had sensed the violence and vengeance that were part of Mr. Grant's temperament. Of course, he couldn't get any money back from her, but she was frightened of his retribution, whatever it might be.

The matron considered blackmailing Dr. Craig-Dunlop. She rejected this idea only because the doctor was in a position to counterblackmail her.

There was really only one thing for Matron Ivy Braddock to do.

Back in the comforting serenity of Applebank Cottage, Clare sat beside Sam in front of the fire and stared into the flames. She hadn't been able to contact Annabel, but Miranda and Buzz had been thrilled to hear the news of Elinor's rescue. It had been difficult to stop Buzz from traveling over that night to look after her old friend.

Elinor was sleeping in the spare room; Steve, the driver, was staying at the Bath Arms; and Sam—who had insisted on sticking around—said he'd sleep on the living room sofa.

Six-year-old Josh, too excited by the arrival of his father to be able to sleep, kept coming down in his pajamas to ask for a glass of water. Every time he appeared, Clare felt the usual pangs of guilt. Yet again she worried whether Josh would prefer to live alone with a happy mother, or with his father and an unhappy mother.

"Now that the fuss has died down," Sam said, "what happened to *you?*"

"I didn't expect to hear that crash—I suppose you broke the French window. I panicked and started to run toward the front door. That damned matron tried to stop me. I honestly can't remember much about it. I'm sorry—I know I should have waited for the three toots."

Sam grinned. "If you'd just looked surprised, she'd have rushed to investigate and then you could have simply walked out of the front door, as planned."

"Things didn't happen as planned."

"No," Sam said. He paused for a moment before adding, "They almost never do, do they?"

Clare thought how strange it was that the animosity between them had dissolved. For nearly four years, she had bitterly resented Sam's ability to thwart her and been resentful of his power. She remembered Gilda, who had worked with her at the Chelsea shoe shop, saying long ago. "Don't tell *me* you've fallen out of love with that husband of yours! If you had, you'd be indifferent, you wouldn't give a damn about him."

As Sam watched the firelight flicker on Clare's small, neat features, he thought: This is the moment to give it my last try. Aloud he said softly, "I don't know how to say this . . . I want to say I'm sorry I've been such a bastard. I reckoned if I didn't give you any money, and I didn't let you have any evidence, and I didn't let you divorce me, then you'd come back to me."

"That's the way you train dogs, not wives," Clare said tartly.

"Okay. I was wrong. I admit it."

"Thanks," Clare replied bitterly. She added, "I've never understood why you won't let me go. What's the difference between me and your other ex-wives?"

"Josh, for a start."

"I realize that no other man can replace a father—not even a bad one," Clare said, still bitter. "But that's not enough reason to return to you. I have my life to lead. I am not merely Josh's mother."

"I never expected you to be able to manage on your own. I really admire you for that. . . . This bakery is a great idea. You could build it into a chain. Even the name's right." Clare had called her business ABUNDANCE.

Clare said, "I've no intention of building it up into a chain. That's how a man *would* see a successful business! I've looked into men's territory and I didn't like what I saw. I don't want the worry of a big business. I don't want that treadmill! I just want to enjoy my little business and do something useful while I earn my living." She pushed her dark hair out of her eyes and added, "I don't want the sort of life that Miranda leads. It was relatively easy for me to leave for four weeks in Switzerland—but I bet Miranda can't just drop everything and go skiing."

Sam tried a new tack. "I never realized how much I enjoyed being with you—until you'd gone, Clare. And I miss Josh every single goddamn day." Persuasively he continued, "Clare, won't you let me have *one* more chance? Remember that Josh is *our* son, not just yours." He saw Clare wince and pressed on what was clearly her Achilles' heel. "Clare, we *both* should be deciding what's best for Josh."

"You forgot that Josh was your son when it came to paying the bills for him!" Clare cried. "You didn't seem to care *then* what was best for Josh. Don't talk to me of reconciliation. Our marriage clearly wasn't important to you!"

Sam looked into her eyes. "I promise you, Clare, that our marriage *is* important to me. Would I have dropped everything and flown halfway around the world to rescue your grandmother if that weren't the case?"

"I'm grateful. But not that grateful," Clare said. Briefly she remembered. "You had your squalid little adventures, Sam. You thought that what I didn't know wouldn't hurt me. Well, it didn't hurt me, but—I told you before—*it hurt our marriage.* Instead of protecting the ship we were building, you deliberately screwed holes in it—and then looked surprised when it leaked."

"But it hasn't sunk."

"You've been trying to get me into bed ever since we got back here. I remember your tactics. But if you and I made love, it would legally wipe out the last three and a half years. In ten minutes, we would be legally reconciled, so if it didn't work, I'd have to start all over again—and, incidentally, the lawyer's bills would start again. So I can't risk it, even if I wanted to, *which I don't*. I'm in love with another man!" Clare thought she might as well let him have it between the eyes. "I now have a very happy, steady relationship with a thoughtful, gentle, concerned lover."

Sam said, "And would this thoughtful, gentle, concerned lover of yours have had the guts to smash jaws for your grandmother?"

At seven the next morning, when it was still dark, Josh crept into bed beside Clare and said, "I fink she's woken up."

Clare leapt out of bed and listened outside the spare room door. She heard weak sobbing. She entered and switched on the light.

Elinor turned toward the door, her thin fingers clutching the sheet. "Clare!" she whispered in surprise. "Where am I? How wonderful to see you, dear child."

Clare knelt by the bedside, took the frail blue-veined hands in hers, and kissed them. "You're safe now, darling. This is where I live. You're never going back to that dreadful place again. Buzz is coming to help me look after you."

"Clare, I've missed you so much."

"And I've missed you. I've been stupid and stubborn."

"So have I."

"I'm so sorry, darling Gran. Will you forgive me?"

"If you forgive me."

"Let's not waste any more time, not one more day."

"Not one more day," whispered Elinor as Clare bent to hug her.

Almost weeping, Clare felt she had to explain. "Darling, if you'd answered any of my letters, I would have come rushing to you. I wrote you sad letters, angry letters, and self-pitying letters. But Adam made it clear that you would only see me after I had made a formal apology. I felt more hurt each time he told me."

Elinor whispered, "I wish I'd known. I missed you so. And I missed Josh."

Clare felt remorseful. Elinor had missed three and a half years of the life of her only great-grandchild, who looked so like Daddy Billy's boyhood photos.

Elinor stroked Clare's hair. "But none of it matters now. All that matters is that we're together again."

At ten o'clock, the doctor left Elinor, after prescribing a low dosage of Valium during the next few days while she was weaned from her medication and detoxified.

Just after his departure, Clare answered insistent rings at the front door. Miranda stood on the doorstep, her head still bandaged. Behind her was Buzz.

Speechless, Clare held out her arms to her sister: they hugged in silence.

"How's Nell?" Buzz asked urgently.

"She's going to be fine, especially now that you're both here," Clare said.

After a happy, tearful reunion at Elinor's bedside, they left her to rest.

As the three women drank coffee in the kitchen, Miranda looked puzzled. "Clare darling, I never understood why you were broke. Adam told us you were getting an income from the trust, but that you wouldn't see Gran, and wanted nothing to do with Annabel or me because we sided with Gran."

"Adam told *me* that you and Annabel didn't want to see me," Clare said. "And I didn't get a penny from the trust—my allowance stopped as soon as I left Saracen."

Briefly Miranda wondered how she could ever have allowed herself to care for Adam. She said, "We've got to nail him, fast."

"Sam's on the phone discussing it with some London lawyers."

"I wish I could be more help," Miranda said. "But I'm still getting bad headaches and it's hard for me to concentrate. I'm also having trouble with my memory—I can't remember a thing about my crash."

Hearing a car draw up outside, Clare glanced casually past the pots of geraniums on the window ledge. "What's a London taxi doing here?"

Buzz peered out the window. "Cor, I do believe that's Annabel."

"No, it can't be," Clare said. "Goodness . . . what a wonderful coincidence!"

Miranda darted to the kitchen window and, as Clare ran along the passage to the front door, called angrily to her, "You can't expect *me* to believe this is a coincidence! How *dare* you arrange this!"

Bewildered, Clare turned and said, "What's the matter? I haven't seen Frog for almost four years! I haven't arranged anything."

"Oh, no? Do you expect me to believe that on the first day I see you in over three years, Annabel just *happens* to show up? How dare you try to fix up this clumsy reconciliation behind my back."

"Oh, do shut up, Miranda. I haven't a clue what you're talking about. What *is* your problem?" Clare asked crossly. "Or are you still feeling the effects of your accident?"

"Not at all," Miranda said angrily. "And if you open that door to her, I swear I'm leaving!"

"Stop that! You've always had a flair for dramatics, but this is not the time," Clare said. "Look, I don't know what's happened between the two of you, but you'll just have to sort it out fast. This is too important." She moved forward and opened the front door.

Standing on the doorstep, Annabel burst into tears. "Oh Clare, you *are* here! I was afraid I might have been given an old address. It's so *good* to see you again! I've missed you so!"

"Come inside quickly, darling!" Clare shivered against the cold as she tugged Annabel, babbling happily, along the passage and into the warm kitchen.

Annabel abruptly stopped chattering when she saw Miranda.

Miranda glared. "I don't know how you have the gall to show your face here!"

Annabel sobbed, "Oh, Miranda, you don't know what's happened . . . Adam didn't love me . . . "

"Oh, I knew *that*," Miranda said stonily.

"He didn't love either of us . . . "

"What *are* you talking about?" Clare asked.

Miranda said, "Adam's been having a love affair with me for several years, and with both me *and* Annabel for several months."

"*Both* of you?" Clare looked astonished. "*Adam!* I can't believe it!"

"It's worse than that," Annabel sobbed. "Adam likes *boys*, too!"

The other three women were stunned into silence. Buzz raised her arms in a perplexed gesture.

Then Miranda said contemptuously, "Annabel, you must be out of your mind!"

"No, believe me. I didn't want to accept it either, so I went to a pub where homosexuals hang out. I was told Adam would be there, and he was. I wish . . . I've tried . . . to pretend to myself that I imagined it. *But I know I didn't.* Roger told me Adam's always been like that—so if you don't believe me, ask *him.*"

"Roger who?" Miranda snapped.

"Sonia's nephew. The Roger who taught us all the twist," Annabel said.

Miranda was scornful. "Everyone in London knows that Roger's that way. Plenty of men are. I know some of my friends are *but not Adam.*"

"Yes he is!" Annabel insisted, and again started to cry. "I know how you feel—because I know how I felt. And there was nobody I could talk to about it—nobody I could really trust, who could explain what was going on. I felt so lonely."

"I'm going to phone Roger," Clare decided. "Do you have his number?"

Annabel nodded. Buzz hurried over and hugged her. "My poor lamb."

Clare returned to a silent kitchen. A tearful Annabel sat at the kitchen table staring. From the other side, Miranda scowled suspiciously at Annabel.

"Roger says it's true." Clare spoke quietly. "And I believe him. He and Adam had . . . well . . . a fling some time back. He said he wasn't Adam's first either."

Miranda burst into tears.

Clare said gently, "Annabel, why don't you telephone Scott?"

All the misery she felt was in Annabel's expressive eyes. "I can't . . . I feel . . . too much of a fool." She started to weep again. "I said terrible things to Scott . . . I've made such a fool of myself."

Miranda lifted her head and painfully admitted, "I think we've both made fools of ourselves. But don't be too proud to admit to Scott that you lost your head over a man who doesn't give a damn about you. I know Scott still loves you. Phone him."

Annabel hesitated, then nodded. "All right, I will. But it's five in the morning in New York."

"I should wait a bit, until you're feeling calmer," Clare suggested.

Humbly Annabel said, "Thank you for saying that, Miranda." But she knew she had to say more than that, to start to repair the wound she had slashed in her relationship with Miranda. She knew what she ought to say—but she hesitated. Then Annabel forced herself to say the two words that have, in their time, undoubtedly altered history and the destiny of the human race—two simple words that those who wish to hear them find so easy to expect yet those who wish to say them find so difficult to deliver. Slowly and painfully Annabel said, "I'm sorry, Miranda."

Miranda hesitated, then said. "Thank you. I'm sorry too. Now let's forget it. We've all been hurt by Adam."

"I think we all need a strong cup of tea," Buzz suggested, "before we start repairing the damage Adam's caused. That man had you three exactly where he wanted you!"

As Buzz put the kettle on, Clare said, puzzled, "What I don't understand is why Adam should want to cut me off from my family."

"I think I know," Miranda said. "I also know why he put Gran in that vile place. Adam has been siphoning money away from the trust, using some method that's legal; this has probably taken longer than a straightforward theft. If so, it would explain why Adam separated us and encouraged us to quarrel. He did it to distract us—while he quietly embezzled our money."

"*What?* But I don't understand—if he's stealing the money, why were we sent those huge checks?" Annabel asked.

"What we had was a drop in the ocean, compared to the total," Miranda said. "And while Adam was so kindly arranging for us to have as much money as we wanted, it never occurred to us that he was stealing the rest."

The three sisters looked sadly at each other in silence: all felt cheated, humiliated, and angry.

"I feel such a fool," Annabel said quietly.

Clare nodded. "Me too."

"You aren't alone," Miranda said wryly. "I could kick myself when I remember the *acres* of print I've read about my hotshot business brain. How *could* I have been so gullible for so long?" She did not complicate the situation by adding that Adam was fighting her for control of her business.

"I'd better telephone the Bath Arms," Clare said. "We have only one spare room and Gran's sleeping in it. Sam's sleeping on the sitting room sofa."

"And where's Josh?" Miranda asked, suddenly remembering.

"At school," Clare said. She hoped that her son had not forgotten his aunts.

Miranda said, "Does Josh like being in the country? *You* seem a lot less anxious, more relaxed."

"Yes, Josh loves it. And I'm happy with my life."

"We can see you are," Annabel said wistfully.

"You look much better, Annabel," Clare said quickly. "When your face was thinner, it looked elegant, but . . . you look far prettier now."

Miranda nodded. "Clare's right. Sickening to see you look so ravishing without one spot of makeup!"

Annabel wrinkled her tiny nose and said in a pleased voice, "Do you *really* think so?"

When her sisters had taken their baggage to the local inn, Clare told Sam what they had discussed.

"Don't kick yourself too hard," Sam said. "It sounds as if Adam is an experienced con man, and like all of them, he knows how to flatter women and gain their confidence. The bastard's good-looking, charming, sophisticated, and self-assured. He zeroed in on each of your vulnerable areas; he pressed the buttons of your insecurities; he had you all running around in circles, doing exactly what he wanted. Now you must stop reacting and start acting. Now we have to strike back."

Clare said, "Adam doesn't know he's been rumbled. We'd better let him think that we're still quarreling with each other."

"Our weak point there is Annabel. Where does Adam think she's been for the last few days?"

"I've no idea. Ask her."

Later, Annabel explained. "I couldn't face Adam . . . or speak to him . . . after I saw him with that boy. So I wrote a note, said I was coming down with flu and didn't want him to catch it, and was going to a health farm for a week—of course, no health farm would have let me in with flu, but it was the first lie that jumped into my mind. In fact, I stayed at the Park Lane and sat in my bedroom shaking and crying, until I thought to phone Sam's secretary to get Clare's address."

At six o'clock that evening, Clare went to deliver a fresh loaf of bread to a woman in bed with arthritis. She refused Sam's offer to drive her, saying that it was only a short trip and she wanted some fresh air. While she was away, Sam could put Josh to bed.

Josh, who at six considered himself too old to be bathed by his mother, was thrilled to let Sam bathe him.

When the cork floor of the bathroom was awash with water, Sam, in his shirtsleeves, went down to the kitchen for a mop. As a key turned in the front door, he called out, "Clare? I've managed to get Josh *into* the bath, but it's not so easy to get him out."

Hearing an unexpectedly heavy tread, Sam looked up just as the best-looking man he had ever seen stooped to avoid the lintel over the kitchen door.

"Where's Clare?" David asked casually.

"My wife is out," Sam said equally casually. Clare hadn't mentioned that this son of a bitch looked like the hero of a spaghetti western.

The two men stared at each other in silence, like dogs, stiff-legged, sniffing each other before a fight.

So *this* was why Clare hadn't phoned him as usual yesterday evening, David thought. When he'd rung her, the line had always been engaged. The big man with dark curly hair and his shirtsleeves rolled up over muscular arms seemed more of a charmer than David had expected. He looked friendly, easy to talk to.

"If you're David, why don't you get the hell out of here?" Sam said, making the situation clear. He added, "If you want to see my wife, come back another day. There's a lot going on here." Sam knew that, without Romeo hanging around, he could operate much more effectively on Clare. He'd better get the bastard out before she returned.

"As I came to see Clare, I'll wait till she gets back." David had phoned late that afternoon to find out why he hadn't heard from Clare; Josh answered and, totally overexcited by the presence of so many relatives, explained that his daddy had arrived. David had come to see what was going on.

Sam said, "Clare and I have a lot to talk about. You're in the way." He took an aggressive step toward David, who did not retreat.

"I'll wait for Clare," David repeated. "If Clare wants me to leave, then she can say so."

They both heard Josh yell from the bathroom, "Dad, where's the *mop!*"

"I'll be up in a minute, son," Sam yelled back. To David he said, "I want you *out* of here, *now!*"

From the darkness outside, both men heard the garden gate wheeze open and the asthmatic twang of a bicycle bell.

Whistling, Clare opened the back door to the kitchen to find Sam and David now staring at each other with the alert, focused, intent expression of two wrestlers about to pounce.

"David! *What's happened?*" Clare exclaimed.

"Nothing yet," Sam said, not taking his eyes off David.

"Why didn't you tell me he was coming?" said David without taking his eyes off Sam.

"Because it's none of your goddamn business!" Sam roared.

"Because I didn't expect him," Clare said. "I tried to ring you this morning, but you were out."

"Does this guy have to stay?" Sam asked.

"Do you want me to go, Clare?" David asked, equally truculent.

"Stop it, both of you!" Clare ordered. "You're behaving like five-year-olds."

"Get the hell out of here," Sam growled to David. "You're in the way. There's no reason for you to stay."

"Yes there is. I want to marry Clare," David said.

"You've never once said so!" Clare cried.

"Clare happens to be married already." Sam glared.

Josh appeared, naked and dripping, in the doorway from the hall. He took no notice of David or Clare but, hero worship imprinted on his face, ran straight to Sam, who swung him up in his arms and hugged him.

"You haven't finished my barf." Josh gave Sam a sloppy kiss.

"Well, will you?" David asked Clare. "Marry me, I mean?"

Hesitantly Clare looked from one man to the other.

CHAPTER 28

Thursday, 30 January 1969

A*FTER A RESTLESS NIGHT,* Elinor woke early. Buzz made her a cup of tea and provided a cheerful stream of gossip about her cruise with Bertha Higby.

Then Elinor asked how things were at Saracen.

Buzz hesitated.

Elinor whispered, "*What's happened?*"

Eventually Buzz said, "That Adam, he sold it."

"*Sold my home?*"

"Someone had to tell you sometime, Nell."

Elinor said nothing, but two tears rolled down her cheeks. Finally she whispered, "What's happened to the staff?"

"Oh, they was well looked after, that I will say! I don't know what's happened to 'em all, because I ain't been back yet."

"At least we're all together again," Elinor murmured. "That's the most important thing."

Buzz comforted her for the next two hours, answering Elinor's halting questions about events of the past year. When it was nearly time for Clare to appear with the breakfast tray, Elinor dried her eyes and tried to look cheerful.

When a smiling Clare arrived, she said, "Annabel and Miranda have gone to London for the day, on business."

"Is it about Adam?"

"Yes."

"He's stolen my money, hasn't he?"

"Don't you tell her no lies," Buzz said.

Hesitantly Clare replied, "It might not all have gone. We don't know yet. But even if it *has* disappeared, you'll still have an income from future book sales."

"If I get any of the money back, I want it divided equally between the five of us," Elinor said weakly. "I should have done that in the first place."

At about the same time, Dr. Craig-Dunlop, wearing a Paisley silk dressing gown and pajamas, left the stateroom and reported to the radio room, where he was shown how to use the receiver.

The little doctor's black-fringed eyes widened as he listened to the faint but agitated voice of Sister Parks, his deputy matron.

"Calm down, Sister Parks," he said when he could get a word in. "If I understand correctly, some relatives of Mrs. O'Dare have removed her from the nursing home, but you do not know whether or not this was with her consent. It's certainly without *our* consent, and we therefore cannot be responsible for what happens to Mrs. O'Dare. That is our official attitude, Sister Parks." His calm, firm voice obviously reassured her, for she seemed less agitated. "Has Mr. Grant been informed? No? Splendid! As Mrs. O'Dare has been removed by her own relatives, who produced proof of their identity before they did so, I can see no reason to inform Mr. Grant until I return. . . . Yes, naturally I'll come back straightaway."

He thought swiftly. The cruise ship was due to arrive in Jamaica on Friday afternoon, in some thirty hours. God knows how long it would take him to get back to England from Kingston. He might have to hang around until he could get a seat on a plane to New York. There he might have a further long wait: flights to London didn't leave every five minutes. He said, "I'll get back as soon as I can, Sister Parks, but my arrival depends on connections and availability of seats. I won't be there for at least two days—probably longer. I suspect the earliest you'll see me is Sunday evening . . . Yes, the second of February."

When Sister Parks had brought him fully up-to-date, the doctor concluded, "As for Matron Braddock, she did the most extraordinary thing. Completely cleared out her room, went off in a taxi, without a word to anyone, and she left with a broken arm. Perhaps Matron Braddock also had slight concussion after her unfortunate fall. Perhaps officially we had better say that Matron is taking a long-overdue holiday and that we expect her return at the end of the month. There is no need to say more than that to anyone."

He gave a little cough. "Because of Mrs. O'Dare's notoriety, you may hear from newspaper snoopers. Do not speak to strangers, Sister Parks. Tell Patricia to be very careful when she answers my telephone. Give *no* information to *anyone* about Mrs. O'Dare, except for my lawyer. I think it wise to inform him of this exasperating incident as soon as possible, and I would appreciate it if you give him the details. Now I want to speak to Orderly Gibson . . . Well, *get him!*" The doctor started to bite his left thumbnail.

After an aggrieved speech from the orderly, the doctor placated him. "What impudence! It sounds as if you were unduly provoked, Gibson. We will consult my lawyer as soon as I return, regarding assault *and* libel *and* slander. . . . Yes, I promise you. In the meantime, I don't think you should go to the police, or speak to anyone else. After all, *we* mustn't libel or slander anyone. I know that I can rely on your support in this highly embarrassing situation. Do you agree?"

There was silence at the other end of the radiophone.

"I'll make it worth your while," the doctor said wearily.

Silence.

"You'll have a job for life, Gibson."

"Can I have that in writing?" asked the white-coated orderly.

Like many of the legal offices in Lincoln's Inn, that of William Owen, financial specialist lawyer, looked like an overworked headmaster's study. The lawyer sat behind a desk piled high with papers and red box files. He was a bulky man with sallow skin and frizzy gray hair. Next to him sat his consultant accountant, Richard Fraser, who specialized in fraud; he had the pink cheeks and solemn young face of a well-scrubbed choirboy.

Sitting opposite the desk between Annabel and Sam, Miranda felt very tired; her head ached.

Mr. Owen said, "From what you tell me, there are three distinct areas of complaint. Firstly, the seemingly unnecessary detention of your grandmother in the nursing home. Secondly, the possible embezzlement of monies from the trust. Thirdly, the possible purchase of SUPPLYKITS shares by persons at present unknown, upon Adam Grant's instructions, with money that may not rightfully belong to the purchaser but to the Dove Trust."

"Can our grandmother sue the nursing home?" Annabel asked.

Mr. Owen lifted his eyebrows and peered over his spectacles. He did not look optimistic. "Even before I know the full facts, I can tell you that it might take ten years of arduous legal work to be able to reclaim a relatively small amount of money. I probably won't advise such a waste of time and energy."

"What about any embezzlement from the trust?" Miranda asked.

"Surely the trustees must account for all funds?" Annabel added.

Miranda shook her head. "STG warned me that Adam and Paul Littlejohn are probably acting within the law and if that's so, nobody has any power legally to query the actions of the trust."

"But why doesn't Adam have to answer our questions?" Annabel said. "*He* organized the trust."

"If Adam Grant is unwilling to give you information," Mr. Owen replied, "you may, as trust beneficiaries, decide to go to court to seek information about the trust. But to force the information from him through the courts would take a long time."

Richard Fraser leaned forward. "From what you say, it sounds as if this operation was carefully planned, years ago. If so, the money will be accounted for on paper by scurrilous documentation—investments in companies that fail or shares that drop like stones. We'll be able to trace where each sum went when it left the Dove Trust bank accounts. But if fraud is involved, that cash will have quickly been transferred again—to numbered Swiss bank accounts that are untraceable."

William Owen looked over his half-glasses. "Adam Grant is probably the only person who knows where that money is. Undoubtedly, he keeps some written record of what's happening to it—because nobody can keep track of vast sums of money and complicated bank transfers without some record. But I expect his summary is carefully hidden. He probably keeps it in a small unobtrusive notebook—something that he could either carry around with him or leave in a small safe. *If* you could get your hands on it, then we could go to the police—but it's no use going to them without such evidence. Though I do advise you to contact the authorities now, so that they can act immediately should you find any hard evidence."

"Then all we have to do is find that summary?" Annabel asked.

Miranda snapped, "Adam's hardly likely to hand it to us on a plate."

Richard Fraser took the two sisters and Sam to a modern building near Victoria—the fraud squad base—where he introduced them to Detective Inspector Walter Piper; in a navy pin-striped suit and expensive pale blue shirt, he looked more like a young trainee banker than a policeman. He took notes as Miranda told her story. When she had finished, the inspector said, "From what you say, and adding a few guesses based on my experience, we're looking at this sort of situation." Carefully he summarized, "In July 1965, STG set up an offshore Bermuda trust, administered by their associate accountants in Bermuda. The protector of the trust was Paul Littlejohn, a partner of STG. At the same time, Elinor O'Dare signed a general power of attorney in favor of Adam Grant of STG, to be used in event of her illness.

"Unlike Paul Littlejohn, a South African subject living in Bermuda, Grant was based in Britain, subject to British law. So in August 1966, he persuaded Mrs. O'Dare to substitute Paul Littlejohn for himself in the power of attorney held by Grant. Probably a clause in the transfer deed stated that the power of attorney was subject to the law of Bermuda and not British law.

"Mrs. O'Dare also signed papers absolving Adam Grant and STG from any further responsibility for Mrs. O'Dare's affairs.

"In March 1967, Grant left STG to start his own firm. Elinor O'Dare transferred her business from STG to Grant's new office. In February 1968, Paul Littlejohn—who is probably Grant's accomplice—left STG to set up his own firm in Bermuda, to which he transferred the Dove Trust. As the protector, Littlejohn had the power to remove existing trustees and appoint other trustees.

"By February 1968, Mrs. O'Dare had started treatment for paranoia in the Lord Willington Nursing Home. Paul Littlejohn was therefore able to use his power of attorney to strip her of her personal fortune, including a chateau in France. At this point, those two villains would have been able to simply siphon off all funds. Paul Littlejohn controlled the Dove Trust, as well as Mrs. O'Dare's personal fortune, but Adam Grant probably controlled Littlejohn.

"It also appears that Adam Grant, a director of SUPPLYKITS, has acquired control of forty-six percent of the shares of that company, possibly using funds from the Dove Trust. We'll be able to trace back the recent purchases, and if they were paid for with money from the Dove Trust, then those shares rightly belong to the trust. If other trust money has disappeared, then the trust might *also* claim the shares that rightly belong to Grant."

When Inspector Piper was finished, Miranda asked, "Where do we start?"

"Contact Mrs. O'Dare's literary agent, to ensure that no further royalties are forwarded to the Dove Trust until it has been investigated. You can't do anything else until you have proof of illegality."

"Can we prosecute?"

"You can't prosecute unless you find some hard evidence, because in 1966, when your grandmother signed the trust deeds, she also signed papers saying that she no longer wished Adam Grant or STG to handle her affairs and absolved both parties from any future responsibility for her affairs. She also voluntarily signed her application to enter this nursing home. So where's the crime?" The inspector shrugged his shoulders. "But I'll check our records to see whether Mr. Grant has done anything like this before."

Sam asked, "What do we do if we get hard proof?"

"Bring it to us as fast as possible—there's always someone available to take emergency action."

In her pale gray drawing room, Miranda collapsed into an armchair. She was exhausted; she also felt that the white dagger slicing through her head was about to split it in two.

"Help yourselves." She wearily waved her hand toward the drinks tray. "I've been trying to think. I've no idea where Adam might keep a small notebook. It could be *anywhere*."

Sam poured himself a generous whiskey. "Not 'anywhere' because it's very valuable. Where would you hide a twenty-carat, blue-white marquise diamond? *Not anywhere.*"

"I doubt he carries it around with him," Miranda mused. "What happens if he takes off his jacket and the notebook falls out? . . . It wouldn't be safe from pickpockets. It wouldn't be safe while he . . . slept."

Annabel volunteered, "Sometimes I fetched things from Adam's pockets—cigarettes, keys, that sort of thing. He'd never have asked me to do such a thing if he kept something secret and precious in his pockets."

"Do you think it might be in a bank vault?" Miranda asked Sam.

"Unlikely," Sam said. "It sounds as if Adam has to keep it handy to make entries."

"He's unlikely to keep it in his SUPPLYKITS office." Miranda continued to think aloud. "We have the usual petty theft problems, so none of the staff are supposed to keep valuables in their desks."

"Maybe he keeps the notebook in an office safe?" Sam asked.

"No, our only safe is in the accountant's office," Miranda said. "And we regard it as a serious burglary risk. We use it as little as possible."

"Adam has his own safe—in his apartment," Annabel volunteered. "It's not particularly secret. It's built into the window wall in his sitting room, and it's hidden by a curtain. . . . Oh my God, I gave him my jewelry to keep safe, and it's still there!"

Miranda smiled grimly. "Maybe. I've also seen that safe. Adam keeps cash in it—but not very much—and a few valuable bits and pieces: his father's gold cigarette case, things like that. Last Christmas I gave him a Cartier watch which he put in that safe. I noticed he never wore it: he always wears that old Omega."

"Maybe the notebook is hidden in his home but not in his safe," Sam said. "It's probably in a private sort of room—his bedroom or bathroom. And it's probably in something immovable rather than something like a briefcase that can be stolen."

Annabel said, "I think I know where it is."

Miranda and Sam looked at her.

"No, really. A couple of weeks ago, when Adam left for work, I was still in bed, doing the newspaper crossword. I wanted an eraser—I'm not very good at crosswords—so I went to that Georgian desk opposite the fireplace. As I pulled the desk flap down, Adam opened the bedroom door—he'd forgotten something. He made a lot of fuss about my going to his desk. But where would you look for an eraser if not in a desk? I wasn't rifling through the drawers, you understand."

"This notebook, or file, wouldn't be lying around in a drawer," Sam said.

"How about a *secret* drawer?" Annabel suggested.

Miranda nodded. "Any good eighteenth-century desk has at least one secret drawer, because they didn't have wall safes then."

"D'you remember Gran showing us how to measure the depth of each desk drawer with a ruler? Any drawer that's shorter than the desk space it seems to occupy probably has a secret compartment behind it."

"There are probably plenty of other hiding places in his bedroom," Sam said. "How can we get in there?"

Miranda said, "You mean . . . "

"Can we break into the house?" Sam asked impatiently. "What staff are there? What burglary precautions?"

"His apartment's on the top two floors of an old house in Cadogan Place,"

Miranda said. "There are double locks and chains on the front door, sliding steel shutters on the windows. There might be some sort of access to the roof, but I bet it's barred."

In a quiet voice, Annabel said, "There's no need to break in. I still have the keys. Adam thinks I'm at a health farm. As far as he is concerned, our relationship hasn't altered."

"The Trojan horse!" Sam exclaimed, delighted. "When would be the best time for you to get in—when you can be *sure* that Adam won't be there?"

"That's easy," Miranda said triumphantly. "The SUPPLYKITS EGM takes place tomorrow, at nine A.M., at the Connaught Rooms—miles away from Cadogan Place. Adam can't afford to miss that meeting. He has a starring role."

CHAPTER 29

Friday, 31 January 1969

A*NGUS MACLAYNE TURNED* up the collar of his heavy city overcoat and hurried down the steps from the VC10, an hour late. London was almost as cold as New York, he thought, stifling a yawn.

Although eight A.M. in London, it was still only three A.M. New York time. Angus, unable to sleep in the plane, had gone over his notes of the international banking conference that had taken him to New York.

He crunched wearily through the gritty snow to the airport bus, which smelled of stale cigarette smoke. Although he carried only hand baggage to avoid delay, there were too few customs officers, so it was eight forty-five when he hurried to his black Daimler, waiting for him at the terminal entrance: there was still enough time to get to the meeting.

The voice of Maria Callas—"*In mia man' alfin' tu sei*"—throbbed with exultant emotion in Clare's pink kitchen. David, who had eaten little, pushed away his breakfast plate and said, "I wish you'd sit down and talk about this seriously, Clare."

"If people bother to bicycle through the snow for my bread," Clare said, tying her baker's apron, "I'm going to serve them as usual."

"But your damned husband will turn up tonight! I want an answer from you before then!"

Clare looked lovingly at him, but there was also determination in her look. Quietly she said, "I may be able to answer you tonight, but I may not. We've been together now for two years, sharing meals, hopes, concerns; sharing my son, sharing my bed. All that time I've loved you—even when you were in one of your 'difficult' moods, when you didn't want me or anyone else. I have loved you, and you have known it, the whole time. And I've known that you loved me as well, even when it didn't seem that way."

"Then why won't you say you'll marry me?"

"Because all the time we've been together, I've never felt that you were really mine; you've been like some partly domesticated animal—there beside me for months, and then one day—gone! Back to the wilds, or to whatever place your demons drive you. . . . But now you're afraid of losing me, and you don't want that, and I'm very glad. I don't want you to lose me. Nevertheless, I can't accept your ultimatum: there are too many things to be considered. You, and our love for each other, are incredibly important to me, but in the time I've had to wait for you to decide what *you* want to do, I've grown stronger, more sure of myself, increasingly aware of my absolute need *to decide for myself* what's best for me. I need time to make that decision. I can't decide by this evening."

"Fine. How long do you need?"

"I don't know. I may decide by tomorrow, but I may need longer. I might need a week, I might need much longer than that. But I think this is as important as you do—and that's why I'm not going to be rushed into a decision. I hope you'll allow me the time I need, and not put me under pressure. And also I hope you know that I really do love you, David."

"How can I believe that, when you won't say yes?"

"You *know* I love being with you, David; I love doing things with you; I love learning from you. And I simply love sleeping with you." A dreamy look came into her eyes, and she hugged herself. "I can't imagine anything more luxurious than snuggling with you under the patchwork quilt upstairs, knowing that it's snowing outside. Except waking up in the middle of the night and putting my arm out to you—and feeling that wonderful warm lump beside me."

"So how are you going to feel if you wake up and the warm lump beside you turns out to be Sam? You have to decide whether you want me or a square-jawed Superman who gets his way with his fists."

Clare hesitated. At Elinor's rescue, she had secretly found Sam's fight-now-talk-later, he-man side almost irresistible. Now, being fought over by two men made her feel like a medieval damsel with white hands and a wimple. To Clare's surprise and chagrin, two aggressive, battling rivals for her hand made her feel exultant and powerful, sneakily, guiltily thrilled to bits.

Turning away from the oven, she looked intently at David and said, "We're not the only ones concerned."

"Josh likes me—you know he does—and I'm growing very fond of him," David said. "As a matter of fact, I was quite hurt when he—"

"Ran to his dad? Josh ignored *me* as well," Clare said ruefully. "Whether or not *I* think his father deserves it, *Josh loves his father*. And I'm *glad* he's loyal to his father—painful though it is."

"So Josh is going to decide who you'll spend the rest of your life with?" David asked. "What will happen to *you* in twelve years' time when Josh leaves you—with never a backward look—to play in some college band or work his way to India with the rest of his mates? How are you going to feel *then* when you wake up in the dark and feel for the warm lump?"

Clare sat down abruptly. This is what made her decision so difficult. Where did her duty lie? With Josh. And where did her heart lie? With David. But suppose she went back to Sam and it didn't work out? Briefly she recalled what her life had been before David appeared.

No, she preferred not to think of it! Life was never, never, *never* going to be like that again for her. She wasn't going to drop the reins of her own life again. Clare was damned if she was going to be overinfluenced by Sam, David, or *anyone*.

Anyway, she told herself, she didn't believe that Sam was going to turn over a new leaf.

But if that wasn't his intention, then why had he bothered to come here? Sam had traveled halfway around the world—no doubt at great inconvenience, for Clare knew how carefully his life was structured—to help solve her family problems and to see her. It certainly looked as if he was serious.

Feeling ambivalent and confused, Clare said, "It's no use. The arguments just go round and round in my mind, until I'm back where I started."

David zipped his windproof wine jacket. From the chair beside him, he picked up his sheepskin gloves and flat tweed cap. "Let me know when you decide."

"You'll be back this evening?" Clare asked anxiously. She pushed back her chair and ran to him.

David hesitated. He knew he ought to say no, that he'd come back only if she agreed to marry him. On the other hand, given David's absence, that bastard Sam would move in as fast as a greased lizard.

He said, "I'll see what the weather's like when I've finished work."

He left without kissing her.

The driver half turned to Angus. "Sorry about this, sir. Looks as if we might be here for some time." The Daimler was stuck in a seemingly immovable traffic jam at Hammersmith Broadway.

Through lightly falling snow, Angus peered impatiently at the conglomeration of honking, static vehicles feeding in from five converging roads. "I'll get to Holborn quicker if I take the underground," he decided. "You go on to the Connaught Rooms and wait for me there."

Carrying his briefcase, Angus slipped and stumbled through translucent brown slush, dodging past cars, lorries, and taxis, toward the blue sign that hung above the station. He was no longer confident of arriving in time for the meeting. He wondered briefly whether to dangle a few fivers in front of one of the motorbike riders who were weaving their way neatly through the traffic. Angus decided against it—better late than never—and hurried to the ticket office.

At a quarter to ten, Adam hurried across the well-swept pavement of Cadogan Place and lowered himself into his black Porsche.

Annabel, wearing a black balaclava and ankle-length wolf-skin coat, watched the Porsche dart away and turn left into Pont Street.

She slipped from the inconspicuous gray BMW Sam had hired and stumbled across the wet road toward the old red brick building that seemed suddenly forbidding. When she turned the key in the lock, the black door to the communal entrance hall swung open.

Why shouldn't it? There's no reason why Adam should have changed the locks, Annabel reassured herself as she heaved aside the old-fashioned metal-barred door to the elevator.

And her key also opened the front door to Adam's apartment. Annabel crept into the hall, her wet boots making tracks across the navy carpet.

A dark shape leapt from the floor at her.

She jumped back, alarmed. But it was only Pitch, Adam's huge black cat. He sprang at Annabel's crimson boots, clawing the toes. She bent to stroke his silky head and whisper reassurance, then looked up. The silence seemed threatening.

Ahead was the door to the recently redecorated living room, which stretched the depth of the house with windows at both ends. To Annabel's left was the dining room, and to her right, the kitchen.

Adam's apartment was as handsome, impersonal, and tightly controlled as its owner. His fashionable decorator had done a slick job: The walls were painted in carefully chosen tones of plum, aubergine, and gray blue; the carpet and upholstery were navy. Eastern antiques were mixed with the latest clear-plastic, inflatable armchairs and white pedestal tables.

Suddenly, upstairs, a vacuum whined.

Annabel started. Mrs. Price must be cleaning the bedroom. What a nuisance, she thought—the Georgian desk was there. Annabel had imagined herself going directly to the desk and searching it thoroughly.

Because she reckoned that the desk was the most likely hiding place, she couldn't summon up much enthusiasm for searching elsewhere. But perhaps she should search the living room while Mrs. Price was occupied in the bedroom above it. Or should she just march upstairs, whistling, and use some excuse to get rid of Mrs. Price?

Annabel decided to go straight to the desk. Decisively she turned right, toward the staircase.

At the top of the stairs, she stumbled over Pitch, who crouched, invisible, against the navy-blue carpet. The cat's yellow eyes glared up at her, as if he knew what she was doing and wanted to protect his master's territory.

As Annabel entered the bedroom, she saw the large black backside of Mrs. Price, who was picking bits of white china from the floor. She stood up, turned, and gave a squawk as she saw Annabel. "Oh madam, I'd no idea you were back. Mr. Grant didn't say. That dratted, clumsy cat just knocked over an ashtray!"

"Mr. Grant doesn't know I've returned," Annabel said cheerfully. "It was bitterly cold in Norfolk at the health farm, so I decided to return to town."

"You were lucky to get here, madam. On the early morning news, they said there was blizzards in southeast England."

"Yes, terrible blizzards," Annabel said hastily.

"You must have left very early, madam. Before six. In the dark."

"Yes. But the train arrived on time." Annabel wanted to say, "Go *away*."

"Shall I unpack for you, madam?"

"I stupidly left my suitcase on the train." Annabel gave an embarrassed laugh and embroidered her lie. "I've already telephoned the lost property office. . . . Luckily, a porter handed it in. I have to go and collect it this afternoon."

"What a nuisance, madam. Would you like me to go for you? Or I could telephone Mr. Grant's secretary. She could have the suitcase picked up."

"You're very kind," Annabel said. "But . . . er . . . er . . . I have to personally sign for it, you see, and produce identification—prove that it's mine." Firmly she added, "What I would like now is a hot bath."

"I haven't finished the bathroom yet, madam."

"Then please leave it until tomorrow. Leave this room as well." Annabel had regained her confidence: Why had she been so frightened?

"Shall I take your boots to dry, madam? They look very wet. They need stuffing with newspaper."

"Thank you. I'll let you have them after my bath."

"Would you care for a cup of tea to warm you up, madam?"

Go away! Go away! Annabel thought, but aloud, said calmly, "No thank you, Mrs. Price, that will be all."

Motionless, Annabel listened as Mrs. Price padded downstairs. Then she ran to the bedroom door and turned the key in the lock. She flung her fur coat on the floor. In the bathroom she shoved the plug in the tub and went through the charade of preparing a bath; while the taps were running, she could take the drawers out without being heard.

Adam's bathroom was above the kitchen, his study above the dining room. His bedroom also ran the width of the house; one end, which overlooked Cadogan Place, was used as a sitting area. Here navy sofas were grouped around a zebra skin before a marble fireplace in which a log fire quietly burned; dark blue shelves on either side of the fireplace held a collection of Thai water jars.

On the opposite wall stood a George III mahogany bureau bookcase. Above four narrow drawers, a sloping desktop could be pulled down to provide a writing surface; above it, a glass-fronted bookcase contained a collection of eighteenth-century drinking glasses.

On trembling legs, Annabel ran toward this splendid piece of furniture.

Miranda wore a plain orange suit, not so short-skirted as the rest of her clothes. She felt nervous but excited. Waiting in the impressive pillared entrance hall of the Connaught Rooms, she had already peeped into the cream hall and seen SUPPLYKITS shareholders sitting in rows, some stamping snow from their shoes, some reading newspapers. The city press had been having a great deal of fun, and there had been a lot of speculation and broad hints—for Miranda's private relationship with Adam was guessed on Fleet Street. Today's headlines had read: SUPPLYKITS BOARDROOM CONTROL BATTLE (*The Times*), IT'S MIRANDA V. ADAM! (*Daily Mail*), NEW BOSS AT SUPPLY-KITS? (*Daily Express*), and WHOOPS, IT'S D-DAY FOR CITY SWEETHEART, MIRANDA (*Daily Mirror*).

Miranda, who quite enjoyed a fight, knew that she was about to battle as fiercely as a mother tiger for her wounded cub; the neglected KITS needed all her protection, care, and attention to nurse it back to health.

From behind her, Lord Brighton said, "Nearly time to start—it's five to ten." Together, they moved slowly toward the hall.

"*Miranda!*"

Miranda twisted her head backward as she heard her name shouted.

To her astonishment, she saw the wild red-gold hair and unmistakable Viking-sized figure of Angus Maclayne rushing toward her from the street entrance.

"*Angus!* What are *you* doing here?"

"Thought I'd never make it," he panted. "I'm here to vote."

"But you aren't registered as a shareholder!"

Angus grinned. "Yes I am."

"How? Why?" Miranda puzzled. "I don't understand."

"I've been keeping an eye on your shares. Didn't like it when your holding dipped to forty-five percent and you lost your majority," Angus said. "So I started buying."

"*How many shares do you own?*" Miranda asked urgently.

"Four point eight, which still won't give you a majority vote. . . . I had hoped to get five point one percent."

"Angus . . . how can you own four point eight percent? Unless . . . "

Angus nodded. "Highland Croft Holdings is indirectly owned by my family."
Miranda flung her arms around him. She mumbled into his still-damp overcoat, "You're *wonderful*, Angus. I love you for thinking of this! Four point eight is all I need!"
Behind her, Lord Brighton coughed. "We should move in."
As Miranda's orange figure appeared on the platform, cameras flashed and a rustle of excitement swept through the hall.
Walking confidently across the platform, Miranda felt exultant. It looked as if she controlled the votes. Behind her back, she crossed her fingers.
Miranda took her seat next to Lord Brighton. She and Adam Grant, sitting on his Lordship's other side, ignored each other.

Annabel could just peer behind the back of the desk, which stood against the wall; nothing was attached to it. She pulled down the sloping top of the central section of the desk. The writing surface, thus revealed, was covered by worn black leather. Centered at the rear was a tiny classical doorway with carved pillars on either side and a pediment above it; on either side of this were pigeonholes, with drawers beneath.
Her hands shaking, Annabel removed each drawer and laid it on the navy-blue carpet in the order of its removal: she had to be careful to put the drawers back correctly or Adam would immediately spot that someone had been tampering with his desk.
With a tape measure borrowed from Miranda, she measured each drawer: all were the same width and the same depth. Damn!
Annabel closed the sloping top and looked carefully at its beautifully inlaid design of musical instruments. Perhaps if she pressed some part, it would activate a hidden mechanism.
Suddenly she realized that she couldn't hear the bathwater.
She scrambled to her feet and ran toward the bathroom.
The bath had overflowed. Water seeped gently over the navy carpet.
"*Damn!*" As soon as one drop leaked through the kitchen ceiling, Mrs. Price would be up with mops and pails; she would see the desk drawers scattered over the carpet.
Annabel sloshed across the carpet. Quickly she turned off the taps and pulled out the plug—her big mistake. She threw all the towels she could see, plus Adam's dressing gown, on the floor and then stamped on the bundle to soak up the water.
Trembling more violently, she ran back to the desk.
Halfway there, she changed her mind and ran back to the bathroom. She turned on the taps above the handbasin, which she did not plug: running taps were still necessary to camouflage any odd noises she might make.
Annabel glanced at her watch. "*Damn!*" Ten-fifteen already. And her knees were knocking.

In the cream-colored assembly hall, the shareholders, quiet but expectant, looked up at Lord Brighton as he outlined the reason for the meeting. Miss Miranda O'Dare wished to regain control of the KITS cosmetics business by separating it from the complex of companies into which her original business had developed. The KITS shops had been losing money since the group went public; therefore, this sale might be no great loss to the holding company.
Should the shareholders agree to the price that their independent assessors had

decided was reasonable, Miss O'Dare would pay this price for KITS. Should it be decided that Miss O'Dare could not buy the company, then Miss O'Dare would resign from SUPPLYKITS as soon as her contract expired, in three months.

Mr. Adam Grant had also offered to buy KITS, at ten percent above any price that Miss O'Dare offered to pay.

Lord Brighton concluded his speech by saying that every member of SUPPLYKITS worked hard, but nobody worked harder than Miss O'Dare, KITS' founder. As "the face of the firm," Miss O'Dare was perceived by the public to be responsible for the easy and continued success of the company, and therefore, in his opinion, SUPPLYKITS could not afford to lose Miss O'Dare. They could not afford to lose her services or the publicity generated by Miss O'Dare's presence. Nor could they afford to have any rival company acquire the services of Miss O'Dare. And should she leave, he felt certain, the share price would fall.

For these reasons, Lord Brighton recommended that the shareholders refuse Mr. Adam Grant's offer. He also recommended that they show their appreciation for Miss O'Dare's work by accepting Miss O'Dare's offer and agreeing to sell the cosmetics chain KITS to Miss O'Dare for the independent valuation price of fourteen thousand pounds. Lord Brighton moved that Miss O'Dare's offer be accepted.

Carefully Annabel ran her hands around each empty drawer space in the desk. She touched the backs, the sides, and the bottoms, hoping to feel a piece of wood move—very, very slightly—when it shouldn't.

"*Ah!*"

At the base of the left-hand bank of drawers, the bottom moved ever so slightly. Annabel pushed it backward, then edged her nails under the base panel.

The thin wooden panel lifted easily.

She had been right to start her search at the desk!

Gently she lifted the panel and pulled it toward her: attached to the end was a box ten inches wide by two inches deep.

Annabel ran her thumb lightly over the top of the box: it yielded. She slid it aside and looked into the secret compartment.

From the second row of seats at the Connaught Rooms, a tall, thin man with a ginger mustache stood up. "Mr. Chairman, I don't go along with what you suggest."

Lord Brighton said, "Do I understand that you object to the company's acceptance of Miss O'Dare's offer to purchase KITS?"

"No, I'm all for that," said the man with the ginger mustache, "but like you said, we all know how hard Miranda—I mean Miss O'Dare—has worked to pay our dividends. Why don't we show a bit *more* appreciation than you suggest? Why don't we *give* KITS to her?"

There was a buzz of noise in the hall. A woman in a beige raincoat quickly stood up and, without addressing the chair, pointed out that Miss O'Dare was well paid for her work; personally, she *expected* Miss O'Dare to work hard for the company; personally, *she* was a canteen manageress, and she *also* worked hard for her pay, and nobody gave *her* gifts worth thousands of pounds. So she opposed the suggestion. She sat down to cries of agreement.

Lord Brighton settled the matter by reminding the meeting that, by law, no proposal of which the shareholders had not been advised by letter could be brought up for consideration.

Annabel stared at the contents of the secret drawer: a battered silver King Edward III sixpence. Clearly, Adam did not know of the existence of this drawer; that sixpence may have lain in it for over two hundred years.

Annabel was bitterly disappointed. She sat back on the heels of her crimson thigh boots and checked her watch. Ten forty-five already. She looked at the desk. Was there any point in searching it further?

She glanced upward. Something *might* be hidden behind the pediment above the doorway in the center of the desk; something *might* be attached to the underside of the base.

Annabel dragged the desk chair closer to the desk and stood on it. Carefully she felt over the top of the bookcase. Her hand came away covered by dirt: obviously, Mrs. Price's feather duster didn't move above eye level.

Then she jumped down from the chair and lay flat on the floor to peer beneath the desk. As she couldn't see clearly, she felt over the entire undersurface; had Adam lodged a notebook there, her fingers would certainly have felt it.

Again disappointed, Annabel sat back on her heels and studied the tiny classical doorway with pillars on either side. She opened it.

Inside were two shelves and, at the top, a very small drawer, too shallow to take anything but visiting cards and rings. Annabel gently withdrew the drawer: it contained only a crumpled old-fashioned white five-pound note.

She bit her lip. She had been so certain that this desk was Adam's hiding place. Before returning the little drawer, she carefully put her hand in the opening and pressed each wooden side; none yielded.

But something didn't feel right.

It was then Annabel realized what she should do.

In the Connaught Rooms, Lord Brighton, as chairman, made sure that anyone who wished to speak was allowed to do so.

Then the votes were taken and counted.

A rustle ran through the room. Reporters flipped their notebooks. Shareholders whispered excitedly to one another. Tension rose.

Adam glared at Miranda, and she glared back.

The shareholders voted in Miranda's favor. The majority was small, but Miranda didn't mind because KITS would be sold back to her for fourteen thousand pounds: the resolution was passed.

But the meeting was not yet finished.

Annabel again studied the little doorway inside the desk. That central structure didn't feel as secure as it should. She took hold of the scrolls of the Ionic pillars on either side of the doorway and tugged them toward her.

She was either about to break a valuable antique or . . .

As Annabel held her breath, the entire little doorway slid toward her: it was a box unit, measuring about ten inches wide and deep by twelve inches high, and it left a space of the same size in the desk.

Trembling now with excitement, she pushed her hand to the back of this space:

there was a little trough in which she could feel several small items.

From it Annabel eagerly withdrew three small, battered black leather notebooks and an envelope.

The black notebooks contained page after page of neat figures in Adam's handwriting. The envelope contained a certificate and a crumpled handwritten letter.

Holding her breath, willing herself to concentrate on what she was doing, Annabel carefully replaced the central section of the desk; then, one by one, she started to replace the little drawers.

Behind her, there was a sudden *crack!*

She jumped and gasped with fright.

But it was only the sound of a smoldering log.

At the SUPPLYKITS EGM, Adam Grant, tight-lipped, stood up. As was appropriate, he offered his resignation from the board of directors of SUPPLYKITS.

Mr. Grant's resignation was accepted.

The meeting was then dissolved. Reporters, wearing unbelted raincoats, rushed toward the platform and a glowing Miranda.

As Annabel crept downstairs, Mrs. Price appeared in the kitchen doorway.

Seeing that Annabel was wearing her fur coat, Mrs. Price said, "Going out again, madam? In *this* weather?" Broom in hand, she advanced to the bottom of the stairs.

"A hair appointment," Annabel said rapidly. "Dare not skip an appointment with Leonard himself, not even in this weather!" Her heart thudded against her black skinny-rib sweater as she added, "I'm afraid I've made rather a mess of the bathroom, Mrs. Price. I'll explain to Mr. Grant that it was my fault."

"Was it the overflow stuck, madam? That's happened to Mr. Grant a couple of times." Now Mrs. Price stood before the front door.

Annabel thought wildly, Get out of my way. *Please! Get away from that front door!* In a worried voice, she said, "Would you mind making *quite* sure I turned all the taps off? I might have left the basin tap running. Awful of me."

Mrs. Price scooted upstairs. She didn't want her kitchen ceiling falling down again.

Annabel flung herself through the front door and waited, trembling, for the elevator, pressing the button anxiously over and over. She couldn't hear it coming up. Damn! Someone must have left it open down below.

She dashed to the end of the passage, clattered down the service stairs, and ran out to the street and headed for Sam's car, parked farther up the road, next to the wrought-iron railings of the garden. Before she reached it, Annabel slipped on the slush and almost fell.

Sam was feeling apprehensive as he waited. Annabel had been in Adam's home for nearly two hours, and there was no way of knowing when the SUPPLYKITS meeting would end. Just then Annabel ran across the road toward him, and Sam could see from her excited face that her search had been successful. He switched on the engine purposefully, and they were gone.

They arrived at the lawyer's office just after midday. Sam and Annabel watched impatiently as the big Rank Xerox dark brown photocopier slowly copied each page of the black notebooks. The machine gave off a slight smell of ozone as the paper went through the heat fuser. Obviously, the copier was one of the older models.

"Can't it go faster?" Annabel asked, then added nervously, "*Must* I take those notebooks back to Adam's apartment?"

"If we want to be safe—yes," Sam said regretfully. "We don't want Adam to realize they're missing. If he suspects that we've enough evidence to put him in jail, he'll immediately whisk off whatever cash is left, remove all evidence, and disappear."

Annabel fidgeted with a fingernail, then remembered that she was supposed to be at the hairdresser. She went to the cracked mirror in the dingy cloakroom and began to comb her hair, flattened by the balaclava, into a thick lion's mane that would rival even that of Baby Jane Holzer. Mrs. Price would definitely see a change.

Heart thudding, Annabel opened Adam's front door. She could hear the news on the radio in the sitting room, which meant that he was in. Her heart sank as she slowly entered the room.

"Where the hell have you been?" Adam asked irritably. A glass of whiskey in one hand, he sat in one of the transparent inflatable armchairs.

"I told you in my note. I've been at the St. Ivory health farm."

"You said *a* health farm. You didn't say which one," Adam said crossly. "Suppose someone had wanted to get in touch with you? Suppose something had happened to your grandmother?"

"I'm so sorry," Annabel said. "I just didn't think . . . " Her voice trailed away.

"Well, hurry up. I've just told Mrs. Price to serve lunch." Adam did not kiss her.

Annabel wondered if she could endure lunch, knowing that proof of her theft was a few feet away, in her scarlet leather shoulder bag. She decided to replace the documents immediately; it would be a risk, but Adam was sitting down with a fresh drink, and she'd be able to do it in three minutes.

"I'll just take off my wet boots," she said.

Taking her bag with her, Annabel hurried upstairs to the bedroom. By the time she reached the top of the stairs, her knees were weak with fear.

She shut the bedroom door, but did not dare lock it. Moving quickly to the desk, she pulled out the sloping desktop.

Slowly she edged out the elaborate central box.

Hands trembling, she opened her bag and replaced the notebooks and envelope, then edged the box back into place and closed the desk flap.

A wave of relief swept over her, only to be replaced by terror as she turned away from the desk.

Adam was standing in the doorway, watching her.

"Looking for stamps?" he asked pleasantly. "Second drawer down on the left-hand side. I've brought you a Campari and soda—tell me if you want more Campari in it. And do hurry down, darling. Mrs. Price is getting tetchy. You know she likes to leave promptly at three o'clock."

"She's had a trying morning. I'm afraid I flooded the bathroom again." With a great effort, Annabel took the drink, and Adam left the room. She collapsed on the sofa and, with shaky hands, tugged her boots off.

Had he seen her?

If so, why hadn't he said anything?

He couldn't have. It was too unbearable to think about.

Downstairs, Adam carefully closed the door of the living room. He needed time to think. There was only one thing Annabel could have been looking for in that desk. Her face told him that she'd found the notebooks. Had she hidden them in her clothes? Or in her purse? Was she about to deliver them to someone outside? Annabel wasn't smart enough to be in this alone. And she certainly wasn't smart enough to understand what was in those notebooks. Someone who did know how important they were had clearly sent Annabel here to steal them . . . and that person must be waiting somewhere outside. Adam could search her purse, he could search her person; he could certainly find and remove the notebooks—but that unknown someone would still come after them.

He had to think clearly, control his momentary panic. Okay—his next move should be to convince Annabel's accomplice that he *didn't* have the notebooks. But how could that be arranged?

Suppose Annabel was given all the space she needed to take anything she wanted out of this house? And then suppose she was mugged—and her purse stolen—before she had a chance to give those notebooks to anyone else? She'd have to be beaten up a little to make the mugging look convincing . . . but the bitch deserved it. . . .

Yes, that was it.

He had to keep calm—there were still a lot of things to work out. He needed to arrange for someone to follow Annabel until she was in a relatively quiet spot where she could be jumped. Maybe he needed two people, in case her accomplice was lurking outside his front door. In that case, they would *both* have to be taken care of. Maybe three men would be needed. . . . Mike would be able to arrange it. God, he hoped he'd be able to get hold of Mike. . . .

And maybe he'd better drop everything and get out of the country without waiting until the rest of the money had been funneled out. Most of the money was out there, waiting for him. . . . He didn't think there was anything the police could hold him for, but then everyone caught in some sharp practice thought that. If he got out fast, he'd be taking no chances. . . . But suppose the airports were already being watched? . . . Steady, steady—no need to panic. *There was no need to worry.* If someone got hold of the notebooks, that someone still wouldn't know *where* the money was, or *how* to get it. No, he had nothing to fear, so long as he kept his head. . . .

Still, it wouldn't be a bad idea to arrange for the notebooks to be "stolen," and to let them rough up that bitch Annabel while they were about it—that would teach the little whore a lesson . . . and if her accomplice was also beaten up, then Adam would discover who he was. Maybe she'd been reconciled to that smart-ass husband of hers—Mr. Hotshot Reporter . . . He'd get them both, mess up both their pretty faces . . . *Yes.*

Now that he'd decided what to do, all that remained was to locate Mike. Obviously, it would take Mike some time to make these arrangements, so he would have to keep Annabel here until Mike's people were in place. But he knew the perfect way to stall Annabel. . . . What better way to kill time than by giving the bitch a fuck she'd never forget?

Adam reached for the telephone. As he listened to the rings, he nervously tugged his hair over his left eye, then jerked his head up to flip it back into place.

"Mike? Thank God I've reached you. I'm in trouble. . . . I knew you would. . . . Look, I need you to take care of someone for me. . . . I promise, I wouldn't ask you if it wasn't absolutely necessary. . . . No, I only want you to frighten someone. . . . Thanks. . . . Right now, as a matter of fact. . . . I'm sorry. . . . Thanks. . . . Well, it's Annabel O'Dare. . . . You bloody well just said you *would!* Mike, I'm sunk if you don't! When I explain later, you'll see there's no alternative for me—short of pushing her out of the window, or jumping myself. . . . No, no, of course I won't!"

Quickly Adam explained that he had just seen Annabel deliberately steal carefully hidden documents that could put him behind bars. "What she's nicked are details of some bank transactions. It won't do her a blind bit of good because she doesn't know where to find the bank account numbers." Adam's voice sounded increasingly desperate as he whispered, "I've *got* to find the bastard she's working with. I've *got* to find out who's after my notebooks . . . and I've *got* to scare Annabel so badly that she'll refuse to do it again—*or* involve the police. . . .

"Why don't *I* frighten her? Because, Mike, it's more frightening if someone else does it. Shows them I have powerful friends. Makes Annabel feel that even if *I'm* put behind bars, she'll still be vulnerable. . . . Yes, of *course* I know it's also safer for me. Look, I want this done by someone else for exactly the same reason Toby Sutch gets other people to do this sort of thing.

"Mike, I swear I *need* you on this. . . . I swear you'll understand when I tell you the whole story. . . . As a matter of fact, I'm scared stiff. If I can't frighten her off, I'll have to leave the country for good. . . . Thanks, Mike. . . . How long will you need to arrange it? . . . Yes, yes, I can keep her here for another couple of hours. Thanks." Triumphantly Adam replaced the receiver.

They ate a pleasant but not very enterprising meal of green pea soup, grilled Dover sole, and a too stiff chocolate mousse, followed by a perfect, ripe Camembert.

Over lunch, Adam chatted agreeably about nothing much: John Lennon's blossoming romance with Yoko Ono; whether the Americans actually would land a man on the moon; whether Golda Meir would be Israel's first woman prime minister; whether Annabel wanted to stay in that evening or dance at Sybilla's.

To Annabel, every minute seemed to stretch to an hour. She felt ashamed, confused—and worried because she knew that she wasn't a very good actress. A screen test in L.A. had once confirmed this.

As he finished his coffee, Adam stared across the table at her elaborate coiffure. He said, "I know you've spent the entire morning at the hairdresser having your hair put up like Marie Antoinette's. But I feel an irresistible impulse to tear it all down."

Smiling, he stood up, walked around to Annabel's seat, drew her chair back for her, took her firmly by the wrist, and led her to the stairs.

It was a quarter to three. Mike had said not before five o'clock, by which time it would be dark.

CHAPTER 30

Friday, 31 January 1969

FIRMLY ADAM LED Annabel up the stairs. She had no choice but to follow him. She dared not suddenly act out of character: should she seek excuses to avoid going to bed with him, it would be the first time. Adam, whose reactions were as fast and instinctive as those of his damned huge cat, would immediately guess that there was another reason for Annabel's refusal.

He would ask questions, silky smooth and casual at first but gradually becoming sharper, faster, and more pointed. Annabel knew that she would become flustered; she would allow herself to be led into the trap of contradicting herself—and then that many-toothed trap would snap shut! She had watched Adam do this to others—why not to her?

And though the apartment was warm, and Adam's hand was warm, Annabel felt her body chill and the hair prickle on the back of her neck. His strong, insistent fingers firmly clasped her wrist as they climbed the stairs: his hand felt like a handcuff, impossible to unshackle.

Annabel dreaded what was about to happen. She could not bear Adam to touch her, could not bear to think that she had ever *allowed* him to touch her; she could not bear to think that once she had willingly offered her body to him—willingly opened herself, her mind and her affection. Without much hope, she longed for some distraction, some possibility of escape, some means of putting off this humiliation. On the other hand, she was anxious to get this final ordeal finished—and escape.

Adam was now leading her toward his bedroom as he would a call girl—for a little light entertainment on a wintry afternoon. The only way Annabel's situation differed was that the call girl would be paid and would probably feel indifference, for it was something she had chosen to do, and in a way, she would feel wanted.

Of course, Adam would probably prefer a call boy.

Briefly Annabel remembered the moment at the pub when he had given a lingering kiss to that boy and, for the first time, she had seen Adam's emotions not under his usual firm control: she had seen him openly relaxed and happy. Before that moment, she hadn't understood why he had insisted, so successfully, that Miranda keep their long affair a secret—but now she knew what might have happened if those two had become engaged: blackmail. The boy he had kissed was unlikely to be the only one. Annabel supposed that discarded male lovers felt as bruised, battered, and resentful as female ones—and might similarly seek revenge, especially accompanied by wads of cash.

As Adam opened his bedroom door, Annabel felt revulsion and self-disgust. Standing aside to let her enter, he released his grip on her wrist. She smelled his erotic, country smell as she passed before him, and it made her nearly nauseous.

She watched Adam's big black cat jump from the bed and run forward; he rubbed sinuously against Adam's leg. Pitch was as wary and as independent as his master, and Adam was fond of Pitch, primarily because Pitch seemed determined not to be fond of Adam. Pitch might stretch out on the ocelot cover of Adam's bed, but when Adam climbed into the bed, Pitch jumped off.

Outside, against a bleak, pale sky, the witch fingers of the trees in Cadogan Place bent beneath the weight of snow still on their branches. Adam drew the curtains. He said, "I won't switch on the lights." The firelight threw flickering shadows over his thin, taut face, making his dark eyebrows seem longer, more saturnine.

He sat on an armchair and pulled Annabel to him until she stood between his knees. His warm hands slowly traveled up her legs, over sheer black nylon.

Adam said, "You're wearing tights!"

"It's a very cold day." Wearily Annabel thought that she must be the only woman in London not allowed to wear tights when it was snowing. But Adam like to peel off lace bikinis, suspender belt, high-heeled shoes, and stockings, in that order. Sometimes he did not peel them all off.

"Naughty, naughty." Adam unzipped Annabel's black suede miniskirt. She felt his hands beneath her black skinny-rib sweater. "Dear me, nothing at all," he said. He pulled up her sweater, and when her face was hidden and her arms trapped, he licked her nipples.

When she was naked except for her black tights, Adam said, "*Don't move!*" He stood up and walked toward the Georgian desk.

Annabel suddenly felt very frightened.

Adam opened a drawer and produced a pair of scissors. He turned and said, "You're shivering! Surely you can't be cold with this roaring log fire?"

"I'm . . . excited," Annabel gulped. She found it difficult to breathe.

Adam returned, sat, and again pulled her to him. "I told you never to wear tights. So I'm cutting these into stockings." He hooked one finger over the waistband and drew it toward him. The scissors flashed in the firelight. Adam pulled at each thigh and snipped until the jagged tights dangled down Annabel's legs.

She felt him stroke her hair.

"You're so silky," he murmured. "Some women are like an old saucepan scourer down there." Adam never let a woman forget that she was not the only one.

Annabel felt him lick her: sick at heart, she felt her body melt, respond.

He looked up and whispered, "You're very tense. Are you frightened?"

"Yes," Annabel breathed truthfully.

"I'm not surprised," Adam said. "You've disobeyed my orders. *Don't move.*"

Again he moved toward the antique desk. And again Annabel felt terrified. Her heart seemed to leap up into the back of her mouth. She swallowed with difficulty. She held her breath. *Was* this some cat-and-mouse game?

Adam returned with a Victorian baby's hairbrush, very soft and backed by ivory.

"First I'll brush your bush, and then you can do it to me." He stroked her pubic hair lightly, slowly, rhythmically.

"Adam . . . Can't we just . . . go to bed?" Annabel had now faced the fact that bed was unavoidable and the sooner she got into it, the sooner she would be able to get out of it.

Adam put down the hairbrush and said, "Of course we're going to bed. Turn around."

Annabel did so.

Adam stood up and pulled the pins from her elaborately disheveled coiffure; he pushed both hands into the long fair strands at the base of her skull and started to shake her hair free.

He said, "Your neck is rigid. You're *very* tense! What's the matter?"

"Nothing," Annabel quavered. "I'm just tired. I know it's only three in the afternoon—but that's just how I feel."

"I know what to do to women who are too tired." He carried her to the bathroom, where he pulled off her shredded tights; together, they stood naked beneath the warm shower. He carefully soaped her body all over, watched her nipples harden. With difficulty, Annabel smiled at him.

Adam played the warm hand spray over each smooth surface and crevice of her body; then he wrapped her in a bathtowel and carried her to his bed.

"A pretty picture," he said, looking at Annabel's plump white body on the ocelot bedspread.

He moved to one of the side tables; they were antique Thai chests with elaborate silver locks, and upon each one, in an eighteen-inch-high pewter holder, stood a huge, thick aubergine candle, which he now lit.

Adam's skilled lovemaking was never mechanical because he was genuinely interested in having a woman at his mercy—hooked on him. He liked to maneuver his women partners into a sexual relationship in which they became increasingly subordinate to him in bed and eventually gave over to him total responsibility for their erotic response.

Unlike most men, Adam had developed his gift of imagination, and put it to use. Fantasy was an important part of his lovemaking because he saw that it excited women. He was adept at playing Rhett Butler, Lewis Carroll or Petruchio; master and slave girl, doctor and nurse, vicar and choirgirl, teacher and schoolgirl.

Adam was especially attractive to the woman who liked the fantasy of being "forced" to have sex with some authority figure: this exonerated her childish feelings of guilt and her wickedness for thinking sexy thoughts. When his partner eventually confided them, Adam always acted out her own fantasies, which aroused her even more.

Whatever their wishes, there were few women who did not stagger, dazed by pleasure, from Adam's long bedroom.

Annabel, however, felt only cold apprehension as, lying on Adam's bed, she watched him go back to the bathroom and return carrying thick white towels. She looked up at his well-muscled body, at the shadow of hair that ran from his neck to his thick penis, and she thought: Oh God, he's going to give me a massage.

She wouldn't be able to get away for at least another hour!

Adam picked up a cut-glass bottle of baby oil; he warmed some in his hands.

It was warm and still in the bedroom. Annabel listened to the soft strains of "The Swans of Tuonela": Sibelius always made her feel as if she were in a cozy, dark hut, in the middle of a quiet, snowy forest, while hungry wolves howled faintly on a distant skyline.

She lay face down on the bed as Adam started to rub his oiled hands slowly over every inch of her body, movements that were firm but fluid, and never hurt.

Using the entire surface of his hands, keeping his fingers together, he blended each movement into the next. His stroking seemed one smooth and continuous motion as he moved silently from one part of her body to the next, always keeping to the same rhythm and pressure, always repeating each movement three times. Adam smoothed her body until it felt supple as satin. Annabel felt her eyes close and her thoughts drift away. Slowly his hands traveled upward.

Then she felt his tongue on her spine, gently moving up it . . . down . . . and up again.

"Feel better?" Adam's voice caressed her as softly as his hands. Gently he pried her thighs apart and stroked them, first with his fingertips, then with his tongue. He turned her over. As his lips touched her breast, Annabel quivered with pleasure. She breathed, half panting now, as if she had been running.

As his head bent over her, she felt his warm breath just before his lips touched hers; she felt her own lips part before the moist, insistent tip of his tongue; she felt his tongue thrust deep into her mouth. Softly Annabel groaned. It was not only as if Adam were playing her like a fine violin but as if the entire Philharmonic string section were playing arpeggios over every quivering inch of her body, the chords ascending, then descending, in rapid succession, without stop.

Adam knew so well the responses of her body, how to gradually excite her to frenzy, so that she neither knew where she was, or with whom, nor cared who knew it or might observe them.

As she groaned with pleasure, Annabel forgot that this man had clawed and shredded her emotions, had sought to ruin her family and might have succeeded. She knew only that the animal smell of his body, so close to hers, made her lose all grip on reason, and the hard force of that muscular weight against her softness made her forget everything but their swiftly rising passion.

How could I *do* this? Annabel thought fleetingly, and then she did.

Just after four o'clock, Miranda appeared at the offices of Owen and Fraser. The orange suit that she had worn to the EGM was very crumpled; she looked a little dazed and very happy: clearly, Angus had found New York educational, but Miranda was too pleased to feel jealous.

She was shown into a room with a large oval table in the center, strewn with paper. Behind a pile of documents, Sam sat beside Richard Fraser.

"You're late," Sam said crossly. "And so's Annabel. It's after four. God knows why the traffic comes to a standstill all over this island whenever it rains or snows! You'd have thought that by now they'd have all gotten used to the idea that this is normal British weather."

"Sorry, Sam. Everything went as planned at my end." Miranda smirked. "Did Annabel find anything?"

"She found three notebooks in Adam's desk. She left here at one o'clock to put them back where she found them." Sam nodded toward the papers piled on the table. "These are photostats." He did not mention the envelope hidden in his jacket pocket.

With a smile, Richard Fraser said, "We've got what we need to prove your case."

"*What have you found?*"

"The notebooks contain details of each financial transaction, as Grant moved the money from one bank account to another, until it became untraceable. They clearly show which bank account each sum of money eventually reached."

Sam added, "He seems to have five final bank accounts in which the money accumulates; they are referred to as accounts A, B, C, D, and E. Unfortunately, the notebooks don't give the account numbers or address of the banks; they might all be in a single Swiss bank—or scattered in five different places throughout the world. There's no way of telling from the notebooks."

"Of course," Richard Fraser went on, "Grant could remember the names of the banks and their addresses: it's not difficult to remember that your A account is in Bank Leu, Zurich. But he must have some record of the numbers of these five bank accounts, because without the correct number, you cannot have access to a numbered bank account."

Sam said, "So although we now have hard evidence to convict Adam of embezzlement, we can't get the money back until we find where it is. So there's still a missing bit to our puzzle. Now we've got to look for a list of five numbers."

"I'm glad we can nail the bastard," Miranda said. "But I'm worried about Annabel. What could have happened to her?"

"Her cab's probably stuck in a traffic jam," Sam grunted.

"But if you say she left here around one o'clock, she should have got to Cadogan Place by . . . two at the latest," Miranda calculated. "So she should have been back here by three—no matter how bad the traffic!"

"Maybe someone was there," Sam said. "Maybe Adam turned up, and she hasn't yet been able to put the stuff back in the desk. She said once Adam yelled at her when he saw her open it."

"I suppose we couldn't telephone . . . ?"

"If Adam's not there, then we can. But if he's there—why would *you* be telephoning him, Miranda? Why would *you* telephone Annabel? And how could *I* know that Annabel's there?"

"She might have phoned you."

Sam shook his head. "By now that matron has reported back to Adam," he said, assuming incorrectly. "So he knows how Clare and I took Elinor from the nursing home. We gave our real names and showed our passports. It's clear that we suspect dirty work. So *I* can't exactly telephone him for a friendly chat!"

"Annabel might have had an accident," Miranda worried.

"You women blow a raindrop into a storm," Sam said. "If I telephone the police, they'll think I'm crazy. 'My sister-in-law should have been back an hour ago—so I thought I'd better report her as a missing person.' " Seeing Miranda's dubious expression, he relented and picked up the telephone. "Still, if she's been in an accident, the police'll know about it."

Richard Fraser said, "We've still got work here, Sam. Let Miranda call the police while we finish listing these documents."

Just after five-thirty, Fraser looked up from the boardroom table and said, "It looks as if most of the trust money has been transferred to these five accounts. There seems to be about seventeen percent of the original sum left in the trust."

"How did he manage to shift it?" Miranda asked.

"Most of the money was sent to a Hong Kong firm of investment brokers, who deducted three percent in various ways, then passed the remainder to bank accounts A, B, C, and D. Grant never sent further money to these brokers until the previous amount had been passed to the A, B, C, or D accounts: that's one reason why it's taken a long time to process the money."

"Adam didn't trust them?" Miranda said.

"Why should he?" Fraser replied. "The Hong Kong brokers take a commission of three percent for legally laundering the money. I expect they'll be able to produce 'records' to account for every penny; on paper, it'll look as though they're mighty unlucky stockbrokers: either the firms they invest in go bankrupt, or the stock dives shortly after they've invested in it. Although not *all* the money passed to them has been lost. They still hold some of it—as a stockbroker easily might—in the account referred to as E. I would guess that's a genuine investment account, to give a little plausibility to their cover story."

"The fraud squad should be interested in this Hong Kong outfit," Sam said.

Fraser said laconically, "Probably nothing they can do about it because it's outside U.K. jurisdiction. But I expect they can now pick up Grant." He pulled over the telephone and dialed. "Detective Inspector Piper? . . . The O'Dare case. I'm looking at clear evidence that you can smack him with. I'll need a couple of days to get it in order and check it carefully, but by Monday morning I should have enough for you to act on. . . . The photostats of his account books . . . Yes, all in Grant's handwriting, according to Miss O'Dare. . . . No, we haven't any bank statements yet. . . . I *know* you need to see that the money ends up in a bank statement in Grant's name—but in the meantime, surely you won't let Grant leave the country? There's certainly enough stuff, right in front of me, for you to ask him for help with your inquiries. . . . Okay, I'll bring it straight over to you. . . . Certainly, with one of the family to lodge the complaint."

"Come on, let's go." Sam stood up.

Miranda protested, "It's nearly six o'clock. I'm worried about Annabel—she should have been back here three hours ago! I don't like to leave without her. Can't Detective Inspector Piper do something about finding her?"

Richard Fraser shook his head. "He's fraud squad. And you've already notified the police."

"Look, we're all worried," Sam admitted. "But what can we do except tough it out? And move in on Adam as fast as possible?"

"I'm going round to Adam's place now," Miranda said. "*Don't* try to talk me out of it!"

Sam sighed and turned to Fraser. "You take this stuff to Piper's office. We'll meet you there as soon as possible. I can't let Miranda go by herself."

After the door had shut behind the accountant, Sam said, "Before we leave, I think you should have a swift look at these." He pulled two creased sheets of paper from his pocket and handed them to Miranda.

Miranda scanned the first document. She looked puzzled. "This is my birth certificate. How did *you* get it? Why give it to me now?" She glanced at it again. "Hang on. . . . This *isn't* my birth certificate!"

Mystified, Miranda once again scanned the white sheet of paper, with its royal crest, headed: "Certificate of Birth." She read aloud, " 'Name, Miranda Patricia. Sex, girl. Name of mother, Patricia Doreen Kettle. Name of father, William Montmorency O'Dare. Date of birth, seven November 1941. Place of birth and registration district, St. Pancras. Subdistrict, southwest St. Pancras. Certified to have been compiled from records . . .' "

Miranda looked at Sam.

"This birth certificate says that Daddy Billy was my *father!* What rubbish!"

Sam said nothing.

Miranda looked again at the certificate. "Miranda Patricia O'Dare is *my* name all right, but who is this woman called Patricia Doreen Kettle? *She* isn't my mother! And this isn't my birthday!"

Sam shrugged his shoulders. "Look at the other paper."

The second sheet of paper bore the letterhead of Swithin, Timmins and Grant; it was handwritten and dated 17 March 1942. Slowly Miranda read: "My dear Elinor, I beg you to do nothing hasty. Miranda is now Billy's only surviving child, and so she might, one day, have a claim to Larkwood, together with the entire estate. Because of this, I advise you on no account to destroy her genuine birth certificate. Yours, in haste, devotedly, Joe."

Miranda looked up and said, "So if these documents aren't forgeries or jokes, I am Daddy Billy's daughter, not his granddaughter. But if this Patricia Doreen Kettle was my mother, then . . . Edward and Jane weren't my parents . . . *and I'm not related to Elinor!*"

CHAPTER 31

Friday, 31 January 1969

SAM AND MIRANDA hurried from the lawyer's office through lightly falling snow. Miranda impatiently brushed snowflakes from her face and beckoned to her driver, waiting at the opposite curb in her silver Mercedes.

Before the driver could pull over, a taxicab shrieked to a stop in front of her. The driver jumped out and hurried around to open the door for his passenger, but before he could reach it, the door opened.

The passenger collapsed onto the trampled, grimy snow at Miranda's feet.

"*Annabel!*" Miranda recognized the wolfskin coat and crimson boots. She knelt in the snow beside her sister.

The driver said to Sam, "I wanted to take the lady to St. George's Casualty, guv, but she made me bring 'er 'ere."

Annabel's face was unrecognizable. Her swollen left eye-lid was badly torn, leaving the top of her eyeball exposed; the eye was cut and bloody. Her flattened nose was clearly broken. Two front teeth were missing from her open, bleeding mouth.

"*What happened?*"

"I picked 'er up at the junction of Cadogan Lane and Pont Street. She was staggering about. Matter o' fact, I thought she'd 'ad a bit too much to drink. Then I saw the blood."

"Thank you. She'll be okay with us." Sam thrust notes into his hand.

"Hey, wait a minute, guv. You gotta give me your name and address. Sorry, but we 'ave to report this sort of thing to the police."

The casualty ward doctor bent over Annabel. "Bad bruising on the face . . . left eye cut . . . Looks as if there's a loss of one muscle, which will have to be restitched. The two front teeth can be dealt with later. Fractured nasal septum . . . Fractured left radius and ulna . . . Fractured fifth, sixth, and seventh ribs on the left side . . . severe abrasion on stomach, chest, and legs." He stood up. "I can't cope with all this. Nurse, please call the emergency eye doctor and get an orthopedic specialist to look at the fractured forearm. Clean her up and get her to the operating theater fast. Give her a normal anesthetic, but with a muscle relaxant."

Sam telephoned C1, the Major Crimes Branch of the Metropolitan Police, from the hospital pay phone. He doubted that Annabel's mugging was a coincidence. If he was right, this case was no longer merely a case of fraud. It was also assault and battery, grievous bodily harm, and attempted—perhaps actual—murder.

After talking to C1, Sam checked his watch: 7:30 P.M. in London meant 2:30 P.M. in New York. He called Scott's office.

Annabel lay in the operating room, her hair tucked beneath a green plastic cap, as the medical team—the ophthalmic surgeon, the orthopedic surgeon, the casualty doctor, the hospital emergency anesthetist, the nursing sister, and two nurses—prepared to go about their business.

After the anesthesia was administered, the orthopedic surgeon cleared up and stitched the abrasions; then Annabel's fractured left arm was gently put back in place and set in plaster, and her ribs strapped back. These matters were dealt with quickly and easily, but the eye operation was a far more delicate matter.

"We're looking at major trauma to the eye," the ophthalmic surgeon said after his initial examination. "I'm going to just clean up initially. She's lost that left eye muscle and may lose her left eye. She's had a nasty laceration, and there's a lot of abrasion as well as damage to the cornea. If I can save the eye, she'll need at least one further major operation, when the bruising and lacerations have subsided. At this stage, I can't say whether her sight will be impaired indefinitely."

The eye operation took over an hour. Afterward, the ophthalmic surgeon removed his gloves and ran his hands over his face wearily. He washed, then again donned his dinner jacket; without being asked, the sister tied his black bow tie. He hurried off.

After Annabel's nose was set, she was given a sedative injection. It was ten P.M. when she was wheeled into a dimly lit ward filled with other recovering emergency patients.

At three in the morning, she became conscious of the pain: it hurt to breathe. She felt such pain in her head that she winced with each labored breath.

Upon hearing her groan, the nurse sitting by her bedside spoke reassuringly. "You're in hospital, Mrs. Svenson. You've had an accident. You're going to be all right. Your family are waiting outside. We had to give you an injection before we tidied you up, and the effects are wearing off now, which is why you're waking up."

"I . . . can't . . . see." Her words were slurred and muffled, almost as though she were drunk.

"That's because your left eye is bandaged, and your right eye is very swollen."

She fed Annabel a little water from a cup with a spout. As the water dribbled into her mouth, Annabel retched. The nurse sponged her lips and continued to soothe her until Annabel drifted into an uneasy sleep.

Saturday, 1 February 1969

As soon as Miranda opened her eyes, she reached for the ivory telephone at her bedside.

"It's only seven o'clock. The hospital said you couldn't call before nine," Angus sleepily reminded her.

"I'd forgotten." In the pale winter sunlight, Miranda sighed, then stretched luxuriously. "Well, well, well," she said softly.

"I've been practicing," Angus murmured smugly.

"No more practice needed." Gently she pinched his rather large ear. "I'm a jealous woman."

"So now will you marry me?"

Miranda propped herself on one elbow. "Hold on, darling, give me time to collect my thoughts." She was delighted by his proposal. The big obstacle clearly no longer existed: she would be happy to stay in bed with Angus for the rest of the week, and to live with him for the rest of her life. She was confident that they would live happily ever after, for all the reasons she had originally become engaged to him. But she couldn't think about the future until she had resolved the present. But she wasn't going to risk hurting Angus or herself again by making up her mind in a hurry—although now that it was behind her, she could admit to herself how much she had regretted breaking off their engagement.

By ten A.M., Annabel was vaguely aware of nurses' voices, of squashy rubber-soled shoes treading a rubber floor, china clinking, a radio playing soft music. She could smell antiseptic.

Her right hand was warm. It was being held in somebody else's hand.

Annabel whispered, "Scott?"

"I've been here for over an hour, angel."

"Please . . . don't . . . leave me."

"Never again."

"I'm so . . . sorry."

"So am I!" During his long flight, Scott had been able to think of nothing but Annabel and their marriage. He had eventually decided that there were no innocent partners in a troubled marriage, and if one spouse pointed an accusing finger at the other, it was probably an unrealistic way to solve the problems and save the marriage.

Annabel had not been his wife and partner: he had always expected her to be his second lieutenant, to submerge her individuality to his needs, and to be displayed—Scott's status symbol. He suspected that if she hadn't fallen for that bastard Adam, she'd have fallen for someone else—someone who was prepared to make the effort to make her feel that he cared for her as a person and not as a supportive prop to his self-image as a smart and successful career man.

Scott kissed Annabel's hand. In a frenzied whisper, he told her what he had been longing to say: "I thought my job was a good enough reason to neglect everything else, angel. I didn't mean for it to suck up all my time and energy.

Things are going to be different, Annabel. I want to be successful, but I also want my life."

In spite of her woozy state, Annabel could feel his warmth and tenderness. She could feel the difference between Scott's loving attention and the skillful but detached and uninvolved attention she received from Adam.

She whispered, "Scott, I'm so ashamed."

"So am I. In future, I'll be looking after you." He rested his cheek on her arm, which lay on the bedclothes.

"What's . . . happened . . . to me?" Annabel asked.

"A couple of guys mugged you and snatched your purse. The police have to ask you a few things, later. You've got a broken arm and ribs, and . . . they reset your nose. It will look exactly the same—the surgeon swore it would."

"My eyes feel funny."

"They punched your face, angel."

"Are my eyes going to be all right?"

Scott hesitated. "Of course."

"You're such a bad liar, Scott."

After a moment, he said, "Your right eye will be fine."

Annabel's soft sobs hurt her broken ribs.

"You'll certainly be able to see," Scott said. "And it doesn't matter to me . . . Oh Christ, I shouldn't have told you."

"*I want to know*. . . . I don't want to be treated like a child anymore."

"You won't be." Scott again kissed her hand. "In fact, if you still want it . . . I know I've always argued that New York was no place to bring up a child . . . But what the hell—other people do it. Why shouldn't we?"

Annabel stopped crying.

"Can you remember what happened, madam?" the unseen policeman asked quietly.

"Not much," Annabel whispered. "But I'll try."

Just after five o'clock, Annabel had left Adam's home, explaining that she was late for a dress fitting. As she hurried along, her crimson boots occasionally slipped on the slush. She turned left into Pont Street, where she thought she could probably get a cab. There was nobody in sight and very little passing traffic.

Annabel was vaguely aware that a small woman in dark clothes had emerged from the recessed door of a flower shop—already closed for the night—on the corner of Cadogan Lane. As Annabel hurried past, this woman suddenly leapt toward her. Expertly she thrust her left index and middle fingers up Annabel's nostrils, which jerked her head backward. At the same time, the woman hooked her right foot around Annabel's left boot and tugged it forward. Annabel's arms circled wildly as she slipped on the slush.

Desperately she tried to regain her balance but failed. She crashed backward.

From behind, she heard a car draw up. In the light of the streetlamp, she looked up and saw two men with stockings pulled over their heads, flattening their features into terrifying, inhuman shapes.

As the two men jerked Annabel to her feet, twisting her so that she faced the street, she felt the woman grab her red shoulder bag, then saw her jump into the car, take the wheel, and rev the engine.

With a thug on either side of her, Annabel was held in midair. Her elbows pinioned to her body, she was dragged to the rear of an old Morris Minor parked in Cadogan Lane.

As one of her attackers swiftly and roughly searched her, the other hissed, "We've got a message for you. Remember for the future—if you *make* trouble, you *get* trouble!" He drew back his fist, then smashed it in Annabel's jaw.

He continued to hit her with a professional boxer's skill and a steady rhythm as the second man held her more or less upright. Annabel felt agonizing pain in her kidneys; her left ribs seemed to explode. She felt a blow to her chest, then could no longer breathe as her nose was smashed. After the first punch in her eye, she began to lose consciousness.

"Better leave it at that," she heard the second man grunt as she passed out. "You know what happened last time."

In her bronze Reliant Scimitar, Miranda drove Sam to Wiltshire, where Josh was waiting for his dad. Sam had spent the night at the hospital, and felt as stiff and stale as yesterday's bread, but he had promised Josh that he would see him over the weekend. And Miranda wanted to talk to Elinor about the birth certificate.

Jet lag was now catching up with Sam, but Miranda's fast driving over snowy roads in the sports car was sufficiently suspenseful to keep him awake.

Clare waited for them, alone in her kitchen. Elinor and Buzz were having their afternoon nap on the twin beds in the guest room. Josh had happily scuttled off to a Cubs meeting. David, who had to attend the annual meeting of the Kennet and Avon Canal Trust, wasn't due to arrive until evening.

Clare had told David about Annabel's horrific assault, and that she had lost her left eye, but the doctor had warned her not to tell the two older women yet: such a shock might well delay her grandmother's recovery. Although Elinor was still too weak to leave her bed and still spoke in a whisper, she was recovering faster than the doctor had expected; she was responding well to the Parentrovite injections, and her old vitality was returning.

Shortly after three P.M., the Scimitar slid to a halt in front of Applebank Cottage.

Seeing the weary faces of the occupants, Clare asked no questions as she placed the white tureen of mulligatawny soup on the kitchen table.

Sam fell asleep at the table after the cheese omelet and before Clare could serve her apple tart with apricot glazing.

Miranda yawned and said, "I didn't get much sleep last night either. Mind if I have a nap on Josh's bed?" She disappeared.

Clare gently woke Sam and led him upstairs to her bedroom.

At six o'clock, Sam opened his eyes. He could hear faint classical music. The green chintz curtains hadn't yet been closed, and in the firelight, he could see the snow beating silently from the darkness against the windowpanes.

He stretched out a hand, groped for the bedside light, and knocked a brass alarm clock to the floor.

Clare ran upstairs, opened her bedroom door, and flicked on the light switch.

"I'm still a clumsy son of a bitch," Sam said apologetically. He sat up in bed, rubbing his bruised face and black eye.

Clare stared at the crisp black curls that covered his big chest and at the purple bruises inflicted on his arms by Matron Braddock.

"Sit down a minute," Sam said sleepily. He patted the patchwork quilt.

As she perched on the side of the bed, Clare suddenly felt filled with gratitude. "Sam, I can't thank you enough. Maybe we could have done it by ourselves, but . . . you made everything happen so fast. You dealt with that vile nursing home . . . the lawyer . . . the accountant . . . the police . . . the hospital . . . You've been wonderful."

In the firelight, Sam leaned forward and gently kissed the tip of her nose. He put his arms around her, pulled her against his chest, and started kissing her neck. Softly he said, "I have to get back to work the day after tomorrow."

Clare gently pulled away from him, feeling anything but gentle. How *dare* Sam press his advantage and try to seduce her! And yet as she felt indignation rise . . . at the same time . . . although her head was telling her what to do, her body was contradicting the message.

Sam leaned forward, kissed the space between her eyebrows, and tightened his arms around her. Slowly Clare stopped resisting. As she inhaled his familiar acrid odor and remembered the first time she had been aware of his pungent eroticism, she felt as irresistibly drawn to Sam as a pin to a magnet. She remembered how secure she had felt when first encircled by the powerful strength of these muscular, bruised arms. Even as she weakened, she was furious and bewildered. Why didn't she feel this magnetism between herself and David, who was so much better a man than Sam, so much more caring? Why was she even *speaking* to Sam when she knew how hurt David would be if he could see her now?

At this very moment, David was probably collecting Josh from the church hall at Warminster. Tomorrow he was going to help Josh with the work he'd missed, when he was late returning to school after their skiing holiday.

Clare whispered, "I *hate* you, Sam, you manipulative bastard."

"Yes, baby," Sam murmured as he gently kissed her hairline.

"Let me *go*, you bastard," Clare hissed, trying to pull away from him.

Sam laughed and kissed her hard on the mouth.

Briefly, Clare tried to remind herself of the way Sam had made her suffer during the past three and a half years, but her memories faded as she felt again the dynamism and protective strength that had first attracted her to him. She didn't want to be independent and sensible; she wanted to lay her head on Sam's hard, hairy chest and feel his arms around her—and know that everything was going to be taken care of by him—just for a few moments.

As her resolve melted and she yielded, somewhere at the back of her head, Clare realized that there was a kernel of truth in Elinor's world of romance.

Later, as Sam slept, Clare lay awake watching the firelight flicker on the ceiling. She felt guilty, treacherous, and miserable.

Just half an hour earlier, after they had made love, she had whispered to Sam, "Why do you *really* want me back? Tell me the truth."

Sam had hugged her hard against his big chest; his crisp, curly hair had tickled her nose as he murmured, "Because I love you."

But Clare knew that the real reasons were not quite so romantic: Sam missed his son, his wife, and family life more than he had ever expected. As a dog becomes accustomed to its basket, Sam had grown used to having Clare around; she made him laugh, she ran his home and his social life, she entertained his clients and took care of all the tedious background trivialities of life; this left Sam free to concentrate on the work he loved.

Clare sighed. Just now Sam had really tried his best. But it had felt as if he was trying. At one point, he had whispered, "What *more* do I have to do? I've been hanging on the chandeliers trying to please you."

And Clare had whispered back, "That's exactly why it isn't going to work, Sam. Because I know you're trying, and so am I. But David and I don't *need* to try."

"What the hell does *he* do that I don't?"

Hesitantly Clare had tried to explain, without hurting Sam. "David accepts me the way I am—the way my body *and* my mind work. David accepts my feelings, so I don't have to twist them to suit his prejudices: he may feel differently—but he isn't going to insist that I agree."

"You mean he's better than me in the sack."

"That just shows you haven't been listening!" Clare felt her indignation grow. "I left you because you didn't *listen* to me, Sam, and you never took me seriously! When I talked to you about something that was important to me, you made the appropriate comments—*but I knew you weren't really hearing me*, because you carried on reading the paper or whatever. That told me that reading the paper was more important than what I had to say!" She sat up in bed. "I felt you weren't really there, that you had removed yourself—to where I couldn't bother you."

"Are you telling me you walked out on me because I didn't *listen* to you?"

In the firelight, Clare lifted her hands in a hopeless gesture. "Sam, you have a conveniently short memory. I left you because I found you in bed with a girl—again."

Sam started to lose his temper. What was the point of bringing up all that again? And if Clare felt so strongly about it—how come they were in bed together? He snapped, "You didn't miss anything. I gave you your orgasms, didn't I? Could one quick fuck in the wrong cunt change so much between *us?*"

Clare snapped back, "Promiscuity devalues the coinage of love." She was adamant. She had learned the hard way that a dishonest sexual relationship could alter a woman's entire life for the worse, because one couldn't separate sex from the rest of reality.

Suddenly Clare knew without a doubt which man she wanted to spend the rest of her life with. Certainly her conscience still told her to take Josh back to his father and let Sam have another chance to prove himself a good husband. But she had already confronted the agonies of conscience over depriving Josh of a father. Why should she endure that again?

And why should she risk going back to Sam? Why should she risk this new, happy life she had struggled so hard to build up—in the hope that he would keep his promise, when he had broken so many promises before?

"I didn't mean that." Sam groped for the words that would reach Clare. "Honey, I'm sorry."

Gently she shook his arm off. She had made her decision, and nothing was going to alter it. Sam was still basically selfish, and David was still basically the unselfish man who had encouraged her to develop her own personality. David was kind and gentle, compassionate and thoughtful. He was a considerate person, and Sam was an inconsiderate person, which is why Sam was a bad lover. Clare remembered that it was this quality in David that had quieted her sexual anxiety. And David's gentle consideration had also lulled the uncertainty within her that had made it difficult for her to stand on her own feet and solve her own problems.

Now as she watched Sam sleep, Clare hoped to God that David would be gentle, compassionate, and understanding when she told him that she had just been to bed with Sam.

At six o'clock that evening, Miranda heard Buzz, in the cottage's only bathroom, singing tunelessly, "All the nice girls love a sailor . . . "

She made a tray of tea and took it up to the guest room. Elinor was sitting in bed pouring Scrabble letters back into the bag.

"I won!" she said triumphantly, then looked anxious. "You don't think Buzz would cheat to let me win?"

"Never," lied Miranda as she poured the tea. She handed a cup to Elinor and said softly, "I have something very important to ask you, Gran. Who is Patricia Kettle?"

With a trembling hand, Elinor slowly put down her cup. "She . . . she had some secretarial job at the War Office." She was clearly making an effort to sound casual. "She was killed in an air raid—sometime in 1943, I think."

"I need to know more than that, darling." Miranda's voice was gentle but determined. She pulled the crumpled birth certificate and Joe Grant's letter from her pocket and handed both to Elinor.

Elinor looked at them sadly. "After all these years . . . " she said. "I suppose . . . you'd better be told what happened." She looked down at her cup of cooling tea, but what she saw was the front room of her home in Earls Court Square, on Christmas Eve, 1941.

Elinor, wearing the dark green uniform of the Women's Voluntary Service, switched off the wireless. Cheerful news, for a change. In Washington, Churchill was deciding policy with Roosevelt, for after the Japanese surprise attack on the American fleet at Pearl Harbor, the United States had entered the war.

In London, still under threat of German invasion, life seemed to consist either of devastating air raids or of clearing up after them. Like everyone else, Elinor did not get enough sleep, rarely ate a proper meal, and often worked seven days a week, from dawn to long after dark, for the unpaid W.V.S. did any dirty work that seemed to be nobody else's job: they had cared for the exhausted troops evacuated from Dunkirk; they supervised evacuees; they housed and fed the bombed-out; they dislocated their own lives to smooth those of other people.

The O'Dares now lived, ate, and slept in the living room, which arrangement minimized housework, and there was coal only for one fire. On the right of the fireplace opposite the door stood the Morrison shelter—a table-height, four-poster double bed made of iron with metal mesh sides. Inside this shelter slept Clare, nearly three years old, and Annabel, who was a year younger. Elinor also slept in the Morrison, and when there was a raid, Billy left his camp bed to join them.

Objects tended to accumulate along the deep, flat top of the Morrison: Elinor's sewing machine, the notes for her next home-nursing class, a pile of mending, and, tonight, a small Christmas tree that Billy had bought for an exorbitant sum in a pub, and a battered cardboard box.

As Elinor lifted the lid of the box, she smiled with disbelief. Carefully she picked up the golden-haired china angel, with wings of real feathers. "Billy, *look! Nothing* seems to be broken!" The fragile gold and silver balls, the folded, crinkly multicolored paper bells, the brightly colored concertina paper chains, lay waiting to be used again on the Christmas tree.

"Why bother with Christmas decorations this year?" Billy asked, from the worn orange-flowered armchair by the fireplace. "The babies won't understand what Christmas is all about. I'm not sure that *I* do. Can't think why you hung up those stockings." He jerked his head to the two red stockings that dangled from the end of the Morrison.

"Stop being an old bear," Elinor said cheerfully. "You're going to play Santa Claus tonight, just as you've always done." She added winningly, "And you're the best-looking Santa in London."

"I always feel a complete fool," Billy grumbled, but he smiled at Elinor and added, "I must admit, girl, you don't look too bad yourself, all things considered. After all, Marjorie is the same age as you, but her skin looks like the Nile Delta."

Although she was past forty, Elinor's looks had worn well and her coloring had not faded. Her creamy skin was unlined; her pink cheeks looked as if she still lived in the country; her blue eyes sparkled; and her hair still waved, honey gold. Of course, her figure had thickened: wartime meals were based on bread and potatoes.

The doorbell rang.

Automatically both adults looked to the window, but the blackout curtains were drawn—no chink of light was showing. So it couldn't be an air-raid warden, about to complain.

Elinor kicked away the sandbag kept at the bottom of the door to cut out drafts. Shivering in the bitter chill of the hall passage, she groped her way to the front door. "Who is it?"

"I'm a friend of Billy," said a woman's voice: it was too dark to see her.

"Come in quickly, out of the cold." After shutting the door, Elinor switched on the hall light and looked at her visitor, who cradled a baby, wrapped in a blanket, in one arm, and carried a small, battered suitcase with the other.

Astonished, Elinor said, "I remember you! Once I saw you speak to my husband in a pub in Whitehall."

It had been on that day Annabel was born. Elinor remembered the distraught face of this girl and her slim-as-a-bulrush, brown-coated figure. She remembered the girl's almost visible aura of depression, her pleading face, and the stooped shoulders that seemed to signal dejection. She remembered that the girl had laid her head on Billy's sleeve. He had roughly shaken her off.

"Who's that?" Billy, clutching the *Daily Telegraph*, opened the front room door.

"Pat! What the hell are you doing *here?*" Billy backed into the room; the woman followed him. To Elinor, he seemed at once startled, truculent, and nervous.

The girl looked at Billy, who wore a shabby knitted cardigan and carpet slippers, no tie. Wearily she said, "You don't look so much of a ladykiller at home, Billy." Her voice was devoid of expression and of hope. "I told you I'd bring her if you didn't turn up." Turning to Elinor, she said abruptly, "It's his." She nodded her head toward the blanket-wrapped bundle in her arms.

"How dare you come here! How dare you make these ridiculous accusations!" Billy blustered.

"Shhhh! You'll wake the girls!" Elinor said automatically as her heart shriveled.

For years, Elinor had subconsciously dreaded just such a scene, had known that Billy would be caught out one day. She was surprised it hadn't happened before. She did not find it difficult to believe the girl, and her words had the surrealist inevitability of a scene déjà vu, although this tired young creature was not the tough, hard-bitten predator Elinor had half expected to appear someday.

Standing in the middle of the room, still clutching the bundle, the young woman started to cry in a soft, hopeless wail. "I *know* Shorty told you I'd had the baby, Billy. He visited me in hospital—brought me two eggs. Every day, I hoped you'd come yourself." She burst into fresh tears. "*Not once!*"

"What the hell do you want?" Billy asked roughly.

"I couldn't stay at the hospital no longer, Billy. I can't go back to the hostel with a baby. I can't go home. My dad would kill me. *I don't know what to do.* Won't you come and look after us, Billy? Remember all those times you promised?"

Billy said, "You have no right to come here and cause trouble between my wife and me."

At his formal tone of voice, the girl's face hardened. She turned to look at Elinor.

Elinor stared back. The threadbare brown coat could not disguise this child's figure; she was clearly unaware of the aura of sexuality that she so strongly projected, and that was probably what had attracted Billy. Elinor was irritatingly aware that her own green W.V.S. uniform made her look dumpy.

The girl said to Billy, "Why do you want to stay with *her?*" She jerked her head toward Elinor.

With a nervous, shaking hand, Elinor pointed to the chimneypiece, upon which stood two silver-framed photographs: Edward, aged seven, and Edward and Jane on their wedding day.

She said, "Billy and I have been married for twenty-three years. That is Billy's son. Billy's granddaughters are sleeping in this room. We are Billy's family, and he will never leave us." Her voice rang with a quiet confidence that she did not feel, although Elinor knew that Billy depended on her strength, ability, and ingenuity to look after him in wartime and still provide him with his home comforts: Billy liked to be looked after; Billy did not want to find himself responsible for this wilting woman-child and her helpless, dependent infant.

"*But you can't dump me!*" Pat Kettle pleaded. "It's your job to look after us, Billy. There's nobody else."

This was a fatal error. Billy took a hesitant step behind Elinor.

"You can't pretend we don't exist!" Miss Kettle wailed. The baby in her arms started to cry. "*Tell me what to do, Billy!* I can't look after a baby and earn my living at the same time!" She looked beseechingly at Billy. "It's *your* baby—whatever you like to think. You *know* I've never been with another man! *I love you, Billy!*" She appealed to Elinor. "*It's his baby as much as mine!* Why should I have all the responsibility? *He's* got a home and someone to look after it—I haven't."

Raising his voice above the baby's yells, Billy said, "I'm not admitting it's mine." He turned to Elinor. "I admit . . . Well, you saw for yourself that she threw herself at me. But it only happened a couple of times. And it . . . was never anything serious. And if it hadn't been for her bloody stupid religion, she could have taken precautions! *That* was her responsibility!"

At this point, the noise woke Annabel, who started to cry. Clare woke up and bawled in sympathy. Billy clapped his hands over his ears and turned away from the two women, toward the window.

Almost incredulous, the girl stared at his rejecting back. "Well, *I* can't cope any longer," she said, and laid the blanket-wrapped baby on top of the Morrison shelter. Then, sobbing, she hurried from the room.

A small, clenched fist thrust up from the wailing, jerking bundle, which rolled toward the edge of the Morrison.

As Elinor jumped forward to stop the baby from falling to the floor, she heard the front door bang.

Defensively Billy said, "Stupid bitch." To break the angry silence, he turned on the wireless. The Andrews Sisters sang cheerfully about the Boogie Woogie Bugle Boy from Company B.

With the baby in one arm, Elinor switched off the wireless. She glared at Billy. "There's some dried milk in the larder. Make me a jugful. Quickly. This baby is hungry."

She would pretend that this baby was Edward and Jane's third daughter; a six-week baby couldn't be passed off as a ten-month baby, but her new birth date would have to be before Jane's death. So Elinor would have to keep this infant away from the neighbors for a bit; then she would say that the baby had been born prematurely, had been tiny at birth and was still small for her age, and had been kept in hospital for months . . . Luckily, Annabel and Clare were too young to remember anything strange about the arrival of this sister . . . It would be easy to pretend.

"What happened to . . . my mother?" Miranda whispered.

"I never saw Miss Kettle again," Elinor said apologetically. "I've no idea whether Billy still carried on with her after that. I doubt she'd have let him. We never spoke of it again."

"She abandoned me. My *mother* abandoned me," Miranda said with disbelief.

"She was very young and clearly at the end of her tether. Be generous," Elinor said.

"No!" Miranda's voice was almost a shriek; her face was ashen white. "Please, I don't want this. I want my sisters and I want you to be . . . *I love you*, Gran! I want to be part of *your* family. You're the one who has always looked after me, the one I've always loved!"

"So you are," Elinor said firmly. She held out her frail arms and pulled Miranda against her. "Some people are born into a family and some people are chosen. I chose you long ago, Miranda, and I love you every bit as much as I love Annabel and Clare." She stroked Miranda's hair. "They are your sisters, and I trust you never to tell them otherwise."

"But then I'll by lying to Clare and Annabel," Miranda cried. "I can't look them in the eyes and know that I'm hiding something so important from them!" She stepped back from Elinor. "I'm not going to lie to them," she said. "I'm not going to deceive them. *And I'm not going to lie to myself!* Then I *really* won't know who I am!" She started to sob. "How can I behave normally, as a sister, if

I know I'm lying to them all the time? . . . *You've* always been able to shut your eyes to what you don't want to see, or put on your rose-colored spectacles so that you only see what suits you in life. But *I* want to face up to life, and deal with what's unpleasant, rather than hide or ignore it. I can't live with the people I love, knowing that I'm acting a lie all the time—deceiving them. *I can't do that!* I could never behave naturally with them and I would have no peace of mind—I couldn't stand it. It would always be on my conscience."

"Please, darling," Elinor implored, "you've always been impetuous as well as straightforward. This time please listen to me. Annabel and Clare were too young to know. If I deceived you and your sisters, it was because I love you all very much, and I love you all the same. It's often thought best not to let an orphan know she's adopted, but to raise her as one of the family; that is what I did with you."

"But Gran, you can't imagine how I feel. It's as though someone had suddenly pushed me over a cliff, and I'm falling into a void. I feel rootless. My life is never going to be the same again. I don't belong anywhere. . . . "

"Nonsense. You belong with us, as you always have." Elinor's thin hand stroked Miranda's arm. "Because although this sounds important—*it isn't.* It doesn't change anything: you're still an O'Dare—still one of the family . . . *our* family. What happened was upsetting for me at the time, but if it hadn't happened, then I wouldn't have had my third granddaughter—so I'm glad it did!"

Miranda bit her lower lip. "Nevertheless, I can't keep something like this from my . . . from Clare and Annabel."

"There's a difference between being dishonest and being discreet," Elinor said. "Everyone is morally entitled to guard their privacy to protect themselves; everyone does that, all the time. Nobody blabs their secrets to the world. Sometimes discretion—and I refuse to call it 'dishonesty'—is the best policy."

"But they're not 'the world'! They're . . . my sisters . . . and I want them to know the truth."

"Then I would prefer that you didn't tell them yet. I don't want them to be distressed on your behalf: we've had enough upsets recently in this family. Besides, there's nothing to be gained by telling them the truth. Not now."

Miranda stared at her. "How can *you* judge that? You, who always ran from the truth if it didn't suit you! You, who lied in so many ways—by omission, by insinuation. Gran, you lied to everyone, most especially to yourself. *Why did you do it?*"

Elinor paused before she spoke again; the pain was evident in her voice. "Why does anyone lie? Fear. I was afraid of violence, afraid of the deeper unhappiness—perhaps despair—that I would feel if I had to admit to myself that my life was unhappy; I was afraid of having to face the world alone—every woman's fear—and of being unable to cope. I'm afraid I'm not very brave, Miranda."

Miranda said nothing; her face reflected mute confusion.

Elinor pressed her argument persuasively: "Miranda, you can't see this thing objectively right now—nobody in your position could. So please promise me that you won't say anything to anyone yet."

"Gran, Gran, how can I let you decide anything about this? You're as subjective as I am. *How can I trust your judgment?*"

"I'm only asking you to give yourself time, to think more calmly about the matter."

After reflection, Miranda nodded her head slowly. "All right. I'll agree to that."

"And should you eventually decide that they should be told, then let *me* tell them. . . . " Elinor persisted.

"Okay," Miranda responded wearily.

"And let *me* choose the time and the place to tell them. Just promise me that, darling."

With great reluctance, Miranda said, "Yes, if that's what you want."

Elinor sighed with relief. She had managed to postpone this unhappy matter, but what was more important was that she had managed quickly to persuade Miranda that this hurtful revelation was of no consequence—and that was certainly true.

Miranda threw her head back and stared unhappily at her grandmother. "There's another thing I also feel ashamed about. All my life I've howled for my fair share of whatever was going—I felt it was my moral right. I felt cheated when I was left out of something because I was the youngest. I even insisted that I was morally entitled to inherit one third of all your money. I always made a point of *that!* And now I realize I'm not entitled to a single penny! Adam knew that. Why else would he have my birth certificate? It gave him proof I wasn't entitled to any of the Dove Trust. Oh, Gran, I've been such a greedy little bitch! How could you stand me?"

"Hush, darling. I don't want to hear any more of this nonsense. The youngest child often feels left out, and I always understood how you felt. All *any* child is entitled to is a good education and perhaps a start in life, and luckily I was able to give you that. As to the rest . . . Who knows whether I'm going to have *any* money to leave anybody? But we're none of us going to be homeless and starving. And, anyway, that's not what matters right now." She tightened her arms around Miranda, and Miranda felt like a little girl again, being comforted in Elinor's arms.

Then Elinor slowly said, "Perhaps I *also* need that peace of mind of which you spoke."

CHAPTER 32

Saturday, 1 February 1969

MIKE WORE HIS black leathers with the jacket unzipped; he stood, legs astride, before the pine log fire in Adam's study. His face was white, and his clear, wide-apart gray eyes reflected his fury—and his horror.

Adam brandished the *Evening Standard*. " '*Society beauty loses eye*'!" he shouted. "I told you to *scare* her—not half kill her! You can't hush up this sort of thing, you know!"

"I'm just as worried as you are. How do you suppose *I* feel?" Mike had rarely seen his brother so angry. Bad-tempered, yes, but not this towering fury. Unlike

Mike, whose self-control could easily snap if he was sufficiently provoked, Adam usually kept his feelings under tight control.

"*How the hell did it happen?*"

"These people aren't always controllable—*you* know that, Adam! One of the reasons they do it is because they *enjoy* it. They don't *want* to stop."

Adam roared, "You didn't even get my notebooks back!"

"There were *no* notebooks in Annabel's purse, just the usual junk," Mike again insisted. "Her clothes were searched as well—they found nothing."

Adam didn't bother to mention that the notebooks were upstairs in his desk, as usual. He felt chagrined that he hadn't checked on them before having Annabel beaten up. He had a sudden thought. "I'd better make sure that Elinor doesn't find out about this! Of course she doesn't read the papers, but there's a TV stuck in front of her bloody bed! It could mean trouble!" As he spoke, he snatched up the telephone and dialed the long-distance operator.

When connected, Adam brusquely addressed the receptionist: "Get me Matron Braddock. . . . What do you *mean*, she's resigned? . . . Then give me Dr. Craig-Dunlop!"

The receptionist stammered, "Dr. Craig-Dunlop is cruising in the Caribbean, on his winter vacation."

"When will he return?" Adam's voice was harsh.

"Dr. Craig-Dunlop has already left the cruise ship," quavered the receptionist. "He's flying back to Britain as fast as he can. I'll telephone your office as soon as he arrives, Mr. Grant."

Adam could have kicked himself. He should have checked on Elinor every single goddamn day. Why hadn't the doctor told him that he was going on a cruise? Why hadn't someone told him that the matron was leaving? My God, if you wanted anything done, you had to do it yourself.

Sharply he asked, "And in the meantime, *who* is in charge of the nursing home? . . . Then tell the assistant matron that I want to speak to her immediately. . . . To discuss one of her patients, of course. . . . Mrs. O'Dare."

The receptionist stammered, "We have strict instructions not to talk about Mrs. O'Dare."

Adam was almost speechless with anger. "*I* am Mrs. O'Dare's lawyer!" His voice dropped as, carefully, he asked, "Is Mrs. O'Dare dead?"

There was a long pause.

"Well, is she or isn't she?" Adam growled, his anxiety once more surfacing.

"No. Mrs. O'Dare hasn't passed away," said the receptionist reluctantly. "But I can't tell you more than that."

Clearly there was a lot more to be told. Something odd was happening at the Lord Willington, and Adam was sure he would get more information from this stupid bitch at the desk than from the assistant matron. He barked, "I'm coming down to Eastbourne immediately unless you tell me what's happened to Mrs. O'Dare."

The terrified receptionist didn't want this bullying lawyer yelling at her in person. She blurted out, "That wouldn't do any good—Mrs. O'Dare's no longer here!"

"*What do you mean, she isn't there?*" Adam bellowed.

Prudently the receptionist pulled the line from the switchboard.

Adam turned to Mike. "I've been cut off. Deliberately, I suspect. I wonder what the *hell* is happening."

Mike was astonished by the speed with which his brother's interest had switched from the frightening problem of Annabel's injuries to trouble at Elinor's nursing home. Why should it matter so much to Adam where Elinor was? And it was obvious that Adam had hoped she was dead. *Why?*

The answer had to be money, Mike figured. He'd probably rigged her will—something like that. What a cold-blooded bastard his brother was.

Adam tapped a finger against his teeth as he considered what to do. He decided, "I'd better get down to the nursing home and check what's happened." He looked at his watch. "Six o'clock." Snatching up the telephone, he said, "The quickest way to Eastbourne is by train. When's the next express?"

Having gained this information, Adam turned to Mike. "You can take me to Victoria Station on your bike!" he ordered. "The next train leaves in fifteen minutes, so get going, you lazy bastard!"

Mike stared, surprised. Normally Adam would never deign to ride a motorbike. He didn't understand why Mike chose to drive a bike—like a greaser—when he had a perfectly good, new E-Type that could go far faster than all his two-wheeled monsters. Adam didn't seem to realize that a motorbike was no longer a poor man's transport method: Bikes were dangerous and exciting. A man who rode a bike was a man ready for action. And even the most expensive Ferrari was a vanishing dot in the rearview mirror of a fast bike.

But apparently, Adam did realize that during the rush hour, no transport was faster for weaving in and out of London traffic than a motorbike.

"Come *on!*" Adam urged brusquely, hurrying toward the door. In the hall, he pulled on his overcoat and waited impatiently as Mike buckled his German officer's black leather trench coat—liberated from the original owner by their uncle, in Munich, in 1945. "Hurry!" Adam snapped.

Both brothers clattered down the back stairs rather than wait for the slow, wheezing elevator. As he did so, Mike fastened his helmet strap and pulled on his leather gloves: if he came off, he preferred to sacrifice the leather and not his skin.

Outside, it was already dark. The weak morning sunshine had dissolved the slush, and the roads were now dry.

"For Christ's sake, *get moving!*" Adam snarled.

The bike didn't start at Mike's first kick.

"Mike the Bike!" Adam jeered. Even Adam knew that only legendary racer Mike Hailwood was known as Mike the Bike. He also knew that his brother didn't like to be teased about his bikes.

Mike, on edge after hearing the bad news about Annabel, turned his head and said, "Don't take your bloody bad temper out on me!"

"*I'll say whatever I bloody well like to you, and you'll bloody well do whatever I tell you to do!*" Adam yelled.

As always, Mike was bewildered by Adam's abrupt change of mood. He understood the hard shell into which Adam retreated when the world became too threatening; he also understood the depth of feeling in Adam that lay hidden from the rest of the world. But Mike never understood why his brother always chose to vent his vile moods on him—of all people.

Mike kicked the starter again. The bike merely coughed.

"Why doesn't this fucking machine *work?*" Adam screamed. He kicked the side panel.

"*Don't kick my bike,*" Mike growled. After years of being at Adam's mercy, being humiliated by him, being the recipient of his bad-tempered kicks and snarls, Mike was finally pushed to violent action. He decided it was time that Adam stopped treating him like a dog. It was time—more than time—that he taught Adam a lesson. He would show him that he *wasn't* always in the superior position. *For once, Mike would be in control.* He was going to give Adam the fright of his life.

The black Egli Vincent with the nickel-plated frame started on the third kick. Listening to the thundering noise from the throbbing 1,000cc V twin, Mike smiled to himself. The Vincent engine was tuned to Black Lightning Specification, capable of doing a hundred and forty miles an hour.

Mike turned from Cadogan Place, then left onto Pont Street. With a roar, the bike shot ahead into Belgrave Square, a central garden encircled by cream, classical buildings.

"*Hey!*" Half deafened by the noise from the exhaust, Adam yelled over Mike's shoulder, "*This is a one-way street! You just turned the wrong way!*"

Mike smiled. He knew that at this time of night, there was never much traffic in Belgrave Square.

The Egli tore at increasing speed around the black-spiked railings that surrounded the central garden.

"*What the fuck do you think you're doing?*" Adam screamed into the wind.

His brother's terrified reaction made Mike grin. The euphoria went right to his head, like a glass of fizzing champagne on an empty stomach. His bike throbbed beneath him, leaping ahead.

The harsh wind on Adam's face forced tears from the corners of his eyes. The buildings were leaning out at him. No, the bike was leaning in. He felt dizzy and frightened. As the Egli swerved to avoid a sedate limousine, Adam screamed, and his arms tightened around Mike's waist.

Mike laughed. He could still hear an enraged horn behind them as, with a thunder of exhaust, he slid out of Belgrave Square. He knew it seemed to Adam that he was handling the Egli with violence—even savagery; Adam probably thought that he wasn't completely in charge of his machine, though Mike knew that he was.

Leaving the square, Mike should have turned right, toward Victoria Station. Instead, he turned left.

"*This isn't the way to Victoria Station! Where the fuck do you think you're going?*" The wind flung Adam's words back into his mouth.

At this point, Adam seriously considered throwing himself from the Egli, but that would be even more dangerous, with all the traffic, on this dark night, than clinging to his brother.

As the bike picked up speed, Mike felt increasingly exhilarated. Adam, who never spared a thought for other people, now knew what it felt like to be at someone else's mercy, to endure violence, to be terrified.

Ahead of the Egli loomed a high triumphal arch with elaborate gates. Mike headed toward these closed gates, as if to smash straight into them.

Adam screamed.

At the last minute, the Egli swerved.

Now, to Adam's left, shadowed trees threatened him from beneath old-fashioned lamplight; to his right loomed the spike-topped walls of Buckingham Palace.

"Lean in with me!" Mike yelled over his shoulder.

The Egli started to slalom. In terrifying fashion, the gleaming monster wove in and out of the moving vehicles. The shrieks of protesting horns could be heard even above the howl of the bike. Adam ducked his head behind Mike's body and clung to him, concentrating simply on staying alive and thinking only from one moment to the next.

With a powerful roar, the bike zoomed around the statue in front of Buckingham Palace and up the Mall, where Mike took the Egli up to maximum speed.

Adam's cheeks were forcibly drawn back, and his breath torn from his mouth. The crenellated walls of St. James's Palace blurred past on his left. In front of the Egli, traffic lights were red.

Mike did not reduce speed.

Adam shut his eyes.

Just as the Egli reached the lights, they switched to amber. The Egli roared on, at full throttle.

Adam, surprised to find himself still alive, opened his eyes to see, ahead, the stately gray curve of Admiralty Arch.

With a squeal of tires, Mike viciously decelerated, turning into Trafalgar Square. Briefly the Egli's front wheel left the ground.

Adam's brain began functioning again as the bike slowed down. *"What do I have to do to get you to stop? What do you want?"* he yelled to a background cacophony of loud bangs as the engine backfired on the overrun, and flames flashed from the exhaust.

Mike swung the bike to the right, calling over his shoulder, "Ten percent of what you're getting from the Dove Trust."

"Bugger that!" yelled Adam. *"No!"*

Mike grinned. So he had guessed correctly. Adam *was* milking the trust. He flicked his wrist and the speed increased.

They were circling Trafalgar Square now. In the square, the base of Nelson's Column was guarded by four enormous bronze lions in a semicircle of iron posts. Behind this were two pools, their fountains of bronze mermaids and dolphins floodlit from below. Naturally, no tourists or slick-selling touts were hanging about after dark in the cold, but there was plenty of traffic around the square. The Egli thundered past weary, double-decker, red buses and licorice-black taxis.

Adam again wondered whether it was more dangerous to stay on the bike or hurl himself off. He half decided to throw himself off, knowing that Mike would have to slow down when he turned right—*if* he turned right—at the top of the square.

But as the Egli climbed uphill toward the top, Adam saw the row of posts that protected the stone steps leading down into the square; to hit one of those iron guards with his head would mean a funeral march.

He decided to hang on tight and remember what a good driver Mike was—although it was no use thinking that Mike wouldn't put himself at risk, because a biker did that all the time.

Mike swerved to the right. The Egli dodged between two posts.

Adam—beyond screaming—gurgled hoarsely as the motorbike slithered down the shallow steps to the square.

A crowd of pigeons fluttered into the air as the Egli bounced from the steps, then passed the ornamental pools, thundered past the dark, crouching lions, and bumped onto the road again.

Again Mike flicked the bike to the right. Dear God, Adam thought. He's going to do that nightmare stunt *again!*

He leaned forward and yelled into Mike's ear, "*All right! Ten percent. You win!*"

Mike grinned into the wind. He knew Adam wouldn't give him a penny, but Mike wasn't serious about the money. He didn't want it. What he wanted was to be in control and have Adam begging for mercy—just once.

"You're sure you *really* want to give me ten percent?" Mike teased over his shoulder as the Egli again circled the square.

"*Yes!*"

"Sure?"

"*Yes! Yes!*"

"I don't believe you!" Mike's laugh was torn by the wind. He was really enjoying this ride.

As the Egli tore past the top of the square for the second time, it continued straight ahead. Like a howling black and silver bullet, the motorbike shot past the policeman at the traffic lights. Then Mike turned left, into the Strand.

On Adam's right shone the lights of Charing Cross Station. The bike's acceleration made him feel nauseous. He hoped he wouldn't vomit . . .

Hell, what did it matter if he did?

The first set of lights were green.

The second set of lights were green.

Adam's heart thudded against his chest as the Egli thundered toward the third set of traffic lights, where the road was divided by central iron railings.

The third set of lights were green.

As the bike charged on, Adam ducked his head and glimpsed the silvery metal portico of the Savoy Hotel. Top-hatted porters in green uniform stood before revolving doors.

Mike slammed the bike to the left, curved around the island of the Aldwych, then drove back toward the Savoy.

At this point, the downpour that had been threatening all afternoon suddenly started. Mike immediately slowed down.

Adam, relieved, hunched his back, but couldn't prevent the rain from streaming down the back of his neck. He dared not let go with one hand to turn up his coat collar. He would *kill* Mike when he finally stopped!

As they approached the brilliantly lit cul-de-sac where the Savoy Hotel stood, the traffic lights changed to green, which allowed the Egli right-of-way.

Not noticing that the lights had changed, a majestic maroon Bentley slowly drew out of the cul-de-sac onto the main road.

Mike hurriedly swerved to the right to avoid the tank-tough Bentley. He then swerved again to avoid the central line of iron railings that divided the road.

In front of the Egli, an Italian businessman had just paid his taxi fare. Without looking, from force of habit he mistakenly opened the right-hand passenger door.

The Egli charged into the open door of the taxi.

The door ripped from its hinges. The plump Italian was flung back into the interior of the cab, with a broken thumb. Mike and Adam were hurled into the air over the door of the taxi.

Head-on, Adam crashed into an ornate pale blue lamppost. He was thrown backward onto the pavement.

The Egli slid down the Strand on its left side, the footrest and handlebars raising a shower of sparks from the road.

After that, nothing seemed to happen for a long time.

Mike lay on his back in the road, between the cab and his bike. As he tried to sit up, pain shot through his left arm and leg, and he fell back. He clapped his right arm to his left and touched shredded flesh and sticky blood: the arm of his jacket had been ripped off. He fumbled for his left thigh and felt the shredded remains of his trouser leg. But his kneecap was still there. He tried again, unsuccessfully, to bend his knee.

Slowly Mike lifted his head and looked around. The Egli lay on its left side, wheels still spinning. "Shit!" At least his broken leg would mend, but he realized that his irreplaceable bike was a write-off.

As rain streamed down on him, he painfully pulled himself up on his right elbow. Where was Adam? He twisted his body to the right so that he could see behind him.

About seven feet behind, Adam lay, inert, on the road.

In spite of the rain, passersby with coat collars turned up gathered on the pavement. A woman screamed, "Someone get the police!" A man in black bowler hat and fashionable overcoat hurried toward Mike, who was now crawling down the middle of the road.

Mike shook his head to the offer of help; with gritted teeth, he inched his way toward his brother. Soon he was near enough to see that the top of Adam's head was missing and his neck lolled at an odd angle. Blood and dark splotches of brain splattered the pavement.

With hoarse groans, Mike started to cry.

A policeman came up to him and draped his black rain cape over Mike, but Mike shook it off. When the ambulance arrived, he was huddled by the side of the road, hugging Adam in his arms and rocking him back and forth. Tears ran down his filthy, bloodied, torn face.

The two paramedics gently pried Mike's arms away from Adam's body. One said, "It's all right, mate, we'll look after him now."

"Be careful of him," Mike said through sobs. "He's my *brother*." "Course we will, mate. Leave him to us."

Rain slashed down as the two paramedics slid Adam onto the stretcher. As they lifted him, his left arm flopped over the side, and Mike glimpsed a gleam of gold.

"His watch! I'd better look after his watch for him," he said. Adam was fond of that watch for some reason. He'd never forgive Mike if someone nicked it on the way to the hospital.

The paramedics glanced at each other. The poor sod couldn't accept that his brother was a goner. The policeman unstrapped the Omega watch, replaced Adam's arm on the stretcher, and handed the watch down to Mike. "They'll be right back for you, sir," he said. Once again he covered Mike with his black rain cape.

Mike glanced at the watch and turned it over. In the light of the streetlamp that had killed his brother he noticed five lines of figures engraved on the back of it.

Mike felt sick; then he felt faint. He put the watch down beside him on the stone curb and flopped on the pavement. He still hoped that this scene was as unreal as it seemed to him. He still hoped that he would have the chance to tell Adam how sorry he was for trying to frighten him.

When the paramedics returned to load Mike on the stretcher, he forgot about the watch. It lay under the lamplight, on the blood-streaked curbstone, and the raindrops fell softly upon it.

CHAPTER 33

Tuesday, 1 April 1969

"DARLING GRAN, MAY I phone you back?" Miranda looked at the pile of folders on her desk. "I have a directors' meeting in ten minutes, and Adam left so much to straighten out—as if I hadn't enough work!"

"I hope you're allowing enough time for the wedding preparations," Elinor reminded her anxiously.

"Oh, Angus is organizing our wedding. I'm not allowed to do a thing. He won't even tell me where we're going on our honeymoon. Even the doctor who gave me my shots wouldn't tell me. Just smiled as he said, 'This one's anticholera—you can't be too careful in Brighton.' "

"I can't help wishing that you and Clare were having a double wedding."

"You know Clare and David would hate a grand wedding. And besides, you're only allowed your *first* wedding in church." Miranda glanced at her watch. "Darling, can't this wait until I see you on Saturday?"

"I had the feeling that you might be so busy you'd cancel Saturday. I'm really just calling to make sure you don't."

"I must admit I thought of it. I reckon I could almost catch up, given an uninterrupted working weekend."

"Not this weekend," Elinor said firmly. "You promised to drive Annabel down here, and it's the last time we'll all be together for goodness knows how long. Scott arrives on Monday to take her for her final checkup at St. George's, and then they're both flying back to New York."

"Well, if you insist," Miranda said reluctantly, "I *will* be there."

"I do, Miranda," Elinor said. "This is important. I have something to tell you all, something I should have told you long ago. It's a story . . . a rather special story."

"Darling, you've been telling stories for forty—"

"I know," Elinor's quiet voice interrupted, "but this is *my* story, Miranda, and I can't live alone with it any longer."

A touch of *Wuthering Heights*, Miranda thought, sighing. "I may be the first bride to walk down the aisle of St. Margaret's, Westminster, with a briefcase in her hand, but of course I'll come if it's important to you."

Saturday, 5 April 1969

"Only another five minutes," Miranda said as she swung the Reliant Scimitar off the main road toward Clare's cottage. She added, "Now remember, Annabel, in front of Gran, you *don't* mind wearing that eye patch."

"Of course not. I adore wearing the goddamn thing. It gives me an air of mystery, like the man in the Hathaway shirt ads." Annabel paused. "Actually, you know, I do rather like the eye patch because it reminds me that I'm *not* as I was before. Oh, I know the plastic surgeon has promised me the scars will go away, and I know the glass eye will look every bit as natural as the one I lost, but in an odd way, that mugging freed me. It's freed me to be myself—and I'm only just starting to find out who I am, because up to now I've hidden behind an eight-by-ten glossy print. And you know what? So far my real self has been *quite* a surprise to me."

"We're all proud of the new, grown-up Annabel—especially Gran."

"She certainly seems back to normal—tough as old boots."

"Buzz says she wakes up happy every morning, just because she's not in that grim nursing home."

"I still don't understand why she won't sue that awful doctor," Annabel said.

"Craig-Dunlop is bound to have covered himself legally, and it would just drag on and on in the courts, as Mr. Owen told us," Miranda reminded her. "It's much better for Gran to try and forget the whole thing, and look forward to something pleasant. She and Buzz are planning a trip to the south of France. They want to find a small farmhouse, where they can start a new life and put this behind them."

"Oh, I wish we all could." Annabel sighed. "There are just so many unanswered questions. I suppose Adam's watch hasn't turned up yet?"

"No. One of the ambulance paramedics remembers a policeman unstrapping it from Adam's wrist and handing it to Mike, but since then there's been no sign of it. Mike probably dropped it on the street, which means anything could have happened to it. Someone may have walked off with it, or it might have been destroyed, in which case some Swiss bank will hang on to all that money! I can't bear to think of it!"

"I don't understand why our lawyers are offering that huge reward, especially since nobody's even certain that those bank account numbers were engraved on the back of the watch. It's only guesswork by Angus."

"I'd bet on it. Those numbers *must* be written down somewhere," Miranda said. "The detectives found nothing in Adam's home or office. Besides, it really is more than guesswork by Angus. He says that those numbers have to be written down somewhere. Some people engrave them on backs of signet rings, or maybe inside a pocket watch. We've checked all of Adam's jewelry and found nothing. No, it must be that watch; he was always so protective of it. And who knows? Maybe it'll turn up."

"I suppose we should be grateful that Adam didn't get *all* Gran's money," Annabel said ruefully.

"No, there's still about seventeen percent left in the trust—a little over one and a half million pounds," Miranda replied. "Plus, the lawyers think the trust will be awarded all of Adam's shares in SUPPLYKITS in lieu of the money he so clearly stole: the trust will then own forty-six percent of the company, which is worth about two and a half million pounds. Plus, the royalties on Gran's novels keep coming in, so there really is plenty. In American dollars, what's left in the trust should total at least ten million."

"That's all well and good," said Annabel, "but I *still* don't understand why the trust wasn't protected, when we were told it was insured for millions."

"Because Adam was careful to do nothing overtly illegal," Miranda explained, yet again. "His taking money from the trust and squirreling it away in some secret place was obviously not Gran's intent, but the fact remains that she gave him her power of attorney, a document that virtually said, 'I hereby authorize Adam Grant to do anything he likes with everything I own.' "

"I wonder whether Adam would have been able to get away with it if he'd been dealing with men, not women," Annabel mused.

"Probably not," Miranda said. "God knows men aren't any smarter, but most of them are brought up to be self-reliant, to look after themselves more, and not to always be so dependent . . . and trusting."

After lunch, when Josh had gone out to play, Elinor looked at the expectant faces around the table and knew that there would never be a better moment to tell them.

Quietly, she related the truth of Miranda's parentage.

"The dirty dog," Buzz said.

Clare looked at Miranda's wary face and slowly said, "It doesn't alter anything between us, you know."

Annabel added, "Of course not."

Then they all started talking at once. Everyone hugged Miranda.

Eventually, Elinor said, "At first I didn't want you to know about this . . . unpleasantness, but Miranda insisted, and when she did I realized there was something else you had to be told." She took a deep breath, "You all think I don't want to talk about what happened with Adam—but I *do*. All my life, I've allowed myself to ignore the lessons I should have learned and to forget the ones I should have remembered. Well, *not this time!* I can't. I can't go on pretending that bad things don't happen, that the happy ending will always come along. Not after this. Not after I've seen my family almost destroyed. All because I couldn't deal with reality and always, always refused to face unpleasant facts. I now see that if, ostrich-like, you pretend not to see your own problems, then you can't solve them."

An astonished silence greeted this firm speech: Elinor had clearly regained her old strength.

"Don't be too hard on yourself, Gran," Annabel said. "We've survived."

"Only just! You and I could have been killed! I almost lost my reason, not to mention most of my money. *Your* money. Miranda lost control of her business. Buzz found herself with no home and no income. And Clare was almost lost to me forever. *How did I let that happen?*"

"Don't blame yourself, Nell," Buzz said. "*Nobody* noticed what was happening because Adam was a con man, and nobody spots a successful con man—until it's too late. And he was very good—he could have fooled anyone."

Elinor slowly shook her head. "I mustn't hide behind excuses. Not this time, and not ever again. I could have stopped all this before it started, and *I know why I didn't*."

Everyone stared at Elinor.

"You see, I didn't trust myself to handle my own problems," she explained. "If any man said, 'This isn't the sort of thing that a woman understands,' then I immediately decided that I didn't understand it, and let him handle it."

Gently Clare said, "Gran, I'm so pleased that you can finally admit this."

"I always expected a man to look after me," Elinor went on. "I always believed that a man would know best. Now I know how wrong I was, and I regret it. It's harmed all of you."

"Nonsense, darling!" Annabel cried. "You've never hurt us. And you've always given us everything we needed."

Elinor looked around the table. "Yes, everything. Except the truth. *That's* why Annabel and Miranda expected a perfect Prince Charming. I now realize that happiness is not hoping for protection by an illusory, perfect man, but in discovering the surprising strength of one's imperfect self—that inner core, the 'real me' that every woman senses. Only Clare always said I confused romance with reality. When she fought me, I was determined not to let her win. . . . I *couldn't* let her win, because losing would mean tearing down the facade that I'd carefully erected to conceal the truth of my life—most especially from myself—because my reality was so painful."

"Surely not after Daddy Billy died?" Annabel asked.

"*Especially* after Billy died." Elinor paused, then continued quietly: "It's time I also told you the truth about Billy's death, time I stopped remembering a fake life and started to live a real one . . . in the real world."

Elinor paused again. She knew it would take all her ability as a storyteller and all her strength as a survivor to tell this, her most difficult story, because she had lived the lie for so long that she had almost come to believe it. But now the truth had to be told—without sentiment, without romance.

"On the day Billy died," Elinor began, "I'd visited my publishers in London. They'd called me there for press interviews, but there was also another reason they wanted to see me. When I arrived at their office, I found that Joe Grant was also there. Unsavory stories were being spread, stories that threatened my good name and ultimately threatened my growing success as a writer. Apparently, they were being spread by Billy—silly rumors to get him attention and sympathy rather than harming me. For the most part, no one had paid attention to them.

"However, the latest story was not so easily dismissed. It didn't come from Billy, but it involved him, and it was ugly. It seems he had bothered a young girl . . . No, that's not quite it." She hesitated, determined to tell the story straight. "It seems he had *molested* a young girl, or at least attempted to do so. Apparently Billy offered to photograph her, then tried to take off her clothes. Afterwards, when the girl made trouble and threatened to contact me through my publisher, Billy confessed to Joe Grant, who tried to hush up the situation; he decided I had better be warned. In fact I already knew. Maybe not about this one, but there had been others. I had even once confronted Billy. He denied it, of course. And of course I tried hard to believe him."

In the silence of her kitchen, Clare said, "Gran, does that matter now? It all happened so long ago . . ."

"It mattered then," Elinor said, "because I knew I would have to speak to Billy about it. I had to make him realize his danger—the danger for all of us. But in order to do that, he would have to admit his folly to me, and to himself. I knew it would be almost impossible, but I *had* to try. I was too depressed to talk to him when I got back from London that evening, and anyway, he wasn't home when I returned, exhausted, at ten—an hour before the pubs closed. Neither was Buzz." She looked at her friend. "Remember, you were spending your summer holiday with us at Starlings and had gone to a church whist party that night? So I went straight to bed. But I was woken just before midnight . . . " Elinor's eyes closed.

She could almost hear the slow, ponderous stumbling as Billy pulled himself up the stairs, and the high-pitched, unearthly sound that had wakened her. She had leapt from her bed and run to the landing. A disheveled Billy stood halfway up the stairs. His right hand clutched the fluffy white nursery cat by its hind legs; it was the cat's anguished, terrified howls that had roused Elinor. Billy's other hand was stretched out to Annabel, who stood frozen in fright only a few steps above him.

Annabel said quietly, "Yes, I remember. Daddy Billy was tormenting Snowball. And you pulled me away and told me to go back to bed and stay there. I heard noises, but I was too frightened to leave my bed again."

"That's what I wanted," Elinor said. "What happened next was my secret and I thought that if no one ever knew about it, then it wouldn't be true, that it never really happened, you see.

"But it did happen, of course. As soon as Annabel was gone, I grabbed the cat from Billy's hand. As I did, he reached out, clutching at me. His hand caught in the lace on my nightgown, and he pulled me toward him. I smelled the brandy on his breath. I felt his anger, his belligerence; I knew in that moment that I had to be free of him. I couldn't live with his lies and my disgust and the fear—always the fear. Fear that he would hurt you girls. Fear that others would know the truth. And perhaps the worst fear was that he would be taken away from me and imprisoned.

"In that moment, I made up my mind. With all my strength, I pushed him away from me, down the stairs. The lace on my nightgown tore as he fell backward, but he didn't manage to pull me with him. I watched as he stumbled and grasped for a hold but missed it. I watched his bloodshot eyes as they opened wide with the realization that I wanted him to die. For a moment, I almost felt sorry for him. For a moment, I thought of the wonderful man I had fallen in love with, and regretted what I had done. But it was too late." Elinor paused once more, remembering how Billy had crashed downstairs, turned a final half-somersault, then landed on his back, his eyes closed.

She shook her head sadly. "I had seen plenty of dead men; I was sure he was dead. I didn't want to touch him. I decided that the sensible thing to do was to leave him lying in the hall. I remember that my mind was very clear, that for once in my life, I felt completely in control. I decided to forget reality and rewrite the entire scene in my mind, then memorize it according to my new script, hoping that in time it would be the only version I'd remember."

Elinor recalled that she had stared at Billy and felt relief, fresh as a sea breeze playing around her head. She had drawn a deep breath and allowed herself the luxury of her true feelings; for just a few moments, she allowed herself to hate Billy for what he had done to their marriage . . .

Miranda leaned back in her chair and shook her head, still trying to understand why it was so important for them all to hear this story. Puzzled, she asked, "So you just went back to bed?"

Elinor shook her head again and said with difficulty, "No. As I looked at Billy . . . his eyelids slowly opened." Once again she forced herself to remember the terror she had felt as Billy's pouchy, red-veined eyes glared maliciously at her. "Just you wait," he croaked, and then started to vomit. As she stared down at him, Elinor, horrified, also thought of the many times she had had to clean up Billy's mess before someone else saw it. She remembered the many times she had dutifully tended him and served him.

And for one bewildering moment, Billy's malicious stare reminded her of something else, something buried—fragments of a memory she had thought long forgotten. Her head felt as if a storm were raging inside it, whirling her thoughts around like fluttering and panicking birds. For as Billy's eyes stared up at her, Elinor felt again the total despair and helplessness she had felt when her father looked at her with the same contemptuous malevolence.

Violent rage suddenly consumed her. She wanted to howl to primitive gods, for she felt cheated: she had grasped at release, she had acted in vengeance, she had been granted her freedom—but now it was being snatched back . . .

"What *did* you do, Gran?" Miranda persisted.

Elinor started, blinked, and looked in a dazed way at the four faces around the kitchen table. She said quietly, "I ran upstairs and grabbed a pillow from my bed. Then I rushed downstairs and . . . I held it over Billy's face." The pillow had hidden Billy's angry eyes as he heaved in protest. When his body started to jerk and writhe in its final struggle, Elinor called on a reserve of strength she had never known she possessed, holding the pillow over his face with the entire weight of her body. Gradually Billy heaved less, until only his arms, protruding beyond the pillow, twitched occasionally. Eventually all movement ceased.

Elinor said, "I don't know how long I stayed that way. I remember I didn't remove the pillow until the grandfather clock struck one." She had stood up wearily, her body suddenly drained of all strength, and looked with distaste at the vomit-smeared pillowcase. She removed it from the pillow; she would have to wash it. She felt perfectly calm.

Clare's kitchen was completely still as the women sat in stunned silence.

Finally Elinor spoke again. "I was terrified that Annabel might have heard something, might even have seen me . . . do it."

"No," Annabel said, "I saw nothing. I just remember that you brought Snowball up to my bedroom, and the gardener took him to the vet the next morning."

"After I put Snowball in your bed, I stayed until you fell asleep," Elinor said. "Luckily, Buzz hadn't wakened—her bedroom was at the far end of the house, over the kitchen quarters. I remember very clearly the calm with which I sprinkled a bottle of brandy over Billy's body, washed the pillow, then repaired the tear in my nightgown as best I could.

"I lay in bed, awake nearly all night, terrified of what I had done, longing to wake Buzz but afraid to involve her in what was . . . a murder."

Elinor looked slowly around the room, her eyes resting briefly on each face, searching for some reaction.

Clare thought fleetingly of the silver-framed photograph at Elinor's bedside and wondered how, every night, Gran could have slept beside that smiling face, knowing that she had killed him. Then Clare realized suddenly that the bright-eyed young man in that photograph was the perfect husband Gran chose to remember; her carefully crafted fantasy had blanked out the debauched, middle-aged drunkard—the bully she had murdered.

Buzz said, "I can't say I'm sorry, Nell. Billy was a vicious blighter; he tried to bugger up everything you tried to do for them kids. In my view, he died because you had to protect them—from him."

"That's what I tell myself," Elinor murmured. "But I also know that I . . . did what I did . . . to protect *myself.*"

"I still reckon Billy deserved it," Buzz said firmly.

"Poor darling," Annabel said. "You must have been scared stiff."

"No," Elinor said. "At first I was too angry to be scared. I didn't care if they caught me—although, in those days, you were hanged for murder. Later, of course, I *was* frightened, and that fear has never really left me. I'd tremble and my heart would thump every time I saw Sergeant Watson bicycle up the drive on what, thank God, always turned out to be some trivial matter." She looked at Buzz. "I longed to talk to you about it. I never dared. I was terrified of telling anyone. But I've always wondered whether . . . "

Slowly Buzz nodded. "Yes. I knew."

"*How?*"

"I got back fairly early from the church social and was asleep before eleven, so I woke at six that morning and went downstairs to get a cup of tea. I actually found Billy before the maid came downstairs. And I saw the one thing you had overlooked—a piece of your lace nightgown still clutched in Billy's hand. I pried it loose and burned it, so no one would ever know."

Miranda said urgently, "Why are you telling us this now, Gran, after keeping your secret for so many years? As you once told me, everyone is morally entitled to guard their privacy to protect themselves."

Elinor looked levelly at her. "Because I want you all to see—and see me acknowledge—the danger of self-deception. And perhaps I can only truly admit this to myself, and absolve myself, by telling you—who have seen how destructive it was for us all. That—and my deference.

"I hope each of you now understands how important it is to trust yourself and stand up for yourself; I should have done so earlier. I should have confronted Billy or left him; I would have managed somehow, I would have stood on my own two feet—but I didn't trust myself to try." She looked around the table, then said earnestly, "If, at the beginning, I'd made it clear to Billy that I wasn't going to put up with his self-indulgent ill-treatment, then perhaps it wouldn't have escalated—as bad behavior always does when it's unchecked."

"I know what you mean," Clare said, thinking of Sam.

Buzz said soothingly, "Well, now we all know what happened, I see no reason ever to mention it again. It's all in the past."

"The past is always a part of the present," Elinor said. "And these three must never forget it."

Clare pushed her chair back, hurried around the table to her grandmother, and hugged her. "I'm proud of you for facing the truth at last."

Earnestly Miranda said, "*I'm* proud of you, Gran, because you've always fought and survived, all your life. Although you've never believed it, you've *always* been capable of looking after yourself. You never needed anyone to protect you, Gran—you only thought you did."

After a moment, Annabel said hopefully, "And now we've all learned to stand on our own two feet, haven't we?"

Miranda sighed. "It was an expensive experience."

Quietly Elinor said, "All profitable experience is expensive."

"Not as expensive as the folly of misplaced trust," Clare said.

"Talking of which," Miranda said ruefully, "there's certainly one thing that we've all learned at last . . . "

"Oh yes," Clare sent her a wry smile. "We've finally realized that . . . Daddy doesn't know best."

Epilogue

Liberty: freedom from arbitrary or despotic control;
the power to do as one pleases; the power of choice;
independence; the quality or state of being free.

ACKNOWLEDGMENTS

As always there are many people whom I wish to thank for their kind help in getting this book before your eyes, and the person to whom I'm most grateful is my kind and considerate "Mission Control," Nikki Manwaring.

In New York, I much appreciated the hard work of Michael Korda, Chuck Adams, Jack McKeown, Sandi Gelles-Cole, Victoria Meyer, Frank Metz, and Sandi Mendelson. I am also, as always, grateful to my agents, Morton Janklow and Anne Sibbald.

I must also thank the Laurey Girls Agency, who took so much trouble to obtain temporary typists who could read my handwriting (in particular I appreciated the charm and ability of Maria Dubow), Ronald Colon, who provided the typewriters, and Anthony J. Barbaro for his banking expertise.

I am also grateful to Judy Licht, Paul Smirnoff, John Parsons, Judy Tygard, Christine Tomlinson, Bob O'Brien, Carol Ann Sullivan and Catherine O'Shea of TV Channel 5.

In Los Angeles I must thank Bill Haber, Joanne Brough and Judy Hilsinger; in Canada, Richard Pearce.

In Britain, as always I am grateful for the patience, understanding and cheerful support of my British publishers, William Armstrong and Peter Carson, as well as George Sharp and Jacqueline Graham-Pelham; I would also like to thank Debbie Gill, Jenny Page and Dido Armstrong for their help.

In Monaco, I would like Nikki Manwaring, Nicole Proetta and Kristina Gonzales de Linares to know how much I appreciated their organization, typing, enthusiasm, attention to detail and general support. I am also very grateful to Roselyn Haudberg, Jane Dubuisson, Suzanne Proetta, Mary George, Paula Whittam, Eva Cleydon and Diego Gonzales de Linares for their help in producing the manuscript.

I was lucky enough to have the final manuscript read and criticized by Geraldine Cooke, Pete Williams and Dr. Georges Sandulescu.

I must also thank Maurice Baird Smith, who taught Miranda to fly, and Gill Brooks of the Cannes Flying School; Ariane Davies-Gilbert, who gave Elinor her Elizabethan candied flower recipe; Elizabeth Barker, who was Miranda's stockbroker; Wendy Williams who designed the garden at Starlings; Ian Melrose who advised Mike on his motorbikes; Alexander Plunket Greene who gambled with Adam, and Annie Trehearne who advised Miranda on fashion and publicity.

For professional advice on legal matters, I am indebted to Sir Patrick Lawrence, Charles Chatwin, John Dewhurst, Charles Doughty and William Easun. For advice on accounting and finance I am grateful to Richard MacLellan, Stephen Ainsworth and Peter Alexander; for advice on Lloyds I am grateful to David Larner; for advice on business procedure I was lucky enough to be helped by Jennifer d'Abo and Jonathan Bevan.

For advice on fraud, I much appreciated the advice, sagacity and wit of Walter (Wally) White of the Fraud Squad. For medical information I am grateful to Dr. John Cardwell, Dr. Dennis Friedman, Dr. Jonathan Gould, Dr. Margaret Reinhardt and Marion Symes.

For technical information on World War I (including advice on nurses' underwear) I am most grateful to Malcolm Brown, as well as the Imperial War

Museum and the RAF Museum at Hendon. I am also grateful to Trevor Williams and John Bryant of the League Against Cruel Sports and Nick Symes for his musical advice.

Others who have helped are Sharon Flynn of Rank Xerox, Diane Kane of British Airways, Claude Laughier and Geoff Osman.

As always, I am indebted to my son Sebastian Conran for esoteric information on such subjects as old motor coaches and atom bombs, vintage motor bikes and Hong Kong massage parlors; and to my son Jasper Conran for fashion advice, criticism and moral support.

Finally I would like also to thank Isabel Carr, Julia de Biere, Elizabeth Chatwin and Patrick Seale for their advice and encouragement. I would also like particularly to thank Bettina Culham (who typed my first novel) and Vanessa Gayle (who typed my second novel), who have kept an eye on me ever since.

About The Author

SHIRLEY CONRAN is the highly successful author of *LACE,* which was not only an international bestseller and a *New York Times* bestseller for three months but was one of the most successful television miniseries ever aired. Her other bestselling books include *LACE 2, CRIMSON,* and *SAVAGES.*